THE ROUGH GUIDE TO

PERU

This tenth edition updated by
Steph Dyson, Sara Humphreys and Todd Obolsky

In memory of Dilwyn Jenkins

Contents

VIEW OF MACHU PICCHU

Introduction to
Peru

Trekking through the awe-inspiring Andes to the world-famous Inca citadel of Machu Picchu is the main draw for most travellers to Peru but, truth be told, this takes in only a fraction of the treasures that lie within one of South America's most diverse countries. Peru is home to a staggering array of landscapes – puzzling geoglyphs in the arid plains of Nazca, two of the world's deepest canyons outside the colonial city of Arequipa, the lush Amazon rainforest in the east and excellent surf in the northwest – offering boundless potential for adventure. Peru's Andean cultures are some of the most exciting in the Americas, with tucked-away highland towns that explode into colour on market day, and vibrant local fiestas that have been celebrated with unbridled enthusiasm for centuries – a heady mix of ancient beliefs with colonial Catholic customs.

Peru's immense wealth of sights and experiences has its roots in one of the world's richest heritages, topped by the **Inca Empire** and its fabulous **archeological gems**, not to mention the monumental adobe temples and pre-Inca ruins along the desert coast. While Machu Picchu is undoubtedly one of the world's most important archeological sites, Peru is home to a host of other riches – and important new discoveries are constantly being unearthed.

With Peru boasting access to the highest tropical mountain range in the world as well as one of the best-preserved areas of virgin Amazon rainforest, its **wildlife** is as diverse as you'd expect, and sights such as jaguars slinking through the jungle, caimans sunning themselves on riverbanks and dazzling macaws gathering at Amazon clay-licks are all within the visitor's grasp. For those looking for adrenaline-fuelled fun, a host of **outdoor activities** are on offer, from trekking ancient trails and whitewater rafting to paragliding, bungee-jumping and ziplining above the forest canopy.

MIRAFLORES, LIMA

Equally, a trip to Peru could focus on more restful pursuits. Widely touted as one of the world's **culinary hotspots**, the country – and Lima in particular – offers a cornucopia of exotic tastes to appeal to curious palates, as well as a laidback, vibrant dining scene, ranging from backstreet cevicherías to gourmet restaurants. And in the big cities, you can expect buzzing **nightlife** too.

Despite it all, simple, unaffected pleasures remain in place. The country's prevailing attitude is that there is always enough time for a chat, a ceviche or another drink. Peru is accepting of its visitors – it's a place where the resourceful and open-minded traveller can break through barriers of class, race and language far more easily than most of its inhabitants can. Even the Amazon jungle region – covering nearly two-thirds of the country's landmass, but home to a mere fraction of its population – is accessible for the most part, with countless tour operators or community associations on hand to organize trips to even the furthest-flung corners. Now all you have to do is figure out where to start.

Where to go

You're most likely to arrive in the buzzing and at least fitfully elegant capital, **Lima**; a modern city, it manages effortlessly to blend traditional Peruvian heritage with twenty-first-century glitz. **Cusco** is perhaps the most obvious place to head from here. A beautiful and bustling colonial city, it was once the ancient heart of the Inca

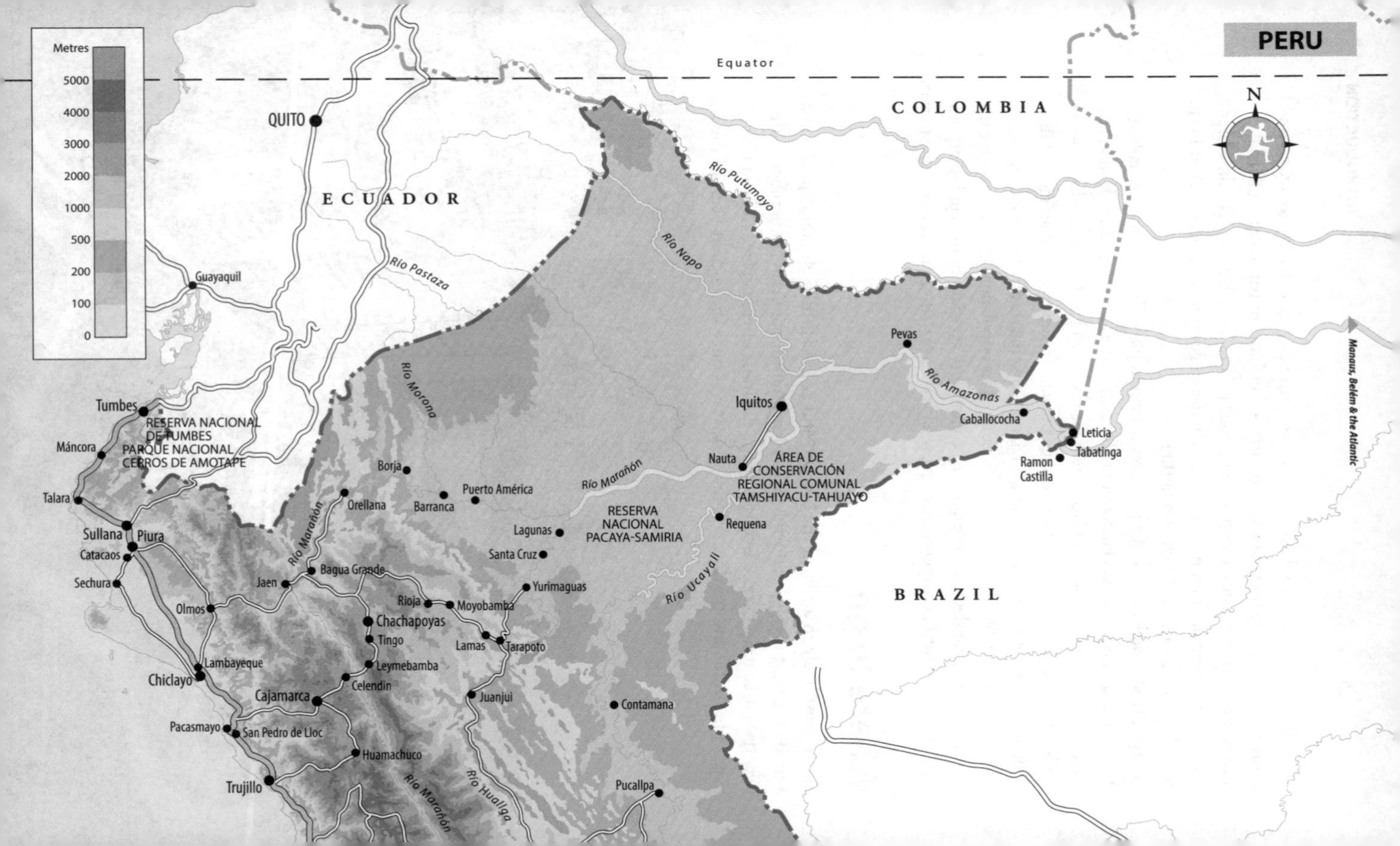
PERU
Metres
5000
4000
3000
2000
1000
500
200
100
0
Equator
COLOMBIA
ECUADOR
BRAZIL
N
QUITO
Guayaquil
Río Pastaza
Río Putumayo
Río Napo
Río Morona
Manaus, Belém & the Atlantic
Pevas
Río Amazonas
Iquitos
Caballococha
Leticia
Tabatinga
Ramon Castilla
Nauta
ÁREA DE CONSERVACIÓN REGIONAL COMUNAL TAMSHIYACU-TAHUAYO
Río Marañon
Borja
Puerto América
Barranca
Orellana
RESERVA NACIONAL PACAYA-SAMIRIA
Requena
Lagunas
Santa Cruz
Río Ucayali
Yurimaguas
Tumbes
RESERVA NACIONAL DE TUMBES
PARQUE NACIONAL CERROS DE AMOTAPE
Máncora
Talara
Sullana
Piura
Catacaos
Sechura
Olmos
Jaen
Río Marañon
Bagua Grande
Rioja
Moyobamba
Chachapoyas
Tingo
Lamas
Tarapoto
Leymebamba
Celendin
Lambayeque
Chiclayo
Cajamarca
Juanjui
Contamana
Pacasmayo
San Pedro de Lloc
Huamachuco
Trujillo
Río Marañon
Río Huallga
Pucallpa

PACIFIC OCEAN
BOLIVIA
CHILE
LIMA
LA PAZ
Chimbote
Casma
Caraz
Huaraz
PARQUE NACIONAL DE HUASCARÁN
Tingo María
Huánuco
Pozuzo
Oxapampa
Cerro de Pasco
La Merced
Satipo
Canta
La Oroya
Tarma
Huancayo
Huancavelica
Ayacucho
Lunahuaná
Cañete
Pisco
RESERVA NACIONAL DE PARACAS
Ica
Nazca
Chala
Camaná
Mollendo
Arequipa
Cotahuasi
CAÑÓN DE COTAHUASI
CAÑÓN DEL COLCA
Chivay
Sicuini
Juliaca
Puno
Juli
Yunguyo
Moquegua
Ilo
Tacna
Arica
Lago Titicaca
Río Ucayali
Atalaya
R. Tambo
Río Ene
Río Urubamba
Sepahua
PARQUE NACIONAL ALTO PURÚS
Río de las Piedras
PARQUE NACIONAL DEL MANÚ
Manu
Boca Manu
Alto Madre de Dios
Madre de Dios
Boca Colorado
Iñapari
Iberia
Puerto Heath
Puerto Maldonado
RESERVA NACIONAL TAMBOPATA
PARQUE NACIONAL BAHUAJA-SONENE
Río Iñambari
R. Tambopata
Kiteni
Shintuya
Pillcopata
Machu Picchu
Pueblo
Urubamba
Quillabamba
Pisac
Paucartambo
Cusco
Urcos
Abancay
0
250
kilometres

FACT FILE

- **Potatoes** are native to what is today southern Peru – they were domesticated here around 7000 to 10,000 years ago. Today there are over 3000 varieties of potato grown in the country.
- Peru is home to the largest segment of the **Amazon rainforest** after Brazil, with over 60 percent of Peruvian territory covered in dense forest.
- **Guinea pigs** (*cuy*) are widely consumed in Peru; it is said approximately 65 million guinea pigs are eaten every year.
- The Cañón de Cotahuasi is one of the world's **deepest canyons**, with a depth of over 3500m – twice that of the Grand Canyon.
- Peru's **population** is an estimated 32 million, almost a third of whom live in Lima, the country's capital and South America's second biggest city.
- The **Cerro Blanco** sand dune is the **highest** in the world at 2070m above sea level and 1176m from base to summit.

Empire, and is surrounded by some of the most spectacular mountain landscapes and palatial ruins in Peru, and by magnificent hiking country. The world-famous **Inca Trail**, which culminates at the lofty, mist-shrouded Inca citadel of **Machu Picchu**, is just one of several equally scenic and challenging treks in this region of Peru alone.

Along the **coast**, there are more fascinating archeological sites as well as glorious beaches and sparky towns. South of Lima are the bizarre **Nazca Lines**, which have mystified since their discovery some seventy years ago, as well as the beguiling desert landscapes of the **Reserva Nacional Paracas** and the wildlife-rich haven of the neighbouring **Islas Ballestas.** If that all sounds too active, you could always duck away to spend a day knocking back pisco at the many **Ica Valley bodegas.**

North of Lima lie the great adobe city of **Chan Chan** and the **Valle de las Pirámides**. The surfing hangouts of **Puerto Chicama** and trendy **Máncora** beach are big draws along this stretch, but almost all of the coastal towns come replete with superb beaches, plentiful nightlife and great food.

For high mountains and long-distance treks, head for the stunning glacial lakes, snowy peaks and little-known ruins of the **sierra** north of Lima, particularly the ice-capped mountains and their valleys around **Huaraz**, but also the more gentle hills, attractive villages and ancient sites in the regions of **Cajamarca** and **Chachapoyas.** The central sierra is crammed with tradition and glorious colonial architecture, at its peak in **Ayacucho** and **Huancayo**; the region around **Tarma** is also worth exploring, offering a variety of landscapes, from jungles and caves to waterfalls and stupendous terraced valleys.

If it's wildlife you're interested in, there's plenty to see almost everywhere, but **the jungle** provides startling opportunities for close and exotic encounters. From the comfort of tourist lodges in **Iquitos** to river excursions around **Puerto Maldonado**, in the **Reserva Nacional Tambopata**, the fauna and flora of the world's largest tropical forest can be experienced first-hand here more easily than in any other Amazon-rim country. Not far from Iquitos, the **Reserva Nacional Pacaya-Samiria** is a remote and extremely beautiful, though less-visited region; while close to Cusco, just below the cloud forest, the **Reserva Biósfera del Manu** is another wildlife hotspot.

FIESTA DE LA VIRGEN DEL CARMEN, PAUCARTAMBO

When to go

Picking the best time to visit Peru's various regions is complicated by the country's physical characteristics; temperatures can vary hugely across the country. Summer (*verano*) along the **desert coast** more or less fits the expected image of the southern hemisphere – extremely hot and sunny between December and March (especially in the north), cooler and with a frequent hazy mist, known as *garúa*, between April and November – although only in the polluted environs of **Lima** does the coastal winter ever get cold enough to necessitate a sweater. Swimming is possible all year round, though the water itself (thanks to the Humboldt Current) is cool-to-cold at the best of times; to swim or surf for any length of time you'd need to wear a wetsuit. Apart from the occasional shower over Lima it hardly ever rains in the desert. The freak exception, every few years, is when the shift in ocean currents of **El Niño** causes torrential downpours, devastating crops, roads and communities all down the coast.

In **the Andes**, the seasons are more clearly marked, with heavy rains from December to March and a warm, relatively dry period from June to September. Inevitably, though, there are always some sunny weeks in the rainy season and wet ones in the dry. A similar pattern dominates **the Amazon Basin**, though rainfall here is heavier and more frequent, and it's hot and humid all year round. Confusingly, the rainy season in both the Andes and the Amazon basin is referred to locally as winter (*invierno*).

Taking all of this into account, the **best time to visit** the coast is around January while it's hot, and the mountains and jungle are at their best after the rains, from May until September. Since this is unlikely to be possible on a single trip there's little point in worrying about it – the country's attractions are broad enough to override the need for guarantees of good weather.

PERU TEMPERATURES AND RAINFALL

	Jan	Feb	Mar	Apr	May	Jun	July	Aug	Sep	Oct	Nov	Dec
LIMA												
Max/min (ºC)	26/19	27/19	26/19	24/18	22/16	20/15	19/15	18/15	19/15	20/15	22/16	24/18
Rainfall (mm)	1	0	5	0	0	0	0	0	5	0	0	0
CUSCO												
Max/min (ºC)	19/7	19/7	19/6	20/5	20/3	20/0	19/0	20/2	20/4	21/6	21/6	19/6
Rainfall (mm)	145	134	107	43	9	2	4	9	22	39	72	123
IQUITOS												
Max/min (ºC)	31/22	31/22	31/22	31/22	30/22	30/22	30/21	31/21	32/21	32/22	32/22	31/22
Rainfall (mm)	266	210	317	292	292	190	187	174	210	254	287	301

Author picks

Our intrepid authors have travelled to every corner of Peru, trekking across Andean plateaus, whitewater rafting through some of the world's deepest canyons and paddling down narrow creeks in the Amazon jungle. Here are some of their highlights:

Beach life Around 2000km long, Peru's desert coastline is one huge beach. Of the resorts, Máncora (see page 417) is very crowded these days but still pretty (more so out of season), while tranquil Punta Sal (see page 420) is stunning and Lobitos (see page 415) is an increasingly popular surf hangout.

Canyons and condors Colca (see page 174) is great for the stunning new resorts for wealthier travellers, but Cotahuasi (see page 183) is exactly what the more adventurous types coming to Peru are looking for: quiet and relatively unvisited with spectacular scenery and pre-Inca settlements tucked up next to the river and high up on the cliff.

Lima's nightlife Limeños can't help but move to music, and the best *peñas* and *salsadromos*, like *Las Brisas del Titicaca* (see page 92), bring out that impulse in travellers. Whether drinking at *Ayahuasca* (see page 90) or taking on the lively rock scene, prepare to do so until the wee hours.

Inca citadels A masterpiece of architecture and engineering that blends in with its environment, Machu Picchu (see page 255) is the country's greatest archeological attraction, but Peru abounds in strikingly perpendicular sites like Choquequirao (see page 266) and Pisac (see page 236).

River trips Glide along the Amazon on a luxury riverboat from Iquitos (see page 467), or sling up a hammock on a cargo boat in Pucallpa (see page 463), and drift down the Ucayali.

Trekking Peru offers endless hiking opportunities, with most people heading to the glacial landscapes around Cusco (see page 202) or the Cordillera Blanca mountains near Huaraz (see page 324).

Wildlife encounters While the colourful clay-licks, jaguars and tapirs in the reserves of Manu and Tambopata grab headlines, it's hard to beat paddling up to pink river dolphins, giant otters and monkeys in a dugout in Pacaya-Samiria (see page 477).

> Our author recommendations don't end here. We've flagged up our favourite places – a perfectly sited hotel, an atmospheric café, a special restaurant – throughout the Guide, highlighted with the ★ symbol.

HAMMOCKS ON AN AMAZON CARGO BOAT

CAÑÓN DE COTAHUASI

25 things not to miss

It's not possible to see everything that Peru has to offer in one trip – and we don't suggest you try. What follows, in no particular order, is a selective taste of the country's highlights: colourful towns, awe-inspiring ruins, spectacular hikes and exotic wildlife. Each highlight has a page reference to take you straight into the Guide, where you can find out more. Coloured numbers refer to chapters in the Guide section.

1 HIKING TO MACHU PICCHU

See page 255

With mysterious temples and palaces nestling among hundreds of terraces, this fabulous Inca citadel is awe-inspiring. Alongside the classic Inca Trail, the Salcantay and Lares treks provide equally spectacular, multi-day ways to get there.

2 PERUVIAN WILDLIFE

See page 510

Whether spotting a three-toed sloth in the Amazon treetops or crossing paths with a *vicuña* while hiking in the Andes, Peru's sheer variety of flora and fauna never fails to amaze.

3 MARCAHUASI

See page 101

At an altitude of 4000m, the little village of Marcahuasi makes an excellent overnight trip from Lima. The mysterious rock shapes in the nearby plateau must be seen to be believed.

4 TEXTILES

See pages 214 and 228

Peru has been producing fine cotton and woollen textiles for over three thousand years, from the ayahuasca-inspired designs of Shipibo cloth, to the intricate Andean weavings picked up in highland markets.

5 LAGUNAS DE LLANGANUCO

See page 331

Part of the Parque Nacional Huascarán National Park, these pristine turquoise and emerald blue lagoons are hidden in a glacial valley in the Cordillera Blanca.

6
7
8

6 A TRADITIONAL FESTIVAL

See page 36

Take in one of Peru's renowned fiestas, a riot of music, dancing and outlandish costumes, such as Puno's Fiesta de la Candelaria, or Paucartambo's Fiesta de la Virgen del Carmen.

7 KUÉLAP

See page 390

The ruined citadel of Kuélap is one of the most fascinating archeological sites in the Andes.

8 LAGO TITICACA

See page 186

While the lake's floating Islas de los Uros steal the limelight, less-visited Amantile and Taquile offer fascinating cultural insights into island life.

9 PISCO SOUR

See page 88

Deservedly the national drink of Peru, the pisco sour refreshes thanks to its limes with crushed ice – and can also pack the kick of a mule.

10 PRE-INCA CRAFTWORK

See pages 76, 126 and 403

The country's top museums boast stunning displays of beautifully ornate ceramics, textiles and gold adornments crafted by ancient civilizations such as the Nazca, Lambayeque and Chimú.

11 CAÑÓN DEL COLCA

See page 174

Twice the depth of the Grand Canyon, the enormous Cañón del Colca is one of Peru's biggest attractions.

12 PARACAS AND ISLAS BALLESTAS

See page 115

Rocky islets teeming with bird and marine life and a beguiling coastal desert landscape make this an unmissable day-trip.

13 CEVICHE

See page 33

Seafood ceviche is a popular alternative version of Peru's national dish, which is typically made from fresh fish soaked in lime juice and chillies.

14 SLEEPING IN THE SELVA

See pages 446 and 447

The evocative sounds and sights of the jungle are a highlight of any trip, whether you opt for a luxury lodge, a village homestay or a shelter in the rainforest.

15 LIMA FINE DINING

See page 87

The upmarket neighbourhoods of Miraflores and Barranco tempt with some outstanding gourmet treats, with inventive twists to Peru's culinary traditions, and exotic ingredients.

11

12

13

14

15

16 CORDILLERA BLANCA

See page 324

The Cordillera Blanca mountain range offers some of the best hiking and climbing in South America.

17 AREQUIPA

See page 154

This white stone city, beautiful and intriguing, is watched over by the seasonally snow-capped volcano of El Misti.

18 AYACUCHO

See page 294

Bustling streets, impressive churches, passionate religious processions and unique artesanía make this Andean city a standout.

19 SACSAYHUAMAN

See page 229

The zig-zag megalithic defensive walls of this Inca temple-fortress are home to the annual Inti Raymi Festival of the Sun.

20 CHAVÍN DE HUANTAR

See page 337

Dating back over 2500 years, this large temple has many striking stone carvings and gargoyles, both externally and within its subterranean chambers.

18
19
20

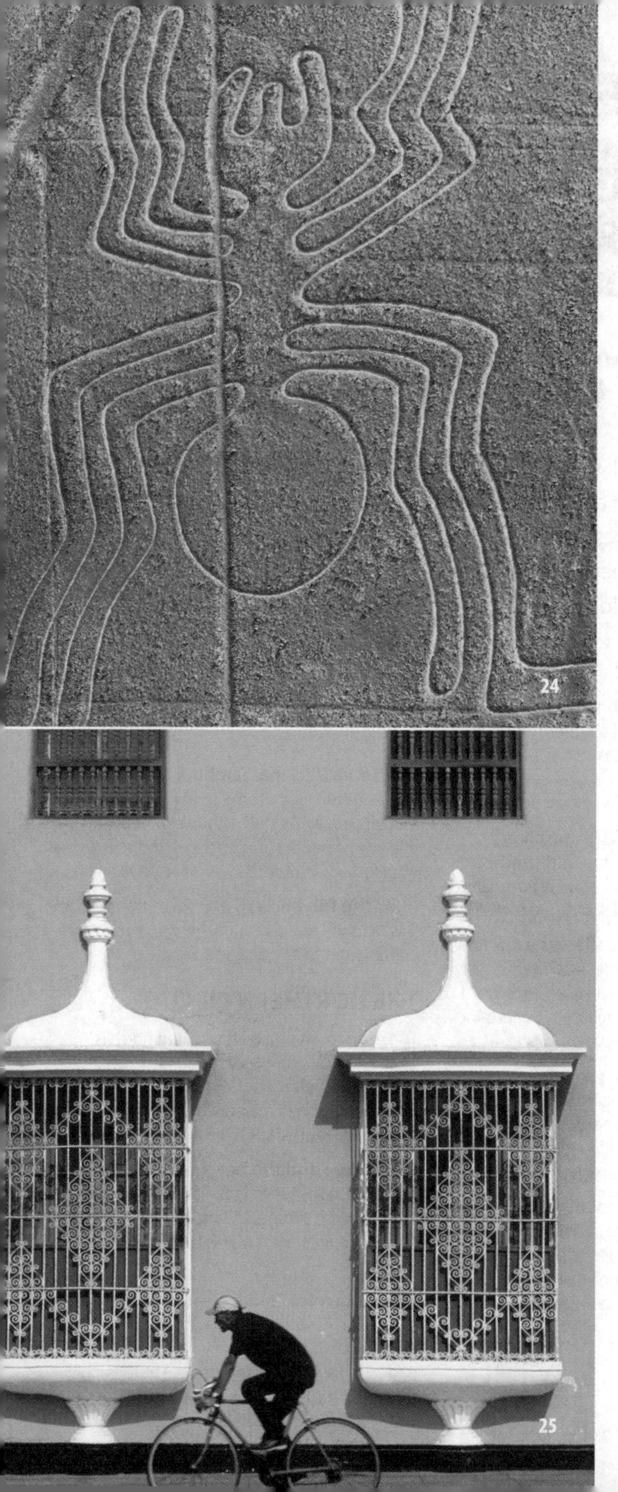

21 IQUITOS

See page 467

The steamy Amazonian capital oozes character: from the floating port of Belén, to the rubber-boom era mansions and laidback bars that overlook the Río Amazonas.

22 MÁNCORA

See page 417

Peru's most popular surfer hangout features gorgeous beaches and buzzing nightlife; those who want better surf and fewer crowds will find Lobitos, 50km south, more up their street.

23 VALLE DE LAS PIRÁMIDES

See page 407

Over twenty adobe pyramids built by a pre-Inca civilization surround a sacred mountain at Túcume in the northern deserts.

24 LAS LÍNEAS DE NAZCA

See page 131

Take a flight to fully appreciate these intricate symbols, etched into the deserts of southern Peru.

25 TRUJILLO

See page 350

Though it doesn't attract the hype of Lima or Cusco, Peru's third city charms with its colonial architecture and cosmopolitan atmosphere.

Itineraries

First-time visitors will inevitably try to fit in most of the major sites of the south; for those with ample time on their hands, the northern circuit offers an offbeat array of destinations to suit all tastes. You could also base an entire trip around keeping your adrenaline count high, from scaling Andean peaks, to rafting rapids or surfing the waves.

THE GRAND TOUR

Taking in the main attractions of the capital, Lima, and the highlights of southern Peru, this tour can be covered in just over two weeks, but could very easily absorb an extra week or two, especially if you add on a jungle excursion.

❶ **Lima** Spend a couple of days exploring the city's colonial centre, its museums and art galleries, making pit-stops in its lively bars, cafés and high-quality restaurant scene. See page 54

❷ **Paracas and the Islas Ballestas** A few hours south of Lima, this beachside area offers boat trips to islands of penguins and sea lions, great beaches, desert scenery, a scattering of pre-Inca sites and fine seafood. See page 115

❸ **Nazca** Located in an attractive desert valley, Nazca sits next to a huge plain on which an ancient civilization etched enormous animal figures, as well as geometric shapes and perfectly straight lines. See page 132

❹ **Arequipa and canyon country** Arequipa is a stunning city with a colonial heart, built of white volcanic stone. The rugged regions around the city offer access to two of the world's deepest canyons – Colca and Cotahuasi. See page 154

❺ **Puno and Lago Titicaca** One of the most desolate yet scenic corners of Peru, Puno sits at the edge of the enormous Lago Titicaca. Take in its lively and vibrant music and festivals scene, and visit the lake's peaceful islands. See page 188

❻ **Cusco** Capital of the Inca Empire, Cusco today embodies outdoor activities, great dining, lively nightlife and craft shopping as much as it does ancient history. See page 204

❼ **Reserva Nacional Tambopata** By taking a short return flight from Cusco to Puerto Maldonado, you're only a couple of hours' boat ride away from the jungle lodges and spectacular wildlife in this tropical reserve. See page 444

❽ **Machu Picchu** Easily accessible from Cusco, this magnificent Inca citadel makes a fitting culmination to any trip. See page 255

THE NORTHERN CIRCUIT

The main focus of the little-visited north is beaches and surfing, coastal archeology and a chain of ancient mountain citadels and tombs, with the option of a jungle trip tagged on for those with more than two weeks to spare.

❶ **Máncora and the beaches** Máncora is the trendy focus of several fabulous sandy beaches – all good for surfing, fishing and diving, as well as Cabo Blanco and Lobitas further south. See page 417

❷ **The Mochica Trail** The ancient Mochica civilization developed an important centre around the Huacas del Sol y de la Luna (see page 363) and is also in evidence at the richly endowed tombs of El Señor de Sipán and the Valle de las Pirámides. See page 407

3 **Ventanillas de Otuzco** A huge pre-Inca necropolis of *ventanillas* (windows) where Cajamarca chieftains were once buried in niches cut into volcanic rock. See page 380

❹ **Cajamarca to Chachapoyas bus ride** If you fancy a hairy adventure – with sick bags included – take the bus from Cajamarca to Chachapoyas, an epic twelve-hour journey along knife-edge single track roads edged by plunging mountain valleys. See page 385

❺ **Chachapoyas and Kuélap** Inland and high up in the northern Andes, the Chachapoyas region abounds in waterfalls, cliff-bound mausoleums and little-explored trails and is home to Kuélap, a mountain citadel with 20m-high walls. See pages 384 and 390

❻ **Into the Amazon Basin** Escape into the jungle with a yoga or ayahuasca retreat, go hummingbird spotting with a birdwatching tour or travel as far as Reserva Nacional Pacaya-Samiria or Iquitos for a taste of the Peruvian rainforest. See page 430

ADVENTURE ACTIVITY CIRCUIT

Peru is an adventure-holiday destination par excellence, with countless mountain routes to trek, bike or ride across, rivers to raft down and waves to surf. What follows is a small selection for an action-packed three weeks.

❶ **Cusco and around** Base yourself in Cusco and book an adrenaline-filled four-day rafting and camping trip down the Río Apurímac, finishing off with a soak in the hot springs of Cconoc. See page 204

❷ **Into the Valle Sagrado** Heading out from Cusco into the Valle Sagrado, you can whizz along ziplines, go bungee jumping or take on one of the challenging multi-day hikes to Machu Picchu. See page 235

❸ **Huaraz** Fly to Lima, where you can stop off for a spot of paragliding before heading north by bus to Huaraz, the springboard for exploring some of Peru's highest mountains. See page 312

❹ **Into the Cordillera Blanca** Mountain-bike the scenic Callejón de Huaylas, canoe the rapids of the Río Santa before climbing one of the snow-capped peaks of the Cordillera Blanca. See page 324

❺ **Playa Chicama** A day's bus ride further north takes you to Playa Chicama, one of the country's top surf spots, featuring the world's longest left-breaking wave. See page 372

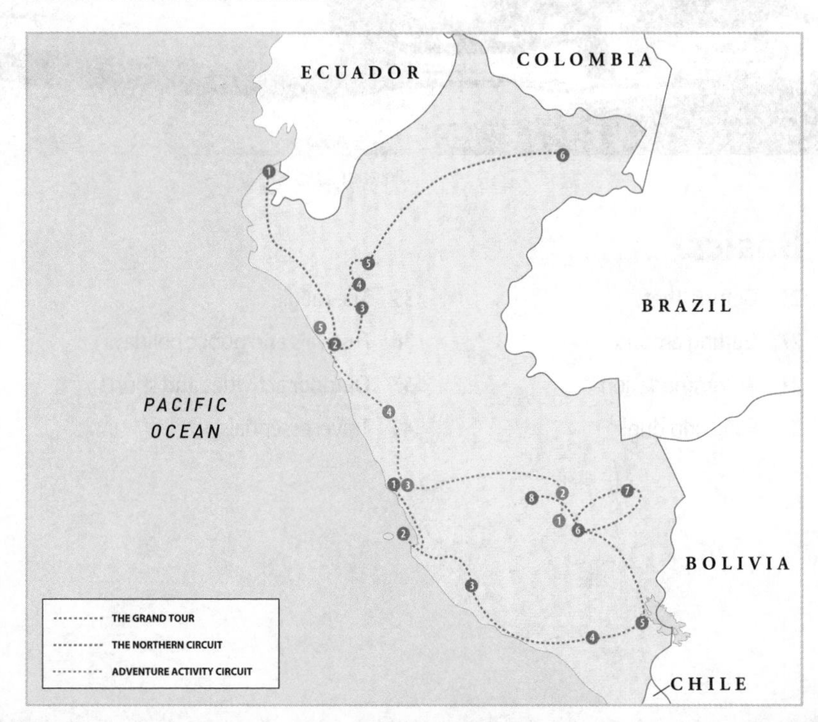

BUS IN THE ANDES

Basics

Getting there

Unless you're travelling overland through South America, you'll need to fly to reach Peru. Although prices vary depending on the time of year, how far in advance you buy and the type of ticket, the main airlines seem to hold fares fairly steady and tickets can easily be bought online. Apart from Christmas and to a lesser extent Easter, high season is roughly from late May to early October.

You can sometimes cut costs by going through a specialist **flight or travel agent**, who, in addition to dealing with discounted flights, will occasionally also offer special student and youth fares and a range of other travel-related services such as insurance, car rental, tours and the like.

Most people arrive at Jorge Chávez airport in Lima (see page 78). There's an airport hotel (T 017 112 00, W ramada.com), but it's a fair distance to downtown areas of Lima – Miraflores, San Isidro, Barranco – or even the old Lima Centro. A taxi to downtown Lima takes 35 to 55 minutes (S/55). Inside the airport is the official Taxi Green service (W taxigreen.com.pe). It is strongly advised to use this service and not take one of the local taxis outside the airport, which have a reputation for robbing passengers. Alternatively, use the safe new bus transfer to Miraflores (W airportexpress.com).

Flights from the UK

As there are no **direct flights** from the UK to Peru, getting there always involves switching planes somewhere in Europe or America. From Heathrow you can expect the journey to take anywhere between 16 and 22 hours, depending on the routing and stopovers. The permutations are endless, but the most common routes are **via Amsterdam** or **Paris** on KLM (W klm.com), **via Madrid** on Iberia (W iberia.com), **via Frankfurt** on Lufthansa (W lufthansa.com) or **via Miami**, **Atlanta**, **Dallas, Houston** or **Toronto** on one of the North American airlines.

Fares (usually £500–1100) vary almost as much as route options, and the closer to departure you buy, the higher the price is likely to be, so it is worth **booking in advance**. KLM and Iberia tend to offer the most competitive rates.

There's also a wide range of **limitations** on the tickets (fixed-date returns within three months etc), and options such as "open-jaw" flights are available (flying into Lima and home from Río, for example). Having established the going rate, you can always check these prices against those on offer at **discount flight outlets** and other travel agents listed in the press.

It's best to avoid buying international air tickets in Peru, where prices are inflated by a **high tax** (and are not cheap to begin with). If you're uncertain of your return date, it will probably still work out cheaper to pay the extra for an **open-ended return** than to buy a single back from Peru.

Flights from the US and Canada

Nearly all flights to Peru from the US go **via Miami**, **Houston or Atlanta**. Delta (W delta.com), and American Airlines (W aa.com) are the traditional carriers serving Peru from the US. A number of airlines fly from Miami to Lima, including American, Copa (W copaair.com), Avianca (W avianca.com) and LATAM (W latam.com); the fare is usually US$600–1000 return. Fares **from New York** (via Miami) cost no more than fares from Miami.

Flights **from Toronto** straight to Lima start at about Can$800 with LATAM (W latam.com); it can be a little cheaper when flying from Montréal via Toronto.

There is a huge variety of **tours and packages** on offer from the US and Canada to Peru, starting from around US$1500 for a two- to three-day package and ranging up to US$4000–5000. You'll also find a number of packages that include Peru on their itineraries as part of a longer **South American tour**.

Flights from Australia, New Zealand and South Africa

Scheduled flights to Peru from Australia and New Zealand are rather limited and tend to involve changing planes, usually in the US.

LATAM (W latam.com) flies **from Sydney** to Lima via Auckland, Miami, or Santiago de Chile, while Delta (W delta.com) flies from Sydney to Lima via the US; Air Canada flies via Montréal and Toronto; the cheapest tickets for any of these starts at about Aus$2200. American Airlines (W aa.com) flies regularly **from Melbourne** via Sydney and the US (stopovers available) with fares starting a bit higher at about Aus$2800.

Air New Zealand (W airnewzealand.com) flies to LA **from Auckland and Wellington** but has no specific connections to Peru. Qantas (W qantas.com.au) has flights from Auckland to Santiago de Chile

A BETTER KIND OF TRAVEL

At Rough Guides we are passionately committed to travel. We believe it helps us understand the world we live in and the people we share it with – and of course tourism is vital to many developing economies. But the scale of modern tourism has also damaged some places irreparably, and climate change is accelerated by most forms of transport, especially flying. All Rough Guides' flights are carbon-offset.

from where there are connecting flights to Lima; prices start from about NZ$1600. **Round-the-world (RTW)** tickets including Peru are usually a good investment.

All flights from South Africa to Lima involve making connecting flights. Lufthansa flies from Johannesburg to Frankfurt where there's a change for Lima flights via São Paulo, or with COPA Airlines, New York or Panama City (around ZAR15,000). South African Airways (W flysaa.com) flies to Lima from Cape Town via Johannesburg, with a changeover in São Paulo (ZAR9500–22,000).

Buses from neighbouring countries

Peru shares borders with five other South American countries: Brazil, Ecuador, Colombia, Bolivia and Chile. **From Brazil**, you can drive directly into Peru via Puerto Maldonado on the Transoceanic Highway; Puerto Maldonado is just two to three hours out from the border.

Arriving in southern Peru **from Bolivia** entails catching a bus, either directly or in stages, from La Paz across the altiplano to Copacabana or Desaguadero, both near Lago Titicaca, and on to Puno, or even straight through to Cusco, though this last option is taxing. **From Chile** it's a similarly easy bus ride, across the southern border from Arica to Tacna, which has good connections with Lima and Arequipa.

From Ecuador, there are two routes, the most popular being a scenic coastal trip, starting by road from Huaquillas, crossing the border at Aguas Verdes and then taking a short bus or taxi ride on to Tumbes, from where there are daily buses and flights to Chiclayo, Trujillo and Lima. An alternative – and also rather scenic – crossing comes into Peru from Macará in Ecuador over the frontier to La Tina, from where there are daily buses to Peru's coast.

Boats from neighbouring countries

It's possible to take a boat ride up the Amazon from the **three-way frontier** between Brazil, Colombia and Peru (see page 480) to Iquitos. This is a twelve-hour to three-day ride depending on the type of boat. **From Leticia**, just over on the Colombian side of the three-way frontier, there are speedboats up the Río Amazonas more or less daily to Iquitos. Taking the slow boat is usually a memorable experience – you'll need a hammock (unless you book one of the few cabins) and plenty of reading material.

AGENTS AND OPERATORS

Adventure tours or customized packages are often good value, but always check in advance exactly what's included in the price. Other specialist companies organize **treks** and **overland travel**, often based around some special interest, such as the rainforest, birdwatching, indigenous culture or Inca sites.

Abercrombie & Kent UK T 01242 386 500, W abercrombiekent.co.uk. With long-established contacts with the best authentic and luxury hotels and specialists in everything from art to archeology, A&K also offers a "guardian angel" service out of Cusco on customized trips, which means someone is on hand 24/7 for any requests, big or small.

Adventure Associates Australia T 02 6355 23022, W adventureassociates.com. Tours and cruises to Central and South America, including Peruvian Amazon river cruises.

Adventure Travel New Zealand T 0800 269 000 or T 04 494 7180, W adventuretravel.co.nz. Off-the-beaten path treks to Machu Picchu, tours around Lago Titicaca, food tours of Lima, as well as family trips and adventures by bike and kayak.

Adventure World Australia T 1 300 295 049, W adventureworld.com.au. Agents for a vast array of international adventure travel companies that operate trips to every continent, with near a dozen options for Peru.

Backroads US T 1 800 462 2848 or T 510 527 1555, W backroads.com. Cycling, hiking and multi-sport tour offerings including Cusco/Machu Picchu.

Classic Journeys US T 1 800 200 3887, W classicjourneys.com. Offers cultural walking adventures and family trips to Machu Picchu.

Dragoman UK T 01728 888 081, W dragoman.com. Extended overland journeys in expedition vehicles through the Americas, covering Machu Picchu, Titicaca, Arequipa, Colca, Nazca and other sites in Peru.

Exodus UK T 0203 553 6321, W exodus.co.uk. Adventure-tour operators taking small groups on tours to South America, usually incorporating Peru's main destinations. They also provide specialist programmes including adventure, activity and walking trips.

Explore Worldwide UK ⓣ 01252 883 505, ⓦ explore.co.uk. Big range of small-group tours, treks and expeditions on all continents, including the Amazon, Cusco and Lago Titicaca areas of Peru.

Mountain Travel Sobek US ⓣ 1 888 831 7526, ⓦ mtsobek.com. Hiking, river-rafting and trekking in Peru.

Nature Expeditions International ⓣ 1 877 659 7520 or ⓣ 954 693 8852, ⓦ naturexp.com. Offers luxury wildlife, adventure and cultural tours in 35 countries around the world.

North South Travel UK ⓣ 01245 608 291, ⓦ northsouthtravel.co.uk. Friendly, competitive travel agency, offering discounted fares worldwide. Profits are used to support projects in the developing world, especially the promotion of sustainable tourism.

On the Go Tours UK ⓣ 020 7371 1113, ⓦ onthegotours.com. Eight- to 21-day tours in Peru; highlights include treks to Machu Picchu and the Amazon.

Overseas Adventure Travel US ⓣ 1 800 995 1925, ⓦ oattravel.com. Offers a wide variety of adventure trips around the planet, including some South American combinations, like Machu Picchu and the Galápagos. Good for solo travellers, with no or low single supplements.

Peru For Less US ⓣ 1 877 269 0309 or ⓣ 1 817 230 4971, UK ⓣ 0203 002 0571; ⓦ peruforless.com. Specializes in travellers who seek worry-free, fully customizable tours and services combined with personalized attention from their Peru tour experts – budget, luxury or boutique.

Real World UK ⓣ 0113 2625329, ⓦ realworldholidays.co.uk. South America specialists providing personalized tours of Peru for individuals, couples and small groups. As well as visits to the usual suspects, they have good and up-to-date local knowledge to help you get off the beaten track.

Select Latin America UK ⓣ 020 7407 1478, ⓦ selectlatinamerica.co.uk. Specializes in bespoke journeys to all parts of Peru, including Huaraz, the northern coast and Iquitos, with meticulous planning. Good rates for small boutique accommodation and local guides that are experts in culture, wildlife, archeology or birdwatching.

STA Travel UK ⓣ 0333 321 0099, US ⓣ 1 800 781 4040, Australia ⓣ 134 782, New Zealand ⓣ 0800 474 400, South Africa ⓣ 0861 781 781; ⓦ statravel.co.uk. Worldwide specialists in independent travel; also student IDs, travel insurance, car rental, rail passes and more. Good discounts for students and under-26s.

The Surf Travel Co Australia ⓣ 02 9222 8870; ⓦ surftravel.com.au. Packages and advice for catching the waves (or snow) in the Pacific region, including main sites on the Peruvian coastline such as Chicama, Pacasmayo and Punta Huanchaco.

Trailfinders UK ⓣ 0207 368 1200, Republic of Ireland ⓣ 01 677 7888; ⓦ trailfinders.com. One of the best-informed and most efficient agents for independent travellers.

Travel CUTS Canada ⓣ 1 800 667 2887, ⓦ travelcuts.com. Canadian youth and student travel firm with a twenty-day Peru option.

USIT Republic of Ireland ⓣ 01 602 1906, Australia ⓣ 1 800 092 499; ⓦ usit.ie. Ireland's main student and youth travel specialists.

World Expeditions Australia ⓣ 02 8270 8400 or ⓣ 02 8631 3300, New Zealand ⓣ 09 368 4161, UK ⓣ 0800 0744 135 or ⓣ 020 8875 5060, US/Canada ⓣ 1 800 567 2216 or Canada ⓣ 1 613 241 2700; ⓦ worldexpeditions.com. Adventure company offering several programmes focused on the Peruvian jungle.

Getting around

With distances in Peru being so vast, many Peruvians and other travellers are increasingly flying to their destinations, as all Peruvian cities are within a two-hour flight of Lima. Most Peruvians, however, still get around the country by bus, a cheap way to travel with routes to almost everywhere. In a few cases, it's possible to arrive by train – an interesting and sought-after experience itself – though these trips are considerably slower than the equivalent bus journeys.

By plane

There's a good **domestic air service** in Peru these days. Some places in the jungle can only sensibly be reached by plane, and Peru is so vast that the odd flight can save a lot of time. There are three main established airline companies: LATAM (ⓦ latam.com), a Chilean-owned company, which flies to all of the main cities and many smaller destinations; StarPerú (ⓦ starperu.com), a Peruvian airline that began operating in 2005; and Avianca (ⓦ avianca.com). More recently, Peruvian Airlines (ⓦ peruvian.pe) has set up to compete with these three, along with Bolivian-run Amaszonas (ⓦ amaszonas.com) and Andes Air (ⓦ andesair-corp.com).

Most tickets for all these domestic airlines can be booked and bought online as well as from travel agents or airline offices in all major towns. The most popular domestic routes cost upwards of S/215 (US$80) and are generally cheaper if booked well in advance. In high season some Lima–Cusco flights are fully booked months in advance. Less busy routes tend to be less expensive per air mile

ADDRESSES

Addresses are frequently written with just the street name and number: for example, Pizarro 135. Officially, though, they're usually prefixed by Calle, Jirón or Avenida (abbreviated to C, Jr and Av in listings throughout this guidebook). The **first digit** of any street number (or sometimes the first two digits) represents the block number within the street as a whole. Note that in Cusco some streets have two street names in order to honour Inca/Quechua heritage – the official Spanish name and an Inca/Quechua equivalent. This is not, however, a challenge for foreigners as the default names are still the official ones.

and can be booked the day before. On all flights it's probably wise to **confirm your booking** two days before departure.

Flights are often cancelled or delayed, and sometimes they even leave earlier than scheduled – especially in the jungle where the weather can be a problem. If a passenger hasn't shown up **an hour before the flight**, the company may give the seat to someone on the waiting list, so it's best to be on time whether you're booked or are merely hopeful. The luggage allowance on internal flights can range from 10 to 16kg, so pack lightly.

Note that there is a "gringo tax" on internal flights. The cheapest fares offered by Avianca ("Promo" and "Econo") and LATAM for Lima to Cusco, for example, are for Peruvians only, but it isn't always obvious. You may be charged up to US$170 at the airport if you can't show papers to prove that you are a Peruvian resident. Make sure you read the small print carefully before purchasing your ticket.

By bus

Peru's **buses** are run by a variety of private companies, all of which offer remarkably low fares, making it possible to travel from one end of the country to the other (over 2000km) for under US$35. Long-distance bus journeys cost from around US$2 per hour on the fast coastal highway, and are even cheaper on the slower mountain and jungle routes. The condition of the buses ranges from the efficient and relatively luxurious Cruz del Sur fleet that runs along the coast, to the older, more battered buses used on local runs throughout the country. Some of the better bus companies, including Cruz del Sur (W cruzdelsur.com.pe), offer excellent onboard facilities including sandwich bars and video entertainment. The major companies generally offer two or three levels of service, and many companies run the longer journeys by night with a **bus-cama** (comfortable, deeply reclining seat) option. Cruz del Sur operates an excellent website with timetables and ticket purchase option (credit cards accepted). Oltursa (W oltursa.pe) and Movil Tours (W moviltours.com.pe) are also reputable companies, and have services to most major destinations throughout the country.

As the only means of transport available to most of the population, buses run with surprising regularity, and the coastal Panamerican Highway and many of the main routes into the mountains have now been paved (one of ex-President Fujimori's better legacies), so on such routes services are generally **punctual**. On some of the rougher mountainous routes, punctures, arguments over rights of way and, during the rainy season, landslides may delay the arrival time by several hours.

Peru is investing in a series of **terminal terrestres**, or *terrapuertos*, centralizing the departure and arrival of the manifold operators. Lima does not have this facility and, in any case, you should always double-check where the bus is leaving from as some companies operate from their individual terminals around town. If you can't get to a bus depot or *terminal terrestre*, you can try to catch a bus from the exit roads or **police checkpoints** on the outskirts of most Peruvian cities, though there's no guarantee of getting a ride or a seat.

For intercity rides, it's best to **buy tickets in advance** direct from the bus company offices; for local trips, you can buy tickets on the bus itself. On long-distance journeys, try to avoid getting seats right over the jarring wheels, especially if the bus is tackling mountain or jungle roads.

By taxi

Taxis can be found anywhere at any time in almost every town. Any car can become a taxi simply by sticking a taxi sign up in the front window; a lot of people, especially in Lima, take advantage of this to supplement their income, although beware – robberies in illegal taxis are not unheard of, and it's certainly not advisable to use them, especially if you're a single female traveller. It's always best to call a reliable taxi company (your hotel or restaurant can do so for you). Whenever you get into a taxi, always fix the price in advance (in nuevo soles rather than in

US dollars) since few of them have **meters**. Taxi drivers in Peru do not expect **tips**.

Relatively short journeys in **Lima** generally cost around S/5–10 (US$2–4), but it's cheaper elsewhere in the country. Radio taxis, minicabs and airport taxis tend to cost more. Even relatively long taxi rides in Lima are likely to cost less than S/20 (US$7), except to and from the airport, which ranges from S/35 to S/55 (US$10–21); prices depend on how far across the city you're going and how bad the traffic is.

By mototaxi

In many rural towns, you'll find small cars – mainly motorcycle rickshaws, known variously as **mototaxis**, all competing for customers. They are cheap, starting at S/1 for short rides, if slightly dangerous and not that comfortable, especially if there's more than two of you or if you've got a lot of luggage. In a rural town, you might find normal car taxis (eg Toyotas) and mototaxis competing for business; a ride across town might cost S/5–8 in a normal taxi but only S/2–3 in a mototaxi.

By colectivo

Colectivos (shared taxis) are a very useful way of getting around that's peculiar to Peru. They connect all the coastal towns, and many of the larger centres in the mountains. Like the buses, many are ageing imports from the US – huge old Dodge Coronets – though, increasingly, fast new Japanese and Korean minibuses run between the cities.

Colectivos tend to be faster than the bus, though they are often as much as twice the price. Most **colectivo cars** manage to squeeze in about seven people including the driver (three in the front and four in the back), and can be found in the centre of a town or at major stopping places along the main roads. If more than one is ready to leave it's worth bargaining a little, as the price is often negotiable. **Colectivo minibuses**, also known as combis, can squeeze in twice as many people, or often more.

In the cities, colectivos have an appalling reputation for **safety**. There are crashes reported in the Lima press every week, mostly caused by the highly competitive nature of the business. There are so many combis covering the same major arterial routes in Lima that they literally race each other to be the first to the next street corner. They frequently crash, turn over and knock down pedestrians. Equally dangerous is the fact that the driver is in such a hurry that he does not always wait for you to get in. If you're not careful he'll pull away while you've still got a foot on the pavement, putting you in serious danger of breaking a leg.

By train

Peru's spectacular **train journeys** are in themselves a major attraction, and you should aim to take at least one long-distance train ride during your trip, especially as the trains connect some of Peru's major tourist sights. At the time of writing, the **Central Railway**, which climbs and switchbacks its way up from Lima into the Andes as far as Huancayo on the world's highest standard-gauge tracks, only runs about twice a month between April and September (see page 283).

There are two rail companies operating out of Cusco. PeruRail (W perurail.com) offers passenger services inland from Puno on Lago Titicaca north to Cusco, from where another line heads out down the magnificent Urubamba Valley as far as Machu Picchu Pueblo. On the Cusco-to-Machu Picchu line there is also Inca Rail (W incarail.com).

The trains move slowly, allowing ample time to observe what's going on outside. For all train journeys, it's advisable to buy **tickets** a week or two before travelling and even further in advance during high season.

By car

Driving around Peru is generally not a problem outside of Lima, and allows you to see some out-of-the-way places that you might otherwise miss. However, road traffic in Lima is abominable, both in terms of its recklessness and the sheer volume. Traffic jams are ubiquitous between 8 and 10am and again between 4 and 7pm every weekday, while air pollution from old and poorly maintained vehicles is a real health risk, particularly in Lima and Arequipa.

If you bring a car into Peru that is not registered there, you will need to show (and keep with you at all times) a **libreta de pago por la aduana** (proof of customs payment) normally provided by the relevant automobile association of the country you are coming from. **Spare parts**, particularly tyres, should be carried, along with a tent, emergency water and food. The chance of **theft** is quite high – the vehicle, your baggage and accessories are all vulnerable when parked.

International driving licences are valid for six months in Peru, after which a permit is required from the Touring y Automóvil Club del Perú, Av Trinidad Moran 698, Lince, Lima (Mon–Fri 8.30am–5.30pm, Sat 9am–1pm; ⓣ01 611 9999, ⓦtouring-peru.com.pe).

Renting a car costs much the same as in Europe and North America. The major rental firms all have offices in Lima, but outside the capital you'll generally find only local companies are represented. You may find it more convenient to rent a car in advance online – expect to pay from around US$40 a day, or US$200 a week for the smallest car. In the Amazon cities it's usually possible to rent **motorbikes** or **mopeds** by the hour or by the day: this is a good way of getting to know a town or being able to shoot off into the jungle for a day.

By boat

There are no coastal **boat services** in Peru, but in many areas – on Lago Titicaca and especially in the jungle regions – water is the obvious means of getting around. From Puno, on Lago Titicaca, there are currently no regular services to Bolivia by ship or hydrofoil – though check with the tour agencies in Puno – but there are plenty of smaller boats that will take visitors out to the various islands in the lake. These aren't expensive and a price can usually be negotiated down at the port.

In the jungle areas **motorized boats** come in two basic forms: those covered speedboats with individual seats and a large outboard motor (*deslizadores/rápidos*) and those uncovered narrow wooden dugout canoes with a slow, noisy **peque-peque** engine; the outboard is faster and more manoeuvrable, but they cost a lot more to run. Your best option is to **hire a canoe** along with its guide/driver for a few days. This means searching around in the port and negotiating, but you can often get a *peque-peque* canoe from around S/150–240 (US$50–80) per day, which will invariably work out cheaper than taking an organized tour, as well as giving you a choice of guide and companions. Obviously, the more people you can get together, the cheaper it will be per person.

Lanchas, the plodding cargo boats that ply the Amazon a few times a week between the major ports, are cheap (some of them even include meals in the ticket price) and take a few days. Iquitos boats travel to Pucallpa and Yurimaguas, others connect the Colombian/Brazilian border with Peru and Manaus, Brazil.

On foot

Even if you've no intention of doing any serious hiking, there's a good deal of walking involved in checking out many of the most enjoyable Peruvian attractions. Climbing from Cusco up to the fortress of Sacsayhuaman, for example, or wandering around at Machu Picchu, involves more than an average Sunday afternoon stroll. Bearing in mind the rugged terrain throughout Peru, the absolute minimum **footwear** is a strong pair of running shoes. Much better is a pair of hiking boots with good ankle support.

Hiking – whether in the desert, mountains or jungle – can be an enormously rewarding experience, but you should go properly equipped and bear in mind a few of the **potential hazards**. Never stray too far without food and water, and keep something warm and something waterproof to wear. The weather is renowned for its dramatic changeability, especially in the mountains, where there is always the additional danger of altitude sickness. In the jungle the biggest danger is getting lost.

In the mountains it's often advisable to hire a **pack animal** to carry your gear. Llamas can only carry about 25–30kg and move slowly; a *burro* (donkey) carries around 80kg and a mule – the most common and the best pack animal – will shift 150kg with relative ease. Mules can be hired at about S/90 a day, and they normally come with an *arriero*, a muleteer who'll double as a guide. It is also possible to hire mules or horses for **riding** but this costs a little more. With a guide and beast of burden it's quite simple to reach even the most remote valleys, ruins and mountain passes, travelling in much the same way as Pizarro and his men did over four hundred years ago.

Hitching

Hitching in Peru usually means catching a ride with a truck driver, who will almost always expect payment. Always agree on a price before getting in as there are stories of drivers stopping in the middle of nowhere and demanding unreasonably high amounts (from foreigners and Peruvians alike) before going any further. Hitching isn't considered dangerous in Peru, but having said that, few people, even Peruvians, actually hitch. Trucks can be flagged down anywhere but there is greater choice around markets, and at police controls or petrol stations on the outskirts of towns. **Trucks** tend to be the only form of public transport in some less accessible regions, travelling the roads that buses won't touch and serving remote communities, so you may end up having to sit on top of a pile of potatoes or bananas.

Hitchhiking in **private cars** is not recommended, and, in any case, it's very rare that one will stop to pick you up.

Organized tours

There are hundreds of **travel agents** and **tour operators** in Peru, and reps hunt out customers at bus terminals, train stations and in city centres. While they can be expensive, **organized excursions** can be a quick and relatively effortless way to see some of the popular attractions and the more remote sites, while a prearranged trek of something like the Inca Trail can take much of the worry out of camping preparations and ensure that you get decent campsites, a sound meal and help with carrying your equipment in what can be difficult walking conditions.

Many **adventure tour companies** offer excellent and increasingly exciting packages and itineraries – ranging from mountain biking, whitewater rafting, jungle photo-safaris, mountain trekking and climbing, to more comfortable and gentler city and countryside tours. Tours cost US$60–300 a day and, in Cusco and Huaraz in particular, there's an enormous selection of operators to choose from (note that most tour operators in Peru charge in US dollars). **Cusco** is a pretty good base for hiking, whitewater rafting, canoeing, horseriding or going on an expedition into the Amazonian jungle with an adventure tour company; **Arequipa** and the **Cañón del Colca** offer superb hiking; **Huaraz** is also a good base for trekking and mountaineering; **Iquitos**, on the Río Amazonas, is one of the best places for adventure trips into the jungle and has a reasonable range of tour operators. Several of these companies have branches in Lima, if you want to book a tour in advance. Reliable tour operators are listed in the relevant sections throughout the Guide.

Accommodation

Peru has the typical range of Latin American accommodation, from top-class international hotels at prices to compare with any Western capital down to basic rooms or shared dorms in hostels. The biggest development over the last ten years has been the rise of the mid-range option, reflecting the growth of both domestic and international tourism. Camping is frequently possible, sometimes free and perfectly acceptable in most rural parts of Peru, though there are very few formal campsites.

Note that accommodation denominations of hotel, *hostal*, *residencial*, *pensión* or *hospedaje* are almost meaningless in terms of what you'll find inside. Virtually all upmarket accommodation will call itself a **hotel** or, in the countryside regions, a **posada**. In the jungle, **tambo lodges** can be anything from somewhere quite luxurious to an open-sided, palm-thatched hut with space for slinging a hammock. Technically speaking, somewhere that calls itself a **pensión** or **residencial** ought to specialize in longer-term accommodation, and while they may well offer discounts for stays of a week or more, they are just as geared up for short stays. There's no standard or widely used **rating system**, so, apart from the information given in this book, the only way to tell whether a place is suitable or not is to walk in and take a look around – the proprietors won't mind this, and you'll soon get used to spotting places with promise.

Many of the major hotels will request a **credit card number** to reserve rooms in advance; be careful, since if you fail to turn up they may consider this a "no-show" and charge you for the room anyhow. Always check beforehand whether the quoted price includes **IGV tax** (as a tourist, if you register your passport and tourist card with the hotel, they don't charge you this tax, which is currently eighteen percent). It's not advisable to pay **travel agents** in one city for accommodation required in the next town; by all means ask agents to make reservations but do not ask them to send payments as it is always simpler and safer to do that yourself.

The **prices** quoted for accommodation throughout the Guide are for the **cheapest double room in high season**, except where noted, and usually include breakfast and wi-fi; prices are always per night, even if there's a minimum stay.

Hotels

Peru's cheaper **hotels** are generally old – sometimes beautifully so, converted from colonial mansions with rooms grouped around a courtyard. They tend to be within a few blocks of a

ACCOMMODATION ALTERNATIVES

These useful websites provide some often interesting alternatives to standard hotel and hostel accommodation:

CouchSurfing couchsurfing.org.

Vacation Rentals by Owner vrbo.com.

Airbnb airbnb.com.

town's central plaza, general market or bus or train station. For a night in a no-frills place, expect to pay around S/60.

You can find a good, clean single or double room in a **mid-range hotel** (generally three-star), with a private bathroom, towels and hot water, for S/75–180 (US$25–60). Quality hotels, not necessarily five-star, but with good service, truly comfortable rooms and maybe a pool or some other additional facility, can be found in all the larger Peruvian resorts as well as some surprisingly offbeat ones. Out of season some are relatively inexpensive, at S/150–250 (US$50–80).

There are quite a few **five-star hotels** in Peru (usually costing upwards of S/800 or US$265 for a double room), nearly all in Lima, Arequipa, Cusco, Trujillo and Iquitos. Even **four-star hotels** (S/530–800 or US$160–265) offer excellent service, some fine restaurants and very comfortable rooms with well-stocked minibars.

A little haggling is often worth a try, and if you find one room too pricey, another, perhaps very similar, can often be found for less: the phrase "Tiene un cuarto más barato?" ("Do you have a cheaper room?") is useful. Savings can invariably be made, too, by **sharing rooms** – many have two, three, even four or five beds. A double-bedded room ("con cama matrimonial") is usually cheaper than a twin ("doble" or "con dos camas").

Hostels

Not to be confused with "hostales" which are simple guesthouses, most of Peru's **hostels** are unaffiliated to Hostelling International (see hihostels.com or hostellingperu.com.pe), though there are dozens spread throughout Peru, including in Arequipa, Cusco, Iquitos, Lima, Puno, Tumbes and Trujillo. Most of the hostels that are linked to Hostelling International don't bother to check that you are a member, but if you want to be on the safe side, you can visit one of Peru's issuing offices in Lima, Cusco, Máncora or Arequipa (see hostellingperu.com.pe/socio_en.html).

While not the standardized institution found in Europe, Peru's hostels are relatively cheap and reliable; expect to pay S/21–30 (US$7–10) for a bed (the most expensive ones are in Lima and Cusco). All hostels are theoretically open 24 hours a day and most have cheap cafeterias attached. They are always great places to meet up with other travellers and tend to have a party scene of their own.

Camping

Camping is possible almost everywhere in Peru, and it's rarely difficult to find space for a tent; since there are only one or two organized campsites in the whole country (costing between S/10–15 per person), it's also largely free. Moreover, camping is the most satisfactory way of seeing Peru, as some of the country's most fantastic destinations are well off the beaten track: with a tent – or a hammock – it's possible to go all over without worrying if you'll make it to a hostel.

It's usually okay to set up camp in the fields or forest beyond the outskirts of settlements, but ask **permission** and advice from the nearest farm or house first. Apart from a few restricted areas, Peru's enormous sandy coastline is open territory, the real problem not being so much where to camp as how to get there; some of the most stunning areas are very remote. The same can be said of both the mountains and the jungle – camp anywhere, but ask first, if you can find anyone to ask.

Reports of **robberies**, particularly along such popular routes as the Inca Trail, are not uncommon, so travelling with someone else or in groups is always a good idea. There are a few basic precautions that you can take: let someone know where you intend to go; be respectful, and try to communicate with any locals you may meet or who you are camping near (but be careful who you make friends with en route).

Standard **camping equipment** is easy to find in Peru, but good-quality gear can be difficult to obtain. Several places sell, rent or buy second-hand gear, mainly in Cusco, Arequipa and Huaraz, and there are some reasonably good, if quite expensive, shops in Lima. It's also worth checking the noticeboards in the popular travellers' hotels and bars for equipment that is no longer needed or for people seeking trekking companions. Camping Gaz butane canisters are available from most of the above shops and from some *ferreterías* (hardware stores) in the major resorts. A couple of essential things you'll need when camping in Peru are a mosquito net and repellent, and some sort of water treatment system.

Food and drink

Peruvian cuisine is rated among the best in the world and is currently experiencing a period of flourishing self-confidence and great popularity overseas. The country's chefs are adept at creating innovative new fusions with its fantastic wealth of food products, most of which are indigenous.

As with almost every activity, the style and pattern of eating and drinking varies considerably between the three main regions of Peru. The food in each area, though it varies depending on the availability of different regional ingredients, is essentially a *mestizo* creation, combining indigenous cooking with four hundred years of European – mostly Spanish – influence.

Guinea pig (*cuy*) is the traditional dish most associated with Peru, and you can find it in many parts of the country, especially in the mountain regions, where it is likely to be roasted in an oven and served with chips. It's likely however, that you may encounter more burgers and pizza than guinea pig, given that fast food has spread quickly in Peru over the past two decades.

Snacks and light meals

All over Peru, but particularly in the large towns and cities, you'll find a wide variety of traditional **fast foods** and snacks such as *salchipapas* (chips with sliced sausage covered in various sauces), *anticuchos* (a shish kebab made from marinated lamb or beef heart) and empanadas (meat- or cheese-filled pies). These are all sold on street corners until late at night. Even in Peru's villages you'll find cafés and restaurants that double as bars, staying open all day and serving anything from coffee and bread to steak and chips, or even lobster. The most popular sweets in Peru are made from either *manjar blanco* (sweetened condensed milk) or fresh fruit.

In general, the **market** is always a good place to stock up – you can buy food ready to eat on the spot or to take away and prepare – and the range and prices are better than in any shop. Most food prices are fixed, but the vendor may throw in an orange, a bit of garlic or some coriander leaves for good measure. Smoked meat, which can be sliced up and used like salami, is normally a good buy.

Restaurants

All larger towns in Peru have a fair choice of **restaurants**, most of which offer a varied menu. Among them there are usually a few **Chinese** (*chifa*) places, and nowadays a fair number of **vegetarian** restaurants too. Most establishments in larger towns stay open daily from around 11am until 11pm, though in smaller settlements they may close one day a week, usually Sunday. Often they will offer a **set menu**, from morning through to lunchtime, and another in the evening. Ranging in price from S/10 to S/25, these most commonly consist of three or four courses: soup or other starter, a main dish (usually hot and with rice or salad), a small sweet or fruit-based third plate, plus tea or coffee to follow. Every town, too, seems now to have at least one restaurant that specializes in *pollo a la brasa* – spit-roasted chicken.

Seafood

Along the coast, not surprisingly, **seafood** is the speciality; the Humboldt Current keeps the Pacific Ocean off Peru extremely rich in plankton and other microscopic life forms, which attract a wide variety of fish. **Ceviche** is the classic Peruvian seafood dish and has been eaten by locals for over two thousand years. It consists of fish, shrimp, scallops or squid, or a mixture of all four, marinated in lime juice and chilli peppers, then served "raw" with corn, sweet potato and onions. *Ceviche de lenguado* (sole) and

TIPPING

In budget or average restaurants **tipping** is normal, though not obligatory and you should rarely expect to give more than about ten percent. In fancier places you may well find a **service charge** of at least ten percent as well as a **tax** of eighteen percent (IGV) added to the bill. In restaurants and *peñas* where there's live music or performances a **cover charge** is generally also applied and can be as high as US$5 a head. Even without a performance, additional cover charges of around US$1 are sometimes levied in the flashier restaurants in major town centres.

ceviche de corvina (sea bass) are among the most common, but there are plenty of other fish and a wide range of seafood is utilized on most menus. You can find ceviche, along with fried fish and fish soups, in most restaurants along the coast from S/15–25.

Escabeche is another tasty fish-based appetizer, this time incorporating peppers and finely chopped onions. The coast is also an excellent place for eating **scallops** – known here as *conchitas* – which grow particularly well close to the Peruvian shoreline; *conchas negras* (black scallops) are a delicacy in the northern tip of Peru. Excellent **salads** are also widely available, such as *huevos a la rusa* (egg salad), *palta rellena* (stuffed avocado), or a straight tomato salad, while *papas a la Huancaína* (a cold appetizer of potatoes covered in a spicy, light cheese sauce) is great too.

Mountain food

Mountain food is fairly basic – a staple of potatoes and rice with the meat stretched as far as it will go. *Lomo saltado*, or sliced prime beef sautéed with onions and peppers, is served everywhere, accompanied by rice and French fries. A delicious snack from street vendors and cafés is *papa rellena*, a potato stuffed with vegetables and fried. **Trout** is also widely available, as are cheese, ham and egg sandwiches. *Chicha*, a **corn beer** drunk throughout the sierra region and on the coast in rural areas, is very cheap with a pleasantly tangy taste. Another Peruvian speciality is **pachamanca**, a roast prepared mainly in the mountains but also on the coast by digging a large hole, filling it with meats and vegetables, thereafter placing stones and lighting a fire over them, then using the hot stones to cook a wide variety of tasty meats and vegetables.

Jungle food

Jungle food is quite different from food in the rest of the country. **Bananas** and **plantains** figure highly, along with *yuca* (a tuber rather like a yam), rice and plenty of fish. There is **meat** as well – mostly chicken supplemented occasionally by **game** (deer, wild pig or even monkey). Every settlement big enough to get on the map has its own bar or café, but in remote areas it's a matter of eating what's available and drinking coffee or bottled drinks if you don't relish the home-made *masato* (cassava beer).

Drinking

Beer, wines and spirits are served in almost every bar, café or restaurant at any time, but there is a **deposit** on taking beer bottles away from a shop (canned beer is one of the worst inventions to hit Peru in recent years – some of the finest beaches are littered with empty cans).

Nonalcoholic drinks

Soft drinks range from mineral water, through the ubiquitous Coca-Cola and Fanta, to home-produced favourites like the gold-coloured Inka Cola, with rather a home-made taste, and the very sweet Cola Inglesa. **Fruit juices** (*jugos*), most commonly papaya or orange, are delicious and prepared fresh in most places (the best selection and cheapest prices are generally available in a town's main market), and you can get **coffee** and a wide variety of herb and leaf **teas** almost anywhere. Surprisingly, for a good coffee-growing country, the coffee in cafés outside Lima, Cusco and Arequipa leaves much to be desired, commonly prepared from either *café pasado* (previously percolated coffee mixed with hot water to serve) or simple powdered Nescafé. Increasingly it's possible to find great coffee in larger towns where certain cafés prepare good fresh espresso, cappuccino or filtered coffee. *Starbucks* (complete with wi-fi) can be found in several of Peru's cities and is everywhere you turn in Lima.

Beer and wine

Most **Peruvian beer** – except for *cerveza malta* (black malt beer) – is bottled lager almost exclusively brewed to five percent alcohol content, and extremely good. Traditional Peruvian beers include Cristal, Pilsen and Cusqueña (the last, originating from Cusco, is generally preferred, and has even reached some UK supermarkets in recent years). In Trujillo on the north coast, they drink Trujillana beer, again quite similar; and in Arequipa they tend to drink Arequipeña beer. There are several new lager beers now on the market, including the Brazilian brand Brahma. Peru has been producing **wine** (*vino*) for over four hundred years. Among the better ones are Vista Alegre (the Tipo Familiar label is generally OK) – not entirely reliable but only around S/8 a bottle – and, much better, Tabernero or Tacama Gran Vino Reserva (white or red) from about S/30–45 a bottle. A good Argentinian or Chilean wine will cost from US$15 upwards.

Spirits

As for **spirits**, Peru's main claim to fame is **pisco**. This is a white-grape brandy with a unique, powerful and very palatable flavour – the closest equivalent elsewhere is probably tequila. Almost anything else is available as an import – Scotch **whisky** is cheaper here than in the UK, but beware of the really cheap whisky imitations or blends bottled outside Scotland which can remove the roof of your mouth with ease. The jungle regions produce a sugar-cane rum, **cashassa** (basically the Peruvian equivalent of Brazilian *cachaça*), also called *aguardiente*, which has a distinctive taste and is occasionally mixed with different herbs, some medicinal. While it goes down easily, it's incredibly strong stuff and is sure to leave you with a hangover the next morning if you drink too much.

The media

English language, or non-Spanish, magazines and newspapers are hard to find in Peru; some are available in Miraflores, Lima, and they can occasionally be found in airports or bookshops in Cusco. BBC World Service and VOA can be picked up if you have the right receiver.

There are many poor-quality newspapers and magazines available on the streets of Lima and throughout the rest of Peru. Many of the **newspapers** stick mainly to sex and sport, while **magazines** tend to focus on terrorism, violence and the frequent deaths caused by major traffic accidents. Meanwhile, many get their news and information from **television** and **radio**, where you also must wade through the panoply of entertainment-oriented options.

Newspapers and magazines

The two most established (and establishment) **daily newspapers** are *El Comercio* (Ⓦ elcomercio.pe) and *Expreso* (Ⓦ expreso.com.pe), the latter having traditionally devoted vast amounts of space to anti-Communist propaganda. *El Comercio* is much more balanced but still tends to toe the political party of the day's line. *El Comercio*'s daily *Seccion C* also has the most comprehensive cultural listings of any paper – good for just about everything going on in Lima. In addition, there's the sensationalist tabloid *La República* (Ⓦ larepublica.pe), which takes a middle-of-the-road to liberal approach to politics; and *Diario Ojo* (Ⓦ ojo.pe), which provides interesting tabloid reading.

International newspapers are fairly hard to come by; your best bet for English papers is to go to the British Embassy in Lima (see page 96), which has a selection of one- to two-week-old papers, such as *The Times* and *The Independent*, for reference only. US papers are easier to find; the bookstalls around Plaza San Martín in Lima Centro and those along Avenida Larco and Diagonal in Miraflores sell *The Miami Herald*, the *International Herald Tribune*, and *Newsweek* and *Time* magazines, but even these are likely to be four or five days old.

One of the better weekly **magazines** is the fairly liberal *Caretas* (Ⓦ caretas.com.pe), generally offering mildly critical support to whichever government happens to be in power.

Television and radio

Peruvians watch a lot of **television** – mostly football and soap operas, though TV is also a main source of news. Many programmes come from Mexico, Brazil and the US, with occasional eccentric selections from elsewhere and a growing presence of manga-style cartoons. There are nine main terrestrial channels; the government-run channel 7 has the most cultural and educational content. **Cable and satellite TV** is increasingly forming an important part of Peru's media, partly due to the fact that it can be received in even the remotest of settlements.

Alternatively, you can tune in to **Peruvian radio stations**, nearly all of which play music and are crammed with adverts. International pop, salsa and other Latin pop can be picked up most times of the day and night all along the FM wave band, while traditional Peruvian and Andean folk music can usually be found all over the AM dial. Radio Moda (97.3FM) mainly plays latino and reggaeton; Radio Planeta (107.7FM) plays rock and pop in English while Studio 92 (92.5FM) plays popular hits from rap to latino; RPP Noticias (89.7FM) and Radio Capital (96.7FM) are best for the news, while Radio Felicidad (88.9FM) and Radio Mágica (88.3FM) play old school 70s and 80s tracks. A useful website is Ⓦ radios.com.pe.

Festivals and public holidays

Public holidays, Carnival and local fiestas are all big events in Peru, celebrated with an openness and gusto that gives them enormous appeal for visitors; note that everything shuts down, including banks, post offices, information offices, tourist sites and museums. The main national holidays take place over Easter, Christmas and during the month of October, in that order of importance. It is worth planning a little in advance to make sure that you don't get caught out.

In addition to the major regional and national celebrations, nearly every community has its own saint or patron figure to honour at town or **village fiestas**. These celebrations often mean a great deal to local people, and can be much more fun to visit than the larger countrywide events. Processions, music, dancing in costumes and eating and drinking form the core activities of these parties. In some cases the villagers will enact **symbolic dramas,** and in the hills around towns like Huaraz and Cusco, especially, it's quite common to stumble into a village fiesta, with its explosion of human energy and noise, bright colours and a mixture of pagan and Catholic symbolism.

Such celebrations are very much **local affairs**, and while the occasional traveller will almost certainly be welcomed with great warmth, none of these remote communities would want to be invaded by tourists waving cameras and expecting to be feasted for free. The dates given below are therefore only for established events that are already on the tourist map, and for those that take place all over the country.

PUBLIC HOLIDAYS

Jan 1 New Year's Day.

March/April Easter; Semana Santa (Holy Week). Maundy Thursday and Good Friday are national holidays, Easter Monday is not.

May 1 Labour Day.

July 28–29 National Independence Day. Public holiday with military and school processions.

Oct 8 Anniversary of Battle of Angamos.

Nov 1–2 All Saints' Day, and Day of the Dead (All Souls' Day).

Dec 8 Immaculate Conception.

Dec 25 Christmas Day.

FESTIVALS

Feb Carnaval. Wildly celebrated immediately prior to Lent, throughout the whole country.

Feb 2 Virgen de la Candelaria. Celebrated in the most spectacular way in Puno (known as the folklore capital of the country) with a week of colourful processions and dancing.

March/April Semana Santa (Holy Week). Superb processions all over Peru (the best are in Cusco and Ayacucho), the biggest being on Good Friday and Easter Saturday night.

Late May/early June Q'oyllor Riti. One of the most breathtaking festivals in Peru; thousands of people make the overnight pilgrimage up to Apu Ausangate, a shrine located on a glacier just outside of Cusco.

Early June Corpus Christi. Takes place nine weeks after Maundy Thursday and involves colourful processions with saints carried around on floats and much feasting. Particularly lively in Cusco.

June 24 Inti Raymi (Winter Solstice). Cusco's main Inca festival, Inti Raymi – Quecha for "resurrection of the sun" – is based on an Inca ritual, and one of the largest festivals in all South America, drawing visitors from the world over. Meant to welcome the sun god and request his next return, the event is celebrated in the fortress of Sacsayhuaman (see page 217).

June 29 St Peter's Day. Fiestas in all the fishing villages along the coast.

July 15–18 Virgen del Carmen. Celebrated in style in the town of Paucartambo, on the road between Cusco and Reserva Biósfera del Manu. Dancers come from surrounding villages as Spanish colonists, wearing ugly blue-eyed masks and long beards for the celebration. There's a smaller celebration in the Valle Sagrado town of Pisac.

Aug 13–19 Arequipa Week. Processions, firework displays, plenty of folklore dancing and craft markets in Arequipa.

Aug 30 Santa Rosa de Lima. The city of Lima stops for the day to worship its patron saint, Santa Rosa.

Late Sept Spring Festival. Trujillo festival involving dancing, especially the local *marinera* dance and popular Peruvian waltzes.

Oct 18–28 Lord of Miracles. Festival featuring large and solemn processions (the main ones take place on Oct 18, 19 & 28); many women wear purple.

Nov 1–7 Puno Festival. Celebrates the founding of Puno by the Spanish and of the Inca Empire by Manco Capac. Particularly colourful dancing on the fifth day.

TOP 5 TREKS

Ausangate See page 268
The Chiquián Loop See page 341
Choquequirao See page 266
The Inca Trail See page 251
The Llanganuco-to-Quebrada Santa Cruz Loop See page 332

Outdoor activities and sports

Few of the world's countries can offer anything remotely as varied, rugged and stunningly beautiful as Peru when it comes to ecotourism, trekking, mountain biking and river rafting. Apart from possessing extensive areas of wilderness, Peru has the highest tropical mountain range in the world, plus the Amazon rainforest and a long Pacific coastline, all offering different opportunities for outdoor activities and adventure. Football is Peru's sport of passion, closely followed by women's volleyball; they field a remarkably good team, often contending at the very top international levels. Bullfighting has a strong heritage both in Lima and small Andean villages.

Trekking and climbing

The most popular areas for **trekking and climbing** are: north and south of Cusco; the Cañón del Colca; and the Cordillera Blanca. But there are many other equally biodiverse and culturally rich trekking routes in other *departamentos*: Cajamarca and Chachapoyas both possess challenging but rewarding mountain trekking, and the desert coast, too, has exceptional and unique eco-niches that are most easily explored from Lima, Trujillo, Chiclayo, Nazca, Pisco, Ica and Arequipa, cities which have some tourism infrastructure to support visits.

The main tours, treks and climbs have been listed throughout the Guide in their appropriate geographical context. Chapter Six, which includes Huaraz and the Cordillera Blanca, contains further information on climbing, mountaineering and trekking in the Andes, or **Andinismo**, as it's long been known. The Cusco and Arequipa chapters also contain extensive listings of tour and trek operators as well as camping and climbing equipment rental.

TREKKING AND CLIMBING INFORMATION

Regional trekking resources can also be found in the relevant chapters of the Guide.

Asociación de Guías de Montaña del Peru (AGMP) Parque Ginebra 28-G Ancash, Huaraz (T 043 421811, W agmp.pe). Base

A WALK ON THE WILD SIDE: COMMUNITY-BASED TOURISM AND ECOTOURISM IN PERU

Peru's Ministry of Culture and Tourism (MINCETUR) is making **community-based tourism** (*turismo rural comunitario*) a priority through 2025. This covers a wide range of activities, but generally this pertains to tourism experiences specifically run by and for the benefit of local villages and families, often indigenous ones. The heart of some CBT programmes lies in homestays of one or a couple of days (*turismo vivencial*) whereby the visitor gets to truly experience what a villager's typical day is like, and may involve chores, working on traditional handicrafts, or preparing meals; other options may involve standalone activities like building a new (simple) lodging. iPerú offices and municipal tourist desks can usually provide a list of participating communities with contact persons; the programme is particularly strong around Cusco, Arequipa and Puno, but there may be options for areas such as Uros and the Cañón del Colca as well. You can check out the site W turismoruralcomunitario.com.pe but note that the English version is not always accessible.

Ecotourism is most developed in the Amazon rainforest region of Peru, particularly around Manu, which is considered one of the most biodiverse regions on Earth; Iquitos in the northern jungle and the Tambopata region around Puerto Maldonado are similar ecotourism hotspots. These areas, and others in Peru's extensive rainforest, all support a wide choice of operators leading tours up various rivers to **jungle lodges**, which themselves function as bases from which to explore the forest on foot and in smaller, quieter canoes. Naturally, the focus is on wildlife and flora; but there are often **cultural elements** to tours, including short visits to riverside communities and indigenous villages, and sometimes even mystical or healing work with jungle shamans. Prices vary and so does the level of service and accommodation, as well as the degree of sustainability of the operation.

Ecotourism is very much alive in the Peruvian **Andes** too, with several tour operators offering expeditions on foot or on horseback into some of the more exotic high-Andes and cloud-forest regions.

NATIONAL PARKS AND RESERVES

Almost ten percent of Peru is incorporated into some form of **protected area**, including fourteen national parks, fifteen national reserves, nine national sanctuaries, four historical sanctuaries, twelve reserved zones, six buffer forests, two hunting reserves and an assortment of communal reserves and national forests.

The largest accessible protected area is the **Reserva Nacional Pacaya-Samiria**, an incredible tropical forest region in northern Peru. This is closely followed in size by the **Reserva Biósfera del Manu** , another vast and stunning jungle area, and the **Reserva Nacional Tambopata–Candamo and Parque Nacional Bahuaja-Sonene**, again an Amazon area, with possibly the richest flora and fauna of any region on the planet. Smaller but just as fascinating to visit are the **Parque Nacional Huascarán** in the high Andes near Huaraz, a popular trekking and climbing region, and the less-visited **Reserva Nacional Pampas Galeras**, close to Nazca, which was established mainly to protect the dwindling but precious herds of *vicuña*, the smallest and most beautiful member of the South American camelid family.

Bear in mind that the parks and reserves are enormous zones, within which there is hardly any attempt to control or organize nature. The term "park" probably conveys the wrong impression about these huge, virtually untouched areas, which were designated by the **National System for Conservation Units (SNCU)**, with the aim of combining conservation, research and, in some cases (such as the Inca Trail) recreational tourism.

In December 1992, the **Peruvian National Trust Fund for Parks and Protected Areas (PROFONANPE)** was established as a trust fund managed by the private sector to provide funding for Peru's main protected areas. It has assistance from the Peruvian government, national and international non-governmental organizations, the World Bank Global Environment Facility and the United Nations Environment Program.

VISITING THE PARKS

There's usually a small **charge** (usually around S/30 a day) to visit the national parks or nature reserves; this is normally levied at a reception hut on entry to the particular protected area. Sometimes, as at the Parque Nacional Huascarán, the cost is a simple daily rate (1 day S/10; 2 days S/65 includes camping fee); at others, like the Reserva Nacional Paracas on the coast south of Pisco, you pay a fixed sum to enter (S/10), regardless of how many days you might stay. The fee was significantly increased for 2018, for all parks, to S/30 for one day, S/60 for two or three days, or S/150 for entry for four days or more. For really remote protected areas, like Pacaya-Samiria, or if for some reason you enter an area via an unusual route, it is best to check on permissions – for Pacaya-Samiria you can pay the fee within the reserve itself. Most frequently visited National Parks will have an official hut for registration and payment of entry fees. For details, check with the protected areas national agency **SERNANP** at C Diecisiete 355, Urb El Palomar, San Isidro, Lima (T 01 717 7500, W sernanp.gob.pe) or at the local tourist office.

for the Huaraz and Cordillera Blanca mountain guides association (see page 328).

Club de Montañismo Camycam W camycam.org. A well-run, reliable mountain climbing organization set up in 1994.

Club de Andinismo de la Universidad de Lima Av Javier Prado Este, Lima 33 T 01 348 0086, W ulima.edu.pe/departamento/vida-deportiva-ulima/andinismo. Peru's leading mountaineering club.

Canoeing and whitewater rafting

Peru is hard to beat for **canoeing** and **whitewater rafting**. The rivers around Cusco and the Cañón del Colca, as well as Huaraz and, nearer to Lima, at Lunahuana, can be exciting and demanding, though there are always sections ideal for beginners. **Cusco** is one of the top rafting and canoeing centres in South America, with easy access to a whole range of river grades, from II to V on the Río Urubamba (shifting up grades in the rainy season) to the most dangerous white-water on the Río Apurímac (level VI). On the Río Vilcanota, some 90km south of Cusco, at Chukikahuana, there's a 5km section of river that, between December and April, offers constant level-V rapids. One of the most amazing trips from Cusco goes right down into the **Amazon Basin**. It should be noted that these rivers can be very wild and the best canoeing spots are often very remote, so you should only attempt river running with reputable companies and knowledgeable local guides.

The main companies operating in this field are listed in the relevant chapters. Trips range from half-day excursions to several days of river adventure, sometimes encompassing both mountain and jungle terrain. **Transport, food and accommodation** are generally included in the price where relevant; but the costs also depend on levels of service and whether overnight accommodation is required.

Cycling

In Peru, **cycling** is a major sport, as well as one of the most ubiquitous forms of transport available to all classes in towns and rural areas virtually everywhere. Consequently, there are bike shops and bicycle-repair workshops in all major cities and larger towns. Perhaps more importantly, a number of tour companies offer **guided cycling tours,** which can be an excellent way to see the best of Peru. Huaraz and Cusco are both popular destinations for bikers. Perhaps the first stop for information is the quite comprehensive site for Cicloturismo Peru (Ⓦcicloturismoperu.com), home to details not only on bike rentals and tours, but also shops, events, maps, heart rate calculator, moon calendar and emergency road assistance. For additional information contact the Federación Peruana de Ciclismo, Av San Luis 1308, Villa Deportiva La Videna, San Luis, Lima Centro (Ⓣ01 346 3493, Ⓦfedepeci.org).

Surfing

People have been **surfing** the waves off the coast of Peru for thousands of years and the traditional *caballitos de totora* (cigar-shaped ocean-going reed rafts) from the Huanchaco and Chiclayo beach areas of Peru are still used by fishermen who ride the surf daily. Every year around twelve thousand surfers come to Peru whose best beaches – Chicama, Cabo Blanco, Punta Rocas – rival those of Hawaii and Brazil. Good websites to find out more about the scene include: Ⓦperusurfguides.com, Ⓦperuecosurf.com and Ⓦvivamancora.com/english/surf.htm.

Diving and fishing

For information on **diving** and **fishing** contact the Spondylus dive school, with offices in Máncora (Av Piura 216 Ⓣ01 7349 6932) and Lima (C Grimaldo del Solar 238, Miraflores Ⓣ01 478 7151); they offer courses and info on nearby beach accomodation as well. Aquasport, Conquistadores 805, San Isidro, Lima (Ⓣ01 221 1548) or Av República de Panamá 505 in Barranco (Ⓣ01 207 2560 ext 105), Ⓦaquasport.pe), stocks a good range of watersports gear.

Football

Peru's major sport is **football** and you'll find men and boys playing it in the streets of every city, town and settlement in the country down to the most remote of jungle outposts. The big teams are **Cristal**, **Alianza** and **El U** in Lima and **Ciencianco** from Cusco. The "Classic" game is between Alianza, the poor man's team from the La Victoria suburb of Lima, and El U ("U" from "Universitario"), generally supported by the middle class. To get a flavour for just how popular football is in Peru try a visit to the *Estadio Restaurant* in Lima (see page 86), which has great murals, classic team shirts and life-size models of the world's top players.

Volleyball

Volleyball (*vóley*) is a very popular sport in Peru, particularly the women's game. The national team frequently reaches World Cup and Olympic finals, and they are followed avidly on TV. Even in remote villages, most schools have girls' volleyball teams. For more information, check out Ⓦvivevoley.com.

Birding

The **birding** community looks on Peru as one of the top three destinations in the world, due to avian population density and the country's amazing diversity in terms of geography and topography, with more than 1700 species living here. The Reserva Biósfera del Manu – home to nearly one thousand species on its own – and the Tambopata and Pacaya-Samiria reserves, are fine locations to start from. Peru Birding Tours (Ⓣ01 994 996 309, Ⓦperubirdingtours.com), established in 2010, has a full calendar of multi-day birding trips all over the Peruvian map (and has expanded into other South American countries). Kolibri Expeditions (Ⓣ01 652 7689, Ⓦkolibriexpeditions.com) has more offerings of shorter duration (some just a day); these are listed on Birding Peru (Ⓦbirding-peru.com), which contains a 2000-bird strong directory with location notes, and hundreds of photographs as well.

Bullfighting

Although **bullfighting** is rightly under threat from the pro-animal lobby, and has diminished significantly in popularity in the twenty-first century, in many coastal and mountain haciendas (estates), organized bullfights are still often held at fiesta times. In a less formal way they happen at many of the village fiestas, too – often with the bull being left to run through the village until it's eventually caught and mutilated by one of the men. This is not just a sad, upsetting sight, it can also be dangerous for unsuspecting tourists who happen to wander into a seemingly evacuated village. The Lima bullfights in October (see page 68), in contrast, are a very serious business; even Hemingway was impressed.

Travel essentials

Costs

Peru is certainly a much **cheaper** place to visit than Europe or the US, but how much so will depend on where you are and when. As a general rule low-budget travellers should – with care – be able to get by on around S/45–120/US$15–40/£10–26/€13–34 per day, including transport, board and lodging. If you intend staying in mid-range hotels, eating in reasonable restaurants and taking the odd taxi, S/150–270/US$50–90/£33–60/€42–77 a day should be adequate, while S/300–600/US$100–200/£65–130/€85–170 a day will allow you to stay in comfort and sample some of Peru's best cuisine.

In most places in Peru, a good **meal** can still be found for under S/25 (US$8.50), **transport** is very reasonable, a comfortable **double room** costs S/60–180 (US$20–60) a night, and **camping** is usually free, or under S/15 (US$5) per person. Expect to pay a little more in the larger towns and cities, especially Cusco and Lima, and also in the jungle, as many supplies have to be imported by truck. In the villages and rural towns, on the other hand, some basic commodities are far cheaper and it's always possible to buy food at a reasonable price from local villages or markets.

In the more popular parts of Peru, costs vary considerably with the **seasons**. Cusco, for instance, has its best weather from June to August, when many of its hotel prices go up by around 25–50 percent. The same thing happens at **fiesta** times – although on such occasions you're unlikely to resent it too much. As always, if you're travelling alone you'll end up spending considerably more than you would in a group of two or more people.

Tipping (see page 33) is expected in restaurants (ten percent) and upmarket hotels, but not in taxis.

BARGAINING

You are generally expected to **bargain** in markets and with taxi drivers (before getting in). Nevertheless, it's worth bearing in mind that travellers from Europe, North America and Australasia are generally much wealthier than Peruvians, so for every penny or cent you knock them down they stand to lose plenty of nuevo soles. It's sometimes possible to haggle over the price of hotel rooms, especially if you're travelling in a group. Food, except at markets, and shop prices, however, tend to be fixed.

Student and youth discounts

It's also worth taking along an international **youth/student ID card**, if you have one, for the occasional reduction (up to fifty percent at some museums and sites). Cards generally cost US$20–25, but, once obtained, they soon pay for themselves in savings. Full-time students are eligible for the International Student ID Card (ISIC) or ITIC, Youth, VIP, YHA or Nomads card, most of which entitle the bearer to special air, rail and bus fares and discounts at museums, theatres and other attractions. For US citizens there's also a **health benefit**, as you can purchase low-cost travel insurance coverage, which includes emergency medical and hospital coverage, plus a 24-hour hotline to call in the event of a medical, legal or financial emergency.

You only have to be 26 or younger to qualify for the International Youth Travel Card, which carries the same benefits. Teachers qualify for the International Teacher Card, offering similar discounts. All these cards are available in the UK, US, Canada and South Africa from STA (W statravel.com) and from Hostelling International (W hihostels.com) in Australia and New Zealand. Several other travel organizations and accommodation groups also sell their own cards, good for various discounts.

Crime and personal safety

The biggest problem for travellers in Peru is arguably **theft**, for which the country once had a bad reputation. While Peruvian pickpockets are remarkably ingenious, as far as violent attacks go, you're probably safer here than in the backstreets of Miami, Sydney, Durban or London; nevertheless, muggings do happen in certain parts of Lima (eg in the main shopping areas, La Victoria district, Barranco late at night and even occasionally in the parks of Miraflores), Cusco, Arequipa and, to a lesser extent, Trujillo.

Theft

While the overall situation has improved, **robbery** and **pickpocketing** are still real dangers; although you don't need to be in a permanent state of paranoia and watchfulness in busy public situations, common sense and general alertness are still recommended. Generally speaking, **thieves** (*ladrones*) work in teams of often **smartly dressed** young men and women, in crowded markets, bus depots and train stations, targeting anyone who looks like they've got money. One of them will distract your attention (an old woman falling over in front of you or someone splattering an ice cream down your jacket) while another picks your pocket, cuts open your bag with a razor or simply runs off with it. Peruvians and tourists alike have even had earrings ripped out on the street.

Bank **ATMs** are a target for **muggers** in cities, particularly after dark, so visit them with a friend or two during daylight hours or make sure there's a policeman within visual contact. **Armed mugging** is rare but does happen in Lima, and it's best not to resist. The horrific practice of "strangle mugging" has been a bit of a problem in Cusco and Arequipa, usually involving night attacks when the perpetrator tries to strangle the victim into unconsciousness. Again, be careful not to walk down badly lit streets alone in the early hours.

Theft from cars and even more so, theft of car parts, is rife, particularly in Lima. Also, in some of the more popular **hotels** in the large cities, especially Lima, bandits masquerading as policemen break into rooms and steal the guests' most valuable possessions while holding the hotel staff at gunpoint. Objects left on restaurant floors in busy parts of town, or in unlocked hotel rooms, are obviously liable to take a walk.

Precautions

You'd need to spend the whole time visibly guarding your luggage to be sure of keeping hold of it; even then, though, a determined team of thieves will stand a chance. However, a few simple **precautions** can make life a lot easier. The most important is to keep your ticket, passport, travellers' cheques and , money on your person at all times (under your pillow while sleeping and on your person when washing in communal hotel bathrooms). **Money belts** are great for travellers' cheques and tickets, or a holder for your passport and money can be hung either under a shirt or from a belt under trousers or skirts. Some people go as far as lining their bags with chicken wire (called *maya* in Peru) to make them knife-proof, and wrapping wire around camera straps for the same reason (putting their necks in danger to save their cameras).

Cities are most dangerous in the early hours of the morning and at **bus or train stations** where there's lots of anonymous activity. In rural areas robberies tend to be linked to the most popular towns (again, be most careful at the bus depot) and treks (the Inca Trail for instance). Beyond that, **rural areas** are generally safe. If you're camping near a remote community, though, it's a good idea to ask permission and make friendly contact with some of the locals; letting them know what you are up to will usually dissolve any local paranoia about tomb-robbers or kidnappers.

The only certain precaution you can take is to **insure** your gear and cash before you go. Take refundable travellers' cheques, register your passport at your embassy in Lima on arrival (this doesn't take long and can save days should you lose it) and keep your eyes open at all times. If you do have something stolen, report it to the tourist police in larger towns, or the local police in more remote places, and ask them for a certified **denuncia** – this can take a couple of days. Many insurance companies will require a copy of the police *denuncia* in order to reimburse you. Bear in mind that the police in popular tourist spots, such as Cusco, have become much stricter about investigating reported thefts, after a spate of false claims by dishonest tourists. This means that genuine victims may be grilled more severely than expected, and the police may even come and search your hotel room for the "stolen" items.

Terrorism

You can get up-to-date information on the **terrorism** situation in each region from the Peruvian embassies abroad (see page 43) or your embassy in Lima (see page 96). Essentially, though, **terrorism** is not the problem it was during the 1980s and 1990s when the two main **terrorist groups** active in Peru were the Sendero Luminoso (the Shining Path) and Tupac Amaru (MRTA).

The police

Most of your contact with the **police** will, with any luck, be at frontiers and controls. Depending on your personal appearance and the prevailing political climate, the police at these posts (Guardia Nacional and Aduanas) may want to **search your luggage**. This happens rarely, but when it does, it can be very thorough. Occasionally, you may have to get off buses and **register documents** at the police controls which regulate the traffic of goods and people from one *departamento* of Peru to another. The controls are usually situated on the outskirts of large towns on the main roads, but you sometimes come across a control in the middle of nowhere. Always stop, and be scrupulously polite – even if it seems that they're trying to make things difficult for you.

In general the police rarely bother travellers but there are certain sore points. The possession of (let alone trafficking of) either soft or hard **drugs** (basically marijuana or cocaine) is considered an extremely serious offence in Peru – usually leading to at least a ten-year jail sentence. There are many foreigners languishing in Peruvian jails after being charged with possession, some of whom have been waiting two years for a trial – there is no bail for serious charges.

Drugs aside, the police tend to follow the media in suspecting all foreigners of being **political subversives** and even gun-runners or terrorists; it's more than a little unwise to carry any Maoist or **radical literature**. If you find yourself in a tight spot, don't make a statement before seeing someone from your embassy, and don't say anything without the services of a reliable translator. It's not unusual to be given the opportunity to pay a **bribe** to the police (or any other official for that matter), even if you've done nothing wrong. You'll have to weigh up this situation as it arises – but remember, in South America bribery is seen as an age-old custom, very much part of the culture rather than a nasty form of corruption, and it can work to the advantage of both parties, however irritating it might seem. It's also worth noting that all police are **armed** with either a revolver or a submachine gun and will shoot at anyone who runs.

Tourist police

It's often quite hard to spot the difference between **Policía de Turismo (tourist police)** and the normal police. Both are wings of the Guardia Civil, though the tourist police sometimes wear white hats rather than the standard green. Increasingly, the **tourist police** have taken on the function of informing and assisting tourists (eg in preparing a robbery report or *denuncia*) in city centres.

If you feel you've been ripped off or are unhappy about your treatment by a tour agent, hotel, restaurant, transport company, customs, immigration or even the police, you can call the 24-hour **Tourist Protection Service** hotline for the tourist police in Lima (☎01 423 3500 or free at ☎0800 22221, or at the airport, ☎01 517 1841). There are also **Policía de Turismo** offices throughout the country, including all major tourist destinations, such as Cusco, Arequipa and Puno.

Customs and etiquette

The most obvious cultural idiosyncrasy of Peruvians is that they **kiss** on one cheek at virtually every meeting between friends or acquaintances. In rural areas (as opposed to trendy beaches) the local tradition in most places is for people, particularly women, to **dress modestly** and cover themselves (eg longish skirts and T-shirts or blouses, or maybe traditional robes). In some hot places men may do manual labour in shorts, but they, too, are generally covered from shoulder to foot. Travellers sometimes suffer **insults** from Peruvians who begrudge the apparent relative wealth and freedom of tourists. Remember, however, that the terms "gringo" or "mister" are not generally meant in an offensive way in Peru.

Punctuality has improved in Peru in the last twenty years or so, but for social happenings can still be very lax. While buses, trains or planes won't wait a minute beyond their scheduled departure time, people almost expect friends to be an hour or more late for an appointment (don't arrange to meet a Peruvian on the street – make it a bar or café). Peruvians stipulate that an engagement is *a la hora inglesa* ("by English time") if they genuinely want people to arrive on time, or, more realistically, within half an hour of the time they fix.

Try to be aware of the strength of **religious belief** in Peru, particularly in the Andes, where churches have a rather heavy, sad atmosphere. You can enter and quietly look around all churches, but in the Andes especially you should remain respectful and refrain from taking photographs.

Electricity

220 volt/60 cycles AC is the standard **electrical current** all over Peru, except in Arequipa where it is 220 volt/50 cycles. In some of Lima's better hotels you may find 110 volt sockets to use with

standard electronic devices (though you'll need a converter for high-powered items like electric shavers). Don't count on any Peruvian power supply being one hundred percent reliable and, particularly in cheap hostels and hotels, be very wary of the wiring (especially in electric shower fittings).

Entry requirements

Currently, EU, US, Canadian, Australian, New Zealand and South African citizens can technically stay in Peru as tourists for up to 183 days without a visa. However, the situation does change periodically, so always check with your local Peruvian embassy some weeks before departure. Passports are typically stamped with a ninety-day allowance for visitors to stay in the country, though sometimes not; if you do plan for several weeks, make sure the official is aware of that fact. Extensions of this period are no longer given.

A Migraciones office is the place to sort out new visas if you've **lost your passport** (having visited your embassy first) and to get passports re-stamped.

Student visas (which last twelve months) are best organized as far in advance as possible through your country's embassy in Lima, your nearest Peruvian embassy or the relevant educational institution. **Business visas** only become necessary if you are to be paid by a Peruvian organization, in which case ask your Peruvian employers to get this for you.

PERUVIAN EMBASSIES AND CONSULATES

An up-to-date list of Peruvian diplomatic missions can be accessed in Spanish on Ⓦ rree.gob.pe.

AUSTRALIA

Peruvian Embassy 40 Brisbane Ave, 2nd floor, Office 1B, Barton 2606 ACT, Canberra Ⓣ 02 6273 7351, Ⓦ embaperu.org.au

Peruvian Consulate 157 Main St, Croydon, Melbourne Ⓣ 03 9725 4655, Ⓦ consulperuau.org.

Peruvian Consulate Suite 1001, 84 Pitt St, Sydney Ⓣ 02 9235 0300, Ⓦ consulperuau.org.

CANADA

Peruvian Embassy 1901–130 Albert St, Ottawa Ⓣ 613 233 2721.

NEW ZEALAND

Peruvian Embassy Level Eight, Cigna House, 40 Mercer St, Wellington Ⓣ 04 499 8087.

SOUTH AFRICA

Peruvian Consulate 200 Saint Patricks St, Muckleneuk Hill, Pretoria Ⓣ 012 440 1030.

UK

Peruvian Embassy 52 Sloane St, London SW1X 9SP Ⓣ 020 7235 1917.

US

Peruvian Embassy 1700 Massachusetts Ave NW, Washington, DC Ⓣ 202 833 9860.

Health

No inoculations are currently required for Peru, but a **yellow fever vaccination** is sometimes needed to enter the jungle, as well as being generally recommended. It's always advisable to check with the embassy or a reliable travel agent before you go. Your doctor will probably advise you to have some **inoculations** anyway: typhoid, cholera, rabies and, again, yellow fever shots are all sensible precautions, and it's well worth ensuring that your polio and tetanus-diphtheria boosters are still effective. Immunization against hepatitis A is also usually recommended.

In case you don't get your shots before you leave for Peru, there is a useful 24-hour vaccination service at the Sanidad de la Fuerza Aérea on the first floor of Jorge Chávez airport in Lima (Ⓣ 01 575 1745); remember to bring your passport as you will need to show it before getting the vaccination (S/85).

Yellow fever

Yellow fever breaks out now and again in some of the jungle areas of Peru; it is frequently obligatory to show an inoculation certificate when entering the Amazon region – if you can't show proof of immunization you'll be jabbed on the spot. This viral disease is transmitted by mosquitoes and can be fatal. Symptoms are headache, fever, abdominal pain and vomiting, and though victims may appear to recover, without medical help, they may suffer from bleeding, shock, and kidney and liver failure. The only treatment is to keep the patient's fever as low as possible and prevent dehydration.

Malaria

Malaria is quite common in Peru these days, particularly in the Amazon regions to the east of the country, and it's very easy to catch without prophylactics. If you intend to go into the jungle regions, malaria tablets should be taken – starting a few weeks before you arrive and continuing for some time after. Make sure you get a supply of these, or whatever is recommended by your doctor in advance of the trip. There are several commonly recommended malarial **prophylactics** recommended for the Peruvian jungle regions; some are more expensive than others and some are not recommended for prolonged periods. You should investigate your options with your GP, ideally more than a month prior to your departure for Peru. To avoid getting bitten in the rainforest wear long sleeves, long trousers, socks and a mosquito-proof net hat and sleep under good mosquito netting or in well-proofed quarters. For more information check out Ⓦcdc.gov/travel/regionalmalaria.

Dengue fever

Like malaria, **dengue fever** is another illness spread by mosquito bites; the symptoms are similar, plus aching bones. Dengue-carrying mosquitoes are particularly prevalent during the rainy season, with urban jungle areas often the worst affected; they fly during the day, so wear insect repellent in the daytime if mosquitoes are around. The only treatment is complete rest, with drugs to assuage the fever – unfortunately, a second infection can be fatal.

Diarrhoea

Diarrhoea is something everybody gets at some stage, and there's little to be done except to drink a lot of water and bide your time. You should also replace salts either by taking oral rehydration salts or by mixing a teaspoon of salt and eight teaspoons of sugar in a litre of purified water. You can minimize the risk by being sensible about what you eat, and by not drinking **tap water** anywhere. Peruvians are great believers in herbal teas, which often help alleviate cramps.

Dysentery and giardia

If your diarrhoea contains blood or mucus, the cause may be dysentery (one of either two strains; see below) or giardia. Combined with a fever, these symptoms could well be caused by **bacillic dysentery** and may clear up without treatment. If you're sure you need it, a course of antibiotics such as tetracyclin or ampicillin (travel with a supply if you are going off the beaten track for a while) should sort you out, but they also destroy "gut flora" which help protect you, so should only be used if properly diagnosed or in a desperate situation. Similar symptoms without fever indicate **amoebic dysentery**, which is much more serious, and can damage your gut if untreated. The usual cure is a course of metronidazole (Flagyl), an antibiotic which may itself make you feel ill, and should not be taken with alcohol.

Similar symptoms, plus rotten-egg-smelling belches and gas, indicate **giardia**, for which the treatment is again metronidazole. If you suspect you have any of these illnesses, seek medical help, and only start on the metronidazole (250mg three times daily for a week for adults) if there is definitely blood in your diarrhoea and it is impossible to see a doctor.

Water and food

Water in Peru is better than it used to be, but it can still trouble non-Peruvian (and even Peruvian) stomachs, so it's a good idea to only drink **bottled water** (*água mineral*), available in various sizes, including litre and two-litre bottles from most corner shops or food stores. Stick with known brands, even if they are more expensive, and always check that the seal on the bottle is intact, since the sale of bottles refilled with local water is not uncommon. Carbonated water is generally safer as it is more likely to be the genuine stuff. You should also clean your teeth using bottled water and avoid raw foods washed in local water.

Apart from bottled water, there are various methods of **treating water** while you are travelling, whether your source is tap water or natural groundwater such as a river or stream. **Boiling** is the time-honoured method, which is an effective way to sterilize water, although it will not remove any unpleasant tastes. A minimum boiling time of five minutes (longer at higher altitudes) is sufficient to kill microorganisms. In remote jungle areas, **sterilizing tablets** are a better idea, although they leave a rather bad taste in the mouth. Pregnant women or people with thyroid problems should consult their doctor before using iodine sterilizing tablets or iodine-based purifiers. There are also several portable **water filters** on the market. In emergencies and remote areas in particular, always check with locals to see whether the tap water is OK (*es potable?*) before drinking it.

Peruvian **food** cooked on the street has been frequently condemned as a health hazard, particularly during rare but recurrent **cholera outbreaks**. Be careful about anything bought from street stalls, particularly seafood, which may not be that fresh. **Salads** should be avoided, especially in small settlements where they may have been washed in river water or fertilized by local sewage waters.

The sun

The sun can be deceptively hot, particularly on the coast or when travelling in boats on jungle rivers when the hazy weather or cool breezes can put visitors off their guard; remember, **sunstroke** can make you very sick as well as burnt. Wide-brimmed hats, sunscreen lotions (factor 60 advisable since the sun high up in the Andes is deceptively strong) and staying in the shade whenever possible are all good precautions. Note that suntan lotion and sunblock are more expensive in Peru than they are at home, so take a good supply with you. If you do run out, you can buy Western brands at most *farmacias*, though you won't find a very wide choice available, especially in the higher factors. Also make sure that you increase your water intake, in order to prevent **dehydration**.

Altitude sickness

Altitude sickness – known as *soroche* (see page 207) in Peru – is a common problem for visitors, especially if you are travelling quickly between the coast or jungle regions and the high Andes. The best way to prevent it is to eat light meals, drink lots of coca tea and water and spend as long as possible acclimatizing to high altitudes (over 2500m) before carrying out any strenuous activity. Anyone who suffers from headaches or nausea should rest; more seriously, a sudden bad cough could be a sign of **pulmonary edema** and demands an immediate descent and medical attention – altitude sickness can kill. People often suffer from altitude sickness on trains crossing high passes; if this happens, don't panic, just rest and stay on the train until it descends. Most trains are equipped with oxygen bags or cylinders that are brought around by the conductor for anyone in need. **Diamox** is used by many from the US to counter the effects of *soroche*. It's best to bring this with you from home since it's rarely available in Peruvian pharmacies.

Insects

Insects are more of an irritation than a serious problem, but on the coast, in the jungle and to a lesser extent in the mountains, the **common fly** is a definite pest. Although flies can carry typhoid, there is little one can do; you might spend mealtimes swatting flies away from your plate but even in expensive restaurants it's difficult to monitor hygiene in the kitchens.

A more obvious problem is the **mosquito**, which in some parts of the lowland jungle carries malaria. Repellents are of limited value – it's better to cover your arms, legs and feet with a good layer of clothing. Mosquitoes tend to emerge after dark, but the daytime holds even worse biting insects in the jungle regions, among them the **manta blanca** (or white blanket), so called because they swarm as a blanket of tiny flying insects. Their bites don't hurt at the time but itch like crazy for a few days afterwards. **Antihistamine creams** or tablets can reduce the sting or itchiness of most insect bites, but try not to scratch them – if it gets unbearable go to the nearest *farmacia* for advice. To keep hotel rooms relatively insect-free, buy some of the spirals of incense-like **pyrethrin**, available cheaply everywhere.

HIV and AIDS

While Peru does not have as bad a reputation for **HIV** and **AIDS** (also known as **SIDA** in Latin America) as neighbouring Brazil, they are a growing problem in South America and you should still take care. All hospitals and clinics in Peru are supposed to use only sterilized equipment.

Contraception

Condoms *(profilacticos)* are available from street vendors and some *farmacias*. However, they tend to be expensive and often poor quality, so bring an adequate supply with you. **The Pill** is also available from *farmacias*, officially on prescription only, but frequently sold over the counter. You're unlikely to be able to match your brand, however, so it's far better to bring your own supply. It's worth remembering that if you suffer from moderately severe **diarrhoea** on your trip the Pill (or any other drug) may not be in your system long enough to take effect.

Pharmacies

For **minor ailments** you can buy most drugs at a pharmacy (*farmacia* or *botica)* without a prescription. Antibiotics and malaria pills can be bought over the counter (it is important to know the correct dosage), as can antihistamines (for bite allergies) or medication for an upset stomach (try Lomotil or Streptotriad). You can also buy Western-brand **tampons** at a *farmacia*, though they are expensive, so it's better to bring a good supply. For any serious illnesses, you should go to a doctor or hospital; these are listed throughout the Guide, or ask your hotel or the local tourist office for the best clinic around.

Alternative medicines

Alternative medicines have a popular history going back at least two thousand years in Peru and the traditional practitioners – *herbaleros, hueseros* and *curanderos* – are still commonplace. **Herbaleros** sell curative plants, herbs and charms in the streets and markets of most towns. They lay out a selection of ground roots, liquid tree barks, flowers, leaves and creams – all with specific medicinal functions and sold at much lower prices than in the *farmacias*. If told the symptoms, a *herbalero* can select remedies for most minor (and apparently some major) ailments. **Hueseros** are consultants who treat diseases and injuries by bone manipulation, while **curanderos** claim diagnostic, divinatory and healing powers, and have existed in Peru since pre-Inca days.

MEDICAL RESOURCES

UK AND IRELAND

Hospital for Tropical Diseases Travel Clinic ⊕ 0203 447 5999, ⊕ thehtd.org/travelclinic.aspx.
MASTA (Medical Advisory Service for Travellers Abroad) ⊕ masta.org for the nearest clinic.
Tropical Medical Bureau Ireland ⊕ 0353 12715 272, ⊕ tmb.ie.

US AND CANADA

Canadian Society for International Health ⊕ 613 241 5785, ⊕ csih.org. Extensive list of travel health centres.
CDC ⊕ 1 800 232 4636, ⊕ cdc.gov/travel. Official US government travel health site.
International Society for Travel Medicine ⊕ 1 404 373 8282, ⊕ istm.org. Has a full list of travel health clinics.

AUSTRALIA, NEW ZEALAND AND SOUTH AFRICA

The Travel Doctor – TMVC ⊕ 1300 658 844, ⊕ traveldoctor.com.au. Lists travel clinics in Australia, New Zealand and Thailand.

Insurance

Insurance is definitely a sound idea for a destination like Peru. Most worldwide policies offer a range of options to cover different levels of adventurous activities. Some of the extreme sports, including kayaking and bungee jumping, may not be covered by standard policies.

Internet

Peru has good **internet** connections, with cyber-cafés, internet cabins and wi-fi in the most unlikely of small towns. There is wi-fi virtually everywhere in Lima and Cusco, including at hotels, hostels, restaurants and cafes, closely followed by Arequipa, Huaraz, Puno, Iquitos and Trujillo. Wi-fi is generally free, while the rate is typically S/3 an hour at internet cafés, though thirty- and fifteen-minute options are often available.

Language lessons

You can learn **Peruvian Spanish** all over Peru, but the best range of schools is in Lima, Cusco, Arequipa and Huancayo. Check the relevant Directory sections in the Guide.

Laundry

Mid- to high-end hotels frequently offer a **laundry** service and some basic hotels have communal washrooms where you can do your own washing. It's no great expense to get your clothes washed by a *lavandería* (laundry) on the street, normally upwards of S/3 per kg.

LGBTQ travellers

Homosexuality is pretty much kept underground in what is still a very macho society, though in recent years Lima has seen a liberating advance, and anyone cross-dressing can walk around with relative

ROUGH GUIDES TRAVEL INSURANCE

Rough Guides has teamed up with ⊕ WorldNomads.com to offer great travel insurance deals. Policies are available to residents of over 150 countries, with cover for a wide range of adventure sports, 24-hour emergency assistance, high levels of medical and evacuation cover and a stream of travel safety information. Roughguides.com users can take advantage of their policies online 24/7, from anywhere in the world – even if you're already travelling. And since plans often change when you're on the road, you can extend your policy and even claim online. Roughguides.com users who buy travel insurance with ⊕ WorldNomads.com can also leave a positive footprint and donate to a community development project. For more information, go to ⊕ roughguides.com/travel-insurance.

freedom from abuse. However, there is little or no organized LGBTQ scene. **The Peruvian Homosexual and Lesbian Movement** can be contacted at C Mariscal Miller 828, Jesús María, Lima (ⓦfacebook.com/mholperu). There are few specialist LGBTQ organizations, hotel facilities, restaurants or even clubs (where they exist they are listed in the relevant sections of the Guide). Further information can be accessed at the following websites: ⓦpurpleroofs.com, ⓦglobalgayz.com, ⓦperuesgay.com and ⓦgayperu.pe.

Living and working in Peru

There is a certain amount of **bureaucracy** involved if you want to work (or live) officially in Peru. Your only real chance of **earning money** here is by teaching English in Lima, or, with luck, teaching English or working in an expat bar in Arequipa or Cusco. In the more remote parts of the country it may sometimes be possible to find board and lodging in return for a little building work or general labour.

For biology, geography or environmental science graduates there's the chance of free board and lodging, and maybe a small salary, if you're willing to work very hard for at least three months as a **tour guide** in a jungle lodge, under the Resident Naturalist schemes. One or two lodges along the **Río Tambopata** offer such schemes and other research opportunities. For more details, it's best to contact lodges such as the *Tambopata Research Centre* (see page 445) directly. Arrangements need to be made at least six months in advance. There are plenty of charities where you can help out, including the Arequipa-based not-for-profit **Traveller Not Tourist** organization (ⓦtravellernottourist.org) that helps volunteers work directly to support children in poverty.

Teaching English

There are two options if you'd like to teach English in Peru: find work before you go, or just wing it and see what you come up with while you're out there, particularly if you already have a degree, teaching experience or a relevant ELT or TEFL qualification. The British Council website (ⓦbritishcouncil.org) has a list of English-teaching vacancies and Overseas Jobs Express (ⓦoverseasjobs.com) also lists jobs.

STUDY AND WORK PROGRAMMES

AFS Intercultural Programs US ⓣ1 800 237 4636, Canada ⓣ1 800 361 7248, Australia ⓣ1300 131 736, NZ ⓣ0800 600 300, SA ⓣ0861 237 468; ⓦafs.org. Intercultural exchange organization with programmes in over 50 countries.

American Institute for Foreign Study US ⓣ1 866 906 2437, UK ⓣ020 7581 7300, Australia ⓣ1300 889 067; ⓦaifs.com. Language study and cultural immersion, as well as au pair and Camp America programmes.

BUNAC US ⓣ1 866 220 7771, UK ⓣ0333 999 7516; ⓦbunac.org. Organizes working holidays in a range of destinations for students.

TCV (The Conservation Volunteers) UK ⓣ01302 388 883, ⓦtcv.org.uk. One of the largest environmental charities in Britain, with a programme of national and international working holidays (as a paying volunteer).

Council on International Educational Exchange (CIEE) US ⓣ1 207 553 4000, ⓦciee.org. Leading NGO offering study programmes and volunteer projects around the world.

Earthwatch Institute UK ⓣ01865 318 838, US ⓣ800 776 0188, Australia ⓣ03 9016 7590; ⓦearthwatch.org. Scientific expedition project that spans over fifty countries, with environmental and archeological ventures worldwide.

Mail

The Peruvian **postal service** – branded as Serpost – is reasonably efficient, if slightly irregular and a little expensive. Letters from Europe and the US generally take around one or two weeks to arrive – occasionally less – while outbound letters to Europe or the US seem to take between ten days and three weeks. Stamps for postcards and airmail letters to the UK, the US and to Australia, New Zealand and South Africa cost around S/3–7.

Be aware that **parcels** take about one month to arrive and are particularly vulnerable to being opened en route – in either direction – and expensive souvenirs can't be sure of leaving the building where you mail them. Never send money through the Peruvian post!

Maps

Maps of Peru fall into three basic categories. A standard **road map** should be available from good map-sellers just about anywhere in the world or in Peru itself from street vendors or *librerías*; the Touring y Automóvil Club de Perú, Av Trinidad Morán 698, Lince Lima (ⓣ01 611 9999, ⓦtouringperu.com.pe), is worth visiting for its good route maps. **Departmental maps**, covering each *departamento* (Peruvian state) in greater detail, albeit often very out of date, are also fairly widely available. **Topographic maps** (usually 1:100,000) cover the entire coastal area and most of the mountainous regions of Peru. In Lima, they can be bought from the Instituto

USEFUL NUMBERS AND DIALLING CODES

USEFUL TELEPHONE NUMBERS

Directory enquiries ⊕ 103
Operator ⊕ 100
Emergency services ⊕ 105
Fire ⊕ 116
International operator ⊕ 108

CALLING HOME FROM ABROAD

To make an international call, dial the international access code (in Peru it's +51 then the destination's country code, before the rest of the number. Note that the initial zero is omitted from the area code when dialling the UK, Ireland, Australia and New Zealand from abroad.
Australia + 61
New Zealand + 64
UK + 44
US and Canada + 1
Republic of Ireland + 353
South Africa + 27

Geográfico Nacional (ⓦ ign.gob.pe), and the Reise Know-How maps, available in bookstores, are quite reliable and regularly updated.

Money

The **currency** in Peru is the **nuevo sol**, still simply called a "sol" on the streets, and whose symbol is S/. The sol remains relatively steady against the US dollar, and at time of writing, the exchange rate for the nuevo sol was roughly US$1 = S/3.2, £1 = S/4.4 Aus$1 = S/2.5, NZ$1 = S/2.3, €1 = S/3.8.

Dollars are also accepted in many places, including smart hotels, tour companies, railway companies and classy restaurants. The main supermarkets in Lima also take dollars, as do some taxi drivers (especially those picking up from airports).

ATMs are common in all of Peru's cities and main towns, with the BCP (Banco de Crédito del Peru) probably being the most common, but all the main banks' ATMs seem to work well with standard credit and debit cards. Travellers' cheques and cash dollars or euros can be cashed at **casas de cambio**. Cash can be changed on the street, sometimes at a slightly better rate than the banks or casas de cambio, but with a greater risk of being short-changed.

Opening hours

Most **shops** and **services** in Peru open Monday to Saturday 9am to 5pm, or 6pm. Many are open on Sunday as well, if for more limited hours. Of Peru's **museums**, some belong to the state, others to institutions and a few to individuals. Most charge a small admission fee and are open Monday to Saturday 9am to noon and 3 to 6pm.

Peru's more important **ancient sites** and ruins usually have opening hours that coincide with daylight – from around 7am until 5pm or 6pm daily. Smaller sites are rarely fenced off, and are nearly always accessible 24 hours a day. For larger sites, you normally pay a small admission fee to the local guardian – who may then walk around with you, pointing out features of interest. Only Machu Picchu charges more than a few dollars' entrance fee – this is one site where you may find it worth presenting an ISIC or FIYTO student card (which generally gets you in for half-price).

Churches open in the mornings for Mass (usually around 6am), after which the smaller ones close. Those which are most interesting to tourists, however, tend to stay open all day, while others open again in the afternoon from 3 to 6pm. Very occasionally there's an admission charge to churches, and more regularly to monasteries (*monasterios*).

Phones

It's easy to make **international calls** from just about any town in the country, either with a pre-paid phonecard or via a telephone cabin, which can be found in all town centres. **Mobiles** are expensive to use, but almost everyone seems to have one these days. Using your own mobile almost always works out to be the most expensive form of telephone communication, but it may be worth checking with your provider before departure (your phone needs to run on GSM/GPRS band). It is certainly cheaper to buy a local mobile phone and sim card (available in shops everywhere from around S/105–135 or US$35–45) and use this for in-Peru calls. The most popular mobile company is Telefonica Movistar, with Claro as number two.

Phonecards (eg Telefónica Tarjeta 147) are the cheapest way to communciate by phone either domestically or internationally; indeed, inter-national calls from a fixed phone often work out cheaper than ones to Peruvian mobiles or between Peruvian cities. Each card has directions for use (in Spanish) on the reverse and most are based on a scratch-card numeral basis. You can buy phonecards from corner shops, *farmacias* or on the street from cigarette stalls in the centres of most towns and cities. With free wi-fi available in most places, Skype is probably the most convenient form of long-distance calling.

Photography

The light in Peru is very bright, with a strong contrast between shade and sun. This can produce a nice effect and generally speaking it's easy to take good **photographs**. One of the more complex problems is how to take photos of people without upsetting them. You should always talk to a prospective subject first, and ask if she/he minds if you take a quick photo (*"una fotita, por favor?"* – "a little photo please"); most people react favourably to this approach even if all the communication is in sign language, although don't be surprised if you're asked for a sol or two.

Digital photography is by far the most common format for Peruvians and travellers alike. Digital cameras, memory cards, batteries and accessories are now widely available pretty much everywhere in Peru. Most internet cafés can also help download memory cards. Camera film is expensive to buy, and not readily available outside of the main cities; colour Kodak and Fuji films are easier to find, but black-and-white film is rare.

Senior travellers

Senior travellers in reasonable health should have no problems in Peru. Anyone taking medication should obviously bring enough supplies for the duration of the trip, though most drugs are available over the counter in Lima and other cities. The altitude is likely to be the most serious concern, so careful reading of our section on altitude sickness (see page 207) becomes even more crucial; so does taking great care with what food you eat (see page 44).

As far as accommodation for senior travellers goes, most middle- to top-range hotels are clean and comfortable; it's mostly a matter of clearly asking for what you need when booking or on arrival at the hotel. This is particularly true if you have special requirements such as a ground-floor room.

Shopping

Peru is one of those places where you want to buy something from virtually every street corner. Apart from all the fine alpaca sweaters and blankets, there are baskets, musical instruments, paintings and a whole raft of quite well-known **artesanía** (craft goods).

Of course, most Peruvians live in cities with massive supermarkets and a pharmacy on each street corner. **Shopping centres** are springing up all over Lima, each more or less a replica of the other. Traditional craft goods from most regions of Peru can be found in **markets** and independent shops in Lima. Woollen and alpaca products, though, are usually cheaper and often better quality in the mountains – particularly in Cusco, Juliaca and Puno; carved gourds are imported from around Huancayo; the best places to buy ceramic replicas are Trujillo, Huaraz, Ica and Nazca; and the best jungle crafts are from Pucallpa and Iquitos.

If you get offered an "ancient" pot or necklace, remember that **Peruvian law** stipulates that no items of archeological or historical value or interest may be removed from the country. Many of the **jungle crafts** which incorporate feathers, skins or shells of rare Amazonian animals are also banned for export – it's best not to buy these if you are in any doubt about their scarcity. If you do try to export anything of archeological or biological value, and get caught, you'll have the goods confiscated at the very least, and may find yourself in a Peruvian court.

Time

Peru keeps the same hours as **Eastern Standard Time**, which is five hours behind GMT.

Tourist information

These days, **iPerú** (T 01 574 8000, W peru.info) is the key government source of tourist information. They have offices in most major cities, often operating in parallel with a local municipal service. They will provide information by email and their website is useful.

GOVERNMENT WEBSITES

Asociación Peruano de Tursimo Receptivo e Interno Ⓦ apoturperu.org.
Australian Department of Foreign Affairs Ⓦ dfat.gov.au.
British Foreign & Commonwealth Office Ⓦ gov.uk.
Canadian Department of Foreign Affairs Ⓦ international.gc.ca.
Instituto Geográfico Nacional Ⓦ ign.gob.pe.
Irish Department of Foreign Affairs Ⓦ foreignaffairs.gov.ie.
New Zealand Ministry of Foreign Affairs Ⓦ mfat.govt.nz.
Peru Ministerio de Cultura Ⓦ cultura.gob.pe.
US State Department Ⓦ state.gov.
South African Department of Foreign Affairs Ⓦ dirco.gov.za.

Travelling with children

South Americans hold the family unit in high regard and **children** are central to this. Prices can often be cheaper for children; tours to attractions can occasionally be negotiated on a **family-rate** basis and entry to sites is often half-price or less (and always free for infants). Children under 10 generally get half-fare on local (but not inter-regional) buses, while trains and boats generally charge full fare if a seat is required. Infants who don't need a seat often travel free on all transport except planes, when you pay around ten percent of the usual fare.

Travelling around the country is perhaps the most difficult activity with children. **Bus and train journeys** are generally long (twelve hours or more). Crossing international borders is a potential hassle; although Peru officially accepts children under 16 on their parents' **passports**, if they have their own it will serve to minimize problems.

Health

Most types of nappies, creams, wet-wipes and children's medication can be bought easily in main **chemists** and larger supermarkets in Lima, Arequipa and Cusco, but outside these places it's wise to arrive prepared. Consult your doctor before leaving home regarding health matters. **Sunscreen** is important, as are sun hats (cheap and readily available), and you might consider a parasol for very small children. Conversely, it can get cold at night in the Andes, so take plenty of **warm clothing**. In the mountains, the **altitude** doesn't seem to cause children as many problems as it does their elders, but they shouldn't walk too strenuously above 2000m without full acclimatization.

The major risk around the regions is a bad stomach and **diarrhoea** (see page 44) from water or food; you should be ready to act sooner than usual when treating children under 10 with rehydration salts. In **Lima**, where the water is just about good enough to clean your teeth, but not to drink, the issues for local children are mainly bronchial or asthmatic, with humid weather and high pollution levels causing many long-lasting chest ailments. This shouldn't be a problem for any visiting children unless they already have difficulties.

Food and drink

The **food and drink** in Peru is varied enough to appeal to most kids. Pizzas are available almost everywhere, as are good fish, red meats, fried chicken, chips, corn on the cob and nutritious soups, and vitamin supplements are never a bad idea. There's also a wide range of **soft drinks**, from the ubiquitous Coca-Cola and Sprite to Inka Cola (now owned by Coca-Cola). Recognizable commercial **baby food** (and nappy brands) is available in all large supermarkets. **Restaurants** in Peru cater well for children and some offer smaller, cheaper portions; if they don't publicize it, it's worth asking.

Hotels

Like restaurants, **hotels** are used to handling kids; they will sometimes offer discounts, especially if children share rooms or beds. Lower- to mid-range accommodation is the most flexible in this regard, but even expensive places can be helpful. Many hotels and hostels have collective rooms large enough for families to share at reasonable rates.

Travellers with disabilities

Peru is not well set up in terms of access infrastructure for welcoming **travellers with disabilities** (even the best buses have mostly ordinary steps), but nevertheless, in a moment of difficulty many Peruvians will support and help. **Airlines** have facilities and will assist in most of Peru's airports.

While there are still few hotels or resorts that are well designed enough to ensure access for all, Peru, and Lima in particular, has made progress in recent years. The hotel chain Sonesta Posadas del Inca (Ⓦ sonesta.com) caters well for disabilities and has places in Lima, Lago Titicaca/Puno and the Valle Sagrado; other pioneers in Peru include the travel agency Apumayo Expediciones (Ⓦ apumayo.com), Rainforest Expeditions (Ⓦ perunature.com) and InkaNatura Travel (Ⓦ inkanatura.com). Accessible Journeys (Ⓦ disabilitytravel.com), meanwhile, offers tours specifically designed for travellers with physical disabilities, including a thirteen-day trip to Lima, Cusco, the Valle Sagrado, Machu Picchu and Nazca.

Women travellers

Machismo is well ingrained in the Peruvian male mentality, particularly in the towns, and female foreigners are almost universally seen as liberated and therefore sexually available. On the whole, the situations female travellers will encounter are more annoying than dangerous, with frequent comments such as *qué guapa* ("how pretty"), intrusive and prolonged stares, plus whistling and hissing in the **cities**. Worse still are the occasional rude comments and groping, particularly in crowded situations such as on buses or trains. Blonde and fair-skinned women are likely to suffer much more of this behaviour than darker, Latin-looking women.

Mostly these are situations you'd deal with routinely at home but they can seem threatening without a clear understanding of Peruvian Spanish and slang. To avoid getting caught up in something you can't control, any provocation is best ignored. In a public situation, however, any real harassment is often best dealt with by loudly drawing attention to the miscreant.

In the predominantly indigenous, **remote areas** there is less of an overt problem, though surprisingly this is where physical assaults are more likely to take place. They are not common, however – you're probably safer hiking in the Andes than walking at night in most British or North American inner cities.

If you're **camping**, it's a good idea to get to know the locals, which can give a kind of acceptance and insurance, and may even lead to the offer of a room – Peruvians, particularly those in rural areas, can be incredibly kind and hospitable.

Lima and around

LA CATEDRAL, PLAZA MAYOR

Lima and around

Crowded into the mouth of the arid Rimac river valley, with low sandy mountains closing in around its outer fringes, Lima is a boisterous, macho sprawl of a city, full of beaten-up cars chasing Mercedes and 4WDs: this is a place where money rules, with an irresistible, underlying energy. Somehow, though, it still manages to appear relaxed and laidback in the barrios and off the beaten track, and the noisy, frenetic craziness of it all is mellowed somewhat by the presence of the sea and beaches. A large part of the city's appeal is its fascinating mix of lifestyles and cultures: from the snappy, sassy, criolla style to the more easy-going attitude of Lima's poorer citizens. Even if you choose not to spend much time here, you can get a good sense of it all in just a few days: Limeño hospitality and kindness are almost boundless once you've established an initial rapport.

Considered the most beautiful city in Spanish America during the sixteenth and seventeenth centuries and long established as Peru's seat of government, Lima retains a certain elegance, particularly in colonial Lima Centro. Though no one will ever accuse Lima of being beautiful today, the city still brims with culture and history, though it may not be obvious at first. Top of its list of attractions are some excellent **museums** – the best of which should definitely be visited before setting off for Machu Picchu or any of Peru's other great Inca ruins – as well as fine Spanish **churches** in the centre, and some distinguished **mansions** in the wealthy suburbs of Barranco and Miraflores. Add to this some outstanding **restaurants** and hedonistic **nightlife**, and you'll find there's plenty to explore in Peru's distinctive capital.

As a transport and communications hub, Lima also makes a good base for exploring the surrounding region, and the immediate area offers plenty of reasons to delay your progress on towards Arequipa or Cusco. Within an hour's bus ride south is the coastline – often deserted – lined by a series of attractive **beaches**. Above them, the imposing fortress-temple complex of **Pachacamac** sits on a sandstone cliff, near the edge of the ocean. In the neighbouring **Rimac Valley** you can visit the pre-Inca sites of **Puruchuco** and **Cajamarquilla**. To the north, meanwhile, the oldest stone pyramids in the world sit abandoned in the desert of **Caral**.

Lima

Laid out across a wide, flat, alluvial plain, Lima's buildings fan out like a concrete phoenix in long, straight avenues and roads from its centre. The old colonial heart, **Lima Centro**, is of both architectural and cultural interest as well as being the seat of government and religion. South of here, along and just inland from the ocean clifftop, the modern heart of **Miraflores**, where most tourists stay, buzzes with shoppers by day and partiers by night. East along the coast a few kilometres, what was once a separate seaside suburb and artists' quarter, **Barranco**, still boasts both tradition and a vibrant atmosphere. Between Miraflores and Lima Centro, jammed between the Paseo de la República and the Avenida Arequipa main roads that connect them, rise the skyscraping banks of **San Isidro**, Lima's commercial centre.

To the west, the city reaches a fine finger of low-lying land pointing into the Pacific; this is **Callao**, the rather down-at-heel port area, close to the airport. The **shantytowns** that line the highways, meanwhile, continue to swell with new arrivals from the high Andes, responsible in large part for the dramatic surge in Lima's population in recent years.

MUSEO LARCO

Highlights

❶ **Huaca Pucllana** A vast pre-Inca adobe pyramid mound in the middle of suburban Miraflores, this is a good place to get your bearings and a taste of ancient Lima. See page 68

❷ **Parque Kennedy** The central park in downtown Lima's Miraflores district draws locals and tourists alike to its small craft market every evening, and there are some fun cafés and restaurants located along its edges too. See page 70

❸ **MATE** The most modern of Lima's museums, celebrating the city's best known photographer of fashion, travel and night-time debauchery, Mario Testino. See page 73

❹ **Fisherman's Wharf** At the southern end of Lima's cliff-hemmed beaches, a small wooden jetty is home to the fishermen of Chorrillos, whose morning catch is landed just in time for the ceviche kiosks next door to prepare inexpensive, but fantastically fresh, fish lunches. See page 74

❺ **Museo Larco** One of the city's most unusual museums, and the largest private collection of Peruvian archeology, containing more than 400,000 excellently preserved ancient ceramics, including an extensive erotic section. See page 76

❻ **El Cordano** One of Lima's last surviving traditional bar/restaurants, bustling with locals. See page 86

HIGHLIGHTS ARE MARKED ON THE MAP ON PAGE 58

1

Lima's **climate** seems to set the city's mood: in the height of summer (Dec–March) it fizzes with energy and excitement, though during the winter months (June–Sept) a low mist descends over the arid valley in which the city sits, forming a solid grey blanket – what Limeños call **garúa** – from the beaches almost up to Chosica in the foothills of the Andes; it's a phenomenon made worse by traffic-related air pollution, which dampens the city's spirit, if only slightly.

Brief history

When the Spanish first arrived here in 1533, the valley was dominated by three important **Inca**-controlled urban complexes: **Carabayllo**, to the north near Chillón; **Maranga**, now partly destroyed, by the Avenida La Marina, between the modern city and the Port of Callao; and **Surco**, now a suburb within the confines of greater Lima but where, until the mid-seventeenth century, the colourfully painted adobe houses of ancient chiefs lay empty. Now these structures have faded back into the sandy desert terrain, and only the larger pyramids remain.

The sixteenth and seventeenth centuries

Francisco Pizarro founded **Spanish Lima**, nicknamed the "City of the Kings", in 1535. The name is thought to derive from a mispronunciation of Río Rimac, while others suggest that "Lima" is an ancient word that described the lands of Taulichusco, the chief who ruled this area when the Spanish arrived. Evidently recommended by communities in the mountains as a site for a potential capital, it proved a good choice – apart perhaps from the winter coastal fog – offering a natural harbour nearby, a large well-watered river valley and relatively easy access to the Andes.

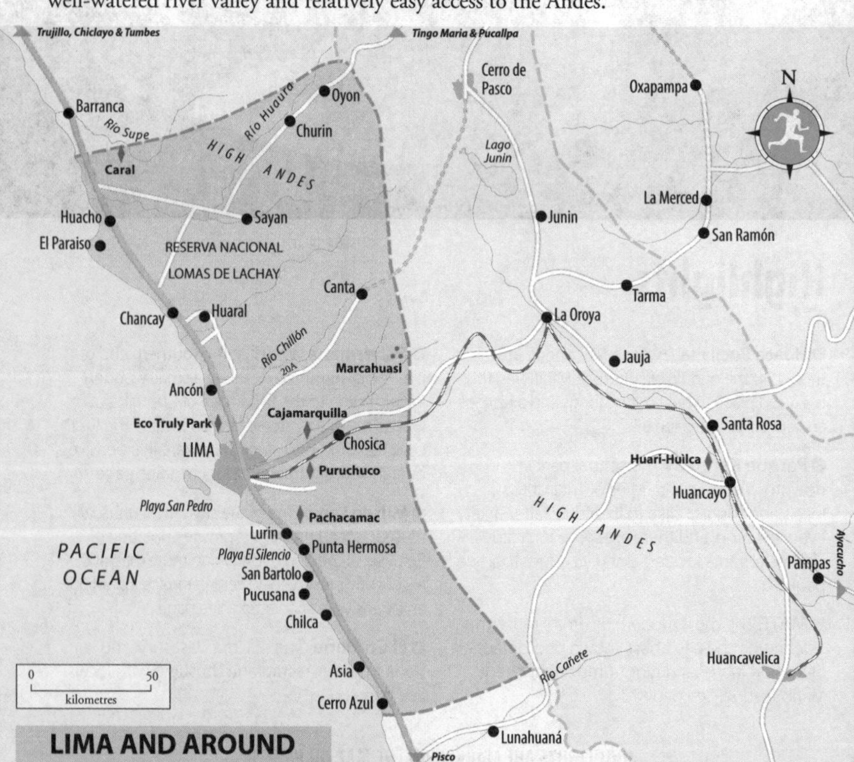

LIMA ORIENTATION

Lima Centro, the old city, sits at the base of a low-lying Andean foothill, Cerro San Cristóbal, and focuses on two plazas, separated by some five blocks along the **Jirón de la Unión**, a major shopping street: the colonial **Plaza Mayor** (often still called the Plaza de Armas), separated from the Río Rimac by the Palacio de Gobierno and the railway station; and the more modern **Plaza San Martín**. The Plaza Mayor is fronted by the Catedral and Palacio de Gobierno, while there's greater commercial activity around Plaza San Martín. The key to finding your way around the old part of town is to acquaint yourself with these two squares and the streets between.

From Lima Centro, the city's main avenues reach out into the sprawling suburbs. The two principal routes are **Avenida Venezuela**, heading west to the harbour area around Callao and the airport, and perpendicular to this the broad, tree-lined **Avenida Arequipa** stretching out to the coastal downtown centre of **Miraflores**, 7 or 8km from Lima Centro. Running more or less parallel to Avenida Arequipa, the **Paseo de la República**, more fondly known in Lima as **El Zanjón** (the Great Ditch), is a concrete, three-lane highway connecting central Lima with San Isidro and Miraflores, and almost reaching Barranco. Most visitors make Miraflores their base, with Lima Centro and Barranco also good options.

Since the very beginning, Lima was different from the more popular image of Peru in which Andean peasants are pictured toiling on Inca-built mountain terraces. By the 1550s, the town had developed around a large **plaza** with wide streets leading through a fine collection of elegant mansions and well-stocked shops run by wealthy merchants, rapidly developing into the capital of a Spanish viceroyalty which encompassed not only Peru but also Ecuador, Bolivia and Chile. The **University of San Marcos**, founded in 1551, is the oldest on the continent, and Lima housed the Western Hemisphere's headquarters of the Spanish Inquisition from 1570 until 1820. It remained the most important, the richest, and the most alluring city in South America until the early nineteenth century.

Perhaps the most prosperous era for Lima was the **seventeenth century**. By 1610 its **population** had reached a manageable 26,000, made up of forty percent Africans (mostly slaves); thirty-eight percent Spanish people; no more than eight percent pure indigenous people; another eight percent (of unspecified ethnic origin) living under religious orders; and less than six percent *mestizo*, today probably the largest proportion of inhabitants. The centre of Lima was crowded with shops and stalls selling silks and fancy furniture from as far afield as China. Rimac and Callao both grew up as satellite settlements – initially catering to the very rich, though they are now fairly run down.

The eighteenth century

The **eighteenth century**, a period of relative stagnation for the city, was dramatically punctuated by the tremendous **earthquake of 1746**, which left only twenty houses standing in the whole city and killed some five thousand residents – nearly ten percent of the population by that point. From 1761 to 1776 Lima and Peru were governed by **Viceroy Amat**, who, although more renowned for his relationship with the famous Peruvian actress **La Perricholi**, is also remembered for spearheading Lima's rebirth. Under his rule, the city lost its cloistered atmosphere, and opened out with broad avenues, striking gardens, Rococo mansions and palatial salons. Influenced by the Bourbons, Amat's designs for the city's architecture arrived hand in hand with other transatlantic reverberations of the Enlightenment, such as the new anti-imperialist vision of an independent Peru.

The nineteenth and twentieth centuries

In the **nineteenth century** Lima **expanded** still further to the east and south. The suburbs of Barrios Altos and La Victoria were poor from the start; above the beaches at Magdalena, Miraflores and Barranco, the wealthy developed new enclaves. These were originally separated from the centre by several kilometres of farmland, at that time

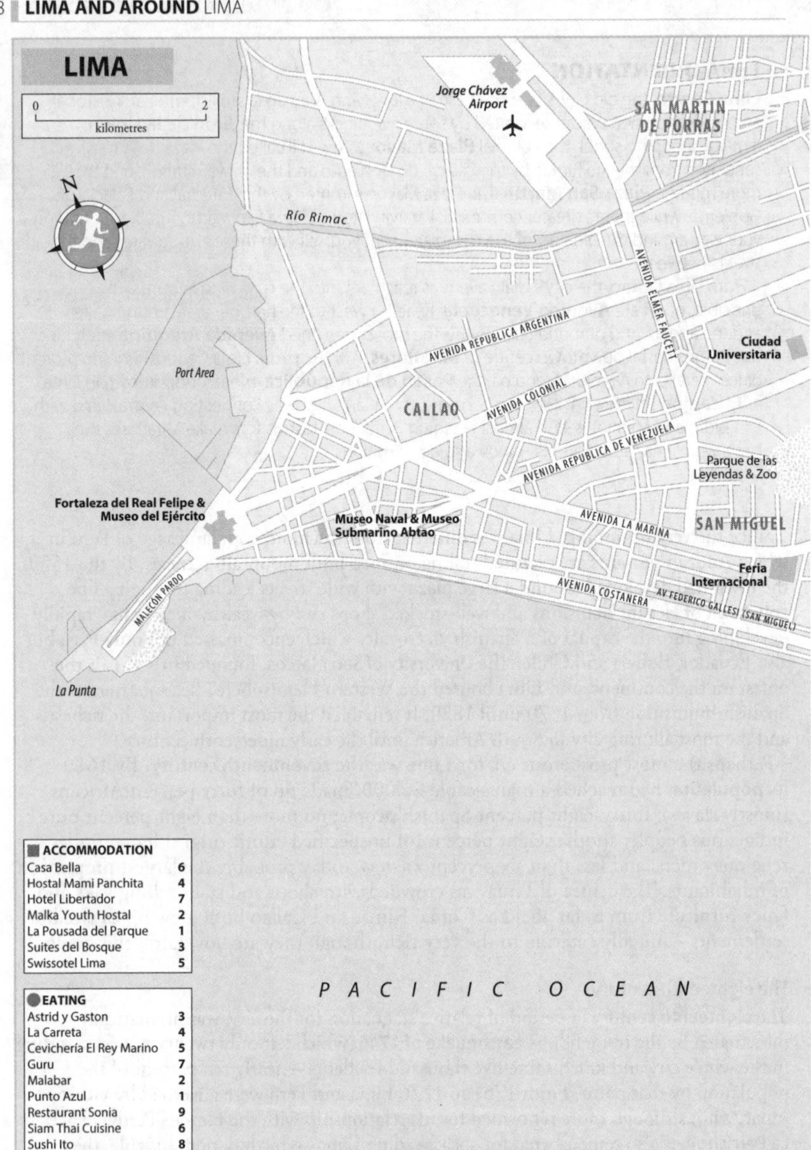

HIGHLIGHTS

1. Huaca Pucllana
2. Parque Kennedy
3. MATE
4. Fisherman's Wharf
5. Museo Larco
6. El Cordano

SHOPPING

Big Head	2
Jockey Plaza	1
Peru Bike	3

DRINKING & NIGHTLIFE

La Cueva	3
Las Brisas del Titicaca	2
Delfus Taberna	4
Karamba	1
Kimbara	5

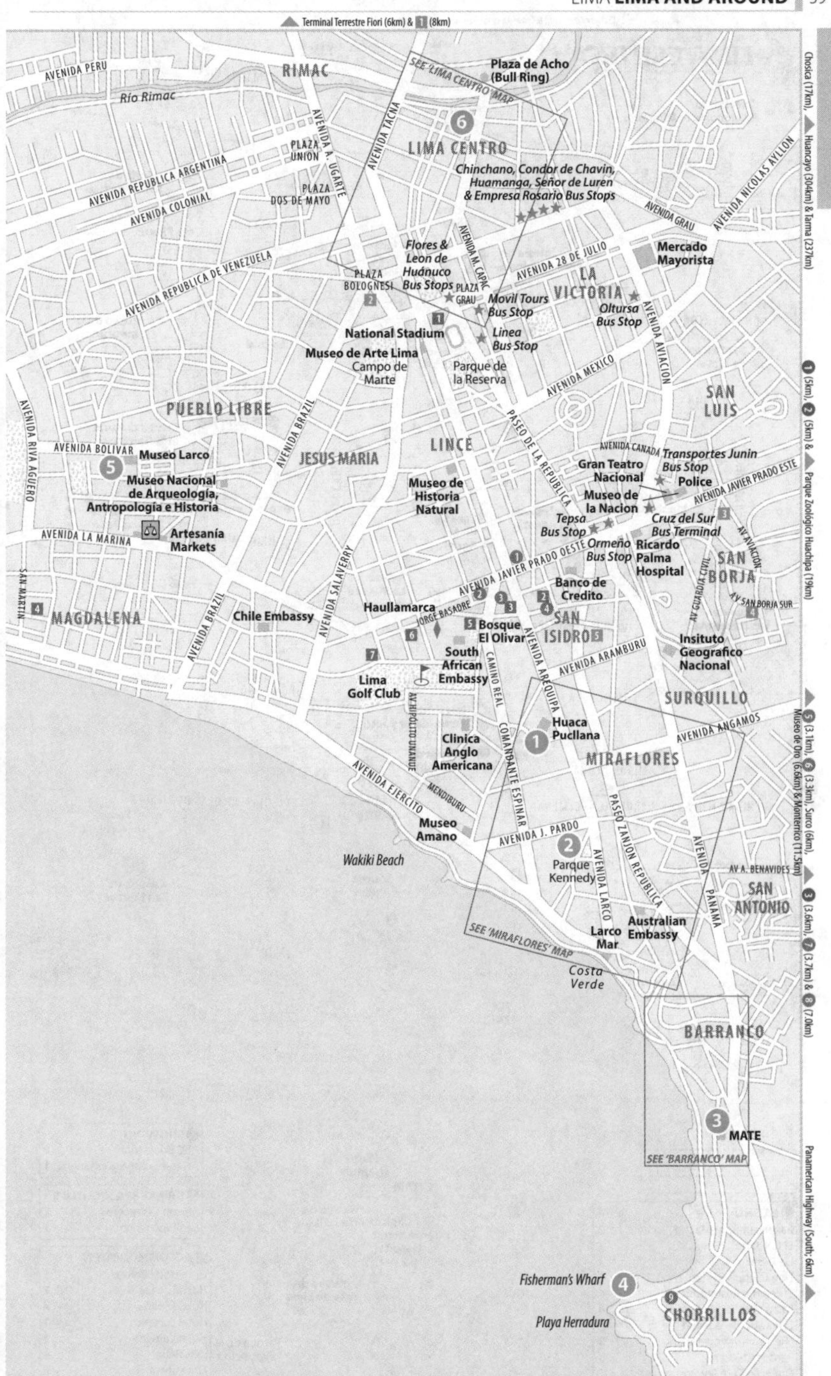
Terminal Terrestre Fiori (6km) & 1 (8km)
Chosica (17km), Huancayo (304km) & Tarma (237km)
1 (5km), 2 (5km) & Parque Zoológico Huachipa (19km)
5 (3.1km), Museo de Oro 6 (3.3km), Surco (6km), (6.6km) & Monterrico (11.5km)
3 (3.6km), 7 (3.7km) & 8 (7.0km)
Panamerican Highway (South; 6km)
RIMAC
AVENIDA PERU
Río Rimac
Plaza de Acho (Bull Ring)
SEE 'LIMA CENTRO' MAP
LIMA CENTRO
PLAZA UNION
PLAZA DOS DE MAYO
AVENIDA TACNA
AVENIDA A. UGARTE
AVENIDA REPUBLICA ARGENTINA
AVENIDA COLONIAL
Chinchano, Condor de Chavin, Huamanga, Señor de Luren & Empresa Rosario Bus Stops
AVENIDA NICOLAS AYLLON
AVENIDA GRAU
Mercado Mayorista
AVENIDA REPUBLICA DE VENEZUELA
Flores & Leon de Huánuco Bus Stops
AVENIDA M. CAPAC
AVENIDA 28 DE JULIO
LA VICTORIA
PLAZA BOLOGNESI
PLAZA GRAU
Movil Tours Bus Stop
Oltursa Bus Stop
AVENIDA AVIACION
National Stadium
Linea Bus Stop
Museo de Arte Lima
Campo de Marte
Parque de la Reserva
AVENIDA MEXICO
SAN LUIS
PUEBLO LIBRE
AVENIDA BRAZIL
PASEO DE LA REPUBLICA
AVENIDA RIVA AGÜERO
AVENIDA BOLIVAR
Museo Larco
JESUS MARIA
LINCE
AVENIDA CANADA
Transportes Junin Bus Stop
Gran Teatro Nacional
Police
Museo Nacional de Arqueología, Antropología e Historia
Museo de Historia Natural
Museo de la Nacion
AVENIDA JAVIER PRADO ESTE
Cruz del Sur Bus Terminal
Tepsa Bus Stop
AVENIDA LA MARINA
Artesanía Markets
AVENIDA SALAVERRY
Ormeño Bus Stop
Ricardo Palma Hospital
AV AVIACION
SAN BORJA
AVENIDA JAVIER PRADO OESTE
AV GUARDIA CIVIL
SAN MARTIN
Banco de Credito
AV SAN BORJA SUR
MAGDALENA
Chile Embassy
Haullamarca
JORGE BASADRE
SAN ISIDRO
Bosque El Olivar
Insituto Geografico Nacional
AVENIDA AREQUIPA
South African Embassy
AVENIDA ARAMBURU
Lima Golf Club
CAMINO REAL
AV. HIPÓLITO UNANUE
SURQUILLO
Huaca Pucllana
AVENIDA ANGAMOS
Clinica Anglo Americana
COMANDANTE ESPINAR
MIRAFLORES
AVENIDA EJERCITO
MENDIBURU
PASEO ZANJON REPUBLICA
Museo Amano
AVENIDA J. PARDO
AVENIDA PANAMA
Wakiki Beach
Parque Kennedy
AVENIDA LARCO
AV. A. BENAVIDES
SAN ANTONIO
Australian Embassy
Larco Mar
SEE 'MIRAFLORES' MAP
Costa Verde
BARRANCO
MATE
SEE 'BARRANCO' MAP
Fisherman's Wharf
Playa Herradura
CHORRILLOS

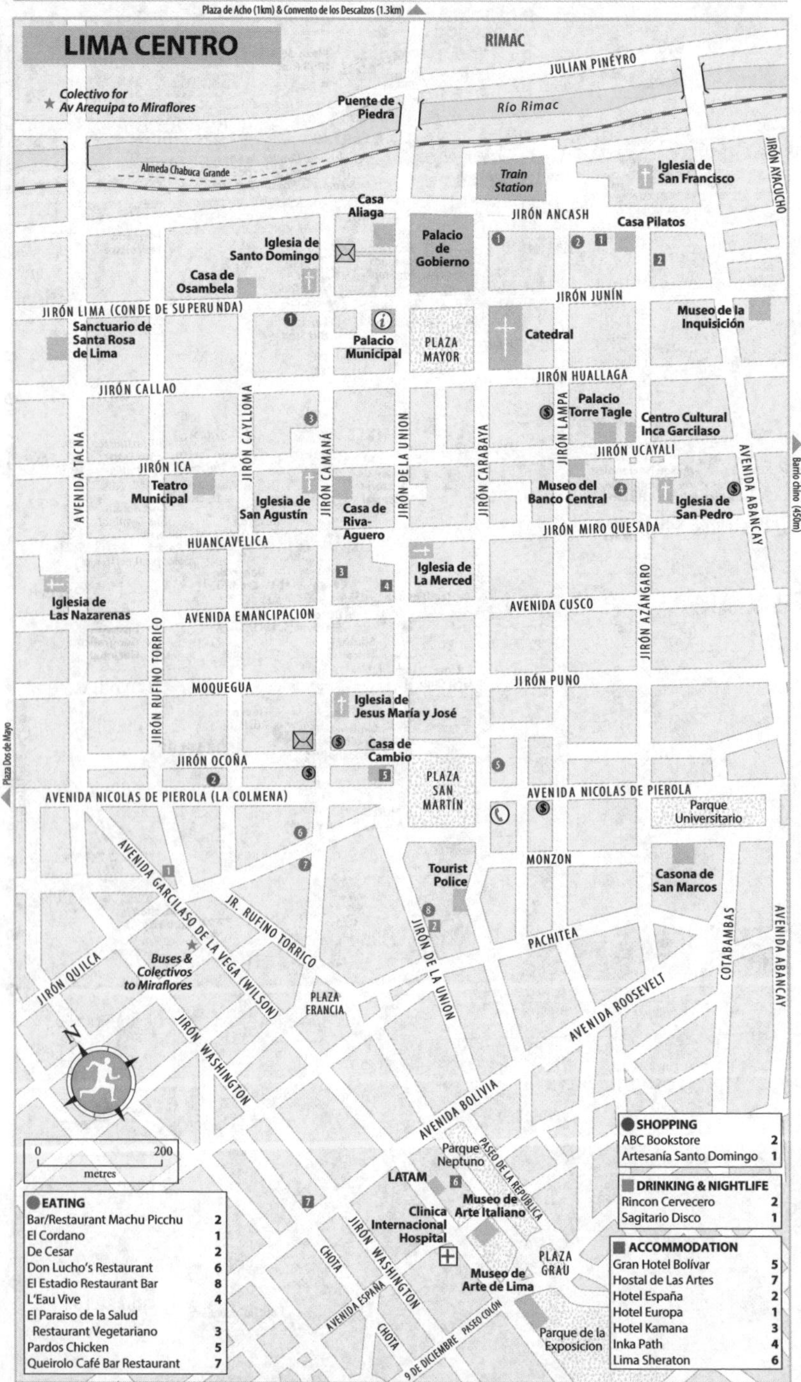

SHOPPING

ABC Bookstore	2
Artesanía Santo Domingo	1

DRINKING & NIGHTLIFE

Rincon Cervecero	2
Sagitario Disco	1

ACCOMMODATION

Gran Hotel Bolívar	5
Hostal de Las Artes	7
Hotel España	2
Hotel Europa	1
Hotel Kamana	3
Inka Path	4
Lima Sheraton	6

EATING

Bar/Restaurant Machu Picchu	2
El Cordano	1
De Cesar	2
Don Lucho's Restaurant	6
El Estadio Restaurant Bar	8
L'Eau Vive	4
El Paraiso de la Salud Restaurant Vegetariano	3
Pardos Chicken	5
Queirolo Café Bar Restaurant	7

still studded with fabulous pre-Inca *huacas* and other adobe ruins. Lima's first modern facelift and expansion occurred between 1919 and 1930, revitalizing the central areas. Under orders from **President Leguia**, the Plaza San Martín's attractive colonnades and the *Gran Hotel Bolívar* were erected, the Palacio de Gobierno was rebuilt and the city was supplied with its first drinking-water and sewerage systems.

Modern Lima

Lima's rapid **growth** has taken it from 300,000 inhabitants in 1930 to over nine million today, mostly accounted for by massive immigration from the provinces into the *pueblos jovenes* ("young towns", or **shantytowns**) now pressing in on the city. The ever-increasing traffic is a day-to-day problem, yet **environmental awareness** is rising almost as fast as Lima's shantytowns and neon-lit, middle-class suburban neighbourhoods, and the air quality has improved over the last ten years.

The country's **economy** is booming even in the face of serious slowdowns in some of Peru's traditional markets, namely Europe and the US. Lima's thriving middle class enjoy living standards comparable to, or better than, those of the West, and the elite ride around in chauffeur-driven Cadillacs and fly to Miami for their monthly shopping. The vast majority of Lima's inhabitants, though, endure a constant struggle to put either food on the table or the flimsiest of roofs over their heads.

Lima Centro

With all its splendid architectural attractions, **Lima Centro** might well be expected to have a more tourist-focused vibe than it does. In reality, though, the neighbourhood is very much a centre of Limeños' daily life. The main axis is formed by the parallel streets – Jirón de la Unión and Jirón V Carabaya – connecting the grand squares of the **Plaza San Martín** and **Plaza Mayor**. Here the roads are narrow and busy, bringing together many of the city's office workers with slightly downmarket shops and their workers. There are many fine buildings from the colonial and Republican eras, overhung with ornate balconies, yet apart from a few – notably the **Palacio de Gobierno** and **Torre Tagle** – these are in a poor state of repair. To the north you'll find the somewhat run-down **Rimac suburb**, home to the city's bullring. South of the two main plazas, some lavish parks and galleries are within walking distance.

Plaza Mayor

The heart of the old town is **Plaza Mayor** – also known as the Plaza de Armas, or Plaza Armada as the early conquistadores called it. There are no remains of any indigenous heritage in or around the square; standing on the original site of the palace of Tauri Chusko (Lima's indigenous chief at the time the Spanish arrived) is the relatively modern Palacio de Gobierno, while the cathedral occupies the site of an Inca temple once dedicated to the puma deity, and the Palacio Municipal lies on what was originally an Inca envoy's mansion.

Palacio de Gobierno

Plaza Mayor • **Changing of the guard** Mon–Sat warm-up at 11.45am, start at noon • **Tours** Sat & Sun; pre-register at Ⓔ scuadros@presidencia.gob.pe or call Ⓣ 01 311 3908 ext 378 (Mon–Fri 9am–6pm) • Free • Ⓦ presidencia.gob.pe

The **Palacio de Gobierno** – also known as the Presidential Palace – was the site of the house of **Francisco Pizarro** (see page 490) long before the present building was conceived. It was here that he spent the last few years of his life, until his assassination in 1541. As he died, his jugular severed by the assassin's rapier, Pizarro fell to the floor, drew a cross, then kissed it; even today some believe this ground to be sacred.

The **changing of the guard** takes place outside the palace – it's not a particularly spectacular sight, though the soldiers look splendid in their scarlet-and-blue uniforms. There are guided **tours** in English and Spanish, which include watching the changing of the guard; to go on a tour you have to register with the Departamento de Actividades at least 24 hours in advance. The tour also takes in the imitation Baroque **interior** of the palace and its rather dull collection of colonial and reproduction furniture.

La Catedral and Museum of Religious Art and Treasures

Plaza Mayor • **Catedral** Daily 9am–5pm • Free • ⓣ 01 427 9647 • **Museum** Mon–Fri 9am–5pm, Sat 9am–1pm, Sun 1–5pm • S/10 • ⓦ museocatacumbas.com

Southeast across the square, less than 50m from the Palacio de Gobierno, the squat and austere **Catedral**, designed by Francisco Becerra, was modelled on a church in Seville, and has three aisles in a Renaissance style. The first stone was symbolically laid here in 1535 on the city's founding; when Becerra died in 1605, the cathedral was still far from completion, with the towers alone taking another forty years to finish. In 1746, further frustration arrived in the guise of a devastating **earthquake**, which destroyed much of the building. Successive restorations over the centuries have resulted in an eclectic style; the current version, which is essentially a reconstruction of Becerra's design, was rebuilt throughout the eighteenth and nineteenth centuries, then remodelled once again after another quake in 1940.

The building is primarily of interest for its **Museum of Religious Art and Treasures**, which contains seventeenth- and eighteenth-century paintings and some superb **choir stalls** – exquisitely carved in the early seventeenth century by Catalan artist Pedro Noguero. Its other highlight is a collection of human remains thought to be **Pizarro's body** (quite fitting since he placed the first stone shortly before his death), which lie in the first chapel on the right. Although gloomy, the interior retains some of its appealing Churrigueresque (or highly elaborate Baroque) decor.

Palacio Municipal

Plaza Mayor • Mon–Fri 8am–4pm • Free

The square-set edifice directly across the plaza from the cathedral is the **Palacio Municipal**, usually lined with heavily armed guards and the occasional armoured car, though actual civil unrest is fairly uncommon. Built on the site of the original sixteenth-century city hall and inaugurated in 1944, it's a typical example of a half-hearted twentieth-century attempt at Neocolonial architecture, designed by Alvarez Emilio Harth Terré and Ricardo de Jara Malachowski, and fronted by grand wooden balconies.

The elegant **interior** is home to the **Pinacoteca Ignacio Merino Museum**, which exhibits a selection of Peruvian paintings, notably those of Ignacio Merino from the nineteenth century. Those with an interest in Peruvian constitutional history should head to the library, where the city's **Act of Foundation and Declaration of Independence** is displayed.

Iglesia de San Francisco

Jr Ancash • Daily 9.30am–5pm; 45min tours at least hourly • S/10, including tour • ⓣ 01 427 1381

Jirón Ancash leads east from the Palacio de Gobierno towards one of Lima's most attractive churches, **San Francisco**, a majestic building that has withstood the passage of time and the devastation of successive earth tremors. A large seventeenth-century construction with an engaging stone facade and towers, San Francisco's vaults and columns are elaborately decorated with Mudéjar (Moorish-style) plaster relief.

The **Convento de San Francisco**, part of the same architectural complex and a museum in its own right, contains a superb library of 25,000 volumes, some dating to the sixteenth century, and a room of **paintings** by (or finished by) Zurbarán, Rubens, Jordaens and Van Dyck. The most impressive of these is the massive version of the Last Supper, painted by Belgian Diego de la Puente, taking up an entire wall with a decidedly Peruvian take on the familiar tableau: the table is oval, the costumes look less than European, and there's *cuy* for the main dish for dinner.

You can take a **guided tour** of the monastery and its subterranean crypt, both of which are worth a visit. The monastery's vast crypts were only discovered in 1951 and contain bones of some seventy thousand people (though the skulls on display are mainly tourist bait).

Casa Pilatos

Jr Ancash 390 • Access Mon–Fri 8am–1pm & 2–5pm, when court is not in session • Free • 01 427 5814

Opposite the Iglesia de San Francisco is the **Casa Pilatos**, today home to the constitutional courts; although you can't enter the building, you can get as far as the central courtyard. Quite a simple building, and no competition for Torre Tagle (see below), it is nevertheless a fine early sixteenth-century mansion, with an attractive courtyard and a stone staircase leading up from the middle of the patio. The wooden carving of the patio's balustrades adds to the general picture of opulent colonialism.

Museo de la Inquisición

Jr Junín 548 • Daily 9am–5pm, by guided tour only • Free • 01 311 7777

Behind a facade of Greek-style classical columns, the **Museo de la Inquisición** was the **headquarters of the Inquisition** for the whole of Spanish-dominated America from 1570 until 1820, and contains the original tribunal room with its beautifully carved mahogany ceiling. Beneath the building, you can look round the **dungeons** and torture chambers, which contain a few gory, life-sized human models, each being put through unbearably painful-looking antique contraptions, mainly involving stretching or mutilating.

Mercado Central and Barrio Chino

The few blocks east of Avenida Abancay are taken over by the **Mercado Central** (Central Market) and **Barrio Chino** (Chinatown). one of the more fascinating sectors of Lima Centro, the Barrio Chino (which can be entered by an ornate Chinese **gateway**, at the crossing of Jirón Ucayali with Capon) houses Lima's best and cheapest *chifa* (Chinese **restaurants**). Many Chinese people came to Peru in the late nineteenth century to work as labourers on railway construction; many others came here in the 1930s and 1940s to escape cultural persecution in their homeland. The shops and street stalls in this sector are full of all sorts of inexpensive goods, from shoes to glass beads, though there is little of genuine quality.

Iglesia de San Pedro

Jirones Ucayali and Azángaro • Mon–Sat 8.30am–1pm & 2–4pm • Free

At the corner of Jirón Ucayali, the **Iglesia de San Pedro** was built and occupied by the Jesuits until their expulsion in 1767. This richly decorated colonial church is home to several religious art treasures, including paintings from the Colonial and Republican periods, and a superb main altar which was built in the late nineteenth century after the Jesuits returned; definitely worth a look around.

Museo del Banco Central de Reserva del Peru

Jr Ucayali 271 • Tues–Sat 9am–5pm • Free • 01 613 2000 ext 22655, bcrp.gob.pe

The **Museo del Banco Central de Reserva del Peru** holds many antique and modern **Peruvian paintings**, as well as a good collection of **pre-Inca artefacts**, including some ancient objects crafted in gold; most of the exhibits on display come from grave robberies and have been returned to Peru only recently. The museum also has a numismatic display and sometimes shows related short films for kids.

Palacio Torre Tagle

Jr Ucayali 323 • Mon–Fri 9am–5pm, book two days in advance • Free • 01 311 2400

The spectacular **Palacio Torre Tagle** is the pride and joy of the old city. A beautifully maintained mansion, it was built in the 1730s and is embellished with a decorative facade and two elegant, dark-wood balconies, with one larger than the other, as is typical of Lima architecture. The **porch and patio** are distinctly Andalucian, with their strong Spanish colonial style, although some of the intricate **woodcarvings** on pillars and across ceilings display a native influence; the *azulejos*, or **tiles**, also show a combination of Moorish and Limeño tastes. In the left-hand corner of the patio you can see a set of **scales** like those used to weigh merchandise during colonial times, and the house also contains a magnificent sixteenth-century **carriage** (complete with mobile toilet). Originally, mansions such as Torre Tagle served as refuges for outlaws, the authorities being unable to enter without written and stamped permission from the owners – now anyone can pop in (afternoons are the quietest times to visit).

Centro Cultural Inca Garcilaso

Jr Ucayali 391 • Tues–Sun 11am–7pm • Free • ⓣ 01 204 2658

By Torre Tagle, you'll find the **Centro Cultural Inca Garcilaso**, built in 1685 as the Casa Aspillaga but restored during the late nineteenth century and again in 2003. It contains an art gallery (mainly temporary photographic or sculpture exhibitions) but is most interesting for its Neoclassical Republican-style architecture.

Casa Aliaga

Jr de la Unión 224 • Tours daily 9.30am–5pm by appointment (outside guide required) • S/30 • ⓦ casadealiaga.com • Book through Lima Tours at ⓣ 01 619 5000 or ⓣ 01 619 6911, or inquire through website about available guides

Heading north from the Plaza Mayor you pass the **Casa Aliaga**, an unusual mansion, reputed to be the oldest in South America, and occupied by seventeen generations of the same family since 1535, making it the oldest colonial house still standing in the Americas. It's also one of the most elaborate mansions in the country, with sumptuous reception rooms full of Louis XIV mirrors, furniture and doors. It was built on top of an Inca palace and is divided stylishly into various salons (note the living room with fireplace and blue *azulejo* tiles) where wood features heavily.

Iglesia de Santo Domingo

Jr Camaná 170 • Mon–Sat 9am–noon & 3–6pm, Sun & hols 9am–1pm • Church free, tombs S/7 • ⓣ 01 427 6793

Just off Plaza Mayor, a block behind the Palacio Municipal, is the church and monastery of **Santo Domingo**. Completed in 1549, Santo Domingo was presented by the pope, a century or so later, with an alabaster statue of Santa Rosa de Lima. The **tombs** of Santa Rosa, San Martín de Porres and San Juan Masias (a Spaniard who was canonized in Peru) are the building's great attractions, and much revered. Otherwise the church is not of huge interest or architectural merit, although it is one of the oldest religious structures in Lima, built on a site granted to the Dominicans by Pizarro in 1535.

Casa de Osambela

Jr Conde de Superunda 298 • Guided tours Mon–Fri 9am–12.45pm & 2–4.45pm • Free; donation appreciated

The early nineteenth-century **Casa de Osambela** has five balconies on its facade and a lookout point from which boats arriving at the port of Callao could be spotted by the first owner, Martín de Osambela. This mansion is home to the Centro Cultural Inca Garcilaso de la Vega, which offers **guided tours** of the building.

Sanctuario de Santa Rosa de Lima

Av Tacna 100 • Mon–Sat 9am–1pm & 3–6pm • Free • ⓣ 01 425 1279

Two traditional sanctuaries (see page 65) can be found on the western edge of old Lima, along Avenida Tacna. Completed in 1728, the **Sanctuario de Santa Rosa de Lima** is a fairly plain church named in honour of the first saint canonized in the Americas. The construction of Avenida Tacna destroyed a section, but in the patio next door you can visit the saint's **hermitage**, a small adobe cell; there's also a 20m-deep well where devotees drop written requests.

Iglesia de San Agustín

Jirones Ica and Camaná • Daily 8–11am & 4.30–8pm • Free • ⓣ 01 427 7548

The southern stretch between the Plaza Mayor and Plaza San Martín is the largest area of Old Lima, home to several important churches, including **San Agustín**, founded in 1592. Although severely damaged by earthquakes (only the small side-chapel can be

EARTHQUAKES AND MIRACLES

Despite its small size and undistinguished appearance, the **Iglesia de las Nazarenas** (daily 6am–noon & 4–8.30pm; free; ⓣ 01 423 5718), on the corner of Avenida Tacna and Huancavelica, has an unusual history. After the severe **1655 earthquake**, a mural of the Crucifixion, painted by an Angolan slave on the wall of his hut and originally titled *Cristo de Pachacamilla*, was the only structure left standing in the district; this also occurred during the quake of 1687. Its survival was deemed a miracle – the cause and focus of popular processions ever since – and it was on this site that the church was founded in the eighteenth century. The widespread and popular **processions for the Lord of Miracles**, to save Lima from another earthquake, take place every spring (Oct 18, 19, 28 & Nov 1), and focus on a silver litter, which carries the original mural. **Purple** is the colour of the procession and many women in Lima wear it for the entire month.

visited nowadays), the church retains a glorious **facade**, one of the most complicated examples of Churrigueresque–Mestizo architecture in Peru; it originally had a Renaissance doorway, traces of which can be seen from Jirón Camaná.

Casa de Riva-Aguero

Jr Camaná 459 • Daily 10am–1pm & 2–5pm • S/3 • ⓣ 01 626 6600

Across the road from San Agustín, the **Casa de Riva-Aguero** is a typical colonial house, built in the mid-eighteenth century by a wealthy businessman and later sold to the Aguero family. Its patio has been laid out as a **Museo de Arte y Tradiciones Populares**, displaying crafts and contemporary paintings from all over Peru.

Iglesia de la Merced

Jr de la Unión 621 and Av Miro Quesada • Mon–Sat 8am–noon & 5–8pm, Sun 7am–noon & 5–8pm; cloisters daily 8am–noon & 5–6pm • Free • Guided visits ⓣ 01 427 8199

Perhaps the most noted of all religious buildings in Lima is the **Iglesia de la Merced**, two blocks south of the Plaza Mayor. Built on the site where the first Latin Mass in Lima was celebrated, the original sixteenth-century church was demolished in 1628 to make way for the present building, whose ornate granite facade, dating back to 1687, has been adapted and rebuilt several times – as have the broad columns of the nave – to protect the church against tremors.

By far the most lasting impression is made by the **Cross of the Venerable Padre Urraca** (La Cruz de Padre Urraca El Venerable), whose silver staff is witness to the fervent prayers of a constantly shifting congregation, smothered by hundreds of kisses every hour. If you've just arrived in Lima, a few minutes by this cross may give you an insight into the depth of Peruvian belief in miraculous power. Be careful if you get surrounded by the ubiquitous sellers of candles and religious icons around the entrance – **pick-pockets** are at work here.

Iglesia de Jesus María y José

Jr Camaná 765 and Jr Moquegua • Daily 7am–1pm & 3–7pm • Free

Close to the Plaza San Martín stands the **Iglesia de Jesus María y José**, home of Capuchin nuns from Madrid in the early eighteenth century; its particularly outstanding interior contains sparkling Baroque gilt altars and pulpits.

Plaza San Martín

A large, grand square with fountains at its centre, the **Plaza San Martín** is almost always busy by day, with traffic tooting its way around the perimeter. Nevertheless, it's a place where you can sit down for a few minutes – at least until hassled by street sellers or shoeshine boys.

Ideologically, the Plaza San Martín represents the sophisticated, egalitarian and European spirit of intellectual liberators like San Martín himself, while remaining well and truly within the commercial world. The plaza has attracted most of Lima's major **political rallies** over the past hundred years, and rioting students, teachers or workers and attendant police with water cannons and tear gas are always a (rare) possibility here.

Plaza Dos de Mayo

The city's main rallying point for political protests is **Plaza Dos de Mayo**, linked to the Plaza San Martín by the wide Avenida Nicolás de Piérola (also known as La Colmena). Built to commemorate the repulse of the Spanish fleet in 1866 – Spain's last attempt to regain a foothold in South America – the plaza is markedly busier and less visitor-friendly than Plaza San Martín. It sits on the site of an old gate dividing Lima from the road to Callao.

Casona de San Marcos

Av Nicolás de Piérola 1222 • Mon–Sat 9am–5pm • S/5 • T 01 619 7000, W ccsm-unmsm.edu.pe

East of Plaza San Martín, Avenida Nicolás de Piérola runs towards the **Parque Universitario**, site of South America's first university. Right on the park itself, the **Casona de San Marcos** is home to the Centro Cultural de San Marcos and the Ballet de San Marcos. Once lodgings for the Jesuit novitiate San Antonio Abad (patron saint of everything from animals to skin complaints), it's a pleasant seventeenth-century complex with some fine architectural features including colonial cloisters, a Baroque chapel, a small **art and archeology museum**, exhibitions and a great café. The **amphitheatre** in the park is sometimes used for free public performances by musicians and artists.

Museo de Arte Italiano

Paseo de la República 250, Parque Neptuno • Tues–Sun 10am–5pm • S/6 • T 01 321 5622

South of Plaza San Martín, Jirón Belén leads down to the Paseo de la República and the shady **Parque Neptuno**, home to the pleasant **Museo de Arte Italiano**. Located inside a relatively small and highly ornate Neoclassical building that's unusual for Lima, built by the Italian architect Gaetano Moretti, the museum exhibits oils, bronzes and ceramics by Italian artists, and offers welcome respite from the hectic city outside.

Parque de la Exposición

Entrance at corner of Paseo Colón and Av Wilson • Free

The extensive, leafy **Parque de la Exposición** was originally created for the International Exhibition of Agricultural Machines in 1872. Conspicuously green for Lima, the park is where lovers meet at weekends and students hang out amid greenery, pagodas, an amphitheatre, a small lake and organized music and dance performances at fiesta times. The park stretches a couple of hundred metres down to Avenida 28 de Julio, from where it's just a few blocks to the Estadio Nacional and **Parque de la Reserva** (see page 67).

Museo de Arte de Lima

Paseo Colón 125 • Tues–Fri & Sun 10am–7pm, Sat 10am–5pm • S/30 • T 01 204 0000 ext 212, W mali.pe

Within the park, a couple of minutes' walk south of the Museo de Arte Italiano, is the commanding **Museo de Arte de Lima**, housed in the former International Exhibition Palace, which was built in 1868. The museum holds interesting permanent collections of colonial art, as well as many fine crafts from pre-Columbian times, and also hosts frequent international exhibitions of modern photography and video as well as contemporary Peruvian art. Film shows and lectures are offered on some weekday evenings (check the website, *El Comercio* newspaper listings or posters in the lobby).

Casa Museo José Carlos Mariátegui

Jr Washington 1946 • Mon–Fri 9am–1pm & 2–5pm, Sat 9am–1pm • Free

Not far from the Parque de la Cultura Peruana is the **Casa Museo José Carlos Mariátegui**, an early twentieth-century one-storey house – home for the last few years of his life to the famous Peruvian political figure, ideologist and writer Mariátegui –

which has been restored by the Instituto Nacional de Cultura. The period furnishings reveal less about this man than his writings, but the house is kept alive in honour of one of Peru's greatest twentieth-century political writers.

Parque de la Reserva

Between the Paseo de la República and Av Arequipa • Tues–Sun & hols 3–10.30pm; fountains go off at 7.15pm, 8.15pm & 9.30pm • S/4 • ⓦ circuitomagicodelagua.com.pe

The **Parque de la Reserva**, next to the Estadio Nacional, was superbly and imaginatively refurbished in 2007. Within the park, near blocks 5–8 of Avenida Arequipa, is the splendid array of themed water features which comprises the **circuito mágico del agua**, or "magical water circuit". It's a popular haunt, boasting fifteen colourful and well-lit **fountains**, some of which spurt some 80m into the air. Watch out for the Fuente de Fantasía, which moves to music, and the Cupula Visitable, which you can climb inside of (expect to get drenched), as well as the beautiful water pyramid and the Tunel de Sorpresas (Tunnel of Surprises), which you can walk through. It all makes for one of Lima's most memorable evening attractions, especially for kids who can run through the spouts.

Puente de Piedra

It's a short walk north up Jirón de la Unión from the Plaza Mayor to the **Puente de Piedra**, the stone bridge that arches over the Río Rimac – usually no more than a miserable trickle – behind the Palacio de Gobierno. Initially a wooden construction, the current brick structure was built in the seventeenth century, using egg whites with sand and lime to improve the consistency of its mortar.

Rimac

The function of the Puente de Piedra was to provide a permanent link between the centre of town and the Barrio of San Lázaro, known these days as **Rimac**, or, more popularly, as **Bajo El Puente** ("below the bridge"). This district was first populated in the sixteenth century by African slaves, newly arrived and awaiting purchase by big plantation owners; a few years later Rimac was beleaguered by outbreaks of leprosy. Although these days its status is much improved, Rimac is still one of the most run-down areas of Lima. It can be quite an aggressive place after dark, when drug addicts and thieves abound, and it's **dangerous** to walk this area alone at any time of day. Take a taxi direct to where you want to go.

Museo Taurino de Acho

Jr Hualgayoc 332 • Mon–Sat 9am–4.30pm • S/5 • ⓣ 01 482 3360

Rimac is home to the **Plaza de Acho**, Lima's most important **bullring** (see page 68), which also houses the **Museo Taurino de Acho**, or Bullfight Museum, containing some original **Goya engravings**, several related paintings and a few relics of bullfighting contests.

The Alameda de los Descalzos and Paseo de Aguas

A few blocks to the right of the bridge, you can stroll up the **Alameda de los Descalzos** (though best not to do so alone, even in daylight), a fine tree-lined walk designed for courtship, and an afternoon meeting place for the early seventeenth- to nineteenth-century elite (the railings were added in 1853). Along the way stands the **Paseo de Aguas**, built by Viceroy Amat in the eighteenth century. It leads past the foot of a distinctive hill, the **Cerro San Cristóbal**, and, although in desperate need of renovation, it still possesses twelve appealing marble **statues** brought from Italy in 1856, each one representing a different sign of the zodiac.

At the far end of the Alameda is a fine Franciscan monastery, **Convento de los Descalzos** (daily 9.30am–12.30pm & 2–5pm; S/7, usually including a 40min tour; ⓣ01 481 0441), dating from 1592 and housing a collection of colonial and Republican paintings from Peru and Ecuador; its chapel – **La Capilla El Carmen** – possesses a

BULLFIGHTING IN LIMA

Bullfighting has been a popular pastime among a relatively small, wealthy elite from the Spanish Conquest to the present day, despite some 185 years of independence from Spain. Pizarro himself brought out the first *lidia* bull for fighting in Lima, and the controlling families of Peru – the same families who breed fighting bulls on their haciendas – maintain the tradition. They invite some of the world's most renowned bullfighters from Spain, Mexico and Venezuela, offering them significant sums for an afternoon's "sport" at the prestigious **Plaza de Acho** in Rimac. Events are held mostly on Sunday afternoons in October and November.

beautiful Baroque gold-leaf altar. The monastery was built in what was then a secluded spot beyond the town, originally a retreat from the busy heart of the city at the base of Cerro San Cristóbal. Now, of course, the city runs all around it and way beyond.

Lima's suburbs

The old centre of Lima is surrounded by a number of sprawling **suburbs**, or *distritos*, which spread across the desert between the foothills of the Andes and the coast. A short drive south of Lima Centro lies the lively district of **Miraflores**, a slick, fast-moving mini-metropolis, which has become Lima's business and shopping zone, with a coast walk watched over by expensive apartments. South of Miraflores begins the oceanside suburb of **Barranco**, one of the oldest and most attractive parts of Lima, above the steep sandy cliffs of the **Costa Verde**, hosting a small nightlife enclave. Sandwiched between Lima Centro and Miraflores is plush **San Isidro**, boasting both the city's main commercial and banking sector and a golf course surrounded by sky-scraping apartment buildings. West of here, **Pueblo Libre** is older, an established home to several good museums. To the east lies **San Borja**, a more recently constructed district with another fine museum, the Museo de la Nación. The city's port area, **Callao**, is an atmospheric if rather old and unsavoury zone tapering into the western peninsula of **La Punta**, with its air of slightly decayed grandeur. Lima city's sprawl means that there are massive urban areas to the north, the south, and into the western foothills of the Andes, where the upmarket suburb of **Monterrico** is found.

Miraflores

As far as Lima's inhabitants are concerned, **Miraflores** is the major focus of the city's action and nightlife, its streets lined with cafés and the capital's flashiest shops. **Larco Mar**, a modern commercial complex built into the cliffside at the bottom of Miraflores' main svenue, adds to its swanky appeal. Although still connected to Lima Centro by the long-established Avenida Arequipa, which is served by frequent colectivos, another generally faster road – Paseo de la República (also known as the Vía Expressa and El Zanjón) – provides the suburb with an alternative route for cars and buses.

Most of Lima's popular city **beaches**, like the surfers' hangout of **Playa Wakiki**, are directly below the sea-facing cliffs of Miraflores, visible from Larco Mar and accessible on foot, down a long, hill-hugging stairway, from **Parque Kennedy**.

Huaca Pucllana

General Borgoño 800 • Mon & Wed–Sun 9am–4.30pm • S/12 • T 01 617 7138, W huacapucllanamiraflores.pe/english • A 5min walk from Av Arequipa, on the right as you come from Lima Centro at block 44

A good place to make for first is the **Huaca Pucllana**, a pre-Columbian temple, tomb and administrative centre in the middle of suburban Miraflores. One of a large number of *huacas* and palaces that formerly stretched across this part of the valley, little is known about the Huaca Pucllana, though it seems likely it was named after a pre-Inca chief of the area. It has a hollow core and is believed to have been constructed in the shape of an enormous frog, symbol of the rain god, who spoke to priests through a tube connected to the cavern at its heart. The site may well have been the mysterious

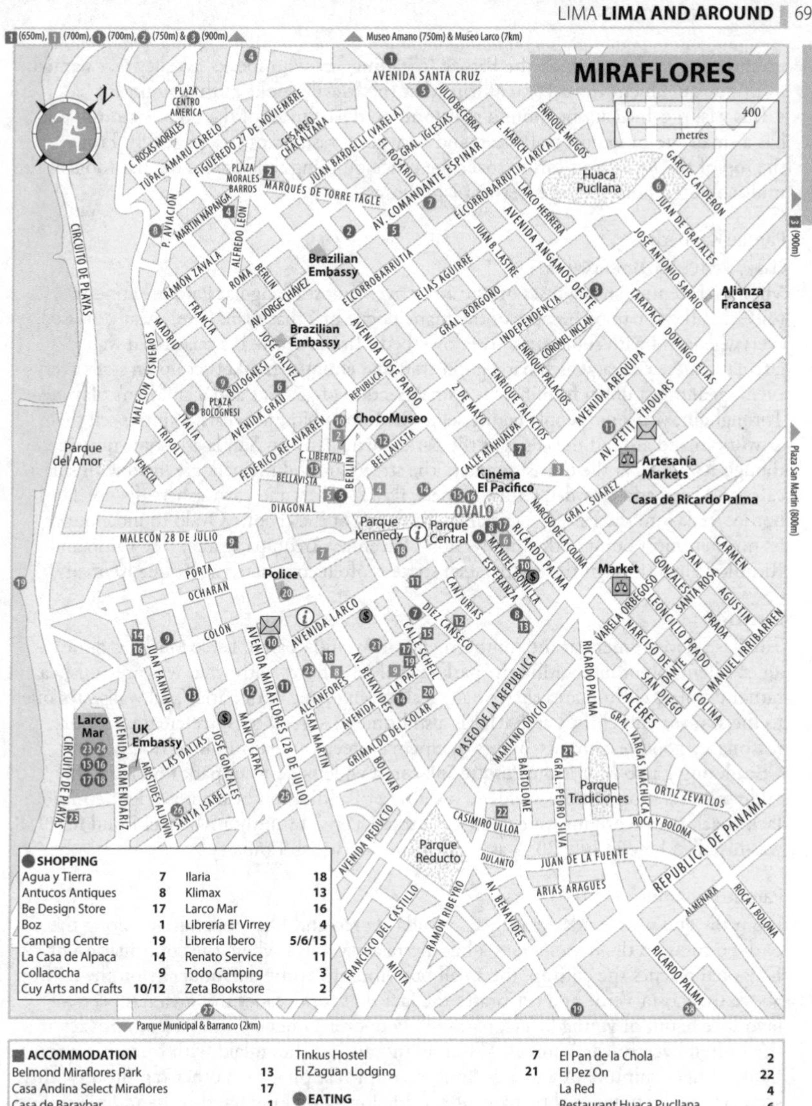

ACCOMMODATION

Belmond Miraflores Park	13
Casa Andina Select Miraflores	17
Casa de Baraybar	1
Casa del Mochilero	2
Colonial Inn	5
Embajadores Hotel	14
Explorer's House	4
Faraoña Grande Hotel	10
HI Hostel Lima	22
Hospedaje Flying Dog	11
Hospedaje Tinkus	19
Hostal Buena Vista	20
Hostal El Patio	12
Hostal Martinika	3
Hostal Pariwana	8
Hotel Antigua Miraflores	6
Miraflores Colón Hotel	16
Pensión José Luís	23
Radisson Decapolis Miraflores	9
Sonesta Posadas del Inca Miraflores	15
Tierra Viva Miraflores Larco	18
Tinkus Hostel	7
El Zaguan Lodging	21

EATING

ámaZ	25
Arabica Espreso Bar	10
Aromia	13
Bio Leben	21
Las Brujas de Cachiche	9
Café Café	14
Café Haiti	15
Café Verde	5
Central	26
Club Suizo	28
D'nnos Pizza	7
El Kapallaq	27
La Lucha Sanguchería	16
Maido	20
Mama Lola	18
Mangos	23
La Mar	3
El Mercado	1
El Pan de la Chola	2
El Pez On	22
La Red	4
Restaurant Huaca Pucllana	6
Restaurant Tai-i Vegetariano	11
La Rosa Nautica	19
Scena Restaurant Bar	12
El Señorio de Sulco	8
Tanta	24
La Tiendacita Blanca	17

DRINKING & NIGHTLIFE

Downtown Vale Todo	7
La Emolientería	5
Habana Café Bar	6
Jazz Zone	9
Legendaris	2
Lola Bar	8
Nebula	3
The Old Pub	4
Peña Sachún	1
Satchmo	9

unknown oracle after which the Rimac (meaning "he who speaks") Valley was named; a curious document from 1560 affirms that the "devil" spoke at this mound.

This vast pre-Inca adobe mound continues to dwarf most of the houses around and has a small site museum, craft shop and very good restaurant (see page 88). From the top of the *huaca* you can see over the office buildings and across the flat roofs of the multicoloured houses in the heart of Miraflores.

Parque Kennedy

C Diagonal and C Schell • Market daily 6–9pm

Miraflores' central area focuses on the attractive, almost triangular **Parque Kennedy** (or Cat Park, so named because of the many docile cats that roam here), neatly grassed everywhere and with some attractive flowerbeds. In the centre is a raised and walled, circular concrete area, which has a good **craft and antiques market** set up on stalls every evening; and just down from here is a small section of gardens and a children's play area. Throughout, you'll see people taking selfies with the ubiquitous cats. Painters sell their artwork in and around the edges of the park, particularly on Sundays – some quite good, though it's aimed at the tourist market. The streets around the park are lined with smart cafés and bars, and crowded with shoppers, flower-sellers and car-washers. Its northern border feeds into the Parque Central, culminating at the chaotic Óvalo roundabout at its northernmost point at the intersection of avenues Arequipa, Larco, José Pardo and Ricardo Palma (though the entire green space is often considered as Parque Kennedy).

Larco Mar

The flash development at the southern end of Avenida Larco, **Larco Mar**, has done an excellent job of integrating the park end of Miraflores with what was previously a rather desolate clifftop area. Essentially a shopping zone with patios and walkways open to the sky, sea and cliffs, Larco Mar is also home to several bars, ice-cream parlours, reasonably good restaurants, a host of cinema screens and a couple of trendy clubs.

Bordering Larco Mar is the **Parque Salazar**, a wide pedestrian park unremarkable aside from its most famous resident: a statue of Paddington bear (in a bright Union Jack coat), whose origins were cited as "darkest Peru" by author Michael Bond in 1958, was installed here in July 2015 as a gift from the British Embassy.

Parque del Amor

From the end of Avenida Arequipa, avenidas Larco and Diagonal fan out along the park en route to the ocean about a kilometre away. Near where the continuation of Diagonal reaches the clifftop, the small but vibrant **Parque del Amor** sits on the clifftop above the Costa Verde and celebrates the fact that for decades this area has been a favourite haunt of young lovers, particularly poorer Limeños who have no privacy in their often overcrowded homes. Winding mosaic benches inlaid with romantic quotes flank a huge sculpture of a loving Andean couple clasping each other rapturously; this scene is usually populated by pairs of real-life lovers walking hand-in-hand or cuddling on the clifftop, especially at sunset and on Sunday afternoons.

Casa de Ricardo Palma

General Suarez 189 • Mon–Fri 9am–12.45pm & 2.30–5pm • S/6 • 01 617 7115 or 01 445 5836, ricardopalma.miraflores.gob.pe

Miraflores' only important mansion open to the public is the **Casa de Ricardo Palma**, where Palma, Peru's greatest historian, lived for most of his life. Located between Avenida Arequipa and the Paseo de la República, just behind the artesanía markets on Petit Thouars (see page 96), the nineteenth-century house has some architectural merit, but is mostly visited for an insight into Palma's lifestyle, through the household furnishings, and his mind, through first editions of his written works and some diary extracts. The set of spacious rooms includes a music room, bedrooms, patio and bathroom, all of which can be explored.

Museo Enrico Poli

Lord Cochrane 466 • S/60 per person; minimum five people • By appointment only; call ⓣ 01 422 2437 or ⓣ 01 654 4531 or ask in person

The **Museo Enrico Poli** contains some of the finest pre-Inca archeological treasures in Lima, including ceramics, gold and silver. The highlight of this private collection is the treasure found at **Sipán** in northern Peru, in particular four golden trumpets, each over a metre long and over a thousand years old. As contact is difficult (the phone is rarely answered, and there's no message service), going to ask in person may be the easiest way to arrange a visit.

Museo Amano

C Retiro 160, by block 11 of Av Angamos Oeste • Tues–Sun 10am–5pm, Mon by appointment • S/30 • ⓣ 01 441 2909, ⓦ museoamano.org

The private **Museo Amano** merits a visit for its fabulous exhibition of beautifully displayed textiles, mainly Chancay weavings (among the best of pre-Columbian textiles) but also including works from ten other Peruvian civilizations like the Chavin and the Huari. In addition, check out the display of tools used to create the fabrics, as well as some 400 different textile types in the viewable storage facility room.

ChocoMuseo

C Berlín 375 • Daily 11am–7.30pm • Free • ⓣ 01 445 9708, ⓦ chocomuseo.com/#peru

A museum, café and gift store, Lima's **ChocoMuseo** explores the history and process of chocolate making in Peru; the knowledgeable guides can answer all your questions, leading you around a model cacao tree, sacks of real cacao beans to run your fingers through and taste tests of every stage from cacao to chocolate. Detailed plaques in English and Spanish explain the process from bean to cup. The tour finishes with some samples and a bit of a sales pitch, but the products – chocolate tea, liqueurs, fresh hot chocolate and raw chocolate (using unroasted cacao) – are all delicious. There are also free chocolate-making workshops. Other branches can be found at the Plaza de Armas (Jr Carabaya 191) and bordering Parque Kennedy (C Diagonal 344).

Parque Reducto

Av Benavides, by Paseo de la República

The greatest attraction of the **Parque Reducto** is arguably the Saturday-morning organic food and sustainable products **market** (8am–noon), which takes place along its southern edge. There's also a good kids' play area, and a **museum** (Mon–Sat 7am–5pm; free) dedicated to the Municipality of Miraflores and the Peruvian army, in particular to the latter's battle against invading forces from Chile – the 1881 Battle of Miraflores. Exhibits include war memorabilia, photographs, small cannons and guns.

Barranco

Some 3km south of Larco Mar and quieter than Miraflores, **Barranco** overlooks the ocean and is scattered with old mansions, including fine colonial and Republican edifices, many beginning to crumble through lack of care. This was the capital's seaside resort during the nineteenth century and is now a kind of Limeño Left Bank, with young artists, writers, musicians and intellectuals taking over some of the

LIMA FROM THE AIR

To see Lima from a completely different perspective, jump off the coastal cliffs in Miraflores (from Parque Raimondi, next to Parque del Amor) on a tandem **paragliding flight**. Flights take around ten to fifteen minutes, and you're in the safe hands of expert guides and teachers Mike Fernandez, from Aeroextreme (Tripoli 345, Dpto 503, Miraflores; ⓣ 01 242 5125 or ⓣ 999 480 954, ⓦ aeroextreme.com), and Jorge Hernández and Eduardo Reátegui of Paragliding Peru (ⓣ 01 495 3396, ⓦ paragliding-peru.com/en/tandem-flights.com) throughout. No previous experience necessary, and you don't need to reserve. Prices hover around S/260 including equipment and HD video card; for Paragliding Peru this includes insurance.

older properties. Only covering three square kilometres, Barranco is quite densely populated, with some 40,000 inhabitants living in its delicately coloured houses. The area's primary attractions are its **bars, clubs and cafés**, and there's little else in the way of specific sights, though you may want to take a look at the clifftop remains of a **funicular rail-line**, which used to carry aristocratic families from the summer resort down to the beach.

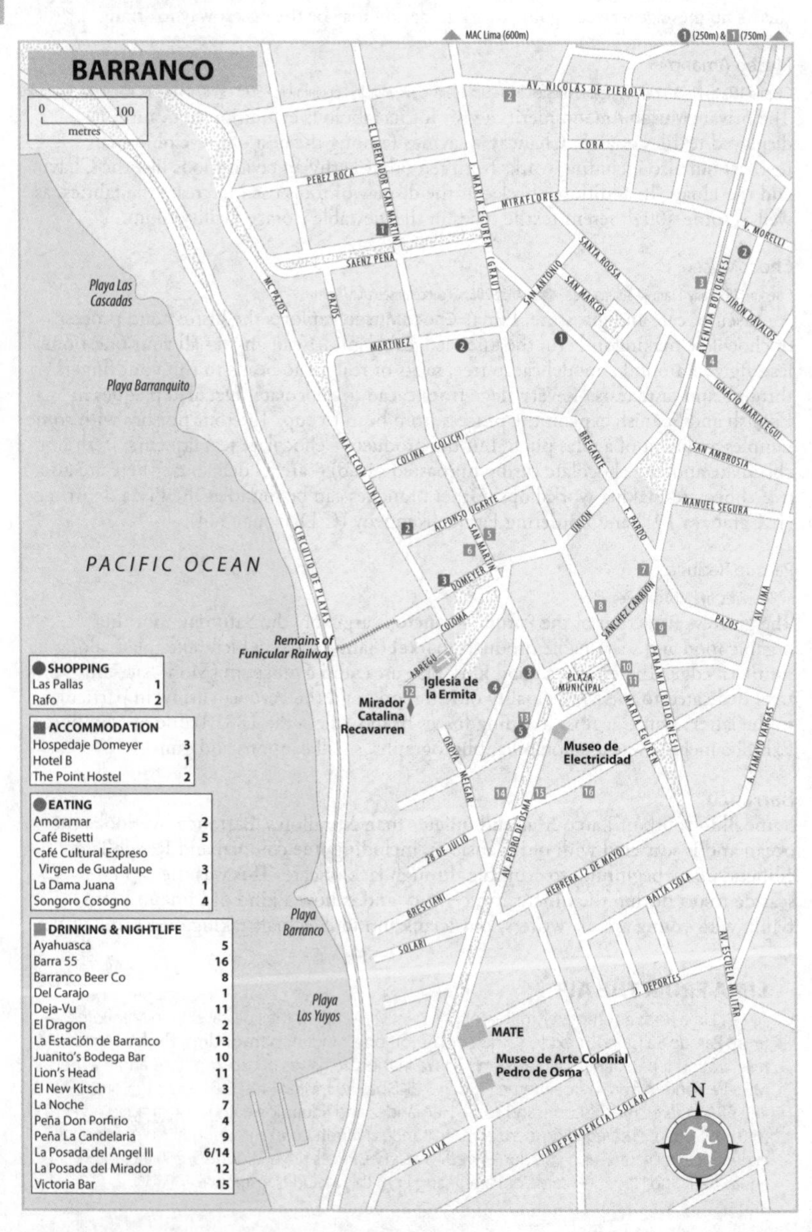

Plaza Municipal de Barranco and south

The small but busy and well-kept **Plaza Municipal de Barranco** is the hub of the area's **nightlife**: the bars, clubs and cafés clustered around the square buzz with frenetic energy after dark, while retaining much of the area's charm and character. A few museums near here are worth a browse: the **Museo de Electricidad** (Pedro de Osma 105; currently closed, but expected to reopen by 2019); the **Museo de Arte Contemporáneo**; the **Museo de Arte Colonial Pedro de Osma**; and the gallery devoted to photographer Mario Testino, **MATE**.

Museo de Arte Contemporáneo (MAC Lima)

Av Miguel Grau 1511 • Tues–Sun 10am–6pm • S/10 • T 01 514 6800, W maclima.pe

A stone's throw from Miraflores, and opened only five years ago, the spare, white-walled **MAC Lima** shows a worthy collection of Latin American and European artists only begun in the 1950s. It includes works from some less exhibited schools like geometric art and constructivism, in addition to abstract expressionism and pieces with a more surreal or pop art inclination.

Museo de Arte Colonial Pedro de Osma

Av Pedro de Osma 421 • Tues–Sun 10am–6pm • S/20 • **Tours** 5 daily Wed–Sat; 1hr • Free with entry • T 01 467 0141, W museopedrodeosma.org

The oft-overlooked **Museo Pedro de Osma** wonderfully details the process by which the **Cusco school** of religious painting developed in the seventeenth and eighteenth centuries. As the country came under European control, Flemish and Italian painting masters arrived in the 1570s. As a means of spreading the story of Christianity to Peruvians – used to worshiping the gods of sky, earth and underworld – these painters had local artists literally recreate notable works from copies printed on small cards. After years of "straight" copies, you can see Peruvian aesthetics introduced in the subjects' dress and ornamentation, and eventually in their facial features.

The painting and sculpture pieces are presented in the gorgeous main building full of stained-glass windows commissioned by the former mayor of Barranco in 1906; the collection belonged to his son, Pedro de Osma Gildemeister, who passed away in 1967. The handsome property also holds a **gallery** of furniture and portraits of the family, a room housing colonial silver jewellery and another gallery displaying art from the southern Andes.

MATE

Av Pedro de Osma 409 • Tues–Sun 10am–7pm • S/25 • T 01 200 5400, W mate.pe

Perhaps the best antidote for Lima's heavy dosage of churches and ancient civilizations is this **MATE**, a museum devoted to **Mario Testino**, famed photographer of high-fashion models and celebrity nightlife. The prints, many from shoots for Vanity Fair or Vogue, are all blown up to gigantic size; there's a separate exhibit of his warm, intimate shots of the late Princess Diana in 1997, which were to be her last official portraits. In addition, there's a looping ten-minute film/slideshow of a Testino interview backed with hundreds of photos from the permanent collection, all fading into one another in a technicolour blur.

Iglesia de la Ermita and around

One block inland of the funicular, the impressive **Iglesia de la Ermita** (Church of the Hermit) sits on the cliff, with gardens to its front. Local legend says that the church was built here after a miraculous vision of a glowing Christ figure on this very spot. Beside the church is the **Puente de los Suspiros**, a pretty wooden bridge crossing a gully – the Bajada de Baños – which leads steeply down to the ocean, passing exotic dwellings lining the crumbling gully sides. A path leads beside the church along the top edge of the gully to the **Mirador Catalina Recavarren**, boasting lovely sea views. There's a uniquely situated pub, *La Posada del Mirador* (see page 91), at the end of the path, as well as some other pleasant cafés and bars, buzzing on weekend evenings.

Costa Verde and Chorillos

Down beside the pounding rollers lies the **Costa Verde** beach area, so named because of vegetation clinging to the steep sandy cliffs. The Circuito de Playas highway follows the shore, heading southeast from Lima's less inviting northern districts, past Miraflores and Barranco, towards **Chorrillos**. The sea is cold here, but the surfers still brave it. Chorrillos' **Fisherman's Wharf** (S/1) is always an interesting place for a stroll, surrounded by pelicans and, early in the day, fishermen unloading their catch, which is delivered immediately to the neighbouring market. The outdoor restaurants here (which close by mid-afternoon) compete vigorously for customers; all of them are pretty good and, not surprisingly, have a reputation for serving the freshest **ceviche** in Lima.

San Isidro

Unless you're shopping, banking or looking for a disco, there are few reasons to stop off in **San Isidro** aside from its galleries (see page 76). The exception is to take a stroll through the **Bosque El Olivar** – 150m west from Avenida Arequipa, along Calle Choquehuanca – one of Lima's relatively few large, open, green spaces. A charming grove first planted in 1560, it's now rather depleted in olive trees but you can still see the old press and millstone, and the grove has developed its own **ecosystem**, which is home to over thirty different **bird species** including doves, flycatchers and hummingbirds. There's also a stage where concerts and cultural events are often held.

Huallamarca

Nicolás de Rivera 201, just off Av El Rosario • Tues–Sun 9am–5pm • S/5

A few blocks northwest of the Bosque El Olivar and a few north of Lima Golf Club, the impressive reconstructed adobe *huaca*, **Huallamarca**, is now surrounded by wealthy suburbs. Like Pucllana (see page 68), this dates from pre-Inca days and has a small **museum** displaying the archeological remains of ancient Lima culture, such as funerary masks and artwork found in the *huaca* – including textiles oddly reminiscent of Scottish tartans.

Museo de Historia Natural Jesús María

Av Arenales 1256, Jesús María • Mon–Fri 9am–5.15pm, Sat 9am–4.30pm, Sun 10am–4.30pm • S/7 • **Tours** S/25 per group (in Spanish), S/40 per group (in English or Portuguese) • T 01 619 7000

The workaday suburb of **Jesús María**, west of San Isidro and Lince, south of Lima Centro, has only one real attraction: the little-visited, but quite fascinating, **Museo de Historia Natural Jesús María**. The museum presents a comprehensive if dusty overview of Peruvian wildlife and botany. One highlight is the sun fish: one of only three known examples of this colourful fish that can be found in the American coastal waters. There are also great **gardens** with botany displays, as well as a **geology** section.

Pueblo Libre

The quiet backstreets of **Pueblo Libre**, a relatively insalubrious suburb lying between San Isidro and Callao, on the western edge of Lima, is now home to two of Lima's major **museums**. These are quite tucked away, so you should definitely take a taxi.

Museo Nacional de Arqueología, Antropología e Historia del Peru (MNAAHP)

Plaza Bolívar, San Martín and Antonio Pola • Daily 8.45am–5pm • S/10 • T 01 321 5630, W mnaahp.cultura.pe • **Tours** S/20 • Phone a week in advance on T 01 321 5630, ext 5255

First among Pueblo Libre's attractions is the **Museo Nacional de Arqueología, Antropología e Historia del Peru**, which has a varied collection of pre-Inca artefacts and a number of historical exhibits relating mainly to the Republican period (1821 until the late nineteenth

HUACA PUCLLANA

LIMA'S ART AND PHOTOGRAPHY GALLERIES

Lima's progressive culture of **art and photography** is deeply rooted in the Latin American tradition, combining indigenous ethnic realism with a political edge.

Centro Cultural PUCP Av Camino Real 1075, San Isidro ⊕01 616 1616. Art gallery hosting visiting exhibitions by foreign artists. Daily 10am–10pm.

Centro Cultural Ricardo Palma Av Larco 770, Miraflores ⊕01 617 7263. Hosts fixed and changing exhibitions of paintings, photographs and sculpture on one side of a space that also features performances. Daily 9am–10pm.

Corriente Alterna Av de la Aviación 500, Miraflores ⊕01 242 8482. Visual art school with accomplished student presentations. Mon–Fri 9am–7pm, Sat 9am–1pm.

Enlace Arte Contemporáneo Av Camino Real El Bosque 291, San Isidro ⊕01 222 5714. Hope for a peek at works by surrealist Hugo Salazar or photorealist Christian Bendayán, from Callao and Iquitos, respectively. Mon–Sat 11am–8pm.

Galeria L'Imaginaire Av Arequipa 4595, Miraflores ⊕01 610 8000. Usually exhibits Latin American painters and sculptors. Mon–Sat 5–9pm.

Revolver Galería Av El Bosque 291, San Isidro ⊕01 608 0884. Installations and photography exhibitions in a modern space. Tues–Sat 11am–8pm.

Sala Cultural del Banco Wiese Av Larco 1101, Miraflores ⊕01 446 5240. A contemporary, international art gallery in the Banco Weise in the heart of downtown Miraflores. Mon–Sat 10am–2pm & 5–9pm.

century). The liberators San Martín and Bolívar both lived here for a while. Although there's plenty to see, most more of the museum's immense collection is in storage, though some has permanently shifted to the Museo de la Nación (see page 78).

Renovated displays give a detailed and accurate perspective on Peru's prehistory, a vision that comes as a surprise if you'd previously thought of Peru simply in terms of Incas and Conquistadors. The galleries are set around two colonial-style courtyards, with exhibits including stone **tools** some 8000 years old, Chavín-era **carved stones** engraved with felines and serpents, and the Manos Cruzados or Crossed Hands stone from Kotosh, evidence of a mysterious cult from some five thousand years ago. From the Paracas culture there are sumptuous **weavings** and many excellent examples of deformed heads and trepanned **skulls;** a male mummy, "frozen" at the age of 30 to 35, has fingernails still visible and a creepy, sideways glance fixed on his misshapen head. The **Nazca**, **Mochica** and **Chimu cultures** (see page 486) are represented, too, and there are of course exhibits devoted to the **Incas.** The national history section shows off some dazzling antique clothing, extravagant furnishings and other period pieces, complemented by early Republican paintings.

Museo Larco

Av Bolívar 1515 • Daily 9am–10pm • S/30 • ⊕01 461 1312, ⓦmuseolarco.org • Walking from MNAAHP, follow the blue path painted on the pavement north up Av Sucre, turn left on C Cordova, then head west for ten blocks on Av Bolivar

Within a fifteen-minute walk of the district's other museum is one of Lima's most striking attractions, the **Museo Larco** (the familiar name for the **Museo Rafael Larco Herrera**) which contains hundreds of thousands of excellently preserved **ceramics**, many of them Chiclin or Mochica pottery from around Trujillo. The museum houses the largest collection of Peruvian antiquities in the world and is divided into three sections: the **main museum**, which contains an incredible range of household and funerary ceramics, textiles, ornaments and jewellery, including bold silver and gold head and neck pieces; the **warehouse museum**, with shelf after shelf stacked with 40,000 ceramics; and the **erotic art museum**, holding a wide selection of sexually themed pre-Inca artefacts – mainly from the explicit Mochica culture – which tends to attract the most interest.

The mansion itself is noteworthy as a stylish *casa Trujillana*, in the style of the northern city where this collection was originally kept. The grounds are abundant in colourful flora, strewn with bougainvillea and pink trumpet flowers, the structures bound by climbing flowering vines; a smallish green lawn gives way to the café beneath a pergola covered in drooping green ferns.

Callao

Isolated on a narrow, boot-shaped peninsula, **Callao** forms a natural annexe to Lima, looking out towards the ocean. Originally founded in 1537 and quite separate from the rest of the city, Callao was destined to become Peru's principal treasure-fleet port before eventually being engulfed by Lima's other suburbs during the course of the twentieth century. Still the country's main commercial harbour, and one of the most modern ports in South America, Callao lies about 14km west of Lima Centro. These days the community is a crumbling but attractive and atmospheric area full of restaurants and once-splendid houses. The suburb is rife with slum zones and nameless areas infamous for prostitution and gangland killings, making it virtually a **no-go area** for visitors. If you travel here, hire a taxi to take you around.

Fortaleza del Real Felipe

Av Saenz Peña, 1st block, Plaza Independencia • Daily 9.30am–3.30pm; museum Tues–Sat 9am–4pm • S/15 • ⓣ 01 429 0532, ⓦ realfelipe.com

Away from Callao's rougher quarters and dominating the entire peninsula is the great **Fortaleza del Real Felipe**, built after the devastating earthquake of 1764, which washed ships ashore and killed nearly the entire population of Callao. This is a superb example of the military architecture of its age, designed in the shape of a pentagon. Although built too late to protect the Spanish treasure-fleets from European pirates like Francis Drake, it was to play a critical role in the **battles for independence**. Its firepower repulsed both Admiral Brown (1816) and Lord Cochrane (1818), though many Royalists (Peruvians loyal to the Spanish Crown) starved to death here when the stronghold was besieged by the Patriots (those patriotic to Peru but keen to devolve power from the Spanish colonial authorities) in 1821, just prior to the Royalist surrender. The fort's grandeur is marred only by a number of storehouses, built during the late nineteenth century when it was used as a customs house. Inside, the **Museo del Ejercito** (Military Museum) houses a good collection of eighteenth- and nineteenth-century arms, and has various rooms dedicated to Peruvian war heroes.

Museo Naval

Av Jorge Chávez 123, off Plaza Grau • Tues–Sat 9am–3pm, Sun 9am–noon • S/3 • ⓣ 01 429 4793 ext 6794,

If your interest in military matters has been piqued by the Fortaleza, head for the **Museo Naval**, displaying the usual military paraphernalia, uniforms, paintings, photographs and replica ships. Outside is the **Canon del Pueblo**, a large gun installed in a day and a night on May 2, 1866, during a battle against a Spanish fleet; it is also claimed to have deterred the Chilean fleet from entering Lima during the War of the Pacific in 1880.

Museo Submarino Abtao

Av Jorge Chávez 120, waterside • Tours Tues–Sun 9.30am–4.30pm; 30min • S/12 • ⓣ 01 453 0927, ⓦ submarinoabtao.com

From the same building as the Naval Museum, there's also access to the nearby **Museo Submarino Abtao**, or Submarine Museum, actually a real sub that literally opened its hatches in 2004 to allow public access for guided tours, including a simulated attack by an enemy submarine. A Sierra-type vessel, this torpedo-firing battle sub was built in Connecticut, US, between 1952 and 1954, when it first arrived in Peru. You can touch the periscope, visit the dorms and enter the engine and control rooms, which were responsible for over five thousand submersions during 48 years of service.

La Punta

One of Callao's six districts, out at the end of the peninsula, is **La Punta** (The Point); once a fashionable beach resort, it's now overshadowed by the Naval College and Yacht Club. Many of its old mansions, slowly crumbling, are very elegant, though others are extravagant monstrosities. Right at the peninsula's tip, the land is very low-lying, and the surf feels as

1

though it could at any moment rise up and swallow the small rowing-boat-dotted beach and nearby houses. An open and pleasant **promenade** offers glorious views and sunsets over the Pacific and the nearby offshore islands such as **Fronton** (with its small, isolated prison), **San Lorenzo** (with evidence of human occupation, fishing and the use of both cotton and maize going back to 2500 BC) and **Isla Palomino** (with a colony of sea lions).

Museo de la Nación

Av Javier Prado Este 2466, San Borja • Daily 9am–5pm • Free • ⓣ 01 476 9878

The **Museo de la Nación**, situated in the suburb of **San Borja** just east of San Isidro, is Lima's largest modern museum, with exhibitions covering most of the important aspects of Peruvian archeology, art and culture, including regional dress from around the country, and life-sized and miniature models depicting life in pre-Conquest times. Frequent high-profile temporary exhibits, displayed in vast salons, are usually worth the trek out of town.

Museo de Oro

Av Alonso de Molina 1100, Monterrico • Daily 10.30am–6pm • S/33 • ⓣ 01 345 1292, ⓦ museoroperu.com.pe • Taxi from Miraflores or Lima Centro S/12–15 one way

Housed in a small, fortress-like building set back in the shade of tall trees and owned by the high-society Mujica family, the **Museo de Oro** is located along Avenida Javier Prado Este, in the suburb of **Monterrico**. As it's difficult to find and quite far from Miraflores and Lima Centro, it's best to take a taxi.

The upper floor holds some excellent **tapestry** displays, while the ground level boasts a vast display of **arms and uniforms**, which bring to life some of Peru's bloodier historical episodes. The real gem, however, is the basement, crammed with original and replica pieces from **pre-Columbian** times. The pre-Inca weapons and wooden staffs and the astounding Nazca yellow-feathered poncho designed for a noble's child or child high-priest are especially fine. Look out for the **skull** with a full set of pink quartz teeth.

ARRIVAL AND DEPARTURE — LIMA

Most visitors arrive in Lima by **plane**, landing at the Jorge Chávez airport, or by **bus**, concluding their long journeys either in the older, central areas of the city, or in one of the modern terminals en route to the busy commercial suburb of San Isidro, or close to the Avenida Javier Prado Este. **Driving** into the city is only for the truly adventurous: the roads are highly congested and the driving of a generally poor standard.

BY AIR

Jorge Chávez airport is 7km northwest of the centre (ⓣ 01 511 6055, ⓦ lap.com.pe). Many hotels, even mid-range ones, will arrange for free or relatively inexpensive airport pick-up; otherwise, the best way into town is to take a taxi.

Facilities You'll find an ATM at the top of the stairs by the internet cabins at the north end of the aiport building, and another by baggage claim. There are 24hr exchange counters with reasonably competitive rates in both the arrivals baggage reclaim area and near the departure gates, but you'll get slightly better rates in the centre of Lima or Miraflores.

Official taxis The quickest way into the city is by taxi, which will take around 45min to Lima Centro or downtown Miraflores. The simplest way is to book or find on arrival an official taxi from the Taxi Green kiosk (ⓣ 01 484 2734), or official drivers with laminated badges inside the terminal. To most parts of Lima the cost is S/55. Returning to the airport is cheaper and should be S/40 from Miraflores.

Non-official taxis It is possible – though not easy without good Spanish – to negotiate with non-official taxi drivers outside the terminal building and agree a price as low as S/35; however the streets here are quite rough and have a reputation for theft. If you don't use the official service, it's very important to fix the price in Peruvian soles with the driver before getting in. It can be in US$, if required, but the important thing is to be clear about both the amount and the currency. Take extra care when looking for a taxi outside the perimeter at the roundabout or on the road into Lima, as there are often thefts in these areas.

Domestic airline contacts Aeroica (ⓣ 01 444 3026, ⓦ aeroica.net); Aeroparacas (ⓣ 01 449 4768, ⓦ aeroparacas.com); LATAM (ⓣ 01 213 8200, ⓦ latam.com); Star Peru (ⓣ 01 705 9000, ⓦ starperu.com); TACA Peru (ⓣ 01 213 6060, ⓦ Taca.com); TANS (ⓣ 01 241 8510).

International airline contacts Aerolineas Argentinas (ⓣ 0800 52200, ⓦ aerolineas.com); Air Canada (ⓣ 0800 52073, ⓦ aircanada.com); Air France

(T 01 213 0200, W airfrance.com); American Airlines (T 01 211 7000 or T 0800 40350, W americanairlines.com); Avianca (T 01 444 0747, T 01 444 0748 or T 0800 51936, W avianca.com); Continental Airlines (T 01 221 4340 or T 0800 70030, W continentalairlines.com); Delta Airlines (T 01 211 9211, W delta.com); Iberia (T 01 4417801, W iberia.com); KLM (T 01 213 0200, W klm.com); Japan Airlines (T 01 221 7501, W jal.com); LATAM Chile (T 01 213 8200 or T 0801 11234, W latam.com).

Destinations Arequipa (1 daily; 1hr 20min); Chiclayo (1 daily; 1hr 40min); Cusco (several daily; 1hr); Iquitos (2 daily; 2hr); Jauja for Huancayo (1 weekly; 30min); Juliaca for Puno (1 daily; 2hr); Piura (1 daily; 2hr); Pucallpa (1 daily; 1hr); Rioja/Moyabamba (1 weekly; 2hr); Tacna (1 weekly; 2hr 30min); Tarapoto (1 weekly; 1hr 30min); Trujillo (1 daily; 1hr); Tumbes (1 daily; 2hr 30min).

BY BUS

Lima doesn't have one bus terminal, but multiple individual private bus companies with their own offices and depots in different locations (see below). Whichever terminal you arrive at, your best bet, particularly if you have luggage, is to hail a taxi and fix a price – about S/8–20 to pretty much anywhere in Lima.

Long-distance and inter-regional buses The bus terminals of the main operators – Cruz del Sur, Ormeño and Tepsa – are on Av Javier Prado Este. Plenty of buses and colectivos pass by here (those marked Todo Javier Prado), and can be picked up on Av Javier Prado or where Av Arequipa crosses this road. Many operators have alternative depots in the suburbs, to avoid the worst of Lima Centro's traffic.

Local and intercity buses Some of the smaller buses serving the area north of Lima depart from the Terminal Terrestre Fiori, block 15 of Av Alfredo Mendiola in San Martín de Porres; other companies arrive at small depots in the district of La Victoria, including those that connect with the Central Sierra and jungle regions; some arrive on the Paseo de la República, opposite the Estadio Nacional. Other common arrival points nearby include Jr García Naranjo, C Carlos Zavala (in the Cercado district) and Av Luna Pizarro.

Destinations Arequipa (12 daily; 14–16hr); Chincha (8 daily; 2–3hr); Cusco (10 daily, some change in Arequipa; 17–22hr); Huacho (12 daily; 2–3hr); Huancayo (12 daily; 6–8hr); Huaraz (10 daily; 9–10hr); Ica (every 15min; 3–4hr); La Merced (8 daily; 7–8hr); Nazca (10 daily; 6hr); Satipo (2 daily; 12–14hr); Pisco (6 daily; 3hr–3hr 30min); Tacna (6 daily; 18–20hr); Tarma (8 daily; 6–7hr); Trujillo (10 daily; 8–9hr).

BUS OPERATORS

The best and most reliable bus companies – Cruz del Sur, Ormeño, Tepsa and Oltursa – can deliver you to most of the popular destinations up and down the coast, and to Arequipa or Cusco. Cruz del Sur is the best choice – if not the cheapest – for the big destinations. Below is a list of bus companies and the destinations they serve. Note that the addresses given below are of the companies' offices, and buses often depart from elsewhere: always check which terminal your bus is departing from when you buy your ticket.

Chanchamayo Manco Capac 1052, La Victoria T 01 470 1189. Tarma, La Oroya, San Ramon and La Merced.

Chinchano Av Carlos Zavala 171, La Victoria T 01 427 5679. The coast as far as Cañete, Chincha and Pisco.

Cial Av Abancay 947 and Av República de Panamá 2469–2485, Santa Catalina, La Victoria T 01 207 6900, W expresocial.com. North coast including Máncora, Cajamarca and Huaraz.

Civa Av Paseo de la República 569, La Victoria T 01 418 1111. The coast, plus northern inland stops.

El Condor Av Carlos Zavala 101, Lima Centro T 01 427 0286. Trujillo and Huancayo.

Condor de Chavín Montevideo 1039, La Victoria T 01 428 8122. Callejón de Huaylas, Huaraz and Chavín.

Cruz del Sur Av Javier Prado Este 1109 and Nicolás Arriola, San Isidro/La Victoria T 01 3115050, W cruzdelsur.com.pe. Chiclayo, Trujillo, Máncora, Piura, Tumbes, Ica, Nazca, Tacna, Arequipa, Puno, Cusco, Huaraz, Huancayo and Ayacucho.

Empresa Huaral 131 Av Abancay, Lima Centro T 01 428 2254. Huaral, Ancon and Chancay.

Empresa Rosario Jr Ayacucho, La Victoria 942 T 01 534 2685. Huánuco and La Unión.

Flores Buses Calles Paseo de la República and 28 de Julio, La Victoria T 01 424 3278. North and south coast, plus Arequipa and Puno.

Huamanga Jr Montevideo 619 and Luna Pizarro 455, La Victoria T 01 330 2206. Ayacucho, Chiclayo, Moyobamba, Yurimaguas and Tarapoto; you'll probably need to change buses at Pedro Ruiz for Chachapoyas.

León de Huánuco Av 28 de Julio 1520, La Victoria T 01 424 3893. Cerro de Pasco, Huánuco, Tarma and La Merced.

Libertadores Av Grau 491, Lima Centro T 01 426 8067. Ayacucho, Satipo and Huanta.

Linea Paseo de la República 979, La Victoria T 01 424 0836. Buses to all north coast destinations as far as Piura, plus Huaraz and Cajamarca.

Lobato Buses 28 de Julio 2101–2107, La Victoria T 01 4749411. Tarma, La Merced and Satipo.

Mariscal Caceres Av 28 de Julio 2195, La Victoria T 01 474 7850. The coast and some other sectors, including Huancayo.

Movil Tours Paseo de la República, opposite the Estadio Nacional, La Victoria T 01 716 8000; other depot at Av Carlos Izaguirre 535, Los Olivos. Huaraz, Tarapoto and Chachapoyas.

1

PLAYING IN TRAFFIC

Mind your Ps and Qs when walking around the city. **Traffic**, besides contributing to smog, is a beast that can barely be tamed. Only the most major of intersections sports a traffic light; everywhere else there are either hopeful stop signs, small road bumps before the crossing, or nothing, as drivers move into the fray, tapping on their horns and slowing only slightly. In the evening on the main roads, traffic officials attempt to create détente between automobile and pedestrian, with only limited success.

Oltursa Av Aramburu 1160, La Victoria 01 708 5000. Máncora and Tumbes, down south all the way to Arequipa, as well as to Cusco, Huancayo and Huaraz.

Ormeño Av Javier Prado Este 1059, on the border of San Isidro and La Victoria 01 472 1710; some buses also pass through the depot at Carlos Zavala 177, Lima Centro 01 427 5679, grupo-ormeno.com.pe. One of the first Peruvian bus companies. Good for big national and international services along the coast to Tacna and Arequipa and Puno, and also Cusco and into Ecuador, Bolivia, Brazil, Argentina and Chile.

Palomino Av 28 de Julio 1750, La Victoria 01 428 6356. Cusco via Nazca and Abancay.

Señor de Luren Manco Capac 611, La Victoria 01 479 8415. Nazca.

Soyuz/Peru Bus Av Carlos Zavala y Loyaza 221 and Av Mexico 333, La Victoria 01 4276310 or 01 2661515. Nazca, Ica and the coastal towns en route.

Tepsa Av Javier Prado Este 1091, on the border of San Isidro and La Victoria 01 617 9000. Serves the whole coast, north and south (Tacna to Tumbes) as well as Cajamarca, Huancayo, Abancay, Cusco and Arequipa.

Transportes Junin Av Nicolás Arriola 240, C Av Javier Prado, La Victoria 01 326 6136. Tarma, San Ramon, La Merced and the Selva Central.

Transportes Rodríguez Av Paseo de la República 749, La Victoria 01 428 0506. Huaraz, Caraz and Chimbote.

INFORMATION

TOURIST INFORMATION

Some of the commercial tour companies (see page 80) are also geared up for offering good tourist information, notably Fertur Peru and Lima Vision.

Airport Información y Asistencia al Turista, run by i-Peru, has a kiosk at the airport (01 574 8000).

Lima Centro The main public municipal office of Información Turística is hidden away in a small office behind the Palacio Municipal on the Plaza Mayor at C Los Escribanos 145 (daily 9am–5pm; 01 315 1505 or 01 315 1300 ext 1542).

Miraflores There's a small tourist information kiosk in the central Parque Kennedy (daily 9am–2pm & 2.30–7pm). Maps, leaflets and information can also be obtained from the Central de Información y Promoción Turística, Av Larco 770 (Mon–Fri 9am–1pm & 2–5pm; 01 446 3959 ext 114, miraflores.gob.pe and regionlima.gob.pe). There are other kiosks on the corner of Av Petit Thouars and Enrique Palacios, close to the craft stores – the Petit Thoars Mercado Indio – and also in Larco Mar (01 445 9400, iperuLarcoMar@promperu.gob.pe).

San Isidro The office of Información y Asistencia al Turista is run by i-Peru from Jorge Basadre 610 in San Isidro (Mon–Fri 8.30am–6pm; 01 421 1627, peruinfo.org).

LISTINGS

Published monthly, the *Peru Guide* gives up-to-date information on Lima, from tours and treks to hotels, shopping, events and practical advice; it's readily available in hotels, tour and travel agents, and information offices.

MAPS

Buy city maps from kiosks in Lima Centro or the better bookshops in Miraflores; the best is the *Lima Guía "Inca" de Lima Metropolitan* (US$15).

TRAVEL AGENTS AND TOURS

For standard tours, tickets, flights and hotel bookings, the best agencies are below. A number of companies also organize specialist outdoor activities in and around Lima (see page 82).

Class Adventure Travel San Martín 800, Miraflores 01 444 1652, cat-travel.com. Organizes excellent tours and packages including Lima culinary tours, Nazca and desert experiences.

Fertur Peru Jr Junín 211, Lima Centro 01 427 2626, fertur-travel.com; or in Miraflores at Schell 485 01 242 1900. Top service in tailor-made visits around Peru, as well as overland, air or other travel needs and accommodation.

Highland Tours Av Pardo 231, Oficina 401, Miraflores 01 242 6292, highlandperu.com. Offers tours and will arrange travel around Peru plus accommodation when required.

Lima Tours Jr de la Unión (ex-Belén) 1040, near Plaza San Martín, Lima Centro ☎01 619 6900, limatours.com.pe. One of the more upmarket companies, with an excellent reputation.

Lima Vision Jr Chiclayo 444, Miraflores ☎01 447 7710, limavision.com. A variety of city tours, plus a range of archeological ones: Pachacamac, Nazca and Cusco.

Marilí Tours Av Primavera 120, Oficina 306, Chacarilla ☎01 241 0142, marilitours.com.pe. Tours to most of Peru, including Cusco, Madre de Dios, Puno and the northern desert region.

Overland Expeditions Jr Emilio Fernández 640, Santa Beatrice ☎01 424 7762. Specialize in the Lachay Reserve.

Paracas Tours Av Rivera Navarette 723, San Isidro ☎01 222 2621, paracastours.com.pe. Quite an accommodating air-ticketing service from a small office.

Tour Guide Peru ☎01 997 898 502, tourguideperu.com. A small outfit with a very professional service that includes transportation, personalized culinary tours, both around Lima and in coordination with trips to Cusco and Lake Titicaca.

GETTING AROUND

BY COLECTIVO

Colectivos vary in appearance, but are usually either microbuses (small buses) or combis (minibuses); both tend to be crowded and have flat rates (from around S/1). Quickest of all Lima transport, combi-colectivos race from one street corner to another along all the major arterial city roads; microbuses generally follow the same routes, albeit usually in a more sedate fashion.

Avenida Arequipa colectivos The Av Arequipa colectivos start their route at Puente Rosa in Rimac, running along Tacna and Garcilaso de la Vega in the centre before picking up on Av Arequipa, which will take you all the way down to Miraflores via Diagonal to C José González, before starting the route back to the centre up Larco.

Barranco colectivos To reach Barranco from Miraflores, pick up one of the many colectivos or buses (marked Barranco or Chorrillos) travelling along Diagonal, which is one-way.

BY BUS

The modern Lima Metropolitana bus system (☎01 203 9000, metropolitano.com.pe) connects Chorrillos and Barranco in the south with Independencia to the north of the city. Much of the route follows a dedicated track in the centre of the Paseo de la República, and the bus track can be accessed via the road bridges across the multi-lane freeway. There are "regular" and "expreso" buses (every 10min; daily 6am–9.50pm). Tickets (*tarjeta inteligente*) can be bought at the station entry points, mainly from machines. You can catch other (non-Lima Metropolitana) buses to most parts of the city from Av Abancay in the centre; to catch a bus to a destination covered in this chapter look for the suburb name (on a sign atop the bus windshield).

BY TAXI

Taxis are a fast and cheap way to get around Lima, and can be hailed pretty well anywhere on any street at any time.

Official taxis Official taxis are based at taxi ranks and licensed by the city authorities (most but not all their cars have taxi signs on the roof; some of the larger taxi companies are radio-controlled). Short rides cost S/5–10 for ten blocks or so, say from Parque Kennedy in Miraflores to Barranco, while longer rides will set you back S/10–25, for example from Miraflores to Lima Centro or the Museo de Oro in Monterrico. Taxis can be rented for the day from about S/150. You should always fix the price to your destination in soles before getting in, and pay (in soles only) at the end of your journey. Reliable 24hr taxi companies include: Taxi Seguro ☎01 536 6956; Taxi Amigo ☎01 349 0177; and Taxi Movil ☎01 422 6890.

Unofficial taxis Unofficial taxis abound in the streets of Lima; they're basically ordinary cars with temporary plastic "taxi" stickers on their front windows, and are cheaper than official taxis, but use at your own risk.

BY CAR

Driving in Lima is incredibly anarchic. It's not too fast, but it is assertive, with drivers, especially *taxistas*, often

DOUBLE-DECKER TOURS OF LIMA

Mirabus (☎01 476 4213, mirabusperu.com) operates a fleet of double-decker buses, with an **open roof** on the upper deck, for exploring the sites in and around Lima. They offer day- or night-tours of Lima, colonial tours of the city, and trips out to places like the Pachacamac archeological site (see page 97) some 30km south of the city centre. **Tickets** (ranging from S/10 to S/75) can be bought from the tourist information kiosk adjacent to Parque Kennedy, Miraflores' central park (see page 70).

finding gaps in traffic that don't appear to exist; this means you have to be brave as a visitor to take the wheel. Given the city's size and spread, however, this is still an option, particularly if you want to visit sites just north or south of the city (such as Caral, Pachacamac or the beaches).

Car rental Budget, Av Larco 998, Miraflores (T 01 444 4546, W budgetperu.com); Hertz, Cantuarias 160, Miraflores (T 01 447 2129, W hertzperu.com.pe).

Van and driver hire Backpacker Van Express, Av Comandante Espinar 611, Miraflores (T 01 447 7748); Transporte Manchego Turismo (T 01 420 1289 W manchegoturismo.com.pe); LAC Dolar, Av La Paz, Miraflores (T 01 717 3588).

BY BIKE

Bike Tours of Lima C Bolívar 150, Miraflores T 01 445 3172, W biketoursoflima.com. Bilingual themed bike tours, as well as bike rentals, from S/20 for 2hr to S/50 for a full day.

Greenbike Av Larco 383, Miraflores T 01 255 9607, W greenbikeperu.com. Private and shared bike tours, and rental options ranging from 1hr (S/15) to full day (S/45) to 24hr (S/55).

ACCOMMODATION

There are three main areas in which to stay. Most travellers on a budget end up in **Lima Centro**, in one of the traditional gringo dives around the Plaza Mayor or the San Francisco church. These are mainly old buildings and tend to be full of backpackers, but they aren't necessarily the best choices in the old centre, even in their price range; most are poorly maintained. If you can spend more and opt for mid-range, you'll find some interesting old buildings bursting with atmosphere and style, albeit with fewer opportunities for carousing. If you're into nightlife and want to stay somewhere with a downtown feel, with access to the sea, choose the **Miraflores** neighbourhood, home to most of Lima's nightlife, culture and shops. However, most hostels here start at around S/50 per person, and quite a few hotels go above S/350. Some higher-end hotels aimed at foreigners give their prices in US$; they are listed here in that format if so. The trendy ocean-clifftop suburb of **Barranco** is increasingly the place of choice for the younger traveller. Apart from the bohemian, hipster vibe and the clubs and restaurants, though, the area has few sights. Other suburban options include **San Isidro**, mainly residential but closer to some of the main bus terminals; and **San Miguel**, a mostly rather down-at-heel suburb, close to the clifftop and extending from Miraflores towards La Perla and Callao.

ADVENTURE TRIPS AND TOURS FROM LIMA

Many of Lima's travel agents (see page 80) can organize trips to the most popular destinations; the operators below specialize in adventure tours. There's a huge range of trips on offer, from paragliding above the city (see page 71) to trekking and mountain biking.

TREKKING

For advice on **trekking and mountain climbing** and trail maps, visit the Trekking and Backpacking Club, Jr Huascar 1152, Jesús María (T 01 423 2515), the Asociación de Andinismo de la Universidad de Lima, based at the university on Avenida Javier Prado Este (T 01 437 6767; meets Wed evenings).

Most trekking companies run multi-day trips to the Cordillera Blanca and Colca, as well as around the Cusco area and along the Inca Trail.

Incatrek Av Pardo 620, Oficina 11, Miraflores T 01 242 7843, W incatrekperu.com. This outfit sometimes runs tours to Lima's Museo de Oro, the ancient site of Caral, Ica and Paracas, Tarma, Oxapampa, Pozuzo and Satipo.

Peru Expeditions C Colina 151, Miraflores T 01 447 2057, W peru-expeditions.com. A professional, helpful company specializing in adventure travel, particularly on the coast (Paracas and Ballestas, Nazca) plus Arequipa and Colca. Offers trekking, mountain biking and 4WD tours.

Rainforest Expeditions Av Larco 1116, Dep-S, Miraflores T 01 719 6422, W perunature.com. Arguably Peru's best eco-tourism operator, with three lodges in the Peruvian Amazon; check website for toll-free telephone details.

DIVING AND BOAT TRIPS

Motor Yachts Contact through Ecocruceros, Av Arequipa 4960, of 202, Miraflores T 01 226 8530, W islaspalomino.com. Offers trips from Lima to the nearby islands, Islas Palomino, to see marine mammals, including a sea lion colony; a pleasant trip in clear weather.

Nature Expeditions T 946 096 753, W nature-expeditions-peru.com. Diving and scuba are popular sports in Peru – this is the best operator for trips.

CATCH A COLECTIVO

Almost every corner of Lima is linked by the ubiquitous, regular and privately owned **colectivos**. Generally speaking, colectivos chalk up their **destination or route** on the windscreen and shout it out as they pull to a stop. So, for instance, you'll see "Todo–Arequipa" or "Tacna–Arequipa" written on their windscreens, which indicates that the colectivo runs the whole length of Avenida Arequipa, connecting Lima Centro with downtown Miraflores. The driver will call out the destination sing-song style, competing with market-stall holders and the like for the attention of prospective passengers.

LIMA CENTRO

★ **Gran Hotel Bolívar** Jr de la Unión 958 ⊕01 619 7171, ⊕granhotelbolivar.com.pe; map p.60. This old, elegant and luxurious hotel is well located and full of old-fashioned charm, dominating the northwest corner of the Plaza San Martín. Even if you don't stay here, you should check out the cocktail lounge (famous for its Pisco Sour Cathedral) and restaurant, which host live piano music most nights (8–11pm). Great-value online deals; breakfast and wi-fi not included. S/245

Hostal de Las Artes Chota 1460 ⊕01 433 0031; map p.60. At the southern end of Lima Centro, this clean, gay-friendly place is popular with travellers, located as it is in a large, attractive house. Some rooms have a private bathroom, and there's also a dorm with shared bathroom; avoid the downstairs rooms, which can be a little gloomy. English is spoken and there's a book exchange, as well as a nice patio. Dorms S/30, doubles S/70

Hotel España Jr Azángaro 105 ⊕01 428 5546, ⊕hotelespanaperu.com; map p.60. A converted nineteenth-century Republican-style house very popular with backpackers, this secure hostel has rooms available with or without private bathroom. There's also a dorm with shared bathroom. Amenities include a nice courtyard and rooftop patio, internet connection, book exchange and safe; breakfast not included. Dorms S/25, doubles S/65

Hotel Europa Jr Ancash 376 ⊕01 427 3351; map p.60. One of the best-value budget pads, conveniently located opposite the San Francisco church, with a lovely courtyard. It's a good place to meet fellow travellers and as such is very popular and fills up quickly. No breakfast or wi-fi. Dorms S/25, doubles S/38

Hotel Kamana Jr Cámana 547 ⊕01 426 7204, ⊕hotelkamana.com; map p.60. An adequate, small hotel in the heart of Lima Centro, with friendly staff. All of the nicely furnished rooms come with TVs and showers. Facilities include a 24hr café, room service, security-guarded entrance, wi-fi and money exchange. S/190

Inka Path Jr de La Unión 654 ⊕01 426 1919, ⊕hotelinkapath.com; map p.60. About as central as you could wish for, *Inka Path* has very comfortable, if overly minimal, rooms. Beds are queen size and bathrooms private, with 24hr hot water. S/200

Lima Sheraton Paseo de la República 170 ⊕01 315 5000, ⊕sheratonlima.com; map p.60. A top-class, modern international hotel – concrete, tall and blandly elegant, though past its heyday. It also boasts a casino, a spa and a good restaurant. S/470

★ **La Pousada del Parque** Parque Hernan Velarde 60, Santa Beatriz ⊕01 433 2412, ⊕incacountrylaposadadelparque.com; map p.58. A wonderful boutique hotel in a large, quiet and stylish house close to Lima Centro and the Parque de La Exposición, but just south of the centre's busy sectors. The rooms are excellently kept and well furnished, and there are good breakfasts. Internet access available. S/150

MIRAFLORES

Belmond Miraflores Park Av Malecón de la Reserva 1035 ⊕01 610 4000 or US toll-free ⊕800 237 1236, ⊕belmond.com; map p.69. Conspicuously modern hotel for the area, with a day spa, great restaurant, pub-style bar and lovely views over Miraflores, the city and the Pacific. In short, total luxury. US$350

★ **Casa Andina Select Miraflores** C Schell 452 ⊕01 416 7500, ⊕casa-andina.com; map p.69. Occupying seven floors, this popular, well-appointed place is close to Parque Kennedy and most of Miraflores' shops and nightlife, with rooms decently sized and sleekly decorated. It's hard to beat for value at the top end; all rooms have private bathrooms, wi-fi and TV, and the price includes an exceptional buffet breakfast. S/760

Casa de Baraybar C Toribio Pacheco 216 ⊕01 441 2160, ⊕casadebaraybar.com; map p.69. Located between blocks 5 and 6 of Av El Ejercito, this hotel has ten spacious rooms, all with comfortable beds, private bathroom and cable TV. You can benefit from a ten to twenty percent daily discount if you stay for a few nights. S/205

Casa del Mochilero Jr Cesareo Chacaltaña 130A, 2nd floor ⊕01 444 9089, ⊕pilaryv@hotmail.com; map p.69. Within walking distance of central Miraflores, this place has bunk-bed rooms. Though none too big, rooms do come with hot water and cable TV, and there are kitchen facilities too. The very friendly and helpful staff can arrange airport pick-up. Dorms S/17, doubles S/50

1

Colonial Inn Av Comandante Espinar 310 ⓣ01 241 7471; map p.69. Great service and exceptionally clean, if slightly away from the fray of Miraflores. Light sleepers should ask for a room away from the (very busy) road. The English spoken by the staff is hit and miss. No breakfast. US$100

Embajadores Hotel Juan Fanning 320 ⓣ01 242 9127, ⓦembajadoreshotel.com; map p.69. Part of the Best Western chain, this is located in a quiet area of Miraflores, just a few blocks from Larco Mar and the seafront. Small but pleasant, the hotel has comfortable rooms and access to a mini-gym, small rooftop pool and restaurant. US$71

Explorer's House Av Alfredo Leon 158 ⓣ01 241 5002, ⓦexplorershouselima.com; map p.69. A short walk from the action of Parque Kennedy and close to the sea, this ramshackle hostel has a homely feel, thanks to the cheerful owner (who speaks good English). Basic breakfast, guest kitchen, wi-fi and hot water are all included. Some doubles have private bathroom and cost a little more. Book ahead as it is small and popular. Dorms S/28, doubles S/80

Faraoña Grande Hotel C Manuel Bonilla 185 ⓣ01 446 9414, ⓦfaraonagrandhotel.com; map p.69. A secure, quite modern hotel in a central part of this busy suburb; there's a rooftop pool (Dec–April) and a pretty good restaurant with Peruvian, international and vegetarian dishes. Live piano music daily in the bar 7–10pm. S/620

HI Hostel Lima Casimiro Ulloa 328 ⓣ01 446 5488, ⓦhihostels.com; map p.69. A great deal, this is the top-rated HI hostel in the capital. It's located just over the Paseo de la República highway from Miraflores in the relatively peaceful suburb of San Antonio, in a big, fairly modern and stylish house with a pool. There's also a restaurant and bar with views to the garden, and they can pick you up from the airport. Dorms S/51, doubles S/185

★ **Hospedaje Flying Dog** Av Diez Canseco 117 ⓣ01 242 7145, ⓦflyingdogperu.com; map p.69. A clean and homely, B&B-style backpackers' hostel right in the middle of Miraflores. Most rooms are shared but the maximum size is four beds; you also have the option of a double with private bathroom. There's an open kitchen facility and cable TV lounge, as well as internet access. Price includes breakfast. It has an annexe over the road at Lima 457 (ⓣ01 444 5753). Dorms S/40, doubles S/110

Hospedaje Tinkus Av La Paz 608 ⓣ01 242 0131, ⓦhospedajetinkus.com; map p.69. Well located just a few blocks from Av Larco in central Miraflores, *Tinkus* is a good-value option. The lobby is larger and more salubrious-looking than the rooms, though the larger ones aren't too bad. Staff are friendly, there's laundry service, and the breakfast is worthwhile. S/180

Hostal Buena Vista Av Grimaldo del Solar 202 ⓣ01 447 3178, ⓦhostalbuenavista.com; map p.69. Located in a distinctive house in downtown Miraflores, the *Buena Vista* offers large rooms with private bathroom, and there's also outside space in the form of gardens and rooftop patios. Staff are friendly and helpful, and a buffet breakfast is included. US$60

★ **Hostal El Patio** Av Diez Canseco 341 ⓣ01 444 2107, ⓦhostalelpatio.net; map p.69. A very charming, family-friendly and secure little place right in the heart of Miraflores, with comfy beds and private – albeit small – bathrooms. More expensive mini-suites and full suites are also available, and it's often fully booked, so reserve in advance. US$55

Hostal Martinika Av Arequipa 3701 ⓣ01 422 3094, ⓔmartinika@terra.com.pe; map p.69. Very reasonably priced and centrally located within the greater city area – it's close to the boundary of Miraflores and San Isidro – though a little noisy in the mornings. It's also comfortable and friendly, offering fairly large rooms with private bathroom. Airport pick-up available. S/150

★ **Hostal Pariwana** Av Larco 189 ⓣ01 242 4350, ⓦpariwana-hostel.com; map p.69. With a wide, grand stairway entrance including spectacular stained-glass window, this converted mansion is a veritable backpackers' haven and a great meeting place for young travellers. It's also in a lovely location, overlooking the main park in Miraflores. There are dorms as well as private rooms, mainly with shared bathroom, plus games, free internet, kitchen access, rooftop terrace, tours and a good bar and café, which serves very tasty late breakfasts. Dorms S/39, doubles S/132

Hotel Antigua Miraflores Av Grau 350 ⓣ01 201 2060, ⓦantiguamiraflores.com; map p.69. Within walking distance of downtown Miraflores, the *Antigua* is an expanding mock mansion with professional and helpful service, and spacious, well-appointed and very quiet rooms. There's also a small restaurant with reasonable food. Good breakfast included. US$146

Miraflores Colón Hotel C Colón 600 ⓣ01 610 0900, ⓦmiraflorescolonhotel.com; map p.69. Located near the corner of C Juan Fanning, rooms here are spacious, clean and equipped with bathtubs – bathrooms with jacuzzi and hydro-massage baths are also available. Breakfast not included. US$83

Pensión José Luís Francisco de Paula de Ugarriza 727 ⓣ01 444 1015; map p.69. Comfortable, modern house, in a good location within walking distance of central Miraflores and the ocean, and popular with English-speaking travellers. Most rooms have city views, and all come with private bathroom, basic breakfast and wi-fi. S/120

Radisson Decapolis Miraflores Av 28 de Julio 151 ⓣ01 625 1200, ⓦradisson.com/miraflores.pe; map p.69. Entering the *Radisson* resembles boarding a spaceship: lobby and bars alike have a sci-fi ambience. The rooms are as modern and luxurious as you'd expect from this famous chain. No breakfast included in the rate, but they do have a restaurant, a year-round rooftop pool and a fitness centre. S/480

Sonesta Posadas del Inca Miraflores C Alcanfores 329 ☎01 241 7688, sonestapimiraflores.com; map p.69. This understatedly plush, excellently run and modern downtown hotel offers cable TV, a/c and a decent 24hr restaurant (breakfast not included). Airport pick-up is available. US$125

Tierra Viva Miraflores Larco C Bolivar 176 ☎01 637 1003, tierravivahoteles.com; map p.69. Sleekly decorated in white and pale tones with bright multicoloured accents, this hotel of quiet luxury is very good value. Great location, and the breakfast buffet is served adjacent to an airy terrace overlooking the city. S/260

BARRANCO

Hospedaje Domeyer Jr Domeyer 296 ☎01 247 1413; map p.72. Close to the Plaza Municipal and nightlife of Barranco, this is a beautiful old mansion from the outside with a bohemian, colourful interior. Shared and private rooms available, most of them small but comfortable, with hot water and cable TV. Price includes breakfast. Dorms S/50, doubles S/150

★ **Hotel B** Av Sáenz Peña 204 ☎01 206 0800, hotelb.pe; map p.72. A boutique hotel with a strong personality, *Hotel B* showcases both traditional and modern art by mostly Peruvian artists, curated by one of the owners (who has a gallery next door). Every room and suite in this converted Belle Époque mansion is different, but all are spacious, white and light with high ceilings, some with freestanding bathtubs. The breakfast buffet and afternoon teas in the "library" are exceptional in variety and quality; and many Limeños drop by just for a drink in the chic-casual restaurant-bar. US$315

The Point Hostel Malecón Junín 300 ☎01 247 7997, thepointhostels.com; map p.72. A B&B hostel with twelve rooms created by two *mochilleros* (backpackers) in a colonial house with relaxing gardens; the shared kitchen and billiard room are further bonuses. There's often music playing, sometimes live jams among travellers, sometimes rock and reggae CDs, but rarely so loud it interferes with others' sleep. The managers are helpful and offer sensible travel information. Breakfast not included. Dorms S/34, doubles S/90

SAN ISIDRO

Casa Bella Las Flores 459 ☎01 421 7354, casabellaperu.net; map p.58. A modern hotel located one block from the Country Club and Golf Club in San Isidro (behind *Los Delfines Hotel*), offering exceptionally pristine rooms with state-of-the-art finishes in a redesigned mansion from the early 1930s. Staff can help with tours and tickets. S/240

Hotel Libertador Los Eucaliptos 550 ☎01 518 6300, libertador.com.pe; map p.58. A top-class hotel in this well-to-do Lima suburb, with service and room standards as excellent as you'd expect. The website offers much better prices than you'll get in person. S/290

Malka Youth Hostal Los Lirios 165 ☎01 442 0162, youthhostelperu.com; map p.58. *Malka* is cheerful and intimate as well as being good value for this part of the city, and the staff are quite helpful. However, there's only a simple breakfast included. There are several airy rooms, one with views over the garden, and a few with private bathrooms that cost a bit more. Dorms S/35, doubles S/112

Suites del Bosque Av Paz Soldan 165 ☎01 616 2121, suitesdelbosque.com; map p.58. Though essentially a business hotel with conference centre, the suites themselves are smartly furnished, complete with dining/living room, cable TV, internet access, heating and a/c. There's also a restaurant and bar, a jacuzzi and great buffet breakfasts. S/290

Swissotel Lima Vía Central 150, Centro Empresarial Real ☎01 421 4400, swissotellima.com.pe; map p.58. Located in the quiet residential district near banks, bus depots and some department stores and supermarkets, this is luxurious accommodation with all the modern conveniences you'd expect, aimed largely at the business traveller. S/650

SAN MIGUEL

Hostal Mami Panchita Av Federico Gallesi 198 ☎01 263 7203, mamipanchita.com; map p.58. A very approachable hostel in lovely gardens with a well-appointed, shared dining room, TV lounge and bar. Both English and Dutch are spoken, and they also offer airport pick-up (just 20min away). Price includes breakfast. S/160

EATING

Lima boasts some of the best **restaurants** in the country, serving cuisines from all over the world. What makes traditional **Peruvian dishes** (see page 88) so special is the combination of diverse cultural ingredients (Andean, Spanish, Italian, African and Chinese in particular) alongside varied indigenous edible plants. Regardless of class or status, virtually all Limeños eat out regularly – and a meal out usually ends up as an evening's entertainment in itself. Many of the more upmarket places fill up very quickly, so it's advisable to **reserve in advance**. In recent years a large number of **cafés** have sprung up around Miraflores and Barranco, many offering free wi-fi and providing snacks as well as coffee. Lima Centro is less well served by cafés, though there are a few appealing options.

CAFÉS

LIMA CENTRO

Bar/Restaurant Machu Picchu Jr Ancash 318; map p.60. A busy place opposite San Francisco church, serving inexpensive snacks such as omelettes and sandwiches or even *cuy picante* (spicy guinea pig); it offers cheap, set-menu lunches and it's a good spot for meeting up with other travellers. Daily 9am–6pm.

★ **El Cordano** Jr Ancash 202 ⓣ01 427 0181, ⓦrestaurantecordano.com; map p.60. Across the street from the Palacio de Gobierno, this is one of the city's last surviving traditional bar/restaurants with mirrored walls, racks of bottles and old-style waiters, who are curt but efficient – even charming, in an old-fashioned way. Worth visiting if only to soak up the atmosphere, sample the excellent ham sandwiches and see first-hand the exquisite late nineteenth- and early twentieth-century decor. Mon–Sat 8am–9pm.

El Paraiso de la Salud Restaurant Vegetariano Jr Cámana 344 ⓣ01 428 4591; map p.60. Offering a delivery service, this vegetarian place does good breakfasts, as well as yoghurt, juice, salads, wholemeal breads and smoothies. It's a large space but gets busy at lunch, when it serves delicious plates such as steamed broccoli and lentil tortillas. Mon–Sat 8am–10pm.

Queirolo Café Bar Restaurant Jirones Cámana 900 and Quilca ⓣ01 425 0421, ⓦbodegaqueirolo.com; map p.60. This is a classic meeting place for poets, writers and painters, and is worth a visit just for the splendour of its old Lima Cason-style architecture and bohemian atmosphere. It serves comida criolla, sandwiches, beer and pisco; great for inexpensive but good-quality set lunches. Mon–Sat 9am–2am.

MIRAFLORES

Arabica Espreso Bar General Recavarren 269 ⓣ01 447 0904; map p.69. A narrow space with small patio and coffee-roasting equipment out back, this place serves arguably the best coffee in Lima. There are great cakes, too, as well as free wi-fi. Mon–Fri 8am–10pm, Sat 10am–11pm, Sun 2–9pm.

Aromia C Libertad 415 ⓣ01 447 5017; map p.69. The quaint, cosy and white *Aromia* serves strong coffee drinks, with a few sweets and toasts on the card as well. You can sit at a table undisturbed for as long as you like. Mon–Sat 8am–9pm, Sun 9am–8pm.

Café Café Pasaje Martir Olaya 250 ⓣ01 445 1165; map p.69. Located just off Diagonal in downtown Miraflores, this is a hip, LGBTQ-friendly coffee shop that plays good rock music and serves a variety of sandwiches, salads, paellas, pastas and Peruvian dishes, as well as cocktails. Mon–Thurs 9am–1am, Fri–Sun 9am–3am.

Café Haiti Diagonal 160 ⓣ01 446 3816; map p.69. The most popular meeting place for upper-middle-class Limeños, based near the Cinema El Pacífico in the heart of Miraflores. It offers excellent snacks, such as stuffed avocado or *ají de gallina*, and a decent range of soft and alcoholic drinks, although it's not cheap. Daily 8am–2am.

Café Verde Av Santa Cruz 1305 ⓣ01 652 7682; map p.69. One of the best places for coffee in Lima is this small café, which roasts on site. Mon–Sat 7am–9pm.

El Pan de la Chola Av La Mar 918 ⓣ01 221 2138; map p.69. Perhaps Lima's buzziest new *panaderia* (bakery), the shop offers half a dozen speciality artisan breads and wonderful pastries – like the pear frangipane (S/10) – alongside great coffee and a small menu of toasts, sandwiches and salads. The space is big enough for you to sit and savour your chewy purchases. Mon–Sat 8am–10pm, Sun 9am–6pm.

BARRANCO

★ **Café Bisetti** Av Pedro de Osma 116 ⓣ01 713 9565; map p.72. On the Plaza Municipal, this place serves really excellent coffees – which can be prepared by any of eight different methods – and very good snacks. The dark chocolate slice and the blondie are incredible. It's a large space with plenty of tables and a pleasant garden, and they also roast coffee on the premises. Occasional live music on Sat and movies on Sun. Mon–Thurs 8am–9pm, Fri–Sun 9am–10pm.

RESTAURANTS

LIMA CENTRO

De Cesar Jr Ancash 300 ⓣ01 428 8740; map p.60. Great little café/restaurant and bar right in the heart of old Lima, with a buzzing atmosphere. The spacious interior is sometimes a bit dark but the food is fine and cheap, the service very friendly and the range of breakfasts and juices all but endless. Daily 7.30am–10pm.

Don Lucho's Restaurant Jr Quilca 216; map p.60. Just off the Plaza San Martín, this is a busy lunchtime spot with a fan-cooled interior, popular with local office workers and offering fast service and decent set-menu meals, with a ceviche option, for under S/10. Daily 7.30am–6pm.

El Estadio Restaurant Bar Jr de la Unión 1047–1049, Plaza San Martín ⓣ01 428 8866, ⓦestadio.com.pe; map p.60. A restaurant with a strong football theme with walls covered in sports paraphernalia: fascinating even for those only remotely interested in the sport. You can even take your picture next to a life-size bust of Pele. Both the food and bar are excellent; there's karaoke on Thurs and rock bands Sat nights. Mon–Wed 12.15–11pm, Thurs 12.15pm–midnight, Fri & Sat 12.15pm–3am, Sun 12.15–6pm.

HIGH DINING IN LIMA

It may come as a surprise to some, but these days Lima is considered the pinnacle of **fine dining** in South America. In 2017, Britain's *Restaurant* magazine declared that Lima was home to two of the world's top ten restaurants, and a whopping ten of Latin America's top fifty. The winners covered not only Peruvian (see page 88) but also **world cuisines**. Below are some of our favorites, running the gamut from "quite reasonable, really" to "how on earth are we going to pay for this?"

ámaZ Av La Paz 1079, Miraflores ⓣ01 221 9393, ⓦamaz.com.pe; map p.69. Almost everything has a link to the Amazon at this restaurant located below the Hilton hotel. Count on S/100 per person for starter and main, with a drink. Check out the unusual ingredients ahead of time in the *glosario* section of the website. Mon–Thurs 12.30–11pm, Fri & Sat 12.30pm–midnight, Sun noon–4pm.

Astrid y Gastón Av Paz de Soldán 290, San Isidro ⓣ01 442 2777, ⓦastridygaston.com; map p.58. A trendy, colonial-style signature restaurant run by the world-renowned Peruvian chef Gastón Acurio. It's stylish and expensive (expect to spend from around S/200 per person for the a la carte menu, more for the tasting menu), with dishes blending Peruvian criolla and Mediterranean-style cooking. Mon–Sat 1–3pm & 7–11pm, Sun 12.30–3.30pm.

Central C Santa Isabel 376, Miraflores ⓣ01 242 8515, ⓦcentralrestaurante.com.pe; map p.69. A truly spectacular night is in store for diners who come to Central, with wave after wave of ultra-creative plates from master Virgilio Martinez. His creations are based on Peruvian biodiversity, with ingredients from the high Andes (alpaca heart), low rivers (piranha skin) and everywhere in between. Your only choices are the full or vegetarian menu, and either 17 or 11 courses (around S/560 and S/530 respectively). Reserve at least couple of months in advance. Mon–Sat 12.45–3pm & 7.45–11.15pm.

Maido C San Martin 399, Miraflores ⓣ01 446 2512, ⓦmaido.pe; map p.69. A modern take on Japanese food with a Peruvian twist – a fusion called Nikkei – from this top award-winner. Plan on S/370 per person for the Nikkei Experience menu. Mon–Sat 12.30–4pm & 7–11pm, Sun 12.30–5pm.

Malabar Av Camino Real 101, San Isidro ⓣ01 440 5200, ⓦmalabar.com.pe; map p.58. The appearance of ingredients such as nasturtiums, beef tongue, marrow bone and emu on the menu point to this being anything but a run-of-the-mill fancy restaurant. Strong earth-to-table ethos and cultural sensibility. Count on spending S/40–64 for main dishes, with desserts like purple corn cake with purple corn beer sorbet going for S/28. Mon–Sat 12.30–3.30pm & 7–11pm.

L'Eau Vive Jr Ucayali 370 ⓣ01 427 5612; map p.60. The pink, balconied building opposite the Palacio Torre Tagle, this interesting restaurant serves superb French and Peruvian dishes cooked by nuns. It offers a reasonable set menu at lunch and dinner, and closes after a chorus of *Ave Maria* most evenings. Mon–Sat 12.30–3pm & 7.30–9.30pm.

Pardos Chicken Jr Carabaya 821 ⓣ01 428 1168, ⓦpardoschicken.pe; map p.60. Yes, Pardos is a chain, but they serve some of the tastiest *pollo ala brasa* east of the Pacific. Around S/25 will get you a very meaty half bird, plus potatoes, sauces and a small salad. Other outposts in Miraflores at C Santa Cruz 898, Av Benavides 730 and in Larco Mar. Daily noon–11pm.

MIRAFLORES

Bio Leben C Alcanfores 416 ⓣ01 241 0507; map p.69. A great vegetarian restaurant, and a cheerful place to shelter from the bustle of the Miraflores streets. Mon–Sat 8am–10pm, Sun 10am–6pm.

Las Brujas de Cachiche Av Bolognesi 472 ⓣ01 477 1883; map p.69. Very trendy and expensive (main plates S/50–135), this top-class restaurant and bar serves mainstream Peruvian dishes as well as a range of pre-Columbian and *novo andino* meals, such as seafood ceviche and maize-based dishes made using only ingredients available more than a thousand years ago. Mon–Sat noon–midnight, Sun 12.30–4.30pm.

Club Suizo Genaro Iglesias 550, La Aurora, Miraflores ⓣ01 445 9180, ⓦclubsuizoperu.com; map p.69. Located level with block 17 of Av Benavides, this fine place offers exquisite Swiss cuisine, including extravagant fondues combining four cheeses, in a very pleasant environment. Daily 9am–6pm.

D'nnos Pizza Comandante Espinar 408 ⓣ01 219 0909, ⓦpizza.com.pe; map p.69. This flashy, brightly lit restaurant offers some of the best pizza in Lima (S/22 for individual, S/50 for a medium to serve 2 or 3), as well as relatively fast service and delivery. Daily noon–midnight.

El Kapallaq Av El Reducto 1505 ⓣ01 444 4149; map p.69. Recently opened in a new, 1950s-style renovated

1

PERUVIAN CUISINE

Widely acclaimed as one of the world's great culinary destinations (see page 87), Lima is a paradise for food enthusiasts. As well as a wide array of delicious meat-, rice- and vegetable-based **criolla dishes**, you'll come across the highly creative **novo andino cuisine**, often pairing alpaca steaks with ingredients from lush Andean farms, and best appreciated in Lima's finest restaurants. Below are a few specialities.

Arroz con Pato a la Chiclayana From northern Peru, this is a dish of duck and rice prepared as in the city of Chiclayo, with oranges, spices, beer, brandy, peas and peppers. It's such a popular dish you'll probably come across it in all regions of the country.

Asado A good cut of beef roasted in a red sauce, usually served with *pure de papas* (smooth, garlicky mashed potatoes).

Cabrito a la Norteña This traditional goat feast has made its way to Lima from the northern coast of Peru; the dish incorporates a sauce made with *chicha de jorra* (rustic maize beer), yellow chillies, *zapallo* squash, onions and garlic, plus *yuca* and lots of fresh coriander, served with rice.

Ceviche Seafood is particularly good in Lima, with ceviche – raw fish or seafood marinated in lime juice and served in dozens of possible formulas with onions, chillies, sweetcorn and sweet potatoes. A must-try (see page 89).

Chicken broaster The staple at the thousands of *pollo ala brasa* restaurants found in every corner of Peru: essentially, spit- or oven-roasted chicken with chips, and often a very meagre salad on the side.

Chorros a la Chalaca These spicy mussels are best sampled near the port area of Callao.

Cuy This is the Inca word for guinea pig, a common food for Andean country folk, but also something of a delicacy which can be found everywhere from backstreet cafés to the best restaurants in Lima, Cusco and Arequipa. There are various ways to prepare *cuy*, but *chactado* (deep-fried) is one of the most familiar.

Pisco Sour Pisco is Peru's clear, grape-based brandy, which forms the heart of the national drink – pisco sour. The pisco, crushed ice, fresh lime juice, plus a sweetener and egg white, are whisked together and finished with a dash of bitters. It's refreshing and often surprisingly potent.

Tiraditos Similar to ceviche, though the fish, in more manageable, bite-sized slices, comes in a citrus sauce of varying ingredients.

house on the border between Miraflores and Barranco, this excellent restaurant focuses on a fusion of north-coast and Lima seafood cuisine. Service and food are both excellent. Advance booking necessary. Mon–Sat 11am–5pm.

★ **La Lucha Sanguchería** Diagonal and Pasaje Martir Olaya ⓣ01 241 5953; map p.69. The best place to discover what makes a Peruvian *sanguch* (S/15) so much more than a plain sandwich. The crispy, panini-like buns come with a variety of meaty fillings and creamy sauces – the La Lucha and the *chicharrón* are both delicious (extra for rustic potato wedges). No bookings taken; expect to queue for a seat. Mon–Thurs & Sun 8am–1am, Fri & Sat 8am–3am.

Mama Lola Av Diez Canseco 119 ⓣ01 241 6335; map p.69. Right in the heart of Miraflores, near the bottom end of the park, this welcoming trattoria and pizzeria buzzes at night with locals and tour groups. Mama Lola serves great Italian dishes such as onion soup and spinach ravioli with ricotta, as well as Peruvian dishes like tacu tacu, black beans and seafood. Daily 11.30am–11pm.

Mangos Larco Mar ⓣ01 242 8110; map p.69. On the terrace at dusk, under a heat lamp and perched above the twinkling car lights of the Panamericana Sur, *Mangos* is the place to be, with a chatty clientele and a DJ spinning on weekend evenings. And the food – ceviche, anticuchos, salads, meaty mains – doesn't disappoint, especially with one of the strong pisco drinks. Daily 8am–1am.

Restaurant Huaca Pucllana General Borgoño, block 8 ⓣ01 445 4042; map p.69. Tasty, international cuisine with a French flavour and quality Peruvian dishes, including *novo andino* and excellent traditional *cuy*, *cabrito* (goat) and various fish options. The service is outstanding, and the restaurant has an elegant terrace that looks out onto the ancient monument of the Huaca Pucllana (see page 68). Mon–Sat 12.30pm–midnight, Sun 12.30–4pm.

Restaurant Tai-i Vegetariano Av Petit Thouars 5232 ⓣ01 242 6654; map p.69. Handily located opposite the artesanía markets, this veggie standby offers simple, inexpensive and satisfying food in the shape of set-lunch menus, plus a range of great Asian dishes. Daily 8am–8pm.

La Rosa Nautica Espigon 4, Costa Verde ⓣ01 447 5450; map p.69. With excellent ocean views thanks to its pier location, this is one of Lima's more expensive seafood restaurants. The menu offers a wide range of Latin American and European dishes. Jazz performances every Thurs evening. Daily 12.30pm–12.30am.

Scena Restaurant Bar C San Francisco de Paula Camino 280 ⓣ01 241 8181; map p.69. Ultramodern in design, this restaurant's dishes are a fusion of flavours based on the chef's own interpretation of *cocina Peruana*, with good meat and fish. Mon–Fri 12.30–4pm, Sat 7.30pm–12.30am.

El Señorio de Sulco Malecón Cisneros 1470 ⓣ01 441 0183; map p.69. Specializing in Peruvian cuisine, including *novo andino*, this restaurant uses the finest ingredients to prepare mainly traditional dishes, many cooked in earthen pots. This type of meal can be found on street stalls all over Peru, but here the chef is top quality – and this is reflected in the prices. Mon–Sat 12.30–11.30pm, Sun 12.30–4.30pm.

Tanta Larco Mar ⓣ01 446 9357; map p.69. Friendly staff serve extremely well executed updated versions of Peruvian classics like *lomo saltado*. Daily noon–1am.

La Tiendacita Blanca Av Larco 111 ⓣ01 445 1412; map p.69. Located right on the busiest junction in Miraflores, this is a popular meeting place, with a superb range of Peruvian and Swiss foods, including fondue, plus (pricey) cakes and pastries. Live piano music. Daily 7am–midnight.

BARRANCO

Amoramar Jr García y García 175 ⓣ01 619 9595; map p.72. Classy, roomy and largely open-air restaurant with an extensive menu of fish dishes and substantial salads, but also quinoa platters with tuna, and stir-fry meals. Tues–Thurs 12.30–4pm & 8–11pm, Fri & Sat 12.30–4pm & 8pm–midnight, Sun 12.30–4pm.

★ **Café Cultural Expreso Virgen de Guadalupe** Av Prol San Martín 15A ⓣ01 252 8907; map p.72. A unique, atmospheric restaurant and bar situated right beside the Puente de los Suspiros, serving typical international and Peruvian food inside an ornate nineteenth-century railway carriage. Live music at weekends. Daily 5pm–midnight.

La Dama Juana Av República de Panamá 230 ⓣ01 248 7547; map p.72. *La Dama Juana,* with super colourful patterns and atmospheric lighting, aims to be a place that evokes the old Peru. It succeeds, too, with its homestyle

TOP SPOTS FOR CEVICHE

City dwellers can be fanatical about their favourite **ceviche** spots, and you may be too after a representative sampling of venues and dishes. Note that though many spots will serve ceviche throughout normal dining hours, the true Limeño way is to have it for lunch only.

La Mar Av La Mar 770, Miraflores ⓣ01 421 3365, ⓦlamarcebicheria.com; map p.69. Easily Lima's trendiest and liveliest cevichería, *La Mar* is stylish, swanky and very, very busy. Noisy but with great salsa music and strong pisco sours, the restaurant serves a wide range of ceviche in all sorts of regional styles. Look for the innovative combinations such as the *tiradito laqueado* with slivers of tuna in a fantastic sauce incorporating honey and tumbo. No bookings taken; get there before 12.30pm to avoid the queues. Tues–Thurs noon–5pm, Fri–Sun noon–5.30pm.

El Mercado Av Hipolito Unanue 203, Miraflores ⓣ01 221 1322, ⓦrafaelosterling.pe; map p.69. Locals love this place, tricked out to look old and authentic, with its blackboard of specials and ten-page menu (includes non-ceviche items). Casual and fun. Tues–Sun 12.30–5pm.

El Pez On C San Martin 537, Miraflores ⓣ01 713 0860, ⓦelpez-on.com; map p.69. Local chain started in 2000. Largely traditional-type ceviche options in a number of sizes, with soups and some criolla and *chaufa* dishes thrown in for good measure. Mon–Thurs noon–10pm, Fri & Sat noon–11pm, Sun noon–5pm.

Punto Azul Avenidas Javier Prado and Petit Thouars, San Isidro ⓣ01 221 3747; map p.58. One of a chain of excellent and unpretentious cevicherías, this one is unusual in that you eat outside at tables overlooking one of Lima's busiest junctions. Mon–Sat 11am–4pm.

La Red Av La Mar 391, Miraflores ⓣ01 441 1066, ⓦlared.com.pe; map p.69. A little less flash and more traditional than *La Mar* nearby, opt for *La Red* if the former is booked up. The menu is much more extensive, and you'll get a very similar experience for less cash. Daily noon–5pm.

Restaurant Sonia C La Rosa 173, Chorillos ⓣ01 251 6693, ⓦrestaurantsonia.com; map p.58. This spot on the cliff above the Chorillos fish market offers more unusual fare, with black clams and octopus on the menu. It's great for ceviche and tiraditos, but also does other Peruvian favourites extremely well. The proprietors were responsible for creating *pescado a la Chorillana* (corvina in a sauce of onions and tomatoes), now a nationally known recipe. Daily noon–5pm.

1

dishes and an evening buffet and dance show. Daily 12.30–4pm & 7.30–10pm.

Songoro Cosongo Jr Ayacucho 281 ⓣ01 247 4730; map p.72. Another fine traditional Peruvian restaurant in the heart of Barranco. Daily 11am–10pm.

SAN ISIDRO

La Carreta Av Rivera Navarrete 740 ⓣ01 442 2690, ⓦrestaurantelacarreta.com; map p.58. One of Lima's best *churrascarías* (Brazilian-style steakhouses), close to San Isidro's Centro Comercial. Designed to resemble an old hacienda, this place also serves the usual Peruvian dishes, and there's a spectacular bar with quality wines. Daily noon–midnight.

SURQUILLO

Cevichería El Rey Marino Clara Barton Lte. 10, La Calera ⓣ01 448 8667; map p.58. Located close to block 43 of Av Aviación, this is a brilliant and unpretentious cevichería with very friendly service and good Peruvian music. Daily 11am–6pm.

SURCO AND MONTERRICO

Guru Av Benavides 4518, Surco ⓣ01 240 3710; map p.58. If you like spice, this is the place. A small but excellent curry and kebab house, located in the district of Surco, but easily accessible by taxi from Miraflores. Daily noon–10pm.

Siam Thai Cuisine Av Caminos del Inca 467, Surco ⓣ01 372 0680; map p.58. Superb Thai food in a delightful, tranquil environment with small indoor gardens and very reasonable service and prices. Best to take a taxi (S/12 from Miraflores). Daily 11.30am–10.30pm.

Sushi Ito Av El Polo 740, Monterrico ⓣ01 435 5817; map p.58. Located in the Centro Comercial El Polo, this is an excellent, posh sushi restaurant serving *sashimi* and *temaki*, among other dishes. Mon–Sat noon–4pm & 7pm–midnight.

DRINKING AND NIGHTLIFE

Lima's nightlife is less traditional than in cities such as Cusco and Arequipa, with **Barranco** the trendiest and liveliest place to hang out. The city has an exciting scene, with the majority of its popular **bars** and discos located out in the suburbs of San Isidro and Miraflores. In the summer months (Jan–March) the party sometimes carries on down the coast to the resort of **Asia**, 110km south (see page 100), where there are some surprisingly sophisticated nightclubs. As far as the **live music scene** goes, the great variety of traditional and hybrid sounds is one of the best reasons for visiting the capital, with folk group *peñas*, Latin jazz, rock, reggae and reggaeton all popular. All forms of **Peruvian music** can be found here, some – like **salsa** and **Afro-Peruvian** (see page 508) – better than anywhere else in the country. Even Andean folk music can be close to its best here (though Puno, Cusco and Arequipa are all more probable contenders).

Entrance charges and policies Most clubs charge an entrance fee of around S/20–50, which often includes a drink and/or a meal. Many clubs have a members-only policy, though if you can provide proof of tourist status, such as a passport, you usually have no problem getting in.

Listings The daily *El Comercio* provides the best information about music events, and its Friday edition carries a comprehensive nightlife supplement – easy to understand even if your Spanish is limited. Things are at their liveliest on Friday and Saturday nights.

BARS

Ayahuasca Av Prol San Martín 130, Barranco ⓣ01 247 6751; map p.72. A fantastic venue, this place is based in a lovingly restored mansion with several interesting bar areas; it's not cheap but the drinks are inventive and there are great snacks too. Very busy after 10pm at weekends. Mon–Sat 8pm–3am.

Barra 55 Av 28 de Julio 206, Barranco ⓦfacebook.com/barr55; map p.72. Casual and unpretentious yet trendy, this space doles out really competent cocktails; unusually for Lima, they carry more than a dozen types of gin. Tapas are available, and a swinging soul or jazz band provides a background soundtrack on the weekend. Tues–Thurs 6pm–midnight, Fri & Sat 6pm–2.30am.

Barranco Beer Co Av Grau 308, Barranco ⓣ01 247 6211, ⓦbarrancobeer.com; map p.72. The award-winning cervezas on draft are all housemade at this roomy rustic tavern, with the Avena Buena oatmeal stout and the Pale X especially refreshing. Futbol often plays on the screens on the second floor. Order a flatbread-style pizza, hang out a while and you'll need nothing else. Tues & Wed noon–midnight, Thurs noon–2am, Fri & Sat noon–3am.

El Dragon Av Nicolás de Piérola 168, Barranco ⓦeldragon.com.pe; map p.72. A dark, often packed and always fun cultural bar, *El Dragon* usually has live music, frequently good Latin rock and jazz. Tues–Sat 8pm–2am.

La Emolientería C Diagonal 598, Miraflores ⓣ01 444 5579; map p.69. Very hip ambience, with plenty of glass, a science-lab inspired bar, wooden interior balcony and two floors of colour and artwork. The staff and drinkers are young and cool; there are pisco cocktails (S/25) and bar food but their speciality is the *emoliente*, a hot Peruvian "medicinal" herbal drink, with (S/15) or without pisco. Mon–Fri noon–1am, Sat noon–2.30am, Sun 5.30pm–1am.

SELF-CATERING

Lima offers plenty of options for DIY lunches. **Surquillo market** (daily 6.30am–5.30pm), a couple of blocks from Miraflores – along Calle Gonzales Prada over the Avenida Angamos road bridge, on the eastern side of the Paseo de la República freeway – is a colourful place fully stocked with a wonderful variety of mainly fruits and vegetables, but also cheeses and meats. Pickpockets are at work here, though, so keep your wallet and passport close.

Of Lima's **supermarkets**, Metro has the best range at reasonable prices. You'll find this chain across the city, notably at the San Isidro Comercial Centre, the Ovalo Gutierrez in Miraflores and next to Ripley's on Calle Schell in the centre of Miraflores. All branches accept and change US dollars. The Vivanda chain is generally much larger and carries top line brands (several branches in San Isidro and Miraflores). **Bakeries and delicatessens** can be found in most urban districts – try Avenida Larco in Miraflores, within a few blocks of Larco Mar. *Madre Natura* (Jr Chiclayo 815), off Avenida Comandante Espinar in Miraflores and Avenida La Encalada 300 in Surco, stocks a wide range of **health foods** and ecological products.

Habana Café Bar Av Manuel Bonilla 107, Miraflores ⓣ01 446 3511; map p.69. Live music Fri and Sat (10pm–1am), particularly Cuban, but also great jazz and nostalgic rock. Serves an excellent range of rum and cocktails. Mon–Thurs 11am–1am, Fri & Sat 11am–3am, Sun 6pm–1am.

Juanito's Bodega Bar Av Grau 270, Barranco; map p.72. Probably the most traditional of the neighbourhood's bars; facing onto the Parque Municipal, it's small and basic and offers an excellent taste of Peru as it used to be. The music policy is strictly criolla and traditional Peruvian folk, and the front bar tends to stay open until very late. Closed during World Cup finals, when the owners travel to watch the games. Mon–Sat 11am–2.30am, Sun noon–midnight.

Lion's Head Av Grau 268, Barranco; map p.72. Located on the second floor of the building is this British-style pub with dartboard, pool table, newspapers, sports TV and, of course, English beers. Mon–Sat 4pm–4am.

The Old Pub C Bellavista 247, Miraflores ⓣ01 242 8155; map p.69. The most authentic of the English-style pubs in Lima – it's run by an Englishman – and easy to find, just a block or two from the park in Miraflores, at the far end of Little Italy (San Ramón). There's good music and a dartboard, and sandwiches, salads, chips and roast-beef meals are available. Mon–Sat 4pm–2am, Sun noon–3am.

La Posada del Mirador C Ermita 104, on the clifftop point behind the Puente de Suspiros and church, Barranco ⓣ01 246 1796; map p.72. A popular evening bar – choose your poison from pisco, rum, tequila and whiskey – with great views and a lively atmosphere. Daily 10am–10pm.

Rincon Cervecero Jr de la Unión 1045A, Lima Centro ⓣ01 428 8866, ⓦrinconcervecero.com.pe; map p.60. An original Lima bar but in Germanic style, with satisfyingly large pitchers of draught beer and shots, and a buzzing atmosphere. The kitchen serves original recipes, and they've put on a beer festival here every Oct since 1999. Mon–Thurs noon–midnight, Fri & Sat noon–3am, Sun noon–9pm.

Victoria Bar Av Pedro de Osma 135, Barranco ⓣ01 247 1225; map p.72. Located in a fine old Barranco mansion, now converted into an *albergue* and live music bar, with outside tables and a musical grab bag that lurches from ska and cover bands to DJs. Tues–Sat 7pm–3am.

CLUBS

Deja-Vu Av Grau 294, Barranco ⓣ01 247 6989; map p.72. A popular dance club, with music that mainly ranges from trance to techno, but also live music, mainly rock, sessions at weekends. Best Thurs–Sat. Mon–Wed & Sun 7pm–1am, Thurs–Sat 7pm–3am.

Nebula C Gonzalez Prada 194, Miraflores ⓣ986 154 292; map p.69. For the most part they're stuck in the eighties at *Nebula*, and have been for 17 years now. They do occasionally dip into techno, electronica and more recent incarnations of new-wave and synthpop like Daft Punk and Tame Impala, though. Fri & Sat 10pm–5am.

El New Kitsch Av Bolognesi 743, Barranco ⓣ01 947 298 157; map p.72. A funky and gay-friendly disco-bar with weird decor, known for playing lots of 1970s and 1980s tunes mixed in with newer house; it gets hotter later on. Thurs–Sat 10pm–3am.

LGBTQ BARS AND CLUBS

Since the **LGBTQ scene** is relatively small, there are few gay meeting places, though the main park and **Larco Mar** centre in Miraflores (see page 70) can be cruisey in the evenings. Although there are gay saunas in Miraflores, the busiest in Lima, Baños Turcos 240, is in an isolated part of Lima Centro that is dangerous to reach without a taxi. Lima society has begun to grow more tolerant, but this does depend on which area you're in. The culture, however, is still primarily macho, so, as a visitor, keeping a relatively low profile makes for an easier time. Most clubs here have

LIMA'S DANCE SCENE

Lima's **peñas** – some of which only open at weekends and nearly all located in Barranco – are the surest bet for listening to authentic **Andean folk**, although some of them also specialize in **Peruvian criolla**, which brings together a unique and very vigorous blend of Afro-Peruvian, Spanish and, to a lesser extent, Andean music. These days it's not uncommon for some of Lima's best *peñas* to feature a fusion of criolla and Latin jazz. Generally speaking, *peñas* don't get going until after 10pm and usually the bands play through to 3 or 4am, if not until first light.

Lima is also an excellent place to experience the Latin American **salsa** scene, and there are *salsódromos* scattered around many of the suburbs. They play a mix of tropical music, salsa, merengue and technocumbia. Most are open Friday and Saturday 10pm–3am.

a cover charge that includes a complimentary drink after a certain time, with free entry earlier in the evening.

La Cueva Av Aviación 2514, San Borja ⊕954 113 171; map p.58. A simple LGBTQ club with drag shows and special bear nights. Great shows on Fri and Sat, usually peaking around 3am. Thurs–Sat 10pm–6am.

Downtown Vale Todo Pasaje Los Pinos 160, Miraflores ⊕01 444 6433, ⊛mundovaletodo.com; map p.69. Perhaps a bit past its prime as the best gay club in Lima; now and then there are caged go-go dancing boys, occasional striptease acts and a cruise bar. A primarily young crowd, usually fairly mixed but at its gayest on Sat. Mon–Thurs & Sun 8pm–1am, Fri & Sat 8pm–3am.

Legendaris C Berlín 363, Miraflores ⊕01 446 3435; map p.69. Fashionable *Legendaris* is a large, comfortable club with personalized service, good drinks and shows, particularly on Sat night. Thurs–Sun 10pm–7am.

Lola Bar C Bolivar 197, Miraflores ⊕01 299 2503; map p.69. The clientele of *Miss Lola*, as the bar is sometimes known, are generally mid-twenties and up, casual but sophisticated, and very democratic – they're friendly to every persuasion. Dancing comes naturally with a soundtrack of Spanish radio hits, eighties alternative and current dance favourites; the Coca-Cola wall is a great photo op. Thurs–Sat 10pm–4am.

Sagitario Disco Av Wilson 869, Lima Centro ⊕01 424 4383; map p.60. The longest-established LGBTQ club, in the heart of Lima, has cruising balconies filled with young people – a large number of them gay – and dancing through the night, often until 11am the next day. Daily 8pm–late.

PEÑAS AND SALSÓDROMOS

★ **Las Brisas del Titicaca** Jr Heroes de Tarapaca 168, Lima Centro ⊕01 715 6960, ⊛brisasdeltiticaca.com; map p.58. One of the busiest and most popular venues for tourists in the know and locals alike; excellent bands and yet this is one of the cheapest of the city's *peñas*. Thurs–Sat 8.30pm–5am (shows 10.30pm–2.30am).

★ **Del Carajo** Jr Catalino Miranda 158, Barranco ⊕01 247 7023, ⊛delcarajo.com.pe; map p.72. A lively and popular *peña* playing a range of criolla, Andean and coastal traditional and modern music. Some of Latin America's top criolla muscians play here. Fri & Sat 10pm–3am.

La Estación de Barranco Av Pedro de Osma 112, Barranco ⊕01 247 0344; map p.72. Just across the road from the suburb's main plaza, this established *peña* regularly varies its flavour between folklore, criolla and even Latin jazz or rock at times, with a lively atmosphere most Fri and Sat nights. Tues–Fri 9pm–3am, Sat 10pm–4am.

Karamba Av Industrial 3669, Independencia, 11km north of Plaza Mayor ⊕01 208 0920; map p.58. This is a hectic *salsódromo* based north of Lima Centro in the somewhat seedy Independencia district is split into two levels with its walls painted with coconuts. The club has a hot, tropical feel and pounds out the salsa. Fri & Sat 9pm–5am.

Kimbara Av Petit Thouars 2481, Lince ⊕01 421 7853; map p.58. This is a sprawling, unpretentious choice, with vibrant salsa music, sometimes performed live at weekends. Top Peruvian criolla musicians sometimes play here. Fri & Sat 9pm–6am.

Peña Don Porfirio C Manuel Segura 115, Barranco ⊕01 477 3119; map p.72. Possibly the only traditional-style *peña* left in Lima. Offers dance lessons during the week. Fri 9pm–3am.

Peña La Candelaria Av Bolognesi 292, Barranco ⊕01 247 1314, ⊛lacandelariaperu.com; map p.72. An enormous venue presenting live music and dance from the three regions (coast, Andes and Amazon). Fri & Sat 8pm–2am.

★ **Peña Sachún** Av del Ejercito 657, Miraflores ⊕01 441 4465; map p.69. Very lively and popular tourist restaurant with a good reputation for live folkloric music and criolla dancing. Thurs 8pm–2am, Fri & Sat 9pm–3am.

JAZZ, ROCK AND LATIN JAZZ

Delfus Taberna Av San Martín 587, San Borja ⊕01 997 680 240; map p.58. Live rock music every Fri and

Sat night, with open jam sessions on Tues and Thurs. Wed–Sat 9pm–2am.

Jazz Zone Av La Paz 656, Miraflores ☎01 241 8139; map p.69. Located in the Pasaje El Suche, Jazz Zone offers cutting-edge live Latin or Brazilian rock, salsa and jazz, as well as fine examples of avant-garde Andean folk and occasionally Peruvian ballad singers. Tues–Sat 7pm–2am.

★ **La Noche** Av Bolognesi 307, El Boulevard Pazos, Barranco ☎01 247 1012, lanoche.com.pe; map p.72. This is a top club located at the top end of the Boulevard, and is arguably the best venue in Barranco for meeting people; it gets really packed at weekends. Musically, it specializes in Latin rock and electronica, with free jazz sessions on Mon evenings. Live music (Fri & Sat 10pm–2am) comes with a small entry fee. Mon–Sat 7.30pm–3am.

★ **La Posada del Angel III** Av Prol San Martín 157, Barranco ☎01 247 5544; map p.72. This is the largest of three *Posada del Angel* venues, all within a stone's throw of each other in Barranco. Well known for its Trova and Latino live music sessions, it has a great bar and also serves snacks and meals. All three locations are richly – and kitschly – decorated; the other two are at Pedro de Osma 164 & 218. Tues–Sat 6.30pm–midnight.

Satchmo Av La Paz 538, Miraflores ☎01 444 4957; map p.69. A large, traditional indoor live venue, best at weekends when performances range from Latino and Peruvian criolla music to jazz and blues. It's reasonably priced and food is also available. Fri–Sun 8pm–late.

ARTS AND ENTERTAINMENT

Going to the **cinema** and **theatre** is an important part of Limeño life. Peruvians tend to be well-cultured, with a passion for and understanding of Latin music, fine arts, ancient textiles and traditional Andean dance forms. **Peruvian culture** is very much alive and most locals know dozens of songs and several folk dances, as well as more raucous salsa steps. Lima's **cultural and university centres** are often the best places to catch innovative films, music shows and drama. The best source of **information** about film, theatre, sporting events and exhibitions is the daily *El Comercio*, especially its Friday supplement.

CINEMAS

There are clusters of cinemas around the Plaza San Martín, Jr de la Unión and Av Nicolás de Pierola in Lima Centro, on the fringes of the park in Miraflores, at Larco Mar and in some of the suburban shopping malls. Find the main companies at cinemark-peru.com, cineplanet.com.pe or cinerama.com.pe.

Cinemark Peru Jockey Plaza 12, Av Javier Prado Este 4200, Surco ☎01 437 3707.

Cinemark Plaza Lima Sur 7 Av Prol Paseo de la República, Chorrillos ☎01 251 7702.

Cineplanet Alcazar 1–8 Santa Cruz 814, Miraflores ☎01 624 9500.

Cineplanet Centro Jr de la Unión 819, Lima Centro ☎01 624 9500.

Cineplanet Primavera Av Angamas Este 2684, San Borja ☎01 624 9500.

Cinerama El Pacífico Av Pardo 121, Miraflores ☎01 243 0541.

UVK Multicines Larco Mar 1–12 Parque Salazar, Larco Mar, Miraflores ☎01 446 7336.

CULTURAL CENTRES

Centro Cultural de la PUCP (Universidad La Católica) Av Camino Real 1075, San Isidro ☎01 616 1616. One of the most active cultural centres in Lima, with innovative theatre, cinema and video, as well as art exhibitions, library and cafetería.

Centro Cultural de la UNMSM (Universidad de San Marcos) Av Nicolás de Piérola 1222, Parque Universitario, Lima Centro ☎01 619 7000, ext 5207. Often presents folk music and dance performances. The centre is run by the Universitario de San Marcos (see page 57), on the Parque Universitario, and performances are publicized on the noticeboard at the entrance.

Centro Cultural Ricardo Palma Av Larco 770, Miraflores ☎01 617 7263. Often hosts excellent concerts of Andean music, but doesn't have the same participatory feel as the *peñas* (see page 92). It does, however, boast a library, two exhibition rooms and occasional cinema festivals, plus jazz, dance and theatre performances.

THEATRE, BALLET AND CLASSICAL MUSIC

Lima possesses a prolific and extremely talented **theatre** circuit, with many of its best venues based in Miraflores. In addition to the major theatres, short performances sometimes take place in the bars of the capital's top theatres. The country's major prestige companies, however, are the **National Ballet Company** and the **National Symphony**, both based at the Gran Teatro Nacional, along with the National Youth Symphony Orchestra, the National Chorus and the National Folkloric Ensemble.

Gran Teatro Nacional Jr Prado Este 2225, San Borja ☎01 715 3659, granteatronacional.pe. This grand purpose-built theatre seating 1500 opened in 2012 and hosts orchestral concerts, Broadway shows and other stage experiences.

La Tarumba C Leoncio Prado 225, Miraflores ☎01 446 4660, latarumba.com. Circus theatre of high renown.

Teatro Británico Jr Bellavista 531, Miraflores ☎01 615 3636. One of the more traditional venues in the city, where Shakespeare plays are, naturally, frequently presented.

1

Teatro Municipal Block 3 of Jr Ica, Lima Centro ⓣ01 632 1300. In 2010, twelve years after a fire gutted the structure, this theatre, first opened in 1920, was re-inaugurated with a stunning restoration based on the original plans. Today, it hosts theatrical performances, concerts, and ballet and dance shows.

SHOPPING

When it comes to **shopping**, Lima is the most likely of Peru's towns and cities to have what you're looking for. It's certainly your best bet for **shoes and clothing**, particularly if you want a large selection to choose from. The same is true of **electronic goods**, **stationery** and **music**; Lima also has a good selection of reasonably priced **arts and crafts** markets and shops. The usual **opening hours** are Mon–Sat 10am–7pm, though in Miraflores, the main commercial area, many shops and artesanía markets stay open until 8pm and sometimes later. Some shops, but by no means all, shut for a two-hour lunch break, usually 1–3pm, and many shops shut on Sundays, though the artesanía markets on avenidas La Marina and Petit Thouars tend to stay open all week until 7pm.

ANTIQUES

Antucos Antiques C Esperanza 308, Miraflores ⓣ991469290; map p.69. This friendly shop has good-quality antiques, especially ceramics and glassware.

Collacocha C Colón 534, Miraflores ⓣ01 447 4422; map p.69. Parallel to block 11 of Av Larco, this place has good-quality antiques, as well as arts and crafts.

Rafo Martinez de Pinillos 1055, Barranco ⓣ01 247 0679; map p.72. Quality antiques and a good lunchtime restaurant, too.

ARTS AND CRAFTS

Agua y Tierra Av Diez Canseco 298, Miraflores ⓣ01 444 6980; map p.69. A wide range of ethnic and traditional healing or *curanderos'* artefacts.

Artesanía Santo Domingo Jr Lima Conde de Superunda 221–223, Lima Centro; map p.60. This little square pavement area, just a stone's throw from the Correo Central in Lima Centro, is good for beads, threads and other artesanía items.

Be Design Store Larco Mar, Miraflores; map p.69. Interestingly constructed souvenirs, many with a literary focus.

La Casa de Alpaca Av La Paz 665, Miraflores; map p.69. High-quality but expensive alpaca clothing and unique fabrics, masks and figurines you won't find in the markets. A similar artesanía store is across the road.

Cuy Arts and Crafts Av Larco 1175 & 874, Miraflores; map p.69. Dodge the T-shirts and usual souvenirs and you'll find some good handmade crafts of all kinds.

Las Pallas Cajamarca 212, Barranco ⓣ01 477 4629; map p.72. A fascinating, veritable museum of artesanía, run by a British woman who has spent most of her life collecting fine works and who may be able to show you the rest of her collection (ring for an appointment).

BOOKS

ABC Bookstore Av Colmena 689, Lima Centro; map p.60. Well supplied with all kinds of works in English. The same street (aka Nicolás de Pierola) has a few other shops stocking English-language books.

Librería El Virrey C Bolognesi 510, Miraflores; map p.69. Well-respected shop with a strong selection of native Peruvian authors, some of whom stop by for readings and book launches.

Librería Ibero Larco 199, Av Oscar Benavides 500, Larco Mar & Comandante Espinar 840, by the Ovalo Gutierrez, Miraflores; map p.69. This bookshop has three branches, which generally have a wide range of books and magazines in English.

Zeta Bookstore Comandante Espinar 219, Miraflores; map p.69. Has a small selection of new English paperbacks.

CAMPING, SURF AND SPORTS EQUIPMENT

Big Head Jockey Plaza Shopping Centre, Surco; map p.58. Good surf store. There's another branch on Av Benevides 1836 in Miraflores.

Boz Av Angamos Oeste 1130, between Miraflores and San Isidro ⓣ01 440 1033; map p.69. Specializes in surfing equipment.

Camping Centre Av Benavides 1620, Miraflores ⓣ01 242 1779; map p.69. Has a good range of tents and other equipment in a small space.

Klimax C José González 488, Miraflores ⓣ01 442 1685; map p.69. Good for surf gear.

Peru Bike Parque Nueva Castilla, C A, d-7, Surco ⓣ01 449 8435; map p.58. Good range of bikes and related accessories.

Todo Camping Av Angamos Oeste 350, Miraflores; map p.69. Has a range of tents and other equipment.

JEWELLERY

Ilaria Larco Mar, Miraflores; map p.69. Stocks fine silver jewellery made by Peruvian artisans.

ASTRID Y GASTON, MIRAFLORES

CRAFT-SHOPPING IN LIMA

Lima is a treasure-trove of **Peruvian artesanía**, with woollen goods, crafts and gemstones among the best souvenirs. Artesanía shops tend to cluster in particular areas, and there are some dedicated craft markets too. **Avenida La Paz** in Miraflores boasts several shops selling precious metals, gemstones and antiques, with many places devoted to silverwork and other jewellery. Some of the cheapest traditional crafts in Peru can be found in an artesanía market area en route to Callao, located by the roadside blocks 6–8 of **Avenida La Marina**, in Pueblo Libre. The **Mercado Indio**, on Avenida Petit Thouars north of Avenida Ricardo Palma is much more central, reasonably priced and home to the best craft and souvenir stalls and shops, all well within walking distance of Miraflores centre. **Artesanía Gran Chimu**, Av Petit Thouars 5495, has a wide range of jewellery and carved wooden items, as does **Mercado Artesanal**, Av Petit Thouars 5321. At La Rotunda, the small circular area towards the southern (ocean) end of Parque Kennedy in Miraflores, a small selection of reasonable-quality crafts and antiques is displayed every evening (6–9pm).

PHOTOGRAPHY

Renato Service 28 Julio 442, Miraflores; map p.69. For excellent camera and video equipment. The store is not very obvious from the street.

SHOPPING MALLS

Jockey Plaza Av Javier Prado Este 4200, Surco; map p.58. The largest of the shopping malls, with over two hundred shops including two massive department stores (OE and Ripley), a bowling alley, twelve cinema screens and dozens of restaurant-cafés. Take any colectivo or bus marked "Todo Javier Prado" heading east from the junction of avenidas Javier and Arequipa.

Larco Mar At the clifftop end of Av Larco, Miraflores; map p.69. This compact centre has more than seventy shops complemented by a couple of dozen restaurant-cafés, cinema screens, a few bars, and a bowling alley.

DIRECTORY

Banks and exchange Banco de la Nación, Av Nicolás de Piérola 1065 and Av Abancay 491; Banco de Credito, Jr Lampa 499, Av Larco 1099, Miraflores (well run and with small queues) and Juan de Arona, San Isidro; Banco Continental, Av Larco, Miraflores. Casas de cambio sometimes offer better rates and are often the only places where travellers' cheques will be accepted. Try casa de cambio, Ocoña 211A; or LAC Dollar, Av Camaná 779, 2nd floor (has another office at La Paz 211, Miraflores). In addition there are numerous storefronts along Av Larco, as well as individual money changers on the street (hard to miss, as they're waving stacks of US$).

Embassies and consulates Australia, Av Victor Belaunde 147, Office 1301, Torre Real 3, San Isidro (T 01 222 8281); Brazil, Av José Pardo 850, Miraflores (T 01 421 5660); Canada, C Bolognesi 228, Miraflores (T 01 319 3200); Chile, Av Javier Prado Oeste 790, San Isidro (T 01 710 2211); Ireland, Av Camino Real 390, San Isidro (T 01 222 5252); South Africa, Av Victor Andres Belaunde 147 (office 801), Edificio Real Tres, San Isidro (T 01 440 9996); UK, Torre Parque Mar, Av Larco 1301, 22nd floor, Miraflores (T 01 617 3000); US, La Encalada, block 17, Monterrico (T 01 434 3000).

Health For an ambulance call T 01 440 0200 , but if you can, take a taxi – it'll be much quicker. The following hospitals are well equipped, with emergency departments which you can use as an outpatient, or which you can phone for a house call: Clínica Anglo Americana, Av Salazar, San Isidro (T 01 221 3656); Clínica Internacional, Av Inca Garcilaso de la Vega 1420, Lima Centro (T 01 619 6161); and Clínica Ricardo Palma, Av Javier Prado Este 1066, San Isidro (T 01 224 2224). For anti-rabies vaccinations and emergency treatment contact Antirabico (T 01 337 0383). If you just need to see a doctor, try one of the following: Dr Jorge Bazan works as a "backpackers' medic" and will make house calls to hostels (T 997 352 668, E backpackersdr@yahoo.com); Dr Aste, C Antero Aspillaga 415, Oficina 101, San Isidro (T 01 441 7502), speaks English. The best pharmacy is Boticas Fasa, Av Benavides 847, Miraflores (T 01 612 5000), with 24hr delivery; they accept major credit cards. There's a comprehensive Mifarma pharmacy in Lima Centro at Av Abancay 601. Inka Farma (T 01 619 8000) is a delivery service.

Language schools Hispana Spanish School, C San Martín 377, Miraflores (T 01 446 3045, W hispanaidiomas.com); Ecela, Gen Recavarres 542, Miraflores (T 01 444 2279); Lima School of Languages, Av Grimaldo del Solar 469, Miraflores (T 01 242 7763, W elsol.idiomasperu.com), where you can start any Monday for small-group or private tuition, full- or part-time; El Tulipán, José Galvez 426, Miraflores (T 01 447 7403, W eltulipanperu.com), which offers a good Spanish survival course and free salsa classes Fridays at 7pm.

Laundry Many hotels will do this cheaply, but there are numerous *lavanderías* in most areas; the chain Lavandería Saori, Av Grimaldo del Solar 175, Miraflores (Mon–Sat 8am–7pm, Sun 9.30am–1.30pm; ⓣ 01 444 3830), is fast; LavaQueen, Av Larco 1158, Miraflores, does washing by the kilo at reasonable prices.

Police Peru's Tourist Police are based at Jr Colón 246, Miraflores (ⓣ 01 225 8698 or ⓣ 01 423 3500, or free at ⓣ 0800 22221), and in the Museo de la Nación at Av Javier Prado Este 2465 (ⓣ 01 225 8698).

Post office The main post office is at Pasaje Piura, Jr Lima, block 1 near the Plaza Mayor (Mon–Sat 8am–8pm, Sun 8am–2pm), with another branch in Miraflores, at Av Larco 868 (Mon–Fri 9am–5pm, Sat 8am–5pm). The best bet for sending large parcels is to use KLM (Av Elmer Faucett 2823, Oficina 404, Lima Cargo City, Callao; ⓣ 01 575 5270), with charges about US$15/kilo to Europe. Concas Travel, C Alcanfores 345, Oficina 101, Miraflores (ⓣ 01 241 7516), can arrange larger shipments.

The coast around Lima

Stretching out along the coast in both directions, the **Panamerican Highway** runs the entire 2600km length of Peru, with Lima more or less at its centre. Towns along the sometimes arid coastline immediately north and south of the capital are of minor interest to most travellers, though there are some glorious **beaches**, mostly to the south, with next to no restrictions on beach camping. The best of the beaches begin about 30km out, at the impressively hulking pre-Inca ruins of **Pachacamac**, a sacred citadel that still dominates this stretch of coastline.

Pachacamac

Mon–Sat 9am–5pm, Sun 9am–4pm • S/15, guides S/25 for a small group • ⓣ 01 430 0168 or ⓣ 01 321 5606, ⓦ pachacamac.cultura.pe

Originally one of the most important centres of pilgrimage on the Peruvian coast, **PACHACAMAC** functioned from around the time of Christ as a very sacred location that, even in pre-Inca days, housed a miraculous wooden idol (see below). As one of the few sites used by both pre-Inca and Inca civilizations, it's by far the most interesting of the Rimac Valley's ancient spots, and well worth making time for even

IDOLS AND ORACLES

"Pachacamac" means (more or less) "Earth's Creator", and the site was certainly occupied by 500 AD and probably for a long time before that. When other *huacas* were being constructed in the lower Rimac Valley, Pachacamac was already a temple-citadel and centre for mass pilgrimages. The god-image of Pachacamac was believed to express his or her anger through **tremors and earthquakes**, and was an **oracle** used for important matters affecting the State: the health of the ruler, the outcome of a war and so on. Later this became one of the most famous **shrines** in the Inca Empire, with Pachacamac himself worshipped along with the sun. The Incas built their Sun Temple on the crest of the hill above Pachacamac's own sacred precinct.

In 1533, **Francisco Pizarro** sent his brother Hernando to seize Pachacamac's treasure, but was disappointed by the spoils, which consisted of little more than an intricately carved **wooden idol** representing a two-faced humanoid. This wooden representation of Pachacamac may well have been the oracle itself: it was kept hidden inside a labyrinth and behind guarded doors – only the high priests could communicate with it face to face. When Hernando Pizarro and his troops arrived at the main idol site, it was raised up on a "snail-shaped" (or spiralling) platform, with the wooden carving stuck into the earth inside a dark room, separated from the world by a jewelled curtain. Pizarro ended up burning the complex to the ground, dissatisfied with the relatively small amounts of gold on offer.

As well as earthquakes, Pachacamac's powers extended to the absence or presence of **disease and pestilence**. His wife, or female counterpart, was believed to dominate **plant and fish life**.

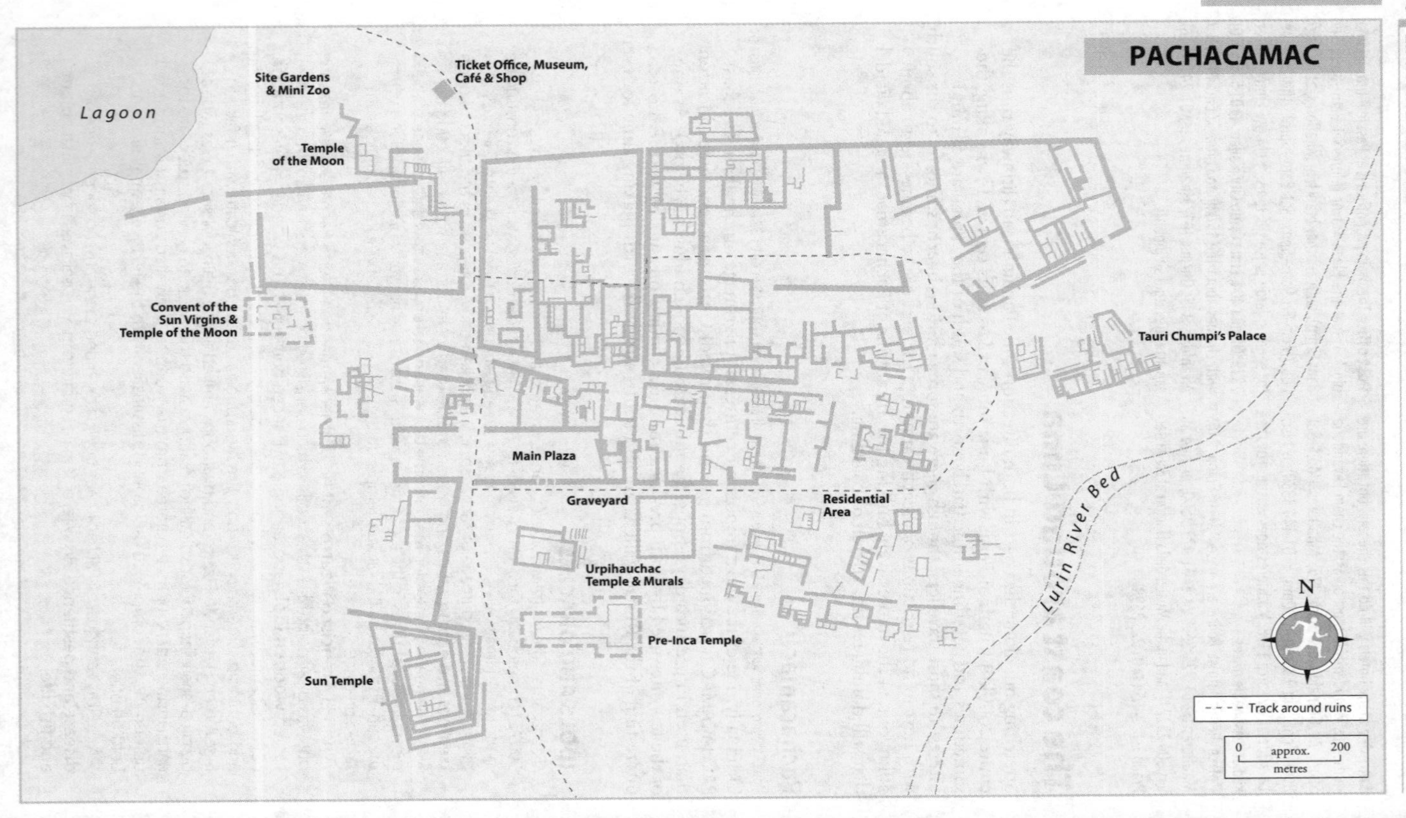
PACHACAMAC
Site Gardens & Mini Zoo
Ticket Office, Museum, Café & Shop
Lagoon
Temple of the Moon
Convent of the Sun Virgins & Temple of the Moon
Tauri Chumpi's Palace
Main Plaza
Graveyard
Residential Area
Urpihauchac Temple & Murals
Pre-Inca Temple
Sun Temple
Lurin River Bed
N
Track around ruins
0
approx.
200
metres

if you're planning to head out to Cusco and Machu Picchu; allow a good two hours to wander around the full extent of the ruins. The site can easily be combined with a day at one or other of the beaches, and it's little problem to get out there from the capital.

The museum

The entry fee for the citadel includes admission to the site **museum**, opened in 2015, which merits a fifteen- or thirty-minute browse on the way in. Definitely take a look at the wooden idol of Pachacamac and the detailed 3D site model, if not a few of the 6500 ceramic pieces in the museum collection, or other objects and textiles. Before the official **tour** you can eye the nice attached gardens, or grab a drink from the café (serves a limited menu of snacks).

The ruins

Entering the ruins, after passing the restored sectors, which include the **Templo de la Luna** (Temple of the Moon) and the **Convento de las Virgenes del Sol** (Convent of the Sun Virgins, or *Mamaconas*), you can see the later Inca construction of the **Sun Temple** directly ahead. Constructed on the top level of a series of pyramidal platforms, it was built tightly onto the hill with plastered adobe bricks, its walls originally painted in gloriously bright colours. From the very top of the Sun Temple there's a magnificent **view** west beyond the Panamerican Highway to the beach (Playa San Pedro) and across the sea to a sizeable yet uninhabited island, which resembles a huge whale approaching the shore. Below the Sun Temple is the **main plaza**, once covered with a thatched roof supported on stilts, and thought to have been the area where pilgrims assembled in adoration. The rest of the ruins, visible though barely distinguishable, were once dwellings, storehouses and palaces.

ARRIVAL AND DEPARTURE — PACHACAMAC

By bus Buses leave every 2hr for Pachacamac from Av Abancay in Lima Centro and around the Parque Universitario on Jr Montevideo at the corner with Jr Ayacucho (1hr). Buses can also be picked up from one of the bus-stop lay-bys on the Panamericana Sur (south direction); the spot where Av Angamos Este crosses the Panamericana is a good bet.

By taxi A taxi to Pachacamac and back from Miraflores can be arranged from around S/100.

By tour Many of the tour agencies in Lima offer half-day tours to the site (see page 80).

Lomas de Lucumo

Taxi from Lima (S/120–180) or Pachacamac (S/15)

Going away from the Pachacamac site via the pueblo of the same name you pick up a hard road heading for the Quebrada Verde area. Within a few kilometres you come across the **Lomas de Lucumo**, a beautiful natural ecosystem at the edge of the desert replete with shrubs and the odd flower thriving on little more than seasonal coastal fog.

Southern beach towns

South from Pachacamac lie some of Lima's most attractive **beaches**. Closest to the ruins, just a couple of kilometres away, is **Playa San Pedro**, a vast and usually deserted strip of sand. Constantly pounded by rollers, however, it can be quite dangerous for swimming. Though much more sheltered, the bay of **El Silencio**, 6km to the south, occasionally suffers from low-level pollution that can appear here from the local beachside developments. You may be better off heading to one of the excellent **seafood restaurants** on the cliff above, or to the smaller, more secluded bays a short drive further down the coast.

Santa María and San Bartolo

At **Punta Hermosa**, about ten minutes on the bus beyond El Silencio, you come to an attractive clifftop settlement and, down below, what's becoming Lima's leading surf resort, **Santa María**, a great family spot, with plenty of hotels and a reasonable beach. Just south of here the surf and beach resort of **San Bartolo** offers hostels, restaurants and reasonably good waves.

Pucusana, Chilca and around

South of San Bartolo lies the fishing village of **Pucusana**, clustered on the side of a small hilly peninsula, which is now perhaps the most fashionable of the beaches – a holiday resort where Limeños actually stay rather than just driving out for a swim.

Continuing south, the road cruises along the coast, passing the long beach and salt pools of **Chilca** after 5km, and the curious lion-shaped rock of **León Dormido** (Sleeping Lion) after another 15km or so.

Asia and further south

Spread out along the roadside from Km 95 to Km 103, **Asia** has turned from a small agricultural town, producing cotton, bananas and corn, to a modern, trendy resort with hotels and fashionable **clubs** alongside its long **beach**. Archeological finds in local graveyards have revealed that this site was occupied from around 2500 BC by a pre-ceramic agricultural community associated also with the earliest examples of a trophy-head cult (many of the mummies were decapitated). About 20km on from Asia is the growing surfers' resort of **Cerro Azul**.

ARRIVAL AND GETTING AROUND — SOUTHERN BEACH TOWNS

By bus Buses to San Bartolo (45min) and Pucusana (35min) can be picked up in Lima from one of the bus-stop lay-bys on the Panamericana Sur (south direction); wait at the spot where Av Angamos Este crosses the Panamericana. Some buses start from the corner of jirones Montevideo and Ayacucho every 2hr, passing Pachacamac, San Pedro, El Silencio, Punta Hermosa and Santa María on the 65km journey. For Asia and Cerro Azul take the Peru Bus (Av Mexico 333, La Victoria; T 01 205 2370, W perubus.com.pe).

ACCOMMODATION AND EATING

Doña Paulina Panamericana Sur, Km 86.5, about 20km south of Chilca on the highway, where it bypasses the town of Mala. At this cafetería, you can sample the best *chicharrones* (chunks of deep-fried pork) in the region. Daily 9am–7pm.

Penascal Surf Hotel Av Las Palmeras 258, San Bartolo T 01 430 7436, W surfpenascal.com. These apartments with oceanfront views are tied to a surfing school that also offers surf trips and Spanish lessons. Rates include breakfast, parking and laundry; lunch and dinner (with vegetarian options) available. S/215

East of Lima

Several destinations in the **foothills of the Andes** are within relatively easy reach in the east, inland from Lima. The most spectacular is the mystical plateau of **Marcahuasi** (see page 101) in the northeast, a weekend trip from the city; much closer to Lima are the impressive sites of **Puruchuco** and **Cajamarquilla**, which are typical of ruins all over Peru and make a good introduction to the country's archeology. The attractive mountain towns of **Tarma, Huancayo** and **Huancavelica**, all interesting destinations, are within a day's easy travelling of the capital, fanning out from northeast to southeast (see Chapter Five).

Puruchuco and around

Between Km 4 and Km 5 of the Carretera Central • Daily 9am–5pm • S/5 • T 01 494 2641 • Take any bus marked Vitarte or Chaclacayo and get off in Villa Vitarte, where the entrance is signposted from the Carretera Central (quite close to the football stadium)

An 800-year-old, pre-Inca settlement, **PURUCHUCO** is a labyrinthine villa. Nearby is the small but interesting **Museo de Sito Puruchuco**, containing a complete collection of artefacts and attire found at the site (all of which bears a remarkable similarity to what many indigenous communities in the Amazon still use today). The name itself means "feathered hat or helmet", and recent building work in the locality discovered that the Puruchuco site was also a massive **graveyard**, revealing greater quantities of buried pre-Incas than most other sites in Peru; in 2004, excavators discovered the oldest identified victim of a gunshot wound in the Americas, dated to the mid-sixteenth century. The villa's original adobe structure was apparently rebuilt and adapted by the Incas shortly before the Spanish arrived. It's a fascinating ruin, superbly restored in a way which vividly captures what life was like before the Conquest.

Very close by, in the Parque Fernando Carozi (ask the site guard for directions), two other ruins – **Huaquerones** and **Catalina Huaca** – are being restored, and at **Chivateros** there's a quarry dating back some twelve thousand years.

Cajamarquilla

Huachipa, Carretera Central • Daily 9am–5pm • S/5 • Take any bus marked Chaclacayo and get off at Santa Clara junction; cross over the river from here and turn right along the signposted road, from where it's 3km to the site

First occupied in the Huari era (600–1000 AD), **CAJAMARQUILLA** flourished under the **Cuismancu culture**, a city-building state contemporary with the better-known Chimu in northern Peru. It was an enclosed city containing thousands of small, complex dwellings clustered around a higher section, probably nobles' quarters, and numerous small plazas. The site was apparently abandoned before the Incas arrived in 1470, possibly after being devastated by an earthquake. Pottery found here in the 1960s by a group of Italian archeologists suggests habitation over 1300 years ago.

Today the site is a vast and almost overwhelming labyrinth of cracked and weathered adobe-built corridors, rooms and small plazas, and feels almost as if it was only recently deserted after a massive earthquake.

ARRIVAL AND DEPARTURE — PURUCHUCO AND CAJAMARQUILLA

Both Puruchuco and Cajamarquilla lie near the beginning of the Central Highway, the road that climbs up behind Lima towards Chosica, La Oroya and the Andes. The two sites are only 6km apart.

By tour The sites are most easily visited on a half-day guided tour from Lima (see page 80).

Parque Zoológico Huachipa

Av Las Torres, Vitarte; close to the Cajamarquilla turn-off • Daily 9am–5.30pm • S/18, children S/11 • T 01 356 3141, W zoohuachipa.com.pe • Take any bus marked Chaclacayo and get off at Santa Clara junction; it's on the right and well signposted before you reach the river and bridge, just a short walk along Av Las Torres

A long way out to the east of Lima in the Vitarte district, the **Parque Zoológico Huachipa** offers a diverse, man-made habitat with lakes and rides, and plenty of animals and birds. It's also fun for kids, with a walk-on pirate boat, a waterworld section, and an imaginative play area. The African savanna district is full of exotic fauna, including zebras and giraffes; there's another dedicated to carnivores (including tigers), a kangaroo enclosure and an aquatic area, not to mention an array of brightly coloured reptiles.

Marcahuasi and around

90km east of Lima • S/20; pay at the San Pedro de Casta tourist office (see page 102) • W marcahuasi.com

Marcahuasi (4100m) is a high plateau that makes a fantastic weekend camping jaunt (take a good sleeping bag – it can get very chilly) and is one of the more adventurous but popular excursions from Lima. Its main attractions are incredible, mysterious **rock formations**, which, particularly by moonlight, take on weird shapes – llamas, human faces, turtles, a hippopotamus and even a human figure known as Peca Gasha, a monument to humanity. Located 40km beyond Chosica, the easiest way to visit this amazing site in the hard-to-access Santa Eulalia Valley is on a day-trip from the capital (see page 80). The second week of October sees the start of the annual **Festival del Agua**, eight days of celebrations with music, dance and festivities. There is no clean water or food at the site, so make sure to take all provisions with you.

San Pedro de Casta

Only a few kilometres from Marcahuasi (2hr 30min–3hr trek), **SAN PEDRO DE CASTA** makes a good overnight stop – unless you choose to camp at Marcahuasi. It's a small and simple Andean village, quaint but without much choice in its limited range of facilities. There is a basic, municipally run hotel in town, and a handful of people rent out rooms in their homes, while others can set you up mules for the trek. Your best bet is to ask around when you arrive.

ARRIVAL AND INFORMATION — MARCAHUASI AND AROUND

By bus There are no direct buses from Lima to Marcahuasi/San Pedro. Instead, take a colectivo to Chosica (50min) from between the 3rd and 4th blocks of Av Paseo Colón, east of Bolognesi in Lima. From C Libertad, a block north of Chosica's Parque Echinique, a local bus departs at 7am and noon for San Pedro (3hr).

Tourist information There's an Oficina de Información on the main plaza in San Pedro de Casta which tends to have erratic opening hours; it is normally open early in the morning and around lunchtime. This is where you will have to pay your S/20 fee for Marcahuasi. If you're looking for a guide, head to *La Cabañita* restaurant on the main square and ask for Jorge.

Tour operator The friendly TEBAC (Trekking and Backpacking Club), Jr Huascar 1152, Jesús María, Lima (943 866 794, angelfire.com/mi2/tebac) runs three-day trips to Marcahuasi and throughout Peru; it's a great source of information on the country, too.

North of Lima

To the north of Lima, the desert stretches up between the Pacific Ocean and the foothills of the Andes. A couple of short trips north of Lima are becoming increasingly popular as long-weekend breaks. One of these is a horseshoe loop connecting the **Chillón and Chancay valleys** via the beautiful town and region of Canta in the foothills of the Andes. Another route, further out from Lima, heads up the Huara Valley from Huacho; although the road can be traced all the way to Huánuco, most people only get as far up into the Andes as **Churin**, where their efforts are pleasantly rewarded with a visit to the hot springs. Further north again, yet still feasible as a day-trip from Lima, the recently discovered pyramids of **Caral** are considered to be the most ancient ruins in the Americas.

The Chillón and Chancay valleys

Leaving Lima and heading north, the Panamerican Highway – or Panamericana Norte – passes through the **Chillón Valley**, dotted with ancient **ruins**, of which the most important are on the south side of the Río Chillón within 3 or 4km of the Ventanilla road. The most impressive is the 2000- to 3000-year-old **Temple El Paraiso**, which was built by a sedentary farming community of probably no more than 1500 inhabitants and consists of three main pyramids built of rustic stones.

From here, the Panamerican Highway passes the yacht and tennis clubs that make up the fashionable beach resort of **Ancón**, about 30km from Lima, then crosses a high, often foggy, plateau from the Chillón to the **Chancay Valley**. Still covered by sparse vegetation, this was a relatively fertile *lomas* area (where plants grow from moisture in the air rather than rainwater or irrigation) in pre-Inca days, and evidence of winter camps from five thousand years ago has been found. The highway bypasses the market town of Huaral and runs through **Chancay**, some 65km north of Lima.

Eco Truly Park

Km 63 on the Panamericana Norte • Lima contact: Paseo Colon 414, Miraflores • ⓣ 01 433 2455, ⓦ ecotrulypark.org • Coastal buses headed for Chancay, Barranca or Chimbote can drop off here

The unique domes of **Eco Truly Park** appear along the beach at Km 63 on the Panamerican Highway, by Chacra y Mar beach. Set at the foot of desert cliffs and close to the pounding ocean, this ashram offers guided tours of their adobe huts and organic gardens, plus yoga and meditation, hikes and workshops on ecology. Always book visits in advance.

Reserva Nacional Lomas de Lachay

Signposted off the Panamericana Norte between Chancay and Huacho, before the police controls at Doña María • ⓣ 968 218 647, ⓔ rnlachay@sernanp.gob.pe • Daily 7am–7pm

North of Chancay, the road passes through stark desert for 20km until at Km 105 you reach the **Reserva Nacional Lomas de Lachay**, a protected area of unique *lomas* habitat some 5000 hectares in extent and around 600m above sea level. Run by the Ministry of Agriculture, the centre maintains the footpaths that thread through the reserve's beautiful scenery. Formed by granite and diorite rocky intrusions some seventy million years ago, the **lomas** – at its best between June and December when it is in full bloom – is home to more than forty types of **bird**, including hummingbird, parrot, partridge, peregrine and even condor; you may also spot various species of reptile and native deer.

ARRIVAL AND DEPARTURE — RESERVA NACIONAL LOMAS DE LACHAY

By tour The easiest way to get to the reserve is with an organized tour from Lima (see page 80).

By car or taxi In a car or taxi from Chancay (S/20 each way; 45min), continue up the Panamericana Norte for about 6km beyond the turning for Sayan and Churin. The turn-off to the reserve is signposted at the top of a hill, but from the road it's still an hour's walk along a sandy track to the interpretive centre at the entrance to the reserve.

El Paraíso and Huacho

A little north of the Reserva Nacional Lomas de Lachay, at Km 133 of the Panamericana Norte, a track turns off onto a small peninsula and leads to the secluded bay of **El Paraíso** – a magical beach perfect for camping, swimming and scuba diving. Crossing bleaker sands, the Panamericana Norte next passes through **HUACHO**, an unusual place with some interesting colonial architecture and a ruined church in the upper part of town, but mostly made up of recent concrete constructions. As it's so close to Lima, it was one of the first towns to be hit by expanding and migratory populations, as well as wealthy Lima families taking on a second home or farmstead.

The Huara Valley

Just beyond Huacho a side road turns east into the **Huara Valley** and the foothills of the Andes to reach **Sayan**, a small farming town where little has changed for decades – the church here has maintained its very attractive colonial interior.

Churin

Further up the valley from Sayan lies **CHURIN**, a small thermal spa town popular with Limeños during holidays, located in the district of Pachangara 210km from Lima. Most of the farmland on the valley floor and the Sayan-to-Churin road was washed away in the 1998 El Niño, and a new, rough road has been carved out between the boulders littering the valley floor. There are two spas in town, both fairly cool, with private and communal baths; the **El Fierro spa** (all baths cost S/2–3) is the hottest and reputed to be the most curative. It's a ten-minute ride by colectivo from town (S/1.50).

Churin is also a good base from which to explore a number of traditional communities as well as archeological **ruins**, such as Ninash, Kutun, Antasway and Kuray. For climbers, there are also some challenging **peaks** in the Cordillera Raura (up to 5700m). The main **festival** here is San Juan, between June 23 and 25, which includes a ritual procession to the river for a cleansing bath, to ensure health in the coming year.

Huancahuasi

Baths S/6

An excellent day-trip from Churin can be made to more thermal baths at **Huancahuasi**. There are two sets of hot baths here, and traditional snacks such as *pachamanca* (meat and vegetables on pre-heated rocks covered with earth and left for a few hours) are prepared outside them. En route to Huancahuasi you'll spot a remarkable, early colonial, carved facade on the tiny church at **Picoy**.

ARRIVAL AND DEPARTURE — THE HUARA VALLEY

By bus There are several buses to Sayan and Churin from Lima daily (6–7hr), the best run by Transportes Estrella Polar, Av Luna Pizarro 330–338, La Victoria (T 01 332 8182; expect to pay around S/14).

By colectivo Colectivos run between Sayan and Huacho every 30min. Colectivos to Huancahuasi leave from Churin church at around 8am (S/12 return; 30min), returning mid-afternoon.

ACCOMMODATION AND EATING

There are many places to stay in Churin, but they all get packed out in the main holiday periods, when prices double. All of the **hotels** are within a couple of blocks of each other in the town centre. Churin has some good **restaurants** and **cafés** too, mostly around the main plaza. Local specialities include honey, *alfajores*, *manjar blanca* and cheeses.

Hotel Las Termas Av Larco Herrera 411, Churin T 01 237 3094. This well-located place has pleasant rooms, good service and a pool, as well as a private terrace and gardens. S/70

Caral

Supe Valley, accessed via Carretera Caral-Las Minas Ambar from Supe Town • Daily 7am–5.30pm • S/10 • T 01 431 2235, W caralperu.gob.pe

North up the coast from Huacho, only the town and port of **SUPE** breaks the monotonous beauty of desert and ocean, until you reach Barranca and the labyrinthine ruins of the Fortaleza de Paramonga (see page 343). Inland from Supe, however, along the desert coast in a landscape that looks more lunar than agricultural, archeologists have uncovered one of the most important finds of the past century. Thought to be the oldest city in the Americas at around five thousand years old, the ancient pyramids of **Caral** are now a **UNESCO World Heritage Site**.

Brief history

From humble beginnings (see page 105), Caral developed into one of the earliest metropolises, representing human achievements that took place four thousand years earlier than the Incas: the stone ceremonial structures here were flourishing a hundred years before the Great Pyramid at Giza was even built.

Archeologists have studied its temples, houses and plazas, and the artefacts unearthed here, to form a picture of the ancient Caral culture, which focused heavily on agriculture and construction. There's evidence of ceremonial functions, too, and music was also important: a collection of coronets and flutes have been found on site.

THE ORIGINS OF CARAL

Before the advent of urban living and stone ceremonial pyramids here, the region was only populated by a few **coastal villages**, each with around a hundred inhabitants. Around 2700 BC it appears that a number of larger villages emerged, principally, it seems, based around the successful domestication and early cultivation of the cotton-bush plant. The early use of **cotton** was nothing short of a bio-technological revolution, not only providing cloth for garments but more importantly permitting the fabrication of nets for fishing in the rich coastal waters, as well as net or woven bags for carrying produce and fish back home to their settlements. The introduction of cotton fishing nets transformed the lives of coastal communities, giving them sufficient protein, more spare time to evolve social and religious practices, and surplus food to trade with neighbouring communities, laying the groundwork for what was to become a thriving urban centre.

The site

The heart of the site covers about 150 acres. There are two large, sunken circular plazas, the base of the tallest mound measuring 154m by 138m, making it the largest pyramid yet found in Peru. Excavations have revealed that this **Piramide Mayor** (main pyramid) was terraced, with a staircase leading up to an atrium-like platform, culminating in a flattened top housing enclosed rooms and a ceremonial fire pit. Some of the best artefacts discovered here include 32 **flutes** made from pelican and animal bones and engraved with the figures of birds and even monkeys, demonstrating a connection with the Amazon region.

The six mounds, or pyramids, are arranged together around a large plaza. Archeologists believe that the pyramids were constructed in a maximum of two phases, which suggests a need for particularly complex social structures for planning, decision-making and the mobilization of a large sector of the population to provide sufficient labour as and when it was required. Around the pyramids is evidence of many residential structures.

ARRIVAL AND DEPARTURE — CARAL

By bus and colectivo Transportes Paramonga (Av Luna Pizarro 251, La Victoria; ⓣ01 423 6338, ⓦturismoparamonga.com.pe) runs buses every day to Supe, usually leaving around 6.20am. From here, if unguided, you'd need to take a colectivo (S/6; 45min); they leave regularly from near the market in Supe centre.

By car Easier to reach with your own car, Caral is connected to the Panamerican Highway by a badly rutted dirt-track road that starts at Km 184 of the highway and continues for 23km to the site.

By tour Mirabus (see page 81) offers a day-trip from around US$80/person, including guide and bus to the site. Caral Tours (C Porta 130, Office 707, Miraflores; ⓣ01 243 3168, ⓦen.caraltours.net) is also recommended, with a slightly higher price. Most trips require at least two people. Note that other operators offer similar trips at roughly three times the price (given in US$ instead of soles), so buyer beware.

Nazca and the south coast

PENGUINS ON ISLAS BALLESTAS

2

Nazca and the south coast

South of Lima, a beautiful dry desert stretches the entire 1330km to Chile. In places just a narrow strip of desert squashed between Andes and Pacific, it is followed diligently by the Panamericana Sur Highway. The region harbours one of South America's greatest archeological mysteries – the famous Líneas de Nazca – as well as offering access to coastal wildlife and stunning, desolate landscapes. Once home to at least three major pre-Inca cultures – the Paracas (800 BC–200 AD), the influential Nazca (100 BC–650 AD) and the Ica (900–1470 AD) – this region of Peru was eventually taken over by the Incas. Today, Nazca and Paracas are very much part of the tourist trail and are often visited en route between Lima and Cusco.

Once beyond Lima's beaches, the first tourist destination of note is the attractive **Valle de Lunahuaná**, well known as a river-rafting centre as well as for its vineyards. Just south of here, the busy town of **Chincha** is the hub of Afro-Peruvian culture, though for most tourists, their first stop south of the capital is the beguiling desert landscape of **La Reserva Nacional de Paracas,** and the nearby coastal resort of El Chaco (more often dubbed Paracas). This is the jumping off point for the **Islas Ballestas**, which offer an exciting mix of wildlife – including vast seabird colonies as well as sea lions, dolphins and sharks – and boat trips.

Hidden in sand dunes just outside the city of **Ica**, the once peaceful desert oasis of Huacachina has been rather taken over by sandboarding and dune-buggies; arguably the glorious pre-Inca ceramic and textiles in Ica's recently renovated **regional museum** are of greater interest, while the **bodegas** in the surrounding vineyards produce some of the country's finest pisco. A couple of hours' drive south, the geometric shapes and giant figures of the **Líneas de Nazca** are etched over almost 500 square kilometres of bleak pampa. Nazca also offers access to the outstanding, rare vicuña reserve of Pampa Galeras (in the Andes above Nazca), as well as to other archeological treasures.

Further south, just before the town of Chala, **Puerto Inca** is a delightfully secluded but still relatively undeveloped beach resort, by the ruins of the one-time coastal port for the nobles of Inca Cusco. Also nearby is a small, unique nature reserve, **Las Lomas de Atiquipa,** where rugged hills are tucked up against the ocean, and precious vegetation sustained by coastal fog. Once past the town of Camaná, south of Chala, the **Panamericana Sur** runs inland to within almost 40km of Arequipa (see Chapter Three), where there's a fast road connection into the city. From here the highway cuts south across undulating desert to the calm colonial town of **Moquegua**, a springboard for the region's archeological heritage, before heading south another 150km to **Tacna**, the last pit stop before the frontier with Chile. A more spectacular route to Tacna follows the coastal **Carretera Costanera.**

GETTING AROUND

THE SOUTH COAST

Transport is not usually a problem along the south coast, with local buses connecting all the towns with each other and with Lima, and express buses ploughing along the Panamericana Sur between Lima and Arequipa day and night.

By bus The best bus companies serving the south coast are Cruz del Sur (01 324 6332, cruzdelsur.com.pe) and Excluciva (01 418 1111, excluciva.com.pe). Not far behind are Oltursa (01 708 5000, oltursa.pe), Ormeño (01 472 1710, grupo-ormeno.com.pe) and TEPSA (01 617 9000). Cheaper, more frequent and less luxurious services from Lima southwards are Soyuz/PerúBus (Av México 333, La Victoria 01 427 6310, soyuzonline.com.pe) and Flores (Av Paseo de la República 627 01 480 0725, floreshnos.pe); the former goes as far as Ica, whereas the latter goes all the way to Tacna. Soyuz/

BODEGA VISTA ALEGRE

Highlights

❶ **Islas Ballestas** Within a morning's boat ride from the town of Pisco, these guano islands with their much-photographed rock arches are home to an impressive range of seabirds and mammalian marine life. See page 116

❷ **Reserva Nacional de Paracas** A beautiful peninsula with beguiling desert landscapes touching the Pacific Ocean; both beaches and sea are a haven for wildlife. See page 117

❸ **Ica's bodegas** A trawl round the vineyards of this desert oasis will allow you to sample plenty of Peru's national beverage, pisco, while gaining insights into the production processes, both old and new. See page 124

❹ **Museo Regional Adolfo Bermúdez Jenkins** One of the best museums outside Lima; in addition to showcasing stunning ancient textiles and pre-Columbian ceramics, it offers a graphic description of the process of mummification. See page 126

❺ **Líneas de Nazca** The world-famous Nazca Lines, including stylized geometric and animal figures, were etched, seemingly impossibly, into a massive desert pampa. See page 131

❻ **Puerto Inca** This small but secluded resort lies in an area of coast teeming with Inca remains as well as offering great access to beaches, coves, fishing and excellent diving. See page 143

HIGHLIGHTS ARE MARKED ON THE MAP ON PAGE 110

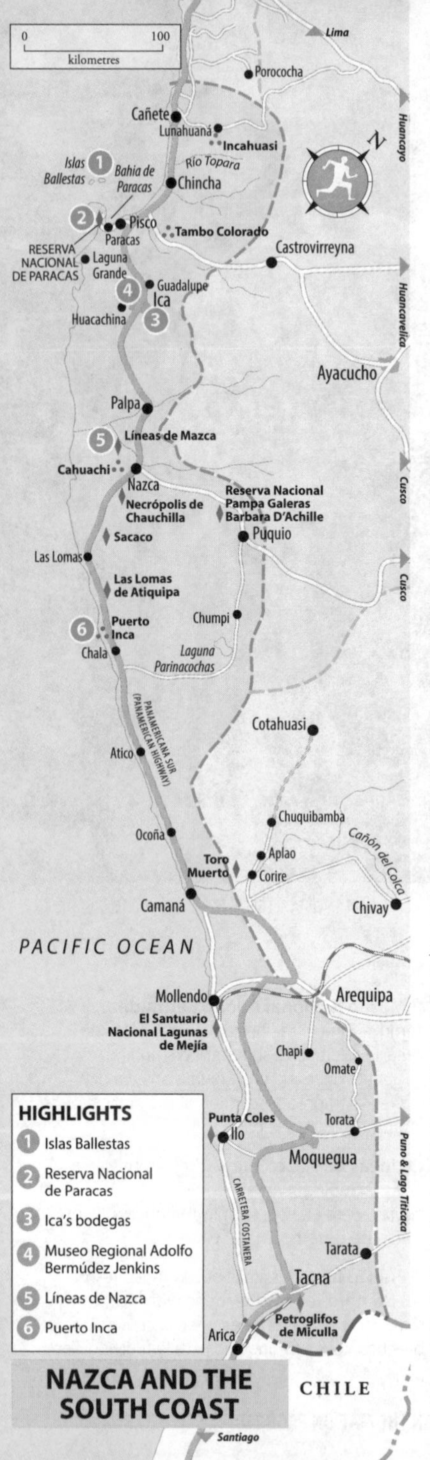

PerúBus buses leave roughly every 10–15min during the day (every 30min at night) and can also be picked up from obvious bus stops along the Panamericana Sur in Lima (for instance, where the highway is crossed by either Av Javier Prado Este or Av Benavides Este).

By colectivo White Mercedes minivans run routes between most of the towns and cities in the south. They are generally safe and comfortable, usually with a/c; the only downside is that they don't have set departure times, only leaving when full. You can generally find them outside the standard bus terminals. Even quicker, though less safe, are the shared taxi colectivos, which can be located along major junctions, such as Pisco, along the Panamericana heading towards Lima.

Lunahuaná

Two hours' or so drive south of Lima, the town of Cañete provides access to the pleasant river-valley resort of **LUNAHUANÁ,** which lies some 35km east, on the road to Huancayo. Relaxed and low key, it is home to several hotels and a large number of tour agencies offering **adventure activities.** Though initially renowned for whitewater rafting, the town's diversions have expanded to include trekking, mountain biking, ATV tours, horseriding, abseiling and ziplining. The place varies in feel considerably depending on whether it is the busy time, mainly Dec–March/April, when the rapids can reach up to class IV. Other peak periods include: the *fiestas patrias* on July 28; the grape harvest in early March which is combined with rafting competitions; and the **Festival del Níspero**, the first weekend in October, which celebrates the popular orangey fruit of the same name (loquat in English), alongside the usual beauty pageants, folk dancing and general carousing. Outside these periods, and midweek in particular, it's empty and laidback. Although numbers of foreign visitors are growing, the town mainly sees a mix of families and a young and sporty crowd from Lima. If your expectations aren't too high, it can be a diverting break to experience some low-key adventure activities; otherwise you may want to save your soles for the Andes proper.

Lunahuaná and the surrounding area consist of beautifully sculpted, dusty mountainsides flanking a narrow, irrigated

ACTIVITIES AROUND LUNAHUANÁ

There are numerous **tour operators** in Lunahuaná, many lining Jr Grau, offering much the same excursions at similar prices. Rafting is the main draw and usually costs S/40–50 for just under an hour on the river – including guide, transport and training – depending on the season (price is reduced in the low season, May–Oct). Other **activities** include rock-climbing, abseiling, hiking, zip-lining, horseriding and ATV or mountain bike tours (from around S/50 upwards). Check the operator's equipment and safety procedures before signing up.

Lunahuaná Rafting Jr Grau 180 ⓣ999 579 709, ⓦlunahuanarafting.com. Rafting – obviously – plus tours for trekking and adventure action, including a trip up to the lovely Reserva Paisajística Nor Yauyos Cochas (see page 290).

Río Cañete Expediciones Jr Grau 284 ⓣ012 841 271, ⓦriocanete.com. Operations are based round riverside *Camping San Jerónimo*, 5km down the valley from Lunahuaná. Offers guided whitewater runs from 5km to 21km, and also a two-day package that includes rafting, hiking and climbing.

2

and fertile green valley floor. As well as possessing abundant **vineyards**, which can be visited on tours (see page 120), the valley is also dedicated to cultivating maize, cotton, rice, avocados, chillies, limes, papayas and bananas.

On the plaza, which hosts a weekend market, stands a fine colonial **church** with a cool interior and a sky-blue wooden vaulted ceiling. Within easy striking distance there's a traditional hanging bridge (*puente colgante*), the local Inca archeological complex of **Incahuasi**, plus rustic **pisco haciendas**, such as the *Bodega Fidelina Candela*, (Anexo Jita, at Km 37, ⓣ012 841 030) dotted along the Cañete-Yauyos road on either side of Lunahuaná.

Incahuasi

8km southwest of Lunahuaná on the main Cañete road • Daily 24hr • Free • **Guided tours** On request (contact the caretaker, ⓣ993 411 655); Spanish only • S/40 for 1–3 people • Any Lunahuaná-Cañete colectivo can drop off/pick up at the site; alternatively take a taxi from Lunahuaná (S/10–15), or visit as part of a tour (see page 120)

Incahuasi was established by the Inca Emperor Pachacuti (1438–71), who created his empire by expanding the territorial base out of the Cusco valley. This was one of his coastal palaces, a hunting lodge and an optimum spot for his administrators and soldiers to control the flow of goods and people in and out of the Andes. What remains are scattered low stone and mud walls in a dominant position overlooking the valley.

ARRIVAL AND DEPARTURE — LUNAHUANÁ

By bus Soyuz/PerúBus (ⓦsoyuzonline.com.pe) or Flores (ⓦfloreshnos.pe) buses heading south from Lima, or north from Pisco, Ica and Nazca, stop in San Vicente (de Cañete), from where you can get a minivan up the valley to Lunahuaná.

By colectivo Minivans bound for Lunahuaná (6am–7/8pm; 50min) depart from Imperial, an eastern suburb of Cañete, dropping you on Jr Grau or the Plaza de Armas. Imperial is a 15min combi ride from outside the Soyuz/PerúBus or Flores bus terminals on the Antigua Panamericana Sur in Cañete.

By taxi Taxis to Lunahuaná from Cañete (S/30) are usually available in the town centre, around the bus stops on the main through-road.

ACCOMMODATION

Camping and the pricier lodgings are strung out along the valley, by the river, above and below Lunahuaná, with cheaper places along Jr Grau and around the plaza. Prices are often hiked for long weekends and holiday periods, when you can expect partying at campsites.

Camping Lunahuaná Entry on the main access road opposite Jr Grau ⓣ945 690 398. A well-set-up campground, with electricity, on the banks of the Río Cañete, busy over weekends and holidays. S/20

★ **La Confianza** Carretera Cañete ⓣ968 213 093, ⓦlaconfianza.com.pe. Out in the countryside, a 15min drive down the valley from town, bungalows and wooden A-frames stand on lush lawns by the river, surrounded by impressive mountains. The restaurant, set in an old bodega, is excellent, offering a well-prepared and -presented range of local dishes. S/230

Hostal Los Portales Jr Grau 503 ⓣ982 913 619, ⓦfacebook.com/lunahuanalosportaleshostal. A quiet spot offering professional service, this neo-colonial hotel on three floors comprises simple, well maintained en-suite doubles with polished floors set around a grand colonnade. Room only. S/100

Hostal Haku Peru Jr Grau 250. Pleasant budget hostel just off the main square, with sparkling tiles and nice pine furniture. Good value. Room only. S/60

Refugio de Santiago C Real 33, Paullo Km 31 ⓣ01 436 2717, ⓦrefugiodesantiago.com. Simply but beautifully furnished light, airy rooms inside a colonial-style house, with an interior courtyard bar and a few acres of gardens with outside tables, this has one of the finest restaurants south of Lima (see page 86). Good-value family rooms. S/151

EATING

★ El Patio 140 Jr Grau 140 ⓣ952 362 618 ⓦfacebook.com/elpatio140. Freshly prepared food made to order at this family-run enterprise, with river shrimp dishes the house speciality (S/40). Try also the local trout, with salad and melt-in-your-mouth *papas doradas* (crispy roast potatoes; S/30). Thurs–Sun 8.30am–9pm.

El Refugio de Santiago C Real 33, Paullo Km 31. This place undoubtedly provides the best cuisine in the valley, served out in the gardens in fine weather. The owner-chef takes great pride in cooking with fresh, home-grown indigenous herbs, fruits and vegetables – don't miss the trout ceviche. Unfortunately, it is not always open to day-visitors, and times vary out of season. Call in advance to check. Mains S/25–72. Mon–Sat noon–8pm, Sun noon–5pm.

Restaurant Valle Hermoso San Jerónimo Km 33.2 ⓣ01 284 1100. A simple, homely place with friendly owners, known as "La Casa del Pis-cuy" on account of its most famous platter: *cuy* marinated in pisco – one of the best dishes in the valley (S/48). The *chicharrón de conejo* (fried rabbit) is also a winner. Daily 9am–5pm.

Chincha

Languishing at the top of a cliff, **CHINCHA** is a relatively rich oasis that appears after a stretch of almost Saharan landscape – and a mightily impressive sand dune. A rather crowded and noisy little coastal centre renowned for its cheap wines and variety of **piscos**, Chincha is a strong cultural hub for **Afro-Peruvian culture.** The town was developed during the early colonial period when Africans (mainly from Guinea) were brought over as slaves to work on the cotton plantations. Chincha is dominated by two roads running north to south; most hotels and restaurants are on the main Panamericana itself. For the passing tourist, Chincha isn't particularly attractive, and musically it's a bit dry outside the festivals. Nearby **El Carmen** has slightly more charm, and at weekends you'll be more likely to come across some Afro-Peruvian music and dance, with the rhythm of the *cajón*, a traditional, boxlike wooden percussion instrument, setting the pace. Swing by the Centro Afroperuano on Calle Tupac Amaru (ⓣ998 785 286, ⓦcentroafroperuano.blogspot.com) to learn more about the area's cultural heritage and to find out what's on.

Las Huacas de Chincha

A taxi from Chincha will take you to the sites for S/40–50, depending on how long you want the driver to wait

The area has a number of ruins, with the **Huacas de Chincha** lying scattered about the oasis. Dominated in pre-Inca days by the Cuismancu (or Chincha) state, activity focused around what were probably ceremonial pyramids. One of these, the majestic **Huaca Centinela** – also known as the little city of Chinchacamac – sits in the valley between the Chincha plateau and the ocean, around thirty minutes' walk from the town, some 8km off the Panamericana. Sadly, all these neglected sites have been heavily eroded, and encroached on by agricultural and residential developments. Not far away,

CHINCHA'S FESTIVALS

The main local festival – **Día Nacional del Pisco** – takes place on the fourth Sunday in July, when things really get lively along this section of the coast. The area is also well known for its traditionally rhythmic music and annual cultural festival, **Verano Negro**, which celebrates Afro-Peruvian culture and stretches over ten days at the end of February. In November, the **Festival de Danzas Negras** is excellent, a vibrant dance event also based on Afro-Peruvian traditions. In both cases the celebrations are liveliest in the district of **El Carmen**, 10km southeast of Chincha.

38km up the main road to Ayacucho (which leaves the Highway at Km 230) is a more impressive Cuismancu ruin, Tambo Colorado (see page 119).

Hacienda San José

Pueblo San José • Daily 9am–6pm • Hacienda and catacomb tours 45min, S/20; free for guests • ⓣ 056 221 458 • Colectivos from C Caqueta (by the market, three blocks west of the Plaza de Armas) bound for El Carmen (30min) will detour via the hacienda if requested. If travelling by bus along the Panamericana Sur, alight at Km 203 and get onto one of the colectivos travelling from Chincha to El Carmen

Don't miss the **Hacienda San José** – now converted into a hotel (see below) – set 9km southeast of Chincha in an extensive plantation. Its morbid history includes the tale of an owner murdered on the house's main steps by his slaves, and it still sports impressive Churrigueresque-domed towers built in the 1680s. The **tours** take in the main hacienda building, the chapel and a section of the extensive, labyrinthine **catacombs** containing prison cells still clearly showing the appalling conditions in which slaves were once shackled; a horrific but important reminder.

ARRIVAL AND DEPARTURE — CHINCHA

By bus Most bus connections to and from Chincha are at the Terminal Terrestre on Av Benavides, close to the big bend in the Panamericana Sur as it enters the urban areas of town from the north. Both Soyuz/PerúBus (Av Benavides 704; ⓣ 056 269 239, ⓦ soyuzonline.com.pe) and Flores (Av San Martin 350) have connections every 20min south with Paracas, Ica and Nazca, and north with Lima.

By colectivo Colectivos and taxis drop off and pick up on the Panamericana Sur, as well as around the big bend in the highway as it enters town from the north and crosses over Jr Santo Domingo.

ACCOMMODATION

Unremarkable, cheap hotels in Chincha are close to the Plaza de Armas and along Avenida Benavides. More appealing options lie outside the town centre.

Casa Albergue Huaranjapo El Carmen, off Panamerica Sur Km 203 ⓣ 998 785 286, ⓦ huaranjapo.com. A welcoming house set in the middle of a large green space with fruit trees. Plenty of options to keep you busy, from a volleyball pitch to an inviting hammock area. S/170

Hacienda San José Signposted off the Panamericana Sur at Km 203 ⓣ 056 313 332, ⓦ casahaciendasanjose.com. A beautifully restored building with a dark history, this old-style hacienda and ex-slave plantation offers the chance to experience the luxury of another era, but also reminds us what this luxury was built upon. Stunning rooms – all but two in modern bungalows – and the grounds are a pleasure to explore, but there's not much to do nearby; come for pure relaxation. Guided tour included (see above) and substantial weekday discounts. US$160

Punto Sur Lodge C Los Eucaliptos s/n ⓣ 056 267 528, ⓦ puntosurlodge.com. Friendly place with thirteen simple, modern rooms. Has a particularly nice pool and garden area. S/130

EATING AND DRINKING

Bodega Naldo Navarro Pasaje Santa Rosa, Sunampe ⓣ 979 096 418. A 100-year-old bodega that's one of the best places for pisco and local sweet wine (*vino dulce*). Based 2km west of Chincha, it offers free guided tours and samples, and occasional musical events. Daily 9am–5pm.

El Batán Panamericana Sur 791 Km 197.5 ⓣ 056 268 050, ⓦ elbatanchincha.com. A petrol station diner right on the Panamericana with gourmet aspirations – and it delivers. International and local creole favourites are all superbly prepared (S/18–45). Great empanadas. Mon–Sat 6.30am–10pm, Sun 6.30pm.

El Refugio de Mamainé Cacerio El Guayabo, El Carmen ⓣ965 941 010. 2km west of El Carmen lies one of the region's best-loved restaurants, run by the gregarious queen of creole flavours, Esther Cartagena. Nothing fancy, and quality can suffer when it's busy, but the food is abundant and affordable and the place oozes character. Local favourites include *carapulcra* (a spicy pork and dried potato stew) and *pollo con sopa seca* (basil pasta with chicken), *tacu tacu* (a fried rice and bean cake) and *cau cau* (tripe stew), all S/18 – S/32. Often live music and dance. Daily 11.30am–5pm.

Pisco and around

Less than three hours by bus from Lima, the old port town of **PISCO** is the gateway to the neighbouring resort town of **Paracas**, 17km away. Pisco is a cheaper and less touristy base for visiting the **Reserva Nacional de Paracas** and the **Islas Ballestas** and the well-preserved Inca coastal outpost of **Tambo Colorado**. The two towns are also decent stop-offs before heading up into the Andes: you can take roads from here to Huancavelica and Huancayo, as well as to Ayacucho and Cusco.

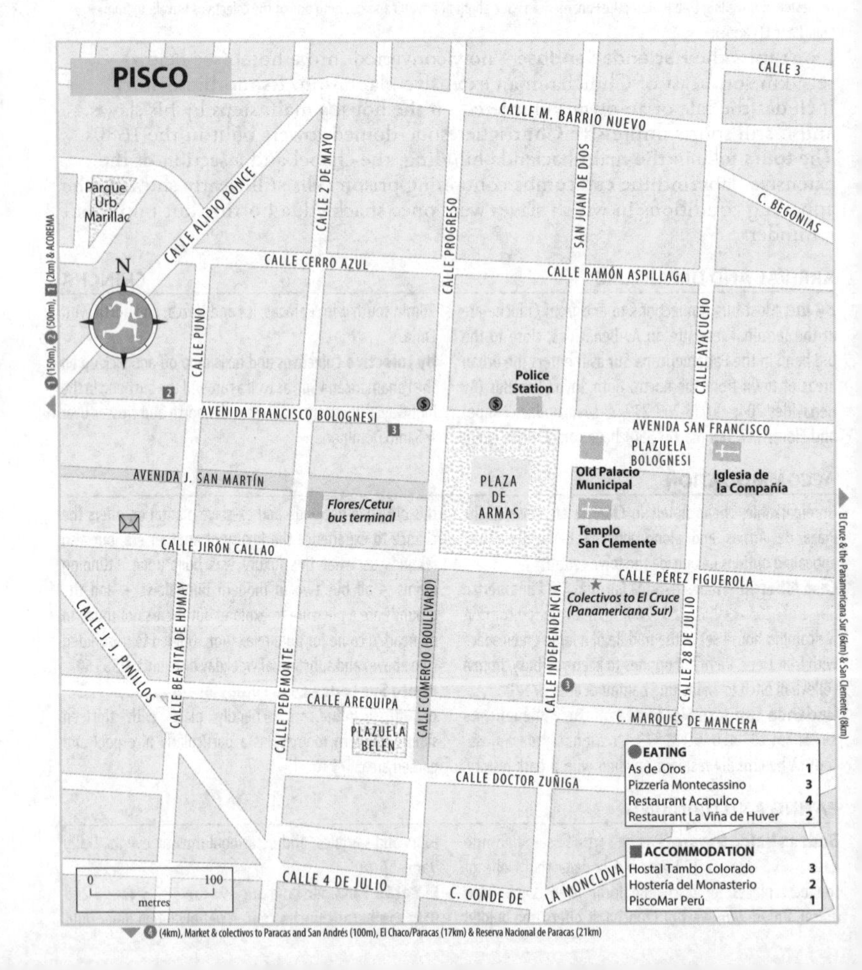

Pisco today, however, is a shadow of its former self. An 8.0 magnitude earthquake hit in the evening of August 15, 2007, devastating the town and the surrounding area. Some 70 percent of the town's buildings were destroyed, hundreds of people were killed and over 15,000 were left homeless. Much of the emergency relief money never made it to the people who most needed it, and it is only the last few years that the government promises of redevelopment have begun to be realised.

The town

Pisco's focus of activity is the **Plaza de Armas,** dominated by the equestrian monument to liberator San Martín, and adjoining **Jirón Comercio** and **Avenida San Martín**; the latter leads down to the sea and the as yet undeveloped new waterfront. Every evening the plaza is crowded with people walking and talking, buying *tejas* (small sweets of pecan nuts and toffee) from street sellers or chatting. The square's most impressive landmark is the Moorish-style **Palacio Municipal** – still awaiting post-earthquake reconstruction and its promised conversion into a museum; it is painted in striking blue and white stripes, in memory of San Martín's colours. The adjacent, uninspiring red-brick building is the new **cathedral**, which was inaugurated in 2012, and replaces the original one that was destroyed in the 2007 earthquake.

Paracas (El Chaco)

PARACAS, to the south of Pisco and only four kilometres north of the national park of the same name, is a decidedly more scenic place to base yourself than Pisco. Its original name is **El Chaco** – though clearly Paracas has more marketing appeal, since it bears the name of the nearby national park – and it was once a spot for wealthy Limeños, whose expensive resort hotels and large private bungalows line the beach close to the entrance to the reserve. However, plenty of reasonably priced hostels and restaurants have appeared of late, though all charge fairly touristy prices. The wharf here, surrounded by pelicans, is the place to board **speedboats** (*lanchas*) bound for the Islas Ballestas (see page 116), and a pleasant spot to sip a pisco sour and watch the sunset. Just before entering the town from the north, you'll pass a bleak concrete obelisk vaguely shaped like a nineteenth-century sailing boat, built in 1970 to commemorate the landing of San Martín here on September 8, 1820, on his mission to liberate Peru from the Spanish.

Swimming in the bay is not recommended, since the water is becoming increasingly polluted – not least from the fishmeal-processing factories that line the shore between Paracas and Pisco, and whose spillages of fish oil are endangering bird and sea-mammal life. However, the new industrial port under construction is likely to pose an even greater threat to the environment.

SEA TURTLES, DOLPHINS AND WHALES

San Andrés, the fishing village midway between Pisco and Paracas, is still known for its **sea turtle** dishes, even though it is now **illegal** to serve them due to the danger of extinction. Warm turtle blood is occasionally drunk in the region, reputedly as a cure for bronchial problems. In order to help save these endangered turtles from extinction, you should avoid turtle dishes and perhaps even consider the merits of reporting any restaurant that offers it to a turtle conservation group. The seas around here are traditionally rich in fish life, and **dolphins** are often spotted. The abundant plankton in the ocean around Pisco and Paracas attracts numerous species of **whale**, and in 1988 a new, small species – the *Mesoplodon peruvianus*, which can be up to 4m long – was discovered after being caught accidentally in fishermen's nets.

Islas Ballestas

20km northwest of Paracas • Park fee S/11; S/17 for a combined ticket with the Reserva Nacional de Paracas; dock tax S/5 • Can only be visited on a boat tour (from S/30, plus park & dock fees; see page 120) or by private charter. Tours depart daily at 8am, plus 10am and noon, depending on demand

The **Islas Ballestas** (one of a whole string of islets and sea stacks that fuelled Peru's guano boom in the mid-nineteenth century) lie off the coast due west of Pisco and although the comparisons to Galápagos seem optimistic, visits nonetheless rarely fail to surprise and impress. These rocky outposts, parts of which have eroded into impressive arches and caves, seem to be alive and moving with a mass of flapping, noisy pelicans, penguins, terns, boobies and Guanay cormorants. The name *Ballesta* is Spanish for crossbow, and may derive from times when marine mammals and larger fish were hunted with mechanical crossbow-style harpoons. There are

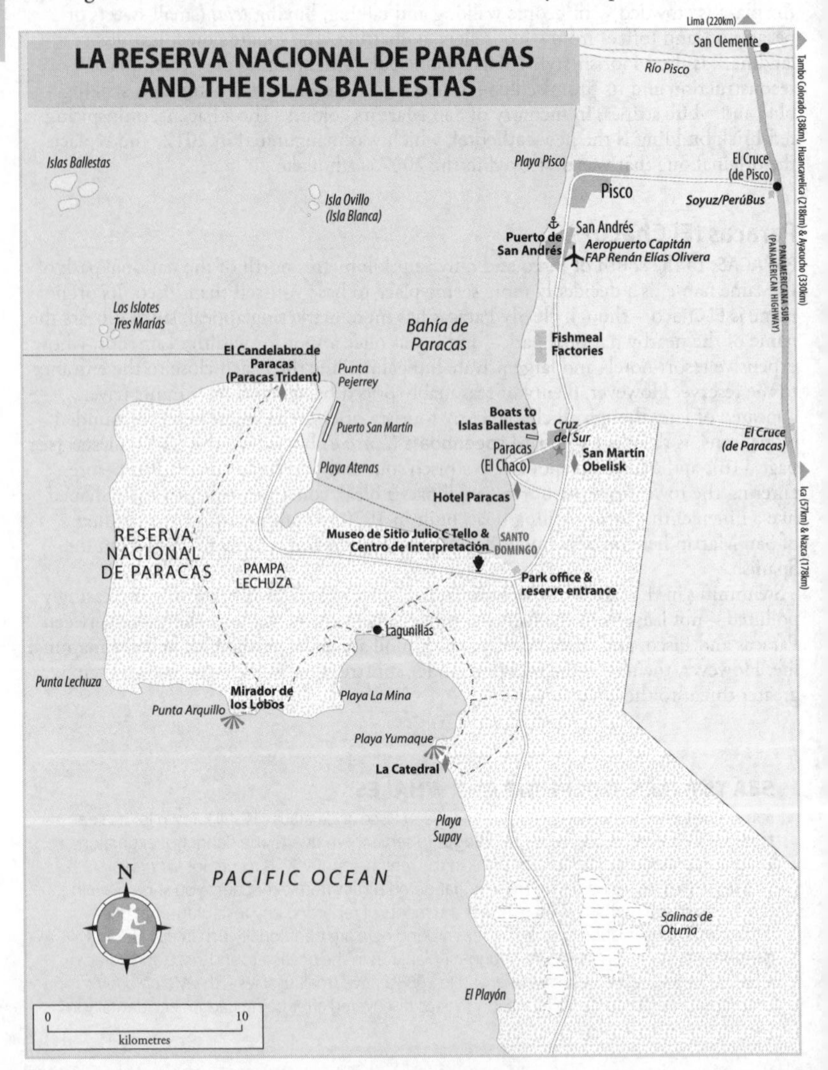

scores of islets, many of them relatively small and none larger than a couple of football pitches together, where abundant wildlife sleeps, feeds and mates. The waters around the islands are equally full of life, sometimes sparkling black with the shiny dark bodies of sea lions and the occasional killer whale. With luck, green or leatherback turtles will make an appearance, or even the endangered sea otters.

The only way to visit is to take one of the two-hour **boat tours** (see page 120), or charter a vessel privately. You can't actually land on the islands – which technically speaking are rocky islets, rather than islands – though you do get close to the wildlife; sometimes too close. The quality of guiding varies, but most guides are knowledgeable and informative about marine and bird life, and nearly all the boats are fast, comfortable and take around 36 passengers. The choppy seas and powerful smell of guano may make it tough for those prone to seasickness. Go early in the morning, when the ocean is usually calmer and you can avoid the extreme heat. Take a broad-brimmed hat (for sale at the harbour) as the boats have no shade and, although some consider it lucky to take a guano hit, the hat at least helps keep it off the face. In winter you'll need to bring warm clothes too.

Reserva Nacional de Paracas

Main entrance 4km south of Paracas • Daily 8am–5.30pm, though you can enter by bike earlier • Reserve S/11; S/17 for a combined ticket with the Islas Ballestas; pay at the park office, located at the entrance • To get to the reserve, take a taxi from Paracas (from S/20 per hr), join an organized tour (from S/40; see page 120), or rent a bike (see page 120)

The **Reserva Nacional de Paracas**, a few kilometres south of Paracas, was established in 1975, mainly to protect the marine environment. Its bleak 1170 square kilometres of pampa are frequently lashed by strong winds and sandstorms (*paracas* means "raining sand" in Quechua), especially in August. Home to some of the world's richest seas (a couple of thousand square kilometres of ocean is included within the reserve's borders), an abundance of marine plankton nourishes a vast array of fish and various marine species, including octopus, squid, whale, shark, dolphin, bass, plaice and marlin. This unique desert is also a staging post for a host of migratory birds and acts as a sanctuary for many endangered species. Schools of dolphins play in the waves offshore; condors scour the peninsula for food; small desert foxes come down to the beaches looking for birds and dead sea lions; and lizards scrabble across the hot sands. People have also been active here – predecessors of the pre-Inca Paracas culture arrived here some 9000 years ago, reaching their peak between 2000 and 500 BC.

Most visitors come on a bus tour either from Paracas or from as far as Lima (usually combined with an early-morning boat trip to the Islas Ballestas). **Tours** stop at the various viewpoints and the visitor centre, and may also call in for lunch at the scenic fishing hamlet of Lagunillas. **Cycling** is encouraged, though the corrugations on the dirt roads can make it a tough ride at times; several places in Paracas rent out bikes. There is a well-marked 30km tourist circuit along a combination of tarred and unsealed roads that follows a clockwise direction from the park entrance, taking in some fossilised shells, the main viewpoints of La Catedral (a collapsed rock arch) and Yumaque, plus a detour to Lagunillas (see page 119), before returning to the entrance via the museum and visitor centre. Add an extra 10km if you want to go to the Mirador de los Lobos, and a further 26km if you're set on visiting El Candelabro de Paracas (see page 118). Think about renting your bike the night before to allow you to make an early start and enjoy cooler cycling conditions.

Several stretches of the main route have parallel dirt tracks that cyclists share with **ATVs** and **dune buggies**, which can also be rented in Paracas, and which some visitors insist on driving onto the beaches and off the main route, leaving unsightly tyre tracks and causing lasting damage to the surface of the desert.

PARACAS BURIAL SITES

It was at and around **Cerro Colorado** that archeologist **Julio C. Tello** made the first major discoveries of the **Paracas culture** and found remains which could be dated as far back as 3000 years. He unearthed **burial sites** with two distinct styles: a deeper, earlier technique, denominated Paracas Cavernas, which saw mummies buried in bottle-shaped tombs at depths of up to 7m below the surface, while on the northern slope, at a site called Wari Kayan, he found shallower gravesites like small rooms where some **mummies** were found seated, facing the sea, among ceramics, weapons and foodstuffs. The **burial cloths** of this Paracas necropolis are the best-known Paracas embroideries, whose intricate and colourful designs are considered among the finest pre-Columbian textile work.

Not far away, Tello unearthed another necropolis, known as **Cabezas Largas**, where several excellent examples were found of the deformed, **elongated craniums** which have also come to be associated with the Paracas of this era. Most mummies were wrapped in vicuña skins or rush matting, and buried along with personal objects like shell beads, bone necklaces, lances, net bags and cactus-spine needles.

Many fine examples of the textiles and trepanated skulls can be seen at the regional museum in Ica (see page 149), and the Museo Larco (see page 76) and Museo Nacional de Arqueología, Antropología e Historia de Perú (see page 74) in Lima.

2

Museo de Sitio Julio C Tello and Centro de Interpretación

At Km 27 of the Carretera Pisco, 2km beyond the reserve entrance and park office • Daily 8am–5pm • interpretive centre free; museum S/6

The reserve's small **museum** is located between the two major Paracas archeological sites of Cerro Colorado and Cabezas Largas, and named after the famous Peruvian archeologist who unearthed them (see above). Depicting human life here over the last 9000 years, the museum displays a modest collection of Paracas artefacts and replicas (mummies, ceramics, funerary cloths and a reconstructed dwelling) since most were transferred to museums in Nazca and Ica following the 2007 earthquake. More interesting is the free **interpretative centre**, which houses fascinating bilingual displays on the geology and ecology of the reserve.

Beyond the necropolis of Cabezas Largas (which remains out of bounds to visitors) are the remains of a Chavín-related settlement, known as **Disco Verde**, though all there is left to see now are a few adobe walls. Also nearby is a beach where dozens of pink flamingoes gather between June and November (they return to the high Andean lakes for breeding Dec–May).

El Candelabro de Paracas

El Candelabro de Paracas (The Paracas Trident), a massive 128-metre-high by 74-metre-wide candelabra carved into the tall sea cliffs and facing out towards the Pacific Ocean, is one of Paracas' main features. No one knows its function or its creator, though Erich von Däniken, author of *Chariots of the Gods*, speculated that it was a sign for extraterrestrial spacecraft, pointing the way (inaccurately as it happens) towards the mysterious Líneas de Nazca that are inland to the southeast; others suggest it was constructed as a navigational aid for eighteenth-century pirates. It seems more likely, however, that it was a kind of pre-Inca ritual object, representing a cactus or tree of life, and that high priests during the Paracas or Nazca eras worshipped the setting sun from this spot. A **trail** leads 13km across the desert from the Museo de Sitio; the first 2km follow the main park road, and then just before the modern port complex of San Martín a sandy side-track leads away from the sea and around the hills on the outer edge of the peninsula towards the trident. However, the best way to appreciate the Candelabro is from a **boat** on the way to the Islas Ballestas, just after you round the headland.

Lagunillas and around

The tiny and likeable fishing hamlet of **Lagunillas**, some 7km from the entrance to the park, consists of a jetty and four pricey restaurants serving fresh *conchitas* (scallops) and other great seafood. Try *La Tía Chela* and *El Ché*, two favourites in the area. Lagunillas is the only place within the Paracas reserve where you can buy a meal and drinks – but there's no accommodation. From here, it's possible to appreciate the unique and very beautiful peninsula, so flat that if the sea rose just another metre the whole place would be submerged. Pelicans hang around the bobbing boats waiting for the fisherman to drop a fish, turkey vultures scavenge for scraps on the beach, and little trucks regularly arrive to carry the catch back into Pisco.

On the peninsula

The peninsula possesses a few lovely coves and **beaches**, including sheltered **La Mina** – just a thirty-minute walk southwest of Lagunillas – and **Yumaque**, an empty stretch of sand 8km by road to the southeast. Beyond La Mina lies a longer sandy beach, **Arquillo**; on the cliffs a few hundred metres beyond there's a **viewing platform** (Mirador de los Lobos) looking out over a large colony of sea lions. On the north coast of the peninsula, off the road to Puerto San Martín, is stony **Playa Atenas**, known for one particular resident, El Griego; from Thursdays to Sundays he serves the best grilled scallops in the area, at a very decent price. From here a path leads north across the headland to the Candelabro and on to **Punta Pejerrey**.

There have been reports of **stingrays** on some beaches, so take care, particularly if you're without transport or company; check first with the fishermen at Lagunillas.

Tambo Colorado

Km 38 up the road to Ayacucho from El Cruce de San Clemente (by Pisco) • Daily 9am–4/4.30pm • S/5 • ⓣ 056 233 881

Some 48km northeast of Pisco, and 327km south of Lima, the ruins at **Tambo Colorado** were originally a fortified administrative centre, probably built by the Chincha before being adapted and used as an Inca coastal outpost. Its position at the base of steep foothills in the Pisco river valley was perfect for controlling the flow of people and produce along the ancient road down from the Andes. You can still see dwellings, offices, storehouses and row upon row of barracks and outer walls, some of them even retaining traces of the red-coloured paints that gave the place its name. The rains (and the earthquake) have taken their toll, and the place is not as visually impressive as some of the stone Inca ruins in the Andean highlands, though a good guided tour (see page 120) can help bring it alive. Even so this is considered one of the best-preserved **adobe ruins** in coastal Peru – roofless, but otherwise fairly intact.

ARRIVAL AND DEPARTURE — PISCO AND AROUND

BY PLANE

4km south of Pisco, the Aeropuerto Capitán FAP Renán Elías Olivera, a military airport, has been upgraded and is likely to start receiving international scheduled flights from 2018.

BY BUS

Cruz del Sur (ⓣ 056 536 636, ⓦ cruzdelsur.com.pe) runs several direct buses between Lima and Nazca via Paracas, where it has a depot at the entrance to the town. Oltursa (ⓣ 994 616 492, ⓦ oltursa.pe) runs one bus a day from Lima to Camaná which also stops in Paracas, next to the *Refugio del Pirata* on Av Paracas. One northbound bus a day from Camaná to Lima makes the same stop. Flores and Cetur (ⓦ floreshnos.pe) share the only bus terminal in the centre of Pisco, on the corner of Av San Martín and C Pedmonte, with local connections north and south.

Destinations from El Cruce de Pisco Ica (numerous daily; 1hr); Lima (every 10min; 3–4hr); Nazca (numerous daily; 3–4hr).

BY BUS AND COLECTIVO

Pisco and Paracas via El Cruce All buses travelling up and down the Panamericana Sur pass through El Cruce (de Pisco) – also known as San Clemente (the name given to the nearby small town) – where the Panamericana meets the turn-off to Pisco. From here, there are regular colectivos to Pisco (S/2; 10min) and on to Paracas (S/5; 25min). On the return trip, colectivos depart from just off the Plaza de Armas in Pisco. From Paracas, colectivos bound for Pisco pass along Av Principal in Paracas, as do shared cars. If there is sufficient demand, cars will go on to El Cruce; otherwise, you will have to change vehicle in Pisco. To continue south along the Panamericana Sur from El Cruce, get a ticket at the Soyuz/PerúBus terminal (056 269 239) at the junction.

Pisco and Paracas via El Cruce de Paracas An alternative route from the Panamericana is 14km further south of El Cruce, at El Cruce de Paracas, where the reserve is signposted west down a turn-off. If arriving from the south, you can either alight here and pay for a taxi to Paracas (S/12–15, though they are not always available after about 2pm), or continue northwards to El Cruce for a more certain connection.

To Tambo Colorado Express buses travelling between the coast and Ayacucho may pick up in El Cruce (see page 119) and be willing to drop you off at the ruins (the road passes by them, 7km after the village of Humay). Alternatively, take a minivan from San Clemente bound for Huancano, further up the road to Ayacucho.

2

GETTING AROUND

On foot Pisco and Paracas are both small enough to explore on foot.

By bike Several places in Paracas rent bicycles for the day until 5.30/6pm. Rates (S/25–40) depend upon seasonal demand and the quality of the bike.

By colectivo Combis between Pisco and Paracas cost S/2.50, and leave Pisco from C Callao just off the Plaza de Armas in Pisco and C 4 de Julio near the market; in Paracas they pick up/drop off from the square or anywhere along the main road in Paracas.

By taxi A private taxi between Pisco and Paracas is around S/15; a shared one is S/3.

INFORMATION

Banks and exchange There is no bank or ATM in Paracas; however, several are dotted in and around the Plaza de Armas in Pisco, where the *cambistas* offer the best exchange rates for dollars. Most hotels and the tour companies (see below) in Paracas accept credit cards and will also change dollars for soles.

Tourist information A small iPerú office sits in the municipal offices on Av Principal, opposite the park in Paracas (daily 7am–4pm). In Pisco limited information (in Spanish) is available at the municipality, at the corner of calles Ramón Aspillaga and López de Alarcón (Mon–Fri 8am–3.30pm).

TOURS AND ACTIVITIES

Tours to the islands and reserve There are more tour companies than you would imagine for such a small place; most operators offer combined package excursions to the Islas Ballestas and Reserva Nacional de Paracas, with bilingual guiding. You can also book through your accommodation, or, out of season, pick up a boat at the jetty on the day itself. Some excursions include a lunch stop at a seafood restaurant in Lagunillas (not included in the price). Check whether park fees are included in the price. Most operators can also organize trips to Tambo Colorado (from S/50).

Desert activities Sandboarding, ATV tours, and dune-buggy rides are offered, though their potentially negative impact on the desert environment has yet to be officially recognised and regulations are lacking (see page 130).

Kite-surfing Paracas is a major centre for kite-surfing with IKO-certified instructors; well established Peruvian-owned Perukite (perukite.com) is located by the *Hilton Hotel* in the Santo Domingo area south of the main town; pricier but highly acclaimed Kangarookite (986 725 376, kangarookite.net), with top-notch gear, lies 300m further south along the beach.

Nazca flyover A flyover of the Líneas de Nazca from Pisco airport is possible, but is much longer and more expensive (around 1hr 40min; around US$/260–300) than from Nazca itself.

Tour operators Reliable companies include Emotion Tour, on the main road next to *Hotel Brisas de Bahía* (946 864 314, emotiontourperu.com); and Zarcillo Connections, by the Cruz del Sur bus terminal (056 536 636, zarcilloconnections.com). From Lima, Haku Tours offers a full-day excursion (US$150), which includes hotel pick-up, entry fees and bilingual guiding, though not lunch (01 444 2077, hakutours.com); the company is a well-run and friendly non-profit operation with a strong social responsibility programme.

ACCOMMODATION

Most people choose to stay in Paracas/El Chaco, where there is a far greater range of accommodation, though Pisco offers much cheaper hotels and a less touristy vibe.

PISCO

Hostal Tambo Colorado Av Bolognesi 159 056 531 379, hostaltambocolorado.com; map p.114. Right by the Plaza de Armas, this is about as good as it gets in Pisco for quality and price. Great staff with plenty of local knowledge who can also organize tours. Rooms aren't exactly stylish but are impeccably clean and comfortable with great showers and surprisingly good wi-fi. Set around a pleasant shady courtyard with an open communal kitchen – though good breakfasts are also available (S/10–12 extra). S/90

Hostería del Monasterio C Bolognesi 326 056 534 119, triher3@hotmail.com; map p.114. Best of the cheapies, this old converted monastery offers classic literature to browse at reception, a small garden, the odd antique and simple, painted brick rooms, with pedestal fans and old-fashioned TVs (but cable service). S/40

PiscoMar C Demetrio Miranda 419 056 385 449, piscomarperu.com; map p.114. Set just back from the beach (though only a couple of top-floor rooms manage a partial sea view), this new hotel offers excellent value for money: sparkling tiled rooms with pedestal fans, comfortable beds and friendly service. S/80

PARACAS

Atenas Backpacker Hospedaje Av Los Libertadores Mz G, Lote 2 971 148 201, bhwj6aix.preview.suite.booking.com. Simple, spotless and cheerfully decorated dorms, double and triples – all with shared bathrooms – at rock-bottom rates. Add to that a sheltered patio common area, a small kitchen complete with Welsh dresser, plus lockers, bike rental and breakfast for S/8. Dorms S/25, doubles S/85

La Hacienda Bahía Paracas Urb Sto Domingo Lote 25 056 581 370, hoteleslahacienda.com. One of the best resort-style hotels along the beach, *La Hacienda* has all the luxuries and comforts necessary for complete relaxation. Rooms have a tiny private terrace and most overlook the huge pool and the sea. Breakfasts are delicious and the restaurant ocean view is a winner. US$260

Hostal Santa María Av Los Libertadores s/n, by the Plazuela Quiñones 056 545 045, hostalsantamariaparacas.com. Just off the main drag, this well-maintained property is a good deal, offering spotless compact rooms, some overlooking the park. Bathrooms and tiled floors sparkle and the rooftop terrace with gazebo is a plus, though breakfast is a let-down. Price includes Islas Ballestas tour for two. S/170

Hotel Paracas Resort Av Paracas 173, 056 581 333, hotelparacasresort.com. A luxurious option that hits all the notes of a high-end resort, with private patios, infinity pools, an excellent bar and restaurant (open to non-residents), all stylishly designed and right by the ocean. US$357

Kokopelli Hostel Paracas Av Paracas 128 056 311 824, hostelkokopelli.com. Clean, cool common areas with colourfully painted walls, a lively bar and the beachfront location make this the most popular backpackers' spot in town. The beds are comfortable in the dorms (4 to 8 beds), and the private rooms (S/35 more for your own bathroom) are light, spacious and welcoming. Dorms S/35, doubles S/115

Paracas Sunset Hotel Av Los Libertadores Mz J1 Lot 1 056 534 473, paracassunset.com. Solid mid-range choice, popular with tour groups. Take a room on one of the upper floors, which share a wide balcony and overlook the garden area, where there's a decent-sized pool and sun loungers. Doubles, triples and family rooms have painted brick walls, tiled floors, wall fans and cable TV. US$95

RESERVA NACIONAL DE PARACAS

Camping There are no facilities beyond the flush toilets at Lagunillas and at a couple of the viewpoints; they are only open park hours – though in low season, sometimes not even then – and use water that has to be brought into the reserve. Over summer weekends and holidays, you can scarcely see the beach for the patchwork of tents, but at other times you can be alone with the birds and the lizards. You should pitch your tent near one of the control points in the low season, for safety reasons. Cost includes park entry. Three days S/20

Intimar Playa Atenas 991 350 656, inti-mar.com. A four-room *hostal* offering absolute peace and quiet, stunning views, great food (and pisco) and plenty of wildlife – including a scallop farm – though at a price. US$120

EATING

Most **restaurants** in both Pisco and Paracas specialize in a wide range of locally caught fish and seafood. Prices are higher in Paracas, and quality is variable. **Nightlife** is restricted to a couple of lively bars in Paracas, with a midnight curfew outside major festivities. Anyone wanting to hit a nightclub will need to head for Pisco.

PISCO

★**As de Oros** Av San Martín 472 056 532 010 asdeoros.com.pe; map p.114. A local classic, around for over forty years; now in a bigger, fancier location with a heavily stocked bar and outdoor seating by a swimming pool – the perfect venue for the occasional Saturday-night disco. Still, nothing has taken away from the flavour; the food – regional creole favourites – is still among the town's best. Try the *parihuela* (S/30), a powerful seafood soup. Tues–Sun noon–11pm.

★**Pizzería Montecassino** C Independencia 191 056 532493, montecassinopizzeria.com; map p.114. If you're tired of seafood, come and bite into a slice of authentic, artisanal thin-crust pizza. Several veggie and vegan options plus the local favourite, the Pisco pizza. Finish off with an espresso. Daily 6–11pm.

Restaurant Acapulco Av Genaro Medrano 620, San Andrés ⓣ056 542 335, ⓣ956 757 575; map p.114. A mere 50m from the main fishermen's wharf at San Andrés –between Pisco and Paracas – it's a traditional and popular seafood restaurant, serving massive fish dishes at reasonable prices (S/20–35). Daily 10am–5pm.

2

Restaurant La Viña de Huver Prolongación Cerro Azul, next to the Parque Zonal ⓣ056 536 456; map p.114. Slightly out of the centre of town, this is one of Pisco's busiest lunch spots, serving excellent, huge and relatively inexpensive ceviche (S/30) and other seafood dishes in a bustling, appealing environment. Mon & Wed–Sun 11am–5.30pm.

PARACAS

Arena Café Av Los Libertadores s/n ⓣ949 052 610. Gleaming new café with extremely comfy seating and an incongruous Eiffel Tower painted on the wall. Dishing up competent breakfasts, burgers and sandwiches at tourist prices (from S/15) and plenty of real coffee. Daily 7am–late.

Il Covo Av Los Libertadores s/n ⓣ056 530 324, ⓦilcovo.pe. The smartest place in town outside the excellent resort hotel restaurants, *Il Covo* serves up great Italian food in a classy dining room. You can't go wrong with anything on the menu, but the pizza (S/30–40) is always a good option. Pricey, with most dishes over S/40, but worth it. Tues–Sat noon–3.30pm & 7.30–11pm, Sun noon–3.30pm.

Restaurant Brisas del Mar El Malecón. The pick of the tourist-priced waterfront options close to El Chaco jetty, serving up fresh fish and shellfish (mains S/28–35). Daily 11am–3pm.

Misk'i Opposite the jetty at El Chaco ⓣ983 474 735. With a mellow backpacker vibe aided by a suitably chilled reggae soundtrack, this casual, cosy bar is *the* place to hang out. Though the wood-fired pizzas, burritos and salads are nothing special, the strong cocktails really hit the spot. Daily 5.30pm–late.

Restaurant Paracas Opposite the pier at El Chaco ⓣ056 535 138. Up on the fourth floor, the view overlooking the pier and harbour are worth the visit alone. The seafood dishes (around S/40) are satisfying, though service can be sluggish when it gets very busy. Daily 8am–11pm.

Pukasoncco Av Libertadores s/n ⓣ949 052 610. A veritable Aladdin's cave of pre-Columbian-style crafts, this unpromising bamboo hut set back from the road also houses a small restaurant. Artist-chef Sanson lovingly prepares healthy local cuisine at moderate prices, with plenty to please vegans. Daily 8am–8pm.

Ica

An old but busy city with around 170,000 inhabitants, **ICA** sits in a fecund valley, close to enormous sand dunes that rise some 400m above sea level and help protect the town from the coastal mists that form over 50km away. Here you can virtually guarantee **sunny weather** most of the year, but, like Pisco, Ica suffered serious damage in the 2007 earthquake.

The surrounding region is famous throughout Peru for its wine and pisco production. The city's foundation (1563) went hand in hand with the introduction of grapevines to South America, and for most Peruvian visitors it is the **bodegas**, or wineries, that are the town's biggest draw. However, the renovated **regional museum**'s superb collections of pre-Columbian ceramics and Paracas, Ica and Nazca cultural artefacts alone would make the city worth an excursion.

Ica's streets and plazas are crowded from early morning to evening with hundreds of **mototaxis**, all beeping their horns to catch potential passengers' attention and making crossing the streets a dangerous affair. It's no wonder that most visitors prefer to bed down at the desert oasis of **Huacachina**, a few kilometres to the southwest, though even there it can get busy and boisterous at weekends. On the edge of Ica is the rather ramshackle suburb of **Cachiche**, known throughout Peru as a traditional sanctuary for white witches (see page 129).

Plaza de Armas

Ica's colonial heart – the **Plaza de Armas**, site of the 1820 declaration of independence from Spain – remains its modern centre, smart and friendly, with the inclusion of an obelisk and fountains. Running east from the plaza, the commercial spine is busy Avenida Grau with the market area parallel, a couple of blocks to the north.

La Iglesia Catedral de la Merced

Plaza de Armas • Daily 8am–3pm • Free

Tucked away on the southwest corner of the plaza **La Iglesia Catedral de la Merced** was first constructed in the eighteenth century, then remodelled in 1814 with a Neoclassical exterior and a Baroque altar and pulpit. The church contains Padre Guatemala's tomb – said to give immense good fortune if touched on New Year's Day.

Museo Científico Javier Cabrera

Jr Bolívar 170, Plaza de Armas • Mon–Sat 10am–1.30pm, 4–7pm by guided tour only – prior appointment preferred; knock on the door if closed • S/35, including tour • 056 227 676 • museodepiedrasgrabadasdeica.com.pe

On the Plaza de Armas, the **Museo Científico Javier Cabrera** (formerly known as the Museo de Piedras Grabadas de Ica) contains a controversial collection of engraved stones, assembled by the late Dr Javier Cabrera, who claimed that the stones are several thousand years old. Few people believe this – some of the exhibits depict

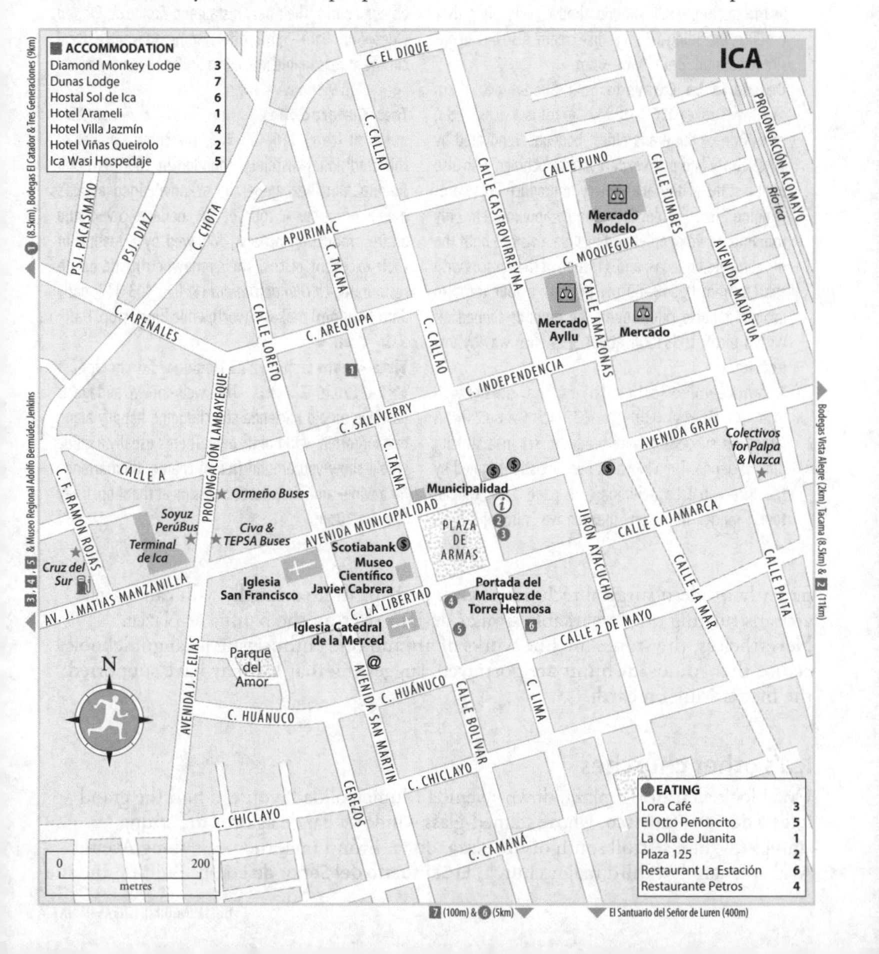

ICA'S BODEGAS

The best way to pass Ica's hot desert afternoons is to wander around the cool chambers and vaults of one or more of the town's **bodegas** or wineries, sampling their wares. Many of the region's best wine and piscos can be tasted in stores on or close to the Plaza de Armas in Ica, but if you have the time, it's well worth visiting the producer haciendas outside the town. The bodegas can loosely be divided into the large-scale **commercial distilleries**, some of which produce decent exportable wine and high-quality pisco, and small artisanal operations, which can produce some great pisco but generally rather undistinguished wine; the **artisanal bodegas** can often be less appealing visually. A half-day visit with a tour operator to two or three vineyards costs around US$30–35, or around S/40 if you contract a local taxi driver. Most bodegas don't charge entry, on the assumption that they'll make money on sales. Microbuses or combis from Ica also pass close to most of the vineyards listed below.

El Catador Fundo Tres Esquinas, 9km north of Ica T 056 403 516 W elcatador.pe. A quality artisanal pisco producer that offers free tours and tasting. What the tour lacks in aesthetics – clambering over piles of rubble – it makes up for in guiding enthusiasm, and in the tasting: you'll sample almost every pisco they produce, including a Baileys-like cream. Also has an on-site restaurant. Daily 9am–6pm.

Destilería La Caravedo Sala Guadalupe, 11km north of Ica T 056 313 963, E tours@lacaravedo.com. One of the area's oldest bodegas, renovated by TV celebrity and pisco expert Johnny Schuler, who also built a state-of-the-art refinery to produce his award-winning Pisco Portón. Tours are by appointment only (minimum two people) and include a visit to both the new and old bodegas, and a tasting of their piscos with snacks (from US$48–60 per person); a tour can also include a horse ride around the grounds topped off with a picnic (US$100). About S/15 each way by taxi from Ica.

Tacama Camino Real s/n, La Tinguiña, 8.5km north of Ica T 056 581 030, ext 1039, W tacama.com. A large and successful wine producer, set in a striking pink hacienda. The vineyards here are still irrigated by the Inca canal La Achirana (see page 126). Guided tours range from an inexpensive nuts-and-bolts option (50min; S/10, S/15 on hol weekends) to a full exposition including tasting three premium wines (2hr; S/130). Time your visit for a weekend afternoon and you'll also be treated to a *marinera con caballo de paso* (traditional dance involving a female dancer and man on horseback). Their new restaurant, *Tambo de Tacama* (Tues–Sun 9am–5pm) offers some top-notch local cuisine at reasonable rates. Taxi S/15 one-way from Ica. Tues–Sun 9.30am–4.30pm.

Tres Generaciones Fundo Tres Esquinas, 9km north of Ica T 056 403 565. The current owner of this traditional distillery, founded in 1856, is Doña Juanita Martinez, generally acknowledged as Ica's queen of pisco. A tour of the bodega covers the entire production process, followed by a tasting of their excellent piscos. Their renowned rustic onsite restaurant, *La Olla de Juanita* (T 056 403 317; daily 9am–4.30pm) makes a worthwhile lunch stop. Daily 9am–6pm.

Vista Alegre Camino a La Tinguiña, 2km northeast of Ica T 056 222 919. This well-known bodega is based in an old hacienda still chugging happily along in a forgotten world of its own. There's usually a guide who'll show you around free of charge, then arrange for a wine- and pisco-tasting session at the shop. Daily 9am–4.30pm.

patently modern surgical techniques and, perhaps more critically, you can watch artisans turning out remarkably similar designs over on the pampa at Nazca. Nevertheless, the stones are fine works of art and one enthusiastic local guidebook claims that "dinosaur hunts are portrayed, suggesting that Ica may have supported the first culture on earth."

Ica's other churches

One block west of the plaza, down Avenida Municipalidad, you can find the grand **Iglesia de San Francisco**, whose stained-glass windows dazzle against the strong sunlight. Quite a stroll south of the plaza, down Jirón Lima, then east along Avenida Ayabaca, stands a third major church, **El Santuario del Señor de Luren**. Built on the site

LA ACHIRANA – AN INCA LOVE TOKEN

Several of Ica's biggest bodegas owe their continued existence to water provided by La Achirana, a **canal** which was built by the Inca Pachacutec (or his brother Capac Yupanqui) as a gift to Princess Tate, daughter of a local chieftain. Apparently, it took 40,000 men just ten days to complete this astonishing feat of engineering, which brings cold, pure water down 4000m from the Andes to transform what was once an arid desert into a startlingly fertile oasis. Obviously a romantic at heart, Pachacutec named it Achirana – "that which flows cleanly towards that which is beautiful".

of a hermitage founded in 1556, the present construction – Neoclassical in style and with three brick-built *portales* – houses the Imagen del Señor de Luren, an image of the town's patron saint, a national shrine and a centre for procession and pilgrimage at Easter as well as on the third Sunday in October.

Ica's mansions

Several **mansions** of note can be found near the plaza, including the **Casona del Marqués de Torre Hermosa**, block 1 of Calle Libertad. Now belonging to the Banco Continental, it is one of the few examples of colonial architecture to survive in this earthquake-stricken city. In the first block of Calle 2 de Mayo, you can find the **Casona de José de la Torre Ugarte**, once home to the composer of the Peruvian national anthem. The **Casona Alvorado**, now belonging to the Banco Latino, at Cajamarca 178, is the region's only example of a copy of the Greco-Roman architectural style, while the **Casona Colonial El Portón**, C Loreto 233, conserves some fine features of colonial architecture.

Museo Regional Adolfo Bermúdez Jenkins

Block 8 of Av Ayabaca, between Av Tupac Amaru and Av J.J. Elias • ⊕ 056 234 383, ext 103 • Tues–Fri 8am–7pm; public hols & Sat 9am–6pm • S/12, extra if you want to take photos • 15min walk from the Plaza de Armas; alternatively take the #17 bus or a mototaxi from the plaza

The **Museo Regional Adolfo Bermúdez Jenkins** is one of the best archeological museums in Peru, whose displays were reinvigorated in 2015 following an injection of foreign funds. While there are exhibits from various ancient cultures, including Paracas, Nazca, Ica, Huari and Inca, the most striking of the museum's collections is its display of glorious **Paracas textiles**, the majority of them uncovered at Cerro Colorado on the Paracas peninsula by archeologist Julio Tello in 1927 (see page 118). Enigmatic in their apparent coding of colours and patterns, these funeral cloths consist of blank rectangles alternating with elaborately woven ones – repetitious and identical except in their multidirectional shifts of colour and position. One priceless piece was stolen in October 2004, so security is tight.

The first room to the right off the main foyer contains a fairly gruesome display of **mummies**, **trepanned skulls**, **grave artefacts** and **trophy heads**, accompanied by equally graphic descriptions of the various processes involved. It seems very likely that the taking of trophy heads in this region was related to specific religious beliefs – as it was until quite recently among the head-hunting Jivaro of the Amazon Basin. The earliest of these skulls, presumably hunted and collected by the victor in battle, come from the Valle de Asia (north of Ica) and date from around 2000 BC.

The main room

The museum's main room is almost entirely devoted to pre-Columbian **ceramics and textiles**, possibly the finest collection outside Lima, beautifully displayed and better contextualised (with bilingual text) than in other museums. Standout exhibits include some spectacular Paracas urns – one with an owl and serpent design painted on one side, and a human face with arms, legs and a navel on the other. There is some exquisite Nazca pottery, too, undoubtedly the most colourful and abstractly imaginative designs found on any ancient Peruvian ceramics. The last wall consists mainly of artefacts from the Ica-Chincha culture – note the beautiful **feather cape**, with multicoloured plumes in almost perfect condition. Also in the main room are several **quipus**, ancient calculators using bundles of knotted strings as mnemonic aids, also used for the recitation of ancient legends, genealogies and ballads. Thanks to the dry desert climate, they have survived better here on the coast than in the mountains, and the Ica collection remains one of the best in the country.

Before leaving, don't forget to check out the excellent **large-scale model** of the Líneas de Nazca round the back of the museum.

ARRIVAL AND DEPARTURE ICA

By bus The main bus companies have their own bus terminals at or around the intersection between Lambayeque and Matias Manzanilla: Cruz del Sur (056 223333), Flores (056 212 266), Ormeño (056 215 600), Soyuz/ PerúBus (056 224 138), TEPSA (056 233806) and Transportes Civa (056 523 019).

Destinations Arequipa (frequent buses daily; 12hr); Lima (frequent buses daily; 4–5hr); Nazca (frequent buses daily; 2–3hr).

By colectivo Colectivos from Nazca drop you off within two or three blocks of the Plaza de Armas, at the same small depots from where they depart back to Nazca. Colectivos to Huacachina leave from Bolívar and Chiclayo.

GETTING AROUND

By taxi and mototaxi Mototaxi rides around town should not cost more than S/3–4. Ordinary taxis cost slightly more.

By microbus For longer journeys to the outlying parts of town, take one of the microbuses, which leave from Jr Lima or Prolongación Lambayeque and have their destinations up on their windscreens.

INFORMATION AND TOURS

Tourist information The Dircetur office is on Av Grau, half a block from the Plaza de Armas, and can provide you with a map of the town and information (in Spanish) on local attractions (Mon–Fri 8am–12.30pm & 2–4.30pm; 056 238710, ext 29).

Tour operators A number of tour operators in Ica or Huacachina (see page 120) can take you on a city tour, to visit various bodegas, on dune-buggy ride or on a trip south to Nazca or north to Paracas. However, none are outstanding and prices are high; you are better off letting your accommodation sort a reliable taxi driver or guide, or getting advice from other travellers.

FIESTAS IN ICA

There are several important **fiestas** in Ica throughout the year. The best is in **March** after the grape harvest (*vendimia*), when there are open-air concerts, fairs, handicraft markets and *caballo de paso* meetings (horse dressage – where Peruvian Paso horses are trained by riders to dance and prance for events or competitions), though unfortunately you're also likely to see cockfighting taking place. Over the **Semana de Ica** (June 12–19), based around the colonial founding of Ica, there are more festivities, including religious processions and fireworks, and again in the last week of September for the **Semana Turística**. On the fourth Sunday of July, the nationwide **Día Nacional de Pisco**, a big celebration for the national brandy (rather than the town of the same name), is an excuse for more drinking and merrymaking, which mostly takes place in the bodegas south of Lima, particularly around Ica. The more recently instituted **Día Nacional de Pisco Sour** (first Sat in Feb) gives a further excuse to down the national tipple. As in Lima, **October** is the main month for religious celebrations, with the focus being the ceremony and procession at the church of El Santuario del Señor de Luren (main processions on the third Sun and following Mon of Oct).

ACCOMMODATION

There are plenty of options in Ica, but very little of particular quality or note. For style or range of choice, most people go to Huacachina (see page 129) or one of the other out-of-town places.

IN TOWN

2

Diamond Monkey Lodge Urb Santa Margarita A-15 ⓣ955 951 555, ⓔdiamondmonkeylodge@hotmail.com; map p.123. A popular place offering simple, clean rooms with shared hot-water bathrooms (en-suite for S/15 more) plus ample breakfasts. It's located on a main road, close to a supermarket, restaurants and the regional museum. Welcoming owner Danilo also runs great local tours. S/70

Dunas Lodge C Bolívar 634 ⓣ975739334, ⓔjavier_vivar1@hotmail.com; map p.123. Central and good value, with rooms on two floors set round a flower-filled garden and central gazebo. Book a lighter upstairs room with shared balcony. Friendly service. S/79

Hostal Sol de Ica Jr Lima 265 ⓣ056 232 243, ⓦhotelsoldeica.com; map p.123. Well located, this recently renovated hotel combines rustic chic with comfort: expect the usual amenities plus phone and bedside lights. The best (and quietest) rooms overlook the lovely pool and garden area. Includes a substantial buffet breakfast. S/249

Hotel Arameli Jr Tacna 239 ⓣ056 239 107; map p.123. Plain rooms off a prison-like corridor with private hot-water bathrooms. Spacious for the price with firm beds and simple wooden furniture, plus the place is clean, central and very friendly. Room only. S/60

Ica Wasi Hospedaje Fermin Tauguis 194 and Luis Medina ⓣ966 787 343, ⓦicawasihostel.com; map p.123. Cheerful hosts offer great service and attention to detail. Two eight-bed dorms and two en-suite doubles are spotless and bright, and the rooftop terrace is a real winner. No kitchen though. The location is close to the plaza, but removed enough to afford a little peace and quiet. Excellent information on tours. Dorms S/20, doubles S/70

OUT OF TOWN

Hotel Villa Jazmín Los Girasoles Mz C-1, Lote 7 ⓣ056 258 179, ⓦvillajazmin.net; map p.123. In a quiet neighbourhood on the outskirts of Ica, this is one of the most pleasant and peaceful places to stay. A large, solar-heated pool, surrounded by sun loungers and all the little luxuries of a higher-end hotel. Rooms are tastefully designed and spacious. S/230

★ **Hotel Viñas Queirolo** Carretera a Los Molinos s/n ⓣ056 254 119, ⓦhotelvinasqueirolo.com; map p.123. First-class luxury in the vineyards of the bodega Queirolo, an unbeatable rural setting and beautiful, well-furnished rooms, some with vineyard views. The pool area is the perfect place to try their wines and the restaurant serves superb food at decent prices. S/420

EATING

In your haste to try out the region's piscos, don't miss out on Ica's famous **sweets**, which can be sampled round the Plaza de Armas: *tejas* (pecan nuts enveloped in *manjar blanco*, soft caramel, and covered in fondant) and *chocotejas* (coated in chocolate rather than fondant). Note also that some of Ica's best food can be sampled in the bodega restaurants (see page 124).

IN TOWN

Lora Café Jr Lima 135, Plaza de Armas ⓣ056 216 153; map p.123. If you're tired of the traditional *café pasado*, lounge on the sofa here and enjoy a decent latte, espresso or cappuccino (from S/6), though the cakes are less enticing. Daily 7.30am–10.30pm.

El Otro Peñoncito Jr Bolívar 255 ⓣ056 233 921; map p.123. Less than a block from the plaza, this stylish, yet homely restaurant has walls tastefully adorned with artwork from Andean cosmology by an Iqueño artist; their speciality is *pollo iqueño* – chicken stuffed with spinach and pecan nuts topped with a pisco sauce. Daily noon–11pm.

Plaza 125 Jr Lima 125, Plaza de Armas ⓣ056 211816; map p.123123. No-nonsense place with formica-top tables serving a good-value set lunch and inexpensive mains (S/15–28), such as vegetables with noodles in ginger sauce. You can even purchase a glass of local wine. Friendly service. Daily 8am–11pm.

Restaurante Petros Jr Libertad 173, Plaza de Armas ⓣ056 212 509; map p.123. This agreeable open-fronted café is a top breakfast spot – coffee aside – offering fruit salad and cheese and spinach omelette (S/18) along with the expected dishes. And for other meals choose from traditional chicken, beef and fish dishes, plus beans galore (mains S/20–37). Daily 7am–late.

OUT OF TOWN

★ **Restaurant La Estación** Panamericana Sur Km 307, ⓣ056 237 164; map p.123. Its location at the rear of a petrol station may not inspire much faith, but inside they cook up some of the best local and creole Peruvian food around. The dishes are abundant and delicious; don't miss the *tacu tacu con mariscos* (a fried cake of rice and beans with a seafood sauce) and the *picamuseo de piedrante de pallares* (broad beans). Daily 8am–6pm.

THE WITCHES OF CACHICHE

In the down-at-heel suburb of Cachiche, history and mythology have merged into a legend of a local group of **witches**. The story dates back to the seventeenth century, when Spanish witches were persecuted for their pagan beliefs during the Inquisition. Seeking religious refuge, the witches emigrated to Lima, where they were also persecuted for their beliefs, before finally settling in the countryside, in particular the Ica Valley, in a village called Cachiche. The Cachiche witches operated in secret until the 1980s, when there was a renewed interest in alternative health practices; even the Peruvian presidents of the 1980s and 1990s openly consulted them about health matters. The popularity of Cachiche healing methods grew even more when a powerful congressman appeared, dramatically, to be cured of a terminal illness on TV by a Cachiche witch. Similar to witchcraft and shamanism along the Peruvian coast, Cachiche practices involve the use of San Pedro, a psychedelic cactus containing mescaline.

Huacachina

According to myth, the lagoon at **HUACACHINA**, almost 5km southwest of Ica, was created when a princess stripped off her clothes to bathe. As she looked into a mirror and saw that a male hunter was watching her, she dropped the mirror, which then became the lagoon. More prosaically, during the late 1940s, the **lagoon** became one of Peru's most elegant and exclusive resorts, surrounded by palm trees, sand dunes and waters famed for their curative powers. Since then, as with several other desert oases in the area, the lake's subterranean water source has dried up, and although the lagoon is artificially maintained by an alternative, diverted water source, it is no longer the size it once was and its legendary curative powers are a thing of the past. The placid green waters are increasingly threatened by pollution due to Ica's expanding population and overdevelopment at the resort itself – you'd be wiser to head for one of the hotel pools if you need a dip to combat the searing midday heat.

For all that, however, the oasis is still quite picturesque, and makes a perfect lunch stop if you visit midweek in low season. Should you decide to spend the night, note that although the settlement is still small, the growing backpacker atmosphere and associated clubs has changed the focus from relaxation to **adventure sports** and **parties.** Street noise can be a problem almost everywhere in the oasis, and the refuse is piling up. Climb the dunes at the end of the lake and take in the views from the top early in the morning, before it gets too hot and prior to the noisy dune-buggy runs (see page 130).

ARRIVAL AND INFORMATION — HUACACHINA

By mototaxi or taxi From Ica, all taxis drop off and pick up passengers at the entrance to the lagoon, within 100m of the lake edge. Taxis to/from Huacachina cost S/10; mototaxis cost S/6.

Tourist information A small tourist information kiosk stands at the taxi drop-off point, but it is only open at weekends and during holiday periods. For accommodation or a tour operator, take a stroll around and make your choice based on what you see, not what taxi drivers recommend – they work on a commission basis.

ACCOMMODATION

Banana's Adventure Av Perotti s/n ⓣ056 237 129, ⓦbananasadventure.com. The most popular hostel in town for good reason – friendly, helpful staff, clean rooms (shared and private bathrooms) and great gardens, bar and chillout area. The restaurant is average, but affordable. Prices include a choice of tour and breakfast. Dorms S/65, doubles S/150

★ **La Casa de Bamboo** Av Perotti next to Hostería Suiza ⓣ056 776 649, ⓔlacasadebamboo1@gmail.com. Compact family-run place on three floors, perfect for those looking to escape the party, without paying a fortune. Rooms are small and simple, but light and cool – some with a tiny balcony. The owners are great, the garden restaurant/café is a treat, and wi-fi is good. Breakfast extra. Dorms S/30, doubles S/90

Hostería Suiza Av Perotti 264 ⓣ056 238 762, ⓦhosteriasuiza.com.pe. Comfort well in line with the higher price paid; it is cosy and quiet, located at the far end

FUN ON THE DUNES

Daytime fun in Huacachina revolves around **adrenaline activities** on the dunes: namely careering over them at breakneck speed in a sci-fi-type **dune-buggy** (*arenero*), or **sand-boarding** down near perpendicular dunes at speeds of up to 70kph. This occurs principally in the morning (around 8am) and late afternoon (around 4pm) to avoid the hottest part of the day. The most popular tour lasts around two hours and involves a combination of frenetic dune-buggy rides and sand-boarding, though some operators also offer a more sedate drive over the sand. Rates hover around S/40, including board rental (a better board can be rented at extra cost) plus S/3.70 dune "entry". Sand-boards can be rented all over Huacachina for around S/10 per hour from the cafés and hotels along the shoreline. Make sure the board is waxed, otherwise you won't be moving far on the sand.

SAFETY

With numerous buggies and sand-boards flying about, countless tour operators, and no regulation, it goes without saying that **safety** is a concern. Over the years, the occasional serious **accident**, and even fatality, has occurred. Generally, operators that work with the hotels are likely to be more reliable than the cheaper independent guys who pick up their clients in the street. Check the state of your buggy in advance – especially the seat belts and helmets. When sand-boarding, zig-zag down the dunes to ensure that you descend at a manageable speed. Note that although board rental outlets exist by the steep dunes that enclose the lagoon, sand-boarding is actually **forbidden** here, precisely because of the risk of flying into or onto concrete.

ENVIRONMENTAL CONCERNS

While dune-buggy rides and sand-boarding are undeniably great fun, they are also potentially **damaging to the environment.** In addition to contributing to **noise pollution** and creating **eyesores** with their tyre tracks, dune-buggies – and sand-boards, to a lesser extent – threaten the fragile desert ecology. They destabilize the dunes and threaten the limited wildlife that exists in such a climate – often in tufts of grass, or even surviving beneath the surface of the sand. In Huaucachina in particular, the loose sand that sprays up as a result of these activities is helping to silt up the lagoon.

of the lake, with a touch of old-world elegance. One of the nicest swimming pool areas around. S/249

Hotel El Huacachinero Av Perotti s/n ⓣ056 217 435, ⓦelhuacachinero.com. A nice choice with the better (and quieter) rooms giving onto the spacious green garden and pool, affording good views of the dunes, and a calm, pleasant atmosphere. Rooms are on the basic side, but all have fan or a/c, and some have cable TV. US$80

★ **Upcycled Hostel** Road to Huacachina, 800m before the oasis ⓣ982 054 725, ⓦfacebook.com/theupcycledhostel. A 15min walk or short mototaxi hop from Huacachina, this secluded walled property with a chilled vibe is full of superlatives: friendly, helpful staff, spotless facilities – much made from recycled materials – comfy dorms and doubles with fans, and plenty of space to lounge round the garden and pool, in the sun or shade. Add to that bike rental, well-priced tasty comfort food, and a generous breakfast (included), and you've got a pretty perfect hostel. Dorms S/57, doubles S/110

EATING

La Casa de Bamboo Av Perotti next to Hostería Suiza ⓣ056 776 649. True to its simple, healthy and friendly style, there is no pretension, just great food: delicious vegetarian dishes, superb espresso and a Thai curry that everybody loves – all at comfortable prices (S/15–30). The go-to spot for those with a sweet tooth. Daily 8am–10pm.

Restaurant Rumi Wasi Road to Huacachina, 700m from the oasis ⓣ056 235 518. Low-key venue on the way to Huacachina. Best-loved for the *chancho al palo*, a Peruvian version of spit-roasted pig. Rumi Wasi has achieved nationwide fame after several appearances at Mistura, Peru's biggest culinary festival. Tues–Sun noon–6pm.

Wild Olive Trattoría and Guesthouse Malecón s/n ⓣ956 000 326. A popular choice with a pleasant waterfront setting, offering well-prepared standard Italian food: paninis, bruschettas, salads, pizzas and mix 'n' match pasta dishes (mains S/22–35). The raised terrace is the perfect spot for an evening cocktail (S/15). Also runs an excellent adjoining hostel, so breakfast (S/18) is available too. Daily 8am–11pm.

Las Líneas de Nazca

One of the great mysteries of South America, **Las Líneas de Nazca** (Nazca Lines) are a series of animal figures and geometric shapes, some up to 200m in length, drawn across some five hundred square kilometres of the bleak, stony **Pampa de San José**. If you plan to visit the Lines by air or on foot, you'll have to spend at least one night in Nazca, though you'll need more time to really do the area justice. If you're staying over, you'll probably base yourself in **Nazca Town**. When it comes to visiting the Lines, by far the best way is by **air** (see page 135). If you're keen to keep your feet on the ground, and costs down, make for the **mirador** (viewing tower), 23km north of Nazca. Two other viewing towers nearer Palpa afford views of the lesser known, though more numerous, **Líneas de Palpa**, many of which were produced by the older Paracas culture (see below).

The Nazca Lines are a combination of straight lines continuing for many kilometres in some cases across the sandy, stone-strewn plateau; others look like trapezoidal plazas, perfectly created by clearing the stones from the surface for the required pattern. Around seventy other "lines" are actually stylized line drawings of birds and animals (some over fifty metres wide), believed to symbolize both astrological phases and possible ancient Nazca clan divisions, with each figure representing, perhaps, the totem of a particular sub-group of this pre-Inca society and that clan's animal ally in the spirit world. Theories discussing their purpose and origin are as varied as the patterns themselves.

ARRIVAL AND DEPARTURE — LAS LÍNEAS DE NAZCA

Approaching from Ica in the north, you first have to cross a wide desert plain and pass through a couple of valleys, including Palpa, before arriving at the Pampa de San José and the Nazca Lines proper. The Lines themselves begin on the tableland above the small town of Palpa, about 90km south of Ica on the Panamericana Sur, and around 50km north of the town of Nazca.

By bus/minivan It's best to visit the Lines with a tour from Nazca (see page 138), since the guide will help make sense of the mass of geological etchings, but if you want to travel independently, take a local bus or minivan from Nazca (S/2). There are regular departures from near the *óvalo* at the corner of the Panamericana and Jr Lima on the outskirts of Nazca. They'll let you off at the main *mirador* on the road between Palpa and Nazca. It's usually easy enough to flag down a bus back to town.

By colectivo/taxi A taxi to the Lines from Nazca town costs S/30, and it will wait and bring you back again. Colectivos link the airstrip with Jirón Bolognesi and Av Grau in town. It's also fairly easy to get a colectivo back from the Nazca Lines.

Palpa

PALPA is a one-street town, but there are several archeological sites in the area, a small municipal **museum** on the Plaza de Armas, and incipient signs of tourism infrastructure.

Geoglyphs and petroglyphs known as the **Líneas de Palpa**, just as puzzling as the more famous Nazca Lines, are to be found etched into or scattered round the surrounding hillsides; one of a killer whale (orca), was only confirmed as recently as 2017. The geoglyphs can be viewed on a flight from Nazca (see page 135) but since the main sites are elevated, rather than on flat land, several are clearly visible from viewing towers near Palpa. Recent research suggests that at least fifty of these plant-, animal- and human-like shapes predate the Nazca Lines and were produced by the Paracas culture in 600–100BC.

If you happen to be in town around August 15, your visit will coincide with the annual **Fiesta de la Naranja** (Orange Festival), which sees a few days of processions, dancing, singing and drinking.

Las Líneas de Palpa and other sites

The best-known of the geoglyphs, collectively referred to as **Las Líneas de Palpa**, can be viewed from a *mirador* (S/2) just over a kilometre north of the town centre. Known

THEORIES ABOUT THE LÍNEAS DE NAZCA

Las Líneas de Nazca remain one of the world's biggest archeological mysteries and attract thousands of visitors every year to Peru's south coast. Theories abound as to their purpose and creation.

MARIA REICHE

The greatest expert on these mammoth desert designs was **Maria Reiche**, who escaped from Nazi Germany to become a tutor in Peru in the 1930s and worked at Nazca almost continuously from 1946 until her death in 1998. Standing on the shoulders of US scientist Paul Kosok, a colleague of hers, she believed that the Lines were an **astronomical calendar** designed to help organize planting and harvesting around seasonal changes rather than the fickle shifts of weather. When certain stars lined up with specific lines, shapes or animals, it would signal a time for planting, the coming of the rains, the beginning or end of summer, the growing season or the time for harvesting. It also gave the elite high priests, who possessed this knowledge, a large element of control over the actions of the populace. In a desert area like Nazca, where the coastal fog never obscures the night sky, there was a strong emphasis on relating earthly matters to the movements of the heavens and how they in turn relate to nature's cycles. Reiche's theories are thought to have established some alignments, many of which were confirmed by the computer analysis (particularly those for the solar solstices) of astronomer Gerald Hawkins (world famous for "decoding" Stonehenge in England), who himself spent much of the 1960s working on the Nazca Lines. Much, however, was left unexplained, and this has allowed more recent theorists to fill out the picture.

THEORIES OF RITUALS

Toribio Mejía Xesspe, a Peruvian archeologist, actually "discovered" the site in 1927 and believed that the Lines were made for walking or dancing along, probably for ritual purposes.

In 2000, Dr Anthony Aveni, a leading archeoastronomer, agreed that at least some of the Nazca Lines were **pathways** meant to be walked in rituals, perhaps consciousness-changing like labyrinths, but also relating to the acquisition of water. A statistically significant number of the Lines point towards a section of the horizon where the sun used to rise at the beginning of the

locally as the **Reloj Solar** (solar clock), it contains geometric lines that form a pattern visible on the lower valley slopes. It's said that during the equinox, seers can tell from the Reloj Solar what kind of harvest there will be. Six kilometres to the south of Palpa, on the Panamericana Sur, another *mirador* (S/3) gives you a fine view of the anthropomorphic figures of the *Familia Real de Paracas* (Royal Family of Paracas), which includes the striking *Dios Oculado*, the main Paracas God, recognisable by its prominent, bulging eyes.

A trickier site to locate, some 8km by navigable dirt track northeast from Palpa, are the **Petroglifos de Casa Blanca**, where human figures and cubic shapes have been etched onto one sunken but upright stone. Roughly 3km further on is a series of rock engravings on the scattered volcanic boulders, known as the **Petroglifos de Chicchictara**. The images depict two-headed snakes, a sunburst, a moon and animals.

ARRIVAL AND DEPARTURE — PALPA

By bus/colectivo All local buses and colectivos running between Ica and Nazca can drop off and pick up passengers on the Panamericana Sur, which bisects the town of Palpa.

Nazca and around

The colonial town of **NAZCA** spreads along the margin of a small coastal valley, just south of the eponymous Lines, overlooked from afar by the towering 2000m peak of **Cerro Blanco**, one of the highest sand dunes in the world. The river running through the town is invariably dry, but the valley remains green and fertile through the rainy season, suggesting that perhaps they were created to help worship or invoke their gods, particularly those related to rain. According to Aveni, air and ground surveys revealed that "most of the straight lines on the pampa are tied to water sources".

IT'S IN THE WATER

In 2003, David Johnson (University of Massachusetts) proposed that the ancient Nazcans mapped the desert to mark the surface where **aquifers** appeared. His work suggested that large underground rivers run under the pampa and many of the figures are connected to this, creating a giant map of what's happening under the earth. Zigzag lines indicate a lack of underground water, while trapezoids point towards the source of it. Archeological research also suggests that Nazca experienced a serious drought around 550 AD, at the same time as the main ceremonial centre – Cahuachi – was abandoned on the plain, and more or less contemporaneous with the construction of the trapezoid spaces where evidence of ritual offerings has been found.

MORE IDEAS...

Further theories on the purpose of the Lines include the concept of shamanic flight or out-of-body experience, with the symbolic "flight path" already mapped out across the region. Such an experience is induced by some of the "teacher plants", such as the mescaline cactus San Pedro, which are still used by traditional healers in Peru. Visually, there are clear links and similarities between the animal figures found on the plain and those elaborately painted onto Nazca's fine ceramics. Animal totems or spirit helpers are commonly used, even today, by traditional Peruvian healers to communicate with the "other world".

Most of the above theories are fairly compatible; taken together, they form a matrix of interrelated explanations – agro-astronomical, environmental, spiritual and ritual. However, just how the ancient Nazca people ever constructed the Lines is possibly the biggest mystery of all – not least since they can't even be seen from the ground. In the early 1970s the populist writer Erich von Däniken claimed that the Lines were built as runways for alien spaceships. Less controversially, perhaps, in the 1980s a local Nazca school tried building its own line and from its efforts calculated that a thousand patient and inspired workers could have made them all in less than a month.

continued use of ancient Nazca subterranean aqueducts, and the town is an enjoyable place to stay.

In addition to the world-famous Líneas de Nazca (see page 131), there are plenty of fascinating local sites, like the pre-Inca and Inca remains of **Los Paredones** and the **Acueductos de Cantalloc**. Others, such as the ancient Nazca ceremonial and urban centre of **Cahuachi** and the early Huari and Nazca graveyard at **Chauchilla** lie a little further away in the desert, only reachable by car or with a tour group.

If you're hoping to catch a **fiesta**, the *patronales* make September a good time to visit, when the locals venerate the Virgen de Guadalupe (Sept 8) with great enthusiasm. In May, the religious and secular festivities of the Fiesta de las Cruces go on for days.

Museo Didáctico Antonini

Av de la Cultura 600 • Daily 9am–7pm • S/15 • ☎ 056 523 444

The town's best museum, the fascinating **Museo Didáctico Antonini**, is an Italian pre-Columbian archeological research and study centre, which lies a couple of blocks east of the main plaza, and is a must-see attraction. The museum presents excellent interpretative exhibits covering the evolution of Nazca culture, a good audiovisual show and scale-model reconstructions of local remains such as the Templo del Escalonado at Cahuachi. The museum complex is extensive and includes an archeological park that contains the Acueducto de Bisambra (fed by the reservoir higher up the valley) and some burial reconstructions.

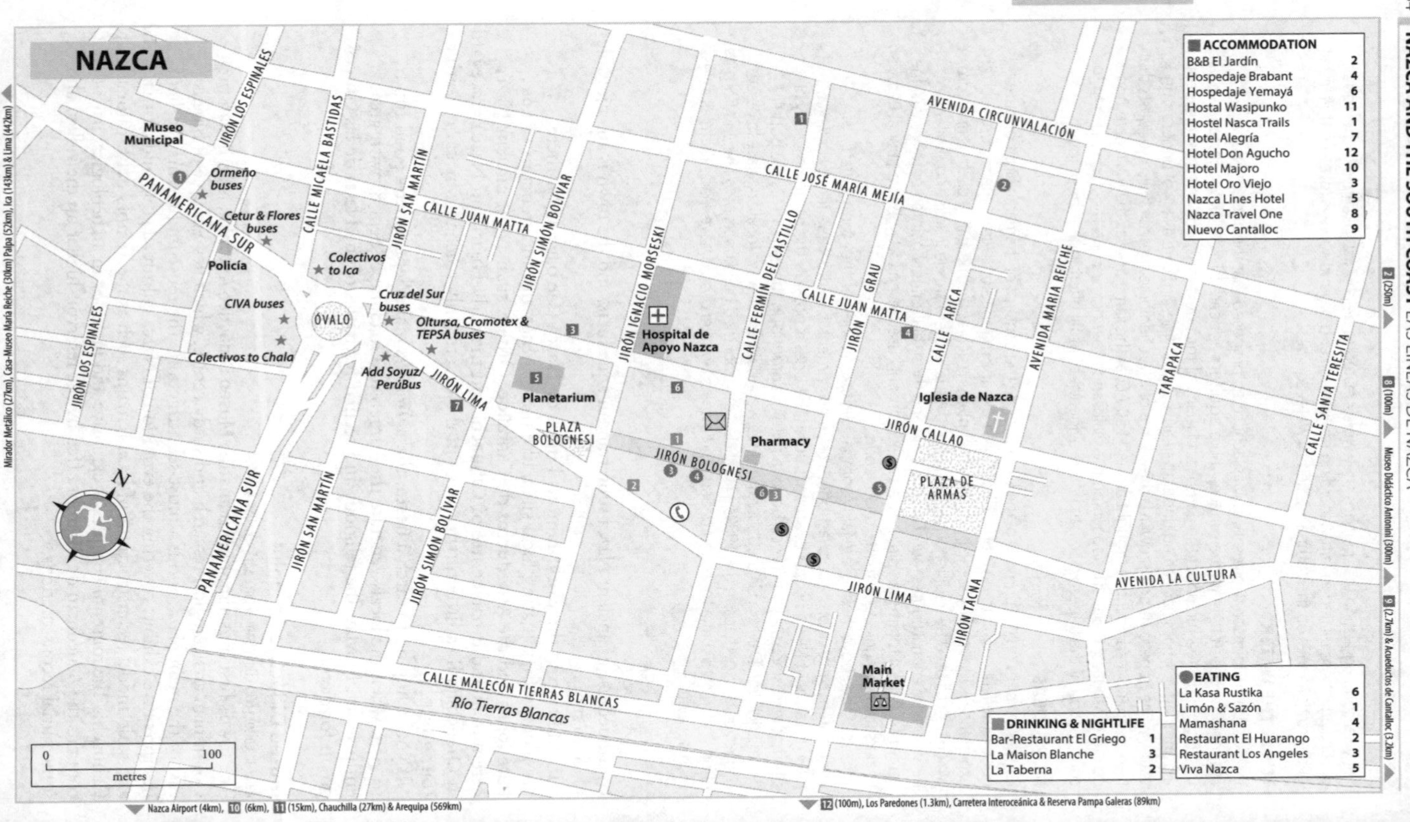
NAZCA
ACCOMMODATION
B&B El Jardín 2
Hospedaje Brabant 4
Hospedaje Yemayá 6
Hostal Wasipunko 11
Hostel Nasca Trails 1
Hotel Alegría 7
Hotel Don Agucho 12
Hotel Majoro 10
Hotel Oro Viejo 3
Nazca Lines Hotel 5
Nazca Travel One 8
Nuevo Cantalloc 9
EATING
La Kasa Rustika 6
Limón & Sazón 1
Mamashana 4
Restaurant El Huarango 2
Restaurant Los Angeles 3
Viva Nazca 5
DRINKING & NIGHTLIFE
Bar-Restaurant El Griego 1
La Maison Blanche 3
La Taberna 2
2 (250m)
8 (100m)
Museo Didáctico Antonini (300m)
9 (2.7km) & Acueductos de Cantalloc (3.2km)
12 (100m), Los Paredones (1.3km), Carretera Interoceánica & Reserva Pampa Galeras (89km)
Nazca Airport (4km), 10 (6km), 11 (15km), Chauchilla (27km) & Arequipa (569km)
Mirador Metálico (27km), Casa-Museo Maria Reiche (30km) Palpa (52km), Ica (143km) & Lima (442km)
CALLE SANTA TERESITA
TARAPACA
AVENIDA LA CULTURA
AVENIDA MARIA REICHE
AVENIDA CIRCUNVALACIÓN
CALLE ARICA
Iglesia de Nazca
JIRÓN CALLAO
PLAZA DE ARMAS
JIRÓN TACNA
JIRÓN LIMA
Main Market
JIRÓN GRAU
CALLE JUAN MATTA
CALLE JOSÉ MARÍA MEJÍA
CALLE FERMÍN DEL CASTILLO
Pharmacy
Hospital de Apoyo Nazca
JIRÓN IGNACIO MORSESKI
JIRÓN BOLOGNESI
PLAZA BOLOGNESI
Planetarium
JIRÓN SIMÓN BOLÍVAR
CALLE MALECÓN TIERRAS BLANCAS
Río Tierras Blancas
Oltursa, Cromotex & TEPSA buses
Cruz del Sur buses
Add Soyuz/ PerúBus
JIRÓN SAN MARTÍN
Colectivos to Ica
ÓVALO
CALLE MICAELA BASTIDAS
JIRÓN LOS ESPINALES
Ormeño buses
Cetur & Flores buses
Policía
CIVA buses
Colectivos to Chala
PANAMERICANA SUR
Museo Municipal
metres
0
100
N

Planetario del Hotel Nazca Lines

Hotel Nazca Lines, Jr Bolognesi 147 • Presentations daily at 7.30pm in English, 8.30pm in Spanish • S/20 • ⓣ 056 522 293

If you're expecting a regular **planetarium** showing, you're likely to come away disappointed. However, as an informative introduction to the various theories regarding the meaning of the Nazca Lines (see page 132), this 45-minute illustrated talk is worth attending. In particular, it focuses on the astronomical calendar of Maria Reiche – who spent her later years living in the hotel. To finish off, you'll be taken outside to peer through a telescope at a few constellations.

Mirador Metálico

Km 420 of the Panamericana Sur • Daily 8am–5.30pm • S/3 • Regional buses and minivans that run between Nazca and Ica will drop off and pick up passengers

Around 27km north of Nazca, a tall metal **mirador** (viewing tower) has been built above the plain, right by the Panamericana. Unless you've got the time to climb up onto one of the hills behind – known as the *mirador natural* – or take a flight over the Lines (see below), this is the best view of the Líneas de Nazca you'll get, though only two and a half geoglyphs are visible: the hands, the tree and half of the lizard. However, with a good guide, it is worth coming out to the *mirador* in addition to booking a flight because you'll learn more about the Lines than you will with a flight alone.

Casa Museo Maria Reiche

Km 416 of the Panamericana Sur • Daily 8am–6pm • S/5

The rather neglected **Casa Museo y Mausoleo Maria Reiche**, about 3km north of the *mirador* on the Panamericana Sur, consists of three main rooms stuffed with displays of photos, drawings and ceramics relating to the Líneas de Nazca and the studies of **Maria Reiche**, the renowned Nazca Lines researcher (see page 132). Housed in her old adobe home, the museum includes one room dedicated solely to Reiche's personal possessions, showing the spartan reality of her daily life here, right down to her flip-flops. However, unless you're passionately curious about her life and come with a knowledgeable guide, this is one sight that can be missed.

FLYING OVER THE LÍNEAS DE NAZCA

A pricey but spectacular way of seeing the Lines – and arguably the only way to fully appreciate them – is to **fly** over them. Flights can be arranged with **tour companies** in Nazca (see page 138) or directly at the Nazca airstrip (where they depart), about 2km southwest of Nazca (at Km 447 on the Panamericana), and **cost** US$50–200 per person depending on the season, the size of the group, how long you want to spend buzzing around (eg if you want to include the Líneas de Palpa as well) and how much demand there is on the day. The **duration** of the standard flight, which takes you over twelve of the best known geoglyphs, and sometimes over the Acueducto de Cantalloc, is around thirty minutes. Rates usually include transfer to and from your accommodation, but do not include the S/30 airport tax. You will also need to present your passport at the airport. In high season, you can feel as though you're on a conveyor belt of people being squeezed in and out of planes. Bear in mind that the planes are small and bounce around in the changeable air currents, which can cause motion sickness; on an early morning trip, you'll usually get a calmer flight and a better **view**, since the air gets hazier as the day progresses.

Many hotels and tour agencies (see page 138) will book a flight for you and arrange transport to the airport from your hotel. Make sure they book with one of the reputable airlines with a good safety record as there have been fatal accidents with some carriers over the years. The three preferred airlines all have offices at Nazca Maria Reiche Airport on Km 452, Panamericana Sur: Aero Nasca (ⓣ 056 522688 ⓦ aeronasca.com); AeroParacas (ⓣ 01 641 7000, ⓦ aeroparacas.com; also has offices in Lima, Paracas and in Nazca Town); and Movil Air (ⓣ 01 716 8005, ⓦ movilair.com.pe; also has offices in Lima and Ica).

Los Paredones and the Cantalloc sites

S/10 covers entry to all four sites

A popular short excursion from Nazca takes in the adobe Inca ruins of **Los Paredones**, the ancient **Acueducto de Cantalloc** and two lots of geoglyphs: **El Telar** and **Las Agujas**. Though you'll get more out of the sites on a tour (see page 138), since information on the ground is sparse, it is possible to hike around all four places from Nazca – around 12km, though you'll need to be prepared for the heat and dust.

Los Paredones

1.5km due south of Nazca • Daily 8am–6pm• S/10 joint ticket • 20min walk from Nazca, heading down C Arica from the Plaza de Armas

Once an Inca trade centre where wool from the mountains was exchanged for cotton grown along the coast, the adobe buildings at **Los Paredones** are now in a bad state of repair and the site is dotted with *huaqueros*' (grave robbers') pits, but if you follow the path to the prominent central sector you can get a good idea of what the town must have been like. Overlooking the valley and roads, it's in a commanding position – a fact recognized and taken advantage of by local cultures long before the Incas arrived. If you're lucky, you might also catch sight of a burrowing owl perching among the ruins, on the lookout for prey.

Los Acueductos de Cantalloc

3.5km east of Nazca on the road to *Hotel Nuevo Cantayoc* • Daily 8am–6pm • S/10 joint ticket

The **Acueductos de Cantalloc** comprise a quietly impressive series of inverted conical spirals laboriously constructed out of stone, like swallow-holes, in the fields. Each around 4m across, they function as air vents for a vast underground **canal system** that siphons desperately needed water from rivers higher in the valley. The spirals allowed walking access to the bottom, which, in turn, allowed the drawing of water and maintenance of the aqueduct. Designed and constructed by the Nazca, the aqueducts are still in use today and play an essential role in the continuing agriculture in the Valle de Nazca. It's worth going down into the openings and poking your head or feet into the canals, where you can sometimes see small fish swimming in the flowing water.

El Telar and Las Agujas

3km and 4km southeast of Nazca off the Carretera Interoceánica • Daily 8am–6pm • S/10 joint ticket • Turn off the Carretera Interoceánica through the barrio of Buena Fé for El Telar; for Las Agujas the *mirador* is just south of the Carretera Interoceánica, 4km from Los Paredones

A couple of natural viewpoints allow you to make reasonable sense of the giant geoglyphs of **El Telar** (the loom) and **Las Agujas** (needles), which consist of trapezoids and spirals theorized to represent Nazca textiles and weaving.

El Necrópolis de Chauchilla

7km east of the Panamericana Sur at Km 469 • Daily 6am-6pm • S/8 • Drive 20km south of Nazca along the Panamericana Sur to Km 469, then take the signed dirt road east beside the Poroma riverbed for 7km; best visited on a tour

Some 27km southeast of Nazca, the **Necrópolis de Chauchilla** certainly rewards the effort it takes to visit. The desert landscape of this atmospheric site rolls gently down towards a small dry riverbed and copses of *huarango* trees on the northern side. To the south are several rain-destroyed adobe pyramids, difficult to discern against the sand. Among the shards of pottery and bones strewn around the site are around a dozen restored open tombs, sheltered from the scorching sun by wooden shelters, containing remarkable seated mummies, cloaked in well preserved textiles, some with their long braided hair and even their nails intact. Further up the track, near Trancas, there's a small ceremonial **temple** – Huaca del Loro – and beyond this at Los Incas, you can find the **Petroglifos de Quemazón**. These last two are not usually included in the standard tour, but if you hire your own guide, you can negotiate with them to take you there for a little extra.

Cahuachi

20km west of Nazca town • Daily 8am–5.30pm • Free, though at the time of writing access was limited on account of restoration work • No public transport; best visited on a tour

The ancient centre of Nazca culture, **Cahuachi** lies to the west of the Lines, about 20km from the city and some 45km from the Pacific. Cahuachi is typical of a Nazca ceremonial centre in its use of natural features to form an integral part of the structure. Their everyday homes showed no such architectural aspirations – indeed there are no major towns associated with the Nazca, who tended to live in small clusters of adobe huts.

The landscape between Nazca Town and the distant coastline is a massive, very barren desertscape – almost always hot, dry and sunny. It's hard to imagine how ancient peoples managed to sustain such an advanced civilization here; but, as in northern Peru, it had much to do with a close religious and technical relationship with natural water sources, all the more important because of their scarcity. The site consists of a religious citadel split in half by the river, with its main temple (one of a set of six) constructed around a small natural hillock. Adobe platforms step the sides of this twenty-metre mound and though badly weathered, you can still make out the general form. Separate courtyards attached to each of the six pyramids can be distinguished, but their exact purpose is unknown.

Templo Escalonado

The only section of Cahuachi to have been properly excavated so far is the **Templo Escalonado**, a multilevel temple on which you can see wide adobe walls and, on the temple site, some round, sunken chambers. A hundred metres away, from the top of what is known as the main pyramid structure, you can look down over what was once the main ceremonial plaza, though it's difficult to make out now because of the sands.

El Estaquería

Quite close to the main complex is a construction known as **El Estaquería**, the Place of the Stakes, retaining a dozen rows of *huarango* log pillars. *Huarango* trees (known in the north of Peru as *algarrobo*) are the most common form of desert vegetation. Their wood, baked by the sun, is very hard, though their numbers are much reduced nowadays by locals who use them for fuel. The Estaquería is estimated to be 2000 years old, but its original function is unclear, though other such constructions are usually found above tombs. The bodies here were buried with ceramics, food, textiles, jewellery and *chaquira* beads. Italian archeologist Giuseppe Orefici has worked on Cahuachi for over thirty years and has uncovered over three hundred graves, one of which contained a tattooed and dreadlocked warrior. Also around 2000 years old, he's a mere whippersnapper compared with other evidence Orefici has unearthed relating to 4000-year-old pre-ceramic cultures.

ARRIVAL AND GETTING AROUND — NAZCA AND AROUND

By bus Most people arrive in Nazca by bus from Lima, Arequipa or Cusco. Nearly all bus companies have depots or offices around the *óvalo* (roundabout) at the northern entry to town, most on Av Los Incas or Jr Lima. If you want to travel to one of the nearby sites, take one of the cheaper, stopping buses such as PerúBus or Flores.

Bus companies Cruz del Sur (T 056 720 440, W cruzdelsur.com.pe); Soyuz/PerúBus (T 056 521 464, W soyuzonline.com.pe); Ormeño (T 056 522 058, W grupo-ormeno.com.pe); Civa (T 056 523 019); Flores (Lima T 01 332 1212, W floreshnos.net); TEPSA (T 056 521 515, W tepsa.com.pe); Oltursa (T 056 522 265, W oltursa.pe).

Destinations Arequipa (several daily; 9–11hr); Chala (several daily; 3hr); Cusco (several daily; 14–16hr); Lima (several daily; 7–8hr); Puquio (several daily; 5–6hr).

By colectivo Cars (S/15) and minivans (S/20) leave from near the *óvalo*, connecting Nazca with Ica to the north and Chala to the south. Minivans for Puquio (2hr 30min), via Pampa Galera (2hr) leave from the Vista Alegre district.

By taxi Taxis and *mototaxis* are cheap; you shouldn't pay more than S/5 for the car or S/2 for the mototaxi for any destination in town.

2

NAZCA CERAMICS

In 1901, when Max Uhle "discovered" the Nazca culture, it suddenly became possible to associate a certain batch of beautiful **ceramics** that had previously been unclassifiable in terms of their cultural background: the importance of Nazca pottery in the overall picture of Peru's pre-history asserted itself overnight. Many of the best pieces were found in Cahuachi.

Unlike contemporaneous Mochica ware, Nazca ceramics rarely attempt any realistic imagery. The majority – painted in three or four earthy colours and given a resinous surface glaze – are relatively stylized or even completely abstract. Nevertheless, two main categories of subject matter recur: naturalistic designs of bird, animal and plant life, and motifs of mythological monsters and bizarre deities. In later works it was common to mould effigies to the pots. During Nazca's decline under the Huari-Tiahuanaco cultural influence (see page 486), the artistry and designs were less inspired. The style and content of the early pottery, however, show remarkable similarities to the symbols depicted in the **Líneas de Nazca**, and although not enough is known about the Nazca culture to be certain, it seems reasonable to assume that the early Nazca people were also responsible for the drawings on the Pampa de San José. With most of the evidence coming from their graveyards, though, and that so dependent upon conjecture, there is actually little to characterize the Nazca and not much is known of them beyond the fact that they collected heads as trophies, that they built a ceremonial complex in the desert at Cahuachi, and that they scraped a living from the Nazca, Ica and Pisco valleys from around 100 BC–600 AD.

REPRODUCTION CERAMICS

Several local workshops in the Barrio San Carlos, south of the river in Nazca, produce high-quality **reproduction Nazca ceramics** and are usually happy to demonstrate techniques to passing tourists; visits to these workshops are included on some tours.

Taller Artesanía "Andrés Calle Flores" Pasaje Torrico 240 ⓣ056 522 319. The best-known pottery workshop, this family-run enterprise – now in its third generation – will demonstrate the ceramic-making process from moulding to polishing. Daily 9am–5pm.

Ceramicas LASC Pasaje López 125. Masters of the craft show and explain how Nazca ceramics were made. Daily 9am–5pm.

INFORMATION AND TOURS

Tourist information There is an excellent iPerú tourist information desk at the airport (ⓣ979 980 622), which can provide you with a photocopied map of the town and surrounding area.

Activities Popular half-day excursions include: the Mirador Metálico, the Casa-Museo Maria Reiche, and sometimes the Palpa viewing towers; Los Paredones, the Acueductos de Cantalloc and El Telar; Cahuachi via the scenic Acueducto de Ocongalla; the Necrópolis de Chauchilla plus a ceramics or gold workshop in town. You can also hike up Cerro Blanco (a tough 2–3hr climb) and sandboard down, pausing at the summit to take in the expansive views (S/110); the trail starts at Km 23 on the road to Puquio.

Tour operators The following Nazca-based operators can provide general information, as well as tours and activities. Prices per person are from around S/60–90 in high season, usually for a minimum of two people. Costs can be much cheaper when negotiated in Nazca, and in low season, than when booked online. Ballestas Nasca-Lines, Jr Bolognesi 395 (ⓣ949 679 692) is a good budget option offering flexible itineraries round local sites. Edunas Tours, Jr Bolognesi 307 (ⓣ056 523189, ⓦedunastoursperu.com), specialises in adventure trips; Great Nazca Tours, Pasaje Bisambra 255 (ⓣ056 523 100, ⓦgreatnazcatours.com), focuses on organizing flights over the Lines but also runs excursions to Chauchilla; Mystery Peru, C Simon Bolívar 221 (ⓣ056 522 379, ⓦmysteryperu.com), offers tours countrywide. Wander down Jr Bolognesi to find other operators.

ACCOMMODATION

IN TOWN

★ **B&B El Jardín** C José María Mejia 01 ⓣ056 522 956, ⓔel.jardin.nasca@gmail.com; map p.134. A home turned B&B with colourful local decoration and a hammock-strewn stone-paved garden to relax in and enjoy your sumptuous breakfast. Rooms have balconies overlooking the garden, plus there is a small pool. It's a bit of a stroll to the centre, but this friendly, attractive spot is worth it. S/130

Hospedaje Brabant C Juan Matta 878 ⓣ 056 524 127, ⓦ brabanthostal.com; map p.134. An excellent budget choice a block from the plaza. Plenty of young travellers, decent wi-fi and a terrace with hammocks to sip a beer and watch the sunset over the city. TV lounge, laundry and luggage storage are other pluses. You get what you pay for: it's very basic but clean. Dorms S/20, doubles S/45

Hospedaje Yemayá Jr Callao 578 ⓣ 056 523 146, ⓦ hospedajeyemaya.com; map p.134. Another well-located budget option near the plaza, Yemayá is a little dark in the corridors, but the rooms are impeccable and cool, and have fans for hot nights. The rooftop terrace and free airport shuttle are welcome extras. Breakfast S/12. S/50

Hostel Nasca Trails C Fermin Del Castillo 637 ⓣ 056 522 858, ⓦ nascatrailsperu.com; map p.134. Excellent budget choice, with clean rooms, comfortable beds and decent showers. Wi-fi is quick and there is a gravel-covered patio with some slumping sofas and hammocks. The extremely friendly owners run quality tours. S/55

Hotel Alegría Jr Lima 166 ⓣ 056 522 702, ⓦ hotelalegria.net; map p.134. This popular hotel has en-suite rooms with a/c set around an attractive garden with a fine pool; it also runs a café that serves tasty, affordable meals and has an on-site travel agency that can arrange tours and bus connections. Late check-out, parking and buffet breakfast. S/180

Hotel Don Agucho Av San Carlos 100 ⓣ 056 522 048, ⓦ hoteldonagucho.com.pe; map p.134. An attractive hacienda-style place with white-washed walls and wooden balustrades overlooking a pool and leafy courtyard. Comfortable rooms with a/c and a minibar lead off cactus-filled passages. Decent buffet breakfast. S/150

Hotel Oro Viejo Jr Callao 483 ⓣ 056 523 332, ⓦ hoteloroviejo.net; map p.134. An excellent mid-range option with big rooms around a well-maintained courtyard and a very welcome pool considering the heat in Nazca. Good buffet breakfast. Conveniently located close to bus stations. S/200

★ **Nazca Lines Hotel** Jr Bolognesi 147 ⓣ 056 522 293, ⓦ dmhoteles.pe; map p.134. Luxurious hotel, offering spacious, well-appointed rooms with minibar, a/c and safe, a well-kept pool and an excellent restaurant. S/250

Nazca Travel One Pedagógico 181 ⓣ 956 948 167, ⓦ nascatravelonehostel.com; map p.134. Popular budget choice on a quiet road. Small but spotless en-suite twins and doubles with flat-screen TVs. The inclusion of breakfast as well as free transfers to bus stations and the airport makes this particularly good value. S/70

Nuevo Cantalloc 3km from Nazca on Route 26 to Cusco, close to the Acueductos de Cantalloc ⓣ 056 522 264, ⓦ hotelnuevocantalloc.com; map p.134. Located 15min from the town centre in an old hacienda, this is not a five-star resort as advertised on its website, but rather a tranquil hotel spread over six hectares of pools, fine gardens, and sports facilities, with a range of wildlife roaming free (for the most part). US$110

AROUND NAZCA

★ **Hostal Wasipunko** Km 462, Panamericana Sur, Pajonal ⓣ 056 631 183, ⓦ wasipunko.com; map p.134. A delightful, rustic hostel set in an impressive green oasis in the desert, 15km south of Nazca, with its own small ecological and archeological museum. Rooms are set around a courtyard, and the restaurant specializes in tasty pre-Inca dishes using local produce. In addition to conventional tours, they offer birdwatching, hiking and community-based activities. Camping S/25, doubles S/243

Hotel Majoro Km 447, Panamericana Sur ⓣ 056 522 481, ⓦ hotelmajoro.com; map p.134. It's an idyllic place to relax outside Nazca, but close to the airstrip. The rooms lack some style, but the grounds are stunning, with a fabulous pool, and resident peacocks. The hotel also runs tours, including to wildlife havens on the nearby coast. US$120

EATING

Eating in Nazca offers more variety than you might imagine given the town's small size. Most places are in or around Jr Bolognesi and Jr Lima. There's also a small **market** on Jr Lima, opposite the Banco de la Nación.

★ **La Kasa Rustika** Bolognesi 372 ⓣ 998 996 754, ⓦ lakasarustika.com.pe; map p.134. Currently the top culinary spot in town, offering an extensive menu of delicious international and Peruvian dishes to suit all wallets: from S/18 for a juicy lasagne to S/45–48 for a house speciality beef dish, such as a succulent marinated *lomo al pobre* with plantain, egg and *tacu-tacu* (beans and rice). Plenty of seafood too, excellent service and a lively bar. Mon 11.30am–11pm, Tues–Sun 7am–11pm.

Limón & Sazón Av Los Incas 202 ⓣ 056 522 540; map p.134. Refined *cevichería*, complete with garden seating, serving a great selection of classic Peruvian seafood dishes, beautifully presented. Most mains S/20–35. Daily 9am–6pm.

Mamashana Jr Bolognesi 270 ⓣ 056 521 286; map p.134. A solid choice with a varied menu and well prepared dishes. The pizzas are decent, but they're best at creole fusion dishes – try the classic *lomo saltado* or the innovative shrimp in *aguaymanto* sauce (S/45). The open upper deck is particularly pleasant. Most mains S/20–35. Daily 10am–11pm.

Restaurant El Huarango C Arica 602 ☎ 056 522 141; map p.134. Offering a covered rooftop patio and a great ambience, this place serves delicious food, mostly traditional coastal Peruvian dishes such as *ají de gallina* (chilli chicken) but also including some more international cuisine. Daily 11am–11pm.

2

Restaurant Los Angeles Bolognesi 266; map p.134. Nice, inexpensive family-run restaurant with a wide range of freshly cooked foods, from burgers and omelettes to pizza, and more traditional Peruvian dishes (S/18–25). Mon–Sat 9.30am–9pm.

Viva Nasca C Bolognesi 464 ☎ 994 562 477; map p.134. Small and over-lit, this typical Peruvian sandwich restaurant has friendly staff and delicious sandwiches and house burgers. Soothe the throat with a fresh juice after a day in the desert. Mon–Sat 9am–11pm.

DRINKING AND NIGHTLIFE

What little nightlife exists is mainly based around restaurants and bars, particularly on Jr Lima, the Plaza de Armas and Jr Bolognesi.

Bar-Restaurant El Griego Jr Bolognesi 287 ☎ 056 521 480; map p.134. Friendly local eating-house with fine food and decent drinks at reasonable prices. Breakfasts are tasty and evenings can be fun when there's more of a bar atmosphere. Daily 10.30am–late.

La Maison Blanche Jr Bolognesi 388 ☎ 056 522 361; map p.134. Great for daytime crêpes and coffee, and the patio is perfect for a cold beer at night. Sandwiches are hit and miss, and service can be sluggish, but staff are friendly and the piscos top notch. Good wi-fi. Daily 10am–11pm.

La Taberna Jr Lima 321; map p.134. Serves a good selection of local and international dishes, plus a variety of drinks; its walls are covered with graffiti, scrawled over the years by passing travellers. Live folk music most evenings. Daily 11am–midnight.

La Reserva Nacional Pampa Galeras Barbara D'Achille

Km 89 of the Nazca–Cusco road • Daily: reserve 8am–5pm; museum 8am–1pm & 2–5pm • Free • Take a minivan bound for Puquio, which leaves from a stop (*paradero*) in Vista Alegre, Nazca; get off at the *puesto de control* Pampa Galeras • Further information from Andres Flores at SERNANP, C Grau 494, Nazca, ☎ 056 522 770, ⓔ aflores@sernanp.com.pe

Some 90km inland from Nazca, the **Reserva Nacional Pampa Galeras Barbara D'Achille** is one of the best places in Peru to see the **vicuña**, a llama-like animal with very fine wool, though you should also keep an eye out for tarucas (north Andean deer), rheas (the Andean answer to the ostrich) and condors when wandering along one of the reserve's several trails.

Vicuña have lived for centuries in the area of the reserve, which contains more than four thousand of the creatures, though they are not easy to spot. When you do notice a herd, you'll see it move as if it were a single organism. The animals flock together and move swiftly in a tight wave, bounding gracefully across the hills. The males are strictly territorial, protecting their patches of scrubby grass by day, then returning to the rockier heights as darkness falls. Try to visit on June 24 for the **Chaccu**, a rowdy traditional roundup and shearing of the vicuña that needs hundreds of helping hands.

At the reserve entrance there's a small but informative **museum** and several **kiosks** selling snacks and a few basic provisions. Camping and basic dormitory **accommodation** with limited solar-powered electricity is available, as well as kitchen access. Since the reserve is at 4000m, you'll need to bring a warm sleeping bag. Note that while it is relatively easy to get to the reserve by minivan, transport is often full when passing by and may therefore not stop to pick you up when you leave.

La Panamericana Sur

From Nazca, the **Panamericana Sur** continues for about 1000km to the border with Chile. Apart from the sizeable, unappealing towns of Chala and Camaná, the highway only passes the occasional fishing village or squatter settlement until it reaches the

LAGUNA DE PARINACOCHAS

Scenically situated at the foot of *Nevado Sarasara*, amid glorious sierra scenery some 140km south off the Nazca–Cusco road lies **Laguna de Parinacochas**, a large and beautiful body of water named after the many **flamingoes** that, thanks to its shallow and saline nature, live and breed there. The lake remains brackish on account of the build-up in concentration of mineral salts due to evaporation and the lack of outflow. A haven for wildlife, Parinacochas attracts a host of resident and migratory water birds, including several species of ducks, geese, coots and avocets; on the surrounding pampa you can also spot vicuña, guanaco and taruca as well as the more prosaic grazing cattle belonging to the local villagers. Scattered along the shore are some **Inca ruins**, where several families have now set up home. The ruins, known as Incahuasi, were part of a strategic Inca administrative centre at the meeting of the cross-coastal route west from Arequipa, and the Andean-coastal road from Cusco.

PRACTICALITIES

Access is via a sinuous tarred road that heads south at Puquio, with the main route continuing over the Andes to Cusco via Abancay. In the dry season, if you have a good GPS and your own 4x4 transport (in a convoy of at least two vehicles), you can negotiate a spectacular Andean route from Parinacochas to Cotahuasi (see page 183). A twice-daily colectivo (3hr) bound for Pausa leaves Puquio from Av Mariscal Castilla and passes by the lake.

Arequipa turn-off. From here, the highway heads inland and southeast, across the Desierto de la Clemesí – arguably the northernmost section of the Atacama Desert – to Tacna, with the pisco-producing town of Moquegua the main place worthy of a detour. The desert landscape immediately south of Nazca is stunningly bleak and there's relatively little of specific interest in the 170km of sand and bare rock between Nazca and Chala, a tatty fishing village that serves the mines in the area. If you can, stop at the unexpected patch of green that is **Yauca,** a slender valley dedicated entirely to the production of olive oil, some 123km south of Nazca. Some of the olive trees are ancient, supposedly all grown from a single plant stolen from the gardens of San Isidro in Lima in the 1500s.

Sacaco

2km north of Km 539, Panamericana Sur • Daily 9am–3pm (the onsite caretaker will open up) • Donations (S/5–10 per person) encouraged • ⓣ 054 482 057 • Get off a Nazca–Chala bus or colectivo at the signposted turn-off, from where it's 2.2km, shadeless walk north up a sandy track to the site

The remarkable paleontological site of **Sacaco** gives access to fossilized whale remains sitting in the desert near a small museum about 96km south of Nazca, just after south of the turn-off to Las Lomas. One fossilized whale skeleton is housed within the museum building itself, alongside an impressive collection of shark teeth and interpretative material about the geology and paleontology of the region. The fossils date back several million years to when the area – now 8km from the coast – was underwater. The site is included in some tours from Nazca.

Las Lomas de Atiquipa

Panamericana Sur Km 600; turn inland and 2km further is the village of Atiquipa. To go further you need a 4WD • Daily 8am–5pm • Community donation • ⓦ conservamospornaturaleza.org/area/lomas-de-atiquipa • You can camp, or stay in a community hostel (S/30 per person; S/100 including meals)

Near the village of **ATIQUIPA** is a small **reserve** protecting one of the most impressive remaining examples of a unique micro-climate that once stretched all along the Peruvian coast, and is now reduced to a few enclaves north and south of Lima. The *lomas* are small hills right on the coast which trap the fog coming in off the sea and so support a low, bushy forest and a surprising amount of wildlife. The vegetation is at its best between July and November. A heroic job of reforestation and promotion of this area has been done locally and some basic accommodation is now available, or visitors can stay at the rustic but well-appointed beachside house just before the reserve at **Playa Jihuay**; the Fundación Jihuay, based there, also takes on conservation volunteers.

Puerto Inca

Open access • Free • To get to the ruins, take a taxi from Chala (about S/20 each way; specify a time for pickup), or catch an Arequipa-bound bus along the Panamericana Sur and ask to be dropped off at Km 610; it's an easy 2.5km walk downhill from here to the beach

The ruins of **Puerto Inca**, the Incas' main port for Cusco, stand 7km northwest of Chala. There's an excellent **beach** here, and fine diving and fishing. The ruins are expansive and interesting, although with only a little information, and are just a short stroll up past the *Puerto Inka* hotel and beach. Within a half-day's walk there are caves, grottos, hidden coves, rock formations and plenty of opportunity for getting lost in the desert coastline, birdwatching or even spotting Humboldt penguins if you're patient and lucky enough.

ACCOMMODATION AND EATING — LA PANAMERICANA SUR

Cabaña Molles Km 601, Panamericana Sur ☎ 997 571 952. A delightful, rustic, fully furnished house at the back of the beach, with views across the bay and capacity for eight people. Solar power provides limited electricity and hot water. No wi-fi and limited mobile phone coverage. S/209

Hotel Puerto Inka Km 610, Panamericana Sur ☎ 054 635 362, puertoinka.com.pe; or contact in Arequipa at C Arica 406a, Yanahuara ☎ 054 252 588. This resort-like hotel – with pool, children's playground, volleyball court and games room – is spread out across several bungalows overlooking the sea, by the beach; with a decent restaurant, it makes a good lunch stop. Also has parking and a campsite. No wi-fi, and salt-water showers. Daily 7am–8.30pm. Camping S/10, bungalows S/190

The Moquegua region

The **MOQUEGUA** region – bare, volcanic terrain, streaked with fertile, narrow valleys, on the edge of the Desierto de Clemesi is traditionally and culturally linked to the Andean region around Lake Titicaca; many ethnic Colla and Lupaca from the mountains live here. The local economy today is based on copper mining, fruit plantations and wine, including excellent **pisco**. Historically, this area is an annexe of the altiplano, which was used as a major thoroughfare first by the Tiahuanaco and later the Huari peoples. Few non-Peruvians visit the region, and the frequent harsh, dusty winds can easily put visitors off seeking out its little-visited sights, from wine and pisco bodegas and volcanoes to petroglyphs and archeological remains. Some are reachable with local transport from Moquegua; for others you'll need a vehicle, or the help of a local tour company (see page 120).

Moquegua

Though rather flavourless, **MOQUEGUA** nevertheless possesses an attractive **Plaza de Armas** shaded by fig trees, a restored neoclassical **cathedral**, and a handful of restored **colonial houses** with wooden balconies. The place comes alive at the end of November when the *semana turística* and celebration of the town's foundation (Nov 25) coincide.

Museo Contisuyo

Jr Tacna 294, half a block north of the Plaza de Armas • Daily 8am–1pm & 2.30–5.30pm • Free • ☎ 053 461 844, museocontisuyo.com

2

MOQUEGUA'S BODEGAS

Initially established during the colonial era, Moquegua's **bodegas** have various lines in piscos (including italia and mosto verde), cognacs, aniseed liqueurs and sweet wines. Sign up with a tour operator such as Descubre Moquegua (in Spanish T 980 309 287, W descubremoquegua.wixisite.com/agenciaturistica) or hire a taxi driver (S/30).

Bodega Biondi Km 1143, Panamerica Sur T 053 461 889. Consistently ranked among the best producers in Peru, particularly well known for its aromatic varieties, Moscatel and Albilla. Mon–Fri 8am–2pm & 3–5pm.

Bodega Norvil C Ayacucho 1370 T 053 461 229. Welcoming bodega run by Alberto Villegas Vargas, grandson of the original founder Norberto Villegas Talavera, one of the town's benefactors. Mon–Sat 8am–noon & 2–5pm.

Bodega Paredes (or Parray y Reyes) Fundo la Chimba, on the road to Rayo T 053 461 972. Produces fine piscos from quebranta and italia grapes. You can also visit the vineyards on horseback and stay in their onsite accommodation. Daily 9am–noon & 3–5pm.

The **Museo Contisuyo** exhibits a worthwhile collection of archeological relics from the region, including stone arrow points, ceramics, textiles, gold and silver objects and specimens from the Tiahuanuco and Huari civilisations, as well as the local ancient coastal Chiribaya and Tumilaca cultures. Though small, the displays are well presented in Spanish and English.

ARRIVAL AND GETTING AROUND MOQUEGUA

Moquegua is a busy nodal point for two important roads into the Andes: the **Carretera Transoceánica**, connecting Ilo on the coast to Puno and Juliaca, and the **Carretera Binacional to Desaguadero**, and the Bolivian border, which shears off from the former around 90km northeast of Torata.

BY BUS

The bus terminal covers blocks 2 and 3 of Av Ejercito, several long blocks from the centre, so it's worth hopping in a combi or taxi to get there (S/3–5).

Bus companies Many reliable companies, based in the main bus terminal, serve Lima, Tacna, Arequipa, Puno and Desaguadero, as well as some less comfortable, cheaper options. Transportes Moquegua (T 953954710) has the most frequent connections with Arequipa and Tacna.

Destinations Arequipa (frequent daily; 3hr); Desaguadero (several daily 5hr); Lima (several daily; 18hr); Puno (several daily; 5–6hr); Tacna (frequent daily; 2hr 30min).

BY COLECTIVO

Colectivos for Tarata leave from outside the stadium, Estadio 25 de Noviembre. Minivans to Omate, Ilo, Arequipa and other locations leave from outside the main bus terminal.

BY CAR

Car rental Try Explorer Rent a car, Av San Antonio, Edif. E López Albújar, Block 8, of. 402 (T 053 463 180 W explorerrentacar.com). Rentals start at around S/300 a day.

INFORMATION

Tourist information The tourist office is at C Ancash 275 (T 053 461191), while Dircetur is at C Ayacucho 344 (T 053 464 053). There's also a tourist information kiosk in the main bus terminal (Mon–Sat 9am–5pm).

Website W moqueguaturismo.gob.pe.

ACCOMMODATION AND EATING

Bandido Pub C Moquegua 333 T 989 471 272. One of the few bars in town, where they play good music and serve wood-fired pizzas and a reasonably priced set menu (S/12), plus pisco and other drinks. Mon–Sat 7.30pm–late

Residencial Moquegua C Cusco 454 T 053 462 316, W residencialmoquegua.com. Light, airy rooms – singles and doubles – are impeccably maintained, some with large windows and small balcony. Great service. S/83

Restaurante Moraly C Lima and C Libertad T 053 463 084. Traditional, stylish and centrally located restaurant with a reputation for great breakfasts and attentive service. Note that the tasty set-lunch menu (S/15) sells out quickly. Daily 7am–7pm.

Torata

About 24km up the valley from Moquegua, on the main road to Puno – easily reachable by bus or colectivo – **TORATA** is a picturesque district and settlement of country homes made with traditional *mojinete* (slanted and gable ended) roofs. The legacy of the colonial period also includes an imposing church (rebuilt after the 2001 earthquake), and several old stone mills; the village's renowned artisanal bread can be sampled in the local restaurants.

Cerro Baúl

13km from Moquegua along the main road to Puno • Daily 8am–5.30pm • S/3.50 • Take a colectivo from Moquegua bound for Torata; the start of the path to the summit is signposted

One of the bigger sites in the region is the archeological remnant of a Huari (600–1100 AD) citadel that is easily visited by taxi from Moquegua. Sitting atop an imposing truncated hill – **Cerro Baúl**, after which the ruins are named – a few kilometres northeast of Moquegua, this commanding site once offered its ancient inhabitants a wide view around the Moquegua valley, allowing them to control the flow of goods and people at this strategic point.

Toquepala

30km southeast of Moquegua • Restricted access because the caves are on mine land; contact the PR department of the mine (southernperu.com) or a local guide, such as José Durand (952 842 473) to acquire a permit

In the hills southeast of Moquegua, the mysterious caves of **Toquepala** (at 2500m) – occupied by a group of hunter-gatherers from the Archaic era around nine thousand years ago – are fascinating if rather remote. They contain roughly drawn rock paintings of cameloid animals, hunting scenes and Andean religious symbols.

Los Geoglifos de Chen Chen

4km south of Moquegua • 7am–5pm • Free • Take the road east towards Toquepala, which leaves the Panamericana Sur between Km 98 and 97, just south of the town centre; alternatively a taxi from Moquegua will cost S/10

Best appreciated in the early-morning or late-afternoon light, the little-seen **Geoglifos de Chen Chen** constitute one of the most important remains of the Tihuanaco culture in the area, etched into the earth between 700 and 950AD. The geoglyphs are mainly large Nazca-like representations of camelids, scattered around the hillsides, visible from the road to Toquepala.

Omate and around

130km north of Moquegua • Minivans leave regularly from outside the bus terminal in Moquegua

A long but doable drive (2hr 30min) from Moquegua is the remote town of **OMATE**, on the back mountain road to Arequipa. Surrounded by unique and impressive terrain formed by rock, volcanic ash and sands, it's also famous for its crayfish. Check out the natural **Baños Termales de Ullucán** at 3100m (daily 6am–5pm; S/2), a quick 10km taxi ride from Omate. Also in the sierra are the majestic Ubinas (5673m, with a 350m crater) and Huaynaputina (4800m) **volcanoes**. Visiting these requires your own vehicle or going on a tour (see page 120).

La Carretera Costanera

Running parallel to the Panamericana Sur, the 400km **Carretera Costanera** provides an alternative littoral route between Camaná and Tacna. Though transport is not as straightforward as on the main highway, this at times truly spectacular and hair-raising coastal desert road more than compensates for the inconvenience, affording fabulous **views** of rugged cliffs, pounding surf and the occasional valley oasis. Apart from the journey itself, there are few spots worth lingering at, beyond a couple of minor **nature reserves** which are struggling to stave off the effects of pollution, encroaching ad-hoc developments and government indifference. For either reserve you need decent binoculars to get the most out of a visit. Approaching from the north, the first is the lagoon-based wetland area, **El Santuario Nacional Lagunas de Mejía**, located just south of the unappealing resort town of **Mollendo,** which you'll find crammed with beach-loving Arequipeños in the summer months (Dec–March). The second protected area is **Reserva Punta Coles**, a tiny headland known for its seal and seabird population, just outside the important port and beach resort of **Ilo,** which lies roughly midway between Mollendo and Tacna.

El Santuario Nacional Lagunas de Mejía

19km south of Mollendo, 4km south of Mejía • Daily 6am–5pm; office (*caseta*) daily 8am–5pm • S/30 • ⓣ 968 218 434 • Buses between Mollendo and Ilo pass in front of the entrance; alternatively hop on one of the combis that shuttle between Mollendo and Cocachacra (mainly in the morning)

El Santuario Nacional Lagunas de Mejía is an unusual ecological niche consisting of almost seven square kilometres of wetland – reed beds, saline marshes and lagoons – separated from the Pacific Ocean by just a sand bar, which is often covered in masses of **seabirds**. The reserve provides an important habitat for many thousands of migratory birds (Sept–March, best in Jan & Feb). Of the 200 species sighted at Mejía, such as occasional flamingos, spoonbills and ibis, around 72 are permanent residents, including nine species of heron; the best time for birdwatching is early in the morning.

Ilo

About 95km southwest of Moquegua, and halfway between Mollendo and Tacna on the desert coast, lies the busy port of **ILO**. With a population of over 67,000 inhabitants and an economy based around fishing and mining, its strategic and economic importance is likely to increase further once the international agreement allowing Bolivia access to the Pacific here becomes a reality. Though Ilo doesn't see many foreign visitors, it's a pleasant enough place to stop off for lunch, followed by a wander round the Plaza de Armas and along the neatly landscaped *malecón costero* (seaside promenade). Military buffs might consider popping in at the small **naval museum** by the Capitanía. With even more time to spare, consider setting aside 2–3 hours to visit at least one of Ilo's two worthwhile attractions just outside town: an archeological museum and a nature reserve.

Museo de Sitio "Chiribaya"

Municipalidad El Algarrobal, 12km east of Ilo • Mon– Fri 8am–3.30pm, Sat & Sun 9am–2pm• S/5 • ⓣ 053 290 033, ext108 • No public transport; a taxi from Ilo costs around S/30 return

The **Museo de Sitio "Chiribaya"** mainly showcases exhibits from the pre-Hispanic local culture of the same name, including textiles, ceramics, utensils and mummies – notably of a dog, probably cherished for taking care of a llama herd. The museum also offers **views** over the Valle de Algarrobal and the old Hacienda Chiribaya (1000–1350 AD).

Punta Coles

6km southwest of Ilo • Mon– Fri 8am tour (1hr, in Spanish) by appointment with SERNANP • Free • SERNANP, Bello Horizonte H-12, Ilo, ⓣ 053 471 805; contact Brian Oblitas in advance, ⓔ boblitas@sernanp.gob.pe • Take a colectivo to Playa Pozo LIzas and walk the remaining 600m, or take a taxi (S/5)

Hidden behind a high wall, the small rocky headland nature reserve **Punta Coles** is topped by a black-and-white striped lighthouse. Only accessible via a **guided tour** arranged in advance with the local SERNANP office, it's a bit of a hassle to visit, but is a worthwhile diversion for nature enthusiasts whose Spanish is up to the task. On the other hand, you can see the same species more easily and in greater numbers – though alongside many more tourists and at greater cost – further up the coast at Paracas (see page 115). In addition to seals and penguins, expect to spot cormorants, boobies, pelicans and the strikingly smart Inca terns.

2

ARRIVAL AND GETTING AROUND

CARRETERA COSTANERA

MOLLENDO

By bus/colectivo Flores buses operate frequent services between Arequipa and Mollendo. Colectivo minivans leave across from the market behind the main terminal in Arequipa, and in Mollendo, from the Terminal Terrestre just outside town (S/15). From Tacna or Moquegua, take an Arequipa-bound bus, getting off at El Fiscal; from there, colectivos leave regularly for Cocachacra, on the coast, where another car or a combi will take you on to Mejía or Mollendo. To go south, you can either head back to the Panamericana Sur, or go to Ilo by combi, where you can easily connect with Moquegua and Tacna by bus or minivan.

Destinations Arequipa (frequent daily; 2–3hr); Ilo (several daily; 2hr).

ILO

By bus Some of the long-distance buses arrive at or leave from their various terminals along Matará and Moquegua, a couple of blocks from Ilo's main plaza, though most are in the process of moving to the new bus station on Av Panamericana. Buses to Bolivia leave from the corner of Matará and Junín.

Bus companies Cruz del Sur (T 053 482 071) and TEPSA (T 053 481 051) share a terminal at the corner of Matará and Jr Moquegua. In the Terminal Terrestre: Oltursa (T 053 570 390); Cial (T 053 630 511); Civa (T 053 483 555); Flores (T 053 482 512).

Destinations Arequipa (frequent daily; 4hr); Desaguadero (2 daily; 7hr); Lima (several daily; 18hr); Moquegua (several daily; 2hr); Puno (several daily; 7hr); Tacna (several daily; 2hr30min).

ACCOMMODATION AND EATING

MOLLENDO

Hostal La Cabaña C Comercio 240 T 054 534 671. Inexpensive rooms in a down-at-heel but lovely wooden building with verandas and patio; the family rooms with shared bath and the en-suite doubles both have hot water (although water pressure is an issue), and service is average. Rooms overlooking the plaza, though noisy, have a glimpse of the sea. Cheaper midweek. Breakfast not included. S/100

Hostal Plaza C Arequipa 209 T 054 532 460. The most expensive option near the plaza, but it feels calmer and better cared for. The rooms are also cleaner and more welcoming than most options in town and the service is friendly. No breakfast. S/105

Marco Antonio C Comercio 258 T 054 534 258. A modern, stylish design is backed up by a tasty seafood-focused menu. Good for a midday ceviche, or the daily lunchtime special, or a more elaborate *corvina* in seafood sauce. Daily 9am–10pm.

ILO

Hotel VIP Jr 2 de Mayo 608 T 053 481 492, W viphotelilo.com. This is a very modern five-storey hotel whose bar and restaurant area on the top floor has pleasant views over the nearby port; rooms are carpeted and well equipped with TV, fridge-bar and good bathrooms. S/180

Sargoloco Cevichería C Moquegua 506 T 953 682 100. They make a killer ceviche (S/20–30) and serve up a good range of other seafood dishes. Near the plaza and popular, so service is slow at times. Daily 9am–5pm.

Tacna and around

Over two hours south of Moquegua and five times larger, **TACNA**, at 552m above sea level, is the last stop in Peru. If you're coming from or going over the border with **Chile** (see page 151) the city makes a surprisingly pleasant break; it has an attractive, tidy centre, with a more Chilean than Peruvian feel about it – and indeed Tacna was part

2

of Chile until as recently as 1929. Notably, it is a designated **Zona Franca** (a tax- or duty-free zone – with plenty of contraband in the mix), where visitors can stock up on a range of tax-free electronic, sports and other luxury items. The thriving cross-border trade means there are plenty of well-priced business hotels and several decent restaurants to choose from, though you'll struggle to find a bed if your visit coincides with the annual Feria Internacional de Tacna (FERITAC) held during the last week of August in the Parque Perú; this giant **trade fair** includes shows, craft and traditional food stalls, and a lot of queuing. The *semana turística* at the end of October provides another excuse to party and additionally features folk singing, dancing and sporting competitions.

Brief history

Founded as San Pedro de Tacna in 1535, just three years after the Spanish first arrived in Peru, Tacna was established by Virrey Toledo as a *reducción de indigenas*, a forced concentration of normally scattered coastal communities, making them easier to tax and exploit as labour. Almost three hundred years later, in 1811, Francisco Antonio de Zela began the first struggle for independence from Spanish colonialism here. The people of Tacna suffered Chilean occupation from May 1880 until the Treaty of Ancón was signed in August 1929, following the results of a local referendum. The town's importance in Peruvian conflicts against both Spain and Chile is acknowledged in its sobriquet, the "Ciudad Heroica", which soon becomes apparent once you've taken note of the various military-themed museums and monuments scattered around town. The most strident of these stands around 10km northwest of Tacna (15min by taxi; S/8 one way), on Cerro Intiorko, where some eight steel sculptures of **Campo de Alianza** stand in memory of the Guerra del Pacífico's war heroes; a small *museo de sitio* (daily 8am–5pm; free) houses some old uniforms, arms and missiles left over from the historic battles.

The town centre

With no Plaza de Armas, the main focus of activity in this sprawling city is the elongated **Paseo Cívico** – which tapers into **Avenida San Martín**. At the centre of the ersatz plaza stands an ornamental *pileta*, designed by Gustave Eiffel, while the nearby Arco Parabólico was erected in honour of the Peruvian dead from the Guerra del Pacífico. Fronting the plaza is the **Catedral de Nuestra Señora del Rosario**, also designed by Eiffel, in 1870 (though not completed until 1955). Two blocks south, the **Alameda Bolognesi** is an attractive, palm-lined avenue constructed in 1840; bristling with businesses, it's also dotted with busts of local dignitaries and a fine marble statue of Cristóbal Colón (Christopher Columbus).

The city museums

Tacna possesses several small, niche-interest museums, none of which are must-see attractions. The text-heavy **Museo Histórico Regional de Tacna** (Jr Apurímac 202; Mon–Sat 9am–6pm; free) focuses on the nineteenth-century war with Chile. In contrast, the attractive colonial-era **Casa de Zela** (C Zela 542; Mon–Sat 8am–5.30pm; S/1.50) chronicles the life of Francisco Antonio de Zela, who is credited for mounting the first Peruvian resistance against the Spanish in 1811. His efforts ended in failure, and resulted in his eventual death in prison in Panama. On the corner of Calle Albarracín and Avenida 2 de Mayo, the **Museo Ferroviario** was being renovated at the time of writing, but will attract rail enthusiasts when it eventually reopens; it contains locomotives, machinery and documents mainly relating to the Tacna–Arica line, but also a collection of train-themed stamps from around the world. On Avenida Grau, the small **Parque de la Locomotora** is dedicated exclusively to housing an antique locomotive which carried Peruvian troops to the historic battle of Morro de Arica in 1879.

Petroglifos de Miculla

Km 20–25 road to Palca from Tacna • Visitor centre daily 8am–5pm • S/1 • Taxis charge S/30–40 including wait time; alternatively take a colectivo from outside the Tacna Centro mall to the thermal baths in Pachía and get out at the *desvío*, from where it's a 2.5km walk

One of the largest collections of petroglyphs in South America, **Los Petroglifos de Micullla,** lies a mere fifteen-minute drive outside town. Around 1500 engravings are on boulders sprinkled across an area of around twenty square kilometres. Beyond the small **interpretive centre** at the entrance, a **walking circuit** – which includes two swing bridges suspended above the stones, and a couple of viewing towers – allows you to get close to around 500 of the etchings. Most depict humans carrying out everyday activities, such as hunting or transporting goods; others suggest more ceremonial or ritualistic activities, with the cults of water and fertility prominent themes. Animals, plants and constellations also feature in smaller numbers. Although traces of human habitation in the area date back to 5000 BC, experts estimate the carvings to be from between 500 BC and 1500 AD, but are unsure about their function. Some theorists posit that the glyphs are forms of communication between people crossing on the trade routes between the coast and the altiplano, while others believe the rock art to be of more spiritual or ceremonial significance.

If you have more time, and a sense of adventure, consider visiting the fabulously vivid **cave paintings** of Vila Vilani, another forty-minute drive up the valley, near Palca – ask the tourist office in Tacna for the contact details of the local community guides, who can accompany you from the village of Vilvilani on the two-hour hike (one-way) to the caves.

Tarata and Ticaco

85km by road north of Tacna, on the way to Puno • Baños termales de Putina daily 5.30am–4.30pm • S/6 for the main pool, S/8 per 30min for the private pool • Colectivos from the Terminal Bolognesi and from a bus stop (*paradero*) in the Alto de Alianza district run regularly to Tarata – take a taxi to either place.

A popular day trip from Tacna – using local transport or on a tour (see below) – explores the area round **TARATA,** a small town in a surprisingly verdant, picturesque Andean setting, some two hours north by road. It's an area where Tihuanaco, Aymara and Inca cultures have all made their presence felt – traces remain in the petroglyphs, rock paintings, burial sites, spectacular agricultural terracing and other archeological ruins that can be visited on any excursion. Add to that waterfalls, views of snow-capped volcanoes and delicious thermal pools and you potentially have an idyllic day out.

One of the highlights is to hike the two kilometres up the valley from the village of **TICACO** – itself 10km further up the road from Tarata – along a well preserved stretch of the Qhapaq Ñan (Inca Highway), to the **thermal baths**. Nestled in a narrow valley, the baths consist of one outdoor pool and several hotter, private indoor pools. Avoid the crowds by visiting early in the morning, on a weekday, or, better still stay overnight in Tarata; in addition to the attractive, rustic *Tarata Lodge y Mirador* (@taratalodgeymirador.com), the town has a couple of basic lodgings.

ARRIVAL AND GETTING AROUND — TACNA AND AROUND

BY BUS/COLECTIVO

Most long-distance buses arrive at and leave from the Terminal Terrestre Nacional, on Manuel Odria on C Hipólito Unanue (T 052 427 007). The terminal is 1.5km from the city centre – a 25min walk, or short bus or taxi ride away; take a taxi after dark. Next door, the Terminal Terrestre Internacional accommodates buses to and from Arica in Chile. Flores buses (for Ilo, Moquegua and Arequipa) leave from their own stop on Av Saucini, round the back of the main bus station. Occasional minivans bound for Desaguadero and the Bolivian border leave from Terminal Collasuyo on Av Albarracín, in the Alto de Alianza district. Shorter-distance local buses for the interior of the region leave from the Terminal Bolognesi on Av Circunvalación (T 052 411 786); Tarata buses depart from here, though more frequent minivans leave from a bus stop (*paradero*) in the Alto de Alianza district.

Destinations Arequipa (several daily; 6hr); Arica, Chile (frequent daily; 1–2hr); Cusco (several daily; 14–16hr); Desaguadero (1 daily at 6.30pm; 8hr); Ilo (frequent daily; 2hr 30min); Lima (frequent daily; 20–21hr); Moquegua (several daily; 2–3hr); Nazca (frequent daily 13–14hr); Puno (several daily; 8–9hr).

BY PLANE

The airport, Aeropuerto Carlos Ciriani Santa Rosa, is out on the Panamericana Sur at Km 5 (T 052 572 072). The airlines that fly here have offices in town: LATAM, Apurímac 101 (T 01 213 8200); Peruvian Airlines, Av Bolognesi 670 (T 052 412 699).

Destinations Arequipa (seasonal; 45min); Lima (daily; 1hr 45min).

BY TRAIN

For a more sedate ride to or from Arica, Chile, travel by train. In Tacna, the train station is two blocks from the Plaza de Armas on Av Albarracín and Av 2 de Mayo (ticket office 8am–5pm; T 052 611 824). There are two daily departures (6am & 4.30pm from Tacna, 10am & 8.30pm from Arica; 1hr 15min; S/18).

BY TAXI

Taxis can be stopped anywhere in the centre with ease at any time of day and the fare for destinations within the city should not be any more than S/5–7.

INFORMATION

Tourist information The main iPerú office is at Av San Martín 491 (Mon–Sat 8.30am–6pm, Sun 8.30am–1pm; T 052 425 514), and there are iPerú information desks at the bus terminal (Mon–Sat 8.30am–1pm, 2.30–6pm), airport and Santa Rosa border control (Mon–Sat 7am–7pm).

CROSSING THE CHILEAN BORDER

The **border with Chile** (open 24hr) is just under 40km south of Tacna, at Santa Rosa on the Peruvian side, and Chaculluta on the Chilean side. Travellers only make one stop to carry out immigration and customs formalities for both countries: at Santa Rosa for those entering Peru, and at Chaculluta for those entering Chile. Arica, the first town in Chile, lies around 20km beyond the border, with hotels, restaurants, banks and excellent bus and air services to the rest of the country. Note that Chile is one hour ahead of Peru from mid-May to mid-August, but two hours ahead when daylight saving operates from mid-August to mid-May.

By bus and colectivo Frequent buses (approx 5am–8pm; S/12) and colectivos (approx 5am–10pm; S/20) to Arica leave from the Terminal Terrestre Internacional on Hipólito Unanue, in Tacna (T 052 427 007). In Arica, buses and colectivos leave for Tacna from the Terminal Internacional on Av Diego Portales 1002 (Chile T 056 58 341390).

By train There are now two daily train services between Tacna and Arica (see page 150). Immigration formalities are carried out in the waiting room of the two train stations 30min prior to departure, and at the other end on arrival.

ACCOMMODATION

Casa Andina Select C Billinghurst 170 T 052 580 340, W casa-andina.com; map p.148. This new addition to Peru's high-class chain provides top-notch service and has all the business amenities you'd expect– rooftop pool, top-class restaurant, gym and spa – while light, well-appointed rooms boast the usual trimmings: minibar, safe, desk, tea- and coffee-maker, plus sparkling bathrooms. S/290

Gold Infinity C Deustua 346 T 052 425 816, W hotelgoldinfinitytacna.com; map p.148. Grander than it sounds, and with (a light) breakfast included, decent beds and monsoon showers in some of the bathrooms, this new budget hotel is a good deal. S/85

Hostal Hogar C 28 de Julio 146 T 052 426 811, W hostalhogartacna.com; map p.148. This reliable option has clean, tidy secure rooms with slightly old-fashioned furnishings and cable TV. It is centrally located, half a block from the Plaza de Armas. No breakfast. S/80

Hotel Tambo Real C Hipolito Unanue 180 T 052 426 562, W hoteltamboreal.pe; map p.148. Modern, business-oriented hotel but with family rooms too, offering excellent value for money and a central location. Beds are supremely comfortable and the compact rooms fit in a wardrobe, desk, and bedside tables with phone. Enjoy great city views with your buffet breakfast in the sunny sixth-floor cafeteria. S/150

Nice Inn C Hipólito Unanue 147 T 052 280 152, E nice_inn@yahoo.com; map p.148. Literally a stone's throw from the centre, this crisp, new hotel has bright rooms – some with patio – helpful staff, and a tasty continental breakfast. S/138

EATING

Bocadeli Pasaje Vigil 68; map p.148. Traditional hole-in-the-wall joint where locals flock at lunchtime for an inexpensive two-course *menú del día* (S/13) or a la carte mains (S/22–26). Does breakfasts (from S/9) and fresh juices, too. Mon–Sat 9am–10pm.

Restaurante Mar Adentro Av Pinto 28 T 052 426 027; map p.148. A dressed up *cevichería* with modern stone walls, skylights and pot plants; the higher than average prices are well worth it. Go for the *fuente fría* (S/75) – a mixed platter to share – or order their delicious fish of the day in a seafood sauce (S/35). Daily 11am–4pm.

Restaurante Uros Av San Martín 608 T 052 421 851, W restauranteuros.com; map p.148. If you're fed up with seafood and craving some meat, this is the place to come. Not as good as it thinks it is, but this atmospheric restaurant with smart waiters, sophisticated decor and ambiance delivers succulent slabs of hot-stone Andean meat – the sides are less impressive. Mains around S/40. Mon–Sat 11am–11pm, Sun 11am–5pm.

Arequipa and Lago Titicaca

TAQUILE, LAGO TITICACA

Arequipa and Lago Titicaca

While the southern coast of Peru boasts all manner of intriguing cultural sites, the adjacent interior of the south is much better known for its extremely beautiful geographical features. The Andes take hold here, punctuated by spectacular lakes, towering volcanoes and deep, stark canyons – a landscape well suited to adventurous outdoor pursuits like trekking, canoeing, climbing or mountain biking. The region has two distinct areas: one focused around Arequipa, not far removed from the coast, though high above sea level; the other, surrounding Lago Titicaca, high in the east at the northern end of the immense Altiplano, which stretches deep into Bolivia. Both are detached from the rest of the country, something reflected as much in political leanings as their landscapes, themselves unique in Peru.

Arequipa, second city of Peru and a day's journey from Lima, sits poised against an extraordinary backdrop of volcanic peaks. Located 2335m above sea level, the city enjoys a distinctly poetic appearance. If you're coming from the north, it's one of the last places to really merit a lengthy stop before continuing on south to the **Chilean border** (see page 151). White local stone from the surrounding mountains has been heavily incorporated into the city's buildings and was a major factor in Arequipa's *centro histórico* being designated a UNESCO World Heritage site. Trekkers from across the world are attracted by the startlingly varied countryside within the city's reach: from the gorges of both the **Cañón del Colca** – massive but dwarfed by the volcanoes on either side of the valley – and the more distant **Cañón de Cotahuasi**, to the unsettling isolation of the **Valle de los Volcanes**.

Further inland from Arequipa, you'll probably want to spend time at the world's highest navigable lake, **Lago Titicaca**. The surrounding area is renowned for its folk dances and Andean music and this is an obvious place to break a journey from Arequipa to Cusco or into **Bolivia**. Visit and stay on one of the islands, or on the mainland, to experience life in a very traditional Andean household or get to know its main town and port – **Puno**, a high, quite austere city with a cold climate and incredibly rarefied air.

Arequipa

With a population of well over a million, **AREQUIPA** maintains a rather aloof attitude towards the rest of Peru. Most Arequipeños consider themselves to be distinct, if not culturally superior, and resent the idea of the nation revolving around Lima.

Situated at the foot of an occasionally snow-tufted volcano – **El Misti** (5821m) – and close to four other prominent volcanoes, Arequipa has long been famous for having one of the most beautiful settings and pleasant climates of all Peru's cities. Despite a disastrous earthquake in 1687, it's still endowed with some of the country's finest colonial **churches** and **mansions**, many of which were constructed from white and pinkish-white volcanic *sillar*, cut from the surrounding mountains – the reason, some say, why the city is dubbed "La Ciudad Blanca".

Characterized by arched interior ceilings, Arequipa's architectural beauty comes mainly from the colonial period. In general, the style is stark and almost clinical, except where Baroque and *mestizo* influences combine, as seen on many of the fine sixteenth- to eighteenth-century facades. A huge number of religious buildings are spread about

MIRADOR CRUZ DEL CÓNDOR, CAÑÓN DEL COLCA

Highlights

1 Arequipa Carved out of striking white *sillar* rock, the city's *centro histórico* boasts a majestic collonaded Plaza de Armas, an imposing cathedral and the evocative, labyrinthine Monasterio de Santa Catalina, against the glorious backdrop of El Misti. See page 154

2 La Calera Wallow, swim and relax in the fantastic hot springs of La Calera, a short distance from Chivay at the head of the Valle del Colca. See page 177

3 Mirador Cruz del Cóndor A breathtaking viewpoint on the canyon rim offers sightings of wild condors swooping above and below. See page 178

4 Hiking in the Cañón del Colca Trek into the heart of the arid Cañón del Colca; visit the popular pools of verdant Sangalle oasis, or seek out less well-known hot springs, cascading falls and a bubbling black geyser. See page 179

5 Cañón de Cotahuasi One of the deepest canyons in the world, this remote valley – accessible by overnight bus – boasts soaring condors, Inca ruins, spectacular mountains and dramatic waterfalls. See page 183

6 Islas Taquile and Amantani These islands on Lago Titicaca offer a genuinely fascinating glimpse of what life must have been like five hundred years ago. See pages 196 and 198

HIGHLIGHTS ARE MARKED ON THE MAP ON PAGE 156

the old colonial centre. The architectural design of the **Monasterio de Santa Catalina**, a convent complex enclosing a complete world within its thick walls, constitutes perhaps the city's main appeal to travellers. Further out, but still within walking distance, you can visit the attractive suburbs of **San Lázaro**, **Yanahuara** and **Cayma**, this last being renowned for its dramatic views of the valley.

One of the best months to visit Arequipa is August, when the city commemorates its foundation with a whole month of cultural, sporting and entertainment events; Semana Santa is also celebrated in style (see page 170).

Brief history

Arrowheads and rock art are proof of human occupation around Arequipa for over ten thousand years. This began with early groups of hunter-gatherers arriving here on a seasonal basis for several millennia from 8000 BC to around 1000 BC, when horticulture and ceramic technology began to appear in small settlements along streams and rivers. Initially influenced by the Paracas culture and later by the Tiahuanaco-Huari, two major local groups emerged sharing the area: the **Churajone** living in the far northwest section of the Arequipa region, and the **Chuquibamba** who thrived higher up in the Andean plateaus above Arequipa until the arrival of the Incas.

Etymologists wrangle over the origin of the name Arequipa, though it is most commonly thought to derive from the **Quechua** phrase "*ari quepay*", meaning "Let's

stop here". According to local legend, this is exactly what the fourth Inca emperor, **Mayta Capac**, said to his generals on the way through the area following one of his conquest trips.

Colonial development

The Incas were not alone in finding Arequipa to their liking. When a lieutenant of **Pizarro** officially "founded" the city in 1540, he was moved enough to call it Villa Hermosa, or Beautiful Town. Later *Don Quixote* author Miguel de Cervantes extolled the city's virtues, saying that it enjoyed an eternal springtime. The lovely white stone lent itself to extravagant buildings and attracted skilled architects to the city.

The wool trade

During the eighteenth and nineteenth centuries, this mountainous region became an important source of sheep and alpaca **wool exports**, largely to the UK. Connected to the rest of Peru only by mule track until 1870, Arequipa was slow to become the busy provincial capital it is today. A railway connecting the city with Puno in the highlands and Matarani on the coast was built in 1876, while money made mainly from exports kept the economy growing enough to establish an electric urban tramway in 1913 and then a road up to Puno in 1928.

Political upheaval

The city has a reputation for being *the* centre of **right-wing political power**; while populist movements have tended to emerge around Trujillo in the north, Arequipa has traditionally represented the solid interests of the oligarchy. Important politicos, such as Francisco Javier de Luna Pizarro, who was president of Congress on many occasions in the nineteenth century, came from Arequipa. Sánchez Cerro and Odría both began their **coups** here, in 1930 and 1948 respectively, and Belaúnde, one of the most important presidents in pre- and post-military coup years, sprang into politics from one of the wealthy Arequipa families.

Modern Arequipa

By 1972 the city's population had reached 350,000. Twenty years later it passed half a million, with many people arriving from the Andean hinterland to escape the violence of Peru's civil conflict. Since 1990, the city's population has doubled due to the continued rural-urban migration of families looking to make a better living in the city.

The **social extremes** are quite clear today; despite the tastefully ostentatious architecture and generally well-heeled appearance of most townsfolk in the touristy areas, there is much poverty in the city, and in the region more generally. Social polarization came to a head in 2002, when the city's streets were ripped up in mass political protests against President Toledo's plans to sell off the local electric utilities.

Plaza de Armas

The **Plaza de Armas**, one of South America's grandest, is very much the focus of the city's social activity in the early evenings, dotted with palms, flowers and gardens. At its heart sits a bronze fountain, topped by an angel fondly known as *Turututu* because of the trumpet it carries. The east and west sides of the plaza are dominated by fine granite portals and colonial-style wooden balconies, while the southern edge is taken up by a municipal building.

La Catedral

Plaza de Armas • **Cathedral** Mon–Sat 7–10am & 5–7pm, Sun 9am–1pm • Free • **Museum** Mon–Sat 10am–4.10pm • S/10, plus S/5 for the optional guide • T 054 213 149, W museocatedralarequipa.org.pe

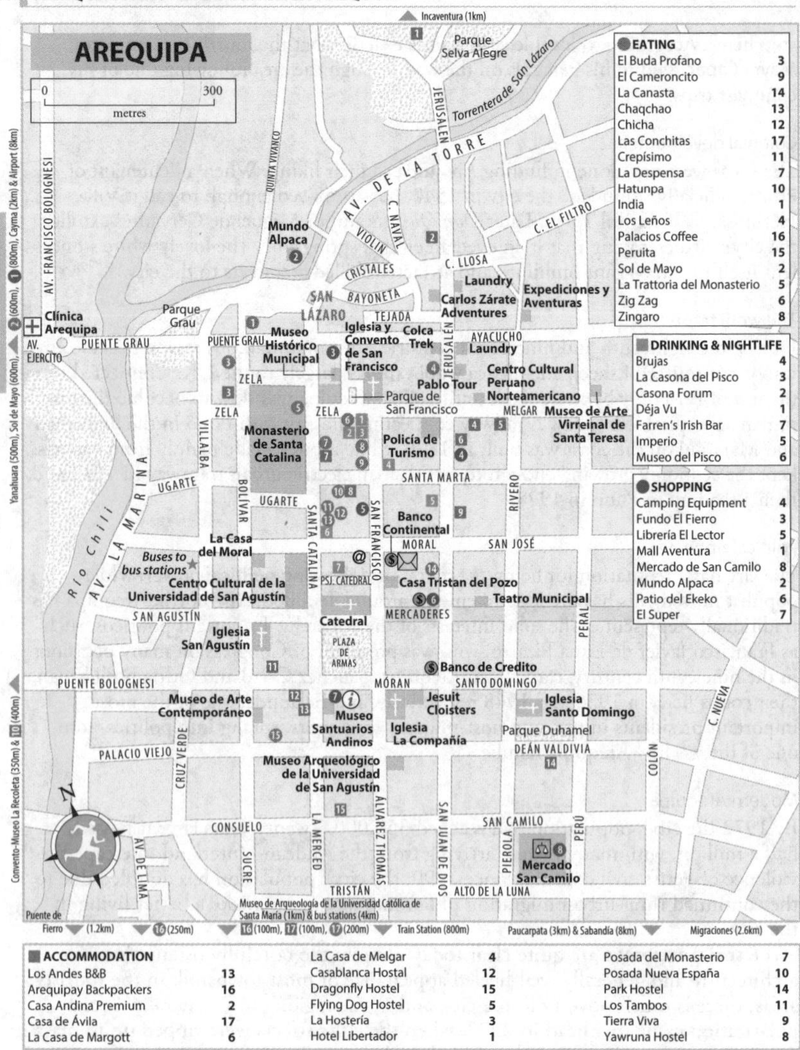

The arcades and elegant white facade of Arequipa's seventeenth-century **Catedral** demand attention, even drawing your eyes away from El Misti towering behind. Displaying some French influence in its Neo-Renaissance style, it looks particularly beautiful when lit up in the evenings. Consecrated in 1556, the cathedral building was subsequently gutted by fire in 1844 and restored in 1868 by Lucas Poblete, before coming to grief again in 2001 when its impressive Neoclassical towers were seriously damaged in an earthquake.

The cathedral's pulpit was brought over from Lille in France in 1879, while the large organ with a height of 15m, shipped over to Peru in 1854, is one of the largest in South America. Entry to the adjacent **Museo de la Catedral**, which houses impressive religious artefacts, grants access to the **bell tower** from where there are wonderful views of the city and beyond.

Iglesia de La Compañía de Jesús

Calles General Morán and Álvarez Thomas • Mon–Fri 9am–12.30pm & 3–7.30pm, Sat 9am–12.30pm, Sun 10am–12.30pm • Free • 054 212 141

On the southeast corner of the Plaza de Armas, opposite the Catedral, and more exciting architecturally, sits the elaborate **Iglesia de La Compañía de Jesús**. The original church, built in 1573, was destroyed eleven years later by an earthquake. The present structure was completed in 1660, when the magnificently sculpted **doorway**, with a locally inspired zigzagging *mestizo*-Baroque stone relief, was crafted using only shadow to outline the figures of the frieze. Inside, by the main altar, hangs a *Virgin and Child* by Bernardo Bitto, which arrived from Italy in 1575.

3

Jesuit cloisters

Cloisters open 24hr • **Capilla de San Ignacio de Loyola** Mon–Sat 9am–1pm & 3–6pm, Sun 9am–1pm • S/5 • 054 212 141

The adjacent **cloisters** exhibit similarly superb carving from the early eighteenth century. In the first cloister, squared pillars support white stone arches and are covered with intricate reliefs showing angels, local fruits and vegetables, seashells and stylized puma heads. The second cloister is, in contrast, rather austere, although it is home to the stunning seventeenth-century **Capilla de San Ignacio de Loyola,** whose cupola depicts images of warriors, angels and Evangelists, along with parrots, fruits and flowers with Spanish and Arab influences. Both cloisters now house **shops** and **cafés**.

Iglesia Santo Domingo

Calles Santo Domingo and Rivero • Daily 7.30am–9.30am & 3.30–6pm • Free

Two blocks east of the main plaza, you'll find the exquisitely restored **Iglesia Santo Domingo**, originally built in 1553 by Gaspar Báez, the first master architect to arrive in Arequipa. Most of what you see today was built between 1650 and 1698, but suffered major damage during the earthquakes of 1958 and 1960. The large main door represents an interesting example of Arequipa's *mestizo* craftwork – an indigenous face amid a bunch of grapes, leaves and cacti – and the side door is said to be the oldest in the city.

Casa de Tristan del Pozo

C San Francisco 108 • Mon–Fri 9am–1pm & 4–6pm, Sat 9am–1pm • Free • 054 215 060 ext 252

Opposite the northeast corner of the cathedral stands a particularly impressive colonial mansion, **Casa de Tristan del Pozo**, also known as La Casa Rickets. Built in 1738 as a seminary, it later became the splendid residence of the Rickets family, who made their fortune from the wool trade in the late nineteenth century. The building boasts an extremely attractive traditional courtyard and façade, whose stonework above the main door depicts Christ's genealogy. Now owned and lavishly restored by the Banco Continental, the mansion houses three art galleries.

Centro Cultural de la Universidad Nacional de San Agustín

C Santa Catalina 101 • Mon–Fri 8am–8.30pm • Free • 054 204 482

North of the Plaza de Armas, the Casa Arróspide (also known as the Casa Iriberri) forms part of the **Centro Cultural de la Universidad Nacional de San Agustín**. This attractive 1743 colonial building houses three main **art galleries** displaying mainly works by Peruvian artists that change regularly. It also hosts the occasional musical, theatrical or literary event.

La Casa del Moral

C Moral 318 • Mon–Sat 9am–5pm • S/5 • 054 285 371

The seventeenth-century **Casa del Moral** (literally "Mulberry House") has been lovingly restored and refurbished with period pieces. Its most engaging feature is a superb stone gateway, carved with motifs that are similar to those on Nazca ceramics – puma heads with snakes growing from their mouths – surrounding a Spanish coat of arms. The mansion's name comes from the ancient *mora* tree, whose wizened trunk – dead some 100 years – still stands defiantly in the central patio.

Iglesia San Agustín

Calles Bolívar and San Agustín • Daily 8am–12.30pm & 5–8pm • Free

One block west of the Plaza de Armas, the elegant 1575 **Iglesia San Agustín** has one of the city's finest Baroque facades, a late eighteenth-century addition. Its old convent cloisters are now attached to the university, while inside only the unique octagonal sacristy survived the 1868 earthquake.

Monasterio de Santa Catalina

C Santa Catalina 301 • Mon & Thurs–Sun 9am–5pm, Tues & Wed 9am–8pm • S/40; guides are optional at around S/20 for two people (1hr), S/5 to join a larger group • ⓣ 054 221, ⓦ santacatalina.org.pe

Two blocks north of the Plaza de Armas the vast walls of the **Monasterio de Santa Catalina** shelter a convent that housed almost two hundred secluded nuns and three hundred servants from the late sixteenth century until 1970, when it opened some of its outer doors to the public. The most important and prestigious religious building in Peru, its enormous complex of rooms, cloisters and tiny plazas takes an hour or two to explore. Some twenty nuns still live here today, though they worship in the main chapel only outside opening hours.

Originally the concept of Gaspar Báez in 1570, though only granted official licence five years later, the convent was funded by the Viceroy Toledo and the wealthy María de Guzmán, who later entered the convent with one of her sisters and donated all her riches to the community. The most striking feature is its predominantly Mudéjar style, adapted by the Spanish from the Moors, but which rarely found its way into their colonial buildings. The quality of the design is emphasized and harmonized by a superb interplay between the white stone and brilliant colours in the ceilings, the strong sunlight and deep-blue sky above the maze of narrow interior streets.

Los locutorios

After entering, turn left along the first corridor to a high vaulted room with a ceiling of opaque *huamanga* stone imported from the Valle de Ayacucho. Beside here are the **locutorios** – little cells where on holy days the nuns could talk, unseen, to visitors.

Claustro Novicias and Claustro de los Naranjos

The **Claustro Novicias** (Novices Cloister) beyond the *locutorios*, is built in solid *sillar*-block columns, with antique wall paintings depicting the various qualities to which the devotees were expected to aspire and the Litanies of the Rosary. Off to the right, the **Claustro de los Naranjos** (Orange Tree Cloister), painted a beautiful blue with birds and flowers over the vaulted arches, is surrounded by a series of paintings showing the soul evolving from a state of sin to the achievement of God's grace. In the *Sala de Profundis*, one of the side rooms, dead nuns were mourned, before being interred within the monastic confines.

La lavandería

Calle Córdoba runs from the Claustro de los Naranjos past a new convent, where the nuns now live. The road continues as Calle Toledo, a long, very narrow street that's the oldest part of the monastery and connects the main dwelling areas with the **lavandería**, or communal washing sector, brought to life with permanently flowering geraniums. There are several rooms off here worth exploring, including small chapels, prayer rooms and a kitchen. The *lavandería* itself, perhaps more than any other area, offers a captivating insight into what life must have been like for the closeted nuns; open to the skies and city sounds yet bounded by high walls. Twenty halved earthenware jars stand alongside a water channel, and it also has a swimming pool with sunken steps and a papaya tree in the lovely garden.

Plaza Zocodober and Sor Ana's rooms

Broad Calle Granada brings you from the *lavandería* to the **Plaza Zocodober**, a fountain courtyard, to the side of which is the *bañera*, where the nuns used to bathe. Around the corner, down the next little street, are **Sor Ana's rooms**. By the time of her death in 1686, 90-year-old Sor Ana was something of a phenomenon, leaving behind her a trail of prophecies and cures. Her own destiny in Santa Catalina, like that of many of her sisters, was to castigate herself in order to offer up her torments for the salvation of other souls – mostly wealthy Arequipan patrons who paid handsomely for the privilege. Sor Ana was beatified by Pope John Paul II in the 1990s.

Don't forget to climb the adjacent steps up to the *mirador*, which affords a fine view of the surrounding streets and rooftops – a pleasure not granted to the nuns.

The refectory and main chapel

The **refectory**, immediately before the main cloisters, is deceptively plain, with its exceptional star-shaped stained-glass windows shedding dapples of sunlight through the empty space. Nearby, confessional windows look into the **main chapel**, but the best view of its majestic cupola is from the top of the staircase beside the cloisters. A small room underneath these stairs has an intricately painted wall niche with a Sacred Heart centrepiece. The ceiling is also curious, illustrated with three dice, a crown of thorns and some other, less recognizable items. Within the quite grand and lavishly decorated **main chapel** itself, but not part of the tour these days, are the lower choir room and the tomb of Sor Ana.

El Claustro Mayor

The **Claustro Mayor (Main Cloisters)** is covered with murals on an intense ochre base with cornices and other architectural elements in white stone; the murals follow the life of Jesus and the Virgin Mary. Although the cloisters were originally a communal dormitory, their superb acoustics now make them popular venues for classical concerts and weddings and the space can absorb up to 750 people standing or 350 seated around tables.

Museo Histórico Municipal

Plaza de San Francisco 407 • Mon–Fri 8am–3pm • S/10 • ☎ 054 221 017

Just above the Monasterio de Santa Catalina, the small, leafy Plazuela de San Francisco, usually buzzing with students and townspeople, is where you'll find Arequipa's city museum, the **Museo Histórico Municipal**. It devotes itself principally to local heroes – army chiefs, revolutionary leaders, presidents and poets (including the renowned Mariano Melgar). Amidst the rather dull collection of memorabilia, is a more interesting display of photographs of the city showing earthquake damage over the years. However, the university's museums are of greater interest (see page 196).

Iglesia y Convento-Museo de San Francisco

Plaza de San Francisco • **Church** Mon–Sat 7.15–9am & 4–8pm, Sun 7.15am–12.45pm & 6.15–8pm • Free • **Convent/museum** Mon–Sat 9am–noon & 3–6pm • S/5 • ☎ 054 223 048

The Plaza de San Francisco is home to a striking Franciscan complex, dominated by a convent and the **Iglesia de San Francisco**. Yet another of Gaspar Báez's projects, this one dating back to 1569, it shows an interesting mix of brick and *sillar* work both inside and on the facade. Original paintings by Baltazar del Prado once covered the central nave, but the earthquake of 1604 destroyed these. However, the nave retains its most impressive feature – a pure-silver altar. Adjoining the church are rather austere convent cloisters and the very simple **Capilla de la Tercera Orden**, its entrance decorated with modest *mestizo* carvings of St Francis and St Clare, founders of the first and second orders.

Museo de Arte Virreinal de Santa Teresa

C Melgar 303 • Mon–Sat 9am–5pm • S/20 • ⓣ 054 281 188, ⓦ museosnatateresa.org

Located in the monastery of the same name, the **Museo de Arte Virreinal de Santa Teresa** has thirteen exhibition spaces set around beautiful cloisters dating from 1750 to 1753. The monastery's most valuable piece is the **custodia**, in Room 6, decorated with more than 2000 pearls and 250 precious and semi-precious stones including diamonds, rubies and amethysts, which continues to be used every year during Semana Santa (Holy Week) processions. Among the other objects on display are antique Chinese porcelain ceramics dating back to the era of Emperor Wanli (1573–1619), thought to have been family bequests to the monastery for taking in the young women. Nuns still live here – if you're visiting around noon you will hear them ring the monastery bells as they enter the premises to pray, though the **chapel** is only open for mass.

Convento-Museo La Recoleta

C La Recoleta 117 • Mon–Sat 9am–noon & 3–5pm • S/10 • ⓣ 054 270 966

The **Convento-Museo La Recoleta** is located on the western side of the Río Chili, which runs its generally torrential course through Arequipa from Selva Alegre, dividing the old heart of the city from what has become a more modern downtown sector, including Yanahuara (see page 164) and Cayma (see page 164). This large Franciscan monastery stands conspicuously alone on Callejón de La Recoleta, just ten to fifteen minutes' walk west of the Plaza de Armas, in an area undergoing renovation.

The stunning major and minor cloisters were built in 1651; in 1869 it was converted to an Apostolic Mission school administered by the Barefoot Franciscans. Although the place gives you a flavour of monastic life, it is the archeology and natural history **exhibitions** that really draw people here. They comprise two rooms of pre-Columbian artefacts including textiles and ceramics; an Amazon room showing artefacts from various indigenous groups and examples of forest flora and fauna; a religious and modern art gallery displaying both Cusqueña and Arequipeña classical works; plus a renowned historic **library** with some 23,000 sixteenth- and seventeenth-century volumes.

Museo Santuarios Andinos

C La Merced 110 • Mon–Sat 9am–6pm, Sun 9am–3pm • S/20; optional guide, fee negotiable • ⓣ 054 215 013, ⓦ ucsm.edu.pe/museo-santuarios-andinos

The **Museo Santuarios Andinos**, part of the Universidad Católica de Santa María, is arguably the most important museum in Arequipa today, with displays of some nineteen Inca mummies and a range of archeological remains. After an introductory video (available in several languages), most visitors head for the main exhibit: **Juanita** – or her occasional replacement mummy Sarita – the ancient 13-year-old "princess" uncovered in her icy ritual grave on September 8, 1995, by an expedition that included archeologists Johan Reinhard and José Chávez, along with the well-known *Andinista*

Miguel Zárate. Her gravesite, located at the incredible altitude of 6380m on Volcán Ampato, is estimated to be about 500 years old. It is thought that Juanita was sacrificed to the Apu Ampato and killed, after a time of fasting and herbal sedation, with a blow to the head by a five-pointed granite mace. The museum also contains fine examples of grave goods such as textiles, precious metals and ceramics.

Museo de Arqueología de la Universidad Católica de Santa María

C Cruz Verde 303 • Mon–Fri 8.30am–4pm • Free; donations expected • ⓣ 054 221 083, ⓦ ucsm.ed.pe

Distinct from Santuarios Andinos, but also a university affiliate, is the **Museo de Arqueología de la Universidad Católica de Santa María**. This museum has eight rooms concentrating on items from pre-Conquest cultures such as the Huari, Tiahuanuco, Chancay and Inca, and boasts around a thousand different pieces including stone weapons, ceramics, textiles, grave goods, as well as other worked and ancient stone, wood and metal objects. Explanations in Spanish only.

Museo Arqueológico de la Universidad Nacional de San Agustín

C Álvarez Thomas 200 • Mon–Fri 9am–4pm • S/2 • ⓣ 054 288 881, ⓦ unsa.edu.pe

The largest of Arequipa's archeological museums, the **Museo Arqueológico de la Universidad Nacional de San Agustín** has good collections of everything from mummies and replicas of Chavín stones to Nazca, Huari and Inca ceramics, as well as colonial paintings and furniture. There are more than 14,000 pieces held here at the university campus.

Casa-Museo Mario Vargas Llosa

Av Parra 101 • Mon–Sat 9am–2.30pm (last entry); by appointment, for a guided 2hr tour (in Spanish) • S/10 • ⓣ 054 283 574

A recent addition to the city's museum scene is the renovated childhood home of Peru's literary giant and renowned Arequipeño, the **Casa-Museo Mario Vargas Llosa.** It's a high-tech, interactive, multimedia romp (sadly only in Spanish) through the colourful life and achievements of the Nobel laureate. Sixteen rooms stuffed full of memorabilia are enhanced by 3D videos and holograms.

Museo de Arte Contemporáneo

C Sucre 204 • Mon–Sat 10am–3pm • S/3 • ⓣ 054 221 068

Recently relocated, the permanent exhibits of the **Museo de Arte Contemporáneo** are spread over four spacious rooms, displaying all manner of artwork, including photographs, from the mid twentieth century onwards.

San Lázaro

The oldest quarter of Arequipa – and the first place the Spanish settled in this valley – is the barrio of **San Lázaro**, an uncharacteristic zone of tiny, winding pedestrianized streets stretching around the hillside at the top end of Calle Jerusalén – all an easy stroll north from the plaza. You will be rewarded with some good views of El Misti.

Mundo Alpaca

Av Juan de la Torre 101, San Lázaro • Mon–Fri 8.30am–6.30pm, Sat 9am–6.30pm, Sun 9am–5.30pm • Free guided tour • ⓣ 054 202525, ⓦ mundoalpaca.com.pe

Exerting only mild pressure to purchase, **Mundo Alpaca** – a retail outlet for pricey alpaca knitwear (see page 170) – puts on free short guided (or self-guided) **tours** at the back of the shop. You'll learn to distinguish one camelid from another – several are grazing on the lawn – and follow the process from sorting the fibres to dying the wool and watching expert Andean weavers at work. Also on display are some fine prize-winning textiles and paintings.

Yanahuara

Until the late nineteenth-century railway boom, which brought rural migrants to Arequipa from as far away as Cusco, **Yanahuara** was a distinct village. It is now built up, though it still commands stunning views across the valley, above all from the elegant **mirador** (viewing point) on the pretty municipal plaza. There are also one or two fine **restaurants** in this sector.

To get here, catch a bus or colectivo from the junction of Puente Grau and Calle Santa Catalina, or walk from San Lázaro (see page 163).

Iglesia Yanahuara

Plaza Yanahuara • Mon–Fri 9am–noon & 4–8pm, Sat 9.30am–2.30pm • Free • ⓣ 054 253 664

The small **Iglesia Yanahuara** on the tranquil main plaza dates to the middle of the eighteenth century, and its Baroque facade is particularly fine, with a stone relief of the Tree of Life incorporating angels, flowers, saints, lions and hidden indigenous faces.

Cayma

These days, the upmarket suburb of **Cayma**, to the north of Yanahuara, reflects the commercial, even flashy side of Arequipa, with large shops and even one or two nightclubs. However, views of the northern volcanoes are still impressive from Cayma – earning it the sobriquet of "El Balcón de Arequipa", especially from the rooftop of the **Iglesia de San Miguel.**

Puente de Fierro

South of the city centre, Arequipa's very impressive black-iron viaduct, or **Puente de Fierro** – also known as the Puente Bolívar – provides a great vantage point for views over the city to El Misti. Designed by Gustave Eiffel, it has successfully spanned the city's bubbling **Río Chili** and withstood the test of Arequipa's severe earthquakes and tremors for well over a century.

ARRIVAL AND DEPARTURE — AREQUIPA

Arequipa is a popular stopping-off point between Lima and the Titicaca, Cusco and Tacna regions, and is a hub for most journeys in the southern half of Peru. From Arequipa you can continue to Cusco, or Lago Titicaca by bus, plane, or even on a three-day luxury train excursion with Peru Rail (see ⓦ perurail.com). **Bolivia** is also within a day's bus journey, while Tacna and the **Chilean frontier** (see page 151) are even more accessible from Arequipa by road.

BY PLANE

Flights by LATAM (ⓦ latam.com), Peruvian Airlines (ⓦ peruvian.pe), Viva Air (ⓦ vivaair.com) and Avianca (ⓦ avianca.com) land at Arequipa's Aeropuerto Alfredo Rodríguez Ballón, 8km northwest of town (ⓣ 054 443 464). Staff at the taxi counter will organize a ride to the centre for S/30 (30min).

Destinations Cusco (several daily; 1hr); Lima (frequent daily; 1hr 30min); Tacna, with Peruvian Airlines (1 daily; 30min).

BY BUS

Most long-distance buses use the Terminal Terrestre (ⓣ 054 427 798) about 4km south from the centre of town, or the newer Terrapuerto next` door. Regular buses for the city centre (*centro histórico*) leave from outside the bus station via Av La Marina, west of the city centre (30–40min); get off at the Puente Bolognesi, three blocks from the Plaza de Armas. Buses to the bus terminals pass along C Cruz Verde. A taxi to the plaza from either bus station is about S/10.

Destinations Andagua (2 daily; 10hr); Aplao (hourly; 3hr); Cabanaconde (6 daily; 5hr); Chivay (8 daily; 4hr); Cotahuasi (4 daily; 9–10hr); Cusco (several daily; 9–11hr); Ica (5 daily; 4hr 30min–5hr); Ilo (every 4hr daily; 4hr); Lima (frequent daily; 14–17hr); Moquegua (frequent daily; 3–4hr); Nazca (frequent daily; 5–6hr); Puerto Maldonado (2 daily; 16hr); Puno; (frequent daily; 6hr); Tacna (frequent daily; 5hr).

BUS OPERATORS

Del Carpio Terminal Terrestre (T 054 427 049) or Terrapuerto (T 054 430 941). Services to the Valle de Majes, Aplao and Pampacolca; also to Mollendo and Mejía.
Civa Terminal Terrestre (T 054 432 208). Services to Ayacucho, Cusco, Puno and Lima.
Cromotex Terminal Terrestre (T 054 451 555) and Terrapuerto (T 054 509 910). Services to Cotahuasi, Cusco, Lima and Tacna.
Cruz del Sur Terminal Terrapuerto (T 054 720 444, W cruzdelsur.com.pe). Services to Lima, Nazca, Paracas, Ica, Cusco, Tacna and Puno.
Flores Terminal Terrestre (T 054 431 646). Services to Tacna, Mollendo, Moquegua and Ilo.
Moquegua Turismo Terminal Terrapuerto (T 054 431 545). Services to Tacna and Moquegua.
MovilTours Terminal Terrapuerto (T 054 342 654). Services to Lima, Nazca, Ica and Cusco.
Oltursa Terminal Terrapuerto (T 054 423 152). Services to Lima, Nazca, Paracas, Ica and Tacna.
Ormeño Terminal Terrapuerto (T 054 427 788). Services to Puno.
Reyna Terminal Terrestre (T 054 425 812). The best services to Chivay and Cabanaconde; also to Cotahuasi and Puerto Maldonado via Juliaca, and daily overnight service to Andagua.
TEPSA Terminals Terrestre and Terrapuerto (T 054 424 135). International services, as well as to Lima.
Transportes Trébol Terminal Terrestre (T 958 608 646). Daily overnight bus to Andagua (10hr).
Turismo Alex Av Olímpico 203 (T 054 202 863). Services to Andaray and Chuquibamba.

GETTING AROUND

On foot The centre of Arequipa is compact and it's easy enough to walk around, especially as several areas are pedestrianized.
By taxi Recommended firms include Aló 45 (T 054 454 545, W taxialo45.com.pe), Taxi Mundo (T 054 200 900, T taximundo.com) and Taxitel (T 054 200 000). If you take a taxi off the street, make sure it has an official licence plate (with a yellow stripe).
By car Though most people travel by bus or take a tour, car rental (with or without *chófer*) for the brave is possible. Some companies rent out 4WD vehicles, including GyG at Palacio Viejo 214 (T 054 212 213, W gygrentacar.com) or at the airport (T 054 344834); DGA Rent a Car at Palacio Viejo 302A (T 054 281 741, W rentacar.com), and Atix Rent a Car at C Ugarte 216 (T 054 224 327, W atixrentacar.com).

INFORMATION

Tourist information The main iPerú office is on the Plaza de Armas (Mon–Sat 9am–6pm, Sun 9am–1pm; T 054 223 265, E iperuarequipa@promperu.gov.pe), with a branch at the airport that meets incoming flights (daily 6am–3pm; T 054 299 191). Those intending to visit the Cañón del Colca should swing by the helpful Autocolca office at C Puente Grau (daily 8.30am–5.30pm; 116 T 054 203 010).

TOURS AND ACTIVITIES

Taking a **guided tour** is the easiest way to negotiate the otherwise quite difficult region around Arequipa, though it's easy enough to get to the Cañon del Colca – the area's most visited attraction – using local transport. It's tricky to get around here in a number of ways – the sheer terrain is inhospitable, massive and wild, and the altitude changes between Arequipa city and, say, Chivay, can affect you for a couple of days (mountain sickness with headaches), which makes driving your own rented car dicey until you're properly acclimatized.

CITY TOURS

All operators tend to offer similar packages, with city tours lasting around three hours and usually including the Monasterio de Santa Catalina, La Compañía de Jesús, La Catedral, Iglesia San Agustín and the Yanahuara *mirador*. City walking tours cost around S/60–70. Several companies offer tips-only "free" walking tours, leaving from various central locations at 10am or 3pm; they usually involve some pisco and/or chocolate tasting as well as a tour of historical sights.
Bus tour Portal San Agustín 111 T 054 203 434, W bustour.com.pe. Offers a half-day open-top bus tour of the city and its outskirts – it starts from C Ugarte 211, and includes stops such as Puente Grau, Yanahuara and Carmen Alto, as well as the old mill at Sabandia and the Mansion del Fundador (see page 171). The tour (S/45) takes a circular route, departing twice daily at 9am & 2pm.

COUNTRYSIDE TOURS

Most companies also offer one- to three-day trips out to the Cañón del Colca (S/100–1500 per person) or to the petroglyphs at Toro Muerto (from S/200 per person, depending on group size). Trips to the Valle de los Volcanes and the Cañón de Cotahuasi are only offered by a select few companies (private tours from S/600 upwards). Specialist adventure activities, such as rafting in the Cañón del Colca, mountaineering or serious trekking can cost anything from S/400 to S/2000 for a three- to six-day outing. Of course, all prices vary according to the season, the quality you demand (in terms of guiding, food, transport to start point – using public transport considerably cuts your costs – and whether you have *arrieros* with mules to carry your gear) and the size of the group. Mountain-bike tours, whizzing down a volcano costs around S/150.

Carlos Zárate Adventures C Jerusalén 505 054 202 461, zarateadventures.com. Established by internationally renowned guide, Carlos Zárate, this is a good expedition outfitter and leading trekking and climbing company with decades of experience, and professional, qualified guides – hence the higher prices. Activities include rock climbing and canoeing in the usual places such as Colca, El Misti and Cotahuasi, mountain-biking, canyon and abseiling too, but they also offer ascents of nevados Mismi and Coropuna.

Colca Trek C Jerusalén 401B 054 206 217, colcatrekperu.com. A well-established company operating its own lodge in the Cañón del Colca, which acts as a base for hikes and climbs in the area. Also organizes trips to Cotahuasi, plus rafting and biking, and also has equipment for rent.

Expediciones y Aventuras C Rivero 504 054 284 289, expedicionesyaventuras.com. Adventure activities specialist offering rafting down the ríos Chili and Majes; canoeing in the Colca and Cotahuasi canyons; sandboarding and rock climbing, and even body boarding along the Pacific Coast. It also arranges downhill and cross-country mountain biking trips, including to Volcán Chachani (6057m).

Incaventura Av Gutemberg 405, Alto Selva Alegre 054 266 853, incaventura.com. Well-regarded specialists in climbing and trekking, who can organize expeditions to all the big volcanoes round Arequipa but also further afield such as the Inca Trail and Salkantay trek, for a minimum of two people.

Pablo Tour C Jerusalén 400A 054 203 737, pablotour.com. This reliable well-established company pioneered tourism in the Cañón del Colca in the 1990s, and has since been operating tours to Cabanaconde and the surrounding areas. It offers a four-day Colca adventure package involving mountain biking, hiking and rafting as well as trips to the Cañón de Cotahuasi, the Valle de los Volcanes and to the source of the Río Amazonas. Its registered mountain guides have the latest equipment.

ACCOMMODATION

Arequipa is awash with hostels and has a wide selection of accommodation in all price ranges, with most options within a few blocks of the Plaza de Armas.

HOTELS

Casa Andina Premium C Ugarte 403 054 226 907, casa-andina.com; map p.158. Previously housing the city's old *Mint* this upmarket hotel just a stone's throw from the Monasterio de Santa Catalina features a range of rooms, from modern superiors with standard business-style decor to lavishly furnished senior suites (S/670) set around a beautiful colonial courtyard. S/460

Casa de Ávila Av San Martín 116, Vallecito 054 213 975, casadeavila.com; map p.158. Simply furnished but comfortable rooms (with cable TV) set around a delightful shady and peaceful garden. Guests enjoy a convivial atmosphere, and fun Spanish or cooking classes (S/70) held on weekdays. S/175

★ **La Casa de Margott** C Jerusalén 304 054 229 517, lacasademargott.com; map p.158. Friendly family-run *hostal* offering compact rooms (singles, doubles and triples) featuring a cosy mix of red brick and white *sillar*. A couple boast small balconies and there's a shaded rooftop terrace open to all. S/120

★ **La Casa de Melgar** C Melgar 108 054 222 459, lacasademelgar.com; map p.158. This lovely eighteenth-century colonial building was once home to the Bishop of Arequipa. Set around several pretty plant-filled courtyards and gardens, spacious rooms feature fine parquet floors, antique furnishings and modern comforts. Breakfast is served in a bright blue courtyard, home to lofty cacti. S/160

Casablanca Hostal C Puente Bolognesi 104 054 221 327, casablancahostal.com; map p.158. With rather a monastic feel, this otherwise agreeable place right by the main plaza is constructed from volcanic blocks of stone. It features eight spacious en-suite rooms with lovely parquet floors. Some rooms have shared balconies overlooking the street, and there's a semi-open rooftop terrace. S/145

★ **La Hostería** C Bolívar 405 054 289 269, lahosteriaqp.com.pe; map p.158. A real gem boasting a pretty flower-filled courtyard and fountain, plus an attractively furnished interior with carved wooden benches, a piano and old curios. Superior rooms (S/340) are more stylish and spacious and worth the extra. All rooms have minibars and soft down bedding. The "Roman bath" and sauna are not to be missed. S/290

Hotel Libertador Plaza Bolívar s/n 054 215 110, libertador.com.pe; map p.158. The city's grand five-star hotel and conference centre boasts efficient service and well-appointed rooms with all the trimmings in a quiet neighbourhood a short walk north of town. Breakfast can be enjoyed in the dining area, in the palatial grounds, or by the large pool. S/452

Posada del Monasterio C Santa Catalina 300 ⓣ054 206 565, ⓦhotelessanagustin.com.pe; map p.158. Housed in a welcoming eighteenth-century *casona* (mansion), once part of the Monasterio de Santa Catalina, this pleasant hotel with stone walls, vaulted ceilings and antiques offers comfortable, modern rooms – carpeted or with faux-wooden floors – with orange bedspreads. S/211

Posada Nueva España C Antiquilla 106, Yanahuara ⓣ054 252 941, ⓦhotelnuevaespana.com; map p.158. Charming old house west of the Río Chili, in a safe and quiet neighbourhood, a 10min walk from the centre. Three floors of brightly painted, simple en-suite rooms (sleeping one to four) set round a small courtyard, with pleasant roof terrace and friendly service. S/95

Los Tambos Puente Bolognesi 129 ⓣ054 600 900, ⓦlostambos.com.pe; map p.158. A top central choice with modern rooms enlivened by warm earthy tones and autumnal abstract paintings. All rooms have flatscreen TV, large windows and double glazing – which cuts out any street noise. Impeccable service, free airport transfers and a la carte breakfasts are other pluses. Good online reductions. S/289

Tierra Viva C Jerusalén 202 ⓣ054 234 161, ⓦtierravivahoteles.com; map p.158. This fine mid-range choice offers 24 bright, well-appointed, carpeted rooms. The comfortable beds have orthopaedic mattresses draped with alpaca blankets, and the modern amenities include flatscreen TV, desk and safe. S/243

HOSTELS

Los Andes B&B La Merced 123 ⓣ054 330 015, ⓦlosandesarequipa.com; map p.158. A stone's throw from the Plaza de Armas, this is a decent budget choice – if a little institutional in feel – with a large, open-plan kitchen for self-caterers, a breezy terrace plus TV lounge. Accommodation is in dorms and spacious rooms with parquet flooring or carpets, shared or (for an extra S/55) private bathrooms. Dorms S/26, doubles S/65

Arequipay Backpackers Pasaje O'Higgins 224 ⓣ054 234 560, ⓦarequipaybackpackers.com; map p.158. A fun, friendly, brightly painted hostel with lots of common rooms: for movies, PlayStation, pool, darts or ping pong, plus a patio with hammocks and barbecue. Slightly cramped dorms have sturdy beds, lockers and shared bathrooms. Simple private rooms share bathrooms. Dorms S/25, doubles S/72

Dragonfly Hostel C Consuelo 209 ⓣ054 384 524, ⓦdragonflyhostels.com; map p.158. Abounding in bright murals and bean bags with colourfully decorated dorms and private rooms – both with clean shared bathrooms – this place has a chilled vibe with hammocks, ping pong and pool table to amuse. Dorms S/30, doubles S/95

★ **Flying Dog Hostel** C Melgar 116 ⓣ054 231 163, ⓦflyingdogperu.com; map p.158. Clean and welcoming rooms give onto colourful courtyards dotted with cacti. The cavernous bar is a good spot to meet fellow travellers, and there's a kitchen for self-caterers, too. Breakfast is served in a pretty patio area, and the place does all the usual hostel services well. Private bathroom costs an extra S/24. Dorms S/28, doubles S/75

Park Hostel C Deán Valdivia 238A ⓣ04 212275, ⓦparkhostel.net; map p.158. With more of a cheap hotel than a backpacker vibe, this popular converted house serves both local and international travellers in a central yet non-touristy street. Rooms are basically furnished, though with snug duvets. Socializing happens on the roof terrace, littered with chairs, tables and sunloungers. Also

AREQUIPAN DELICACIES

Arequipa's restaurants are famous across Peru for a range of delicious dishes that make use of local food resources such as *rocoto* (an indigenous type of pepper), guinea pig, peanuts, maize, potatoes, chillies and river shrimps. The city's specialities include:

Adobo Typically eaten for breakfast in Arequipa. This is a pork dish where the meat and bones are soaked and cooked in maize-beer sediment or vinegar, onions, garlic, boiled small *rocotos* and chillies.

Chupe de camarones River shrimp casserole incorporating squashes, cheeses, chillies and potatoes.

Cuy chactado The name comes from the flat, round stone – or *chaquería* – which is placed on top of a gutted and hung guinea pig to splay it out flat in a large frying pan, while cooking it in ample olive oil; it is usually served with toasted maize and a sauce made from chillies and the herb *huacatay* (black Andean mint).

Ocopa A cold appetizer that originated in this city but can be found on menus across Peru. It is made with potatoes, eggs, olives and a fairly spicy yellow chilli sauce, usually with ground peanuts added.

Rocoto relleno A spicy Andean pepper usually stuffed with minced pork meat and blended with garlic, tomato paste, eggs and mozzarella.

has a kitchen and small games/DVD room. Avoid the noisy rooms round reception. Dorms S/30, doubles S/85

★**Yawruna Hostel** C Ugarte 202 ⓣ941 312 69, ⓦjawrunahostel.com; map p.158. This recently renovated first-floor hostel has kept its colonial charm – moulded high ceilings, decorative tiled floors and wooden balustrades – but with modern arty touches too, especially on the fabulous plant-filled roof-terrace and bar. Both private and dorm rooms are en suite, with flatscreen TVs. Room only. Dorms S/25, doubles S/100

EATING

As it's not too far from the Pacific, the town's better restaurants are also renowned for their excellent fresh seafood. **Picanterías** – traditional Peruvian eating houses serving spicy seafood – are particularly well established here.

CAFÉS

La Canasta C Jerusalén 115 ⓣ054 204 025, ⓦlacanastabagueteria.pe; map p.158. This popular bakery tucked away off C Jerusalén offers a range of tasty, artisanal, organic goodies, including empanadas, sandwiches, cakes and quinoa and cheese croissants (S/4–13) – to take away or eat in the cosy courtyard café. Mon–Sat 8.30am–8pm.

★**Chaqchao** C Santa Catalina 204 ⓣ054 234 572, ⓦchaqchao-chocolates.com; map p.158. A chocaholic's paradise specializing in chocolate and only chocolate, every which way: from lip balm and soap to cakes, bars or hot drinks that you can enjoy on their small balcony. Daily chocolate-making classes (S/65). Daily 9.30am–11pm.

★**Crepísimo** C Santa Catalina 208 ⓣ054 206 620, ⓦcrepisimo.com; map p.158. This popular two-storey restaurant with a sunny patio out back boasts over one hundred types of sweet and savoury crêpes (S/15–26), plus a good lunch deal (S/32), which includes salad, crepe, dessert and drink. It's a great spot to linger at any time of day with craft beer on tap, loose-leaf teas plus a book exchange and board games. Daily 8am–11pm.

★**La Despensa** C Santa Catalina 302 ⓣ054 222 104, ⓦfacebook.com/ladespensa.aqp; map p.158. It's hard to fault this charming interior café, offering a fine array of light meals and snacks; it's great for artisanal breads, flavoursome quiches, fresh salads and mouth-watering cakes (S/6–15). Drinks score just as highly be it a macchiato, a glass of wine, juice or craft beer. Mon–Sat 10am–9pm, Sun 10am–4.30pm.

Palacios Coffee Av Lima 201, Vallecito ⓣ958 965 393, ⓦfacebook.com/TostaduriaPalaciosCoffee.com; map p.158. This gourmet coffee roasting parlour has a small café serving delicious cups from beans sourced from all over Peru, topped off with some fabulous latte art. Mon–Fri 10am–8.30pm, Sat 4–8.30pm.

RESTAURANTS

El Buda Profano C Bolívar 425 ⓣ997 228 590, ⓦelbudaprofano.com; map p.158. This vegan sushi restaurant is such a hit – with vegans and carnivores alike – that you may have to wait to claim one of only a handful of small wooden tables. Try the tasting menu for two (S/50), or a ceviche Serrano, made with beans and mushrooms (S/13). If that all sounds too healthy, indulge yourself with a choco-maki dessert. Daily noon–9pm.

El Cameroncito C San Francisco 303A, ⓣ054 202 080, ⓦconsorciobongourmet.com; map p.158. One of several restaurants under the same roof, but that doesn't detract from the quality; expect ample portions of swordfish, sea bass, crab or shrimps, and efficient service. Prices may be touristy (S/34–55), but worth it. The double billing of ceviche with *chaufa de mariscos* (fried rice and seafood) is a winner. Daily 11am–11pm.

Chicha C Santa Catalina 210 ⓣ054 287 360, ⓦchicha.com.pe; map p.158. One of renowned chef Gastón Acurio's top-quality restaurants; set in a fine colonial mansion, you can dine at a table set with crisp white linen, or at more informal courtyard tables. Dishes range from Arequipan regulars such as *rocoto relleno* to more esoteric fare such as Alpaca curry with quinoa (most mains S/40–60). Mon–Sat noon–11pm, Sun noon–6pm.

★**Las Conchitas** Av San Martín 200 ⓣ054 223 672; map p.158. This small and friendly local hangout off the tourist beat serves excellent fresh fish and seafood dishes at very reasonable prices. The crab empanadas (S/6) are delicious, as are the ceviche (S/24) and steamed fish with *yuca* or rice. Tues–Sun 10am–5pm.

Hatunpa C Ugarte 208 ⓣ054 212 918; map p.158. This cheap and cheerful restaurant attracts a young foreign crowd with its potato-based dishes (S/14–21). Everything on the menu features potatoes with a topping of choice, including meat or veggies. The food is cooked in front of your eyes in the little open-plan kitchen. Mon–Sat 12.30–9.30pm.

India C Bolívar 502 ⓣ958 095 318, ⓦfacebook.com/restauranteindiaarequipa; map p.158. Winning no awards for ambiance, this Indian-Peruvian enterprise scores highly on spice – and it can be hot – and flavour. Curries, masalas, vindaloos and kormas are all there (S/15–28) but the jalfrezis in particular hit the sensory spots. Mon–Sat 1–9pm.

Los Leños C Jerusalén 407 ⓣ054 281 818; map p.158. This little place with stone walls and wooden tables rustles up a handful of pasta dishes and decent wood-fire oven pizzas (from S/23) served on rustic wooden boards. The Provençal pizza topped with aubergines, peppers, onion and black olives is particularly good. Daily 5–11pm.

Peruita Palacio Viejo 321 ⓣ054 212 621; map p.158. This Italian-owned and -run pizzeria with chequered red-and-white tablecloths serves wood-fire-oven pizzas (from S/22). Also featuring pasta, ravioli and lasagne, and there's an excellent-value menu del día on weekdays (S/10–15). Service can be desultory, though. Mon–Fri 1–3pm & 5.30–10.30pm, Sat 5.30–10.30pm.

Sol de Mayo C Jerusalén 207, Yanahuara ⓣ054 254148, ⓦrestaurantsoldemayo.com; map p.158. This Arequipan institution has been dishing up well-prepared traditional cuisine for over a century. Most tables are set within and around attractive gardens, and live Andean folk music plays every afternoon. The place is popular with tour groups – so pick your day and book a (garden) table in advance; and expect tourist prices (mains from around S/38). A 15min walk (S/6 taxi ride) from the city centre. Daily 11am–6pm.

★ **La Trattoria del Monasterio** C Santa Catalina 309 ⓣ054 204 062, ⓦlatrattoriadelmonasterio.com; map p.158. Located within the grounds of the Monasterio de Santa Catalina, this is one of the city's best restaurants. The interior is warm and welcoming with three intimate dining areas while the cuisine offers superb fusion dishes that combine the best of Italian and Peruvian flavours. The ravioli and fettuccine are all home-made, and the creamy *Arequipa risotto* with lima beans, peas and shrimps is divine. Mon–Sat noon–3pm & 7–11pm, Sun noon–3pm.

★ **Zig Zag** C Zela 210 ⓣ054 206 020, ⓦzigzagrestaurant.com; map p.158. A wonderful restaurant, with a cosy vaulted interior, specializing in sizzling, volcanic-stone-cooked meats and fish. The "Alpine" menu includes Swiss favourites such as cheese fondue (S/92 for two people) and there's a great-value three-course lunch menu at S/57. The bar-lounge area with snug fireplace is perfect for a digestif. Daily noon–11pm.

Zingaro C San Francisco 309 ⓣ054 217662, ⓦzingaro-restaurante.com; map p.158. In the heart of town, this smart restaurant with bare-brick walls serves some innovative Peruvian dishes. The menu includes trout fillet stuffed with mint and bacon (S/48) and alpaca *lomo saltado* (S/33), while the extensive wine list has over three hundred bottles, which you can sample in their convivial wine bar area. Daily noon–11pm.

DRINKING AND NIGHTLIFE

Most of Arequipa's nightlife in the historical centre takes place on or around calles San Francisco and Zela, which are lined with bars, pubs and clubs that get particularly busy Thursday to Saturday. For a younger, more local vibe, and cheaper drinks, head for the scene on Avenida Dolores, but take a taxi and arrange to be picked up later.

BARS

Brujas C San Francisco 300, ⓣ959 339 860; map p.158. Relaxed bar with a cosy wooden interior and low lighting; a great spot for those wanting to enjoy a beer and a chat without their voices being drowned out by pumping music; though when football's on the big screen, it can get noisy. Daily 6pm–3am.

★ **La Casona del Pisco** C San Francisco 319A ⓣ054 231 809, ⓦcasonadelpisco.com; map p.158. This classy gastro-bar has four ancient earthenware jugs used to store pisco in the first of several vaulted rooms where tastings take place. There's a patio with outdoor heaters, an open-fronted glass kitchen in the back garden and a terrace with spectacular views of the Iglesia de San Francisco. A range of live music Thurs–Sat. Mon–Wed noon–11pm, Thurs–Sat noon–1am.

Farren's Irish Bar Pasaje Catedral 107 ⓣ054 201 239; map p.158. Classic Irish bar tucked away behind the cathedral, providing predictable comforts: Guiness, imported beers, including Old Speckled Hen and Abbot Ale (S/20), and football-match screenings. Tues–Sat 10am–midnight.

Museo del Pisco Calles Santa Catalina and Moral ⓣ054 281 583, ⓦmuseodelpisco.org; map p.158. With dozens of labels to choose from, it's the perfect spot for a pisco sour, particularly if you're after a quiet place where you can socialize over a drink or two. Also offers cocktail-making classes. Daily 5pm–midnight.

CLUBS AND LIVE MUSIC

Casona Forum C San Francisco 317 ⓣ054 204 294, ⓦcasonaforum.com; map p.158. This three-storey complex houses some of Arequipa's best nightspots: the mellow *Zero Pub & Pool*, with pool; the basement *Forum* disco, *the* place to see and be seen among young *Arequipeños*, with a lively tropical decor including palm trees, pools and a large artificial waterfall; and *Retro*, which favours classic rock, and where live groups hit the stage nightly at 10pm. Tues–Sat 7pm–late.

Déja Vu C San Francisco 319B ⓣ054 221 904, ⓦdejavuaqp.com; map p.158. The appealing terrace, with sofas and views over town, make *Déja Vu* a particularly pleasant spot for a sundowner. It morphs into a club at night, with big-name DJs mainly playing an eclectic mix of salsa and dance music on the ground floor and electronica on the first floor. Free dance classes Thurs and Fri. There's a S/10 cover charge on weekends after 11.30pm. Mon–Wed & Sun 11am–3am, Thurs–Sat 11am–5am.

Imperio C Jerusalén 201A ⓣ972 419 693; map p.158. Well-established LGBTQ nightspot, offering dancing until dawn plus drag acts and themed nights. Fri & Sat 9pm–late.

3

3

FESTIVALS IN AREQUIPA

Though Arequipa abounds in cultural **festivals** throughout the year, **August** is arguably the liveliest month to visit when the city celebrates its foundation with an exhausting month-long calendar of events. Highlights include Peru's biggest **trade fair**, the ten-day **Feria Internacional de Arequipa** (wfia.pe), out at the convention centre by Cerro Juli; skip the agricultural machinery and corporate stands, and head for the craft and food stalls, dancing, folk music, competitions and demonstrations – from karaoke to dog shows. The month-long **Feria de Artesanía**, based in and around the Fundo de Ferro (see page 170) attracts exhibitors from across Peru and even further afield; you can count on artisans competing in wood turning, stone carving, metalwork and ceramics, plus parades, beauty pageants and a **mountaineering race** up El Misti. On the main day, August 15, the streets transform into a riot of colour, as a massive **parade** – the Corso de Amistad (Friendship Procession) – of elaborate floats, dance troupes and marching bands progresses noisily through town.

Semana Santa is also fun in Arequipa, culminating in an effigy of **Judas** being burnt in the rural suburb of Paucarpata on Easter Sunday, and finishing off later with an extravagant **fireworks** display.

ENTERTAINMENT

Alianza Francesa C Santa Catalina 208 ⓣ054 215 579, ⓦafarequipa.org.pe. Regular French film showings (with subtitles, usually in Spanish), art exhibitions and occasional theatre or music.

Centro Cultural Peruano Norteamericano Melgar 109 ⓣ054 391 020 ⓦcultural.edu.pe. Hosts workshops, films, photography exhibitions and theatre.

Instituto Cultural Peruano-Alemán C Ugarte 207 ⓣ054 218 567, ⓦicpa.org.pe. The Peruvian-German culture institute shows good films in Spanish and German and frequent classical music recitals.

Teatro Municipal C Mercaderes 239 ⓣ054 282 303. Outside Arequipa's anniversary programme (see above), when the theatre hosts various performances and musical competitions the theatre only puts on occasional, generally musical events.

SHOPPING

The centre of the alpaca textile industry, Arequipa is also a great place to pick up other souvenirs and gifts. Inevitably, quality and prices vary from the chic shops along Calle Santa Catalina and tucked away in Pasaje Catedral to the small hole-in-the-wall workshops on Puente Bolognesi, which sell leather goods and musical instruments, especially guitars. East of the Plaza de Armas, the busy pedestrianized Calle Mercaderes is worth browsing for its eclectic mix of clothes shops, cafés and fast-food outlets, punctuated by the odd splash of colonial architecture.

Camping Equipment C Jerusalén 300 ⓣ054 213 384; map p.158. A number of tour agencies rent out camping gear. Otherwise, there are several camping stores clustered on C Jerusalén, among them this decently stocked shop selling various essentials including tents, walking boots and torches. Mon–Sat 9am–1pm & 3–8pm.

Fundo El Fierro C San Franciso 415; map p.158. Tucked away under the arches round the courtyard of this former prison is a collection of shops displaying a real rag-bag of often indifferent artesanía, though there are finds to be had. The selection is best in August during the annual craft fair (see above). Individual shop opening hours are erratic but theoretically daily 9am–6pm.

Librería El Lector C San Francisco 213 Cercado ⓣ054 288677, ⓦellector.com.pe; map p.158. Stocks a wide range of English-language books, including many on the history and wildlife of Peru. Mon–Sat 9am–8pm.

Mall Aventura Av Porrongoche 50, Paucarpata, 3km southeast of the centre; map p.158. With plenty of choice in terms of clothing, food, electronic and household items, the largest of the city's malls contains several big-brand stores, including outdoor gear specialists Tatoo. The newer Mall Aventura in Cayma is nearer, only a 15min walk west of Puente Grau along Av Ejercito. Both daily 10am–10pm.

Mercado de San Camilo Nicolás de Piérola, Block 4; map p.158. Arequipa's main market is one of the largest and liveliest in Peru. Its stalls are crammed with everything from llama meat, vegetables and herbs to inexpensive artesanía, shoe repairs, juices and cheap food. Daily 7am–6pm.

Mundo Alpaca Av Juan de la Torre 101, San Lázaro ⓣ054 202525, ⓦmundoalpaca.com.pe; map p.158. In addition to housing exclusive Sol de Alpaca garments, this place is a factory outlet for the whole Michell group, so you'll find handmade woollen rugs alongside shawls and sweaters. Mon–Fri 8.30am–6.30pm, Sat 9am–6.30pm, Sun 9am–5.30pm.

Patio del Ekeko C Mercaderes 141 ⓣ054 215 861, ⓦelekeko.pe; map p.158. A plush mall with silverware, artesanía, clothing – including a branch of Kuna (chic alpaca knitwear) and quality food: a good place to buy gifts. Mon–Sat 10am–9pm, Sun 11am–8pm.

El Super Portal de la Municipalidad 130 ⓣ054 202 573, ⓦelsuper.com.pe; map p.158. Located right on the main square, this is the city's most central supermarket. Mon–Sat 8.30am–10pm, Sun 9am–8pm.

DIRECTORY

Consulates There are several honorary or full consuls in Arequipa for the UK and other European countries, as well as for Peru's bordering South American neighbours. For up-to-date contact details check ⓦembassypages.com/peru.

Immigration Migraciones, Urb. Quinta Tristan, 2nd park, Distrito José Bustamante y Rivero ⓣ054 421 759 (Mon–Fri 8am–4pm, Sat 8am–noon). It's 4km from the centre; a taxi should cost S/8–10

Health For hospital treatment and a 24hr pharmacy, head for Clínica Arequipa at Puente Grau and Av Francisco Bolognesi (24hr; ⓣ054 599 000, ⓦclinicaarequipa.com.pe); Inka Farma is at Mercaderes 214 (7am–midnight).

Language schools Arequipa is a good place to linger and learn Spanish. Recommended schools include Ceica Peru, C Los Arces 257A (ⓣ054 250 722, ⓦceica-peru.com) and Rocio Language Classes, Ayacucho 208, Oficina 22 (ⓣ054 224 568, ⓦspanish-peru.com); both offer Spanish courses to suit all levels.

Laundry There are plenty of laundry places on C Jerusalén to the north of the main plaza; charges are around S/5 a kilo.

Banks and exchange For foreign cards the best are Banco de Crédito at C San Juan de Dios 125 and Scotiabank at C Mercaderes 410; Banco Continental is at C San Francisco 108.

Police Policía de Turismo, C Jerusalén 315A (24hr; ⓣ054 239 888).

Post office Serpost is at C Moral 118 (Mon–Fri 8am–8pm, Sat 8am–7pm).

Around Arequipa

Though the spectacular countryside immediately surrounding Arequipa is gradually being taken over by the growing tentacles of urbanization, there are still one or two oases of calm within half an hour's bus ride from the centre, worth a diversion if you've time to spare. Most people visit these sites on an **organized trip** with one of the tour companies in Arequipa (see page 165), but it's much cheaper by **public transport**.

Around 8km southeast of the centre, the main attraction of the village of **Sabandia** is its renovated seventeenth-century colonial **mill** (daily 9am–6pm; S/10) fronted by lawns happily grazed by alpacas and llamas. Slightly further out, to the southwest and nestled in the fertile Valle de Socabaya, stands the historic **Mansión del Fundador** (daily 9am–5pm; S/15; ⓣ054 213 423). Once owned by the original founder of Arequipa, Don Garcí Manuel de Carbajal, it now houses a colonial museum with period furnishings and attractive gardens. Both sights are reachable by public bus, from Avenida de la Paz and Avenida de la Independencia, respectively.

Climbing the enticing and majestic cone of **El Misti**, however, is a whole different level of undertaking (see page 173). So too is reaching the **Reserva Nacional de Salinas y Aguada Blanca** – Arequipa's nearest protected area – to enjoy herds of roaming vicuñas and migratory birdlife, and beyond, the ancient rock paintings of the **Cuevas de Sumbay.** These last two destinations can be visited en route to or from the Cañón del Colca, but even when the sun is out the wind can be bitter, temperatures may barely top freezing, and public transport is very infrequent, so you need to be well prepared.

Reserva Nacional de Salinas y Aguada Blanca

117km north of Arequipa, by main road • Centro de Interpretación daily 8.30–noon • Free • You can take a bus bound for Chivay; alternatively, a daily 7am bus leaves from Grifo Chambilla in the suburb of Paucarpata for San Juan de Tarucani and passes the Laguna de Salinas, returning to Arequipa around 3pm (confirm the return time when you get off)

Covering some 3000 square kilometres of plateau behind El Misti is the **Reserva Nacional de Salinas y Aguada Blanca**, the largest protected area in this region, located at 4000m above sea level. A cold and dry *puna* (a high Andean ecological zone

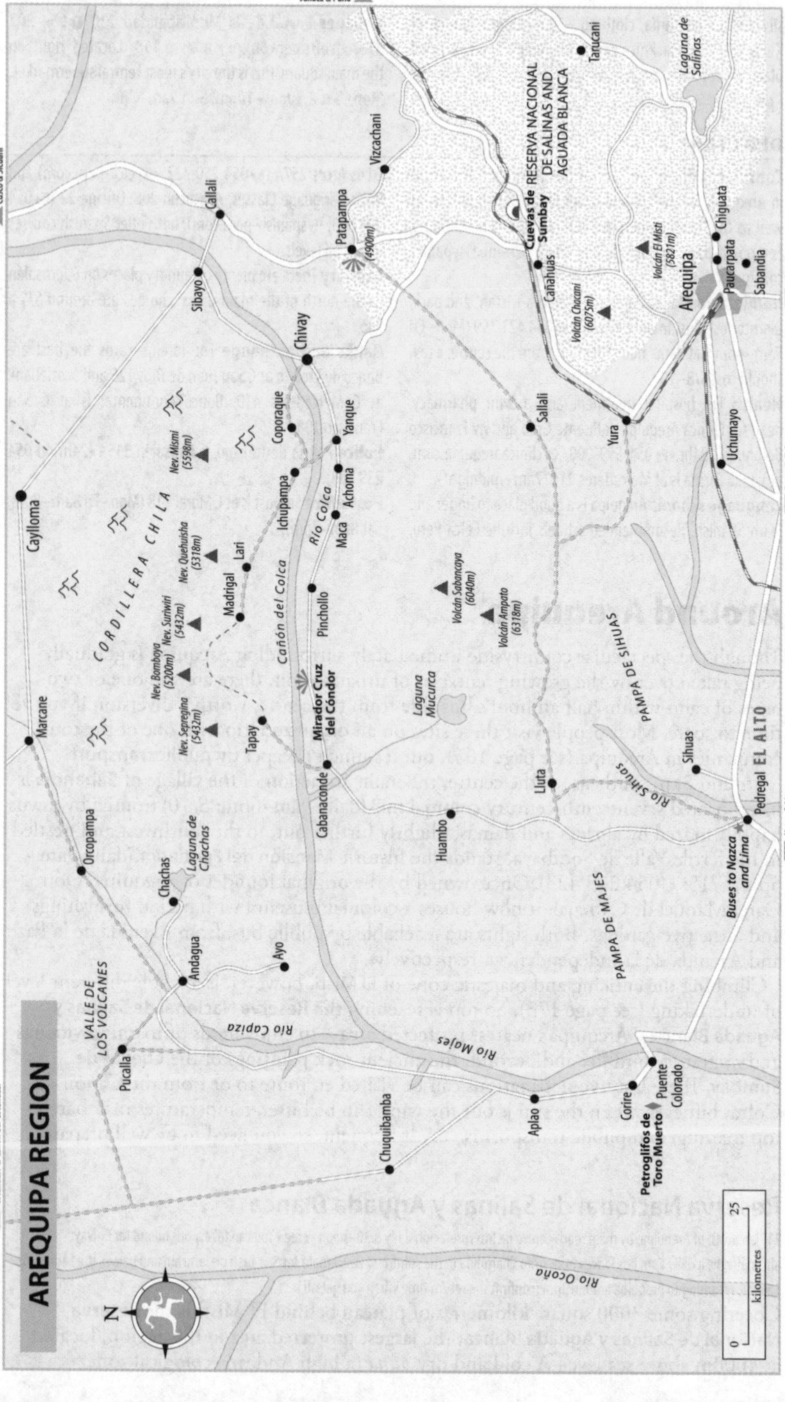

3

AREQUIPA REGION
Juliaca & Puno
Cusco & Sicuani
Cotahuasi & Cañon del Cotahuasi
Chapi
Tacna & Chile
Nazca & Lima
RESERVA NACIONAL DE SALINAS AND AGUADA BLANCA
Laguna de Salinas
Tarucani
Vizcachani
Cuevas de Sumbay
Patapampa (4900m)
Callali
Sibayo
Chivay
Cañahuas
Volcán El Misti (5821m)
Volcán Chacani (6075m)
Chiguata
Paucarpata
Sabandia
Arequipa
Yura
Uchumayo
Sallali
Coporaque
Yanque
Achoma
Ichupampa
Maca
Lari
Madrigal
Pinchollo
Río Colca
Cañón del Colca
Nev. Mismi (5598m)
Nev. Quehuisha (5318m)
Nev. Suriwiri (5432m)
Nev. Bomboya (5200m)
Nev. Sepregina (5432m)
CORDILLERA CHILA
Caylloma
Marcane
Orcopampa
Chachas
Laguna de Chachas
Andagua
Ayo
VALLE DE LOS VOLCANES
Pucalla
Río Capiza
Río Majes
Chuquibamba
Aplao
Corire
Puente Colorado
Petroglifos de Toro Muerto
Mirador Cruz del Cóndor
Tapay
Cabanaconde
Laguna Mucurca
Huambo
Volcán Sabancaya (6040m)
Volcán Ampato (6318m)
Lluta
PAMPA DE SIHUAS
Sihuas
Río Sihuas
PAMPA DE MAJES
EL ALTO
Pedregal
Buses to Nazca and Lima
Río Ocoña
0 kilometres 25
N

CLIMBING EL MISTI

If you feel compelled to climb **El Misti** (5821m), 20km northeast of Arequipa, bear in mind that it's considerably further away and higher than it looks from Arequipa. That said, it's a perfectly feasible two-day hike. Though non-technical, it can be a gruelling ascent, not least because much of the climb is through sand or scree – walking poles are recommended – though you should be rewarded by magnificent views of the surrounding volcanoes and a chance to peer inside a crater or two. The altitude too makes it tough, and about a quarter of those who attempt the climb don't make the summit, often because they are not fully acclimatized. If you are an experienced mountaineer, it's possible to tackle the volcano on your own (with IGN map Characato) but you are strongly advised to seek the assistance of a qualified guide, since every year someone gets lost in the area. Either contact the guiding association office directly (Pasaje Desaguadero 126, San Lázaro Ⓔ agmp-arequipa@pasadeguias.com.pe), or go with a recommended tour operator (see page 165). To spend the night on El Misti, you'll need at the very least food, water (there's none on the mountain), warm clothing, boots and a good sleeping bag. Your main enemies will be the altitude and the cold night air, and during the day you'll need to wear some kind of hat and sunblock as the sunlight is particularly strong. There is likely to be snow on the summit during the wettest months (Jan–March), in which case crampons and ice axes may be needed. Note that unless the agency offers porter service, you will need to carry your tent, sleeping bag and water as far as base camp. Most agencies begin the climb for the summit at night, to arrive just after sunrise or at least by mid-morning, to avoid the hottest part of the day. All-inclusive trip prices with the most professional operators range from US$150 to US$220 per person. A personal porter (10–15kg maximum) costs around US$75–95. There are three main routes to the summit; the most popular two are:

THE AGUADA BLANCA ROUTE

Arguably the "easiest" route and the one most popular with agencies, though independent hikers will need a permit to cross the reserve, and will need to pay for private 4WD transport to/from the trailhead. Base camp is at Monte Blanco at 4800m, a four- to five-hour hike from the drop-off point at the reservoir in the Reserva Nacional de Salinas y Aguada Blanca (3700m), which in turn is a two-and-a-half-hour drive from Arequipa. The ascent usually takes five to six hours, and the descent back to the trailhead a mere two hours.

THE GRAU ROUTE

Popular because you can take public transport here; colectivos marked "Chiguata" leave every twenty minutes from Avenida Sepulveda in Arequipa and will drop you at the trailhead (3400m). From here there's a four- to six-hour hike to base camp at Campo Pirámides Alto (4610m). From base camp it's another breathless five to seven hours to the summit, followed by a two-hour descent.

located above the treeline), it's a great place to spot groups of wild vicuñas, while its reservoirs – El Farile and Aguada Blanca – are known for their excellent trout fishing. You'll cross the reserve on the way to Chivay or Cusco from Arequipa. The **Laguna de Salinas**, which fills with brackish waters during the rains, hosts three types of flamingoes, among other birdlife, and can be reached via a daily bus from the suburb of Paucarpata, or on a private tour.

Las Cuevas de Sumbay

Off Km 88 off the main Arequipa–Chivay road • Daily 9am–4pm • S/5

Really only reachable with your own transport, the entrance to **Las Cuevas de Sumbay** is signposted at Km 88 on the main road from Arequipa towards Chivay and also Cusco, down a bad track to the near-deserted village of Sumbay (4532m), about 1.5km away. Here you'll need to ask around for the custodian who can lead you to the caves, down into a small canyon just before the bridge. The caretaker will have to unlock a gate to give you access to the site. Although small, the main Sumbay cave contains a series of 8000-year-old rock paintings representing shamans, llamas, deer, pumas and vicuñas. The surrounding countryside is amazing in itself: herds of alpacas roam gracefully around the plain looking for *ichu* grass to munch, and vast sculpted rock strata of varying colours mix smoothly together with crudely hewn gullies.

El Cañón del Colca

Some hundred and sixty kilometres north of Arequipa the **CAÑÓN DEL COLCA** is one of the country's most extraordinary natural sights. Called the "Valle de las Maravillas" (Valley of Marvels) by the Peruvian novelist Mario Vargas Llosa, it is in places nearly twice the depth of Arizona's Grand Canyon and is claimed by some to be one of the deepest canyons in the world at more than 1km from cliff edge to valley bottom. That said, it is deemed to be slightly shallower than its more remote rival, the Cañón de Cotahuasi (see page 183). In places the canyon's sides are so steep that it is impossible to see the valley bottom, while the higher edges of Colca are punctuated with some of the finest examples of pre-Inca terracing in Peru, attributed in the main to the Huari cultural era. Craggy mountains, huge herds of llamas and traditionally dressed Andean farmers complete the picture. After Machu Picchu, the Cañón del Colca is Peru's most visited attraction; one of its main draws – beyond the area's outstanding natural beauty – is the **Mirador Cruz del Cóndor**, where several condors, symbols of the Andes, can be seen flying most mornings. Colca is also a popular **trekking** and canoeing destination (best in the dry season, May–Sept).

The canyon was formed by a massive geological fault between the two enormous volcanoes of Coropuna (6425m) and Ampato (6318m): the Río Colca forms part of a gigantic watershed that empties into the Pacific near Camaná. To the north of Colca, meanwhile, sits the majestic **Nevado Mismi**, a 5597m-high snow-capped peak that belongs to the Chila mountain range, and which, according to most current experts' thinking, is the source of the Amazon.

Many tourists do a long day's haul or an overnight trip to the canyon from Arequipa, neither of which really does justice to the place. There are a number of beautifully sited rustic lodges and upmarket hotels sprinkled around the canyon, which make it perfect for a longer stay. Besides, hikers keen to explore the depths of the canyon or the surrounding peaks will definitely need several days.

The standard bus tour takes you along the sinuous road that skirts the canyon's southern rim, stopping off at various viewpoints, including the Mirador Cruz del Cóndor, and a couple of the villages to look at their splendid churches; it also usually includes a visit to the **hot springs** at La Calera. Although the canyon's main access point is the diminutive provincial capital of **Chivay,** the sleepier town of **Cabanaconde,** some 56km west, makes a better base for descending into the canyon, as well as offering its own fabulous mirador across the canyon. It is also possible to hire local guides, mules and muleteers there.

Brief history

Francisco Pizarro's brother, Gonzalo, was given this region in the 1530s as his own private *encomienda* (colonial Spanish landholding) to exploit for economic tribute. In the seventeenth century, however, Viceroy Toledo split the area into *corregimientos* that concentrated the previously quite dispersed local populations into villages. This had the effect of a decline in the use of the valley's agricultural terracing, as the locals switched to farming the land nearer their new homes.

The *corregimientos* created the fourteen main settlements that still exist in the valley today, including Chivay, Yanque, Maca, Cabanaconde, Coporaque, Lari and Madrigal. Most of these villages still boast unusually grand, Baroque-fronted **churches**, underlining

CAÑÓN DEL COLCA – BOLETO TURÍSTICO

Exploring any part of the Cañón del Colca requires you to buy a **Colca Boleto Turístico** (general tourist ticket), which costs S/70 and is valid for a week. It grants you access to the Mirador Cruz del Cóndor, other main *miradores* and all the major churches in the valley. It also covers entry to the Reserva Nacional de Salinas y Aguada Blanca and the Valle de los Volcanes. Tickets are sold at the Autocolca office on the main square in Chivay (T 054 203 010, W autocolca.pe), or in **Pinchollo** (see page 178) and **Cabanaconde** (see page 181) on the main plaza. Don't worry if you can't locate the ticket sales points; someone waving a receipt book will inevitably track you down, sometimes the moment you step off the bus.

the importance of the region's silver mines during the seventeenth and eighteenth centuries. During the Republican era, Colca's importance dwindled substantially and interest in the zone was only rekindled in 1931 when aerial photography revealed the astonishing landscape of this valley to the outside world – particularly the exceptionally elaborate terracing on the northern sides of bordering mountains.

Chivay and around

Surrounded by some of the most impressive and intensive ancient terracing in South America, **CHIVAY**, 163km north of Arequipa and just under four hours by bus from there, lies at the heart of fantastic hiking/mountain biking country. Although not a particularly appealing town, nor a good place from which to observe the canyon, Chivay is nevertheless bustling with tourists and serves as the main base for exploring the canyon area.

The town possesses a notable **market**, located along Avenida Salaverry, where you'll also find a slew of artesanía shops. The town has a growing range of accommodation options, restaurants and bus services for these visitors, making it a reasonable place to stay while you acclimatize to the altitude. The only attraction as such is the **planetarium**, where most evenings there are presentations in English and Spanish (S/20).

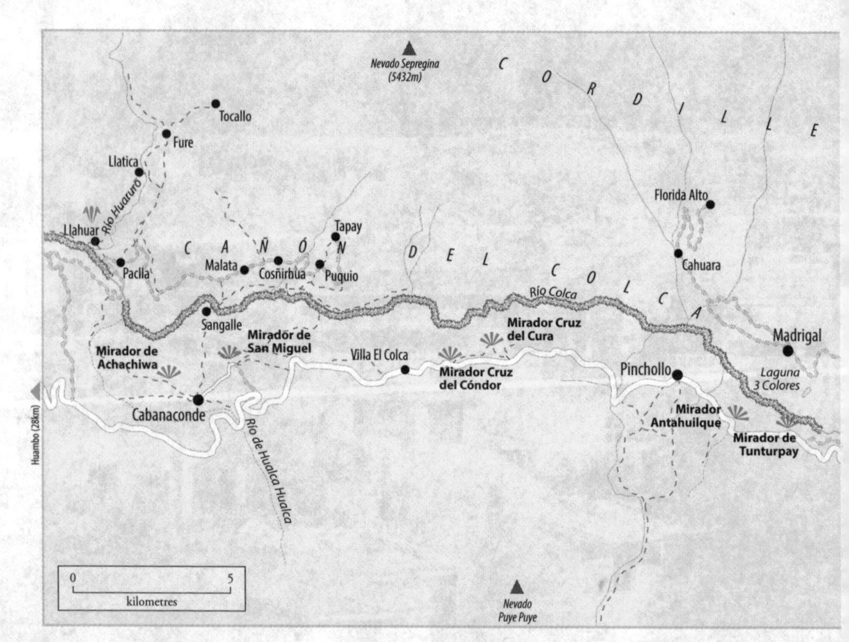

Unless climbing Volcán Mismi is on the agenda, serious trekkers will soon want to move on, probably to **Cabanaconde** (see page 180).

La Calera

Hot springs Daily 4am–7pm • S/15 • Colectivos leave frequently from the main square in Chivay

Just 4km northeast of Chivay, the tiny settlement of **LA CALERA** boasts one of Chivay's main attractions – a wonderful series of **hot-spring pools**, fed by the bubbling, boiling brooks that emerge from Volcán Cotallumi at an average natural temperature of 85°C, though it's a considerably cooler 38°C by the time the water fills the hottest pool. Said to be good for curing arthritis and rheumatism, these clean and well-kept thermal baths are not to be missed, though they can get busy. There's also a **small museum** on site with models and artefacts demonstrating local customs, such as making offerings to the *Pachamama*, Mother Earth. Just beyond the baths, a zipline (Ⓦcolcaziplining.com; S/50–150) offers high-octane thrills.

The canyon's southern rim

In the 56km between Chivay and Cabanaconde, which bookend the canyon, are some of the best and most breath-taking viewpoints from the canyon's **southern rim** into the depths of the ravine, and some of the most appealing, if pricey, lodgings, centred on the village of **Yanque.**

Yanque

From Chivay, the first village the road winds through is **YANQUE.** The mountains to the southwest are dominated by the glaciers of Ampato and Hualca, and sometimes Volcán Sabancaya can be seen smoking away in the distance. Yanque boasts a fine white *sillar* **church**, a small archeology **museum**, some low-key **thermal baths** (daily 4am–7pm; S/10) down by the river, horseriding facilities, mountain-bike rental and, after Maca, some of the area's best-preserved pre-Inca ruins. The village lies directly on

a fault line and is subject to frequent tremors: the visible effects can be seen in various land movements, abandoned houses and deep fissures around the area. Every morning, shortly after sunrise, local dancers perform the traditional Wititi **dance** in the main square, to entertain tour groups.

Maca

The road from Yanque continues on through a very dark tunnel until just beyond **MACA**, a small community which sits on the lower skirts of the Volcán Sabancaya and the Nevado Hualca Hualca, some 23km west of Chivay. Immediately after this tunnel, a number of hanging pre-Inca tombs – *las chullpas colgantes* – can be seen high up in seemingly impossible cliff-edge locations, facing some of the best examples of agricultural terracing in Peru across the valley.

Mirador Cruz del Cóndor

Cañón del Colca boleto turístico S/70 (see page 176); all tours come here and public buses will stop briefly

The **Mirador Cruz del Cóndor** is the most popular point for viewing the canyon – it's around 1200m deep here – and you can almost guarantee seeing several condors circling up from the depths against the breath-taking scenery. The condors are best spotted from 7 to 9am; the earlier you get there the more likely you are to have fewer other spectators around. These days it's a popular spot, and most mornings there will actually be more tourists here than in the Plaza de Armas in Arequipa.

The gateway to the mirador, the settlement of **Pinchollo,** has a small museum and a tourist information office with photos and a model representing the canyon.

TREKKING IN AND AROUND THE CAÑÓN

There are dozens of trekking routes in the Cañón del Colca, but if you're planning on descending to the **canyon floor**, even if just for the day, it's best to be fit and prepared for the altitude – it's tough going and becomes quite dangerous in sections. Make sure you are well acclimatized– even a bus trip to Chivay can bring on altitude sickness (see page 207) if you've only recently arrived from sea level. If you start trekking from Cabanaconde you can organize guides, *arrieros* (muleteers) and mules at most of the recommended lodgings (see page 181); it will be cheaper than paying for a tour from Arequipa. Hiking solo down in the canyon is fine for experienced hikers, though it's a good idea to buy a sketch map from your accommodation (Pachamama and Valle del Fuego have decent enough maps, with trail descriptions).

TREKS FROM CABANACONDE

Mirador Achachiwa Walk A fifteen-minute stroll from the plaza in Cabanaconde takes you past the bullring to the Mirador Achachiwa, a good spot for spotting condors, without the crowds, and viewing the western end of the valley from above.

Basic Colca Trek The classic route from Cabanaconde to the bottom of the canyon starts just beyond *La Casa de Santiago* (see page 181). The descent from here follows an incredibly steep path, quite dangerous in parts, down to the *Oasis* (see page 182), a rustic lodge and campsite right in the bottom of the canyon; it takes one and a half to two hours to descend and four or five to get back up. Many people stay the night.

The Tapay Trail This well-used trekking route connects Cabanaconde with the small settlement of Tapay via the *Oasis* (see page 182). It is a two- to four-day return hike through fine scenery, immense canyons, tiny hamlets such as Cosñirhua (2350m) and Malata as well as various Inca and pre-Inca ruins.

Cabanaconde to Llahuar A zig-zagging path descends from just left of the Mirador Achawiwa; cross the river and take in the bubbling geyser to the right of the bridge before doubling back and bearing westwards alongside the river to Llahuar; overnight there and soak in the hot springs. Strenuous day-hikes from there can take you to waterfalls at Huaruro or Fure; the hamlet at the latter also has a homestay option (though the family is not always there).

Cabanaconde to Laguna Mucurca There is a popular eight-hour hike from Cabanaconde that culminates at Laguna Mucurca (4000m). At its end point the astonishingly beautiful Volcán Ampato is reflected in the lake's crystalline waters.

The Ampato Trail From Laguna Mucurca the adventurous, fully acclimatized and well prepared can trek all the way around snow-capped Ampato (4–6 days). The Ampato Trail has one very high pass – around 4850m at the crossing of two trails on Cerro Quenahuane, above the Quebrada Condori – and most of the walking is at over 4200m. Local guides are a good idea and you will need food and camping equipment. Be prepared for snow and ice; the weather can change very fast. On the last downhill leg of the trek you can choose to follow trails back to Achoma, Maca or Cabanaconde.

THE COLCAS DE CHICHINIA TREK

A relatively easy two-hour walk from the village of **Coporaque** (15min by car or bus from Chivay, on the opposite side of the Cañón del Colca to Maca and the Mirador Cruz del Cóndor), takes in the **Colcas de Chichinia**, a semi-intact set of pre-Inca Huari tombs; today they lie exposed at the foot of the cliffs on Cerro Yurac Ccacca (also known as Cerro San Antonio). A path leads out a couple of blocks just below the plaza in Coporaque, crossing the stream as you leave the settlement behind and climbing steadily towards a prominent, pink rocky outcrop. The tombs are just below the 4000m contour line. To the southwest, a partly tumbled down, but still impressive **Huari village** can be clearly seen stretching from the tombs down to a major *tambo*-style (Quechua for house or resting place) building on the bottom corner, which commands views around the valley. To get back to Coporaque, you can either drop down to the road, tracing it back up to the settlement, or follow the small aqueduct that contours round the hill from the *tambo* back to where you started.

HATS IN THE CAÑÓN DEL COLCA

The indigenous communities of the Cañón del Colca form two distinct ethnic groups: the Aymara-speaking **Collaguas** and the Quechua-speaking **Cabanas**. Traditionally, both groups used different techniques for deforming the heads of their children. The Collaguas elongated them and the Cabanas flattened them – each trying to emulate the shape of their respective principal *apu* (mountain god). Today it is the shape of their **hats** (taller for the Collaguas and round, flat ones for the Cabanas), rather than heads, which mainly distinguishes the two groups.

Cabanaconde and around

The small but growing town of **CABANACONDE** (3300m), 56km west of Chivay, is the best base from which to descend into the canyon. An impressive high wall and painted gateway mark the town's eighteenth-century cemetery. Cabanaconde is also home to several semi-destroyed stone buildings and doorways from the late colonial (or Viceregal) era. If you can make it for the **Fiesta de la Virgen del Carmen** (usually between 14–18 July), you'll see the bullring in action and the town in the throes of a major religious festival and party.

The main reason to visit Cabanaconde, though, is to trek down into the canyon, with most visitors heading for the verdant **Valle de Sangalle**, an oasis of palm and fruit trees lying at the heart of the canyon.

Valle de Sangalle

It's a three-hour walk down a stony path from Cabanaconde to Sangalle, and as you slowly wind your way down the canyon the view becomes increasingly impressive, with the emerald-green Río Colca gushing through the valley. Even more rewarding is the swimming pool of *Oasis Paraíso Camping Lodge* – visible from the path and a refreshing welcome after the tiring trek down the canyon.

ARRIVAL AND DEPARTURE — CAÑÓN DEL COLCA

BY BUS

From Arequipa Buses from Arequipa stop off at the terminal in Chivay, a 10min stroll from the main plaza; some continue on to Cabanaconde along the southern rim of the canyon via Yanque and Maca (sit on the right for the views). There are three main companies – Reyna (☎054 430 612), Andalucía (☎988 060 516) and Turismo Milagros (☎054 298 090), which collectively offer eight daily departures from Arequipa to Chivay (3hr 30min). Six of these buses continue on to Cabanaconde (another 1hr 30min), all arriving at (and leaving from) the main plaza; agencies in the plaza sell tickets. Ask at the iPerú office in Arequipa for the bus timetable. Private minivans to Chivay leave from outside the main bus terminal in Arequipa. A tourist minivan service, with hotel pick-up, bilingual guiding and stops en route runs between Arequipa (leaving 3–3.30am) and Cabanaconde, returning to Arequipa at 9.30am for around US$16 one-way. Book online through Pachamama or La Casa de Santiago in Cabanaconde (see page 181).

From Puno 4M Express (☎054 452 296, 4m-express.com) operates daily tourist services from Puno to Chivay leaving around 6am (5hr 30min; US$50 one way), returning at 1.15pm, and from Cusco to Chivay at 7am on Tues, Thurs & Sat (9hr; US$65 one way), returning Mon, Wed & Fri at 7am; trips include bilingual guiding and photo stops along the way. Rutas del Sur (C Jerusalén 519, ☎951 024 750) also runs daily tourist buses between Chivay and Puno for US$35.

GETTING AROUND

By bus The buses to/from Arequipa will drop off/pick up passengers in the villages along the canyon's southern rim at Yanque, Maca, Pinchollo and at the Mirador Cruz del Cóndor. You may also be able to negotiate a ride on one of the tour buses. There are also colectivos between Chivay and Cabanaconde. Regular combi connections also spray out from Chivay to the villages along the northern rim of the canyon and up the valley to Sibayo. From the square at Cabanaconde, there is a daily truck at 7am that descends into the canyon bound for Tipay; it returns to Cabanaconde from Tipay at around 9am, picking up passengers along the way.

INFORMATION AND TOURS

Tourist information Autocolca on the Plaza de Armas in Chivay (Mon–Sat 8.30am–5.30pm, Sat 8.30am–1pm; ⓣ 054 531 143) can supply information and a map of the local area.

Tours Guides for the region can usually be organized via your accommodation (see below); hiking guides are best organized in Cabanaconde.

Services There's a BCP ATM on the main plaza in Chivay and another ATM just opposite the market, although it's probably wise to bring some spare cash from Arequipa. Cabanaconde has no ATM.

ACCOMMODATION

CHIVAY

Casa Andina Huayna Capac s/n ⓣ 054 531 020, ⓦ casa-andina.com; map p.178. For top-quality accommodation in Chivay this tranquil oasis in the heart of town is arguably the place to choose. Stone walkways lead to a series of tastefully decorated rustic rooms in thatched bungalows, with electric blankets and heaters. Don't miss out on the planetarium. S/340

La Casa de Mama Yacchi Coporaque, 7km west of Chivay ⓣ 054 531 004, ⓦ lacasademamayacchi.com; map p.178. A picture-perfect building with thatched roof, pretty flowers and pre-Inca ruins in the front garden. Rooms are basic but some have wonderful views (make sure to book one well in advance). There are no TVs and no wi-fi, but cosy hammocks and a communal log fire– perfect for those who want to get away from it all. Horseriding and hiking trips on offer. S/230

Hostal La Pascana del Inka Av Siglo XX 106 ⓣ 054 531 001, ⓦ lapascanadelinka.com; map p.178. Located just by the main square, this yellow budget hotel provides simple en-suite rooms, with flatscreen TV, that give onto shared balconies with wooden banisters and brightly painted murals. A local restaurant providing tasty *comida típica* is attached. S/140

Hostal Rumi Wasi C Sucre 714 ⓣ 054 480 091; map p.178. Friendly place with a six-bed dorm and modest en-suite rooms of various configurations, from singles to family-size, with cable TV. Plenty of blankets provided but no heating. There's a semi-open rooftop terrace to lounge on and a popular pancake breakfast is served. Use of kitchen, bike rental and horseriding. Dorms S/25, doubles S/80

Hotel La Casa de Anita Plaza de Armas 607, ⓦ facebook.com/hotellacasadeanitacolca; map p.178. Excellent refurbished hotel comprising simple but sparkling en-suite rooms with extremely comfortable beds decked out with crisp white sheets. Rooms have heating and cable TV; service is attentive. S/120

Hotel Pozo del Cielo Huascar s/n ⓣ 054 346 545, ⓦ pozodelcielo.com.pe; map p.178. Located at the edge of town, the rooms here have character: cosy, with low ceilings, wooden beams, decorated with wooden statuettes and local fabrics; each has an armchair or sofa, most have views, and all have a TV, electric blankets and a wall heater. Take a look at several rooms before committing. S/315

YANQUE

★ Colca Lodge Spa & Hot Springs Fundo Puye s/n ⓣ 054 282 177, ⓦ colca-lodge.com. This wonderful lodge with natural underfloor heating has smart rooms with rustic furniture in a beautiful, manicured, riverside setting. The junior suites, with stylish bathrooms, are worth the splurge. The hotel owns an alpaca ranch just across the river where guests are invited to learn about the friendly creatures while the open-air steaming-hot thermal pools are a treat, especially after a long hike. US$178

Killawasi Lodge C Caravely 408 ⓣ 054 691 072, ⓦ killawasilodge.com. Fourteen ample, light suites made of stone and wood, with private terraces. The *Quinoa Restaurant* is a top place to eat – reserve early – offering a variety of fine trout, alpaca and chicken dishes (from S/35). Service is top-notch. US$105

Samana Wasi C Labrador 207 ⓣ 959 521 804, ⓦ casasamanawasi.com. Welcoming family-run B&B offering basic accommodation (rooms for two to four people) but an opportunity to learn more about local customs and way of life. S/115

Tradición Colca Carretera Principal ⓣ 054 424 926, ⓦ tradicioncolca.com. This French-run place offers clean, well-kept rooms with private bathroom on the main road. The great facilities include three jacuzzis, a sauna, indoor pool and astronomy dome, though the necessary expertise is not always to hand. Staff can organize local treks as well as horseriding trips. Dorms S/65, doubles S/180

CABANACONDE

★ La Casa de Santiago C Grau ⓣ 054 203 737 or ⓣ 959 611 241, ⓦ lacasadesantiago.com. A peaceful guesthouse with rooms set around a pleasant garden area with seating, perfect for reading or soaking in the surrounding mountain views. There's all-day tea, and breakfast is served in a large, light communal area. Local guides, mules and *arrieros* can all be arranged here for canyon hikes and further afield, plus there's trekking equipment for rent. S/120

Hostal Valle del Fuego Calles Grau and Bolívar ⓣ 054 668 910, ⓦ valledelfuego.com. This backpackers' pad is run by friendly Yamil, who welcomes guests with a potent pisco sour. Rooms include two welcoming dorms with bare-brick walls, as well as simple doubles, most with mountain views. A little patio with colourfully painted stone walls, laundry facilities and a camping area just out of town. You can hire horses, mules and rent mountain bikes. An atmospheric restaurant, dotted with couches and old curios, serves great pizzas. Camping S/10, doubles S/80

3

Hotel Kuntur Wassi On the hill above the Plaza de Armas 054 233 120, arequipacolca.com. A comfortable, if overpriced, hotel sitting atop the plaza, whose name translates as "The House of the Condor". The lobby has a water feature and a splash of greenery, while the attractive rooms with clay tiles feature open-fronted wardrobes built using natural materials. Bathrooms have solar-heated showers, and the lovely bar-restaurant boasts views over town and beyond. S/248

Pachamama C San Pedro 209 054 767 277, pachamamahome.com. A popular backpacker pad offering simple, snug rooms, with or without bathroom, tucked away behind a cosy restaurant with candlelit tables where pizzas and other comfort foods are prepared in a wood-fire oven. A good place to linger over a drink or two. Plenty of hiking support. Dorms S/25, doubles S/50, en-suite doubles S/60

La Posada del Conde C San Pedro s/n 054 631 749, posadadelconde.com. In the centre of town, just a short walk from the main square, this place offers darkish olive-green rooms with private bathroom. The restaurant serves good local dishes, with mains at about S/25. S/80

IN THE CAÑÓN

Wherever you trek in the canyon, you'll find a friendly place to lay your head, provided you're not concerned about home comforts. In addition to the listings below, there are homestays available in the hamlets of Coshñirwa and Tapay.

La Casa de Roy San Juan de Chuccho 054 794 198, lacasaderoy@hotmail.com. Hard to contact in advance, but a welcoming family guesthouse offering simple stone and wooden cabins, with shared facilities, spots to pitch a tent, and splendid vistas from the dining terrace, where you can enjoy candlelit dinners. No electricity. S/20

Llahuar Lodge Valle Confluence of the ríos Colca and Huaruro 956 271 333, llahuar.lodge@hotmail.com. Perched precariously on the mountainside, this "lodge" is all about the location and the views, not home comforts: tiny wooden huts, or adobe rooms share rustic bamboo bathrooms, a diminutive riverside garden and hot pools, plus a cosy-cum-cramped balcony bar-restaurant where you can order the set-menu dinner. Breakfast extra. Dorms S/20, doubles S/50

Oasis Paraíso Camping Lodge Valle de Sangalle, 3–4hr hike from Cabanaconde 054 398 439, oasisparaisoecolodge.com. Though it can get rather overrun with tourists these days, at other times the lush garden area with swimming pools is a delight. Meals are served in the open-fronted restaurant, made local fresh produce. It's happy hour 4–6pm. Dorms S/50, doubles S/82

EATING

CHIVAY

Aromas Caffee Plaza de Armas 301 054 796 512, facebook.com/coffeeshopinperu; map p.178. This small coffee joint is a great spot to grab a refreshing frappuccino (S/8) on a hot day or a warming hot chocolate (S/6) on a nippy evening. Seating is at little wooden tables – just enough space to fit your slab of cake or toasted sandwich. Mon–Sat 8am–10pm, Sun 9am–10pm.

Los Portales C Arequipa 603 054 531 101, losportalesdechivay.com; map p.178. This popular restaurant buzzes with tour groups at lunchtime for its decent eat-all-you-can buffet (S/28). There's plenty to choose from, including quinoa- and meat-based dishes, plus veggie options and soups. Daily 11am–2.30pm.

Q'anka C Salaverry 105, 2nd floor 980 961 879, facebook.com/qankachivay; map p.178. Full marks for decor here, with walls decorated with masks and tables adorned with mud vases. House specialities are hot-stone steaks, with a particularly succulent *lomito de alpaca* (S/35), and pizzas (S/20) also served sizzling on hot stones. Daily 11am–9pm.

Urinsaya C Francisco Bolognesi 1026 054 531 235; map p.178. Tucked away off a dusty side road, this pleasant restaurant, featuring a large condor mural and thatched roof, offers a very good buffet lunch for S/35; you'll need to avoid the tour groups. Occasional live folkloric bands liven up the scene. Daily 9am–3pm.

YANQUE

Alpaca Chef Colca Manzanayoc s/n 054 035 783, alpacachef_chivay@hotmail.com. This thatched restaurant has a pleasant interior with terracotta floors, colourful Andean tablecloths and a clay oven. Reservations one day in advance, and meals will set you back about S/35. Daily 10am–3pm.

Cañón de Cotahuasi and around

Free of coach parties and tourist hordes thus far, the remoter and deeper **CAÑÓN DE COTAHUASI** has plenty to offer the adventurous traveller, including spectacular waterfalls, rewarding hiking, thermal baths and pre-Columbian ruins. One of the reasons for fewer visitors – beyond the greater distance from Arequipa: some 375km to the northwest – is the fact that for the final few hours the road is unpaved. What's more, the buses from Arequipa all travel overnight, thereby depriving you of seeing the magnificent **snow-capped peaks** of Coropuna and Solimana on the way.

To reach the canyon from Arequipa, you branch off the main road to Lima at the junction of El Alto, heading up the fertile **Valle de Majes**, through the agricultural towns of Corire – access point to the impressive **Petroglífos de Toro Muerto** – and Aplao. While the canyon is another five to six hours by bus skirting the western flank of Coropuna, to the eastern side of the *nevado* lies the extraordinary cones-and-craters landscape of the **Valle de los Volcanes,** also reachable on a tough multi-day hike from Cabanaconde in the Cañón del Colca (see page 180), or via a back road with your own 4WD transport from Chivay.

Petroglifos de Toro Muerto

Just west of the village of La Candelaria • Daily 6am–6pm • S/5 • Take the hourly bus from Arequipa to Corire (3hr); ask to get off at the desvío a Toro Muerto and walk (30min) or catch a taxi from Corire (10–15min; approx S/30–40 including waiting time). Return buses to Arequipa leave from the Plaza de Armas in Corire

The **Petroglifos de Toro Muerto** consist of carved boulders strewn over a kilometre or two of hot desert. More than a thousand rocks of all sizes and shapes have been crudely, yet strikingly, engraved with a wide variety of distinct representations. No archeological remains have been directly associated with these images but it is thought that they date from between 1000 and 1500 years ago; they are largely attributed to the **Huari culture** (which may have sent an expeditionary force in this direction around 800 AD), though with probable additions during subsequent Chuquibamba and Inca periods of domination in the region. The engravings include images of humans, snakes, llamas, deer, parrots, sun discs and simple geometric motifs. Some of the figures appear to be dancing, others with large round helmets look like spacemen – obvious material for the author Erich Von Däniken's extraterrestrial musings (he based his book *Chariots of the Gods* on several archeological sites in Peru).

ACCOMMODATION AND EATING — PETROGLIFOS DE TORO MUERTO

CORIRE

Hostal Willy's Plaza Principal, avenidas Progreso and Morán ☎054 472 046. The basic rooms all have hot water, TV and chintzy bed linen, although don't be surprised to see paint peeling off the walls here and there. Room only. S/40

Hotel El Molino Av Progreso 121 ☎054 472 056, ✉hotelmolinocorire@hotmail.com. The tiled rooms here are kept clean and bright with regular touch-ups of paint. All are en suite, and some have a TV and a fridge. Staff can help organize trips in the local area. S/80

Laguna Azul Río Majes, 1km east of Corire ☎959 918 541. This laidback, wood-and-thatch riverfront restaurant serves tasty crayfish dishes (April–Dec); when the river water level rises (Jan–April) the restaurant retreats a few metres and specializes in seafood. Mains from S/25. Daily 8am–4/5pm.

APLAO

Majes River Lodge Valle de Majes, 10km north of Aplao ☎054 660 219, majesriver.com. This welcoming place specializing in rafting and kayaking on the Río Majes is run by a warm and welcoming couple. The simple rooms overlook a swimming pool area, while at the back of the premises is a wine cellar (guests here at the right time can even take part in the grape harvest) that brims with character and is packed with old curios. S/100

Valle de los Volcanes

Following some 65km of the Río Andagua's course, the **VALLE DE LOS VOLCANES** (Valley of the Volcanoes) skirts along the presently dormant Volcán Coropuna, the highest volcano in Peru (6425m) and the highest peak in southern Peru. At first sight just a pleasant Andean valley, this is in fact one of the strangest geological formations you're ever likely to see. A stunning lunar landscape, the valley is studded with extinct craters varying in size and height from 10 to 300m. About 200,000 years ago, these small volcanoes erupted when the lava fields were degassed (a natural release of volcanic gas through soil, volcanic lakes and volcanoes) – at the time of one of Coropuna's major eruptions.

The best overall view of the valley can be had from Volcán Anaro (4800m), looking southeast towards the Chipchane and Puca Maura cones. The highest of the volcanoes, known as Los Gemelos (The Twins), are about 10km from Andagua, the main settlement in the area, and your best chance of stocking up on some supplies. To the south, Volcán Andomarca has a pre-Inca ruined settlement around its base.

ARRIVAL AND INFORMATION — VALLE DE LOS VOLCANES

By bus Buses to Andagua (10hr) from Arequipa's Terminal Terrestre leave daily between 3 and 4pm with Reyna, and 5 and 6pm with Transporte Trébol.

By private vehicle If you have your own 4WD transport, you can take the back route from Chivay via Sibayo, Caylloma and Orcopampa

On foot You can trek to the Valle de los Volcanes from Cabanaconde (5–6 days); this expedition will require mules, a guide and cook. Treks can be organized through one of the tour agencies in Arequipa, or, for less, in Cabanaconde.

Information and maps The Municipalidad on the main square at Andagua provides tourist information (Mon–Fri 8am–4pm); also check vallevolcanesperu.com. To explore the 65km main section of the valley in any detail you'll need to get two adjacent IGN maps from the Instituto Geográfico in Peru (ign.gob.pe) or contact the guiding association (see page 165) in Arequipa; Pablo Tour (see page 166) also has detailed maps of the area for sale.

ACCOMMODATION

There are several simple lodgings round Andagua or you can usually pay someone to camp on their land outside the village.

Hostal El Trébol 15 de Agosto 106, Andagua 959 214355, hostal_trebol_andagua_castilla@hotmail.com. Probably the best option in the area, with twelve simple en-suite rooms with hot water. Room only. S/40

Cañón de Cotahuasi

First declared a protected zone in 1988, the magnificent and remote **CAÑÓN DE COTAHUASI** was finally designated as the sierra's largest protected area in 2005 with the catchy title of La Reserva Paisajística Subcuenca del Cotahuasi. One of the world's deepest canyons, along with nearby Colca and the Grand Canyon in the US, it is around 3500m deep in places and over 100km long. Formerly, the only foreigners visiting the area were white-water rafting enthusiasts and hardcore mountaineers, but the heavy commercialism of the Cañón del Colca is encouraging an increasing trickle of travellers to seek out this less visited region. It's a wonderful area to spend several days, wandering through traditional hamlets made from adobe and thatch, taking in Huari and Inca ruins, waterfalls, spectacular panoramic vistas, sightings of condors and thermal baths, to soothe the aching limbs.

Cotahuasi

The canyon's attractive main settlement, **Cotahuasi** (2684m), boasts quaint narrow streets and a small seventeenth-century church. It has a variable climate but isn't particularly cold and is rapidly developing a name as an adventure travel destination, offering by far the best local facilities: a handful of simple lodgings, a few basic restaurants and a couple of tour operators provide ample support. However, in almost all the hamlets dotted round the valley there is the possibility of finding a bite to eat or staying with a local family – enquire at the Municipalidad. Time your visit for the end of April/beginning of May, culminating in the anniversary of the foundation of La Unión on May 4, and the valley's biggest festivities will be in full swing, including sporting competitions, traditional music and dancing – listen out for the *waca waccra*, the giant wind instrument made from bull's horns – parades and bull fights. Make sure you sample some *chimbango*, the local homebrew made from fermented figs.

Upriver from Cotahuasi

Continuing north up the broad, flat valley to the village of **Alca**, just beyond the canyon's most developed **hot springs** at Luicho, the road forks. To the right, it heads towards the village of **Pucya,** from where it's a 2km hike uphill to the canyon's most intact pre-Huari **ruins** of Maukallacta, which later became an Inca staging post on the highway from Cusco to coastal Puerto Inca. Nearby too is a *mirador* that overlooks the **bañadero del cóndor** where these vast birds can be seen bathing during the rainy season (Dec–March), though year-round they can be spotted wheeling on thermals higher up the mountain slopes. Further up the valley, heading pretty well northwest, you end up at the astonishingly beautiful plateau of Lauripampa, from where you can walk down into the canyon or admire the spread of massive *puya raimondii* – the world's largest bromeliad.

Zig-zagging north from Cotahuasi, a dirt road climbs to the pueblo of **Pampamarca**, where the locals weave lovely alpaca blankets. Above the pueblo a short trail leads to a distant view of the Catarata de Uskune below, on one side of the valley; on the other side, a more demanding uphill slog takes you past Huari *chullpas* to the natural **rock formations** of the Bosque de Piedras de Huito, where you'll also have views across to the snow-capped summits of Solimana and Firura. Downhill from Pampamarca you'll find the **thermal springs** of Josla, an ancient spa that's a joy for tired legs after a long hike.

Downriver from Cotahuasi

A narrow, dusty road, clinging to the rock face at times, heads down the valley from Cotahuasi to the tiny village of **Quechualla**. Signposted off the main road, 10km west of Cotahuasi, a short path leads to the lower valley's main attraction, the **Catarata de Sipia,** ferocious falls that plunge dramatically some 150m into an abyss. Further on, the **Bosque de Cactus de Judío Pampa** is an impressive "forest" of **cacti;** reminiscent of the set for a spaghetti western, some candelabra-like specimens top 15m, and are home to the increasingly rare long-snouted bat. Beyond Quechualla, you can walk down to the end of the dirt road at Ushua, which overlooks one of the deepest segments of the canyon.

ARRIVAL AND DEPARTURE — CAÑÓN DE COTAHUASI

By bus Cromotex, Reyna and Immaculada Concepción each offers an overnight bus service from Arequipa (9–11hr) to Cotahuasi, which arrive at the bus station a 15min walk from the centre of the village. There is also a Sunday departure from Lima by Transportes López (9am; 26–28hr), returning to Lima on Tuesdays (7am). Guided tours to Cotahuasi are also offered by some Arequipa tour operators (see page 165).

GETTING AROUND

Every hour (daily 6am–6pm) a combi leaves from the top end of Cotahuasi's main street bound for the village of Alca. A combi leaves Alca for Puyca at 5am and 3pm, returning 7am and 1pm (1hr 30min). A daily combi leaves at 6am from Cotahuasi bus station for Quechualla (2hr), passing the Catarata de Sipia and the cactus forest, returning from Quechualla at 8.30am. On Monday, Friday and Sunday an extra combi runs to Quechualla at 1.30pm. A daily minibus for Pampamarca leaves the bus station at 4pm (2hr), returning from Pampamarca at 7am. Transport for Toro leaves the bus station at 5am on Monday, Wednesday and Friday (1hr 30min), and other combis leave the bus station between 5 and 7am destined for other mountain villages.

INFORMATION AND TOURS

Tourist information The Municipalidad on C Centenario runs a tourism desk, which can happily supply you with information (in Spanish) and a tourist map of the valley.

Tours There are a couple of small, local operators along the village's main street, C Arequipa. Try Purek Tours at no. 103 (T 054 698 081, E cotahuasitours@gmail.com); owner Milko (T 967 789 989) is a mine of information.

ACCOMMODATION AND EATING

3

Hatunhuasi Hotel C Centenario 307–309, Cotahuasi T 054 581 054, W hatunhuasi.com. This small, family-run hotel features eleven simple, clean tiled-floor rooms giving onto a garden area (grab an upstairs room). The owner can cook meals upon request. S/60

★ **Hotel Valle Hermoso** C Tacna 106, Cotahuasi T 054 581 057, W hotelvallehermoso.com. A very pleasant guesthouse with rooms set around a lovely garden area – some with a balcony overlooking avocado, orange and fig trees and a couple of grazing llamas. The rooms have individual touches, such as lamps with old irons as stands, and breakfast includes home-made jams and bread, as well as freshly squeezed juice. S/100

Linda Cotahuasina C Arequipa 117, Cotahuasi T 054 660 113. Unlike most restaurants in Cotahuasi where food is pre-cooked and served as part of a menu, friendly owner Carmen prepares everything to order, with a handful of tasty meat dishes and vegetarian meals as required. Daily 6am–11pm.

El Sabor de Mi Tierra C Independencia 106. Guinea pig and trout (S/10) are the mainstays of this small a la carte menu, to be enjoyed in a sunny courtyard. Daily 7–4pm (closed one day per week).

Lago Titicaca

An undeniably calming and majestic sight, **LAGO TITICACA** is the world's largest high-altitude body of water. At 284m deep and more than 8300 square kilometres in area, it is fifteen times the size of Lake Geneva in Switzerland and higher and slightly bigger than Lake Tahoe in the US. An immense region both in terms of its history and the breadth of its magical landscape, the **Titicaca Basin** makes most people feel like they are on top of the world. Usually placid and mirror-like, the deep blue water reflects the vast sky back on itself. All along the horizon – which appears to bend away from you – the green Andean mountains can be seen raising their ancient backs towards the sun; over on the Bolivian side it's sometimes possible to make out the icecaps of the Cordillera Real mountain chain. The **high altitude** (3827m above sea level) means that recent arrivals from the coast should take it easy for a day or two, though those coming from Cusco will already have acclimatized.

La Reserva Nacional del Titicaca was established in 1978; over a hundred varieties of bird have been recorded, and the lake is home to 25 species of native fish and fifteen types of amphibian. It's often seen as three separate regions: Lago Mayor, the main, deep part of the lake; Wiñaymarka, the area incorporating various archipelagos that include both Peruvian and Bolivian Titicaca; and the Golfo de Puno, essentially the bay enclosed by the peninsulas de Capachica and Chucuito. The villages that line its shores depend mainly on grazing livestock for their livelihood, since the altitude limits the growth potential of most crops. These days, **Puno** is the largest settlement and port in the whole of Lago Titicaca. Densely populated well before the arrival of the Incas, the lakeside Titicaca region is also home to the curious and ancient tower-tombs known locally as **chullpas**: rings of tall, cylindrical stone burial chambers, often standing in battlement-like formations. These were built by the Kollas, an Aymara-speaking people who preceded the Incas and once dominated the lake; the examples at **Sillustani,** northwest of Puno, are included on most tourist circuits in the region (see page 194).

There are over seventy islands in the lake, the largest being the **Isla del Sol** (Island of the Sun), an ancient Inca temple site on the Bolivian side of the border; Titicaca is an Aymara word meaning "Puma's Rock", which refers to an unusual boulder on the island. The island is best visited from Copacabana in Bolivia (see page 201), or trips can be arranged through one of the tour companies in Puno (see page 191).

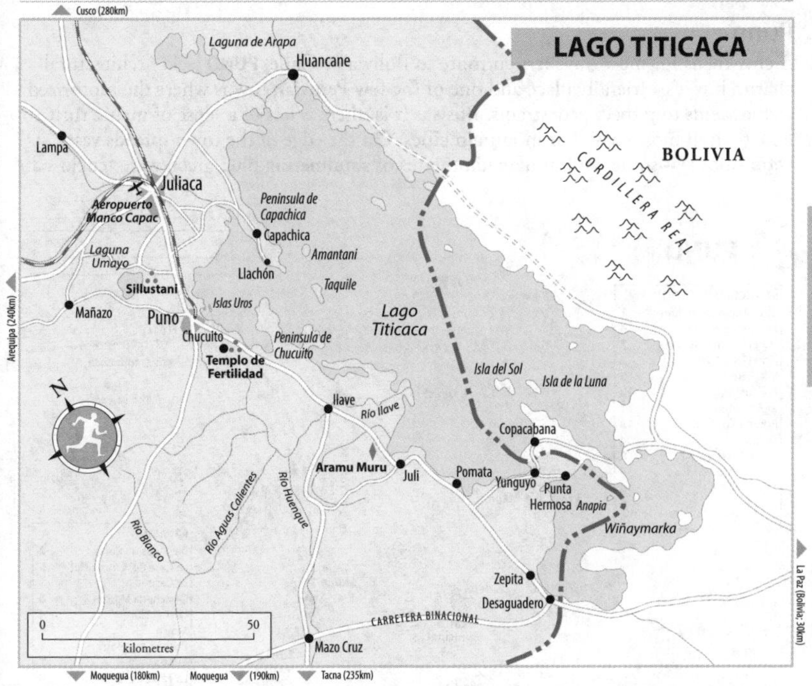

On the Peruvian side of the lake you can visit the unusual **Islas de los Uros**. These floating platform islands are built out of reeds – weird to walk over and even stranger to live on, they are now a major tourist attraction. More spectacular by far are two of the populated, fixed islands, **Amantani** and **Taquile**, where the traditional lifestyles of these powerful communities give visitors a genuine taste of pre-Conquest Andean Peru.

Brief history

The scattered population of the region is descended from two very ancient Andean ethnic groups – the **Aymara** and the **Quechua**. The Aymara's Tiahuanaco culture predates the Quechua's Inca civilization by over three hundred years and this region is thought to be the original home for the domestication of a number of very important plants, not least the potato, tomato and the common pepper.

TITICACA'S AQUATIC INHABITANTS

Not surprisingly, **fish** are still an important food source for Titicaca's inhabitants, including the islanders, and for the ibises and flamingoes that can be seen along the pre-Inca terraced shoreline. The most common fish – the **karachi** – of which there are a number of species, is a small finger-sized specimen. **Trout** arrived in the lake from North America in the 1930s while **pejerrey** (silverside or kingfish) established themselves two decades later. While these introduced species thrived at the cost of native fish, all are now struggling from a combination of fluctuating water levels due to **climate change**, **overfishing,** and **pollution.** In even deeper trouble is the critically endangered endemic **Titicaca water frog** – unappealingly nicknamed the "scrotum frog" on account of its loose folds of skin; over 10,000 specimens were found dead in 2016, though the exact cause of their demise remains a mystery. Whether the world's largest truly aquatic frog survives to reap the rewards of the recent multi-million-dollar pledge between Bolivia and Peru to clean up the lake by 2025 remains to be seen.

Puno

A crossroads for most travellers en route to Bolivia or Chile, **PUNO** lacks architectural charm, but it's a friendly place and one of the few Peruvian towns where the motorized traffic seems to respect pedestrians. Busy as it is, there is less of a sense of manic rush here than in most coastal or mountain cities. On the edge of the town spreads vast **Lago Titicaca** – some 8400 square kilometres of shimmering blue-green water enclosed

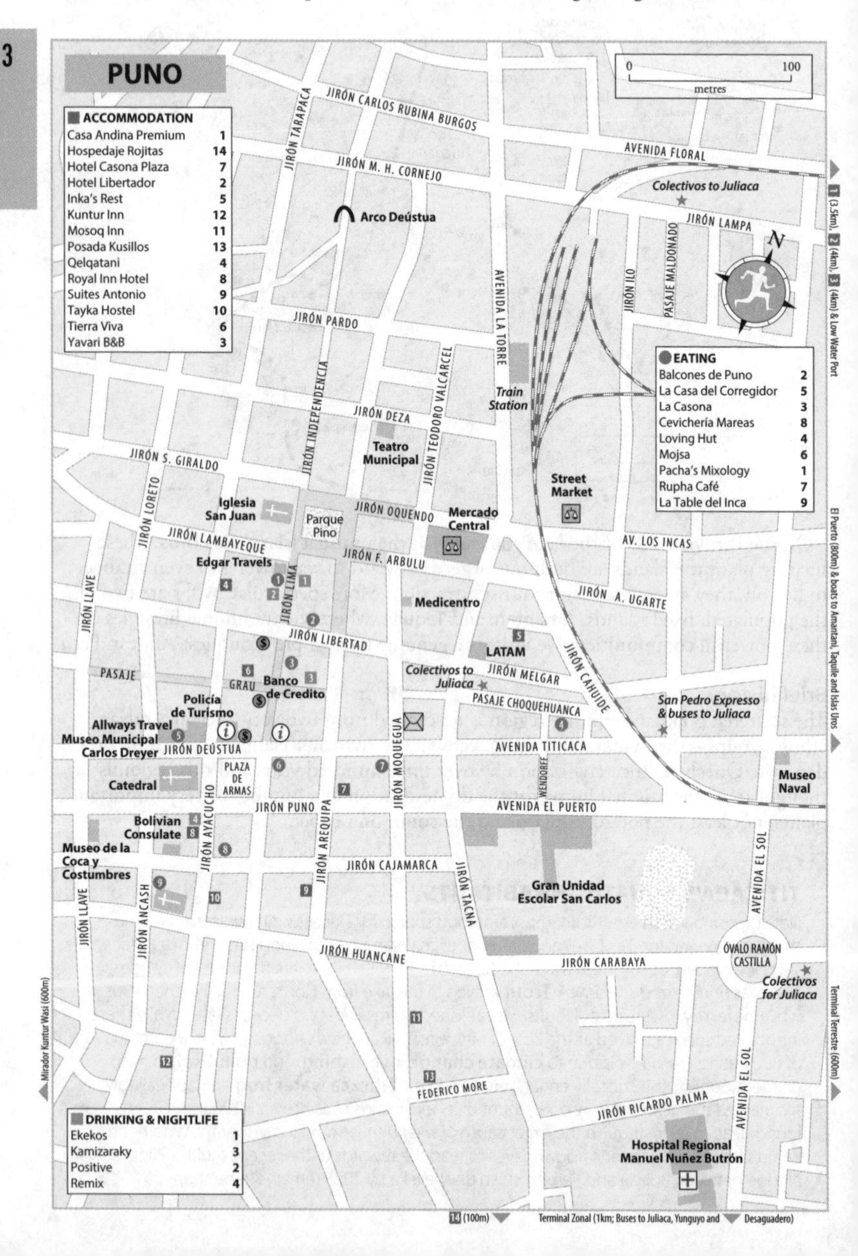

by white peaks. Puno's port is a vital staging-point for exploring the northern end of the lake, with its floating islands just a short distance away by boat.

There are three main points of reference in Puno: the spacious **Plaza de Armas**, the **train station** several blocks north, surrounded by a lively **street market** on Saturdays, and the vast, strung-out area of old, semi-abandoned docks at the ever-shifting **Titicaca lakeside port**. It all looks impressive from a distance, but the town-based attractions are few and quickly visited.

The climate here is generally dry and the burning daytime sun is in stark contrast to the icy evenings (temperatures frequently fall below freezing in the winter nights of July and August). Sloping corrugated-iron roofs bear witness to the heavy rains that fall between November and February.

Brief history

Puno is immensely rich in living traditions – in particular its modern interpretations of folk dances – as well as fascinating pre-Columbian history. The **Pukara culture** emerged here some three thousand years ago, leaving behind stone pyramids and carved standing stones contemporaneous with those of Chavín 1600km further north. The better-known **Tiahuanaco culture** dominated the Titicaca basin between 800 and 1200 AD, leaving in its wake the temple complex of the same name just over the border in Bolivia, plus widespread cultural and religious influence. This early settlement was conquered by the Incas in the fifteenth century.

The first Spanish settlement at **Puno** sprang up around a silver mine discovered by the infamous Salcedo brothers in 1657. The camp forged such a wild and violent reputation that the Lima viceroy moved in with soldiers to crush and finally execute the Salcedos before things got too out of hand. The Spanish were soon to discover the town's wealth – both in terms of tribute-based agriculture and mineral exploitation based on a unique form of slave labour. In 1668 the viceroy made Puno the capital of the region, and from then on it became the main port of Lago Titicaca and an important town on the silver trail from **Potosí** in Bolivia. The arrival of the railway, late in the nineteenth century, brought another boost, but today, it's a relatively poor, rather grubby sort of town, by Peruvian standards, and a place that has suffered badly from droughts and poor water management over the years.

La Catedral

Plaza de Armas • Daily 7am–noon & 3–6pm • Free

The seventeenth-century **Catedral** is surprisingly large, with an exquisite Baroque facade from 1657 and, unusually for Peru, a very simple and humble interior, in line with the local Aymaras' austere attitude to religion. Local men and women are often seen sitting on the church steps, sometimes in traditional dress, watching life go by in the square.

Museo Municipal Carlos Dreyer

Jr Deustua 458 , Plaza de Armas • Mon–Sat 9am–7pm • S/15

Opposite the Catedral's north face, the two-floor **Museo Municipal Carlos Dreyer** is well worth a visit. It contains a unique collection of archeological pieces, predominantly from the Pukara and Inca periods, including ceramics, golden objects from Sillustani, some textiles and stone sculptures, mostly removed from the region's *chullpas*.

Museo de la Coca y Costumbres

C Llave 581 • Mon–Sat 9am–7pm • Free • ⓣ 051 209 420, ⓦ museodelacoca.com

This recently relocated and expanded **Museo de la Coca y Costumbres** provides a text-heavy (in Spanish and English) tour through the agricultural, spiritual, socio-cultural and medicinal functions of coca in pre-Inca and Inca societies. It then examines the conquistadors' initial reaction and the leaf's subsequent uses – and abuses – in

PUNO FESTIVALS

Famed as the **folklore capital** of Peru, Puno is renowned throughout the Andes for its music and dance – around 400 dances are said to exist in the region. The best time to experience this wealth of traditional cultural expression is during the first two weeks of February for the **Fiesta de la Virgen de la Candelaria**, a great folklore dance festival, boasting incredible dancers wearing devil masks and a range of extravagant colourful costumes; the festival climaxes on the second Sunday of February. If you're in Puno at this time, it's a good idea to reserve hotels in advance (hotel prices can double).

The **Festival de Tinajani**, usually around early July, is set in the bleak altiplano against the backdrop of a huge wind-eroded rock in the Cañón de Tinajani. Off the beaten trail, it's well worth checking out for its raw Andean music and dance, plus its large sound systems; ask at the tourist offices in Puno or Cusco for details.

Just as spectacular, the **Semana Jubilar** (Jubilee Festival) occurs in the first week of November, partly on Isla Esteves, and celebrates the Spanish founding of the city and the Incas' origins, which legend says are from Lago Titicaca itself. Even if you miss the festivals, you can find a group of musicians playing brilliant and highly evocative music somewhere in the labyrinthine town centre on many nights of the year.

cocaine production. Don't miss out on the "*costumbres*" costume display and video, which gives you a flavour of the glorious Fiesta de la Virgen de la Candelaria (see above).

Iglesia San Antonio

Jr Ayacucho • Mon–Sat 8am–6pm • Free

The **Iglesia San Antonio**, two blocks south of the plaza, is colourfully lit inside by ten stained-glass circular windows. The church's complex iconography, set into six wooden wall niches, is highly evocative of the region's mix of Catholic and indigenous beliefs.

Mirador Kuntur Wasi

High up on a hillside, the **Mirador Kuntur Wasi** is named after the large, unmissable metal condor (Kuntur in Quechua) that seemingly hovers above the city. To reach this spectacular viewpoint, you climb more than six hundred steps from the top of Calle Llave. At this altitude, you need to take it steady, and there are plenty of benches on the way, but you'll be well rewarded at the top with stupendous views across the bustle of Puno to the serene blue of Titicaca and its unique skyline. Though the late afternoon sun makes for better photos, it is generally considered safer early in the morning. If you are determined to catch the late afternoon light, go in a group, preferably with a local, carrying very little of value with you.

Yavari

Moored by the *Hotel Libertador*, Isla Estévez, Sector Huaje, or cruising Lake Titicaca as a B&B (see page 193) • Museum when moored daily 8am–6pm • By donation • ⓣ 051 369 329, ⓦ yavari.org

The nineteenth-century British-built steamship **Yavari** provides a fascinating insight into maritime life on Lago Titicaca over 150 years ago and the military and entrepreneurial mindset of Peru in those days. Designed by James Watt, it was delivered by boat from England to Arica on the coast, and then carried 560km by mule in over 1300 different pieces, taking a total of six years. Having started life as a Peruvian navy gunship complete with bullet-proof windows, it ended up delivering mail around Lago Titicaca, and at times had to use llama dung as fuel. In 2015 the *Yavari* was certified for passenger use and today travels the lake as a unique B&B. When moored it functions as a museum. At the time of writing, it was closed for refurbishment, and it was unclear when it would reopen.

ARRIVAL AND DEPARTURE

BY PLANE

The closest airport to Puno is Aeropuerto Manco Capac (T 051 328 226) near the unappealing city of Juliaca, about 49km north of Puno. Several flights arrive and depart daily for Lima with LATAM (W latam.com) and Avianca (W avianca.com). Rossy Tours (T 051 366 709, W rossytours.com) offers colectivo taxis from the airport, dropping passengers off at their hotels in Puno for S/15 per person, although reliability is sometimes an issue. All Ways Travel (see page 191) offers a pricier, reliable private service

BY TRAIN

If you're coming in from Cusco by train, you'll arrive at the station at Av la Torre 224 (T 051 369 179). Taxis leave from immediately outside the station and will cost about S/5 to anywhere in the centre of town. Trains from Cusco leave Wed, Fri & Sun at 7.30am, arriving in Puno at 6pm the same day; trains to Cusco leave Puno Mon, Thurs & Sat at 7.30am arriving in Cusco at 6pm. Tickets from US$200 are available from agents or direct from PeruRail (T 084 581 414, W perurail.com).

BY BUS

Buses from Arequipa, Cusco, Tacna, Moquegua, Copacabana and La Paz use the Terminal Terrestre at Jr Primero de Mayo (T 051 364 733). Buses and minivans from local provincial destinations such as Juliaca or along the edge of Lake Titicaca come in at the Terminal Zonal, Av Costanera 451, Barrio Progreso. Ignore anyone who offers you help, unless you have already booked with them (there are thieves operating as touts for hotels or tours).

Destinations Arequipa (frequent daily; 6hr); Chivay (2 daily; 5hr 30min); Copacabana (frequent daily; 2–3hr); Cusco (frequent daily; 6hr); Desaguadero (several daily; 3hr); La Paz (frequent daily; 5–6hr); Lima (a few daily via Arequipa; 20hr); Moquegua (several daily; 7hr); Tacna (several daily; 9hr).

BUS OPERATORS

4M Express Jr Arequipa 736 T 051 452 296, W 4m-express.com. Tourist bus with one daily service to/from Chivay (for the Cañón del Colca), inclusive of hotel pickup, bilingual commentary and photo stops en route.

Cruz del Sur Terminal Terrestre and Jr Lima 394 T 051 205 824, W cruzdelsur.com.pe. Services to Arequipa and Cusco.

Expreso Turismo San Martín Nobleza Terminal Terrestre T 951 677 730. Serves Moquegua and Tacna.

Inka Express Jr Tacna 346 T 051 365 654, W inkaexpress.com. Daily tourist bus between Cusco and Puno, including lunch, bilingual guiding and stops at several archeological and cultural sites en route.

Ormeño Terminal Terrestre T 051 352 780, W grupo-ormeno.com.pe. Services to Arequipa, Lima and La Paz via Desaguadero.

Tour Perú Terminal Terrestre and Jr Tacna 285. T 051 206 088, W tourperu.com.pe. Serves Arequipa, Cusco, Copacabana and La Paz (Bolivia).

Tour Rutas del Sur Jr Lima 440 T 951 024 750, W tourrutasdelsur.com. Daily tourist bus to Chivay (Cañón del Colca), inclusive of pick-up and photo stops en route.

Transportes Internacional Titicaca Bolivia Terminal Terrestre and Jr Tacna 285, 104 T 051 363 830, W titicacabolivia.com. Serves Copacabana and La Paz (Bolivia).

Transzela Terminal Terrestre T 051 353 822, W transzela.com. Serves Cusco, Arequipa and Copacabana (Bolivia)

BY COLECTIVO

Colectivos from Desaguadero and Yunguyo serve the Terminal Zonal. Combis from Juliaca terminate here but also stop off at a number of places in town, including the corner of Jr Lampa close to Pasaje Maldonado.

BY BOAT

The main port, used by boats from Bolivia as well as the Islas de los Uros, Taquile and Amantani, is a 20min walk from the Plaza de Armas, down Av Titicaca. A taxi or mototaxi to and from the port costs S/5–7.

INFORMATION

Tourist information iPerú is on the Plaza de Armas, at jirones Lima and Deústua (Mon–Sat 9am–6pm, Sun 9am–1pm; T 051 365 088, E iperupuno@promperu.gob.pe). They will send a list of community tourism contacts and prices in advance on request (see page 192). iPerú also operates a kiosk at the Terminal Terrestre (daily 6am–8pm), while the airport branch opens for incoming flights.

TOURS

Prices quoted below are per person for a minimum of two people. The trip to **Sillustani** normally involves a 3–4hr tour by minibus (from US$20), but can easily be done via public transport. Most other tours involve a combination of visits to the nearby **Islas de los Uros**, **Taquile** and **Amantani**, from around US$85 for an overnight stay, including transportation, unless you organize it yourself through a community association (see page 192).

3

ARRANGING A HOMESTAY – TURISMO VIVENCIA

For many visitors, the region round Lago Titicaca offers a unique opportunity to learn about ancient Andean cultures: communities' traditions and their modern-day challenges and adaptations. Sadly, tours to local communities, especially on the islands, often result in a highly unsatisfactory voyeuristic experience for the tourist and an **exploitative** one for the community concerned. If you have the time and Spanish, try to organize a visit with a **local community organization** – Taquile, Amantani and the Islas de los Uros each have one, or enquire at the island community transport offices down at the main jetty in Puno. The iPerú office in Puno can also provide you with contact details and prices of all registered community tourism initiatives, and help you get in touch with families and/or villages offering **homestays** (*turismo vivencial*) both on the islands and on the neighbouring peninsulas of Capachica and Chucuito. Spending a night (or preferably longer) with a family as the only foreigners in a home/village, rather than as part of a tour group, is a wholly different, and more satisfactory experience all round. Overnight stays usually cost around S/60–80 per person, including basic meals and lodging and an opportunity to join in daily agricultural or fishing activities (sometimes at extra cost) and undertake guided walks; some homestays are pricier and costed in US dollars. Alternatively, book through a **reputable tour operator**, such as those listed below, to ensure that more of your money goes to directly to the families/communities. Don't be swayed by the numerous touts selling cheap guided tours and trips on the streets of Puno; and if your hotel offers a tour, check their ethical credentials too.

All Ways Travel Jr Deústua 576 051 353 979, titicacaperu.com. This reliable socially responsible tour company runs the usual tours or homestays to Uros and Sillustani (US$140), and offers trips to the wildlife haven of Anapia, close to the Bolivian border, where it works with locals on a sustainable tourism project. Also arranges stays in a remote community on Taquile and on the Peninsula de Capachica.

Edgar Adventures Jr Lima 328 051 353 444, edgaradventures.com. Edgar leads a number of off-the-beaten-track tours such as Titicaca Express, which visits remote parts of Taquile island, thereby avoiding the crowds. Several tours combine kayaking with cultural visits (US$130).

ACCOMMODATION

There is no shortage of **accommodation** in Puno for any budget, but most of it is bland compared with Arequipa or Cusco. The city centre can get quite loud and busy, especially at weekends. Upmarket hotels tend to have more peaceful locations, usually outside town along the shores of Lago Titicaca, which can make for a very relaxing stay, while the real shoestring choices are around the port and market areas. There are big discounts in low season. To organise a homestay on the Peninsula de Capachica, especially round Llachón, or on the Peninsula de Chucuito, contact iPerú (see above).

CENTRAL PUNO

Hospedaje Rojitas Jr Chucuito 252 948 035 125, kenyr486@hotmail.com; map p.188. Unpromising exterior but this friendly shoestring place does the basic job of providing a bed – mattresses variable – for the night in a clean room with shared bathroom possessing hot water. Room only. Per person S/25

Hotel Casona Plaza Jr Puno 280 951 751 814, casonaplazahoteles.com; map p.188. Not the four-star lodging it purports to be, but it's a sound choice nevertheless, with spacious carpeted rooms and comfy beds piled high with pillows. Tasty buffet breakfast. S/180

Inka's Rest Pasaje San Carlos 158 051 368 720, inkas-rest-pe.book.direct; map p.188. This intimate hostel has myriad rooms tucked away on various floors; the simple dorms all have shared bath, while there are doubles, and suites for larger groups. Other draws include a games room and kitchen for guests' use. Dorms S/26, doubles S/60

★ **Kuntur Inn** Jr Ayacucho 708 051 351 209, hotelkun.turinn@hotmail.com; map p.188. This friendly, spick-and-span place offers nicely decorated rooms with faux-parquet floors. Colourful rugs add some character, while splashes of red paint brighten the rooms. All rooms are en suite with flatscreen TV, and some have lake views. S/111

Mosoq Inn C Moquegua 673 051 367 518, mosoqinnperu.com; map p.188. Nothing fancy but the basics are done well: good beds, warm rooms with mounds of blankets and room heater. The breakfast buffet is particularly good. S/180

Posada Kusillos Jr Federico More 162 ⓣ 051 364 579, ⓔ kusillosposada@yahoo.es; map p.188. This small, homely place has ten simple but pleasant en-suite rooms and two little patios. Wicker baskets and the owner's collection of masks from around the world adorn the communal areas. S/110

Qelqatani Jr Tarapacá 355 ⓣ 051 366 172, ⓦ qelqatani.com; map p.188. A short walk from the main plaza, this place has hallways furnished with couches, paintings and pot plants. Rooms are warm and cosy – though some are noisy. S/160

Royal Inn Hotel Jr Ayacucho 438 ⓣ 051 364 574, ⓦ royalinnhoteles.com; map p.188. Central and upmarket, aimed at the business community, featuring carpeted, warm rooms with solid beds with headboards, minibar, safe, phone and room service. Suites with jacuzzis and hydro-massage showers. Friendly, professional service. S/330

Suites Antonio Jr Arequipa 840 ⓣ 051 351 767, ⓦ sanantoniosuitespuno.com; map p.188. Paintings of life on Lago Titicaca brighten up the public areas of this hotel, and there's a communal area with fireplace, and free infusions on each floor. Carpeted rooms vary – some are brighter than others – and service is friendly. S/130

Tayka Hostel Jr Ayacucho 515 ⓣ 051 351 427, ⓦ taykahostel.com; map p.188. Excellent budget option with simple, cheerfully painted rooms for one to four people, including a four-bed dorm with proper beds. Also a kitchen, games room with pool table and luggage storage. Dorms S/25, doubles S/60

★ **Tierra Viva** Jr Grau 270 ⓣ 051 368 005, ⓦ tierravivahoteles.com; map p.188. One of central Puno's best hotels, offering welcoming, carpeted rooms with king-size beds draped with alpaca blankets. Walls are decorated with *quipus*, a set of hanging Inca cords that were used in a similar way to an abacus. The corridors are embellished with fabrics from the island of Taquile, and the slightly more spacious superior rooms (S/260) have tea- and coffee-making facilities and fridge. S/220

3

AROUND PUNO

★ **Casa Andina Premium** Av Sesquicentenario 1970 ⓣ 051 363 992, ⓦ casa-andina.com; map p.188. On the shores of Lago Titicaca, this peaceful hotel offers accommodation in 45 smartly furnished rooms – balcony and lake view S/50 extra – with modern amenities. The hotel restaurant is excellent and the lovely outdoor area is particularly appealing on a crisp sunny day. S/340

Hotel Libertador Isla Esteves s/n ⓣ 051 367 780, ⓦ libertador.com.pe; map p.188. Located on a private island linked to the mainland by bridge, the real draw here is the excellent view of Lago Titicaca from the restaurant's floor-to-ceiling glass panels. Otherwise, the hotel decor is rather outmoded, though rooms are comfortable. S/450

Yavari B&B ⓣ 051 369 329, ⓦ yavari.org; map p.188. The stunning British-built *Yavari* gunship (see page 190) offers accommodation in four cabins but was being renovated at the time of writing. Check the website for progress.

EATING

Balcones de Puno Jr Libertad 354 ⓣ 051 365 300, ⓦ balconesdepuno.com; map p.188. This restaurant hosts well-performed daily folkloric dance shows (7.30–9pm) featuring incredible traditional costumes. Choose your night if you want to avoid the tour groups. Food is delicious – consider alpaca medallions accompanied by quinoa cooked with milk and cheese risotto-style with stir-fried vegetables and gooseberry sauce (S/40), followed by flambéed quinoa and strawberry ice cream. Daily 10am–10pm.

La Casa del Corregidor Jr Deústua 576 ⓣ 051 351 921, ⓦ cafebar.casadelcorregidor.pe; map p.188. Located within a beautifully restored building, the flower-filled patio is a top spot for an afternoon *chichi*, or fresh juice; at night, the atmospheric bar with trendy lampshades, cushioned seating and walls plastered with vinyl discs serves pub grub and is ideal for a beer or cocktail. Mon–Sat 9am–9pm.

La Casona Jr Lima 423, 2nd floor ⓣ 051 351 108, ⓦ lacasona-restaurant.com; map p.188. Large family-run restaurant in the heart of town; walls are adorned with old irons and typewriters, and the menu includes local dishes like trout in crispy *kiwicha* (Andean cereal) with passionfruit sauce and fennel mash (S/34). Daily noon–9pm.

Cevichería Mareas Jr Cajamarca 448 ⓣ 051 777 000; map p.188. Seafood and fresh fish travel daily from Ilo on the coast to this bustling cevichería. The menu includes a range of tasty ceviches, some using lake fish (S/11), as well as other seafood dishes. Daily 9am–4pm.

Loving Hut Jr Choquehuanca 188 ⓣ 051 353 523, ⓦ lovinghut.com/pe; map p.188. This simple, inexpensive vegan restaurant gets particularly busy at lunchtime, and offers freshly prepared dishes at very reasonable prices. The lunch menu will set you back S/15; individual dishes from around S/8. Mon–Fri 11am–8pm, Sat 11am–6pm.

★ **Mojsa** Jr Lima 635, 2nd floor, Plaza de Armas ⓣ 051 363 182, ⓦ mojsarestaurant.com; map p.188. It translates as "delicious" in Aymara, and they wouldn't be lying. Popular, cosy restaurant with wooden interiors offers DIY salads, tasty *causa escabechada* (mashed potato, grilled trout and a peppery sauce; S/20) and alpaca steak with quinoa *pesque*. Most mains S/32–38. Daily noon–9.30pm.

Pacha's Mixology Jr Lima 370; map p.188. Handy bar-cum-breakfast hole-in-the wall joint with intimate wooden tables. You can get an omelette or plate of pancakes for under S/10, salads and snacks too. Beers are S/8 and a glass of wine S/12. Daily 8am–late.

Rupha Café Jr Moquegua 338; map p.188. Pleasant upstairs spot – perfect for breakfast (until noon), all-day waffles (S/10), empanadas, baguettes (S/9–13) or a slice of cake, or more substantial burger and chips. Service is brisk and reliable. Mon–Sat 7am–9.30pm, Sun noon–9.30pm.

★ **La Table del Inca** Jr Ancash 239 ⓣ 994 659 357, ⓦ facebook.com/latabledelinca; map p.188. White tablecloths and napkins yet a relaxed, intimate ambiance and – best of all – mouth-watering dishes exquisitely presented. A small selection of French-Peruvian fusion cuisine (mains S/40, or a three-course menu for S/80). Leave room for the chocolate fondant dessert. Mon–Fri noon–2pm & 6–9.30pm, Sat & Sun 6–9.30pm.

DRINKING AND NIGHTLIFE

Nightlife centres around Jirón Lima, a pedestrian precinct where the locals, young and old alike, hang out, parading up and down past the hawkers selling woollen sweaters, craft goods, cigarettes and sweets.

Ekekos Jr Lima 355, 2nd floor ⓣ 051 365 986; map p.188. *Ekekos* offers snacks, meals, drinks, cable TV, books and games; it also shows films and favours a soundtrack of rock, salsa, reggae, trance and techno music. Daily 6pm–late.

Kamizaraky Jr Grau 158; map p.188. A dark, cavernous bar with live music on weekend nights from 9pm – otherwise expect pop videos. Rock is the mainstay although bands also play reggae, country, jazz and blues. Cocktails from S/15. Daily 5pm–midnight.

Positive Jr Lima 378 ⓣ 051 950 329; map p.188. This place has bags of character – the walls are plastered with travellers' notes and coins, and it hums with custom in the evenings. It's a great spot for a beer (S/15), though the food is average. Daily 8am–late.

Remix Jr Puno 517; map p.188. Close to the cathedral, this cosy two-storey pizza-bar is simple in its tastes: rock and pizza – oven-fired (which keeps the place warm) by the slice or the whole thing (from S/12). Mon–Sat 5–9.30pm.

ENTERTAINMENT

Teatro Municipal Corner of jirones Arequipa and Deza ⓣ 051 351 019. Puno's modern Teatro Municipal hosts folklore music, dance and other cultural events. For details of what's on, check at iPerú (see page 191).

Sillustani

Lago Umayo, 30km northwest of Puno• Daily 8.30am–5.30pm • S/15 • Take a Juliaca-bound combi from Puno's Jr Lampa and Pasaje Maldonado (every 20min); ask to be let off at the Desvío Sillustani (20min), from where you can catch a colectivo to Sillustani (20min) via the hamlet of Atuncolla. Out of season, it can be a long wait between colectivos.

Scattered all around Lake Titicaca you'll find *chullpas*, gargantuan stone towers up to 10m in height in which the ancient Kolla people, who dominated the region before the Incas, buried their dead. Some of the most spectacular are at **SILLUSTANI**, set on a little peninsula in Lago Umayo 30km northwest of Puno. This ancient temple/cemetery consists of a ring of stones more than five hundred years old – some of which have been tumbled by earthquakes or, more recently, by tomb robbers intent on stealing the rich goods (ceramics, jewellery and a few weapons) buried with important mummies. Two styles predominate at this site: the honeycomb *chullpas* and those whose superb stonework was influenced by the advance of the Inca Empire. The former are set aside from the rest and characterized by large stone slabs around a central core; some of them are carved, but most are simply plastered with white mud and small stones. The later, Inca-type stonework is more complicated and in some cases you can see the elaborate corner-jointing typical of Cusco masonry. The onsite museum has been under renovation for years.

Lampa

Just under 80km northwest across the pampa from Puno, beyond the unappealing city of Juliaca, is the low-key town of **LAMPA,** known as the "Ciudad Rosada" on account of its appealing pink stone colonial buildings. Once a strategic crossroads between Cusco,

ABADOSELSANTISIMOSACRA
ELATARILALINPIACONSEF
NDENVESTRASERNORACON
VIDASINMANCHANIDEVD
EPECADOORIGINALMEN
DESVS MARCAIJOSEF

Arequipa and the mines in Potosí in present-day Bolivia, it's now a tranquil backwater. The handsome Plaza de Armas boasts a colonnaded pink Municipalidad, and just west of the square a small private **museum** (Mon–Fri 8am–6pm; S/5 donation) hosts an eclectic collection of pre-Inca, Inca and colonial artefacts. If closed, seek out the owner-curator at the nearby shop. Also ask directions to see the *casona* with the Juego de Oca, a decorative, circular mosaic representing a Spanish "board game", inlaid in the outside patio.

Iglesia de Santiago de Apóstol

Plaza de Armas • Daily 9am–noon & 2–4pm • S/10 for a recommended guided tour (in Spanish)

The town's main attraction is its imposing late seventeeth-century Virreinal church, made from pink *sillar*, and featuring an intricately carved façade. The interior is equally impressive, laden with Cusqueño paintings, and boasting an intricately carved pulpit. Even more extraordinary, the church houses a domed vault topped by an unlikely metal replica of Michelangelo's Pietá; this copy was, in turn, copied from a plaster replica – now housed in the Municipalidad – that was used as a model by restoration experts when repairing the marble original in the Vatican after it had been badly vandalized in 1972. Other curiosities include a reproduction of *The Last Supper*, a leather effigy of Christ, a series of labyrinthine catacombs and various collections of skeletons.

ARRIVAL AND DEPARTURE — LAMPA

By combi Take a combi from Puno bound for Juliaca (50min); once in Juliaca, take a mototaxi to the *paradero* de Lampa, where colectivo cars or combis leave (30min).

Islas de los Uros

The artificially made floating **ISLAS DE LOS UROS** have been inhabited since their construction centuries ago by Uros communities retreating from more powerful neighbours like the Incas. They are now home to a dwindling and much-abused indigenous population. Although there are over forty of these islands, most guided tours limit themselves to visiting one or two of a handful of them, including the largest, **Huacavacani**, where several families live alongside a floating Seventh-Day Adventist missionary school.

The islands are made from layer upon layer of **totora reeds**, the dominant plant in the shallows of Titicaca and a source of food (the inner juicy bits near the roots), as well as the basic material for roofing, walling and fishing rafts. During the rainy season (Dec–March) it's not unusual for some of the islands to move about the surface of the lake. Solar panels have brought limited electricity to the islands.

ARRIVAL AND TOURS — ISLAS DE LOS UROS

By boat It is easy to visit independently; go to the Islas de los Uros office on the main jetty (daily 6am–4.30pm). Colectivo boats leave hourly from around 8am (S/10 return). They also run 2hr 30min–3hr tours (from S/25–30), usually stopping at two islands. For homestays, which can feel very staged, contact one of the islands directly: Asociación Utama (T 951 668 861, E ncoilalujano@yahoo.es); Uros Titicaca Lodge (T 951 926 553, W urostiticacalodge.com); Uros Titino T 979 252 836).

Taquile

One of Titicaca's non-floating islands, **TAQUILE** is a peaceful place that sees fewer tourists than the Uros, though it has a population of over 2000. Located 25–30km across the water from Puno it lies just beyond the outer edge of the Golfo de Chucuito. Taquile is arguably the most attractive of the islands hereabouts, measuring about 1km by 7km, and looking from some angles like a huge ribbed whale, large and bulbous to the east, tapering to its western tail end. The horizontal

THE UROS

There are only a few hundred **Uros** people living on the islands these days – only two to three families per island, and a lot of the population is mixed-heritage, with Quechua and Aymara blood. When the Incas controlled the region, they considered the Uros so poor – almost subhuman – that the only tribute required of them was a section of hollow cane filled with lice.

Life on the islands has certainly never been easy: the inhabitants have to go some distance to find **fresh water**, and the bottoms of the reed islands rot so rapidly that fresh matting has to be constantly added above. Islands last around twelve to fifteen years and it takes two months of communal work to start a new one.

More than half the islanders have converted to **Catholicism** but the largest community is dominated by its Adventist school. Fifty years ago the Uros were a proud **fishing people**, in many ways the guardians of Titicaca, but the 1980s, particularly, saw a rapid devastation of their traditional values. However, things have improved over recent years and you do get a glimpse of a very unusual way of life. Note that lots of the people you may meet actually live on the mainland, only travelling out to sell their wares to tourists.

striations are produced by significant amounts of ancient terracing along the steep-sided shores. Such terraces are at an even greater premium here in the middle of the lake where soil erosion would otherwise slowly kill the island's largely self-sufficient agricultural economy, of which potatoes, corn, broad beans and hardy *quinoa* are the main crops. Without good soil Taquile could become like the Islas de los Uros, depending almost exclusively on tourism for its income. Today, the island is still fairly traditional. There is no grid-connected electricity on the island, though there is a solar-powered community loudspeaker and a growing number of individual houses with solar lighting; it's therefore a good idea to take a torch, matches and candles.

The island has two main ports: **Puerto Chilcano Doc** (on the west or Puno side of the island) and **El Otro Puerto** (on the north side, used mostly by tour agency boats because it has an easier and equally panoramic access climb). Arriving via Puerto Chilcano Doc, the main heart of the island is reached via 525 gruelling steps up a steep hill from the small stone harbour; this can easily take an hour of slow walking. When you've recovered your breath, you will eventually appreciate the spectacular view of the southeast of the island where you can see the hilltop ruins of **Uray K'ari**, built of stone in the Tiahuanaco era around 800 AD; looking to the west you may glimpse the larger, slightly higher ruins of **Hanan K'ari**. On arrival, before climbing the stairs, you'll be met by a committee of locals who delegate various local families to look after particular travellers – be aware that your family may live in basic conditions and speak no Spanish, let alone English (Quechua being the first language).

Brief history

The island has been inhabited for over ten thousand years, with agriculture being introduced around 4000 BC. Some three thousand years ago it was inhabited by the Pukara culture and the first stone terraces were built here. It was dominated by the Aymara-speaking Tiahuanaco culture until the thirteenth century, when the Incas conquered it and introduced the Quechua language. In 1580, the island was bought by Pedro González de Taquile and so came under Spanish influence.

During the 1930s the island was used as a safe place of exile/prison for troublesome characters such as former president Sánchez Cerro, and it wasn't until 1937 that the residents – the local descendants of the original inhabitants – regained legal ownership by buying it back.

WEAVING AND KNITTING ON TAQUILE

Although they grow abundant maize, potatoes, wheat and barley, most of Taquile's population of 1200 people are also weavers and knitters of fine **alpaca wool**, renowned for their excellent cloth. You can still watch the locals drop-spin, a common form of hand-spinning that produces incredibly fine thread for their special cloth. The men sport black woollen trousers fastened with elaborate waistbands woven in pinks, reds and greens, while the women wear beautiful black headscarves, sweaters, dark shawls and up to eight skirts at the same time, trimmed usually with shocking-pink or bright-red tassels and fringes. You can tell if a man is married or single by the colour of his **woollen hat**, or *chullo*, the former's being all red and the latter's also having white; single men usually weave their own *chullos*. The community authorities or officials wear black sombreros on top of their red *chullos* and carry a staff of office.

ARRIVAL AND TOURS — TAQUILE

By boat Check departures at the Taquile office by the main jetty (daily 6am–6pm); they operate departures at 7.20am, returning at 2pm (2hr 30min; S/25 return, including S/8 island fee). Alternatively, you can go on an organized trip with a tour company (see page 192).

Tour guides There are some indigenous Taquileño tourist guides, many of whom now speak some English, so it's not essential to book a visit to Taquile via a travel agent in Puno. Once you arrive at the island, ask around at the port or head to the main square and ask there.

ACCOMMODATION

Homestays Munay Taquile, a community association with an office at the port in Puno (T 051 351 448, W taquile.net) arranges all-inclusive homestay experiences – including return transport via the Islas de los Uros, all food, lodging and activities – for US$75 per person. Another seven island associations offer daytime activities or B&B experiences in islanders' homes (from around S/45 per person for lodgings, plus S/20 for each meal); iPerú can provide a complete list. Alternatively, book through one of Puno's tour agencies (see page 191). If you arrive at the port on spec, you may be able to fix something there and then, but don't bank on it. Sleeping bags, a torch and toilet paper are recommended, and fresh fruit and vegetables are appreciated by the host islanders.

EATING

Restaurants Away from the plaza there are more than twenty restaurants, or eating houses, dotted around the island, most serving the classic local dish of *sopa de quinoa* or *pejerrey* fish with French fries.

Amantani

Like nearby Taquile, **AMANTANI**, a basket-weavers' island and the largest on the lake, has managed to retain some degree of cultural isolation and autonomous control over the tourist trade. Amantani is the less visited of these two islands and consequently has fewer facilities and costs slightly more to reach by boat. Of course, tourism has had its effect on the local population, so it's not uncommon to be offered drinks, then charged later, or for the children to sing you songs without being asked, expecting to be paid. The ancient **agricultural terraces** are excellently maintained, and traditional stone masonry is still practised, as are the old Inca systems of agriculture, labour and ritual trade. The islanders eat mainly vegetables, with meat and fruit being rare commodities, and the women dress in colourful clothes, very distinctively woven.

The island is dominated by two small hills: one is the **Templo de Pachamama** (Mother Earth) and the other the **Templo de Pachatata** (Father Earth). Around February 20, the islanders celebrate their main festival with half the 5000-strong population going to one hill, the other half gathering at the other. Following ancient ceremonies, the two halves then gather together to celebrate their origins with traditional and colourful music and dance.

ARRIVAL AND DEPARTURE — AMANTANI

By boat Boats for Amantani usually leave Puno's main jetty daily round 8am, sometimes via the Islas de los Uros, returning to Puno around 3.30pm (3hr), sometimes via Taquile (S/30 return, including S/8 island fee). Check with the captain beforehand. You can also go on an organized trip with one of the tour companies listed (see page 192), but the agencies are at least twice as expensive. There are less frequent but shorter boat transfers to Amantani from Llachón on the Peninsula de Capachica.

ACCOMMODATION AND EATING

Homestays Other than *Kantuta Lodge*, six other islander families/community associations offer homestays (from S/45 per person including lodging and meals); ask for the full list of options and prices from iPerú. Alternatively, enquire at the Amantani office at the port in Puno (daily 6am–5pm; ⊕973 209 209), or organize something in advance via a tour operator (see page 192).

Kantuta Lodge ⊕051 630 238, ⓦkatutalodge.com. Two-storey family lodge offering ten solar-powered, very basic double rooms with modern bathrooms – though don't expect everything to work all the time. Fabulous views from the terrace, and from most rooms. Rates include all meals and activities. Per person **US$35**

3

South to Bolivia

The most popular routes to Bolivia involve overland road travel, crossing the frontier either at **Yunguyo** or at **Desaguadero** – the former being more popular and more agreeable (see page 201). En route to either you'll pass by some of Titicaca's more interesting colonial settlements, each with its own individual style of architecture. The lakeside stretch between Puno and the Bolivian frontier at Desaguadero is known – also for linguistic reasons – as the **Corredor Aymara**. This sector is full of fascinating but unfortunately slowly decaying colonial relics, particularly the **fine churches** of Chucuito, Acora, Ilave, Juli, Pomata and Zepita. If you've time, it's worth stopping off to look round at least a couple of these.

Chucuito

CHUCUITO, 20km south of Puno, is dwarfed by its intensive hillside terracing and the huge igneous boulders poised behind the brick and adobe houses. It was once a colonial town and the main plaza retains the **pillory** (*picota*) where the severed heads of executed criminals were displayed. Close to this there's a **sundial**, erected in 1831 to help the local Aymara people regulate to an 8am to 5pm work day. The base is made from stones taken from the Inca Templo de Fertilidad. Also on the plaza is the **Iglesia Santo Domingo**, constructed in 1780 and displaying a very poor image of a puma.

Templo de Fertilidad

Located behind the *Hotel Taypikala*, the **Templo de Fertilidad** remains Chucuito's greatest treasure. Inside the temple's main stone walls are around a hundred stone phalluses, row upon row jammed within the temple space, ranged like seats in a theatre. Some of the larger ones may have had particular ritual significance, and locals say that women who have difficulty getting pregnant still come here to pray for help on the giant phalluses.

ARRIVAL AND DEPARTURE — CHUCUITO

By bus/colectivo Colectivos from Puno (every 15min; 25min) drop passengers off at Chucuito's Plaza de Armas. Buses between Puno and the frontier (at Yunguyo and Desaguadero) drop off and pick up on the main road, one block from the Templo de Fertilidad.

ACCOMMODATION

La Arboleda Jr Tarapaca 675 ⊕992 009 455, ⓦarboledachucuito.com. English is spoken in this friendly family B&B, which lies two blocks from the Plaza de Armas and offers three double rooms plus a flower-filled walled garden where you can enjoy the afternoon sun. **S/180**

THE GATEWAY OF AMARU MURU

Coming from Puno, beyond the bridge over the Río Ilave, the road cuts 60km across the plain towards Juli, passing by some unusual rock formations scattered across the altiplano of the Titicaca basin, many of which have ritual significance for the local Aymara. The most important of these is **Aramu Muru**, a gateway-like alcove carved into the rock and said by indigenous mystics to serve as a dimensional link to the ancestors, a belief shared by new agers, who view it as the Andean "star gate", a kind of link to non-Earthly beings and other worlds; it is very hard to find without a local guide or tour leader.

★ **Hotel Posada Santa Barbara** Jr Glorieta 115 ⓣ982 388 184, ⓦhotelposadasantabarbara.com. Run by a welcoming Peruvian-German couple who also run a riding stables, this is a fabulous place to unwind, on horseback or soaking up the lake views from the terrace. Rooms are a fine mix of stone and timber (some with fireplaces) and there's a snug bar-restaurant too. Dorm S/50, doubles S/165

Titilaka Distrito Platería, Peninsula de Chucuito ⓣ01 700 5106, ⓦtitilaka.com. This luxurious, award-winning lodge sits at the tip of the peninsula on Lago Titicaca. It boasts stunning lake-view rooms, with stylishly furnished interiors adorned with local artwork. Rates include all transfers, gourmet meals and activities. S/3918

Juli

A few kilometres on from the Aramu Muru rock (see above) is the relatively large town of **JULI**, notable for its large Sunday **market**. Now bypassed by a new road, it nestles attractively between gigantic round-topped and terraced hills. Juli is also known as Pequeña Roma (Little Rome) because of the seven prominent mountains immediately surrounding it, each one of them of spiritual significance to the indigenous inhabitants in terms of magic, healing and fertility. Perhaps because of this, the **Jesuits** chose Juli as the site for a major missionary training centre. The Jesuits' political and religious power is reflected in the almost surreal extravagance of the church architecture, particularly evident in the abundant gold leaf inside the **Iglesia de San Pedro**, on the Plaza de Armas.

ARRIVAL AND DEPARTURE — JULI

By bus Buses/colectivos from Puno's Terminal Zonal (every 30min; 2hr) drop off/pick up at the Plaza de Armas.

Pomata

Twenty kilometres south of Juli lies the historic town of **POMATA**, with its pink granite **Iglesia de Santiago Apóstol**, built in 1763. Outside the church, in a prominent location overlooking the lake, is a circular stone construction known as **La Glorieta**; crumbling today, it's still the site where local authorities meet for ceremonial purposes. Pomata's name is derived from the Aymara word for "puma", which are carved all over the fountain in the Plaza de Armas and outside the church. The **Fiesta de la Virgen de Rosaria** on the first Sunday of October is a splendid celebration with processions, music and folk dancing, as well as the usual drinking and feasting.

ARRIVAL AND DEPARTURE — POMATA

By colectivo From Puno's Terminal Zonal, catch a colectivo to Yunguyo (services leave every 20min or so), and hop off in Pomata (2hr 30min).

Anapia and Yaspique

Seldom visited, the islands of **ANAPIA** and **YASPIQUE** form part of an eight-island **archipelago** tucked away close to the Bolivian border. The islands sit in Titicaca's Lago Menor (Wiñaymarca), cut off from the main body of water by the Peninsula de

CROSSING INTO BOLIVIA

Tourist buses between Puno and La Paz travel via the lakeside resort of Copacabana, crossing at Yunguyo. However, the more direct route between La Paz and Puno is to cross via the less pleasant border town of Desaguagero, which is inevitably busier, and often involves more hassle. Note that Bolivia is an hour ahead of Peru, and that for both routes the Peruvian border is open 8am–6pm Peruvian time, while the Bolivian border is open 7am–7pm Bolivian time (+1 from Peru), so make sure you time your arrival well. When exiting Bolivia or Peru, you will need to hand in your Tarjeta de Migración (TAM) that you filled in on arrival in the country; if you have overstayed your visa you will need to pay a fine, before being allowed to leave. US citizens will need to pay for a visa for Bolivia (US$165 at the time of writing), for which you'll need to provide two passport photographs and a completed form, best done in advance.

VIA YUNGUYO–COPACABANA

From Puno take a bus, such as Ormeño from the Terminal Terrestre, or catch a colectivo from the Terminal Zonal (every 20min; 2hr 45min). The actual border is about 2km away from Yunguyo; take a mototaxi (10min; S/2). From Kasani on the Bolivian side there are regular colectivos to Copacabana (20min).

Changing money There are a handful of casas de cambio in Yunguyo, but most are at the border itself.

VIA DESAGUADERO–LA PAZ

From Puno catch a colectivo to Desaguadero from the Terminal Zonal (every 20min; 3hr). Once in Bolivia, you can pick up a colectivo to La Paz (3–4hr). though transport dries up mid-afternoon.

Changing money There are a few casas de cambio in town, more at the border.

Copacabana. Flat Anapia is the largest island and main population centre; Yaspique is much smaller and a **vicuña sanctuary** as well as a place for the islanders to rear their sheep and cattle. Sailing across to Yaspique from Anapia is usually one of the activities offered to tourists.

ARRIVAL AND ACCOMMODATION — ANAPIA

By colectivo and boat Buses or colectivos between Puno and Yunguyo can drop you off at Punta Hermosa (30min outside Yunguyo), where colectivo boats leave for Anapia twice a week on Tues and Sun between noon and 1pm (1hr 30min), returning the same day; private boat transport can be hired for around S/150.

Homestays Contact José Flores of the Anapia tourism association (T 951 089 797, E asovanperu@hotmail.com) to arrange a homestay (from S/55 for food and accommodation, extra for activities and transport). Alternatively, contact All Ways Travel in Puno (see page 192).

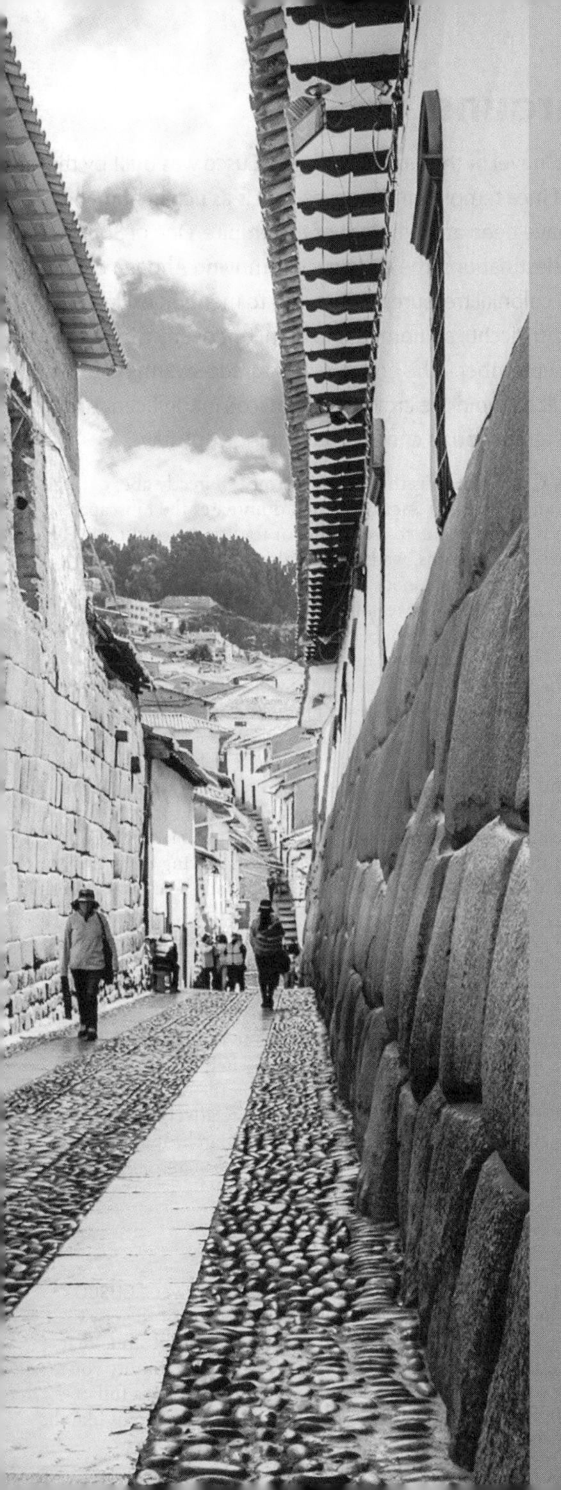

Cusco and around

HATUN RUMIYOC, CUSCO

Cusco and around

Known to the Incas as the "navel of the world", colourful Cusco was built by the Spanish on the remains of Inca temples and palaces, and is as rich in human activity today as it must have been at the height of the empire. One of South America's biggest tourist destinations, the city boasts a thriving Andean culture, and Inca architecture and colonial treasures galore, not to mention exclusive access to the mighty Machu Picchu, an unmissable highlight of any trip to Peru. In high season – June to September – the entire Valle Sagrado swarms with visitors. It might be difficult to avoid the crowds, but Cusco's magnificent history and ancient feel may well tempt you to consider extending your stay.

Enclosed between high hills, Cusco's heart is the **Plaza de Armas**. Directly above it, the imposing ceremonial centre and fortress of **Sacsayhuaman** dominates the hillscape. Once the Incas' capital, Cusco is now home to a rich mix of traditional culture, lively nightlife and an endless variety of museums, walks and tours.

The wider region of Cusco is mainly mountainous, with several peaks over 6000m, all of which the Incas considered sacred. The entire region is **high altitude** and even the city of Cusco sits at 3399m, an altitude which needs to be treated with respect, particularly if arriving by air from sea level. Within easy access of the city, there are dozens of enticing destinations. The **Valle Sagrado** of the Río Urubamba is the obvious first choice, with the citadel of **Machu Picchu** as the ultimate goal, but there are hundreds of other magnificent Inca ruins – **Pisac** and **Ollantaytambo** in particular – set against glorious Andean panoramas.

The Cusco mountain region boasts some of the country's finest **trekking**. The **Inca Trail** (Camino Inca) to Machu Picchu is by far the best known and most popular, but there are excellent **alternative trails** all starting less than a day's overland travel from Cusco. The stunning Inca remains of **Choquequirao**, in the Río Apurímac area, is arguably the best alternative archeological destination, with tours leaving from Cusco more or less daily. **Salcantay** to the north, and **Ausangate**, visible on the city's southern horizon, are also appealing options.

East of Cusco, the Andean mountains slope steeply down into the lowland **Amazon rainforest**, where protected areas are helping to maintain some of the world's most biodiverse wilderness areas. In particular, the Reserva Nacional Tambopata, or the slightly nearer Parque Nacional del Manú, are among the best and most accessible ecotourism destinations. South of Cusco are the pre-Inca sites at **Tipón** and **Pikillacta**, nearly as spectacular as those in the Valle Sagrado but far less visited.

The **best time to visit** Cusco and the surrounding area is during the dry season (May–Sept), when it's warm with clear skies during the day but relatively cold at night. During the wet season (Oct–April, with the heaviest rains Dec–March) it doesn't rain every day, but when it does, downpours are heavy.

Cusco

Nestling majestically in the belly of a highland valley and fed by two rivers, **CUSCO**'s unique layout was designed by the Incas in the form of a puma. Many of the city's finest Inca architectural treasures were so skilfully constructed out of local stone that they are still in great shape today, and the city is ripe for exploring: one minute you're walking down a shadowy, stone-walled alley, the next you burst onto a plaza full of brightly dressed dancers from the countryside, joining in what, at times, seems like the endless carnival and religious **festival celebrations** for which Cusco is famous.

CHOQUEQUIRAO

Highlights

❶ **San Blas** Take in the scene of Cusco's vibrant artists' quarter from a bench beside the church in Plazoleta San Blas. See page 218

❷ **Whitewater rafting** An adrenaline-pumping trip down one of Cusco's whitewater rivers through jaw-dropping Andean scenery is an unmissable experience. See page 222

❸ **Pisac** Standing at this Inca citadel offers a splendid vista along the Valle Sagrado and down onto the beautiful little market town of the same name. See page 236

❹ **Trek to Machu Picchu** The Inca Trail is just one of many breathtaking hikes in the Andes around Cusco; plenty of spectacular alternative treks have opened in recent years. See pages 251 & 266

❺ **Machu Picchu** Words never adequately describe this awe-inspiring Inca citadel; magically set against forested mountain peaks and distant glacial summits, it's dwarfed only by the sky. See page 255

❻ **Choquequirao** In a spectacular mountainous setting, these remote intact ruins are every bit as impressive as Machu Picchu – without the crowds. See page 266

❼ **Paucartambo festival** During the Fiesta de la Virgen del Carmen this normally quiet town transforms into a colourful, haunting display of music and surreal outfits. See page 270

HIGHLIGHTS ARE MARKED ON THE MAP ON PAGE 206

Nearly every site you'll want to visit is within walking distance of the main **Plaza de Armas**, and you can easily cover the main features of each quarter of the city in half a day. You should be able to see most of Cusco town in two or three active days, perhaps allowing a little extra time for hanging out in the bars and shops en route.

Arriving in Cusco is always an exhilarating experience. If coming straight from sea level, there's the physical effect of the **altitude** (see page 207), but, more than that, there's a sense of historic imperial glory reflected in people and architecture alike from the moment you step into the city.

Brief history

The Valle de Cusco and the Incas are synonymous in many people's minds, but the area was populated well before the Incas arrived on the scene and built their empire on the toil and ingenuity of previous peoples such as the **Killki**, who dominated the region from around 700–800 AD.

Building Cusco

According to Inca legend, Cusco was founded by **Manco Capac** and his sister Mama Occlo around 1200 AD but it wasn't until **Pachacuti** assumed leadership of the Incas in 1438 that Cusco became the centre of an expanding empire as the Incas took religious and political control of the surrounding valleys and regions.

Pachacuti masterminded the design of imperial Cusco, which was conceived in the form of a puma, a sacred animal, with **Sacsayhuaman** as its head. The overall

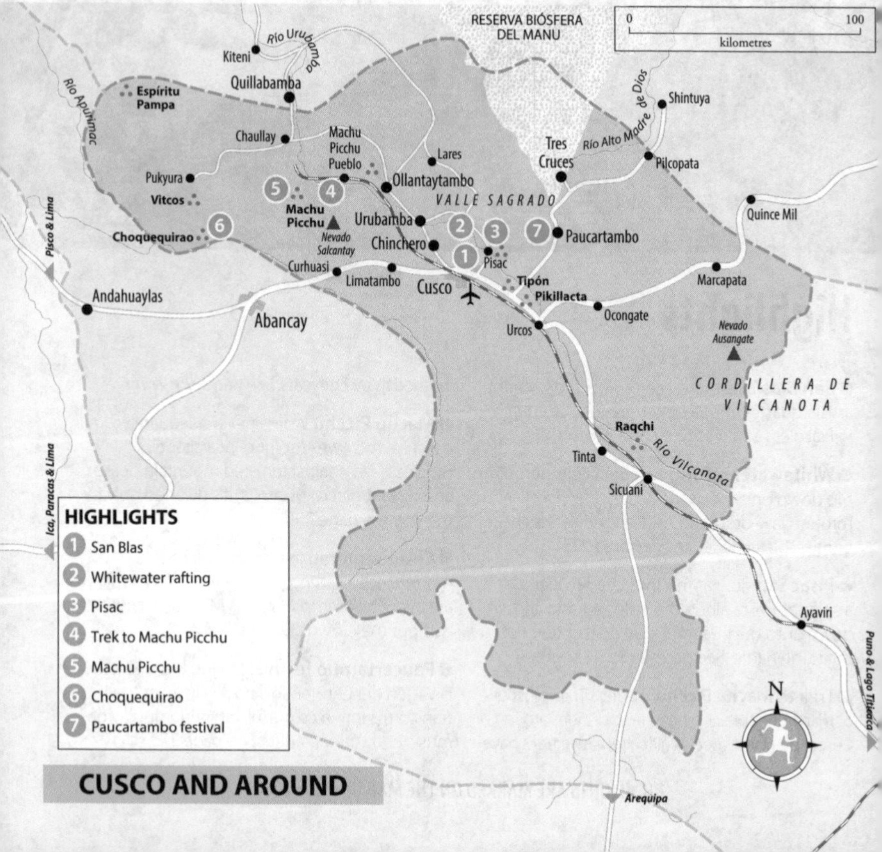

ALTITUDE SICKNESS

Soroche, or **altitude sickness**, is a reality for many people arriving in Cusco by plane from sea level and needs to be treated with respect. It's vital to take it easy, not eating or drinking much on arrival, even sleeping a whole day just to assist acclimatization (**mate de coca** – a herbal coca leaf tea is a good local remedy). After three days at this height most people have adjusted sufficiently to tackle moderate hikes at similar or lesser altitudes. Anyone considering hiking the major mountains around Cusco will need time to adjust again to their higher base camps.

If you do encounter altitude-related health problems, many hotels and restaurants have **oxygen cylinders** to help; alternatively, for serious cases, head for one of the medical centres (see page 229).

achievement was remarkable: stone palaces and houses lined streets which ran straight and narrow, with water channels to drain off the heavy rains. The city was so solidly built that much of ancient Cusco is still visible today.

The Spanish Conquest

Once **Francisco Pizarro** reached the capital on November 15, 1533, he lost no time in looting the place before founding the Spanish city officially on March 23, 1534. The place was divided up among 88 of Pizarro's men who chose to remain there as settlers. **Manco Inca**, a blood relative of Atahualpa – who was murdered by Pizarro – was set up as a puppet ruler, but following almost two years of humiliation and abuse by the colonists, he had had enough. Determined to oppose the invaders, Manco fled to the Valle Sagrado to muster an army for what is known as the **Great Inca Rebellion.** Despite laying siege to Cusco for months with over 100,000 warriors, the Incas were eventually defeated, inexplicably, in a counterattack on Sacsayhuaman by fewer than 200 Conquistadors, forcing Manco to flee once more. Though power battles amongst the colonial elite rumbled on for years to come, Spanish-controlled Cusco never again came under such serious threat from the indigenous population.

Post-Conquest Cusco

The great **earthquake** of 1650 devastated much of the city. After this dramatic tremor, remarkably illustrated on a huge canvas in La Catedral de Cusco, **Bishop Mollinedo** was largely responsible for the reconstruction of the city, and his influence is also closely associated with Cusco's most creative years of art, including the **Escuela Cusqueña** (see page 212) paintings exhibited in museums and churches around the city.

The modern age

In spite of the city's cultural heritage, Cusco only received international attention after the "discovery" of **Machu Picchu** during Hiram Bingham's archeological expedition in 1911 (see page 255). With the advent of air travel and global tourism, Cusco was slowly transformed from a quiet colonial city in the remote Andes into a major international tourist centre.

Orientation

Despite the seemingly complex street structure, it doesn't take long to get to grips with central Cusco. The area **south of the Plaza de Armas to Q'orikancha** starts along the broad **Avenida Sol** running downhill and southeast from the corner of the plaza by the university and Iglesia de la Compañía towards the Inca Templo del Sol at Q'orikancha, and on to the airport in the south.

Running uphill and southwest from the top of Avenida Sol, the area encompassing **Plaza San Francisco** and the Mercado Central follows Calle Mantas past the Plaza and

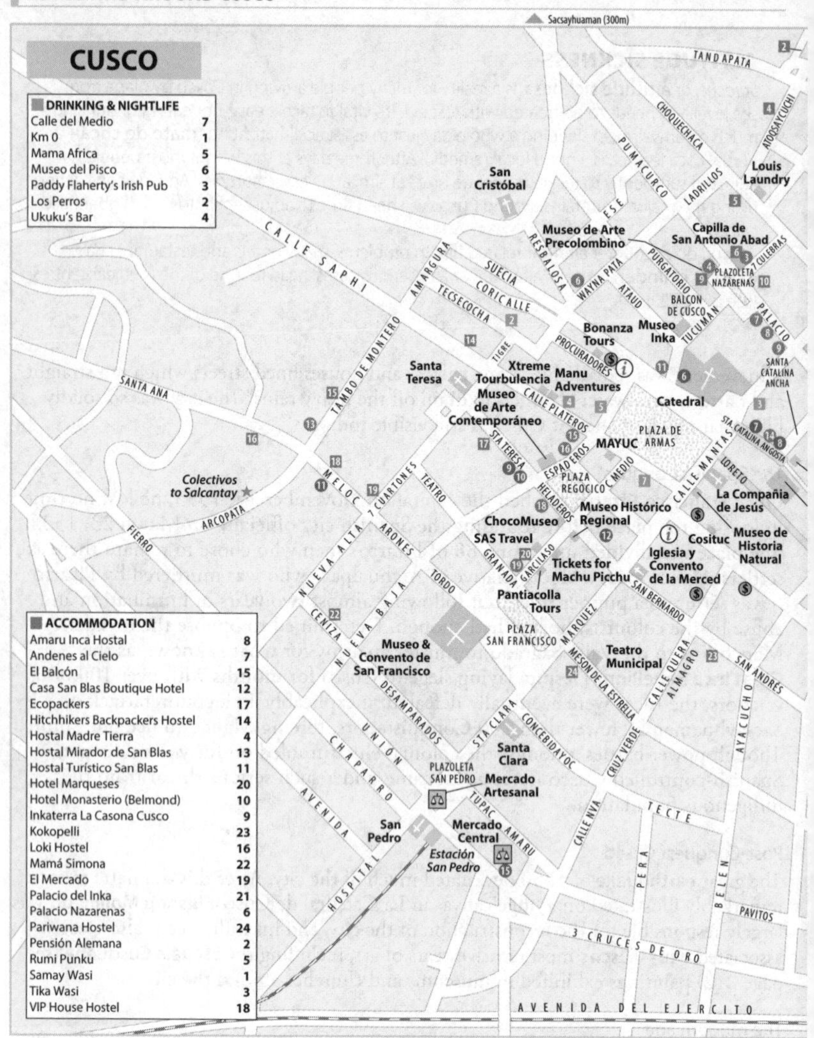

the Iglesia de Santa Clara, before continuing towards the Mercado Central and the Estación San Pedro.

Just one block west of the central plaza, you'll find the smaller, leafier, neighbouring **Plaza Regocijo**, which has Inca origins and is home to some of the city's finest mansions as well as the modest Palacio Municipal.

From the northeast corner of Plaza de Armas, Calle Triunfo heads steeply uphill through a classic Inca stone-walled alley before leading through cobbled streets towards the artesan barrio of **San Blas**. One route here from the Plaza de Armas takes you via the tiny but elegant **Plazoleta Nazarenas**.

Heading northwest along **Calle Plateros**, uphill from Plaza de Armas, you'll pass through some really charming streets that lead towards the fortress of **Sacsayhuaman** above the city.

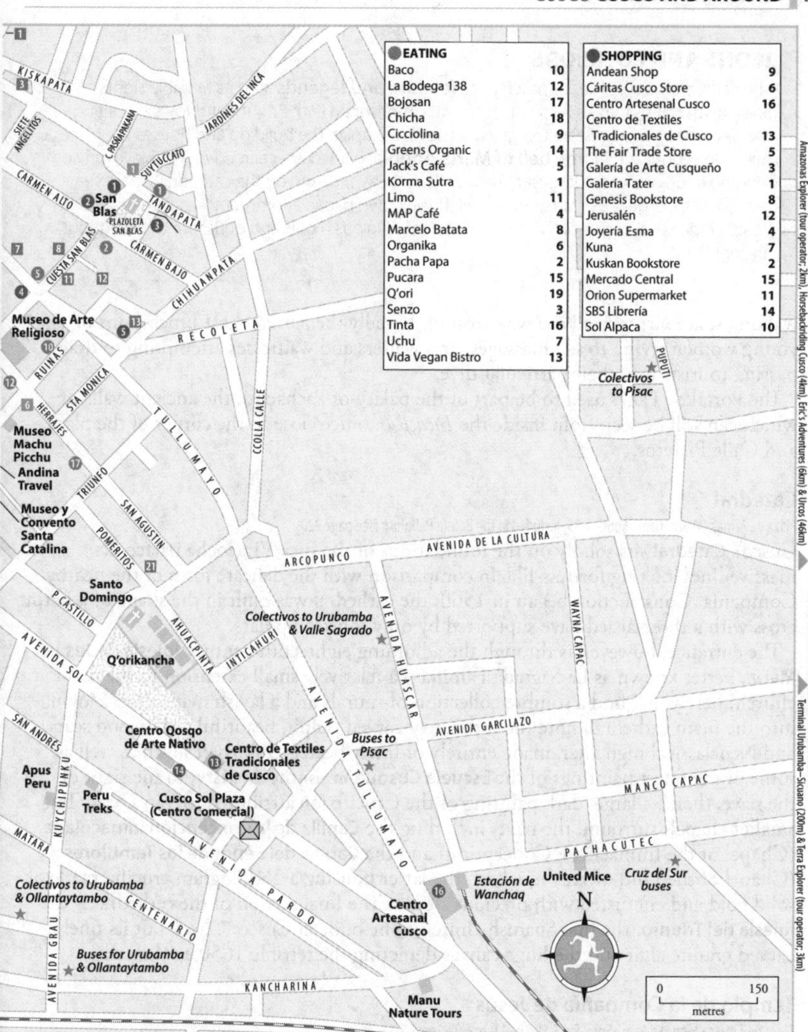

Plaza de Armas

Cusco's modern and ancient centre, the **Plaza de Armas** – whose location corresponds roughly to that of the ceremonial *Huacapata,* the Incas' ancient central plaza – is the natural place to get your bearings. It's always busy, its northern and western sides filled with shops and restaurants. Its exposed northeastern edge is dominated by the squat **Catedral** while the smaller **Templo de la Compañía de Jesús**, with its impressive pair of belfries, sits at the southeastern end.

Portal de Panes

Plaza de Armas

Circling the plaza, the **Portal de Panes** is a covered cloister pavement, with overhanging buildings, supported by stone pillars or arches that create a rain-free and sun-shaded

ICONS AND FOLKLORE

The cathedral's appeal lies as much in its **folklore and legends** as in its tangible sights. Local myth claims that an Andean chief is still imprisoned in the right-hand tower, awaiting the day when he can restore the glory of the Inca Empire. The building also houses the huge, miraculous gold and bronze **bell of María Angola**, named after a freed African slave girl and reputed to be one of the largest church bells in the world. And on the cathedral's massive main doors, indigenous craftsmen have left their own pagan adornment – a carved puma's head – representing one of the most important religious motifs and gods found throughout ancient Peru.

walking space virtually all the way around. Usually the *portales* host processions of young women trying to sell massages, and waiters and waitresses attempting to drag passing tourists into their particular dive.

The Portal de Panes used to be part of the palace of Pachacuti, the ancient walls of which can still be seen from inside the *Inca Rail* office close to the corner of the plaza and Calle Plateros.

Catedral

Plaza de Armas • Daily 10am–6pm • S/25; included in the Boleto Religioso (see page 220)

Cusco's **Catedral** sits solidly on the foundations of the Inca Viracocha palace, its massive lines looking fortress-like in comparison with the delicate form of the nearby Compañía. Construction began in 1560; the cathedral was built in the shape of a Latin cross with a three-aisled nave supported by only fourteen pillars.

The entrance, however, is through the adjoining eighteenth-century **Iglesia de Jesús María**, better known as La Sagrada Familia – a relatively small extension to the main church; here you'll find a sombre collection of murals and a lavish main altar. Moving into the main cathedral, note the intricately carved pulpit, beautiful cedarwood seats and Neoclassical high altar, made entirely of finely beaten embossed silver, as well as some of the finest paintings of the **Escuela Cusqueña**. In the **Sacristy**, to the right of the nave, there's a large, dark painting of the Crucifixion attributed to Van Dyck. Ten smaller chapels surround the nave, including the **Capilla de la Concepción Inmaculada** (Chapel of the Immaculate Conception) and the **Capilla del Señor de los Temblores** (Chapel of the Lord of Earthquakes), the latter housing a 26-kilogram crucifix made of solid gold and encrusted with precious stones. The final section of the cathedral is the **Iglesia del Triunfo**, the first Spanish church to be built in Cusco. Check out its finely carved granite altar and the huge canvas depicting the terrible 1650 earthquake.

Templo de la Compañía de Jesús

Plaza de Armas • Mon–Fri 9am–5pm, Sat & Sun 9–11am & 1–5pm • S/15

Looking downhill from the centre of the plaza, the **Templo de la Compañía de Jesus** dominates the Cusco skyline. First built over the foundations of Amara Cancha – originally Huayna Capac's Palace of the Serpents – in the late 1570s, it was resurrected over fifteen years after the earthquake of 1650, which largely destroyed the original version, itself constructed in a Latin cross shape with two belfries. The **interior** is cool and dark, with a grand gold-leaf altarpiece; a fine wooden pulpit displaying a relief of Christ, high vaulting and numerous paintings of the Escuela Cusqueña; and a transept ending in a stylish Baroque cupola. The gilded altarpieces are made of fine cedarwood and the church contains interesting oil paintings of the Peruvian Princess Isabel Ñusta. Its most impressive features, though, are the two majestic **towers** of the main facade, a superb example of Spanish-colonial Baroque design, which has often been described in more glowing terms than the neighbouring Catedral's. On the left-hand side of the church, the **Capilla de la Virgen de Lourdes**, restored in 1894, is used mostly as an exhibition centre for local crafts, as well as for dances and readings.

Museo Inka

Cuesta del Almirante 103, C Ataúd and C Córdoba del Tucumán • Mon–Fri 8am–6pm, Sat 9am–4pm • S/10 • ⓣ 084 237 380

North of the cathedral you'll find one of the city's most beautiful colonial mansions, **El Palacio del Almirante** (the Admiral's Palace). This palace now houses the **Museo Inka**, which boasts 10,000 catalogued specimens and features excellent exhibits of mummies, trepanned skulls, Inca textiles, a set of forty green-turquoise figurines from the Huari settlement of Pikillacta and a range of Inca wooden *queros* (slightly tapering drinking vessels). There are also displays of ceramics, early silver metalwork and gold figurines, but it's the spacious, organized layout and the imaginative, well-interpreted presentation that make this one of the best museums in Cusco for understanding the development of civilization in the Andes. Frequent temporary exhibitions are held here, too, including live alpaca spinning and weaving demonstrations by local women.

Constructed on Inca foundations – this time the Waypar stronghold, where the Spanish were besieged by Manco's forces in 1536 – the **building** itself is noteworthy for its simple but well-executed Plateresque facade, surmounted by two imposing Spanish coats of arms and a mullioned external balcony.

Convento de Santa Catalina de Sena

Leading southeast from the Plaza de Armas, Callejón Loreto separates La Compañía church from the tall, stone walls of the ancient Temple of the Sun Virgins, or **Acllahuasi,** where the Sun Virgins used to make *chicha* beer for the Lord Inca. Today, the Acllahuasi building is occupied by the **Convento de Santa Catalina de Sena**, built in 1610, with its small but grand side-entrance half a short block down Calle Santa Catalina Angosta; thirteen sisters still live and worship here in isolation.

Museo y Convento de Santa Catalina

C Santa Catalina Angosta 401 • Mon–Sat 8.30am–5.30pm, Sun 2–5pm • S/8

Inside the convent, the **Museo y Convento de Santa Catalina** features a splendid collection of paintings from the **Escuela Cusqueña** (see page 212), as well as an impressive Renaissance altarpiece and several gigantic seventeenth-century tapestries depicting the union of indigenous and Spanish cultures. The blending of cultures is a theme that runs throughout much of the museum's fascinating artwork and is particularly evident in the Cusqueña paintings. Another common feature of much of the Cusqueña art here is the disproportionate, downward-looking, blood-covered head, body and limbs of the seventeenth-century depictions of Christ, which represent the suffering and low social position of the Andean peoples and originate from early colonial days when the indigenous population was not permitted to look Spaniards in the eyes.

Another highlight of the museum, on the first floor at the top of the stairs, is a large fold-up chest containing miniature three-dimensional religious and mythological images depicting everything from the Garden of Eden to an image of God with a red flowing cape and dark beard, and a white dove and angels playing drums, Andean flutes and pianos.

Museo Machu Picchu

Santa Catalina Ancha 320 • Mon–Sat 9am–6pm • S/20 • ⓣ 084 255 535

A number of artefacts that Hiram Bingham unearthed during the 1911 expedition to Machu Picchu are now on display at the **Museo Machu Picchu**. There are a number of informative videos too – it's worth heading here before travelling to the ruins to get a clearer idea of what lies behind the Inca marvel that is Machu Picchu, though if you have done your "homework" before arriving in Cusco it's not a must-see. The exhibition includes over 350 pieces that were returned to the city from the University of Yale in 2010, along with local Inca artefacts that were unearthed during the restoration of the delightful eighteenth-century Casa Concha, in which the museum is housed today.

THE ESCUELA CUSQUEÑA

Colonial Cusco evolved into an exceptional centre for architecture and art. The era's paintings in particular are curious for the way they adorn human and angelic figures in elaborate lacy garments and blend traditional and ancient with colonial and Spanish elements. They are frequently brooding and quite bloody, and by the mid-seventeenth century had evolved into a recognizable school of painting.

The **Cusqueña art movement** dedicated itself to beautifying church and convent walls with fantastic and highly moralistic painting, mainly using oils. It is best known for portraits or religious scenes with dark backgrounds, serious (even tortured-looking) subjects and a profusion of gold-leaf decoration. Influences came from European émigrés – mainly Spanish and Italian – notably Juan de Illescas, Bernardo Bitti and Mateo Pérez de Alessio. At the close of the seventeenth century, the school came under the direction of **Bishop Manuel Mollinedo**. Bringing a number of original paintings (including some by El Greco) with him from his parish in Spain, the bishop was responsible for commissioning **Basilio Santa Cruz**'s fine 1698 reproduction of the *Virgen de la Almudena*, which still hangs behind the choir in Cusco's Catedral. He also commissioned the extraordinarily carved cedarwood pulpit in the Iglesia de San Blas.

The top Cusqueña artists were **Bernardo Bitti** (1548–1610), an Italian who is often considered the "father of Cusqueña art" and who introduced the Mannerist style to Peru, and **Diego Quispe Tito Inca** (1611–81), a *mestizo* painter who was influenced by the Spanish Flamenco school and whose paintings were vital tools of communication for priests attempting to convert the indigenous population to Catholicism. Bitti's work is on display in the Museo Histórico Regional, while some of Quispe's works can be seen in rooms off the second courtyard in the Museo de Arte Religioso del Arzobispado in Cusco (see page 219). The equally renowned **Mauricio García** (painting until the mid-eighteenth century) helped spur the form into a fuller *mestizo* synthesis, mixing Spanish and indigenous artistic forms. Many of the eighteenth- and nineteenth-century Cusqueña-*mestizo* works display bold compositions and colours.

By the eighteenth century the style had been disseminated as far afield as Quito in Ecuador, Santiago in Chile and even into Argentina, making it a truly South American art form and one of the most distinctive indigenous arts in the Americas.

Q'orikancha

Av Sol and C Santo Domingo • Mon–Sat 8.30am–5.30pm, Sun 2–5pm • S/15 • T 084 249 176

The main Inca temple for worship of major deities and a supreme example of Inca stonework underlying colonial buildings can be found just a short walk from the Plaza de Armas, through the Inca walls of Callejón Loreto, then along the busy Pampa del Castillo. You can't miss **Q'orikancha**, with the Convento de Santo Domingo rising imposingly from its impressive walls, which the Conquistadors made lower to make way for their uninspiring seventeenth-century Baroque church – a poor contrast to the still-imposing Inca masonry of the foundations and chambers of the Templo del Sol.

Brief history

Prior to the Incas, the Huari culture had already dedicated the site with its own sun temple, known as Inticancha (*inti* meaning "sun" and *cancha* meaning "enclosure"). Before the Conquistadors set their gold-hungry eyes on it, Q'orikancha must have been even more breathtaking, consisting as it did of four small sanctuaries and a larger temple set around a central courtyard. This whole complex was encircled on the inside walls by a cornice of gold, hence the temple's name (Q'orikancha means "golden enclosure").

Q'orikancha's position in the Valle de Cusco was carefully planned. Dozens of *ceques* (power lines, in many ways similar to ley lines, though in Cusco they appear to have been related to imperial genealogy) radiate from the temple towards more than 350 sacred *huacas*, special stones, springs, tombs and ancient quarries. In addition, during every summer solstice, the sun's rays shine directly into a niche – the **tabernacle** – in

CUSQUEÑA

which only the Inca emperor (often referred to as *the* Inca) was permitted to sit. Mummies of dead Inca rulers were seated in niches at eye level along the walls of the actual temple, the principal idols from every conquered province were held "hostage" here, and every emperor married his wives in the temple before assuming the throne. The niches no longer exist, though there are some in the walls of the nearby Templo de la Luna, where mummies of the emperor's concubines were kept in a foetal position.

Punchau golden sun disc

Still visible today, there's a large, slightly trapezoidal niche on the inside of the curved section of the retaining wall, close to the chamber identified as the Templo del Sol, where there once stood a huge, gold disc in the shape of the sun, **Punchau**, which was worshipped by the Incas. Punchau had two companions in the temple: a golden image of creator god **Viracocha**, on the right; and another, representing **Illapa**, god of thunder, to the left. Below the temple was an artificial garden in which everything was made of gold or silver and encrusted with precious jewels, from depictions of llamas and shepherds to the tiniest details of clumps of earth and weeds, including snails and butterflies. Not surprisingly, none of this survived the arrival of the Spanish.

Museo Arqueológico de Q'orikancha

Av Sol • Daily 9am–6pm • Entry by the Boleto Turístico (see page 220) • It's a 2min walk downhill from the complex reception to the underground museum entrance on block 3 of Av Sol

Though one of Cusco's smaller and less interesting museums, the on-site **Museo Arqueológico de Q'orikancha** does contain a number of interesting pieces. The first section is pre-Inca, mainly stone and ceramic exhibits; the second is Inca, with wooden, ceramic and some metallurgic crafts; in the third, archeological excavations are illustrated and interpreted; and the fourth houses a mummy and some bi-chrome ceramics of the Killki era (around 800 AD), which reflect the art of the pre-Inca Huari culture.

From the museum you can access the **garden**, which, though little more than an open, grassy space just outside the main walls of Q'orikancha, it has a particularly beautiful pre-Inca spring and bath that dates from the Huari period, providing evidence of the importance of Q'orikancha before the Incas arrived on the Andean scene.

Centro de Textiles Tradicionales del Cusco

Av Sol 603, just below Q'orikancha • Daily 7.30am–8pm • Free • ☎ 084 228 117

The **Centro de Textiles Tradicionales del Cusco** is a non-profit organization dedicated to recovering and sustaining traditional weaving traditions and techniques while helping weavers to make a sustainable living from their craft. As well as selling high-quality textile products (see page 228), the centre houses a fascinating small **museum** on the art of traditional Andean weaving. It comprises four small rooms crammed with exquisite textiles: from hats and headdresses, to ponchos, skirts and shawls. The bilingual displays explain in detail the processes involved as well as shedding light on the cultural significance of the various designs and motifs.

Iglesia y Convento de la Merced

Plazoleta Espinar, C Mantas • Mon–Sat 8am–noon & 2–5pm • Convent S/10; church free • ☎ 084 231 821

Ten minutes' walk southwest of the Plaza de Armas the **Iglesia y Convento de la Merced** sits peacefully amid the bustle of one of Cusco's more interesting quarters. First raised with Pizarro's financial assistance on top of the Inca site Limipata in 1536, it was rebuilt some 25 years after the 1650 earthquake in a rich combination of Baroque and Renaissance styles by such local artesans as Alonso Casay and Francisco Monya. Two of the most famous Conquistadors are buried here: Gonzalo Pizarro (brother of Francisco) and Diego de Almagro (see page 492).

The facade is exceptionally ornate and the roof is endowed with an unusual Baroque spire. The monastery's highlight, however, is a breathtaking 1720s **monstrance** standing a metre high and crafted by Spanish jeweller Juan de Olmos, who used over 600 pearls, more than 1500 diamonds and upwards of 22kg of solid gold. The monastery also possesses a fine collection of **Cusqueña paintings**, particularly in the cloisters and vestry, and an exceptionally gorgeous pale-stone cloister.

Museo y Convento de San Francisco

Plaza San Francisco • Mon–Sat 9am–6pm; church open daily (in between masses) 5–8pm • S/10; S/5 for the bell tower • ☎ 054 221 361

Southwest of the city centre lies the **Plaza San Francisco,** frequently filled with food stalls that couldn't be squeezed into the Mercado Central or along Calle Santa Clara. The square's southwestern side is dominated by the simply adorned **Museo y Convento de San Francisco**, built between 1645 and 1652. Inside, two large cloisters boast some of the better colonial paintings by local masters such as Diego Quispe Tito, Marcos Zapata and Juan Espinosa de los Monteros, the last being celebrated for his massive works on canvas, one or two of which are on display here.

Templo de Santa Clara

C Santa Clara, between plazas San Francisco and San Pedro • Currently closed to visitors

The small but beautiful **Templo de Santa Clara** was originally built around a single nave in 1558 by *mestizo* and indigenous craftsmen under the guidance of the architect Brother Manuel Pablo. Partly restored in 2005, it contains a gold-laminated altar, small mirrors covering most of the interior, and a few canvases, although it remains closed to visitors.

4

Templo de San Pedro

C Santa Clara and C Chaparro • Mon–Sat 7.30am–5.30pm • Free

In the busy market area next to the Estación San Pedro stands the sixteenth-century colonial **Templo de San Pedro**, whose steps are normally crowded with Quechua market traders. The interior is decorated with paintings, sculptures, gold-leaf and wooden carvings and an elaborate, carved pulpit. Relatively austere, with only a single nave, the church's main claim to fame is that somewhere among the stones of its twin towers are ancient blocks dragged here from the small Inca fort of Picchu.

Mercado Central

C Santa Clara and C Chaparro • Daily 6am–6pm

The covered Mercado Central bustles with custom at most times of the day, especially in the mornings. Stalls sell every imaginable practical item, from plentiful and exotic foodstuffs to herbalist kiosks that stock everything from lucky charms to jungle medicines. The food stalls at the bottom end of the indoor market offer some of the best and cheapest **street meals** in Peru, while the juice stalls at the top end serve up a delicious range of tropical smoothies.

Plaza Regocijo

A block southwest of the Plaza de Armas, **Plaza Regocijo**, today a pleasant garden square sheltering a statue of Colonel Francisco Bolognesi, a famous Peruvian war martyr, was originally the Inca *cusipata*, an area cleared for dancing and festivities beside the Incas' ancient central plaza – hence its other name, Plaza Cusipata. It is dominated on its northwestern side by an attractively arched municipal building housing the **Museo de Arte Contemporáneo**, with a traditional Inca rainbow flag – not to be confused with the gay pride colours – flying from its roof. On the southwest corner of the plaza stands an impressive mansion, home to the Museo Histórico Regional y Casa Garcilaso.

Museo Histórico Regional y Casa Garcilaso

Plaza Regocijo and C Heladeros • Daily 8am–5pm • Entry by Boleto Turístico (see page 220) • T 084 223 245

Once the residence of **Garcilaso de la Vega**, a prolific half-Inca (his mother may have been an Inca princess), half-Spanish poet and author, the mansion now known as the **Museo Histórico Regional y Casa Garcilaso** is home to significant regional archeological finds and much of Cusco's historic art.

Fascinating **pre-Inca ceramics** from all over Peru are displayed here, as well as a number of **Inca artefacts** such as *bolas*, maces, architects' plumb-lines and square water-dishes used for finding horizontal levels on buildings. The museum also displays some gold and silver llama statuettes found in 1996 in the Plaza de Armas when reconstructing the central fountain and golden pumas and figurines from Sacsayhuaman.

The main exhibition rooms upstairs house mainly period furniture and a multitude of **Cusqueña paintings**, including a room devoted to the work of de la Vega. The paintings span the range from the rather dull (religious adorations) to the utterly spectacular. As you progress through the works you'll notice the rapid intrusion of cannons, gunpowder and proliferation of violence appearing throughout the eighteenth century, something which was reflected in Cusco art as a microcosm of what happened across the colonial world – emanating from Europe as part of the general march of technological "progress".

Museo de Arte Contemporáneo

Plaza Regocijo • Mon–Sat 9am–6pm • Entry by Boleto Turístico (see page 220)

The **Museo de Arte Contemporáneo**, in the municipality building on Plaza Regocijo, is somewhat underwhelming, but as it's included in the *Boleto Turístico* you may want to poke your head in if you're in the area. At the time of going to press, it was in the process of being reorganized, and so displays were lacking in coherence.

ChocoMuseo

Garcilaso 210, 2nd floor, off Plaza Recocijo • Daily 9am–7pm • Free; workshops S/75 for 2hr • T 084 244 765, W chocomuseo.com

Round the corner from Plaza Regocijo, the **ChocoMuseo** has a range of interpretative displays on the history of cacao, starting with the Maya's love of this plant in Central America. The museum also organizes **workshops** on chocolate making and tours to cacao plantations in the Cusco region, and allows you to see artisanal chocolate production first-hand in the on-site **factory**, from cacao bean to chocolate bar. More chocolate in various forms can be sampled in the **café**, or purchased in the **shop**.

Iglesia de Santa Teresa

C Siete Cuartones • Daily 6am–6pm • Free

The **Iglesia de Santa Teresa** is an attractive but neglected church with stone walls, the upper half of which have paintings featuring the eponymous saint. Inside, the small brick ceiling has a beautifully crafted dome and there's a gold-leaf altar inset with paintings. The small **chapel** next door is worth a look for its intricately painted walls (featuring yet more images of Sta Teresa), usually beautifully candlelit.

Plazoleta Nazarenas

Just up the hill behind Cusco's cathedral, lies the charming and peaceful **Plazoleta Nazarenas,** surrounded by attractive whitewashed colonial buildings with wooden balconies, housing a clutch of upmarket hotels and restaurants. On the northeastern side of Plaza Nazarenas, the ancient, subtly ornate stone **Capilla de San Antonio Abad**

FIESTAS IN THE CUSCO REGION

As the imperial capital during Inca times, Cusco was the most important place of pilgrimage in South America, a status it retains today. During Easter, June and Christmas, the city centre becomes the focus for relentless **fiestas and carnivals** celebrated with extravagant processions blending pagan pre-Columbian and Catholic colonial cultures.

Around Jan 20 Adoración de los Reyes (Adoration of the Magi). Ornate and elaborate processions leave from Templo de San Blas and parade through Cusco.

Last week of Jan Pera Chapch'y (Festival of the Pear). A harvest festival in San Sebastián, 4km southeast of Cusco, with lively street stalls and processions.

First week of March Festival de Durasno (Festival of the Peach). Food stalls and folk dancing in Yanahuara and Urubamba.

Holy Week Semana Santa. On Easter Monday there's a particularly splendid procession through Cusco, with a rich and evocative mix of Andean and Catholic iconography. The following Thursday a second procession celebrates the city's patron saint, El Señor de los Temblores (Lord of Earthquakes), and on Good Friday, street stalls sell many different traditional dishes.

May 2–3 Cruz Velacuy, or Fiesta de las Cruces (Festival of the Cross). All church and sanctuary crosses in Cusco and the provinces are veiled for a day, followed by traditional festivities with dancing and feasting in most communities. Particularly splendid in Ollantaytambo.

Weekend before Corpus Christi Qoyllur Rit'i (Snow Star, or Ice Festival). Held on the full-moon weekend prior to Corpus Christi in the isolated Valle de Sinakara, above the road from Cusco to the Amazon town of Puerto Maldonado. Live music continues for days, several processions, and bands and dancers from various communities make an annual pilgrimage to recharge spiritually. As it involves camping at around 4600m at the foot of a glacier, it's only for the adventurous; some tour operators organize trips, but it's primarily a Quechua festival, with villagers arriving in their thousands in the weeks running up to it.

Corpus Christi (nine weeks after Easter) Imposed by the Spanish to replace the Inca tradition of parading ancestral mummies. Saints' effigies are carried through the streets of Cusco, even as the local *mayordomos* (ritual community leaders) throw parties and feasts combining elements of religiosity with outright hedonism. The effigies are then left inside the cathedral for eight days, after which they are taken back to their respective churches, accompanied by musicians, dancers and exploding firecrackers.

June 16–22 Traditional folk festivals in Raqchi and Sicuani.

June 20–30 Fiesta de Huancaro. An agricultural show packed with locals and good fun, based in the Huancaro sector of Cusco (S/6–8 taxi ride from Plaza de Armas, or go down Av Sol and turn right at the roundabout before the airport).

June 24 Inti Raymi. Popular, commercial fiesta re-enacting the Inca Fiesta del Sol in the grounds of Sacsayhuaman, with several days of street dancing in the build-up

July 15–18 Virgen del Carmen. Dance and music festival celebrated all over the highlands, but at its best in Paucartambo.

July 28 Peruvian Independence Day. The key date of the "Fiestas Patrias", nationwide celebrations spread over several days either side of July 28, not least in Cusco.

Sept 14–18 Señor de Huanca. Music, dancing, pilgrimages and processions take place all over the region but are especially lively in Calca, with a fair in the Valle Sagrado.

was connected to a religious school before becoming part of the university in the seventeenth century. The chapel now forms part of the *Hotel Monasterio* (see page 224), and is technically only open to hotel guests, although you may be able to take a peek inside if you ask nicely at reception. Just a few steps north is the exclusive *Belmond Palacio Nazarenas*, where nuns lived until 1977, when they moved to smaller quarters. Separating the two hotels is the narrow Inca passage of Siete Culebras (Seven Snakes) that leads onto Choquechaca.

Museo de Arte Precolombino (MAP)

Plazoleta Nazarenas • Daily 8am–10pm • S/20 • 084 233 210

At the top end of the Plazoleta Nazarenas, the unmistakeable **Casa Cabrera**, an eighteenth-century mansion built on top of a ninth-century temple pyramid, houses the excellent **Museo de Arte Precolombino (MAP)**. The museum boasts many masterpieces dating from 1250 BC to 1532 AD, including gold and other precious metals and jewellery, ceramics and wood carvings displayed in chronological order. Some of the most impressive exhibits, exquisite gold and silver ornaments of the Larco Collection, have come from the Museo Larco in Lima (see page 76). There's also an interesting display exploring the history of urban architecture in this Inca imperial capital city. Frequent temporary exhibitions are held here and the museum courtyard also hosts the excellent MAP Café (see page 226).

Barrio San Blas

Originally known as T'oqokachi ("salty hole"), the **San Blas** barrio was the first parish to be established by the Spanish in Cusco and one of twelve administrative sectors in the Inca capital. After the Conquest it became the residence for many defeated Inca leaders. It rapidly grew into one of the more attractive districts in the city, reflecting strong *mestizo* and colonial influences in its architecture and high-quality **artesanía** – even today it's known as the *barrio de los artesanos* (artesans' quarter). Hit hard by the 1950 earthquake, it has been substantially restored, and in 1993 it was given a major face-lift that returned it to its former glory. The process of rebuilding continues, with many old houses being converted to hostels, shops and restaurants.

Templo de San Blas

Cuesta de San Blas • Daily 8am–6pm • S/10; included in the Boleto Religioso (see page 220).

The highlight of the **Templo de San Blas** is an incredibly intricate pulpit, crafted from a single block of cedarwood in a complicated Churrigueresque style; its detail includes a cherub, a sun disc, faces and bunches of grapes, believed to have been carved by indigenous craftsman Juan Tomás Tuyro Tupac in the seventeenth century.

4

Calle Suytuccato

Outside the Templo de San Blas, along **Calle Suytuccato** (the continuation of Cuesta San Blas), there are several art workshops and galleries, the most notable of which is **Galería Olave**, at no. 651 (Mon–Sat 8am–6pm). The **Museo de Cerámica** (daily 10am–6pm), Carmen Alto 133, is worth checking out for its pottery.

Plazoleta San Blas

At the San Blas barrio's centre, on the southeast side of the Iglesia San Blas, lies the **Plaza San Blas**, with 49 gargoyles set on a fountain that's laid out in the form of a *chakana*, or Inca cross, with four corners and a hole at its centre. On the *plazoleta*, the **Museo Taller Hilario Mendivil** (Mon–Sat 10am–6pm) contains a number of Cusqueña paintings, as well as some interesting murals and religious icons.

Museo de la Coca

Plaza San Blas 618, 2nd floor • Daily 9am–7pm • S/10 • T 084 501 020

The **Museo de la Coca** holds a small but fascinating exhibition (in English and Spanish) about the importance of the coca leaf in both legend and everyday life in times past and present, from trepanning skulls and foretelling the future, to its use in making Coca-Cola and – inevitably – cocaine. The text is interspersed with ancient artefacts showing the chewing of coca leaves, including a replica of the skeleton of a 7-year-old boy that was found in a volcano.

Hathun Rumiyoq

An extension of the Cuesta de San Blas between calles Choquechaca and Palacio

One of the main streets in ancient Cusco, the narrow alley of **Hathun Rumiyoq** provides classic examples of superb Inca **stonework**: the large cut boulders on the museum side, about halfway along, boast one that has twelve angles in its jointing with the stones around it. Not just earthquake-resistant, it is both a much-photographed piece of masonry and a work of art in its own right.

Museo de Arte Religioso del Arzobispado

C Triunfo and Palacio • Daily 8am–6pm • S/10; included in the Boleto Religioso (see page 220) • T084 231 615

At the end of Hathun Rumiyoq, and just one block from the Plaza de Armas, along Calle Triunfo, you'll find the broad doors of the **Museo de Arte Religioso del Arzobispado**, housed in a superb Arabesque-style mansion built on the impressive foundations of Hathun Rumiyoq palace. Once home to Brother Vicente de Valarde and the marquises of Rocafuerte, and later the archbishop's residence, the museum now contains a significant collection of **paintings**, mostly from the Escuela Cusqueña. There are stunning mosaics in some of the period rooms, and other significant features include the elaborate gateway and the intricate gilding on the chapel's altar.

ARRIVAL AND DEPARTURE — CUSCO

The majority of visitors arrive either by plane from outside the country, via Lima, or by bus from Lima, Arequipa or Puno. The **airport and main bus station** (Terminal Terrestre) are both located in the southeast of the city, downhill from the Plaza de Armas and Cusco's bustling heart. Buses, colectivos and taxis are readily available to connect with hotels.

BY PLANE

Aeropuerto Internacional Velasco Astete T084 222 611. The airport is about 5km southeast of the city centre. A taxi to the centre is S/25–35, though you can get a taxi *to* the airport for a lot less. Regular microbuses also leave from outside the airport car park (45min; S/0.80), travelling along Av Sol to Ayacucho, two blocks from the Plaza de Armas. Note that the airport is full of tour touts, who should be avoided, and that flights are often delayed or cancelled in the case of bad weather. There are, however, ATM facilities and limited internet access. A new airport is under faltering construction at Chinchero, 30km by road northwest of Cusco.

Airlines LATAM (W latam.com), Avianca (W avianca.com), Peruvian Airlines (W peruvian.pe), Star Perú (W starperu.com), Viva Air (W vivaair.com) and Amaszonas (W amaszonas.com) serve the airport. In addition to desks at the airport, LATAM, Star Perú and Avianca all have offices just uphill from the post office on Av Sol.

Destinations Arequipa (2 daily; 1hr); Iquitos (1 Mon, Wed & Sat July–Nov); 2hr 30min; Juliaca (1 daily, except Fri; 55min); La Paz (1 or 2 daily; 1hr); Lima (more than 30 daily; 1hr); Pisco (1 Thurs & Sun); Puerto Maldonado (3 daily; 45min–1hr).

BY TRAIN

Estación Wanchaq If you're coming in by train from Puno, you'll arrive at Estación Wanchaq in the southeast of the city; you can hail a taxi on the street outside (around S/5 to the centre), or turn left out of the station and walk about 100m to Av Sol, from where it's a 15–20min walk to the Plaza de Armas in the heart of the city centre.

Trains to Machu Picchu All Machu Picchu trains (see page 254) start and finish outside Cusco city, either at Poroy (15min by taxi from Cusco), Urubamba (1hr 30min by bus from Cusco), or Ollantaytambo (2–2hr 30min by car or colectivo from Cusco, in the Valle Sagrado). Two rail companies offer the Machu Picchu service: PeruRail and Inca Rail. The former runs trains from Poroy, Urubamba and Ollantaytambo, while Inca Rail only operates from Ollantaytambo, in the Valle Sagrado (see page 235).

Train tickets Tickets are sold online for both companies, and at the trains stations they serve. PeruRail's main ticket office is on the Plaza de Armas at Portal de Carnes 214 (daily 7am–10pm), with other offices on Plaza Regocijo and at Av Sol 409 operating the same hours. PeruRail also has an office at the airport (Mon–Fri 6am–8pm, Sat & Sun 6am–noon; call centre T084 581 414, W perurail.com), selling Puno and Machu Picchu tickets. To travel to either Puno or Machu Picchu you should buy tickets well in advance for high season. Inca Rail, which only runs trains from Ollantaytambo, has an office on the Plaza de Armas at Portal de Panes 105 (Mon–Fri 7am–10pm, Sat & Sun 7am–8pm; T084 233 030 W incarail.com). Note that in the rainy season (Dec/Jan–April) on account of possible landslides on the route, trains from Poroy are suspended, and a bus-and-train service is offered.

Destinations Machu Picchu Pueblo (6 daily; 3hr) via Ollantaytambo; more departures from Ollantaytambo (see page 245); Puno (daily at 7.30am: Mon, Wed, Fri & Sun; 10hr, with tourist stops; US$225 one way).

BY BUS

Inter-regional and international buses With the exception of Cruz del Sur (see page 220), all inter-regional and international buses arrive at and depart from the Terminal Terrestre at Av Vallegos Santoni, block 2 (T084 224 471), southeast of the centre, close to the Pachacutec monument and roundabout (*óvalo*) and roughly halfway

CUSCO TOURIST TICKETS

There are two tourist tickets available in Cusco: the principal one is the **Boleto Turístico del Cusco** (S/130; students S/70 with ISIC card), which is valid for ten days and a vital purchase for most visitors. It's the only way to get into some of the city's and region's main attractions, covering some sixteen destinations including the **archeological sites** of the Valle Sagrado (Pisac and Ollantaytambo) as well as Sacsayhuaman, Qenko, Tambo Machay, Puka Pukara, Chinchero, Moray, Pikillacta and Tipón. The ticket also affords free entry to **museums** in Cusco including the Museo de Arte Popular, Museo de Sitio Q'orikancha, the Museo de Arte Contemporáneo and the Museo Histórico Regional. It does not, however, give entry to the cathedral, or Q'orikancha main temple site. It comes with useful **maps** and other information, including opening times. A number of cheaper **boletos parciales** (partial tourist tickets) cost S/70 and take in fewer sights (although note their validity is only two days). Tickets can be bought from COSITUC at Av Sol 103 (T 084 227 037; daily 8am–6pm).

In addition, there is a Boleto Integral del Circuito Religioso Arzobispal, or **Boleto Religioso** (S/30), which grants access to the Catedral, and the templos de San Blas and San Cristóbal, as well as to the Museo de Arte Religioso in the Palacio Arzobispal. The ticket can be purchased at any of the participating religious sights, though you can also buy single entry tickets. Students with ISIC cards get substantial **discounts** at many sights not covered by the tourist tickets, and for activities with some tour companies.

between the Plaza de Armas and the airport. Taxis from here to the city centre cost S/10–15, or you can walk from the centre in about half an hour. Alternatively, catch a microbus marked "Correcaminos" which drops passengers off at C Almagro between Sol and Bernardo. If you're travelling to the bus station from the centre, take a colectivo from C Ayacucho, between San Andrés and Av Sol. Cruz del Sur buses operate both from the Terminal Terrestre and from their own independent depot at Av Industrial 121 in Cusco's Bancopata suburb.

Valle Sagrado buses and colectivos Regular buses and colectivos travel to Pisac (every 15min; 45min–1hr) and Calca (every 15min; 1hr 30min) from C Puputi s/n, while colectivos to Urubamba (every 20min; 1hr 30min) leave from C Pavitos passing through Chinchero (35min). Note that departure points for buses and colectivos change regularly – check with the tourist office for the latest departure locations.

Destinations Abancay (several daily; 5hr); Andahuaylas (several daily; 9–10hr); Arequipa (several daily; 10hr); Ayacucho (several daily; 18hr); Copacabana, Bolivia (several daily; 10hr); Desaguadero (several daily; 9hr); Ica (frequent daily; 16hr); Ilo (2 daily; 15hr); Juliaca (several daily; 5hr); La Paz, Bolivia (several daily; 12hr); Lima (frequent daily; 21hr); Nazca (frequent daily; 13hr); Puerto Maldonado (several daily; 10hr); Puno (several daily; 6hr); Río Branco and São Paolo, Brazil (1 weekly; 18hr & 3–4 days); Tacna (2 daily; 11hr); Quillabamba (10 daily; 7–9hr).

BUS OPERATORS

Civa Terminal Terrestre T 084 249 961. Services to Arequipa, Lima and Puerto Maldonado; also to Desaguadero on the Bolivian border.

Cruz del Sur Av Industrial 121, Bancopata & Terminal Terrestre T 084 480 010, W cruzdelsur.com.pe. Abancay, Arequipa, Lima, Nazca, Puerto Maldonado and Puno.

Expreso Los Chankas Terminal Terrestre T 084 262 909. Services to Abancay, Andahuaylas, Ayacucho and Puerto Maldonado.

Expreso Turismo San Martín T 984 612 520. Services to Arequipa, Desaguadero, Puno and Tacna.

Movil Tours Terminal Terrestre T 084 267 863, W moviltours.com.pe. Services to Abancay, Arequipa, Ayacucho, Lima, Nazca and Puerto Maldonado.

Oltursa Terminal Terrestre T 084 608 313, W oltursa.pe. Services to Abancay, Arequipa, Ica, Lima and Nazca.

Ormeño Terminal Terrestre T 084 241 426, W grupo-ormeno.com.pe. Buses to Lima, Río Branco and São Paulo (Brazil).

TEPSA Terminal Terrestre T 084 224 534 W tepsa.com.pe. Services to Arequipa, Ica, Lima, Nazca and Puerto Maldonado.

Transzela Terminal Terrestre T 084 238 223, W transzela.com.pe. Services to Arequipa, Copacabana and La Paz (Bolivia), Puerto Maldonado and Puno.

Turismo Ampay Terminal Terrestre T 084 224 899. Services to Abancay and Quillabamba.

GETTING AROUND

On foot Cusco's centre is small enough to walk around. Although the expanding city sprawls down the valley, most of the main sights are within a 10–15min walk of the Plaza de Armas.

By taxi Taxis can be waved down on any street, particularly on the Plaza de Armas, Av Sol and around Plaza San Francisco, although it's advisable to call a reliable company in advance as scams are common; rides within

Cusco centre cost around S/4–5, slightly more for outlying suburbs and around S/70–80 to Sacsayhuaman, Qenko and Tambo Machay for a 4hr round trip. To book a taxi try Aló Cusco (T 084 222 222), Taxi Turismo (T 084 245 000) or Oqarina (T 084 255 000).

By bus and colectivo The city bus system is incredibly difficult to fathom, though it's cheap, fast and has several networks extending across the entire city. Buses are mainly minibuses with destinations displayed on the windscreen. Most useful are the buses that run up and down Av Sol every few minutes during daylight hours; they can drop off passengers or be hailed on virtually any corner along the route.

By bike Eric Adventures (see page 223) rents out bikes for US$25–45/day, including helmet, gloves and repair kit.

By car and motorbike Some of the more remote and scenic valleys can be reached by car or motorbike with a map rather than a guide. The following organize car and motorbike rental: Manu, Av Sol 520 (T 084 233 382, W manurentacar.com); Peru Moto Tours, Saphi 578 (T 084 232 742, W perumototours.com); Cusco Moto Tour Peru, Saphi 592 (T 084 227 025).

INFORMATION

Tourist information iPerú is at Portal de Harinas 177 on the Plaza de Armas (Mon–Fri 9am–7pm, Sat & Sun 9am–1pm; T 084 596 159 E iperucusco@promperu.gob.pe); they also have a couple of kiosks in the main hall of the airport as well as at arrivals (daily 6am–5pm; T 084 237 364 E iperucuscoapto@promperu.gob.pe). The Cuscoperu website is another good source of information: W cuscoperu.com. Dircetur, the regional tourism directorate on C Manta s/n (Mon–Sat 9am–noon & 2–8pm), also offers tourist information.

TOURS

Tours in and around Cusco range from a half-day city tour to a multi-day adventure down to the Amazon, at prices ranging from US$40 to over US$200 a day. The majority of operators and agents are by the Plaza de Armas, along Portal de Panes, Portal de Confiturias and Portal Comercio, up Procuradores and along calles Plateros and Suecia. Although prices vary, many are selling places on the same tours and treks, so always hunt around: check that the company is registered, exactly what's provided, the qualifications and experience of the guides, and whether they speak English, the maximum group size, and if insurance is included. To avoid mix-ups and disappointments, try to book with the service provider rather than an agent. Note also that a cheap tour may mean that the company is cutting corners – possibly as regards safety, or in relation to porters' welfare, or equitable payment to communities; ensure you ask questions. Avoid the **tour touts** at the airport or in the plazas in Cusco. For popular treks you need to **book well in advance** (at least six months ahead – nine months is preferable – for the Inca Trail). The companies listed below have been around for some time; a couple of Lima-based operators are included since they work in the Cusco area (see page 80).

TOUR GUIDES

If you wish to contract a guide privately, which can be cheaper than going through a tour company, get in touch with the Asociación de Guías Oficiales de Turismo (C Heladeros 157, Oficina 34F, second floor, T 084 233457, W agrotur-cusco.com). Contact details of individual guides are on the website (in Spanish); although it doesn't indicate which are mountain guides and which are general tourist guides, or even their specialism – though you can make an online enquiry – the website does indicate which languages the guides speak.

TOUR OPERATORS

Amazonas Explorer Av Collasyo 910, Miravalle T 084 252 846, W amazonas-explorer.com. High-end green, ethical international tour operator offering top-notch guiding and professional service. The usual group treks offered, including seven days Choquequirao to Machu Picchu (US$2599), plus custom tours from biking to kayaking and even stand-up-paddle down the Río Urubamba.

Andina Travel Plazoleta Santa Catalina 219 T 084 251 892, W andinatravel.com. Reputable Andina is constantly working at opening and developing new alternatives to remote areas, including Quillatambo. Part of the profits goes towards community projects. A reliable backpacker choice.

Apumayo Expediciones Jr Ricardo Palma 11, Urb. Santa Monica, Wanchaq T 084 246 018, W apumayo.com. Expert, responsible operators offering great multi-adventure activities such as mountain biking and rafting on the Río Apurimac and a nine-day rafting trip down to Amazonía. Also offers unusual historical, archeological or cultural tours and workshops – such as weaving and learning to play pre-Hispanic instruments; also tours for disabled people (with wheelchair support for visiting major sites). They run both customized trips and tours on set dates.

Apus Perú Cuichipunco 366 T 950 301 125, W apus-peru.com. Ethical tour company committed to sustainable tourism with links to the weaving NGO Threads of Peru, so can offer special interest tours to communities to learn about weaving and/or farming practices, as well as the usual treks and day tours.

Aspiring Adventures Apartado 611 T 084 224 514, W aspiringadventures.com. Offers half- and one-day

ACTIVITIES AROUND CUSCO

The Cusco region and nearby cloud forest and lowland Amazon provide a fantastic range of **activities**, from river-based ecotourism and whitewater kayaking to mountain biking, hiking and horseriding, not to mention white-knuckle experiences of the spiritual (and pseudo-spiritual) variety. Many **jungle trip operators** are based in Cusco (see pages 221 and 450).

HIKING AND HORSERIDING

The mountains to the south and the north of Cusco are full of amazing **trekking trails**, some of them little touched, most of them still rarely walked (see page 266). Less adventurous **walks** or **horse rides** are possible to Qenko, Tambo Machay, Pukapukara and Chacan, in the hills above Cusco and in the nearby Valle Sagrado (see page 235).

MOUNTAIN BIKING

The Valle Sagrado offers some great mountain-biking terrain, with adrenaline-filled downhill routes favoured on account of the altitude. In addition to the epic hairpin-bend-filled paved road descent from the Abra Málaga pass high above Ollantaytambo – often included as part of the Inka Jungle Trail (see page 269) – other cross-country routes take in various Inca sites in the Valle Sagrado. The companies listed for Cusco (see page 221) and Ollantaytambo (see page 250) all have decent bikes and gear (including helmets, gloves, knee and elbow pads) and offer professional mountain-bike guiding, though the levels of cultural knowledge and interest can vary among guides.

WHITEWATER RAFTING

Cusco is also a great **whitewater rafting** centre, with easy access to classes II to V around Ollantaytambo on the Río Urubamba and classes I to III between Huambutio and Pisac, on the Río Vilcanota. From Calca to Urubamba the river runs classes II to III, but this rises to V in the rainy season. Calca to Pisac (Huaran) and Ollantaytambo to Chilca are among the most popular routes, while the most dangerous are further afield on the Río Apurimac (May–Nov). The easiest stretch is from Echarate to San Baray, which passes by Quillabamba. Costs range from around US$40 to about US$200 a day, with price usually reflecting quality, but it's always recommended to use a reputable and well-established rafting company such as Terra Explorer or **Mayuc** (see page 223). Remember that most **travel insurance policies** exclude this kind of adventure activity, and always ensure that you are fully equipped with a safety kayak, helmets and lifejackets.

BUNGEE JUMPING

Bungee jumping is big in Cusco. One of the tallest bungee jump facilities in the Americas (122m) is offered by Action Valley Cusco, Santa Teresa 325 (T 084 240 835, W actionvalley.com; US$74 including transport from Cusco), just 11km outside the city; Action Valley activities also include rampaging around on an ATV or paragliding.

CANOPY ZIPLINE

Ziplining has become a popular activity in recent years in Peru. Located 15km from Machu Picchu, Cola de Mono (T 084 786 973, W canopyperu.com), just 2km from the town of Santa Teresa, was Peru's first zipline and is today one of South America's highest. With over 2500m of cables in seven sections and with speeds reaching 60km/hour, this is the place to give it a go (US$50 for the 2hr tour). Set in wonderful scenery with nearby hot springs, it's tempting to overnight here, as some do, on the way to Machu Picchu (see page 269).

HEALING PLANT RETREATS

Although less prevalent than around Iquitos (see page 478), it is possible to take part in ayahuasca and San Pedro retreats in the Valle Sagrado, especially round Pisac and Urubamba. One benefit of this is that mosquitoes and other bugs are less prevalent in the Andes than in the Amazon. Neither ayahuasca nor San Pedro is for the faint-hearted; the effects (not always pleasant) of both plants can last for many hours. Choose your retreat carefully – each shaman is different and the retreats vary in length and intensity; what's more, inevitably in such a touristy area, there are sharks about.

4

gastronomic and "Alternative Cusco" tours to learn more about the city's hidden attractions, unique trips to religious fiestas such as Qoyllur Riti where entranced costume dancing goes on for days, and other four- to fourteen-day mountain biking, cultural, family and generalist tours on set dates.

Eric Adventures Urb Santa María A1-6, San Sebastián ⊕084 272 862, ⊕ericadventures.com. A good selection of tours, from the Inca Trail to kayaking, canyoning, rappelling, paragliding and mountain biking. They also rent out bikes, kayaks, camping gear and 4WDs, and have a good reputation for rafting (US$55).

Explorandes Paseo Zarzuela Q-2 Huancaro ⊕084 238 380, ⊕explorandes.com. Operating since 1975, award-winning Explorandes is very professional and offers a range of tours and treks across Peru. In the Cusco area, these include the Inca Trail, Salcantay and Choquequirao (five-day trek US$742) treks. They also offer mountain climbing, mountain biking, stand-up paddle, kayaking and rafting expeditions (see page 222).

Horsebackriding Cusco Urb. Balconcillo K-10 ⊕966 747 459, ⊕horsebackridingcusco.com. Organized outfit taking good care of their horses, offering tours from US$65 (including hotel pickup) around four of the ruins above Cusco, to US$160, for a full-day outing. Also runs multi-day camping and riding trips to the Valle Sagrado, including to Machu Picchu.

MAYUC Portal Confiturias 211, Plaza de Armas ⊕084 232 666 (or toll free from US and Canada ⊕1 888 493 2109), ⊕mayuc.com. Highly reliable operator with the experience to organize any tour or trek of your choice, from the classic Inca Trail to the Salcantay trek. Whitewater rafting is their speciality, with standard scheduled three-day/two-night excursions to the Río Apurímac from US$490.

Mountain Lodges of Peru Av Emilio Cavenencia 225, Office 3220, San Isidro, Lima 27 ⊕001 421 6952, ⊕mountainlodgesofperu.com. MLP organizes trekking and equestrian trips (following the Lares and Salcantay routes) in comfort and style, from around US$3000. It offers the only lodge-to-lodge trek to Machu Picchu, staying in luxury, but collaborating closely with local communities (one of which shares lodge ownership). Immersion in cultural, natural and archeological attractions provided.

Peru Treks Av Pardo 540 ⊕084 222 722, ⊕perutreks.com. Experienced and responsible family-run business that only offers the classic four-day Inca Trail (US$650), in groups of four to sixteen on set dates. The company is committed to ethical and sustainable practices, taking porter welfare seriously and supporting community projects.

SAS Travel C Garcilaso 270 ⊕084 256 324, ⊕incatrailperutrek.com. One of the most reliable and professional tour and trek operators in Cusco, SAS specializes in the Inca Trail (four days from US$690), but also offers the Salcantay and Lares treks, popular day-trips, as well as the main jungle destinations. All good value.

Terra Explorer Urb. Santa Ursula D4, Distrito de Wanchaq ⊕084 237 352, ⊕terraexplorerperu.com. Top-notch adventure travel agency specializing in high-end trips, including trekking, rafting expeditions, lake and adventure kayaking plus mountain biking. They also organize family trips.

United Mice Av Pachacuteq 424 ⊕084 221 139, ⊕unitedmice.com. Specializing in the Inca Trail, this company is professional, yet reasonably priced (some discounts for students), with good, English-speaking guides and small groups (six maximum). Food is of a high standard. Also offers four-day treks to Ausangate and Choquequirao (US$699).

X-treme Tourbulencia Plateros 364 ⊕084 224 362, ⊕x-tremetourbulencia.com. Wide-ranging tours and adventure expeditions, promoting sustainable tourism and environmental protection: Inca Trail, Salcantay, Lares, Choquequirao and Ausangate (US$699), as well as the four-day Inka Jungle Trail (US$400) and trips throughout the Valle Sagrado; with student discounts.

ACCOMMODATION

Cusco offers a plethora of excellent accommodation options for all budgets, many within a short walk of the Plaza de Armas. You can find slightly pricier and more high-end places in the area east of the Plaza around San Blas and Choquechaca in the artists' quarter.

HOTELS & GUESTHOUSES

Amaru Inca Hostal Cuesta de San Blas 541 ⊕084 225 933, ⊕amaruhostal.com; map p.208. Located in a colonial building around a couple of flower-filled patios with benches, this guesthouse has a calm atmosphere in the heart of San Blas. Warm and spotless rooms are bright with carved wooden beds and parquet floors S/205

★ **Andenes al Cielo** Choquechaca 176 ⊕084 222 237, ⊕andenesalcielo.com; map p.208. A great option in the heart of Cusco offering spacious, tastefully decorated rooms with hardwood floors or carpets that give onto a pleasant courtyard, and a roof terrace. The two deluxe rooms (S/392) feature wooden beams and fireplaces, as well as balconies with street views. Substantial discounts in low season. S/245

★ **El Balcón** Tambo de Montero 222 ⊕084 236 738, ⊕balconcusco.com; map p.208. This lovely guesthouse, set in a leafy garden with wooden benches, offers tasteful, rustic rooms adorned with woven fabrics and local materials. The lengthy shared balcony affords lovely views over the city rooftops. Staff are exceptionally friendly. S/226

Casa San Blas Boutique Hotel Tocuyeros 566, San Blas ⊕084 254 852, ⊕casasanblas.com; map p.208. In the picturesque part of San Blas, this lovely boutique hotel offers twelve thematically decorated rooms with sturdy wooden beds that give onto the leafy interior courtyard. The suites boast city views. Doubles S/484, suites S/687

Hostal Madre Tierra Atoqsaycuchi 647A, San Blas ☎084 248 452, hostalmadretierra.com; map p.208. High up in the district of San Blas, this snug little place features only six en-suite, rustic rooms of various configurations. An excellent breakfast is served communally in the open-plan kitchen area. S/156

Hostal Mirador de San Blas C Chichahuampa 515 ☎084 235 054; map p.208. Solid, inexpensive choice; smallish, cosy rooms – some set into the rock – have parquet floors and comfy beds. Some rooms offer great city views, but can be noisy. S/120

Hostal Turístico San Blas Cuesta San Blas 526 ☎084 225 781, sanblascusco.com; map p.208. In an excellent location, this place offers really good value: warm en-suite rooms, with hot showers and comfortable beds plus a varied buffet breakfast and a fire-warmed lounge area. Service is pleasant and efficient too. S/180

Hotel Marqueses C Garcilaso 256 ☎084 264 249, hotelmarqueses.com; map p.208. A charming three-star hotel in a beautiful sixteenth-century colonial house; much of the original architecture has been preserved, along with some impressive frescoes. The en-suite rooms are warm and inviting, with dark antique furniture, and staff are exceptionally friendly and helpful. Works with SAS Travel (see page 223). S/300

Hotel Monasterio (Belmond) C Palacio 136, Plazoleta Nazarenas ☎084 604 000, belmond.com; map p.208. Set around four stunning sixteenth-century monastery cloisters are 122 opulent rooms and suites with marble bathrooms. The interiors are laden with colonial-era antiques and paintings, as well as hand-woven alpaca throws and state-of-the art modern comforts: espresso machines, underfloor heating and oxygen enriched a/c to fight high altitude. Spa and butler service too. US$595

★ **Inkaterra La Casona Cusco** Plazoleta Nazarenas 167 ☎084 234 010, inkaterra.com; map p.208. Outstanding five-star hotel in a sixteenth-century manor house dripping with colonial art and furnishings, enhanced by top-class service and dining. Eleven sumptuous suites boast a stone fireplace, heated flooring and a large marble bathroom, filled with hand-made toiletries. US$535

★ **El Mercado** 7 Cuartones 306 ☎084 582 640, elmercadocusco.com; map p.208. A stylish hotel brimming with character and located on the site of a former market, with market-themed touches throughout, from wicker baskets to weighing-scale decorations. In the evenings a voguish bonfire is lit in the internal patio. Rooms are contemporary with quirky paintings and modern amenities. S/730

Palacio del Inka Plazoleta Santo Domingo 259 ☎084 604 000, palaciodelinkahotel.com; map p.208. Located opposite the Q'orikancha, this sumptuous hotel is set in a renovated mansion with a spacious lobby with genuine Inca stonework. Rooms are grand, the buffet breakfast is excellent and there's a spa too. S/725

★ **Palacio Nazarenas** Plazoleta Nazarenas 144 ☎084 604 000, belmond.com; map p.208. This former palace and convent makes a classy hotel with 55 plush rooms and suites set around seven cloistered, landscaped courtyards. Supremely comfortable rooms are enriched with oxygen, to ease the change of altitude. Other highlights include the inviting outdoor heated pool – the only one in Cusco – set around a pretty courtyard, home to the *Senzo* restaurant (see page 226). S/1960

Pensión Alemana Tandapata 260 ☎084 226 861, pension-alemana-cuzco.com; map p.208. This German-run guesthouse offers well-appointed, light rooms, some of which are set around a flower-filled garden. The location is particularly peaceful, high up in San Blas – there are nice views over town from some of the rooms, too. S/210

★ **Rumi Punku** Choquechaca 339 ☎084 221 102, rumipunku.com; map p.208. A welcoming establishment built on the site of an old Inca temple in one of Cusco's most attractive streets. En-suite rooms are set around a series of pretty courtyards with hanging potted plants, and are stylish for the price, with hardwood floors. There's a cosy lounge area with TV and fireplace, as well as a Finnish sauna, hot tub and gym. S/350

Tika Wasi Tandapata 491 ☎084 231 609, tikawasi.com; map p.208. It's Quechua for "the house of flowers" – it does indeed have a pretty garden area which is a perfect spot to sit back and relax with a book in hand. The decor of the uniquely and heavily themed rooms will either grab you or not. Good value. S/254

HOSTELS

Ecopackers Santa Teresa 375 ☎084 231 800, ecopackersperu.com; map p.208. A central and modern hostel with female-only and mixed dorms sleeping four to eighteen, with light wooden beds and lockers set around an attractive courtyard. There are sunbeds, table tennis and billiards. Dorms S/33, doubles S/120

Hitchhikers Backpackers Hostel Saphi 440 ☎084 260 079, hhikersperu.com; map p.208. A small intimate hostel with a series of itsy-bitsy courtyards and walls decorated with pretty photos of Inca crafts. All rooms are en suite, including dorms, and woolly blankets are provided. Dorms S/28, doubles S/84

Kokopelli San Andrés 260 ☎084 224 473, hostelkokopelli.com; map p.208. This popular hostel has four- to twelve-bed dorms, with pricier rooms set further away from the happening bar. Facilities include a billiards table, table football, a mini cinema with comfortable lounge chairs and plenty of events from rock'n'roll nights to Peruvian pisco soirées. Dorms S/25, doubles S/140

Loki Hostel Santa Ana 601 ☎084 243 705, lokihostel.com; map p.208. A friendly, lively hostel with dorms and doubles set around the courtyard of a beautifully restored colonial building. Facilities include a TV room, table tennis and a small gym. The comfortable dorms have under-bed lockers, and there are plenty of activities including bingo, karaoke, quiz nights and beer pong. Dorms S/21, doubles S/90

★ **Mamá Simona** Ceniza 364 ⓣ084 260 408, ⓦmamasimona.com; map p.208. Welcoming internal patio-lobby featuring armchairs, fun murals and colourful beanbags. Doubles and dorms have lovely parquet floors and light wooden beds, and are kept spick and span. There's also a shared kitchen. Dorms S/30, doubles S/80

Pariwana Hostel Av Meson de la Estrella 136 ⓣ084 233 751, ⓦpariwana-hostel.com; map p.208. The dorms and private rooms at this pleasant hostel are set around a pretty patio embellished with flowers and colourful beanbags. The atmosphere is welcoming and laidback, and there are plenty of activities and events to meet other travellers including yoga, beer pong and Sunday barbecue (S/15) as well as a busy bar and restaurant. Dorms S/27, doubles S/130

Samay Wasi Atoqsaycuchi 416 ⓣ084 253 108, ⓦsamaywasiperu.com; map p.208. High up in San Blas this place offers four- and six-bed en-suite dorms. The real winners here, however, are the private rooms – welcoming and cosy with exposed stone walls and wonderful city views from the top-floor balcony. There's a guests' kitchen and free airport and bus pick-up if you stay two or more nights. Dorms S/33, doubles S/82

VIP House Hostel C Meloc 422 ⓣ084 238 688, ⓔviphousecusco@outlook.com; map p.208. Run by chilled, friendly guys, this unlikely hostel – long corridors and dark rooms with heavy, rather dated furniture – is a real find. Dorms are spacious with warm bedding and lockers, while the lounge areas are relaxing places and the free informative tour of Cusco is a star extra. Shared and private bathrooms. Dorms S/30, doubles S/100

EATING

Local cuisine Cusco prides itself on its traditional dishes, which have evolved this century into a *novo andina* cuisine, fusing the best ingredients of the Andes with exquisite Mediterranean and even Argentinian influences.

Self-catering The central market by the Estación San Pedro (Mon–Sat 6am–6pm, Sun 7am–4pm) sells a wonderful variety of meats, tropical and imported fruits, local vegetables, Andean cheeses and other basics. The market also has a wide range of hot-food stalls, where you can get superb, freshly squeezed juices.

Where to eat There are literally hundreds of places to eat in Cusco, many of excellent quality, ranging from cheap-and-cheerful pizza joints to fine gourmet establishments. Many of the best restaurants and bars are within a block or two of the Plaza de Armas and uphill towards San Blas; the more central places serve anything from a toasted cheese sandwich to authentic Andean or criolla dishes. *Quintas* – basic local eating houses – serve mostly traditional Peruvian food, full of spice and character.

CAFÉS AND RESTAURANTS

Baco Ruinas 465 ⓣ084 242 808; map p.208. A stylish and atmospheric bistro-cum-restaurant, decorated with quirky paintings. The menu includes great alpaca burgers, as well as pizzas with imaginative toppings such as lamb with rocket (mains S/32–36), along with home-made desserts (from S/18); there's a long wine list, too. Daily 3–11pm.

★ **La Bodega 138** Herrajes 138 ⓣ084 260 272, ⓦfacebook.com/labodega138; map p.208. Set over two floors, this popular spot with wooden tables serves great salads (S/26), and wood-fired pizzas (S/39) – try smoked trout and capers – and calzones, along with delectable desserts. Over thirty beers are on offer, including local brews. Excellent service too. Cash only. Daily noon–10.30pm.

Bojosan C San Agustín 275 ⓣ084 246 502; map p.208. With an open kitchen that aims to recreate Japanese ambience and cuisine, this little udon bar is a top spot for a warming bowl of noodles on a cold Cusco evening. Choose from seven types of udon (S/20–25) including beef, duck, chicken, seaweed and pork, accompanied by Japanese green tea, beer or sake. Mon & Tues–Sun 12.30–3.30pm & 6.30–10.30pm.

Chicha Plaza Regocijo 261, 2nd floor ⓣ084 240 520, ⓦchicha.com.pe; map p.208. Renowned chef Gastón Acurio is behind one of the city's best restaurants – expect excellent ceviche, *causa*, and grilled octopus as well as meat favourites including *lomo saltado* and pork *adobo* in a relaxed atmosphere (most mains S/38–60). Daily noon–10.30pm.

★ **Cicciolina** C Triunfo 393 ⓣ084 239 510, ⓦcicciolinacuzco.com; map p.208. This award-winning restaurant serves delicious Mediterranean and Peruvian dishes with a twist, including tagliolini tinted with squid ink and sautéed with prawns and coconut milk (S/39). The bustling tapas bar, with chilli and garlic strands dangling from the ceiling, offers sandwiches, salads and wine by the glass, while the adjacent fine dining room is a tad smarter with white linen tablecloths. The ground-floor bakery serves home-made breads and superb breakfasts (S/16). Daily 8–11am, noon–3pm & 6–10pm.

Greens Organic Santa Catalina Angosta 135, 2nd floor ⓣ084 243 379, ⓦcuscorestaurants.com; map p.208. A busy restaurant with recycled Coke bottles as lamps serving innovative *novo andina* and Mediterranean dishes, using organic ingredients from their own farm. Vegetarian options are plentiful too, such as wraps (S/30), or seasonal vegetable curry (S/42). And try the quinoa brûlée or mango ravioli dessert (from S/23). Daily 8am–11pm.

★ **Jack's Café** Choquechaca and Cuesta San Blas ⓣ084 254 606; map p.208. This excellent backpacker café serves consistently good dishes in a welcoming cosy interior. The all-day breakfasts are particularly good, as are the hearty soups and tasty sandwiches for under S/20. For lunch try the Mediterranean salad with grilled veg, avocado and greens (S/19). Though it's a pleasant spot to sit back and read a book with a tea in hand, get ready to queue at meal times. Daily 7.30am–11.30pm.

Korma Sutra Tandapata 909 ⓣ 084 233 023; map p.208. It's not every day you see crispy tandoori guinea pig (S/24) on the menu, though Cusco's main curry house also serves Indian favourites, including samosas (S/12), chicken tikka masala (S/27) and lamb rogan josh (S/30). Mon–Sat 1–10pm.

★ **Limo** Portal de Carnes 236, 2nd floor ⓣ 084 240 668, ⓦ cuscorestaurants.com/restaurant/limo; map p.208. Just beside the cathedral, this stylish place is one of Cusco's best restaurants with lovely views over the plaza. The speciality here is fish, in sushi (S/20), ceviche (S/45) and other creatively presented dishes including superb tuna tartare (S/52). The drinks menu features pisco-based cocktails (S/20). Daily 11am–11pm.

MAP Café Plazoleta Las Nazarenas 231 ⓣ 084 242 476, ⓦ cuscorestaurants.com; map p.208. Located in the pretty courtyard of the Museo de Arte Precolombino, this smart restaurant with soft lighting and mellow background music serves creatively presented Peruvian dishes; the signature mushroom *capchi* soup consists of Andean mushrooms, fava beans, potatoes and cheese, topped with soft pastry and crispy black quinoa (S/34). Daily 11.30am–3pm & 7–10pm.

Marcelo Batata Palacio 121, 2nd floor ⓣ 084 222 424; map p.208. This popular restaurant with black and red undertones has a wonderful rooftop terrace with panoramic views over Cusco – a great spot for a post-prandial beer (S/8) or a pisco sour (S/18). The international menu includes grilled lamb ribs served with mash (S/44) and spicy pork *adobo* (S/43). Daily 12.30–11pm.

Organika C Resbalosa 410 ⓣ 084 237 186; map p.208. A small, friendly café dishing up nicely presented, freshly made sandwiches alongside more innovative mains such as trout with pineapple, using organic ingredients. Daily 9am–9.30pm.

Pacha Papa Plazoleta San Blas 120 ⓣ 084 241 318, ⓦ cuscorestaurants.com; map p.208. Probably the barrio's busiest restaurant, set around an attractive, shady inner courtyard; it serves Peruvian favourites including alpaca and *cuy*, as well as grilled lamb. Has nightly live Andean harp music. Mains from S/40. Daily 11.30am–10pm.

Pucara Plateros 309 ⓣ 084 222 027; map p.208. This cosy restaurant with wooden interiors and dim lighting is a great spot to try reasonably priced local dishes in a pleasant setting. The quinoa soup is particularly good (S/15), and the menu includes Peruvian favourites such as *causa rellena* (stuffed potato with tuna salad; S/18), along with a range of tasty desserts (S/9). Daily noon–10pm.

Q'ori Sara Garcilaso 290; map p.208. Hole-in-the-wall joint aimed squarely at the local market: expect vast, filling plates laden with rice or noodles plus some protein for very little: three-course set menus for lunch and dinner (S/10) plus a glass of *chicha morada*. Mon–Sat 7am–9.30pm, Sun 11am–4pm.

Senzo Palacio Nazarenas, Palacio 144 ⓣ 084 582 222, ⓦ belmond.com; map p.208. The setting is exquisite, in the hotel's cloisters, overlooking the outdoor pool area. The mainly Peruvian menu includes *chupe de paiche*, a traditional jungle fish soup, and some mouth-watering ice creams and sorbets, such as eucalyptus and quinoa. Starters from S/50, mains S/63–106. Daily 5am–4pm & 7–10.30pm.

★ **Tinta** C Espaderos 136, ⓣ 084 234 136; map p.208. Small arty restaurant with ambient lighting and walls covered floor-to-ceiling with quality artwork – most of it for sale. Service is attentive but relaxed and dishes are innovative – try the alpaca steak in *aguaymanto* ("Andean gooseberry") sauce (mains from S/30). Occasional and varied live music at weekends. Daily 9am–10pm.

Uchu Palacio 135 ⓣ 084 246 598; map p.208. This steakhouse, tucked away on a little courtyard just off C Palacio offers succulent, sizzling steaks served hot on stone slabs (S/47) in a smart if rather kitsch interior. Daily 12.30–10pm.

★ **Vida Vegan Bistro** Tambo de Montero 508, Santa Ana ⓣ 978163793; map p.208. This intimate, buzzing bistro is not to be missed. The small kitchen turns out delicious, creative veggie and vegan dishes – try the quinoa mushroom risotto in hot pepper sauce. Everything is beautifully presented – often adorned with a fresh flower – and served by cheery, efficient staff. Mains S/15–25. Mon, Tues & Thurs–Sun noon–10pm.

DRINKING AND NIGHTLIFE

Apart from Lima, no Peruvian town has as varied a nightlife as Cusco. The Plaza de Armas is a hive of activity until the early hours, even during the week. Most venues in the city are simply **bars** with a dancefloor and sometimes a stage, but their styles vary enormously, from Andean folk spots with panpipe music to reggae or jazz joints, as well as more conventional **clubs**. Most places are within staggering distance of each other, and sampling them is an important part of any stay in Cusco. The action generally gets going between 10 and 11pm, lasting until 2 or 3am.

★ **Calle del Medio** C del Medio 113 ⓣ 084 248 340, ⓦ calledelmediorestaurante.com; map p.208. The restaurant's welcoming bar–lounge is decked out in recycled furniture plus a touch of retro, with colourful pisco jars lining the bar. Barmen exclusively rustle up pisco-based drinks (S/22). The small balcony overlooking the plaza is the perfect spot for a sundowner. Daily 11am–3am.

Km 0 Tandapata 100, San Blas ⓣ084 238 239; map p.208. This cosy itsy-bitsy bar and restaurant is decked out in warm red undertones; the walls are packed with paintings and customers sip on cocktails at high wooden tables enjoying the live music shows (daily 10.30pm–midnight), which include an eclectic mix of latino, blues, jazz, reggae and rock'n'roll of varying standards. Daily 6pm–2am.

Mama Africa Portal de Panes 109, 3rd floor, Plaza de Armas; map p.208. Right on the main square, this is a popular club that goes on until the early hours of the morning. The main musical flavour is pop, though salsa classes are offered 9–11pm. The second floor bar/club, *Mushrooms*, plays house and electronica, although it's a bit seedy. Fri & Sat cover charge S/10–20. Daily 9pm–5am.

★ **Museo del Pisco** Santa Catalina Ancha 398 ⓣ084 262 709, ⓦmuseodelpisco.org; map p.208. With three types of pisco from over forty bodegas, this is Cusco's pisco bar par excellence, offering tastings and live music – criolla, jazz, rock and blues – daily (9.30–11pm). Tapas (S/16) and more substantial mains accompany the drinks. Mon–Wed & Sun noon–12.30pm, Thurs–Sat noon–1am.

★ **Paddy Flaherty's Irish Pub** C Triunfo 124 ⓣ084 225 361, ⓦpaddysirishbarcusco.com; map p.208. At 11,156ft, this place proudly boasts it's the highest Irish-owned pub on the planet. Its cosy wood-panelled interior decked with Irish-themed decorations makes for a warm, busy atmosphere, especially at weekends, when the Guinness flows. Expect pub grub – shepherd's pie and burgers (all under S/20) – on the menu. Daily 10am–late.

Los Perros Tecsecocha 436 ⓣ084 241 447; map p.208. This trendy, intimate hangout in red and black undertones is a great spot to linger over a beer or a cocktail. Bright paintings enliven the walls, and you've board games and books to entertain. The snacks are tasty too, including chilli rolls and spicy wonton. Daily 11am–midnight.

Ukuku's Bar Plateros 316 ⓣ084 254 911, ⓦukukusbar.com; map p.208. A highly popular venue with one of the best atmospheres in Cusco, teeming with energetic revellers most nights by around 11pm, when the music gets going. There's a small dancefloor, a seating area and a long bar, with music ranging from live Andean folk to DJs or taped rock. Daily 8pm–late.

ENTERTAINMENT

Alliance Française Av de la Cultura 804 ⓣ084 243 887, ⓦafcusco.org.pe. Runs a full programme of events including music, films, exhibitions, theatre and music.

Dance Performances Centro Qosqo de Arte Nativo, Av Sol 604 ⓣ084 227 901. During major fiestas you'll encounter colourfully costumed folk-dancing groups in the streets; at other times, the Centro Qosqo is the only place that offers regular folkloric dance shows. Entrance with the Boleto Turístico or S/25 per show. Daily 6.30–8pm.

Teatro Municipal Mesón de la Estrella 149 ⓣ084 231 847. The municipal theatre of Cusco occasionally holds folkloric shows and events. Check with the tourist office for an updated schedule.

SHOPPING

Areas Most of the touristy artesanía and jewellery shops are concentrated in streets like Plateros around the Plaza de Armas and up Triunfo, though calles Herraje (first right as you head towards San Blas) and San Agustín have slightly cheaper but decent shops with leather and alpaca work. It's worth heading off the beaten track, particularly around San Blas or the upper end of Tullumayo, to find outlets hidden in the backstreets.

Markets The main street-market day for artesanía is Saturday (10am–6pm). The Mercado Central, selling fresh produce, is at San Pedro (see below). Out of town there are good markets for artesanía at Pisac and Chinchero; both have craft stands daily, although the main market days are Sunday and Thursday, respectively (see pages 236 & 244), when *campesinos* from the surrounding villages descend into the Valle Sagrado to sell fresh fruit and veg produce.

Prices and haggling In the markets and at street stalls you can often get up to twenty per cent off, and even in

HOW TO DISTINGUISH BABY ALPACA FROM ACRYLIC

When wandering round the markets and tourist shops in Cusco, you'll receive countless assurances from vendors that the sweater, scarf or shawl that you are eyeing up is "100 percent **baby alpaca**" when it is often only brushed **acrylic**. So how do you tell the difference? The most obvious way is **price**; if the price sounds too good to be true, it probably is. You also need to feel the item: acrylic and baby alpaca will both be smooth on the outside but true baby alpaca will also be **smooth on the inside** – unlike the acrylic – and it will be **cooler to touch** than the fake article. Weight too can give some clue, as baby alpaca is **heavier** than the artificial fibre. Finally, consider the colours; **natural dyes** are usually used on baby alpaca fibres, so expect more muted tones than you get from synthetic dyes. Taking all these qualities into account should help improve your chances of ending up with the genuine article.

the smarter shops it's quite acceptable to bargain a little. If you're worried about carrying an expensive purchase around town, it's fine to ask the shopkeeper to bring the goods to your hotel so that the transaction can take place in relative safety.

ALPACA

Andean Shop Santa Teresa 321 ⓣ 084 244 873, ⓔ 1andeanshop@gmail.com; map p.208. This pleasant shop sells top-quality baby alpaca scarves and other clothing accessories. Daily 9am–9pm.

Kuna Portal de Panes 127 ⓣ 084 243 191, ⓦ kuna.com; map p.208. One of the best places to buy alpaca products, this shop with branches throughout Peru specializes in upscale alpaca fashions, with high-quality scarves, jumpers, hats and coats. Daily 9am–10pm.

Sol Alpaca Santa Teresa 317 ⓦ solalpaca.com; map p.208. With several branches across town, and elsewhere in Peru, this upmarket shop is a safe bet if you're after genuine alpaca wool – prices are high, but so is the quality.

BOOKS AND MAPS

Genesis Bookstore Santa Catalina Ancha 307 ⓣ 084 257 971; map p.208. Sells books in English, particularly guides, history books and material on birds or wildlife; it's also a post office agent and has stationery. Daily 9am–9pm.

Jerusalén C Heladeros 143 ⓣ 084 235428; map p.208. When you need new reading matter for a long bus journey, this is the place to go: second-hand books in English for sale or to exchange (2 for 1). Mon–Sat 10am–2pm, 4–8pm.

Kuskan Bookstore Plaza San Blas 630A ⓣ 084 253 320; map p.208. This store has some fascinating books in English, particularly focusing on travel, culture and biodiversity. Daily 8am–8pm.

SBS Librería Av Sol 864 ⓣ 084 248 106; map p.208. Part of an international chain with a good range of books; of interest to trekkers, it sells topographical maps of the Cusco region. Mon–Fri 9am–8.30pm, Sat 9.30am–1.30pm & 4–8pm.

CAMPING EQUIPMENT

Renting or buying camping equipment is easy in Cusco, but you may be asked to leave your passport as a deposit on more expensive items; always get a proper receipt. For basics such as pots, pans, plates and so on, try the Saturday morning market in Monjaspata, less than half a block from the bottom end of the Mercado San Pedro, while others such as buckets, bowls and sheets are sold in various shops along nearby C Concebidayoq, and C Procuradores, off the Plaza de Armas.

CRAFTS, ANTIQUES AND JEWELLERY

Cáritas Cusco Store Cuesta del Almirante 211 ⓣ 084 237 842, ⓦ caritascuscostore.com; map p.208. A worthy place to spend your soles as seventy percent of the sale from the textile products goes back to the rural artisan.

Centro Artesanal Cusco Last block of Av Sol and Tullumayo; map p.208. A plethora of stalls selling a range of crafts as well as blankets and other accessories. Daily 8am–8pm.

★ **Centro de Textiles Tradicionales de Cusco** Av Sol 603 ⓣ 084 228 117, ⓦ textilescusco.org; map p.208. A not-for-profit organization that aims to keep weaving traditions alive by promoting fine textiles by local communities and artisans. Prices are a bit higher than in shops but are also of superior quality and the profits go to the women who work on each piece. Mon–Fri 7.30am–8.30pm, Sat & Sun 8.30am–7.30pm.

The Fair Trade Store C Chiwampata 515 ⓣ 084 257 270 ⓦ facebook.com/FairTradeStoreCusco; map p.208. Some beautifully crafted weavings and accessories – bags, belts and shawls – in alpaca, baby alpaca ad sheep's wool, with eighty percent of the sale going to the community. Mon–Sat 10am–8pm.

Galería de Arte Cusqueño Plazoleta San Blas 114 ⓣ 084 237857; map p.208. A range of antiques, from furniture to textiles. Mon–Sat 10am–1pm & 4–8pm.

Galería Tater Suytuccato 705B ⓣ 084 506 228; map p.208. Artist Tater Camilo Vera Vizcarra displays his work at his gallery in San Blas – ceramics are available for purchase. He also has a ceramic workshop at Tungasuca Z4 in Urb. Tupac Amaru. Mon–Sat 10am–2pm & 4–8pm.

Joyería Esma Hatun Rumiyoc 120 ⓣ 084 260 824; map p.208. A fun little shop selling hand-designed Peruvian jewellery. Mon–Sat 9.30am–8pm.

FOOD

Mercado Central Plazoleta San Pedro; map p.208. The best place for generally excellent and very cheap food – including all the main typical Peruvian dishes like *cau cau* (tripe), rice with meat and veg, and *papas a la huancaína* (see page 34). Mon–Sat 6am–6pm, Sun 7am–4pm.

Orion Supermarket Meloc 417; map p.208. Central supermarket offering a range of goods, from foodstuffs to toiletries. It also has a branch at Belén 494. Daily 8am–10.30pm.

DIRECTORY

Banks and exchange Numerous banks and ATMs are dotted around the Plaza de Armas and along Av Sol; the small Scotiabank on the Plaza de Armas allows you to withdraw up to S/4000 against a credit card on presentation of your passport. Several casas de cambio line Portal Comercio at the Plaza de Armas, whereas street *cambistas* can be found on blocks 2 and 3 of Av Sol, around the main banks.

Consulates Bolivia, Av Oswaldo Baca 101 (T 084 231 845); Brazil, Jr Las Gardenias D13, 3rd floor (T 084 221 390); UK, Jr Los Geranios 2G, Mariscal Gamarra (T 084 224 135); US, Av El Sol 449 (T 084 231 474).

Health The Hospital Regional is on Av de la Cultura (T 084 231455, 084 223030 or 084 223691). Among the city's best private clinics are CIMA, Av Pardo 978 (T 084 255 550, W cima-clinic.com); Clínica San José, Av Los Incas 1408B (T 084 253 295, W sanjose.com.pe) and the Clínica Peruano Suiza, Av Perú K3, Urb. Quispicanchis (T 084 242 114 W cps.com.pe).

Immigration Migraciones, Av Sol 610 (Mon–Fri 8am–4pm, Sat 8am–noon; T 084 222 741).

Language schools Amigos Spanish School, Zaguan del Cielo B-23 (T 084 225 053, W spanishcusco.com), is a non-profit institution which funds education and food for local young people through its teaching of Spanish; family stays can also be organized. Staff speak English, Dutch, German, French and Japanese. Amauta Spanish at Suecia 480 (T 084 262 345, W amautaspanish.com) also has a good reputation and offers group and individual Spanish lessons.

Laundry There are scores of laundries all over Cusco, especially round San Blas, most charging S/3–4 per kilo.

Police The main police station is on Plaza Tupac Amaru Wanchaq. The 24hr Policía de Turismo is on C Saphi 510 (T 084 249 654).

Post office The main office is at Av Sol 800 (Mon–Sat 7.30am–8pm; Sun 9am–2pm).

Inca sites near Cusco

The megalithic fortress of **Sacsayhuaman**, which looks down onto the red-tiled roofs of Cusco from high above the city, is the closest and most impressive of several historic sites scattered around the Cusco hills. However, there are four other major Inca sites in the area. Not much more than a stone's throw beyond Sacsayhuaman lie the great *huaca* of **Qenko** and the less-visited Salapunco, thought by some to be a temple to the moon. A few kilometres further on, at what almost certainly formed the outer limits of the Inca's home estate, you come to the small, fortified hunting lodge of **Pukapukara** and the stunning imperial baths of **Tambo Machay**.

4

Sacsayhuaman

On the hilltop just over 1km north of the Plaza de Armas • Daily 7am–6pm • Entry by Boleto Turístico (see page 220)

The walled complex of **SACSAYHUAMAN** forms the head of Cusco's puma (the Inca city was designed in the shape of a puma), whose fierce-looking teeth point away from the city. The name Sacsayhuaman is of disputed origin, with different groups holding that it means either "satiated falcon", "speckled head" or "city of stone".

Once the site of a bloody battle between Inca leaders and the Spanish Conquistadors, today the most dramatic event to take place at Sacsayhuaman is the colourful – if overly commercial – **Inti Raymi festival** in June (see page 217). However, throughout the year, you may stumble across various **sun ceremonies** being performed here by local mystics.

Brief history

It was the **Emperor Pachacuti** who began work on Sacsayhuaman in the 1440s, although it took nearly a century of creative work to finish it. Various types of rock were used, including enormous diorite blocks from nearby for the outer walls, Yucay

SACSAYHUAMAN IN NUMBERS

The chronicler Cieza de León, writing in the 1550s, estimated that some twenty thousand men had been involved in Sacsayhuaman's construction: **four thousand** cutting blocks from quarries; **six thousand** dragging them on rollers to the site; and another **ten thousand** working on finishing and fitting the blocks into position. According to legend, some **three thousand** lives were lost while dragging just one huge stone.

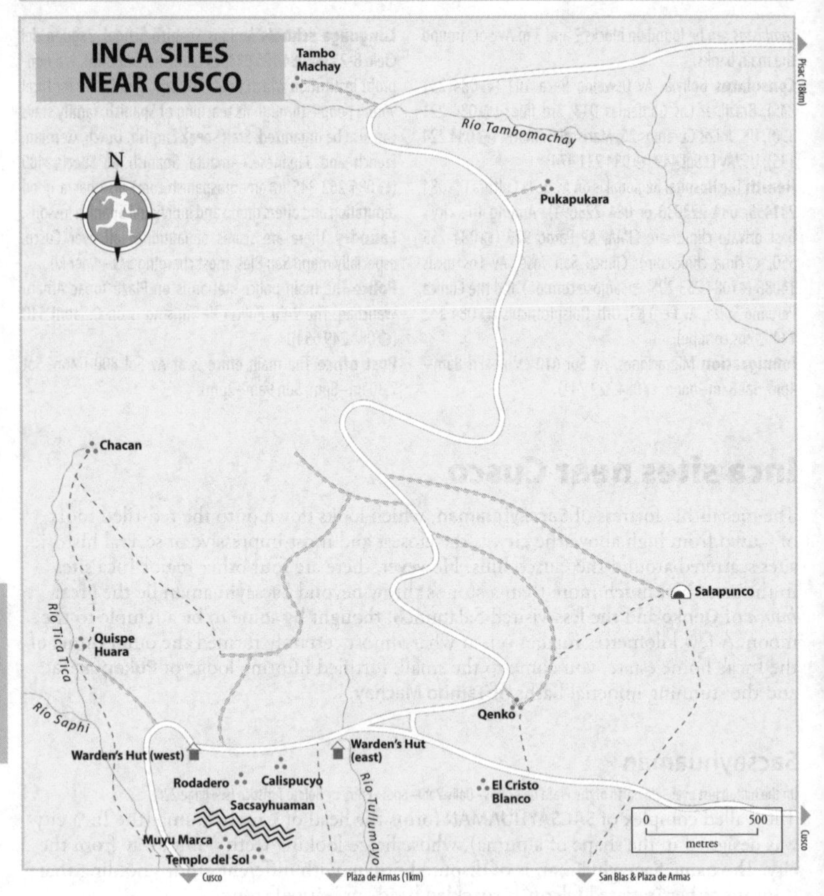

limestone from more than 15km away for the foundations, and dark andesite, some of it from over 30km away at Rumicolca, for the inner buildings and towers. First, boulders were split by boring holes with stone or cane rods and wet sand; next, wooden wedges were inserted into these holes and saturated to crack the rocks into more manageable sizes; finally, the blocks were shifted into place with levers. With only natural fibre ropes, stone hammers and bronze chisels, it would have been an enormous undertaking.

During the fateful **battle of 1536**, Juan Pizarro, Francisco's son, was killed as he charged the main gate in a surprise assault, and a leading Inca nobleman, armed with a Spanish sword and shield, caused havoc by repulsing every enemy who tried to scale Muyu Marca, the last tower left in Inca hands. Having sworn to fight to the death, he leapt from the top when defeat seemed inevitable, rather than accept humiliation and dishonour. After the battle the esplanade was covered in indigenous corpses: food for vultures and inspiration for the Cusco coat of arms, which, since 1540, has been bordered by eight **condors** "in memory of the fact that when the fortress was taken these birds descended to eat the natives who had died in it". The Conquistadors wasted little time in dismantling much of the place, using the stones to build Spanish Cusco.

The walls

Protected by such a steep approach from the town, the fortress only needed **defensive walls** on one side. Nevertheless, this "wall" is one of South America's archeological treasures, actually formed by three massive, parallel stone ramparts zigzagging together for some 600 metres across the plateau just over the other side of the mountaintop from Cusco city and the valley below. These zigzag walls, incorporating the most monumental and megalithic stones used in ancient Peru, form the boundary of what was originally designed as a "spiritual distillation" of the ancient city below, with many sectors named after areas of imperial Cusco.

Little of the inner structures remain, yet these enormous ramparts stand twenty metres high, quite undamaged by past battles, earthquakes and the passage of time. The strength of the mortarless stonework – one block weighs more than three hundred tonnes – is matched by the brilliance of its design: the **zigzags**, casting shadows in the afternoon sun, not only look like jagged cats' teeth, but also seem to have been cleverly designed to expose the flanks of any attacking force. Recently, however, many sacred and ritual objects excavated here have caused archeologists to consider Sacsayhuaman as more of a **ceremonial centre** than a fortress, the distinctive, jagged form of these outer walls possibly symbolizing the important deity of lightning.

The towers and temple

Originally, the inner "fort" was covered in buildings, a maze of tiny streets dominated by three major towers. The tower of **Muyu Marca**, whose foundations can still be seen clearly, was round, over 30m tall and with three concentric circles of wall, the outer one roughly 24m in diameter. An imperial residence, it apparently had lavish inner chambers and a constant supply of fresh water, carried up through subterranean channels. The other two towers – **Salla Marca** and **Paunca Marca** – had rectangular bases about 20m long and were essentially warriors' barracks, and all three were painted in vivid colours, had thatched roofs and were interconnected by underground passages: in its entirety, the inner fortress could have housed as many as ten thousand people under siege. At the rear of this sector, looking directly down into Cusco and the valley, was a **temple dedicated to the sun**, reckoned by some to be the most important shrine in the entire Inca Empire and the most sacred sector of Sacsayhuaman. Excavation of these sites continues, but it's still very difficult to make out anything but the circular tower base.

4

The Rodadero, Qocha Chincanas and Calispucyo

In front of the main defensive walls, a flat expanse of grassy ground – the esplanade – divides the fortress from a large outcrop of volcanic diorite. Intricately carved in places, and scarred with deep glacial striations, this rock, called the **Rodadero** ("sliding place"), was the site of an Inca throne. Originally there was a stone parapet surrounding this important *huaca*, and it's thought that the emperor would have sat here to oversee ceremonial gatherings at fiesta times, when there would have been processions, wrestling matches and running competitions. On the far side of this huge outcrop are larger recreational sliding areas, smoothed by the many centuries of Inca – and now tourists' – backsides.

From here you can see another large circular space called **Qocha Chincanas**, possibly an Inca graveyard, and on its far side the sacred spring of **Calispucyo**, where ceremonies to initiate boys into manhood were held. Excavations here have uncovered crystals and shells (some of the latter all the way from Ecuador), a sign usually associated with water veneration.

Qenko

On a hilltop 2km northeast of the Plaza de Armas • Daily 7am–5.30pm • Entry by Boleto Turístico (see page 220)

The large limestone outcrop of **QENKO** was another important Inca *huaca*. This great stone, carved with a complex pattern of steps, seats, geometric reliefs and puma designs, illustrates the critical role of the rock cult in the realm of Inca cosmological beliefs (the surrounding foothills are dotted with carved rocks and elaborate stone terraces). The name of this *huaca* derives from the Quechua word *quenqo*, meaning "labyrinth" or "zigzag", and refers to the patterns laboriously carved into the upper, western edge of the stone. At an annual festival priests would pour sacrificial llama blood into a bowl at the serpent-like top of the main zigzag channel; if it flowed out through the left-hand bifurcation, this was a bad omen for the fertility of the year to come. If, on the other hand, it continued the full length of the channel and poured onto the rocks below, this was a good omen.

The stone may also be associated with solstice and equinox ceremonies, fertility rites and even marriage rituals (there's a twin seat close to the top of Qenko which looks very much like a lovers' kissing bench). Right on top of the stone, two prominent round nodules are carved onto a plinth. These appear to be mini versions of **intihuatanas** ("hitching posts" of the sun), found at many Inca sacred sites – local guides claim that on the **summer solstice**, at around 8am, the nodules' shadow looks like a puma's face and a condor with wings outstretched at the same time. Along with the serpent-like divinatory channels, this would complete the three main layers of the Inca cosmos: sky (condor), earth (puma) and the underworld (snake).

The tunnels and caves

Beneath Qenko are several **tunnels and caves**, replete with impressive carved niches and steps, which may have been places for spiritual contemplation and communication with the forces of life and earth. It's been suggested that some of the niches may have been where the **mummies** of lesser nobles were kept.

The amphitheatre

At the top end of the *huaca*, behind the channelled section, the Incas constructed an impressive, if relatively small, semicircular **amphitheatre** with nineteen vaulted niches (probably seats for priests or nobles) facing in towards the impressive limestone. At the heart of the amphitheatre rises a natural **standing stone**, which from some angles looks like a frog (representative of the life-giving and cleansing power of rain) and from others like a puma, both creatures of great importance to pre-Conquest Peru.

Salapunco and around

Yet another sacred *huaca*, though off the beaten track around 1km northeast of Qenko, the large rock outcrop of **SALAPUNCO** – also known as the Templo de la Luna and locally called Laqo – contains a number of small caves where the rock has been painstakingly carved. You can see worn relief work with puma and snake motifs on the external rock faces, while the caves hold altar-like platforms and niches that were probably used to house mummies. The largest of the caves is thought to have been a venue for ceremonies celebrating the full moon, as it sometimes is today, when an eerie silver light filters into the usually dark interior. Close to Salapunco lies another site, **K'usilluchayoq**, which has more rock carvings.

Chacan and Quispe Huara

An important but little-visited Inca site, **CHACAN** lies about 5km from Sacsayhuaman on the opposite side of the fortress from Qenko and the road to Tambo Machay. Chacan itself was a revered spring, and you can see a fair amount of terracing, some carved rocks and a few buildings in the immediate vicinity; like Tambo Machay, it demonstrates the importance of water as an ever-changing, life-giving force in Inca religion. A pleasant but more difficult walk (10min) leads down the Tica Tica stream

PERUVIAN WOMAN WEAVING IN CHINCHERO, EL VALLE SAGRADO

to **Quispe Huara** ("crystal loincloth"), where a two- to three-metre-high pyramid shape has been cut into the rock. Close by are some Inca stone walls, probably once part of a ritual bathing location. It's easy to get lost visiting these two sights – you're better off going with a guide (see page 221).

Pukapukara

By the roadside 11km along the Cusco–Pisac road, 600m beyond the village of Huayllacocha • Daily 7am–6pm • Entry by Boleto Turístico (see page 220)

A relatively small ruin, **PUKAPUKARA**, meaning "Red Fort", is around 11km from the city, impressively situated overlooking the Valle de Cusco, right beside the main Cusco–Pisac road. A good example of how the Incas combined recreation and spirituality along with social control and military defence, Pukapukara is well worth the trip.

Although in many ways reminiscent of a small European castle, with a commanding **esplanade** topping its semicircle of protective wall, Pukapukara is more likely to have been a hunting lodge for the emperor as well as a defensive position. Thought to have been built by Inca Pachacutec it could also have had a sacred function, as it has excellent **views** towards the *apu* of Ausangate. Such a strategic location meant it was ideally placed to keep tabs on the flow of people and produce from the Valle Sagrado to Cusco.

Tambo Machay

On the Cusco-Pisac road, 350m further on from Pukapukara, on the opposite side of the road • Daily 7am–6pm • Entry by Boleto Turístico (see page 220)

One of the more impressive Inca baths, at 3765m **TAMBO MACHAY**, or Temple of the Waters, is thought to have been a place for ritual as well as possibly also for physical cleansing and purification. Situated at a spring near the Incas' hunting lodge, its main structure lies in a sheltered gully where superb Inca masonry again emphasizes their fascination with water.

The ruins basically consist of three tiered **platforms**. The top one holds four trapezoidal niches that were likely used to place statues of gods; on the next level, underground water emerges directly from a hole at the base of the stonework, and from here cascades down to the bottom platform. On this platform the spring water splits into two channels, both pouring the last metre down to ground level. This may have been a site for **ritual bathing**; the quality of the stonework suggests that its use was possibly restricted to the higher nobility, who perhaps used the baths only on ceremonial occasions.

About 1km further up the gully, you'll come to a small **grotto** where there's a pool large enough for bathing, even in the dry season. While it shows no sign of Inca stonework, the hills to either side of the stream are dotted with stone terraces and caves, one or two of which still have remnants of walls at their entrance. In Inca, *machay* means "cave", suggesting that these were an important local feature, perhaps as sources of water for Tambo Machay and Pukapukara.

ARRIVAL AND DEPARTURE INCA SITES NEAR CUSCO

BY TAXI

If you don't want to go on a guided tour or hire a guide privately (see page 221), you could hire a taxi driver – ask your lodgings for a recommendation; a day tour of all these sights, including wait time, costs around S/70–90. You could also take a taxi from the centre of Cusco up to Tambo Machay (S/25–30; 15min), and make your way down on foot from there.

ON FOOT

These sites are an energetic day's walk from Cusco, but you'll probably want to devote a whole day to Sacsayhuaman and leave the others until you're more adjusted to the rarefied air.

Sacsayhuaman Although it looks relatively close to central Cusco, it's quite a steep 40min, 1km climb up to the ruins of Sacsayhuaman from the Plaza de Armas.

The simplest route is up C Suecia, then right along the narrow cobbled street of Wayna Pata to Pumacurco, which heads steeply up to a small café-bar with a balcony that commands superb views over the city. It's only another 10min from the café, following the signposted steps all the way up to the ruins. By now you're beyond Cusco's built-up areas and walking in countryside, and there's a well-worn path and a crude stairway that takes you right up to the heart of the fortress.

Qenko An easy 20min walk from Sacsayhuaman. Head towards the Cusco–Pisac road along a track from the warden's hut on the northeastern edge of Sacsayhuaman, and Qenko is just across the main road; the route is straightforward but poorly signposted.

Salapunco Walk for 20min uphill and through the trees above Qenko, to the right of the small hill, along the path (keeping the houses to your right), then come out onto the fields and turn right. It's also possible to walk down to the Plaza de Armas from nearby K'usilluchayoq via interconnecting trails that initially go through some new barrios above the main Cusco–Pisac road, then down to San Blas.

Chacan Chacan can be safely, though not easily, reached in the dry season (May–Sept) by following the main road from the Rodadero at Sacsayhuaman for about 50m; turn left on the dirt track, walk for about 30min or so until you see a small artificial lagoon on your left. Continue up the road for another 5–10min; you will see a path on your left. Follow this path for about 15min until you reach Chacan.

Quispe Huara A difficult walk leads from Chacan down the Tica Tica stream (keep to the right-hand side of the stream and stay well above it) to Quispe Huara. You really need a local map or guide to find your way with any certainty.

Pukapukara Between one and two hours' cross-country walk, uphill of Sacsayhuaman – 4km as the condor flies – and Qenko (longer if you keep to the sinuous main road).

Tambo Machay Walk for less than 15min along a signposted track that leads off the main road just north of Pukapukara.

ON HORSEBACK

Horsebackriding Cusco (see page 223) offers a tour (around 3hr), incorporating four of these sites (US$65, including hotel pickup but not the Boleto Turístico).

El Valle Sagrado

EL VALLE SAGRADO (Sacred Valley), or Vilcamayo to the Incas, about 30km northwest of Cusco, traces its winding, astonishingly beautiful course from here down towards Urubamba, Ollantaytambo and eventually **Machu Picchu** (see page 255), the most famous ruins in South America and a place that – no matter how jaded you are or how commercial it seems – is never anything short of awe-inspiring. The steep-sided river valley opens out into a narrow but very fertile alluvial plain, which was well exploited agriculturally by the Incas. Even within 30km or so of the valley, there are several microclimates allowing specializations in different fruits, maizes and local plants. The **river** itself starts in the high Andes south of Cusco as the Río Vilcanota until it reaches the Valle Sagrado; from here on downriver it's known as the Río Urubamba, a magnificent and energetic torrent which flows right down into the jungle to merge with other major headwaters of the Amazon.

Standing guard over the two extremes of the Valle Sagrado, the ancient **Inca citadels** of Pisac and Ollantaytambo perch high above the stunning Río Vilcanota–Urubamba and are among the most evocative ruins in Peru. **Pisac** itself is a small, pretty town with one of Peru's best artesanía markets, just 32km northeast of Cusco, close to the end of the Río Vilcanota's wild run from Urcos. Further downstream are the ancient villages of **Calca**, **Yucay** and **Urubamba**, the last of which has the most visitors' facilities and, like Pisac, is developing a reputation as a spiritual and meditation centre, yet somehow still retains its traditional Andean charm. As you move along the valley the climate becomes milder and you see pears, peaches and cherries growing in abundance. In July and August vast piles of maize sit beside the road waiting to be used as cattle feed.

At the far northern end of the Valle Sagrado, even the magnificent ancient town of **Ollantaytambo** is overwhelmed by the astounding temple-fortress clinging to the sheer cliffs beside it. The tiny town, though very touristy, is a very pleasant place to spend some time, with a decent choice of restaurants, and it is a convenient location in the heart of great trekking country. It makes an ideal base from which to take a tent and trek above one of the Urubamba's minor tributaries, or else tackle one of the **Salcantay** trails.

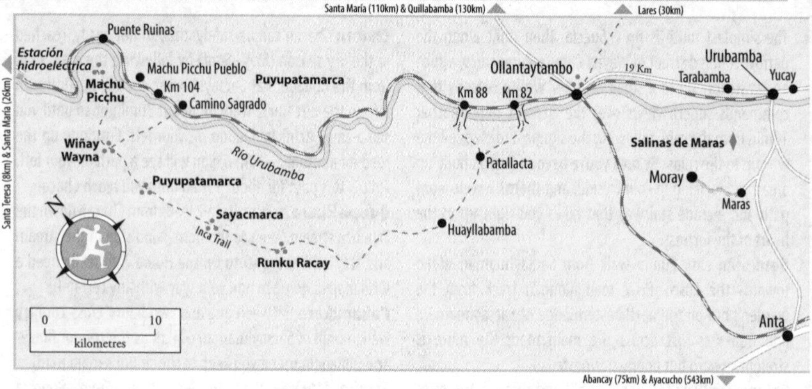

Beyond Ollantaytambo the route becomes too tortuous for any road to follow. Here, the valley closes in around the rail tracks and the Río Urubamba begins to race and twist below **Machu Picchu** itself (see page 255).

Pisac

A vital Inca road once snaked its way up the canyon that enters the Valle Sagrado at **PISAC**, and the ruined **citadel**, which sits at the entrance to the gorge, controlled a strategic route connecting the Inca Empire with Paucartambo, on the borders of the eastern jungle. Less than an hour from Cusco by bus, the town is now most commonly visited – apart from a look at the citadel – for its **market**, though in recent years it has also been attracting travellers interested in spiritual cleansing, including experiences with San Pedro and ayahuasca.

The main local **fiesta** – Virgen del Carmen (from around July 15–18) – is a good alternative to the simultaneous but more remote Paucartambo festival of the same name (see page 270), with processions, music, dance groups, the usual firecracker celebrations and food stalls around the plaza.

Plaza Constitución

Apart from the road and river bridge, the hub of Pisac activity is around **Plaza Constitución**, which is dominated by an ancient and massive *pisonay* tree. Here you'll find most of the restaurants and the few hotels that exist, as well as the **market** and the town's concrete **church**, the Iglesia San Pedro Apóstol, named after Pisac's patron saint.

GETTING TO AND AROUND THE VALLE SAGRADO

The Valle Sagrado and Machu Picchu need to be approached differently, though it is quite possible, even logical, to start in one and then move on to the other. There are three main **transport hubs** in the Valle Sagrado – **Pisac, Urubamba and Ollantaytambo** – all easily reached by buses, colectivo minibuses or taxis from Cusco. Travelling up and down the valley between them is simple enough; pick up a colectivo, taxi or local bus to follow the one main road that hugs the valley floor, keeping fairly close to the Río Vilcanota/Urubamba. **Machu Picchu** (see page 255) is further down the valley and is generally accessed on foot – typically the Inca Trail hike – or by rail, though an increasingly common option for budget travellers these days is to take a circuitous and mountainous route by minivan from Cusco or Ollantaytambo to **Santa Teresa** – beyond Machu Picchu – followed by a two- to three-hour hike back along the rail tracks to Machu Picchu Pueblo (see page 260)

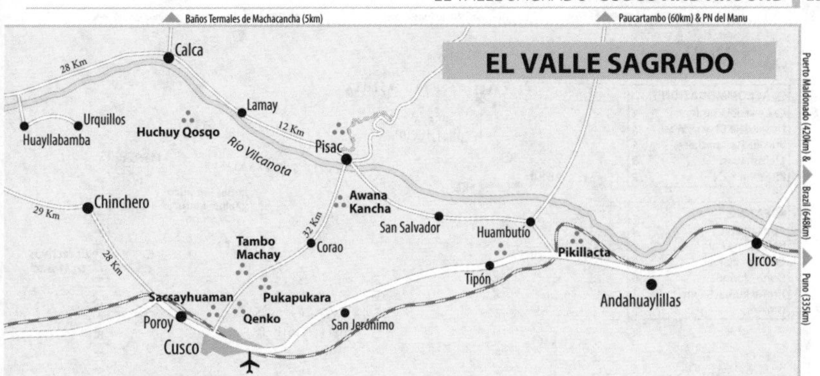

Mercado de Pisac

Plaza Constitución • Craft market daily 8am–5pm

The thriving **market** is held in and around the town's main square, where you can buy hand-painted ceramic beads and pick up the occasional bargain. There are a number of excellent artesanía stands open daily, selling all manner of goods from baby alpaca blankets to jumpers, but as tourism has increased so the quality and authenticity of many of the wares has declined. The best day to visit the market is **Sunday**, when locals descend from surrounding mountain villages to sell their fresh produce.

4

Jardín Botánico Felipe Marín Moreno

C Grau 485 • Daily – no set hours • S/10 • ⓣ 984 718 347

Tucked away from the noisy market scene, this walled **botanical garden** is a delightful oasis of calm and colour. Established in 1917, it contains a mixture of native and non-native plants, including 200 varieties of potato and a collection of cacti. The owner José will happily give you a tour when around – usually on weekends. If it's not open, go to the café *El Encanto* on Calle San Francisco, which has a large floor-to-ceiling window overlooking the garden.

Museo Comunitario de Pisac

Avenidas Amazonas and Federico Zamalloa• Mon–Fri & Sun 8am–1pm & 2–5pm • Free • ⓣ 974 757 466

The small **Museum Comunitario de Pisac** contains interesting displays (though only in Spanish) on the area's history and culture; exhibits include archeological artefacts and textiles made by local Quechua communities, such as Chahuaytire. This is also the place to enquire if you are interested in visiting remote villages or organizing a homestay in the area.

The fortress

3.5km by road northeast of Pisac • Main road entrance: daily 7.30am–5pm; trail entrance in town daily 8am–4pm • Entry by Boleto Turístico (see page 220) • A taxi from Pisac to the ruins costs S/25; alternatively, take a combi bound for Maska from outside the bus station (every 20min), and ask to get off at the *desvío a Maska* (20min). From the turn-off, walk 5min up the tarred road to the entrance and a further 30min uphill to the Templo del Sol; bearing left along the wooden railings after 10min takes you to the lower ruins. You can return the same way or go down the well signed hiking trail back to Pisac (45min)

Set high above a valley floor patchworked by patterned fields and rimmed by centuries of terracing amid giant landslides, the **fortress** displays magnificent stonework – water ducts and steps have been cut out of solid rock – and **panoramas**. The citadel takes around an hour and a half to **climb up to** via a well-signposted, steep path – only attempt it if you're fit and already well adjusted to the altitude.

From the saddle on the hill, you can see over the Valle Sagrado to the north: wide and flat at the base, but towering towards the heavens into green and rocky pinnacles.

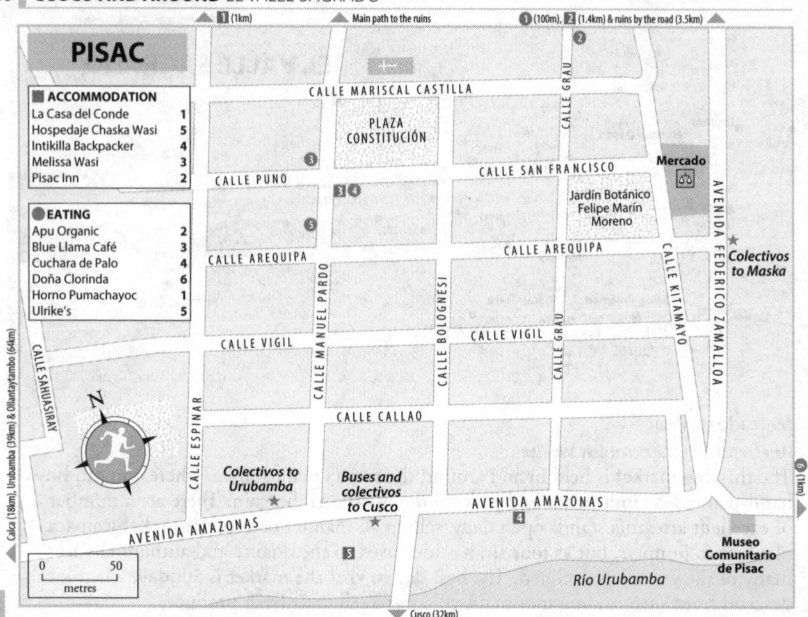

To the south, the valley closes in, but the mountains continue, massive and steep-sided, casting shadows on one another. Below the saddle, a semicircle of buildings is gracefully positioned on a large natural balcony under row upon row of fine stone terraces thought to represent a partridge's wing (*pisac* meaning "partridge").

Templo del Sol

In the upper sector of the ruins, the citadel's **Templo del Sol** (Temple of the Sun) is the equal of anything at Machu Picchu, and more than repays the exertions of the steep climb (20–30min from the car park). Reached by many of the dozens of paths that crisscross their way up through the citadel, it's poised in a flattish saddle on a great spur protruding north–south into the Valle Sagrado. The temple was built around an outcrop of volcanic rock, its peak carved into an Intihuatana, **"hitching post"** for the sun. The hitching post alone is intriguing: the angles of its base suggest that it may have been used for keeping track of important stars, or for calculating the changing seasons with the accuracy so critical to the smooth running of the Inca Empire. Above the temple lie still more ruins, largely unexcavated, and among the higher crevices and rocky overhangs several ancient burial sites are hidden.

ARRIVAL AND GETTING AROUND — PISAC

By bus Buses from Cusco are much slower than colectivos (every 30min; 1hr 30 min).

By colectivo Colectivo minibuses to Pisac leave from C Puputi in Cusco (every 15min; 45min), dropping passengers off on Av Amazonas to the west of town. Return colectivos and buses for Cusco leave from the same place. Combis for Urubamba via Calca pick up passengers at the bridge, and at the petrol station (*grifo*) on Av Amazonas, west of the bridge.

On foot To hike up to the citadel from the village (1hr 30min–2hr), start on the path that leads off uphill from Plaza Constitución, along the left flank of the church.

By taxi Taxis cost S/60–70 one-way from Cusco (45min).

INFORMATION

Tourist information The municipal tourist office is on Plaza Constitución, and in particular can help arrange community-based tourism (☎984 883 265; Mon–Sat 8am–5pm, Sun 8am–1pm).

INCA FIESTAS

Around the end of September and start of October every year local **fiestas** and celebrations take place around Lamay and Calca, which date back at least to early Inca times. The main local ritual theme for the festival is **water**, and there are strong links to a mythic experience high in the hills and tied to the moving shadows of **Nevado Pitusiray**: every year around the beginning of October, the mountain casts shadows over neighbouring peaks and cliffs. Over several days the shadow of Pitusiray, considered to be a solar clock, moves in a dynamic and very clear representation of a prostrate Inca being leapt upon and transformed by a black puma or jaguar; it has to be seen to be believed. With this visual effect on the landscape in mind, a festival is now held on the first Sunday in October and based at the **Inca ruins of Urco**, also dedicated to water, which are located a 2km walk above the village of Calca. For information on the festival ask at the Cusco tourist information offices (see page 221).

ACCOMMODATION

The only time when accommodation in Pisac may be hard to find is in **September**, when the village fills up with pilgrims heading to the nearby sanctuary of Huanca, home of a small shrine which is held very sacred by local inhabitants. In and around Pisac there's a surprising selection of places to stay.

★ **La Casa del Conde** Andenes de Chihuanco s/n ⓣ966 366 474, ⓔlacasadelcondepisac@gmail.com; map p.238. You can't beat this delightful stone guesthouse set in lovely gardens, overlooking the Valle Sagrado. Simple rooms (for one to four people) are of stone, with wooden floors, cheerful Andean decor and snug duvets. The welcoming hosts are happy to arrange excursions. S/265

Hospedaje Chaska Wasi Av Amazonas s/n ⓣ957 593 387, ⓔchaskawasi@hotmail.es; map p.238. This pleasant *hospedaje* is Pisac's best budget option, with warm and welcoming rooms set around a large courtyard. There's a kitchen for guests' use and an outdoor lounge gazebo with cushioned seating. Breakfast extra. Dorms S/35, doubles S/120

Intikilla Backpacker Av Amazonas 153 ⓣ984992424; map p.238. Bare-bones bunkhouse at rock-bottom rates, with shared or private rooms – all with shared bathrooms and a communal sofa and TV on each floor. Breakfast extra. Dorms S/15, doubles S/45

★ **Melissa Wasi** Sector Matará ⓣ084 797 589, ⓦmelissa-wasi.com; map p.238. A lovely place to stay with a large garden and great views. Eight nicely decorated rooms share a spacious, fire-warmed living room. Three self-catering duplexes with fireplace sleep four and are good value. All have satellite TV. The restaurant is built around natural rock, and the owners' son, a shaman, hosts ayahuasca ceremonies, too. There's a barbeque area and children's playground. Bungalows S/420, doubles S/310

Pisac Inn Plaza Constitución 333 ⓣ084 203 062, ⓦpisacinn.com; map p.238. An excellent option right in the heart of town, offering eleven lovely – if overpriced – rooms featuring wooden furniture and rustic lamps with leather lampshades. Also has a small TV loungeand a good restaurant, *Cuchara de Palo*. S/238

EATING

Apu Organic C Grau 534 ⓣ988 338 141; map p.238. Enjoy freshly prepared organic vegetarian and vegan dishes in this small café with New Age decor. Omelettes, lentils, lava cake – all pretty tasty. Mon, Tues & Thurs–Sun 10.30am–4.30pm.

Blue Llama Café Plaza Constitución 352 ⓣ084 203 135, ⓦFacebook.com/bluellamapisac; map p.238. Plenty of blue and llamas feature in the humorous decor of this cheerful café, which has wonderful views over the market from its little balcony. Good comfort traveller food from breakfasts (around S/12) soups and sandwiches (S/15–23), to pasta dishes and local trout. Daily 7am–8pm.

Cuchara de Palo Plaza Constitución 333 ⓣ084 203 062, ⓦpisacinn.com/restaurant; map p.238. This cosy restaurant with a fireplace serves nicely presented Andean dishes both in the dining area and on the small patio. The menu includes quinoa soup, *lomo saltado*, and tasty trout with potato cakes (mains S/30–45). Pizzas are cooked on Sunday in the clay oven. Daily 7.30am–8.30pm.

Doña Clorinda La Rinconada, 1km east of town ⓣ084 203 051; map p.238. Popular with Cusco families and tour groups, this pleasant restaurant offers ample seating in an open-fronted area with tables spilling out onto the garden. Expect Andean cuisine, with a number of quinoa-based dishes, beef and trout, plus some vegetarian options. Quality can suffer when they're busy. Mains S/25–30. Daily 9am–5pm.

Horno Pumachayoc Av Federico Zamalloa s/n ⓣ984 012 575; map p.238. Tasty hand-made empanadas (S/6) are the order of the day, made with natural local ingredients. The dough is proudly made from seven types of flour, including quinoa and coca, and you've five different fillings to choose from, including cheese and tomato and tropical fruits. Wash it down with a glass of *chicha morada* (S/4). Daily 6am–6pm.

Ulrike's C Pardo 613 ⓣ 084 203 195; map p.238. This German-run place with colourful partitioned dining areas is a reliable, inexpensive bet, serving mainly international dishes and a few local offerings: all-day breakfasts, bagels, soups, curries, salads and Peruvian *causas*. Mains from S/15. The set *menú del día* is good value at S/28. Daily 8am–9pm.

Huchuy Qosqo

3.5km west of Lamay, high up the mountainside • Daily 24hr • Free • Take a colectivo between Piscac and Urubamba to Lamay; then it's a 2hr uphill hike: cross the bridge over the Río Vilcanota west of town and follow the 3km zig-zagging path up to the ruins.

The first significant village between Pisac and Urubamba is **Lamay**, just 12km from Pisac, and the access point for the little-known and seldom visited ruins of **Huchuy Qosqo;** these are spread across a natural platform cut into the mountainside, high above the village, yet out of sight, on the other side of the Río Vilcanota. After Ollantaytambo and Pisac, this was the most important Inca **fortress** in the Valle Sagrado, though the ruins are not as well preserved. Meaning "Little Cusco" in Quechua, on account of the similarity in layout with Cusco, it was built on the orders of Viracocha. Then it was known as Qapyqawama ("the place to see lightning" in Quechua), a name which becomes obvious once you take in the stunning panoramic views along the valley from the settlement's natural vantage point. Most impressive is the Inca terracing, but you can also make out a number of stone and adobe buildings including a *kallanka* (great hall), some irrigation channels and, below the main site, some restored *qolqas* (granaries for storing meat and crops). Note the two-tier construction, which helped to keep the contents cool.

It was at Huchuy Qosqo that Gonzalo Pizarro – brother of Francisco – was said to have found Viracocha's mummified remains, which he ordered to be burned, though the ashes were later gathered up and hidden by the Incas, to be revered in secret.

Calca and around

Roughly midway between Pisac and Urubamba lies the village of **Calca,** notable only for its proximity to the popular **Baños termales de Machacancha** (daily 7am–6pm; S/10), 7km northeast of town and reached by frequent combi or an hour and a half's signposted walk. Situated under the hanging glaciers of Nevado Sahuasiray, this place was favoured by the Incas for the fertility of its soil, and you can still see plenty of maize cultivation here. The baths consist of three covered pools averaging 40 degrees centigrade.

ACCOMMODATION — CALCA AND AROUND

IFK Lodge (formerly Qawana Lodge) Km 57.2 Carretera Pisac–Urubamba ⓣ 084 632 086, ⓦ ifk.pe. It's hard to beat this rustic lodge's wonderful riverside location, overlooking the gushing Río Urubamba, with comfortably furnished rooms with views to match. There's a decent a-la-carte restaurant, massage available and bike rental on request, but a ridiculously early check-out time. S/345

Yucay

The small strung-out town of **Yucay,** 3.5km east of Urubamba, had its moment in Peruvian history when, under the Incas, Huayna Capac, father of Huascar and Atahualpa, had his palace here. You can admire the ruined but finely dressed stone walls of another **Inca palace** (probably the country home of Sayri Tupac, though also associated with an Inca princess) on the Plaza Manco II, one of the town's two grassy spaces either side of the church. There are several good lodgings here if you prefer quieter surroundings to bustling Urubamba.

ACCOMMODATION AND EATING **YUCAY**

La Casona de Yucay Av San Martín 104 ⊕ 084 201 116, whotelcasonayucay.com. Recently refurbished colonial mansion where Simón Bolívar himself has stayed. With an onsite spa and 55 refurbished rooms boasting down duvets, lots of natural light and lovely garden or mountain views, this is a supremely relaxing spot. S/450

Yucay Plaza Inn Av San Martín 202 ⊕ 964 791 018, ⊕ Facebook.com/yucayplaza. Excellent budget hotel opposite the church; rooms – some with mountain views – are spartan but sparkling with bedside lamps and spotless bathrooms. The communal lounge has TV and wi-fi access. S/100

Tawa Restaurante C Garcilaso, Plaza Manco II ⊕ 084 632 261, ⊕ tawarestaurante.com. Stylish Peruvian and international cuisine with quinoa featuring in many dishes, from chowders to pizzas, salads to risotto (*quinotto*). Mains S/32–50. The dining room has plenty of natural light but the mountain views from the garden are even nicer. Daily 12.30–9.30pm.

Urubamba

About 80km from Cusco via Pisac or around 60km via Chinchero, **URUBAMBA** is only a short way down the main road from Yucay's Plaza Manco II, and it is here that the Río Vilcanota becomes the Río Urubamba (though many people still refer to this stretch as the Vilcanota). While it has little in the way of obvious historic interest, the town has good **facilities,** and is often used as a base for day-trips to Machu Picchu in preference to far more touristy Ollantaytambo just up the valley. It is appealingly situated in the shadow of the beautiful, though shrinking, Chicón and Pumahuanca glaciers. At weekends there's a large **market** on Jirón Palacio, while on Wednesdays, Fridays and Sundays the new Mercado de Productores is heaving with **livestock** of all shapes and sizes being traded – an event which often spills onto the main road. It's also worthwhile visiting Cerámicas Seminario (Av Berriozábal 405 ⊕ 084 201 002, ⊕ ceramicaseminario.com; daily 8am–7pm), which gives visitors an insight into ancient **pottery** techniques and has a wide range of products for sale, many of which you see on restaurant tables across the country.

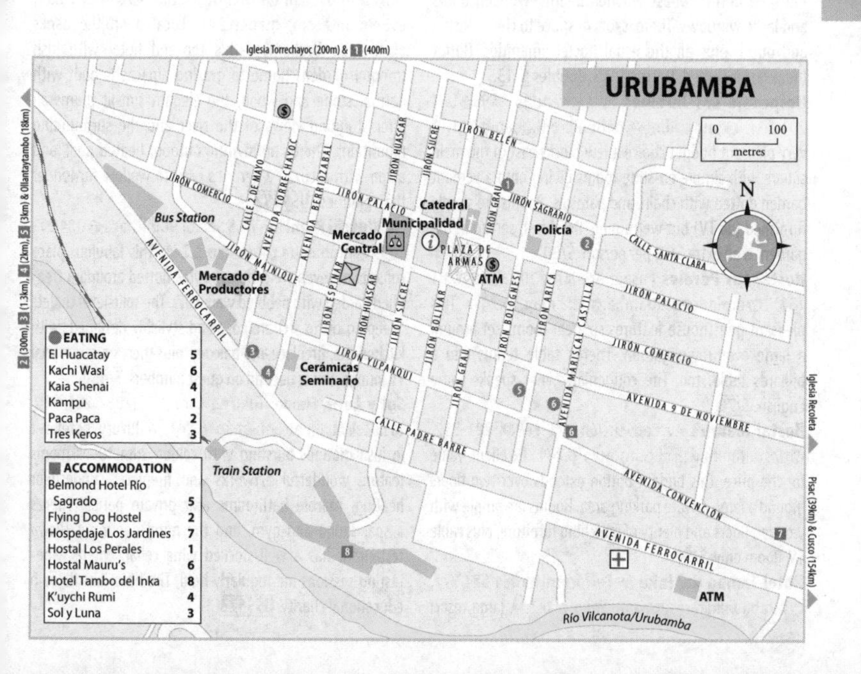

Plaza de Armas

The laidback and attractive **Plaza de Armas** has palm trees and pines surrounded by interesting topiary. At the heart of the plaza is a small fountain topped by a maize plant sculpture, but everything defers to the red sandstone **Iglesia San Pedro**, with its stacked columns below two small belfries. The church's cool interior has a vast, three-tier gold-leaf altar, and at midday light streams through the glass-topped cupola.

ARRIVAL AND INFORMATION — URUBAMBA

By bus The bus station is to the west of the town centre. Buses connect Pisac with Urubamba (every 20min; 2hr); for Calca (40min) and Chinchero (50min), catch a Cusco-bound bus; they run until 8pm (every 20min; 1hr 30min).

By colectivo Colectivos also arrive and depart from the bus station, with frequent services from Cusco (from C Pavitos every 20min from about 5–6am; 1hr 30min) and Pisac (on Av Amazonas; 45min). Colectivos also run regularly between Urubamba and Ollantaytambo (every 10–15min; 30min).

By taxi Taxis from Cusco to Urubamba charge around S/90; taxis from Urubamba to Ollantaytambo cost S/20.

By train Peru Rail runs two trains a day to Machu Picchu at 6.50am and 10.30am (3hr; from US$95 one way).

Tourist information A small municipal tourist office operates just off the Plaza de Armas on C Palacios (Mon–Fri 8.30am–4.30pm), offering a map and limited information in Spanish, with a tendency to tell you to take a tour.

ACCOMMODATION

IN URUBAMBA

★ Flying Dog Hostel Camino a Cotahuincho s/n ⊕977 743 011, ⊛flyingdogperu.com; map p.241. A mere 10min walk from the bus station, this hostel is a real delight: a converted old house with bags of character in a lovely garden with fabulous mountain views. Whitewashed en-suite rooms (including the four-bed dorms) boast wooden beams, wooden floors and large windows. There is lots of space to chill – inside and out – plus all the usual hostel amenities. Buffet breakfast included. Dorms S/35, doubles S/135

Hospedaje Los Jardines Av Convención 459 ⊕084 201 331, ⊜tourjardines@hotmail.com; map p.241. A very pleasant budget choice a few blocks east of the main square with simple en-suite rooms giving onto a verdant garden dotted with chairs and parasols. Rooms are simply furnished (no TV) but welcoming. Breakfast, served in the garden, is an extra S/12 per person. S/80

Hostal Los Perales Pasaje Arenales 102 ⊕084 201 151, ⊛ecolodgeurubamba.com; map p.241. This pleasant guesthouse features six neat rooms set around a large overgrown garden. There's table tennis and a billiards table, too. The congenial owner speaks some English. S/70

Hostal Mauru's Av Convención 113 ⊕084 201 352, ⊛hostaltambodelsol.com; map p.241. Excellent value for the price, this budget option extends over two floors around a large private parking area. Rooms are ample with wooden floors and plenty of matching furniture, plus cable TV. Room only. S/90

Hotel Tambo del Inka Av Ferrocarril ⊕084 581 777, ⊛tambodelinkaresort.com; map p.241. A large resort hotel with over a hundred rooms, mainly well-appointed bungalows, and a conference centre, a pool, spa, fitness centre and tennis courts in extensive grounds by the river. S/1256

OUTSIDE URUBAMBA

★ Belmond Hotel Río Sagrado Km 75.8, Carretera Urubamba-Ollantaytambo ⊕084 201 631, ⊛belmond.com; map p.241. Located on the banks of the Río Urubamba, this top-end hotel with lush tranquil gardens home to grazing alpacas is built with natural stone and wood; the elegant sun-lit rooms all offer stunning views of the river and the surrounding mountains. There's an inviting outdoor heated pool, and a spa with Jacuzzi, where it's easy to wallow for longer than planned. US$582

★ K'uychi Rumi Km 71.5 Sector Rumichaca ⊕084 201 169, ⊛urubamba.com; map p.241. This fabulous place consists of seven welcoming *casitas* dotted around a tree-filled garden with pebbled walkways. The split-level chalets (sleeping up to six) are cosy and stylishly designed, with kitchenette, fireplace and balcony, plus there's a communal TV lounge. Prices depend on guest numbers. S/450

Sol y Luna Fundo Huincho Lote A5, ⊕084 201 620, ⊛hotelsolyluna.com; map p.241. A luxury hotel set in lush grounds bursting with colour; sumptuous rooms feature wonderful artworks and fireplaces, underfloor heating, marble bathrooms and private patios. There's a spa, sauna and gym, and the hotel's gourmet *Wayra* restaurant has a well-stocked wine cellar, where wine-tasting sessions are regularly held. The hotel has its own educational charity. US$523

EATING

El Huacatay Jr Arica 620 ⓣ084 201 790, ⓦelhuacatay.com; map p.241. An excellent choice, with tables set around a leafy garden area that is the perfect spot to linger over a refreshing juice. The innovative fusion cuisine uses local produce, incorporating Mediterranean, Asian and Peruvian influences, such as ricotta croquettes (S/24) and green lima bean salad with duck prosciutto (S/24). Mon–Sat 1–9.30pm.

Kachi Wasi Av Mariscal Castilla 921 ⓣ084 214 989, ⓦfacebook.com/kachiwasirestaurante; map p.241. Enthusiastically run local café-restaurant, offering a ridiculously inexpensive *menu del día* (S/8) and a small selection of well-prepared popular local mains, such as the ubiquitous *lomo saltado* and *chicharrones* (S/22–30). Also does drink offers. Daily 8am–10pm.

Kaia Shenai Av Berriozabal 111 ⓣ084 201 387; map p.241. Child-friendly and specializing in organic and veggie dishes, along with invigorating juices and smoothies. The atmosphere is welcoming and laidback, with leafy lounge areas and colourful decor. A la carte items are a little pricey for the portion size though the daily set menu makes up for that (S/20–24). The menu includes *quinotto* (quinoa risotto with vegetables; S/24) and quesadillas (S/12). Tues–Sun noon–9pm

Kampu Jr Sagrario 342 ⓣ974 955 977; map p.241. This laidback place a stone's throw from the main square has chairs splattered with paint and seating at wooden tables in a series of little dining areas. The eclectic menu, scribbled on a chalk board, includes a range of tasty curries (S/30–40). Mon–Wed & Fri–Sun 1–9pm.

Paca Paca Av Mariscal Castilla 640 ⓣ084 201 181; map p.241. A great choice, with clay-oven pizzas (S/24) and a particularly tasty *lomo a las cuatro pimientas* (loin of beef with four-pepper sauce) or quinoa risotto; (S/40) served in a pleasant setting with painted wooden furniture and quirky decor. Tues–Sun 1–9pm.

★ **Tres Keros** Av Torrechayoc s/n ⓣ084 201 701; map p.241. Superb restaurant not to be missed. The atmospheric interior features candle-lit tables, a glowing fireplace, and walls adorned with beautiful ceramic plates. Home-made dishes use fresh local produce combined with high-quality imported ingredients – the *lomo saltado* (S/42) is mouth-watering, as is the trout (S/38), while veggie options include home-made pastas with pesto and curries. Mon & Wed–Sun 12.30–3.30pm & 6.30–9.30pm.

Around Urubamba

Because of its convenient location and plentiful facilities, Urubamba makes an ideal base from which to explore the mountains and lower hills around the Valle Sagrado, which are filled with sites of jaw-dropping splendour. The eastern side of the valley is formed by the **Cordillera Urubamba**, a range of snowcapped peaks dominated by the summits of Chicón and Verónica. Many of the ravines can be hiked, alone or with local guides (found only through the main hotels and hospedajes) and on the trek up from the town you can take in stupendous views of Chicón.

Moray

10km by road/track southwest of Urubamba • Daily 7am–6pm • Entry by Boleto Turístico (see page 220) • Take a Chinchero- or Cusco-bound bus from Urubamba; get off at the *desvió a Maras*, where colectivos charge around S/20–25 per car to Moray

A stunning Inca site, part agricultural and part ceremonial centre, **Moray** lies about 5km west of Maras village on the Chinchero side of the river, within a two- to three-hour walk from Urubamba. The ruins are deep, bowl-like depressions in the earth, the largest comprising seven concentric circular stone terraces, facing inward and diminishing in radius like a multi-layered roulette wheel.

Salinas de Maras

5km walk northeast from Moray and 4km north of Maras • Daily 7am–6pm • S/10 • Combis leave Urubamba for Maras roughly hourly (7am–4pm; 35min), when full.

The **Salinas de Maras** (Maras salt pans) are still in use after more than four hundred years, and these days are a popular stop on many a Valle Sagrado tour, so get there early to avoid the crowds. If on foot, cross the river by the footbridge in Maras village, turn right, then, 100m downstream along the riverbank, turn left past the cemetery and up the canyon along the salty creek. After this you cross the stream and follow the path cut into the cliffside to reach the salt pans, which are soon visible if still a considerable uphill hike away. The trail offers spectacular views of the valley and mountains, while the Inca salt pans themselves are set gracefully against an imposing mountain backdrop. Bags of the pinkish salt are sold as souvenirs. A **scenic trail** (about an hour's walk) leads down through the salt pans and on to the Río Urubamba below, where there's a footbridge across to the village of Tarabamba, which is on the road for Urubamba (6km) or Ollantaytambo; colectivos pass every twenty minutes or so in both directions.

Chinchero

CHINCHERO ("Village of the Rainbow"), an old colonial settlement with a great market, lies 3762m above sea level, 28km (40min) northwest of Cusco and off the main road, overlooking the Sacred Valley, with the Vilcabamba range and the snowcapped peak of Salcantay dominating the horizon to the west. The bus ride here takes you up to the Pampa de Anta, once a huge lake but now relatively dry pasture, surrounded by snowcapped *nevados*. The town itself is a small, rustic place, where the local women, who crowd the main plaza during the market, still wear traditional dress. Largely built of stone and adobe, the town blends perfectly with the magnificent display of Inca architecture, ruins and megalithic carved rocks, relics of the Inca veneration of nature deities. The best time to visit is on September 8 for the lively traditional **fiesta**. Failing that, the Sunday-morning **market** in the lower part of town, reached along Calle Manco II, is smaller and less touristy than Pisac's but has attractive local craftwork for sale, weavings in particular. The town's "Awayricch'arichiq" weaving association – located on Calle Manzanares, close to the market area – is one of the main contributors to Cusco's Centro de Textiles Tradicionales de Cusco (textilescusco.org; see page 214).

4

Plaza Principal

Uphill from the market, along the cobbled steps and streets, you'll find a vast **plaza**, which may have been the original Inca marketplace. It's bounded on one side by an impressive wall reminiscent of Sacsayhuaman's ramparts, though not as massive – it too was constructed on three levels, and ten classical Inca trapezoidal niches can be seen along its surface. On the western perimeter of the plaza, the raised Inca stonework is dominated by a carved **stone throne**, near which are puma and monkey formations. There's also a small two-room **museo de sitio** displaying historical artefacts and some Cusqueña paintings.

Iglesia de Chinchero and Complejo Arqueológico

Complejo arqueológico Daily 7am–6pm • Entry by Boleto Turístico (see page 220)

Dating from the early seventeenth century, the colonial adobe **Iglesia de Chinchero** was built on top of an Inca temple or palace, perhaps belonging to the Inca emperor **Tupac Yupanqui**, who particularly favoured Chinchero as an out-of-town resort – most of the area's aqueducts and terraces, many of which are still in use today, were built at his command. The church itself boasts frescoes and **paintings**, which, though decaying, are still very beautiful and evocative of the town's colonial past. Many pertain to the **Escuela Cusqueña** and celebrated local artist Mateo Cuihuanito, **the** most interesting depicting the forces led by local chief Pumacahua against the rebel Tupac Amaru II in the late eighteenth century. Though the well-preserved Inca stonework lies all around the area of town the official **Complejo arqueológico** lies behind the church.

ARRIVAL AND DEPARTURE **CHINCHERO**

By colectivo Colectivos to Urubamba leave from Cusco's C Pavitos, passing through Chinchero (every 20min; 35min). In Urubamba they leave from the bus station.

By taxi Taxis from Cusco to Chinchero charge around S/50.

ACCOMMODATION AND EATING

★ **La Casa de Barro** C Miraflores 147 084 306 031, lacasadebarro.com. This homely lodge is an excellent place to base yourself as you explore the Valle Sagrado. Cheerful rooms with mellow lighting and woolly blankets are warm and welcoming, while the restaurant, open to non-guests, serves excellent creole and international dishes in a cosy setting with fireplace. S/255

Hospedaje Encanto de Chinchero C Simacucho s/n 984 800 077. A friendly lodging offering great value for money: rooms have comfortable beds, wardrobes, gleaming floors and large windows, with either shared or private bathrooms. Guests can use the kitchen and make use of free bikes, though bikes and cars are also available for rent. Breakfast not included. S/100

Ollantaytambo and around

The picturesque little town of **OLLANTAYTAMBO** with its cobblestone streets and ancient irrigation canals serves as an excellent base for trekking and biking. Coming down the valley from Urubamba the river runs smoothly between a series of impressive Inca terraces that gradually diminish in size. Just before the town, the rail line reappears and the road climbs a small hill to an ancient **plaza**.

As one of the region's tourist hotspots, and a popular overnight stop en route to Machu Picchu, Ollantaytambo can get very busy in high season, making it hard to escape the scores of other travellers. At heart, though, it's a small but still very traditional settlement, worth enjoying over a few days, particularly during its highly colourful **fiestas**, when local folk-dancing takes place in the main plaza. Many women still wear traditional clothing, and it's common to see them gather in the plaza with their intricately woven *manta* shawls, black-and-red skirts with colourful zig-zag patterns and inverted red and black hats.

Beyond Ollantaytambo, the Valle Sagrado becomes a subtropical, raging river course, surrounded by towering mountains and dominated by the snowcapped peak of Salcantay; the town is also a popular base for **rafting** trips (see page 222).

Brief history

The valley here was occupied by a number of pre-Inca cultures, notably the Chanapata (800–300 BC), the Qotacalla (500–900 AD) and the Killki (900–1420 AD), after which the Incas dominated only until the 1530s, when the Spanish arrived.

The legend of Ollantay

Legend has it that **Ollantay** was a rebel Inca general who took arms against Pachacutec over the affections of the Lord Inca's daughter, the Nusta Cusi Collyu. More prosaically, historical evidence shows that a 14km canal, that still feeds the town today, was built to bring water here from the Laguna de Yanacocha, which was probably Pachacutec's private estate. The later Inca Huayna Capac is thought to have been responsible for the trapezoidal Plaza Maynyaraqui and the largely unfinished but impressive and megalithic temples.

OLLANTAYTAMBO'S FIESTAS

Ollantaytambo's vibrant **fiestas** are a sight to behold, particularly the Fiesta de la Cruz (Festival of the Cross), Corpus Christi and **Ollantaytambo Raymi** (generally on the Sunday after Cusco's Inti Raymi), and at Christmas, when locals wear flowers and decorative grasses in their hats. The **Fiesta del Señor de Choquekillca** celebrates the patron saint of Ollantaytambo over several days to coincide with Pentecost (the seventh Sunday after Easter): it's the usual heady mix of indigenous and Catholic customs involving non-stop dancing, elaborate costumes, processions and general partying. On the **Fiesta de Reyes**, around January 6, there's a solemn procession around town of the three *Niños Reyes* (Child Kings) – sacred effigies – one of which is brought down from the sacred site of Marcaquocha, about 10km away in the Patacancha Valley, the day before.

4

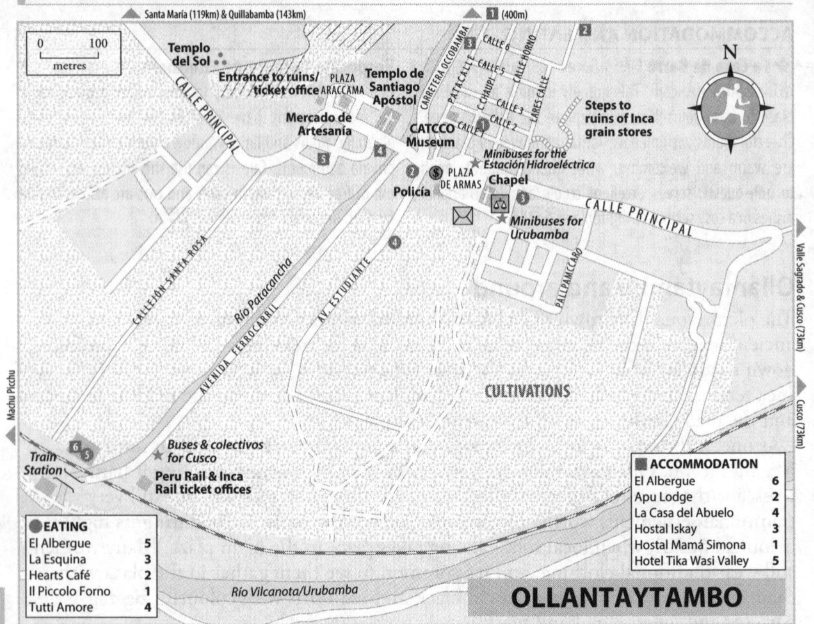

4

A strategic location

Ollantaytambo was built as an Inca **administrative centre** rather than a town and is laid out in the form of a maize corn cob: it's one of the few surviving examples of an **Inca grid system**, with a plan that can be seen from vantage points high above it, especially from the hill opposite the fortress. An incredibly fertile sector of the Urubamba Valley, at 2800m above sea level and with comfortable temperatures of 11–23°C (52–73°F), good alluvial soils and water resources, this area was also the gateway to the **Antisuyo** (the Amazon corner of the Inca Empire) and a centre for tribute-gathering from the surrounding valleys.

As strategic protection for the entrance to the lower Valle de Urubamba and an alternative gateway into the Amazon via the Pantiacolla Pass, this was the only Inca stronghold to have successfully resisted persistent Spanish attacks.

Rebel Inca Manco

After the unsuccessful siege of Cusco in 1536–37 (see page 207), the rebel Inca **Manco** and his die-hard force withdrew here, with **Hernando Pizarro** (one of Conquistador leader Francisco's brothers), some seventy horsemen, thirty foot-soldiers and a large contingent of Andean forces in hot pursuit. As they approached, they found that not only had the Incas diverted the Río Patacancha, making the valley below the fortress impassable, but they had also joined forces with neighbouring Amazonian groups to form a massive army. After several desperate attempts to storm the stronghold, Pizarro and his men uncharacteristically slunk away under cover of darkness, only to return with reinforcements; Manco was forced to retreat further down the valley to Vitcos and Vilcabamba, and in 1540, Ollantaytambo was entrusted to Hernando.

Plaza de Armas

The **Plaza de Armas** is the centre of civic life. Backstreets radiating from here are littered with stone water channels, which still come in very handy during the rainy season, carrying the gushing streams tidily away from the town and down to the Río Urubamba.

Plaza Mañya Raquy

Downhill from the Plaza de Armas, just across the Río Patacancha, is the old Inca **Plaza Mañya Raquy**, dominated by the fortress. Market stalls fill the plaza plus a few artesanía shops and cafés nearby, mainly opposite the attractive small church, the **Templo de Santiago Apóstol**. Built in 1620, it has an almost Inca-style stone belfry containing two great bells supported on an ancient timber. The church's front entrance is surrounded by a simple yet appealing *mestizo* floral relief.

The fortress

Daily 7am–5pm • Entry with Boleto Turístico (see page 220)

ACTIVITIES AROUND OLLANTAYTAMBO

Ollantaytambo is surrounded by stunning countryside and skyscraping mountain peaks, and offers a wealth of interesting **day-trip** options.

WALKING

It's easy enough just to choose a path leading up into the hills to the east and see where you get to, remembering, of course, that you will need a tent or have to get back to town by nightfall. Any route will provide a good **hike**, bringing you into close contact with local people in their gardens. There are also a number of organized **tours**, available from Ollantaytambo (see page 250) as well as from agents in Cusco.

TREKKING

The area around Ollantaytambo is perfect for trekking into the hills. Here you can do hikes of half a day to a week or more; all have Inca ruins along the way. For a half or full day, try heading up the Río Patacancha from town to the little-visited Inca ruins of **Pumamarca**, on the left of the river where the Río Yuramayu merges with the Patacancha under the shadows of Nevado Helancoma. From here the main track follows the right bank of the Río Patacancha through various small peasant hamlets – Pallata, Colqueracay, Marcacocha, Huilloc and Patacancha – before crossing the pass, with the Nevado Colque Cruz on the right-hand side. It then follows the ríos Huacahuasi and Tropoche down to the valley and community of **Lares**, just before which are some Inca baths. Beyond the village are several more ruins en route to Ampares, from where you can either walk back to Urubamba, travel by road back to Cusco, or head down towards Quillabamba. It's at least a two-day walk one way from Ollantaytambo to Ampares, and you'll need camping equipment and food, as there are no facilities at all on the route. Other good day hikes are to **Intihuatana** (see page 259) whereas multi-day hikes can also be launched from nearby Chilca (Km 77).

HORSERIDING

The Inca **quarries of Cachiqata** can be reached in four hours on horseback with a Cusco or Ollantaytambo tour company (see pages 221 and 250). It's also possible to camp here and visit the site of an **Inca gateway** or **Intihuatana**. There are also the nearer ruins of **Pinkuylluna**, less than an hour away by horse, or the **Pumamarca** Inca ruins about half a day away.

MOUNTAIN BIKING

Most options include a shuttle to the mountaintop and a whizz downhill. The most popular route is the 50km, 1500m zig-zagging descent from the dramatic pass and **continental divide** at **Abra Málaga** (en route to Paucartambo and the Estación hidroeléctrica) down to Ollantaytambo, but there are plenty of thrills to be had descending a similar route but off-road. You can even combine one trail with a visit to the traditional village of **Patakancha** and a weaving workshop (see page 250).

RIVER RAFTING

Ollantaytambo is a centre for **river rafting**, organized largely by KB Tambo Tours (see page 250). Alternatively, arrange a rafting trip with one of the Cusco-based tour companies (see page 221). The river around Ollantaytambo is Class II–III in the dry season and III–IV during the rainy period (Nov–March).

As you climb up through the **fortress**, the solid stone terraces and the natural contours of the cliff remain frighteningly impressive. Above them, huge red granite blocks mark the unfinished **Templo del Sol** near the top, where, according to legend, the internal organs of mummified Incas were buried. A dangerous path leads from this upper level around the cliff towards a large sector of agricultural terracing which follows the Río Patacancha uphill. From up above you can see down to the large Inca plaza and the impressive stone aqueducts which carried the water supply. Between here and the river you see the **Andenes de Mollequasa terraces** which, when viewed from the other side of the Valle de Urubamba (a twenty-minute walk up the track from the train station), look like a pyramid.

Around Ollantaytambo

High up over the other side of the Río Patacancha, behind Ollantaytambo, are rows of ruined buildings of **Pinkuylluna** originally thought to have been prisons but now considered likely to have been **granaries**. In front of these, it's quite easy to make out a gigantic, rather grumpy-looking **profile of a face** carved out of the rock, possibly an Inca sculpture of Wiraccochan, the mythical messenger of **Viracocha**, the major creator-god of Peru (see page 506). According to sixteenth- and seventeeth-century histories, such an image was indeed once carved, representing him as a man of great authority; this particular image's frown certainly implies presence, and this part of the mountain was also known as Wiraccochan Orcco ("peak of Viracocha's messenger"). From here, looking back towards the main Ollantaytambo fortress, it's possible to see the mountain, rocks and terracing forming the **image of a mother llama** with a young llama, apparently representing the myth of Catachillay, which relates to the water cycle and the Milky Way. *The Sacred Valley of the Incas – Myths and Symbols* (available in most Cusco bookshops), written by archeologists Fernando and Edgar Salazar, is a useful companion for interpreting the sites in this part of the valley.

ARRIVAL AND DEPARTURE — OLLANTAYTAMBO AND AROUND

BY TRAIN

Though a handful of the trains that connect Cusco with Ollantaytambo and Machu Picchu start at Poroy, (20–30min by taxi from Cusco), most visitors now travel by bus (see below) from Cusco to Ollantaytambo, which is the main departure point for the train to Machu Picchu. The station is a few hundred metres down Av Estación (also known as Av Ferrocarril), about a 10min walk southwest of the main plaza.

Companies PeruRail and Inca Rail both offer the Ollantaytambo–Machu Picchu Pueblo route (roughly 1hr 30min), with slight variations in prices and timings, depending on the company, service level, season, day of the week and time of day. Perurail offers a more frequent service (20 daily). Each company offers online booking, though they also have ticket offices in central Cusco (see page 219) and at the station in Ollantaytambo. Return tickets from Ollantaytambo to Machu Picchu start at around US$110.

Tickets To be on the safe side, it's important to buy tickets well in advance (weeks ahead during high season) online – from a tour agency in your home country (see page 26) or in Cusco (see page 221), or direct from one of the train companies listed here.

BY BUS

Afternoon buses to Cusco (1hr 30min) leave regularly from the small yard just outside the train station, often coinciding with the train timetable. In the mornings, buses depart mainly from Ollantaytambo's main plaza.

BY COLECTIVO/COMBI

Colectivos from Cusco's C Pavitos travel to Ollantaytambo. Heading back to Cusco, car and minibus colectivos leave from by the train station (1hr 40min–2hr; S/15 and S/10 respectively). Combis bound for Urubamba leave frequently from outside the market, just off the Plaza de Armas (every 10–15min; 30min).

BY TAXI

Taxis between Cusco and Ollantaytambo charge about S/90. You can pick up a taxi back to Cusco in Ollantaytambo outside the train station.

FOOD AND FLOWERS AT THE MARKET, PISAC

LEGIO PARTICULAR
ESCOLARIZADO DE NIVEL
MARIO y SECUNDARIA
EINSTEIN PISAC
WORLD MUSIC
ethno art
COLORS
Látex Mate

INFORMATION AND TOURS

Tourist information The Municipalidad operates a small tourist office during government working hours (Mon–Fri 8am–1pm & 2–5pm; also weekends June–Sept).

Tour operators KB Tambo Tours, C Principal s/n (084 204 133, kbtours.com.pe), is by far the most experienced operator in the area, specializing in rafting (from US$45). They also organize trekking, horseriding and mountain biking tours (see page 247). Note that there are several other websites and agencies with similar names and domain names.

Awamaki (awamaki.org) Not-for-profit organization that runs day-visits to the Quechua weaving village of Patakancha (US$85), as well as cookery and wood-carving workshops (US$50) and village homestays.

ACCOMMODATION

★ **El Albergue** Ollantaytambo train station 084 204 014, elalbergue.com; map p.246. Located in the train station, this gem of a place offers rustic yet stylishly furnished rooms that give onto a leafy garden of fruit trees daily visited by hummingbirds. Paintings by North American owner Wendy Weeks brighten up the premises, and the organic farm with chickens, sheep, pigs, alpaca and a vegetable garden supplies the hotel restaurant (see below) with fresh produce. S/288

★ **Apu Lodge** Lares s/n 084 797 162, apulodge.com; map p.246. Tucked away at the end of a quiet pedestrian street, this tranquil lodge is set in a lovely verdant area surrounded by mountains. Local Andean-themed paintings decorate rooms featuring wooden floorboards, a dresser and en-suite bathrooms. Most look over the town's rooftops to the city ruins, and locally made yogurt and granola are served for breakfast. The hotel regularly hosts writers and yoga groups, too. S/190

La Casa del Abuelo Convención 143 084 434 107, lacasadelabuelo78@gmail.com; map p.246. Right in the centre of town, this place offers smallish tiled rooms with puffy duvets and monsoon showers. Some have tiny balconies. Room 301 is cosy, under a slanted roof. S/150

Hostal Iskay Patacalle s/n 084 204 004, hostaliskay.com; map p.246. A lovely little place offering seven rustic rooms on an old Inca site, all with private bathroom and some with bare stone walls. Check out a couple of rooms before committing. They rent out bikes and guests can share the kitchen, though a buffet breakfast is included. S/120

Hostal Mamá Simona Av Ocobamba s/n 084 436 383, mamasimona.com; map p.246. A short walk north of town, by a rushing stream, this peaceful hostel offers comfortable four- and six-bed dorms with sturdy beds and colourful blankets. There's a fully equipped kitchen, a garden with hammocks and a barbecue set for guests, along with all-day coca tea and lockers for those wanting to leave their belongings as they head to Machu Picchu. Dorms S/45, doubles S/125

Hotel Tikawasi Valley Convención s/n 084 204 166, tikawasi-valley.hotelvallesagrado.com; map p.246. This pleasant hotel offers two beautiful Inca rooms with original walls and niches adorned with statuettes. These cost S/65 more than the standard rooms, which are welcoming too, although how often do you get to sleep in a historical Inca room? S/180

EATING

★ **El Albergue** Ollantaytambo train station 084 204 014 elalbergue.com; map p.246. This pleasant restaurant is without a doubt Ollantaytambo's best – ingredients are sourced directly from the farm at the back, including quinoa, corn and potatoes, and the interior is warm and pleasant. The menu includes delicious *causitas* (S/23) with three toppings, namely guacamole, grilled trout and *ají de gallina*. There are plenty of vegetarian options too, and guests can also reserve a *pachamanca* meal in advance. This is also a great spot to grab some freshly made sandwiches for the train journey to Machu Picchu Pueblo. Daily 5.30am–3.30pm & 6–9pm.

La Esquina Plaza de Armas; map p.246. Baked goods fresh from the oven every day, including empanadas (S/6),

SUSPENDED IN THE SKY

An audacious and innovative addition to tourism, or an eyesore on the Valle Sagrado mountainside? What's indisputable is that the **Sky Lodge** (naturavive.com) – three transparent octagonal pods fixed to the mountainside by cables and suspended 400m above the floor of the Valle Sagrado – is a tremendous feat of engineering, and a unique experience. It goes without saying that this is neither for the faint-hearted nor anyone suffering from vertigo, as the overnight (or lunchtime) package involves negotiating a **via ferrata** (climbing ladder) and/or a series of **ziplines**. S/1335 per person includes a night in the capsule – breakfast and dinner are brought up to you – and either the zipline or via ferrata experience, though you can opt for both.

breads and brownies (S/7), while the coffee is sourced from a local artisanal producer. Salads (S/13), soups (S/10) and sandwiches (S/12), as well as all-day breakfasts (S/9), are on offer. Daily 7.30am–9pm.

Hearts Café Av Ventiderio s/n; map p.246. This wonderful little café serves chunky soups, huge salads, and a range of international dishes (mains from S/16), including plenty of veggie options. The bread is freshly baked and the cakes are all home-made. Profits go to the local community. Daily 7am–8.45pm.

Il Piccolo Forno C del Medio 120 ☎996 400 150; map p.246. This Italian-Peruvian owned place is a great spot for a pizza (S/15), lasagne (S/23) or one of the many delectable desserts that can be consumed at little wooden tables. The shelves are lined with jars of pasta sauces and packets of local coffee – available for purchase – and there are plenty of gluten free options, too. Tues–Sun 1–9pm.

Tutti Amore Av Estación s/n; map p.246. This little ice-cream joint produces over eighty flavours a year, solely using local produce including all manner of seasonal fruits. S/5 per scoop or two for S/8. Daily 8am–5pm.

The Inca Trail

Even though it's just one among a multitude of paths across the Andes, the fabulous treasure of Machu Picchu (see page 255) at the end of its 43km path makes the **INCA TRAIL** one of the world's most famous treks. Most people visit the site on a day-tour by train from Cusco, Ollantaytambo or Urubamba (see page 254), or by staying overnight in Machu Picchu Pueblo (see page 260), but if you're reasonably fit and can dedicate four days to the experience, arriving along the Inca Trail – or one of the alternative routes – offers the most atmospheric and satisfying option.

The downside of the trail's popularity is that you have to **book** six to nine months in advance since only 500 permits are awarded per day and that includes porters and guides as well as tourists. What's more, you can only hike with a **licensed tour operator**, generally in a **tour group**, though some agencies organize bespoke tours, which are inevitably more expensive. Either way, hiking the Inca Trail does not come cheap and involves tough altitude trekking at times, but this is rewarded by spectacular scenery, deep valleys, glaciated mountain peaks and remote Inca structures.

The Classic Inca Trail is **four days** and the most common tour length offered by tour agencies. There are numerous **campsites** along the trail, though where you stay the night will ultimately be decided by your trail guide. Note also that the trail is **closed in February**, which is usually the wettest month, for annual maintenance and repair. More recently a shorter two-day tour is being offered – sometimes referred to as the Camino Sagrado de los Incas – which gives you a flavour of the trail, but without any camping (see page 262).

INFORMATION

Acclimatization It's important to make time to acclimatize to the altitude (see page 207) before tackling the Inca Trail or any other high Andean trek, especially if you've flown straight up from sea level.

Costs For the Classic Inca Trail most prices range US$650–900, depending on the season, number of people in the group, quality of equipment and service. If you want the best, including luxuries such as inflatable mattresses or gourmet cuisine, expect to pay more. Make sure also that your agency adheres to the regulations governing proper wages and conditions for porters (at least US$15 per day, and carrying no more than 20kg); not all do, and especially not if they're offering the cheapest rates. Even then, you should tip your porters as well as your guide. Most companies offer good value; some agency rates include transport and entry to the Inca Trail and Machu Picchu (S/345) in their price, but for others these are extra, so check before booking.

Porters and equipment Trekking companies will organize porters and maybe mules to help carry equipment, including tents, food, rubbish and sometimes even portable toilets, since the trail facilities are often not pleasant, though consider that the porters will have to carry out the waste. The amount of personal luggage, which includes your sleeping bag and mat, is usually 4–5kg, so most trekking companies offer the possibility of hiring, or sharing in the hire of a private porter; the rate is normally about US$80 for the four-day trek.

Rules and restrictions The sanctuary authorities (the Unidad de Gestión del Santuario Histórico de Machu Picchu) have imposed a limit of a maximum of five hundred people a day on the Inca Trail (including trekkers, porters, cooks and guides). In addition, it is mandatory for trekkers to go with a tour or licensed guide (see page 221): the old days of going it alone are gone.

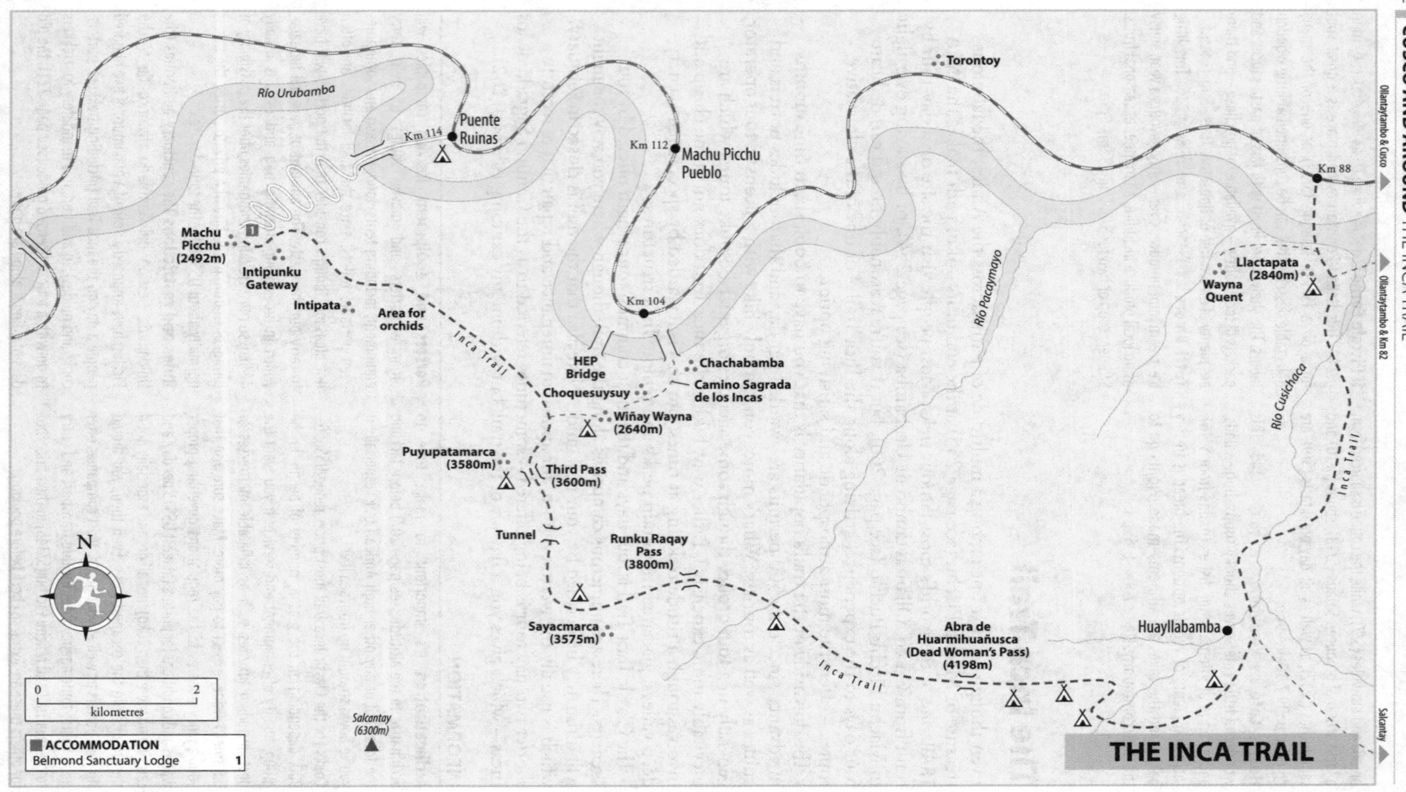
THE INCA TRAIL
Ollantaytambo & Cusco
Ollantaytambo & Km 82
Salcantay
Torontoy
Río Urubamba
Km 114
Puente Ruinas
Km 112
Machu Picchu Pueblo
Km 88
Machu Picchu (2492m)
Intipunku Gateway
Intipata
Area for orchids
Inca Trail
Km 104
Río Pacaymayo
Llactapata (2840m)
Wayna Quent
HEP Bridge
Chachabamba
Camino Sagrada de los Incas
Choquesuysuy
Wiñay Wayna (2640m)
Río Cusichaca
Puyupatamarca (3580m)
Third Pass (3600m)
Tunnel
Runku Raqay Pass (3800m)
Sayacmarca (3575m)
Abra de Huarmihuañusca (Dead Woman's Pass) (4198m)
Huayllabamba
N
0
2
kilometres
Salcantay (6300m)
ACCOMMODATION
Belmond Sanctuary Lodge 1

Websites Check machupicchu.gob.pe for background on Machu Picchu, the Inca Trail and alternative sites like Choquequirao (see page 266).

When to go Choose your season for hiking the Inca Trail carefully. May is the best month to venture on a hike here, with clear views, fine weather and verdant surroundings. Between June and September it's usually a pretty cosmopolitan stretch of mountainside, with travellers from all over the globe converging on Machu Picchu the hard way, but from mid-June to early August the trail is simply very busy (and the campsites noisy), especially on the last stretch. From October until April, in the rainy season, it's less crowded but also, naturally, quite a bit wetter.

The main trail

The usual **starting point** for the Inca Trail is a small station at the hamlet and bridge at Q'orihuayrachina, at **Km 88** on the rail line from Ollantaytambo and Poroy. Some tours arrive here by car and start at Km 82, where the road stops. The train stop is hailed by the guards and a small footbridge sees you across the tumbling Río Urubamba. Once over the bridge, the main path leads to the left through a small eucalyptus wood, then around the base of the Inca ruins of Llactapata – worth a visit for archeology enthusiasts, though most people save their energy for the trail and other archeological remains ahead – before crossing and then following the Río Cusichaca upstream.

It's a good two hours' steep climb to **Huayllabamba**, the only inhabited village on the route, before you embark on the most difficult climb on the whole trail, nearby Warmiwañusqa – which translates as the ominous-sounding **Dead Woman's Pass**. This section of the valley is rich in Inca terracing, from which rises an occasional ancient stone building.

Many groups spend their first night at Huayllabamba campsite, but others wanting to gain distance and time for the second day generally use one of three commonly used **campsites**: one at Llulluchayoc, also known as **Three White Stones**, where the trail crosses the Río Huayruro; another slightly higher site, just below Llulluchpampa; or, slightly higher again, actually on the pampa where there's plenty more camping space – a good spot for seeing rabbit-like *viscachas* playing among the rocks. All of these campsites are on the trail towards the first and highest pass, but only the top one is within sight of it.

4

The first pass

It takes five hours or so to get from Huayllabamba to the Abra de Huarmihuañusca, **the first pass** (4200m) and the highest point on the trail. This is the hardest part of the walk, though the views from the pass itself are stupendous, but if you're lingering to savour them, sit well out of the cutting wind (many a trekker has caught a bad chill here). From here the trail drops steeply down into the Valle de Pacamayo where, by the river, there's an attractive spot to **camp**, and where you can see playful **spectacled bears** if you're very lucky.

The second pass

A winding, tiring track up from the Pacamayo Valley takes you to the **second pass** – Abra de Runku Racay – just above the interesting circular ruins of the same name.

INCA TRAIL WILDLIFE

Acting as a bio-corridor between the Cusco Andes, the Valle Sagrado and the lowland Amazon rainforest, the **Santuario Histórico de Machu Picchu** possesses over 370 bird species, 47 mammal species and over seven hundred butterfly species. Some of the more notable residents include the **cock-of-the-rock** (*Rupicola peruviana*, known as *tunkis* in the Quechua-speaking Andes), **spectacled bear** (*Tremarctos ornatus*) and condor (*Vultur gryphus*). In addition, there are around three hundred different species of orchid hidden up in the trees of the cloud forest.

About an hour beyond the second pass, a flight of stone steps leads up to the Inca ruins of **Sayacmarca**. This is an impressive spot to **camp**, near the remains of a stone aqueduct that supplied water to the ancient settlement.

The third pass

From Sayacmarca, you make your way gently down into increasingly dense cloud forest where delicate orchids and other exotic flora begin to appear among the trees. By the time you get to the **third pass** – which, compared with the previous two, has very little incline – you're following a fine, smoothly worn flagstone path where at one point an astonishing tunnel, carved through solid rock by the Incas, lets you avoid an otherwise impossible climb.

The trail winds down to the impressive ruin of **Puyupatamarca** – "Town Above the Clouds" – where there are five small stone baths and, in the wet season, constant fresh running water. There are places to **camp** actually on the pass (above the ruins), commanding stunning views across the Valle de Urubamba and, in the other direction, towards the snowcaps of Salcantay (Wild Mountain): this is probably one of the most magical camps on the trail, given good weather, and it's not unusual to see deer feeding here.

Wiñay Wayna

It's a very rough, two- or three-hour descent along a non-Inca track to the next ruin, a citadel almost as impressive as Machu Picchu, **Wiñay Wayna** – "Forever Young" – another place with fresh water. Consisting of only two major groups of architectural structures – a lower and an upper sector – Wiñay Wayna's most visible features are **stone baths** with apparently as many as nineteen springs feeding them, all set amid several layers of fine Inca terracing. Nearby there's also a small waterfall created by streams coming down from the heights of Puyupatamarca. Much like today, it is

THE TRAIN JOURNEY TO MACHU PICCHU

A train journey through the Valle Sagrado, flanked by towering mountains and offering glimpses of sparkling snow-capped peaks, is one of the finest train journeys in the world, enhanced by very good service and comfortable, well-kept carriages.

The longest of the train options, only offered occasionally by PeruRail, rumbles out of **Poroy**, fifteen to twenty minutes by taxi from the centre of Cusco (others leave from Urubamba and Ollantaytambo) before dropping rapidly down into the **Valle de Urubamba** via several major track switchbacks.

Ollantaytambo's pretty train station – the starting point for most train passengers these days – is right next to the river, which the train follows, as it winds its way down the valley, stopping briefly at Km 88, where the **Inca Trail** starts (see page 251). The tracks then follow the Río Urubamba as the valley becomes more enclosed (which is why there's no road) and the mountains become more and more forested, as well as steeper and seemingly taller. The end of the line is the station at **Machu Picchu Pueblo** (also known as **Aguas Calientes**), a busy resort town crowded into the valley just a short bus ride from the ruins themselves (see page 260). From Cusco (Estación de Poroy) the journey takes over three hours; it's around an hour and a half from Ollantaytambo. Whichever route you're taking, buy **tickets** well in advance online or at the respective rail offices in Cusco (see page 219).

Budget travellers taking the circuitous minivan route via Santa Teresa (see page 216) can take one of the infrequent trains from the hidroeléctrica, approaching Machu Picchu Pueblo from the other side of the valley (3 daily; 35min; US$33). Times broadly coincide with the workers' shifts at the power station and the arrival and departure times of the minivans from/to Cusco). Most travellers, however, prefer to walk the scenic 11km route alongside the rail tracks (see page 262).

believed that Wiñay Wayna was used by Incas as a washing, cleansing and resting point before arriving at the grand Machu Picchu citadel.

This usually marks the spot for the **last campsite** but with only 150 camping spots available per night, only some trekkers will be based here; otherwise you may have to descend to Machu Picchu Pueblo for your last night, which would be a serious anticlimax.

To reach Machu Picchu for sunrise the next day from Wiñay Wayna, you'll be up very early with a torch to avoid the rush.

Intipunku to Machu Picchu

A well-marked track from Wiñay Wayna takes a right fork for about two more hours through sumptuous vegetated slopes to the stone archway entrance called **Intipunku** (Gateway of the Sun), from where you get your first sight – and the classic view – of Machu Picchu, which is a stupendous moment, however exhausted you might be.

Machu Picchu

Daily 6am–5.30pm • S/152; child or student S/77 (with valid university ID card – not ISIC; see page 40); combined entry with Huayna Picchu or Montaña Machu Picchu S/200; child, or student S/125 (with valid university ID card – not ISIC) • machupicchu.gob.pe • See also page 257

MACHU PICCHU is one of the greatest of all South American tourist attractions: beautiful stone architecture enhanced by the Incas' exploitation of local 250-million-year-old rocks of grey-white granite with a high content of quartz, silica and feldspar, set against a vast, scenic backdrop of dark-green forested mountains that spike up from the deep valleys of the Urubamba and its tributaries. The distant glacial summits are dwarfed only by the huge sky. The site's mysterious origins are central to its enduring appeal, but even without knowing too much about its history or archeology, or the specifics of each feature, it's quite possible to enjoy a visit to Machu Picchu: for many, it's enough just to absorb the mystical atmosphere.

4

Brief history

The name Machu Picchu apparently means simply Old or Ancient Mountain. With many legends and theories surrounding the position of the site, most archeologists agree that its **sacred geography and astronomy** were auspicious factors in helping the Inca Pachacuti decide to build this citadel here at 2492m. It's thought that agricultural influences as well as geo-sacred indicators prevailed, and that the site secured a decent supply of sacred coca and maize for the Inca nobles and priests in Cusco.

The "discovery" of Machu Picchu

Never unearthed by the Spanish conquerors, for many centuries the site of Machu Picchu lay forgotten – though local people and settlers knew of its existence – until it was uncovered on July 24, 1911 by the US explorer **Hiram Bingham**. It was a fantastic find, not least because the site was still relatively intact, without the usual ravages of either Spanish Conquistadors or tomb robbers. Accompanied only by two locals, Bingham left his base camp around 10am and crossed a bridge so dodgy that he crawled over it on his hands and knees before climbing a precipitous slope until they reached the ridge at around midday. After resting at a small hut, he received hospitality from a local peasant who described an extensive system of terraces where they had found good fertile soil for their crops. Bingham was led to the site by an 11-year-old local boy, Pablito Álvarez, but it didn't take him long to see that he had come across some important ancient Inca terraces – over a hundred of which had recently been

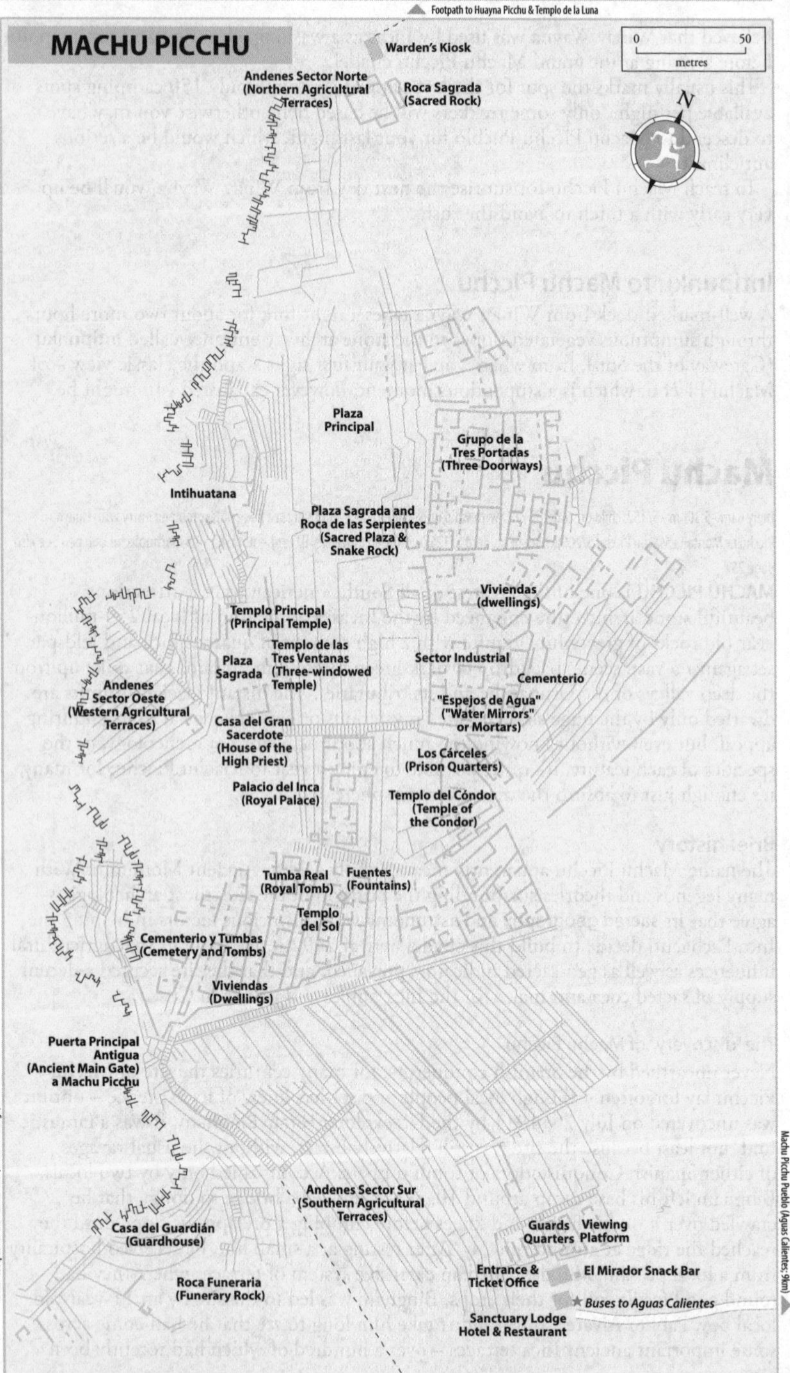
MACHU PICCHU
Footpath to Huayna Picchu & Templo de la Luna
0
50
metres
N
Warden's Kiosk
Andenes Sector Norte
(Northern Agricultural Terraces)
Roca Sagrada
(Sacred Rock)
Plaza Principal
Grupo de la Tres Portadas
(Three Doorways)
Intihuatana
Plaza Sagrada and Roca de las Serpientes
(Sacred Plaza & Snake Rock)
Viviendas
(dwellings)
Templo Principal
(Principal Temple)
Templo de las Tres Ventanas
(Three-windowed Temple)
Plaza Sagrada
Sector Industrial
Cementerio
Andenes Sector Oeste
(Western Agricultural Terraces)
Casa del Gran Sacerdote
(House of the High Priest)
"Espejos de Agua"
("Water Mirrors" or Mortars)
Los Cárceles
(Prison Quarters)
Palacio del Inca
(Royal Palace)
Templo del Cóndor
(Temple of the Condor)
Tumba Real
(Royal Tomb)
Fuentes
(Fountains)
Templo del Sol
Cementerio y Tumbas
(Cemetery and Tombs)
Viviendas
(Dwellings)
Puerta Principal Antigua
(Ancient Main Gate) a Machu Picchu
footpath to the Puente Inca (Inca Drawbridge)
Andenes Sector Sur
(Southern Agricultural Terraces)
Guards Quarters
Viewing Platform
Casa del Guardián
(Guardhouse)
Entrance & Ticket Office
El Mirador Snack Bar
Roca Funeraria
(Funerary Rock)
Buses to Aguas Calientes
Sanctuary Lodge Hotel & Restaurant
Machu Picchu Pueblo (Aguas Calientes; 9km)
Montaña Machu Picchu, Inti Punku (Sun Gate), Inca Trail and Wiñay Wayna

MACHU PICCHU TICKETS AND REGULATIONS

There's no doubt that in high season, with well over five thousand visitors a day, Machu Picchu is struggling to absorb its tourists without it being a total scrum. Due to its popularity and attempts to limit visitor numbers because of the potential environmental impact, **booking ahead** is recommended, and essential if you want to climb Huayna (Wayna) Picchu or Montaña Machu Picchu, as well as visit the main ruins. Since 1 July 2017, the citadel has been operating a two-shift entry system, allowing just over three thousand entries for each shift – 6am to noon and noon to 5.30pm – in an attempt to minimize the stress on the site. For Huayna Picchu, only four hundred tickets are allocated per day, again in two waves: 7 to 8am and 10 to 11am; for the lengthier, more demanding hike up Montaña Machu Picchu, eight hundred tickets are available daily, allowing visitors up 7 to 8am and 9 to 10am.

The website Ⓦ machupicchu.gob.pe allows you to check availability and prices (see also page 255) and purchase online using a Visa credit card, though the English version of the website can be temperamental. Alternatively, book via a travel agency or in person in Cusco at the INC office on C Garcilaso s/n (cash and cards accepted; Ⓣ 084 236 061;,Mon–Sat 7am–8pm) or – in low season –at the INC office in Machu Picchu Pueblo (cash only; Ⓣ 084 582 030; see page 260). Note, however, that once tickets have been purchased for a specific date and time, they cannot be changed. At the time of going to press, only an official student ID card with an expiry date – valid until a time after the intended visit (as well as a passport), and not an ISIC card, was necessary for a student discount, and this could only be negotatied in person (not online).

Theoretically, since 1 July 2017, all visitors now also need to be accompanied by a **guide** (rates around S/180 for a small group); however, at the time of going to press, this was not being enforced since there were insufficient certified guides to go round. Check for the latest news before you leave Cusco.

Bear in mind also that **food and drink** are not allowed into the ruins – though most people manage to smuggle a few snacks and a bottle of water in their day sack. Large backpacks or bags have to be deposited at the entrance. Tickets only allow for one re-entry into the site during the period of their validity; since the only toilet (expect a long queue) and restaurant facilities are outside the site entrance, plan your one exit accordingly.

cleared of forest for subsistence crops. On further exploration, Bingham found the fine white stonework and began to realize that this might be the place he was looking for.

Origins of Machu Picchu

Bingham first theorized that Machu Picchu was the lost city of **Vilcabamba**, the site of the Incas' last refuge from the Spanish conquistadores. Not until another American expedition surveyed the ruins around Machu Picchu in the 1940s did serious doubts begin to arise over this assertion, and more recently the site of the Incas' final stronghold has been shown to be Espíritu Pampa in the Amazon jungle (see page 272).

Meanwhile, it was speculated that Machu Picchu was perhaps the best preserved of a series of **agricultural centres** that served Cusco in its prime. The city was conceived and built in the mid-fifteenth century by **Emperor Pachacuti**, the first to expand the empire beyond the Valle Sagrado towards the forested gold-lands. With crop fertility, mountains and nature so sacred to the Incas, an agricultural centre as important as Machu Picchu would easily have merited the site's fine stonework and temple precincts. It was clearly also a **ritual centre**, given the layout and quantity of temples; but for the Incas it was usual not to separate things we consider economic tasks from more conventional religious activities. So, Machu Picchu represents to many archeologists the most classical and best-preserved remains in existence of a citadel used by the Incas as both a religious temple site and an agricultural (perhaps experimental) centre.

THREATS TO MACHU PICCHU

This most dramatic and enchanting of Inca citadels, suspended on an extravagantly terraced saddle between two prominent peaks, is believed to be in danger of **collapse**. The original Inca inhabitants temporarily stabilized the mountainside, transforming some of the geological faults into **drainage channels**. They also joined many of the construction stones together, using elaborate multi-angled techniques, making them more resistant to both tremors and landslides. Nevertheless, these spots remain weak, and significant damage can be seen on nearby buildings. The Instituto Nacional de Cultura (INC), which administers Machu Picchu, acknowledges the problems, but correcting them is an ongoing process. The decision to spread the visitor load over two shifts, initiated in 2017, is aimed at reducing the stress on the site, just as the refusal to increase the number of bus transfers from Machu Picchu Pueblo has been justified on the grounds of minimizing the environmental impact on the area; increasing the overall daily limit of visitors to over six thousand, however, would seem to be a retrograde step.

The ruins

Though more than 1000m lower than Cusco, Machu Picchu seems much higher, constructed as it is on dizzying slopes overlooking a U-curve in the Río Urubamba. More than a hundred flights of steep stone steps interconnect its palaces, temples, storehouses and terraces, and the outstanding views command not only the valley below in both directions but also extend to the snowy peaks around Salcantay. Wherever you stand in the ruins, you can see spectacular **terraces** (some of which are once again being cultivated) slicing across ridiculously steep cliffs, transforming mountains into suspended gardens.

Though it would take a lot to detract from Machu Picchu's incredible beauty and unsurpassed location, it is a zealously supervised place, with the site guards frequently blowing whistles at visitors who have deviated from the recently instituted one-way routes around the ruins. The best way to enjoy the site – while avoiding the ire of the guards – is to hire a **guide** (see page 221) in advance, or at the entrance to the site, or buy the **map** from the ticket office to help you plan your itinerary.

El Templo del Sol

The **Templo del Sol** (Temple of the Sun), also known as the Torreón, is a wonderful, semicircular, walled, tower-like temple displaying some of Machu Picchu's finest granite stonework. Constructed to incorporate polyhedrons and trapezoidal window niches, the temple's carved steps and smoothly joined stone blocks fit neatly into the existing relief of a natural boulder that served as some kind of altar and also marks the entrance to a small cave. A window off this temple provides views of both the June solstice sunrise and the constellation of the Pleiades, which rises from here over the nearby peak of Huayna Picchu. The Pleiades are still a very important Andean astronomical symbol relating to crop fertility: locals use the constellation as a kind of annual signpost in the agricultural calendar, giving information about when to plant crops and when the rains will come.

La Tumba Real

Below the Templo del Sol is a cave known as the **Tumba Real** (Royal Tomb), despite the fact that no graves or human remains have ever been found there. In fact, it probably represented access to the spiritual heart of the mountains, like the cave at the Templo de la Luna (Temple of the Moon; see page 260).

La Roca Funeraria

Retracing your steps 20m or so back from the Templo del Sol and following a flight of stone stairs directly uphill, then left along the track towards Intipunku (see page 260), brings you to a path on the right, which climbs up to the thatched **warden's hut**. This hut is associated with a modestly carved rock known as the **Roca Funeraria** (Funerary Rock) and a nearby graveyard where Hiram Bingham (see page 255) found evidence of many burials, some of which were obviously royal.

La Plaza Sagrada

Arguably the most enthralling sector of the ruins, the **Templo de las Tres Ventanas** (Three-Windowed Temple), part of the complex based around the **Plaza Sagrada** (Sacred Plaza) is located back down in the centre of the site, the next major Inca construction after the Templo del Sol. Dominating the southeastern edge of the plaza, the attractive Templo de las Tres Ventanas has unusually large windows looking east towards the mountains beyond the valley of the Río Urubamba. From here it's a short stroll to the **Templo Principal** (Principal Temple), so called because of the fine stonework of its three high main walls, the most easterly of which looks onto the Plaza Sagrada. Unusually (as most ancient temples in the Americas face east), the main opening of this temple faces south, and white sand, often thought to represent the ocean, has been found on the temple floor, suggesting that it may have been allied symbolically to the Río Urubamba: water and the sea.

The Intihuatana

A minute or so uphill from the Templo Principal along an elaborately carved stone stairway brings you to one of the jewels of the site, the **Intihuatana**, also known as the **"hitching post of the sun"**. This fascinating carved rock, built on a rise above the Sacred Plaza, is similar to those created by the Incas in all their important ritual centres, but is one of the very few not to have been discovered and destroyed by the Conquistadors. This unique and very beautiful survivor, set in a tower-like position, overlooks the Plaza Sagrada, the Río Urubamba and the sacred peak of Huayna Picchu.

The Intihuatana's base is said to have been carved in the shape of a map of the Inca Empire, though few archeologists agree with this. Its main purpose was as an **astro-agricultural clock** for viewing the complex interrelationships between the movements of the planets and constellations. It is also thought by some to be a symbolic representation of the spirit of the mountain on which Machu Picchu was built – by all accounts a very powerful spot both in terms of sacred geography and its astrological function. The Intihuatana appears to be aligned with four important **mountains**: the snowcapped mountain range of La Verónica lies directly to the east, with the sun rising behind its main summit during the equinoxes; directly south, though not actually visible from here, sits the father of all mountains in this part of Peru, Salcantay, a few days' trek away; to the west, the sun sets behind the important peak of Pumasillo during the December solstice; and due north stands the majestic peak of Huayna Picchu. The rock evidently kept track of the annual cycles, with its basic orientation northwest to southeast, plus four vertices pointing to the four cardinal points.

La Roca Sagrada

Following the steps down from the Intihuatana and passing through the Plaza Sagrada towards the northern terraces brings you in a few minutes to the **Roca Sagrada** (Sacred Rock), below the access point to Huayna Picchu. A three-metre-high and seven-metre-wide lozenge of rock sticking out of the earth like a sculptured wall, little is known for sure about the Roca Sagrada, but it is thought to have had a ritual function; its outline is strikingly similar to the Incas' sacred mountain of Putukusi, which towers behind it in the east.

Huayna Picchu

The prominent peak of **Huayna Picchu** juts out over the Valle de Urubamba at the northern end of the Machu Picchu site, and is easily scaled by any reasonably energetic

SUNRISE OVER MACHU PICCHU

It's easy enough to get into the site before **sunrise**, since the sun rarely rises over the mountains to shed its rays over Machu Picchu before 7am. Make your way to Intihuatana (the "hitching post of the sun") before dawn for an unforgettable sunrise that will quickly make you forget the hike through the pre-dawn gloom – or the tedious bus queues, if you're coming up from Machu Picchu Pueblo. Bring a torch if you plan to try it.

person with a head for heights. The record for this vigorous and rewarding climb is 22 minutes, but most people take at least an hour. Access to this sacred mountain is restricted to four hundred people a day (the first two hundred are expected to get back down by 10am so that the second two hundred can then go up); you will need to book well in advance. From the summit, there's an awe-inspiring **panorama**, and it's a great place from which to get an overview of the ruins suspended between the mountains among stupendous forested Andean scenery.

El Templo de la Luna

Accessed via a small track about one-third of the way up Huayna Picchu (so it can only be visited if you have a ticket for climbing the peak), the stunning **Templo de la Luna** (Temple of the Moon) is hidden in a grotto hanging magically above the Río Urubamba, some 400m beneath the pinnacle of Huayna Picchu. It's at least another 45 minutes each way and not that easy going at times, with rock ladders in places. Once you reach the temple, you'll be rewarded by some of the best stonework in the entire complex, the level of skill hinting at the site's importance to the Inca.

4

The temple's name comes from the fact that it is often lit up by the moonlight, but some archeologists believe the structure was probably dedicated to the spirit of the mountain. The temple's main sector is in the mouth of a natural **cave**, where five niches are set into an elaborate white-granite stone wall. In the centre of the cave stands a rock carved like a throne, beside which five cut steps lead into the darker recesses, where you can see more carved rocks and stone walls, nowadays inaccessible. Immediately to the front of the cave is a small **plaza** with another cut-stone throne and an altar. Outside, steps either side of the massive boulder lead above the cave, from where you can see a broad, stone-walled **room** running along one side of the cave boulder. More buildings and beautiful stone sanctuaries lie just down a flight of steps from this part of the complex.

Intipunku

If you don't have a ticket for Huayna Picchu, head back to the warden's hut on the other side of the site and take the path below it, which climbs gently for forty minutes or so, up to **Intipunku**, the main entrance to Machu Picchu from the Inca Trail. This offers an incredible view over the entire site, with the unmistakeable sugar-loaf shape of Huayna Picchu in the background.

Machu Picchu Pueblo

Many people base themselves at the cramped resort town of **MACHU PICCHU PUEBLO** (previously known as **Aguas Calientes**) – connected to Machu Picchu itself by bus – in order to visit the ruins at a more leisurely pace or in more depth. Though its warm, humid climate and surrounding landscape of towering mountains covered in cloud forest make it a welcome change from Cusco, its brash commercialism is pretty unappealing – despite the recent addition of a cultural **sculpture trail** round the place. The town's explosive growth has pretty well reached the limits of the valley here; there's very little flat land that hasn't been built on or covered in concrete. Not surprisingly, this boom town has a lively, bustling feel and enough restaurants and bars to satisfy a small army.

The thermal baths

Top end of Av Pachacutec, 400m from the main plaza • Daily 5am–8pm • S/20

The main attraction in these parts – apart from Machu Picchu itself – is the natural **thermal baths**, which are particularly enjoyable after a few days on the Inca Trail or a hot afternoon up at Machu Picchu, although they can get very crowded. If you head there before dawn, you'll enjoy cleaner water and only have to share them with a handful of locals.

Putukusi

A **trail** up the sacred mountain of **Putukusi** starts just outside town, a couple of hundred metres along the railway tracks towards the ruins. The walk offers stupendous views of the town and across to Machu Picchu; allow an hour and a half each way. Note it is not for the faint-hearted as the trail is very steep in parts (some sections have been replaced by rock ladders) and very narrow. When wet the trail is closed for safety reasons.

Museo de Sitio Manuel Chávez Ballón

Km 22, at the old train station of Puente Ruinas, 1.7km from the town • Daily 9am–5pm • S/22 • 958 194 475 • Tickets sold in combination with the Machu Picchu ticket, or separately at the museum itself on presentation of your passport • A 40min walk along the road to the ruins

If you've not overdosed on Machu Picchu, you may like to drop by this small, well-designed **museum,** which is usually blissfully free of tourists. Although the contents are not as impressive as in some of the Cusco museums, they are well presented (in English). On display are more than 250 artefacts retrieved from excavations of Machu

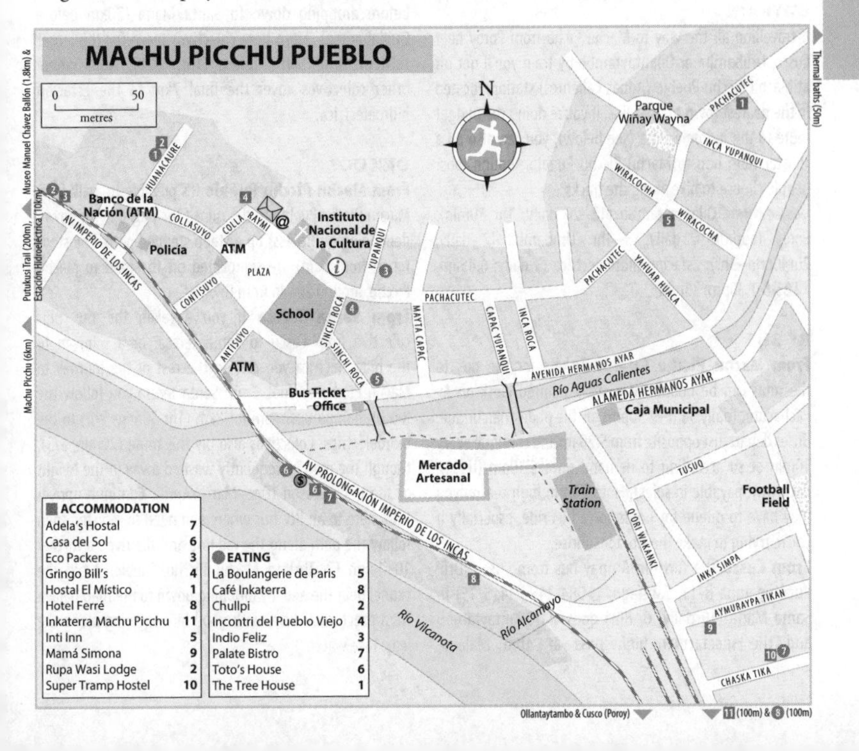

CAMINO SAGRADO DE LOS INCAS

The **Camino Sagrado de los Incas**, a truncated Inca Trail, starts at Km 104 of the railway line, 8km from Machu Picchu. The same costs and regulations regarding trail permits apply (see page 251), but you only have one full day of hiking (around 12km) and avoid camping. The route involves a steep climb (4–6hr) via the ruins of Chachabamba to reach Wiñay Wayna (see page 254). Here most groups picnic before joining the remainder of the Inca Trail, which takes another two hours to complete. After soaking up the majestic vistas of Machu Picchu from Intipunku (the Sun Gate), you descend to spend the night in Macho Picchu Pueblo; the ruins are visited the following morning before you leave on the afternoon train.

Picchu and sites along the Inca Trail in recent decades. Exhibits include many **tools** used to build the citadel – some specifically crafted to cut particular types of rock. A small **botanical garden** is attached.

Mariposario Wasi Pillpi

By the municipal campsite, 1.2km from town • Daily 8am–6pm • S/10 • ⓣ 973 621 266 • A 20min walk along the road to the ruins

For nature enthusiasts who can speak some Spanish, this **butterfly sanctuary** offers short but enthusiastic tours of its facility, giving you the chance to get close to its thirty odd species. A small, locally run non-profit enterprise, it aims to research and educate people about lepidoptera, and their importance to local biodiversity. At the same time, it hopes to increase the butterfly population through a reproduce-and-release programme.

4

ARRIVAL AND GETTING AROUND — MACHU PICCHU PUEBLO

BY TRAIN

If travelling all the way to Machu Pichu from Poroy near Cusco, Urubamba or Ollantaytambo by train you'll get off at Machu Picchu Pueblo (Aguas Calientes) station, located in the nearest town to the ruins. If you're doing the budget route to the hidroeléctrica (see below), you can also do a shorter train hop to Machu Picchu Pueblo, though most people choose to hike along the tracks.

Destinations Ollantaytambo (12–20 daily; 1hr 30min); Poroy (approx 4 daily; 3–4hr; Urubamba (2 daily; 2hr40min–3hr); Estación hidroeléctrica (3 daily: 6.45am, 12.35 & 1.30pm; 35min).

BY BUS

From Machu Picchu Pueblo Tickets for the bus to the ruins can be bought at a small painted kiosk on Av Pachacutec (daily 5am–9.50pm), by the pedestrian bridge. Buses depart just opposite from 5.20am and continue every 10min or so according to demand until 5.30pm (US$12 each way, payable in soles). Note that in high season you may have to queue for hours for a bus ride, especially if you're trying to make the site for sunrise.

From Cusco The Turismo Ampay bus from Cusco (Urb. Pucutupampa B-11, Santiago; ⓣ 084 245 734; S/15) to Santa María (10 daily; 6–8hr) goes via Ollantaytambo and the spectacular high pass at Abra Málaga, before dropping down to Santa María (20km before Quillabamba). From here colectivos leave for the larger settlement of Santa Teresa (1hr; S/20), from where other colectivos cover the final 7km to the Estación hidroeléctrica.

ON FOOT

From Machu Picchu Pueblo It's possible to walk from Machu Picchu Pueblo to the ruins (2hr-plus up, 1hr down, depending on fitness) up a steep stepped path. The steps (open from 5am) are signposted off the road to Machu Picchu, around 20min from town.

From Santa Teresa If you've taken the bus plus colectivo from Cusco to Santa Teresa, or a minivan to the hidroeléctrica you can do the rest of the journey to Machu Picchu on foot. From Santa Teresa you follow the Río Urubamba upstream for 8km (1hr 30min–2hr) to the hidroeléctrica. Colectivos also ply this route (20min; S/3), though the road is frequently washed away in the height of the rainy season (Dec–March/April). Continue upriver from here to an INC hut where you need to register, then follow the path along the rail line and the river, a further 10–11km (2–3hr) to Machu Picchu Pueblo. Avoid the tunnel near the end, by dropping down to the road below. It's a spectacular hike, with good birdwatching along the way; take water.

INFORMATION AND TOURS

Tourist information iPerú is at Av Pachacutec s/n (T 084 211 104; E iperumachupicchu@promperu.gob.pe; daily 9am–1pm & 2–6pm).

Machu Picchu Tickets The INC (Instituto Nacional de Cultura) office just off the main square at Av Pachacutec 123 (T 084 211 196; daily 5.45am–8.30pm) sells tickets for Machu Picchu entry for cash only (see page 257). If you stay overnight in Machu Picchu Pueblo before visiting the site, buy your ticket as soon as you arrive in town as this will save you time in the morning; the same goes for your bus ticket (see page 262).

Banks and services BCP on Av Los Incas 600, next to *Toto's*, Banco de la Nación at Av Los Incas 540 by the police station and Caja Municipal by the Mercado Artesanal all have ATMs, but sometimes run out of money, especially at weekends. The Panamericana pharmacy on the main plaza (daily 8am–9pm) can provide for basic medicinal needs.

ACCOMMODATION

MACHU PICCHU PUEBLO

Although there is an overwhelming choice of places to stay in Machu Picchu Pueblo, there can be a lot of competition for lodgings during the high season (June–Sept), when large groups of travellers often turn up and take over entire hotels. Coming to town on an early train will give you more choice at the budget end, but for the better places, especially in high season, you should book in advance.

HOTELS AND GUESTHOUSES

Adela's Hostal Av Prolongación Imperio de los Incas s/n T 084 211291, W adelashostalmachupicchu.online; map p.261. This small budget option by the train station features cheerily painted rooms with bright bedspreads. There are only eight rooms – some have great river views – which lends the place an intimate feel S/130

Casa del Sol Av Imperio de los Incas 608 T 084 211 118, W casadelsolhotels.com; map p.261. Set on seven floors, this modern hotel boasts welcoming rooms with wooden floors, cosy armchairs and hand-woven framed fabrics from Ayacucho. Bathrooms feature rain showers and stone sinks, and the double-glazing ensures peace and quiet from the honking train and street noise. The spa has a steam room and jacuzzi. S/1292

Gringo Bill's Colla Raymi 104 T 084 211 046, W gringobills.com; map p.261. This intimate establishment is one of the most interesting choices: the bar-restaurant plus rooms painted with orchid designs form an appealing complex built into the hillside, with pebbled walkways and wooden balustrades. Other draws include the small open-air jacuzzi, leafy terrace, barbecue facilities and laundry service. S/240

Hostal El Místico Av Pachacutec 814 T 084 211 051, W elmisticomachupicchu.com; map p.261. This pleasant guesthouse features ten rooms spread across three floors with a little lounge area on each; walls are decorated with psychedelic paintings, and the friendly owner, who runs a jewellery shop right next door, organizes complimentary mystical tours around town. S/108

Hotel Ferré Av Imperio de los Incas 634 T 084 211 337, W hotelferremachupicchu.com; map p.261. A newly built hotel that is very comfortable indeed and prices – for Machu Picchu – are very reasonable; rooms are spick and span and all feature fridge, TV and safe. The interior rooms can be a bit dark; river-view rooms are without a doubt worth the extra S/60 – room 306 is particularly appealing. S/320

Inkaterra Machu Picchu Km 110 by the rail line on the western edge of the settlement T 084 211 122, Lima T 01 610 0400, W inkaterra.com; map p.261. This smart award-winning and eco-friendly hotel features well-appointed rooms set in a large plot of tropical gardens and cloud forest with jacuzzi and a small pool, and a cosy lobby area scattered with books and fireplaces. The grounds boast over 200 bird species and 370 orchids while the excellent restaurant serves tea from the hotel's very own tea plantation. US$602

Inti Inn Av Pachacutec s/n T 084 211 137, W grupointi.com; map p.261. On the town's main drag, this pleasant option has recently been renovated. The corridors are atmospherically lit with low lighting, and the interiors feature stone floors and wooden beams. Rooms are comfortable although they can get a little noisy. S/464

★ **Rupa Wasi Lodge** Jr Huanacaure 105 T 084 211 101, W rupawasi.net; map p.261. The eco-friendly owners of this lovely lodge have done a great job at integrating the accommodation with the surrounding environment. Wooden en-suite rooms are set on a slope in a lush tropical garden, and some feature small balconies with pretty views. The attached restaurant, *The Tree House*, serves superb Peruvian dishes with a twist, and they offer 2hr cooking classes too (US$70/person). S/240

HOSTELS

Eco Packers Av Imperio de los Incas 136 T 084 211 121, W ecopackersperu.com; map p.261. A popular place with dorms and doubles giving onto narrow corridors that wind their way up to the rooftop terrace with billiards table and cable TV. Dorms have tightly packed wooden beds, while the en-suite doubles are more comfortable – quieter rooms lie at the back. Dorms S/43, doubles S/150

Mamá Simona Amuraypa Tikan 104, Las Orquideas T084 436 757, W mamasimona.co; map p.261.

4

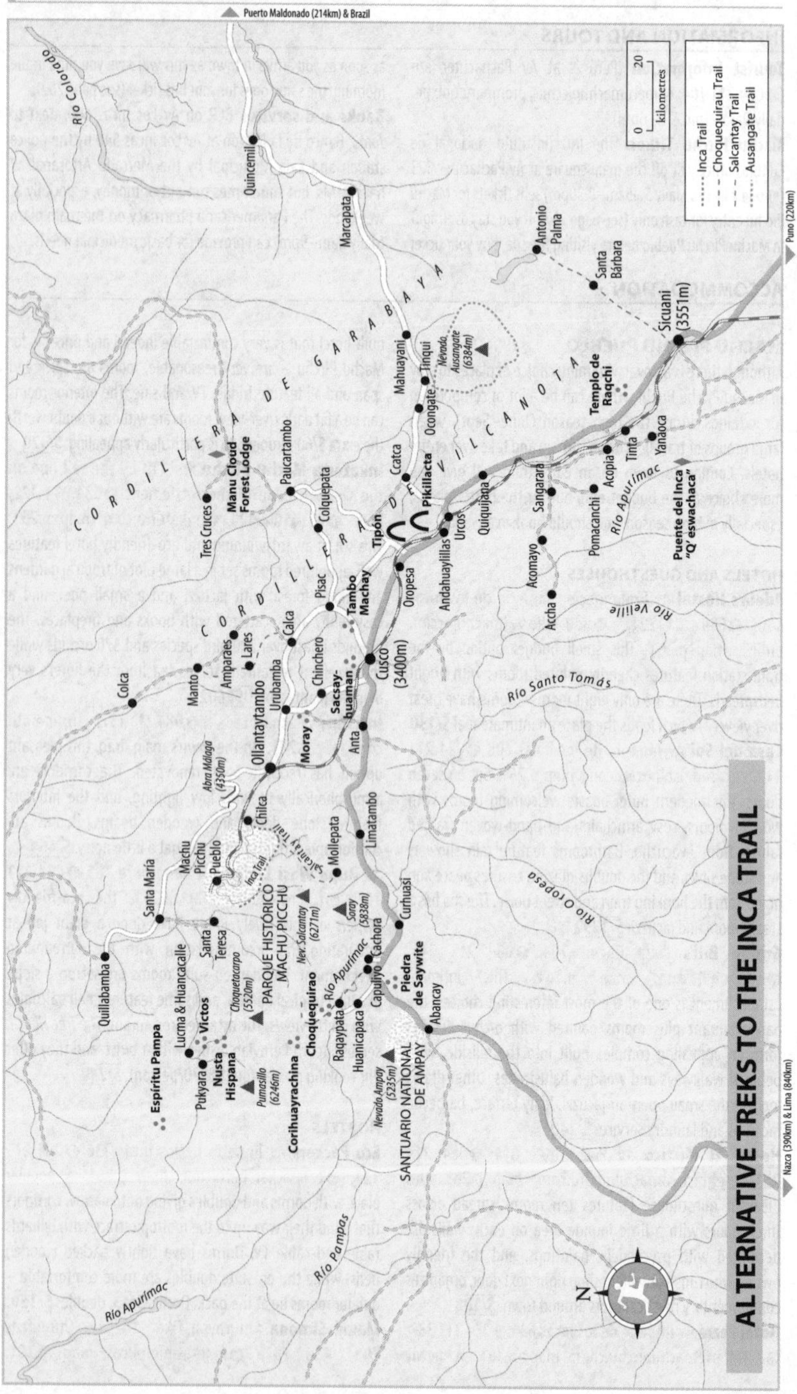

ALTERNATIVE TREKS TO THE INCA TRAIL

Puerto Maldonado (214km) & Brazil
Nazca (390km) & Lima (840km)
Puno (220km)
Río Colorado
Río Apurímac
Río Pampas
Río Oropesa
Río Santo Tomás
Río Velille
CORDILLERA DE GARABAYA
CORDILLERA DE VILCANOTA
Quillabamba
Colca
Espíritu Pampa
Santa María
Lucma & Huancacalle
Pukyara
Victos
Nusta Hispana
Santa Teresa
Machu Picchu Pueblo
Abra Málaga (4350m)
Manto
Amparaes
Lares
Tres Cruces
Manu Cloud Forest Lodge
Quincemil
Pumasillo (6246m)
Choquetacarpo (5520m)
PARQUE HISTÓRICO MACHU PICCHU
Inca Trail
Salcantay Trail
Chilca
Ollantaytambo
Urubamba
Calca
Paucartambo
Corihuayrachina
Choquequirao
Nev. Salcantay (6271m)
Moray
Chinchero
Pisac
Colquepata
Río Apurímac
Raqaypata
Mollepata
Soray (5838m)
Sacsay-huaman
Tambo Machay
Marcapata
Huanicapaca
Capuliyo
Cachora
Limatambo
Anta
Cusco (3400m)
Tipón
Nevado Ampay (5235m)
SANTUARIO NATIONAL DE AMPAY
Piedra de Saywite
Curhuasi
Abancay
Oropesa
Ccatca
Mahuayani
Pikillacta
Ocongate
Tinqui
Andahuaylillas
Urcos
Nevado Ausangate (6384m)
Quiquijana
Acomayo
Accha
Sangarara
Antonio Palma
Pomacanchi
Acopia
Templo de Raqchi
Santa Bárbara
Tinta
Yanaoca
Puente del Inca "Q' eswachaca"
Sicuani (3551m)
N
0 20 kilometres
Inca Trail
Choquequirau Trail
Salcantay Trail
Ausangate Trail
4

Sparkling new hostel decked out in the chain's characteristic bright colours, and with all the essential amenities: activity desk, laundry, shared kitchen, board games, TV room and great staff. Superior dorm beds enjoy reading lights and power points. Dorms S/45, doubles S/150

Super Tramp Hostel Chaska Tika, at Plaza de la Cultura 084 435 830, supertramphostel.com; map p.261. Brightly painted murals cover a range of dorms, for eight to twelve. Doubles, all with shared bath, are small but comfortable. The great little rooftop terrace has recycled furniture, a communal kitchen, a lounge area with cable TV, book exchange, and an onsite burger restaurant. Dorms S/30, doubles S/85

AROUND MACHU PICCHU PUEBLO

Belmond Sanctuary Lodge Right by the ruins of Machu Picchu 084 211 038, belmond.com; map p.252. This exclusive lodge is the only accommodation adjacent to the ruins, allowing easy access to the citadel at sunrise. Set amid lush gardens, most rooms have mountain views and some feature private terraces. Other indulgences include a jacuzzi nestled among greenery from where there are views of the citadel, and a massage meditation temple that overlooks cloud forest. Activities on offer include birdwatching and orchid walks. Full board. S/3385

EATING

There are scores of restaurants in Machu Picchu Pueblo; don't be surprised to be harassed by waiters trying to entice you in as you walk down the street. Most establishments offer pretty average fare; the restaurants outlined below are particularly worth seeking out.

★ **La Boulangerie de Paris** Jr Sinchi Rica 084 797 798, laboulangeriedeparis.net; map p.261. This French-run bakery is the best spot in town to grab a freshly baked croissant or a pain au chocolat. As well as all manner of sweet delights there are plenty of savoury snacks too, including quiche (S/10.50) – it's a great place to stock up on goodies for a picnic. Daily 5am–9pm.

★ **Café Inkaterra** Km 110 by the rail line on the southeastern edge of the settlement 084 211 122, inkaterra.com; map p.261. Tucked away behind the train station, this atmospheric café and restaurant overlooking the murmuring Río Vilcanota serves excellent international and Peruvian dishes in a welcoming thatched-roof building. Mains from S/25. Daily 11am–9pm.

Chullpi Av Imperio de los Incas 140 084 211 350, chullpirestaurant.com; map p.261. Serving Peruvian and *novoandina* (see page 225) dishes, this smartish establishment serves creatively presented dishes. There are plenty of meat and fish options including alpaca medallions grilled in port sauce and fresh trout fillet served with mash. The S/65 menu consisting of three courses will ensure you leave with a full belly. Daily 11am–10pm.

Incontri del Pueblo Viejo Av Pachacutec s/n 084 211 072; map p.261. This Italian- and Peruvian-owned place serves traditional Italian dishes such as home-made tagliatelle (S/33) and gnocchi *al ragú* (S/30). The handmade pastas are kneaded right in front of customers' eyes, and the pizza dough is left to leaven for 24hr, resulting in delicious thin-crust pizzas (S/25) that are cooked in a wood-fire oven. There are great organic beers from Peru and beyond, too. Daily noon–10pm.

★ **Indio Feliz** Lloque Yupanqui 103 084 211 090, indiofeliz.com; map p.261. Despite the outmoded name, this French-owned restaurant bursts with character; the walls are plastered with business cards and the premises jam-packed with curios. Customers enjoy the excellent French–Peruvian cuisine in a series of rooms with pretty hand-painted furniture. The excellent three-course set menu is S/65. Daily noon–10pm.

Palate Bistro Chaska Tika, at Plaza de la Cultura 084 435 830; map p.261. This cosy burger joint adjacent to *Super Tramp Hostel* serves excellent burgers with fries (S/20); there are veggie burgers too, as well as pizzas (S/20). They also prepare Machu Picchu lunch boxes for S/30. Tues–Sun noon–10pm.

Toto's House Av Imperio de los Incas 084 211 020; map p.261. A vast but warm and welcoming restaurant with great views of the river and a crackling open fire to grill meats; they offer an expensive but quite good buffet lunch every day (noon–4pm; S/60). Daily noon–10pm.

★ **The Tree House** Jr Huanacaure 105 084 435 849, thetreehouse-peru.com; map p.261. The menu at one of the town's best restaurants is scribbled on blackboards while large jars of fermented piscos line the bar shelf. The cuisine is *novoandina* with a touch of international, with dishes such as quinoa, tabbouleh, and falafel (S/32) and *tournedos de alpaca* (grilled alpaca wrapped in bacon) in Andean chimichurri dressing (S/52). Or try the raw food menu with sushi (S/35) and fruit rolls (S/35). You can also order a lunch box for Machu Picchu outings, with free delivery to any hotel in town (S/37). Daily 4.30–10pm.

Alternative treks to the Inca Trail

A number of **alternative trekking routes** have been developed by Cusco-based adventure tour operators (see page 221) in response to the desperate over-demand for the Inca Trail. The most popular of these is **Choquequirao**, and like the Inca Trail, this trek ends at a fabulous ancient citadel, though the actual hiking is much harder. Hikes around the sacred glaciated mountain of **Salcantay** are also well developed and, to some extent, overlap with and link to the Inca Trail itself. Much less walked, but equally breathtaking, is **Ausangate**, another sacred snow-covered peak (with a convenient looping trail) that on a clear day can be seen from Cusco dominating the southern horizon. A shorter, popular trek is the route from Ollantaytambo to **Lares** (see page 268). As for **cost**, these treks are similar in price to the Inca Trail, starting from a minimum of about US$100–120 a day.

Choquequirao

An increasingly popular though more challenging alternative to the Inca Trail, the hike to **Choquequirao** can be made with a trekking tour of **four to five days;** these tours tend to leave Cusco on demand and pretty much daily during tourist season. Not quite as spectacular as Machu Picchu, this is still an impressive Inca citadel – whose name in Quechua means "Cradle of Gold" – in part due to its awe-inspiring and isolated setting. Sitting among fine terraces under the glaciated peaks of the Salcantay range, less than half the original remains have been uncovered from centuries of vegetation, making a visit here similar to what Hiram Bingham may have experienced at Machu Picchu when he stumbled on the site back in 1911 (see page 255). This will inevitably change if the long-planned cable car project ever gets off the ground, which aims to transport an alarming 150,000 visitors to the site annually along an ambitious 5km route.

Brief history

Located 1750m above the Río Apurímac and 3104m above sea level in the district of Vilcabamba, Choquequirao is thought to have been a **rural retreat** for the Inca emperor as well as a **ceremonial centre**. It was built in the late fifteenth century – on earlier Huari constructions – and almost certainly had an important political, military and economic role, controlling people and produce between the rainforest communities of the Ashaninka (see page 517), who still live further down the Río Apurímac, and the Andean towns and villages of the Incas. It's easy to imagine coca, macaw feathers, manioc, salt and other Ashaninka products making their way to Cusco via Choquequirao.

Hiram Bingham came to Choquequirao in 1910 on his search for lost Inca cities. Regardless of the exquisite stonework of the ceremonial complex and the megalithic agricultural terracing, Bingham – as have many archeologists since – failed to see just how important a citadel Choquequirao actually was. Evidence from digs here suggest that a large population continuously inhabited Choquequirao and nearby settlements, even after the Spanish Conquest.

The trek to Choquequirao

The most **direct route** up is along the Abancay road from Cusco – about four hours – to Cachora in Apurímac, over 100km from Cusco and some 93km north of Abancay; from here it's a further 30km (15–20 hours) of extremely tough but stunningly beautiful trekking to the remains of the Choquequirao citadel. It's possible to hire mules and muleteers in Cachora. A longer and even more **scenic route** involves taking a twelve-day hike from Huancacalle and Pukyura and then over the Pumasillo range, through Yanama, Minas Victoria, Choquequirao and across the Apurímac ending in Cachora.

Taking the direct route, the first two hours are spent hiking to Capuliyoc, the actual trailhead, where, at 2915m, there are fantastic panoramas over the Valle del Apurímac. Preferably find a tour operator (or taxi in Cachora if you're hiking independently) that will take you here, to save having to hike 13km of not especially interesting terrain. The trail descends almost 1500m from here to Playa Rosalina on the banks of the Río Apurímac, where it's possible to camp the first night. The second day has the most gruelling uphill walking – about five hours as far as Raqaypata and a further two or three to Choquequirao itself.

The site

27km due north of Abancay • Daily 7am–4pm • S/55

Consisting of nine main sectors, the **site** was a political and religious centre, well served by a complex system of aqueducts, canals and springs. Most of the buildings are set around the main ceremonial courtyard or plaza and are surrounded by well-preserved and stylish Inca agricultural terracing.

The return journey

You can go in and come out the same way, or as an alternative, leave Choquequirao via a different, more or less circular, route following the path straight down from the ruins to the river bridge at San Ignacio. The small town of **Huanipaca**, with colectivos for Abancay, is a further two to three hours' steep uphill walk from here. Alternatively, Choquequirao can be approached this way (it's a faster route than via Cachora) and, in a reverse circular route, you can then exit via Cachora.

Salcantay

Irregular colectivos to Salcantay leave from Cusco's C Arcopata (2hr 30min–3hr) with mostly morning departures; you can take a ride in a truck from Mollepata as far as Soraypampa (thereby cutting out the first few hours of the usual trek), for around S/20.

NEVADO SALCANTAY (6271m) is one of the Cusco region's main *apus*, or gods. Its splendid snowcapped peak dominates the landscape to the northwest of Cusco and it makes for relatively peaceful trekking territory. The main route joins the Machu Picchu train line and the Valle de Urubamba with the lesser-visited village of Mollepata in the Río Apurímac watershed. The trek usually takes from **five to seven days** and offers greater contact with local people, a wider range of ecological niches to pass through and higher paths than the Inca Trail: a good, though challenging, option for more adventurous and experienced trekkers who have already acclimatized.

The trail

Most people start on the Urubamba side of Machu Picchu at Km 82, where the Inca Trail also starts (see page 251). From here you can follow the **Inca Trail path** up the Valle de Cusichaca, continuing straight uphill from the hamlet of Huayllabamba, ignoring the main Inca Trail that turns west and right here, up towards Abra de Huarmihuañusca – Dead Woman's Pass. Throughout the trail, the landscape and scenery are very similar to the Inca Trail, though this route brings you much closer to the edge of the glaciers. The trail is steep and hard, up to the high pass at 5000m, which takes you around the southern edge of **Salcantay glacier**, before descending directly south to the village of **Mollepata**.

The trek is increasingly approached **in reverse**, with guides and mules hired at Mollepata, where there is less competition for them than there is on the Huayllabamba side; this route means you finish up in the Valle de Urubamba, between Machu Picchu and Ollantaytambo. There are no official **camping** sites en route, but plenty of good tent sites and several traditional stopping-off spots.

Lares

There are several options for trekking in the **Valle de Lares**, lasting two to five days, and all offer splendid views of snow-capped peaks and green valleys. The hikes allow you to experience village life in the Andes, though it's increasingly a more tourist-oriented version. You'll pass through communities where you can stay with local families and purchase traditional crafts. The **hot springs** in Lares make for a relaxing end to any trek in the area. Some tour operators sell a three-day Lares trek with a day-trip to Machu Picchu on the fourth day, but do not be misled; in most cases you will still need to travel for two to five hours by bus and/or train before arriving at Machu Picchu Pueblo from the end point of your trail.

Ausangate

The start point of the trail (S/10), Tinqui, is reached by bus from Cusco via Urcos; departures are from the Paradero Livitaca in Cusco, close to the Coliseo Cerrado (infrequent; 3–4hr).

An important mountain god for the Incas, **AUSANGATE** is still revered daily by locals. One of the most challenging and exciting treks in southern Peru, this **five-day trail** is also relatively quiet: you'll see very few people, apart from the occasional animal herder, once you leave the start and end point for the trek at the village of **Tinqui** at 3800m.

The **Ausangate Circuit** explores the Cordillera Vilcanota, weaving around many peaks over 6000m. Ausangate, the highest peak at 6384m, remains at the hub of the standard trail. Many of the camps are over 4600m and there are two passes over 5000m to be tackled. A good **map** is essential – the best is the *PERU Topographic Survey 1:100,000–28-T*, available from the Instituto Geográfico Nacional in Lima (ign.gob.pe) or the CBS bookstore in Cusco (see page 228) – and a local **guide** strongly recommended. The management at Tinqui's *Hostal Ausangate* (974 327 538) can arrange guides, mules and a muleteer (*arriero*). Some **supplies** are now available at the trailhead, but it's still safer to bring everything you need with you from Cusco.

4

The trail

The **first day**'s uphill walking from Tinqui brings you to a natural campsite on a valley floor almost 4500m above sea level close to the hot springs near Upis with tremendous views of Nevado Ausangate. **Day two** requires about six hours of walking, following the valley up and over the high pass of Arapa (4800m) into the next valley. Head for the camping area at the red-coloured lake of Jatun Pucacocha; from here you can see and hear Nevado Ausangate's western ice-falls against a backdrop of alpaca herds.

Day three tackles the highest of all the passes – Palomani (5170m) – early on. From here there are views over Ausangatecocha, and the trail undulates, passing the Ausangate base camp en route. From Palomani it is three or four hours' walk to the next campsite, offering some of the best views towards the glaciated peak itself.

Day four continues downhill towards the Valle de Pitumarca, which you follow left uphill to a campsite beyond Jampa, a remote settlement way off the grid, but just this side of the magical Campa Pass (5050m), where centuries' worth of stone cairns left by locals and travellers adorn the landscape honouring the mountain god. From here enjoy the spectacular views towards the snowcapped peaks of Puka Punta and Tres Picos.

Day five takes you uphill again through the pass and down beside Lake Minaparayoc. From here it's a three- or four-hour descent to the campsite at Pacchanta where there are some welcoming **hot springs**, traditionally enjoyed by trekkers as they near the end of this trail. Beyond Pacchanta, it's another three-hour walk back to Tinqui for road transport to Cusco.

Some tour operators in Cusco now include an optional diversion on this circuit to take in **Vinicunca** (aka Rainbow Mountain), whose fabulous multi-coloured striations have only recently been revealed to the world thanks to melting glaciers. Unfortunately, this has also prompted a profusion of heavily marketed day-trips to the peak from

Cusco, for which many clients are ill prepared – given that the mountain is over 5200m high – which in turn are putting huge environmental pressures on the area.

The Inka Jungle Trail

The **Inka Jungle Trail** takes three to four days, starting with a bus journey from Cusco – which you can join in Urubamba or Ollantaytambo – and involves a mixture of hiking and mountain biking; it's ideal for people who want activity but without spending too much money (rates from around US$300) and would rather avoid the train fare to Machu Picchu. It takes the "back route" to Machu Picchu, through some breathtaking scenery via the untouristy small settlements of Santa María and Santa Teresa. The name is a misnomer, as the trail runs through cloud forest rather than jungle, but is clearly aimed at marketing the thrills of the various optional side-activities available en route, such as ziplining and/or rafting. Accommodation can involve a combination of homestays, camping and cheap local hostels, depending on the tour operator.

The first day of the tour you'll go by private bus to Abra Málaga (4300m), the high mountain pass beyond Ollantaytambo, before going on an exhilarating four-hour (60km) downhill **bike ride** to Santa María. This can be cancelled in the rainy season if conditions are dangerous; even in the dry months, make sure your company provides helmets, breakdown support, high-visibility vests and so on. Day two usually involves a **long hike** through sub-tropical forest – or sometimes rafting – to Santa Teresa, via a dip in the superb **hot springs** of Cocalmayo (daily 5am–11pm; S/10), 4km outside Santa Teresa. The third day often entails an **adventure activity** at Cola de Mono (@colodemonoperu.com), usually a two- to three-hour zipline adventure (make sure you get a full safety briefing before setting off and that harnesses are checked, and that platforms between ziplines are not overcrowded – there was a fatality here in 2015). Day three involves **hiking** to Machu Picchu Pueblo via the hidroeléctrica and along the railway line (see page 262) while the final day takes you to the ruins themselves.

Independent travellers should note that Cola de Mono also offers great camping (in your own or a rented tent) and treehouse accommodation, while Santa Teresa also has some basic inexpensive lodgings and restaurants.

Towards the Amazon Basin

The two major places to visit **northeast of Cusco** are **Paucartambo**, 108km from Cusco, and **Tres Cruces**, another 60km beyond Paucartambo. The road between the two follows the **Valle de Kosñipata** (Valley of Smoke), then continues through cloudy tropical mountain scenery to the mission of Shintuya on the edge of the

NEW RE-DISCOVERIES

Major Inca sites are still being uncovered in this jungle region. In April 2002 British explorer **Hugh Thomson** – author of *The White Rock* (see page 521) – and American archeologist **Gary Ziegler**, following rumours of a **lost city**, led an expedition, which came across an Inca city in the virtually inaccessible valley bottom at the confluence of the ríos Yanama and Blanco in the Vilcabamba region. Apparently seen briefly by **Hiram Bingham** nearly a hundred years ago, its coordinates were never recorded and this settlement of forty main buildings set around a central plaza had not been brought to the attention of archeologists since. Although very difficult to access – due to river erosion – there appears to have been an Inca road running through the valley, probably connecting this site to the great Inca citadel of **Choquequirao** (see page 266). This settlement is believed to have been Manco Inca's hideout during his rebellion against the Conquistadors, which lasted until his execution in Cusco in 1572 (see page 207).

4

Reserva Biósfera del Manu (see page 447). Legend has it that the Kosñipata enchants anyone who drinks from its waters at Paucartambo, drawing them to return again and again.

The area along the Río Urubamba from Machu Picchu onwards, to the **north**, is a quiet, relatively accessible corner of the Peruvian wilderness. As you descend from lofty Abra Málaga, high above Ollantaytambo, the vegetation along the valley turns gradually into **forest**, thickening and getting greener and lusher by the kilometre, as the air gets steadily warmer and more humid. Most people heading down here get as far as the town of **Quillabamba**, but the road continues deeper into the rainforest where it meets a navigable river at **Ivochote** (see page 453). It's relatively easy to visit the hilltop ruins of the palace at **Vitcos**, a site of Inca blood sacrifices, and possible – though an expedition of six days or more – to explore the more remote ruins at **Espíritu Pampa**, now thought to be the site of the legendary lost city of Vilcabamba.

Paucartambo

Eternally spring-like because of the combination of altitude and proximity to tropical forest, the small town of **PAUCARTAMBO** (Village of the Flowers) is located some 130km from Cusco in a wild and remote Andean region, and guards a major entrance to the **rainforest of Manu**. A silver-mining colony, run by slave labour during the seventeenth and eighteenth centuries, it's now a popular destination that is at its best in the dry season between May and September, particularly in mid-July when the annual **Fiesta de la Virgen del Carmen** takes place (see below); visitors arrive in their thousands and the village is transformed from a peaceful habitation into a huge mass of frenzied, costumed dancers. Even if you don't make it to Paucartambo for the festival, you can still see the ruined *chullpa* burial towers at **Machu Cruz**, an hour's walk from Paucartambo; ask in the village for directions. Travellers rarely make it here outside festival time, unless en route to the rainforest by road.

FIESTA DE LA VIRGEN DEL CARMEN

Paucartambo spends the first six months of every year gearing up for the **Fiesta de la Virgen del Carmen**. It's an essentially female festival: tradition has it that a wealthy young woman, who had been on her way to Paucartambo to trade a silver dish, found a beautiful (if bodyless) head that spoke to her once she'd placed it on the dish. Arriving in the town, people gathered around her and witnessed rays of light shining from the head, and henceforth it was honoured with prayer, incense and a wooden body for it to sit on.

The energetic, hypnotic **festival** lasts three or four days – usually July 16–19, but check with the tourist office in Cusco (see page 221) – and features throngs of locals in distinctive **traditional costumes**, with **market stalls** and a small **fair** springing up near the church. Clamouring down the streets are throngs of intricately costumed and masked **dancers and musicians**, the best known of whom are the black-masked **Capaq Negro**, recalling the African slaves who once worked the nearby silver mines. Note the grotesque blue-eyed masks and outlandish costumes acting out a parody of the white man's powers – **malaria**, a post-Conquest problem, tends to be a central theme – in which an old man suffers terrible agonies until a Western medic appears on the scene, with the inevitable hypodermic in his hand. If he manages to save the old man (a rare occurrence) it's usually due to a dramatic muddling of prescriptions by his dancing assistants – and thus does Andean fate triumph over science.

On Saturday afternoon there's a **procession of the Virgen del Carmen** itself, with a brass band playing mournful melodies as petals and emotion are showered on the icon of the Virgin – which symbolizes worship of Pachamama as much as devotion to Christianity. The whole event culminates on Sunday afternoon with the **dances of the guerreros** (warriors), during which good triumphs over evil for another year.

Plaza Principal

The beautiful main **plaza**, with its white buildings and traditional blue balconies, holds concrete **monuments** depicting the characters who perform at the fiesta – demon-masked dancers, malaria victims, lawyers, tourists and just about anything that grabs the imagination of the local communities. Also on the plaza is the rather austere **church**, restored in 1998 and full of large Cusqueña paintings. It's also the residence of the sacred image of the **Virgen del Carmen**, unusual in its indigenous (rather than European) appearance. When the Fiesta de la Virgen del Carmen is on, hotels in town are always fully booked and their prices hiked, but it's possible to rent out spaces in local residents' homes or find a site to **camp**. It is always best to take a tent, in case all rooms are full. Tour operators in Cusco (see page 221) can book a hotel for you although note that you'll need to do so several months in advance.

ARRIVAL AND INFORMATION — PAUCARTAMBO

By bus/colectivo Coletivos and Transportes Gallito de las Rocas (☎ 084 226 895) buses leave from the Terminal San Jerónimo (☎ 084 272 459), a S/10-15 taxi ride from the centre of Cusco. There are frequent minivan and infrequent bus departures to Paucartambo (daily 8am, 9am & 3pm; 3–4hr) and onwards to Pilcopata (see page 449), the first major settlement (4–5hr on from Paucartambo) as you go down into the jungle. Buses generally stop off in Paucartambo's marketplace.

Tourist information During festival times, a tourist information point can usually be found near the stone bridge which leads over the river into the main part of town, en route to the plaza.

Tres Cruces

The natural special effects during sunrise at **TRES CRUCES** are in their own way as magnificent a spectacle as the Fiesta de la Virgen del Carmen (see page 270). At 3739m above sea level, on the last mountain ridge before the eastern edge of the Amazon forest, the **view** is a marvel at any time – provided it isn't raining or foggy: by day a vast panorama over the start of a massive cloud forest with all its weird and wonderful vegetation; by night an enormous star-studded jewel. Seen from the highest edge of the **Reserva Biósfera del Manu**, the **sunrise** is spectacular, particularly around the southern hemisphere's winter solstice in June: multicoloured, with multiple suns, it's an incredible light show that can last for hours. There is no **accommodation** at Tres Cruces; **camping** is one option – so take a warm sleeping bag, a tent and enough food; alternatively, at Paucartambo and solstice festival times, when the place can fill up with hundreds of people, colectivos run from Paucartambo to arrive before dawn.

ARRIVAL AND DEPARTURE — TRES CRUCES

By bus Transport to Tres Cruces (S/10 entry) can be a problem, except close to the winter solstice and the Paucartambo fiesta in July. Although there are daily departures from Cusco to Paucartambo (see page 270), from here colectivos to Tres Cruces (1hr 30min–2hr) are irregular; enquire at one of the Paucartambo's hospedajes.

By tour Cusco tour operators (see page 221) can organize a trip.

Vitcos and Espíritu Pampa

Lying at the edge of the jungle, the archeological site of Vitcos is where ruler-in-exile Manco Inca settled after fleeing Cusco and Ollantaytambo; he was subsequently murdered here in 1544 by Spanish Conquistadors. Nearby is Espíritu Pampa (formerly Vilcabamba), the last refuge of the Inca Empire that fell to the Spanish in 1572. The easiest way to see the **Vitcos and Espíritu Pampa ruins** is on a guided tour with an adventure tour company (see page 221). If you'd rather travel more independently, it is possible to travel to Vilcabamba, the jump-off point to the ruins, by bus, although expedition-type preparation is required: you should hire a local **guide** (best done through Cusco tour operators) and possibly even mules. There are no services or facilities as such at either location, and neither is staffed by permanent on-site wardens, but the trail is relatively clear and the trekking not as demanding as on some of the Andean routes; plus, the scenery is stunning, and varied – since you dip into subtropical forest. Although the INC has only recently begun to clear some of the site, the absence of impressive ruins is outweighed by the feeling of getting well off the beaten track.

Vitcos

In 1911, after stumbling over Machu Picchu, **Hiram Bingham** set off down the Valle de Urubamba to Chaullay, then up the Valle de Vilcabamba to Pukyura, where he expected to find more Inca ruins. What he found – **VITCOS** (known locally as Rosapata) – was a relatively small but clearly palatial ruin, based around a trapezoidal plaza spread across a flat-topped spur. Down below the ruins, Bingham was shown by local guides a spring flowing from beneath a vast, **white granite boulder** intricately carved in typical Inca style and surrounded by the remains of an impressive Inca temple. This fifteen-metre-long and eight-metre-high sacred white rock – called Chuquipalta by the Incas – was a great oracle where **blood sacrifices** and other religious rituals took place. According to early historical chronicles, these rituals had so infuriated two Spanish priests who witnessed them that they exorcized the rock and set its temple sanctuary on fire.

Espíritu Pampa

4

The lost city of **Espíritu Pampa** was the last refuge of the Incas, and was brought to international attention in Hiram Bingham's book *The Lost City of the Incas*. After briefly exploring some of the outer ruins at Espíritu Pampa, Bingham erroneously deduced that they were post-Conquest Inca constructions built by Manco Inca's followers since many of the roofs were Spanish-tiled. Believing that he had already found the lost city of **Vilcabamba** at Machu Picchu, Bingham paid little attention to these sites.

Given the inaccessibility of the ruins, Espíritu Pampa remained covered in thick jungle vegetation until 1964, when serious exploration was undertaken by US archeological explorer **Gene Savoy**. He found a massive ruined complex with over sixty main buildings and some three hundred houses, along with temples, plazas, wells and a main street. Clearly this was the largest Inca refuge in the Vilcabamba area, and Savoy rapidly became convinced of its identity as the true site of the last Inca stronghold. More conclusive evidence was subsequently provided by the English geographer and historian John Hemming who, using the historical chronicles, was able to match descriptions of Vilcabamba, its climate and altitude, precisely with those of Espíritu Pampa.

It is only in recent years that excavations have begun in earnest at the site, with the most exciting discovery to date being the treasure-laden tomb of a major Huari dignitary – now referred to as the "Señor de Wari"; not only was the burial chamber a trove of beautifully crafted objects, including a stunning silver death mask, breastplate and necklaces inlaid with semi-precious stones, but it provided evidence to suggest that in constructing Espíritu Pampa Huari, the Incas were building upon a site that had already been developed by the Huari some extent. High-quality replicas of the finds are on display at the Huari site of Pikillacta (see page 275).

ARRIVAL AND DEPARTURE — VITCOS AND ESPÍRITU PAMPA

By colectivo Catch a colectivo or a Turismo Ampay bus (10 daily; 6–8 hr) from Cusco to Quillabamba. From here hop on another colectivo to Espíritu Pampa (2–3hr). From Espíritu Pampa it's just 5km to Vitcos.

By tour Tours are best arranged through one of the companies in Cusco (see page 221).

SCENIC ROUTES TO PUNO AND LIMA

Even if you aren't planning to spend time around Lago Titicaca, the rail journey south to **Puno** (see page 188) is worth taking, though it's far more expensive than the bus. The journey starts in the Cusco region and takes around twelve hours, covering a soul-stirring route that climbs slowly through stunning green river valleys to a desolate landscape to the pass, beyond the town of Sicuani. From here it rolls down onto the altiplano, a flat high plain studded with adobe houses and large herds of llama and alpaca, before reaching Lago Titicaca and its port city of Puno.

If **Lima** is your destination, consider the twenty-hour direct highland road route northwest from Cusco through Abancay and then down to the coast at Nazca. Known as the Nazca-Cusco Corridor, it offers access to a range of potential stopovers on the way: the archeological sites of Choquequirao and Sahuite; the city of Abancay and protected mountain forest area of Ampay; the thermal baths at Chaullanca and the alpaca and vicuña centre at Puquio; and, of course, the mysterious archeological sites around Nazca itself.

South from Cusco

The first 150km of the road (and rail) south from Cusco towards Lago Titicaca (see page 186) passes through the beautiful valleys of Huatanay and Vilcanota, from where the legendary founders of the Inca Empire are said to have emerged. A region outstanding for its natural beauty and rich in magnificent archeological sites, it's easily accessible from Cusco and offers endless possibilities for exploration or random wandering. The whole area is ideal for **camping and trekking**, and in any case, only the rustic towns of **Urcos** and **Sicuani** are large enough to provide reasonable accommodation.

About 20km east of Vilcanota the superb Inca remains of **Tipón** sit high above the road, little visited but extensive and evocative. Closer to the road, the Huari city of **Pikillacta** is easier to find and worthy of an hour or two. Beyond Urcos but before Sicuani, a rather dull transport hub of a town, the great **Temple of Raqchi** still stands unusually high as a monument to Inca architectural abilities.

ARRIVAL AND GETTING AROUND — SOUTH FROM CUSCO

By bus As the trains are slow, infrequent, expensive and don't stop at all towns, most people travel on one of the frequent, and cheaper, buses or minibuses. Many of the bus options are inter-regional carriers (see page 220). The best option is offered by Inka Express, Urb. El Óvalo, Av La Paz C-23 (T 084 247 887, W inkaexpress.com), which has quality buses linking Cusco with Puno, but also offers opportunities to stop off at some of the tourist sites below, including Tipón and Raqchi, en route, with a bilingual tour guide.

San Sebastián

Around 5km south of Cusco by road, you pass through the suburb – and former independent pueblo – of **SAN SEBASTIÁN**. It has an impressive **church**, ornamented with Baroque stonework, six Neoclassical columns and two squat belfries. It was apparently built on the site of a chapel erected by the Pizarros in memory of their victory over Diego de Almagro. These days the Fiesta de San Sebastián is celebrated with processions and prayers throughout the month of January, providing a colourful spectacle.

Oropesa

Around 30km south of Cusco lies picturesque **OROPESA**, traditionally a town of bakers. Its adobe **church** boasts a uniquely attractive three-tiered belfry with cacti growing out of it, and is notable for its intricately carved pulpit and the beautiful, Cusqueña-esque interior murals - probably painted between between 1580 and 1630. In early Inca days Oropesa was home to a well-known rebel clan, the Pinaguas, who had to be subdued by Pachacutec before he could safely build his country residence at Tipón.

Tipón ruins

3.5km by road, north of Tipón • Daily 7am–6pm • Entry by Boleto Turístico (see page 220) • Colectivos leave from Cusco's Pampa de Castilla (1hr 30min), dropping you off at the main square in Tipón; from here it's a 40min walk up to the ruins.

Both in setting and architectural design, the **Tipón ruins** are one of the most impressive Inca sites.

The lower ruins

Well hidden in a natural shelf high above the Valle de Huatanay, the **lower sector** of the ruins is a stunning sight: a series of neat agricultural terraces, watered by stone-lined channels, all astonishingly preserved and many still in use. The impressive stone terracing reeks of the Incas' domination over an obviously massive and subservient labour pool; yet at the same time it's clearly little more than an elaborate attempt to increase crop yield. At the back of the lower ruins, water flows from a stone-faced "mouth" around a **spring** – probably an aqueduct subterraneously diverted from above. The entire complex is designed around this spring, reached by a path from the last terrace.

The reservoir and temple block

Another sector of the ruins contains a **reservoir** and **temple block** centred on a large volcanic rock – presumably some kind of *huaca*. Although the stonework in the temple seems cruder than that of the agricultural terracing, its location is still beneficial. In contrast of the temple, the construction of the reservoir is sophisticated, as it was originally built to hold nine hundred cubic metres of water which gradually dispersed along stone channels to the Inca "farm" directly below.

The upper ruins

Coming off the back of the reservoir, a large, tapering stone **aqueduct** crosses a small gully before continuing uphill – about thirty minutes' walk – to a vast zone of **unexcavated terraces** and dwellings. Beyond these, over the lip of the hill, you come to another level of the upper valley literally covered in Inca terracing, dwellings and large stone storehouses. Equivalent in size to the lower ruins, these are still used by locals who have built their own houses among the ruins. So impressive is the terracing at Tipón that some archeologists believe it was an Inca **experimental agricultural centre,** much like Moray (see page 243), as well as a citadel.

Pikillacta

Daily 7am–6pm • Entry by Boleto Turístico (see page 220) • Beside the main road (ask the bus driver to drop you off)

About 7km south of Oropesa, the pre-Inca ruins of **Pikillacta**, alongside those of Rumicolca, can be seen alongside the road. After passing the Paucartambo turn-off, near the ruins of an ancient storehouse and the small red-roofed pueblo of **Huacarpay,** the road climbs to a ledge overlooking a wide alluvial plain and **Laguna Lucre** (now a weekend resort for Cusco's workers). At this point the road traces the margin of a stone wall defending the pre-Inca settlement of Pikillacta.

Spread over an area of at least fifty hectares, Pikillacta, or "The Place of the Flea", was built by people of the Huari culture around 800 AD, before the rise of the Incas. Its unique, geometrically designed **terraces** surround a group of bulky two-storey constructions: apparently these were entered by ladders reaching up to doorways set well off the ground in the first storey – very unusual in ancient Peru. Many of the walls are built of small cut stones joined with mud mortar, and among the most interesting finds here were several round turquoise **statuettes.** These days the city is in ruins but it seems evident still that much of the site was taken up by barrack-like quarters. When the Incas arrived early in the fifteenth century they modified the site to suit their own purposes, possibly even building the aqueduct that once connected Pikillacta with the ruined gateway of Rumicolca, which straddles a narrow pass by the road, fifteen minutes' walk further south.

While here, make sure you check out the new **exhibition** space, which displays beautifully crafted replicas of the stunning silver death mask and breastplate – among other items – of the "**Señor de Wari**", a major Huari, whose luxurious burial chamber was excavated at the site of Espíritu Pampa in 2010 (see page 272).

Rumicolca

Daily 24hr • Free • Right beside the main road (ask the bus driver to drop you off)

The massive defensive passage of **Rumicolca** was initially constructed by the Huari people and served as a southern entrance to – and frontier of – their empire. Later it became an **Inca checkpoint**, regulating the flow of people and goods into the Cusco Valley: no one was permitted to enter or leave the valley via Rumicolca between sunset and sunrise. The Incas improved on the rather crude Huari stonework of the original **gateway**, using regular blocks of polished andesite from a local quarry. The gateway still stands, rearing up to twelve solid metres above the ground, and is one of the most impressive of all Inca constructions.

Andahuaylillas

Catch a bus from opposite Cusco's Hospital Regional to Urcos or from opposite the Estadio General to Sicuani and ask the driver where to get off (every 30min; 1hr) • Andahuaylillas church 7.30am–5.30pm • S/15; ticket grants access to Huaro church

In the tranquil and well-preserved village of **ANDAHUAYLILLAS**, an adobe-towered church sits above an attractive **plaza**, fronted by colonial houses. Built in the early seventeenth century on the site of an Inca temple, the **Iglesia de San Pedro** has an exterior balcony from which the priests would deliver sermons. While it's fairly small, with only one nave, it possesses some magnificent provincial colonial art. Huge **Cusqueña canvases** decorate the upper walls, while below are some unusual murals, slightly faded over the centuries; the ceiling, painted with Spanish flower designs, contrasts strikingly with the great Baroque altar.

Huaro

45km southeast of Pisac • Catch an Urcos of Sicuani-bound bus (every 30min; 1hr) • Church 8am–noon & 1–5pm • S/15; ticket grants access to Andahuaylillas church

To the south, the road leaves the Río Huatanay and enters the Valle de Vilcanota. **HUARO**, crouched at the foot of a steep bend in the road 3km from Andahuaylillas, has a much smaller **church** whose interior is completely covered with colourful **murals** of religious iconography; the massive gold-leaf altarpiece dominates the space.

Urcos

49km southeast of Pisac • Buses to Urcos leave from Av de la Cultura opposite Cusco's Hospital Regional; alternatively take a Sicuani-bound bus from opposite the Estadio General and ask the driver where to get off (every 30min; 1hr10min)

The uninspiring town of **URCOS** rests on the valley floor, surrounded by weirdly sculpted hills. It shares its name with the nearby **Laguna de Urcos**; according to legend, the Inca Huascar threw his heavy gold chain into these waters after learning that strange bearded aliens – Pizarro and his crew – had arrived in Peru. Between lake and town, a simple **chapel** now stands atop a small hillock, containing several excellent Cusqueña paintings.

The main reason to stop here is to enjoy the town's excellent, traditional **Sunday market**, which takes over the Plaza de Armas.

VIRACOCHA'S HUACA

One of the unusually shaped hills surrounding Urcos is named after the creator-god **Viracocha**, as he is said to have stood on its summit and ordered beings to emerge from the hill, thus creating the town's first inhabitants. In tribute, an ornate **huaca**, with a gold bench, was constructed to house a statue to the god, and it was here that the eighth Inca emperor received a divinatory vision in which Viracocha appeared to him to announce that "great good fortune awaited him and his descendants". In this way, the emperor obtained his imperial name, **Viracocha Inca**, and also supposedly his first inspiration to conquer non-Inca territory, though it was his son, Pachacuti, who carried the empire to its greatest heights.

Templo de Raqchi

22km northwest of Sicuani • Daily 7am–5pm • S/15 • Sicuani-bound buses pass here (every 20min; 3hr)

Between Urcos and Sicuani the road passes through **SAN PEDRO DE CACHA**, the nearest village (4km) to the imposing ruins of the **Templo de Raqchi**, built in honour of Viracocha, the Inca creator-god. The temple was supposedly built to appease the god after he had caused the nearby volcano of Quimsa Chata to spew out fiery boulders in a fit of anger, and even now massive **volcanic boulders** and ancient lava flows scar the landscape as a constant reminder.

With its adobe walls still standing over 12m high on top of polished stone foundations, and the **site** scattered with numerous other buildings and plazas, such as barracks, cylindrical warehouses, a palace, baths and aqueducts, Raqchi was clearly an important **religious centre**. Today the only ritual left is the annual **Festival de Raqchi** (second week of June), a dramatic, untouristy fiesta comprising three to four days of folk music and dance – performed by groups congregating here from as far away as Bolivia to compete on the central stage. The performances are well staged, but the site, in a boggy field, can be mayhem, with hundreds of food stalls, a funfair, Quechua women selling *chicha* maize beer – and their drunken customers staggering through the tightly knit crowds.

Sicuani

115km southeast of Cusco on the road to Puno • Several buses run daily between Sicuani and Cusco (3hr) as well as Puno (4–5hr);

About 20km southeast from Raqchi, **SICUANI** is capital of the province of Canchis and quite a thriving agricultural and market town, not entirely typical of the settlements in the Valle de Vilcanota. Its busy **Sunday market** is renowned for cheap and excellent woollen goods. Although not a particularly exciting place in itself – with too many tin roofs and an austere atmosphere – the people are friendly and it makes an excellent **base for trekking** into the vast Nevada Vilcanota mountain range which separates the Titicaca Basin from the Valle de Cusco.

Continuing south towards Puno and Lago Titicaca (see page 186), the Valle de Vilcanota begins to close in around the line as the tracks cross **Abra La Raya** (4300m), which marks the continental divide between the Pacific and Amazonian basins, before dropping down into the desolate *pampa* that covers much of inland southern Peru.

The Central Sierra

RESERVA PAISAJÍSTICA NOR YAUYOS COCHAS

5

The Central Sierra

Peppered with traditional towns and cities sitting in remote valleys, the green and mountainous Central Sierra region boasts some of Peru's finest archeological sites and colonial buildings. Although significantly fewer travellers make it here compared with hotspots like Cusco and Machu Picchu, anyone with the time to spare will find this region a worthwhile destination in its own right, rather than just somewhere to stop en route to the central selva (see page 454). As well as fantastic mountain scenery, this amalgam of regions in the central Peruvian Andes offer endless walking country, a caving opportunity and a gateway into the country's Amazon rainforest.

The most attractive hub in the Sierra Central is the laidback town of **Tarma**, which has a relatively pleasant climate influenced by the cloud forest to the east, and is a major nodal point for pioneers from the jungle, traders and, to a lesser extent, tourists. To the north, **Huánuco** serves as a good base for exploring some of Peru's most interesting archeological remains, and **Tingo María** is the gateway to the jungle ports of Pucallpa and Tarapoto. To the southwest of Tarma lies the largest city in the northern half of the Central Sierra, **Huancayo**, high up in the Andes. South of Huancayo are the two most traditional of all the Central Sierra's towns: **Ayacucho** – one of the cultural jewels of the Andes, replete with colonial churches and some of Peru's finest artesan crafts – and **Huancavelica**. Immediately north of Huancayo lies the astonishing **Jauja Valley**, which has beautiful scenery, striped by fabulous coloured furls of mountain.

GETTING AROUND — THE CENTRAL SIERRA

Most people will travel this region by bus. Bar unpredictable events like landslides in the rainy season (Dec–March) or miners' union strikes, a car or bus will get over the Andes faster than the train (see page 283). All buses from Lima have to travel by the often-congested Carretera Central, up past some large mines and over the high pass at Ticlio before descending to La Oroya. The train follows the same route. Once up in the Sierra Central, apart from the Lima–Huancayo and Huancayo–Huancavelica railways, the only option for travel is by road. The area is well served by bus and most of the larger towns have colectivo cars or combis connecting them, which have a more informal service and lack fixed departure times.

BY BUS

Cruz del Sur and Móvil Tours run buses between Lima and Huancayo, Ayacucho and Abancay. Other companies connect main centres within the Central Sierra. Turismo Central joins Huancayo with Huánuco, Tingo Maria and Pucallpa. If you're travelling to Cusco from Ayacucho it's quicker to catch a combi via Andahuaylas and Abancay.

BY COLECTIVO

There are colectivo services between most neighbouring major towns and cities in the Central Sierra. In Huancayo they tend to leave from the Terminal Los Andes on Av Ferrocarril; in Lima they start and end at Yerbadero.

BY TRAIN

The world-famous Lima-to-Huancayo railway line ("El Tren de la Sierra") currently runs trains from Lima to Huancayo about once a month (usually Thurs, Fri or Sat, departing at 7am) between March and November; it's a – quite literally – breathtaking 11hr journey.

Information Precise itineraries, up-to-date prices and tickets can be obtained from FCCA (Ferrocarril Central Andino) by phone or online (T 01 226 6363 ext 222, W ferrocarrilcentral.com.pe) or in person at the Lima office (Av José Galvez Barrenechea 566, 5th floor, San Isidro).

Altitude sickness You're more likely to suffer from *soroche* – altitude sickness (see page 207) – if you enter the Central Sierra by train, due to the relatively slow climb through the high Ticlio Pass (over 4800m). To avoid breathlessness and headaches, or the even worse effects of *soroche*, it's advisable to take the first few days over 3000m pretty easy before doing any hiking or other strenuous activities.

Tickets There are two classes of ticket: Touristic (S/1000 return; S/750 one way) and Classic (S/700 return; S/500 one way), although prices are cheaper if travelling one-way from Huancayo rather than from Lima.

CRAFTS IN AYACUCHO

Highlights

❶ **Tarma** An attractive little colonial town, known as La Perla de los Andes, is famous for its fantastic Easter Sunday procession and associated flower "paintings" that carpet the roads. See page 282

❷ **Lima–Huancayo train journey** The last remaining working rail line in the region, this breathtaking high-altitude train journey is one of the finest in the world. See page 283

❸ **San Pedro de Cajas** This scenic and remote village is home to many craftspeople who produce some of Peru's superb modern weavings. See page 284

❹ **Reserva Paisajística Nor Yauyos Cochas** Spectacular cascades, natural dams and blue lagoons in this stunning reserve bursting with flora and fauna. See page 290

❺ **Ayacucho** One of the most traditional and architecturally fascinating cities in the Peruvian Andes – renowned for around forty impressive churches, boisterous religious fiestas and a vibrant tradition of crafts. See page 294

❻ **Tantamayo** The origins of the towering, multi-floored ruins at this vast and remote site remain a puzzle for archeologists, who believe them to date back at least 1200 years. See page 307

HIGHLIGHTS ARE MARKED ON THE MAP ON PAGE 282

5

Tarma and around

Vehicles take four to six hours to cross the high pass at Ticlio from Lima, after which they drop in less than an hour to the unsightly and mining-contaminated town and pit stop of **La Oroya**. Just beyond here the road splits three ways: north to **Cerro de Pasco** and **Huánuco**; south to **Huancayo**, **Huancavelica** and, for the travel-hardened, **Ayacucho**; or, eastwards towards **Tarma**, which is just another hour or two further.

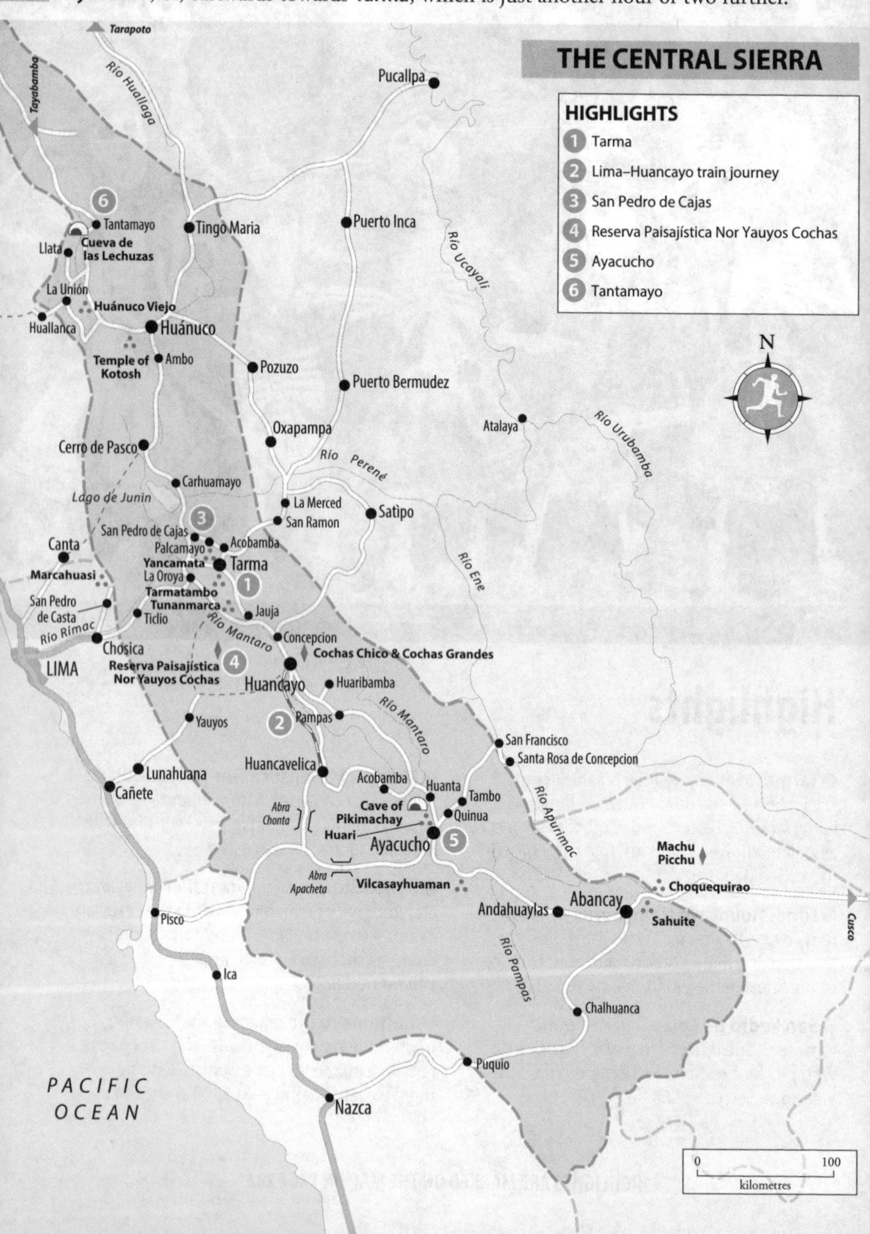

THE ANDES RAIL LINE

The original opening of the Lima-to-Huancayo **rail line** into the Andes in the late nineteenth century had a huge impact on the region and was a major feat of engineering. For President Balta of Peru and many of his contemporaries in 1868, the iron fingers of a rail line, "if attached to the hand of Lima would instantly squeeze out all the wealth of the Andes, and the whistle of the locomotives would awaken the Indian race from its centuries-old lethargy". Consequently, when the American rail entrepreneur **Henry Meiggs** (aptly called the "Yankee Pizarro") arrived on the scene, it was decided that coastal guano deposits would be sold off to finance a new line, one that faced technical problems (ie, the peaks and troughs of the Andes) never previously encountered by engineers. The man really responsible for the success of this massive project was the Polish engineer, Ernest Malinowski. Utilizing timber from Oregon and the labour of thousands of Chinese workers (the basis of Peru's present Chinese communities), Malinowski's skill and determination finished Meiggs's rail line, over a thirty-year period. An extraordinary accomplishment, it nevertheless produced a mountain of debt that bound Peru more closely to the New York and London banking worlds than to its own hinterland and peasant population.

Known locally as "La Perla de los Andes", **TARMA** is by far the nicest mountain town in this part of Peru, with warm temperatures and an abundance of wild and farmed flowers, sitting on the edge of the Andes almost within spitting distance of the Amazon forest. The town makes a good living from its traditional textile and leather industries, and from growing flowers for export. Although connected with the **Juan Santos Atahualpas rebellion** in the 1740s and 1750s, today Tarma is a quiet place, disturbed only by the flow of trucks climbing up from the Amazon Basin loaded with timber, coffee, chocolate or oranges. The town is particularly famous for an Easter Sunday procession, starting from the main plaza; the streets are covered by carpets of dazzling flowers depicting various local, religious or mythic themes.

The scenery **around Tarma** constitutes one of Peru's most beautiful Andean regions, with green rather than snow-capped mountains stretching down from high, craggy limestone outcrops into steep canyons forged by Amazon tributaries powering their way down to the Atlantic. It's nevertheless always a good idea to check with your embassy in Lima for up-to-the-minute intelligence on this area, since the occasional terrorist column has been known to be active in its remoter sectors (see page 498).

Yancamata

6km north of Tarma • Taxi colectivos to the turn off for Tupin (S/1.50) leave from Tarma's Mercado Modelo (every 15min; 10min). From here it's a 5min walk to the main plaza and the trailhead. Alternatively (and most recommended) contact *Casa Hacienda La Florida* or *Hostal IN* for a guide

A tough, 900m (2–3hr) climb along a litany of small trails brings you to the marvellous hilltop pre-Inca ruins of **Yancamata.** A former Xauxa fortress, built at 4080m above sea level, it would have provided excellent surveillance opportunities thanks to its panoramic views south towards modern-day Tarma and northwest across San Pedro de Cajas. The buildings were constructed using dry stone, and many are two- and even three-storeys high. The path is not particularly obvious, so it's best to go with a tour; remember to bring plenty of water.

Acobamba

12km north of Tarma • Church daily 8am–6pm • Free • Taxi colectivo (S/2) from the Mercado Modelo in Tarma (every 15min; 15min); tell the driver you're heading to the church and he will tell you where to get off, as it's 1km after the town centre

Within day-tripping distance from Tarma is the small settlement of **ACOBAMBA**, home of the **Sanctuary of the Lord of Muruhuay**, a small church built in 1972 around a rock painting where a vision of Christ on the cross led to this site becoming a major centre of pilgrimage. Some of the restaurants by the church serve excellent *cuy* and *pachamanca*.

Palcamayo to San Pedro de Cajas

25km north of Tarma, via Acobamba • Taxi colectivos to Palcamayo (S/4) and San Pedro de Cajas (S/8) run here from Av Francisco de Paula Otero (known as "el Ovalo") and Jr Moquegua in Tarma (every 30min; 45min)

The rural village of **PALCAMAYO** makes an interesting day-trip from Tarma, though it's better appreciated if you camp overnight. From here it's an hour's climb to **La Gruta de Huagapo**, the country's deepest explored **caves**; if dry they are generally accessible for about 180m without specialized equipment, or up to 1.8km with a guide and full speleological kit. Colectivos continue 20km along the same road west to the beautiful village of **SAN PEDRO DE CAJAS**, where craftspeople produce superb-quality weavings. An example of how landscapes can influence local art forms, the village lies in a valley neatly divided into patchwork field-systems – an exact model of the local textile style.

Tarmatambo

10km south of Tarma • Taxi colectivos (S/1.50) leave when full for Jauja from Terminal Terrestre Caroline (30min) in Tarma and drop you off on the road outside of Tarmatambo (ask to get dropped off at Tarmatambo). From there, it's a 5min walk to the municipal building and a further 10min walk to the site • Guides cost S/5–10 for lower site and S/20 for upper ruins

Overlooking Inca and more modern terraces that still use a complex system of Inca canals to irrigate their crops, the village of **TARMATAMBO** is worth a visit, particularly if timed to coincide with the lively **Taita Inti** festival, similar in style to Inti Rami in Cusco (see page 217). Held on the 24th of June in the former ceremonial plaza – now the football pitch – festivities see locals dressed as *Chaskis* running along the **Capac Ñan** ("The Great Road" in Quechua), the old Inca highway that still links the village with others in the valley.

Situated on the southwestern edge of the town, the **Complejo Archeológico Tarmatambo** comprises the remains of an administrative Inca centre. Ruins are at the base and the top (a gruelling 1–2hr climb) of Cerro Pirhua, and while buildings have been absorbed into crop land, you can still make out a row of 32 *colcas* or store rooms. It's best to ask at the municipal building in the village for a guide, as most of the site is hard to distinguish from the surrounding farmland.

Tarmatambo is also home to the visually unremarkable **Iglesia Juan Bautista**, thought to be one of the oldest in South America.

ARRIVAL AND DEPARTURE — TARMA AND AROUND

By bus The Terminal Terrestre is on Av Vienrich. Cruz del Sur (064 400 440) leave daily for Lima, while Móvil Tours (989 000 038) have three daily services. Molina Unión (964 616 028) has daily departures for Satipo.

Destinations Lima (several daily; 6hr); Satipo (1 daily, 3am; 4hr).

By colectivo Colectivos serving San Pedro de Cajas stop off at Av Francisco de Paula Otero and Jr Moquegua (every 30min 8am–4pm; 1hr 30min). To get to Huánuco from Tarma, catch a colectivo to Cerro de Pasco (every 30min 5am–3pm; 2hr) from Terminal Terrestre Caroline, Av Vienrich 664 and change to one for Huánuco (every 30min; 3hr). Combis and colectivos leave from this same terminal for Huancayo (every 30min; 3hr) and Jauja (every 30min; 1hr 30min).

INFORMATION AND TOURS

Tourist information Municipal office on the plaza at Jr Arequipa 257 inside the Centro Civico, first floor (Mon–Fri 8am–1pm & 3–6pm; 064 321 010).

Tours Max Aventura at Jr Dos de Mayo 682 (064 323 908, maxaventuraperu.com) organizes a range of full-day tours; the most popular is to the Valle de las Flores (S/45), which takes in a number of sights including San Pedro de Cajas (see above), as well as to the Bosque Geológico de Huayllay (S/65), an imposing array of natural stone pillars.

ACCOMMODATION

TARMA

Hostal El Vuelo del Condor Jr Dos de Mayo 471 064 317 554, hotelelvuelodelcondor.com. This comfortable guesthouse a few steps from the Plaza de Armas is an excellent budget option. The en-suite rooms are warm and welcoming, as are the staff, and there's wi-fi throughout. S/60

Hostel IN Jr Chanchamayo 484 064 408 659, hostelin@bambino.pe. A firm budget choice, rooms are spotless en-suites with fast wi-fi. Bring earplugs, or ask for a room on the top floor: the downstairs gym has late-night classes. The owner offers tours and treks in the vicinity. No breakfast; prices halve out of high-season. S/80

AROUND TARMA

Casa Hacienda La Florida Km 39, Carretera Central 01 518 8429 or 064 341 041, haciendalaflorida.com. Some 6km from Tarma on the Acobamba road towards Chanchamayo, this family-run, eco-friendly hacienda is a working farm; guests can help milk the cows in the early morning, and the farm's own yogurt is served for breakfast. It's also a cultural centre, with art exhibitions and occasional literary readings. Rooms are welcoming and comfortable, decked out with rustic furniture and local artefacts, while there's also accommodation in one-bed adobe houses with balconies and wood-burning stoves. They can arrange home-cooked meals as well as guided tours to all the nearby archeological ruins. Camping S/18, doubles S/232, adobe houses S/300

Hacienda Santa María Sacsamarca, 1.2km from Tarma 01 445 1214 or 064 321 232, haciendasantamaria.com. This beautiful hacienda features comfortable rooms with hand-painted wallpaper, set around a courtyard. The barn has been converted into a welcoming living area decorated with Peruvian rugs, while the Salón de los Recuerdos, or Room of Memories, houses antique furniture and curios, including paintings and old irons. S/240

EATING

Check out the Mercado Modelo (daily 6am–8pm), which has cheap stalls serving local dishes for about S/10. There are many *chifa* restaurants or *pollerías* located within a couple of blocks' radius of the Plaza de Armas.

Coffee and Friends Jr Huancayo 347 064 408 761. A friendly coffee house with the best cakes in town, all made in house; try the *pie de maracuya* (passionfruit pie) – it's divine. There's a wide range of coffee, plus fresh fruit tea infusions (S/8), and delicious empanadas (S/6). Not to be missed in Tarma. Daily 9.30am–2pm & 5–10.30pm.

★ **Daylo** Av Castilla 118 064 323 048. This place proved so popular it had to relocate to larger premises; the extensive menu includes excellent freshwater trout ceviche served with yucca (S/23.50), plus grilled or crispy trout (S/20) and plenty of other beautifully presented local dishes. Daily noon–11pm.

South of Tarma

The bustling city of **Huancayo** is the natural hub of the mountainous and remote region **south of Tarma**. Nearby **Jauja Valley** is significantly more beautiful, less polluted and friendlier. Further afield, **Ayacucho** is a must for anyone interested in colonial architecture, particularly fine churches; while **Huancavelica** offers a slightly darker history lesson – the area has suffered from extreme exploitation both in colonial times, with the mines, as well as in the 1980s and 1990s when terrorism was at a peak. The area is still occasionally visited by remnants of the Shining Path terrorist group (see page 498), but there have been no related problems for tourists in recent years. The trip out here by train (some 130km south of Huancayo), one of the world's highest railway journeys, passes through some stark yet stunning landscapes; the train journey to Huancavelica is a much cheaper but still dazzling trip.

Huancayo

A large commercial city with over 360,000 inhabitants, **HUANCAYO** (3241m) is the capital of the Junín *departamento*. An important market centre thriving on agricultural produce and dealing in vast quantities of wheat, the city makes a good base for exploring the Mantaro Valley and experiencing the region's distinct culture. While the area is rich in pre-Columbian remains, and the cereal and textile potential of the region has long been exploited, the city itself is mostly relatively modern, with very little of architectural or historical interest. It is still a lively enough place with a busy market and even some nightlife at weekends. It's also worth trying to time your trip to coincide with the splendid **Fiesta de las Cruces** each May, when Huancayo erupts in a succession of boisterous processions, parties and festivities.

Brief history

The region around Huancayo was dominated by the Huanca people from around 1200 AD, and the Huari culture before that, though it wasn't until Pachacuti's forces arrived in the fifteenth century that the Inca Empire took control. Occupied by the Spanish from 1537, Huancayo was formally founded in 1572 by Jeronimo de Silva, next to the older and those days relatively small town of Jauja (see page 291). In 1824, the **Battle of Junín** was fought close to Huancayo, when patriotic revolutionaries overcame royalist and Spanish forces. Apart from the comings and goings of the Catholic Church, Huancayo remained little more than a staging point until the rail line arrived in 1909, transforming it slowly but surely during the twentieth century into a city whose economy was based on the export of agrarian foodstuffs and craft goods.

More so than any other Peruvian city – except perhaps Ayacucho – Huancayo was paralysed in the years of **terror during the 1980s and 1990s**. As home to a major army base, it became the heart of operations in what was then a military emergency zone. In 1999, an extensive army operation captured the then leader of **Sendero Luminoso**, Oscar Ramírez Durand, who had taken over from Abimael Guzmán in 1992.

Plaza de la Constitución

Plaza de la Constitución – named in honour of the 1812 Liberal Constitution of Cádiz – is where you'll find monuments in honour of Mariscal Ramón Castilla (who abolished slavery in Huancayo in 1854), surrounded by ornamental plants of local origin, like *quishuar* and *retama*. The square is flanked by the Neoclassical **Catedral de la Ciudad de Huancayo** (daily 7.30–9.30am & 5–7.30pm; free) and some of the town's major public buildings and offices.

Calle Real

Calle Real is the main drag running on the western edge of Plaza de la Constitución; it's here you'll find the **Capilla La Merced** (daily 9am–noon & 3–6.30pm; free), a colonial church, once the site for the preparation and signing of the 1839 Peruvian Constitution.

Plaza Huamanmarca

Plaza Huamanmarca sits at the heart of the city and is the oldest plaza, founded with the town back in 1572. On April 22, 1882, three local heroes – Enrique Rosado Zárate, Vicente Samaniego Vivas and Tomás Gutarra – were shot here by the Chilean army. Today the square is surrounded by public buildings and the Municipality, the latter making it a focal point for protestors.

Museo del Colegio Salesiano

Prolongación Arequipa 10 • Mon–Fri 9am–1pm & 3–6pm, Sat 9am–noon • S/5 • ⓣ 064 247 763

The **Museo del Colegio Salesiano**, in the residential northern district of El Tambo, is an excellent natural history museum with almost a thousand exhibits of local flora and fauna as well as archeological objects, fossils, paintings, sculptures and a selection of interesting rocks and minerals.

Feria Dominical market

Blocks 2–12, Av Huancavelica • Sun 8am–6pm

Established in 1572 to assist the commerce of the local population, the market still sells fruit and vegetables, as well as a good selection of woollen and alpaca clothes and blankets, superb weavings and some silver jewellery. Like most Peruvian city markets, it is the hub of activity early in the morning.

Parque de la Identidad de Huanca

2km northeast of the city centre in Urbanización San Antonio • Taxi S/5–6 each way (more with a wait), or take a colectivo for Cochas (S/1), which should pass within a few streets of the park

A 6000 square metre park, **Parque de la Identidad de Huanca** has plenty of grassy spaces, plus a model of a giant gourd - one of the typical regional artesanía products, a *mirador* (viewing platform), some shady pergolas, cacti and extensive dry-stone walks mimicking the building style of pre-Inca cultures in the region. The entire park was created in honour of the local Huanca (also spelled "Wanka") style of music.

ARRIVAL AND DEPARTURE — HUANCAYO

By bus Most buses from Lima, including Oltursa (ⓣ 064 601 504, ⓦ oltursa.pe), use the Terminal Terrestre, Av Evitamiento Norte s/n, El Tambo, although Oltursa also have a ticket office at Ayacucho 289 (ⓣ 064 212 170). Cruz del Sur has its own terminal at Av Ferrocarril 151 (ⓣ 064 223 367, ⓦ cruzdelsur.com.pe) and another office at Ayacucho 281 (ⓣ 064 235 650), offering buses to Lima. Móvil Tours (Ayacucho 205; ⓣ 064 584 857) sell tickets for Lima, with buses leaving from the Terminal Terrestre Los Andes, next door to the Crus del Sur terminal. Expreso Molina (Jr Angaraes 334; ⓣ 064 224 501) serves Ayacucho and has one daily bus to Huancavelica; for the latter, Ticllas (Av Ferrocarril 1590; ⓣ 987 255 966) has the most frequent departures. Turismo Central (Jr Ayacucho 274; ⓣ 064 589 561), has buses to Lima, Huánuco, Tingo María, Pucallpa and Satipo.

Destinations Ayacucho (5 daily; 7hr); Huancavelica (hourly; 3–4hr); Huánuco (3 daily; 7hr); Lima via Jauja (several daily; 6–7hr); Pucallpa (1 daily; 15hr); Satipo (1 daily; 5–6hr); Tingo María (1 daily; 8–10hr).

By colectivo Most colectivos leave from the Terminal Terrestre Los Andes on Av Ferrocarril.

Destinations Chanchamayo (every 30min; 3hr); Jauja (every 30min; 40min); La Oroya (every 15min; 1hr 30min); Tarma (every 15min; 1hr 30min–2hr); Satipo (hourly; 5hr). Colectivos for Huancavelica leave from the corner of Av Ferrocarrill and Av Huanuco (every 15min; 3hr), although drivers are known to take this route dangerously fast.

By train The station for Lima trains is on Av Ferrocarril 461, within walking distance of the city centre; buy tickets online (ferrocarrilcentral.com.pe). For Huancavelica, head to the Estación de Chilca, Av Leoncio Prado 1750 (064 216 662, Mon–Fri 5.30am–2pm). Tickets can be bought the day prior to travel or from 5.30am on the day. From central Huancayo, a taxi to the Estación de Chilca costs S/6.

Destinations Huancavelica (Mon, Wed & Fri 6.30am; 5hr 30min); Lima (once monthly March–Nov; 11hr).

By plane Flights from Lima to Huancayo (5 daily; 1hr) land at Aeropuerto Francisco Carle in Jauja, 45km northwest of the city, served by LC Perù (Av Ayacucho 322; 064 214 514), Peruvian Airlines (Jr Loreto 883; 01 716 6000) and LATAM (inside Plaza Vea mall, Av Ferrocarril 1057; 01 213 8200). Colectivos to Huancayo (30min; S/7) and Jauja (5min; S/4) meet incoming flights.

GETTING AROUND

By taxi or bike The easiest and safest way of getting around is by taxi (S/5 for most destinations) – or on foot in the very centre; a safe bet is Radio Taxi (064 242 424) or Taxi Line (064 212 121). You can also cycle – Incas del Perú (see below) charges US$10/half day or US$15/full day.

INFORMATION AND TOURS

Tourist information Dircetur, Jr Pachitea 201, inside the station for Lima-bound trains (Mon–Fri 8am–1pm & 2.30–5.30pm; 064 222 575).

Tour operators and guides Pioneers in the region and run by the affable and knowledgeable Lucho, Incas del Perú (José Gálvez 420; 064 223 303, incasdelperu.org) are your one-stop shop for maps and information about the region, mountain treks in the Cordillera Huaytapallana, plus mountain biking and horseriding tours, cultural classes and languages lessons. Archeologist Eduardo, at *Guesthouse Samay* (Jr Florida 285; 064 655 937, samayperu.com), organizes trips to local sites and villages, all with a cultural focus. He also offers language classes and can arrange bike, motorcycle and car hire.

ACCOMMODATION

HUANCAYO

Accommodation in Huancayo ranges between old-fashioned, city-centre hotels and hostels and those offering a more familial setting on the city's outskirts. It's hard to find any rooms with views; for that you need to get out of town.

La Casa de la Abuela Prolongación Cusco 794 and José Gálvez 420 064 234 383, incasdelperu.org; map p.286. Run by Incas del Perú and a 15min walk from the plaza, this backpacker favourite offers accommodation in a large dorm room with woven Peruvian blankets and en-suites, as well as simple doubles with private bath. There's a living room with TV and small kitchen for guests' use, plus a pleasant garden with hammocks and the resident dog and cat. Dorms S/35, doubles S/80

Guesthouse Samay Jr Florida 285 064 655 937, samayperu.com; map p.286. This sprawling guesthouse has basic bedrooms, some with en-suite, a large living room and kitchen and the extensive local knowledge of owner and archeologist Eduardo, who runs tours (see above). There's also secure parking. S/98

★ **Posada Junco y Capuli C Julio** C Tello 414, El Tambo 064 244 368; map p.286. Tucked away in the north of town (but still only a 15min walk to the plaza), this is a lovely budget *posada* with neat and tidy rooms with wooden floorboards, flat-screen TV, private bath and delicious breakfast of fresh fruit, eggs, juice and coffee. S/85

OUTSIDE HUANCAYO

Tuki Llajta Hotel Av Centenario s/n, San Gerónimo de Tunan 064 797 107, tukillajta.com; map p.286. Perched on a hillside to the north of Huancayo overlooking the town, this friendly hotel offers accommodation in spacious rooms, all of which are equipped with fireplaces – a welcome addition on cooler nights. Food is served in the dining area with large windows that look out over the city. It's a great spot to escape the chaos of Huancayo. The helpful staff organize tours, too. S/180

EATING

La Cabaña C José Gálvez 420 064 223 303; map p.286. This cosy restaurant with wooden benches is packed with curios and odds and ends including rows of lanterns, old radios, jukeboxes and wine demijohns. The menu features

Peruvian and international dishes, including sandwiches (S/15), grilled meats (S/25) and the house speciality – huge, woodfired pizzas (S/35). Daily 5pm–midnight.

Coqui Café Jr Puno 296 and Centro Comercial Real Plaza; map p.286. This popular café-bakery serves all manner of cakes (S/6), sandwiches (S/10), coffees (S/3.50) and salads (S/18) in their highly popular location just a few steps behind the cathedral. Mon–Sat 7am–10pm, Sun 7am–1pm & 6–10pm.

Detrás de la Catedral Jr Ancash 335 ⓣ 064 212 969; map p.286. Nestled away on a small side-street just behind the cathedral, this is a great central restaurant offering Peruvian staples (S/18) and pasta dishes (S/22). Mon–Sat noon–10pm, Sun noon–5pm.

★ **Govindas** Jr Cusco 289 ⓣ 064 145 168; map p.286. For vegetarians or those craving a nutritious alternative to meat, *Govindas* takes vegetarian food at shoestring prices to a whole new level. Sample tasty feasts for just S/7, including dishes such as *papa a la Huancaina* followed by kidney bean stews with green bean tempura or rocoto chilli stuffed with quinoa, plus a pudding and a drink. Mon–Sat 9am–5pm.

★ **Leopardo** Jirones Huánuco and Libertad ⓣ 064 235 488, ⓦ leopardorestaurante.com; map p.286. This well-established restaurant (so popular there are three by the same owners on the same crossroads) has been serving traditional Peruvian dishes for more than thirty years. Choose from seafood and ceviche (S/25–50) at one restaurant, a la carte meat dishes (S/25–S/50) at another, or budget menus (S/14) at the other. Daily 7am–6pm.

La Tullpa Jr Atahualpa 145, El Tambo ⓣ 064 253 649, ⓦ latullpa.com; map p.286. A popular local restaurant with seating both indoors and out in the interior patio, offering all manner of trout dishes, from tasty *ceviche* (S/36) to fillet (S/27), along with chicken (S/21) and *cuy* dishes (S/33). Daily 11am–5pm.

SHOPPING

Casa del Artesano C Real 495; map p.286. The main craft market in Huancayo, prices are higher than if you go directly to the villages where they're produced. There's a much smaller range here too, but it's still a good option for buying locally-made gourds and textiles. Daily 10am–6pm.

DIRECTORY

Banks and exchange BCP, C Real 519 or BBVA, C Real 631. To change dollars, try your hotel or the street *cambistas* along C Real.

Health Hospital Regional, Av Daniel Carrión 1552 ⓣ 064 23 35 21.

Language schools Incas del Perú, José Gálvez 420 (ⓣ 064 223 303, ⓦ incasdelperu.org) and Samay, Jr Florida 285 (ⓣ 064 655 937, ⓦ samayperu.com) for Spanish and Quechua.

Police Tourist Police, Av Ferrocarril 580 ⓣ 064 202 022.

Post office SERPOST, Centro Cívico Foco 2, Plaza Huamanmarca (Mon–Fri 8am–8pm, Sat 8am–6pm).

Around Huancayo

There is plenty to see in the area around Huancayo, including the ancient **Wari Willka Sanctuary** just south of the city, and the stunning eighteenth-century **Convento de Santa Rosa de Ocopa**. It's well worth heading to **Cochas Chico and Cochas Grandes** for a morning or afternoon to see skilled craftsmen making beautiful, intricately carved gourds that make for great souvenirs, while the **Complejo Arqueológico Arwanturo** is perfect for a half-day trip, with archeological ruins and expansive views of Huancayo and the Mantaro Valley. The surrounding countryside also offers excellent hiking opportunities in the gloriously underexplored **Cordillera Huaytapallana** and the **Reserva Paisajística Nor Yauyos Cochas**.

Wari Willka Sanctuary and Museum

6km south of Huancayo • Tues–Sun 9am–1pm & 2.30–5.30pm • S/3 • ⓣ 064 363 230 • Combi colectivos (S/1.50) shuttle south along Av Giráldez (every 10min; 30min), and taxis run from Huancayo S/15–20

Near the present-day pueblo of **HUARI** stands the **Wari Willka sanctuary** (also known as Warivilca or Huarivilca) constructed by the Waris between 700 and 1200 AD, and subsequently occupied by the Huanca people (1200–1460 AD) and then probably by the Incas. The grounds are thought to have been used as a religious sanctuary where sacrifices – including of children and dogs – took place. The interesting little **museum** in the town square houses a collection of ceramic fragments and a mummy of a young woman (circa 600–700 AD) in her twenties, whose injuries indicate she was probably sacrificed.

Convento de Santa Rosa de Ocopa

25km northwest of Huancayo • Tours Mon & Wed–Sun 9am, 10am, 11am, 3pm, 4pm & 5pm; 1hr • S/8 • Colectivos (S/3.50) to Concepción from C Mantaro (every 10min; 50min) from where it's another colectivo to Santa Rosa (20min)

Founded in 1725, the **Convento de Santa Rosa de Ocopa** took some twenty years to build. The church was the centre of the Franciscan mission into the Amazon, until their work was halted by the Wars of Independence (see page 493), after which the mission villages in the jungle disintegrated and most of the indigenous people returned to the forest. **Guided tours** take in the convent's two pretty cloisters and a range of rooms, including a canteen with brightly coloured wall paintings, a small printing press, a library with 20,000 titles and a couple of rooms displaying stuffed birds, anacondas, crocodiles and other species from the jungle.

A trip to the *convento* can be conveniently combined with a visit to the nearby village of **SAN JERÓNIMO**, about 12km west, well known for its workshops of fine silver jewellery (daily 8.30am–8pm).

Cochas Chico and Cochas Grandes

6km northeast of Huancayo • Colectivos (S/1.50) pass along Av Giráldez towards Cochas (every 10min; 40min); ask to be dropped off near the craft market

A good half-day trip from Huancayo is to the local villages of **Cochas Chico and Cochas Grandes**, whose speciality is crafted, carved gourds. You can buy straight from the main cooperative (in a rather over-the-top tourist centre in Cochas Chicos) or from individual artisans; expect to pay anything from S/4 up to S/2500 for the finer gourds, and if you are ordering some to be made, you'll have to pay half the money in advance. The etchings and craftsmanship on the more detailed gourds are incredible in their microscopic depth, creativity and artistic skill. On some, whole rural scenes – like the harvest, marriage and shamanic healing – are represented in tiny storyboard format. The less expensive have common geometric designs, or bird, animal and flower forms etched boldly across their curvaceous surfaces.

Cordillera Huaytapallana

About 29km northeast of Huancayo • Accessible on a private tour from Huancayo (see page 288)

To the northeast of Huancayo lies the **Cordillera Huaytapallana** mountain range, punctuated by the snow-blanketed peaks of Lazuhuntay (5557m) and Yanahucsha (5530m). Here the landscape is peppered with beautiful emerald lagoons, deep gorges and scenic rivers, including the River Shullcas that flows towards Huancayo. **Trekking** here, expect altitudes of up to 4800m and a beautiful landscape, among the most elevated in the Central Andes, home to vicuñas and dozens of species of birds.

Complejo Arqueológico Arwaturo

13km west of Huancayo • Daily 24hr • Free • Take a combi from C Sta Isabel and C Julio C Tello in Huancayo to the plaza in Chupaca (30min; S/1.50) and then a colectivo (15min; S/2) from C Apolaya and C Flores; ask to be dropped off at the site

Accessed from a dirt road around 1.2km before you reach Laguna Ñahuimpuquio, **Complejo Arqueológico Arwanturo** is a Huana-built archeological site that was later used by the Incas. Ruins have been found across three main parts of the hill, although the most easily identifiable section is the row of 16 partially ruined storerooms on the ridge, a ten-minute walk up the stairs from the road. From here, you're also treated to panoramic views across the patchwork fields of the **Mantaro Valley** and, on a clear day, the snow-sheathed crests of the Cordillera Huaytapallana.

Reserva Paisajística Nor Yauyos Cochas

70km west of Huancayo • Accessible on a private tour from Huancayo (see page 288)

Occupying an area of 2213 square kilometres, the **Reserva Paisajística Nor Yauyos Cochas** is located in the Junín region between 2500 and 5700m above sea level. The main attractions here are the spectacular cascades, natural dams and blue lagoons that the River Cañete forms at its source. There are excellent birdwatching opportunities, plus beautiful views of Uscho Canyon. The landscape reserve also harbours a plethora of Andean flora and fauna, including vicuñas, Andean foxes and herons. The reserve can be visited as part of a full-day **tour** from Huancayo; it's also possible to camp here.

Jauja

Forty kilometres northwest of Huancayo is **JAUJA**, a little colonial town that was the capital of Peru before the founding of Lima. Surrounded by some gorgeous countryside, Jauja is a likeable place, whose past is reflected in its unspoilt architecture. A much smaller and more languid town than Huancayo, its streets are narrow and picturesque, and its inhabitants friendly. Today, Jauja is more renowned for its traditional and well-stocked Wednesday and Sunday markets.

Capilla de Cristo Pobre

Between calles San Martín and Colina • Ask permission from the sisters in the convent next door to enter

The Gothic **Capilla de Cristo Pobre** shares some similarities with Notre Dame de Paris and has a tenuous claim to fame: it was the first concrete religious construction in the Central Sierra.

Laguna de Paca

10–15min by colectivo (S/1.50) from Terminal Terrestre in Jauja, or take a mototaxi (S/5–10) • Boats S/5–10 per hr

If you fancy exploring the landscape around Jauja, try renting a boat on the nearby **Laguna de Paca** and rowing out to the Isla de Amor; according to local legend, this lake is the home of a mermaid who lures men to their death. The shoreline is lined with cafés serving decent trout meals, and, at weekends, *pachamanca* (meat and vegetables placed in a hole in the earth on preheated hot rocks and covered with soil for slow cooking) is served.

Tunanmarca

Colectivos (S/2.50) leave from the Terminal Terrestre (every 30min; 30min) and drop you 1km short of the ruins; for a small fee, they'll drop you closer; or take a taxi from Jauja (S/25 return)

Some 17km northwest of Jauja, just outside the town of Concho, are the archeological remains of **Tunanmarca**. The settlement was home to an estimated population of 25,000 between 1300 and 1500 AD and boasts circular constructions as well as aqueducts and other pre-Inca water works. Located on a mountain pass surrounded by waterfalls at 3900m, Tunanmarca is one of three pre-Inca defensive constructions. It is thought to have been the main base for the Xauxa culture, centred high up in the Valley of Yanamarca, to the north of the fertile Mantaro Valley.

ARRIVAL AND INFORMATION — JAUJA

By bus Buses serve the Terminal Terrestre on Av Ricardo Palma. Lima-bound buses from Huancayo pick up passengers in Jauja, with most departures in the early mornings or just after lunch.

Destinations Cerro de Pasco (hourly; 4hr); Huancayo (several daily; 45min); Lima (several daily; 6hr).

By colectivo Colectivos use the Terminal Terrestre on Av Ricardo Palma, with frequent services to Huancayo (every 15min; 45min).

Tourist information At the Municipality, Jr Ayacucho 856 on the main plaza (Mon–Fri 8am–1pm & 2–5pm; ☎ 064 362 075 ext 213).

ACCOMMODATION AND EATING

Hotel Manco Capac Jr Manco Capac 575 ☎ 064 403 932. A few blocks north of the city centre, this pretty guesthouse has large, elegant rooms with wooden shutters and en-suites, while the double upstairs has its own private balcony. Breakfast is ample and service friendly. S/150

El Mantaro Jr Tarapacá 680 ☎ 980 560 258. This atmospheric restaurant with black-and-white prints of old Jauja offers a good-value set menu at lunch for S/7–16; food is served in two rooms, and there's frequent live music. Daily 11am–5pm.

Huancavelica

Remote **HUANCAVELICA**, at 3676m, is almost purely indigenous in its ethnic make-up, which is surprising considering its long colonial history and fairly impressive array of Spanish-style architecture. There's little of specific interest in the town itself, except the Sunday market, which sells local food, jungle fruits and carved gourds. Local mines (see below) are also an attraction.

Brief history

Originally occupied by hunter-gatherers from about 5000 years ago, the area then turned to sedentary cultivation as the local population was, initially, taken over by the Huari people around 1100 AD, a highly organized culture that reached here from the Ayacucho Valley. The Huanca people arrived on the scene in the fifteenth century, providing fierce resistance when they were attacked and finally conquered by the Inca. The weight of its colonial past, however, lies more heavily on the region's shoulders.

After mercury deposits were discovered here in 1563, the town began producing **ore** for the silver mines of Peru, replacing expensive imports previously used in the mining process. In just over a hundred years, so many indigenous labourers had died of mercury poisoning that the pits could hardly keep going: after the generations of locals bound to work by the *mitayo* system of virtual slavery had been literally used up and thrown away, the salaries required to attract new workers made many of the mines unprofitable. Today, some of the mines are working again and the ore is taken by truck to Pisco on the coast.

Plaza de Armas

Huancavelica's main sights are around the **Plaza de Armas**, where you'll find the two-storey Cabildo buildings, the **Iglesia Catedral de San Antonio de Padua**, and, at the heart of the square, a stone pileta in octagonal form incorporating two waterspouts, each portraying an indigenous face, water gushing from their respective mouths.

Iglesia Catedral de San Antonio de Padua

Plaza de Armas • Mon–Sat 7–8am & 5.30–6.30pm, Sun 5.30–10am & 5.30–6.30pm

Construction of the **Iglesia Catedral de San Antonio** started in 1673, and it took a hundred years to complete. These days it's home to the sacred image of the city's patron

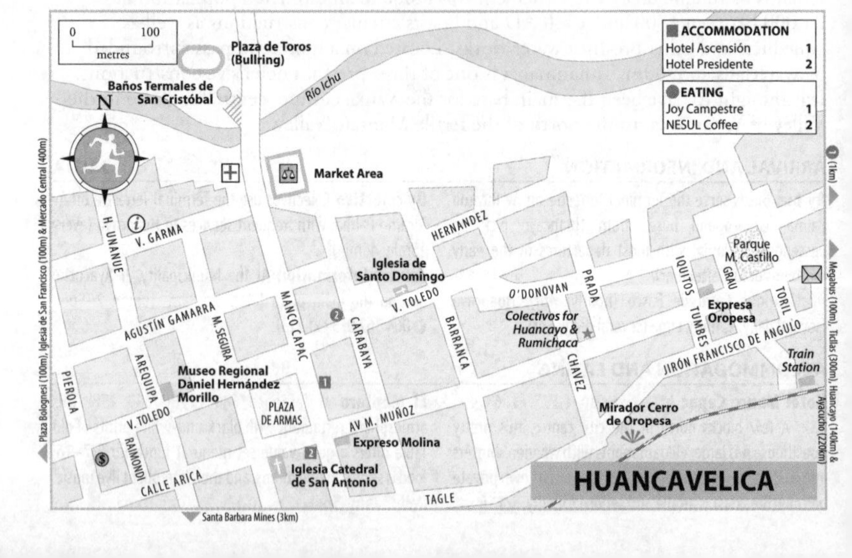

ANDES TRAVEL WARNING

Serious accidents on the **Huancayo–Ayacucho** road, where buses have veered off the single-lane road and rolled down into the river below, make this route particularly dangerous. The **Huancayo–Huancavelica–Ayacucho** stretch of road was once a no-go as it curves its way through isolated mountain plains, making buses an easy target for muggers; however, the safety of this route has increased significantly in recent years. Now, travellers can hop on the "El Macho" train from Huancayo to Huancavelica (5hr 30min) or a faster but more nail-biting colectivo (3hr), before taking another to Rumichaca (3hr) and catching an Ayacucho-bound bus coming from the coast (a further 3hr). Whichever route you choose through the Andes, it's recommended to travel during the day.

– Nuestra Señora de las Mercedes – and an elaborate gold-leaf altar, carved from wood. The silver sheets on display beside it are from the Cusqueña and Huamanguina schools (see page 212).

Iglesia de San Francisco

Plaza Bolognesi • Open daily for Mass • Free

The **Iglesia de San Francisco**, which along with Santo Domingo is connected to the cathedral via an underground passage, was built on the Plaza Bolognesi in 1774 by the Franciscan Order. It survived the nineteenth-century war with Chile, when it was commandeered by the Peruvian army, who sold its fine collection of musical instruments to finance the war effort. Today, the steps of San Francisco are the site, on December 24 and 25, of the awe-inspiring, traditional scissor-dancing performances (*danza tijera*), generally done by men wielding a pair of thick, metal scissors in their right hands.

Iglesia de Santo Domingo

Jr Carabaya • Sun 10.30–11.30am • Free

Santo Domingo is a church and convent complex founded in 1601. The entrance is made from red stone brought from the Pucarumi quarry, while inside there are fine paintings and a Baroque altar with gold-leaf adornment.

Museo Regional Daniel Hernández Morillo

Plazuela San Juan de Dios • Tues–Sun 8.30–11am & 2.30–5pm • S/2 • ⓣ 067 753 420

The small **Museo Regional Daniel Hernández Morillo** sits in the Instituto Nacional de Cultura building one block from the Plaza de Armas, and contains archeological exhibits, fossils from the Tertiary period, petrified marine species and displays on pre-Inca Andean cultures. As well as the archeology and anthropology section, this museum also boasts a room of popular art, showing paintings and objects depicting local culture.

Baños Termales de San Cristóbal

Av 28 de Abril • Mon–Wed & Fri–Sun 5am–4pm • S/2 for large pool, S/4 for private

Four blocks north of the Plaza de Armas are the **Baños Termales de San Cristóbal**, natural hot springs on the hill north of the river. There's a communal swimming pool as well as smaller, private baths, and the waters are naturally heated to 18–22°C.

Santa Barbara mines

3km southeast of town • About 1hr 30min by foot from Huancavelica (the return hike is downhill and faster), or you can take a taxi (S/5–10 return, more for waiting)

The Mina de la Muerte, as the **Santa Barbara mines** tend to be called around Huancavelica, have become a slightly macabre attraction in their own right. The shield of the Spanish Crown sits unashamedly engraved in stone over the main entrance to this ghostly settlement, which has long-since closed and the mine shafts blocked off due to high levels of mercury and toxic gases. It's possible to wander around the old machinery and soak up the eerie ambience, but as with all mines, some sections are dangerous and not visitor-friendly, and it's best to ask local advice before setting off.

ARRIVAL AND DEPARTURE — HUANCAVELICA

By bus Megabus at Av Muñoz 994 (067 451 411) connects Lima with Huancavelica, while Expresa Oropesa, at Av Muñoz 610 (067 368 427), has buses from Ica and Lima; Ticllas, at Av Muñoz 686 (067 355 323), has the most frequent services to Huancayo. Expreso Molina, at Av Muñoz 100 (067 481 236) has daily services to Lima, Huancayo and Ayacucho. Buses were once held up and robbed on the Huancavelica–Ayacucho route; nowadays it's a slow but safer slog to Ayacucho along a very narrow, winding, yet beautiful road.

Destinations Ayacucho (daily at 9pm or midnight; 7–9hr); Huancayo (hourly; 3–4hr); Ica (1 daily; 8hr); Lima (3 daily, evening departures; 11hr).

By colectivo Colectivos leave when full from the corner of Av Muñoz and Jr Prada (3–4hr) for Huancayo. To reach Ayacucho, take a colectivo or minivan to Rumichaca (they leave when full; 2–3hr), and from here, switch to one of the Ayacucho-bound buses coming from the coast, or a waiting colectivo (every 2–3hr; 3hr).

By train Estación Huancavelica, Av Agusto B Leguía (067 452 938). "El Macho" train travels from Huancayo to Huancavelica Mon, Wed & Fri at 6.30am and returns at 6.30am Tues, Thurs and Sat (S/9–S/13; 5hr 30min).

INFORMATION AND TOURS

Tourist information Dircetur, Jr Victoria Garma 444 (Mon–Fri 8am–1pm & 2.30–5pm; 067 452 938).

Tours Turismo Andino organizes tours in and around Huancavelica; it has an office in Huancayo at C Real 261 (064 224 419, turismo-andino.com).

ACCOMMODATION

Hotel Ascensión Jr Manco Cápac 481 067 453 103, hotelascension@hotmail.com; map p.292. Right on the Plaza de Armas, this is one of the city's best options, offering sturdy beds with locally woven blankets and chocolate-coloured furnishings. Use of heaters an extra S/20 per day. S/60

Hotel Presidente Plaza de Armas 067 452 760, huancavelicaes.hotelpresidente.com.pe; map p.292. This is a clean and well-established place with large, modern-styled rooms all with private baths and heaters on request. Room service available and buffet breakfast included. S/280

EATING

Joy Campestre Av Los Incas 870 067 454 101; map p.292. Probably the best restaurant in town, the bestseller is *pachamanca* (S/25), a hearty stew of meat and vegetables baked in hot stones under the ground, only prepared on Sun. There are plenty of other options, such as soups and chicken dishes. Mains around S/16. Daily 8.30am–5.30pm.

NESUL Coffee Jr Virrey Toledo 210 965 076 018; map p.292. From oreo frappes to Irish coffees via all the normal coffee suspects, this cosy café specialises in cakes, local breakfasts and warming *abrigadores* (pisco mixed with fruit, honey and spices). Coffee from S/4. Mon–Thurs 8am–10.30pm, Fri & Sat 9.30am–10.30pm, Sun 9am–9pm.

Ayacucho

Roughly halfway between Cusco and Lima, **AYACUCHO** ("Purple Soul", in the Quechua language) sits in the Andes around 2800m high in one of Peru's most archeologically important valleys, with evidence such as ancient stone tools found in nearby caves at Pikimachay, which suggests that the region has been occupied for over 20,000 years. Its **climate**, despite the altitude, is pleasant all year round – dry and temperate with blue skies nearly every day – and temperatures average 16°C (60°F). The surrounding hills are covered with cacti, broom bushes and agave plants, adding a distinctive atmosphere to the city.

Despite the political problems of the last few years, most people on the streets of Ayacucho, although quiet and reserved (seemingly saving their energy for the city's boisterous **fiestas**),

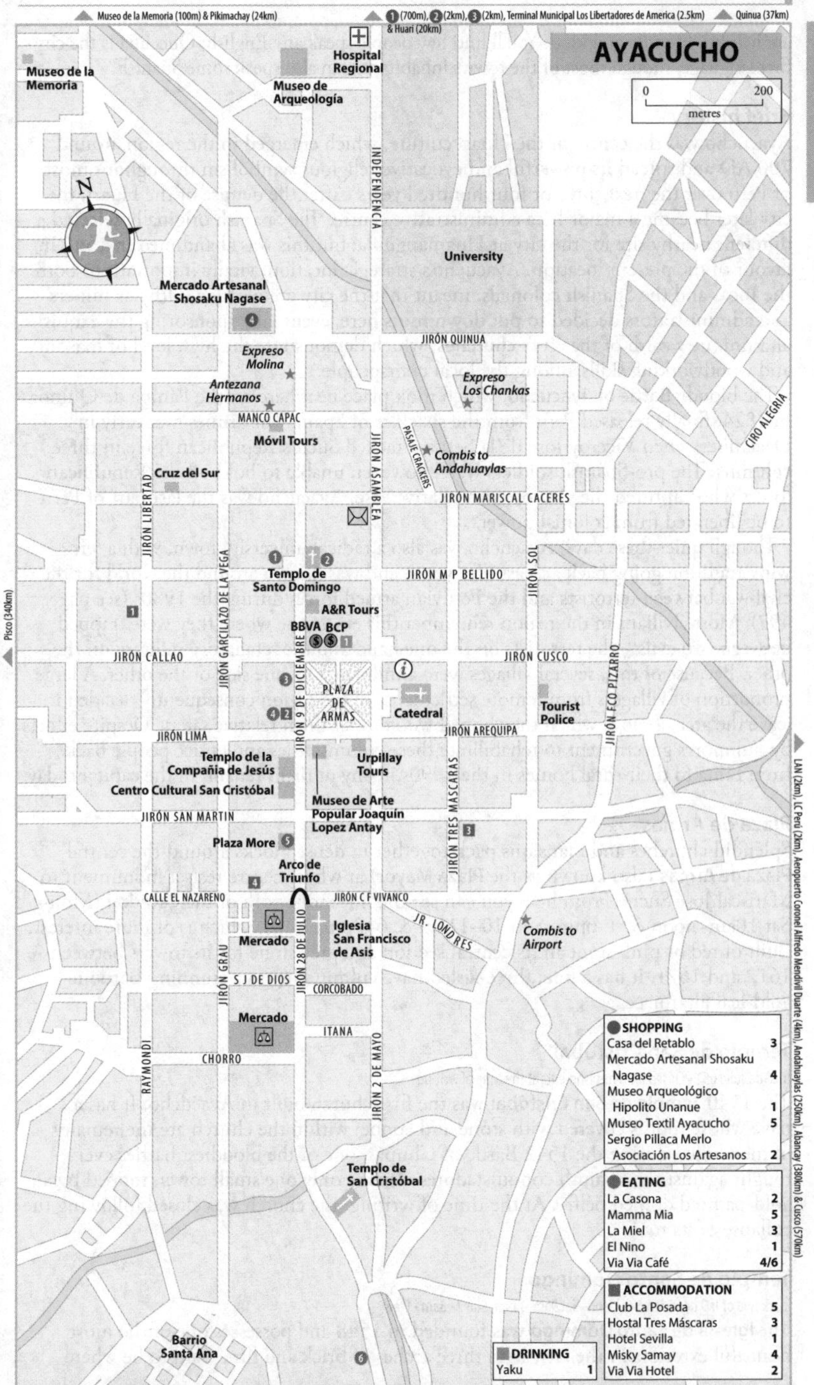
AYACUCHO
0 200 metres
Museo de la Memoria (100m) & Pikimachay (24km)
1 (700m), 2 (2km), 3 (2km), Terminal Municipal Los Libertadores de America (2.5km) & Huari (20km)
Quinua (37km)
Pisco (340km)
LAN (2km), LC Perú (2km), Aeropuerto Coronel Alfredo Mendivil Duarte (4km), Andahuaylas (250km), Abancay (380km) & Cusco (570km)
5 (200m), 5 (200m), Vilcasayhuamán (120km) & Intihuatana (145km)
Vilcasayhuamán (120km) & Intihuatana (145km)
Museo de la Memoria
Hospital Regional
Museo de Arqueología
University
Mercado Artesanal Shosaku Nagase
Expreso Molina
Antezana Hermanos
Expreso Los Chankas
Móvil Tours
Combis to Andahuaylas
Cruz del Sur
Templo de Santo Domingo
A&R Tours
BBVA
BCP
PLAZA DE ARMAS
Catedral
Tourist Police
Templo de la Compañia de Jesús
Centro Cultural San Cristóbal
Urpillay Tours
Museo de Arte Popular Joaquín Lopez Antay
Plaza More
Arco de Triunfo
Iglesia San Francisco de Asis
Mercado
Mercado
Combis to Airport
Templo de San Cristóbal
Barrio Santa Ana
INDEPENDENCIA
JIRÓN QUINUA
MANCO CAPAC
PASAJE CRACKERS
CIRO ALEGRIA
JIRÓN ASAMBLEA
JIRÓN MARISCAL CACERES
JIRÓN LIBERTAD
JIRÓN GARCILAZO DE LA VEGA
JIRÓN M P BELLIDO
JIRÓN SOL
JIRÓN CALLAO
JIRÓN 9 DE DICIEMBRE
JIRÓN CUSCO
JIRÓN FCO PIZARRO
JIRÓN LIMA
JIRÓN AREQUIPA
JIRÓN SAN MARTIN
JIRÓN TRES MASCARAS
CALLE EL NAZARENO
JIRÓN C F VIVANCO
JR. LONDRES
JIRÓN GRAU
S J DE DIOS
JIRÓN 28 DE JULIO
CORCOBADO
ITANA
CHORRO
RAYMONDI
JIRÓN 2 DE MAYO
SHOPPING
Casa del Retablo 3
Mercado Artesanal Shosaku Nagase 4
Museo Arqueológico Hipolito Unanue 1
Museo Textil Ayacucho 5
Sergio Pillaca Merlo Asociación Los Artesanos 2
EATING
La Casona 2
Mamma Mia 5
La Miel 3
El Nino 1
Via Via Café 4/6
ACCOMMODATION
Club La Posada 5
Hostal Tres Máscaras 3
Hotel Sevilla 1
Misky Samay 4
Via Via Hotel 2
DRINKING
Yaku 1

are helpful, friendly and kind. You'll find few people speak any English; Quechua is the city's first language, though most of the town's inhabitants can also speak some Spanish.

Brief history

Ayacucho was the centre of the Huari culture, which emerged in the region around 700 AD and spread its powerful and evocative religious symbolism throughout most of Peru over the next three or four hundred years. After the demise of the Huari, the city later became a major Inca administrative centre. The Spanish originally selected a different nearby site for the city at Huamanguilla; but this was abandoned in 1540 in favour of the present location. Ayacucho's strategic location, vitally important to both the Incas and the Spanish colonials, meant that the city grew very wealthy as miners and administrators decided to put down roots here, eventually sponsoring the exquisite and unique wealth of the city's **churches**, which demonstrate the high level of masonry and woodworking skills among the local craftspeople.

The bloody **Battle of Ayacucho**, which took place near here on the Pampa de Quinoa in 1824, finally released Peru from the shackles of Spain. The armies met early in December, when Viceroy José de la Serna attacked Sucre's Republican force in three columns. The pro-Spanish soldiers were, however, unable to hold off the Republican forces who captured the viceroy with relative ease. Ayacucho was the last part of Peru to be liberated from colonial power.

Though quiet these days, Ayacucho was also a radical university town, with a left-wing tradition going back at least fifty years, and was known around the world for the civil war between terrorists and the Peruvian armed forces during the 1980s (see page 497). Most civilians in the region remember this era as one where they were trapped between two evils – the terrorists on the one hand and the retaliatory military on the other. Because of this, several villages were annihilated by one side or the other. A large proportion of villagers from remote settlements in the region consequently decided to leave the area, a move which they hoped would offer them relative safety. Despite efforts by Fujimori's government to rehabilitate these communities and entice people back from Lima to their rural homes in the 1990s, many of them remain in the capital today.

Plaza de Armas

Splendid churches and mansions pack together in dense blocks around the central **Plaza de Armas** (also known as the **Plaza Mayor**) at whose centre rests a monument to Mariscal José Sucre. From here you can see the fine stonework of the **Catedral** (Mon–Sat 10am–noon & 4–6pm, Sun 10–11am & 6–7pm; S/10), which is of more interest. Built of red or pink stone in its central section and grey stone for its towers between 1612 and 1671, it has a fine, three-aisled nave culminating in a stunning Baroque gold-leaf altarpiece.

Templo de San Cristóbal

Jr 28 de Julio 651 • Closed for refurbishments at the time of writing

The 1540 **Templo de San Cristóbal** was the first church built in Ayacucho. It has a nave whose roof is covered with stone and adobe; within the church are the remains of men killed during the 1542 Battle of Chupas, one of the bloodiest battles ever fought against the Spanish conquistadores. There's only one small tower, topped by a gold-painted domed belfry. At the time of writing, the church was closed following the collapse of its roof.

Templo de Santo Domingo

Block two of Jr 9 de Diciembre • Mon–Sat 9am–noon, Sun 7–8am • Free

The **Iglesia de Santo Domingo** was founded in 1548 and possesses one of the most beautiful exteriors in the city, with three arches of brick and lime, said to be where

heretics were hanged and tortured during the Spanish Inquisition. Inside, the church houses a Baroque and Churrigueresque gold-leaf altar and two images – *El Señor del Santo Sepulcro* and *La Virgen Dolorosa* – only brought out for the Easter processions.

Templo de la Compañia de Jesús

Block one of Jr 28 de Julio • Mon–Sat 6.30–7.30am, 11am–noon & 6.30–7.30pm, Sun 6.30–8am & 11.30am–1pm • Free

The **Templo de la Compañia de Jesús**, built in 1605, is renowned for its distinctive Churrigueresque-style main altar, but even the front exterior facade is one of the city's most complex and colourful, with a red-painted stone entrance held tight between two stout stone towers.

Museo de Arte Popular Joaquín Lopez Antay

Portal Independencia 72 • Mon–Fri 7.30am–1pm & 2–3.45pm • Free

The somewhat diminished **Museo de Arte Popular Joaquín Lopez Antay** is now confined to one room. It showcases some spectacular *retablos* (see page 300) made by acclaimed Peruvian artisan Joaquín López Antay (1897–1981), who was born in Ayacucho and awarded the National Prize of Culture in 1975, shortly before his death.

Museo Arqueológico Hipolito Unanue

Av Independencia 502 • Tues–Sun 9am–1pm & 3–5pm • S/2 • ⓣ 066 312 056

The **Museo Arqueológico Hipolito Unanue** is located in the university's botanical gardens. It's a small museum stuffed full of local archeological finds, mainly ceramics dating from several millennia ago, including a display of miniature pots and other offerings uncovered in a Huari tomb, plus exhibits from Chavín, Huarpa, Nazca and Inca cultures.

Museo de la Memoria

Prolongacióm Libertad 1229 • Mon–Fri 9am–1pm & 3–6pm, Sat 9am–1pm • S/2 • ⓣ 066 317 170

The harrowing **Museo de la Memoria** focuses on the socio-political violence inflicted by the Shining Path revolutionary movement in the 1980s and 1990s (see page 498). The little museum is home to a number of displays including photographs of the dead and missing, as well as artworks on the conflict and a replica of a torture cell. Most labels and descriptions have been translated into English. A wall chart details the history of ANFASEP, the non-profit organization that runs the museum. Mothers and wives of the deceased and missing meet here regularly to share their experiences and lend support to one another. You can purchase the women's handmade clothes and crafts in the little shop upstairs.

ARRIVAL AND GETTING AROUND — AYACUCHO

By plane Most overseas visitors arrive in Ayacucho by plane from Lima (4 daily; 1hr 5min) at Aeropuerto Coronel Alfredo Mendívil Duarte (ⓣ066 527 092), 4km out of town. The route is covered by LAN, at Jr 9 de Diciembre 107 (ⓣ066 310 998) and LC Perú, at Jr 9 de Diciembre 139 (ⓣ066 312 151). The #9 combi (every 15min; 20min) leaves from outside the airport and arrives two blocks from the plaza; in the opposite direction, take the #9 heading east from Jr Carlos F Vivanco and Jr Dos de May (every 15min; 20min). A taxi is about S/6.

By bus Most buses use the Terminal Municipal Los Libertadores de America at Av Pérez de Cuellar s/n (ⓣ066 312 666), although they generally have ticket offices on or around Jr Manco Copac, four blocks from the Plaza de Armas. The well-established Cruz del Sur, however, serves Lima from its own terminal at Jr Mariscal Cáceres 1264 (ⓣ066 312 813). Móvil Tours, Jr Manco Copac 276 (ⓣ956 383 670) travels to Lima and Cusco (via Andahuaylas); Antezana Hermanos, Jr Manco Capac 273 (ⓣ066 311 348) has departures for Lima, plus daily buses to Ica and Huancayo; Expreso Los Chankas, Jr Manco Copac 513 (ⓣ943 779 330) serves Cusco. Expreso Molina, Jr 9 de Diciember 457 (ⓣ066 319 989) serves Huancavelica and Huancayo, the route directly to Huancayo via Huanta having seen a number of fatal accidents occurring over the

FESTIVALS AND MUSIC IN AYACUCHO

In February or March, expect wild celebrations for **Carnaval**, with endless processions of local dancers on the square and throughout town at weekends in the month leading up to the event. If you can be in Ayacucho for **Semana Santa**, the Holy Week beginning the Friday before Easter, you'll see fabulous daily processions, pageants and nightly candlelit processions centred on the Catedral. But beware of the beautiful procession of the **Virgen Dolorosa** (Our Lady of Sorrows), which takes place the Friday before Palm Sunday: historically, pebbles were fired at the crowd (particularly at children and foreigners) by expert slingers so that onlookers took on the pain of La Madre de Dios, and so supposedly reduced her suffering. Nowadays, it's more likely to be paper pellets.

past few years (see page 293). To get into town from the Terminal Municipal, catch a taxi (10min; S/7).

Destinations Abancay (2 daily; 7–8hr); Andahuaylas (2 daily; 5–6hr); Cusco (2 daily, 7pm & 8.30pm; 12–16hr); Huancavelica (1 daily, 9pm and onwards to Huancayo; 8–9hr); Huancayo (3 daily; 10hr); Huanta (3 daily; 1hr); Ica (1 daily; 6hr); Lima (several daily; 8–9hr).

By combi colectivo Minivans to Andahuaylas leave from Pasaje Cáceres just off Jr Mariscal Cáceres, with departures hourly from 7.30am until 4.30pm (4–5hr). For Abancay, change at Andahuaylas.

INFORMATION AND TOURS

Tourist information The helpful iPeru office is located at Jr Cusco 108, just off the Plaza de Armas (Mon–Sat 9am–6pm, Sun 9am–1pm; ⊕066 318 305, ⊕iperuayacucho@promperu.gob.pe). There's also a tourist information kiosk at the airport (6–7.30am & 4–5.30pm).

Tour operators One of the easiest ways to visit the sites around Ayacucho is to take a guided tour. A number of companies offer half-day tours to Pikimachay and Huari (see page 301) for about S/40, Quinua for about S/35, Vilcasayhuamán and Intihuatana for about S/65, and the beautiful natural pools of Millpo for S/90. Operators include A&R Tours, Jr 9 de Diciembre 130 (⊕066 311 300, ⊕viajesartours.com) and Urpillay Tours, Portal Independencia 67 (⊕066 315 074, ⊕ayacuchoviajes.com).

ACCOMMODATION

Finding a room in Ayacucho is easy enough outside the Easter period when, because of the colourful religious festivals, the town is bursting at the seams with visitors from Lima and elsewhere.

★ **Club La Posada** San José Mz P Lote 17 ⊕970 219 308; map p.295. Sat high above the city in the Santa Ana neighbourhood, a 20min walk from the Plaza, this hotel has spectacular views of the valley from its two shady terraces. Large rooms are decorated with locally made textiles and all are en-suite. BBQ facilities and a vast living area are available to guests; wi-fi only in communal areas. S/80

★ **Hostal Tres Máscaras** Jr Tres Máscaras 194 ⊕066 312 921, ⊕hoteltresmascaras.galeon.com; map p.295. This lovely guesthouse has plenty of character – big rooms give onto a lush garden area with prickly pears, apple and orange trees, cacti and bougainvillea, to name a few, while ceramics and the odd curio are displayed in the corridor. Cheapest rooms include shared bath, and dorm-style accommodation can be arranged if you speak with the owner. Two parrots, two chirpy dogs and a cat further add to the atmosphere. Breakfast S/8–10. Dorms S/30, doubles S/55

Hotel Sevilla Jr Libertad 635 ⊕066 314 388, ⊕hotelsevillaperu.com; map p.295. The real attraction here is the beautiful courtyard dotted with dozens of pretty potted plants and beautiful wooden chests. Rooms are large, with fridges, and are decorated with local or fussy paintings. S/125

Misky Samay Jr Carlos F. Vivanco 145 ⊕066 313 335, ⊕miskysamay.com; map p.295. Located just across from the Mercado Central and tucked away in a little courtyard lined with shops, this place offers simple rooms with private bath and powerful showers at a very good price. Breakfast S/6. S/70

Via Via Hotel Portal Constitución 4 ⊕066 312 834, ⊕viaviacafe.com; map p.295. The rooms at this popular place, all named after continents and regions of Ayacucho, give onto a bustling courtyard where meals from the *Via Via Café* are served; expect large bathrooms, local textile wall-hangings and more spacious family rooms set over two floors. There's a book exchange, all-day water and tea, and local crafts and souvenirs on sale in support of NGOs and a local women's association. S/190

EATING

Food is surprisingly good in Ayacucho, with the city's distinctive cuisine including *puca picante*, (pork seasoned with yellow chilli and toasted peanuts), and the local *chorizo* (prepared with minced pork soaked in yellow chilli and vinegar, then fried). The Mercado Central is good for juices and sandwiches in the morning; in the second covered area, you'll be confronted with cages of live guinea pigs and rabbits awaiting their fate.

La Casona Jr Bellido 463 ☎066 312 733; map p.295. This place gets particularly busy at lunchtime for its good-value set lunch of local dishes for S/13; a la carte mains start at S/15. Service can be slow. Mon–Sat 11am–5pm & 6.30–9.30pm, Sun 11am–5pm.

Mamma Mia Plaza More, Jr 28 de Julio 262 ☎945 374 419; map p.295. On the pretty Plaza More, home to a number of restaurants, this is one of the city's few options for pizzas (S/25–50) and pasta dishes (S/20–30). The setting is pleasant, and there are plenty of cocktails to choose from too. Mon–Sat 4pm–10.30pm.

La Miel Portal Constitución 11–12 ☎066 317 183; map p.295. Right on the main square, this is a popular spot that buzzes at all times of day for its tasty cakes (S/6–8), freshly squeezed juices (S/7) and good coffees. Daily 10am–10pm.

El Nino Jr 9 de Diciembre 205 ☎066 314 537; map p.295. One of Ayacucho's most appealing restaurants offers seating on a terrace with views of the Iglesia de Santo Domingo – a great spot for a pisco sour (S/15) as the sun sets. The seating area is decorated with local masks, and the menu is heavy on meat dishes, although at about S/40 a pop it doesn't come cheap. Daily 4pm–midnight.

★ **Via Via Café** Portal Constitución 4 ☎066 312 834, Ⓦviaviacafe.com; map p.295. With wonderful views of the main plaza, this is one of the city's best restaurants, offering local and international dishes including a particularly good *quinoto*, or quinoa risotto (S/18), as well as a selection of alpaca dishes (S/25). There are great fruit and vegetable juices (S/7) too, and inventive home-made ice-cream flavours (S/3 per scoop). There's regular live acoustic music, too (Thurs–Sat 7–11pm). Their other local at Alameda Bolognesi, a 15min walk south, has the same menu but with prices on average S/5 cheaper. Daily 7am–11pm.

DRINKING

Yaku Portal Union 30 ☎066 283 644; map p.295. This first-floor bar spills out onto a terrace overlooking the Plaza de Armas, with table football and long, convivial wooden benches. The food's not the best; locals come here instead to drink a wide selection of local and international beers and to choose from the ample cocktail menu. Mon–Sat 8am–11.30pm.

SHOPPING

Many visitors come to Ayacucho for its thriving **craft industry**, which is focused on intricately woven rugs and *retablos* (little wooden boxes containing elaborate three-dimensional religious scenes made from potato mixed with plaster of Paris). You can find these in the craft markets, but it's more interesting and less expensive – even though the products are far higher quality – to visit the actual **craft workshops** and buy from the artisans themselves.

Casa del Retablo Asociación Los Artesanos, Mz F Lote 1 ☎980 249 255, Ⓦcasadelretablo.strikingly.com; map p.295. The most famous *retablo* craftsman is Silvestre Ataucusi Flores, whose workshop comprises a museum displaying some of his finest creations, a showroom where you can buy one (S/75–S/500) and a room where he'll demonstrate how he transforms the humble potato into the spectacular *retablos* depicting scenes of Andean life. Daily, call ahead.

Mercado Artesanal Shosaku Nagase Av Maravillas 101; map p.295. Stocking a range of textiles, alabaster carvings (known in Peru as Huamanga stone carving) and *retablos*, you can also find some of the crafts from Casa del Retablo and Sergio Pillaca here. Daily 9am–7.30pm.

Museo Arqueológico Hipolito Unanue Av Independencia 502 ☎066 312 056; map p.295. Opposite the museum entrance, this exhibition displays local crafts, all with contact details for purchasing the items or visiting the artisan's workshop. Tues–Sun 9am–1pm & 3–5pm.

Museo Textil Ayacucho San José, Santa Ana neighbourhood, take the stairs left of the church ☎988 193 132; map p.295. Not only does this museum show the different process of turning plants into natural dyes and fibres into yarn, but they've got a wonderful collection of textiles on display, including "3D" designs. The weaver who runs the museum, Santos Huarcaya Huaman, can take you to his and other local artisans' workshops. Mon–Sat 9am–4pm.

Sergio Pillaca Merlo Asociación Los Artesanos Mz G Lote 3, half a block east of the Casa del Retablo ☎966 622 425; map p.295. Ring ahead and this craftsman, who specialises in alabaster carving, will be happy to show you around his workshop. Hours vary, call ahead.

DIRECTORY

Banks and exchange There's a BBVA at Portal Unión 24 and a BCP at Portal Unión 28, both on the Plaza de Armas, plus several exchange shops.

Health Hospital Regional, Av Independencia 355 (T 066 312 180).

Laundry LHL, C Garcilazo de la Vega 265.

Police Tourist Police Jr Sol 280 (daily 8am–9pm; T 066 315 845).

Post office SERPOST, Jr Asamblea 293 (Mon–Fri 8am–6pm, Sat 8am–4pm).

Around Ayacucho

Although the city itself is certainly the main pull, there are some quite fascinating places **near Ayacucho** that are possible to visit. Having said that, it's always a good idea to check with the tourist office (see page 299) beforehand on whether or not it's safe to travel in the rural environs of Ayacucho. At the time of writing, the region had been politically stable for over sixteen years, but the situation is open to change and some villages are more sensitive than others.

GETTING AROUND — AROUND AYACUCHO

By colectivo Colectivos for Huanta leave from the new Terminal Terrestre Totora, 4km northeast of town; those for Huari have their own stop closer to the centre of town, although at the time of writing, it was likely that they would also move to the new terminal. The tourist information office can advise on this. Colectivos for Intihuatana and Vilcasayhuamán leave from the Terminal Terrestre Zona Sur, at Av Cusco 362, 2km from the main square.

By taxi Taxi is the easiest way to get between the centre and the two bus terminals; a taxi to either should cost S/7–10.

By car If you have your own transport or rent a vehicle, you'll need good maps (see page 47).

Huari

20km north of Ayacucho, on the road to Huancayo • **Huari museum** Tues–Sun 9am–1pm & 3–5pm • S/3 • Colectivos (40min; S/4–5) for Quinua, stopping at Huari, leave from C José Santos Chocano and C Ricardo Palma in Ayacucho; alternatively, take a tour (see page 299)

The ancient city of **Huari** (sometimes written "Wari") covers about 20 square kilometres. Historians claim it used to house some 50,000 people just over a thousand years ago, making it one of the largest urban areas in ancient Peru. You can still make out the streets, plazas, some reservoirs, canals and large structures. The small site **museum** displays skulls and stone weapons found here in the 1960s.

Pikimachay

24km northwest of Ayacucho • Free • Take a colectivo (40min; S/3.50) for Huanta from Ayacucho's Terminal Terrestre Totora and asked to be dropped off at the cave; alternatively, take a tour (see page 299)

In the cave of **Pikimachay**, on the road to Huanta, archeologists have found gigantic animal remains (dated to 15,000 BC), tools and evidence of guinea pig and llama domestication. Although these remains have since been taken further north to the town of Huanta, it's still worth the steep thirty-minute hike to enter the cave, which locals claim was used as a hideout by the Shining Path in the 1980s and 1990s.

Quinua

37km northeast of Ayacucho • Colectivos (1hr; S/4–5) leave from C José Santos Chocano and C Ricardo in Ayacucho

The charming and sleepy village of **QUINUA** is a colectivo ride away from Ayacucho through acres of tuna cactus, which is abundantly farmed here for both its delicious fruit (prickly pear) and the red dye (cochineal) extracted from the *cochamilla* larvae that thrive at the base of the cactus leaves. The site of the historic nineteenth-century **Battle of Ayacucho**, just outside town on the pampa, is marked by a striking obelisk, unmistakeable at 44m tall. There are many **artisans** working in Quinua: to look around their workshops, just take a wander along Avenida San Martín or Jirón Sucre, on the latter of which you can find the workshop of acclaimed ceramicist Mamerto Sánchez.

Intihuatana and Vilcasayhuamán

98km and 118km south of Ayacucho • Daily 9am–5pm • Intihuatana S/2; Vilcasayhuamán S/5 • Take a combi (every 2hr, 6am–4pm; 3hr; S/17) from Ayacucho's Terminal Terrestre Zona Sur, Av Cusco 362, to Vilcasayhuamán, which will pass through Vischongo from where you can hike to Intihuatana; alternatively, take a tour (see page 299)

About 98km south of Ayacucho (a 2hr drive plus a 40min walk from the community of Vischongo) lies **Intihuatana**, an archeological complex with a palace, an artificial lake and a stone bath. Fine Inca stonework in terracing and palatial doorways has led investigators to believe it was a getaway for Inca royalty. Another 25km south from Intihuatana is the more spectacular **Vilcasayhuamán**, a pre-Conquest construction with a Temple of the Sun, Temple of the Moon and a ceremonial pyramid. Vilcasayhuamán was an Inca administrative centre once home to 30,000 people around 1400–1500 AD. The central plaza was the focus for ceremonies. Around it stood the Sun Temple (Templo del Sol) – now the site of the colonial church, San Juan Bautista – and the Ushnu, a truncated pyramid on whose upper platform is a large, carved stone, thought to have once been covered with gold leaf, where the Inca sat while presiding over religious ceremonies. It's possible to visit both sites in one day (leaving at 6am from Ayacucho and taking the final combi back from Vilcasauhuamán at 4pm), although if you also want to include a trip to the nearby Bosque de Puyas Raimondi and Laguna Pumaccocha, consult the iPerú office in Ayacucho (see page 299) for information about transport and accommodation.

East to Cusco

It takes 15 to 18 hours to travel from Ayacucho to Cusco via **Andahuaylas** and **Abancay**, a distance of almost 600km.

Andahuaylas and around

It's a 250km, beautiful drive along a paved road from Ayacucho, across mountain passes and through several valleys to **ANDAHUAYLAS**, a small town that serves as the airport for the larger Abancay. There's little to see or do here, despite the backdrop of splendid highland scenery. The main church, **Catedral de San Pedro**, reflects a plain colonial style and the nearby plaza possesses a *pileta* cut from a solid piece of stone. Another fine example of *sillar* stone construction, the **Puente Colonial El Chumbao** road bridge gives access to the Nazca road and the airport. Further afield, 110km south and close to the town of **PAMPACHIRI**, the fairy-tale, conical stone roofs of the **Casa de Piedra Ayamachay**, the star attraction of the **Bosque de Piedras de Pampachiri**, can be visited from the city.

Sondor

21km from Andahuaylas • Free • Take a combi (every 15min; 45min; S/1) from Av Los Chancas and Av Andahuaylas to the site

The archeological remains of **Sondor** lie in the mountains about 2km beyond Laguna Pacucha at 3200m. Recent excavations here have identified that the site was inhabited since around 1500 BC, although most of the buildings date from Chanka or Inca occupation. The site is believed to have served administrative, agricultural, military and ceremonial purposes; trapezoid niches in Puka Corral, once housing mummies and other human remains and ceramic offerings uncovered in Muyu Muyu, a sacred site, support this theory.

This region – the province of Cotabambas, and specifically the village of Coyllurqui – is also home to the **Yáwar Fiesta**, a dramatic and bloody festival that takes place at the end of July. The mythic re-enactment used to involve capturing a live condor and tying it to the back of a bull, the latter representing the Conquistadors and the condor being indigenous to Peru. Legend says that the condor kills the bull, but in real life, the bull would (obviously) kill the condor. Nowadays, the bull alone features in the festivities.

ARRIVAL AND INFORMATION **ANDAHUAYLAS AND AROUND**

By bus The Terminal Terrestre is at Av Malecón Mil Amores 235 and Av José Gátvez. Expreso Los Chankas (983 727 655) serves Cusco, Ayacucho and Lima.

Destinations Ayacucho (daily 11am & 8.30pm; 7hr); Cusco (daily 8pm & 8.30pm; 5hr); Lima (daily 1pm & 3pm; 14–16hr).

By combi colectivo The quickest way to get to Ayacucho is by combi, which leave from the smaller terminal a few doors down from the Terminal Terrestre; to get to Cusco catch a combi to Abancay, and then a bus or another combi from there.

Destinations Abancay (every 30min; 4hr); Ayacucho (hourly; 4–5hr).

Tourist information Dircetur is located at Jr Túpac Amaru 364 (Mon–Fri 8am–1pm & 2.40–5.30pm; 983 662 811, dirceturandahuaylas.gob.pe); they have maps and information about visiting Sondor and the Bosque de Piedras de Pampachiri.

ACCOMMODATION

El Parque Hotel Av Andahuaylas 270 083 421 831. The best budget option in town, a short walk from the Plaza de Armas. All rooms are en-suite and well-sized, with comfortable beds and decent pillows, plus powerful and – more importantly – hot showers. Wi-fi is good; no breakfast. S/80

Abancay and around

About 150km east of Andahuaylas is **ABANCAY**, a large, bustling town at 2378m above sea level. Despite few sights or tourist facilities (with Cusco so close, the town hosts relatively few tourists), it's nevertheless worth a stop as it's within striking range of a number of stunning sites, not least **Choquequirao** (see page 266). From Abancay, the rest of the journey to Cusco is a little less than 200km, usually taking four to five hours and passing through archeologically interesting terrain en route, such as **Sahuite**.

Santuario Nacional de Ampay

Accessed from a track about 6km north of Abancay • S/10 • Take a taxi from Abancay (S/15)

The **Santuario Nacional de Ampay** is a protected area boasting forests, orchids and bromeliads, as well as plenty of falcons, foxes, spectacled bears and *viscachas*. The forest here is almost 60 square kilometres of protected land mostly covered in endangered *intimpa* trees and containing waterfalls, glaciers and swampy areas, accessed via a number of trails, including a stretch of Inca road that join up with Choquequirao (see page 266). It's possible to hike a two-day circuit through the park, starting at Karkatera and finishing in the small **visitor centre** at the entrance, with the hike reaching heights of 5235m at Nevado Ampay, the glacial peak that dominates the landscape here.

Sahuite

45km northeast of Abancay on the road towards Cusco • S/10 • Take a combi (30–45min; S/7–8) towards Curahuasi from Av Nuñez and Av Inca, and asked to be dropped off at Sahuite; alternatively, take a taxi (S/10)

Shortly before crossing into the *departamento* of Cusco, the road goes through the village of **CARAHUASI** where the community of Concacha (3500m) houses the archeological complex of **Sahuite**, comprising three massive, beautifully worked granite boulders, the best of which graphically depicts an Inca village (though the boulders have been defaced in recent years).

ARRIVAL AND INFORMATION **ABANCAY AND AROUND**

By bus The Terminal Terrestre is on Av Pachacutec. Cruz del Sur (083 324 877) serves Lima, via Nazca and Ica; Móvil Tours (965 398 413) has departures for Lima, via Nazca and Ica, and Cusco; Oltursa (083 324 708) goes to Lima.

Destinations Cusco (daily 6am & 11am; 5hr); Lima (several daily; 15–17hr); Nazca (several daily; 8–10hr); Puquio (several daily; 9–10hr).

By combi The quickest way to Ayacucho from Abancay is by combi via Andahuaylas; these leave from the Terminal Terrestre. Services to Cusco leave from Av Nuñezand Av Inca, some of which are direct; for others, you'll need to swap onto a Cusco-bound combi in Curahuasi.

Destinations Andahuaylas (every 45min from 6am–3pm; 3hr); Cusco (every 15min from 5am–6pm; 3hr 30min).

Tourist information There's a tourist information point at the Terminal Terrestre (Mon–Sat 8am–1pm & 2.30–5.30pm); Dircetur is located at Av Arenas 121 (Mon–Fri 8am–1pm & 2.30–5.30pm; 083 321 664, dirceturapurimac.gob.pe); they can provide information and maps for the Santuario Nacional de Ampay and information and recommendations for tour agencies for visiting Choquequirao.

ACCOMMODATION

El Peregrino Apart Hotel Jr Andrés Avelino Cáceres 390 **083 502 610, aparthotelperegrino.com.** This modern hotel just a short walk from the main square offers comfortable tiled apartments with fully equipped kitchenette and living area. The premises are kept clean, there's wi-fi throughout, and staff are friendly. S/120

West of Abancay

Cusco is four or five hours east of Abancay; travelling west it's a relatively short hop to **Puquio** and from there down to Nazca on the coast, or even direct to Lima. The small town of **Chalhaunca** sits beside a popular thermal bath at a crossroads below Abancay, just before the serious mountain climbs start on the route to Puquio.

Chalhuanca

85km southwest of Abancay • Catch a combi from Av Brasil in Abancay (every 10min; 2hr)

CHALHUANCA is a small town in a deep valley a couple of hours downhill from Abancay en route towards Puquio and Nazca. Its main attraction as a stopping point rests in the clean, and reputedly healing, hot thermal springs of **Pincahuacho**, just 5km away (taxi from the main plaza S/5–8).

Puquio

180km southwest of Abancay • Take a Nazca- or Lima-bound bus from Abancay and hop off here (6hr)

PUQUIO lies 180km west, over the Andes, from Chalhaunca. It is a base for exploring alpaca and vicuña land – particularly Pampas Galeras (see page 38). The area is rich in small volcanoes, Huari agricultural terraces still used by the local population and even condor-viewing points within a day or so of the town, most notably the Mirador de de Mayobamba in the Sondondo Valley, where it's possible to observe between fifteen and thirty condors on a normal day. For **tours** of the region, contact the Cámara de Turismo del Valle del Sondondo (camaraturismovallesondondo@gmail.com), who can put you in touch with local agencies.

North of Tarma

North of Tarma there are two main routes. Closest is the steep road which heads northeast down from the Andes into the Central Selva of Chanchamayo and beyond to a large region with its own possible but adventurous overland routes. The other goes back up to the crossroads just before La Oroya and heads north, passing the **Reserva Nacional de Junín**, before reaching Cerro de Pasco and continuing on to **Huánuco**, another important gateway to the **jungle region** (see page 308), and interesting for its nearby archeological remains, such as **Tantamayo** and **Kotosh**, as well as **Huánuco Viejo** near **La Unión**.

Reserva Nacional de Junín

The **Reserva Nacional de Junín** is located some 85km northwest of Tarma on the La Oroya-to-Cerro de Pasco road; this is an excellent trip if you've got the time and your own vehicle. Located at around 4100m above sea level on the Pampa de Junín, the reserve is made up of a vast section of wetlands, packed with aquatic birds, while its 53 square kilometres are also home to plenty of *viscachas*. It's

FIESTAS IN HUÁNUCO

If you can, you should aim to be in Huánuco around August 12, when the **anniversary of the city's founding** begins and the city's normal tranquillity explodes into a wild fiesta binge. **Peruvian Independence Day** (July 28) is also a good time to be here, when traditional dances like the *chunco* take place throughout the streets. From December 24 through January 19, particularly on January 7–9, you may end up witnessing the **Dance of the Blacks** (El Baile de los Negritos) in which various local dance groups, dressed in colourful costumes with black masks (representing the slaves brought to work in the area's mines) run and dance throughout the main streets of the city; food stalls stay open and drinking continues all day and most of the night.

possible to **wild camp** here (always asking local permission first), but there are no facilities at all.

Huánuco and around

The charming modern city of **HUÁNUCO**, more than 100km east of the deserted Inca town of the same name, and around 400km from Lima, sits nestled in a beautiful Andean valley some 1900m above sea level. It's a relatively peaceful place, located on the banks of the sparkling Río Huallaga, which depends for its livelihood on forestry, tea and coca. Founded by the Spaniard Gómez de Alvarado in August 1539, the city contains no real sights, save the usual handful of fine old churches and a small museum. There are plenty of fascinating excursions in the area – notably, the 4000-year-old **Temple of Kotosh**.

Iglesia de San Francisco

Plaza de Armas • Daily hours of Mass only • Free

The sixteenth-century **Iglesia de San Francisco** houses the tomb of the town's founder and shows a strong indigenous influence, its altars featuring richly carved native fruits – avocados, papayas and pomegranates. It also displays a small collection of sixteenth-century paintings.

Iglesia de la Merced

C Hermilio Valdizan • Daily hours of Mass only • Free

The **Iglesia de la Merced** lies some three blocks south and west from the Plaza de Armas. It was built in 1566, in the Romantic style, and it's worth a visit if only for its spectacular Neoclassical gold-leaf altarpiece; there are also two notable Cusqueña-style (see page 212) religious paintings on display.

Iglesia de San Cristóbal

C Damaso Beraun • Daily hours of Mass only • Free

The **Iglesia de San Cristóbal**, three blocks west of Plaza de Armas, has some fine gold-leaf altarpieces, and is said to be built on the site where the chief of the Chupacos tribe once lived and where Portuguese priest Pablo Coimbra celebrated the first Mass in the region, on August 15, 1539.

Museo Regional de Leoncio Prado

Jr Dos de Mayo 680 • Mon–Fri 9am–1pm & 4–6pm • S/3

Located in the former house of Peruvian war hero Leoncio Prado, the **Museo Regional de Leoncio Prado** has a decent selection of regional archeological finds, including pottery, most of which is in fragments, and delicate ornaments unearthed at the Temple of Kotosh, including a tiny fragment of bone carved into the shape of a zoomorphic, bird-like figure. Outside, on the patio, there's a scale model of Kotosh.

5

The Temple of Kotosh

Daily 9am–5.15pm • S/5 • Taxi from Huánuco S/5

Just 6km from Huánuco along the La Unión road, the fascinating, though poorly maintained, **Temple of Kotosh** lies in ruins on the banks of the Río Tingo. At over 4000 years old, this site predates the Chavín era by more than a thousand years. A more or less permanent settlement existed here throughout the Chavín era (though without the monumental masonry and sculpture of that period) and Inca occupation, right up to the Conquest.

The most remarkable feature of the Kotosh complex is the **crossed-hands symbol** carved prominently into the stone of the temple walls – the gracefully executed insignia of a very early culture about which archeologists know next to nothing, although this is only a replica: the original now lies in the **Museo Nacional de Arqueología, Antropología e Historia del Peru** in Lima (see page 74). A second pair of crossed hands were uncovered three years after the initial discovery in 1960, with archeologists positing that the two may represent a male/female duality. The site today consists of three sacred stone-built enclosures in generally poor condition; but with a little imagination and/or a good local guide, it is both atmospheric and fascinating to explore one of the most ancient temple sites in Peru.

ARRIVAL AND INFORMATION — HUÁNUCO AND AROUND

By plane Aeropuerto Alférez FAP David Figueroa Fernandini (☎062 513 066) is 6km out of town, and served by LC Perú, Jr Crespo y Castillo 614 (☎062 280 357) and Star Perú, Jr 28 de Julio 1015 (☎062 519 595). There are three flights daily to and from Lima.

By bus There is no central bus station in Huánuco; each operator uses its own terminal. GM Internacional is at Av 28 de Julio 535 (☎062 519 770) and serves Lima; Turismo Central is at Jr Tarapacá 598 (☎062 624 945 or ☎062 511 806) with buses to Pucallpa and Huancayo.

Destinations Huancayo (3 daily; 7–9hr); Lima (several daily; 8–10hr); Pucallpa (3 daily; 11hr).

By colectivo Colectivos are the best way to get from Huánuco to Tingo María; they leave and drop off from the first block of C Prado. There are more bus options to Pucallpa from Tingo María, so it may be worth hopping onto a colectivo to Tingo and finding a bus there. Colectivos to La Unión leave from block four of Jr Tarapacá (daily 3am–5pm; 4hr). For Tantamayo, Tours Express Chavín, Jr San Martin 546 (☎955 902 607) leave every 2hr or so (4–5hr).

Tourist information There's a Dircetur office at Jr Bolívar 381 (Mon–Fri 8am–1pm & 3–5pm; ☎062 512 980).

ACCOMMODATION

Casa Hacienda Shismay Shismay, 19km east of Huánuco ☎962 367 734, shismay.com. Built in 1859 by German immigrants, this wonderful hacienda was expropriated by the government in 1970 and lovingly restored; today, profits are shared between the building's maintenance and other community projects, students act as guides to the surrounding sites, and local women prepare meals for guests. Accommodation is in attractively furnished rooms, and there's also a mini museum recreating the hacienda's pre-1970 days and horses to hire for the day. S/180

Gran Hotel Huánuco Jr Damaso Beraun 775, Huánuco ☎062 514 222, grandhotelhuanuco.com. Right on the plaza, this comfortable hotel is in a pretty colonial building shaded by old trees; rooms are spacious and kept clean, with wi-fi throughout. Facilities include a swimming pool and a great restaurant serving local cuisine. S/250

Hostel Sweet Dreams Jr Leoncio Prado 1306, Huánuco ☎062 622 722. A 5min walk from the plaza, rooms aren't the largest, and the cheapest come with the toilet and shower practically in the bedroom, but everything's spick and span and the owner is welcoming and chatty. There's decent wi-fi throughout but no breakfast. Rates practically halve out of high season. S/90

EATING

Café San Ignacio Jr Bolivar 325 ☎062 282 120. This colourful, homely café is a great bet for breakfast or dinner; their selection of sandwiches and cakes are a safe option, but for the more adventurous, there are local dishes: *cau cau* (tripe in a yellow chilli sauce) and *patita de mani* (pigs' feet in a spicy peanut sauce). Fri and Sat see the occasional jazz or rock band playing. Daily 7am–1pm & 4.30–10pm.

La Unión

A small market town high up on a cold and bleak pampa, **LA UNIÓN** is a base for visiting the Inca ruins of Huánuco Viejo, a tough three- to four-hour hike away. The precipitous mountain roads make it a dangerous route to walk; the colectivo (see below) is safer, though no faster. La Unión has a few cafés and a couple of hostels.

Brief history

Virtually untouched by the Spanish conquistadores, the city became a centre of native dissent. Illa Tupac, a relative of the rebel Inca Manco and one of the unsung heroes of the indigenous resistance, maintained clandestine Inca rule around Huánuco Viejo until at least 1545. The Spanish built their own colonial administrative centre – modern Huánuco – at a much lower altitude, more suitable for their unacclimatized lungs and with slightly easier access to Cusco and Lima. Huánuco grew thoroughly rich, but was nevertheless regarded by the colonial Peruvians as one of those remote outposts (like Chile) where criminals, or anyone unpopular with officialdom, would be sent into lengthy exile.

Huánuco Viejo

Take a taxi from Plaza de Armas, La Unión (S/15–20) • Daily 8am–5pm • S/4

Huánuco Viejo (also known as **Huánuco Pampa**) sits high up on the edge of a desolate pampa and is one of the most complete existing examples of an Inca provincial capital and administrative centre. The site gives a powerful impression of a once-thriving city – even though it's been a ghost town for four hundred years. The grey stone houses and **platform temples** are set out in a roughly circular pattern radiating from a gigantic *unsu* (Inca throne) in the middle of a plaza. To the north are the **military barracks** and beyond that the remains of suburban dwellings. Directly east of the plaza is the palace and temple known as Incahuasi, and next to this is the Acllahuasi, a separate enclosure devoted to the Chosen Women, or Virgins of the Sun. Behind this, and running straight through the Incahuasi, is a man-made water channel diverted from the small Río Huachac. On the opposite side of the plaza you can make out the extensive administrative quarters.

Poised on the southern hillside above the main complex are more than five hundred **storehouses** where all sorts of produce and treasure were kept as tribute for the emperor and sacrifices to the sun. Well away from the damp of the valley floor, and separated by a few metres to minimize the risk of fire, they also command impressive views across the plain.

ARRIVAL AND DEPARTURE — LA UNIÓN

By colectivo Colectivos (3am–5pm daily; 4hr) connect Huánuco with La Unión and arrive at the terminal on Jr Comercio. The road is unpaved at points and mostly one-lane.

ACCOMMODATION

Hospedaje Shamu Jr Comercio 1318. One of La Unión's safest bets for a night or two, this place offers simple rooms and is on the same street as a number of dining options. S/50

Tantamayo

About 150km north of Huánuco, poised in the mountainous region above the higher reaches of the Río Marañón, lies the small village of **TANTAMAYO**, with its extensive ruins nearby.

The precise age of the remote **ruins of Tantamayo** is unknown. Its buildings appear to fit into the Tiahuanaco-Huari phase, which would make them some 1200 years old, but physically they form no part of this widespread cultural movement, and the site is considered to have developed separately, probably originating from tribes migrating to the Andes from the jungle and adapting to a new environment over a long period of time. It is also thought that the ruins might reveal archeological links to Chavín de Huantar (see page 337) and Kotosh (see page 306).

The architectural development of some four centuries can be clearly seen – growing from the simplest of structures to complex edifices. The thirty separate, massive constructions make an impressive scene, offset by the cloud forest and jungle flourishing along the banks of the Marañón just a little further to the north. Tall buildings dot the entire area – some clearly **watch-towers** looking over the Marañón, one of Peru's most important rivers and a major headwater of the Amazon. One of the major constructions, just across the Tantamayo stream on a hill facing the village, was named **Pirira** by the Incas who conquered the area in the fifteenth century. At its heart there are concentric circles of carved stone, while the walls and surrounding houses are all grouped in a circular formation – clearly this was once an important centre for religious ritual. The **main building** rises some 10m on three levels, its bluff facade broken only by large window niches and by centuries of weathering.

ARRIVAL AND DEPARTURE — TANTAMAYO

By bus or combi Tantamayo is served by a handful of minivans and combis from Huánuco; these leave from the corner of jirones San Martín and Tarapacá, with Tours Express Chavín departing from Jr San Martin 546 (☎955 902 607); most leave around 6am (and then every 2hr or so; 4–5hr). Several combis and buses also run daily from La Unión to Tantamayo (6–7hr); these pick up and drop off from the terminal on Jr Comercio.

Into the jungle

The **Amazon** is the obvious place to move on to from Huánuco and the surrounding area, unless you're heading back to Lima and the coast. The spiralling descent north is stunning, with views across the jungle, as thrilling as if from a small plane. By the time the bus reaches the town of **Tingo María**, a possible stopover en route to Pucallpa (see page 463) or Tarapoto (see page 394), the Río Huallaga has become a broad tropical river, navigable downstream in shallow canoes or by balsa raft. From Tingo María you can continue the 260km directly northeast on the dirt road through virgin forest, going through the **Pass of Padre Abad**, with its glorious waterfalls, along the way to Pucallpa, jumping-off point for expeditions deep into the seemingly limitless wilderness of tropical jungle (see Chapter Eight) or the partially paved route that winds 480km north through high jungle to reach Tarapoto, a sweltering jungle town with access to both the Amazon and the pre-Colombian ruins rich city of Chachapoyas (see Chapter Seven).

Tingo María

Once known as the "Garden City", because of the ease with which gardens, tropical fruit, vegetables and wild flora grow in such abundance, the ramshackle settlement of **TINGO MARÍA**, 130km north of Huánuco, lies at the foot of the Bella Durmiente (Sleeping Beauty) mountain. According to legend, this is the place where the lovesick Princess Nunash sleeps next to her lover Kunyaq, the sorcerer, who transformed himself into stone for eternity to protect himself from the wrath of Nunash's father. These days the town welcomes more travellers than ever due to the decreased activity in the region's cocaine trade, with the roads on to Pucallpa and Tarapoto from Tingo only very rarely seeing the armed robbery of buses travelling by night.

Despite Tingo María's striking setting, it is a tatty, ugly town. There's little for visitors to see, other than the **Cueva de las Lechuzas** (Owls' Cave; daily 8am–6pm, last entry at 5pm; S/30), the vast, picturesque home to a flock of rare nocturnal parrots (you'll need a torch), 14km out of town. To get here, catch a mototaxi (S/10) or a mototaxi colectivo from the city's Parque Ramón Castilla (S/3). Tingo María's major **fiesta** periods are the last week of June, for the **Fiesta de San Juan**, and October 15, to celebrate the **founding of the city** – both are lively and fun times to be in town, but on no account leave your baggage unattended.

ARRIVAL AND DEPARTURE — TINGO MARÍA

By plane Aeropuerto Tingo María, with its grassy, untarmacked runway that's prone to weather delays, is just across the Río Huallaga from Tingo María and a S/2–S/3 moto ride into the centre. LC Perú, Av Raymundi 571 (965 839 660), has daily flights from Lima.

By bus Each bus company has its own terminal. The following all serve Lima: GM Internacional at Av Raymondi 740 (062 561 895, gminternacional.com.pe); Tepsa, Av Raymondi 686 (989 015 475), the most comfortable service; Transmar, Av Pimentel 147 (062 564 733, transmar.com.pe). Turismo Central, Av Raymondi 967–969 (962 770 476, turismocentral.com.pe) serves Huancayo. Buses being robbed at gunpoint is no longer as common as it once was in the region, particularly between Tingo Maria and Tarapoto, but it's still recommended to travel on daylight services that don't stop en route.

Destinations Huancayo (daily 6.30pm; 8–10hr); Lima (several daily; 10–12hr).

By colectivo Colectivos are considered a safer way of reaching Pucallpa (from Av Raymondi and Jr Callao) and Tarapoto (from blocks one and two of Av Raymondi), with Pizana Express (981 681 772) the most reliable option for the latter. For both destinations, rain can cause landslides, so it's recommended to leave early in the day. For Huánuco, combi colectivos leave from block three of Av Raymondi.

Destinations Huánuco (every 30min; 3hr 30min); Pucallpa (every 30min, 5am–6pm; 5–6hr); Tarapoto (hourly; 10–12hr).

INFORMATION AND TOURS

Tourist information The helpful Dircetur is in the Municipal building, Av Alameda Perú 525 (Mon–Fri 8am–1pm & 2.30–6.15pm; 062 562 351, munitingomaria.gob.pe).

Tours Mecsa Osha Tours, Alameda Perú 164 062 563 430, toursmecsaosha.com.

ACCOMMODATION AND EATING

El Encanto de la Selva Av Alameda Perú 288 062 562 848, elencantodelaselva.com. What this place lacks in atmosphere it makes up for with excellent local food. Their *tacachos* are basically mountains of cooked and mashed plantain served with *cecina* (similar to gammon), chorizo or *chicharrón* (fried pork), plus lashings of pickles. Daily 7.30–10pm.

Green Paradise Hotel Av Raymondi 687 062 406 818, greenparadisehotel.com. This friendly central hotel in a modern block offers smallish but clean rooms with private baths and fans. Breakfast is served on an open-fronted terrace, providing a welcome breeze in Tingo María's heat. S/60

Huaraz, the cordilleras and the Ancash coast

CORDILLERA BLANCA

Huaraz, the cordilleras and the Ancash coast

It is the majestic snow-capped peaks of the Cordillera Blanca that draw most visitors to this region – many of them to follow the area's awesome trekking trails, and some to experience mountaineering in the high Andes (or "Andinismo"). The mountains are accessed via an immense desert coastline, where pyramids and ancient fortresses are scattered within easy reach of several small resorts linked by vast, empty beaches. Between the coast and the Cordillera Blanca sits the barren, dark and dry Cordillera Negra. Sliced north to south by these parallel ranges, the centre of Ancash is focused on the Huaraz Valley, known locally as the Callejón de Huaylas. The city of Huaraz offers most of the facilities required for exploring the valley and surrounding mountains, though there are more rural alternatives.

The *departamento* of Ancash was a rural backwater when it was created in 1839. These days, the main industries are fishing (mainly restricted to Chimbote, Peru's largest fishing port), tourism (everywhere but Chimbote), mining (gold, silver, copper and zinc) and agriculture (primarily the cultivation of wheat, potatoes, maize corn and pulses, but also over forty percent of Peru's commercial marigold flowers). The region has a population of just over one million, with 250,000 of these people living in or around **Chimbote**.

For Peruvian and overseas visitors alike, Ancash offers more in terms of **trekking** and **climbing**, beautiful snowcapped scenery, "alpine" flora and fauna and glaciated valleys than anywhere else in the country. It is also extremely rich in history and **pre-Columbian remains**, and possesses a thriving traditional culture. Given the severe earthquake damage this area suffered throughout the twentieth century, it may lack some of the colonial charm seen in Cusco, Arequipa, Cajamarca and Ayacucho, but more than makes up for it with the majesty and scale of its scenery. At around 3000m above sea level, it is important to acclimatize to the **altitude** before undertaking any major hikes.

Nestling in the valleys, the *departamento*'s capital, **Huaraz** – a six- or seven-hour drive north from Lima – makes an ideal base for exploring the region. It's the place to stock up, hire guides and mules or relax after a breathtaking expedition. Besides being close to scores of exhilarating mountain trails, the city is also relatively near the ancient Andean treasure, **Chavín de Huantar**, an impressive stone temple complex that was at the centre of a culturally significant puma-worshipping religious movement just over 2500 years ago.

Huaraz

Situated in the perfectly steep-sided Callejón de Huaylas valley, **HUARAZ** – 400km from Lima – is the focal point of inland Ancash. Only a day's bus ride from either Lima or Trujillo, it's one of the best places in Peru to base yourself if you have any interest in **outdoor adventure** or just sightseeing. As a market town and magnet for hikers, bikers, canoeists and climbers, the city centre has a naturally lively atmosphere, making it the ideal springboard for exploring the surrounding mountainous region; besides the stunning mountain scenery, the area boasts spectacular ruins, natural thermal baths

VIEW OF CHACRARAJU, CORDILLERA BLANCA

Highlights

❶ **Monterrey and Chancos** Relaxing in either of these two natural thermal baths is both a healthy and a hedonistic experience. See pages 322 & 325

❷ **Cordillera Blanca** Hiking or climbing in this mountainous region is as scenic an adventure as you could hope to find anywhere outside the Himalayas. See page 324

❸ **Las Lagunas de Llanganuco** These calm, turquoise-coloured glacial lakes sit 3850m above sea level, dramatically surrounded by Peru's highest peaks. See page 331

❹ **Huascarán** Dividing the Amazon Basin from the Pacific watershed, this mountain is the highest peak in Peru. See page 332

❺ **Caraz** A quaint, attractive town known for its honey and milk products, quietly settled below the enormous Huandoy Glacier and close to the little-visited ruins of Tumshucaico. See page 333

❻ **Chavín de Huantar** One of the most important ancient temple sites in the Andes – associated with a cult dedicated primarily to a terrifying feline god. See page 337

❼ **The Sechin ruins** A unique temple site whose outer wall is clad with some of the most gruesome ancient artwork to be found in South America. See page 344

HIGHLIGHTS ARE MARKED ON THE MAP ON PAGE 314

and beautiful glacial lakes. The valley is dominated by the **Cordillera Blanca**, the world's highest tropical mountain range, and **Huascarán**, Peru's highest peak. The region is best experienced between May and September when the skies are nearly always blue and it rains very little. Between October and April, however, it's often cloudy and most afternoons you can expect some rain.

Brief history

Occupied since at least 12,000 years ago, the area around Huaraz was responsible for significant cultural development during the Chavín era (particularly 1500–500 BC); the Incas didn't arrive here until the middle of the fifteenth century AD. Following the **Spanish conquest** of Peru, and up until less than a century ago, Huaraz remained a fairly isolated community, barricaded to the east by the dazzling snowcapped peaks of the Cordillera Blanca and separated from the coast by the dry, dark Cordillera Negra. Between these two mountain chains the powerful Río Santa valley, known as the Callejón de Huaylas, is a region with strong traditions of local independence.

For several months in 1885, the people of the Callejón waged a **guerrilla war** against the Lima authorities, during which the whole valley fell into rebel hands. The revolt was sparked by a native leader, the charismatic **Pedro Pablo Atusparia**, and thirteen other village mayors, who protested against excessive taxation and labour abuses. After they were sent to prison and humiliated by having their braided hair (a traditional sign of status) cut off, the local peasants overran Huaraz, freeing their chieftains, expelling all officials and looting the mansions of wealthy landlords and merchants (many of them expatriate Englishmen who had been here since the Wars of Independence).

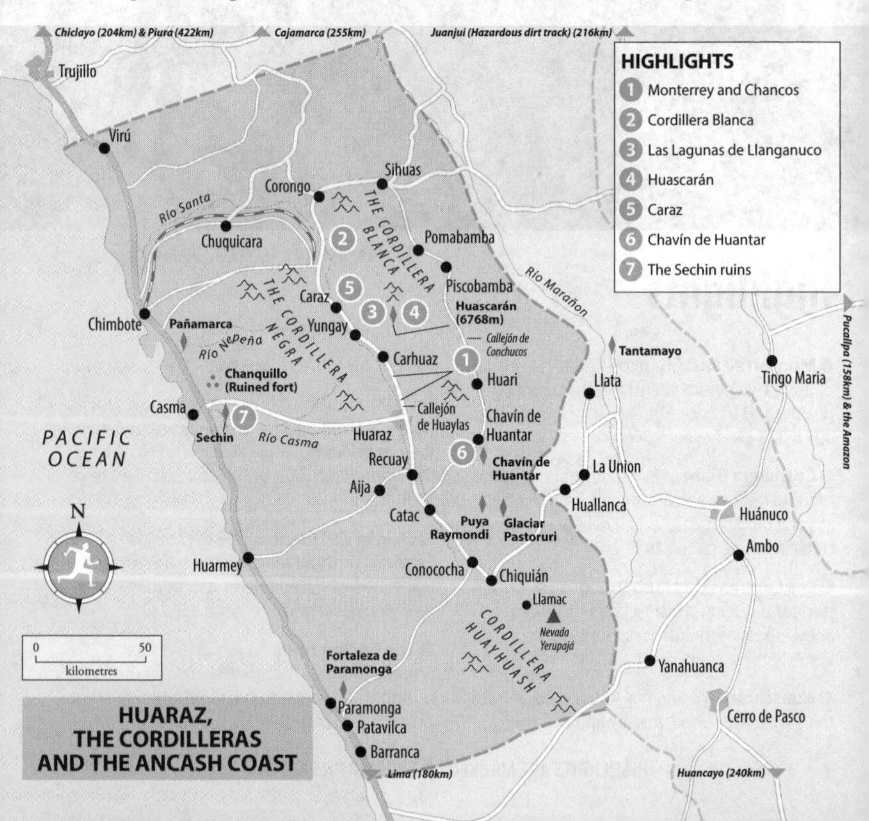

The rebellion was eventually quashed by an army battalion from the coast, which recaptured the city while the locals were celebrating their annual fiesta. Even today, Atusparia's memory survives close to local hearts, and inhabitants of the area's remote villages remain unimpressed by the central government's attempts to control the region.

Downtown Huaraz

Although well over 3000m above sea level, Huaraz has a somewhat cosmopolitan, and very busy, city centre. It developed rapidly in terms of tourism and commerce since the completion of the highway through the river basin from Paramonga, and the opening of mainly US- and Canadian-owned zinc, silver and gold mines in both the Cordillera Negra and the Callejón de Conchucos. Even so, most tourism activity is geared towards goings-on out of town, like trips to Chavín de Huantar or mountaineering expeditions to the glaciated peaks and trekking country that surround Huaraz.

Avenida Luzuriaga is the town centre's north–south axis, where most of the restaurants, nightlife and tour agencies are based. The Parque Ginebra is set just behind Luzuriaga and the **Plaza de Armas**; the plaza is pleasant but something of an afterthought in terms of city planning and not yet fully integrated into the network of roads.

Virtually the entire city was levelled by the **earthquake** of 1970, and the old houses have been replaced with single-storey modern structures topped with gleaming tin roofs. Surrounded by eucalyptus groves and fields, it's still not quite the vision it once was, but it's a decent enough place in which to recuperate from the rigours of hard travel. There are many easy **walks** just outside of town, and if you fancy an afternoon's stroll you can simply go out to the eastern edge and follow one of the paths or streams uphill.

Museo Arqueológico de Ancash

Av Luzuriaga 762 • Daily 9am–5pm • S/5.50 • ☎ 043 421 551

Huaraz's major cultural attraction is the **Museo Arqueológico de Ancash**, facing the modern Plaza de Armas. Fronting attractive, landscaped gardens that are full of stones removed from Recuay tombs and temples, this small but interesting museum contains a superb collection of Chavín, Chimu, Huari, Mochica and Recuay **ceramics**, as well as some expertly trepanned skulls. It also displays an abundance of the finely chiselled stone monoliths typical of this mountain region, most of them products of the Recuay and Chavín cultures. There's also a model of the Cueva del Guitarrero (see page 328), a local site showing evidence of human occupation around 10,000 BC. One of its most curious exhibits is a *goniometro*, an early version of the surveyor's theodolite, probably over a thousand years old and used for finding alignments and exact ninety-degree angles in building construction.

La Catedral

Plaza de Armas • Daily 7am–7pm • Free

On the other side of the Plaza de Armas from the museum stands the **Catedral**. Completely rebuilt after being destroyed in the 1970 earthquake, it has nothing special to see inside, but its vast blue-tiled roof makes a good landmark and, if you look closely, appears to mirror one of the glaciated mountain peaks, the Nevado Huanstán (6395m), behind it.

Santuario del Señor de la Soledad

Plazuela del Señor de la Soledad • Daily 8am–7pm • Free

Uphill in the eastern part of town, at the Parque de la Soledad, is the **Santuario del Señor de la Soledad,** a gleaming church that was rebuilt after two earthquakes, in 1725 and 1970. The modern building houses biblical murals and the powerful sixteenth-century religious image of *El Señor de la Soledad*.

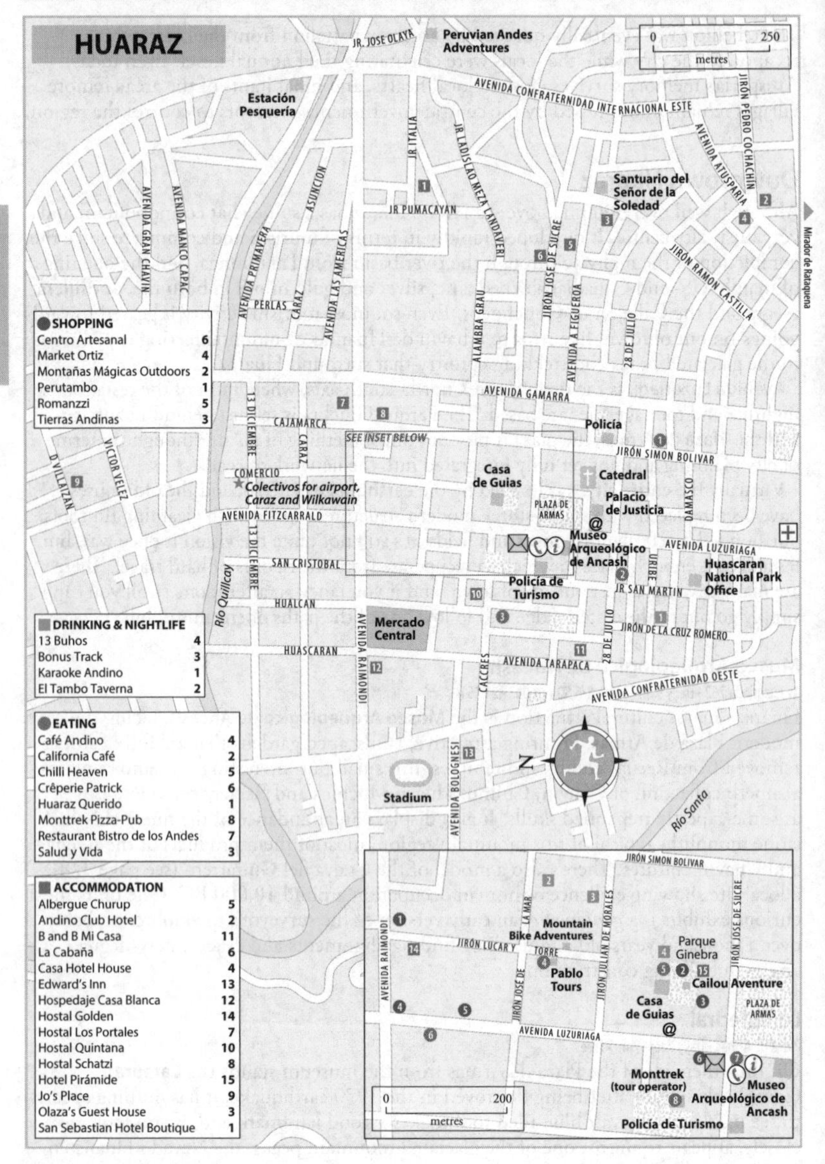

Estación Pesquería

Av Confraternidad Internacional Oeste • Daily 8am–5pm • S/1, includes guided tour • A 15min walk up Av Raimondi then across the Río Quillcay bridge and down Av Confraternidad Internacional Oeste

It is worth the stroll to the regional **Estación Pesquería** (Trout Farm), run by the Ministerio de Pesquería. In a response to the species decline due to overfishing and pollution, it breeds thousands of rainbow trout every year and you can observe the process from beginning to end (more interesting than you might think); much of the excellent trout available in the restaurants of Huaraz comes from here. You can feed the fish, buy some to take back to cook (if you've got the facilities), or sample them at the associated café.

ARRIVAL AND DEPARTURE HUARAZ

BY PLANE

There are daily flights from Lima to Huaraz with LC Perú (01 204 1313, lcperu.pe). The flight lands at a small airstrip close to the village of Anta, some 23km north of Huaraz; from here it's 30min into the city by colectivo (S/2.50) or bus, both of which leave from the main road outside the airstrip, or 25min by taxi (S/35). Colectivos to the airport leave Huaraz from the corner of Jr 13 Diciembre and Av Fitzcarrald before the river.

BY BUS

Most people arrive by bus from Lima or Trujillo. The most comfortable bus service is offered by Cruz del Sur; Movil Tours and Oltursa also offer day and night buses and a range of services. All long-range buses come in at and leave from (or close to) their company's offices. Local buses connect Huaraz with other towns along the valley – Carhuaz, Yungay and Caraz. These can be caught a couple blocks from just over the main river bridge from the town centre, on either side of the main road (Av Fitzcarrald), beside the Río Quillcay. Buses to Chiquián are run by Chiquián Tours from block 1 of C Huascarán, near the market, and leave every hour or so.

Destinations Carhuaz (hourly; 45min); Casma (daily 3–4hr; S/15–20); Catac (hourly; 1hr 20min); Chimbote (daily 4–6hr; S/20–35); Chavín (daily; 2–3hr); Chiquián (daily; 3–4hr); Huánuco (daily; 12–14hr); Huari (daily; 4hr); La Unión (daily; 8hr); Lima (6 daily; 8hr; S/40–80); Piscobamba (daily; 8–10hr); Pomabamba (daily; 8–10hr); Pomacha (daily; 3hr 40min); Sihuas (daily; 10hr); Trujillo (daily 7–9hr; S/35–70).

BUS OPERATORS

Allinbus Jr Lucar y Torre 446 (01 739 0079). Service to Lima.

Empresa 14 Jr Simón Bolívar 407 (043 421 202). Services to Lima and Trujillo.

Cruz del Sur Jr Simón Bolívar 451 (043 380 100). The best services for Lima and Trujillo.

Empresa Huandoy Av Fitzcarrald 261 (043 727 507). Services to Chimbote and Caraz.

Empresa Rapido Av 28 de Julio 202 (043 422 887). Services to Chiquián, Huánuco.and La Unión.

Empresa Sandoval Av Confraternidad Oeste Mza A Lt 6 (043 428 069). Services to Catac, Chavín, Pomacha and Huari.

Movil Tours Av Confraternidad Oeste 451, Independencia (043 422 555). Services to Lima, Chimbote and Trujillo.

Oltursa Av Raimondi 825 (043 423 717). Services to Lima.

Transportes Julio Cesar Jr Simón Bolívar 102 (043 396 443). Services to Lima and Caraz.

Transportes Linea Av Jr Simón Bolívar 450 (043 423 717). Services to Lima, Chimbote and Trujillo.

Turismo Chimbote Services to Trujillo, Caraz and Chimbote.

Turismo Huaraz Jr Caraz 605. Services to Caraz, Piscobamba, Pomabamba and Chimbote.

Yungay Express SRL Av Raimondi 930 (043 424 377). Services to Casma and Chimbote.

BY COLECTIVO

Colectivos Comité 14 run daily services here from Jr Leticia in Lima Centro and also to and from Trujillo. Colectivos also connect all the main towns and villages to the north – Carhuaz (50min), Yungay (1hr 10min) and Caraz (1hr 30min) – at very reasonable rates, departing when full (about every 20min; up to S/10); these can be caught from just over the main river bridge from the town centre, on either side of the main road (Av Fitzcarrald), beside the Río Quillcay. Just before the same bridge, colectivos heading south to Catac (80min; S/4) and Olleros (20–30min; S/8) can be caught daily every 30min from the end of Jr Cáceres, just below the market area.

GETTING AROUND

On foot Much of Huaraz town can be easily negotiated on foot once you've acclimatized to the altitude (3091m); however, some of the more remote sectors should not be walked alone at night since incidents of mugging and rape have, albeit rarely, been reported here.

By colectivo For short journeys within the city, the best option is one of the regular colectivos, which run on fixed routes along avenidas Luzuriaga and Centenario (S/1).

By taxi Taxi rides inside the city are a flat S/3; a trip outside the city might run S/5. A long-distance taxi ride, say from Huaraz to Caraz, would cost at least S/40–70 during daylight, and taxis are also available by the day from around S/100 upwards.

INFORMATION

Tourist information Plaza de Armas (Mon–Sat 9am–6pm, Sun 9am–1pm; 043 428 812, regionancash.gob.pe). The staff are usually helpful and stock photocopies of trekking maps. The Tourist Police (043 421 341)

6

TOURS AND ADVENTURE ACTIVITIES AROUND HUARAZ

The most popular **tours** around Huaraz are to the Lagos Llanganuco (8hr; US$10–15 per person), Chavín de Huantar (9–11hr; US$10–15 per person, including lunch in Chavín) and to the **thermal baths** at Chancos (4hr; from US$8) and Caraz (6hr; from US$10). You can also take a rather commercialized tour to the Pastoruri Glacier, 70km from Huaraz at 5240m (6–8hr return; from US$10 per person). Sadly, the glacier's ice has retreated considerably – it's lost fifty percent of its mass since the mid-1990s – so although worth a visit, it's not as spectacular as it was back in its heyday. A new route around Pastoruri known as the **Ruta del Cambio Climatico** (Climate Change Route) was reopened in 2011; you can get to the edge of the glacier now, but you can't touch it. There are mules available (S/5) to help visitors along the route. It's worth remembering that Pastoruri is very high and can be bitterly cold, so make sure you're well acclimatized to the altitude, and take warm clothing with you.

The Pastoruri tour usually includes a visit to see **Puya raimondii** plants (see page 332) as well.

ADVENTURE ACTIVITIES

In a region as exciting as this in terms of **outdoor adventure**, most people come for something active, namely trekking, climbing, mountain biking, canoeing or even hang-gliding. Adventure activities should really be done in association with reputable **local tour agencies** and/or local guides. Always check on **inclusive costs** (and whether these include entry fees, food, porters etc) and if the guide leading your tour speaks English or another language you understand. Some companies may charge more if they consider their service superior. There's greater price variation in the more adventurous tours, treks, biking, mountaineering, canoeing and river-rafting trips, though tariffs generally start at around US$40–60 per half-day.

Canoeing For canoeing, the most popular section of the Río Santa, which runs along the valley separating the two massive cordilleras, lies between the villages of Jangas and Caraz, navigable between May and October most years with rapids class II and III.

Llama-packing If a three-day trek with llamas carrying your camping equipment appeals, then check out Peru Llama Trek at Av Interoceanica 719 (T 043 421 335, W perullamatrek.com), a llama-packing initiative designed to promote eco-tourism in the region; you can also ask for details in the Casa de Guías, Parque Ginebra 28-G (T 043 427 545 or T 043 421 811).

Mountain biking The Callejón de Huaylas offers one of Peru's most scenic bike rides, with most routes here going over 3500m; Llanganuco (3800m) from Yungay is popular, as is Carhuaz to the Abra de Punta Olímpica (4800m). The sun is very hot here, so always use good sunglasses and sunblock.

Hang-gliding If you fancy hang-gliding, the Huaraz region is an ideal place (mostly around Caraz and Yungay, particularly around the Pan de Azúcar); the best local contact is Alberto Sotelo, contactable through Monttrek (see below).

also have maps and information at the back of the same building by the plaza.

National Institute of Culture Av Luzuriaga 766 (T 043 421 829). The office responsible for ancient monuments provides information about remote ruins.

Website W thehuaraztelegraph.com. The website of the local newspaper, distributed in many of the town's lodgings, is surprisingly helpful for visitors.

TOURS

There are many tour operators in Huaraz who can assist with tours and treks around the city; Pony's Expeditions in Caraz (see page 335) is one of the best.

Caillou Aventure Parque Ginebra T 043 421 214. Rock climbing, trekking, Andinismo (high Andes trekking and climbing) and mountain biking.

Casa das Guías Parque Ginebra 28-G T 043 427 545 or T 043 421 811, W agmp.pe/agmp/index.html. On a quiet little plaza in the streets behind Av Luzuriaga, this is a centre for local guides and mountaineers, with an attached café.

Monttrek Av Luzuriaga 646 (upstairs) T 043 421 124, W monttrek.com.pe. Offers professional climbing, guides, treks, horseriding, river-rafting and snowboarding in the region. It also has a climbing wall, stocks new and used camping and climbing equipment, and the office is a great place to meet other trekkers.

Mountain Bike Adventures Jr Lucre y Torre 530 ⓣ043 424 259, ⓦchakinaniperu.com. Organizes bike tours with mountain bikes to rent as well as a variety of alternative routes for cyclists with particular interests, including cross-country, single track and up- or downhill options. English-speaking guides are available and there's the bonus of a book exchange in the office.

Pablo Tours Av Luzuriaga 501 ⓣ043 421 145, ⓦpablotours.com. One of the best agencies for standard tours, Pablo Tours is particularly good for organized treks and canoeing, but also offers local cultural and city tours. Note that they get booked up very quickly.

Peru Expeditions Psj Santa Teresa 133, Nueva Florida ⓣ943 081 066, ⓦperu-expeditions.org. Longstanding adventure travel company, with regular trips with full board for guests in Cordillera Blanca and Cordillera Huayhuash, with experienced guides, cooks, porters and camp guards.

Peruvian Andes Adventures Jr José Olaya 532 ⓣ043 421 864, ⓦperuvianandes.com. This outfit offers a combination of trekking, climbing and day-trips to sites around the region, plus flights and bus tickets.

ACCOMMODATION

Even in the high season, around August, it's rarely difficult to find accommodation at a reasonable price, though rates do rise during the **Semana Turística** (or Semana del Andinismo) in June and between November and January when many Peruvians tend to visit. There are really three main areas providing accommodation in the urban area: west of the main avenidas Fitzcarrald and Luzuriaga; east of these streets; and another sector, away from the centre, up the Jirón José de Sucre hill to the east. From the Plaza de Armas along Av Luzuriaga there are countless hostels and many smaller places renting out rooms; outside high season it is definitely worth bargaining. There are some peaceful places to choose from out of town, too, some with a garden or **thermal springs**, particularly those around Monterrey.

WEST OF FITZCARRALD AND LUZURIAGA

B and B Mi Casa Av Tarapaca (also known as 27 de Noviembre) 773 ⓣ043 423 375, ⓦmicasahuaraz.jimdo.com; map p.316. Just three blocks west of the Plaza de Armas, this place is distinguished by friendly owners who provide excellent service and have expert cartographical information as well as general tourist info. There's also a dining room serving breakfasts (not included in price), as well as 24hr hot water and private bathrooms. S/85

Edward's Inn Av Bolognesi 121 ⓣ043 422 692, ⓦedwardsinnhuaraz.com; map p.316. One of the most popular trekkers' hostels, and one of the first to cater to them, located just below the market area and offering all sorts of services, including up-to-the-minute tourist information, in a very convivial atmosphere. The rather plain rooms come with private bathroom. The owner, who speaks English, French and Italian, is a highly experienced trekker, climber and mountain rescuer. S/160

Hospedaje Casa Blanca Av 27 de Noviembre 138 ⓣ043 422 602, ⓦcasablancahuaraz.com; map p.316. A comfortable hotel popular with tour groups, with fine wood-beamed ceilings, 24hr reception and a tour desk. It seems a bit out of place on this downmarket street. All rooms have a private bathroom and there's a good restaurant (breakfast not included). S/60

Hostal Quintana Mariscal Cáceres 411 ⓣ043 426 060, ⓦhostal-quintana.com; map p.316. An increasingly popular backpacker joint, less than three blocks from the Plaza de Armas. It is clean, comfortable and well managed, and most rooms have a private bathroom. S/80

EAST OF FITZCARRALD AND LUZURIAGA

Hostal Golden Jr Lucar y Torre 416 ⓣ043 429 412; map p.316. Just a few minutes from the Plaza de Armas, with clan, decently sized, well-decorated rooms with private bathrooms, plus a café/restaurant. S/100

Hostal Los Portales Av Raimondi 903 ⓣ043 428 184; map p.316. A spacious, if dimly lit, three-star hotel, well situated for most bus terminals. Rooms, with well-sprung beds, are clean with private bathrooms, and there's also a large, safe luggage store for trekkers, as well as a restaurant, gym and pool table. S/130

Hostal Schatzi Jr Simón Bolívar 419 ⓣ043 423 074, ⓦhostalschatzi.com; map p.316. A lovely, very friendly little place set around a lush garden patio with small but tidy and nicely furnished rooms; those on the second floor are located on a wraparound wooden balcony with parquetry floors and some views across the garden, town and valley. S/60

Hotel Pirámide Parque Ginebra 22 ⓣ043 428 853, ⓔhotelpiramide_peru@yahoo.es; map p.316. The rooms here, equipped with standard private bathrooms, are a bit boxy but it's a fine choice if you want a leafy plaza and good eating options on your doorstep. Little English spoken. S/50

Jo's Place Jr Daniel Villaizan 276 ⓣ043 425 505, ⓔjosplacehuaraz@hotmail.com; map p.316. Located 10min from the town centre – over the river bridge, on the fourth street on the right – *Jo's Place* is very relaxed, with comfortable rooms and a secure atmosphere making for great value, as well as popularity with backpackers. The staff can help organize tours and there is a large garden, a terrace and views across to the Cordillera Blanca. English newspapers and breakfasts are available. Dorms S/18, doubles S/45

EAST OF AVENIDA GAMARRA

Albergue Churup Jr Amadeo Figueroa 1257, La Soledad ⓣ043 424 200, ⓦchurup.com; map p.316. Just a 5min walk from Plaza de Armas, this great-value establishment has a family atmosphere, a garden, lovely wood-burning stove, laundry, kitchen and left-luggage facilities as well as panoramic views. It also has lots of info on local trekking. Dorms S/55, doubles S/180

★ **Andino Club Hotel** Jr Pedro Cochachín 357 ⓣ043 421 662, ⓦhotelandino.com; map p.316. An uphill hike away from the centre of town, albeit with the reward of beautiful views over the Cordillera Blanca and plush quarters in the best hotel in town. There are a variety of rooms to choose from, with or without terraces and fireplaces, and there's also a gourmet restaurant serving delicious food with a Swiss influence. S/420

★ **La Cabaña** Jr José de Sucre 1224 ⓣ043 423 428, ⓔedgon175@hotmail.com; map p.316. A popular and very friendly *pensión* with safe, comfortable accommodation, a dining room and hot water all day. Rooms have private bathrooms and TV, while guests also have access to kitchen (breakfast not included) and laundry facilities, plus a dining room. S/65

Casa Hotel House C Alejandro Manguina 1467, near C Atusparia ⓣ043 221 028; map p.316. Containing fifteen rooms over four floors, the hotel boasts panoramic views of Huaraz from the roof patio. A pleasant communal area on the ground floor offers a TV, small library, foosball and a billiard table. Rooms come with breakfast and have private bathrooms with 24hr hot water, and there's a laundry available. S/150

Olaza's Guest House Jr Julio Arguedas 1242, La Soledad ⓣ043 422 529, ⓦolazas.com; map p.316. Nice, large rooms here – very clean and with private bathrooms and access to the kitchen and laundry. This place is also a good source of local information; mix with fellow travellers in front of the roaring fire in the communal living space or on the roof terrace with spectacular views. S/120

San Sebastian Hotel Boutique Jr Italia 1124 ⓣ043 426 960 ⓦsansebastianhuaraz.business.site; map p.316. Relatively upscale for Huaraz, the *San Sebastian* offers rooms with fluffy beds, private baths and largely stunning views, centred around a garden courtyard. Amenities include a restaurant that serves Peruvian and American dishes (breakfast included), and the service in general is excellent. S/180

EATING

★ **Café Andino** Lucar y Torre 530 ⓣ043 421 203; map p.316. A popular upstairs café with library and games, serving breakfasts, good coffee, juices and Mexican food. A good place to meet other travellers, trekkers and climbers, or just find a quiet corner in the sprawling space. Daily 11am–10pm.

California Café C 28 de Julio 562 ⓣ043 428 354; map p.316. A good place for wi-fi and mingling with other travellers; the coffee is excellent, there's trekking information on offer and a relaxed atmosphere. Try the all-day American breakfast or waffles, especially if you've worked up an appetite after a few days' hiking. Mon–Sat 7am–10.30pm, Sun 7am–2pm.

Chilli Heaven Parque Ginebra 28; map p.316. The generous servings of spicy curries (Thai and Indian) and Mexican dishes (all around S/30) at this homely, English/Peruvian-owned restaurant will breathe life back into any weary hiker. The authentic tastes make it a popular spot with travellers on the quiet plaza. Daily 8.30am–9.30pm.

Crêperie Patrick Av Luzuriaga 422; map p.316. A centrally located establishment close to the corner with Av Raimondi, *Crêperie Patrick* serves guinea pig, rabbit *al vino* and fondues in addition to excellent crêpes, salads and sandwiches. Daily 4–11pm.

Huaraz Querido Jr Simón Bolívar 961; map p.316. Easily the best spot in town for fresh fish and seafood. The ceviche is generally delicious, but there's a wide range of other sea, lake and farmed fish options (starting at around S/15 a main dish). Daily 9am–6pm.

★ **Monttrek Pizza-Pub** Av Luzuriaga 646 ⓣ043 421 124; map p.316. A spacious place, very popular with trekkers and one of the town's top tour and climbing operators (see page 318). It also boasts a useful noticeboard for contacting like-minded backpackers, as well as maps and aerial photos of the region. The food is delicious and the music good, and there's even a climbing wall. Daily 8am–10pm.

Restaurant Bistro de los Andes Jr Julian de Morales 823 ⓣ043 426 249; map p.316. A great place for breakfast, with seats outside, good yogurt, coffee and pancakes; also popular during the evening. Features a book exchange too. Approx Mon–Sat 7.30am–9pm, Sun noon–9pm.

Salud y Vida Jr Leonisa Lescano 632, near Caceres; map p.316. A dark, simple, good-value place that's filled with locals and worth a visit whether you're vegetarian or not. The standard meat-free stir-fries, salads, soups and soya meat dishes (mains around S/10–15) also feature in the set-menu meals, a steal at S/8, especially for dinner. Mon–Sat 11am–9pm.

FIESTAS IN AND AROUND HUARAZ

Throughout the year various **fiestas** take place in the city and its surrounding villages and hamlets. They are always bright, energetic occasions, with *chicha* and *aguardiente* flowing freely, as well as roast pig, bullfights and vigorous communal dancing, with the townsfolk dressed in outrageous masks and costumes. The main festival in the city of Huaraz is usually in the first week of February and celebrates **Carnival**. In June (dates vary, so check with the tourist office for exact dates), Huaraz hosts the **Semana del Andinismo** (Andean Mountaineering and Skiing Week), which includes trekking, climbing and national and international ski competitions, on the Pastoruri Glacier.

Caraz has its own Semana Turística, usually in the third or fourth week of June. Note that during this month accommodation and restaurant prices in Huaraz and Caraz increase considerably. Other festivals include the **Aniversario de Huaraz**, in July (usually on the 25th), when there are a multitude of civic and cultural events in the city, plus the annual folklore celebrations in the first week of August for Coyllur–Huaraz. The fiesta for the **Virgen de la Asunción** in Huata and Chancas takes place during mid-August. Late September sees the festival of the **Virgen de las Mercedes**, celebrated in Carhuaz, as well as other rural get-togethers you'll often come across en route to sites and ruins in the Callejón de Huaylas.

DRINKING AND NIGHTLIFE

There's a lively nightlife scene in Huaraz, with several **peñas** hosting traditional Andean music, as well as a few **clubs** where locals and tourists can relax, keep warm and unwind during the evenings or at weekends. Nightlife joints start to open from 7pm and can go on until 3am.

13 Buhos Parque Ginebra; map p.316. A popular bar with a chilled, lowdown vibe; note that the cocktails are on the expensive side. Also serves food. Daily 9pm–2am.

Bonus Track Parque del Bombero, Jr Morales 767 ⓣ 955 918 069; map p.316. A more party-like scene can be found here, with walls plastered with album sleeves, photos and country flags. Live music on the weekends. Daily 5.30pm–2am.

Karaoke Andino Jr Teofilo Castillo, Belén, Huaraz; map p.316. Who says Peruvians aren't game for a little lip-synching? Fun spot with Spanish and American tunes on the menu, and some snacks as well. Mon–Sat 6.30pm–3.30am, Sun 6.30pm–midnight.

El Tambo Taverna Jr José de la Mar 776 ⓦ eltambo.negocio.site; map p.316. A restaurant-*peña* serving good drinks, with a great party spirit, a mix of popular sounds and occasional live mu`sic – a blend of Latin, rock and pop. Mon–Thurs 10pm–2am, Fri & Sat 10pm–4am.

SHOPPING

Huaraz is a noted **crafts centre**, producing, in particular, very reasonably priced, handmade leather goods (custom made if you've got a few days to wait around). Other bargains include woollen hats, scarves and jumpers, embroidered blankets and interesting replicas of the Chavín stone carvings. Most of these items can be bought from the stalls in the small **artesanía market** in covered walkways set back off Avenida Luzuriaga (daily 2pm–dusk) or, for more choice, in the **Mercado Modelo** two blocks down Avenida Raimondi from Avenida Luzuriaga. Huaraz is also renowned for its **food**, in particular its excellent local cheese, honey and *manjar blanco* (a traditional sweet made out of condensed milk). These can all be bought in the **food market**, in the backstreets around Avenida José de San Martín (daily 6am–6pm).

Centro Artesanal Next to the post office on the plaza; map p.316. Sells textiles, ceramics, jewellery, stone- and leather-work – most of it made locally in the valley. Mon–Sat 10am–6pm.

Market Ortiz Av Luzuriaga 401; map p.316. One of the best supermarkets in town with everything from wine to trail mix on sale. Daily 8am–9pm.

Montañas Mágicas Outdoors Parque Ginebra 25; map p.316. The most convenient location for stocking up on hiking/trekking/climbing equipment, plus accessories for biking and fishing. The store has got a strong community focus. Mon–Sat 10am–8.30pm.

Perutambo Av Raimondi 820; map p.316. Another natural market with organic and local products, including maca powder, tocosh (ancient penicillin), quinoaand chocolate made with wild Peruvian heirloom peppers. Daily 8am–1pm & 3–9pm.

Romanzzi Av Luzuriaga 465; map p.316. Sweets can be hard to come by in these parts, so this shop does the job, with prepared candy jars (you can customize your own) and sugary frosted cupcakes. Mon–Sat 9am–9pm, Sun 3–9pm.

Tierras Andinas Parque Ginebra; map p.316. Has some fine handicrafts and local artwork. Mon–Sat 10am–5pm.

DIRECTORY

Banks and exchange Banco Wiese, Jr José de Sucre 766; Interbanc, on Plaza de Armas; Banco de Credito, Av Luzuriaga 691; Banco de la Nación, Av Luzuriaga. All banks open Mon–Fri 9am–6pm, with some also Sat 9am–1pm. *Cambistas* gather where Jr Julian de Morales and Av Luzuriaga meet, or try the casa de cambio at Luzuriaga 614 for good rates on dollars.

Health For emergencies, go to the Victor Ramos Guardia hospital at Av Villon and Av Luzuriaga, block 8 (T 043 421 698) or San Pedro Clinic, Huaylas 172 (T 043 428 811). For dental treatment there's the Centro Odontologico Olident, Av Luzuriaga 410–204 (T 043 424 918).

High Altitude Rescue Call T 043 391 163 or T 043 391 669, or via Casa de Guias president Rafael Figueroa at T 941 992 207 (24hr) at off hours, or the Casa during regular hours (see page 329)

Internet and phones California Café, Jr 28 de Julio 562, offers internet plus local, national and international phone calling at very reasonable prices, as does Locutorio Emtelser, Jr José de Sucre 797 (daily 7am–10pm). There are several other internet cafés along Av Luzuriaga and also at Parque Ginebra.

Laundry Lavandería Dennys, Jr la Mar 561, is the best and open until 8pm (closed Sun); otherwise, try Lavandería liz, on the corner of jirones Simón Bolívar and José de Sucre.

Police The Policía de Turismo are on the Plaza de Armas at Jr Larrea y Loredo 724 (T 043 421 341 ext 315); National Police are at Jr José de Sucre, block 2 (T 043 421 330).

Post office Plaza de Armas, Av Luzuriaga 714 (Mon–Sat 8am–8pm).

Around Huaraz

There are a number of worthwhile sights within easy reach of Huaraz. Only 7km north on Carretera 3N (the main road north through the area) are the natural thermal baths of **Monterrey**; higher into the hills, you can explore the inner labyrinths of the dramatic **Templo Wilcahuaín**. On the other side of the valley, **Punta Callan** offers magnificent views over the Cordillera Blanca, while to the south of the city you can see the intriguing, cactus-like **Puya raimondii**.

Monterrey and around

There's no town in **Monterrey** as such, just a street of a few properties, some of which have been converted or purpose-built as hostels or restaurants. At the top end of this street are the **thermal baths**, the reason there's any settlement here at all.

Monterrey thermal baths

Central Monterrey • Daily 6am–4.30pm • From around S/5

The vast **Monterrey thermal baths** include two natural swimming pools and a number of individual and family bathing rooms. Luxuriating in these slightly sulphurous hot springs can be the ideal way to recover from an arduous mountain-trekking expedition, but make sure you are fully acclimatized, otherwise the effect on your blood pressure can worsen any altitude sickness. If you're staying at the wonderful old *Real Hotel Baños Termales Monterrey*, the baths are free. There's also an impressive waterfall just ten minutes' walk behind the hotel and baths.

La Reserva Baños Turcos Sauna

Carretera 3N • Daily 8am–8pm • From around S/5 • T 971 863 202.

About 2km north of Monterrey, **La Reserva Baños Turcos Sauna** is exceedingly pleasant, with both communal and private sauna and steam-room cabins, which feel luxurious due to the fresh branches of mint, chamomile and eucalyptus. There are hot and cold showers to prolong your spa time, and a micro-size cafeteria where you can pick up a healthy fruit salad, a cool drink or a cup of yogurt.

ARRIVAL AND DEPARTURE **MONTERREY**

By colectivo Monterrey is 30min by colectivo (S/1.50) from the centre of Huaraz; services depart frequently (every 10min or so) from the Mercado Central at the corner of avenidas 27 de Noviembre and Raimondi. The trip to

La Reserva, via combi #10 from the central market, costs S/2.50.

By taxi A taxi from Huaraz to Monterrey or La Reserva will run about S/10.

ACCOMMODATION AND EATING

El Cortijo Monterrey Av ⊕ 043 423 813. Arguably the best (only?) barbecue in town, this welcoming place serves great portions, though the service can be slow. Daily 9am–7pm.

★ **Hostal El Patio de Monterrey** Av Monterrey ⊕ 043 424 965, ⊛ elpatio.com.pe. Just a couple of hundred metres from Monterrey's thermal baths and only a few kilometres from Huaraz, this luxurious neo-colonial complex of clean, attractive rooms with iron bedsteads and more expensive bungalows, is based around an attractive patio and lovely gardens. Doubles **US$103**, bungalows **US$180**

Real Hotel Baños Termales Monterrey Av Monterrey ⊕ 043 427 690, ⊛ realhotelmonterrey.com. An old hotel full of character and style and actually attached to the thermal baths (guests have free access). The fine rooms have hot showers and there's a splendid restaurant overlooking the heated pool. They also have bungalows, which cost a bit more. **S/160**

6

Templo Wilcahuaín

Situated some 8km from Huaraz, **Templo Wilcahuaín** (Wilcahuaín Temple) is an unusual two-storey construction, with a few small houses around it, set against the edge of a great bluff. With a torch you can check out some of its inner chambers, where you'll see ramps, ventilation shafts and the stone nails that hold it all together. Most of the rooms, however, are still inaccessible, filled with the rubble and debris of at least a thousand years. The temple base is only about 11m by 16m, sloping up to large, slanted roof slabs, long since covered with earth and rocks to form an irregular domed top. The construction is a small replica of the Castillo at Chavín de Huantar (see page 337), with four superimposed platforms and stairways, and a projecting course of stones near the apex, with a recessed one below it. There was once a row of cat heads carved beneath this, which is a typical design of the Huari-Tiahuanaco culture that spread up here from the coast sometime between 600 and 1000 AD.

ARRIVAL AND DEPARTURE — TEMPLO WILCAHUAÍN

By colectivo Colectivos for Wilcahuaín leave Huaraz from the corner of calles Comercio and 13 de Diciembre.

By taxi If there are four or five of you, a round-trip by taxi will cost about S/20–40.

On foot From Huaraz, follow Av Centenario downhill from Av Fitzcarrald, then turn right up a track (just about suitable for cars) a few hundred metres beyond the *Real Hotel Huascarán*. From here, it's about an hour's winding stroll to the signposted ruins.

Punta Callan

Some 24km west of Huaraz, **Punta Callan** is the classic local viewpoint. No other spot can quite match its astonishing views across the Cordillera Blanca, ideally saved for a really clear afternoon, when you can best see Huascarán's towering ice cap. The grazing land that surrounds the area is as pleasant as you could find for a picnic.

ARRIVAL AND DEPARTURE — PUNTA CALLAN

By bus Punta Callan can be reached in about 2hr on the Casma bus (S/8) from Av Raimondi 336. Ask the driver to drop you off at Callan, shortly before the village of Pira along the road to Casma; from here it's a 20min walk up the path to the promontory. It's a relatively easy walk of a few hours back down the main road to Huaraz. Buses will usually pick up anyone who waves them down en route. Go early in the day, if you want to be sure you can get a bus back.

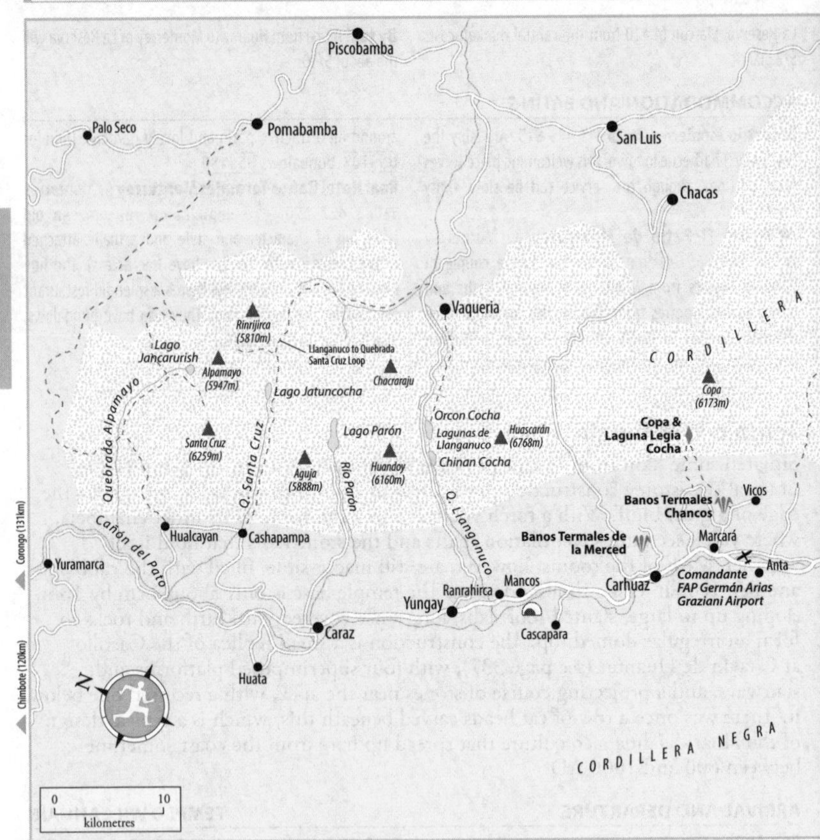

Cordillera Blanca

The **Cordillera Blanca** extends its icy chain of summits for 140 to 160km north of Huaraz. The highest range in the tropical world, the Cordillera consists of around 35 peaks poking their snowy heads over the 6000m mark, and until early this century, when the glaciers began to recede, this white crest could be seen from the Pacific. The **Callejón de Huaylas** is the valley that sits between the Cordillera Blanca and the Cordillera Negra mountain ranges. Under the western shadow of the Cordillera Blanca lie the northern valley Callejón towns, including **Carhauz**, **Yungay** and **Caraz**. Small and rustic, these towns generally boast attractive accommodation and busy little markets, and provide access to ten snow-free passes in the Cordillera Blanca; combining any two of these passes makes for a superb week's trekking. Yungay and Caraz in particular are both popular bases for trekkers.

Of the many mountain lakes in the Cordillera Blanca, **Lake Parón**, above Caraz, is renowned as the most beautiful. Above Yungay, and against the sensational backdrop of Peru's highest peak, **Huascarán** (6768m), are the equally magnificent **Lagunas de Llanganuco**, whose waters change colour according to the time of year and the sun's daily movements, and are among the most accessible of the Cordillera Blanca's three hundred or so glacial lakes.

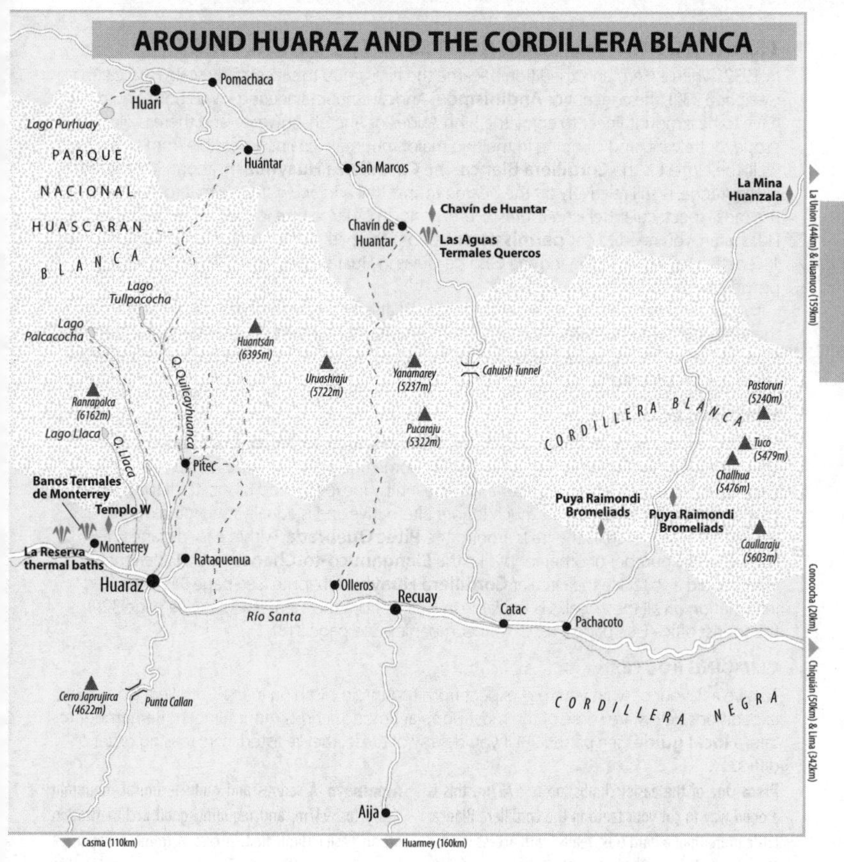

The number of possible **hikes** into the Cordillera depends mostly on your own initiative and resourcefulness. There are several common routes, some of which are outlined below; anything more adventurous requires a local guide or a tour with one of the local operators. **Maps** of the area, published by the Instituto Geográfico Militar, are good enough to allow you to plot your own routes. The most popular hike is the **Llanganuco-to-Quebrada Santa Cruz Loop** (see page 332), which begins at Yungay and ends at Caraz.

Los Baños Termales de Chancos

Chancos, Marcará • Daily 8am–6pm • S/2–5 • Take a bus or colectivo from the first block of Av Fitzcarrald or the market in Huaraz, along the valley towards Yungay or Caraz; get off at the village of Marcará and follow the road uphill for about 4km until you reach the baths

Known traditionally as the Fuente de Juventud (Fountain of Youth), the **Baños Termales de Chancos** (Chancos thermal baths), 30km north of Huaraz, consist of a series of natural saunas inside caves, with great pools gushing hot water in a stream. It is claimed that the thermal waters are excellent for respiratory problems, but you don't have to be ill to enjoy them, and they do serve as an ideal end to a day's strenuous trekking. It's not as nice as it once was (a result of mining activity in nearby Vicos), so if you're pressed for time, opt instead for the baths north of Huaraz near Monterrey (see page 322).

TREKKING AND CLIMBING ROUTES IN THE CORDILLERAS

In 1932, when a German expedition became the first group to successfully scale Huascarán (see page 332), the concept of **Andinismo** – Andean mountaineering – was born. You don't have to be a mountaineer to enjoy the high Andes of Ancash, however, and there is plenty of scope for trekking and climbing in the two major mountain chains accessible from Huaraz as well; the closest is the **Cordillera Blanca**. The **Cordillerra Huayhuash**, about 50km south of that range, is still relatively off the beaten tourist trail and *andinistas* claim it to be one of the most spectacular trekking routes in the world. In order to hike in the Parque Nacional Huascarán, you need to get **permission** first from the park office (Parque Nacional Huascarán, Jr Federico Sal y Rosas 555) and the Casa de Guías in Huaraz (see page 329); both can also provide maps and information.

If you intend to hike at all, it's essential to spend at least a couple of days acclimatizing to the **altitude** beforehand; for high mountain climbing, this should be extended to at least five days. Although Huaraz itself is 3060m above sea level, most of the Cordilleras' more impressive peaks are over 6000m.

TREKKING ROUTES

One of the most popular trekking routes, the **Llanganuco-to-Santa Cruz Loop**, is a well-trodden trail offering spectacular scenery, some fine places to camp and a relatively easy walk that can be done in under a week, even by inexperienced hikers. The **Hualcayan-to-Pomabamba hike** offers a much longer alternative and is equally rewarding. There are shorter walks, such as the trails around the **Pitec Quebrada**, within easy distance of Huaraz, and a number of other loops like the **Llanganuco-to-Chancos** trek. Experienced hikers could also tackle the circular **Cordillera Huayhuash** route (see page 341). Detailed information on all these walks is available in Huaraz from the Casa de Guías (see page 329), the tourist office (see page 318) or tour companies (see page 318).

CLIMBING ROUTES

To give a flavour of what you may expect from mountain climbing in the Cordillera Blanca, the expeditions below are some of the most popular among serious mountaineers. Remember to take a **local guide** (see page 328) if you do any of these; they're listed in increasing order of difficulty.

Pisco One of the easier climbs, up to 5752m, this is a good way to cut your teeth in the Cordillera Blanca. Little more than a hard trek, really, with access via the Llanganuco Valley (3800m), with a duration of only three days. Rated easy to moderate.

Urus A two-day climb reaching heights of around 5500m; access is via Collon to Quebrada de Ishinca and it takes only two days. Rated easy to moderate for the peaks Ishinca and Urus; or moderate to difficult if you tackle Tocllaraju (6034m).

Alpamayo A serious and quite technical mountain rising to 5947m, and requiring good acclimatization on an easier climb first. Access is from Cashapampa (accessible by bus from Caraz), and it usually takes around eight or nine days. Rated as difficult.

Huascarán The south summit at 6768m is the classic route and really requires thorough acclimatization. Access is via Mancos (from where it's an hour by bus to the village of Musho), and it normally demands a good week to tackle effectively. Rated, not surprisingly, as difficult.

Laguna Legia Cocha

From Chancos a small track leads off to the hamlet of Ullmey, following the contours of the Legiamayo stream to the upper limit of cultivation and beyond into the barren zone directly below the glaciers. Keeping about 500m to the right of the stream, it takes ninety minutes to two hours to reach **Laguna Legia Cocha**. Hung between two vast glaciers at 4706m above sea level and fed by their icy melted water, the lake is an exhilarating spot, with the added bonus of amazing views across the Santa Valley to Carhuaz in the north, Huaraz in the south and Chancos directly below. If you leave Huaraz early in the morning, you can enjoy a fine day-trip, stopping at Chancos for a picnic lunch, after walking an hour from Marcará, then returning again the same way.

ORGANIZING A TREK IN THE CORDILLERAS

People die and get lost on these mountains regularly, so ideally you'll be trekking with a **local guide**, perhaps with a tour group, who will ensure you have the right equipment for the terrain and local climatic conditions. If this is not the case, then you need to take responsibility for having good boots, appropriate clothing (including waterproofs), a warm sleeping bag, good mountain tent and other equipment (eg crampons and ice axe).

Wherever you end up, be sure to pay heed to the rules of **responsible trekking**: carry away your **waste**, particularly above the snow line. Note too that you should always use a **camping stove** – campfires are strictly prohibited in Parque Nacional Huascarán, and wood is scarce anyway. Just as important, though, is to realize that the **solar irradiation** in this part of the Andes is stronger than that found in the North American Rockies, European Alps or even the Himalayas. This creates unique glacier conditions, making the ice here less stable and necessitating an **experienced local guide** for the safety of any serious climbing or ice-walking expedition. It's also vital to **be fit**, particularly if you are going it alone.

COSTS

There are three levels of **guide** available: certified mountain guides, who cost upwards of US$80/day; mountain guides undergoing the one-year trial period after training, from US$50/day; and trekking guides, who cost from US$35/day. Note that these costs don't include your transport or accommodation. **Porters** cost between US$20 and US$35/day, depending on whether they are leaders or assistants, and are not supposed to climb over 6000m. **Mule drivers** (*arrieros*) charge from US$18/US$25 a day, plus around US$10/day per animal. Expedition **cooks** usually charge the same as *arrieros*.

INFORMATION

Both the Casa de Guías and the Parque Nacional Huascarán office can give you advice on the best and safest areas for trekking, since this region is not without its **political danger zones**; you also need to obtain permission from them before trekking in the national park. Tour operators offering guided treks can be found in the Huaraz section, and iPerú can also provide substantial list of trekking and mountain guides in the area.

Ideally you should have detailed maps – available from the Casa de Guías – and one or other of the following excellent guidebooks: *Trails of the Cordillera Blanca and Huayhuash*, *Classic Climbs of the Cordillera Blanca* or *The High Andes: A Guide for Climbers* (see page 522).

Carhuaz and around

One of the major towns along the Callejón de Huaylas, **CARHUAZ**, some 30km from both Huaraz and Yungay, has an attractive, central Plaza de Armas, adorned with palm trees, roses and labyrinths of low-cut hedges and dominated by the solid, concrete Iglesia de San Pedro on its south side.

The market

On Sundays the streets to the north and west of the plaza are home to a thriving traditional **market**, where Andean and tropical foodstuffs, herbs and craft (in particular, gourd bowls) can be bought very cheaply. The colourfully dressed women here often sell live guinea pigs from small nets at their feet, and wear a variety of wide-brimmed hats – ones with blue bands indicate that they are married, ones with red bands show that they are single. Many also wear glass beads, on their hats or around their necks, as a sign of wealth.

La Cueva del Guitarrero

24hr • Free • Just over an hour's walk, beyond the sports stadium in Carhuaz and up the stream past the unusual church

In the 1980s, a cave was discovered a few kilometres north of Carhuaz, on the other side of the Río Santa in the Cordillera Negra. Containing the bones of mastodons and llamas and suggesting human occupation dating from as far back as 12,000 BC, it is situated close to a natural rock formation that looks vaguely like a guitar, and the site is now known as the **cave of Hombre Guitarrero** (Guitar Man).

AGOEMA (Asociación de Guias Oficiales Especializados en Montaña de Ancash) Av Luzuriaga 646, 2nd floor ⓣ43 421 124. Based at Monttrek (see page 318), perhaps the most comprehensive place for climbing and trekking info and lists of mountain guides.
Casa de Guías (Mountain Guides) Parque Ginebra 28-G, Huaraz ⓣ43 427 545 or ⓣ43 421 811. The best-organized association of mountain guides in Peru offering plenty of local expertise and the Andean Mountain Rescue Corps on hand.
Mountain Institute Ricardo Palma 100, Pedregal district of Huaraz, south of Av Villón ⓣ43 423 446. A mainly conservation-based organization whose focus is the Peruvian Andes and the Cordillera Blanca in particular.
Turismo Andino Based in the Hotel Andino in Huaraz. Offers very useful assistance to climbers in Cordillera Huayhuash and Cordillera Blanca, plus trekking info.
Trekking and Backpacking Club Jr Los Libertadores 134, Independencia, Huaraz ⓣ943 866 794. Provides information for independent travellers interested in the region's archeology, trekking, backpacking and climbing.

TREKKING GUIDES

Alberto Cafferata Trekking guide contactable through Pony's Expeditions in Caraz (see page 335).
Mérida Roldan Antúnez Av Las Américas 123, Huaraz (ⓣ043 425 155).
Eduardo Figueroa Contactable via *Edward's Inn*, Huaraz (see page 319).
David Gonzáles Castromonte, Pasaje Coral Vega 354, Independencia, Huaraz (ⓣ43 422 213).

HIGH MOUNTAIN GUIDES

High Mountain Guides (members of UIAGM – Unión Internacional de Asociaciones de Guías de Montaña), contactable through the Casa de Guías (see above), include **Javier Monasterio Bilbao, Quique Villafán and Selio VBillón** López, one of the founders of La Asociación de Guías and the Casa de Guías, with 25 years' experience.
Michel Burger Owner of the *Bistro de los Andes* restaurant in Huaraz; offers trekking and fishing through Perou Voyages (ⓦperouvoyages.com).
Rodolfo Reyes Oropeza Malecón Sur Rio Quilkay 734 (Altura de Puente de Piedra), Huaraz (ⓣ043 423 733). Rodolfo has more than seventeen years of experience, and worked with the film crew for the 2003 movie *Touching the Void*, about an ill-fated climb of Siula Grande.

Mancos

On the main valley road between Carhuaz and Yungay; ask your bus or colectivo driver to drop you in the village

Some 9km further north of Carhuaz, over a river, the road comes to the village of **MANCOS**. The village has an unusually attractive plaza, with palm trees and a quaint, modern church with twin belfries sitting under the watchful eye of the glistening glacier of Huascarán. The village's main **fiesta** (Aug 12–16) is in honour of its patron, San Royal de Mancos, and the plaza becomes the focus of highly colourful religious processions, dancing and, later, bullfighting.

ARRIVAL AND DEPARTURE — CARHUAZ

By colectivo Combi colectivos to Huaraz (S/3, 40min), Chancos (S/2) and Caraz (S/2.50) arrive at, and depart from, a stop one block west beyond the market side of the plaza.
By bus Buses to Lima, Huaraz and Caraz leave from a terminal on block 2 of Av La Merced, which is a continuation of the road from the market side of the plaza to the main highway.

ACCOMMODATION AND EATING

El Abuelo Jr 9 de Diciembre 257, by the plaza ⓣ043 394 456, ⓦelabuelohotel.com. A modern, two-storey building with a dining room, comfortable beds and good hot-water supplies. Rooms are stylish without going over the top, and service is attentive as well as friendly. S/218
Casa de Pocha At the foot of Hualcan mountain, about 1.5km above Carhuaz ⓣ943 613 058, ⓦsocialwellbeing.org/swb. A lovely eco-ranch offering accommodation in a traditional adobe lodge with eight spacious rooms under red-tiled roofs. There's a sauna, 12m swimming pool, solar cookers and horseriding, and the hot

springs of La Merced are nearby. The owner speaks Spanish, English, French and Italian. S/130

Hostal La Merced Jr Ucayali 724 043 394 280. This centrally located place has commodious rooms with or without private bathrooms. Rooms are plain and service is good, with a locked room to leave bags in while trekking. S/40

Pakta Jr Comerció 449 043 261 672. Some call this the best restaurant in Carhuaz, with a friendly staff and a varied, fairly ambitious menu split between fish and seafood and Chifa-Peruvian fusion dishes. Daily 8am–11pm.

Los Pinos Jr Amazonas 642 043 261 630. Convivial diner-like spot a short walk from the town's main square. There's a daily changing house meal for S/7, and platters like *lomo saltado* for S/12 (other mains to S/22). Mon–Fri 9.30am–5pm, Sun 10.30am–4pm.

Yungay

Fifty-eight kilometres up the Callejón de Huaylas from Huaraz, and just past Mancos, **YUNGAY** was an attractive, traditional small town until it was obliterated in seconds on May 31, 1970, during a massive earthquake. This was not the first catastrophe to assault the so-called "Pearl of the Huaylas Corridor"; in 1872 it was almost completely wiped out by an avalanche, and on a fiesta day in 1962 another avalanche buried some five thousand people in the neighbouring village of Ranrahirca. The 1970 quake arrived in the midst of a festival and also caused a landslide, and although casualties proved impossible to calculate with any real accuracy, it's thought that over 70,000 people died. Almost the entire population of Yungay, around 26,000, disappeared almost instantaneously, though a few of the town's children survived because they were at a circus located just above the town, which fortunately escaped the landslide. Almost eighty percent of the buildings in neighbouring Huaraz and much of Carhuaz were also razed to the ground by the earthquake.

The new town, an uninviting conglomeration of modern buildings – including some ninety prefabricated cabins sent as relief aid from the former Soviet Union – has been built around a concrete Plaza de Armas a few kilometres from the original site. Yungay still cowers beneath the peak of Huascarán, but it is hoped that its new location is more sheltered from further dangers than its predecessor. The best reason for staying here is to make the trip up to **Las Lagunas de Llanganuco** and **Parque Nacional Huascarán**.

Old town of Yungay

Visible from the main road, before arriving at the new town of Yungay • Daily 8am–6pm • S/2

On the way into town from Carhuaz, a car park and memorial monument mark the entrance to the site of the buried **old town of Yungay**, which has developed into one of the region's major tourist attractions. The site, entered through a large, blue concrete archway, is covered with a grey flow of mud and moraine, now dry and solid, with a few stunted palm trees to mark where the old Plaza de Armas once stood. Thousands of rose bushes have been planted over the site – a gift of the Japanese government. Local guidebooks show before-and-after photos of the scene, but it doesn't take a lot of imagination to reconstruct the horror. You can still see a few things like an upside-down, partially destroyed school bus, stuck in the mud. The graveyard of Campo Santo, above the site, which predates the 1970 quake, gives the best vantage point over the devastation. A tall statue of Christ holds out its arms from the graveyard towards the deadly peak of Huascarán itself, as if pleading for no further horrors.

ARRIVAL AND DEPARTURE — YUNGAY

By bus/colectivo Buses and colectivos all stop and pick up passengers on Jr 28 de Julio en route between Huaraz and Caraz. From Carhuaz (S/2.50). Colectivos for Las Lagunas de Llanganuco (55min; S/5) leave from the same spot, or the Plaza de Armas, usually between 7 and 8.30am.

ACCOMMODATION AND EATING

Café Pilar On the plaza 940 182 631. This large space is good for breakfast and snacks like sandwiches, tamales (maize cakes) and cakes. Daily 8am–8pm.

Hostal Gledel Av Arias Graziani 043 393 048. A very friendly budget hostel at the northern end of town. Upstairs rooms are best, and though all rooms share toilet facilities, the hostel is spotlessly clean and a good place to meet trekkers and climbers. S/20

Restaurant Alpamayo C Carretera Central 255 ⓣ 947 625 258. This place has excellent fish meals including fried trout from local fish farms, but also serves other standard mains. Daily 7am–7pm.

Hotel Rima Rima Jr Miguel Grau 275 ⓣ 043 393 257. Rooms at the *Rima Rima* have large windows and surprisingly low-key, stylish interiors, with colourful tiles in the private bathrooms. Probably the most comprehensive lodgings for miles, this lively spot offers convenient access to trekking guides, local transport, bike rentals and horse tours, along with a restaurant and coffee bar. S/42.50

Hotel Salgado Jr Prado s/n ⓣ 043 393 679. A boxy white exterior hides plain yet cosy rooms, with cable TV. Located on the southern edge of town, with a lovely mountain view. S/35

Parque Nacional Huascarán

Daily 6am–6pm • S/30 for day-visitors, S/60 for two- or three- day visits, $/150 for visits of four days or more • Permission must be obtained from the park office (see page 333 or ⓦ sernanp.gob.pe) or Casa de Guías in Huaraz before trekking or climbing here

Parque Nacional Huascarán is home to the Lagunas de Llanganuco, two stunning, deep-blue lakes, as well as perhaps Peru's most awe-inspiring peak, glaciated Huascarán. On the way up to the level of the lakes you get a dramatic view across the valley and can clearly make out the path of devastation from the 1970 earthquake. The last part of the drive – starkly beautiful but no fun for vertigo sufferers – slices through rocky crevices, and snakes around breathtaking precipices surrounded by small, wind-bent *quenual* trees and orchid bromeliads known locally as *weclla*. Well before reaching the lakes, at Km 19 you pass through the entrance to the national park itself, located over 600m below the level of the lakes; from here it's another thirty minutes or so by bus or truck to the lakes.

Las Lagunas de Llanganuco

At 3850m above sea level, the **Lagunas de Llanganuco** are only 26km northeast of Yungay (83km from Huaraz), but take a good ninety minutes to reach by bus or truck, on a road that crawls up beside a canyon that is the result of thousands of years of Huascarán's meltwater.

The first lake you come to after the park entrance is **Chinan Cocha**, named after a legendary princess. You can rent **rowing boats** by the car park here to venture onto the

LODGES IN THE CORDILLERA BLANCA

The two **lodges** listed below both offer an exciting opportunity to stay in relative comfort right on the edge of the Cordillera Blanca's wilderness. *Lazy Dog Inn* is closer to Huaraz and is right on the edge of Parque Nacional Huascarán. *LLanganuco Mountain Lodge* is also on the edge of the national park, but is much closer to the Lagunas de Llanganuco and Huascarán.

Churup Mountain Lodge Carretera Huaraz, Pitec Km 22 ⓦ churupmountainlodge.com. Up Rte 14A east of Huaraz, *Churup* feels fairly luxurious for a retreat tucked away in the mountains, with bright rooms with fireplaces, an organic veggie garden bordered by streams and natural spring water. Stays include a hearty breakfast and three-course dinner. You could also bunk in the cosy cave dorm, with one wall carved out of the rock, and you can do your laundry for S/8 a kilo. Dorms S/175, doubles S/320

Lazy Dog Inn ⓣ 943 789 330, ⓦ thelazydoginn.com. Some 10km east of Huaraz, it offers transport from the city, or you can take a taxi here (S/20–30); there's a sign at Km 12, a few kilometres beyond Wilcahuaín temple. The cabins are comfortable but you can also stay inside the main adobe-built lodge. The service is excellent and the setting fantastic – it's 30min from Huaraz and borders the Huascarán National Park. There is also the option for "luxury tipi camping" ($35). S/310

Llanganuco Mountain Lodge Keushu Lake, Huandoy ⓦ llanganucomountainlodge.com. A fantastic lodge catering to everyone who wants to stay in comfort by the lake, *Llanganuco Mountain Lodge* is located just underneath the Huascarán and Huandoy glaciers (contact in advance for transport or take a taxi). Accommodation is available in suites, rooms and dorms, and the lodge offers great value and service (the restaurant is excellent) plus a library, games, DVDs and outward-bound activities including adventure trails organized on demand. Dorms S/35, camping/person S/15/, doubles S/315 blue waters (80¢ for 15min), and, if you're hungry, take a picnic from the **food stalls** at the lakeside nearby. The road continues around Chinan Cocha's left bank and for a couple of kilometres on to the second lake, **Orcon Cocha**, named after a prince who fell in love with Chinan. The road ends here and a **loop trail** begins (see page 332). A third, much smaller, lake was created between the two big ones, as a result of an avalanche caused by the 1970 earthquake, which also killed a group of hikers who were camped between the two lakes.

Huascarán

Immediately to the south of the lakes is the unmistakable sight of **Huascarán**, the mountain whose imposing ice-cap tempts many people to make the difficult climb of 3km to the top. Surrounding Huascarán are scores of lesser, glaciated mountains that stretch for almost 200km and divide the Amazon Basin from the Pacific watershed.

The Llanganuco-to-Santa Cruz Loop

The **Llanganuco-to-Santa Cruz Loop** starts at the clearly marked track leading off from the end of the road along the left bank of Orcon Cocha. The entire trek shouldn't take more than about five days for a healthy (and acclimatized) backpacker, but it's a perfect hike to take at your own pace. It's essential to carry all your food, camping equipment and, ideally, a medical kit and emergency survival bag. Along the route there are hundreds of potential campsites. The best time to attempt this trek is in the dry season, between April and October, unless you enjoy getting stuck in mud and being soaked to the skin.

From **Orcon Cocha** the main path climbs the Portachuelo de Llanganuco pass (4767m), before dropping to the enchanting beauty of the Quebrada Morococha (a *quebrada* is a river gully) through the tiny settlement of **Vaqueria**. From here you can move on to Colcabamba and Pomabamba (but only by diverting from the main loop

THE PUYA RAIMONDII

The gigantic and relatively rare **Puya raimondii** plant, reaching up to 12m in height and with a lifespan of around forty years, is found in Parque Nacional Huascarán. Most people assume the *Puya raimondii* is a type of cactus, but it is, in fact, the world's largest **bromeliad**, or member of the pineapple family. Known as *cuncush* or *cunco* to locals (and *Pourretia gigantea* to botanists), it only grows between altitudes of 3700m and 4200m, and is unique to this region. May is the best month to see them, when they are in full bloom and average eight thousand flowers and six million seeds per plant. Dotted about the **Quebrada Pachacoto** slopes (some 50km southeast of Huaraz) like candles on an altar, the plants look rather like upside-down trees, with the bushy part as a base and a phallic flowering stem pointing to the sky. Outside of late April, May and early June, the plants can prove disappointing, often looking like burned-out stumps after dropping their flowers and seeds, but the surrounding scenery remains sensational, boasting grasses, rocks, lakes, llamas and the odd hummingbird.

TOURS

By far the easiest way to see the *Puya raimondii* is on an **organized tour** with one of the companies listed (see page 318). Alternatively, you could take a combi colectivo to Catac, leaving daily every thirty minutes from the end of Jirón Cáceres in Huaraz (roughly S/3.50). From Catac, 45km south of Huaraz, there are a few buses each day down the **La Unión** road, which passes right by the plants. Alternatively, it's possible to get off the combi colectivo 5km beyond Catac at Pachacoto (where there are a couple of cafés often used as pit stops by truck drivers) and hitch from here along the dirt track that leads off the main road across barren grasslands. This track is well travelled by trucks on their way to the mining settlement of Huansala, and after about 15–20km – roughly an hour's drive – into this isolated region, you'll be surrounded by the giant bromeliads. From here, you can either continue on to La Unión (see above), via the Pastoruri Glacier, or return to Huaraz by hitching back to the main road.

trail), which are settlements located in the Callejón de Conchucos – though don't attempt it in the rainy season, when you may well find yourself stranded. Most people prefer to continue on the loop back to the Callejón de Huaylas via Santa Cruz.

Continuing from Vaqueria the main loop trail subsequently heads north up the Quebrada Huaripampa, where you'll probably camp the first night. From here it circles the icecap of **Chacraraju** (6000m) and along a stupendous rocky canyon with a marshy bottom, snowy mountain peaks to the west and Cerro Mellairca to the east.

On the third or fourth day, following the stream uphill, with the lakes of Morococha and Huiscash on your left, you pass down into the **Pacific watershed** along the **Quebrada Santa Cruz**, eventually emerging, after perhaps another night's rest, beside the calm waters of Lake Grande (Lake Jatuncocha). Tracing the left bank and continuing down this perfect glacial valley for about another eight hours, you'll come to the village of **Cashapampa**, which has very basic accommodation, but don't bank on this since it can't be booked in advance. From here it's just a short step (about 2km) to the inviting and very hot (but temperature-controllable) thermal baths of **Huancarhuaz** (daily 8am–5pm; S/3), and there's a road or a more direct three-hour path across the low hills south to Caraz.

The Hualcayan-to-Pomabamba hike

The **Hualcayan-to-Pomabamba hike** is one of the longest in the Cordillera Blanca and requires good acclimatization as well as fitness. It takes at least a week to cover the route's total distance of around 78km – altitudes vary between 3100 and 4850m. Starting at Cashapampa, near Hualcayan (with an archeological complex at 3140m), the route takes seven to ten days, taking in great views of the Cordillera Negra on the first day's uphill, zig-zag, hiking, passing turquoise lakes and with views over the Santa Cruz glacier (6259m). The trail terminates at the village of Pomabamba, where there are thermal baths, a basic hotel and a road.

ARRIVAL AND INFORMATION

By bus You can get to Hualcayan (3100m) and Cashapampa from Caraz by bus (1hr 45min), leaving from the corner of Grau with Santa Cruz, two or three times every morning. Pomabamba is connected by Los Andes bus with Yungay (daily; 4–6hr; S/21); there are sometimes colectivos, too.

PARQUE NACIONAL HUASCARÁN

Parque Nacional Huascarán office Jr Federico Sal y Rosas 555 and Belén, Huaraz (Mon–Fri 8.30am–6pm, Sat & Sun 7–11am; ☎ 043 422 068). If you're going to trek in Parque Nacional Huascarán, you'll need to register here and at the Casa de Guías in Huaraz beforehand.

ACCOMMODATION

Camping Free campsites along the Hualcayan-to-Pomabamba hike include: *Wishcash* (4400m), *Osoruri* (4800m), *Jancanrurish* (4200m), *Huillca* (4200m) and *Yanacollpa* (3850m).

Caraz and around

The attractive town of **CARAZ**, less than 20km down the Santa Valley from Yungay, sits at an altitude of 2285m, well below the enormous Huandoy Glacier. Mainly visited for the access it gives to a fantastic hiking hinterland, it is also well known throughout Peru for its honey and milk products. Palm trees and flowers adorn a colonial-looking **Plaza de Armas**, which has survived well from the ravages of several major earthquakes. The plaza makes the town worth visiting in its own right, especially to escape busy Huaraz. A small daily **market** (6.30am–5pm), three blocks north of the plaza, is usually vibrant with activity, good for fresh food, colourful fabrics, traditional gourd bowls, religious candles and hats. A twenty-minute walk up the hill on the north side of town, dodging house dogs, rewards you with good views over Caraz.

Tumshucaico

Daily 24hr • Free • 15min by taxi from Caraz (S/5–8 one way, more for waiting)

A couple of kilometres northeast of Caraz along 28 de Julio, close to the Laguna Parón turn-off, lie the weathered ruins of **Tumshucaico**, probably the largest ruins in the Callejón de Hualyas. A possible ceremonial centre, dating from the formative period of 1800 BC, replete with galleries and worked stone walls, it may well also have had a defensive function given its dominating position overlooking the valley. These days its edges have been eaten away by the peri-urban growth of Caraz and the extension of local cultivated land.

Huata

Nine kilometres across the Río Santa from Caraz (20min by taxi), set on the lower slopes of the Cordillera Negra, the small settlement of **HUATA** is a typical rural village with regular truck connections from the market area in Caraz. It serves as a good starting point for a number of easy walks, such as the 8km stroll up to the unassuming lakes of Yanacocha and Huaytacocha or, perhaps more interestingly, north about 5km along a path up Cerro Muchanacoc to the small Inca ruins of Cantu.

Laguna Parón

Buses and colectivos (6am; S/5 one way) travel from Caraz market up to Pueblo Parón, from where it's a hike of 9km (3hr) up to the lake. The last transport back from Pueblo Parón to Caraz is usually at noon–1pm. Thus, to make it in a day, tours are the better option

Some 30km, more or less, east of Caraz, the deep-blue **Laguna Parón** (4185m) is sunk resplendently into a gigantic glacial cirque, hemmed in on three sides by some of the

Cordillera Blanca's highest icecaps. A short walk east gives views of the pyramid peak of **Artesonraju**, the supposed inspiration for the Paramount Picture's logo swirling with stars.

ARRIVAL AND DEPARTURE — CARAZ

By bus Most of the bus offices are along jirones Daniel Villar and Cordova, within a block or two of the Plaza de Armas: Chinachasuyo serves Trujillo; Empresa Turismo goes to Lima and Chimbote; Ancash to Lima; Movil Tours to Huraz and Lima; Region Norte runs buses to Yungay, Huaraz and Recuay; and Transporte Moreno to Chimbote.

By colectivo Colectivos for Huaraz leave from just behind the market roughly every 30min (1hr 30min; S/10). Services from Yungay arrive every 15–30min (20min; S/2).

By taxi Taxis are your best bet for visiting the local sites; they can be found most days at the Plaza de Armas.

INFORMATION AND TOUR OPERATORS

Tourist information The office in the Plaza de Armas (Mon–Sat 7.45am–1pm & 2.30–5.30pm; ⊤043 391 029) stocks maps and brochures covering local attractions and some of the hikes (including the relatively demanding 6–8hr Patapata walk).

Pony's Expeditions Jr Sucre 1266, Plaza de Armas ⊤043 391 642, Ⓦponyexpeditions.com. A very professional organization that both fits out and guides climbing, trekking and mountain-biking expeditions in the area. An excellent source of local trekking and climbing information, it also runs treks in other regions, such as the Cordillera Huayhuash, the Inca Trail and Ausangate.

Apu Aventura Psj 9 no. 116 Parque Plazuela La Merced, Barrio Yanachaca ⊤043 391 130, Ⓦwww.apuaventura.pe. Another excellent local option, Apu Aventura organizes guides, porters, cooks and equipment for expeditions in the Cordillera Blanca and elsewhere in Peru.

ACCOMMODATION

★ **Apu EcoLodge** C Jabon Rumi ⊤995 194 288; map p.334. About 2km north of town on the 3N, the eight apartments and bungalows here sleep a minimum of four guests, so it's best for groups, but as a whole, the establishment is like a sort of Peruvian oasis, with plenty of space, an organic garden, a patio with stone oven and fire pit, and a climbing wall and a menagerie of small animals to keep you entertained. S/150

Hostal Chavín Jr San Martín 1135 ⊤043 391 171; map p.334. Close to the plaza, clean and well organized, this hostel is good value, and some rooms have a private bathroom. Breakfast included, and travel assistance also available. S/80

Hostal Perla de los Andes Jr Daniel Villar 179, Plaza de Armas ⊤043 392 007, Ⓔhostalperladelosandes@hotmail.com; map p.334. The balcony rooms at *Perla* have fantastic views onto the Plaza de Armas, but unfortunately suffer from street noise, even late at night. Bring earplugs or choose one of the equally comfortable inside rooms. All have hot water, private bathroom and TV. There's also a very nice breakfast restaurant. S/55

Hostal San Marco Jr San Martín 1133, Plaza de Armas ⊤956 997 170; map p.334. A great place to rest, close to the action. Quiet, light-filled back rooms look onto a courtyard, and boast soft beds, and bathrooms with good hot water. S/50

Los Pinos Lodge Psj 9 #116 Parque Plazuela La Merced, Barrio Yanachaca ⊤043 391 130; map p.334. One of the least expensive options in town, *Los Pinos Lodge* is a youth hostel that also offers camping spaces. There are shared rooms and also private ones. Camping/person S/10 per person, dorms S/20, doubles S/50

Pony's Lodge Jr Sucre 1266, Plaza de Armas ⊤043 391 642; map p.334. Above the tour operator, the conveniently located and recently opened *Pony's* offers rooms with new private baths and hot showers, plus breakfast. S/45

EATING

Café de Rat Jr Sucre 1266 ⊤043 391 642; map p.334. Just down at the bottom southwestern edge of the Plaza de Armas, this café serves decent pasta, pizza, pancakes and vegetarian food, as well as having a dartboard, maps, guidebooks and music. Mon–Sat 8.30am–9pm.

Café La Terraza Jr Sucre 1107 ⊤043 301 226; map p.334. The huge portions of Peruvian, Italian and American staples here are great value, with daily specials of several courses just S/8. Mon–Sat 8.30am–9pm.

Cafétería El Turista Jr San Martín 1133; map p.334. A great place for early morning hot snacks, full breakfasts and coffee. The staff are friendly and the service is good. Daily 6.30am–noon & 5–8pm.

La Pizza del Abuelo Jr Antonio Raimondi 425 ⊤043 968 752 971; map p.334. Just a small stone's throw from the plaza, this Italian café is good for snacks and pasta, and of course, tasty pizzas (S/4 a slice, S/28 whole). Daily 6am–11pm.

Cañon del Pato

One of Peru's most exciting roads runs north from Caraz to Huallanca, reached by daily buses from Huaraz squeezing through the spectacular **Cañon del Pato** (Duck's Canyon). An enormous rocky gorge cut from solid rock, its impressive path curves around the Cordillera Negra for most of the 50km between Caraz and Huallanca. Sheer cliff-faces rise thousands of metres on either side while the road passes through some 39 tunnels – an average of one every kilometre. Situated within the canyon is one of Peru's most important hydroelectric power plants; the heart of these works, invisible from the road, is buried 600m deep in the cliff wall. Unfortunately, the road is often closed for a number of reasons – causes include terrorists, bandits, landslides in the rainy season or just the sheer poor quality of the road surface. Much of the first section has been improved in recent years, but from Huallanca to Chimbote (140km on, after the road branches off west at Yuramarca) it's more like a dry riverbed than a dirt track. Check with the tourist office in Huaraz and local bus companies about the physical and political condition of the road before attempting this journey. Staying on the same track instead will bring you through the valley to Corongo and the Callejón de Conchucos.

Callejón de Conchucos

To the east of the Cordillera Blanca, roughly parallel to the Callejón de Huaylas, runs another long natural corridor, the **Callejón de Conchucos**. Virtually inaccessible in the wet season, and off the beaten track even for the most hardened of backpackers, the valley represents quite a challenge, and while it features the town of **Pomabamba** in the north and the spectacular ruins at **Chavín de Huantar** just beyond its southern limit, there's little of interest between the two. The villages of **Piscobamba** (Valley or Plain of the Birds) and **Huari** are likely to appeal only as food stops on the long haul (141km) through barren mountains between Pomabamba and Chavín.

Brief history

The Callejón de Conchucos was out of bounds to travellers between 1988 and 1993, when it was under almost complete Sendero Luminoso **terrorist control**; many of the locals were forced to flee the valley after actual or threatened violence from the terrorists. The region's more distant history was equally turbulent and cut it off from the rest of Peru, particularly from the seat of colonial and Republican power on the coast. Until the Conquest, this region was home to one of the fiercest ancient tribes – the **Conchucos** – who surged down the Santa Valley and besieged the Spanish city of Trujillo in 1536. By the end of the sixteenth century, however, even the fearless Conchuco warriors had been reduced to virtual slavery by the colonial *encomendero* system.

Pomabamba

The small town of **POMABAMBA**, 3000m up in dauntingly hilly countryside, is surrounded by little-known archeological remains that display common roots with Chavín de Huantar; you can contact Pony's Expeditions in Caraz (see page 335) for further information on these, as well as maps, equipment and advice on trekking in this region. Today the town makes an excellent trekking base; from here you can connect with the **Llanganuco-to-Santa Cruz Loop** (see page 332) by following tracks southwest to either Colcabamba or Punta Unión. Alternatively, for a hard day's hike above Pomabamba, you can walk up to the stone remains of **Yaino**, an immense fortress of megalithic rock. On a clear day you can just about make out this site from the

Plaza de Armas in Pomabamba; it appears as a tiny rocky outcrop high on the distant horizon. The climb takes longer than you may imagine, but locals can point out short cuts along the way.

ARRIVAL AND DEPARTURE — POMABAMBA

By bus Direct Empresa Los Andes buses to Pomabamba leave from the Plaza de Armas in Yungay at 8.30–9am, while bus companies Renzo and El Veloz in Huaraz go to Piscobamba and Pomabamba. Alternatively, you can get here from Huaraz via Chavín, on a bus from Lima that comes north up the Callejón de Conchucos more or less every other day.

ACCOMMODATION

Alojamiento Estrada C Huaraz 209 ☎043 504 615. Located just one block from the small main plaza, this place is basic, but pleasant and clean. S/30

Hotel El Mirador Jirones Moqueca and Centenario ☎043 451 067. Neat little tile-decorated inn, with friendly proprietors and a pleasant view down into the town centre that's the reward for making the short but steep climb up. S/40

Chavín de Huantar

Chavín • Tues–Sun 9am–4pm • S/15 • ☎043 754 042

A three- to four-hour journey from Huaraz, and only 30km southeast of Huari (see page 301), the magnificent temple complex of **Chavín De Huantar** is the most important Peruvian site associated with the **Chavín** cult (see page 340). Although partially destroyed by earthquakes, floods and erosion from the Río Mosna, enough of the ruins survive to make them a fascinating sight and one of the most important ones in Peru's pre-history. Though the **Sala de Exposición** here features ceramics, textiles and stone pieces relating to the cultural influences of the Chavín, Huaras, Recuay and Huari, it is the Chavín culture that evolved and elaborated its own brand of religious cultism on and around this magnificent site during the first millennium BC. This religious cult also influenced subsequent cultural development throughout Peru, right up until the Spanish Conquest some 2500 years later.

The pretty **village** of **CHAVÍN DE HUANTAR**, with its whitewashed walls and traditional tiled roofs, is just a couple of hundred metres from the ruins and has a reasonable supply of basic amenities.

Brief history

The original temple was built here around 900 BC, though it was not until around 400 BC that the complex was substantially enlarged and its cultural style fixed. Some archeologists claim that the specific layout of the temple, a U-shaped ceremonial

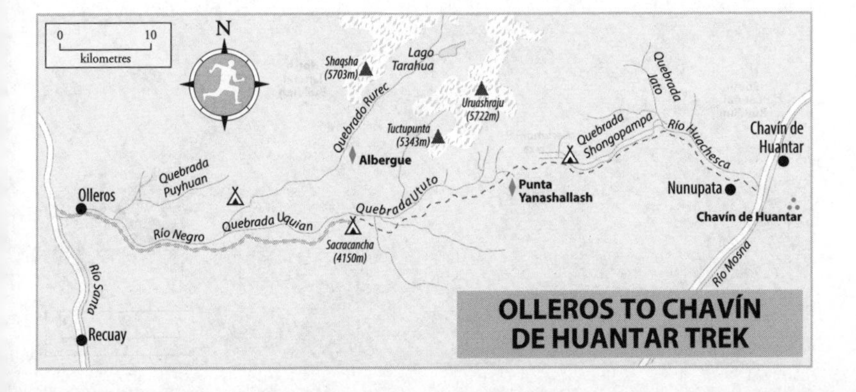

courtyard facing east and based around a raised stone platform, was directly influenced by what was, in 1200 BC, the largest architectural monument in the New World, at Sechin Alto (see page 344). By 300 BC, Sechin Alto had been abandoned and Chavín was at the height of its power and one of the world's largest religious centres, with about three thousand resident priests and temple attendants. The U-shaped temples were probably dedicated to powerful mountain spirits or deities, who controlled meteorological phenomena, in particular rainfall, vital to the survival and wealth of the people.

The temple area

The complex's main temple building consists of a central rectangular block with two wings projecting out to the east. The large, southern wing, known as the **Castillo**, is the most conspicuous feature of the site: massive, almost pyramid-shaped, the platform was built of dressed stone with gargoyles attached, though few remain now.

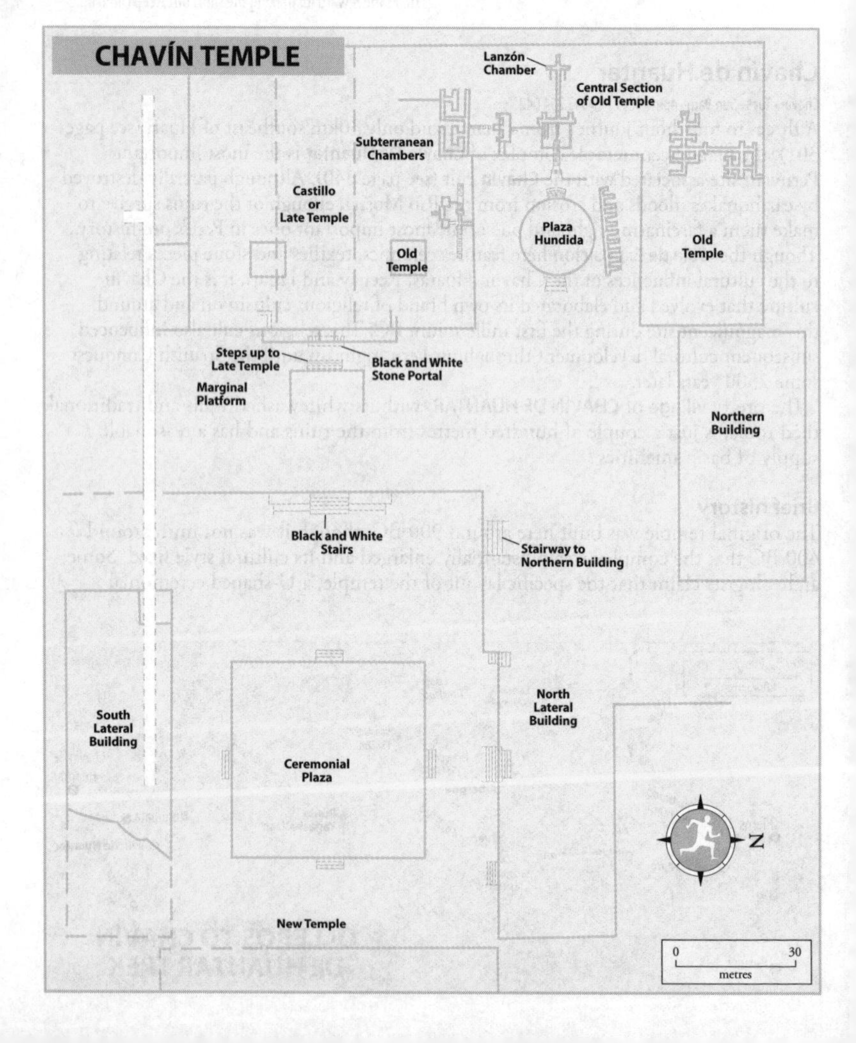

GETTING TO CHAVÍN DE HUANTAR

If you have the time, the journey to **Chavín de Huantar** is almost as rewarding as exploring the archeological site itself; the road has to climb out of the Huaraz Valley and cross over the mountains before dropping quite steeply to the modern-day village and remains of Chavín. The route, as detailed below, is not for the faint of heart. There is also the option of reaching the ruins on foot from Olleros.

THE ROAD FROM HUARAZ

The vast majority of people approach the temple complex from **Huaraz**; buses turn off the main Huaraz-to-Lima road at the town of Catac. From here they take a poorly maintained road that crosses over the small Río Yana Yacu (Black Water River) and then starts climbing to the beautiful lake of **Querococha** (*quero* is Quechua for "teeth", and relates to the teeth-like rock formation visible nearby), which looks towards two prominent mountain peaks – Yanamarey and Pucaraju ("Red Glacier" in Quechua). From here the road, little more than a track now, climbs further before passing through the **Tunél de Cahuish**, which cuts through the solid rock of a mountain to emerge in the Callejón de Conchucos, to some spectacular but quite terrifying views. A couple of the more dangerous and precipitous curves in the road are known as the Curva del Diablo and Salvate Si Puedes ("Save yourself if you can"), from which you can deduce that this journey isn't for the squeamish or for vertigo sufferers.

OLLEROS-TO-CHAVÍN DE HUANTAR TREK

If you are feeling adventurous there is a two- to four-day trail over the hills from **Olleros** to Chavín. It follows the Río Negro up to Punta Yanashallash (4700m), cuts down into the Marañón watershed along the Quebrada Shongopampa, and where this meets the Jato stream coming from the north, the route follows the combined waters (from here known as the Río Huachesca) straight down, southwest to the Chavín ruins another 1500m below. It's quite a **hike**, so take maps and ideally a guide and pack-llamas (see page 328). A good account of this walk is given in Hilary Bradt's *Backpacking and Trekking in Peru and Bolivia* (see page 522).

Some way in front of the Castillo, down three main flights of steps, the **Plaza Hundida**, or "sunken plaza", covers about 250 square metres with a rectangular, stepped platform to either side. Here, the thousands of pilgrims thought to have worshipped at Chavín would gather during the appropriate fiestas. And it was here that the famous Tello Obelisk, now in the Museo de Arqueología, Antropología e Historia in Lima, was found, next to an altar in the shape of a jaguar and bedecked with seven cavities forming a pattern similar to that of the Orion constellation.

Standing in the Plaza Hundida, facing towards the Castillo, you'll see on your right the **original temple**, now just a palatial ruin dwarfed by the neighbouring Castillo. It was first examined by Julio Tello in 1919 when it was still buried under cultivated fields; during 1945 a vast flood reburied most of it and the place was damaged again by the 1970 earthquake and heavy rains in 1983. Among the fascinating recent finds from the area are bone snuff tubes, beads, pendants, needles, ceremonial shells (imported from Ecuador) and some quartz crystals associated with ritual sites. One quartz crystal covered in red pigment was found in a grave, placed after death in the mouth of the deceased.

The subterranean chambers

Behind the original temple, two entrances lead to a series of underground passages and **subterranean chambers**. The passage on the right leads down to an underground chamber, containing the awe-inspiring Lanzon, a prism-shaped 4.5m block of carved white granite that tapers down from a broad feline head to a point stuck in the ground. The entrance on the left takes you into the labyrinthine inner chambers, which run underneath the Castillo on several levels connected by ramps and steps. In the seven major subterranean rooms, you'll need a torch to get a decent look at the carvings and the granite sculptures (even when the electric lighting is switched on), while all around you can hear the sound of water dripping.

Another large stone slab that was originally discovered at Chavín in 1873 – the Estela Raymondi – is now in the same museum as the Tello Obelisk; this was the first and most spectacular of all the impressive carved stones to be found. The most vivid of the carvings remaining at the site are the **gargoyles** (known as *cabeza clavos*) along the outer stone walls of the Castillo sector, guardians of the temple, which again display feline and bird-like characteristics.

ARRIVAL AND INFORMATION — CHAVÍN DE HUANTAR

By bus Empresa Condor de Chavín, Empresa Huascarán, Chavín Express and Empresa Sandoval buses leave Huaraz daily around 6am (3–4hr; S/10–15 one way) for Chavín, while all the tour companies (see page 318) in Huaraz offer a slightly faster, though more expensive, service (3hr; S/35–50 /return). Getting back to Huaraz or Catac, there are buses daily from Chavín, more or less on the hour from 3 to 6pm.

Tourist information There's a small tourist information office on the corner of the Plaza de Armas, next to the

THE CHAVÍN CULT

The **Chavín cult**, whose iconography spread across much of Peru, was not a coherent pan-Peruvian religion, but more of a widespread – and unevenly interpreted – cult of the feline god. Chavín had a strong impact on the Paracas culture and later on the Nazca and Mochica civilizations. Theories as to the origin of its inspiration range from extraterrestrial intervention to the more likely infiltration of ideas and individuals or entire tribes from Central America. There is a resemblance between the ceramics found at Chavín and those of a similar date from Tlatilco in **Mexico**, yet there are no comparable Mexican stone constructions as ancient as these Peruvian wonders. More probably, according to Peruvian archeologist Julio Tello (1880–1947), the cult initially came up into the Andes from the Amazon Basin via the Marañón Valley. The inspiration for the beliefs themselves, which appear through totemic or animistic gods and demons, may well have come from visionary experiences sparked by the ingestion of **hallucinogens**: one of the stone reliefs at Chavín portrays a feline deity or fanged warrior holding a section of the psychotropic mescalin cactus San Pedro, still used by *curanderos* today for the invocation of the spirit world. This feline deity was almost certainly associated with the shamanic practice of visionary transformation from human into animal form for magical and healing purposes, usually achieved by the use of hallucinogenic brews; the most powerful animal form that could be assumed, of course, was the big cat, whether a puma or a jaguar.

CHAVÍN ICONOGRAPHY

Most theories about the **iconography** of Chavín de Huantar's stone slabs, all of which are very intricate, distinctive in style and highly abstract, agree that the Chavíns worshipped three major gods: the moon (represented by a fish), the sun (depicted as an eagle or a hawk) and an overlord, or creator divinity, normally shown as a fanged cat, possibly a jaguar. It seems likely that each god was linked with a distinct level of the Chavín cosmos: the fish with the underworld, the eagle with the celestial forces and the cat with earthly power. Ethnographic evidence from the Amazon Basin suggests that each of these main gods may have also been associated with a different subgroup within the Chavín tribe or priesthood as a whole.

Chavín itself may or may not have been the centre of the movement, but it was at the very least an outstanding **ceremonial focus** for what was an early agricultural society, thriving on relatively recently domesticated foods as well as cotton, and well-positioned topographically to control the exchange of plants, materials and ideas between communities in the Amazon, Andes and Pacific coast. The name "Chavín" comes from the Quechua *chaupin*, meaning navel or focal point, and the complex might have been a sacred shrine to which natives flocked in pilgrimage during festivals, much as they do today, visiting important *huacas* in the sierra at specific times in the annual agricultural cycle. The appearance of the **Orion constellation** on Chavín carvings fits this theory, since it appears on the skyline just prior to the traditional harvest period in the Peruvian mountains.

market, though it doesn't have regular hours. Detailed advice and information on the site and hiking in the area are best obtained from the relevant organizations in Huaraz (see page 318).

ACCOMMODATION AND EATING

It's sometimes possible to **camp** by the Baños Quercos thermal springs (ask for an update at the Huaraz Tourist Office, tour agencies or in Chavín village), 2km up the valley and a 20min stroll from the village.

La Casona Wiracocha 130 043 454 116, lacasonachavin.com.pe. Right next door to the town hall on the plaza, this relatively small hostel offers private bathrooms and has a well-kept patio. S/60

Hotel Inca Wiracocha 170 043 454 021, hotelincachavin.com. A pleasant place with small, well-tended gardens and a very friendly atmosphere; some rooms have private showers. S/65

La Portada C 17 de Enero Sur 311. Housed in an ageing mansion, *La Portada* offers good, simple, local food including soups, meat and rice. The service is very welcoming and there are some tables in the courtyard. Mon–Sat 10.30am–6pm.

Restaurant Chavín Turístico C 17 de Enero Sur 439. As the name suggests, this place has a menu geared towards visitors to town. There is a small central patio garden, service is swift and the ambiance pleasant. Daily 7.30am–8pm.

Restaurant La Ramada C 17 de Enero Sur 577. Centrally located and popular with locals and tourists alike, with fresh trout served most days. Daily 8am–8pm.

North from Chavín

There are buses every hour from Chavín to San Marcos (20min; S/5) and Huari (1hr; S/8), or you can walk to San Marcos in well under 2hr; to continue on to Pomabamba from Huari, there are buses every other day, usually leaving at 9pm (7hr; S/18)

Some 8km north of Chavín is the lovely village of **San Marcos**, a good base for mountain hiking. From San Marcos you can climb up another 300m in altitude to the smaller community of **Carhuayoc**, a 100-year-old village whose population specializes in the production of fine textiles – mainly blankets and rugs (it's a 9hr return journey). About 35km from San Marcos, the town of **Huari** is a good base for a short trek to the scenic Lago Purhuay; it's only 8km from the town and a climb of some 400m, but it usually takes between five and six hours to get there and back.

Cordillera Huayhuash

To the south of Huaraz, the **Cordillera Huayhuash** offers much less frequented but just as stunning trekking trails as those in the Cordillera Blanca. Most treks start in the small town of **Chiquián**, 2400m above sea level. The most popular trek hereabouts is the **Huayhuash Trek** (see page 342), which leaves Chiquián heading for Llamac and the entire Cordillera loop. There is also an alternative trek from Chiquián that is much easier (see below).

The mountains here, although slightly lower than the Cordillera Blanca and covering a much smaller area, nevertheless rise breathtakingly to 6634m at the **Nevada Yerupajá**, some 50km southeast of Chiquián as the crow flies. Yerupajá actually forms the watershed between the Cordillera Huayhuash to the north and the lower-altitude Cordillera Raura to the south. Large and stunning lakes, flocks of alpaca, herds of cattle and some sheep can be seen along the way. High levels of fitness and some experience are required for hiking or climbing in this region and it's always best to tackle it as part of a team, or at the very least to have a **local guide** along. The guide will help to avoid the rather irritating dogs that look after the animals in these remote hills and his presence will also provide protection against the possible, but unlikely, threat of robbery.

Chiquián

A very small and traditional Andean town, **CHIQUIÁN** is quiet (except during the town's festivals), reserved and very pretty. One popular Huayhuash trek from Chiquián follows a route from **Llamac** to Pampa de Llamac (via a very difficult pass), then on to the lake of **Jahuacocha**, where trout fishing is possible. Taking about five days, the scenery on the trek can only be described as breathtaking; the hiking itself is quite hard. The only downside is that you have to walk Chiquián–Llamac twice, and between Rondoy and Llamac a mining company has destroyed much of the beautiful countryside, apparently also polluting the river as well as building a rather ugly road.

THE HUAYHUASH TREK

One of the least-visited and most difficult trails, the **Huayhuash Trek** lies at altitudes between 2750m and 5000m. It covers a distance of 164–186km and takes some fourteen days to hike (give or take a few, depending on your fitness, walking ability and desire). Rated as Class 4 (difficult), the route, as the name suggests, starts and finishes in Chiquián. Note that maps are essential and local guides with mules advisable. It is also possible to do the trek in sixteen days if you'd like to take things a little easier.

Day 1: Chiquián to Llamac This is an easy first-day walk. The wide and clearly marked path takes hikers to the far end of the valley. After crossing three times from one valley to the other, a short way up will lead walkers to Llamac, a typical highland village.

Day 2: Llamac to Matacancha A two-hour descent leads to another little Andean village called Pocpa, from where walkers must take the left bank of the river and start climbing to the campsite. The first mountain that appears is the Ninashanca at 5607m (18,391ft). The camping spot is at the far end of this dry and treeless valley.

Day 3: Matacancha to Janca The first ascent to the Cacananpunta Pass (La Abra Cacananpunta) at 4880m (16,006ft) is difficult and best reached before noon; descent to the camp does not require a major effort.

Day 4: Janca to Carhuacocha This day involves significant trekking up and back down, offering views of almost the entire scenery of the Cordillera Huayhuash. Arriving at the lakeside camp beside Carhuacocha, the Cordillera is clearly visible.

Day 5: Carhuacocha to Carnicero and Rinconada Leaving the lake at Carhuacocha in the morning, the next pass opens out to the Valle Carnicero. A not very steep, and beautiful, climb takes the hiker to the low Rinconada pass that forms visually spectacular rocky scenery.

Day 6: Carnicero to Huayhuash and Altuspata The descent continues to the next valley via the pass of Punta Carnicero (4600m), passing several small lakes and rivers along the way to the village of Huayhuash (4350m) and continuing to Altuspata, which has good camping.

Day 7: Altuspata to Lago Viconga Leaving the Altuspata campsite first thing, the ascent continues towards one of the highest passes on the route, which leads the way to the Lago Viconga. Walking around the lake through the narrow valley one reaches the next camping spot.

Day 8: Lago Viconga to Valle Huanacpatay A very long way and one of the toughest hikes on the route, this is where one crosses the Abra de Cuyoc pass at 5100m (16,728ft) next to the mountain of Nevado Cuyoc and close to Puscanturpa at 5442m (17,854ft). Descending from the pass, a small, steep and difficult corridor leads to the Valle Huanacpatay.

Days 9 and 10: Abra del Diablo Mudo Two days must be set aside for climbing two of the peaks around the Abra del Diablo Mudo pass to reach Huanacpatay (4500m).

Day 11: Huanacpatay to Huatiac Another long trekking day, but downhill overall, takes you from the high Valle Huanacpatay to a lower one at Huatiac (3800m). After a deep descent into the endless valley of the Huallapa River one starts seeing trees and plants, with the trail passing close by Huallapa village.

Day 12: Huatiac to Jahuacocha Leaving the pleasant Huatiac campsite, the trail continues upwards again to the Abra del Diablo Mudo pass at 5000m (16,400ft), an area bereft of plant life. Everything is downhill from the pass until the lake at Jahuacocha and past it, to camp.

Day 13: Jahuacocha to Llamac After almost two weeks the path crosses again into Llamac village. There are two paths from Jahuacocha which lead back to Llamac's campsite: one is direct and very steep and is done in a shorter time, while the second one is longer but with no major or sudden descents.

Day 14: Llamac to Chiquián and Huaraz A repeated stretch, which also formed the first day's hike: a tough but marvellous trek through the Cordillera Huayhuash.

CHIQUIÁN FIESTAS

For about a week starting In late August there are some colourful fiestas in the town, for the **Virgen de Santa Rosa**, during the last day of which there is always a **bullfight**, with the local football stadium being transformed into an arena. The aim of the game is, as with most rural Peruvian bullfights, just to play with the bull (without hurting him) and this is done not only by the *toreador*, but by anyone who feels the urge to get involved (local youth, drunk men); they can challenge the bull with their poncho, which guarantees a lot of excitement and fun, with the public scattering when the irritated bull comes too close.

More information can be obtained from the Casa de Guías in Huaraz. Most people who come this far, though, prefer to do the entire **Huayhuash Trek**, which entails a tough couple of weeks, though the really fit might manage it in ten days at a push.

ARRIVAL AND DEPARTURE — CHIQUIÁN

By bus Chiquián is easily reached by bus with Empresa Rapido (T 04 342 2887), at Jr 28 de Julio 202 in Huaraz (6 daily; 3hr).

ACCOMMODATION AND EATING

After Chiquián it's virtually impossible to buy food, so it's a good idea to get most of this in **Huaraz** or in **Lima**, before arriving, supplementing when you're here with extras such as bread, dry biscuits, dairy products (including good local cheeses), rice and pasta.

Hotel Los Nogales Jr Comercio 1301 T 043 447 121, W hotelnogaleschiquian.com. Friendly and safe, with an inviting bright blue exterior, with a choice of rooms with TV, and with or without private bathroom. There's a cafeteria here, too. S/35

El Refugio de Bolognesi Tarapaca 471. This is the best of a limited set of small restaurants, offering perhaps the nicest set-lunch menus. Daily 7am–7pm.

San Miguel Jr Comercio 233 T 043 447 001. Arranged around a patio, this rustic place has reasonably clean and comfortable beds and a nice little garden. S/40

The Ancash coast

The **Ancash coast** is a largely barren desert strip that quickly rises into Andean foothills when you head east and away from the ocean. Most people going this way will be travelling between Lima and either Huaraz (6–7hr) or Trujillo (8hr). Huaraz is reached by a turn-off from the Panamerican Highway following a well-maintained road that climbs furiously to the breathless heights of the Callejón de Huaylas. There is a small beach resort near **Barranca**, and **Casma** and **Chimbote** have some intriguing archeological sites nearby and offer alternative routes up to Huaraz.

Barranca and around

The only likely reason to stop off at **BARRANCA** is as part of a visit to the nearby **Fortress of Paramonga**, the best preserved of all Peru's coastal outposts, built originally to guard the southern limit of the powerful Chimu Empire. To explore the ruins, it's best to base yourself in the town, where there are a few simple hotels and two or three places to eat.

Five kilometres north of Barranca is the smaller town of **PATAVILCA**, where Bolívar planned his campaign to liberate Peru. The main paved road to Huaraz and the Cordillera Blanca leaves the Panamerican Highway here and heads up into the Andes.

Fortaleza de Paramonga

7km north of Barranca • Daily 9am–1pm & 2–5pm • S/8 • To get from Barranca to Paramonga, take the efficient local bus service, which leaves from the garage at the northern end of town, every hour or so (20min; S/2.50)

The **Fortaleza de Paramonga** (Paramonga Fortress) sits less than 1km from the ocean and looks in many ways like a feudal castle. Constructed entirely from adobe, its walls within walls run around the contours of a natural hillock and are similar in style and situation to the Templo del Sol of Pachacamac (see page 97). As you climb up from the road, you'll see the main entrance to the fortress on the right by the site's small **museum** and ticket office.

Heading into the labyrinthine **ruins**, you'll find the rooms and sections get smaller and narrower the closer you get to the top – and the original **palace-temple.** From here there are commanding views over the desert coast and across vast sugarcane fields, formerly belonging to the US-owned Grace Corporation, once owners of nearly a third of Peru's sugar production. In contrast to the verdant verdure of these fields, irrigated by the Río Fortaleza, the fortress stands out in the landscape like a huge, dusty yellow pyramid.

There are differences of opinion as to whether the fort had a military function or was purely a ritual centre, but as most pre-Conquest cultures built their places of worship around the natural personality of the landscape (rocks, water, geomorphic features and so on), it seems likely that the Chimu built it on an older *huaca* (ancient sacred site), both as a fortified ritual shrine and to mark the southern boundary of their empire. In the late fifteenth century, it was conquered by the **Incas**, who built a road down from the Callejón de Huaylas. Arriving in 1533 en route from Cajamarca to Pachacamac, Hernando Pizarro, the first Spaniard to see Paramonga, described it as "a strong fort with seven encircling walls painted with many forms both inside and outside, with portals well built like those of Spain and two tigers painted at the principal doorways". There are still red- and yellow-based geometric murals visible on some of the walls in the upper sector, as well as some chessboard-style patterns.

ARRIVAL AND ACCOMMODATION — BARRANCA

By bus/colectivo Nearly all buses and colectivos on their way between Lima and Trujillo or Huaraz stop at Barranca. There are several buses daily to Casma (2hr), Chimbote (3hr), Huaraz (4–5hr) and Lima (3hr) from here.

Hotel Jefferson C Jose Olaya 228 ⓣ01 235 2184. An inexpensive establishment with quite comfortable rooms. S/70

Casma and around

The town of **CASMA**, 170km north of Barranca, marks the mouth of the well-irrigated Sechin River Valley. Surrounded by corn and cotton fields, this small settlement is peculiar in that most of its buildings are just one storey high and all are modern. Formerly the port for the Callejón de Huaylas, the town was razed by the 1970 earthquake – the epicentre was just offshore. There's not a lot of interest here and little reason to break your journey, other than to try the local speciality of duck ceviche (flakes of duck meat soaked deliciously in lime and orange juice) or to explore the nearby ruins, such as the temple complex of Sechin, the ancient fort of Chanquillo and the Pañamarca pyramid, 20km north.

Sechin

5km southeast of Casma • Daily: Ruins 8am–5pm; Museo de Sitio Max Uhle 8am–5.30pm • S/5 • A 1hr walk from Casma, south along the Panamericana Norte for 3km, then up the signposted side road to Huaraz for about the same distance. Otherwise take a *mototaxi* (S/5 one way) or a taxi (around US$10–15 return, including a wait of an hour or so). Some local colectivos come here in the mornings from Casma's market area

A partially reconstructed temple complex, the main section of the **Sechin ruins** is unusually stuck at the bottom of a hill, and consists of an outer wall clad with around ninety monolithic slabs engraved with sometimes monstrous representations of particularly nasty and bellicose warriors, along with their mutilated sacrificial victims or prisoners of war. Some of these stones, dating from between 1800 and 800 BC, stand 4m high. Hidden behind the standing stones is an interesting inner sanctuary – a rectangular building consisting of a series of superimposed platforms with a central stairway on either side. The site also contains the small **Museo de Sitio Max Uhle**, which displays photographs of the complex plus some of the artefacts uncovered here, as well as information and exhibits on Moche, Huari, Chimu, Casma and Inca cultures.

Some of the ceremonial centres at Sechin were built before 1400 BC, including the massive, U-shaped **Sechin Alto complex** (21km away near Buena Vista Alta; not accessible via public transport), at the time the largest construction in the entire Americas. Ancient coastal constructions usually favoured adobe as a building material, making this site rare in its extensive use of granite stone. Around 300m long by 250m wide, the massive stone-faced platform pre-dates the similar ceremonial centre at Chavín de Huantar, possibly by as much as four hundred years. This means that Chavín could not have been the original source of the temple architectural style, and that much of the iconography and legends associated with what is known as the Chavín cultural phase of Peruvian prehistory actually began 3500 years ago down here on the desert coast.

Pampa de Llamas and Mpjeque

Daily 24hr • Free • Both sites are best visited from Casma by taxi (around S/30 return)

Several lesser-known archeological sites dot the Sechin Valley, where the maze of ancient sandy roadways constituted an important pre-Inca junction. The remains of a huge complex of dwellings can be found on the **Pampa de Llamas**, though all you will see nowadays are the walls of adobe huts, deserted more than a thousand years ago. At **Mojeque**, you can see a terraced pyramid with stone stairs and feline and snake designs.

Fortaleza de Chanquillo

Daily 24hr • Free • From Casma your taxi should take the turn east from the Panamericana Norte at Km 361; the driver will have to wait since it is unlikely there will be others at the site (S/15 one way, plus S/5–10 for the wait)

Some 12km southeast of Casma lies the ruined, possibly pre-Mochica fort of **Chanquillo**, around which you can wander freely. It's an amazing ruin set in a commanding position on a barren hill, with four walls in concentric rings and watchtowers in the middle, keeping an eye over the desert below. Less than one kilometre below the fort stand thirteen towers in a long, lonely line.

Pañamarca

Daily 24hr • Free • Best reached by taxi from the Plaza de Armas in Casma for around S/20

At Km 395 of the Panamericana Norte, a turn-off on the right leads, 11km on, to the ruined adobe pyramid of **Pañamarca**, an impressive monument to the Mochica culture, dating from around 500 AD. Three large painted panels can be seen here, and on a nearby wall a long procession of warriors has been painted – but all this artwork has been badly damaged by rain.

ARRIVAL AND DEPARTURE — CASMA

By bus Turismo Chimbote buses, at block 1, Av Luís Ormeño, run at least every hour to Lima (6hr) and Chimbote (40min) and Tepsa, leaving from a station on the Panamericana Sur, has a daily Lima bus at 12.15am; for Huaraz, Huandoy buses, Av Luís Ormeño 121 (T 043 411 633), take the fastest normal route, finishing at Caraz. Turismo Erick El Rojo, Av Luís Ormeño 145, has five buses daily to Trujillo.

ACCOMMODATION

Hostal Las Aldas Panamericana Norte Km 347 T 01 422 8523, W lasaldas.com. Some 30km from Casma, this fun hostel is located near a pleasant beach at Playa Las Aldas (turn off the Panamericana Norte at Km 345); some of the bungalows face the ocean and are right on the beach. You can also camp for free here, but they charge a nominal fee for services like access bathroom and parking. S/95

Hostal Gregori C Luís Ormeño 530 T 043 580 073. Very clean and quiet hostel with comfortable rooms in a modern building with an airy and pleasant lobby; service is good too. S/55

Hotel El Farol Tupac Amaru 450 043 411 064, hostalfarol@yahoo.com. Just two blocks from the Plaza de Armas, the only hotel in Casma is friendly and clean, with TVs and private bathrooms, a summer pool and a decent restaurant which sometimes serves ceviche *de pato*. S/70

Chimbote

Elderly locals say that **CHIMBOTE** – another 25km beyond the turn-off to the Pañamarca pyramid – was once a beautiful coastal bay, with a rustic fishing port and fine extensive beach. You can still get a sense of this on the southern Panamericana approach, but the smell and industrial sprawl created by the unplanned fishing boom over thirty years ago undeniably dominates the senses. Chimbote has more than thirty **fish-packing factories**, which explains the rather unbearable stench of stale fish. Despite the crisis in the fishing industry since the early 1970s – overfishing and El Niño have led to bans and strict catch limits for fishermen – Chimbote accounts for more than 75 percent of Peru's fishing-related activity. Most travellers stay in Chimbote one night at most; the town is smelly and offers little of interest to visitors, apart perhaps from some attractive **marble sculptures** which adorn the central Boulevard Isla Blanca.

Chimbote's development constitutes the country's most spectacular **urban growth** outside Lima. Initially stimulated by the Chimbote–Huallanca rail line (built in 1922), a nearby hydroelectric plant and government planning for an anticipated rise in the anchovy- and tuna-fishing industry, the population grew rapidly from 5000 in 1940 to 60,000 in 1961 (swollen by squatter settlers from the mountains). However, Chimbote was virtually razed to the ground during the 1970 earthquake (see page 330).

ARRIVAL AND INFORMATION — CHIMBOTE

By plane The airport, where you can get daily flights to (or from) Lima and Trujillo, can be found at Km 421 (043 311 844 or 043 311 062).

By bus Most important is knowing how to get out of town. Most buses call at and leave from the Terminal Terrestre El Chimbador, a few kilometres south of the city centre on Av de los Pescadores on the Carretera Panamericana. All the coastal buses including Cruz del Sur, travelling north to Trujillo (3hr north) and south to Lima along the Panamerican Hwy stop here; it can be very busy. Also from here, Movil Tours bus to Huaraz, Carhuaz, and Yungay, five times daily, and night buses to Caraz. Turismo Huaraz run direct Chimbote–Huaraz buses, twice daily (one daytime, one at night) from Av Pardo 1713 (043 321 235). Turismo Chimbote, Expresso Huandoy and Trans Moreno all run daily buses to Huaraz via Patavilca and Casma, as well as (mostly nightly) services to Caraz via Huallanca and the Cañon del Pato (on a very rough road) from Jr Pardo, between jirones José Galvez and Manuel Ruiz.

By colectivo Colectivos to Trujillo (2–3hr away) leave regularly from C Enrique Palacios, near the Plaza de Armas, while colectivos to Lima hang around on Manuel Ruiz, one block towards the sea off Av Prado.

Tourist information Bolognesi 421 (Mon–Sat 9am–5.30pm). Can advise on transport to nearby sites and sometimes stocks town and regional maps. Limited information in Spanish can also be found at chimboteonline.com.

ACCOMMODATION

Hostal La Casona de Buenos Aires Av Pacifico Mz L2 Lt 19, Nuevo Chimbote 043 316 726. Located in a southern suburb, a stylish and very comfortable hotel with all modern conveniences and a restaurant. S/60

Real Gran Chimú Av José Galvez 109 043 328 104. A big red box dominating the Plaza 28 de Julio, this hotel is reasonably priced, offering comfortable rooms and mod cons, and its restaurant, though not cheap, serves some of the best food found along this part of the coast; try the ceviche or the criolla dishes such as *aji de gallina*. S/120

The Santa and Viru valleys

The valleys formed by the rivers **Santa** and **Viru** provide relief against the sun-blasted desert on the road north between Chimbote and Trujillo. Despite the bleak terrain and climate the roadside towards Trujillo is fast filling up with new settlements – a kind of ribbon development between two busy markets and population centres. The desert itself, beyond the road, is rarely visited, yet littered with **archeological remains**.

Great Wall of Peru

Daily 24hr • Free • Take any Trujillo bus north from Chimbote along the Panamericana Norte, and get off when you see a bridge over the Río Santa. From here, head upstream for three or four hours and you'll arrive at the best surviving section of the wall, where the piled stone more than 4m high in places

Twenty kilometres north of Chimbote, the Panamericana crosses a rocky outcrop into the Santa Valley, where an enormous defensive wall known as the **Great Wall of Peru** – a stone and adobe structure more than 50km long and thought to be over a thousand years old – rises from the sands of the desert. The enormous structure was first noticed in 1931 by the Shippee-Johnson Aerial Photographic Expedition, and there are many theories about its construction and purpose. Archeologist Julio Tello thought it was pre-Chimu, since it seems unlikely that the Chimu would have built such a lengthy defensive wall so far inside the limits of their empire. It may also, as the historian Garcilaso de la Vega believed, have been built by the Spaniards as a defence against the threat of Inca invasion from the coast or from the Callejón de Huaylas. The wall stretches from Tambo Real near the Río Santa estuary in the west up to Chuqucara in the east, where there are scattered remains of pyramids, fortresses, temples and stone houses.

Further up the valley – albeit far off the beaten track, with no tourism infrastructure whatsoever – lies a double-walled **construction** with outer turrets, discovered by Gene Savoy's aerial expedition in the late 1950s. Savoy reported finding 42 stone-built strongholds in the higher Santa Valley in only two days' flying, evidence that supports historians' claims that this was the most populated valley on the coast prior to the Spanish Conquest. Hard to believe today, it seems more probable if you bear in mind that this desert region, still alive with wildlife such as desert foxes and condors, is fed by the largest and most reliable of the coastal rivers.

Viru

The road between Chimbote and Trujillo runs straight through the Viru Valley's main town – the eponymous **VIRU**, a small place at Km 515 of the Panamericana Norte, with a bridge over the riverbed, which in the dry season looks as though it has not seen rain in decades. The name Viru is believed by many to be the original source of the modern name Peru. According to the chroniclers, the Spanish conquistadores met a raft of fishermen out on the sea here, before landing in Peru. When the Spanish tried to find out from the fishermen where they came from, apparently they said "Viru, Viru".

An impressive cultural centre around 300 AD, when it was occupied by the Gallinazo or Viru people, today the town offers very little to the tourist. The most interesting ruin in the area is the **Grupo Gallinazo** near Tomabal, 24km east of Viru up a side road just north of the town's bridge. Here in the valley you can see the dwellings, murals and pyramids of a significant religious and administrative centre, its internal layout derived from kinship networks (with different clans responsible for different sectors of the settlement). The site covers an area of four square kilometres and archeologists estimate that over ten thousand people sometimes lived here at the same time. You can also make out the adobe walls and ceremonial platform of a Gallinazo temple, on one of the hilltops at Tomabal.

Trujillo and the north

THE CHAN CHAN COMPLEX

Trujillo and the north

Northern Peru is packed with unique treasures – cultural, archeological and natural. Blessed with fewer tourists and better coastal weather than either Lima or the south (particularly in the high season – December to February), the area encompasses city oases along the coast, secluded villages in the Andes – where you may well be the first foreigner to pass through for years – and is brimming with imposing and important pre-Inca sites, some of them only discovered in the last decade or two. For many, the biggest attractions will be the beautiful and trendy beaches or the perfectly formed surf rolling in just offshore. For others, it's the scenery, archeology and chance to get off the beaten tourist trail.

Trujillo is located on the seaward edge of the vast desert plain at the mouth of the Moche Valley. Its attraction lies mainly in its nearby ruins – notably **Chan Chan**, the huge, sacred pyramids of the **Huaca del Sol** and **Huaca de la Luna** and great haul of treasures found at **Huaca El Brujo** – but also partly in the city's colonial centre, and some excellent, laidback outlying beach communities. **Huanchaco**, only 12km from Trujillo, is a good case in point; a fishing village turned surf town fronting on long sandy beaches and with massive ancient ruins just down the road.

There are established bus **touring routes** through the Andean region above Trujillo, all of which present the option of winding through the beautifully situated mountain town of **Cajamarca**. It was here that Pizarro first encountered and captured the Inca Emperor Atahualpa, beginning the Spanish conquest of Peru. Cajamarca is also a springboard for visiting the growing town of **Chachapoyas** and the ruined citadel complex of **Kuélap**, arguably the single most overwhelming pre-Columbian site in Peru. Beyond, there are possible routes down to Amazon headwaters and the jungle towns of **Tarapoto** and even **Iquitos** – long and arduous journeys.

The coastal strip north of Trujillo, up to **Tumbes** by the Ecuadorian border, is for the most part a seemingly endless **desert** plain, interrupted by isolated villages and squatter settlements, but only two substantial towns, **Chiclayo** and **Piura**. Newly discovered archeological sites around Chiclayo possess some of the coast's most important temple ruins, pyramids and nobles' tombs, the latter containing a wealth of precious-metal ceremonial items, and there are some excellent regional museums such as **the Museo Nacional Tumbas Reales de Sipán**, not far from Chiclayo. Northern Peru has the country's best beaches, with party town **Máncora** throbbing at the heart of them and luxurious **Las Pocitas** lazing just next door. To the south are surf getaways **Puerto Chichama**, famous for its curling left, increasingly hipster **Lobitos** and **Cabo Blanco**, whose fishing club once hosted Hemingway, who went there with a team to film parts of the *Old Man and the Sea*. To the north, up to the border with Ecuador, are isolated beach retreats **Punta Sal** and, near Tumbes, **Zorritos**, a growing favourite among Limeño youth.

Trujillo

Just eight hours north of Lima along the Panamerican Highway – also known here as the Panamericana Norte – **TRUJILLO** looks every bit the oasis, standing in a relatively green, irrigated valley bounded by arid desert at the foot of the brown Andes. Despite a long tradition of leftist politics, today Peru's northern capital only sees the occasional street protest, and it is more recognized for its lavish colonial architecture and colourful old mansions. Lively and cosmopolitan, it's small enough to get to know in a couple of days, and is renowned for its friendly citizens. Known as the City of the Eternal Spring, its

MÁNCORA

Highlights

❶ **Complejo Archeológico El Brujo** A day-trip from the city of Trujillo, this collection of *huacas* and enlightening on-site museum are home to resplendant Mochica treasures from 100–800 AD, including the tatooed body of the enigmatic Señora de Cao. See page 370

❷ **Kuélap** Peering over the verdant Utcubamba Valley, this majestic mountaintop citadel rivals Machu Picchu for its setting and archeological interest. See page 390

❸ **Museo Nacional Tumbas Reales de Sipán** An excellent museum whose exhibits include precious objects of gold and silver, plus a replica of the tomb of El Señor de Sipán. See page 403

❹ **Batán Grande** On the eastern edge of the Americas' largest dry forest, and right next to the beautiful Río de la Leche, ancient pyramids act as an impressive monument to the ceremonial heart of Sicán culture. See page 406

❺ **Valley of the Pyramids** Standing in the hot dry desert of northern Peru, this magnificent collection of adobe pyramids from the Sicán culture dates to around 1100 AD. See page 407

❻ **Lobitos and Máncora** Peru's trendiest beach and surf resort, Máncora has warm water, strong sunshine and hot nightlife, while Lobitos is the perfect chilled surf hangout. See pages 415 and 417

HIGHLIGHTS ARE MARKED ON THE MAP ON PAGE 352

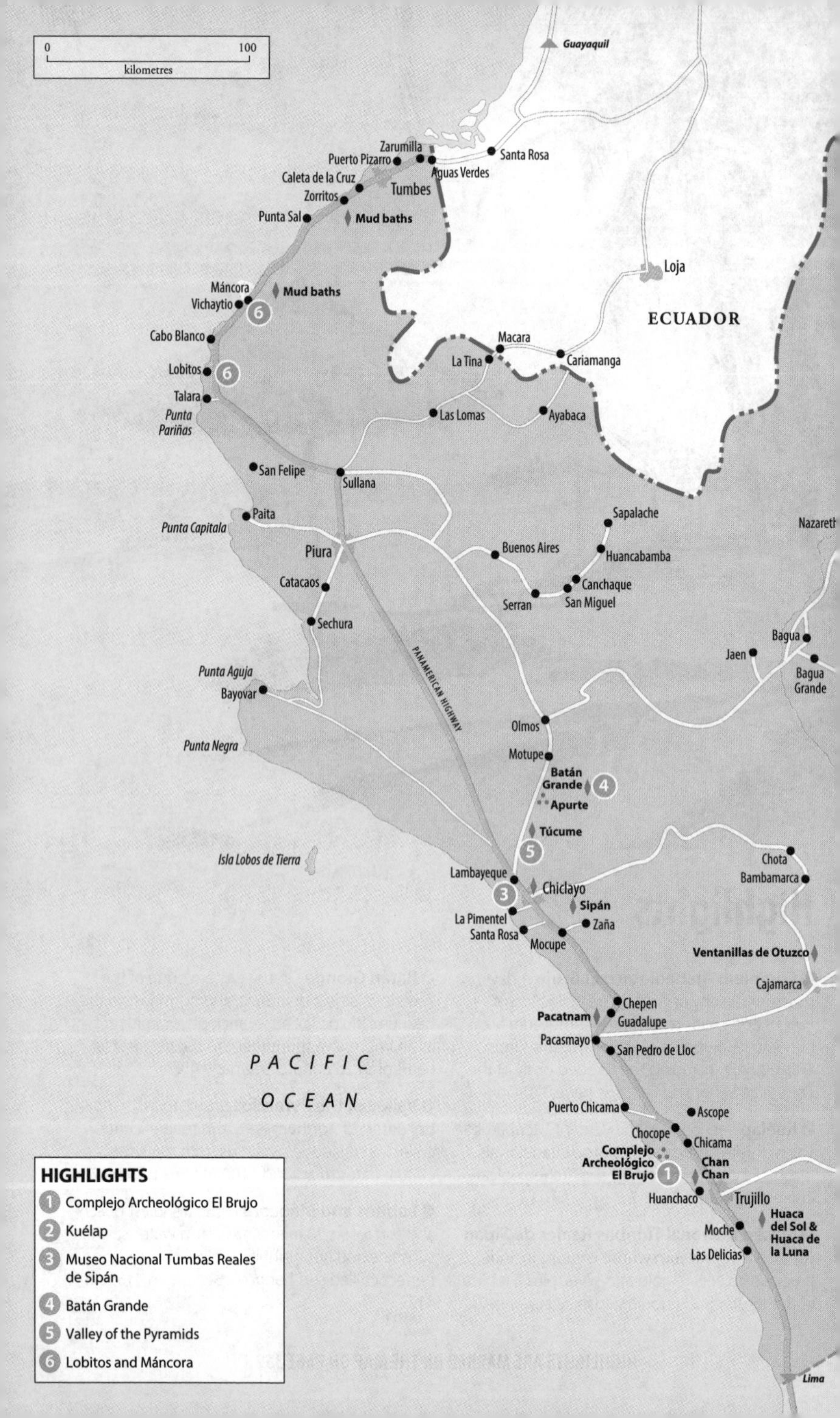
0
100
kilometres
Guayaquil
Zarumilla
Puerto Pizarro
Santa Rosa
Aguas Verdes
Caleta de la Cruz
Tumbes
Zorritos
Punta Sal
Mud baths
Máncora
Mud baths
Vichaytio
6
Cabo Blanco
Loja
ECUADOR
Lobitos
6
Macara
La Tina
Cariamanga
Talara
Punta Pariñas
Las Lomas
Ayabaca
San Felipe
Sullana
Paita
Punta Capitala
Sapalache
Nazareth
Piura
Buenos Aires
Huancabamba
Catacaos
Canchaque
Serran
San Miguel
Sechura
PANAMERICAN HIGHWAY
Bagua
Jaen
Bagua Grande
Punta Aguja
Bayovar
Olmos
Punta Negra
Motupe
Batán Grande
4
Apurte
Túcume
5
Isla Lobos de Tierra
Chota
Lambayeque
Chiclayo
Bambamarca
3
Sipán
La Pimentel
Zaña
Santa Rosa
Mocupe
Ventanillas de Otuzco
Cajamarca
Chepen
Pacatnam
Guadalupe
Pacasmayo
San Pedro de Lloc
PACIFIC
OCEAN
Puerto Chicama
Ascope
Chocope
Chicama
Complejo Archeológico El Brujo
1
Chan Chan
Huanchaco
Trujillo
Moche
Huaca del Sol & Huaca de la Luna
Las Delicias
Lima
HIGHLIGHTS
1 Complejo Archeológico El Brujo
2 Kuélap
3 Museo Nacional Tumbas Reales de Sipán
4 Batán Grande
5 Valley of the Pyramids
6 Lobitos and Máncora

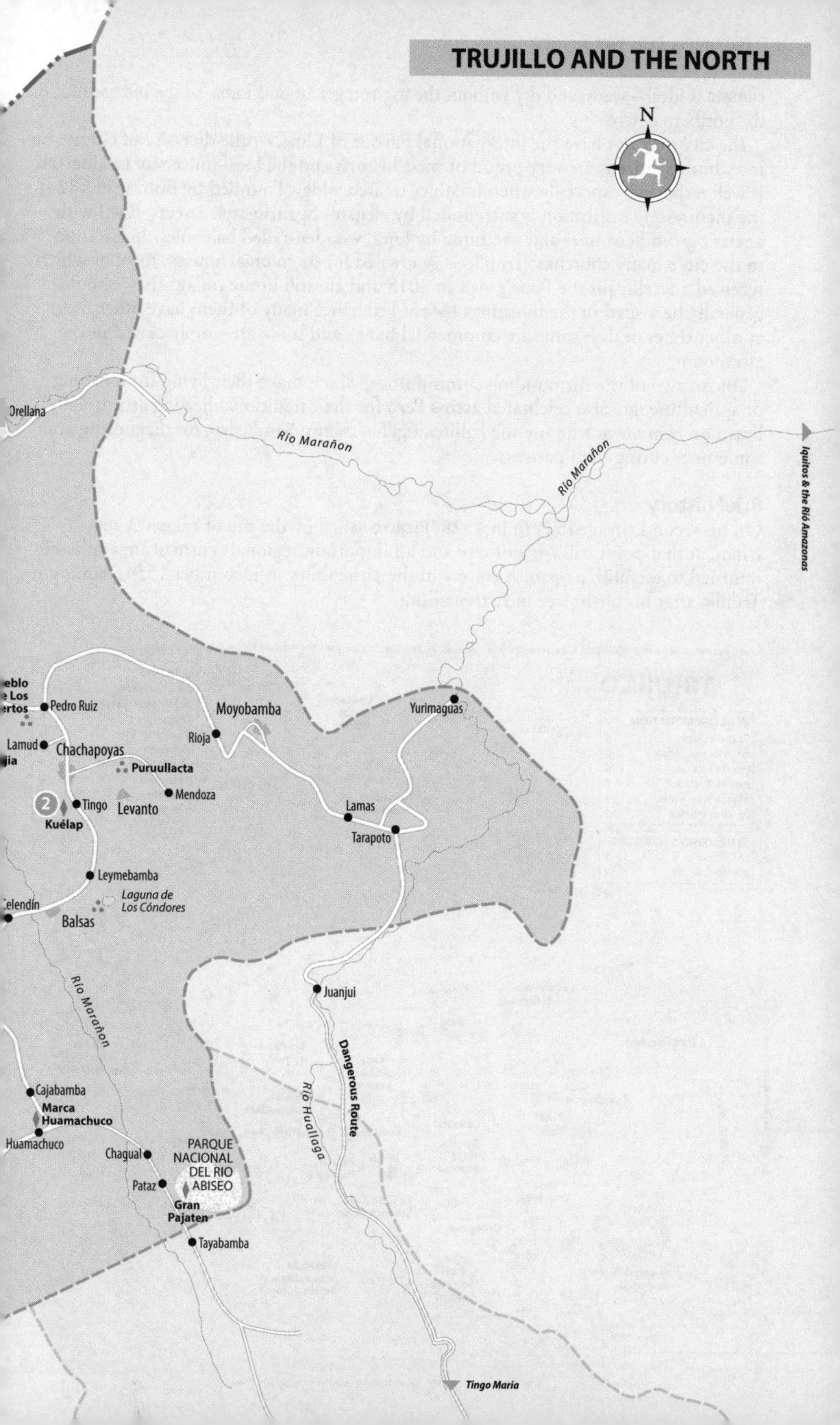

TRUJILLO AND THE NORTH
N
Orellana
Río Marañon
Río Marañon
Iquitos & the Río Amazonas
Pedro Ruiz
Moyobamba
Yurimaguas
Rioja
Lamud
Chachapoyas
Puruullacta
Mendoza
Tingo
Levanto
Kuélap
Lamas
Tarapoto
Leymebamba
Laguna de Los Cóndores
Balsas
Juanjui
Río Marañon
Dangerous Route
Río Huallaga
Cajabamba
Marca Huamachuco
Huamachuco
Chagual
PARQUE NACIONAL DEL RIO ABISEO
Pataz
Gran Pajaten
Tayabamba
Tingo Maria

climate is ideal – warm and dry without the fog you get around Lima, or the intense heat of the northern deserts.

The city may not have the international flavour of Lima, or the diversity of culture or race, but its citizens are very proud of their history, and the local university **La Libertad** is well respected, especially when it comes to archeology. Founded by Bolívar in 1824, the picturesque institution is surrounded by elegant, Spanish-style streets, lined with ancient green ficus trees and overhung by long, wooden-railed balconies. In addition to the city's many **churches**, Trujillo is renowned for its **colonial houses**, most of which received a facelift for the Pope's visit in 2018 and are still in use today. These should generally be visited in the mornings (Mon–Fri), since many of them have other uses at other times of day; some are commercial banks and some are simply closed in the afternoons.

One or two of the surrounding communities, which make their living from fishing or agriculture, are also celebrated across Peru for their traditional healing arts, usually based on *curanderos* who use the hallucinogenic cactus, San Pedro, for diagnosing and sometimes curing their patients.

Brief history

On his second voyage to Peru in 1528, **Pizarro** sailed by the site of ancient Chan Chan, at that point still a major city and an important regional centre of Inca rule. He returned to establish a Spanish colony in the same valley in December 1534, naming it Trujillo after his birthplace in Extremadura.

TRUJILLO ORIENTATION

The heart of Trujillo comprises some twenty blocks of colonial-style architecture around a wide main plaza, **Plaza Mayor** or Plaza de Armas, which is in turn encircled by Avenida España. Radiating from here, the buildings get steadily more modern and less attractive. The main streets of Pizarro and Independencia originate at the plaza; the only other streets you really need to know are San Martín and Bolívar, parallel to Pizarro and Independencia, and Gamarra, the main commercial street lined with shops, hotels and restaurants. The other big avenue, older and more attractive, is **Jirón Pizarro**, where much of the city's nightlife is centred and which has been pedestrianized from Plaza Mayor to the pleasant **Plazuela El Recreo**.

In 1536, the town was besieged by the Inca Manco's forces during the second rebellion against the conquistadores. Many thousands of Conchuco warriors, allied with the Incas, swarmed down to Trujillo, killing the Spanish and collaborators and offering their victims to Catequil, the tribal deity.

After surviving this attack, Trujillo grew to become the main port of call for the Spanish treasure fleets, sailors wining and dining here on their way between Lima and Panama. By the seventeenth century it was a walled city of some three thousand houses covering three square miles. The only sections of those walls that remain are the **Herrera rampart** and a small piece of the facade on Avenida España.

7

APRA

With a restless past, Trujillo continued to be a centre of popular rebellion, declaring its independence from Spain in the Plaza de Armas in 1820, long before the Liberators arrived. The enigmatic leader of the **APRA** – American Popular Revolutionary Alliance (see page 496) – Haya de la Torre, was born here in 1895, and ran for president in the elections of 1931. The dictator, Sánchez Cerro, however, counted the votes (unfairly, some believe), and declared himself the winner. APRA was outlawed and Haya de la Torre imprisoned, provoking Trujillo's middle classes to stage an uprising. Over one thousand people died, many of them APRA supporters, who were taken out to the fields of Chan Chan by the truckload and shot. Even now, the 1932 massacre resonates among the people of Trujillo, particularly the old APRA members and the army, and you can still see each neighbourhood declaring its allegiance, in graffiti, to one side or the other.

APRA failed to attain political power in Peru for another 54 years, until Alan García became president for the first time; but it was the revolutionary military government in 1969 that truly unshackled this region from the tight grip of a few **sugar barons**, who owned the enormous haciendas in the Chicama Valley. The haciendas were then divided up among the worker co-operatives – the Casa Grande, a showcase example, is now one of the most profitable and well-organized agricultural ventures in Peru.

Plaza Mayor

Trujillo's **Plaza Mayor** (also known as the Plaza de Armas) faced an extensive revamp in 2017, but is still packed with sharp-witted shoeshine boys around the central statue – the *Heroes of the Wars of Independence*, a Baroque marble work created by German Edmundo Muller. Legend has it that the statue's centrepiece, an angel with a torch of liberty, has had a rather tough time of it. When the statue was set up, they realized his legs were too long to balance properly and he was promptly shortened by a few centimetres. Then, the more devout ladies of the city found to their dismay that the angel was very noticeably male, and demanded that the offending member be removed.

The two colonial mansions that front it have both been tastefully restored: **Casa Bracamonte**, on Jr Independencia 441 (Mon–Fri 8am–5pm, Sat 8am–noon) is more beautiful outside than in, with interesting cast-ironwork around its patio windows and door knockers in the shape of lions' heads, while the Banco de la Nación-owned **Casa**

TOP ARCHEOLOGICAL SITES NEAR TRUJILLO

One of the main reasons for coming to Trujillo is to visit the numerous **archeological sites** dotted around the nearby Moche and Chicama valleys. In many ways these sites are more impressive than the ruins around Cusco – and most are more ancient too. The pyramids, courtyards and high walls of the various sites are all constructed from adobe bricks; these have suffered from the rains over the last eight hundred years or so, consequently requiring a little imagination to mentally reconstruct them as you wander around. Here are three to aim for:

Chan Chan A gigantic adobe city on the northern edge of Trujillo (see page 366).

Huaca del Sol/Huaca de la Luna Standing alone beneath the Cerro Blanco hill south of Trujillo, these are the largest mud-brick pyramids in the Americas (see page 363).

Complejo Archeolgico el Brujo Set within the sugar-cane plantations of the haciendas in the Chicama Valley, these adobe temples bore fascinating treasures, including the tattooed mummy of the female ruler, the Señora de Cao (see page 370).

Urquiaga (Mon–Fri 9.15am–3.15pm, Sat 10am–1pm; free, you must present a passport; 30min guided tours often available), on Jr Pizarro 446 (also known as Casa Calonge), is said to be where Bolívar stayed when visiting Trujillo; it's also home to some first-class Rococo-style furniture and a small collection of ancient ceramics and national medals.

La Catedral

Plaza Mayor • **Catedral** Daily 7–11.45am & 4–7pm • Free • **Museum** Mon–Fri 9am–1pm & 4–7pm, Sat 9am–1pm • S/4

Plaza Mayor is home to **La Catedral**, built in the mid-seventeenth century, then rebuilt the following century after earthquake damage. Known locally as the Basílica Menor, it's easily spotted by its mustard yellow exterior and houses some colourful Baroque sculptures and a handful of paintings by the Quiteña school (a deeply religious style of painting that originated in eighteenth-century Quito). The paintings that cover the roof of the Cathedral are particularly impressive. To the right of the main doors, the **Museo de Catedral** exhibits a range of eighteenth- and nineteenth-century religious paintings and sculptures. The **tour** (only in Spanish) included in the museum's entry fee explains a little of the history of the rather drab collection in the small room, but also involves a visit into the crypt. Only visitable as part of this tour, it hosts seventeenth- and eighteenth-century paintings, murals depicting funeral rites and a morbid selection of paintings of decapitated martyrs.

Casa Orbegoso

Jr Orbegoso 553 • Closed to the public, only opening for art shows

Between Plaza Major and the Mercado Central stands the most impressive of Trujillo's colonial houses – **Casa Orbegoso**, the home of **Luís José Orbegoso**, former president of Peru. Born into one of Trujillo's wealthiest founding families, Orbegoso fought for independence and became president of the republic in 1833 with the support of the liberal faction. However, he proved to be the most ineffective of all Peruvian leaders, resented for his aristocratic bearing by the *mestizo* generals, and from 1833 to 1839, although still officially president, he lost control of the country – first in civil war, then to the Bolivian army, and finally to a combined rebel and Chilean force. Unfortunately, unless your visit coincides with an art show, you will only be able to appreciate its impeccable yellow-painted exterior, with elaborate window frames and an intricately carved wooden box balcony.

Mercado Central and Mercado Mayorista

Central Jr Ayacucho and Jr Gamarra • **Mayorista** Av Costa Rica • Mon–Sat 7am–5pm

Trujillo's main market, the **Mercado Central** (known locally as the Mercado de los Brujos: the Witches' Market) is only two blocks east of the Plaza Mayor. As well as selling most essentials, such as juices, food and clothing, it has an interesting if rapidly declining line in **herbal stalls** and healing or magical items, not to mention unionized shoe-cleaners. There's a second, much busier market, the **Mercado Mayorista**, further out in the southeast corner of town.

Museo de Arqueología y Antropología

Jr Junín 682 • Mon 9am–2.30pm, Tues–Sat 9am-4.30pm • S/5; 30min guided tours in Spanish included in fee, ask at front desk • ⓣ 044 474 850

The university's excellent **Museo de Arqueología y Antropología** specializes in ceramics, early metallurgy, textiles and feather work. It is located in Casa Risco, a colonial mansion donated by the Peruvian government to the university of Trujillo in 1995. The main hall provides a chronological review of the archeological finds of the north coast and their respective cultures, while four further rooms host temporary exhibitions of current work and new discoveries. Well worth visiting for some solid background information before going on any further tours in the area.

La Casa de la Emancipación

Jr Pizarro 610 • Mon–Sat 9am–1pm & 4–8pm • Free

East of the main plaza stands an impressive mansion, **La Casa de la Emancipación.** Remodelled in the mid-nineteenth century by the priest Pedro Madalengoitia (the reason it's also sometimes known as the Casa Madalengoitia), it is now head office of Banco Continental. The main courtyard and entrance demonstrate a symmetrical design with pinstriped blue and yellow walls, while the room beyond is home to 150 titles written by or about poet César Vallejo, considered one of the most important figures in Peruvian literature. Paintings are usually exhibited in at least one of the rooms, and classical music concerts and film screenings are often held here.

Palacio Iturregui

Jr Pizarro 688 • Daily 8–10.30am • S/5

Two blocks east of the Plaza Mayor is the **Palacio Iturregui**, a striking mid-nineteenth-century mansion. Built by army general Don Juan Manuel de Iturregui y Aguilarte, the house is used today by the city's exclusive Central Club. The room to the right of the entry usually hosts a small but excellent collection of local modern paintings. The highlight of the building is its pseudo-classical courtyard, encircled by superb galleries, with tall columns and an open roof, which provides a wonderful view of the blue desert sky. The club maintains very limited entry hours, but you can pop in any time during the day to appreciate the courtyard and the two rooms just off the courtyard, with the delicate cast-ironwork around the windows very typical of Trujillo.

Plazuela El Recreo

Eastern end of Jr Pizarro

Five blocks from the Plaza Mayor, there's a small, attractive square known as the **Plazuela El Recreo** where, under the shade of some vast 135-year-old ficus trees, a number of **bars** and food stalls act like a magnet for young couples in the evenings. This little plaza was, and still is, an *estanque de agua* – a water distribution point – built during colonial days, but tapping into even more ancient irrigation works.

Monasterio El Carmen

C Colón and C Bolívar • Church 9.30am–10.30am • S/3, pay at the entrance to the monastery

Less than two blocks southeast of where the pedestrianised Jirón Pizarro ends stands the stunning **Monasterio El Carmen**, considered by many to be the most superb

FIESTAS IN TRUJILLO

Trujillo's main **fiestas** turn the town into even more of a relaxed playground than it is normally, with the **marinera** dance featuring prominently in most celebrations. This regional dance originated in Trujillo and is accompanied by a combination of Andalucian, African and indigenous music played on the *cajón* (rhythm box) and guitar. Energetic and very sexual – this traditional dance represents the seduction of an elegant, upper-class woman by a male servant – the *marinera* involves dancers holding handkerchiefs above their heads and skilfully prancing around each other. You'll see it performed in *peñas* all over the country but rarely with the same spirit and conviction as here in Trujillo. The last week in January, sometimes running into February (check with the tourist information office), is the main **Festival de la Marinera**. During this time there's a National Marinera Competition – el Concurso Nacional de Marinera – that takes place over several weeks and features dance academies from all over Peru.

The main **religious fiestas** are in October and December, with October 17 seeing the procession of El Señor de los Milagros, and the first two weeks of December being devoted to the patron saint of Huanchaco – another good excuse for wild parties in this beach resort. February, as everywhere, is **Carnival** time, with even more *marinera* evenings taking place throughout Trujillo. The end of June sees a week-long celebration of the patron saint of the fishermen, San Pedro, which takes place along the coast and is particularly festive in Huanchaco.

religious building in the north of Peru. Built in 1759 but damaged by an earthquake in the same year, its two brick towers were rebuilt using bamboo to stop them toppling over. The church, with its resplendent gold altars, oil paintings inset with gold leaf and original murals, is really quite spectacular. If you show an interest, the guardian will also let you into an adjoining room where oil paintings are being restored.

Casa de los Leones

Jr Independencia 630 • Daily noon–11pm • It is now a restaurant, *Casona Deza* (see page 360); to explore, you will need to order food or drinks

Just one block from the plaza stands the **Casa de los Leones**, a colonial mansion also known as the Casona Ganoza Chopitea, which is larger and more labyrinthine than it looks from the outside. There are two open-air courtyards to explore and the internal walls are decorated with some excellent modern art, while the outside ones showcase original painted murals.

Museo del Juguete

Jr Independencia 705 • Mon–Sat 10am–6pm, Sun 10am–1pm • S/7

Two blocks from the plaza, the **Museo del Juguete** is the only toy museum in Peru, with a 5000-strong private collection by local artist Gerardo Chávez – who also owns the *Museo Café Bar* downstairs (see page 360) – showcasing objects from across the world. The most fascinating are undoubtedly those in the pre-Hispanic room, with Moche ceramic rattles dating back to 100–800 AD.

Mural Mosaico

Av Juan Pablo II and Jesús de Nazareth • Free

Along two exterior walls of the university of Trujillo, artists Rafael Hastings and Carlos de Mar have created the world's largest mosaic mural, completed with the help of thousands of students over the span of more than twenty years. It is an impressive sight, with over 3000 square metres covered in 1cm by 1cm tiles making up a series of images – the early works were mostly pre-Hispanic themed, while the later images range from volcanoes and hurricanes to a levitating sleeper.

ARRIVAL AND DEPARTURE

TRUJILLO

BY PLANE

Aeropuerto Carlos Martínez de Pinillos (044 464 224; daily 7am–9pm) is about 8km from Trujillo, near Huanchaco. LATAM (Jr Almagro 490; Mon–Fri 9am–7pm & Sat 9am–1pm), Avianca (inside Real Plaza, Av César Vallejo Oeste 1345; Mon–Fri 11am–8pm, Sat & Sun 11am–6pm) and LC Perú, Jr Almagro 305 (044 290 299; Mon–Fri 9am–7pm, Sat 9am–1pm) serve the airport. Taxis into the city cost around S/15–20.

Destinations Lima (several daily; 1hr 40min).

BY BUS

Buses arrive from the south at the Terrapuerto on the Panamericana Norte Km 558. From there, a taxi into town costs S/8. Heading north, most bus companies have terminals close to Av España in the southwest, or east along Av America Norte or Av Ejercito. Check with the bus company when buying tickets whether it's best to pick up the bus at the depot or at the terminal south of town.

Bus companies Cruz del Sur, Amazonas 437 (044 261 801) serves Lima, Máncora and Guayaquil; Excluciva, Av Ejercito 285 (044 251 402) is the best luxury service to Lima; Oltursa, Av Ejercito 342 (044 423 597) serves the whole coast up to Tumbes (excluding Piura). Others include Emtrafesa, Av Túpac Amaru 185 (044 484 120), a good and reliable service to Chiclayo (every 30min) as well as Lima, Chimbote, Pacasmayo, Guadalupe, Cajamarca, Piura, Máncora and Tumbes; Linea, Av America Sur 2857 (044 297 000) for Lima, Cajamarca, Chiclayo, Piura and Chimbote; Tunesa, Av César Vallejo 1390 (044 210 725) has departures for Huamachuco; Móvil Tours, Av America Sur 3959 (044 245 523) is the safest and most comfortable for Nueva Cajamarca, Moyobamba, Tarapoto and Chachapoyas, and even runs to Huaraz.

Destinations Cajamarca (several daily; 6–8hr); Chachapoyas (daily; 13hr); Chiclayo (12 daily; 3hr); Guayaquil (daily except Tues; 18hr); Huamanchuco (5 daily; 5hr); Lima (20 daily; 9hr); Piura, via Chiclayo (8 daily; 6hr); Máncora (several daily; 6hr); Tarapoto (daily; 18hr); Tumbes (daily; 10hr).

BY COLECTIVO

Colectivos connecting with towns to the north mostly leave from and end up on Avenida España. If you're arriving by day it's fine to walk to the city centre, though at night it's best to take a taxi (S/5–6).

INFORMATION AND TOURS

Tourist information iPeru office in the depths of the Casona Minka, Jr Independencia 467 (Mon–Sat 9am–6pm, Sun 9am–1pm; 044 294 561, iperutrujillo@promperu.gob.pe) on the Plaza Mayor. The Tourist Police is next door to the Gobierno Regional building, Jr Diego de Almagro 442 (daily 8.30am–10pm, 044 291 705).

Tour operators and guides Most companies offer 3hr tours to Chan Chan and Huanchaco for around S/30 per person (including the site museum, Huaca Arco Iris and Huaca Esmeralda), and to huacas del Sol and Luna from S/30, with a discount for a combined, full-day tour. For Chicama sites, expect to pay S/40. Recommended operators include: Colonial Tours, Jr Independencia 616 (044 291 034, colonialtoursnorteperu.com), who have daily, English-speaking departures for most destinations; Clara Brava's Tours at *Casa de Clara* (see below); and Peru Routes, Av San Martín 455, Office 5 (044 250 000, peruroutes.com). Expect to pay extra for an English-speaking guide.

GETTING AROUND

By taxi Taxis cost less than S/5 for rides within Trujillo and can be hailed anywhere, but for safety and fair, set prices, stick with the official "radio" taxis (that have a telephone number on the roof). At night in particular, it's best to call Sonrisa (044 233 000) or New Takci (044 290 494).

ACCOMMODATION

The best and safest places to stay in Trujillo are around Plaza Mayor in the centre of the old city. However, many people prefer to stay out of the city centre at the nearby beach resort of Huanchaco (see page 364).

★ **Casa de Clara** C Cahuide 495, Santa María 044 243 347; map p.354. Located near Huayna Capac 542, this is very nice bargain accommodation, with private bath and breakfast. Owner Clara, an archeologist, is very well informed about local places of interest, and will help organize reliable and affordable tours. S/60

Enkanta Hospedaje Jr Independencia 341 992 534 141; map p.354. A real favourite among budget backpackers, with tired decoration and furniture but a sociable vibe and shared kitchen. Dorms at the back of the building are quieter thanks to distance from the common area. Breakfast not included. Dorms S/35, doubles S/50

Hotel Colonial Jr Independencia 618 044 258 261, hotelcolonial.com.pe; map p.354. An attractive, colonial-style place with colourfully painted walls, white-trimmed balconies and striped pillars, all around a pleasant green central courtyard. Some English-speaking staff members. Rooms are comfortable and include fans and fast wi-fi; for guaranteed peace and quiet get a room at the back. S/120

★ **Hotel Libertador** Jr Independencia 485 044 232 741, libertador.com.pe; map p.354. Right on the plaza, this place is grand and well-maintained, with excellent service, a pool and a superb restaurant renowned for its criolla dishes. The large, comfortable rooms have mod cons and kingsize beds. S/300

Munay Wasi Hotel Jr Colon 50 044 231 462, munaywasihostel.com; map p.354. Near the edge of the historic centre, the location isn't ideal, but friendly owners, a communal kitchen plus good wi-fi make this a welcome choice for the budget-conscious. It's also impeccably clean. Dorms S/30, doubles S/70

★ **Le Saint Etienne** C Obispe Guillermo Charun 271 044 345 127, lesaint-etienne.com; map p.354. Set in Trujillo's safest neighbourhood and only five blocks from the plaza, this friendly, French-run guesthouse has large, slightly clinical bedrooms, all with private bathrooms and fans. Those on the first and second floor are significantly larger. An ample breakfast is available for S/8. S/115

EATING

Some of the liveliest restaurants are along jirones Independencia, Pizarro, Bolívar and Ayacucho, to the east of Plaza Mayor. Goat and beans is a local speciality, too; if you get the chance, try *cabrito con frijoles*, a truly traditional dish of goat marinated in *chicha* beer and vinegar and served with beans cooked with onions and garlic. There's a good supermarket for general provisions at Pizarro 700.

Café Restaurant El Rincon del Vallejo Jr Orbegoso 311 044 226 232; map p.354. A local institution set in a beautiful old building and the original home of Trujillo's most famous poet, Cesar Vallejo, just next door. Great for traditional local meals, with a different soup (S/19) each day. Quick, quality service. Mon–Sat 7am–11pm, Sun 7am–3pm.

Casona Deza Jr Independencia 630 044 474 756; map p.354. A first-rate Italian restaurant set in a historic building dating back to 1635. There are two gorgeous open-air patios for dining, and the walls are decorated with impressive artwork. Best for a coffee and sandwich during the day to appreciate the building, but also a good choice in the evening for quality pizza (S/27). Mon–Sat noon–11pm.

★ **El Celler de Cler** Jr Independencia 588 044 317 191; map p.354. Opt for an outside table to appreciate the beautifully restored eighteenth-century wooden balcony and atmospheric vistas of Iglesia San Francisco. The house special is their starter of *ceviche de lomo* (beef tartare cooked in lemon juice; S/27) but their juicy *lomo saltado* (S/46) is something else. Service likely the most attentive you'll have in Peru. Mon–Sat 6.30pm–1am, Sun 6.30pm–midnight.

El Chileno Ayacucho 581; map p.354. Outside the market, another classic. It's nothing fancy, just great home-style ice cream (S/4), wonderfully rich and tasty. Daily 8.30am–9.30pm.

★ **Jugería San Agustín** Jr Bolívar 522 044 245 653; map p.354. Trujillo's most famous juice bar is actually best known for its *sandwich de pavo* (turkey sandwich; S/7.50). The original, pint-sized shop serves takeaway downstairs; the new spacious café is around the corner at San Agustín 104. Daily 8am–1pm & 4.15–8.30pm.

El Mochica Bolívar 462 044 295 181; map p.354. A smart restaurant extremely popular with foreign tourists serving exquisite criolla dishes and local cuisine – try their *cabrito con frijoles* (S/29); at the weekend, expect folkloric dance performances. Daily 8am–11pm.

Muya Musquy Jr San Martín 600; map p.354. There are only ten tables – and not enough staff – but their well-flavoured tofu stews, chickpea salads and quinoa burgers are worth the wait at this popular vegan restaurant. Lunch menu from S/8. Mon–Sat 11am–5pm, 7–10pm.

★ **El Patio Rojo** Jr San Martín 883 044 242 339; map p.354. Sample vegetarian ceviche (S/20) or chow down on hearty dishes of quinoa (S/20–28) or vegan cakes (S/5–8) at this hip café. Popular with an alternative crowd for its Thurs pizza nights and occasional live music at weekends. Lunch menu S/9. Mon–Thurs 8am–11pm, Fri & Sat 8am–1am, Sun 10am–4pm.

DRINKING AND NIGHTLIFE

Trujillo has a fairly active nightlife, with several *peñas* and nightclubs celebrating local culture, dance and music, as well as Latin rhythms and the latest global popular sounds. The city is also well known worldwide for its January *marinera* dance fiesta (see page 358) and occasional international dance jamborees.

★ **La Cañana** San Martín 791 044 295 422; map p.354. A highly popular restaurant-*peña* and discotheque that does excellent meals. Expect a great atmosphere and danceable, orchestra-accompanied folklore shows starting after 10pm and carrying on into the early hours. Thurs–Sat 8pm–5am.

Museo Café Bar Jr Independencia 701 044 346 741; map p.354. An old-style, wood-heavy bohemian bar created by local artist Gerado Chavez; go for a beer, a sandwich and long conversations. On Fri and Sat, a live jazz band sets up in the corner. Mon–Thurs 9am–midnight, Fri & Sat 9am–1am.

DIRECTORY

Banks and exchange BCP, Jr Gamarra 562; Scotiabank, Jr Pizarro 699; BBVA Jr Pizarro 620. Exchange dollars at the numerous casas de cambio on Pizarro, between Almagro and Gamarra, or with the *cambistas* (though be very careful, especially after dark) on the corner of Jr Pizarro and Gamarra, or on the Plaza Mayor.

Consulates UK (honorary consul), at Jr Alfonso Ugarte 310 (T 044 245 935).

Health Hospital Belén de Trujillo, Jr Bolívar 350 T 044 245 748 (24hr); Hospital Regional Docente de Trujillo, Av Manseriche 795 T 044 231 581 (24hr).

Immigration Av Larco 1217 (T 044 282 217), for visa renewals.

Language school Trujillo Language School T 044 280 015, W peru-language-school.com.

Laundry Lavanderia El Olivo, Jr Orbegoso 270.

Post office Serpost (Mon–Fri 8am–8pm, Sat 8am–4pm), Jr Independencia 286.

Tourist police Jr Almagro 442 (T 044 291 705).

Around Trujillo

The beaches close to Trujillo have seen a lot of fast and unattractive development recently and though there remain some nice empty stretches, they are somewhat spoilt by the strong smell from the nearby marshes. It's best just to head straight out to **Huanchaco** for beach time. For those in search of sand and seafood south of the city, the villages of **Moche** and **Las Delicias** are within easy reach.

Moche and Las Delicias

From Trujillo (S/1.50; 25min), catch the direct minivan (hourly) marked "Delicias" from the corner of Avenida Los Incas and Suarez; or take a taxi (S/25–30)

After crossing the Río Moche's estuary, 2km south of Trujillo, you'll come across the settlements of **MOCHE** and **LAS DELICIAS**, both within an easy bus ride of the Huaca del Sol and Huaca de la Luna (see page 363). Moche is a small village some 4km south of the city, slightly inland from the ocean, blessed with several **restaurants** serving freshly prepared seafood. Close by, Las Delicias, 5km south of Trujillo, has a long, empty **beach** and a handful of reasonable restaurants. Las Delicias's main claim to fame is that the *curandero* El Tuno once lived at Lambayeque 18, right on the beach.

Museo Arqueológico de la Municipal de Moche

Jr Bolognesi 359 • Mon–Fri 8am–1pm & 2–4pm • S/5

Located on the third floor of the Municipal building on the Plaza de Armas, the **Museo Arqueológico de la Municipal de Moche** is home to the private collection formerly displayed in the (now defunct) **Museo Casinelli.** Simply stuffed with pottery and artefacts spanning thousands of years and collected from local *huaqueros*, the Salinar, Viru, Mochica, Chimú, Nazca, Huari, Recuay and Inca cultures are all represented. Highlights include **Mochica pots** with graphic images of daily life, people, animals and anthropomorphic deities, and an exquisite range of **Chimú silver artefacts**, including a tiny set of panpipes.

Huacas del Moche

5km south of Trujillo • Colectivos (S/1.50) leave from the south side of Ovalo Grau (every 10–15min) at the southern entrance of the Panamericana Norte into Trujillo city. Some go all the way to the Huaca de la Luna, but many prefer to drop you off on the road, within sight, but still a 10–15min walk away

In a barren desert landscape beside the Río Moche, two temples bring ancient Peru to life. Collectively known as the **Huacas del Moche**, these sites make a fine day's outing and shouldn't be missed even if you only have a passing interest in archeology or the ancient civilizations of Peru. The vast **Huaca del Sol** (Temple of the Sun) is the largest adobe structure in the Americas, and easily the most impressive of the many pyramids on the Peruvian coast. Its twin, the **Huaca de la Luna** (Temple of the Moon), is smaller, but more complex and brilliantly frescoed.

Brief history

After more than eighteen years of excavation, Huaca de la Luna is now believed to have been two different temples, developed in two main phases: platform I and three plazas (known collectively as the old temple) around 600 AD; platform III by around 900 AD.

The complex is believed to have been the capital, or most important ceremonial and urban centre, for the Moche culture at its peak between 400 and 600 AD. Although very much associated with the Moche culture and nation (100–600 AD), there is evidence of earlier occupation at these sites, dating back two thousand years to the Salinar and Gallinazo cultures, indicated by constructions underlying the *huacas*. The

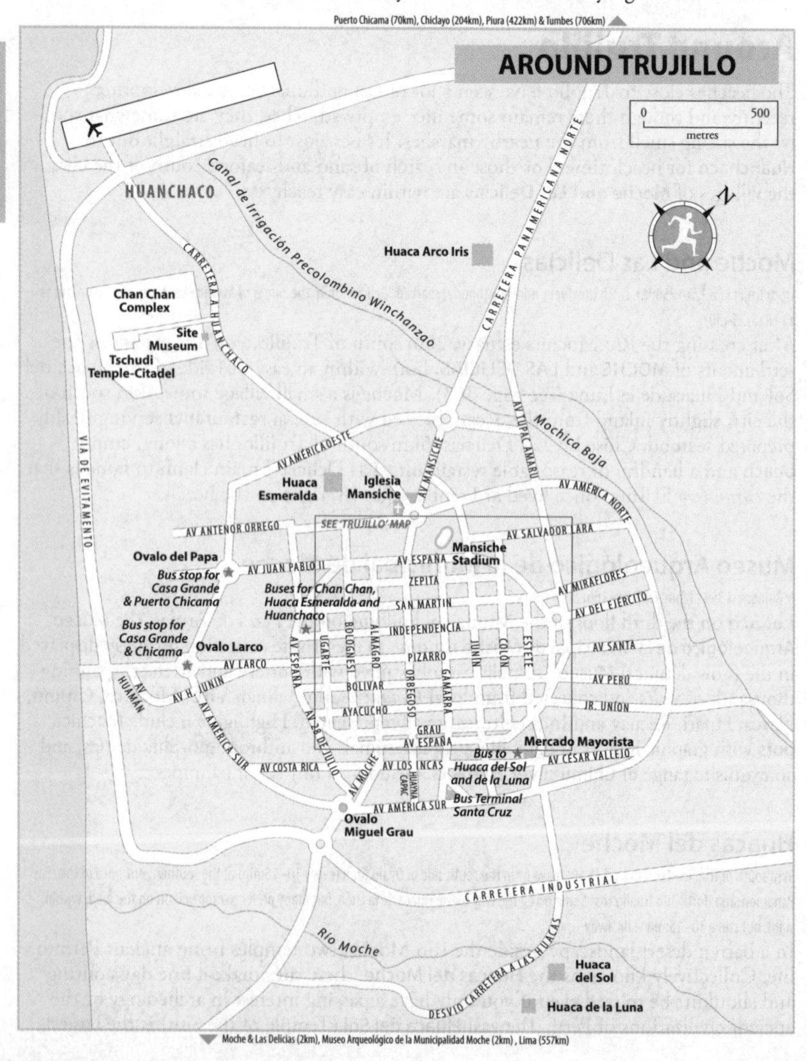

area continued to be held in high regard after the collapse of the Moche culture, with signs of Wari, Chimú and Inca offerings here demonstrating a continued importance. The latest theory suggests that Huaca de la Luna was a ceremonial centre, separated physically from the administrative Huaca del Sol by a large graveyard and an associated urban settlement. Finds in this intermediate zone have so far revealed some fine structures, plus pottery workshops and storehouses; the new buildings housing the gift shop and toilets are re-creations (slightly larger but still using the same materials and colours) of what these buildings would have looked like.

Huaca del Sol

Closed at the time of writing

The **Huaca del Sol** remains off limits to visitors as archeologists are still investigating the area, but it's an amazing sight from the grounds below or from the Huaca de la Luna. Built by the Mochica around 500 AD, and extremely weathered, its pyramid edges still slope at a sharp 77 degrees to the horizon. Although it remains an enormous structure, what you see today is only about thirty percent of the original construction. On top of the base platform is the demolished stump of a four-sided, stepped pyramid, surmounted about 50m above the desert by a ceremonial platform. From the top of this platform you can clearly see how the Río Moche was diverted by the Spanish in 1602, in order to erode the *huaca* and find treasure. They were quite successful at washing away a large section of the site, but found precious little except adobe bricks.

Estimates of the pyramid's brickwork vary, but it is reckoned to contain around 140 million adobe blocks, each marked in any one of a hundred different ways – probably with the maker's distinguishing signs. It must have required a massively well-organized labour supply to put together – Calancha, a Spanish historian, wrote that 200,000 workers were involved. How the Mochica priests and architects decided on the shape of the *huaca* is unknown, but if you look from the main road at its form against the silhouette of Cerro Blanco, there is a remarkable similarity between the two, and if you look at the *huaca* sideways from the vantage point of the Huaca de la Luna, it has the same general outline as the hills behind.

Huaca de la Luna

Daily 9am–4pm • S/10; you can only enter as part of tour; guides available in French, English and Spanish for the 45min tour, tip expected

Clinging to the bottom of Cerro Blanco, just 500m from Huaca del Sol, is **Huaca de la Luna**, a ritual and ceremonial centre that was built around the same time as its neighbour. What you see today is only part of an older complex of interior rooms built over six centuries that included a maze of interconnected patios, some covered and lavishly adorned with polychrome friezes. The **friezes** are still the most striking feature of the site, rhomboid in shape and dominated by an anthropomorphic face surrounded by symbols representing nature spirits, such as the ray fish (symbol of water), pelicans (symbol of air) and serpent (symbol of earth). Its feline fangs and boggle-eyes are stylizations dating back to the early Chavín cult and it's similar to an image known to the Moche as **Ai-Apaec**, master of life and death. The god that kept the human world in order, he has been frequently linked with human sacrifice, and in 1996 archeologists found the dismembered body parts of over seventy sacrificial victims here. Sediment uncovered in their graves indicates that these sacrifices took place during an El Niño weather phenomenon, something that would have threatened the economic and political stability of the nation. Ceramics dug up from the vast graveyard that extends between the two *huacas* and around the base of Cerro Blanco suggest that this might have also been a site for a cult of the dead. Cerro Blanco itself may have been considered a link to Ai-Apaec.

On the northern side of the *huaca* around the Plaza Ceremonial, are the remains of frescoed rooms, discovered in the early 1990s and displaying multicoloured murals (mostly reds and blues). The most famous of these is *The Myths*, the most sophisticated example of Moche mural-art yet uncovered with its chaotic assimilation of warriors in scenes of combat, fishermen with reed boats and even a hairless dog. This side of the temple also

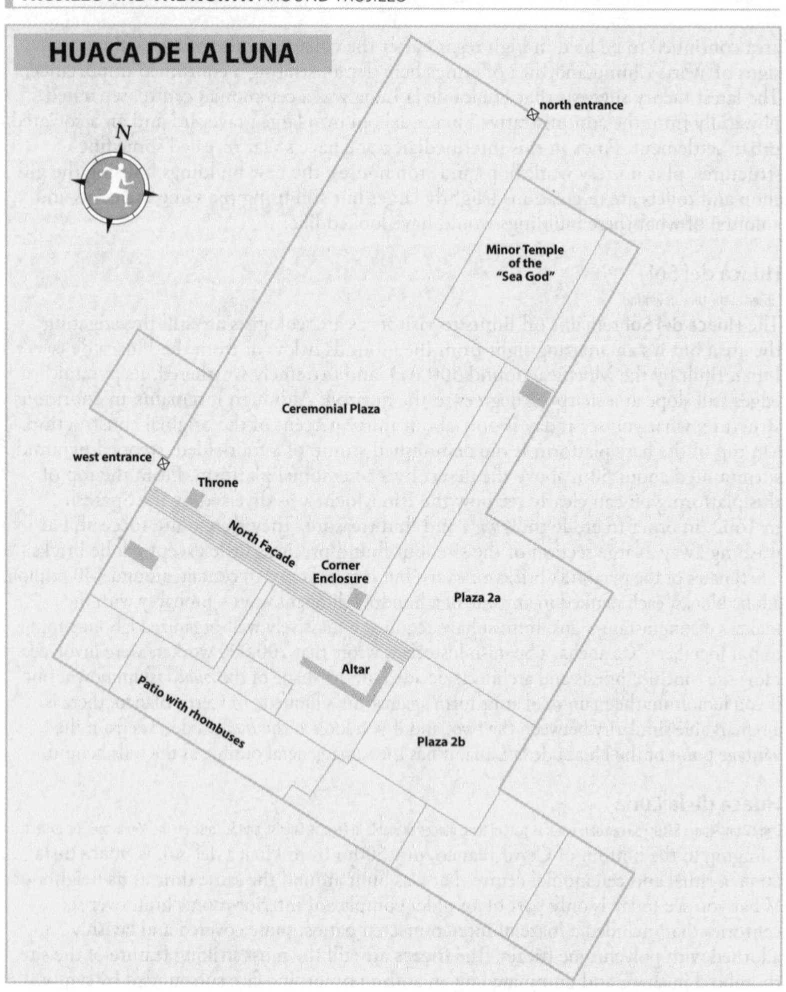

allows you to appreciate its astounding multi-tiered facade; archeologists believe that throughout the centures the old temple was buried and a new, larger one built on top.

Museo Huacas de Moche

Close to the Huaca de la Luna • Daily 9am–4pm • S/5 • 044 221 269 or 971 492 924 • huacasdemoche.pe

The new **Museo Huacas de Moche**, built in a pyramid style to mimic Moche architecture, displays some fine ceramics – check out the warrior duck and the blind shaman – as well as a whole room dedicated to the ceramics and other artefacts uncovered in the tombs of warriors and shamans found in the *huacas*. Similarly interesting is the set of pottery moulds, indicating that ceramics were being produced on a large scale here.

Huanchaco

Although no longer exactly a tropical paradise, **HUANCHACO**, 12km northwest of Trujillo, remains a pleasant beach town, with a thriving surfer and backpacker scene.

Until the 1970s, Huanchaco was a tiny fishing village, quiet and little known to tourists. Today it consists of half-finished adobe houses, concrete hotels and streets slowly spreading back towards Trujillo, although significant damage was caused by flooding in March 2017 and at, the time of research, the town was only just getting back on its feet. It makes an excellent base for visiting many of the sites around the region, in particular the nearby ruins of **Chan Chan**.

A good time to stop by is at the end of June for the **fiesta** of the patron saint of fishermen, San Pedro, when a large *totora* raft comes ashore accompanied by a smaller flotilla of *caballitos* (see page 358). But the best weather here, and the most crowded and expensive time to visit, is between December and March. The town is always lively, with surfers catching the waves, sunbathers on the beach and fishermen hanging around by the pier.

Iglesia Soroco

A 15min walk uphill from the seafront • Mon–Sat 8am–6pm

The town's only historical sight is the old, square **Iglesia Soroco**, perched high on the coastal cliffs. The second church in Peru to be built by the Spanish, it was constructed in 1540 on top of a pre-Inca temple dedicated to the idol of the Golden Fish, and was rebuilt after its destruction during the earthquakes of 1619–70.

The waterfront

Jetty S/0.5; boat trips S/10

Huanchaco's picture-perfect heart is a long pier, where fishermen and tourists jostle for the best positions, while the entrance is crowded with hawkers of trinkets and ice creams. Just next door, stacked along the beach are rows of *caballitos del mar* – the ancient seagoing rafts designed by the Mochica – still used by locals today. They are constructed out of four cigar-shaped bundles of *totora* reeds, tied together into an arc tapering at each end. The fishermen kneel or sit at the stern and paddle, using the surf for occasional bursts of motion. The local boat-builders here are the last who know the craft of making *caballitos* to the original design of the Mochica, and the best can assemble a seaworthy craft in thirty minutes. Some of the fishermen offer ten- to fifteen-minute trips on the back of their *caballitos*.

ARRIVAL AND DEPARTURE — HUANCHACO

By bus or combi Southwest of the Plaza de Armas in Trujillo, where Independencia meets España, you can get a combi with an A on the windshield that takes you directly to Huanchaco. To catch the colourful red and yellow bus, cross Av España and head two blocks further, to Juan Pablo II and Jesús Nazereth (S/1.50; 45min). Returning, board either bus or combi (S/2.50) on the waterfront near the pier; look out for the bus marked 'H Corazón', this takes the shortest route back to where you boarded.

By taxi From Trujillo, taxis are around S/15–20.

INFORMATION AND TOURS

Tourist information An all-in-one stop for info, maps, tours, money exchange and bus tickets, Huanchaco Tours at Av La Rivera 726 (044 462 405, huanchacotours.com).

Tours and surfing classes Check out Muchik Surf School at Independencia 100 (044 633 487, escueladetablamuchik.com), Huanchaco's most established. They have a practice room for learning how to stand on the board before you hit the waves, and also run tours to nearby Puerto Chicama and Pacasmayo.

ACCOMMODATION

The town is well served by the kind of accommodation range you'd normally expect at a popular beach resort. A plethora of new options opened in the wake of the 2017 floods, and many more established ones closed. Unless stated, breakfast isn't included, but practically all have kitchen access. Many families also put people up in private rooms; these can be identified by the signs reading "Alquila Cuarto" on houses, particularly in the summer (Dec–Feb).

★ **ATMA** Palma 442 044 664 507, atmahuanchaco.com. The polar opposite of the party hostels on this side of town, ATMA oozes serenity with daily yoga classes, large dorms and ample relaxed communal space, including an outside patio and sea-facing terrace. There's a kitchen and staff are exceptionally knowledgeable and friendly. Dorms S/22, doubles S/70

Casa Fresh Av La Rivera 322 ⓣ044 462 700, ⓦcasafresh.pe. Located near the beginning of Rivera where the street noise is lower and you'll find the biggest waves. Simple, comfortable rooms with a communal kitchen and rooftop deck with great sea views, perfect for relaxing with a drink. Dorms S/20, doubles S/60

Corazon Verde Av La Rivera 328 ⓣ968 309 066. With only three rooms, this tiny guesthouse feels more like a home than a hostel. Only the double room has sea views and the single's a bit poky, but it's a great place to unwind, with a vibrant cultural space and café downstairs, featuring local artwork, food festivals, pizza nights, yoga classes and a daily menu of healthy vegetarian food. S/120

Frogs Chillhouse Hostel El Pescador 308 ⓣ044 462 223, ⓦfrogsperu.com. The name's a bit misleading – this place is more for partying than chilling – but they've got great facilities, including a kitchen, and large, spotless dorms, many with sea views and all with private baths. There's also a rooftop bar with live (and loud) music practically every night that's also open to the public. Dorms S/20, doubles S/75

★ **Naylamp** Av Victor Larco 1420 ⓣ044 461 022, ⓦhostalnaylamp.com. Set over two distinct areas, with a shady patio with hammocks in the first and, across the road, a communal kitchen and grassy area for camping and socialising. Dorms are large with private baths; doubles are on the small side. Camping S/15, dorms S/20, doubles S/60

Oceano Los Cerezos 105 ⓣ044 461 653. Family run, comfortable and popular among holidaying Peruvians, *Oceano* is a long block away from the beachfront, which can be a blessing on busier days, and has a kitchen on the top floor. The *cremoladas* (a rough sorbet) downstairs are amazing; try the *lúcuma* or the coco. S/50

EATING AND DRINKING

There are restaurants all along the front in Huanchaco, and not surprisingly, ceviche and other seafood are the local specialities, including excellent crab, and you can often see women and children up to their waists in the sea collecting shellfish. Unfortunately, only the bigger, more expensive restaurants make ceviche fresh each day; in the others, it won't kill you, but it also won't be as tasty as it should be. There are plenty of S/10 menus along Los Pinos, while nightlife is focused along the main avenue, La Rivera, south of the pier.

Chocolate Café Av Rivera 752 ⓣ044 626 973. A small and very friendly café, serving tasty snacks and breakfasts (S/12) and good coffee. The staff are a mine of local information. Daily 8.30am–6pm.

Huanchaco Beach Restaurant Malecón Larco 602 ⓣ044 461 484. Fresh fish dishes (ceviche S/39), and excellent views across the ocean and up to the clifftop Iglesia Soroco. Daily 11am–5pm.

Restaurant Big Ben Av Larco 836 ⓣ044 461 378. Serves probably the best and certainly the most expensive seafood dishes (averaging around S/60) in Huanchaco, including excellent crab and sea urchin if you're lucky. Daily 11.30am–5.30pm.

Restaurant El Caribe Atahualpa 100. Just around the corner from the seafront avenue to the north of the pier, this restaurant has great ceviche (S/34) and is very popular with locals. Mon–Sat 10.30am–5pm.

Dulci Nelly Los Pinos 245 ⓣ044 461 392. Indulge your sweet tooth at this titchy bakery and pastelería set just one block back from the main drag. They've got juices which are not too sickly-sweet (S/5) plus cakes, sandwiches and quiches, and freshly baked bread in the mornings and after the afternooon delivery at 5pm. Daily 6am–10pm.

★ **The Lighthouse** Av Rivera and Colon ⓣ972 909 574. Don't miss the mouth-watering buffalo wings and juicy kebabs (S/20–25), cooked over the barbeque right in front of you, in this restaurant, where you lounge on comfy chairs spilling out onto the square beyond. Live music at weekends. Mon–Sat 6.30–11.30pm.

The Chan Chan complex

Daily 9am–4pm • S/10 (see page 370) • ⓣ044 206 304, ⓦchanchan.gob.pe • Taxis from Trujillo cost S/20, or a half-day for around S/75. The orange and yellow Huanchaco-bound microbus (S/1.5) from Av España and Independencia or Pizarro in Trujillo goes past the main Chan Chan sites. Tell the driver where you want to get off

The ruined city of **Chan Chan** stretches across a large sector of the Moche Valley, beginning almost as soon as you leave Trujillo northwards on the Huanchaco road, and ending just a couple of kilometres from Huanchaco. A huge complex even today, its main focus and museum site is the **Nik Am** sector (see page 368), which needs only a little imagination to raise its weathered mud walls to their original grandeur. Not far from Nik Am, **Huaca La Esmeralda** displays different features, being a ceremonial or ritual pyramid rather than a citadel. The third sector, the **Huaca Arco Iris** (or **El Dragón**), on the other side of this enormous ruined city, was similar in function to Esmeralda but has a unique design that has been restored with relish, if not historical perfection.

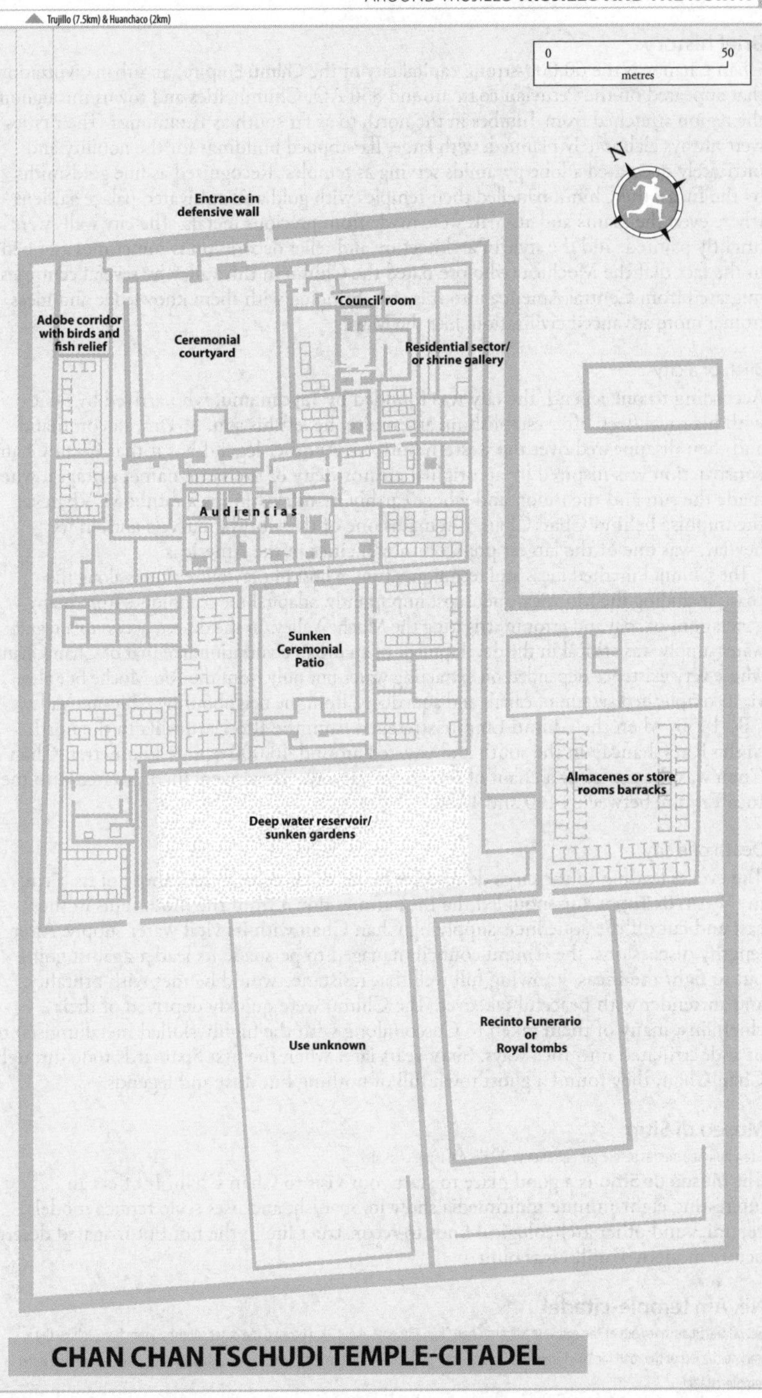
Trujillo (7.5km) & Huanchaco (2km)
Ticket Office (10m)
0 50
metres
N
Entrance in defensive wall
'Council' room
Adobe corridor with birds and fish relief
Ceremonial courtyard
Residential sector/ or shrine gallery
Audiencias
Sunken Ceremonial Patio
Almacenes or store rooms barracks
Deep water reservoir/ sunken gardens
Recinto Funerario or Royal tombs
Use unknown
CHAN CHAN TSCHUDI TEMPLE-CITADEL

Brief history

Chan Chan was the 60,000-strong capital city of the **Chimú Empire**, an urban civilization that appeared on the Peruvian coast around 850 AD. Chimú cities and towns throughout the region stretched from Tumbes in the north to as far south as Paramonga. Their cities were always elaborately planned, with large, flat-topped buildings for the nobility and intricately decorated adobe pyramids serving as temples. Recognized as fine goldsmiths by the Incas, the Chimú panelled their temples with gold and cultivated palace gardens where even the plants and animals were made from precious metals. The city walls were brightly painted, and the style of architecture and relief decoration is sometimes ascribed to the fact that the Mochica (who pre-dated the Chimú in this valley by several centuries) migrated from Central America into this area, bringing with them knowledge and ideas from a more advanced civilization, like the Maya.

Birth of a city

According to one legend, the city was founded by **Taycanamu**, who arrived by boat with his royal fleet; after establishing an empire, he left his son, Si-Um, in command and then disappeared over the western horizon. Another legend has it that Chan Chan's construction was inspired by an original creator-deity of the same name, a dragon who made the sun and the moon and whose earthly manifestation is a rainbow. Whatever the impulse behind Chan Chan, it remains one of the world's marvels and, in its heyday, was one of the largest pre-Columbian cities in the Americas.

The Chimú inherited ideas and techniques from a host of previous cultures along the coast, including the Mochica, and, most importantly, adapted the techniques from many generations of trial and error in irrigating the Moche Valley. In the desert, access to a regular water supply was critical in the development of an urban civilization like that of Chan Chan, whose very existence depended on extracting water not only from the Río Moche but also, via a complicated system of canals and aqueducts, from the neighbouring Chicama Valley.

By 1450, when the Chimú Empire stretched from the Río Zarumilla in the north to the Río Chancay in the south and covered around 40,000 square kilometres, Chan Chan was the centre of a chain of provincial capitals. These were incorporated into the Inca Empire between 1460 and 1480.

Death of a city

The events leading to the city's demise are better documented than those of its birth: in the 1470s **Tupac Yupanqui** led the Inca armies down from the mountains in the east and cut off the aqueducts supplying Chan Chan with its vital water supply. After lengthy discussions, the Chimú council managed to persuade its leader against going out to fight the Incas, knowing full well that resistance would be met with brutality, and surrender with peaceful takeover. The Chimú were quickly deprived of their chieftains, many of them taken to Cusco (along with the highly skilled metallurgists) to be indoctrinated into Inca ways. Sixty years later when the first Spaniards rode through Chan Chan, they found a ghost town full of nothing but dust and legends.

Museo di Sitio

A few hundred metres before the entrance to the Nik Am temple-citadel

The **Museo de Sitio** is a good place to start your visit to Chan Chan. It offers an interesting eight-minute multimedia show in Spanish, and uses scale replica models, ceramics and other archeological finds to reconstruct life in the hot but irrigated desert before modern Trujillo was built.

Nik Am temple-citadel

Get off the Huanchaco bus at the concrete Nik Am/Chan Chan signpost about 2km beyond the outer suburbs. From here, follow the track to the left of the road for 10–15min until you see the ticket office (on the left), next to the high defensive walls around the inner temple-citadel

The best place to get an idea of what Chan Chan must have been like is the **Nik Am temple-citadel**, the only one of nine temples open to the public, even though it's now stuck out in the desert among high ruined walls, dusty streets, gateways, decrepit dwellings and open graves.

Following the marked route around the citadel through a maze of corridors, chambers, and amazingly large plazas, you will begin to form your own picture of this highly organized ancient civilization. For example, in the small courtyard just past the entrance gateway, some 25 seats are set into niches at regular intervals along the walls. By sitting in one niche and whispering to someone in another, you can witness an unusual acoustic effect: this simply designed **council room** amplifies all sounds, making the niches seem like they're connected by adobe intercoms.

Fishing-net motifs are repeated throughout the citadel's design, particularly in the **sunken ceremonial patio** (an antechamber before the entrance to the *audiencias)*, and show how important the sea was to the Chimú people, both mythologically and as a major resource. Dedicated to divinities and designed to receive and hold offerings and tributes brought by worshippers for the ruler, the **audiencias** lead to the **main ceremonial courtyard**, which has been restored with lines that mimic the waves, and also to the corridor of fish and bird designs.

The westernmost point accessible on the site is the burial area, known as the **Recinto Funerario**, and the most sacred part of Nik Am, where the tomb of El Señor Chimo and his wives, plus over a hundred human sacrifices, were found. Beyond the citadel extend large areas of untended ruins that are dangerous for visitors – people have been robbed after wandering off alone.

7

Huaca La Esmeralda

Get off the Huancacho bus at the colonial church of San Salvador de Mansiche, at blocks 14 and 15 of Av Mansiche, then follow the path along the right-hand side of the church for three blocks (through the modern barrio of Mansiche), until you reach the *huaca*

One of the most beautiful, and possibly the most venerated of Chimú temples, **Huaca La Esmeralda** (The Emerald Temple) lies in ruins a couple of kilometres before Nik Am, just off the main Trujillo-to-Huanchaco road. Unlike Nik Am, the *huaca*, or sacred temple, is on the very edge of town, stuck between the outer suburbs and the first cornfields. It was built in the twelfth or early thirteenth century – at about the same time as the Nik Am temple-citadel – and is one of the most important of the *huacas* scattered around Trujillo. Uncovered only in 1923, its adobe walls and decorations were severely damaged in the freak rains of 1925 and 1983. Now you can only just make out what must have been an impressive multicoloured **facade**. All the relief work on the adobe walls is original, and shows marine-related motifs including friezes of fishing nets, a flying pelican, a sea otter and repetitive patterns of geometrical arabesques.

The *huaca* has an unusually complex structure, with two main platforms, a number of surrounding walls and several sloping pathways giving access to each section. From the top platform, which was obviously a place of worship and possibly the cover to a royal tomb, you can see west across the valley to the graveyards of Chan Chan, out to sea, over the cultivated fields around the site and into the primitive brick factory next door. Only some shells and *chaquiras* (stone and coral necklaces) were found when the *huaca* was officially dug out some years ago, long after centuries of *huaqueros* (treasure hunters) had exhausted its more valuable goods. These grave robbers nearly always precede the archeologists. In fact, archeologists are often drawn to the sites they eventually excavate by the trail of treasures that flow from the grave robbers through dealers' hands into the market in Lima and beyond.

Huaca Arco Iris (or Huaca del Dragon)

Due to safety considerations (the outskirts of Trujillo have seen an increase in gang-related crime and muggings recently) it is best to take a taxi (S/10–15).

The **Huaca Arco Iris** (Rainbow Temple) is the most fully restored ruin of the Chan Chan complex and one of the oldest sectors at 1100 years old, located just to the left of the Panamericana, about 4km north of Trujillo in the middle of the urban district of La Esperanza. The *huaca* consists of two tiers: the **first tier** is made up of fourteen rectangular chambers, possibly used for storing corn and precious metals for ritual purposes, while a path slopes up to the **second tier**, a ceremonial platform where sacrifices were held and the gods apparently spoke. From here, there is a wide view over the valley, towards the ocean, Trujillo and the city of Chan Chan.

Several interpretations have been made of the **central motif**, which is repeated throughout the *huaca* – some consider it a dragon, some a centipede and some a rainbow. Most of the main **temple inner walls** have been restored, and they are covered with the re-created central motif. The outer walls are decorated in the same way, with identical friezes cut into the adobe, in a design that looks like a multi-legged serpent arching over two lizard-type beings.

INFORMATION AND TOURS — THE CHAN CHAN COMPLEX

Facilities There's a small interpretive centre at the Nik Am complex entrance, as well as toilets, a cafetería and souvenirs, plus a life-size model of a Chimú warrior in full regalia in the central courtyard.

Guided tours Easily arranged (around S/10 for the museum); guides for the Nik Am complex (S/40 for a group of 1–4 people) are at the Nik Am entrance, and can also take you round the *huacas*.

Tickets Entrance to the three archeological sites of the wider Chan Chan complex and the Museo de Sitio is included on the same ticket (S/10), which is valid for only two days (but you can try asking for an extension if you need more time). There are ticket offices at the Museo de Sitio, the Nik Am temple-citadel and at Huaca Arco Iris.

The Chicama Valley

The **Chicama Valley**, north of the Río Moche and about 35km from Trujillo, is full of **huacas** and ancient sites, the most famous – and impressive – being the **Complejo Archeológico El Brujo**. The valley is also home to the remains of fortresses and an irrigation system possibly dating back nearly 6000 years, to when the Río Chicama was connected to the fields of Chan Chan by a vast system of canals and aqueducts over 90km long. Today, however, the region looks like a single enormous sugar-cane field, although in fact it's divided among a number of large sugar-producing co-operatives, originally family-owned **haciendas** that were redistributed during the military government's agrarian reforms in 1969. Even more laidback than Huanchaco, the isolated seaside village of **Puerto Chicama**, 65km north of Trujillo, offers excellent surfing opportunities.

Complejo Archeológico El Brujo

50km north of Trujillo • Daily 9am–5pm, entry to the museum led in site ticket • S/10 • elbrujo.pe • Free 1hr 20min Spanish-only tour available on request with local guides; tips welcome • From Trujillo, take a bus to Chocope from the Santa Cruz (ex-Chicago) bus terminal on Av America Sur. Once there, take a colectivo to Magdalena de Cao (every 30min; S/1.5), about 5km from the site and the nearest place that local colectivos pass through. From Magdalena, a mototaxi will take you and wait for the return for S/15. It's significantly easier to take a tour from Trujillo or Huanchaco

The **Complejo Archeológico El Brujo**, is a Mochica-built complex of associated adobe temple ruins incorporating the Huaca Cao Viejo to the south, plus the *huacas* Cortada and Prieto, slightly to the north. Most of the recent discoveries have been made in Huaca Cao Viejo, most notably a mummy, known as the Señora de Cao, who was clearly a powerful shamanic leader, with intricate tattoos of spiders, fish and snakes found on her hands and arms. It is after her that the complex is named; "El Brujo" means "The Wizard".

Her body is now on display in the small but excellent onsite **Museo Cao**, alongside other artefacts uncovered from her tomb, including a rich booty of fifteen necklaces of gold, silver and precious stones, 24 half-silver, half-gold *narigueras* (ornaments hooked to the nose

SUGAR AND THE TRUJILLO REGION

Sugar cane was first brought to Peru from India by the Spanish in the seventeenth century and quickly took root as the region's main crop. Until early in the twentieth century, the haciendas were connected with Trujillo by a British-operated rail line, whose lumbering old wagons used to rumble down to Trujillo full of molasses and return loaded with crude oil; they were, incidentally, never washed between loads. Although the region still produces nearly half of Peru's sugar, it has diversified as well. These days, Chicama is also well known for the fine Cascas semi-seco **wine** it produces. The haciendas are renowned, too, for the breeding of *caballos de paso* – **horses** reared to compete in dressage and trotting contests, a long-established sport that's still popular with Peruvian high society.

used by warriors) and even a pot representing the different stages of her life. You'll also find textiles dating back to 3000 BC and a who's who of pottery produced or traded within the region. In a small room next to the main museum, archeologists have constructed a full replica of the Señora de Cao's face, using cutting-edge forensic technology and drawing on the facial structures of Moche descendants still living in the region.

To get to the complex, you have to pass through the nearby village of **MAGDALENA DE CAO** – the ideal place to sample *chicha del año*, an extra-strong form of **maize beer** brewed in the valley.

The huacas

Three main ceremonial *huacas* make up the Huaca El Brujo site: Cortada, Cao Viejo and Prieta. **Huaca Cao Viejo** is the largest pyramid and the only one you can visit, topped by a ceremonial platform some 30m high, from where you can see right across the Chicama Valley and note at least seven earthy "hills"; these are just some of at least 200 *huacas* in the surrounding area. In a small chamber further down is where Señora de Cao's tomb was uncovered; on the surrounding walls, you'll see many original painted murals representing Ai-Apaec, discovered here as recently as 1990. Outside the pyramid, high relief friezes showcase the same grizzly sacrifice rituals as those visible in Huaca de la Luna (see page 363).

Opposite Huaca Cao Viejo, the un-excavated **Huaca Cortada** is named for the way it looks like it's been sliced through the middle, while **La Huaca Prieta** sits at the edge of the ocean, ten minutes' walk west of the main Huaca El Brujo site. It is the oldest of the temples, at around 3000 years old, and there are signs of subterranean dwellings on the top – believed to have housed agriculturists who used fishing nets made from cotton – that have been long since excavated by archeologists Larco Hoyle and Junius Bird.

Puerto Chicama

PUERTO CHICAMA (also known as **Puerto Malabrigo**), 13km northwest of Paijan and 74km north of Trujillo, is a small fishing village that once served as a port for the sugar haciendas (see page 372), but is now much better known as a **surfers**' centre, offering some of the best waves on Peru's Pacific coast. The place is slowly establishing tourism facilities, with a new *malecón* built along the southern stretch of the bay, and most hostels will rent you a surfboard – or know someone who can. The sea here is said to have the longest left-hand breaking surf in the world, often reaching heights of over 2m and running for over 2km, with March the best month. Novice surfers may want to check out the gentler waters of Lobitos (see page 415) or Máncora (see page 417).

GETTING AROUND — THE CHICAMA VALLEY

While there are buses and colectivos serving the Chicama Valley, it is a good day-trip from Trujillo and many people prefer to go on a guided tour to visit El Brujo (see page 370) or to hire a taxi with driver and guide for the day (S/90).

By bus From Trujillo, catch the El Dorado from Terminal Santa Cruz on Av America del Sur to Puerto Malabrigo (every 30min; S/4.50; 2hr).

By taxi You can usually find taxis in Chicama or Chocope that'll take you to the sites for around S/20 an hour.

ACCOMMODATION AND EATING

Hotel Nuevo Amanecer Tacna 104 044 576 045. Set on the northern edge of the beach, this place is spotlessly clean, with somewhat soulless bedrooms but superbly friendly service. Breakfast not included. S/80

Surf House Chicama 044 576 138. Rooms are large and modern and there's a liberal sprinkling of hammocks in this popular surfers' hangout with large kitchen. They rent boards and wetsuits for S/50 for a full day and can arrange classes. S/110

Chicamo Restobar Zona Turistica 986 109 964. One street back from the new *malecón*, this place has surprisingly good Peruvian and international food. Check out their sushi (S/20) and beef or quinoa burgers (S/15). They also rent boards and can organize surfing trips to nearby beaches. Daily noon–4pm & 6–11pm.

Cajamarca

A grand Andean town, **CAJAMARCA** is second only to Cusco in the grace of its architecture and the soft drama of its mountain scenery. The city's stone-based architecture reflects the cold nights up here – charming as it all is, with elaborate stone filigree mansions, churches and old Baroque facades. Almost Mediterranean in appearance, Cajamarca, at 2720m above sea level, squats below high mountains in a neat valley.

Proud and historic, the city has intrinsic interest as the place where Pizarro captured and ransomed the Inca Emperor, Atahualpa, for gold – before killing him anyway. The metal has been an issue here since Pizarro arrived. Today the operations of massive **gold mines** in the region are generating protest; there are grave concerns in the area that the gold industry is polluting the land and groundwater.

Brief history

As far back as 1000 BC the fertile Cajamarca Basin was occupied by well-organized indigenous cultures, the earliest sign of the Chavín culture's influence on the northern mountains. The existing sites, scattered all about this region, are evidence of advanced civilizations capable of producing elaborate stone constructions without hard metal tools, and reveal permanent settlement from the **Chavín** era right through until the arrival of the conquering **Inca** army in the 1460s.

For seventy years after the Incas' arrival in the 1460s, Cajamarca developed into an important provincial garrison town, evidently much favoured by Inca emperors as a stopover on their way along the Royal Highway between Cusco and Quito. With its hot springs, it proved a convenient spot for rest and recuperation after the frequent Inca battles with "barbarians" in the eastern forests. The city was endowed with sun temples and sumptuous palaces, so their ruler's presence must have been felt even when the supreme Inca was over 1000km away to the south in the capital of his empire.

Plaza de Armas

The city is laid out in a grid system centred around the **Plaza de Armas**, which was built on the site of the original triangular courtyard where Pizarro captured the Inca leader Atahualpa in 1532.

La Catedral de Cajamarca

Plaza de Armas • Mon 4–6pm, Tues–Fri 8–11am & 4–6pm, Sat 9–11am • Free

On the northwest side of the plaza is the late seventeenth-century **Catedral de Cajamarca**, its walls incorporating various pieces of Inca masonry, and its interior

ATAHUALPA'S LAST DAYS

Atahualpa, the last Inca lord, was in Cajamarca in late 1532, relaxing at the hot springs, when news came of **Pizarro** dragging his 62 horsemen and 106 foot soldiers high up into the mountains. Atahualpa's spies and runners kept him informed of their movements, and he could easily have destroyed the small band of weary aliens in one of the rocky passes to the west of Cajamarca. Instead he waited patiently until Friday, November 15, when a dishevelled group entered the streets of the deserted Inca city.

For the first time, Pizarro saw Atahualpa's camp, with its sea of cotton tents, and an army of men and long spears. Estimates varied, but there were between 30,000 and 80,000 Inca warriors, outnumbering the Spanish by at least two hundred to one.

SPANISH TRICKERY

Pizarro was planning his coup along the same lines that had been so successful for Cortés in Mexico: he would capture Atahualpa and use him to control the realm. The plaza in Cajamarca was perfect, as it was surrounded by long, low buildings on three sides, so Pizarro stationed his men there, hidden from view. Leaving most of his troops outside on the plain, Atahualpa entered the plaza with some five thousand men, unarmed except for small battle-axes, slings and pebble pouches. He was carried into the city by eighty noblemen in an ornate carriage – its wooden poles covered in silver, the floor and walls with gold and brilliantly coloured parrot feathers. The emperor himself was poised on a small stool, richly dressed with a crown placed upon his head and a thick string of magnificent emeralds around his aristocratic neck. Understandably bewildered to see no bearded men and not one horse he shouted, "Where are they?"

7

A moment later, the Dominican friar, **Vicente de Valverde**, came out into the plaza; with a great lack of reverence to a man he considered a heathen in league with the Devil, he invited Atahualpa to dine with Pizarro. The Lord Inca declined the offer, saying that he wouldn't move until the Spanish returned all the objects they had already stolen from his people. The friar handed Atahualpa his Bible and began preaching unintelligibly to the Inca. After examining this strange object Atahualpa threw it angrily to the floor. As Vicente de Valverde moved away, screaming – "Come out, Christians! Come at these enemy dogs who reject the things of God." – two cannons signalled the start of what quickly became a **massacre**. The Spanish horsemen hacked their way through flesh to overturn the litter and capture the emperor. Knocking down a two-metre-thick wall, many of the Inca troops fled onto the surrounding plain with the cavalry at their heels. Spanish foot soldiers set about killing those left in the square with speed and ferocity. Not one Inca raised a weapon against the Spanish. Atahualpa, apparently an experienced warrior-leader, had badly underestimated his opponents' crazy ambitions and technological superiority – steel swords, muskets, cannons and horsepower.

ATAHUALPA'S RANSOM

Taken prisoner by the Conquistadors after the deaths of 7000 or so of his followers and aware of the Spanish lust for gold, Atahualpa offered to buy his freedom by filling a large chamber with the precious metal, and it took a year for this ransom to be gathered, with priceless objects melted down and turned into bullion. Atahualpa had good reason to fear his captors' treachery, and sent messages to his followers in Quito to come and free him. These messages were intercepted by the Spanish who sentenced him to death by being burnt at the stake. In the end, the sentence was changed to garrotting as Atahualpa accepted a last-minute baptism. The help he sought never came and the Spanish justified murdering the Inca ruler by claiming that Atahualpa won his title by treachery against his own brother and that they, in fact, were freeing the Incas from Atahualpa's 'tyranny'. These events were dramatized in the 1964 British play, *The Royal Hunt of the Sun* and also in the 1969 film version of the play.

distinguished only by a splendid Churrigueresque altar created by Spanish craftsmen. Its Plateresque Baroque facade is the most elaborate of all of Cajamarca's churches.

Iglesia San Francisco and Museo de Arte Religioso

Plaza de Armas • **Church** Mon–Sat 7–11am & 4–7pm, Sun 4–8pm • Free • **Museum** Mon–Sat 10am–noon & 4–6pm • S/5

Opposite the cathedral on Plaza de Armas is the elaborate Plateresque Baroque **Iglesia San Francisco**, in whose sanctuary the bones of Atahualpa are thought to lie, though they were originally buried in the church's cemetery. Attached to the church, the **Convento de San Francisco** houses a **museum** devoted to religious art. For a small fee, a guide will happily take you into the crypt to view the bones of the church's benefactors, the catacombs where the Franciscan monks are seeing out eternity (some entombed as recently as 2001) and several rooms around the attractive cloisters where you can view examples of the Cusco, Cajamarca and Quito schools of art from the sixteenth to eighteenth centuries. See if you can spot the *Cristo de la Columna*, with a four-legged Christ, and Satan's head in the painting depicting San Jerónimo.

La Dolorosa

Plaza de Armas • Mon–Fri 10am–5pm • Free

One of Cajamarca's unique features was that, until relatively recently, none of the churches had towers, in order to avoid the colonial tax rigidly imposed on "completed" religious buildings. The eighteenth-century chapel of **La Dolorosa**, next to Iglesia San Francisco, followed this pattern; it does, however, display some of Cajamarca's finest examples of stone filigree, both outside and in.

El Cuarto del Rescate (Atahualpa's Ransom Room)

Av Amalia Puga 722 • Tues–Sat 9am–1pm & 3–8pm, Sun 9am–1pm • S/5 joint ticket (see above)

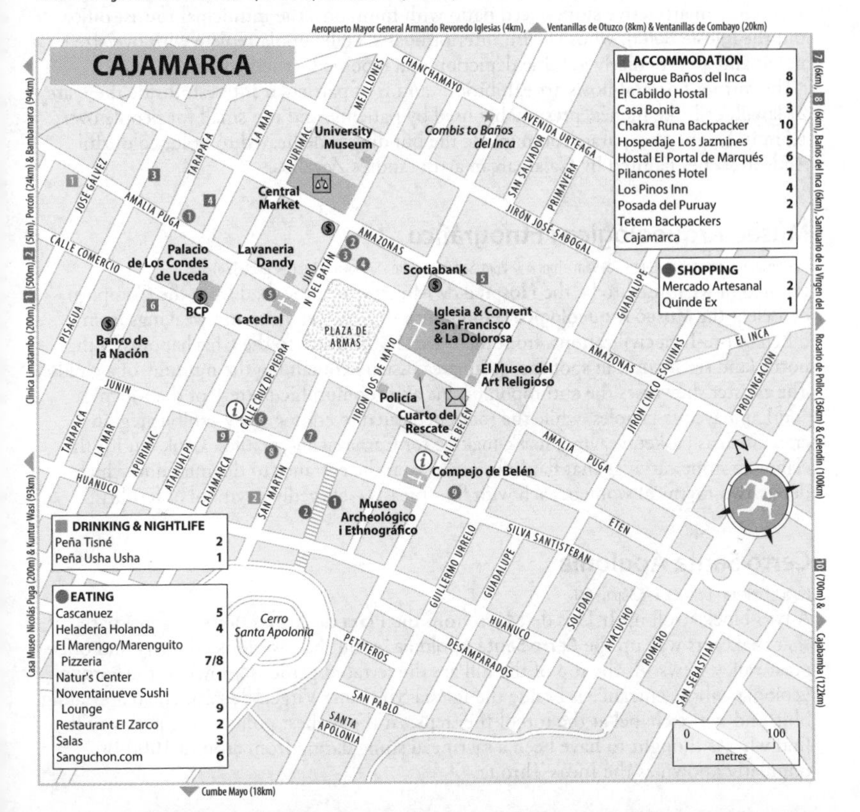

TICKETS IN CAJAMARCA

A single **ticket** (S/5) allows entrance to three of Cajamarca's main attractions, **El Cuarto del Rescate**, the **Museo Arqueológico i Etnográfico** and the **Complejo Belén**, the last of which includes the **Iglesia Belén** and the former **Hospital de Hombres**. The ticket can be bought at either the El Cuarto del Rescate or the complex.

The most famous sight in town, **El Cuarto del Rescate** is the only Inca construction still standing in Cajamarca. Lying just off the Plaza de Armas, across the road from the Iglesia San Francisco, the Ransom Room is a small rectangular room with Inca stonework in the backyard of a colonial building. It has long been claimed that this is the room which Atahualpa, as Pizarro's prisoner, promised to fill with gold in return for his freedom, but historians are still in disagreement about whether this was just Atahualpa's prison cell. There is, however, a line drawn on the wall at the height to which it was supposed to be filled with treasure, and you can also see the stone on which Atahualpa is thought to have been executed. The room's trapezoidal niches and doorways are classic Inca constructions. A painting at the entrance to the site depicts Atahualpa being burnt at the stake – the fate to which he was originally sentenced (see page 374).

Complejo de Belén

C Belén • Tues–Sat 9am–1pm & 3–8pm, Sun 9am–1pm • S/5 joint ticket (see above)

The **Complejo de Belén** (Belén Complex) comprises the former Hospital de Hombres, which has an attractive stone-faced patio with fountains, the municipal tourist office and the **Iglesia Belén**, whose lavish interior boasts a tall cupola replete with oversized angels and a particularly graphic depiction of a bloodied, crucified Jesus.

The former hospital hosts art exhibitions and is of particular interest: inside there are 21 small, cell-like niches, presumably used by patients, and too small for people over 1.5m in height. A separate room inside the building is dedicated to bold, colourful Andean scenes painted by Cajamarcan artist Andrés Zevallos.

Museo Arqueológico i Etnográfico

C Belén and C Santisteban • Tues–Sat 9am–1pm & 3–8pm, Sun 9am–1pm • S/5 joint ticket (see page 376)

Located in what used to be the Hospital de Mujeres, over the road from the Complejo de Belén, the **Museo Arqueológico i Etnográfico** displays ceramics and weavings from different pre-Inca civilizations, from the Nazca in the south to the Chachapoyas in the north (and see if you can spot the Cajamarca ossuary containing the mummy of a child). The cloister showcases the anthropomorphic and zoomorphic pottery of the Mochica and Lambayeque peoples, while the room dedicated to ethnography exhibits regional crafts such as basket weaving, mask-making for Carnaval and textiles. Look out for the elaborate stone carvings that flank the archway at the entrance to the museum, which depict two mythical women, each with four breasts – allegedly a symbol of fertility.

Cerro Santa Apolonia

Parque Ecología • Daily 7am–6.30pm • S/1

A two-block stroll up Jr Dos de Mayo from the Plaza de Armas takes you to a path that snakes its way up the **Cerro Santa Apolonia**, a hill that overlooks the city and offers great valley views. At the top of the hill are the terraced gardens known as the **Parque Ecología**, whose entrance is beside the Iglesia Santisima Virgen de Fatima, an appealing blue-and-white chapel at the top of the steps. At the highest point in the park you'll find what is thought to have been a sacrificial stone dating from around 1000 BC, popularly known as the Inca's Throne.

Casa Museo Nicolás Puga

Av José Gálvez 634 • By appointment only • S/20 • 976 234 433

Set within a beautifully maintained 1780 adobe colonial mansion, the **Casa Museo Nicolás Puga** is a private collection of treasures, complied over decades. Owner Don Nicolás guides you through eight rooms, overflowing with everything from antique European clocks to decocrative altarpieces that were once displayed in the private churches of local haciendas.

Upstairs, the real highlights include the pre-hispanic textiles, some dating back 2000 years to the Nazca and Paracas cultures, plus the incredible display of Mochica *tumbaga* armour (made from a metal alloy of copper mixed with gold) and Chavín stone statues, the latter of which include a seated mummy and a musician playing the flute.

ARRIVAL AND DEPARTURE — CAJAMARCA

BY PLANE

Aeropuerto Mayor General Armando Revoredo Iglesias (076 343 960) is 4km out of town, on Av Arequipa. It is served from Lima by LATAM, Jr Sor Manuela Gil, in the Centro Comerical El Quinde (lan.com; Mon–Sun 10am–9pm), and LC Perú, Jr Comercio 964 (lcperu.pe; Mon–Fri 8am–7pm). The quickest and cheapest way to and from the airport is by taxi (S/10–15).

Destinations Lima (4 daily; 1hr 20min).

BY BUS/COLECTIVO

Most bus terminals are located at or around the third block of Av Atahualpa, a major arterial route running almost directly east out of the city.

Bus companies Cruz del Sur, Av Atahualpa 844 (076 362 024); Civa, Av San Martin de Porres 957 (076 368 186); Tepsa, Jr Sucre 422 (076 363 306); and Línea, Av Atahualpa 306 (076 507 690) all run overnight buses to Lima, with Línea being the most comfortable. Línea also runs services to Chiclayo and Trujillo. Móvil Tours, Av Atahualpa 686 (076 280 093) runs a night service to Chicalyo, where you can find good onward connections to Tumbes via Máncora; Virgen del Carmen, Av Atahualpa 333a (076 606 966), runs direct minibus services to Chachapoyas via Celendín and Leymebamba; Transportes Texas, Av Atahualapa 285 (942 086 348), has hourly minivans to Cajabamba and twice daily departures for Huamachuco.

Destinations Celendín (several daily; 2hr 30min); Chachapoyas (2 daily, 5am & 5pm; 12hr); Chiclayo (7 daily; 6hr); Huamachuco (2 daily, 4am & 3pm; 6hr); Leymebamba (2 daily, 5am & 5pm; 9hr); Lima (at least 10 daily; 16hr); Piura (4 daily; 9hr); Trujillo (5 daily; 6hr); Tarapoto (1 daily, 5am; 18hr).

INFORMATION AND TOURS

Tourist information There's a tourist office in the Complejo de Belén (Mon–Sat 7.30am–1pm & 3–5pm; 076 362 903), while the very helpful staff at iPerú, Jr Cruz de Piedra 601 (Mon–Sat 9am–6pm, Sun 9am–1pm; 076 365 166) are happy to explain how to reach outlying attractions independently. Some English spoken.

Tour operators All the companies offer pretty much the same array of tours, and most of them will pool clients. Catequil Tours, Jr Amalia Puga 689 (076 363 958, catequiltours.com) organizes everything from guided city tours to community tourism in the nearby countryside; Cumbe Mayo Tours, Jr Amalia Puga 635 (076 362 938) offers excursions to all the main sights.

ACCOMMODATION

Most of Cajamarca's accommodation is in the centre of the city, around the Plaza de Armas, although there are also some interesting options slightly out of town.

IN CAJAMARCA

El Cabildo Hostal Jr Junín 1062 976 459 971, elcabildohostal.pe; map p.375. Set around an attractive courtyard filled with greenery and statuary, this rambling old mansion offers a clutch of well-maintained yet somewhat musty rooms with modern showers and polished wooden floors. S/140

Casa Bonita C Pisagua 731 076 363 395, hotelescasabonita.com; map p.375. A charming colonial house with well-kept wooden floors, ceiling beams and an attractive covered patio where visitors can enjoy breakfast. All rooms have private bath, and there's also good internet access. S/160

★ **Chakra Runa Backpacker** Psje Cutervo 129 971 096 916; map p.375. Comfortable and homely, this backpackers' hostel is well-located for both the bus station and the plaza (it's a 10min walk to each). The Peruvian and French hosts are experts on activities in the local area

FIESTAS IN CAJAMARCA

Cajamarca likes to party. Its wildest festival is **Carnaval**, which is celebrated at the beginning of Lent and tends to coincide with the Carnaval in Río. It's a month-long party leading up to eight central days of celebrations, with parades, cultural events, music, dancing and water fights. Anybody is fair game, so if you're in town at the height of celebrations, expect to be soaked with water guns, water balloons, buckets of paint and more. Book accommodation in advance. Another good time to visit Cajamarca is during May or June for the **Festival of Corpus Christi**. Until the early twentieth century this was the country's premier festival, before it was superseded by the traditional Inca sun festival, Inti Raymi, held at Sacsayhuaman in Cusco. Corpus Christi nevertheless actually coincided with the sun festival and is traditionally led by the elders of the Canachin family, who, in the Cajamarca area, were directly descended from local pre-Inca chieftains. The procession here still attracts locals from all around, but increasing commercialism is eating away at its traditional roots. Nevertheless, it's fun, and visited by relatively few non-Peruvian tourists, with plenty of parties, *caballos de paso* meetings and an interesting trade fair – though be warned, you're also likely to come across a bullfight or two.

and can advise on reaching nearby cave paintings and waterfalls. Dorms S/25, doubles S/52

Hospedaje Los Jazmines Jr Amazonas 775 ⓣ076 361 812, ⓦhospedajelosjazmines.com.pe; map p.375. A comfortable hotel in a converted colonial house surrounds a leafy courtyard, with an antique doll collection housed in the latter. The excellent *Espresso Bar* on the premises serves some of the best coffee in town. Rooms are simple en suites. This place is associated with a charity that supports less-able children. S/90

★ **Hostal El Portal de Marqués** C Comercio 644 ⓣ076 368 464, ⓦportaldelmarques.com; map p.375. A formidable stone gateway leads you into the immaculate courtyard of this restored colonial house, surrounded by two floors of modern, carpeted rooms decked out in warm colours and with welcome touches of contemporary art. S/206

Pilancones Hotel Jr Angamos 739 ⓣ076 362 986, ⓦhotelpilanconescajamarca.com; map p.375. Although the surrounding street is somewhat scruffy, everything is perfectly in order in this modern hotel a 10min walk from the plaza. Bedrooms are huge and decorated with Andean textiles; ask for one with a mountain view – they're away from the street noise and have more light. S/160

Los Pinos Inn Jr La Mar 521 ⓣ076 365 992, ⓦlospinosinn.com; map p.375. Tucked away down a quiet street, this mansion combines Old World elegance in the form of gilded mirrors, antique furniture and a rather splendid staircase with Old World kitsch (the suits of armour in the lounge) and modern amenities (cable TV, wi-fi). Choose from the cheaper old wing or the newer bedrooms. Doubles S/120, suites S/280

EATING

Cajamarca is famous for its **dairy** products, including the widest variety of cheese in Peru. It's often served as *choclo con queso*, where you literally get a slab of cheese with a big cob of corn – a delicious snack. Other dishes include *caldo verde* (green broth) – something of an acquired taste – made from potato, egg, herbs and quesillo cheese, and *picante de papas con cuy* (potatoes with peanut and chili sauce with fried guinea pig).

★ **Cascanuez** Jr Amalia Puga 548 ⓣ076 366 089; map p.375. The best coffee and cake in town is served in this refined café. Also good for lunchtime sandwiches, *humitas* and four types of breakfast (S/15–17). Daily 7.30am–midnight.

Heladería Holanda Jr Amalia Puga 657, on the plaza; map p.375. There's a real artisan at work here preparing some excellent ice cream using local milk and fresh tropical fruit. It's hard to go wrong with *maracuyá* (passion fruit) or *lúcuma* (eggfruit). Cones from S/3. Daily 9am–7pm.

El Marengo/Marenguito Pizzeria Jr Junín 1201 ⓣ076 368 045 & Junín 1184 ⓣ076 344 251; map p.375. This tiny pizzeria, warmed by a giant wood-burning oven, is so popular it has two branches practically opposite each other; the latter (*Marenguito*) is actually larger. Both get packed with locals after the best pizza in town (from S/16), washed down with sangria. Daily 5.30–11pm.

Natur's Center Jr Amalia Puga 409; map p.375. Chow down on simple, cheap and hearty vegetarian food at this titchy restaurant where wheat soups and butter bean stews make up the S/5 set lunch menu. There's an extensive selection of vegetarian takes on Peruvian classics (such as *lomo saltado* and *lomo a lo pobre*) on their a la carte. Mon–Thurs 8am–2pm & 5–8pm, Fri 8am–2pm.

★ **Noventainueve Sushi Lounge** Jr Silva Santisteban 157 ⊕076 362 928; map p.375. An incongruously sleek and stylish sushi bar with Japanese decoration and a wide selection of Peruvian-style sashmi and sushi: think prawns, avocado and lashings of cream cheese. Sushi from S/20. Daily 6–11pm.

Restaurant El Zarco Jr del Batán 170 ⊕076 312 241; map p.375. One of the few standout local cafés in Cajamarca, *El Zarco* is always packed with locals. It plays a wide range of mostly Latin music and offers an enormous variety of tasty, large dishes, including excellent trout, served in a refined, 1920s atmosphere. Mains from S/12. Mon–Fri & Sun 7am–11pm.

Salas Jr Amalia Puga 637 ⊕076 362 867; map p.375. Local institution *Salas* has been around since 1947 and is still run by the same family, with a repertoire of regional dishes that's hard to fault. There's *cuy* with potato and rice stew (S/30), *caldo verde* (S/7), dish-of-the-day specials (a steal at S/10), plus sandwiches and light bites. Daily 7am–10pm.

Sanguchon.com Jr Junín 1137 ⊕076 343 066, ⊕sanguchon.com.pe; map p.375. This lively hole-in-the-wall bar specializes in humongous sandwiches. And what sandwiches they are! Choose from overflowing burgers, grilled chicken sandwiches (the Californichicken stands out) or the Vito Corleone if you really want to push the boat out – an epic creation comprising steak, double cheese, eggs and more. Sandwiches S/9–15. Mon–Sat 6–11.30pm.

7

DRINKING AND NIGHTLIFE

Peña Tisné Jr San Martín 265; map p.375. This is neither a real *peña* nor a real bar, but a one-of-a-kind Peruvian experience that should not be missed. Knock on the unmarked door and Don Victor will lead you through his house to his bohemian back garden, full of cosy tables and memorabilia soaked in Cajamarcan history. Everyone is welcome here, from tourists to poets to the mayor. Try the home-made *macerado* – a delicious liquor made from fermenting tomatillo (an exotic fruit) and sugar (pitcher S/16). Daily 9am–midnight.

★ **Peña Usha Usha** Jr Amalia Puga 142; map p.375. The best venue in town for live Peruvian, (especially criolla) music, as well as Cuban troubadour-style performances. A small space is busiest on Fri and Sat but also entertaining during the week when owner Jaime Valera inspires locals and tourists alike with his incredibly talented and versatile guitar playing and singing. Often lit only by candles, this bar has a cosy and inviting atmosphere. Thurs–Sat 9pm–2am.

SHOPPING

Mercado Artesanal Jr Dos de Mayo 255; map p.375. There's a handful of artisans – who you'll see at work – at this collection of stalls, but the rest is mass-produced tat. Daily 10am–7pm.

Quinde Ex Jr Dos de Mayo 264; map p.375. A wonderful little artesanía shop with a good selection of textiles, bags and shawls. Daily 9.30am–1.30pm, 3–6.30pm.

DIRECTORY

Banks and exchange BCP, Jr Del Comercio 675; Banco de La Nación, Jr Tarapaca 647; Scotiabank, Jr Amazonas 750. *Cambistas* are on Jr Amalia Puga on the main plaza.

Hospital Clínica Limatambo, Jr Puno 263, ⊕076 362 241. Private, high-standard care.

Laundry Lavandería Dandy Jr Amalia Puga 545.

Post office SERPOST, at Jr Apurímac 626 (Mon–Fri 8am–7pm, Sat 8am–6pm).

Tourist police Jr del Comercio 1013 (⊕076 354 515).

Around Cajamarca

Within a short distance of Cajamarca are several attractions easily reachable on a day-trip from the city. The most popular trip from Cajamarca is to the steaming-hot thermal baths of **Baños del Inca**, just 6km from the city centre. Further out are the impressive aqueduct at **Cumbe Mayo**, the ancient temple at **Kuntur Huasi** and the "windows" into the world of the dead: the two ancient necropolises of **Ventanillas de Otuzco** and **Ventanillas de Combayo**. On the road to Celendín, there are also the striking mosaics at the **Santuario de la Virgen del Rosario de Polloc**.

Baños del Inca and around

6km east of Cajamarca • Daily 5am–4.45pm, final entrance 3pm • S/3–25 • ctbinca.com.pe • 15min ride from the intersection of Jr Dos de Mayo and Jr Chanchamayo in Cajamarca with combis leaving when full (S/0.80), usually every 10min or so

Many of the ruins around Cajamarca are related to water, in a way that seems to both honour it in a religious sense and use it in a practical way. A prime example of this is the **Baños del Inca**, where the Inca ruler allegedly recuperated from war wounds. The baths, which actually date from pre-Inca times, have long been popular with locals and wallowing in the thermal waters is a glorious way to spend a few hours (mornings are best to avoid the crowds). There's a restored Inca bath within the complex, but the stonework, though very good, is not original. It was from here that the Inca army marched to their doom against Pizarro and co. You can choose between using the public pool (S/3), cleanest on Mondays and Fridays; and little private pools (S/6–25). Sauna (S/10) and massages (S/20) are also on offer and there's a decent guesthouse attached (see page 382).

Ventanillas de Otuzco

8km east of Cajamarca • Daily 9am–6pm • S/5 • Direct combis leave from the corner of Jr Gladiolos and C Tayabamba in Cajamarca (S/1) when full

The **Ventanillas de Otuzco** are a huge pre-Inca necropolis where the dead chieftains of the Cajamarca culture were buried in niches (windows), sometimes metres deep, cut by hand into the volcanic rock. They can be reached either directly by colectivo or via an enjoyable two-hour (one way) walk along the road that follows the river north from outside the Baños del Inca (ask for directions).

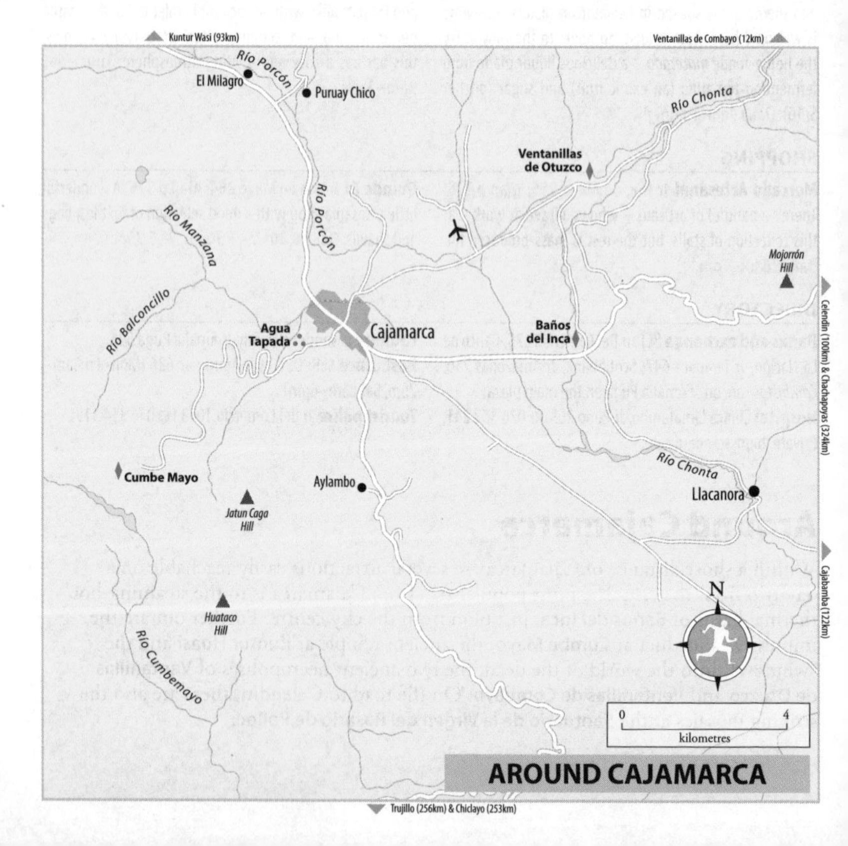

Ventanillas de Combayo

28km northeast of Cajamarca • Daily 9am–4pm • Free • Direct combis leave from block 1 of Jr Pérez in Cajamarca when full (S/5)

Twelve kilometres further east from the Ventanillas de Otuzco are the **Ventanillas de Combayo**, a much larger necropolis of niches carved out of the rock, but far less visited. Colectivos pass nearby but you have to ask the driver to drop you off at the entrance to the site and then walk up; otherwise it's a four-hour walk (one-way) from Otuzco.

Santuario de la Virgen del Rosario de Polloc

36km east of Cajamarca • Daily 8am–6pm • Free, donations appreciated • Take a combi to the outskirts of the village of Polloc with Encañada Tours at Av Atahualapa s/n (opposite the entrance to C Uchuracay) (S/3; 40 min), from where it's a short walk to the church

From its humble beginnings in 2008, the spectacular mosaics of the **Santuario de la Virgen del Rosario de Polloc** are now a real highlight of the region, demonstrating hours of patient work by a brigade of local children from the area who live and study art, woodwork and other crafts in the *albergue* behind the main church building. The project was instigated by Italian priest Don Bosco, but it is his young charges who have since painstakingly created magnificent mosaic friezes depicting religious scenes that wrap the external walls of the school buildings and continue inside the church (make sure you look up as you enter to admire the burst of colour on the ceiling) and into the small square with a statue of the Virgen del Rosario, the patron saint of Polloc, at the centre. There's also a small shop on site (you'll need to ask for it to be opened) where you can buy religious statues in a similar mosaic style.

Cumbe Mayo

18km southwest of Cajamarca • Daily 8am–5pm • Best to visit with a tour operator (S/20–25 per person, including site entry)

Southwest of Cajamarca stands the ancient aqueduct and canal of **Cumbe Mayo**, stretching for over 9km in an isolated highland dale. A twenty-kilometre dirt road winds up here from Cajamarca, affording fantastic views of the city below. From the parking area, the two-kilometre trail loops past the Bosque de Piedras (Forest of Stones), where huge clumps of eroded limestone taper into some fanciful shapes. A little further on, you'll see the well-preserved and skilfully constructed **canal**, built around 1200 BC, making it one of the oldest man-made structures in South America. Dotted along the canal are some interesting **petroglyphs** attributed to the early Cajamarca culture. The amount of meticulous effort which must have gone into crafting the aqueduct, cut as it is from solid rock with perfect right angles and precise geometric lines, suggests that it served a more ritual or religious function rather than being simply for irrigation purposes. Cumbe Mayo originally carried water from the Atlantic to the Pacific watershed via a system of canals and tunnels, many of which are still visible and in some cases operational. To the right-hand side of the aqueduct (with your back to Cajamarca) there is a large face-like rock on the hillside, with a man-made **cave** cut into it. This contains some 3000-year-old petroglyphs etched in typical Chavín style (you'll need a torch to see them) and dominated by the ever-present feline features. If you'd prefer to walk back, ask your tour guide to leave you at the trailhead for the path that drops back down into Cajamarca (2hr 30min).

Kuntur Wasi

93km west of Cajamarca • Daily 9am–5pm • S/5 • Visit via full-day tour (S/250) or take a colectivo (S/10) to the village of San Pablo from Jr Angalamos 1121 in Cajamarca (every hour; 1hr 30min). From here, it's a short mototaxi ride (S/2) to the ruins

Largely destroyed by the ravages of time and weather, **Kuntur Wasi** was clearly once a magnificent temple. You can still make out a variation on Chavín designs carved onto its four stone monoliths. Apart from Chavín itself, this is the most important site in the northern Andes relating to the feline cult; golden ornaments and turquoise were found in graves here. So far, not enough work has been done to give a precise date to the site, although the anthropomorphic carvings indicate they were installed throughout different time periods, suggesting the site was built, inhabited and renovated by various cultures, such as the Chavín, between 1200 and 200 BC. Whatever its age, the pyramid is an imposing ruin amid exhilarating countryside. There's a small site **museum** displaying mostly replicas of pieces uncovered here by archeologists, plus maps of the site and photographs of the first major excavations that were led by a team from the University of Tokyo.

ACCOMMODATION **AROUND CAJAMARCA**

Albergue Baños del Inca Behind the thermal bath complex ⓣ076 348 249, ⓦctbinca.com.pe; map p.375. A number of rooms (doubles and family rooms), as well as two-person bungalows, all comfortable and with their own built-in thermal bathrooms, TV, minibar and living room. Many of the chalets afford stunning views of, and direct access to, the complex of atmospheric steaming baths. Doubles S/60, bungalows S/150

★ **Posada del Puruay** 5km north of the city ⓣ076 367 028, ⓦposadapuruay.com.pe; map p.375. A country mansion converted into a luxury hotel-museum. All rooms have colonial furniture and iron bedsteads, and are decorated in warm ochres and yellows. Besides its sculpted grounds and lovely interior, this gorgeous mansion is notable for its ecological approach (they have their own organic garden) and range of activities for guests, from horseriding to mountain biking. S/255

Tetem Backpackers Cajamarca 500m east along the main road beyond the Baños del Inca complex, on the right ⓣ076 280 042, ⓔtetembackpackerscax@gmail.com; map p.375. Attention's a bit surly and there's no breakfast, but they've got a thermal swimming pool (when it's filled) and communal kitchen. Bedrooms are large – although the cheaper doubles have small beds. Dorms S/26, doubles S/50

South from Cajamarca

It's a long but rewarding journey south from Cajamarca to the small town of **Huamachuco**, jumping-off point for visiting the archeological site of **Marcahuamachuco** and the remarkable, rarely visited and very remote ruins of **Gran Pajatén**. The small colonial town of Cajabamba is the only other place of significance en route, but its main function is as a place to change buses. The road from Trujillo is now paved, making the journey a more comfortable – and shorter – six hours.

Huamachuco

Infamous in Peru as the site of the Peruvian army's last-ditch stand against the Chilean conquerors back in 1879, **HUAMACHUCO**, at 3180m, is a fairly typical Andean market town, surrounded by partly forested hills and a patchwork of fields on steep slopes. The site of the battle is now largely covered by the small airport, while the large Plaza de Armas in the centre of town possesses an interesting colonial archway in one corner, which the Liberator Símon Bolívar once rode through. Now, however, it's flanked by the modern cathedral.

FIESTAS IN HUAMACHUCO

On the first weekend in August the **Fiesta de Waman Raymi** is held at nearby Wiracochapampa, bringing many people from the town and countryside to the Inti Raymi-style celebrations. Other festivals in the region include the **Fiesta de Huamachuco** (celebrating the founding of the city) on August 13–20, a week of festivities including a superb firework display on August 14 and aggressive male *turcos* dancers during the procession.

Marcahuamachuco

10km northwest of Huamachuco • Daily 8am–5.30pm • Free • marcahuamachuco.gob.pe • A taxi will take you 5–6km (S/15–20), then walk the rest of the rough road; or 3hr walk one-way • Ask at your guesthouse for 4WD transport (around S/60 for up to 4 people one way, waiting time extra)

The dramatic circular fort of **Markahuamachuco**, located on top of one of several mountains dominating the town, is considered to be of great archeological significance as the most important site relating to the Markahuamachuco culture, thought to have developed independently of its neighbours. Some 3km long, the **ruins** date back to around 300 BC, when they probably began life as an important ceremonial centre, with additions dating from between 600 and 800 AD. The fort was adopted possibly as an administrative outpost during the Huari-Tiahuanaco era (600–1100 AD), although it evidently maintained its independence from the powerful Chachapoyas nation, who lived in the high forested regions to the north and east of here (see page 384). An impressive and easily defended position, Markahuamachuco is also protected by a massive eight-metre-high wall surrounding its more vulnerable approaches. The *convento* complex, which consists of five circular buildings of varying sizes towards the northern end of the hill, is a later construction and was possibly home to a pre-Inca elite ruler and his concubines; the largest building has been partially reconstructed.

ARRIVAL AND DEPARTURE — HUAMACHUCO

By bus Transportes Texas, Av Atahualapa 285 (942 086 348) have departures for Huamachuco at 4am and 3pm from Cajamarca; alternatively, to reach Cajamarca, take any bus to Cajabamba and change there. Tunesa, Jr Suarez 721 (044 441 157), run services to Trujillo.

Destinations Cajabamba (numerous daily; 1hr); Cajamarca (2 daily; 6hr); Trujillo (5 daily; 5hr).

ACCOMMODATION

Hotel Gran Colonial Jr Castilla 539 944 924 444 hotelgrancolonial.com. Just off the Plaza de Armas, this colonial house may not be grand, but its luridly decorated ten rooms have private baths and are arranged around a pleasant courtyard with fountain. Good restaurant on-site. S/60

Hostal Huamachuco Jr Castilla 354 044 440 599. Close to the Plaza de Armas, this appealing guesthouse attracts younger travellers with its clutch of swing-a-cat singles, doubles and triples, set around a quiet courtyard. S/70

Gran Pajatén

322km to the nearest town, Patáz, from Cajamarca

Discovered in the 1960s, the remote archeological site of **Gran Pajatén** is difficult to reach and rewards those who are successful. Added to the World Monuments list in 2014, and inhabited as early as 200 BC, this important Chachapoyas site consists of sixteen typical circular structures, as well as terraces with elaborate decoration, both built mainly of a slate-type stone. One of the round buildings is thought to have been a temple, another living quarters. Many of the walls features elaborate slate mosaics (similar to those found around Kuélap; see page 390), with geometric and anthropomorphic figures that have been created by the way in which these frequently thin stones are placed in the walls. Some of the buildings had once been elaborately painted in red, yellow, white and black and Mausoleum no. five still retains six curious *pinchidos* (*caoba*-wood sculptures) dangling from the rafters, depicting nude men with elaborate headgear, arms folded over their stomachs and exposed genitalia. Their purpose is unknown and you can see a lifesize example at the Museo de Leymebamba (see page 392).

ARRIVAL AND DEPARTURE — GRAN PAJATÉN

By bus and mule A fairly rough road connects Huamachuco with the village of Patáz, reachable by several combis weekly. In Patáz you can hire mules and guides for the trek to Gran Pajatén, which is a three-day walk one way, making this a true expedition (roughly S/100 per day). The site is only open to those with authorization from the Ministerio de Cultura and SERNANP in Lima; contact sanmartin@cultura.gob.pe or 016 189 393 ext 203 who can help with the formalities.

Chachapoyas and around

The thriving market town of **CHACHAPOYAS**, at 2334m high up in the Andes, is rapidly gaining traction as a springboard for a wealth of nearby pre-Columbian remains. West of Chachapoyas lie the **Pueblo de los Muertos** and **Karajía**, two impressive cliff-face burial centres for the elite of the Chachapoyas. However, the most famous and most worthwhile of all the Chachapoyan archeological remains is **Kuélap**, a huge citadel complex. South of here lie **Balsas** and **Leymebamba,** the latter with its excellent museum. To some extent, the ancient culture lives on in some of the remote, traditional communities like **La Jalca**, 76km south of Chachapoyas. Less than 30km north of Chachapoyas gush the fabulous **Cataratas de Gocta**, which compete with nearby **Catarata Yumbilla** over the title of the tallest falls in Peru.

The town is centred around the tranquil **Plaza de Armas**, surrounded by the cathedral and the municipal buildings and with a colonial bronze fountain as its centrepiece: a monument to Toribio Rodríguez de Mendoza. Born here in 1750, he is considered the main source of Peru's ideological inspiration behind independence from its colonial master, Spain. The town's main church of interest, the **Iglesia de Santa Ana**, Jr Santa Ana 1056, was built in 1569 by the Spanish to ensure the commitment of Chachapoyas' indigenous population to Christianity.

Brief history

In Aymara, Chachapoyas means "the cloud people", perhaps a description of the fair-skinned tribes who used to dominate this region, living in one of at least seven major cities (like Kuélap, Magdalena and Purunllacta), each one located high up above the Utcubamba Valley or a tributary of this, on prominent, dramatic peaks and ridges. Many of the local inhabitants still have a remarkably light-coloured complexion. The Chachapoyas people, despite building great fortifications, were eventually subdued by the empire-building Incas. **Chachapoyas** was once a colonial possession rich with

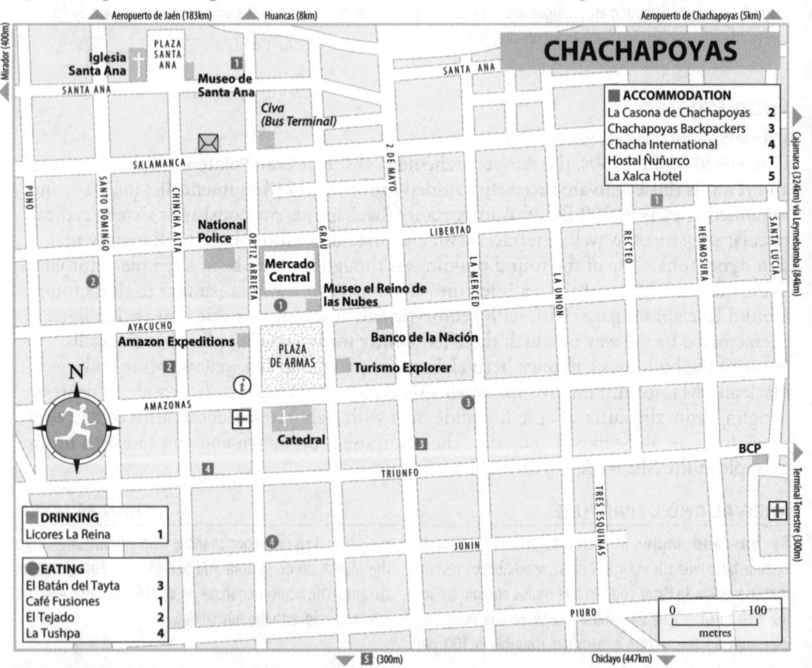

THE TWO ROADS TO CHACHAPOYAS

There are two routes up to Chachapoyas from the south; the far longer and less exciting route is the road leaving the coast from Chiclayo and Piura via Olmos, Jaen and Bagua; this route has fewer and lower passes but is not terribly scenic, and is prone to landslides during the rainy season.

A fascinating **alternative route to Chachapoyas** is the direct scenic route – a precarious one-lane highway (with spots to pull over) from Cajamarca that passes through Celendín and Leymebamba, winding its way up and down several massive valleys and passes. This road is completely paved but there's a reason why the driver's assistant hands out travel sickness bags at the start of the journey: the curves can be nausea-inducing – many locals tend to be sick – and it's best if you have a head for heights, given the sheer drop to one side, which is stunning or terrifying, depending on your outlook. Just to up the risks stake, this scenic route can be taken overnight, although it's advisable to travel during the day as drunk bus drivers are an unfortunate reality. Passing via the market town of Celendin, the road descends into the Marañón Valley and the smaller town of Balsas. Climbing again, the bus reaches heights of almost 4000m, dropping down to Leymebamba and passing along the valley to reach the town of Chachapoyas.

gold and silver mines as well as extremely fertile alluvial soil, before falling into decline during the Republican era.

Museo el Reino de las Nubes

Jr Ayacucho 904 • Mon 3–5.30pm, Tues–Fri 9am–1pm & 3–5pm • Free

Right on the plaza, the small **Museo el Reino de las Nubes** offers an excellent introduction to the various archeological sites in the region. Displays include 1000-year-old textiles, a drum made from reindeer leather (with antlers still attached), a mock up of a Kuélap dwelling and to-scale models of *purunmatshu*, the sarcophagi found at Karajía, plus a collection of mummies, one of which looks like it's laughing. Labels are in Spanish but you can request an English-language booklet at the entrance.

ARRIVAL AND DEPARTURE — CHACHAPOYAS AND AROUND

By plane Aeropuerto de Chachapoyas is 5km northeast of Chachapoyas and served by ATSA Airlines (T 017 173 268, W atsaairlines.com), which has flights to and from Lima on Tues, Thurs and Sat. SAETA, Jr Grau 293 (T 972 657 957), has flights Mon–Sat for Tarapoto. Rainfall (especially Nov–May) can cause long delays; it's safest to book onto the earliest flight of the day. A taxi from the airport costs S/10. Aeropuerto de Jaén, 4hr by road from Chachapoyas, has daily flights with LATAM (T 076 313 777) to Lima.

Destinations Lima (3 weekly to Chachapoyas; daily to Jaén; 1hr 20min); Tarapoto (6 weekly; 20min).

By bus The best of the bus companies, the comfortable Movil Tours at Libertad 464 (T 041 478 545, W moviltours.com.pe), serves Lima, Chiclayo and Trujillo, while Civa at Jr Ortiz Arrieta 279 (T 041 478 048) also runs to Lima and Chiclayo. Buses go via Pedro Ruíz rather than the shorter route via Cajamarca. There are no direct buses for Tarapoto; instead, take a bus or colectivo to Pedro Ruíz and then the Movil Tours bus coming from Piura that passes through Pedro Ruíz at midnight.

Destinations Chiclayo (4 daily; 9hr); Lima (3 daily; 22hr); Trujillo (1 daily; 12hr).

By colectivo Minibuses and shared cars to regional destinations depart from the Terminal Terrestre at block two of Jr Triunfo, around 10 blocks from the Plaza de Armas. Vírgen del Carmen (T 976 015 594) has daily minibuses to Tarapoto and Cajamarca via Leymebamba; Turismo Selva (T 961 659 443) has four departures for Tarapoto; Tours Tella (T 961 769 021) and Trotamundo (T 956 918 759) go to Nuevo Tingo, with the latter also serving San Bartolo; Turismo Días (T 940 159 156) has one daily departure for Jaén; Raymi Express has frequent departures to Leymebamba; Chinata Tours (T 978 041 600), TED (T 950 046 809) and Los Diplomáticos (T 964 509 665) run to Pedro Ruíz when full; Transportes San Roque (T 951 055 805) runs to La Jalca; and shared cars run by Transporte Luya & Lamud (T 962 081 421) run when full to Luya and Lamud between 5am and 6pm.

Destinations Cajamarca (1 daily; 7.30pm; 10–12hr); Jaén (1 daily; 4hr); La Jalca (1 daily; 3hr); Lamud (several daily; 1hr); Leymebamba (6 daily; 2hr 30min); Luya (several daily; 1hr); Pedro Ruíz (numerous daily; 1hr); San Bartolo (1 daily; 2hr); Tarapoto (5 daily; 8hr); Nuevo Tingo (every 30 min; 1hr).

INFORMATION AND GETTING AROUND

Tourist information iPerú's office, Jr Ortiz Arrieta 582 (Mon–Sat 9am–6pm, Sun 9am–1pm; ⊕041 477 292). For advice on archeological sites, try the Direción Regional de Cultura Jr Ayacucho 904 (Mon–Fri 8am–1pm & 3–5.45pm).

By taxi Taxis around town charge a flat rate of S/3; you can flag them down in the street.

ACCOMMODATION

La Casona de Chachapoyas Jr Chincha Alta 569 ⊕041 477 353; map p.384. Another elegant colonial mansion set around a charming courtyard, with chandeliers and a cosy open fire in the living area. Bedrooms have beautiful wooden beams and are elegantly decorated, while hot water is plentiful and an ample American or regional breakfast is included. S/190

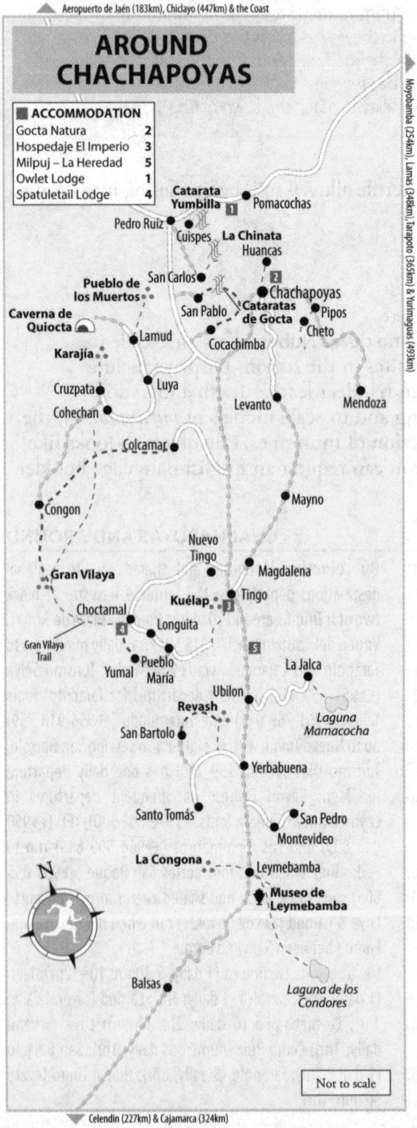

Chachapoyas Backpackers Jr 2 de Mayo 639 ⊕041 478 879, ⓦchachapoyasbackpackers.com; map p.384. This central hostel is the one most warmly recommended by backpackers. The simple, swamp-green rooms (some with own bathrooms) come with funky lamps in the shape of Karajía sarcophagi and guests congregate in the small kitchen. Unfortunately, there are only a few shared bathrooms to go around. Dorm S/20, doubles S/45

Chacha International Jr Triunfo 1098 ⊕948 757 586, ⓔchacha17international@gmail.com; map p.384. Clean rooms and beds with the added luxury of an actual duvet cover. Lacking a bit in atmosphere, but has a decent shared kitchen and an attached language school. Dorm S/18, doubles S/40

Hostal Ñuñurco Jr Ortíz Arrieta 186 ⊕041 477 845, ⓦnunurcotravellers.com; map p.384. Three blocks from the plaza, this rambling guesthouse is run by several friendly, helpful guys who organize tours to nearby sites. Breakfast is simple and the rooms are spacious, tiled and spick and span. There's wi-fi throughout the hotel. S/100

La Xalca Hotel Jr Grau 940 ⊕041 479 106, ⓦlaxalcahotel.com; map p.384. Adding a touch of Old World charm to Chachapoyas' accommodation options, this handsome mansion sports antique furnishings, chandeliers in the lounge and seriously spacious rooms – some carpeted, some tiled – with strangely low beds. Service is professional, and the breakfast buffet features regional specialities such as *humitas*. S/330

AROUND CHACHAPOYAS

ACCOMMODATION
Gocta Natura 2
Hospedaje El Imperio 3
Milpuj – La Heredad 5
Owlet Lodge 1
Spatuletail Lodge 4

Aeropuerto de Jaén (183km), Chiclayo (447km) & the Coast
Moyobamba (254km), Lamas (348km), Tarapoto (365km) & Yurimaguas (493km)
Celendín (227km) & Cajamarca (324km)
Catarata Yumbilla
Pomacochas
Pedro Ruíz
Cuispes
La Chinata
Huancas
San Carlos
Pueblo de los Muertos
Chachapoyas
Cataratas de Gocta
Pipos
Cheto
San Pablo
Caverna de Quiocta
Lamud
Cocachimba
Karajía
Luya
Cruzpata
Cohechan
Levanto
Mendoza
Colcamar
Mayno
Congon
Nuevo Tingo
Magdalena
Gran Vilaya
Kuélap
Tingo
Choctamal
Longuita
Gran Vilaya Trail
Pueblo María
Yumal
La Jalca
Ubilon
Revash
Laguna Mamacocha
San Bartolo
Yerbabuena
Santo Tomás
San Pedro
Montevideo
La Congona
Leymebamba
Museo de Leymebamba
Balsas
Laguna de los Condores
Not to scale

EATING

El Batán del Tayta Jr La Merced 604 ⊕982 777 219; map p.384. A corridor inscribed with messages from happy customers greets you as you enter, and the menu is as eclectic as the decor, running the gamut from steak marinated in *chicha* and coriander rice with duck to imaginative salads and shredded pork wontons. Wash it down with pineapple sangria or one of their signature sours. Mains from S/22. Mon–Sat noon–11pm.

TOURS FROM CHACHAPOYAS

There are numerous tour operators dotted around the Plaza de Armas, all of which offer standard day-trips at standard prices to Kuélap (S/90), Karajía combined with either Pueblo de Los Muertos or the Caverna de Quiocta (S/90), Gocta waterfall (S/60), Yumbilla waterfall (S/197), and Revash combined with the Museo de Leymebamba (S/120); some offer more specialized trips. The above prices cover transport, guide, entrance fees and lunch. Not all companies and guides are certified, however, and not all guides speak English. Below are three certified tour agencies with good reputations and bilingual tour guides.

Amazon Expeditions Jr Ortiz Arietta 508 041 798 718, amazonexpedition.com.pe. Highly professional outfit that runs four-day treks to Gran Vilaya combined with Karajía and Kuélap (S/650), three-day treks to Laguna de los Cóndores (S/850), plus rafting half-day trips with certified guides along the Río Utcubamba, one hour from Chachapoyas (S/100).

Nuevos Caminos In Café Fusiones, Jr Ayacucho 952, nuevoscaminostravel.com. Community-based tours to the coffee farms of the Cooperative Agraria Rodrigues de Mendoza (S/184), plus day and multi-day trips to Catarata Yumbilla (S/197) and other local sights.

Turismo Explorer Jr Grau 509 041 478 162, turismoexplorerperu.com. Experienced, competent operator that also runs popular day-trips to Kuélap, Karajía, Gocta and Revash, as well as multi-day explorations of Gran Vilaya.

7

★**Café Fusiones** Jr Ayacucho 952 960 119 965, caféfusiones.com; map p.384. This bohemian hangout specializes in largely organic "slow food"'. Come here for spicy lentil burgers, thick milkshakes and fresh juices, plus chunky sandwiches, ample breakfasts and great teas and coffees. A book exchange makes it even more linger-worthy. Mains from S/12. Mon, Tues & Thurs–Sun 7am–10.30pm.

El Tejado Santo Domingo 424 041 477 592; map p.384. Really good traditional Peruvian and local cuisine served in a warm, friendly ambience around a patio. The speciality here is several takes on *tacu tacu*, a rice and beans dish. Lunch from S/10. Daily noon–4pm.

La Tushpa Jr Ortiz Arrieta 753 041 477 471; map p.384. A magnet for the carnivorously inclined, this restaurant specializes in meat dishes such as *cuy* (S/25), *chicharrónes* (deep-fried pork), steak and *anticuchos de corazón* (oxheart kebabs). It's not gourmet (the meat can be tough) but it'll do in a pinch. Mains S/15–35. Mon–Sat 1–10pm.

DRINKING

Licores La Reina Jr Ayacucho 544; map p.384. Set around a wide patio, this is the locals' favourite bar for a drink of the boisterously potent *macerado* (cane sugar *aguardiente*, infused with fruit) made on the premises, and guaranteed to put hairs on your chest. Daily 9am–1am.

DIRECTORY

Banks and exchange BCP is on Triunfo, seven blocks from the Plaza de Armas and next to the hospital. Banco de la Nación is at block eight of Ayacucho, where you can change money. Both have global ATMs.

Post office Jr Salamanca 956 (Mon–Fri 8am–7pm, Sat 8am–4pm).

Karajía

46km southwest of Chachapoyas • Daily 8am–5pm • S/5 • It's easiest to go via organized tour (see page 387) from Chachapoyas. Alternatively, catch a shared car to Luya and then one to Cruzpata

A characteristic of the Chachapoyas region are the ancient **sarcophagi**, elaborately painted clay coffins moulded around a cone made of wooden poles, dating back to the fifteenth century and often stuck inaccessibly into horizontal crevices high up along cliff faces to prevent desecration by grave robbers. There are over 250 sarcophagi sites in the region, of which the only accessible one is the **Karajía** site.

From the plaza in the village of Cruz Pata, it's a one-kilometre descent via dirt road and steep steps to the narrow walkway hugging the cliff. Thirty metres above you, you can see a row of six sarcophagi (there were eight but two were destroyed) with heads

CONSERVATION AROUND CHACHAPOYAS

The Amazonas region has one of the largest concentrations of private **conservation projects** in all of Peru, many of which are combining efforts to preserve nature with sustainable, community-led tourism in comfortable lodgings. Most are affiliated with **Conservamos Por Naturaleza** (conservamospornaturaleza.org), an excellent resource for information about sustainable tourism projects in Peru.

★ **Gocta Natura** Cocachimba goctanatura.com; map p.386. Not only does it have the best views of the waterfall from its five boutique cabins, each of which boasts traditional materials and building techniques combined with stylish, modern design, but the hosts have serious conservation credentials. Rocio and Augusto have supported and implemeneted numerous reforestation and education projects in the local area and can organize traditional weaving and cookery workshops in the village. Book well in advance. Meals included. S/890

★ **Milpuj – La Heredad** Km 282, road from Chachapoyas to Leymebamba 991 929 218, peherediarce@gmail.com; map p.386. Hidden away in the dry forest of the Utcubamba Valley, Lola and her son Perico have planted ten thousand native *tara* trees and supported local environmental initiatives since arriving in 2000. Lodgings are in cosy rooms built from traditional materials in their private nature reserve. Activities including bird and wildlife spotting along forest trails (the pampas cat is one of the rarer species), beekeeping and helping out on their organic farm. Meals available. S/189

Owlet Lodge Fernando Belaunde Km 365.5, road towards Tarapoto 984 564 884; map p.386. Set within the grounds of Abra Patricia reserve, home to the rare – once presumed extinct – long-whiskered owlet, just one of over 400 species found here, this lodge has simple but comfortable cabin-style accommodation, plus access to nature trails and an array of hummingbird feeding stations. Prices include all meals; it's also possible to visit the reserve for the day (S/25). They arrange birding tours throughout the north of Peru. S/231

reminiscent of Easter Island's moai. Up to 2m in height, they house the mummies of the most important individuals, such as chieftains, warriors and shamans, as well as their most prized belongings. The two skulls above them and one to the right are thought to be trophy skulls. Walk to the far end of the walkway; from there you'll be able to see another five sarcophagi to the left of the main group – these are far less elaborate and have been thoroughly desecrated. To the left of those there's a solitary sarcophagus, hidden in the shrubbery.

Caverna de Quiocta

46km north of Chachapoyas • S/5, local guide S/40 • Take a colectivo to Lamud (S/5) and motortaxi (S/40 including waiting time) or go with a combined Karajía tour (see page 387)

The **Caverna de Quiocta**, reachable via a muddy, rutted road up from Lamud, is known both for its otherworldly rock formations and mortal remains. The cave is 23m high at its highest point and 55m deep, and consists of five chambers. In the first chamber are skulls and bones, neatly piled on ledges – the remains of a few Chachapoyas people. Overhead, the cave ceiling sparkles with a myriad tiny constellations, actually specs of metal ore. Proceeding deeper into the cave is really muddy going (tour companies stop in Luya to pick up rubber boots); you cross streams, and the deeper you go, the more outlandish the rock formations become, hence the fanciful names of "Beer Mug", "Castles", "Chamber of the Pharaoh" and more. The final chamber features the largest stalagmite formation of them all, looking rather like a Gothic meringue.

Pueblo de los Muertos

30km north of Chachapoyas • S/5 • Take a shared car to Lamud, from where it's a 45min walk down and 1hr 30min walk back up; or S/50 for a taxi (including wait time) • A handful of tour operators combine visits to Pueblo de los Muertos with Karajía during the dry season

The **Pueblo de los Muertos** (City of the Dead), about 3km from Lamud, is where you'll find overgrown roundhouse foundations plus **sarcophagi**, some up to 2m high and carved with human faces. Six were originally found here and three have been put back in their previous sites to stare blankly across the valley from a natural fault in the rock face. Each one has been carefully moulded into an elongated egg-like shape from a mixture of mud and vegetable fibres, then painted purple and white with geometric zigzags and other superimposed designs.

Cataratas de Gocta

Daily 7am–5pm, last entry 2pm • S/10 • Take a colectivo to Cocahuayco and a mototaxi to Cocachimba or San Pablo (S/10), or take a tour from Chachapoyas (S/70; see page 387)

With a cumulative height of 771m, the **Cataratas de Gocta** are some of the tallest falls in the world, although there's much debate over whether nearby Catarata Yumbilla pips them to the post when it comes to the global rankings. Only revealed to the outside world in 2002, local legend says that it is protected by an immense siren-like serpent. Getting to a good viewpoint – from where you can make out the main two tiers of the falls (231m above and another 540m below) – requires some hiking. The walk starts in the hamlet of Cocachimba; from here it's 6km to the base of the falls (you can hire a mule for S/40), but if you want to explore higher or return via San Pablo hamlet on the other side of the valley, you will need at least four to six hours. The hike goes through attractive cloud-forest terrain where *gallitos de la roca* (Peru's emblematic bird) and many other feathered species flit about.

Catarata Yumbilla

35km north of Chachapoyas • Daily 8am–1pm • S/10, S/40 if you want a local guide • Take a colectivo from Chachapoyas to Pedro de Ruíz (S/5; 1hr) then a mototaxi to Quispes (S/10), which will drop you off at the ticket office on the plaza and then take you to the trailhead; or, take a tour from Chachapoyas (see page 387)

A one-and-a-half-hour trek through dense cloud forest from the trailhead, 5km west of Cuispes, brings you out at a series of viewpoints for the **Catarara Yumbilla**, a waterfall of monstrous proportions and considered by some to be the fifth-highest in the world. At 896m, it's certainly taller than nearby Gocta, but, as its three distinct falls often run dry outside of rainy season, many consider it not deserving of the title of tallest in Peru. Either way, it's a spectacular force of nature and the trail leads you past two smaller – but still impressive – waterfalls. The community-run ticket office can also point you in the direction of short treks to visit others in the vicinity.

Kuélap

40km south of Chachapoyas • Daily 8am–5pm • S/20, optional guide for up to twenty people available at the entrance for S/50 • Take a colectivo from Chachapoyas to Nuevo Tingo (S/7; 1hr) from where you board the cable car (S/20 return; 20min) to the ticket office; it's then a 20min walk to the site. Or, take a tour from Chachapoyas (see page 387)

The main attraction for most travellers in the Chachapoyas region is the partially restored ruin of **Kuélap**, one of the most overwhelming pre-Inca sites in Peru, originally inhabited by the Chachapoyas people – a seemingly impregnable stone citadel sitting atop a limestone mountain, with exceptional views of the valleys below. The ruins were discovered by Judge Juan Crisóstomo Nieto in 1843, above the tiny village of **TINGO** in the remote and verdant Utcubamba Valley.

Built sometime between 500 AD and 1493, Kuélap was the strongest, most easily defended of all Peruvian fortress cities, something that can be seen in the narrowing defensive form of the main entry passageways, though walls may have shifted over the centuries due to damage done by the elements.

In 2017, a new teleférico (cable car) was built to connect Tingo Viejo with Kuélap, reducing journey time to only twenty minutes from Tingo Viejo, and virtually sounding the death knell for the tourist enterprises of the communities along the old road to the ruins.

The site

It has been calculated that some 700,000 tonnes of stone were used to build this fortress and to this day, it is not known where the Chachapoyas people obtained it. An estimated four thousand people would have lived here at its height, working mainly as farmers, builders and artisans and living in little, round stone houses.

Kuélap is 700m long and the site's enormous **walls** thrust 20m high, and are constructed from gigantic limestone slabs arranged in geometric patterns, with some sections faced with rectangular granite blocks over forty layers high. The average wall thickness is around 80cm and the largest stone 2m thick.

Inside the ruins lie the remains of some five hundred **round stone houses** which originally sported conical grass roofs; some, thought to be the houses of the nobility, were decorated with a distinctive diamond and zigzag pattern that can still be noted today. The smaller stone circles served a funerary function. Elsewhere, you may spot carved animal heads, condor designs, deer-eye symbols and intricate serpent figures. These are similar in style to the better-known Kogi villages of today's northern Colombia; and, indeed, there are thought to be linguistic connections between the Kogi and the Chachapoyas peoples, and possible links to a Caribbean or even Maya influence. A typical circular house features a stone grinder, a cellar-like hole – some were used as food storage and some for funerary purposes, and a squat, narrow stone tunnel used as a guinea-pig hutch.

The upper part of the citadel features a seven-metre-high watchtower at the north end of the fortress inside which human remains and over 2500 small stones, believed to have been propelled into the air by slingshots in an attempt to hit the clouds and attract rain, have been found, as well as several rectangular buildings, possibly used for ceremonial purposes. At the citadel's south end, there is a unique structure with fine, curved outer walls, which is believed to have been a temple, or at least to have had a ceremonial function. Inside the temple and accessible from the roof is an inverted, truncated cone containing a large, bottle-shaped cavity (known as El Tintero or inkwell), possibly a place of sacrifice, since archeologists have found human bones there and llama remains nearby. Just up from the temple are several more circular houses, believed to have been the dwellings of the priests. If arriving by cable car, look back at the cliff as you start your initial descent into the valley; you'll see a human skull and bones in a hole in the rockface.

ARRIVAL AND DEPARTURE — KUÉLAP

By colectivo and cable car Colectivos run from the Terminal Terrestre in Chachapoyas (5am–5pm) to Nuevo Tingo, where you can buy tickets for the cable car (including a short passage in bus). Cable cars theoretically run daily 8am–5pm, with the final cable car down departing at 3.30pm; however, it's usually closed on Mon for maintenance. Colectivos still shuttle along the winding, precipitous road on a circular anticlockwise route via the village of Choctamal to Malca and the ticket offfice at Kuélap, but this adds an additional hour to your journey. Colectivos run frequently from Tingo Viejo to Chachapoyas.

On foot It's possible to hike up to Kuélap from Tingo Viejo; the 9.8km trail is well signposted but a steep, shadeless slog (around 4hr up and 2hr back down). Leave early to avoid the mid-morning sun, and remember to carry all the water you'll need with you. Alternatively, you can trek up to Kuélap from Pueblo María; it's a 2hr hike up a gently inclining dirt road that passes through Cuchapampa, Quisango and Malcapampa hamlets. It's also possible to take the cable car up and hike back down.

By organized tour The easiest option, although it does mean that you'll be exploring the ruins during the heat of the day with all the other tour groups (see page 387).

ACCOMMODATION

Hospedaje El Imperio Kuélap ☎979 935 592; map p.386. Basic, friendly little place beneath the Kuélap ruins with hot water. Meals (S/8–12) available on request. It's also free to camp next to the nearby INC hostel. S/50

Spatuletail Lodge Kuélap road Km 20, Choctamal ⓣ995 237 268, ⓦmarvelousspatuletail.com; map p.386. A community-run lodge with individually decorated rooms, an orchidarium, telescope observatory and grounds overflowing with bougainvillea, where hummingbirds, including the rare Marvelous Spatuletail, flit. Breakfast an additional S/40. Private tours to Kuélap offered. S/175

Gran Vilaya

54km southwest of Chachapoyas • Colectivos drop you off at the village of Choctamal or Cruz Pata. From here it is expedition-style trekking, with or without horses or mules and with a local guide • 4-day guided treks from Chachapoyas possible (see page 387)

The collection of archeological remains known as **Gran Vilaya** – a superb complex of almost entirely unexcavated ruins scattered over a wide area – are found in the lush mountain valleys west of Chachapoyas. About thirty of these sites are of note, and companies in Chachapoyas run four-day treks into the valley, starting from Cruz Pata and paying a visit to Karajía before crossing a 3000m pass into the splendid Valle Belén. The trek includes staying overnight in very simple accommodation in the villages of Congon and Choctamal en route, visits to important ruins, such as Pirquilla and horse trekking (or hiking, if you prefer) between Congon and the ruins of Lanche, followed by a trek to Choctamal and a visit to Kuélap. This gives you a good taste of Gran Vilaya, but if you're keen on seeing more of the valley's ruins or spending more time in Gran Vilaya, then consider looking for a guide and mules in either Cruz Pata or Choctamal and taking camping gear and food with you.

La Jalca

80km south of Chachapoyas • There are a couple of direct combis from Chachapoyas (leaving at 2pm or 3pm, returning at 5am and 12.30pm), which requires overnighting at one of the very basic guesthouses, but you can also take any Leymebamba-bound combi, get off at the turn-off, and walk up to La Jalca (around 3hr)

Two hours by road from Chachapoyas, the traditional village of **LA JALCA** is within walking distance of a number of ruins. The folklore capital of the region, La Jalca also lays claim to some amazing fourteenth-century stone walls and a seventeenth-century stone-built **church**, with characteristic Chachapoyan zigzags. The houses in the village, built in typical Chachapoyas fashion along the ridge, are lovely, conical thatched-roofed constructions with walls of *tapial*-type mudwork.

Leymebamba and around

The charming cobblestoned village of **LEYMBEBAMBA**, some 80km south of Chachapoyas along the scenic road to Cajamarca, is a good place to break the journey. The land around Leymebamba is rich in archeological sites, the most important being La Congona and Revash. Leymebamba can also be used as a jumping-off point for visiting the spectacular Laguna de los Cóndores, though both destinations can be included in organized tours from Chachapoyas (see page 387).

Museo de Leymebamba

5km south of Leymebamba • Daily 10am–4.30pm • S/15, optional guided tour S/40 for up to 20 people • ⓣ971 104 909 • ⓦmuseoleymebamba.org • Take a mototaxi from the plaza (S/5)

The superb **Museo de Leymebamba** is the home to the 219 Chachapoyas mummies, around 800 years old, from the mausoleum found near the **Laguna de los Cóndores** in 1996. They are remarkably well preserved (some still have eyes) and while many are still wrapped in their original shrouds embroidered with human faces, others – including two babies – are uncovered and seem to be peeking through their fingers at you from behind glass. Other exhibits focus on Chachapoyas and Inca pottery, ritual and household objects and centuries-old weavings. A fascinating display depicts the pick of the region's archeological sites – Karajía, La Petaca, Gran Pajatén – in miniature, and you may also spot two trepanned skulls, a mummified dog and Inca bone flutes, plus a collection of 33 *quipus* (knotted strings used by the Inca to record information) found at Laguna de los Cóndores.

La Congona

5hr return hike from Leymebamba

Up from Leymebamba along a trail that begins at the bottom end of Calle 16 de Julio, **La Congona** is an overgrown site featuring the circular houses of the Chachapoyas as well as a lookout tower which can be climbed for superb views of the valley. Inside the houses there are niches, believed to have been used for storing sacred objects, and many houses feature the distinctive diamond patterns favoured by the Chachapoyas culture. The two-hour trail is reasonably easy to follow but it's not a bad idea to ask for directions before you go, or ask for a guide (around S/100) for the half-day.

Revash

40km north of Leymebamba • Accessed either via 5km uphill hike from the turnoff to the Santo Tomás village or via a level 3km walk from San Bartolo village

Consisting of several red-and-white mudbrick *chullpas* (funerary buildings) that look remarkably like cheerful cottages, **Revash** is a thirteenth-century burial site, built by the Revash culture (contemporaneous with the Chachapoyas people), where skeletal remains were found by archeologists (even if the tombs themselves had been looted) and where rock paintings decorate the cliff behind the tombs. There is some public transport from Chachapoyas to the villages, but it's easiest to take a tour from Chachapoyas (see page 387) that drops you off either at the Santo Tomás or the San Bartolo trailhead.

Laguna de los Cóndores

36km from Leymebamba • S/10 • Accessed via a 3-day, 2-night trek/horseride from Leymebamba (S/550) or from Chachapoyas (S/850)

This gorgeous highland lake, fringed with cloud forest, was the location of a remarkable archeological find in 1996, when some local *campesinos* stumbled upon six Chachapoyas tombs perched on a ledge above the water. They turned out to contain a treasure trove of mummies and funerary objects, which you can view at the Museo de Leymebamba. The lake is a tough but beautiful ten- to twelve-hour uphill trek from Leymebamba; guided three-day treks involve a day's stay at the lake and exploration of the area. Enquire about guides and horses at the museum, *La Casona de Leymebamba* or *Kentitambo* (see page 393), or else join a guided trek from Chachapoyas (see below).

ARRIVAL AND DEPARTURE — LEYMEBAMBA AND AROUND

By bus Three companies run colectivos from Chachapoyas to Leymebamba's Plaza de Armas; of these, Vírgen del Carmen (☎ 990 161 661) and Amazonas Express continue to Cajamarca. Vírgen, with minibuses rather than buses, are theoretically safer, although incidents involving drunk drivers (as the drive from Leymebamba to Cajamarca is now only taken at night) make this journey somewhat hard to recommend. Raymi Express, based in the Terminal Terrestre, has the most frequent Chachapoyas–Leymebamba departures.

Destinations Cajamarca (daily at 10pm; 8–10hr); Chachapoyas (6 daily; 2hr).

ACCOMMODATION AND EATING

La Casona de Leymebamba Jr Amazonas 223 ☎ 957 607 416, casonadeleymebamba.com. Run by the indefatigable Nelly, this beautiful house dates back to 1906, with heavy wooden beams, a tranquil inner courtyard overflowing with flowers and a hanging orchid garden – the owner's passion. Most beds come with antique, carved wooden headboards. The owner can put you in touch with local guides if you wish to visit Revash, the Laguna de los Cóndores or other local attractions. S/230

KentiKafé Opposite the Museo de Leymebamba. By far the best place for coffee or a light meal, this café sits uphill from the Museo de Leymebamba, and besides enjoying the excellent coffee, chunky sandwiches and home-made cakes, you can also observe seventeen different species of hummingbird at feeders strategically placed amid the greenery. Sandwiches from S/8. Daily 8.30am–5.30pm.

Kentitambo Next to KentiKafé ❶971 118 259, ⓦkentitambo.com. Surrounded by lush gardens, this boutique guesthouse consists of just two bungalows, both with king-sized beds, rain showers, and hammocks out front. The hosts are multilingual historians who can tell you all about the Laguna de los Cóndores mummies. **S/550**

SHOPPING

A.M.A.L. Jr San Agustín 429. Right on the plaza, this is the main outlet for the local women's co-operative that specializes in high-quality weavings, scarves and bags. A small selection of their work is also available at the Museo de Leymebamba. Daily 9am–6pm.

Artesania Huamán Jr Bolognesi 550, Anexo Dos de Mayo, in the streets just below the Museo de Leymebamba ❶941 878 830. Having been part of the group who discovered the treasures at Laguna de los Cóndores, artisan Miguel Huamán Revilla now carves wooden replicas of the artefacts, on sale in his tiny workshop. Daily 7am–5pm.

Tarapoto and around

7

TARAPOTO, known as the "City of Palms", is a sweltering, busy jungle town that has become a growing hub for health tourism, especially yoga and ayahuasca, with a motley collection of lodges and centres offering multi-day retreats. It also makes a good base from which to explore the surrounding villages and waterfalls, prepare for a spell in the jungle or do some whitewater rafting on the Río Mayo. It has excellent road connections with the jungle port of Yurimaguas, the starting point for one of Peru's best Amazon river trips to Iquitos (see page 467) via the remote rainforest haven of **Reserva Nacional de Pacaya-Samiria** (see page 476).

Lamas

20km northeast of Tarapoto • Take a colectivo from Jr Urgarge, block 10 (S/5; 30min) or go with a tour with one of the agencies on the plaza for S/35

Surrounded by large pineapple plantations, the small village of **LAMAS**, up in the forested hills near Tarapoto, is very popular with tour groups, which stop at the Plaza de Armas where a statue of Inca leader Pachacutec shaking hands with a conquistador clearly takes great liberties with history. After a visit to the small history museum, visitors are whisked off to the *mirador* overlooking the town before descending to the incongruous-looking brick castle built here by an Italian expatriate in 2005. A final stop involves mingling with the inhabitants of Barrio Wayco, who reputedly are the direct descendants of the Chanka tribe that escaped from the Andes to this region in the fifteenth century, fleeing the conquering Inca army. You can meet them selling their traditional (and not so traditional) handicrafts to tourists. The best month to visit is August, when the village **Fiesta de Santa Rosa de Lima** is in full swing.

Cataratas de Ahushiyacu and Cataratas de Huacamaillo

Ahushiyacu 16km east from Tarapoto • Tours S/30–40 (including transport) • **Huacamaillo** 13km north from Tarapoto • Tours S/70 (including transport)

The forty-metre **Cataratas de Ahuashiyacu** are a scenic local swimming spot; they are situated along the road east towards Yurimaguas, and you can get any Yurimaguas-bound bus or colectivo to drop you off. The **Cataratas de Huacamaillo** are trickier to get to, with a two-hour trek that involves river crossings; this one is easiest done by tour.

ARRIVAL AND DEPARTURE — TARAPOTO AND AROUND

By plane Tarapoto airport is 5km from the centre of town. A mototaxi into town costs S/5–8. LATAM, Jr Hurtado 183, and Peruvian Airlines, Jr Hurtado 277, have four daily flights to Lima, while Viva Air (ⓦvivaair.com), and Star Peru, Jr Pablo de la Cruz 325 have daily flights to Lima, the latter also flying to Iquitos.

Destinations Iquitos (daily; 1hr); Lima (6 daily; 1hr).

By bus Most bus companies operate from the Terminal Terrestre Morales, 1 de Mayo, opposite the cemetery (S/3 by mototaxi from the centre), with departures for Lima, Chiclayo, Pucallpa and Trujillo between 7am and 6pm. To get to Chachapoyas, change at Pedro Ruíz or take a combi (see below). Civa (T 042 522 269) is a good bet for Lima and Pedro Ruíz. while Trans Amazonica (T 942 680 495) has a daily service to Pucallpa at 8.30am. Movil Tours at Av Salaverry 880 (T 042 529 193) is the most comfortable option for Chiclayo, Trujillo and Lima,

Destinations Chiclayo (several daily; 14hr); Lima (several daily, via Pedro Ruíz; 25–30hr); Pucallpa (daily at 8am; 15hr); Trujillo (several daily; 15–18hr).

By colectivo Turismo Selva, Jr Alfonso Ugarte 1128 (T 042 530 100) has combis running to Yurimaguas and directly to Chachapoyas. Pizana Express Tarapoto, Jr Cuzco 556 (T 942 013 618) is the most recommended of the minivans travelling to Tingo Maria. Be aware that, until recently, this road maintained quite the reputation, as cars were held up by armed robbers and badly maintained bridges caused long travel delays. Get up-to-date information on the ground before taking a colectivo south.

Destinations Chachapoyas (5 daily; 8hr); Tingo Maria (daily 3am, 9am if passengers; 12hr); Yurimaguas (every 15min; 2hr).

INFORMATION AND ACTIVITIES

Get chatting to the locals, and you'll be told that Tarapoto is the new place for **health tourism**, with shamanas from Iquitos arriving in droves to offer ayahuasca ceremonies.

Tourist information The Municipal tourist information office on the northwest corner of the Plaza de Armas (daily 7am–11pm; T 042 526 188) isn't hugely helpful; you'll find more useful information in the hostels.

Sacharuna Adventure T 931 828 324, W sacharunadventure.com. Your best bet for immersive cultural tourism in and around San Roque de Cumbaza; they arrange activities including ceramic and chocolate workshops in indigenous communities, hikes and river tours to nearby protected areas.

Tambo Ilusión 15min south of Tarapoto by mototaxi T 942 754 466, W tamboilusion.com. Offer multi-day yoga retreats (including SUP yoga), reiki introduction classes, vegetarian cookery classes and 8-day ayahuasca retreats, all based in their beautiful, rustic *tambos* (small huts) in a 14-hectare nature reserve. They also have 3-day/2-night packages starting at US$360 for two, including hiking, food and accommodation, and can organise 4-day birdwatching tours in the Cordillera Escalera conservation area, where you've a chance of spotting 16 types of hummingbirds (including the endemic Koepcke's hermit) among the 98 species of bird known to reside in the region.

ACCOMMODATION

Bambú Jr Moray 521 T 014 443 964. E tarapoto.bambu@gmail.com. Easily the most popular backpackers' hangout in the area, with friendly policies such as a free laundry load. Rooms are cramped and breakfast isn't included, but there's a communal kitchen and English-speaking staff with plenty of information about visiting the local attractions independently. Dorms S/20, doubles S/40

★ **Chirapa Manta** Camino a San Roque T 997 435 611 W chirapamanta.com. Buried deep within the tropical forest only 30min from Tarapoto, this lodge offers serenity and silence in spades. Expect cosy, well-furnished bedrooms with luxurious cotton curtains and a hammock-slung terrace from which to enjoy the soothing rhythm of the Río Cumbaza. Breakfast, a wholesome mix of fruit salad, pancakes and granola with lumps of roasted cacao, is as divine as the setting. They also offer massages and yoga and work directly with Sacharuna Adventure (see page 395). S/165

Colibri Jr Gregorio Delgado 374 T 997 333 511 E colibri.tarapoto@gmail.com. Set around a leafy patio – where resident opossum Pinky lives – this relaxed hostel has spacious rooms with fans, a large kitchen and a delicious vegetarian breakfast (dorms cost S/5 more with breakfast) of chapattis, cane sugar honey, fruit juice and coffee. Dorms S/30, doubles S/70

★ **El Mirador** Jr San Pablo de la Cruz 517 T 042 522 177, W elmiradortarapoto.com. With its hammock-hung upper terrace overlooking the sea of green in the valley below, this guesthouse is made all the sweeter by its motherly matriarch. Individually decorated rooms are spotless and spacious (particularly the newer a/c doubles), the extensive breakfast features eggs, fruit salad and fresh fruit juice, and your hosts can help you organize tours and transport. S/120

EATING AND DRINKING

Tarapoto has seen a huge boom in **vegetarian** restaurants lately, and there are at least four within a few blocks of the plaza, many of which have cheap lunch menus. The Jr San Pablo de la Cruz Solidus and Jr Lamas intersection is lined with bars pumping loud music and serving jungle-themed cocktails.

Estar Cajue Jr San Pablo de la Cruz 243 T 042 341 052. With a leafy courtyard out front, this sedate café mocks Starbucks, but more importantly it serves an impressive range of coffees (ristretto, cortado, Americano and espresso are all present and correct; S/5), iced coffees, milkshakes and fruit juices. Sustenance is ample, with a range of traditional Peruvian dishes such as *lomo saltado*, sandwiches, crêpes and large breakfasts (S/12). Daily 8.30am–12.30pm & 5.30–10.30pm.

★ **Mamá Julia** Jr Grau 1005 T 042 529 417. It's a ten-minute walk north of the plaza to reach this *cevichería*,

7

but it's worth every step: sit yourself down at the bar and watch as they whip you up a feast of *ceviche de corvina* with *chicharrón de pescado* (S/16), *leche de tigre* (S/8) and dishes combining *causa de pescado* (mashed potato filled with fish), seafood fried rice and ceviche (S/18). Easily the best fish you'll find in the city. Mon 10am–5pm, Tues–Sun 10am–5pm & 7–11pm.

La Patarashca Jr Lamas 261 042 528 810 lapatarashca.com. Atmospherically lit, breezy restaurant shrouded in greenery, specializing in jungle dishes such as *patarashka* (fish steamed in a leaf with tomatoes, garlic, onions and sweet peppers) and smoked wild pork with *patacones* (balls of mashed, fried green plantains). Mains from S/25. Daily 11am–11pm.

★ **Zygo Café** Jr Hurtado 417. An oasis of calm from the noise of the street, this Peruvian-French vegetarian café rises above the competition with its hearty bowls of quinoa, organic goats'cheese and almond salad (S/17), granola breakfast fruit bowls (S/9) and an extensive selection of biodynamic coffee (with home-made vegan milk if you fancy). Tues–Sat 8am–8pm, Sun 9am–2pm.

DIRECTORY

Banks and exchange There are several banks within half a block from the Plaza de Armas, including Scotiabank (Jr Hurtadp 203), BBVA (Hurtado 149) and BCP (block one of Jr Maynas), all with ATMs.

Hospital Jr Morey 503 (042 526 969), in the north of the city.

Laundry Visto Lavandería, Jr Pimentel 510.

Police Policía Nacional, block one of Jr Hurtado (042 522 141).

Post office Jr San Martín 482 (Mon–Fri 9am–5pm, Sat 8am–4pm).

7

Yurimaguas

From Tarapoto it's another 140km north along a paved road to the frontier town of **YURIMAGUAS**. This friendly, bustling market town has little to offer other than its **four ports**, on the Río Huallaga, the busiest being **La Boca**, located thirteen blocks north of the town centre, or a S/2 ride in a mototaxi. The ports provide quick – or more sedate, if desired – access to both the fabulous Reserva Nacional Pacaya-Samiria (see page 476) and, further downriver, Iquitos (see page 467). If you've time to spare while waiting for a boat, consider a half-day trip to scenic Lago Cuipari or a full-day excursion to Balsapuerto, including a boat trip and a hike (with a guide) through the forest to a giant petrolglyph and a waterfall. Both destinations are reachable via a mix of public boats and mototaxis. Ask the tourist office about transport or for advice on a local tour operator.

ARRIVAL AND DEPARTURE — YURIMAGUAS

BY BUS/COLECTIVO

Buses, colectivos (S/20) and combis (2hr; S/10) shuttle between Tarapoto and Yurimaguas several times daily, departing when full. In Yurimaguas, transport leaves from the southern outskirts of town.

BY BOAT

Cargo boats (*lanchas*) and speedboats (*deslizadores/rapidos*) leave here both for Lagunas, which is the main access point for La Reserva Nacional Pacaya-Samiria, and for Iquitos.

Lanchas Transporte Eduardo's cargo boats (065 351 270, 975 156 538) are the most comfortable way to reach Iquitos; pay S/100 to sling up your hammock for the two-day trip (which also stops at Lagunas; 12hr) or pay S/150 per person to share a two-bunk cabin. Boats leave every day or two from La Boca port; arrange details directly with the captain, and don't pay anyone apart from them. The requisite hammocks (from S/30), water and other necessities for the trip are sold at stalls by the port. The scenery en route is electric: the river gets steadily wider and slower, especially once it joins Río Marañón, and the vegetation on the riverbanks more and more dense. En route you can break your journey at the small settlement of Lagunas (12hr), the starting point for trips into Reserva Nacional de Pacaya-Samiria (see page 476). You can also catch a speedboat to Lagunas (around S/50; 5hr).

Deslizadores/rapidos Speed boats leave daily for Lagunas (5hr) and Nauta (16hr), with a road connection to Iquitos. The main operators are: Clever at La Boca port (920 473 568; daily 11.30pm to Lagunas, S/50, then on to Nauta, S/140); Huallagas VIP (956 322 396; Mon–Sat 6.30am to Lagunas, S/50), with an office down the steps at the river end of Teniente César López Rojas; Bravo, at Abel Guerra dock, which operates smaller but cheaper speedboats to Lagunas (065 639 539; daily 7am; S/40).

INFORMATION AND TOURS

Tourist information The municipality runs a helpful tourist office on the corner of the Plaza de Armas (Mon–Fri 7.30am–1pm & 2.30–6pm). They can advise you on the best transport and tour operators for visiting Iquitos and the Reserva Nacional Pacaya-Samiria.

ACCOMMODATION AND EATING

Hospedaje Amazonía C Francisco Bardales 608–610 ⓣ065 353 361. By Plazuela Moralillos, eight blocks from the centre, this excellent shoestring budget option offers really good-value, cheerful small rooms, which pack in a surprising amount of furniture. But even with the fan, the rooms can get hot. S/45

Hotel Río Huallaga C Arica 111 ⓣ065 353 951, ⓔhotelriohuallaga@hotmail.com. Catering to all traveller needs, Yurimaguas' smartest option has plenty of perks – from a swimming pool and sauna, to a small cinema and in-house tour agency. The overpriced a/c rooms are bright, airy and come with fridge and private balcony – make sure you bag one overlooking the river. The decent restaurant serves an ambitious mix of international, regional and classic Peruvian dishes (mains S/25–35) while the top-floor terrace is a prime spot for a sundowner – try the *camu-camu* sour. S/250

★ **Mil Sabores Café & Bistro** Monseñor Atanasio Jáuregui 109 ⓣ065 351 353. This popular local restaurant is a real gem, with tasteful deor, a refreshing lack of blaring TV, and nicely presented, tasty dishes. Enjoy a healthy breakfast (yoghurt, fruit and granola), a lite-bite or a more substantial main of fish, chicken or other meat (S/14–24). Mon–Thurs & Sun 7.30am–2.30pm & 6.30–9.30pm, Fri 7.30am–2.30pm.

The northern desert

The **northern desert** remains one of the least-visited areas of Peru, mainly because of its distance from Lima and Cusco, the traditional hubs of Peru's tourist trail, but it is still an invaluable destination for its distinctive landscape, wildlife, archeology and history.

Northern Peru has some excellent **museums**, besides the stunning, if harsh, coastal beauty of its desert environment, which itself contains the largest dry forest in the Americas, almost entirely consisting of *algarrobo* (carob) trees. The main cities of **Chiclayo** and **Piura** (the first Spanish settlement in Peru) are lively commercial centres, serving not only the desert coast but large areas of the Andes as well. If, like a lot of travellers, you decide to bus straight through from Trujillo to the Ecuadorian border beyond **Tumbes** (or vice versa) in a single journey, you'll be missing out on some unique attractions.

The coastal resorts, such as the very trendy and lively **Máncora** and quieter, posher **Punta Sal** are among the best reasons for stopping. Other options include **Cabo Blanco** and, further south, **La Pimentel**, Chiclayo's closest beach. Whatever the beach experience you're looking for, be it an all-night party, a yoga retreat, a surf vacation or just complete peace and quiet, you can find it somewhere along the Panamericana where the country's warmest and richest seas lap against tropical dry forest. The real treasures of the region, however, are the archeological remains, particularly the **Valley of the Pyramids** at **Túcume** and the older pyramid complex of **Batán Grande**, two immense pre-Inca ceremonial centres within easy reach of Chiclayo. Equally alluring is the **Temple of Sipán**, where some of Peru's finest gold and silver artefacts were found within the last fifteen years.

Pacasmayo and around

Some 10km north of the town of San Pedro de Lloc, which is famous for its stuffed lizards and great ham, the Panamericana passes by the growing port town of **PACASMAYO**; many buses pull in here to pick up passengers and it is a possible stop-off en route between Trujillo and Chiclayo. The town isn't particularly attractive, but beach and promenade are pleasant and the old jetty is considered the largest and most attractive surviving pier on the Peruvian coast. The local surf conditions are good and nearby Poemape has a famous wave that old surfers tell long stories about. There are a few hotels here, handy if you do decide to spend some time to enjoy the surf and the generally chilled atmosphere.

Pakatnamú

Daily 9am–3pm • Free • Take a colectivo or bus from Pacasmayo, then 6km walk from the main highway to the site or take a taxi (S/20–30 with short wait)

A few kilometres north of Pacasmayo, just before the village of Guadalupe, a track leads off left to the well-preserved ruins of **Pakatnamu** (City of Sanctuaries), overlooking the mouth of the Río Jequetepeque. Being off the main road and far from any major towns, the ruins of this abandoned city have survived relatively untouched by treasure hunters or curious browsers. The remains include pyramids, palaces, storehouses and dwellings. The place was first occupied during the Gallinazo period (around 350 AD), then was subsequently conquered by the Mochica and Chimú cultures. It gets very hot around midday, and there's little shade and **no food** or drink available at the site.

ARRIVAL AND DEPARTURE — PACASMAYO AND AROUND

By bus From Trujillo take the regular Emtrafesa, Av Tupac Amaru 185 (044 484 120), service to Chiclayo (every 30min, S/8), which will drop you off at Leoncito Prado and 28 de Julio. From there a taxi to the beachfront will cost around S/5.

Bus companies Most buses stop at the main terminal two blocks north of 28 de Julio. All destinations are served by Emtrafesa, which runs regularly all day.

Destinations Cajamarca (5hr); Chiclayo (1–2hr); Trujillo (2hr).

7

ACCOMMODATION AND EATING

Tabaris Adolfo King, at Ayacucho. A typical family-owned seafood restaurant, known throughout the region for making a killer ceviche and for grilled grouper freshly caught nearby (S/30–40). Daily 8am–9.30pm.

Hotel Pakatnamu Malecón Grau 103 044 522 368. This hotel has an attractive wooden veranda and sea views; rooms are comfortable but simple, with carpet cover, cable TV and private hot showers. The wi-fi doesn't quite reach the bedrooms. S/130

Hotel El Mirador Aurelio Herrera 10 044 521 883, perupacasmayo.com. One of the most popular options among the passing surfer crowd, this large building with wooden balconies has great sea views from the terrace upstairs. The rooms are quite bare, with white brick walls and basic furnishings, but are clean and comfortable. S/100

Chiclayo

The commercial centre of northern Peru, **CHICLAYO** is better famed for its banks than its heritage. Nevertheless, it has its own attractions, even if most of the city is an urban sprawl modernizing and growing rapidly. The city has an incredibly busy feel to it, with people and traffic moving fast and noisily everywhere during daylight hours.

Parque Principal and around

The city's heart is the **Parque Principal**, where there is a futuristic fountain that's elegantly lit at night. You'll also find the Neoclassical **Catedral** (open for mass) here, built in 1869 and with its main doorway supported by Doric columns, and the **Palacio Municipal** (Mon–Fri 8am–7pm, Sat 8am–1pm, free), a Republican edifice built in 1924 and worth visiting for its collection of photography taken by German ethnologist Hans Heinrich Brüning in the late 1800s, capturing the daily life of rural indigenous people. Along Calle San José you'll find the **Convento Franciscano Santa María**, built in the early seventeenth century but destroyed, apart from the first cloister, by El Niño rains in 1961.

La Verónica and the Plazuela Elías Aguirre

Six blocks directly west of the Parque Principal, there's the small, attractive chapel of **La Verónica** (daily 7–10am and 6–8pm; free), on Calle Torres Paz. Built at the start of the nineteenth century, its most notable feature is an altarpiece of silver- and gold leaf. In the **Plaza Elías Aguirre**, just around the corner, there's a statue in honour of the *comandante* of this name, a local hero serving the Republicans in the Battle of Angamos during the War of the Pacific.

ARRIVAL AND DEPARTURE — CHICLAYO

BY PLANE

Aeropuerto José Abelardo Quiñones González is 2km east of town on Av Bolognesi (T 074 236 016; 24hr), and easily reached by taxi for S/4. Flights are with LATAM, C Manuel María Izaga 770 (Mon–Fri 9am–7pm, Sat 9am–1pm; T 074 274 875).

Destinations Lima (daily; 1hr 30min).

BY BUS AND COLECTIVO

All bus services use their own private terminals, while smaller minivans serve closer local destinations and leave from set terminals.

Bus companies Civa, C Bolognesi 714 (T 074 226 471), for Chachapoyas, Lima, Tarapoto, Huancabamba, Máncora, Tumbes and Gayuaquil; Cruz del Sur, C Bolognesi 888 (T 074 224 008), for Lima; Línea, C Bolognesi 638 (T 074 233 497), for good services to Cajamarca, Lima and hourly buses to Piura; Movil Tours, C Bolognesi 195 (T 074 623 302), for Chachapoyas, Bagua, Moyobamba and Tarapoto; Oltursa, at Balta and C María Izaga (T 074 237 789), has an excellent service to Lima, as well as Los Organos, Máncora and Tumbes, with buses leaving from their terminal at Av Vincente de la Vega 101 (T 074 225 611); Transportes Chiclayo, Av Lora y Lora s/n (T 074 223 632) is the best for Piura (every 30 min), Sullana and Talara.

Destinations Batán Grande (several daily; 40min), Cajamarca (10 daily; 6hr); Chachapoyas (2 daily; 9hr); Chongoyape (several daily; 1hr); Ferreñafe (several

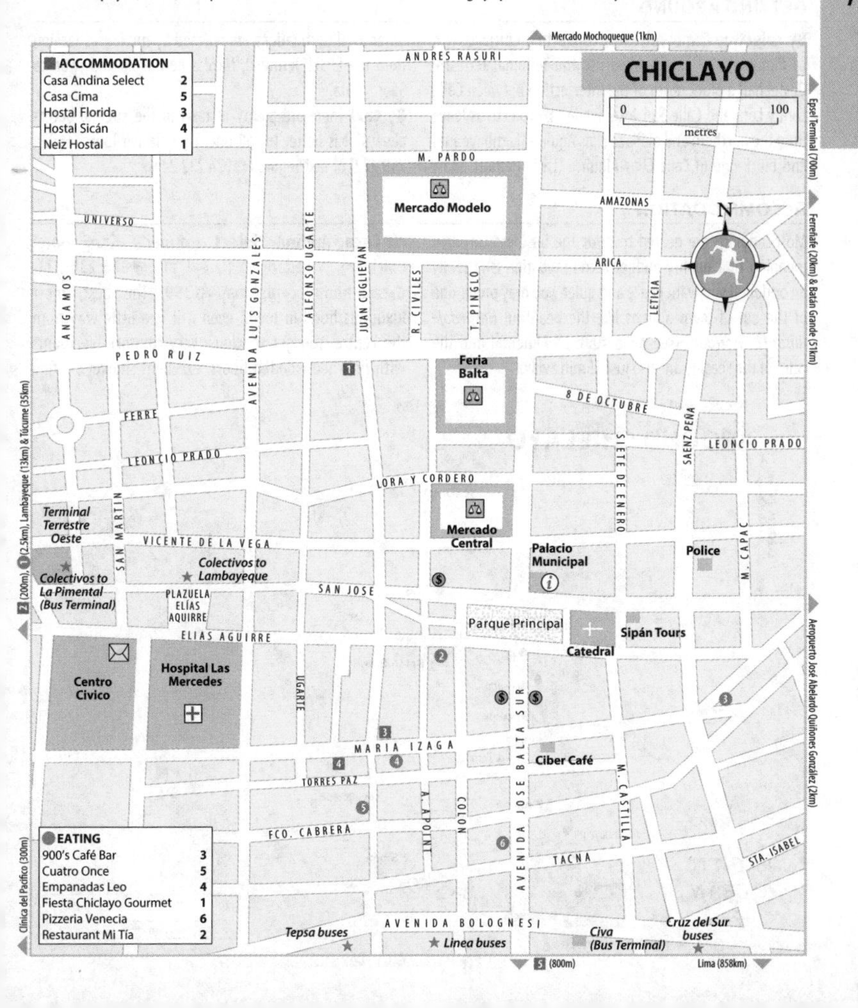

daily; 20min); Huancabamba (3 weekly, 3pm Mon, Wed & Fri; 11hr); La Pimentel (several daily; 15min); Lambayeque (several daily; 20min); Lima (at least 10 daily; 13hr); Piura (every 30 min; 3hr 30min); Sipán (several daily; 25min); Sullana (several daily; 5hr); Talara (several daily; 6hr); Tarapoto (3 daily; 10hr); Trujillo (several daily; 3hr); Túcume (several daily; 45min); Tumbes (8 daily; 7hr).

BY CAR

San José Rent a Car, Av Tumbes Norte 486 (T 072 522 321, W rentacarsanjose.pe).

INFORMATION AND TOURS

Tourist information iPerú has an office in the Palacio Municipal de Chiclayo, C San José 823 (Mon–Sat 9am–6pm, Sun 9am–1pm; T 074 205 703).

Tour operators Tours around the area include trips to Túcume, Batán Grande and the local museums, and last 4–8hr; costs are S/40–75 per person. The best are offered by Sipán Tours, C 7 de Enero 772 (T 074 229 053, W sipantours.com), who also have trips to Reserva Chiparrí, and Chaskiventura, C Manuel Izaga 740, oficina. 207 (T 074 221 282, W chaskiventura-travel-peru.com). Both operators have highly trained, English-speaking guides, with the latter working directly with local community projects, including cotton growers in the Bosque de Pomac (see page 406).

GETTING AROUND

By colectivo Combi colectivos connecting Chiclayo with La Pimentel and Lambayeque use the Terminal Terrestre Oeste, half a block north of the intersection between Calle Lora y Lora and Calle San José, while taxi colectivos leave from the northern end of Plaza Elías Aguirre (Lambayeque) and block one of Calle Elías Alguirre (La Pimental). Most other local destinations are reached by minibuses leaving from the EPSEL Terminal, Nicolas de Pierola and Avenida Sáenz Peña.

By taxi There are plenty of taxis in the streets, but as always, it is better to call one. Try Chiclayo Tours (T 074 799 772) or Taxi Seguro (T 074 232 244).

ACCOMMODATION

Most lodgings are geared towards the business traveller, meaning that quality budget accommodation isn't really an option. If you want peace and quiet, you may prefer one of the out-of-town options like the beautiful *Hospedaje Rural Los Horcones* (see page 409). La Pimental and the calm of the seaside are also just 15min away.

★ **Casa Andina Select** (formerly Gran Hotel Chiclayo) Av Federico Villareal 115 T 074 234 911, W casa-andina.com; map p.399. The best, most luxurious hotel in town, even if it is a little way from the centre. You get spacious, very comfortable rooms with polished wooden floors, excellent showers, a fine

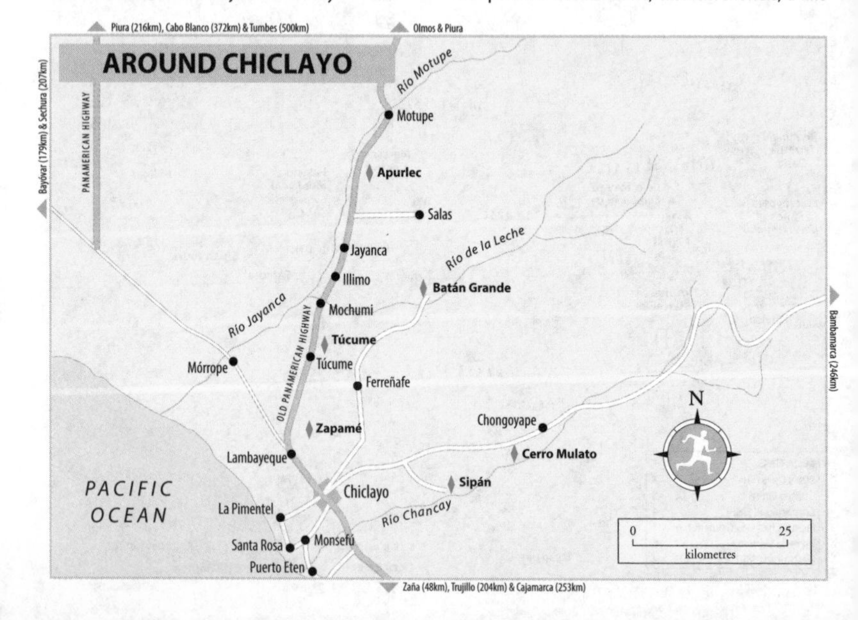

CHICLAYO'S MARKETS

Along with the massive semi-covered **market lanes**, the main focus of activity in town is the **Central Market** (daily 7am–7pm). Known as the Mercado Modelo, the main part of the Central Market is packed with food vendors at the centre, and other stalls around the outside. Here you can find some of the best ceviche in town. This is one of the most complete markets in the north – and a revelation if you've just arrived in the country. A wander into its hidden depths will uncover ray fish, known as *la guitarra*, hanging up to dry in the sun before being made into a local speciality, *pescado seco*, but the most compelling displays are the herbalists' shops, or *mercado de brujos* (witches' market), selling everything from herbs and charms to whale bones and hallucinogenic cacti. Be aware things turn a bit sketchy after dark, so it's not wise to wander here after 7pm.

restaurant, decent swimming pool and even a little casino-bar. S/240

Casa Cima C Los Mangos 161, apt 501, Urb Santa Victoria 074 617 862, einfocima.ingles.cix@gmail.com; map p.399. Located in a quieter, safe neighbourhood, some ten blocks from the plaza, rooms are up in the owner's penthouse, with a terrace offering great views over the city. There are just two rooms (one en-suite), all impeccable and simply comfortable. Helpful hosts Liam and Teófila go above and beyond the call of duty. S/120

Hostal Florida C Juan Cuglievan 608 074 272 632, floridahostal.com; map p.399. Although they're somewhat soulless and most have windows facing into the hallway, the rooms here are a cut above others in this price range, and that's before you include fast internet and a pretty rooftop terrace where breakfast is served. S/95

Hostal Sicán C María Izaga 356 074 208 741; map p.399. Nicely decorated, central and friendly, fans are included (S/10 more for a/c). The quietest beds are at the top. S/65

Neiz Hostal Av Pedro Ruiz 756 074 229 441; map p.399. Solid value, the rooms are clean and big enough, with fans and hot water. There's a lot of clashing gold and green and if you're lucky, swan-shaped towels, but the staff are welcoming and helpful. S/65

EATING

The best thing to do in Chiclayo is eat: some of the most flavourful Peruvian dishes come from this region and reach back deep into their **Moche** heritage. The Moche were among the first cultures to domesticate the local Muscovy duck, and the *seco de pato* stew is a local favourite. Being close to the ocean, seafood is also on every menu, and one local speciality – although definitely an acquired taste – is rehydrated dried fish (*pescado seco*), often prepared from flat ray fish, with potatoes.

900's Café Bar C María Izaga 900 074 209 268; map p.399. Quality and stylish Peruvian food, and some fine cocktails, but really, it's all about the coffee and desserts (S/8.50). There's also live music Thurs through Sat. Mon–Thurs 8am–11pm, Fri & Sat 8am–1pm.

★ **Cuatro Once** C Juan Cuglievan 411; map p.399. This slick restobar, popular among Chiclayo's younger crowd, serves craft beer from over eight Peruvian breweries, with pairing suggestions for the regional nibbles on its menu, including *conchas negras* ceviche (S/25) and *yuquitas con queso* (deep fried yuca oozing cheese; S/20). Mon–Thurs 5pm–midnight, Fri & Sat 5pm–2am.

Empanadas Leo C María Izaga 482 074 651 792; map p.399. With fillings ranging from *lomo saltado* to *chicharrón* (via more traditional cheese and ham), this *empanadería* offers a fresh take on the ubiquitous South American snack, all at reasonable prices (S/7). Daily 9am–1.30pm & 5–11pm.

★ **Fiesta Chiclayo Gourmet** Av Salaverry 1820 074 201 970; map p.399. This is where celebrity chef Hector Solís started his empire, and it remains the best place to eat refined, creative versions of the best local dishes (S/150–200 for three courses). He breeds his own ducks and goats at his nearby farm and serves up stunning food in a fine-dining atmosphere. Don't miss the *ceviche caliente* (S/65), a grouper ceviche flash-grilled in its own juices in an open banana leaf. Daily 10am–10pm.

Pizzeria Venecia Av José Balta 365 074 233 384; map p.399. Just a few blocks down from the Parque Principal, this is the best of Chiclayo's numerous pizza parlours; cosy in the evenings with small tables and a large pizza oven, but fills up quickly. They've got a second restaurant half a block closer to the plaza along Av Balta. Pizzas S/10–25. Mon–Sat 6.45pm–1am, Sun 6.45–10.30pm.

★ **Restaurant Mi Tía** C Elías Aguirre 662 074 205 712; map p.399. You'll find this place easily in the evenings by the queue snaking along outside, but skip that, they're here for the takeaway fast food; instead, head inside and grab a table. The space is quite small, but friendly service and the best traditional Chiclayo food in town makes sharing elbow space well worth it. Try the *arroz*

ATTRACTIONS AROUND CHICLAYO

Most places of interest in the region can be reached independently by taking a **colectivo** from the market area of Chiclayo, but it's a very time-consuming process; you'll find it much easier to see all the archeological sites if you've got your own transport. You'll get the most out of these by going with a knowledgeable local **guide** on an organized tour from Chiclayo. **Taxi** drivers can also be hired by the day or half-day (usually around S/60 for half-day and S/150 full day, but it depends on negotiation and, in particular, how much actual driving time).

con pato (S/23), roast local duck with savoury, coriander-perfumed rice, or any of the goat stews (S/32–40) which get their famous flavour from an overnight marinade in *chicha*. Mon–Sat 8am–11pm, Sun 8am–4pm.

DIRECTORY

Banks and exchange The main banks are concentrated around the Parque Principal. *Cambistas* are on the corners of the Parque Principal, particularly Av José Balta, or there's Casa de Cambio Lucha at Av Balta 679.

Hospital Clínica del Pacifico at Av José Leonardo Ortiz 420 (074 228 585, clinicadelpacifico.com.pe; 24hr).

Internet Ciber Café at C María Izaga 716.

Post office C Elías Aguirre 140, seven blocks west of the plaza (Mon–Fri 8am–8pm, Sat 8am–2pm).

Tourist police Av Sáenz Peña 830 074 238 658 (Mon–Sat 8am–6pm).

7

La Pimentel and around

An attractive beach resort just 11km southwest of Chiclayo, **LA PIMENTEL** is a pleasant settlement with an attractive colonial-style centre around the **Plaza Diego Ferre**. More importantly, though, it offers a decent **beach** for swimming and **surfing** (competitions take place in Dec and Jan). The town is known for its small-scale fishing industry, some of it using the traditional *caballitos del mar* (made from *totora* reeds). For a small fee (S/1) you can access the long pier, nearly 100 years old, that divides the seafront *malecón* in two, where you can watch the fishermen.

More picturesque is the small fishing village of **La Caleta Santa Rosa**, about 5km south of La Pimentel. Here the beach is crowded with colourful boats and fishermen mending nets; the best and freshest **ceviche** in the Chiclayo area is served in the restaurants on the seafront here.

The area known as **El Faro** (the Lighthouse), slightly to the south of La Caleta Santa Rosa, is good for surfing. Continuing from here inland for about 5km, you come to the small town of **MONSEFÚ**, known as the "city of flowers" because of the local cottage industry that supplies blooms to the area. It's also renowned for its fine straw hats, straw-rolled cigarettes and the quality of its cotton, all of which you can buy at the daily **market**.

About 4km south from Monsefú you come to the colonial village of **ETÉN** and its nearby ruined church, the Capilla del Milagro, built following a local's vision of the Christ Child in 1649. Southwest, towards the sea, lie the wide avenues of largely derelict **Puerto Etén**, just another 4km away, where there are abandoned nineteenth-century train carriages.

ARRIVAL AND DEPARTURE — LA PIMENTEL AND AROUND

By bus Buses depart regularly from the Terminal Terrestre Oeste, half a block north of the intersection between C Lora y Lora and C San José in Chiclayo (S/1.5; 20min).

By colectivo Colectivos leave from block one of C Elias Aguirre in Chiclayo and pass along the Av Alfonso Ugarte in La Pimentel S/2; 15min).

ACCOMMODATION AND EATING

Casona del Muelle C Nueva Estación 116 074 484 778. Located in a beautiful old house from the 1920s, with wooden floors and decoration that takes you right back to that era. Rooms are a bit dark, but it's comfortable, the service is great, and you're within spitting distance of the pier. They also have their own seafood restaurant. S/150

★**La Posada** Av Alfonso Ugarte 491 ⓣ074 484 894. Easily the best choice in La Pimentel, with modern, airy and light bedrooms with private baths and most with a balcony overlooking the road or over the garden. There's also a lovely terrace upstairs with city views. It's a short three blocks away from the seafront and beach. **S/120**

La Tienda del Pato Malecón Seoane, next to the Capitanía de Puerto ⓣ944 687 064. The "local's local" (as it has been for thirty years), right on the *malecón*, with great seafood and duck dishes (S/20–40). Daily 11.30am–5pm and 7.30pm–midnight.

Lambayeque

The old colonial town of **LAMBAYEQUE**, 12km from Chiclayo city, must have been a grand place before it fell into decay last century; fortunately, it seems on the road to recovery, helped by its popular museums and vibrant Sunday **markets**. Buildings worth seeing here include the early eighteenth-century **Iglesia de San Pedro**, parallel to the main square between 2 de Mayo and 8 de Octubre, which is still holding up and is the most impressive edifice in the town, with two attractive front towers and fourteen balconies.

The dusty streets of Lambayeque are better known for their colonial *casonas*, such as **La Casa Descalzi** (8 de Octubre 345), which has a fine *algarrobo* doorway in typical Lambayeque Baroque style. **La Casa de la Logia Masónica** (Masonic Lodge), at the corner of calles 2 de Mayo and San Martín, is also worth admiring for its superb balcony, which has lasted for about four hundred years and, at 67m, is thought to be the longest in Peru.

Museo Arqueológico Nacional Brüning

Block 7, Av Huamachuco • Daily 9am–5.30pm • S/8 • ⓣ074 282 110

The modern **Museo Arqueológico Nacional Brüning** is the older of Lambayeque's two museums. Named after its founder Hans Heinrich Brüning, an expert in the Mochica language and culture, the museum has superb collections of early ceramics and the gold that was uncovered from the temples of Túcume and Batán Grande.

Museo Nacional Tumbas Reales de Sipán

Av Juan Pablo Vizcardo y Guzmán 895 • Tues–Sun 9am–5pm • S/10, a guide for up to 10 people S/30 • ⓣ074 283 978

The **Museo Nacional Tumbas Reales de Sipán**, or National Museum of the Royal Tombs of Sipán, is an imposing concrete construction in the form of a semi-sunken or truncated pyramid, reflecting the form and style of the treasures it holds inside. This mix of modernity and indigenous pre-Columbian influence is a fantastic starting-point for exploring the archeology of the valley. You'll need a good hour or two to see and experience all the exhibits, which include a large collection of gold, silver and copper objects from the tomb of **El Señor de Sipán** (see page 404), including his main emblem, a staff known as **El Cetro Cuchillo**, found stuck to the bones of his right hand in his tomb. The tomb itself is also reproduced as one of the museum's centrepieces down on the bottom of the three floors. The top floor mainly exhibits ceramics, while the second floor is dedicated to El Señor de Sipán's ornaments and treasures. There are also extensive displays of the objects unearthed in the tomb of **El Viejo Señor de Sipán**, who was buried far below El Señor de Sipán, and is believed to have preceeded him by 100 years, and which was richly filled with gold masks and delicate shell necklaces.

The Lambayeque Valley has long been renowned for turning up pre-Columbian metallurgy – particularly gold pieces from the neighbouring hill graveyard of **Zacamé** – and local treasure-hunters have sometimes gone so far as to use bulldozers to dig them out; but it's the addition of the Sipán treasures that's given the biggest boost to Lambayeque's reputation, and the museum is now one of the finest in South America

ARRIVAL AND DEPARTURE LAMBAYEQUE

By colectivo From Chiclayo, take the short combi ride north from C San José, opposite the Plazuela Elías Aguirre, six blocks west of Parque Principal (S/2) and ask to be dropped off near the museums. For the return journey, hop on one of the combis that head south along Ruta 1.

EATING

Lambayeque is famous for its sweet pastry cakes – filled with *manjar blanca* (a very popular condensed-milk product) and touted under the unlikely name of *King-Kongs*. In any of the town's streets, you'll be bombarded by street vendors pushing out piles of the cake, shouting "King-Kong! King-Kong!"

El Cantaro C Dos de Mayo 180 ⓣ 074 282 196. An excellent lunchtime restaurant whether you go for the set menus or a la carte; known by most taxi drivers, it's one of the more traditional restaurants in the region, serving ceviche, duck, goat and other local specialities. Mains S/25. Daily 9.30am–4.45pm.

The Temple of Sipán (La Huaca Rajada)

7

Daily 9am–5pm • S/8 • ⓣ 074 434 616 • Combi colectivos to Sipán (25min; S/2–3) leave Chiclayo from the EPSEL Terminal

The **Temple of Sipán**, 33km southeast of Chiclayo, discovered in 1987 by archeologist Walter Alva has proved to be one of the richest **tombs** in the entire Americas. Every important individual buried here, mostly Mochica nobles from around 200–600 AD, was interred lying flat with his or her own precious-metal grave objects, such as gold and silver goblets, headdresses, breastplates and jewellery including turquoise and lapis lazuli, themselves now on show in the **Museo de las Tumbas Reales de Sipán** (see page 403). The most important grave uncovered was that of a noble known today as **El Señor de Sipán**, the Lord of Sipán. He was buried along with a great many fine gold and silver decorative objects adorned with semi-precious stones and shells from the Ecuadorian coast.

There are two large adobe **pyramids**, including the Huaca Rajada, in front of which there was once a royal tomb; the place certainly gives you a feel for the people who lived here almost two millennia ago, and it's one of the few sites in Peru whose treasures were not entirely plundered by either the Conquistadors or more recent grave robbers. There's also a **site museum**, displaying photos and illustrations of the excavation work plus replicas of some of the discoveries.

Pampa Grande and around

Buses to Pampa Grande and Chongoyape leave Chiclayo from the EPSEL Terminal (S/4; 1hr 20min)

Pampa Grande was one of the largest and most active Mochica administrative and ceremonial centres in the region and was populated by thousands. Located in the desert some 20km west of the Temple of Sipán, it can be reached along a dusty path from the town of Pampa Grande. Also worth a visit is the site of **Cerro Mulato**, near the hill town of **Chongoyape**, 80km out of Chiclayo along the attractive Chancay Valley. From Chongoyape, if you've got your own transport, take the dirt road tracing an alternative route through the desert to Cerro Mulato. Here you can see some impressive Chavín **petroglyphs**, and in the surrounding region, a number of Chavín graves dating from the fifth century BC.

Reserva Nacional Chaparrí

Entry S/30 per person, guide for a 3hr tour S/50 for 1–10 people; the lodge costs S/926 for one night, S/1650 for two nights for two people, includes a local Spanish-speaking guide and all meals • ⓣ 984 676 249, ⓦ chaparrilodge.com • Buses to Chongoyape leave Chiclayo from the EPSEL Terminal (S/5; 1hr 20min); tell the driver you are going to Chaparrí and he will let you off at Acoturch, the reserve's main administrative office. Alternately, and more comfortably, the reserve can organize transport for S/480 for the round trip to Chiclayo

Chaparrí was Peru's first privately owned reserve in 1999, and is an inspiring example of a community-run project making great strides in protecting communal

THE SICÁN CULTURE

The **Sicán culture**, thought to descend from the Mochica (see page 487), is associated with the Naymlap dynasty, based on a wide-reaching political confederacy emanating from the Lambayeque Valley between around 800 and 1300 AD. These people produced alloys of gold, silver and arsenic-copper on a scale unprecedented in pre-Hispanic America. The name Sicán actually means "House of the Moon" in the Mochica language. Legend has it that a leader called **Naymlap** arrived by sea with a fleet of balsa boats, his own royal retinue and a green female stone idol. Naymlap set about building temples and palaces near the sea in the Lambayeque Valley. The region was then successfully governed by Naymlap's twelve grandsons, until one of them was tempted by a witch to move the green stone idol. This allegedly provoked a month of heavy rains and flash floods, rather like the effects of El Niño today, bringing great disease and death in its wake. Indeed, glacial ice cores analysed in the Andes above here have indicated the likelihood of a powerful El Niño current around 1100 AD.

The Sicán civilization, like the Mochica, depended on a high level of **irrigation technology**. The civilization also had its own copper money and sophisticated ceramics, many of which featured an image of the flying **Lord of Sicán**. The main thrust of the Lord of Sicán designs is a well-dressed man, possibly Naymlap himself, with small wings, a nose like a bird's beak and, sometimes, talons rather than feet. The Sicán culture showed a marked change in its burial practices from that of the Mochica, almost certainly signifying a change in the prevalent belief in an afterlife. While the Mochica people were buried in a lying position – like the Mochica warrior in his splendid tomb at Sipán (see page 404) – the new Sicán style was to inter the dead in a sitting position. Excavations of Sicán sites in the last decade have also revealed such rare artefacts as 22 "tumis" (semicircular bladed ceremonial knives with an anthropomorphic figure where a handle should be).

The Sicán monetary system, the flying Lord of Sicán image and much of the culture's religious and political infrastructures were all abandoned after the dramatic environmental disasters caused by El Niño around 1100 AD. **Batán Grande**, the culture's largest and most impressive city, was partly washed away, and a fabulous new centre, a massive city of over twenty adobe pyramids at **Túcume** (see page 407), was constructed in the Leche Valley. This relatively short-lived culture was taken over by Chimú warriors from the south around 1370 AD, who absorbed the Lambayeque Valley, some of the Piura Valley area and about two-thirds of the Peruvian desert coast into their empire.

land and changing local attitudes on the value of conservation. Set in over 34,000 hectares of community-owned land, Chaparrí is a birdwatchers' paradise, with over 250 species to be found within its boundaries and seventy endemic species. Among the various terrestrial inhabitants, the stars are the spectacled bears, reintroduced here in the reserve, and while most of the population is scattered a day's hike or more away, it is possible to see some in the recuperation area where rescued bears are prepared for reintroduction into the wild. For the really persistent and lucky, there are a few puma and ocelot around, although they are mostly only seen by the local camera traps. Accommodation is in luxurious rustic cabins with adobe walls and bamboo ceilings, and a stay of a few nights is simply the best way to enjoy the peace and beauty of Peru's least-known ecosystem. Reservations must be made at least a day in advance.

Ferreñafe and around

Combis to Ferreñafe leave Chiclayo from the EPSEL Terminal and colectivo cars leave from C Leoncio Prado 1159 and Av Sáenz Peña (20min; S/2.50). From town, a mototaxi gets you to the museum (10min; S/2)

Founded in 1550 by Captain Alfonso de Osorio, **FERREÑAFE**, 18km northeast of Chiclayo, was once known as the "land of two faiths" because of the local tradition of believing first in the power of spirits and second in the Catholic Church. Curiously, Ferreñafe is also home to more Miss Peru winners than any other town in the country.

Museo Nacional Sicán

Tues–Sun 9am–5pm • S/8 • ⓣ 074 286 469

Ferreñafe is best known for its excellent **Museo Nacional Sicán**, which has an audiovisual introduction and a large collection of exhibits, mostly models depicting daily life and burials of the Sicán people (see page 405), a great introduction before or after visiting the local archeological sites themselves. One central room is full of genuine treasures, including famous ceremonial headdresses and masks. There's also a reconstruction of the surreal tomb of the Señor de Sicán; his body was discovered decapitated, upside down and with huge gauntlets laid out beside him.

Santuario Historico Bosque de Pomac

57km northeast of Chiclayo • Daily 8.30am–5.30pm • S/10, a guide from the interpretative centre, through the forest and to the *huacas*, S/30 • Interpretative centre ⓣ 074 206 434

The site at **Batán Grande** inside the forest sanctuary incorporates over twenty pre-Inca temple pyramids within one corner of what extends to the largest dry forest in the Americas, the **Bosque de Pomac**. There's an **interpretative centre** at the main entrance, which has a small archeological museum with a scale model of the pyramids and a shop, selling local textiles woven from naturally coloured cotton grown here.

7

Part of the beauty of this site comes from its sitting at the heart of an ancient forest, dominated by *algarrobo* trees, spreading out over some 13,400 hectares, a veritable oasis in the middle of the desert. Over eighty percent of Peru's ancient gold artefacts are estimated to have come from here – you'll notice there are thousands of holes, dug over the centuries by treasure hunters. Batán Grande is also known to have developed its own copper-smelting works, which produced large quantities of flat copper plates – *naipes* – that were between 5 and 10cm long. These were believed to have been used and exported to Ecuador as a kind of monetary system.

Brief history

The **Sicán culture** arose to fill the void left by the demise of the Mochica culture around 700 AD (see page 487), and were the driving force in the region from 800 to 1100 AD, based here at Batán Grande. Known to archeologists as the Initial Lambayeque Period, this era was clearly a flourishing one judging by the extent of the pyramids here. Nevertheless, Batán Grande was abandoned in the twelfth century and the Sicán moved across the valley to Túcume (see page 407), probably following a deluge of rains (El Niño) causing devastation, epidemics and a lack of faith in the power of the ruling elite. This fits neatly with the legend of the Sicán leader Naymlap's descendants, who brought this on themselves by sacrilegious behaviour. There is also some evidence that the pyramids were deliberately burnt, supporting this idea.

The site

The main part of the **site** that you visit today was mostly built between 750 and 1250 AD, and comprises the Huaca el Oro, Huaca Rodillona, Huaca Corte and Huaca las Ventanas, where the famous **Tumi de Oro** was uncovered in 1936. The tomb of **El Señor de Sicán** (not to be confused with the tomb of El Señor de Sipán; see page 404), on the north side of the Huaca el Oro, contained a noble with two women, two children and five golden crowns; these are exhibited in the excellent **museum** in Ferreñafe. Huaca las Ventanas, named after the substantial damage caused by the *huaqueros,* is the only pyramid you can climb, offering splendid views across the other pyramids and the striking green of the forest.

Bosque de Pomac

The **Pomac Forest** is the largest dry forest in western South America. A kilometre or so in from the interpretative centre you'll find the oldest *algarrobo* tree in the forest, the **árbol milenario.** Over 500 years old, its spreading, gnarled mass is believed to be magical, with legend stating that when cut off, its branches grew roots and blossomed; the locals still bring offerings to hang from its twisted boughs. The reserve is home to over forty species of birds such as mockingbirds, cardinals, burrowing owls and hummingbirds, and most visitors at least see some iguanas and other lizards scuttling into the undergrowth. Rarer, but still present, are wild foxes, deer and anteaters. There's also a **mirador** (viewing platform) in the heart of the forest, from where it's possible to make out many of the larger *huacas*. The staff at the interpretative centre can direct you to camping zones and can organise food if you contact them in advance.

ARRIVAL AND TOURS **SANTUARIO HISTORICO BOSQUE DE POMAC**

By car Take the northern road from Ferreñafe to reach Batán Grande; it's a 15–20min drive. There are two routes into the forest; one passes the interpretative centre, while another goes via Huaca el Oro, and comes from the nearby village of Illimo, the next settlement north of Túcume. You'll need a decent car, preferably but not essentially 4WD, and a local driver or good map. If you take this route you'll be rewarded by close contact with small, scattered desert communities, mainly goat herders and peasant farmers, many of whose houses are still built out of adobe and lath.

By colectivo Combis to Batán Grande pueblo (10km beyond the site) leave from the EPSEL Terminal in Chiclayo (40min; S/4) – go as early as possible and ask to be dropped at the interpretative centre.

Tours To visit the site in just one day, it's best to take a guided tour from Chiclayo or Ferreñafe.

Túcume

33km north of Chiclayo • Daily 8am–4.30pm • Cost varies depending on the route chosen: Route A museum and *mirador* S/8; Route B museum and Huaca las Balsas S/8; Route C covering all three S/12

The site of **TÚCUME**, also known as the **Valley of the Pyramids**, contains 26 adobe pyramids, many clustered around the hill of **El Purgatorio** (197m), also known as Cerro La Raya (after a ray fish that lives within it, according to legend). Although the ticket office closes at 4.30pm and the museum shortly after this, the site is accessible after these hours (being part of the local landscape and dissected by small paths connecting villages and homesteads), with the main sectors clearly marked by good interpretative signs.

Túcume's modern settlement, based alongside the old Panamerican Highway, lies just a couple of kilometres west of the Valley of the Pyramids, and doesn't have much to offer visitors except a handful of accommodation and eating options (see page 409).

Brief history

Covering more than two hundred hectares, Túcume was occupied initially by the **Sicán culture**, which began building here around 1100 AD after abandoning Batán Grande (see page 406). During this time, known as the Second Lambayeque Period, the focus of construction moved to Túcume where an elite controlled a complex administrative system and cleared large areas of *algarrobo* forest (as is still the case today in the immediate vicinity of the Valley of the Pyramids and Cerro El Purgatorio at Túcume). Reed seafaring vessels were also essential for the development of this new, powerful elite. The Sicán people were clearly expert **seamen** and traded along the coast as far as Ecuador, Colombia and quite probably Central America; to the east, they traded with the sierra and the jungle regions beyond. They were also expert **metallurgists** working with gold, silver, copper and precious stones, and their elaborate funerary masks are astonishingly vivid and beautiful.

At Túcume's peak, in the thirteenth and early fourteenth centuries, it was probably a focus of annual pilgrimage for a large section of the coastal population, whose Sicán leaders were high priests with great agro-astrological understanding, adept administrators, a warrior elite, and expert artisans.

It wasn't long, however, before things changed, and around 1375 AD the **Chimú** invaded from the south. Within another hundred years the **Inca** had arrived, though they took some twenty years to conquer the Chimú, during which time it appears that Túcume played an important role in the ensuing military, magical and diplomatic intrigues. Afterwards, the Inca transported many Chimú warriors to remote outposts in the Andes, in order to maximize the Incas' political control and minimize the chances of rebellion. By the time the **Spanish** arrived, just over half a century later, Túcume's time had already passed. When the Spanish chronicler, Pedro Cieza de León, stopped here in 1547, it was already abandoned and in ruins.

The site

From Túcume's plaza, follow the right-hand road to the site; it's a dusty 2km walk. Alternatively, take a mototaxi or combi colectivo for S/2. At the end of the fields, the road divides: right leads to the museum and ticket office

Today, Túcume remains an extensive site with the labyrinthine ruins of walls and courtyards still visible, if slightly rain-washed by the impact of heavy El Niño weather cycles, and you can easily spend two or three hours exploring. The site has two clearly defined areas: the **North sector** is characterized by large monumental structures; the **South sector** has predominantly smaller and simpler structures and common graveyards. The adobe bricks utilized were loaf-shaped, each with their maker's mark, indicating control and accounting for labour and tribute to the elite. Some of the pyramids – most notably Huaca Las Balsas in the south – have up to seven phases of construction, showing that building went on more or less continuously. Recent excavations unearthing only female remains (except for one decapitated male) have left archeologists speculating that Huaca Las Balsas and the surrounding southern pyramids were presided over by female leaders and their intricate relief designs on the walls representing maritime themes suggest that Huaca Las Balsas was a temple to the cult of water.

El Purgatorio hill

There's a **viewing point**, reached by a twisting path that leads up **El Purgatorio hill**, from where you can get a good view of the whole city. This hill, circular and cone-shaped, at the very centre of the occupied area, was and still is considered by locals to be a sacred mountain. Access to it was restricted originally, though there is evidence of later Inca constructions, for example an altar site. It is still visited these days by the local *curanderos*, healing wizards who utilize shamanic techniques and the psychoactive San Pedro cactus in their weekly rituals, which researchers believe are similar to those of their ancestors and which could be one possible explanation for the name El Purgatorio (the place of the purge).

Museo de Sitio

Daily 8am–4.30pm • ☎ 978 167 851

The award-winning **Museo de Sitio**, at the entrance to the site, was constructed to reflect the style – known as *la ramada* – of colonial chapels in this region, built by local indigenous craftsmen centuries ago and using much the same materials. It's split into three rooms, with the first offering a selection of ceramics from the Lambayeque, Chimú and Inca cultures, including a wide selection of pots depicting monkeys and felines. The next is dedicated to the Templo de la Piedra Sagrada, a temple excavated next to Huaca Larga containing the remains of the Señor de Túcume and 130 human sacrifices that had been drugged with nectandra seeds; the funerary offerings include tiny metal panpipes and trumpets. The final room has a handy timeline showing the different Peruvian cultures in the context of others from around the world. There's also an attractive picnic area, and workshops used by the community to produce crafts, including ceramics made using 2500-year-old techniques. They also hold occasional fairs where they sell crafts or showcase local gastronomy.

HEALING SESSIONS IN SALAS

SALAS is known locally as the capital of folklore medicine on the coast of Peru. Here the ancient traditions of **curanderismo** are so strong that it's the major source of income for the village. Most nights of the week, but especially Tuesdays and Fridays, there'll be healing sessions going on in at least one of the houses in the village, generally starting around 10pm and ending at roughly 4am. The sessions, or *mesas*, are based on the ingestion of the hallucinogenic **San Pedro cactus** and other natural plants or herbs, and they do cost money (anything up to US$200 a night, though the amount is usually fixed and can be divided between as many as five to ten participants). Combining healing with divination, the *curanderos* use techniques and traditions handed down from generation to generation from the ancient Sicán culture.

Salas is 20min by car from Túcume; take a back road for 17km off the old Panamerican Highway at Km 47 (27km north of Túcume). To contact a *curandero* about participating in a session, the best bet is to ask a local tour operator or hotel, such as *Hospedaje Rural Los Horcones*, or a trustworthy taxi driver from Túcume, to take you to the village one afternoon to see what can be arranged.

ARRIVAL AND ACTIVITIES — TÚCUME

By colectivo From Lambayeque, take a combi from the market on the Panamericana Norte (15min; S/2.50). From Chiclayo, take one of the colectivos marked "Túcume" (45min; S/2.50), which leave every 30min or so from a yard on Las Amapolas, just off block 13 of Av Leguía and near the Óvalo de Pescador. Get a taxi here as it's in a rough neighbourhood. Ask for "las pirámides" and the *combi* will drop you on the main road about 1km from the site. A mototaxi from there will cost S/1.50 per person.

Shamanic healing This is a strong local tradition and one renowned healer, Don Victor Bravo, lives very close to the ruins of Túcume; anyone seriously interested in participating in one of his *mesa* ceremonies (see page 409) could try asking for an introduction through the *Hospedaje Rural Los Horcones*.

ACCOMMODATION AND EATING

Hospedaje Las Balsas Augusto B Leguía 149 ⓣ950 207 387. Cheap decor and furnishings match the low price, but rooms are clean with fans and private baths. Just two blocks from the plaza, a good choice for overnighting near the ruins. S/55

Hospedaje Rural Los Horcones North of Túcume archeological site ⓣ951 831 705, ⓦloshorconesdetucume.com. Luxurious rooms plus shower blocks and local home-cooked food available here; buildings are constructed with traditional materials in a style reflecting that of the pyramid site next door. A very good breakfast is included. S/386

Piura

The city of **PIURA** feels very distinct from the rest of the country, cut off to the south by the formidable Sechura Desert, and to the east by the Huancabamba mountains. **Francisco Pizarro** spent ten days in Piura in 1532 en route to his fateful meeting with the Inca overlord, Atahualpa, at Cajamarca (see page 374). By 1534 the city, then known as **San Miguel de Piura**, had well over two hundred Spanish inhabitants, including the first Spanish women to arrive in Peru. As early as the 1560s, there was a flourishing trade in the excellent indigenous **Tanguis cotton**, and Piura today still produces a third of the nation's cotton.

The city has a strong oasis atmosphere, entirely dependent on the vagaries of the **Río Piura** – known colloquially since Pizarro's time as the Río Loco, or Crazy River. At only 29m above sea level, modern **Piura** is divided by a sometimes dry riverbed. Most of the action and all the main sights are on the west bank. With temperatures of up to 38°C (100°F) from January to March, the region is known for its particularly wide-brimmed, finely woven straw sombreros, worn by everyone from the mayor to local goat-herders. You'll have plenty of opportunities to see these in **Semana de Piura** (first two weeks of Oct), when the town is in high spirits. Sweaty and easy-going, Piura is fine as a stopover, but most travellers arrive with the beach in their sights, and would be forgiven for moving rapidly along.

Plaza de Armas

The spacious and attractive **Plaza de Armas** is shaded by tall tamarind trees planted well over a hundred years ago. On the plaza you'll find a "Statue of Liberty", also known as *La Pola* (The Pole), and the **Catedral de Piura** (Mon–Fri 9am–1.30pm & 4.30–6.30pm, Sat 9am–1pm; free), where the town's poorest folk tend to beg. Though not especially beautiful, the cathedral's tasteless gilt altars and intricate wooden pulpit are worth a look. Surrounding the plaza, you'll see some pastel-coloured, low, colonial buildings that clash madly with the tall, modern glass-and-concrete office buildings nearby.

Plaza Pizarro and around

One block towards the river from the Plaza de Armas, along Jirón Ayacucho, a delightful elongated square, called **Plaza Pizarro**, is also known as the Plaza de Tres Culturas. Every evening the Piurans promenade up and down here, chatting beneath tall shady trees. One block east of here is the Río Piura, usually little more than a trickle of water with a few piles of rubbish plus white egrets, gulls and terns searching for food. The riverbed is large, however, indicating that when Piura's rare rains arrive,

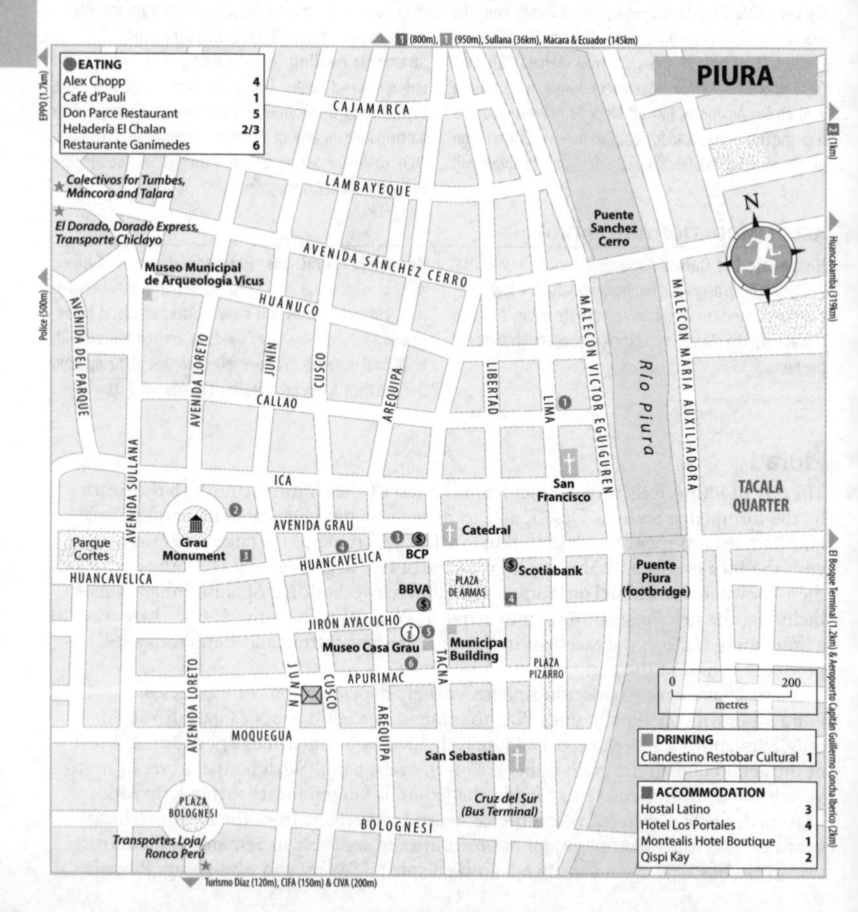

the river rises dramatically; people who build their homes too close to the dry bed regularly have them washed away. Puente Piura bridge connects central Piura with the less aesthetic east-bank quarter of **Tacala**, renowned principally for the quality and strength of its fermented *chicha* beer.

Casa Museo Gran Almirante Grau

C Tacna 662 • Tues–Fri 8am–4pm, Sat & Sun 8am–noon • Free • 073 402 434

A block south of the Plaza de Armas, you'll find the **Casa Museo Gran Almirante Grau**, nineteenth-century birthplace of **Admiral Miguel Grau**, one of the heroes of the War of the Pacific (1879–80), in which Chile took control of Peru's valuable nitrate fields in the south and cut Bolivia's access to the Pacific. The museum, a reconstruction of the house which was destroyed in a 1912 earthquake, includes a model of the British-built ship, the *Huascar*, Peru's only successful blockade runner, as well as various military artefacts.

Museo Municipal de Arqueologia Vicús

Av Sullana and Jr Huánuco • Tues–Sat 9am–5pm, Sun 9am–1pm • Free • **Sala de Oro** Tues–Sat 9am–5pm • S/4

An array of the region's archeological treasures, and in particular the ceramics from Cerro Vicus, is displayed at the **Museo Municipal de Arqueologia Vicús**, one block west of Avenida Loreto. One of the rooms has artefacts uncovered at the necropolis Vicús at Chulucanas while another is dedicated to the archeology of metallurgy. A new addition is the **Sala de Oro**, a separate section of the museum housing over sixty ancient gold objects, including jewellery, cups and pincers.

The market

One block north of Av Sánchez Cerro • Best Mon–Sat 6.30–11am

The town's daily **market**, in the north of the city, is worth a visit for its straw hats, well made in Santo Domingo, and ceramics from the villages of Chulucanas and Simbila, plus a variety of leather crafts.

ARRIVAL AND DEPARTURE — PIURA

BY PLANE

Aeropuerto Capitán Guillermo Concha Iberico (073 378 279) is 2km east of the city. The LAN Perú office is in the Plaza Vea at the Real Plaza shopping centre on Av Sánchez Cerro (977 295 338) and Peruvian Airlines at C Libertad 777 (073 322 385). A taxi into the centre costs S/10–12.

Destinations Lima (9 daily; 2hr).

BY BUS

El Dorado buses from Trujillo and Tumbes, Dorado Express buses from Tumbes, Sullana and Aguas Verdes and Transporte Chiclayo buses all arrive around blocks 11 and 12 of Av Sánchez Cerro. All other buses arrive at their companies' offices.

Bus companies CIFA, C Loreto 1465 (972 894 618) for Machala and Guayaquil; CIVA, C Loreto 1501 (989 141 658), have departures for Huancabamba, Lima and Chiclayo; Cruz del Sur, Av Bolognesi 160 (073 322 889), for Lima, Chiclayo and Trujillo; EPPO, Av Panamericana 243 (073 304 543), the usual choice for Talara, Los Organos and Máncora, but often without a/c; Transportes Loja share a terminal with Ronco Perú at Av Loreto 1241 and have twice-daily departures for Loja, Ecuador; Tepsa, Av Loreto 1195 (073 306 345), for Lima; Transportes Chiclayo, Av Sánchez Cerro 1121 (073 308 455), the most reliable and frequent to Chiclayo; Turismo Díaz, Av Loreto 1485 (073 302 834), for Cajamarca and Tarapoto.

Destinations Cajamarca (2 daily; 9hr); Chiclayo (every 30min; 3hr); Guayaquil (4 daily; 10hr); Huancabamba (2daily 10am & 6pm; 12hr); Lima (8 daily; 13–15hr); Loja, Ecuador (daily 1pm & 9pm; 8–9hr;) Talara and Máncora (every 30min; 1hr 30min–3hr); Tarapoto (daily; 18hr); Trujillo (2 daily; 6–7hr); Tumbes (daily; 4–6hr).

BY CAR

San José Rent a Car, Av Grau 1602 (073 303 240, rentacarsanjose.pe).

BY COLECTIVO

Colectivos, mainly for Tumbes, Máncora and Talara, arrive and depart from the middle of the road at block 11 of Av Sánchez Cerro, a 10min stroll from the centre of town. For Huancabamba, colectivos leave from the El Bosque terminal just beyond the stadium in the east of the city.

GETTING AROUND

By mototaxi The quickest way of getting around the city is by the ubiquitous mototaxi, which you can hail just about anywhere, except the historic centre, for S/2.

By taxi In-town taxi rides are set at around S/5–6; or call Taxi Seguro ⊕073 676 800.

INFORMATION AND TOURS

Tourist information The best choice is iPerú at Jr Ayacucho and C Libertad, just off the corner of the plaza (Mon–Sat 9am–6pm, Sun 9am–1pm; ⊕073 320 249).

Tour operators Piura Tours, C Arequipa 978 (⊕073 326 778).

ACCOMMODATION

There's a range of hotels and hostels in town, with most of the cheaper ones on or around Av Loreto or within a few blocks of Av Grau and the Plaza de Armas.

Hostal Latino Jr Huancavelica 720 ⊕073 335 114, ⊛hostal-latino.com; map p.410. A large, fairly modern and centrally located establishment, close to good dining options. All the usual facilities, including fans, with a/c an additional S/20. The staff at reception are particularly helpful and accommodating. Breakfast not included. S/92

Hotel Los Portales C Libertad 875 ⊕073 321 161, ⊛losportaleshoteles.com.pe; map p.410. A luxury hotel set in a lovely old building; the best rooms are those around an internal courtyard, which are first rate, if overpriced. The restaurant with tall glass doors overlooks the pool and makes for a great place to breakfast. S/470

Montealis Hotel Boutique C Ricardo Espinoza 108 ⊕073 302 750, ⊛montealis-boutiquehotel.com; map p.410. One of the most modern options in town, all rooms are large and well-maintained, with modern artwork on the walls and a/c. Located in a safe and serenely quiet neighbourhood, it's popular with business travellers. S/170

Qispi Kay Los Cedros 187 ⊕974 125775; map p.410. The city's backpacker hostel, it's a great place to meet other travellers thanks to a convivial upstairs terrace and bar. They're a bit short on bathrooms but the breakfast is good. Bring ear plugs: noise carries to the dorms from the terrace upstairs and the gym on the ground floor. Dorms S/32

EATING

Most of Piura's restaurants and cafés are near the Plaza de Armas, with many of the cafés specializing in delicious ice cream. Piura's speciality is a very sweet toffee-like delicacy, called *natilla*, bought from street stalls around the city. There's a **supermarket**, good for general provisions, by the Grau monument.

Alex Chopp C Huancavelica 528 ⊕073 332 538; map p.410. A popular venue with a friendly atmosphere, serving good bottled beers and fine seafood all day. Ceviche S/38–45. Mon–Sat 11am–2am, Sun 11am–midnight.

Café d'Pauli C Lima 541 ⊕073 322 210; map p.410. A small, smart café serving pricey but delicious ice creams, cakes, teas and coffee; don't miss their lemon pie (S/7) and their cheesecake (S/8). Daily 9am–9.30pm.

Don Parce Restaurant C Tacna 646 ⊕073 300 842; map p.410. A graceful old building just off the plaza, with five sunlit rooms that buzz over lunch thanks to a great menu of local classics (average S/30). Particularly well known for their roast pork sandwiches (S/14) and the *ronda criolla*, a mix of four different traditional northern dishes (S/60). Daily 7am–midnight.

Heladería El Chalan Av Grau 452; map p.410. Excellent service in a busy atmosphere; a great choice for breakfast (S/12–14), and for sandwiches, juices and ice creams. They have a newer place just up the road at Grau 179, which only offers ice cream. Daily 7.30am–10.30pm.

Restaurante Ganímedes C Apurímac 468; map p.410. The best in town for vegetarian meals; try the Locro de Zapallo (a pumpkin stew flavoured with Peruvian yello chili) from their excellent lunch menu (S/10). Friendly service, but cash only. They also sell fresh bread throughout the day. Daily 8am–10pm.

DRINKING

In the evenings, you'll find most Piurans strolling around the main streets, mingling in the plazas and drinking in the cheap bars along the roads around Junín.

Clandestino Restobar Cultural C Andrés Avelino Caceres 230; map p.410. It might look closed from the road but it's not: Piura's hippest hangout is open and gets lively with a DJ playing dance classics at weekends. Their sushi is also top-notch (try the ceviche-inspired cream cheese-filled rolls topped with crispy chicken *chicharrón* and raw tuna), especially when washed down with one of their house cocktails – the pina colada is particularly tasty. Mains from S/22. Mon–Sat 7pm–3am.

LA CATEDRAL, TRUJILLO

HOW PIZARRO FOUND ATAHUALPA

It was at Serran, then a small Inca administrative centre in the hills above Piura, that Francisco **Pizarro** waited in 1532 for the return of a small troop of soldiers he had sent up the Inca Royal Highway on a discovery mission. It took the soldiers, led by **Hernando de Soto**, just two days and a night to reach the town of Cajas, now lost in the region around Huancabamba and Lake Shimbe.

At Cajas, the Spaniards gained their first insight into the grandeur and power of the Inca Empire, although, under orders from Atahualpa, the town's two thousand-warrior Inca garrison had slunk away into the mountains. The Spanish were not slow to discover the most impressive Inca buildings – a sacred convent of over five hundred virgins who had been chosen at an early age to dedicate their lives to the Inca religion. The soldiers raped at will, provoking the Inca diplomat who was accompanying De Soto to threaten the troops with death for such sacrilege, telling them they were only 300km from Atahualpa's camp at Cajamarca. This information about Atahualpa's whereabouts was exactly what De Soto had been seeking. After a brief visit to the adjacent, even more impressive, Inca town of Huancabamba – where a tollgate collected duties along the Royal Highway – he returned with the diplomat to rejoin Pizarro. Realizing he had provided the Spanish with vital information, the Inca diplomat agreed to take them to Atahualpa's camp – a disastrous decision that resulted in the massacre at Cajamarca (see page 374).

DIRECTORY

Banks and exchange Find Scotiabank at C Libertad 825 on the Plaza de Armas, BCP at Av Grau 133 and BBVA at Tacna 598. *Cambistas* are at block 7 of Jr Arequipa, near the corner of Av Grau; a safer bet are the casas de cambio between blocks 4 and 7 of Jr Arequipa.

Police Av Sánchez Cerro, block 12 (☎ 073 307 641).

Post office Serpost at Apurimac 657 (Mon–Fri 8am–7pm, Sat 8am–4pm).

Catacaos

Just 12km south of Piura is the friendly, dusty little town of **CATACAOS**, worth a visit principally for its excellent, vast **market** (best at weekends 10am–4pm). Just off the main plaza, the market sells everything from food to crafts, even filigree gold- and silver-work, with the colourful hammocks hanging about the square a particularly good buy.

The town is renowned locally for its **picanterías** (traditional restaurants), which serve all sorts of local delicacies, such as *tamalitos verdes* (little green-corn pancakes), fish-balls, *chifles* (plantain chips), goat (*seco de cabrito*) and the local *chicha* beer. While you're In town you could also try a Peruvian favourite common here; *algarrobina*, a sweet syrup used as a honey substitute, and often mixed into fruit smoothies. Made from the seed pods of the tree that dominates the northern desert, the *algarrobo*, a type of carob, it is reputed to have various health benefits and is available from bars and street stalls.

ARRIVAL AND DEPARTURE — CATACAOS

By colectivo Regular combi colectivos for Catacaos leave Piura when full, usually every 20min or so (S/1.50; 20min), from Av Avelino Cáceras, opposite Open Plaza. Colectivo cars (S/3; 15min) leave when full from Av Loreto 1292, at Óvalo Bolognesi.

EATING

La Chayo San Francisco 497 (near the church) ☎ 073 370 121. Most locals agree that this is one of the best places to get your teeth into Piura cuisine, which tends to be seafood-heavy, but they also have fair bit of turkey and, like most of the northern region, goat and duck, often accompanied by plantain in various forms and frequently cooked with coriander. *La Chayo* still cooks over wood fires, adding an extra smoky flavour. Don't miss the *chicha* – this fermented maize beer is an acquired taste, but is tasty if well made and fresh. Mains S/15–30. Daily 10am–6pm.

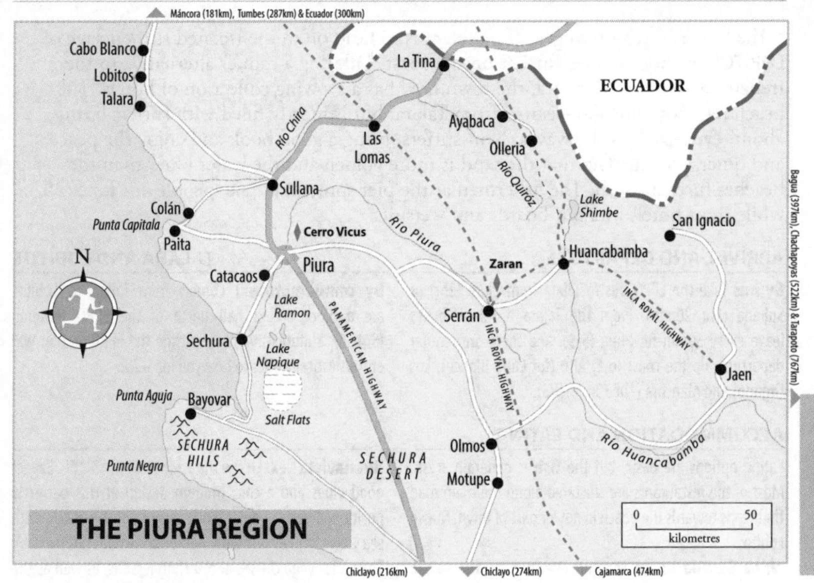

Sullana

Leaving Piura, the Panamericana Norte heads directly north, passing through the large town of **SULLANA** after 40km. This major transport junction has little of interest to travellers, except to connect with the inland route up into the mountains to La Tina and Ecuador. If you do stop, take a quick look at the **Plaza de Armas**, which boasts fine views over the Río Chira, and is the location for the old church of La Santísima Trinidad.

ARRIVAL AND DEPARTURE — SULLANA

By bus EPPO, Panamericana 701 (073 502 522; eppo.com.pe) runs buses every 20min to Talara (1hr 20min), every 30min to Piura (40min) and hourly to Máncora (3hr).

By combi/colectivo There are regular combis from Av Lama to Piura, while the faster colectivos cost slightly more. Combis for the inland border crossing with Ecuador (see page 422) at La Tina leave mornings from Av Buenos Aires and Calle 4 (several daily; 2hr).

Talara and Lobitos

TALARA, 70km further north, has been ruined by recent growth – the trees and cliffs are dotted with plastic bags, fertilizer plants cut the skyline and the smell near the port is overpowering. Until 1940, it was no more than a small fishing hamlet, though its deep-water harbour and tar pits had been used since Pizarro's time for caulking wooden ships. Pizarro had chosen the site for the first Spanish settlement in Peru, but it proved too unhealthy and he was forced to look elsewhere, eventually hitting on Piura. Talara's **oil reserves**, which you'll see being worked on- and off-shore along the coast, were directly responsible for the military coup in 1968. President Belaunde, in his first term of office, had given subsoil concessions to the multinational company IPC, declaring that "if this is foreign imperialism, what we need is more, not less of it." A curious logic, it led to the accusation that he had signed an agreement "unacceptable to true Peruvians". Within two months, and as a direct consequence of the affair, he was deposed and exiled. The new revolutionary government nationalized IPC and declared the Act of Talara null and void.

The only real reason to get off in Talara is to head on to the isolated surf enclave of **LOBITOS** twenty minutes further up the coast. Offering a calmer alternative to the frenzied activity of Máncora, the town now has a growing collection of hotels. The beach receives some day-visitors from Talara, but is mostly filled with surfers lazing about, eyes fixed on the waves. Non-surfers, bring a good book and enjoy the peace and quiet, plus the fact that the sand is more golden and the water bluer than the beaches further south. The fishermen at the pier sometimes take people out for S/25, while most hotels hire out boards and wetsuits.

ARRIVAL AND DEPARTURE — TALARA AND LOBITOS

By bus Take the EPPO bus to Talara from Piura (2hr) or Sullana (1hr 20min). From the Talara terminal, buses leave every 30min for Piura (S/9), and there are regular departures up the coast to El Alto (for Cabo Blanco), Los Organos and Máncora (1hr 30min; S/8).

By combi/mototaxi Combis from Talara to Lobitos are a block and a half north of the EPPO terminal (S/4–5). Mototaxis waiting outside the EPPO station will enthusiastically offer to take you for S/25.

ACCOMMODATION AND EATING

Eating options are basic, but the **fish** is generally fresh. Most of the restaurants are clustered along the main road that leads towards the beach in newer part of town, Nuevo Lobitos.

★ **La Casona** Up on the hill overlooking the beach ⊕996 548 201, ⊕casonadelobitos.com. The patio of this sprawling, slightly run-down, but charming old wooden house has the best views of the waves from its huge terrace. There's a laidback and friendly vibe, drawing surfers and travellers from all over. Breakfast not included. Dorms S/25, doubles S/40

Buenavista Next to the mirador ⊕941 983 266. Expect good vibes and a chic, modern design at this perfectly positioned hotel, a quiet block away from the beach, with sea views from its first-floor bedrooms to boot (S/20 extra). They offer yoga classes and surfing lessons, as well as the rare luxury of a communal kitchen. S/100

Tallakí Café 100m from the main beach car park ⊕989 837 321. A chalk board displays a simple menu comprising cheap breakfasts (S/5), sandwiches, lasagnes and cakes at this chilled café, a stone's throw from the waves. Daily 9am–2pm & 5–9pm.

Cabo Blanco

Thirty kilometres or so north of Talara, there's a turning off the highway to the old fishing hotspot of **CABO BLANCO**. Thomas Stokes, a British resident and fanatical fisherman, discovered the place in 1935, and it was a popular resort in the postwar years. **Hemingway** stayed for a month in 1951 while filming parts of *Old Man and the Sea*, while two years later the largest fish ever caught with a rod was landed here – a 710-kilo black marlin. While the fishing has declined continuously since those glory days, and the famous Cabo Blanco fishing club that housed the celebrities has long since closed down, it is still worth casting a line out there. Most tourism in Cabo Blanco these days, however, is from surfers looking to ride its famous left tube.

From here to Tumbes the Panamericana cuts across a further stretch of desert, for the most part keeping tightly to the Pacific coastline. It's a straight road, except for the occasional detour around bridges destroyed by the 1998 El Niño. To the right of the road looms a long hill, the **Cerros de Amotape**, named after a local chief whom Pizarro had killed in 1532 as an example to potential rebels.

ARRIVAL AND DEPARTURE — CABO BLANCO

By bus Located just over halfway between Talara and Máncora at Km 1137 of the Panamericana Norte, take the EPPO bus from Piura to El Alto (3hr). From here, 50m ahead, white minivans run into Cabo Blanco (every 20min, 7am–7pm; S/2).

ACCOMMODATION AND EATING

Hotel El Merlin Km 1136.5, Cabo Blanco ⊕073 256 188, ⊕elmerlin.webs.com. A really nice place right on the beach, with stone floors, bamboo and *estera* (reeds) for the nine rooms overlooking the ocean. There are kayaks available for use and excellent boat-based fishing trips can be arranged. S/120

Restaurante Cabo Blanco Km 1136.5, Cabo Blanco ☎073 256 121. Just 50m from *Hotel El Merlin*, this place has the best reputation locally for seafood; try the superb ceviches (S/30–45). Tues–Sun 11am–6pm.

Máncora

Once just an attractive roadside fishing port, **MÁNCORA** is now the most fashionable beach in Peru, attracting an international surf crowd. It's a highly welcome and enjoyable stopover when travelling along the north coast, well served by public transport, and spread out along the Panamericana as it lies parallel to a beautiful sandy beach.

As the highway passes through town, it is first called Avenida Piura, lined with stylish restaurants, funky cafés, a few of the cheaper hostels and an obligatory hippie market selling decent crafts and jewellery. Further north it becomes Avenida Grau, where most buses have terminals and where you'll find cheaper local restaurants and, one block away, the food market.

Heading down to the central beach, the bars here are the heart of Máncora's non-stop party, particularly ferocious during the summer months. The main beach has grown considerably thinner over the years as hotels encroach ever closer, and tends to be quite packed, while the waves are full of competing surfers. Those who look for a peaceful patch of sand and prefer the sound of the sea as their soundtrack (instead of thumping *cumbia*) will have to shell out for the pricey but luxurious hotels on Máncora's southern beaches, the palm-lined Las Pocitas or Vichayito, or head north to Punta Sal, Cancas or Zorritos.

ARRIVAL AND DEPARTURE — MÁNCORA

BY BUS

Coming from the south – Lima, Chiclayo or Piura – there are several buses daily. Excluciva has the best service (2nd level, 180° reclining seats and personal TV), as well as Cruz del Sur and Oltursa. From Tumbes, buses and colectivos to Máncora leave frequently from Av Tumbes Norte, but the return is better in one of the minivans.

Bus companies The bus companies are all based on the main street, Av Piura, where you can buy tickets for their selection of daily and nightly services up or down the coast, connecting Tumbes with Lima and the major cities in between. Transportes EPPO, Av Piura 679 (☎073 258 140) has buses hourly to Piura and every 30min to Los Organos, El Alto, Talara and Sullana. Cruz del Sur, Av Grau 208 (☎073 258 232), goes daily to Trujillo, Lima and Guayaquil, while Civa, Av Piura 476 (☎073 290 814), has several daily departures to Lima and Guayaquil. Cifa, Av Grau 313 (☎941 816 863), goes direct to Machala, Guayaquil and Montanita; Oltursa, Av Piura 509 (☎073 258 276) connects with Piura, Chiclayo, Trujillo and Lima.

Destinations Chiclayo (1 daily; 5–7hr); Guayaquil (5–6 daily; 8hr); Lima (several daily; 18hr); Los Organos (every 30min; 30min); Machala (1 daily, 9pm; 1hr 30min once through immigration); Piura (hourly; 3–4hr); Talara (every 30min; 1hr); Trujillo (2 daily; 9–10hr).

BY COLECTIVO

For Tumbes, minivans leave from the lay-by half a block north of the Cruz del Sur office (2hr; S/12–15); these same vans run south to Piura (3hr; S/30) and even to the airport for an extra S/15. The most reliable company is SerTour (☎999 243 768); you can buy tickets from the tour agency opposite El Mero Murique restaurant at Av Piura 392. For those looking to save a few soles, cars and beat-up minibuses shuttle between Máncora and Tumbes from along Av Grau (2hr; S/10–12), stopping anywhere in between.

INFORMATION

Tourist information Municipal Tourist Information at Av Piura 534 (summer daily 8am–1pm & 1.45–9pm; rest of year Mon–Fri 8am–1pm, & 1.45–3.45pm).

Website ⓦvivamancora.com.

ACTIVITIES IN MÁNCORA

Máncora enjoys warm waters that hover between 18°C and 24°C year-round and its position is blessed as the place where northern tropical currents meet with the much, much cooler southern one: at Lobitos, the next beach down the coast from Cabo Blanco (30km south of Máncora), the sea is cold. This geographical position gives Máncora near-perfect surf conditions at times, with barrel waves achieving up to 4m in height. Although fairly safe, there are offshore currents which surfing novices are advised to watch out for (ask one of the surf teachers before venturing out). **Kite-surfing** has also boomed here, and Máncora is now recognized as an international destination for the sport, with the best conditions found between April and November

SWIMMING AND DIVING

When the sea is flat and the wind dies, head to Spondylous Dive School (T 999 891 268, W buceaenperu.com) who have half-day snorkel (US$45) and scuba diving (US$100) tours in the waters near Máncora.

OTHER OUTDOOR ACTIVITIES

Eco Fundo La Caprichosa (Av Grau s/n T 073 258 574, W ecofundolacaprichosa.com) is a lodge set a little way north of Máncora that specializes in adventure activities – they offer ziplining, a monstrous climbing wall, quad bikes, horseriding and plenty of protected forest in which to go hiking and birdwatching.

SURF TOURS AND HIRE

Laguna Surf Camp See page 418. Pilar, a well-loved local, offers trips and lessons, the latter costing S/60 for a 1hr 20min group class.

Surf Point On the beach in front of the Bird House (see page 419). Rent boards and wetsuits for S/20 for the day.

Wild K In front of Casa Mediterranean, Playa del Amor T 941 324 784, W wild-kitesurf-peru.com. One-stop shop for all kitesurfing needs, including rentals (US$60/hr), classes for all levels (US$65/hr) and multi-day safaris to destinations down the coast. They also offer stand-up paddle lessons and board rental (S/70 1hr class; S/30 1hr rental).

ACCOMMODATION

The cheapest hotels in Máncora are along Avenida Piura, with a couple of big **party hostels** near the entrance just after the bridge (with the exception of the infamous *Point Hostel*, out north of town on Playa del Amor). Heading towards the beach, to the north are first a few run-down old **motels** that fill up with party-intent locals over the holidays, while a block or two further on the places become more refined, with some decent, cheaper options set back from the sea – although it's not advised to wander along Playa del Amor or the streets east into town from here at night. Past the pier, to the south, **hotels** become more exclusive and ever pricier as the beach becomes emptier at Las Pocitas and on to palm-lined Vichayito.

Casa Naranja Jr B 116, a 5min walk inland from the southern edge of Av Piura T 073 411 301. A haven of calm – albeit one painted in shocking colours – located a short distance from the main thoroughfare, with modern rooms, a communal kitchen and a pleasant, hammock-filled patio. The owners can help with information about day trips to surrounding beaches. S/90

★ **Laguna Surf Camp** C Acceso Veraniego s/n T 994 015 628, E pilarinmancora@yahoo.es. One of the best for location and price in Máncora; just half a block from the beach, you can hear the sea, but generally not the noise from the parties just up the road. The bamboo and palm-thatched bungalows are set in a calm, hammock-filled area around a small but adequate pool. Amazing breakfasts with generous, tasty portions available at an additional cost. Dorms S/40, doubles S/150

Misfit Hostel Playa del Amor T 969 173 750, W hostelmisfitsmancora.com. The four wooden A-frame huts with decidedly trippy interior murals are the most sought-after budget accommodation in Máncora. A fair bit north of town, and set right on the beach, the vibe is intimate but always festive. Book well in advance. Dorms S/26, doubles S/85

Las Olas Av Piura 135 T 073 258099, W lasolasmancora.com. Practically on the beach, every room has a terrace or balcony (ask for one facing the waves at no extra cost) and direct access to private lounging chairs on the beach. Breakfast is ample, with eggs or fresh fruit salad and freshly squeezed juice. S/190

Psygon Surf Camp Playa del Amor 124 ☎ 994 142 983. With a more relaxed vibe than other party hostels, there are large rooms located around a palm-thatched patio, and a bar that's open daily until midnight (live music on Fri) – just bring ear plugs as there's no escaping the music. They organize surfing classes and bike rental, too. Dorms S/25, doubles S/95

EATING AND DRINKING

Comercial Marlon, between the Global Net and BCP ATMs, has a superb range of groceries, including wholemeal bread, local honey and wines, although prices are high. For fruit, skip the vendors on Avenida Piura and walk to the local **market**, one block behind the Cruz del Sur office. For eating out, there's a surplus of **restaurants** in the centre of town, mainly along the Panamericana. There is a hectic **nightlife** scene based in the bars, beachside hotels, backpacker hostels and on the beach itself, especially during Peruvian holiday times; it's easy to find – just follow the sounds after dark.

★ **El Atelier Vino Bar** Av Piura 360 ☎ 973 906 020, ✉ ateliermancora@gmail.com. A bastion of calm cool on the avenue, this bar could be in any major city, with its kooky decor of recycled wooden crates. It's not just a pretty face: the food is great, with roots in French and Peruvian cuisines. Even if you're not hungry, go for the cheese, wine or cocktails; live music twice a week in summer. Mains S/23–28. Daily 6.30pm–1am.

La Balsa Av Piura 245. This pint- (well, pisco-) sized bar has thumping music and a great selection of home-infused piscos, in flavours from blackberry through to green chili, making their signature sour a lot less sweet than normal mixes. Happy hour 7–11pm. Daily 5.30pm–2am.

The Bird House Beachfront, two doors down from Las Olas. This extremely popular spot is divided into shops, bars and cafés, mostly franchised out, which offer a wide range of international dishes (the breakfasts at *Green Eggs and Ham* are among the best in town, if pricey at S/12), as well as local cuisine (try the fish and seafood at *Surf and Turf* on the ground floor; S/15 set menu); there's also a surf shop, cocktail bar, great smoothies at *Papa Mo's Milk Bar* and a beachside upstairs terrace. Daily 7am–8pm.

★ **Café del Mundo** Av Piura 246. This French-themed café oozes charm and serves up delicious plates of both French and local cuisine. Goat features heavily on the menu: try the *bourguinon de cabrito* (S/35) or *lasagne de cabrito*. The lunch and dinner set menu is a steal at S/15. Daily 8am–11pm.

La Sirena de Juan Av Piura 316 ☎ 073 258 173. A standout on the crowded Av Piura, *La Sirena de Juan* serves impressive food in a stylish two-storey location. Best loved for their tuna steaks, cooked to near-raw perfection. Dishes average S/30–50. Daily 12.30–3.30pm & 7–11.30pm.

DIRECTORY

Banks and exchange Banco de la Nación, block 5 of Av Piura; there are at least five ATMs and plenty of shops offering currency exchange scattered about Máncora.

Health Clínica San Pedro, Grau 636 (☎ 073 258 513).

Laundry Laundry Service at Av Piura 314.

Tourist Police Av Piura 330 (☎ 073 496 925).

Las Pocitas and Vichayito

Las Pocitas 2km southwest of Mancora • **Vichayito** 7.4km southwest of Mancora • Take the rough (old Panamerican) highway on the right just as you leave Máncora; mototaxis will charge S/3–S/8, depending on how far you want to go; alternatively, walk from Máncora along the coast, but take water with you

Máncora's two satellite beaches, **LAS POCITAS** and **VICHAYITO**, are probably what you were hoping for when you planned your trip here. Las Pocitas basically begins once you pass the pier, and the isolation grows as you head south. They make for relaxing alternatives, with good swimming, some surf and lovely coastal scenery, but staying here is pricey.

ACCOMMODATION AND EATING

★ **Kichic** Playa Las Pocitas ☎ 922 104 569, 🌐 kichic.com. Every detail of this tiny boutique hotel is refined; gorgeous and exuding calm, it is set in lush green grounds and has a pool overlooking the beach. The focus here is on rejuvenating the spirit, offering massages, yoga and a healthy menu at the superb vegetarian restaurant. S/900

Arennas Playa Las Pocitas ☎ 016 119 001, 🌐 www.arennasmancora.com. Some of the hotels have excellent restaurants: *Arennas* is a real treat offering creative, gourmet food, superbly presented and prepared. This stylish restaurant sits on a wooden deck next to a large, palm-fringed pool, with the empty beach in the foreground. Daily 7.30am–midnight.

La Poza de Barro

13km east of Máncora • Open access daily 24hr; basic toilets and a changing hut • S/5 • Take a taxi for S/60 (including 1hr wait). The entry road to the mud baths is off the Panamericana, just north of Máncora next to the "Comunidad Máncora Campesino" sign by the bridge

If the beach isn't relaxing enough, you can always head to the local mud baths, or **La Poza de Barro**. Set 11km from the main road and surrounded by hills and *algarrobo* trees, the warm natural bath appeared in the shaft following oil extraction in the 1980s. It's now visited for its cleansing subterranean waters (no sign of oil today).

Punta Sal

Located some 2km along a track from Km 1187 of the Panamericana, **PUNTA SAL**, considered by many to have the best **beach** in Peru, has extensive sands and attractive rocky outcrops, swarming with crabs at low tide. It's a safe place to swim and a heavenly spot for diving in warm, clear waters. In the low season you'll probably have the beautiful beach to yourself; in high season it's a good idea to book your accommodation in advance.

The waters off Punta Sal are known for their high concentration of striped and black marlin. **Fishing trips** can be arranged (a yacht for four costs between US$500 and US$880 with North Shore Peru Expeditions; ⓣ961 770 728, ⓦnorthshore.pe), with prices based on what you're hoping to catch and how far out to sea you wish to go. Between July and October, Punta Sal also makes an excellent base for **whale watching**, as humpbacks come up from the Antarctic to calve. Trips can be arranged with North Shore Expeditions in Punta Sal or Pacifico Adventures in Los Organos (ⓣ073 257 686, ⓦpacificoadventures.com; S/130 per person).

ARRIVAL AND DEPARTURE — PUNTA SAL

By bus From Tumbes, go with the comfortable, air-conditioned minivans that run along the coast; try Sertur, Av Tumbes Norte 302 (ⓣ072 521 455; 1hr; S/25).

By colectivo Colectivo cars leave from in front of the Cruz del Sur office in Máncora (30min; S/5) and drop you off on the highway outside the city. For an extra charge, the driver will take you right to the beach. If not, take a mototaxi there for S/3.

ACCOMMODATION AND EATING

There are a couple of small **bodegas** in Punta Sal, so drinks and general groceries can be bought without leaving the beach area. Most hotels have a restaurant.

Hospedaje Hua Punta Sal ⓣ072 540 043, ⓦhua-puntasal.com. Located towards the middle of the beach, *Hua* is a good mid-range choice, with a wooden main building; some rooms have ocean views. Service is very good, plus there's a restaurant which serves seafood (S/26–40) and great fresh juices during the day and at night whips up pasta and tasty pizzas (S/20–40). S/140

★ **La Pirámide del Mar** ⓣ072 540 006. Sip a pisco sour with the sand between your toes at this relaxed beachside restaurant. Their ceviche and seafood dishes (S/25–30) are straight from ocean to plate, while they've got 18 types of craft beer and a long list of cocktails to sample during their perpetual happy hour. Check out their newest locale on the main road through Punta Sal for even cheaper ceviches (S/10) and delicious desserts. They also rent stand-up paddle and body boards. Daily 9am–10pm.

★ **Yemaya** Panamericana Norte Km 1179 ⓣ981 848 008, ⓦyemayaperu.com. A luxurious boutique hotel past the village of Cancas a few kilometres north of Punta Sal. Just eight bungalows on a spacious plot guarantee absolute peace and individual attention; all meals included at their excellent restaurant overlooking the beach. S/420

Tumbes

About 30km from the Ecuadorian border and 287km north of Piura, **TUMBES**, separated from the rest of Peru by the sluggish brown River Tumbes, is usually a mere pit stop for overland travellers, but offers a few decent restaurants and better money-changing options than at the Ecuadorian frontier. The city has a significant history, and is somewhat friendlier than most border settlements. On top of that, it's close to two distinct and unique forests and protected areas: the **Santuario Nacional los Manglares de Tumbes** and the **Zona Reservada de Tumbes.** The settlement of **Zorritos** is strung out along the seafront and Panamericana some 34km south of Tumbes; as well as a long, empty and quite beautiful beach, this town is the point of access to some ancient, still-working natural mud baths.

The area can get very hot and humid between December and March, while the rest of the year it offers a pleasant heat, compared with much of Peru's southern coast. The sea is warm and mosquitoes can be bothersome between September and January. Locals tend to be laidback and spontaneous, a trait reflected in the local traditions such as **las cumananas**, an expression in popular verse, often by song with a guitar. The verse is expected to be sparky, romantic, comical and even sad, but most importantly, spur of the moment and rap-like.

Brief history

Pizarro didn't actually set foot in Tumbes when it was first discovered by the Spanish in 1527. He preferred to cast his eyes along the Inca city's adobe walls, carefully irrigated

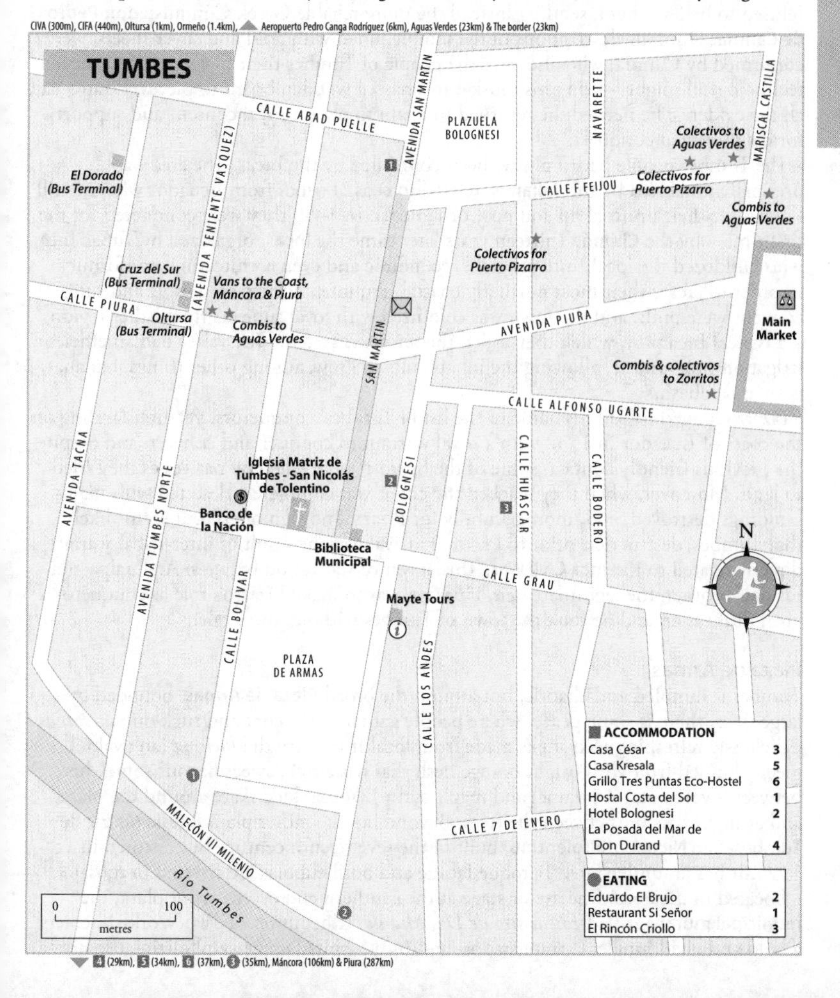

BORDER RELATIONS WITH ECUADOR

Tumbes was the first town to be "conquered" by the Spanish and has maintained its importance ever since – originally as the gateway to the Inca Empire and more recently through its strategic position on the contentious **frontier with Ecuador**. Despite three regional wars (in 1859, 1941–42 and 1997–98), the exact line of the border remains a source of controversy. Maps of the frontier vary depending on which country you buy them in, with the two countries claiming a disparity of up to 150km in some places. The traditional enmity between Peru and Ecuador and the continuing dispute over the border mean that Tumbes has a strong Peruvian army presence and a consequent strict **ban on photography** anywhere near military or frontier installations.

fields and shining temple, from the comfort and safety of his ship. However, with the help of translators, he aimed to learn as much as he could about Peru and the Incas during this initial contact.

The Spaniards who did go ashore made reports of such grandeur that Pizarro at first refused to believe them, sending instead the more reliable Greek Conquistador, **Pedro de Candia**. Dubious descriptions of the temple, lined with gold and silver sheets, were confirmed by Candia, who also gave the people of Tumbes their first taste of European technological might – firing his musket to smash a wooden board to pieces. Pizarro had all the evidence he needed; he returned to Spain to obtain royal consent and support for his projected conquest.

The Tumbes people hadn't always been controlled by the Incas. The area was originally inhabited by the **Tallanes**, related to coastal tribes from Ecuador who are still known for their unusual lip and nose ornaments. In 1450 they were conquered for the first time – by the **Chimú**. Thirteen years later came the **Incas**, organized by Tupac Inca, who bulldozed the locals into religious, economic and even architectural conformity in order to create their most northerly coastal terminus. A fortress, temple and sun convent were built, and the town was colonized with loyal subjects from other regions – a typical Inca ploy, which they called the *mitimaes* system. The valley had an efficient irrigation programme, allowing the inhabitants to grow, among other things, bananas, corn and squash.

Pizarro longed to add his name to the list of Tumbes' conquerors, yet after landing on the coast of Ecuador in 1532 with a royal warrant to conquer and convert, and despite the previous friendly contact, some of the Spanish were killed by natives as they tried to land. Moreover, when they reached the city it was completely deserted with many buildings destroyed, and, more painfully for Pizarro, no sign of gold. It seems likely that Tumbes' destruction prior to Pizarro's arrival was the result of inter-tribal warfare directly related to the **Inca Civil War**. This, a war of succession between Atahualpa and his half-brother, the legitimate heir, Huascar, was to make Pizarro's role as conqueror a great deal easier, and he took the town of Tumbes without a struggle.

Plaza de Armas

Tumbes is jumbled and chaotic, but around the broad **Plaza de Armas**, bounded by large trees, there is some peace, where people gather to sit, chat and suck on *marcianos*, deliciously refreshing iced sticks made from local fruit – try the *lúcuma* (an ovaloid, green-skinned fruit with bright orange flesh that has a rich, sweet flavour somewhere between sweet potato, caramel and maple syrup). Young kids skate around the plaza, and at night bats flit between the trees. Beyond lies the rather plain **Iglesia Matriz de Tumbes–San Nicolás de Tolentino**, built in the seventeenth century but restored in 1995. It has an understated Baroque facade and both cupolas are covered in mosaics.

Located in the amphitheatre or stage at the southern end on the main plaza, the **municipal mural** entitled *Encuentro de Dos Mundos* (Encounter of Two Worlds) depicts a bold and vivid jungle, Conquistador- and Inca-inspired scene symbolizing the first contact between Spain and ancient Peru and in particular the Battle of the Mangroves. Leading off eastwards from the northern edge of the plaza is Calle Grau, an attractive old-fashioned hotchpotch of a street, lined with wooden colonial buildings.

Malecón

The slightly grubby raised **Malecón** promenade runs along the high riverbanks of the Río Tumbes, a block beyond the southern end of the Plaza de Armas. At the western end of the Malecón, you can see a massive Modernist **sculpture**, *Tumbes Paraiso del Amor y el Eterno Verano* (Tumbes Paradise of Love and Eternal Summer), depicting a pair of lovers kissing.

ARRIVAL AND GETTING AROUND — TUMBES

BY PLANE

Aeropuerto Pedro Canga Rodríguez, Av Panamericana Norte 1276 (072 521 688), is 6km north of the city. LATAM, desk ground floor of Costa Mar Plaza, Av San Martin 2601, has flights to and from Lima. A taxi into town (15min) should cost around S/20. Taxis to Punta Sal (1hr) cost around S/90.

Destinations Lima (3 daily; 1hr 45min).

BY BUS

Most buses coming to Tumbes arrive at offices along Av Tumbes Norte (also known as Av Teniente Vásquez), or along Piura.

Bus companies CIFA, Av Tumbes Norte 1010 (972 894 619) for Machala and Guayaquil; Civa, Av Tumbes Norte 518 (072 525 120), and Cruz del Sur, Av Tumbes Norte 319 (072 526 200), are among the best for Lima and Guayaquil, the latter with a weekly service to Bogotá too; El Dorado, Av Tacna 351 (072 635 701), for Piura, Chiclayo and Trujillo; Oltursa, Av Tumbes Norte 948 (072 523 046), for luxurious travel to Lima, Chiclayo and Trujillo, with a ticket office one block north of the plaza at Av Tumbes Norte 305; Ormeño, Av Tumbes Norte 1187 (072 522 894), similar to Oltursa, but also covering Guayaquil and Bogotá.

Destinations Aguas Verdes (hourly; 30min); Bogotá (2 daily; 48hr); Chiclayo (7 daily; 8hr); Guayaquil (5 daily; 6hr); Lima (7 daily; 20–22hr); Machala (hourly; 1hr 30min once through immigration); Máncora (several daily; 1–2hr); Piura (12 daily; 5hr); Puerto Pizarro (hourly; 15min); Trujillo (5 daily; 12hr).

BY MINIVAN AND COLECTIVO

Sertur minivans (more comfortable than combis and colectivos) pull in at Av Tumbes Norte 302 (072 521 455) and leave when full for Máncora, Sullana and Piura. For Zorritos, colectivos leave from Av Mariscal Castilla at C Ugarte (S/4–5; 30min).

BY CAR

San José Rent a Car, Av Tumbes Norte 486 (072 522 321, rentacarsanjose.pe).

BY TAXI AND MOTOTAXI

Taxi Beach (072 504 202) is a recommended firm. You can also hail one of the many mototaxis, which will take you anywhere in the city for around S/2.

INFORMATION AND TOURS

Tourist information iPerú have an office on the plaza at Jr Bolognesi 194 (072 506 721; iperutumbes@promperu.gob.pe; Mon–Sat 9am–6pm, Sun 9am–1pm).

Tour operators Mayte Tours, Jr Bolognesi 196 (072 523 219, maytetours.com), run English-speaking tours to Puerto Pizarro mangrove swamp (S/40) and to local beaches (via the Baños de Barro) from S/80. They also visit Parque Nacional Cerros de Amotape and the Santuario Nacional los Manglares de Tumbes (both S/70).

ACCOMMODATION

The best spots are within a few blocks from the Plaza de Armas; best not go much further abroad as the buildings are run down and the traffic chaotic and noisy. To eascape the city, it's worth considering lodgings in the most attractive beach near Tumbes, Zorritos (see page 425).

Casa César C Huascar 311 072 522 883, casacesartumbes.com; map p.421. Still looking new from a recent renovation, rooms are spacious with comfortable beds and a/c. Good service and a secure parking lot across the road. S/160

Hostal Costa del Sol Av San Martín 275 072 523 991, costadelsolperu.com; map p.421. Located on the Plazuela Bolognesi, the rooms at *Hostal Costa del Sol* are about as luxurious as it gets here, with a/c, private baths and cable TV, plus a garden patio and pool. S/210

Hotel Bolognesi C Bolognesi 221 072 633 837; map p.421. Friendly service and spotless rooms with fan (a/c S/30 more). Hot water, good wi-fi and just 100m from the plaza. S/70

EATING

Tumbes has a handful of good restaurants and is the best place in Peru to try *conchas negras* – the black clams found only in these coastal waters, where they grow on the roots of mangroves.

★ **Eduardo El Brujo** Jr Malecón Benavides 850 ⓣ 972 634 456 ⓦ eduardoelbrujo.com; map p.421. Probably the best reason to stop in Tumbes, thanks to superb seafood with interesting creations you won't easily find outside of Lima, including delectable ceviches of *conchas negras*. Impeccable service, although it does get very busy. Mains S/30–50. Mon–Sat 10.30am–11.30pm, Sun 11am–5pm.

Restaurant Si Señor C Bolívar 115 ⓣ 976 678 640; map p.421. Serves mostly beer and seafood, right on the Plaza de Armas, and is open late into the night. The food is tasty (set menu for S/9), but for freshness, stick to eating at lunch time. Daily 7.30am–3am.

DIRECTORY

Banks and exchange There are a number of banks and ATMs lining the plaza on C Bolívar. *Cambistas* are at the corner of Bolívar with Piura and an official casa de cambio is Cambios Internacionales, Jr Bolívar 259.

Police Av Mayor Novoa and C Zarumilla (ⓣ 072 522 525).

Post office C San Martin 208 (Mon–Fri 9am–6pm, Sat 9am–5pm).

Puerto Pizarro

PUERTO PIZARRO, 13km northeast of Tumbes, is worth a visit if you have time to kill, although the waterfront today is full of rubbish. The boat trips offered to the Isla de Amor (see page 424) can be pleasant; just choose your guide carefully and go at high tide. If, however, you only have time for one mangrove outing, the Santuario Nacional los Manglares de Tumbes (see page 425) is more attractive.

An ancient fishing port, Puerto Pizarro was a commercial harbour until swamps grew out to sea over the last few centuries, making it inaccessible for large boats and permanently disconnecting Tumbes from the Pacific.

ARRIVAL AND DEPARTURE — PUERTO PIZARRO

By combi/colectivo Taxi colectivos leave Tumbes regularly for Puerto Pizarro (S/2.50; 15min) from C Huascar, just across Av Piura, while combis depart from C Feijoó, at Av Castilla (S/1.50; 20min).

By taxi Taxis cost around S/20 from Tumbes.

ACCOMMODATION AND EATING

Hotel Bayside Overlooking Puerto Pizarro ⓣ 072 543 045 ⓦ hotelbayside.com. This hotel is right on the waterfront; it has a pool, private bathrooms, palm trees and a restaurant-café. They can advise on fishing and boat excursions. S/99

Isla de Amor

Boats run to Isla de Amor from Puerto Pizarro; buy tickets (S/70 per boat minimum, more for a more comfortable boat) from the information and ticket booth on the seafront

From Puerto Pizarro you can take slow but pleasant **boat trips** out to the **ISLA DE AMOR**, where there's a bathing beach and a café. The boat operators tell you the history of the area and the mangroves themselves, while pointing out wildlife like the magnificent frigate bird (the late afternoon is the best time to see the birds, as they return home to roost) and the occasional white iguana languishing among the mangroves. The tour will also take you through **mangrove creeks** where you'll see the *rhizopora* tree's dense root system. The centre for the protection of Peru's only indigenous, and **endangered**, **crocodile** (*Crocodylus acutus americano)* is neglected and a bit depressing (S/3.50). There are very few of these crocodiles left in the wild, having been hunted in the past for their skin, and the centre has bred around 225 in captivity. You can see the crocodiles at most life stages, with the largest growing to around 3m.

TUMBES' PROTECTED AREAS

The Tumbes region is well endowed with natural resources, not least the three major **protected areas** of the Santuario Nacional los Manglares de Tumbes, the Parque Nacional Cerros Amotape and the Zona Reservada de Tumbes. These, plus the El Angulo Hunting Reserve, encompass many habitats only found in this small corner of the country. If you're short on time, it is just about possible to travel between them in one day by going with a local tour company. To visit, you have to register at a small SERNANP post. For more info contact the iPerú office in Tumbes (see page 423) or the main SERNANP office in Tumbes (☎072 526 489).

SANTUARIO NACIONAL LOS MANGLARES DE TUMBES

The **Santuario Nacional los Manglares de Tumbes** comprises most of the remaining **mangrove swamps** left in Peru, which are under serious threat from fishing and shrimp farming. The best way to visit the sanctuary is via Puerto 25, fifteen minutes from Aguas Verdes. There are five species of mangrove here, of which the red mangrove is the most common and where the *conchas negras* thrive, although the 1998 El Niño weather introduced large amounts of fresh water into the shell beds here, causing significant damage. The mangroves also contain over two hundred bird species, including eight endemic species, notably the splendid mangrove eagle.

Combis run from Tumbes (on block 4 of Av Mariscal Castillo, just past the market, across from the church) to Aguas Verdes (S/2.50; 30min). From here, head to the iPeru post (☎016 167 300), where they can call a reliable mototaxi which will take you to Puerto 25 for S/10, and later return you to Aguas Verde. At the SERNANP office you need to pay a S/10 entry fee and choose your boat operator. A two- to three-hour trip through the mangroves will cost S/60 and a longer trip (5–6hr) all the way out to Punta Capones, where there is more birdlife, S/120 (price per boat, for up to four people). A short stroll over a raised walkway is available at no cost if you just want a glimpse of the mangroves.

ZONA RESERVADA DE TUMBES

The **Zona Reservada de Tumbes** extends right up to the Ecuadorian border and covers over 75,000 hectares of mainly **tropical forest**. The best route is inland, due south from Tumbes via Pampas de Hospital and El Caucho to El Narranjo and Figueroa on the border, but transport is infrequent, making visits only really possible with a tour. Potential sightings include monkeys, small cats and snakes; but the whole area is under threat from pollution and gold mining, mainly from across the border in Ecuador at the headwaters of the river.

PARQUE NACIONAL CERROS DE AMOTAPE

Home to the best-preserved region of dry forest anywhere along the Pacific coast of South America, the **Parque Nacional Cerros de Amotape** contains six other distinct habitats covering over 90,000 hectares. Access is via Rica Playa at the SERNANP post, 1hr 20min south of Tumbes (36km), but public transport is rare and slow. Essentially, unless you have your own car, you need to go with a tour. Animals here include black parrots, desert foxes, deer, white-backed squirrels, *tigrillos* (ocelots), pumas and white-winged turkeys. Remember to take plenty of **water** (for drinking, washing etc) with you.

Zorritos

Still managing to retain its identity as a quiet fishing village, **ZORRITOS**, 34km south of Tumbes, has become popular with young Limeño sun-seekers. It gets lively over summer, drawing surfers for waves between January and April, and makes for a great alternative to the grey, muggy heat of Tumbes. It's also well situated for day-trips to the nearby relaxing natural mud baths, the **Baños de Barro Medicinal Hervideros.**

ARRIVAL AND DEPARTURE — ZORRITOS

By combi/colectivo Combis and colectivos leave from Av Mariscal Castilla at C Ugarte in Tumbes, and can drop you anywhere along Ruta 1 in central Zorritos (S/4–5; 30min).

CROSSING THE BORDER TO ECUADOR

Crossing the **Peru–Ecuador border** is relatively simple in either direction. You have the choice of crossing at: the busy frontier settlement of **Aguas Verdes**, easily done with little effort thanks to long-distance international buses plying the route; at the crossing between **La Tina** and **Macará**, 112km north of Piura, which is a very pleasant alternative (its main advantage being the scenery en route to Loja); or at the lesser-used, and more long-winded route between **Zumba** and **La Balsa**, a good choice if you're heading directly to Chachapoyas (see page 384).

AT AGUAS VERDES

By bus The best and safest way to enter Ecuador is to take an international bus from Tumbes (or Máncora) to Machala or Guayaquil; the bus waits for you as you do the exit and entry process at the CEBAF (Centro Binacional de Atención Fronteriza) border control. The entry and exit is in the same building and is open 24hr. The bus to Machala is a good option if you plan on heading directly on to other places in Ecuador, as this city has connections to all major destinations in the country.

By colectivo Colectivo cars (S/5; 30min) for the border leave Tumbes from block 4 of Av Mariscal Castillo, just past the market, and leave you in Aguas Verdes. Once here, it is a short stroll across the Puente Internacional (international bridge) and on the other side you take one of the yellow taxis to the CEBAF control point (10min; US$3–5). Get your stamps and head to Huaquillas (the Ecuadorian equivalent of Aguas Verdes) and choose a bus for any Ecuadorian destination.

By taxi A taxi from Tumbes to the border bridge (taxis are not allowed over the two bridges into Huaquillas, Ecuador) costs S/30. Note that the risk of mugging or fraud makes travelling by taxi to the CEBAF control point an undesirable option; it is much easier and more pleasant to just take a direct international bus from Tumbes or Máncora.

Entry/exit stamps The CEBAF border control (T 072 597 900) for both exit and entry stamps is on the Ecuadorian side of the bridge and is open daily, 24hr.

Customs The main Peruvian customs point is actually a concrete complex in the middle of the desert between the villages of Cancas and Máncora, more than 50km south of the border. When it is operating, buses are pulled over and passengers have to get out, often having to show documents to the customs police, while the bus and selected items of luggage are searched for contraband goods. This rarely takes more than 20 minutes.

Banks and exchange Since Ecuador dollarized its currency, exchange has become much easier. Change your remaining nuevos soles to dollars in Tumbes before leaving as the moneychangers by the bridge are a hassle and you open yourself up to fraudulent notes and pickpockets.

7

ACCOMMODATION

★ **Casa Kresala** Barrio El Pacifico T 072 500 801, W casakresala.com; map p.421. In central Zorritos, just off the beach, this is a simple, colourful surfer hostel. Green, shady common areas have hammocks, while private rooms come with silky – and necessary – mosquito nets. They also prepare vegetarian meals. Dorms S/40, doubles S/100

Grillo Tres Puntas Eco-Hostel Av Los Pinos 563 T 072 794 830, W casagrillo.net; map p.421. A few kilometres south of Zorritos, this laidback, HI-affiliated eco-lodge right on the beach has spacious wooden and bamboo cabins. Shaded campsites with hammocks are just 20m from the waves and there's a brand-new swimming pool. Some good vegetarian food at their restaurant and free yoga in the afternoons. Camping S/20, bungalows S/65

La Posada del Mar de Don Durand Caleta Grau, about 2km before Zorritos T 072 630 311; map p.421. Blissfully away from the noise of the Panamericana, this cute guesthouse is mere metres from a deserted beach. Large, light and airy rooms with fans, a large communal kitchen and a barbecue area with hammocks right on the sand conspire to make this place feel like paradise. S/190

EATING

El Rincón Criollo Panamericana Norte 162, next door to the church; map p.421. Decent criolla food at good prices, including mountainous portions of straight-from-the-ocean ceviche (S/16), delicately fried *chicharrón de pescado* (S/16) and a cheap lunch menu. Tues–Sun noon–4pm.

Similarly, when leaving Ecuador, change at your first major Peruvian destination, or at least at an official exchange in Aguas Verdes.

VIA LA TINA AND MACARÁ

By colectivo The crossing is most conveniently approached by combi from Sullana, leaving from the Terminal Terrestre in Avenida Buenos Aires, not far from the main market, departing regularly for La Tina between 6am and 6pm (S/15; almost 2hr). A short mototaxi ride (S/1; 5min) connects small La Tina with the international bridge and immigration facilities.
Macará The Ecuadorian town of Macará, which has a couple of hostels, is located some 4km from the border; mototaxis (10min; 70¢) take people into town. The journey between the border and Macará is extremely hot – if the sun's out, take water to drink. Buses on to Loja (5hr) depart from Macará; there are also buses direct to Loja from Piura (see page 409).
Banks and exchange You can change money in La Tina at the bank (Mon–Fri 9am–4pm) on the Peruvian side.
Entry/exit stamps The Peruvian and Ecuadorian immigration offices are open 24hr; the frontier is based on a river bridge with the Peruvian immigration on the Peruvian end of the bridge. Hand in your tourist card and get an exit stamp in your passport here, then walk over the bridge to the Ecuadorian immigration facility. Coming into Peru you may have to have your completed tourist card stamped by the national police.

VIA LA BALSA AND ZUMBA

By colectivo Firstly, take a colectivo (S/20) or combi (S/10) from Jaén, departing for San Ignacio (2hr) when full from the Terminal Terrestre Sur Jaén, between C La Marina and C Cruz del Chalpón. In San Ignacio, asked to be dropped off for the colectivos to La Balsa (S/15; 1hr 30min–2hr); upon arrival in the latter, you'll be deposited a short distance from the Peruvian immigration office, just before the international bridge that connects Peru with Ecuador. Get your stamps – it's as easy as just walking across the bridge to get to the Ecuadorian side, where you can pick up a *ranchara* ($3; 1hr) or a private taxi ($20; 45min) for Zumba. Here, around nine buses daily connect the town with Loja ($10; 5hr).
Banks and exchange You can change money on both sides of the bridge in La Balsa.
Entry/exit stamps The official opening hours of the Peruvian and Ecuadorian immigration offices are 7.30am–8.30pm although during these hours the officers often wander off for long breaks, so you may have to wait. You'll need to hand in your tourist card and get an exit stamp in your passport in the offices on the Peruvian side of the bridge and walk the short distance across to reach the Ecuadorian immigration facility on the other side.

Baños de Barro Medicinal Hervideros

40km south of Tumbes • Turn off the Panamericana Norte at Bocapan, Km 1214; signpost reads "Parque Nacional Cerros de Amotape"; the baths are about 4km down this road. Walking (2–3hr), taxi or mototaxi from Zorritos (S/30–40 with 1hr wait) are the only alternatives to going with a tour from Tumbes or Máncora

The little-visited **Baños de Barro Medicinal Hervideros** (medicinal mud baths) are reputedly very good for your skin. Surrounded by hills and *algarrobo* trees, this is a peaceful and relaxing spot, with the *pozos de barro* (mud baths) discovered by the archeologist Raymondi in 1882 – though they were almost certainly used for centuries before that. There are several mud baths, with a lower pool for washing down. Temperatures and health effects vary by pool; some of this is noted on small wooden signs showing an analysis of the mud. Make sure to take plenty of drinking water, as there is none at the baths.

The Amazon Basin

AERIAL VIEW OF IQUITOS

The Amazon Basin

The Amazon, the rainforest, the selva, the jungle, the green hell (*el infierno verde*): all attempt to name this huge, vibrant swathe of Peru. Whether you explore it up close, from the ground or a boat, or fly over it in a plane, the Peruvian Amazon Basin seems endless. Well over half of the country is covered by dense tropical rainforest, and this jungle region, sharing the western edge of the Amazon with Colombia, Ecuador and Brazil, forms part of what is probably the most biodiverse region on Earth. Jaguars, anteaters and tapirs still roam the forests, huge anacondas lurk in the swamps, toothy caimans sunbathe along riverbanks, and trees rise like giants from the forest floor. Many indigenous communities still live scattered throughout the Peruvian section of the Amazon, surviving primarily by hunting and fishing.

The jungle of southeastern Peru is plentifully supplied with lodges, guides, boats and flights. Cusco is arguably the best departure point for trips into the **southern selva**, with air and road access to the frontier town of **Puerto Maldonado** – a great base for visiting the nearby forests of **Madre de Dios**, which boast the **Reserva Nacional Tambopata** and the **Parque Nacional Bahuaja-Sonene**, an enormous tract of virgin rainforest close to the Bolivian border. Many naturalists believe that this region is the most biodiverse on the planet, and thus the best place to head for wildlife. Reachable overland from Cusco, the **Reserva Biósfera del Manu** runs from cloud forest on the slopes of the Andes down to relatively lowland forest. For a quicker and cheaper taste of the jungle, you can travel by bus from Cusco via Ollantaytambo to **Quillabamba**, on the **Río Urubamba**, which flows north along the foothills of the Andes, through the dangerous but unforgettable whitewater rapids of the **Pongo de Mainique**.

North of here lies **Pucallpa**, a rapidly growing, industrialized Amazonian town in the **Selva Central**, best reached by scheduled flights or the fully paved road from Lima. Another sector of this scenic central jungle region – **El Valle de Chanchamayo** – is only eight hours by road from Lima, and is blessed with crystalline rivers, Peru's best coffee, numerous protected areas for birdwatching and good road links. Winding fast but precariously down from the Andean heights of Tarma, the Carretera Central is paved all the way to **Satipo**, a jungle frontier town, relatively close to the **Río Tambo**, the jumping-off point for off-the-beaten-track adventures. En route, the road passes through the cloud forest via **La Merced**, from where there are connections to quasi-European **Oxapampa,** the curious Tyrolean settlement of **Pozuzo** , and **Villa Rica**, Peru's Coffee Central.

The main access point to the **northern selva** is **Iquitos**, at the heart of the largest chunk of lowland jungle – the largest city in the world that can only be reached by riverboat or plane. The northern selva can also be reached from the northern Peruvian coast via an adventurous route that takes the Río Huallaga from Yurimaguas (see page 396), a three- to four-day boat journey that can be broken by a visit to the immense **Reserva Nacional Pacaya-Samiria** at the heart of the upper Amazon, a spectacular, little-visited wildlife haven, or via a river journey of similar length from Pucallpa along the Río Ucayali. The northern selva is also the most organized and established of the Peruvian Amazon's tourist destinations, with many reputable companies offering a range of jungle visits, from luxury lodges and cruises (see page 433) to no-frills survival expeditions.

Brief history

Many archeologists believe that the initial spark for the evolution of Peru's high cultures came from the jungle. Evidence from **Chavín**, **Chachapoyas** and **Tantamayo**

RÍO TAMBOPATA

Highlights

❶ **Río Tambopata** You'll be hard-pushed to find anywhere as rich in flora and fauna as the rainforest around some of the lodges on this stunning Amazonian river. See page 444

❷ **Reserva Biósfera del Manu** An excellent place to experience a truly pristine rainforest and spot plenty of jungle wildlife – from giant otters in secluded lakes to caimans sunning themselves on the riverbanks. See page 447

❸ **La Selva Central** Taste Peru's best coffee in Villa Rica or La Merced or discover the country's Tyrolean roots in Pozuzo on a trip around the Selva Central. See page 454

❹ **Iquitos** A fun, vivacious city, boasting some splendid old colonial mansions; ridiculously hot during the day, it has an equally sizzling bar and club scene when the sun goes down. See page 467

❺ **Parque Nacional Pacaya-Samiria** You can't get closer to nature then when being paddled through the tangled mangroves of this seasonally flooded reserve, spotting otters and dolphins in the water, monkeys galore in the treetops. See page 476

❻ **Staying in an indigenous village**. A stay in an indigenous community is an unforgettable experience, whether it be learning traditional skills, joining in everyday tasks, or soaking up the sounds of the forest. See pages 446, 452 & 457

HIGHLIGHTS ARE MARKED ON THE MAP ON PAGE 432

cultures seems to back up such a theory – ancient Andean people certainly had continuous contact with the jungle areas – and the **Incas** were unable to dominate the people, their main contact being peaceful trade in treasured items such as feathers, gold, medicinal plants and the sacred coca leaf. At the time of the **Spanish Conquest**, long-term settlements existed along all the major Amazonian rivers, with people living in large groups to farm the rich alluvial soils.

TAKING A SLOW BOAT IN THE AMAZON

Idling in a hammock on a **slow boat** (*lancha*) while watching the sun dip below the rainforest canopy constitutes many a backpacker's fantasy of adventure travel in the Amazon. The main routes in Peru are between Pucallpa and Iquitos, along the Río Ucayali on a Henry boat (see pages 465 and 471), or between Yurimaguas and Iquitos along the Río Marañon on one of Eduardo's vessels (see pages 396 and 471). Further fluvial adventures down to Brazil or Colombia are also possible from Iquitos (see page 471). Boats generally leave three times a week – less often when the river's low – but are prone to long delays.

Both itineraries involve spending several days (how many largely depends on water levels and the direction of the current) on a passenger-carrying **cargo boat** with several decks. You'll pay S/150 for a bunk in a hot and airless **cabin** for two to four people – unless you're lucky enough to get on a new boat with fans or air conditioning. On the plus side, a cabin is usually safer for your belongings (though you may have to buy a padlock) and provides you with a power point, though you'll also want a hammock for some daytime lolling. Alternatively, you can sleep in a **hammock** for only S/100, though theft can be a hazard so keep a sharp eye on your valuables. Cheap hammocks are easily acquired in the market (along with rope to tie them up): a cloth one should ensure a more comfortable night's snooze. Get to the boat several hours before the scheduled departure to bag a good spot to sling the hammock: on the upper deck, towards the front, away from the throbbing engine and the dining area. During the rainy season, avoid the sides of the boat and protect yourself from being lashed by rain. The captain will usually allow you to stay on the boat the night before departure and, if the boat docks late in the evening, the night you arrive – a good idea given that port areas are not the safest of places after dark.

Food is included in the price but meals are extremely basic, generally unappetizing and repetitive, so you'd be wise to bring extra supplies. A plate, cutlery and a cup are vital on some boats, desirable on others, given that hygiene is not the best. Other **essentials** include a large flagon of water, repellent, sun screen, plastic bags (for rubbish and to keep the rain off your valuables), flip-flops (for the showers) and toilet paper. A mosquito net is also a good idea, though rarely essential once the boat is moving on the river, on account of the breeze. Reading material and a pack of cards complete the list – the days can be long and monotonous on the river, but dispense with any idea of a peaceful trip communing with nature: expect to be cheek by jowl with fellow passengers, periodically subjected to bouts of drunken banter and pounding music (earplugs or headphones are a good idea) but enjoy the adventure.

8

Early colonization

For centuries, the Peruvian jungle resisted major colonization. **Alonso de Alvarado** successfully led the first Spanish expedition, cutting a trail through from Chachapoyas to Moyobamba in 1537, but most incursions ended in utter disaster, defeated by disease, the ferocity of the indigenous peoples, the danger of the rivers, the climate and wild animals. Ultimately, apart from "white-man's" epidemics (which spread much faster than the men themselves), the early Conquistadors had relatively little impact on the populations of the Peruvian Amazon. Only **Orellana**, one of the first Spaniards to lead exploratory expeditions into the region, managed to glimpse the reality of the rainforest, though even he seemed to misunderstand it when he was attacked by a group of blonde women, one of whom managed to hit him in the eye with a blow-gun dart. These "women" are now thought to be the men of the Yagua people (from near Iquitos), who wear straw-coloured, grass-like skirts and headdresses.

The impact of the Church

By the early eighteenth century the **Catholic Church** had made deep but vulnerable inroads into the rainforest regions. Resistance to this culminated in 1742 with an **indigenous uprising** in the central selva led by an enigmatic character from the Andes calling himself **Juan Santos Atahualpa**. Missions were destroyed, missionaries and colonists killed, and Spanish military expeditions defeated. The result was that the central rainforest remained under the control of the indigenous population for nearly a century more.

AMAZON ECOLOGY: THE BASICS

At about six times the size of England, or approximately the size of California, the tangled, sweltering **Amazon Basin** rarely fails to capture the imagination of anyone who ventures beneath its dense canopy. In the **lowland areas**, away from the seasonally flooded riverbanks, the landscape is dominated by red, loamy soil, which can reach depths of 50m. Reaching upwards from this, the **primary forest** – mostly comprising a huge array of tropical palms, with scatterings of larger, emergent tree species – regularly achieves evergreen canopy heights of 50m. At ground level the vegetation is relatively open (mostly saplings, herbs and woody shrubs), since the trees tend to branch high up, restricting the amount of light available. At marginally **higher altitudes**, a large belt of **cloud forest** (*ceja de selva*) sweeps the eastern edges of the Andes, the most biodiverse of the rainforest zones.

The rubber boom

As technology advanced, so too did the possibilities of foreigners conquering Amazonia. The 1830s saw the beginning of a century of massive and painful exploitation of the forest and its population by **rubber barons**. Many of these wealthy men were European, eager to gain control of the raw material desperately needed following the discovery of the vulcanization process. Moreover, during this era the jungle regions of Peru were better connected to Brazil, Bolivia, the Atlantic and ultimately Europe, than they were to Lima or the Pacific coast. The peak of the boom, from the 1880s to just before World War I, had a prolonged and devastating effect. Treating the local indigenous communities as little more than slaves, men like the notorious **Fitzcarrald** (see page 439) made overnight fortunes at the expense of the local populations.

Modern colonization

Nineteenth-century colonialism also saw the progression of the **extractive frontier** along the navigable rivers, which involved short-term economic exploitation based on the extraction of other natural materials, such as timber and animal skins; coupled to this was the advance of the **agricultural frontier** down from the Andes. Both kinds of expansion assumed that Amazonia was a limitless source of natural resources and an empty wilderness – misapprehensions that still exist today.

Coca barons

When the Peruvian economy began to suffer in the mid-1980s, foreign credit ended, and those with substantial private capital fled, mainly to the US. The government, then led by the young Alan García, was forced to abandon the Amazon Basin, and both its colonist and indigenous inhabitants were left to survive by themselves. This effectively opened the doors for the **coca barons**, who had already established themselves during the 1970s in the Valle del Huallaga, and who moved into the gap left by government aid in the other valleys of the *ceja de selva* (cloud forest) – notably the Pichis-Palcazu and the Apurímac-Ene. Over the subsequent decade, illicit coca production was responsible for some ten percent of the deforestation that occurred in the Peruvian Amazon during the entire twentieth century; furthermore, trade in this lucrative crop led to significant corruption and supported the rise of **guerrilla activity**.

The twenty-first century

Clearing the forest for agriculture continues, as does illegal timber extraction, and in Madre de Dios gold mining ravages the jungle (see page 445). By the turn of the century, a massive desert had appeared around Huaypetue, previously a small-time frontier mining town. The neighbouring communities of Amarakaeri (which have been panning for gold in a small-scale, sustainable fashion for more than thirty years) are in danger of losing their land and natural resources. Attempts by NGOs and pro-indigenous lawyers to maintain the boundaries of reserves and communities are constantly thwarted by colonists, who are supported by local government.

GETTING TO THE AMAZON BASIN

By plane Flying to the main jungle towns – Iquitos (2hr), Puerto Maldonado (1hr 40min), Tarapoto (1hr15min) and Pucallpa (1hr) – from Lima is relatively inexpensive (from around US$100 one way) and can save a long bus journey (Iquitos is only reachable by plane or boat). Puerto Maldonado (45min–1hr) and Iquitos (July–Nov; 2hr 30min) are also reachable by plane from Cusco.

By bus or colectivo La Selva Central (La Merced, Oxapampa, Satipo) is easily reachable by paved road from Lima (8–10hr), while Tarapoto and Yurimaguas are also reachable by paved road from Lima (28–30hr), Pucallpa and Cajamarca (15–16hr) via Pedro Ruíz. Parts of the southern selva (Reserva Biósfera del Manu and Quillabamba) are reachable from Cusco by bus (the former involving some boat travel too), while Puerto Maldonado is only 10hr by bus along a good paved road from Cusco and 12hr from Puno.

By boat You can reach Iquitos easily by fast or slow boat from the frontier with Brazil and Colombia (see page 480), or less easily from the border with Ecuador using several boats. From Pucallpa and Yurimaguas upriver, you can also reach Iquitos by slow boat or one or more speed boats.

GETTING AROUND THE AMAZON BASIN

BY BOAT

The three most common forms of river transport are canoes (*canoas*), speedboats (*deslizadoras or rápidos*) and larger riverboats (*lanchas*). Where possible, try and check out the condition of the boat – and the boatman – in advance.

By canoe Canoes can be anything from a small dugout with a paddle, useful for moving along small creeks and rivers, to a large 18m canoe with panelled sides and a *peque-peque* (on-board engine) or a more powerful outboard motor (*fuera de borda*). Travelling in a smaller canoe requires either reliable local guides or a good tour company with professional guides.

By speedboat Speedboats are considerably faster and more manoeuvrable than canoes, but also more expensive. The scheduled ones that ply the Amazon, Ucayali and Huallaga and Marañon are covered and, like the long-distance buses, include basic meals and sometimes even video entertainment in the price.

By riverboat Riverboats come in a range of sizes and vary considerably in their river-worthiness: always have a good look at the boat before buying a ticket or embarking on a journey. The best are the Iquitos-based tour boats, with cabins for up to thirty passengers, dining rooms, bars, sun lounges and even jacuzzis on board. Next best are the

INDIGENOUS PEOPLES OF THE AMAZON

Outside the few main towns of the Peruvian Amazon, there are few sizeable settlements, and the population remains dominated by about fifty **indigenous groups**. For some, the jungle still offers a **semi-nomadic** existence, and in terms of material possessions, they have, need and want very little. These more "traditional" communities are scattered, with groups of between ten and two hundred people, and their sites shift every few years. For **subsistence** they depend on small, cultivated plots, fish from the rivers and game from the forest, including wild pigs, deer, monkeys and a great range of edible birds. The main species of edible jungle fish are *sabalo* or doncella (oversized catfish), *carachama* (an armoured walking catfish), the feisty piranha and the giant *zúngaro* (another type of catfish) and *paiche* – the last, at up to 200kg, being the world's largest scaled freshwater fish. In fact, food is so abundant that jungle-dwellers generally spend no more than three to four days a week engaged in subsistence activities, which, as some anthropologists like to point out, makes them "relatively affluent".

After centuries of **external influence** (missionaries, gold-seekers, rubber barons, cash-crop colonists, cocaine smugglers, soldiers, oil companies, illegal loggers, documentary makers, anthropologists and now tourists), however, most indigenous peoples speak Spanish and live fairly conventional, westernized lives. While many have been sucked into the money-based labour market, however, others, increasingly under threat, have struggled for cultural integrity and **territorial rights**; some – voluntarily isolated or uncontacted – have retreated as far as they are able beyond the world's enclosing frontier. Today they are struggling as their traditional and last remaining hunting grounds are infiltrated by oil companies and loggers.

JUNGLE ESSENTIALS

- Basic first-aid kit including anti-diarrhoea medicine (such as Lomotil or Imodium), plasters, antiseptic cream, rehydration powders etc
- Certificate of inoculation against yellow fever (essential if you're planning on crossing into Brazil overland)
- Malaria pills (start course in advance as directed by your doctor)
- Insect repellent
- Suitable clothing (including socks, loose-fitting lightweight trousers, a long sleeved shirt, and a light fleece/jumper as it can get cold even in the jungle – especially on the river)
- Sunhat
- Toilet paper
- Torch and spare batteries
- Waterproof poncho
- Whistle
- Multipurpose knife (with can and bottle opener)
- Plastic bags for packing and lining your bags (a watertight box is best for camera equipment and other delicate valuables)
- Waterproof matches and a back-up gas lighter
- Gifts for people you might encounter (batteries, knives, fish-hooks and line, and so on)
- Insect-bite ointment (antiseptic cream, antihistamines, tiger balm or *mentol china*)
- Running shoes; trekking sandals (rubber boots for jungle outings are provided by jungle lodges)
- Bottled water, or, better, the means to purify fresh water

larger vessels such as Henry or Eduardo boats (see page 471).

By ferry Since 2017 a comfortable Norwegian-built ferry has operated between Santa Rosa, at the frontier with Brazil and Colombia, and Iquitos, with plans to extend the service upriver to Yurimaguas and Pucallpa in the near future (see page 471).

ON FOOT

Walking is slow and difficult in the forest, and should only be attempted with an experienced tour guide or local person willing to guide you. People rarely get from A to B on foot, since river travel is the fastest and safest route in much of the rainforest. It is easy to get lost in the rainforest, so don't stray more than 100m from your lodge, camp, the river or your guide.

Madre de Dios

A large, forested region, with a manic climate (usually searingly hot and humid, but with sudden cold spells – *friajes* – between June and August, due to icy winds coming down from the Andean glaciers), the **southern selva** has only been systematically explored since the 1950s.

Named after the broad river that flows through the heart of the southern jungle, the still relatively wild *departamento* of **MADRE DE DIOS** is centred on the fast-growing river town of **Puerto Maldonado**, near the Bolivian border and just 180m above sea level. Most visitors come for the nearby **wildlife**, either in the strictly protected **Manu Biosphere Reserve** – still essentially an expedition zone – and the cheaper and easy-to-access **Reserva Nacional Tambopata–Candamo**. Both offer some of the most luxuriant jungle and richest flora and fauna in the world. Another massive protected area, the **Parque Nacional Bahuaja-Sonene**, is adjacent to Tambopata.

Easily accessible from several jungle lodges (or by chartering a boat), **Lago Sandoval** and the huge expanse of **Lago Valencia** are both great wildlife spots east along the Río Madre de Dios and close to the Bolivian border. At the very least, you're likely to spot a few caimans and the strange hoatzin bird, and if you're very lucky, larger mammals such as capybara, tapir or, less likely, jaguar – and at Valencia, you can fish for piranha. A little further southeast lies the **Pampas del Heath**, the only tropical grassland within Peru.

The Río Madre de Dios itself is fed by two main tributaries, the **Río Manu** and the **Río Alto Madre de Dios**, which roll off the Paucartambo Ridge just north of Cusco. West of this ridge, the **Río Urubamba** watershed starts and its river flows on past Machu Picchu and down to the sub-tropical mountain forests around the town of **Quillabamba**, before entering lowland Amazon beyond the rapids of **Pongo de Mainique**.

Puerto Maldonado

A frontier colonist town with strong links to the Cusco region, **PUERTO MALDONADO** has a fervour for bubbly jungle *chicha* music. With an economy originally based on unsustainable lumber and gold extraction, the early twentieth-century rubber boom and highly sustainable Brazil-nut gathering from the rivers and forests of Madre de Dios, Puerto Maldonado has grown enormously from a small, laidback outpost of civilization to a busy market town.

Today, swollen by the arrival of businesses thanks to the Carretera Interoceánica linking Peru to Brazil, it's the thriving capital of a region that feels very much on the threshold of major upheavals.

The town itself is centred around a pleasant Plaza de Armas but has few specific attractions, and most visitors come here primarily to head into the jungle and stay in a **lodge** (see page 445).

The port

Follow Jirón Billinghurst one block towards the river from the main plaza, and head down the steep steps to the main **port** area, situated on the **Río Madre de Dios**, and offering an otherwise rare glimpse of the river. There used to be a lot of boat traffic, ferrying people across the river, now replaced by the **suspension bridge** (Puente Intercontinental), built recently as part of the Carretera Interoceánica.

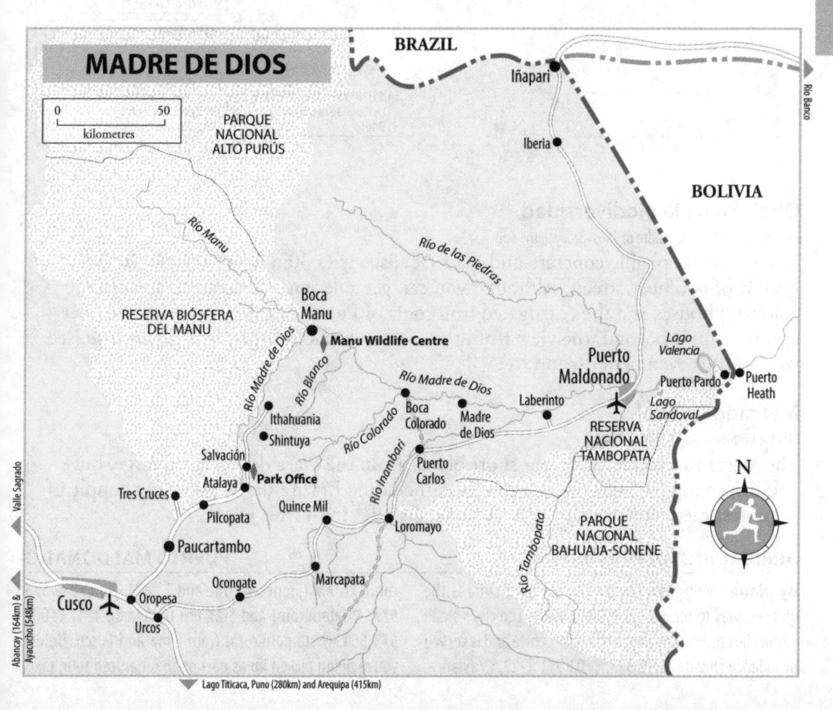

Obelisco de la Biodiversidad

Jirones Fitzcarrald and Madre de Dios • Daily 9am–5pm • S/3

This distinctly phallic concrete-and-glass **Obelisco** rises 30m above the city in the middle of two busy streets. Although you can get a decent a 360-degree view of the colourful houses and the corrugated iron roofs of Puerto Maldonado, with the river and the jungle beyond, the view from the rooftop terrace of the *Hotel Centenario* (see page 440) is even better – and free.

Mercado Central

Block 4 of Jr Ica • Daily 6.30am–5pm

The **Mercado Central**, just eight short blocks from the Plaza de Armas, is large, busy and brimming over with jungle produce, including Brazil nuts; it also has a couple of rainforest medicine practitioners. A few stalls offer fresh fruit juice.

ARRIVAL AND DEPARTURE — PUERTO MALDONADO

By plane Flying from Cusco or direct from Lima is the quickest way to reach Puerto Maldonado. The city's small airport lies some 7km west of the city centre and is served by Avianca (Jr 2 de Mayo 313; ☎ 01 511 8222, 🌐 avianca.com), LATAM (jirones Velarde and 2 de Mayo; ☎ 082 573 677, 🌐 latam.com) and StarPerú (C Velarde 151; ☎ 082 573 564, 🌐 starperu.com) from Lima and Cusco. Unless you're being picked up as part of an organized tour, taxis

(S/15) or mototaxis (S/10) will whisk you off to the city centre.

Destinations Cusco (3 daily; 45min); Lima (3–4 daily; 1hr 40min).

By bus/colectivo All buses serving Peruvian destinations arrive at the Terminal Terrestre, 3.5km northwest of the Plaza de Armas, and a S/8 mototaxi ride from the centre. A dozen bus companies run overnight services to Cusco, including Cruz del Sur (974 338 994, cruzdelsur.com.pe), CIVA (082 574 816, civa.com.pe) and Movil Tours (989 176 306, moviltours.com.pe); the last operates a daytime service too. There are also direct daily departures to Juliaca, with connections to Puno and Arequipa.

Grupo Ormeño buses (kiosk at the bus station; grupo-ormeno.com.pe) pass Puerto Maldonado on Saturdays (8–9am) en route to Río Branco in Brazil (10hr). Several operators offer minivan departures throughout the day from near the Mercado Central to Iñapari, by the Brazilian border (daily 5am–6pm; 3hr 30min; S/25–30): Empresa de Transporte y Turismo Iñapari (Jr Ica 547; 948 000 515) and Turismo Real Dorado (Jr Ica 558; 082 638 531).

Destinations Brazilian border (see page 480); Cusco (frequent daily; 10hr); Juliaca, for Puno (several daily; 12hr).

By boat Puerto Maldonado has two main river ports: the Puerto de la Capitanía on the Río Madre de Dios, at the northern end of León de Velarde, just off the Plaza de Armas, where you can hire boats to take you up the Río Madre de Dios; the other on the Río Tambopata lies at the southern end of León de Velarde, 2km from the plaza; here you can catch the weekly public boat up the Río Tambopata as far as Baltimore (Fri 7am, returning the same day; S/50). Boats to jungle lodges use both docks; some lodges along Río Tambopata take passengers by road (20km) to the village of Infierno and travel up by boat from there. A new municipal dock, the Embarcadero Turístico, on the Río Madre de Dios, is located in the new tourist complex at the end of Jr Billinghurst, though at the time of writing it was not in regular use. Boat travel to Bolivia is not common but can be done; ask at the Capitanía.

GETTING AROUND AND INFORMATION

By mototaxi/motorbike The quickest way of getting around Puerto Maldonado is by mototaxi (S/2–3 in town, S/8 to the airport, but check before getting in) or on a passenger-carrying motorbike (S/1.50–2 in town).

Tourist information The main iPerú office is just off the Plaza de Armas at Loreto 390 (Mon–Sat 9am–6pm, Sun 9am–1pm 082 571 830, iperuptomaldonado@promperu.gob.pe). There's also a small tourist information kiosk at the airport, which is open weekdays for incoming flights. Both offices can provide you with a map of the town and the area.

National park information The SERNANP office at Av Cajamarca 946 (Mon– Fri 8.30am–1pm, 2–5.30pm; 082 571 247) has handouts on the nearby national park and reserve. It also collects entrance fees (S/30 for 1 day; S/60 for 2–3; S/150 for 4 days or more); if you are planning to go independently to one of the reserves, you should pay for a permit here as you may not be able to acquire one at the park entrance. On an organized excursion, your tour operator will usually deal with the permit, though the cost may not be included in the tour price.

8

THE SAGA OF FITZCARRALD

While the infamous rubber baron, **Fitzcarrald** (often mistakenly called Fitzcarraldo), is associated with the founding of Puerto Maldonado, he actually died some twelve years before the event; his story is, however, relevant to the development of this region. While working rubber on the Río Urubamba, Fitzcarrald caught the gold bug after hearing rumours from local Ashaninka and Machiguenga men of an **Inca fort** protecting vast treasures, possibly around the Río Purús. Setting out along the Mishagua, a tributary of the Río Urubamba, he managed to reach its source, and from there walked over the ridge to a new watershed which he took to be the Purús, though it was in fact the Río Cashpajali, a tributary of the Río Manu. Leaving men to clear a path, he returned to Iquitos, and in 1884 came back to the region on a boat called *La Contamana*. He took the boat apart, and, with the aid of over a thousand Ashaninka and other indigenous people carried it across to the "Purús". But, as he cruised downriver, attacked by villagers at several points, Fitzcarrald slowly began to realize that he'd misidentified the waterway– a fact confirmed when he eventually bumped into a Bolivian rubber collector.

Though he'd ended up on the wrong river, Fitzcarrald had found a link connecting the two great Amazonian watersheds. In Europe, the "discovery" was heralded as a great step forward in the exploration of South America, but for Peru it meant more **rubber**, a quicker route for its export and the beginning of the end for Madre de Dios's indigenous peoples. Puerto Maldonado was founded in 1902, and as exploitation of the region's rubber peaked, so too was there an increase in population of workers and merchants, with Madre de Dios ultimately becoming a *departamento* of Peru in 1912. German director **Werner Herzog** thought this historical episode a fitting subject for celluloid, and in 1982 directed the epic *Fitzcarraldo*.

CROSSING INTO BRAZIL AND BOLIVIA

Check your visa and yellow fever certificate requirements for Brazil or Bolivia before arriving in Madre de Dios as both change frequently and visa stipulations vary widely; citizens of some countries, such as the US, will probably need to apply for a visa in advance.

INTO BRAZIL

From Puerto Maldonado to the border Catch a minivan to the border town of Iñapari (see page 439) and get an exit stamp from the Peruvian border post (daily 7am–7pm). It's only 2km from Iñapari to the Brazilian police and customs (colectivos available from the main plaza in Iñapari, though some combis from Puerto Maldonado continue to the border, and even on to Assis in Brazil). Change Peruvian money before leaving Peru; there are *cambistas* just before the frontier. Assis, across the border from Iñapari, has better lodgings than Iñapari (though still basic).

From the border to Brazil Get stamped into Brazil in Assis. From Assis public transport plies the 112km to Brasíleia, a much larger town that also connects via a walkable bridge with the Bolivian free-trade-zone town of Cobija. From Brasiléia, colectivos and buses for Río Branco leave regularly from near the Ponte Augusto do Araujó.

INTO BOLIVIA

By boat It's possible to travel into Bolivia on one of the cargo boats that leave more or less every week from Puerto Maldonado (there are occasional cargo and passenger boats that go all the way to Riberalta, though not during the "dry" months of July–Sept); enquire at the Capitanía. Alternatively, you can hire a boat to take you to Puerto Pardo (around S/600), the last frontier Peruvian settlement. First, get your Peruvian exit stamp from the Puerto Maldonado police and Migraciones offices. From Puerto Pardo it's a short hop by boat to the Bolivian frontier post of Puerto Heath (get your Bolivian entry stamp here) from where you continue by river to Riberalta (a week or so), or take public transport north to Cobija via Chivé. From Riberalta there are land and air connections to the rest of Bolivia.

8

For permits to travel by river into the jungle call at the Capitanía del Puerto on León de Velarde, between avenidas González Prada and 2 de Mayo (Mon–Sat 8am–6pm; ☎082 573 003).

ACCOMMODATION

IN TOWN

Hostal Paititi Jr Velarde 290 and Jr Prada ☎082 574 667; map p.438. Colourful central guesthouse on a busy street, with spacious rooms (a/c or fan) and large windows, and even a small gym. S/152

Hotel Centenario Av 2 de Mayo 744 ☎082 574 731, hotelcentenario.com.pe; map p.438. Modern, business-style hotel several blocks out of the centre, complete with rooftop pool surrounded by greenery and restaurant, plus spick-and-span rooms with shiny floors, cable TV, a/c and swan-shaped towels. Some English spoken. S/185

★ **Tambopata Hostel** Jr González Prada 234 ☎082 574 201, tambopatahostel.com; map p.438. Owned by a professional local guide, this great-value pad has stark, high-ceilinged dorms and private rooms (some en suite) – though with limited privacy. Rooms are screened and there's a communal kitchen and laundry, but the star attraction is the refreshing pool area at the back (complete with hammocks). Runs affordable tours to their own lodge in Tambopata. Dorms S/30, doubles S/70

★ **Wasai Lodge** Parque Grau on Jr Billinghurst ☎082 572 290, wasai.com; map p.438. The best of the higher-end options, offering fine views over the Río Madre de Dios, and an apple-shaped swimming pool with a waterfall and bar set among trees. All rooms are cabin-style with TV and shower, and staff here also organize local tours and run the *Wasai Tambopata Lodge* (see page 446). A new hostel section comprises two small wooden dorms sharing a balcony with river views and bathroom facilities (bed only) and a simple private room, with breakfast included. Dorms S/39, double S/111, cabins S/242

OUT OF TOWN

Fundo Refugio K'erenda Homet Km 2.7 on the Corridor Turístico Tambopata ☎982 743 881, refugiokerenda.com; map p.438. You'll get a warm welcome from this small, family-run private reserve on recovered farmland along the banks of the Tambopata. Accommodation is in three very basic wooden cabins on stilts, surrounded by lush forest, with two cabins overlooking the river. It's very back to nature – no electricity or hot water and beds have mosquito nets – yet so close to town. Food can be prepared or you can use the kitchen. S/160

Passiflora Camp Km 4.8 on the Corridor Turístico Tambopata 966 382 139, corredortambopataaoatam.org/passiflora-camp; map p.438. Set among fruit trees and pleasantly wooded grounds are three rooms (including a two-bed "dorm") in two delightful rustic cabins on stilts with shared bathrooms, and shaded hammock space. There's rewarding birdwatching, and activities such as boat trips and mountain biking can easily be added to the menu (for relatively little cost) by the congenial hosts. Breakfast is included but other meals can be prepared on request. No wi-fi. Dorms S/75, doubles S/97

EATING

Manioc and fish are staple foods in the town's **restaurants**. A variety of river fish is always available, even in ceviche form, though there is some concern in the region about mercury pollution from the unofficial gold mining, so some places will serve farmed fish. Venison (try *estofado de venado*) and wild boar fresh from the forest are often on the menu too.

El Asadazo Jr Arequipa 229, 082 502 697; map p.438. Pleasant semi-open restaurant with small wooden tables backed by a mellow soundtrack, overlooking the main plaza – great for people watching. The food is nothing special but when only S/8 gets you the lunch or dinner of the day, you can't complain. Daily 9am–11pm.

★ **Burgos's House** Av 26 de Diciembre, 082 573 653, burgosrestaurant.com; map p.438. Surrounded by lush greenery, this is the nicest place to eat in town, with an extensive menu of dishes heavily influenced by jungle ingredients (*juanes* with wild pig and criollo salad, grilled fish with star-fruit sauce) and an evening buffet (pick a main and then help yourself to fried *yuca* and sweet potato, salads and more) for S/24 – get there early for it to be fresh. The exotic cocktails (star-fruit sour, for example) pack a punch. Mains S/22–32. Daily noon–3pm & 6–10pm.

La Cabaña del Chato Jr Loreto 385; map p.438. Hands down the best cevichería, getting regular supplies of fresh fish from the Pacific coast, this cheery wooden cabaña is a bit of a squeeze, with only a handful of tables. There are several ceviches on offer (S/10–15): one with a serious kick, "el classico", and a fiery ceviche Amazónico with *cocona*. Daily 9am–2pm.

Los Gustitos del Cura C Loreto 258; map p.438. Run by a Swiss priest, the profits at this pleasant café help fund a local orphanage. The place is particularly good for ice cream (S/3 a scoop), but it also serves tamales and other inexpensive light bites. Daily 8am–8pm.

Pizzería El Hornito Jr Carrión 271 1st floor 082 572 082; map p.438. Overlooking the Plaza de Armas, this is arguably the town's best pizzeria serving up ample portions of wood-fired pizza, calzones and an array of pastas. Only open in the evening, as the oven makes the place, erm, an oven during daytime. Six-piece pizzas from S/22 to S/68 for a twenty-piece "Terminator" size. Daily 6–10pm.

Restaurante El Faro At Wasai Lodge, Parque Grau on Jr Billinghurst 082 572 290; map p.438. Under a breezy open-sided deck with views of the river, you can feast on a good-value buffet breakfast (S/15) and an executive *menú del día* for lunch (S/10); evening dishes are moderately priced (S/20–26), a la carte and well prepared – try the steak in *cocona* sauce. Daily 7–9am, noon–2pm & 6–9pm.

DRINKING AND NIGHTLIFE

There's a surprisingly busy **nightlife** in this laidback town, especially at weekends when folk come from as far as Cusco and Brazil to party. Venues blare out rock, reggaeton, *chicha*, *cumbia* – some spots even have live groups with dancers – or Latin pop. Things tend to really kick off around midnight on Friday and Saturday nights. Many bars are either on or around the plaza.

La Casa de la Cerveza Jirones Velarde and Carrión; map p.438. Popular two-storey watering hole right on the plaza, with a good range of beers and some stronger options if you feel like courting oblivion. Live music on Saturday nights after 9pm. Daily 6pm–late.

Witite Jr Velarde 151; map p.438. This old stalwart, playing the whole range of Latino music, is still one of the best places in town to hit the dancefloor. DJs, drinks specials and entry usually free until midnight. Thurs–Sat 9pm–late.

Around Puerto Maldonado

Madre de Dios boasts spectacular virgin **lowland rainforest** and exceptional **wildlife**. A range of lodges, some excellent local guides and ecologists, plus indigenous cultures are all within a few hours of Puerto Maldonado. Serious **jungle trips** can be made here with relative ease, and this part of the Amazon offers easy and uniquely rewarding access to relatively undisturbed rainforest. Most travellers come to Puerto Maldonado in order to stay in a jungle lodge, either on the Río Madre de Dios or the Río Tambopata. The former offers greater ease of access from Puerto Maldonado, with good wildlife-viewing opportunities nearby on lagos Sandoval and Valencia and Río Heath, while the last is spectacular for its remoteness away from human habitation offering an even better chance of seeing jungle fauna, particularly inside the Reserva Nacional Tambopata proper.

Lago Sandoval

13km east of Puerto Maldonado • S/30 day trip; S/60 for 2–3 days • 40min down the Río Madre de Dios from Puerto Maldonado (over 1hr on the return), plus 40min–1hr 3km walk.

A short way downriver from Puerto Maldonado, within the confines of the Reserva Nacional Tambopata, is **Lago Sandoval**, a large oxbow lake lined with lofty *aguaje* palms. You can walk here from the drop-off point on the Río Madre de Dios; during the rainy season, the 3km track turns into a mudbath and rubber boots are essential. By the lake, a caretaker watches over several large rowing boats that can hold up to a dozen people. There is also an observation tower. The wildlife is at its best early in

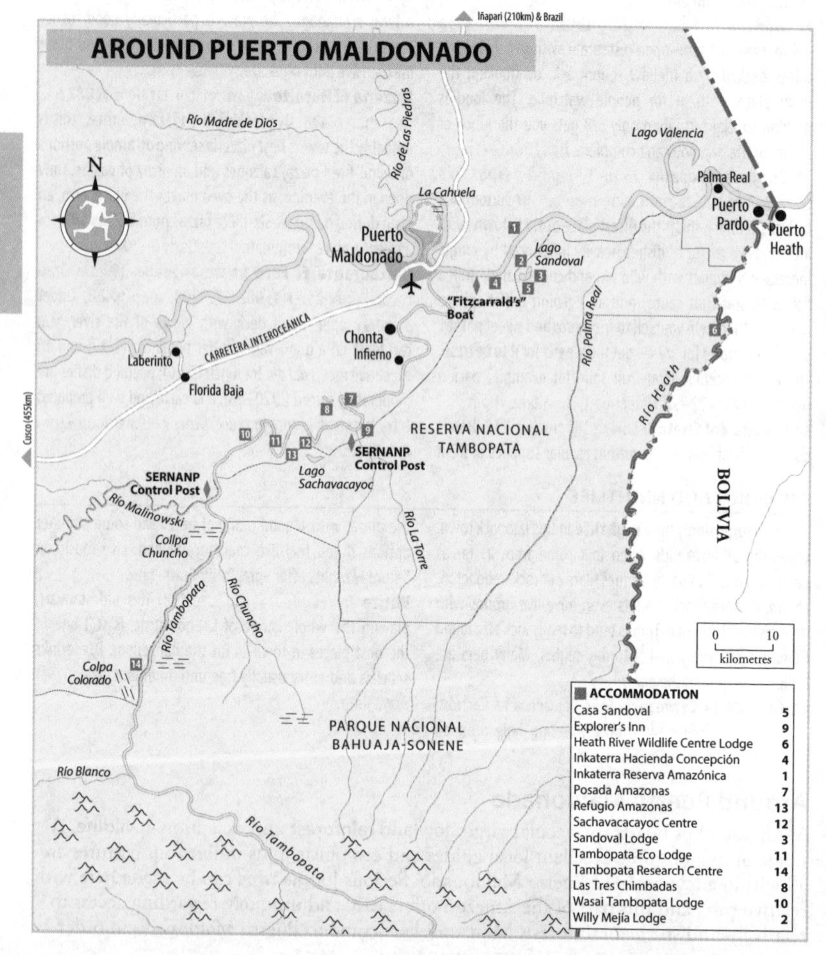

MADRE DE DIOS' INDIGENOUS GROUPS

Off the main Madre de Dios waterways, within the system of smaller tributaries and streams, live a variety of different **indigenous groups**. All are depleted in numbers due to contact with Western diseases and influences, such as pollution of their rivers, environmental destruction by large-scale gold-mining and new waves of exploration for oil. While some have been completely wiped out over the last twenty years, several have maintained their isolation. These groups have recently come to worldwide attention as the international press have highlighted the plight of the "*aislados*" ("the uncontacted").

If you go anywhere in the jungle, especially on an organized tour, you're likely to stop off at a local village for at least half an hour or so, and the more you know about the people, the more you'll get out of the visit, though you'll get a lot more if you organize at least an overnight stay (see page 446). Downstream from Puerto Maldonado, the most populous indigenous group are the Ese Eja (often wrongly, and derogatorily, called "Huarayos" by *colonos*). Originally semi-nomadic hunters and gatherers, the Ese Eja were well-known warriors who fought the Incas and, later on, the Spanish expedition of Álvarez Maldonado – eventually establishing fairly friendly and respectful relationships with both. Under Fitzcarrald's reign, they suffered greatly through the *engaño* system, which tricked them into slave labour through credit offers on knives, machetes, pots and pans, which then took years, or in some cases a lifetime, to work off. Quite often, indigenous people were kidnapped, forced to sign sham contracts and live out short, brutal lives as slaves, only to be replaced by others like themselves when they died from overwork and maltreatment. Although many traditional customs have disappeared, you can still learn a lot by organizing a stay at Palma Real – the largest Ese Eja village in the area, close to the Bolivian border, and within access of the Parque Nacional Bahuaja-Sonene (see page 444).

Upstream from Puerto Maldonado live several indigenous groups, known collectively (again, wrongly and derogatorily) as the "Mashcos" but actually comprising at least five separate linguistic groups – the **Huachipaeri**, **Amarakaeri**, **Sapitoyeri**, **Arasayri** and **Toyeri**. All typically use long bows – over 1.5m – and lengthy arrows, and most settlements will also have a shotgun or two these days, since less time can be dedicated to hunting when they are panning for gold or working timber for *colonos*. Traditionally, they wore long bark-cloth robes and had long hair, and the men often stuck eight feathers into the skin around their lips, making them look distinctively fierce and cat-like. Many Huachipaeri and Amarakaeri groups are now actively engaging with the outside world on their own terms, and some of their young men and women have gone through university education and subsequently returned to their home villages.

the morning, so it helps to stay either next to Lago Sandoval or at one of the nearby lodges (see page 445) that run tours here. There's a fair amount of **birdlife** to be seen, including hoatzins and the occasional toucan, as well as a family of **giant otters**.

You can come here as part of a tour run by a lodge or else you can charter a boat for around S/120 in Puerto Maldonado for several people and have it pick you up later, but since you need a permit from SERNANP in Puerto Maldonado, and can only enter with a guide, a tour is easier.

Lago Valencia and around

56km downriver from Puerto Maldonado along Río Madre de Dios • S/30 • 6–8hr by canoe with a *peque-peque*, or around 2hr in a boat with an outboard motor

Travelling by boat from Puerto Maldonado to the huge body of water that is **Lago Valencia**, you can stop off to watch some gold-panners on the Río Madre de Dios and visit a small settlement of **Ese Eja**; about thirty minutes beyond, you turn off the main river into a narrow channel that connects with the lake.

Towards sunset it's quite common to see caimans basking on the muddy banks, an occasional **puma** if you're lucky, or the largest rodent in the world, a **capybara**. Up in the trees around the channel lie hundreds of **hoatzin** birds, or *gallos* as they are called locally – large, ungainly creatures with orange and brown plumage, long wings and distinctive spiky crests. Some lodges organize full-day tours to the lake that combine birdwatching with some excellent fishing.

WILDLIFE ON THE LAKES

Both Lago Valencia and Lago Sandoval are superbly endowed with **birdlife**. In addition to the hoatzin you might spot kingfishers, cormorants, herons, egrets, pink flamingoes, skimmers, macaws, toucans, parrots and hawks.

Behind the wall of trees along the banks hide **deer**, **wild pigs** and **tapir**, all of them spotted occasionally. If you're lucky enough to catch a rare glimpse of a tapir – most likely at night – you'll be seeing one of South America's strangest creatures; almost the size of a cow, it has an elongated rubbery nose and spiky mane. In fact, the tapir is known in the jungle as a *sachavaca* ("forest cow" – *sacha* is Quechua for "forest" and *vaca* is Spanish for "cow").

There are caimans and larger fish in the lake, but the easiest fish to catch are **piranhas** – all you need is some line, a hook and a chunk of unsalted meat; throw this into the lake and you've got yourself a piranha.

Río Heath and Parque Nacional Bahuaja-Sonene

S/30 day permit fee; S/60 for 2–3 days; S/150 for 4 days or more • Less than 2hr from Lago Valencia in a boat with an outboard motor

Further up from Lago Valencia and skirting the Peru–Bolivia border is the **Río Heath**, a national rainforest sanctuary that passes through the remote **Parque Nacional Bahuaja-Sonene**, which abuts the Reserva Nacional Tambopata. A vast place, it's also superb for wildlife watching and well worth the effort of getting there. The only place to stay in the park is the *Heath River Wildlife Center Lodge*, run by InkaNatura (see page 447), whereas the only way to visit outside a tour is to be accompanied by a guide from one of the Ese Eja communities, such as Palma Real, but you would still need to acquire a reserve permit at SERNANP in advance (see page 439).

Río Tambopata and Reserva Nacional Tambopata

S/30 day entry fee; S/60 for 2–3 days; S/150 for four days or more • Reached by motorized canoe from Puerto Maldonado, or road to Infierno then canoe

Containing some of the world's finest and most biodiverse rainforest, and reachable via the Río Tambopata, one of the tributaries of the Río Madre de Dios, the **Reserva Nacional Tambopata** is one of the most easily accessible parts of relatively pristine Amazon rainforest.

Transformed into a reserved zone in 2000, mainly due to the scientific work of the adjacent *Explorer's Inn* lodge, the area covers around 2750 square kilometres, and is next to the Parque Nacional Bahuaja-Sonene. The expansion of the national park is a major success for conservation in Peru, but despite this there are fears that the government has plans to open up the park in future to gas and oil exploitation.

It's only possible to visit the national park on a **tour** with a licensed operator, or a guide from an indigenous community. Tours organized from Cusco or Puerto Maldonado can enter en route to one of the major macaw **salt-licks** (*colpas*) in the region; **Colpa de Guacamayos**, one of the largest clay-licks in Peru, is particularly spectacular. The licks are the best places to see wildlife in the jungle, since their salts, minerals and clay are highly nutritious, attracting large numbers of birds and animals.

It's technically possible to enter the *zona de amortiguamiento* (buffer zone) independently, after paying the park entrance fee at Puerto Maldonado's SERNANP office, but the vast majority of visitors come in conjunction with a lodge or homestay

ARRIVAL AND DEPARTURE

By boat Travelling independently from Puerto Maldonado can be rewarding, though most of the major river trips are expensive, particularly if you're travelling solo and wish to charter a boat. Visitors are required to obtain permission from the Capitanía del Puerto in Puerto Maldonado (see page 437) – though boatmen and guides generally do this for you and also organize payment of fees for you at entry to any protected areas. From the Tambopata dock there is a weekly boat for cargo and passengers (Fri 7am; S/50) that goes as far as the community of Baltimore, returning to Puerto Maldonado the same day.

TOURS

Compared with independent travel, an organized excursion saves time and offers reasonable levels of comfort. It also ensures that you go with someone who knows the area, probably speaks English and can introduce you to the flora, fauna and culture of the region. Most people book a trip with a tour operator in Cusco (see page 221) before travelling to Puerto Maldonado, or in advance online, though it is possible, and cheaper, to book in Puerto Maldonado itself. Rates can often be negotiated in low season.

Jungle Pro Jr Lambayeque 1445, Puerto Maldonado ⓣ982 613 293, ⓦtoursjunglepro.com. Locally owned, small outfit offering a more personalized service and good guiding. Tours centre on their simple, intimate seven-room lodge, *Casa Sandoval* (see map p.442), on Lago Sandoval, and the *Sachavacayoc Centre* (see map p.442) up the Río Tambopata, where you can explore two oxbow lakes and visit the large macaw clay-lick, Colpa Chuncho. Tours range from three days in Casa Sandoval (US$230 per person sharing) to a five-day trip taking in both locations for US$600 per person sharing.

Inotawa Expeditions Av Aeropuerto, Puerto Maldonado ⓣ082 572 511, ⓦinotawaexpeditions.com. Responsible tour operator with a 22-room lodge in a good location on the Río Tambopata quite close to the Parque Nacional Bahuaja-Sonene. Runs expeditions to Colpa Colorado, the world's biggest macaw salt-lick a further 8hr into the forest from the lodge, as well as specialist birdwatching and fishing tours. Works closely with the community of La Torre. Prices start at US$340 per person for three days, US$500 for six days – park fees extra.

ACCOMMODATION

Prices given for lodges below are per person, per night. Most of them have a three- or four-night **minimum stay**, though; check well in advance.

RÍO MADRE DE DIOS

★ **Inkaterra Hacienda Concepción** C Andalucía 174, Miraflores, Lima ⓣ01 610 0400, ⓦinkaterra.com; map p.442. Around 45min downstream of Puerto Maldonado this intimate lodge offers rustic luxury, and is comprised of fan-cooled, individual bungalows and cheaper rooms at the lodge itself. Nature outings include trips to Lago Sandoval, canopy walkway, caiman-spotting on the river, night walks in the jungle and more. Service is fantastic and the food is very good. The even plusher *Inkaterra Reserva Amazónica* (see map p.442) lies further downriver. US$123

RÍO TAMBOPATA

RAINFOREST EXPEDITIONS LODGES

Rainforest Expeditions (Av Aeropuerto, La Joya Km 6, Puerto Maldonado US freephone ⓣ0877 231 9251, ⓦperunature.com) is the premier tour operator in the area, possessing and/or managing three lodges and a private villa. The lodges are similar in style, with several categories of wood-and-thatch rooms – only some with fan – that open out onto the forest, and mosquito nets over large, comfy beds. Packages can combine stays in more than one lodge.

Posada Amazonas Map p.442. Only 45min by boat from Maldonado (after 45min by road), this thirty-room lodge is fully owned and jointly managed by the Ese Eja indigenous community of Infierno, with whom you can spend time. There's a canopy tower, a series of forest trails and access to a nearby ethno-botanical garden. Spa treatments are available. US$156

Refugio Amazonas Map p.442. Some 4hr away from Puerto Maldonado, the most luxurious, yet family-oriented of the company's three lodges boasts a splendid mix of traditional hut design and extravagant architectural beauty. It has 32 spacious rooms, plus a great dining area and busy bar. Varied activities include: birdwatching, kayaking, canopy climbing and mountain biking. Two nearby lakes are inhabited by otters, and there is an engaging educational trail for kids. US$193

★ **Tambopata Research Centre** Map p.442. The remotest of the Rainforest Expeditions lodges, this recently renovated comfortable 24-room lodge sits in the heart of

MADRE DE DIOS' GOLD

Every rainy season the swollen rivers of Madre de Dios deposit a heavy layer of **gold dust** along their banks, and those who have been quick enough to stake claims on the best stretches have made substantial fortunes. In such areas there are thousands of **unregulated miners**, using large front-loader earth-moving machines, contaminating the rivers with mercury and destroying large sections of the forest – and very quickly.

Gold lust is not a new phenomenon here – the gold-rich rivers have brought Andeans and occasional European explorers to the region for centuries. The Inca Emperor Tupac Yupanqui is known to have discovered the Río Madre de Dios, naming it the Amarymayo ("serpent river"), and may well have sourced some of the Empire's gold from around here.

8

COMMUNITY-BASED TOURISM

As well as standard tours, there are also opportunities to stay with and/or engage in activities with local communities; iPerú can provide pointers, and several local tour operators, such as *Tambopata Hostel* and Inotawa Expeditions, are also promoting this kind of *turismo vivencial*, which is generally cheaper than a conventional lodge stay. Obviously, lodgings may not be as luxurious and the level of guiding can be more variable but you'll generally get a more personalized service and a chance to interact more fully with local people, joining in everyday activities, from fishing to harvesting Brazil nuts, cooking to playing football. Knowledge of Spanish is an advantage. If you can, make arrangements with the community concerned rather than through a third party, which will ensure that the money goes directly to them. In addition to iPerú, the office for indigenous communities, FENAMAD (Federación Nativa del Río Madre de Díos y Afluentes), at 26 de Diciembre 276 (Mon–Fri 8am–noon & 2–5.30pm; 082 572 499), is a good place to start; alternatively enquire at the docks early in the morning about a ride in a colectivo boat to one of the villages.

Comunidad Palma Real Enquire at FENAMAD. On the banks of the Madre de Díos, on the doorstep of the Bolivian border and the Parque Nacional Bahuaja-Sonene. Though not very developed as yet, this welcoming, 500-strong Ese Eja community (S/20 entry) has a breezy, raised, thatched structure where you can sling a hammock, plus shared cold-water ablutions. You'll need a pass from SERNANP if you want to go into the national park, though there's plenty of forest to explore around the village. Including meals (activities extra) S/60 per person.

Hospedaje El Gato Jr Junín cuadra 1 s/n 941 223 676, baltimore.org.pe. Community–run association involving homestays in rustic accommodation for those who want to immerse themselves more in local culture as well as experiencing the surrounding rainforest. Even cheaper if you get there under your own steam via combi plus a 15km hike to the village; ask how at their office. Three-day trip US$206 per person.

8

the reserve, in an area of great bird and mammal diversity. It's located 500m from the world's biggest macaw *colpa*, the Colpa Colorado, and there's an excellent chance of spotting five species of monkey, peccaries, capybara, agouti and even the occasional jaguar. Three night-minimum stay but longer is needed since you'll spend an entire day there and back on the river, spending the first night at *Refugio Amazonas*. Guiding is more personalized as groups are no bigger than six. US$236

OTHER LODGES

Explorer's Inn 082 573 029, explorersinn.com; map p.442. Located within the national reserve some 58km upriver from Puerto Maldonado, this long-standing (since 1975), well-organized lodge sits in an area of staggering biodiversity – 620 bird species have been spotted in the vicinity; with a 38km network of jungle trails and a nearby parrot (not macaw) clay-lick and lake containing giant otters. The food is good, and accommodation is in a series of raised bungalows containing single, twin or triple en-suite rooms spread around a clearing. They also offer specialist birdwatching and ayahuasca programmes. US$128

Tambopata Eco Lodge C Nueva Baja 432, Cusco 084 245 695, tambopatalodge.com; map p.442. Just over the river from the Reserva Nacional Tambopata, nearly 4hr from Puerto Maldonado, this lodge offers comfortable, individual cabin-style accommodation and good food for up to 70. Some of the three- to five-day programmes include camping. Activities include forest walks, kayaking and birdwatching on Lago Condenado, and caiman-spotting at night. Park fees not included in cost. US$169

Las Tres Chimbadas Puerto Maldonado 999 605 519, treschimbadaslakelodge.com; map p.442. On an oxbow lake an hour up the Río Tambopata, just outside the park, this budget family-run lodge has a long, thatched dorm as well as private cabins. Activities include a farming tour with local villagers as well as excursions on the lake – inhabited by giant otters – and rainforest walks. They do day-tours (US$127), but you'll get much more out of the three-day option. Dorms US$76, doubles US$80

Wasai Tambopata Lodge Contact through Wasai Lodge in Puerto Maldonado; map p.442. Four hours or 120km upriver from Puerto Maldonado, this luxurious lodge consists of 21 airy cabins, a pleasant bar and dining area, a hammock-festooned lounge, 20km of walking trails around the lodge and a canopy tower for all-encompassing jungle views. Three- to five-day programmes can include a visit to Lago Sandoval (though it means spending one night in their town lodge; see page 440) as well as exploration of the upper Tambopata and may include kayaking, an adventure circuit (ziplines, etc), or the Chuncho *colpa*. Four-day stays include one night camping. US$103

CHOOSING A LODGE

The quality of the **jungle experience** varies from river to river and from lodge to lodge. Most companies offer full board and include transfers, park fees and guiding, though it is a good idea to verify the level of service online and talk to other travellers. You should also check what's included, and what **extra costs** you'll be liable for once you're there; alcoholic beverage prices can be high. Remember, too, that conditions can be rustic and relatively open to the elements: **sleeping arrangements** range from bunk rooms to luxurious doubles with mosquito nets, solar-powered showers, fans and hammocks. The **size of the lodge** is another consideration – whether you're sharing the forest with a dozen other guests or an awful lot more; ask also about the maximum number of guests per guide. **Food** is generally good, though you may want to take additional snacks. Electricity is likely to be generator-powered – though solar power is on the increase – and tends only to be on at certain times of day, sometimes in selected areas. Note also that since some tours cater for fly-in visitors, to fit with the flights to/from Cusco and/or Lima, the last day of any tour is often only a half-day. Related to this is **travel time** to and from the lodge; the deeper into the forest you go, the greater the travel time and the need for a longer tour in order to get the most from the experience and not feel that you're constantly "on the road". Most lodges require a minimum two- or three-night stay.

LAGO SANDOVAL

Sandoval Lodge InkaNatura, C Manuel Bañon 461, San Isidro, Lima ⓣ01 203 5000, ⓦinkanatura.com; map p.442. On the shores of Lago Sandoval, and accessed by canoe after the 3km walk (see page 442), this lodge (jointly owned by a non-profit organization and several indigenous families) has a privileged location on a small hill surrounded by primary forest. It gives you exclusive access to the lake in the very early morning and late afternoon, best hours for wildlife viewing and photography. The lodge has a large, airy bar-cum-dining room, plus 25 rooms with electricity and hot water. Most groups spend time on the lake or explore the small, well-trodden surrounding trail system with multilingual guides. US$146

Willy Mejía Lodge Jr Velarde 487, Puerto Maldonado ⓣ979 656 310; map p.442. This friendly family-run hostel houses up to twenty guests in bungalow-style accommodation with shared or private facilities (S/40 extra), on the side of Lago Sandoval. Inexpensive meals (S/10–15), guiding services (S/130), and they can get you a permit, with advance notice; if you already have a permit, you can just turn up. S/40

RÍO HEATH

Heath River Wildlife Center Lodge InkaNatura, C Manuel Bañon 461, San Isidro, Lima ⓣ01 203 5000, ⓦinkanatura.com; map p.442. The only eco-lodge on the Río Heath, consisting of ten simple but comfortable rooms, is run by the local Ese Eja indigenous community, and there's some great birdwatching to be had from floating hide nearby, with hundreds of parrots and dozens of macaws flocking to one of the world's most impressive clay-licks. Other attractions include wildlife spotting from the trails around the lodge. US$220

Reserva Biósfera del Manu

Eco-tours in the **RESERVA BIÓSFERA DEL MANU** don't come cheap, but represent good value when you consider its remoteness and the abundance of **wildlife** that thrives in its almost two million hectares of virgin cloud- and rainforest, a uniquely varied environment that ranges from crystalline cloud-forest streams and waterfalls down to slow-moving, chocolate-brown rivers in the dense lowland jungle. Created in 1973 as a national park, it became a UNESCO World Heritage Site in 1987.

The only permanent residents within this vast area are the teeming forest wildlife; a few virtually uncontacted indigenous groups who have split off from their major ethnic units (Yaminahuas, Amahuacas and Matsiguenka); the park guards; and the scientists at a biological research station just inside the park on Cocha Cashu, a beautiful lake.

The reserve is divided into three zones. By far the largest, comprising eighty percent of the park, is **Zone A** (Zona Natural), the core zone, the **Parque Nacional Manu**, which is strictly preserved in its natural state. A few biologists are allowed in for research purposes and several Matsiguenka groups live inside Zone A, some of whom have virtually no contact with outsiders. **Zone B** (Zona Reservada) is a Buffer Zone, ten percent of the park, set aside mainly for controlled research and tourism, with several lodges located here. Boca Manu village marking the boundary between zones A and B. The final ten percent, **Zone C** (Zona Cultural) is a Transitional Zone, an area of human settlement for controlled traditional use, though there is a cluster of lodges at the southern tip of the reserve, near Pilcopata. Tourists are allowed into zones A and B only as part of organized visits with guides, following the basic rules of non-interference with human, animal or vegetable life.

The interior of the protected area is only accessible by **boat**, so any expedition to Manu is very much in the hands of the gods, due to the temperamental jungle environment; the **rainy season** is from December to March, and visits are best organized between May and August when it's much drier, although then temperatures often exceed 30°C (86°F).

Pretty much the only way to visit Manu is by joining an **organized tour** through one of the main Cusco agents or via a local community tourist organization. To reach Zone

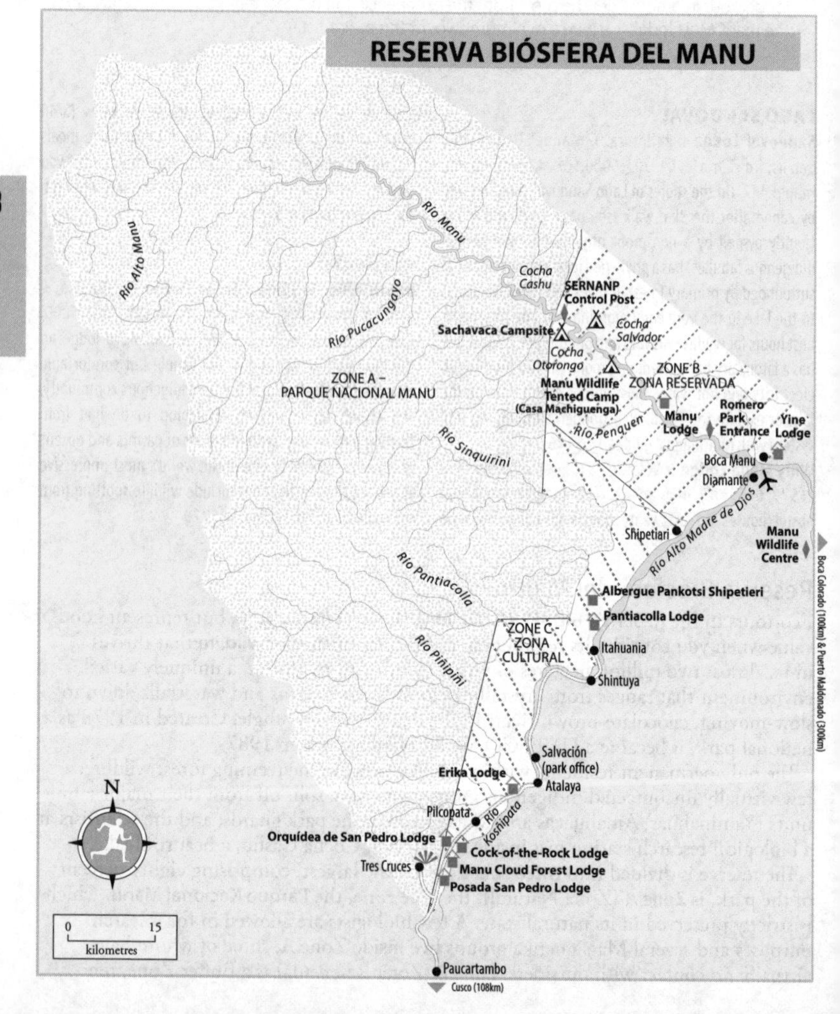

B, tours either enter via the Paucartambo road and then river descent from Cusco (1.5 days travel) – or from Puerto Maldonado (often following a flight from Cusco) using a combination of overland transport by minivan and fast boats (6hr plus), since the **airstrip** at Boca Manu is presently not being used for tourism (the available charter planes are currently monopolized by oil companies). Thus, the first and last day of any tour to Manu will be taken up with travel, which means that you need at least a five-day tour to make the most of the area.

The overland route from Cusco

The road route to Manu from Cusco is highly scenic. The first four- to six-hour stage is to the attractive town of **Paucartambo** (see page 270), over stupendous narrow roads with fine panoramas of the region's largest glaciated mountain of Ausangate. From Paucartambo, it's 25km to the **Tres Cruces** turn-off (see page 271), at the reserve's southern tip. The road drops steeply to the quiet jungle town of **Pilcopata**, a journey of around ten hours from Cusco. From here the terrain is fairly level as it skirts the Río Alto Madre de Dios, which eventually merges with the Río Manu to form the great Río Madre de Dios. Some 20km beyond Pilcopata is the smaller riverside settlement of **Atalaya** and another 20km brings you to the pueblo of **Salvación**, 28km before Shintuya, where the Reserva Biósfera del Manu has an **office** and where your guide will usually be expected to show his permits. From Shintuya, the route continues another 15km or so to the river port of Itahuania, where the road finishes. From here, it's another 55–60km by boat via Río Madre de Dios to the small settlement of Boca Manu, which lies at the confluence of the ríos Alto Madre de Dios and Manu, and at the entrance to Manu's Zona Reservada. The Limonal **ranger station** here is the place to wave your permit. Close by is the indigenous Yiné community of **Diamante.**

Manu Wildlife Centre and around

Some 10km outside the park and further downstream (around 30min–1hr) from Boca Manu along the Río Alto Madre de Dios is the **Manu Wildlife Centre,** a comfortable lodge used by various tour companies (see page 450), which also features mobile canopy towers for watching the local wildlife right up among the treetops. The centre is also close to a superb salt-lick where small parrots and larger, colourful macaws can be seen, and claims to be strategically located in an area of forest that has the highest diversity of microhabitats in Manu: *tierra-firme* (lowland forest that doesn't get flooded), transitional flood plain, *varzea* and bamboo forest are all found close by, and an astounding 530 bird species were recorded in one year alone.

About an hour's walk through the forest there's also a large salt-lick where you can see tapirs and Brocket deer. The **Blanquillo** macaw-and-parrot salt-lick, within the Blanquillo private reserve, is only thirty minutes away by river, with elevated hides from which to watch the wildlife.

Río Manu and around

Heading deep into Zone B of the park, **Río Manu** is perhaps your best bet for spotting such wildlife as jaguar (if you're lucky, you may see one sunning itself on the banks of the river), howler, dusky titi, spider, emperor tamarin, squirrel, capuchin and other monkeys, and giant otters that dwell in Cocha Otorongo and Cocha Salvador – two oxbow lakes typically visited during an extended trip into Manu.

ARRIVAL AND INFORMATION — RESERVA BIÓSFERA DEL MANU

On a tour From Cusco, reaching Zone B of Manu is either a day's journey by bus then at least half a day more by canoe, or a 40min flight to Puerto Maldonado, followed by around 6hr in a combination of minivan and speedboat.

Independent travel It is possible to travel independently on the rivers in the Zona Cultural by picking up a boat at Shintuya or one of the other riverside towns; this won't allow you to enter the reserve but you can hop aboard a cargo-bearing boat from Atalaya, Shintuya and Diamante

MANU WILDLIFE AND FLORA

For **flora and fauna**, Manu is pretty much unbeatable in South America, home to over 5000 flowering plants, 1200 species of butterfly, 1000 types of bird and 200 kinds of mammal. Rich in macaw salt-licks and otter-inhabited lagoons, it's also home to prowling jaguars, thirteen species of monkey and seven species of macaw, and contains several species in danger of extinction, such as the giant otter and the black caiman. The highlight of most organized visits to Manu is the trail network and lakes of **Cocha Salvador** (the largest of Manu's oxbows, at 3.5km long) and **Cocha Otorongo**, both bountiful jungle areas rich in animal, water and birdlife.

OTORONGO OTTERS

The **Cocha Otorongo** lake is known for its resident **giant otters**, one of the world's most endangered species. The otters are also bio-indicators of the environment, since they only live where there is clean, healthy water and a wide choice of fish. Only the oldest female of the group is mated with, so reproduction is very slow – the "queen" otters only have two or three cubs a year, usually around October, which can be expected to live for around thirty years. The top-ranking male otters are responsible for defending the group and do very little fishing, taking the catch from younger males instead.

Although they appear friendly as they play in their large family groups, the otters can be very aggressive, able to keep jaguars at bay and kill caimans that approach their lakeside nesting holes. Canoeing is not permitted, but there is a **floating platform** which can be manoeuvred to observe the otters fishing and playing from a safe distance (though your guide has to book a time for this): 30–50m is good enough to watch and take photos, though as this is Manu's most popular tourist area, you're likely to meet other groups and there can be severe competition for access to the platform.

OTHER WILDLIFE

Other wildlife to look out for includes the plentiful **caimans**, including the 2–3m white alligators and the rarer 3–5m black ones, and you can usually spot several species of **monkey** (including dusky titis, woolly monkeys, red howlers, brown capuchins and the larger spider monkeys, known locally as *maquisapas*). Sometimes big mammals such as **capybaras** or **white-lipped peccaries** (*sajinos*) can be seen lurking in the undergrowth.

GIANT TREES

The flora of Manu is as outstanding as its fauna. Huge **cedar trees** are visible from the trails, covered in hand-like vines climbing up their vast trunks (most of the cedars were removed between 1930 and 1963, before it became a protected area). The giant **catahua trees**, many over 150 years old, are traditionally the preferred choice for making dugout canoes – and some are large enough to make three or four; their bulbous white trunks seem to reach endlessly up to the rainforest canopy.

downriver from Manu to Puerto Maldonado for around S/12 per hr. Most places have a basic hospedaje, where you can spend the night, and the travel itself should guarantee an adventure of sorts and a feel for jungle life. A quicker route between Manu and Puerto Maldonado involves a combination of fluvial and terrestrial transport: catching a boat downriver from Manu to Boca Colorado – an unappealing mining centre on the Río Madre de Dios – then catching a colectivo along the 35km stretch of road to Puerto Carlos on the Río Inambari; after a quick transfer across the river, you can squeeze into a colectivo to Puerto Maldonado.

Tourist information The office for the Parque Nacional del Manu is at Av Cinco Los Chacacomos, F2-4, Larapa Grande, San Jerónimo, Cusco (T 084 274 509, W visitmanu.com). Entrance to the reserve proper (Zone B) is by organized tour; it's virtually impossible to get permission to go it alone.

TOURS AND ACCOMMODATION

A number of **organized tours** compete for travellers who want to visit Manu; however, only a few are authorized to operate within Zone B of the reserve, while others claim to take tourists to Manu but in fact only run tours to the Manu Wildlife Centre, which isn't actually within the reserve, though still provides access to some fine rainforest and

COMMUNITY-BASED TOURISM IN MANU

The most enduring of **community-run ventures** within the Zona Cultural is the *Albergue Pankotsi Shipetieri*, a Matsiguenka-operated initiative, on the Río Alto Madre de Dios (084 225595, alberguepankotsi.com). Accommodation is basic: five simple, open-fronted shelters, each with private bath and three single beds with mosquito nets. Guests have use of a kitchen, if they prefer, or can enjoy local home cooking prepared by members of the community. US$60 a day covers food, lodging and an opportunity to join in and learn from community activities: making cassava beer, fashioning hunting arrows, or walking through the forest learning about the flora and fauna. For other similar options enquire at iPerú in Cusco, or in Puerto Maldonado.

wildlife-viewing opportunities. The options listed below have a good reputation both for the way they treat their tourists and the delicate ecology of the rainforest itself. Most own, or part-own, the lodges they use. Numbers to the reserve are limited annually to around three thousand visitors, so it's a good idea to book well in advance. **Prices include** transport, lodging, park fees, bilingual guides and food, and are quoted per person sharing (a room), unless stated otherwise. See **map** p.448 for lodge locations.

Bonanza Tours C Suecia 343, Cusco 084 507 871, bonanzatoursperu.com. Highly recommended local, family-run operation with a strong environmental and social commitment working out of their own small private lodge and reserve, off the Río Alto Madre de Dios (where they've a camouflaged platform to sleep out on and wait for tapirs), and the community-run *Casa Machiguenga* near Cocha Salvador in the Zona Reservada. All knowledgeable, qualified Amazonian-born guides, particularly keen on birdwatching. Runs affordable four- to eight-day tours. Five days in Zone C US$620, and seven days (Zonas B & C) US$935

InkaNatura Travel C Manuel Bañon 461, San Isidro, Lima 01 203 5000, inkanatura.com. This well-respected champion of sustainable tourism offers customized travel, from four to five days, from Puerto Maldonado, operating from the Manu Wildlife Centre, which they part-own (see page 449). InkaNatura also accommodates people at the *Cock-of-the-Rock Lodge*, 6hr by road from Cusco, in one of the best cloud-forest locations for birdwatching, and its *Manu Wildlife Tented Camp* – whose fully screened "tents" are raised on stilts, with wooden floors and thatched roofs – and is located several hours down Río Manu in Zone B, near an oxbow lake with thirteen monkey species living nearby and a good chance of spotting a jaguar. Five days based at Manu Wildlife Centre US$1880

Manu Adventures C Plateros 356, Cusco 084 261 640, manuadventures.com. One of the first operators to run trips into Manu, with its own vehicles, boats and multilingual guides and three lodges throughout the park that allow visitors to experience different ecological habitats – from the *Orquídea de San Pedro Lodge* in the cloud forest and *Erika Lodge* in Zone C to the *Sajino Campsite* in Zone B (only visited on the longer tours) on the banks of Cocha Salvador – ideal for wildlife spotting. It runs three- to eight-day trips into Manu. Seven days US$845

Manu Expeditions Jr Los Geranios 2G, Urb. Mariscal Gamarra Primero Etapa, Cusco 084 225 990, manuexpeditions.com. Professional British-run company, specializing in ornithological tours. They offer five-, six- and nine-day lodge-based and tented camp expeditions into Zone B and to the Manu Wildlife Centre, as well as specialist birding tours, with top-quality service and naturalist guides. Six days US$2485

Manu Nature Tours Av Pardo 1046, Cusco 084 252 721, manuperu.com. A pioneer in Manu since 1985, this responsible operator part-owns the *Manu Cloud Forest Lodge* as well as *Manu Lodge*, located on an oxbow lake off the Río Manu – the only lodge within Zone B. Tours range from three to nine days, the latter including birdwatching along the 20km of trails around *Manu Lodge*. Tours can include whitewater rafting and mountain biking for an extra fee, and stay in cheaper lodgings for more affordable rates. Eight-day tours US$1953

Pantiacolla Tours C Garcilaso 265, 2nd floor, Office 12, Cusco 084 238 323, pantiacolla.com. An established company with an excellent reputation, knowledgeable guides and two lodges in the reserve: *Posada San Pedro Lodge*, *Pantiacolla Lodge* as well as the basic *Sachavaca Campsite* in the Zona Reservada, even deeper in Zone B, six hours up the Río Manu. It specializes in seven- or nine-day tours of Zone B, complete with birdwatching at clay-licks and animal watching on the oxbow lakes, though offers shorter tours. Five days US$815, seven days US$1550

Río Urubamba and around

Traditionally the home of the Matsiguenka and the Piro, the **Río Urubamba** rolls down from the Incas' Valle Sagrado to the humid lower Andean slopes around the town of **Quillabamba**. The river remains unnavigable for another 80km or so, with regular buses following a dirt road that continues deeper down into the jungle via the settlement of **Kiteni**, where the Río Urubamba becomes navigable again, to the even smaller frontier settlement of **Ivochote**. From here on, the river becomes the main means of transport, through the Amazon Basin right to the Atlantic, interrupted only by the impressive **Pongo de Mainique** whitewater rapids, just a few hours downstream from Ivochote. These rapids are generally too dangerous to pass between November and March.

Most of the Urubamba has been colonized as far as the *pongo*, and much of it beyond has suffered more or less permanent exploitation of one sort or another – rubber, cattle, oil or gas – for over a hundred years. Travel-wise, it still remains a relatively quiet and untouristed region.

Quillabamba

A rapidly expanding market town, growing fat on profits from coffee, tropical fruits, chocolate and, to an increasing extent, narcotrafficking, **QUILLABAMBA** is the nearest Peruvian jungle town that's easily accessible by road from Cusco: the main attraction here is a trip to the Pongo de Mainique rapids. Coming from Cusco, the road, though completely paved, ribbons its narrow, precipitous way over the magical Abra Málaga – the main pass, after Ollantaytambo, before descending into the distinctly warmer, more luxuriant Valle de Urubamba. The town itself, though a good place to stock up on necessities at the market before heading further into the jungle, is unremarkable. However, it does have a pleasant, leafy **Plaza de Armas** and a small **museum**.

A few kilometres out of town, the beautiful waterfalls of **Pacchac** and **Siete Tinajas** (in order of proximity to Quillabamba) are accessed just off the main road; take a combi or colectivo towards Echarati and ask to be dropped off.

8

ARRIVAL AND DEPARTURE QUILLABAMBA

By bus Buses from the terminal on C Lorena in Cusco terminate at Quillabamba's Terminal Terrestre at jirones 25 de Julio and Lima; you can also flag down one of these Quiilabamba-bound buses at Ollantaytambo, on the main road at the entrance to the town.

By colectivo Minibuses and shared cars from Cusco leave from within a couple of blocks of the C Lorena terminal, along C Inca. In Quillabamba they depart, when full, from the block of Jr 25 de Julio closest to the Plaza de Banderas, four blocks along Jr Torre from Plaza Grau from 4am onwards. Shared cars to Kiteni (with onward connections to Pongo de Mainique) leave from the first block of C Palma, by the market.

Destinations Cusco (several daily; 5–6hr); Kiteni (several daily; 5hr); Ollantaytambo (several daily; 2hr 30min–3hr).

ACCOMMODATION AND EATING

Chifa Mio Av San Martín 333. The pick of the town's *chifas* has a very decent selection of rice and noodle dishes (prawn with vegetable hits the spot) with a free wonton soup thrown in and a breezy courtyard location. Mains from S/12. Daily noon–9pm.

Misky Av San Martín 600, next to the market. Billed as an ice-cream and cake shop, it certainly excels at the former – with two dozen delectable flavours, though it's branched out less successfully into burgers and pizza. Daily 8.30am–9pm.

Hostal Alto Urubamba 2 de Mayo 333 084 281 131, hostalaltourubamba.com. One of two decent choices in town, with fan-cooled or a/c rooms encircling a small inner courtyard and helpful staff. S/80

Hostal Don Carlos Jr Libertad 556 084 281 150, hostaldoncarlosquillabamba.com. Just up from the Plaza de Armas, this is a cosy, friendly and popular place. Rooms are smart and face a leafy courtyard but you'll need to find a café for breakfast. S/70

Ivochote and around

The road continues down into the jungle from Quillabamba via Kiteni to the village of **Ivochote**, the staging point for the Pongo de Mainique; look for a boatman in the

Ivochote port area. Boats to the *pongo* tend to set off early in the morning, as travelling there and back takes up much of the day.

Travelling down the river from Ivochote, just before you reach the *pongo* you'll pass the community of **San Idriato**, home to the Israelitas, a Peruvian biblical sect; the men leave their hair long and, like Rastafarians, they twist it up under expandable peaked caps. Across the Urubamba from San Idriato, the small community of **Shinguriato** marks the official entrance to the *pongo* itself.

Pongo de Mainique

The awe-inspiring **Pongo de Mainique rapids** – a very challenging 2km of a (barely) navigable river in the entire Amazonian river system – are hazardous at any time of year, and difficult to pass during the rainy season (Nov–March).

As you approach, you'll see a forested mountain range directly in front of you; the river speeds up, and as you get closer, it's possible to make out the great cut made through the range over the millennia by the powerful Urubamba. Then, before you realize, the boat is whisked into a long **canyon** with soaring rocky cliffs on either side: gigantic volcanic boulders look like wet monsters of molten steel; imaginary stone faces can be seen shimmering under cascades; and the danger of the *pongo* slips by almost unnoticed, as the walls of the canyon will absorb all your attention. The main hazard is a drop of about 2m, which is seen and then crossed in a split second. Now and then boats are overturned at this dangerous drop – although even then locals somehow manage to come upstream in small, non-motorized dugouts.

ARRIVAL AND DEPARTURE — IVOCHOTE AND AROUND

By organized tour If you want to take an organized tour or whitewater-rafting trip down through the *pongo*, it's best to do this in Cusco with one of the rafting companies.

By bus or colectivo To get to Ivochote from Quillabamba, buses and colectivos leave from Quillabamba's northern bus depot (daily 8–10am; 8hr).

By boat Boats regularly take goods and people from the river port at Ivochote to the gas operations and lower Urubamba communities through the *pongo* most days between May and October, and it's often possible to pay a small fee for a ride on one, though you then need to find a way to get back; it's far easier to pay a boatman to take you there and back (from S/80 per person, depending on the number of people you're with and your bargaining powers).

La Selva Central

The obvious appeal of the Selva Central is its ease of overland access and proximity to Lima. Directly east of the capital, the region is endowed with an array of rainforest eco-niches. The large and modern jungle city of **Pucallpa** lies in lowland rainforest, the main point of departure for trips downriver to the larger destination of **Iquitos**, a 1000km, three-day journey.

Closer to Lima yet less explored by foreign tourists, the **Chanchamayo** region – famous for its fantastic coffee – offers stunning forested mountain scenery, fast-running rivers and trees dripping with epiphytes. A steep road descends from Tarma down to the jungle gateway towns of **San Ramón** and **La Merced**, separated by a ten-minute drive. From here you can travel north, visiting the unique Austro-German settlements of **Pozuzo** and **Oxapampa**, both rich agricultural centres located within a mosaic of little-visited protected areas, including the stunningly beautiful **Parque Nacional Yanachaga-Chemillén**. Alternatively, via the coffee-growing area of Villa Rica you can experience the rough and adventurous ride along the **Carretera Marginal** that heads northwards to Pucallpa via Puerto Bermúdez and Puerto Inca on the Río Pachitea.

East from San Ramón and La Merced, an easier paved road heads towards the lower forest region, focused on the frontier town of **Satipo**, where the Ashaninka often come to town to sell produce and buy supplies. Near Satipo are scores of indigenous communities, mainly Ashaninka, and some of South America's finest **waterfalls**; Puerto Prado and Atalaya are also the gateway for adventurous river travel.

El Valle de Chanchamayo

El Valle de Chanchamayo, only 300km from Lima and 750m above sea level, marks the real beginning of the Selva Central, directly east of the capital, via the towns of San Ramón and La Merced.

San Ramón

The settler town **SAN RAMÓN** is more tranquil and less "happening" than its larger and noisier twin La Merced, just ten minutes further by bus down the Valle de Chanchamayo. Founded originally as a fort in 1849, to assist the colonization of the region in the face of fierce indigenous resistance, San Ramón is centred around the leafy **Plaza Mayor** that features a Chinese-pagoda-esque construction. There are several waterfalls within easy reach of town, the most accessible being the 35m drop of **El Tirol**, a S/5 mototaxi ride away.

ARRIVAL AND DEPARTURE — SAN RAMÓN

By bus Direct buses running from Lima and Huancayo in the Sierra stop in San Ramón en route to and from La Merced.

By colectivo Shared cars (S/3) link the twin towns of San Ramón and La Merced throughout the day.

ACCOMMODATION AND EATING

Chanchamayo-Italia Ristorante Jr Tarma 592 ⓣ 964 417 217. The legacy of Italian colonists, this Italian restaurant is excellent for mainly home-made pastas and pizzas as well as good coffee and wine. Mains from S/20. Daily noon–3pm & 6–10pm.

Chifa Felipe Siu C Progreso 434 ⓣ 064 331 078. Based in an attractive, airy space on two storeys and overlooking a small, lush garden, the San Ramón branch of this La Merced institution serves up a vast array of Chinese food – considered the best *chifa* in the region by locals. There are set meals at lunchtimes (around S/12). Mains from S/20. Daily 11.30am–9.30pm.

Hospedaje Oria C Sta Clara 230. The friendly welcome and spotless tiled floors and bathrooms at this excellent budget guesthouse cannot fail to impress, though the quilted pillowcases might not be to everyone's taste. No breakfast. S/55

Santuario Nacional Pampa Hermosa

20km north of San Ramón • No public transport, 4WD needed; you have to book a guided tour at least a day in advance with a tour operator in La Merced (minimum four people) for around S/240 per person. To see the cock-of-the-rock, you'd need to organize a pre-dawn departure

Covering some 110 square kilometres, the **Santuario Nacional de Pampa Hermosa** is an area of verdant virgin cloud forest. Several impressive waterfalls bisect this private reserve's unusually rich vegetation, which includes orchids, royal palms, lianas and giant ferns. It's also home to Peru's national bird, the resplendent vermillion cock-of-the-rock, which can be seen strutting its stuff early in the morning in its *lek* (communal courtship ground). The reserve also boasts what is considered to be the **oldest cedar tree** in South America; fondly known as *el abuelo* (the grandfather), it is a breathtaking and towering sight.

La Merced

The dusty, noisy town of **LA MERCED**, some 8km further down the Valle de Chanchamayo, is larger and busier than San Ramón. It has over twenty thousand inhabitants, a thriving Saturday **market** a couple of blocks behind the main street, and several restaurants and bars crowded around the Plaza de Armas. Here countless tour operators tout for business, offering very similar half-day or day-excursions (S/25–30) aimed primarily at Limeños that pile into the valley for a blast of tropical heat and outdoor adventure over long weekends and holiday

COFFEE FROM THE VALLE DE CHANCHAMAYO

An additional reason to come to La Merced is to sample its celebrated local brew. El Valle de Chanchamayo famously produces some of Peru's best gourmet coffee – smooth, medium-bodied, slightly nutty in flavour – including the world's most expensive bean, **Café Misha**, which sells for US$1400 per kilo. This exclusive bean passes through the digestive system of the coati, a member of the racoon family, which gives the coffee an intense aroma and takes away the bitterness. In La Merced proper, you can organize a tour of the Chanchamayo Highland Coffee factory (Urb. San Carlos, just off the main road towards Oxapampa and Satipo, up a short dirt track; ⊕064 531 198, ⓦhighlandproducts.com.pe) if you phone in advance. Otherwise, its vast retail outlet sells a bewildering array of coffees (including Café Misha), as well as local jams and liqueurs (coffee-flavoured included), honeys, raw cocoa paste and some of the smoothest, most intense coffee ice cream in Peru.

periods; at such times accommodation prices can double. Tours include visits to some of the area's impressive **waterfalls,** such as Bayóz and Velo de la Novia – off the road to Satipo; activities such as abseiling and gentle kayaking in a nearby adventure park; and some rather awkward voyeuristic visits to nearby Ashaninka villages.

Though La Merced holds little intrinsic appeal, you're likely to have to spend some time here as it is the main **transport hub** for the area, where you can clamber into a colectivo to Villa Rica, Satipo or Oxapampa, delving deeper into the Peruvian selva.

8

ARRIVAL AND GETTING AROUND — LA MERCED

By bus La Merced is easily accessible by bus from Lima via Tarma. Movil Tours, from its own terminal on Av Prado Este in Lima (⊕01 768000, ⓦmoviltours.com.pe) offers the most comfortable service, with four overnight and one daytime departure (7–8hr); a similar timetable operates for the return journey to Lima. Buses leave from the Terminal Terrestre (Terminal Royal Bus), located on the main Satipo/Oxapampa road heading northeast out of town, 700m from the Plaza de Armas. Expreso Molina Unión (ⓦmolinaunion.pe), which also operates comfortable buses, has its own terminal on the main road, 1km back towards San Ramón.

Destinations Huancayo (several daily; 5hr); Lima (at least 12 daily; 7–8hr); Oxapampa (2–3 daily; 2hr); San Ramón (many daily; 15–20min); Satipo (several daily; 2hr 30min); Tarma (at least 24 daily; 1–2hr).

By colectivo Colectivo cars link the twin towns of San Ramón and La Merced 24hr daily, leaving from within one block of each town's main plaza, and colectivo cars and slower combis also reach most regional destinations. Colectivos leave from in or around the Terminal Terrestre for Oxapampa, San Ramón, Villa Rica, Puerto Bermúdez (with onward connections to Pucallpa), and Satipo via Pichanaki (where in most cases you'll have to change vehicle).

Destinations Oxapampa (numerous daily; 2hr 30min); Puerto Bermúdez (several daily; 5hr); Satipo (numerous daily; 2hr 30min); Villa Rica (numerous daily; 1hr).

ACCOMMODATION

Aviró Hotel Jr Junín 992 ⊕064 531 394, ⓦavirohotel.com. The flashest of in-town options and overlooking Parque Incarnación, *Aviró* offers vast, white rooms with large windows, fridges, a/c, TVs and equally spacious bathrooms. Receptionists are friendly and breakfast is included. S/150

Fundo San José Av Circunvalación s/n ⊕064 531 816, ⓦfundosanjose.com.pe. High up on the hillside above town, this plush hotel offers quality bungalow accommodation with lovely views across the valley and a great swimming pool. S/255

Hotel Fundo El Paraíso Jr Junín 550 ⊕064 532 245, ⓦhotelfundoelparaiso.com. As close as you get to heaven in La Merced, with spotless tiled en suites overlooking the main plaza, a/c, fans, flatscreen TVs and a warm welcome. No breakfast. S/80

San Miguel Centro Jr Ripamonti 125 ⊕064 531 416. Enquire here, at the office of Ecomundo Ashaninka, about a stay at this welcoming hilltop Ashaninka community only 30min from La Merced, off the road to Satipo. Rudimentary cabin or homestay offered; water can be an issue in the dry season. Meals S/10–15. S/50

EATING

Cafeteria y Chocolatería Chanchamayo Highland Coffee Jirones Ancash and Tarma. If you don't make it to its coffee factory-cum-produce store, you can still pick up some excellent Peruvian coffee, fruit preserves and chocolates at this café, and sample a cup of the brew (S/2.50) or a huge fresh juice (S/3), with tamales and burgers as snacks. Daily 7.30am–10pm.

Chifa Felipe Siu Jr Junín 121. Locals proclaim this to be the best *chifa* in town, and if you taste its glass noodles with shrimp and broccoli, it's difficult to argue with that. The wonton soup and main combos (S/12.50–19.50) are excellent value and the *chicha morada* is unadulterated black corn goodness. Mains around S/20. Daily noon–11pm.

Los Koquis Jr Tarma 376. Set back from the Plaza de Armas, this greenery-festooned, family-run spot serves enormous though average-tasting portions of classics such as *asado de res*; vegetarians might try some *tallarines verdes* (spaghetti in Peruvian-style pesto). Mains S/13–28. Mon–Sat 7am–10pm, Sun 7.30am–3pm.

Shambari Campa Jr Tarma 383. On the Plaza de Armas, this popular restaurant is decorated with early twentieth-century photos of La Merced and produces an array of both traditional dishes (*cecina* – pork – with *juanes* and fried plantains) and jungle flavours, such as river-fish ceviche, *chancho* (wild pig) and *zamaño* (a medium-sized forest rodent). Mains S/19–29. Daily 7am–11pm.

Satipo

A real jungle frontier town, **SATIPO** is the jumping-off point for really off-the-beaten-track river travel into the jungle, but not a town to wander around after dark – narcotrafficking activity along the nearby Río Ene occasionally brings some insalubrious characters here. The settlement was first developed to service colonists and settlers in the 1940s, and continues in similar vein today, providing an economic and social centre for a widely scattered population of over forty thousand colonists and Ashaninka people, with supplies of tools and food, medical facilities and banks.

In the 1940s, the first dirt road extended here from Huancayo, but it wasn't until the 1970s that a road was opened from Lima via La Merced. The later surfacing of the road all the way from Lima encouraged many more settlers to move into the region, but the rate of development is putting significant pressure on the last surviving groups of traditional forest dwellers, mainly the **Ashaninka**, who have mostly taken up plots of land and either compete with the relatively newcomer farmers or live in one of the ever-shrinking zones with very little contact with the rest of Peru. You can often see the Ashaninka in town to stock up and trade, sometimes still dressed in their reddish-brown or cream *cushma* robes.

ARRIVAL AND DEPARTURE — SATIPO

By bus and colectivo Satipo is accessible by direct buses from Lima; Movil Tours, Expreso Molina Unión and Transmar are the best of the half-dozen companies that offer overnight *bus-camas* to Lima. Turismo Central (daily 6.45pm) is the most reliable service to make the arduous overnight journey to Pucallpa via the Carretera Marginal. Buses arrive in Satipo at the Terminal Terrestre, on Jr Leguia, seven blocks from the plaza, as do the vast majority of colectivos, shared cars and pickups. Pickup trucks leave early in the morning for Atalaya.

Destinations Atalaya (1–2 daily; 9hr); Huancayo (at least 10 daily; 6–8hr); La Merced (at least 20 daily; 2hr 30min); Lima (10–12 daily; 10–12hr); Pucallpa (2–3 overnight; 9–12hr).

By colectivo Shared cars to La Merced and Pichanaki depart when full from the corner of jirones Irazola and Bolognesi, a block downhill from the plaza. Shared cars to Puerto Ocopa, Puerto Prado, Atalaya and Puerto Bermúdez depart from Jr Bolognesi.

Destinations Atalaya (several daily; 7–9hr); La Merced (several daily; 2hr30min); Puerto Bermúdez (several daily; 8hr); Puerto Ocopa (several daily; 2hr).

INFORMATION

Visiting an indigenous community If you are considering travelling and staying with an Ashaninka community, you should call in at the La Asociación Regional de Pueblos Indígenas de Selva Central (ARPI SC) on Jr Julio C Tello (☎064 545 175; Mon–Fri 8am–6pm). They can advise on where to go and may help you get in touch with the relevant community members, though you will need some Spanish. They can also advise you about any security issues in the area.

8

ACCOMMODATION

Hostal Palmero Jr Manuel Prado 228 ⓣ064 545 020. The rooms are basic but clean and come with balconies and shared or private (extra S/10) hot showers, but the real treasures are the owners who are happy to share their knowledge of the area and to arrange tours of the local petroglyphs and waterfalls. The location is within half a block of the main plaza. No breakfast. S/30

Hotel Brassia Jr Los Incas 535 ⓣ064 407 440, ⓦhotelesbrassiahotel.com. Clean and secure, this two-star hotel comes with polished parquet floors and fan-ventilated or a/c (for an extra S/10) rooms, cable TV and hot water. Service is very pleasant and they'll even wash your dirty clothes for you. No breakfast. S/60

Hotel San Luis Jr Grau 173 ⓣ064 545 319, ⓦsanluishotelsatipo.com. The nicest of Satipo's digs, this family-run hotel has quiet a/c rooms, some overlooking a small garden and pool at the back. They offer secure parking and even money-changing facilities, but you'll need to go out for breakfast. S/90

EATING AND DRINKING

El Bosque Jr Prado 554. Found inside a large courtyard full of greenery and away from the bustle of the street, this restaurant specializes in grilled meat dishes (the ribs aren't bad at all), as well as jungle dishes such as *doncella* ceviche and *tacacho* (a pork dish) with fried cassava, washed down with overly sweet regional fruit juices. Mains S/20–25. Daily 9am–10pm.

Puntarena Cevichería Jr Irazola 607 ⓣ064 545 401. Excellent seafood and efficient service to be enjoyed in a chilled a/c environment. Choose from tasty *causas* to ceviche and whole fish brought fresh from the Pacific coast. Mains from S/15. Mon–Thurs 8.30am–5pm, Fri–Sun 8.30am–11pm.

Rosemary Restaurant Jirones Las Incas and San Martín. Locally appreciated for its ample bowls of *caldo de gallina* (chicken soup), this informal joint does S/8 breakfasts and lunches – solid portions of fried fish, chicken and chanco (wild pig). Daily 8am–4pm.

Around Satipo

Satipo sits in the middle of a beautiful **valley**, with some spectacular waterfalls within reach; other attractions beyond these tend to be for the very adventurous, with plenty of time to spare.

Puerto Ocopa, Puerto Prado and around

Satipo is the southernmost large town on the jungle-bound Carretera Marginal, and a dirt road continues to **PUERTO OCOPA** (a small river port originally founded by Franciscan missionaries in 1918) and further on to **PUERTO PRADO** which, for the last few years, has been the main port and a strategic location for travelling deeper into the forest along Río Tambo (while the Río Ene is currently best avoided due to narco-activity). If you wish to travel to the Ashaninka settlement of **BETANIA** (S/40), roughly halfway between Puerto Prado and Atalaya, which is known for its natural swimming pools, contact Nely Marcos (ⓣ976 535 254) or enquire at the ARPI SC office in Satipo (see page 457); otherwise, you risk a glacial welcome.

Atalaya and around

Tiny **ATALAYA**, reachable either by boat down the **Río Tambo** or the loggers' road from Satipo (these days passable by pickup truck year-round), is way off the tourist trail: facilities are few and you need to bring all supplies with you. From Atalaya there is usually a daily *rápido* down the Río Ucayali to Pucallpa (S/130, 8–10hr; see below), provided water levels are high enough, while slower cargo boats take two to three days to travel the 450km; enquire in Satipo about the current security situation before embarking.

ARRIVAL AND GETTING AROUND — AROUND SATIPO

By bus and colectivo From Satipo, at least six bus companies make several daily journeys to Huancayo from the Terminal Terrestre (at least 10 daily; 6–8hr). Colectivos run to Puerto Prado via Puerto Ocopa (several daily; 2hr 15min), while pickup trucks depart daily for Atalaya early in the morning (1–2 daily; 8–9hr).

By boat From Puerto Prado motorized canoes leave for the Tambo and Ene rivers. Boats head to Atalaya (around 8hr) and Pucallpa (2–3 days).

Oxapampa

Some 78km by road (2hr) north of La Merced lies the small settlement of **OXAPAMPA**, a pleasant and well-organized town, with broad, relatively traffic-free roads situated on the banks of the Río Chontabamba, some 1800m above sea level in the Selva Alta; wealthy residents from Lima buy land on the outskirts and build holiday ranches here. The area was settled by two hundred immigrants from Prussia and Tyrol in the mid-nineteenth century – pushing the indigenous Yanesha and Ashaninka to the margins – and evidence of these German roots is present both in the language still spoken by some of the descendants, and in the blue eyes and light hair of many inhabitants.

Oxapampa is situated around a beautiful, leafy square, complete with towering araucaría trees, and the frequently cool climate, combined with the vista of mist creeping along the surrounding mountains, gives the town a slightly Alpine feel. This is dairy country, and a good place to feast on local cheeses, yogurts and honey.

Oxapampa's main local **fiesta** takes place at the end of August; on the thirtieth, the town celebrates its founding, while on the following day the traditional **Torneo de Cintas** takes place, when local young men compete on horseback to collect ribbons from a post. At the end of June or in early July you can enjoy **Selvámonos** (selvamonos.org), a fun music and arts festival.

ARRIVAL AND GETTING AROUND — OXAPAMPA

By bus Oxapampa is reached via Movil Tours, Expreso Molina Unión, Lobato and Transportes Merced buses from Lima via La Merced, among others. Transportes Edatur (964 863 041) runs to Huancayo. All buses pull in at the Terminal Terrestre in Jr Loechle, one block off the main road, Av San Martín, and a few blocks from the Plaza de Armas. Overnight departures for Lima leave at around 8pm.

Destinations Huancayo (several daily; 6–7hr); La Merced (several daily; 3hr); Lima (several daily; 10–12hr).

By colectivo Combis and shared cars to La Merced, Villa Rica and Puerto Bermúdez leave throughout the day from the Terminal Terrestre. Two companies operate infrequent combis for Pozuzo (3–4hr) from the Terminal Pozuzo on Jr Ruffner.

Destinations La Merced (numerous daily; 1hr–40min–2hr); Pozuzo (7–8 daily; 3–4hr); Villa Rica (several daily; 1hr 20min).

By mototaxi Getting around town and from the bus station to the centre costs S/1.

INFORMATION AND TOURS

Tourist information For tourist information on Oxapampa and around, try the websites oxapampa.pe and oxapampaonline.com. Peru's protected-area agency SERNANP has a park office in Oxapampa, on the third block of Jr Pozuzo (063 462 544, sernanp.gob.pe) and is happy to advise on how to access the Parque Nacional Yanachaga-Chemillén, as well as accepting your entry fee.

Tour operators There are four tour companies all running similar tours around the region – to Villa Rica, Pozuzo and the waterfalls around La Merced and Chontabamba. A decent bet is Polka Tours, on the first block of Av Mariscal Castilla on the Plaza de Armas (976 006 078); it also has a few mountain bikes for rent.

ACCOMMODATION

★ **Carolina Egg Gasthaus** Av San Martín 1085 063 462 331, carolinaegg.com. A lovely complex of en-suite rooms and wooden bungalows, hidden amidst lush vegetation in a gated property across the main road from the bus station. This is an exceptionally friendly and well-run place (managed by a family descended from the original nineteenth-century colonists); there's a good restaurant during high season and the breakfasts are amazing. Doubles S/220, two-bedroom bungalows S/420

Edelweiss Miraflores Km 53, Lote 58, at the entrance to town 063 462 567, posadaedelweiss.com. A 100-year-old cedarwood house with forty beds based in chalets around a garden, with hammocks and a barbecue. There's also a guest lounge with TV, and a restaurant serving German and Italian dishes. S/140

Hospedaje Esperanza Jr Bolívar 756 063 462 352, hospedajeoxapampa.com. A modern take on the traditional Alpine style, this large four-storey structure overlooking a trimmed lawn boasts plenty of varnished wood and offers superb mountain views from the shared upper floor balconies. Rooms are clean and comfortable: firm beds with frilly bedspreads and private bath. No breakfast. S/80

Hospedaje Ruffner Jr Bolívar s/n, block 5 063 221 002. Handsome, red-brick guesthouse just three blocks from the plaza. Simple rooms come with balconies (facing the street or out back), exposed brick walls and hot showers. Good rates for solo travellers. Breakfast not included. S/70

★ **Ulcumano Ecolodge** Sector La Suiza, Chontabamba (10km south of Oxapampa) 063 462 431, 939 481 099, ulcumanoecolodge.com. This birdwatcher's paradise – a major focus of many guests – sits in a small private reserve, off the grid: no TV, no wi-fi, (almost) no mobile phone coverage, solar-powered energy and biodegradable toiletries The handful of simply furnished spacious wooden chalets boast large windows and glorious views from the balcony across cloud-forested mountains. A fabulous place to immerse yourself in nature. All inclusive. Per person S/229

EATING AND DRINKING

La Casa de Baco In the Miraflores suburb on the way into town at Km 2.5. Easily reached by mototaxi, this great garden restaurant is locally famous for its grilled meat dishes (from S/22), though service is very slow if you arrive when a tour bus is in. The *parilla* mix, which includes chicken, smoked pork and *chorizo*, can generously feed two. Thurs–Sun 11.30am–9.30pm.

La Nonna Jr Grau s/n, cuadra 1. Just off the Plaza de Armas, this is Oxapampa's answer to a trattoria. Think warm ambiance, imaginative pizzas (from S/12), spinach and ricotta lasagne, and more (from S/15), though the food doesn't quite taste as good as it looks. A boon for vegetarians and full of surprises: the wine list even features some nice Chilean reds. Daily noon–3pm & 5–9pm.

Restaurant Típico Oxapampino Jr Mariscal Castilla 063 462 155. Virtually the only place open for breakfast (S/10–15) on a Sunday morning, when you can enjoy a healthy fruit salad, or the full works involving pork with fried plantain, served on checked tablecloths. Other meals range S/20–25, accompanied by plenty of *yuca,* rice and chips, with a smidgen of salad if you're lucky. Daily 8am–9pm.

Vater Otto Jr Bolívar 514 1st floor. Tyrolean-style drinking den that doesn't get going until after 10pm. As well as serving craft beer, imported brews and the regular Pilsen – all modestly priced – the bar overflows with whiskies, aged rums and cocktails. Also with a sibling bar opposite *La Nonna*, more favoured by locals. Thurs–Sun 5pm–midnight.

Parque Nacional Yanachaga-Chemillén

The most used Huampal entrance is 15km south of Pozuzo • Entrance fee S/30, accommodation S/10, payable onsite or at the SERNANP office in Oxapampa • 063 462 544

Some 30km north of Oxapampa is the southern boundary of the **Parque Nacional Yanachaga-Chemillén**, a 1220 square kilometre reserve dominated by dark mountains and vivid landscapes, where grasslands and cloud forest merge and separate, though its lower reaches melt into moist tropical forests. Established as a protected area in 1986, there are some **hiking trails** here and it is possible to camp or stay in a bunkhouse close to each of the park entrances. Best visited in the dry season (May–Sept), there are vast quantities of bromeliads, orchids and cedars, as well as dwarf brocket deer, giant rats and even the odd spectacled bear – especially round the San Alberto sector in June/July – some jaguar and around 427 bird species, including a significant variety of hummingbirds. The reserve is also home to a number of Yanesha and Ashaninka communities, some of which are happy to receive visitors.

There are four entrances to the national park. The most accessible for independent travellers is **Huampal**, by the Oxapampa–Pozuzo road, 15km south of Pozuzo. There's a lovely camping spot, close to the **Cañón de Hunacabamba,** and even a comfortable dorm, kitchen and fireplace, but no trails. The birdlife is bountiful though, including a cock-of-the-rock displaying most afternoons. The San Alberto sector, however, has the best reputation for **birdwatching**, and has a two-hour trail. You can camp overnight here, but need to be self-sufficient. The San Daniel sector centres on a reed-lined **lake** and is known for its aquatic birds and **orchids.** Paujil, in contrast, is the best area for spotting mammals, but the most remote and difficult to access. To really explore the park, you need a guide; if amenable you can engage one of the park wardens on their day off.

ARRIVAL AND INFORMATION PARQUE NACIONAL YANACHAGA-CHEMILLÉN

To Huampal, San Alberto and San Daniel Any Oxapampa–Pozuzo bus can drop you off right at the entrance to the Huampal sector; for San Alberto, a colectivo taxi from the Terminal Pozuzo charges around S/40 return

POZUZO'S TYROLEAN ROOTS

Back in the 1850s, Baron Schütz von Holzhausen of Germany and the then President of Peru, General Ramón Castilla, developed a grand plan to establish settlements deep in the jungle. The original **deal between Germany and Peru** required Peru to build roads, schools and churches; while the Austro-Germans needed to be of Catholic religion, have some kind of office and impeccable reputation.

The first group, comprising two hundred **Tyrolean** and one hundred Prussian immigrants, left Europe in 1857 on the British ship *Norton*, arriving in Lima on July 28. During the overland journey, cutting their way through jungle, almost half the colonists died of disease, accident or exhaustion. The town of **Pozuzo** was founded in 1859 when the area was ripe with virgin forest and crystalline rivers owned by the Yanesha people. Nine years later, a second group of immigrants arrived to reinforce the original population, which had been left, more or less abandoned, by the Peruvian authorities. The colonists began to expand their population and territory; first, **Oxapampa** was founded in 1891 by the Böttger family, then others went on to found **Villa Rica** in 1928.

Today the economy of Pozuzo is based on beef cattle and agriculture; but **lederhosen** are worn for fiestas – and even adapted for school uniforms – and **Tyrolean dances** are still performed, particularly during the annual **festival** on July 25 – creating a peculiar combination of European rusticism (the local dance and music is still strongly influenced by the German colonial heritage) and native Peruvian culture. Moreoever, many of the older generation of this unusual town's present inhabitants speak a nineteenth-century form of German, eat the best sausages in Peru and dance the polka.

for the 15min drive as far as the road goes, then it's a further 50min hike to the park; for San Daniel get off the Oxapampa–Pozuzo bus at Grapanazu (after 15km), followed by a 1hr 30min hike uphill.

To Paujil Reached using a combination of combis, colectivos and then a long (4hr), and costly (S/400–500 – unless anyone's heading that way) motorized canoe trip up the Río Iscozacín from the Yanesha community of the same name, off the Carretera Marginal (see page 463). Sra Sulema Sharaba (T 957 316 163) or Manuel Sottovariano (T 992 481 799) in Iscozacín may be able to help with arrangements.

8

Pozuzo

Some 80km further north from Oxapampa, and down into the rainforest at 823m above sea level, **POZUZO** is a slice of Tyrol-meets-the tropics. Reached via a hair-raising rough and winding dirt road that crosses over (or through) several rivers and streams as it loops down through the greenery, the vista of wooden chalets with sloping Tyrolean roofs has endured ever since the first **Austrian and German colonists** arrived here in the mid-nineteenth century.

Pozuzo is a popular destination for Peruvian, Austrian and German tourists, particularly during the lively festival in the last week of July commemorating the founding of the town. It's a gorgeous little settlement, very unlike any other Peruvian town: it's compact, no more than two blocks wide; its streets – with pavements – are noticeably spotless and orderly; its chalet-style houses sport colourful gardens and flowers in window boxes; mototaxis are few and far between; and it's surrounded by greenery-clad mountains wreathed in low-hanging mist. Mobile and wi-fi coverage are sporadic.

When the road from Oxapampa crosses the river, it first reaches tiny **PRUSIA**, a German settlement linked to Pozuzo proper by the best 3km of paved road in rural Peru. Pozuzo itself is centred around the leafy **Plaza de Armas**, complete with a water, wheel and ship commemorating the colonists' voyage. Other places to explore include the fine **Iglesia San José**, built in stone and wood during 1875; the **Museo Schafferer** (Mon–Sat 9am–1.30pm & 2.30–4pm, Sun 9am–1pm; S/3), which focuses on the colonists' history and displays photos and curios of the indigenous peoples; the very Germanic **Casa Budweiser** with its stylish chimney; and the neat, colourful little **cemetery**. Among the most noteworthy of the **colonists' houses**, perhaps the Casa

Típica Palmatambo and the Casa Típica Egg Vogt are among the most interesting. As for scenic walks, take the turn-off towards the river next to the playschool and cross the **Puente Emperador Guillermo I**; a couple of trails start from the other side of the river, including a fifteen-minute walk up to a chapel that affords fantastic views over the whole of Pozuzo.

ARRIVAL AND INFORMATION — POZUZO

By colectivo Two colectivo companies run between Oxapampa and Pozuzo daily from the Terminal Pozuzo on Jr Ruffner, by the stadium. Between them they make around eight trips a day (3–4hr), but check for times as they often change. Delays due to landslides are common during the rains (Dec–March).

Tourist information For local information, check out pozuzo.pe.

ACCOMMODATION

★ **Albergue Frau Maria Egg** Av Los Colonos 063 287 559, pozuzo.com. Accommodation here is in attractive wooden chalets, with lush gardens surrounding a little pool. The food served is exceptionally good, and Frau Maria can organize hikes to her ancestral home of Casa Palmatambo, cock-of-the-rock spotting by the Pozas de Guacamayo and more. S/150

Hostal Prusia 953 291 084. The gleaming whitewashed exterior overlooks Prusia's small plaza, though it's distinctly darker inside. Rooms in this back-to-basics guesthouse have a dated feel – from the floor tiling to the bathroom fitments and furnishings, but the place is clean and good value, with hot showers. No breakfast. S/60

El Mango C Pacificación 185 063 287 528. This pleasant, wood-built place offers compact, comfortable rooms, a restaurant serving comida criolla and Germanic-Peruvian specialities; the owner is renowned for her smoked sausages and smoked pork. S/80

EATING AND DRINKING

Cervecería C José Egg s/n. Remarkably, Pozuzo has its own microbrewery that produces only one kind of blond beer – the Dörchen. It's a very informal outdoor spot; pick a pew by the vats and ask for a mug of the stuff (S/6). No set hours.

Restaurante Luiz María Av Los Colonos s/n 940 062 803. The pick of Pozuzo's criollo restaurants, with good wi-fi, this friendly place is a good bet for local fare such as *pachamanca de chancho* (a pork dish). The cheap daily menu includes soup and main (S/10–12) but splurge on the *mixto Pozucino* – a pile of juicy sausages, smoked chicken and pork with fried plantains and *yuca* (S/20). Daily 7am–10pm.

Restaurante Típico Prusia Av Cristóbal Johann 110 064 631 251. Ignore the clichéd name as you enter Prusia, and sit down to a meal that includes Pozuzo's famous sausages and smoked pork with fried plantains, *yuca* and delicious home-made cheese, all washed down with *quitoquito* juice. The owner is a descendant of Tyrolean colonists and speaks German. Tyrolean dancing occurs when tour groups visit. Mains from around S/18. Daily noon–10pm.

Around Pozuzo

Reachable from Prusia, the main attraction is the **Catarata Delfín**, which has an 80m drop and is an hour's walk from the hydroelectric plant by the Cañón de Huancabamba, itself a couple of hours' walk from the village; you can swim in the pool beneath the falls. At **Pozas de Guacamayo**, a fifteen-minute walk from Prusia, there's a *lek* (meeting and courtship area) for the cock-of-the-rock, which can be seen most afternoons.

En route to Pozuzo from La Merced, the road passes through the small town of **HUANCABAMBA**, starting point for a four- or five-day trek up into the high Andes on an old Inca road crossing the Cordillera Huaguruncho via the Abra Anilcocha pass (4500m) towards Lago Chinchaycocha and Cerro de Pasco.

Villa Rica and around

The town of **VILLA RICA**, some 36km southeast from Oxapampa, in the *ceja de selva* (cloud forest) next to an immense, shallow reed lake that's ideal for recreational boating, offers overland access to the Pichis and Palcazu valleys, the region's principal producers of coffee. The oversized coffeepot that graces the Plaza de Armas is testimony to the bean's importance in the local economy, and the coffee grown around Villa Rica is considered to be Peru's best.

There's a small place that roasts and grinds its own beans on Jirón San Carlos and Avenida Padre Salas, a couple of blocks from the Plaza de Armas, while the tourist office on the square has details of local *fincas* (coffee farms), a short mototaxi drive out of town, where you can sample local coffee and even stay the night. The annual **Feria del Café** in July/August is the biggest fun-filled week, and not just for coffee-lovers, as there are plenty of cultural and gastronomic events by way of entertainment.

In terms of other attractions, only 12km from town you'll find the **Catarata El Encanto** (the "Spell" or "Enchantment" Waterfall), which has three sets of falls; rainbows frequently appear here, and there are deep, dangerous plunge pools.

ARRIVAL AND INFORMATION — VILLA RICA AND AROUND

By bus Movil Tours, Molina and Lobato all operate direct overnight buses to and from Lima

By combi and colectivo Villa Rica is well connected to Oxapampa (1hr 20min) and La Merced (1hr) by frequent combis and colectivos. Shared cars (accompanied by some scary driving) head up the unpaved Carretera Marginal to Puerto Bermúdez (S/60; 4–5hr), and even Pucallpa (S/100; 8–10hr).

Tourist information The tourist office on the Plaza de Armas (daily 8am–1pm & 2.30–5pm) has information on the local *fincas* and there is a small coffee museum in the Municipalidad.

ACCOMMODATION AND EATING

Finca Santa Rosa 3.5km south of Villa Rica on the road to the Laguna de Oconal ⊕999 788 930, ⊕fincasantarosaperu.com. An excellent place to stay, where you can take guided tours of the coffee farm, go birdwatching or hiking in the forest on the property and stay in simple but comfortable double and triple chalet-like rooms; book one with a balcony from which to soak up the mountain views. S/150

★ **Hospedaje & Restaurante Copaxa** Main street ⊕978 854 582. A top spot to linger over a meal; it offers an international menu (from S/14) including tasty Peruvian and German dishes, such as *spätzle*, goulash and *wienerschnitzel*, which you can enjoy on their semi-open terrace. Service is efficient but friendly. No fixed hours, so advance booking preferred. Simple double rooms available S/80

El Húngaro Av Leopoldo Krausse 253 ⊕964 129 999. Tasty made-to-order Peruvian and central European dishes: tuck into a perfectly seasoned goulash or *lomo saltado* – moderately priced in a clean, unpretentious environment. Tues–Thurs noon–4pm, Fri–Sun 6–9pm.

The Carretera Marginal to Pucallpa

The 360km of largely unmade, yet constantly improving road that is the **Carretera Marginal** provides a rough but adventurous ride northwards from Villa Rica, shadowing the descent of the Río Pachitea as it winds its way into the Río Ucayali, one of the main tributaries of the Río Amazonas. As the road descends from the Selva Alta and enters the Selva Baja, so the temperatures and humidity rise, announcing your arrival in Amazonia proper. After skirting the eastern edge of the Parque Nacional Yanachaga-Chemillén, the first place of note is **Puerto Bermúdez,** whose main claim to fame is that it marks the geographical centre of Peru. A small laidback jungle town off the beaten track, it has a couple of decent places to stay and eat, an ATM, and is a good place for a river trip along the scenic Río Pichis. Seek out the enthusiastic Elvis González, who works at the Municiplidad and is also the local tour operator (⊕941 401 626, ⊕huayruroexpeditions@gmail.com).

Pucallpa

A sprawling, hot and dusty city with over 400,000 inhabitants, and seemingly thousands of mototaxis, **PUCALLPA** is a decent base for travellers who wish to take a boat out on **Yarinacocha** – an oxbow lake a ten-minute mototaxi drive away – or learn more about Shipibo culture. For backpackers, though, Pucallpa is most likely the point of departure for an adventurous river trip down to the Amazon. If you stay a little while, it's difficult not to appreciate the entrepreneurial optimism of this burgeoning jungle frontier city and its unvarnished waterfront activity. The Plaza de Armas features a construction of concrete and glass that is the town's modern **cathedral**; opinions divide as to whether it's cutting edge or hideous. From the southeast corner of the plaza, follow the pedestrianized Jirón Tacna four blocks to the leafy **Parque del Reloj Público** (also Parque San Martín) the city's first main square built in 1950, which overlooks the bustling port on the impressive Río Ucayali. The park's most striking feature is the colourful 25m **clock tower,** whose garish stained-glass panels depicting local themes look particularly attractive when illuminated at night – go early evening before the less salubrious elements of dockside living emerge.

Pucallpa's annual festival for visitors – the **Semana Turística de la Region Ucayali** – is usually held in the last week of September, offering mostly artesanía and forest-produce markets, as well as folklore, music and dance. The festivities kick off again in October for the **Semana Jubilar,** which celebrates the city's foundation, including extravagant parades of decorated floats, more music, dancing and street food, plus the inevitable beauty pageant.

Brief history

Long an impenetrable refuge for the **Cashibo**, Pucallpa was developed as a camp for rubber gatherers at the beginning of the twentieth century. In 1930 the town was connected to Lima by road (850km of it), and since then its expansion has been intense and unstoppable. Sawmills surround the city and spread up the main highway towards Tingo María and the mountains, and there's an impressive floating harbour at the nearby port of **La Hoyada**, where larger commercial vessels dock. In the twenty-first century, the city has been one of the main routes for lumber (much of it illegally culled) travelling from the Peruvian Amazon to Lima and the Pacific coast for export markets. Cattle-ranching is also big around here, putting increasing pressure on the rainforest's ecosystems and biodiversity as well as on indigenous Shipibo, Conibo and Cashibo communities.

Shops and markets

If you have an hour or so to while away in the town itself, both the downtown **food market** on Jirón Independencia and the older central **market** on 2 de Mayo are worth checking out; the latter in particular comprises varied stalls full of jungle produce, and can supply anyone heading downriver by boat with a hammock and other essentials. For **craft shopping**, artesanía can be found at the **Feria Municipal Artesanal** in the pedestrian passageway between Independencia and Libertad, closest to Ucayali. Shipibo women hang out on the plaza in front of *Hotel El Castillo*, selling their distinctive colourful weavings and other trinkets.

Museo Agustín Rivas

Jr Tarapacá 861 • Mon–Fri 10.30am–1pm & 3–5pm, Sat 10.30am–noon • S/4

There are works by the Pucallpa-born wood sculptor **Agustín Rivas** at his house – fantastic, twisted creations featuring humans and jungle creatures, inspired by Rivas' work with ayahuasca (he is also a shaman). The museum keeps erratic hours, though.

"Usko-Ayar" Escuela de Pintura Amazónica

Jr Sánchez-Cerro 465–467 • Mon–Fri 9am–5pm • S/10

The **"Usko-Ayar" Escuela de Pintura Amazónica**, art school and **gallery** established by shaman and painter **Pablo Amaringo**, is definitely worth checking out. He was one of the most internationally renowned exponents of the **Neo-Amazónico** style of painting: bright fluorescent colours and spiritual themes inspired by ayahuasca visions. Many of the pieces by Pablo or his students are for sale. Ask to borrow the 3-D glasses for an enhanced viewing experience.

ARRIVAL AND DEPARTURE PUCALLPA

By air The easiest way to get into town from Pucallpa airport, 5km west of town, is by mototaxi (15min; S/5–6) or taxi (10min; S/20). LATAM at the corner of Jr Tarapacá 805 (061 579 840, latam.com, operates daily flights between Pucallpa and Lima, while Peruvian Airlines (Jr Tarapacá 805 061 579 840) serves both Iquitos and Lima daily. Star Perú, Jr 7 de Junio 865 (061 590 589, starperu.com) flies here daily from Lima and Iquitos three times a week.

Destinations Iquitos (1–2 daily; 1hr); Lima (6 daily; 1hr).

By bus The main bus station is 5km west of town, close to the airport. A mototaxi into town costs around S/6. Most buses arrive here but some of the long-distance ones have a pick-up point in town too. There are direct services between Pucallpa and Lima via the sealed road that passes through Huánuco and Tingo María (at least 12 daily, 16–20hr). The most reliable and comfortable companies are Movil Tours (989 806 845, moviltours.com.pe) and TEPSA (061 506 466, tepsa.com).

By colectivo Selva Express (962 570 752) and Turismo Ucayali (961 075 522), both with offices on Av Centenario, run colectivo services to Tingo María.

By boat The operational port depends mostly on the height of the river and during the high-water season (Jan–April) many boats dock at the public dock (Puerto del Reloj) in front of the park of the same name, which can transform into a mud bath after heavy rain. Henry boats (980 253 420) to Iquitos dock at Puerto Henry, around ten blocks north of the city centre (S/2 by mototaxi). These depart downriver for Iquitos three times weekly (generally Mon, Wed & Fri); the journey takes three days, and it costs S/100 to sling your hammock (buy one at the Pucallpa market) or S/150 per person for a bunk for a cabin for up to four people. Buy your ticket in the unmarked office by the port. Food is included in the price, but see page 433. As for smaller boats, their precise destinations can be identified directly in the port by notices on (or in front of) each boat; you'll need to talk to the captain about prices and schedule.

By speedboat *Rápidos* or *deslizadores* also ply the Ucayali. Provided water levels are high enough, there are daily departures upriver to Atalaya leaving early in the morning and taking all day (S/150). It's also possible to travel downriver to Iquitos by speedboat, in several stages: first to Contamana (5hr), where you could stop off to visit some thermal springs and a macaw clay-lick; then in another boat to Requena (9–10hr), by the Parque Nacional Pacaya-Samiria (see page 476); and finally, taking a third *rápido* to Nauta (2–3hr), on the Río Amazonas, with a road connection to Iquitos.

8

GETTING AROUND AND INFORMATION

By mototaxi Ubiquitous mototaxis charge S/1–2 for short hops in town and S/5–6 to get out to Yarinacocha, the bus station or the airport.

Tourist information The rather dingy Dircetur office at 2 de Mayo 111 (Mon–Fri 8am–4.30pm; 061 575110) is quite helpful if you have some Spanish. An iPerú office has been requested, so may open soon.

ACCOMMODATION

Del Castillo Plaza Hotel Jr Independencia 550 061 573 141, delcastilloplazahotel.com. Overlooking the plaza, this three-star hotel boasts the best location, and has vast, spotless a/c rooms, with bright splashes of colour and towels shaped into swans, though breakfast is disappointing. If you fancy a romantic night with your sweetie, they'll strew flower petals over the bed and deliver a champagne breakfast to your room – for a price. **S/180**

Grand Hotel Mercedes Jr Raimondi 610 061 575 120, granhotelmercedes.com. One of Pucallpa's best upmarket options, *Mercedes* has a great swimming pool, lovely tropical gardens, a reasonable restaurant and bar. The rooms are comfortable and clean, and come with cable TV and fridge. Prices halve in the off-season. **S/310**

Hospedaje Barbtur Jr Raimondi 670 061 572 532. Central cheapie run by a friendly family. Your room may, or may not have a window (and it can be noisy) but it will have cable TV and cold showers. A private bath costs an extra S/10. No breakfast. **S/30**

Hospedaje Komby Jr Ucayali 360 061 571 562, kombypucallpa.com. In spite of being on a busy street a couple of blocks from the plaza, many rooms are quiet as they face an inner courtyard, and the amenities – cable TV, fridges and a pool at the back – make up for the lack of a scenic view. Rooms have fans, or a/c for an extra S/20; airport drop-off is included in the price. **S/80**

Manish Hotel Ecológico Jr Vargas Guerra 300, off Av Centenario, 6km from the centre 061 577 167, manishhotel.com.pe. Though it's the perfect antidote to dusty, frenetic Pucallpa, there's nothing particularly "*ecológico*" about this hotel, beyond its lovely natural surroundings; otherwise, it has all the luxuries of a good resort: swimming pool, gym, spa, hammocks, restaurant and bar, and tasteful a/c wooden rooms or suites for two, or self-catering bungalows for four. **S/230**

EATING

Like all jungle cities, Pucallpa has developed a cuisine of its own; one of the unique dishes you can find in some of these restaurants is *inchicapi* – a chicken soup made with peanuts, manioc and coriander leaves. Try the local speciality *patarashca* (fresh fish cooked in *bijao* leaves).

La Caleza Jr Tacna 665 ⊕ 061 283 259. Great hole-in-the wall *cevichería* and seafood restaurant, a block and a half down the pedestrianized street from the main plaza. Try a filling ceviche and *causa* combo (S/22) or a slab of the mighty Amazonian *paiche* fish in a creamy garlic sauce. Mon–Sat 9am–5pm, Sun 9am–3pm.

Chez Maggy Jr Inmaculada 643 ⊕ 061 754 958. At the massive stone oven at the front of the restaurant, the chefs toil to produce a wide selection of decent pizzas and calzones the size of your head. The tropical sangria or *camu camu* (Amazonian fruit) make excellent accompaniments. Medium pizza from S/20. Daily 5pm–midnight.

Chifa Dragón del Oro Jr Inmaculada 668 ⊕ 061 574 841. The pick of the city's Chinese-Peruvian establishments, with attentive staff, an extensive menu of noodle, rice, meat and seafood dishes and proper, stock-based wonton soup. Portions are ample if a little salty. Mains from S/22. Daily 11.30–3.30pm & 6.30–11pm.

★ **Heladería La Muyuna** Jr Sucre 351. Fabulous, locally made ice cream showcasing regional flavours, such as *camu-camu*, *lúcuma* and soursop fruits and *aguaje* palm. Not to be missed. Daily 10am–11pm.

★ **Pucacha's** Jr Coronel Portillo 658 ⊕ 061 283 259. Two blocks back from the waterfront, this quirky café-bar with arty decor serves up tasty offerings: from tamales, *causas*, soups, salads and crepes to coffees and cakes. Don't miss the good-value *menú del día* (S/12.50). Mon–Sat noon–11.30pm, Sun 3.30–8.30pm.

Yarinacocha

Some 6km from downtown Pucallpa lies **YARINACOCHA**, a large oxbow lake that is the city's biggest attraction. **Dolphins** are a common enough sight if you take a boat out onto the water, and there's rewarding **birdwatching** in the early morning. There are small **Shipibo communities** scattered around the lake's perimeter, some, such as San Francisco, easily reachable by road. The more remote and peaceful **Cashibococha**, a further half-hour west by dirt road is far more scenic, though with fewer facilities.

Puerto Callao

The former lakeside village, **Puerto Callao**, has virtually been swallowed up by the urban sprawl of Pucallpa, save for the delightful topiary-filled Plaza de Armas, with trees pruned into the shapes of wild beasts. While in the plaza, it's worth dropping into the Moroti-Shobo Crafts Cooperative (daily 8am–5pm), staffed primarily by Shipibo women selling **traditional textiles**, but also some ceramics and jewellery. Two blocks down from here the waterfront was – at the time of going to press – still closed off to the public and undergoing major renovations; but follow the dirt road east along the shore if you want to find a boat to take you onto the lake. Local guides and motorized dugouts loiter between the waterside restaurants, which become full-on *chicha*-blaring party places at weekends, complete with hip-gyrating live acts – so time your visit wisely if you're hoping to commune with nature.

ARRIVAL AND DEPARTURE — YARINACOCHA

By mototaxi Though it is served by both buses and colectivos, by far the quickest and easiest way to reach Yarinacocha is to take a mototaxi from Pucallpa (15min; S/5–6).

The northern selva

At the "island" city of Iquitos, by far the largest and most exciting of Peru's jungle towns, there are few sights as magnificent as the **Río Amazonas** when in full flow. Its tributaries start well up in the Andes, and when they join together several hours upstream from the town, the river is already several kilometres wide. The town's

BOAT TRIPS FROM PUERTO CALLAO

The guides lurking near their boats will approach you as you reach the lake with proposals of **boat trips**. The standard hour-long jaunt (S/30 for up to five people) includes **dolphin-spotting** plus a chance to see **sloths** on a small island near the southern lake shore – though make sure you're not dragged along to an animal "rescue centre"; some tours visit the Jardín Etno-Botánico Chullachaqui to learn about **medicinal plants**. A two-hour early morning excursion would be better if you're interested in some **birdwatching**. More adventurous options include two- and three-day ventures down rivers beyond the lake, with overnight stays in **Shipibo villages**, piranha-fishing on the Canal Negro, animal-watching along the Río Ucayali and jungle trekking/camping. Congenial Mario Ojanama (T 961 571 880) – owner of the *Los 3 Hermanos* boat and founder member of the Asociación de Botes Turístico "Los Yacarunas" – and his son run such trips (very little English spoken); it's a bare-bones adventure (around S/200 per day all-inclusive, usually for three days, two nights); a number of other operators offer something similar.

location, only 104m above sea level yet thousands of miles from the ocean and surrounded in all directions by brilliant green forest and hemmed in by the maze of rivers, streams and lagoons, makes for a stunning entry to the **NORTHERN SELVA**.

Much of **Iquitos's** appeal derives from its being the starting point for excursions into the **rainforest**, but the town is an interesting place in its own right, if only for the lively local people and magnificent architecture. It's a buzzing, cosmopolitan tourist town, connected to the rest of the world by river and air only: the kind of place that lives up to all your expectations of a jungle town, from its elegant reminders of the rubber-boom years to the atmospheric shantytown suburb of **Puerto Belén**, one of Werner Herzog's main locations for his 1982 film *Fitzcarraldo*, where you can buy almost anything, from fuel to ayahuasca medicines.

The town has a friendly café and club scene, a couple of interesting museums and beautiful, late nineteenth- and early twentieth-century buildings, and the surrounding region has some great island and lagoon **beaches** (in the low-water season), access to the rainforest and the possibility of continuing down the Amazon into **Colombia or Brazil**. The area has also become something of a **spiritual focus**, particularly for foreigners seeking a visionary experience with one of the many local shamans who use the sacred and powerful hallucinogenic ayahuasca vine in their psycho-healing sessions (see page 478).

Unlike most of the Peruvian selva, the **climate** here is little affected by the Andean topography, so there is no rainy season as such; instead, the year is divided into "high water" (Dec–May) and "low water" (June–Nov) seasons. The upshot is that the weather is always hot and humid, with temperatures averaging 23–30°C (74–86°F) and with an annual rainfall of about 2600mm. Most visitors come between May and August, but the high-water months are perhaps the best time for seeing **wildlife**, because the animals are crowded into smaller areas of dry land, though the low-water months are best for fishing.

Iquitos

Self-confident and likeable, **IQUITOS** is a modern, sprawling city of almost half a million people, built on a wide, flat river plain. Only the heart of the city, around the main plaza, contains older, architecturally interesting buildings, but the river port and market area of **Belén** boasts rustic wooden huts on stilts – a classic image of Iquitos.

If it weren't for the few stalls and shops selling jungle craft goods it would be hard to know that this place was once dominated by **hunter-gatherer peoples** like the Iquito, Yaguar, Bora and Witito, who initially defended their territory against the early Spanish missionaries and explorers.

Brief history

By the end of the nineteenth century Iquitos was, along with Manaus in Brazil, one of *the* great rubber towns, built on the misery and countless deaths of indigenous people who were used by the rubber barons as de facto slaves. From that era of grandeur a number of structures survive, but during the last century the town veered between prosperity (as far back as 1938, when the area was explored for oil) and the depths of economic depression. However, its strategic position on the Amazon, which makes it accessible to large ocean-going ships from the distant Atlantic, has ensured its continued importance. From the 1940s to the 1960s, Iquitos was buoyed by the export of timber, tobacco and Brazil nuts, and dabbling in the trade of wild animals, tropical fish and birds, while from the 1960s, an oil boom helped Iquitos to regain a degree of prosperity, now being further assisted by tourism.

Plaza de Armas

Iquitos has several squares, but the heart of the city is the central **Plaza de Armas**, still weirdly dominated by the towering presence of a bright blue, abandoned and

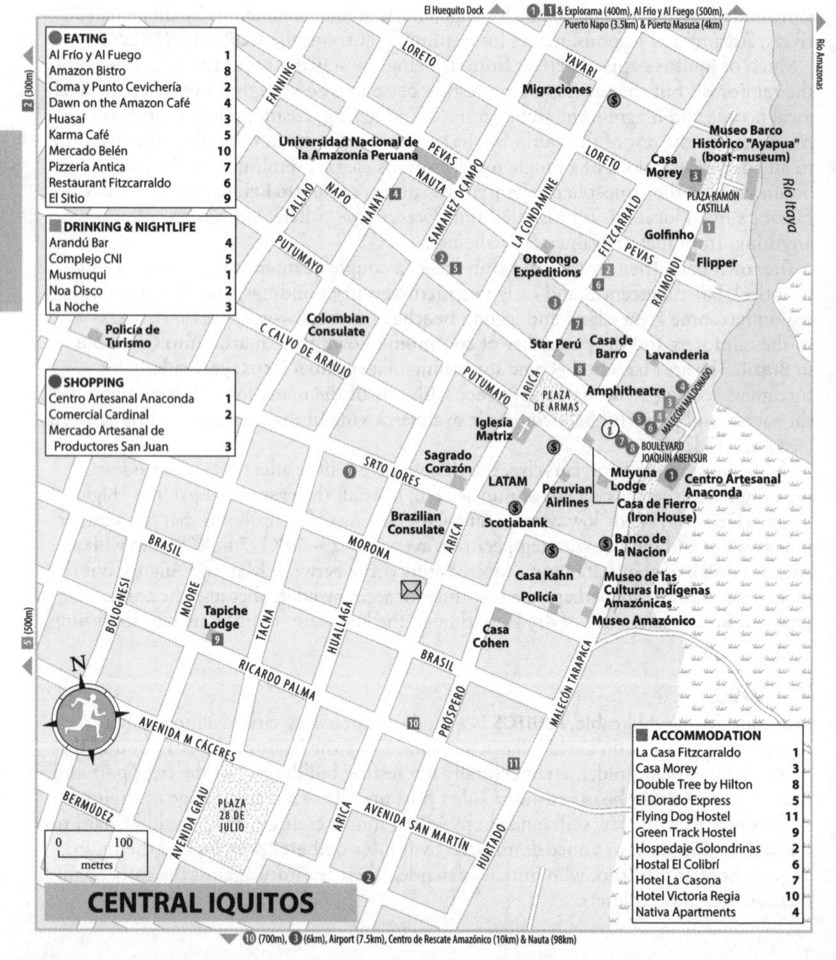

dilapidated high-rise **hotel**, built during the boom of the early 1980s, before the economy slumped and terrorism temporarily slowed tourism in the region. The plaza comes alive at night with hundreds of little lights.

On the southwest side of the plaza, the **Iglesia Matriz** (daily 7am–5pm), the main Catholic church, houses paintings by the Loretano (Loreto is the *departamento* Iquitos is located in) artists Américo Pinasco and César Calvo de Araujo, depicting biblical scenes.

Casa de Fierro

On the southeast corner of the plaza, you'll find the eye-catching **Casa de Fierro** (Iron House), hard to miss with its silvery sides glinting in the afternoon sunshine. Designed by Gustave Eiffel for the 1889 Paris exhibition, it was later shipped in pieces to Iquitos and reconstructed here in the 1890s by one of the local rubber barons. It now houses a pharmacy.

The riverfront

One block southeast of Plaza de Armas are the two best sections of the **old riverfront**, El Boulevard and Malecón Tarapacá, both of which have been recently restored to some of their former glory. **El Boulevard** is the busier of the two areas, especially at night, full of bars and restaurants and with a small **amphitheatre** with live entertainment some nights, from capoeira demonstrations to breakdancing. In the evenings this pedestrian stretch fills with a whirlwind of strolling locals, people playing roulette, tourists having their photos taken with gussied-up llamas and hippie travellers sprawled on benches with their battered rucksacks.

The **Malecón Tarapacá** boasts some fine old mansions, one of which, at no. 262, with lovely nineteenth-century *azulejos* (glazed coloured tiles), is now one of the town's better bakeries. On the corner with Putumayo stands the magnificent, colourfully tiled, military-occupied building (no photos allowed) that was once the Art Nouveau **Hotel Palace** – one of the city's historical icons.

Museo de las Culturas Indígenas Amazónicas

Malecón Tarapacá 332 • Daily 8am–7.30pm • S/15

This excellent two-storey **museum** along the waterfront – not to be confused with the less interesting municipal Museo Amazónico nearby – showcases the culture and rituals of some of the forty different indigenous people of the Amazon Basin, complete with captions in English. Here you can admire the pre-Columbian funerary urns found at Peru's Valencia site, the splendid ceremonial feathered headgear of the Wayana-Apari and the Kaiapo and the totem-pole-like mask of the Tikuna, check out a shrunken head of the kind formerly collected as trophies by the Jivaro, learn about the Matses poison frog ceremony, and much more. It's an absolute must for anyone anthropologically inclined.

Museo Barco Histórico "Ayapua"

Plaza Ramón Castilla • Daily 9am–5pm • S/15 • fundoamazonia.org

Docked by the waterfront across the little Plaza Ramón Castilla from Casa Morey is this triple-decked 1906 **steamer**, the Ayapua (daily 9am–5pm; S/10). Inside the beautifully restored cabins are displays that cover the European exploration of the Amazon, missionaries, the rubber boom and the notorious rubber barons who got rich from it – such as Carlos Fermín, Fitzcarrald and Luis Morey – and the indigenous people mercilessly exploitated because of it.

Casa Cohen

Jirones Próspero and Morona

The quaint, one-storey **Casa Cohen** is a nod to Iquitos' small Sephardic Jewish community that came to the Amazon mainly from Morocco in the 1870s Built in

IQUITOS FIESTAS

Iquitos throws some good annual festivals. The carnival known as **Omagua** (local dialect for "lowland swamp") has grown vigorously over recent years and now involves not only townsfolk, but hundreds of indigenous people as well, with plenty of chanting and dancing. The main thrust of activities is over the weekend before Ash Wednesday, and on Monday the town celebrates with the traditional Umisha dance around a sacred tree selected for the purpose. It's similar to maypole dancing in Britain, though in Iquitos the dancers strike the tree with machetes; when it eventually falls, children dive in to grab their share of the gifts suspended from it.

Perhaps the best time to visit Iquitos, however, is at the end of June (supposedly June 23–24, but actually spread over three or four days), when the main **Fiesta de San Juan** takes place. The focus is on the small artesanía market of San Juan (the patron saint of Iquitos), some 4km from the city centre, before the airport. It's the traditional time for partying and for eating *juanes*, delicious little balls of rice and chicken wrapped in waxy *bijao* leaves; the best place for these is in San Juan itself.

In September/October, the local tourist board organizes what is now the world's longest **international rafting competition,** in hand-built crafts; it takes place over three days, covering 180km and drawing enthusiasts from every continent. At the end of the month there's the **Espíritus de La Selva** (Spirits of the Jungle) festival, which coincides with Hallowe'en and All Souls, and involves street processions with costumes depicting mythological figures, plus the usual communal drinking and eating.

8

1905 and beautifully adorned with ironwork, colourful *azulejos* (tiles) and *pilastras* (mural-covered pillars), it reflects the past days of rubber-boom commerce and glory; these days it's a less-than-glamorous supermarket.

Casa Kahn

Block 1 of Jr Sargento Lores

The **Casa Kahn** is a particularly fine example of the Portuguese tile decoration that adorns many of the late eighteenth- and early nineteenth-century buildings, some of which are brilliantly extravagant in their Moorish inspiration.

Casa Fitzcarrald

Jr Napo 200–212

Once home to the legendary rubber baron of the same name, sadly the **Casa Fitzcarrald** is not open to the public. It was built of adobe and *quincha* (cane or bamboo plastered with mud) and has a central patio with arches, plus ceilings of roughly sawn wood.

Belén

The most memorable part of town – best visited around 7am when it's most active – **Belén** looms out of central Iquitos at a point where the Amazon, until recently, joined the Río Itaya inlet. Consisting almost entirely of **wooden huts** raised on stilts or floating on rafts, it has changed little over its hundred or so years, remaining a poor shanty settlement trading in basics like bananas, manioc, fish, turtles and crocodile meat.

Mercado Belén

1.3km south of the Plaza de Armas, off Jr Próspero • 4–5min in a mototaxi (S/2) from the centre

A somewhat insalubrious grid of pungent, narrow streets lined with produce, the **market** adjacent to the floating shantytown makes for a fascinating wander and a cheap and exotic place to eat (see page 473). Not all of it is pleasant: you may see some dismembered river turtles headed for the soup pot, and one section of the market features cages full of jungle animals, some of which end up in "animal rescue centres" (see page 476). Do not buy any animals or animal products from the market, though – it encourages illegal poaching, and setting them free may introduce disease into the forest.

Ask for directions to **Pasaje Paquito**, the busy herbalist alley in the heart of the market, synthesizing the rich flavour of the place. Here you'll find scores of competing stalls selling an enormous variety of natural jungle medicines, as well as some of the town's cheapest artesanía.

Cementerio General San Miguel Arcángel

Alfonso Ugarte and Av Fanning • Daily 8am–7pm • Free • S/2 mototaxi ride from the centre

One of the oldest in Peru, Iquitos' main **cemetery** is most definitely worth a wander. Containing smaller cemeteries for Jewish, German and even Augustinian friars, it is filled with ornate chapels, lavish mausoleums and colourful tombstones – don't miss the cargo boat or the castle.

ARRIVAL AND DEPARTURE — IQUITOS

BY BOAT

Iquitos is Peru's largest and busiest river port city and there are three main passenger ports, though if you're arriving from Yurimaguas or Pucallpa, you will probably disembark at Nauta – the small river port at the end of the isolated 100km strip of tarred road that runs southwest from Iquitos; by transferring to a minibus here, you'll avoid several extra hours on the river in favour of a 2hr shortcut by road. Puerto Masusa (Av La Marina), 4.5km northeast of the Plaza de Armas, is the departure point for cargo boats (*lanchas*) headed upstream to Yurimaguas, via Lagunas, or downstream to Tabatinga, Brazil and Leticia, Colombia, via Pevas. Occasionally there are also cargo boats all the way to Manaus, Brazil. Henry boats to Pucallpa have their own port on Av La Marina, 3.5km northeast of the city centre. Speedboats (*rápidos*) and the new ferry service between Iquitos and Santa Rosa (Peruvian immigration), Leticia and Tabatinga (the tri-border; see page 480) leave from/arrive at Puerto Napo, on Av La Marina at 28 de Julio, 3km northeast of the city centre. Local boats go from Puerto Bellavista Nanay (see page 476). Tickets for *lanchas* can only be bought from the ports on, or the day before, the day of travel (buy from the boat captain or from the designated office by the dock); speedboat companies have offices in town. On the Yurimaguas–Iquitos route, it's possible to stop off in Lagunas to find guides and excellent, inexpensive tours by indigenous tour operators to the Reserva Nacional Pacaya-Samiria (see page 476). Similarly, there are community-run tours from Bretaña, or Manco Capac, off the Canal de Pinahua, on the south side of the national park. There are tips on travelling by boat in the main jungle listings (see page 435).

To Lagunas and Yurimaguas Motonaves Eduardo, Puerto Masusa (2–3 days; Mon, Wed & Fri at 6pm from S/100; T 065 351 270). Flipper, Raimondi 350 (T 065 766 303), operates a *rápido* from Nauta (Mon, Wed & Fri, returning from Yurimaguas Tues, Thurs & Sat; 12hr; S/160); other speedboat operators have offices in Nauta.

To Requena and Pucallpa Motonaves Henry, Puerto Henry (4–5 days; Mon, Wed & Fri at 6pm; from S/100 T 065 263 948). Flipper also runs a bus transfer and *rápido* service from Iquitos to Requena, on the Río Ucayali, via Nauta (daily 11am; 3hr 30min–4hr; S/80); from Requena another *rápido* service runs as far as Contamana, where you can transfer to another *rápido* to reach Pucallpa.

To Santa Rosa (three-way border) Cargo boats bound for Brazil depart from Puerto Masusa (2.5–3 days; Mon–Sat; from S/80; T 065 250 440). Golfinho, Jr Raimondi 378 (T 065 225 118), Flipper and Transtur, Raimondi 384 (T 065 233 188), have *rápidos* to the border (9–10hr; Tues–Sun at 5am; S/150–170), from Puerto Napo. Ferry Amazonas, Jr Pevas 197 (T 065 233 188, W ferryamazonias.com), runs a comfortable new ferry service (Tues, Thurs & Sat at 5am; 12–15hr; S/160).

BY PLANE

Flights land at Iquitos airport (Aeropuerto Internacional Francisco Secada Vignetta), 8km southwest of town. Flights are met by taxis (S/15–20) and mototaxis (S/10). Iquitos is served by flights from Lima with LATAM, Jr Prospero 232 (T 065 232 421), flights from Lima and Pucallpa with Star Perú, Jr Napo 256 (T 065 236 208) and Peruvian Airlines, Jr Prospero 215 (T 065 480 111); Star Perú also flies to Tarapoto while LATAM operates three flights a week between Cusco and Iquitos.

Destinations Cusco (Mon, Wed & Sat; 2hr); Lima (several daily; 1hr 50min); Pucallpa (1–2 daily; 1hr); Tarapoto (daily; 1hr).

GETTING AROUND

By mototaxi For getting around town, the ubiquitous mototaxis are the best option. They charge around S/8–10 to the airport, and approx S/2 for short hops within Iquitos.

INFORMATION AND TOURS

Tourist information The main iPerú tourist office is at Jr Napo 161 (Mon–Sat 9am–6pm, Sun 9am–1pm; 065 236 144). The staff provide free advocacy should you run into any problems with tour companies. There's also a helpful tourist information kiosk at the airport (daily 8am–9pm; 065 260 251).

National park information The SERNANP office for the Reserva Nacional Pacaya-Samiria office is at Jr Chávez 930–942 (065 223 555). It's good for maps, information on the reserve and permission to enter it (S/30 for one day; S/60 for 2–3 days; S/150 for 4–30 days).

Tours A number of tour companies arrange tours of Iquitos and its environs, and there are also independent guides offering their services (see page 474).

ACCOMMODATION

HOTELS AND GUESTHOUSES

★ **La Casa Fitzcarraldo** Av La Marina 2153 065 601 138, lacasafitzcarraldo.com; map p.468. Hidden within a lush garden that blocks off much of the city's bustle, this characterful, luxurious B&B runs with the theme from Hertzog's film (in fact, the cast and crew were resident here when *Fitzcarraldo* was being filmed). There are only three individually decorated rooms and a bungalow (Mick Jagger had the Blue Room, Klaus Kinski the Green Room and Hertzog took the spacious bungalow), a very clean swimming pool, plus great food, drinks, lovely orchid-rich gardens and a three-level treehouse with panoramic views. S/258

★ **Casa Morey** C Loreto 200 065 231 913, casamorey.com; map p.468. This gorgeous rubber-boom mansion from 1913 – all Georgian chic mixed with Amazonian motifs – has been converted to a boutique hotel with fourteen spacious, light-filled rooms with some period furniture and thoroughly modern bathrooms. The secluded pool with its faux-Grecian columns and fountain is perfect for a quiet swim and visitors and guests alike are welcome to peek into the handsome library. US$95

Double Tree by Hilton Jr Napo 258, Plaza de Armas 065 222 555, doubletree3.hilton.com; map p.468. Iquitos' first five-star hotel, recently refurbished in a contemporary wood-themed design, and taken over by the Hilton chain, is the most central splurgeworthy option. Spacious rooms have floor-to-ceiling windows, some with superb views of the plaza and all the quality amenities and service you'd expect. The standout feature of the pool area is the water cascading off an elevated jacuzzi. Good online offers. Doubles US$156, suites US$172

El Dorado Express Jr Napo 480 065 235 718, doradoexpress.com; map p.468. This small short-stay business-style hotel has a range functional rooms with a/c, set back from the road, a café serving light bites and vegetarian dishes, and guest computers in the lobby. Guests can also use the small pool of the neighbouring Dorado hotel further down the street. Look out for the Francisco Grippa artwork. Doubles S/120, suites S/175

Hospedaje Golondrinas Jr Putumayo 1024 065 236 428, hospedajegolondrinas.com; map p.468. Friendly guesthouse that's nine to ten blocks from the plaza, with a greenery-filled courtyard, large swimming pool, guest kitchen and compact, basic private singles, doubles and triples. Could be cleaner, but really good value for the money and the owners run a rustic jungle lodge. No breakfast. S/54

Hostal El Colibrí Jr Nauta 172 065 241 737, hostalelcolibri@hotmail.com; map p.468. A modern, clean and secure guesthouse stacked up on four floors right in the centre. Double or triple rooms have cable TV, private bath with hot water, a/c (S/20 extra) or fan. There's also a decent breakfast (S/8). A good deal. S/50

Hotel La Casona Jr Fitzcarrald 147 065 223 283, hotellacasonaiquitos.com.pe; map p.468. A stone's throw from the plaza, this is a large, rambling budget hotel with an inner courtyard (a good place to hang out with fellow travellers), psychedelic Shipibo weavings and Bora masks on walls, simple en-suite rooms (some with a/c) and helpful staff. There's a smaller, cheaper branch of *La Casona* across the street. S/105

Hotel Victoria Regia Jr Palma 252 065 231 983, victoriaregiahotel.com; map p.468. One of Iquitos's more luxurious options, this smart hotel is decked out in purples and shades of mustard and the rooms are stylish, with excellent beds and baths in the bathrooms (the suite comes with a jacuzzi). There's also a small pool and two fine restaurants on site. S/372

Nativa Apartments Jr Nanay 144 065 600 270, nativaapartments.com; map p.468. Run by a friendly and helpful family, this secure guesthouse is just a few blocks from the plaza and comes with clean, colourful, small studio apartments with kitchenettes, for long- or short-term let. Tea and coffee available for guests. S/225

8

HOSTELS

Flying Dog Hostel Jr Tarapacá 592 ⓣ065 223 755, ⓦflyingdogperu.com; map p.468. Great hostel in a great location, complete with colourful rooms (some with bathroom), spacious guest lounge with graffitied testimonies from happy travellers, guest kitchen and plenty of *buena onda* (good vibes). Dorms S/28, doubles S/99

Green Track Hostel Jr Palma 516 ⓣ065 600 805, ⓦgreentrack-jungle.com; map p.468. Popular backpacker haunt a short distance from the plaza with all facilities that backpackers have come to expect: a/c guest lounge, security lockers and guest kitchen, as well as an appealing courtyard filled with greenery. Rooms are small and bare, with no lock; dorms are better value though mattresses can be squidgy. As a bonus, *Green Track* has its own jungle lodge (see page 481) in the Reserva Tapiche and the owner is renowned for his efforts to protect the local wildlife. Dorms S/26, doubles S/65

EATING

Food in Iquitos is exceptionally good for a jungle town, specializing in **fish dishes** but catering pretty well to any taste. Unfortunately, many of the **local delicacies** are now in danger of disappearing entirely from the rivers around Iquitos – notably, river turtle and alligator, though the tasty *paiche* fish – the largest scaled fish in the world – is now more readily available due to breeding programmes.

★ **Al Frío y Al Fuego** Av la Marina 138 ⓣ965 607 474, ⓦalfrioyalfuego.com; map p.468. This is an excellent restaurant that floats on the Río Itaya and focuses on imaginative jungle cuisine. Choose from the likes of doncella-filled ravioli, the classic *patarasca* dish and *cecina con tacacho* (smoked pork with fried green plantains), washed down with generously poured fresh tropical juices. Take a mototaxi to the Av La Marina address and catch a boat from the dock downstairs to the restaurant; there's a swimming pool and bar at the restaurant, so you may wish to linger. Most mains from S/40. Mon 6–9pm, Tues–Sat noon–3pm & 6–9pm, Sun noon–3pm.

Amazon Bistro Malecón Tarapacá 268 ⓣ065 600 785; map p.468. Housed in the gorgeous Casa del Fierro, this restaurant combines Old World charm with high ceilings, an imposing bar and an eclectic menu of international dishes. *Patarashka* (fish steamed with manioc in a palm leaf) sits comfortably alongside Argentinian steak, Caesar salad and doncella fish in lemon sauce; the dessert list features profiteroles and tipples include Belgian beer. Very popular with travellers and expats. Daily 8am–midnight.

Coma y Punto Cevichería Jr Napo 488 ⓣ065 225 268; map p.468. This popular lunchtime spot serves some of the city's best ceviche (from S/16) made from various river fish. Other dishes include generous portions of *arroz con mariscos* (seafood rice) and *chicharrón de pescado* (chunks of fried, battered fish). Mains from S/20. Daily noon–5pm.

★ **Dawn on the Amazon Café** Malecón Maldonado 185 ⓣ065 600 057; map p.468. Hugely popular, relaxed spot on the waterfront that runs the gamut from American-style all-day breakfasts and freshly prepared, ample salads (S10) to spicy Mexican fajitas, falafel burgers and grilled fish. Owner Bill is a mine of local information. Mains from around S/20. Mon–Sat 7.30am–10pm.

Huasaí Jr Fizcarrald 131 ⓣ065 242 222; map p.468. Family-run, traditional Peruvian restaurant serving regional dishes – plenty of rice, beans and plantain – always heaving with locals. Serves a fine, huge S/16 lunch *menú* including starter, main and jug of juice, and has a vast array of breakfast combos (S/10–13). Mon–Sat 7am–4pm.

★ **Karma Café** Jr Napo 138 ⓣ065 223 663; map p.468. All psychedelic wall hangings, bean bags and bright colours, with plenty to please vegetarians (falafel burgers, veggie curry) and meat eaters alike, and spice-lovers (Thai curries S/27). Mains from S/15. Also serves voluminous fruit juices and salads, and in the evening the place is packed, especially when there's live music (Thurs–Sun). Daily 9am–late.

Mercado Belén Jirones Prospero and 9 de Diciembre; map p.468. The chaotic Mercado Belén is a great spot for cheap eats, particularly large fresh fruit juices (try the *jugo especial* – jungle juice), and real jungle staples of juicy Amazon grubs on a stick, *sikisapa* – fried leafcutter ants, rice-studded *morcilla* (black pudding) and more. Daily 7am–5pm.

Pizzería Antica Jr Napo, between the plaza and the Malecón ⓣ065 241 988; map p.468. A large space with ceiling fans and driftwood decor, this Italian joint has an extensive menu of wood-fired pizzas (from S/22), pastas and immense calzones, including good veggie options and dishes incorporating local ingredients. Daily noon–midnight.

Restaurant Fitzcarraldo Jr Napo 100 ⓣ065 236 536; map p.468. Inside a historic rubber-boom building right on the Malecón, this fan-cooled, smart restaurant serves some excellent Amazonian dishes, such as grilled fish with *patacones* (skip the tasteless *tiradito*, though), and the not-so-jungly crêpes Suzette for dessert. Mains S/27–35. Daily 8am–midnight.

El Sitio Jr Lores, block 4; map p.468. A very creative, inexpensive snack bar/restaurant specializing in delicious *anticuchos* (kebabs), washed down with fruit juices or beer; best to get there before 9pm, or you'll miss out on the tastiest treats. Skewers from S/8. Mon–Sat 8.30am–1.30pm & 6.30–11pm.

EXPLORING THE JUNGLE AROUND IQUITOS

ORGANIZED TOURS

For tours beyond the limited network of roads and community boats around Iquitos, you'll have to take an organized trip with a lodge operator or agent with a contact from an indigenous community, go on a river cruise, or hire a freelance guide. And tours are indispensable for specialized activities, such as fishing for peacock bass – the holy grail of the Amazon's fish – or visiting the Pacaya-Samiria reserve, since only a few ecologically responsible outfits have permission to operate there. Check out which outfits are registered at the tourist office in Iquitos (see page 472). We list several reliable operators below; each has its own **riverboats** and services. Prices given per person sharing (a room/cabin), unless otherwise stated.

Amazon Voyagers T 0866 725 3255 in the US, W amazoncruise.net. Choose from a range of riverboats, from the more modestly luxurious *Delfín* to the super-opulent *Arias*, with spacious suites, gourmet cuisine and naturalist bilingual guides. Depending on the time of year and water levels, these cruises may pass through the Pacaya-Samiria reserve and along the Amazonas, Yarapa and Ucayali rivers. Four-day cruise from US$1650

Dawn on the Amazon Malecón Maldonado 185 T 065 223 730, W dawnontheamazon.com. Passionate about the local ecology, Bill Grimes and his team are happy to organize custom-made tours depending on your interests – be it day-trips in the surrounding area, or multi-day camping cruises into the Reserva Nacional Pacaya-Samiria, swinging in a hammock on the *Dawn on the Amazon*. Three days US$495

Green Tracks T 970 884 6107 in the US, W greentracks.com. Offers a similar range of boats to Amazon Voyagers, though often with special offers, heading into the Reserva Nacional Pacaya-Samiria. You don't spend all your time on board; guided hikes in the jungle and small-boat wildlife watching excursions are part of the package. *La Perla*'s four-day cruise is the cheapest option. US$1615

INDEPENDENT BOAT TRAVEL

If you're thinking of **hiring a boat** and heading down Río Amazonas or Río Napo, stopping at various small communities en route, it's doable but costly; you'll pay at least US$90–100 per person per day. There's an almost infinite amount of jungle to be rewardingly explored in any direction from Iquitos, and one of the less-visited but nevertheless interesting areas lies east between Iquitos and the Brazilian border; having your own boat allows far greater potential for exploration, since the public boats plying this stretch of the Amazon River rarely stop and certainly don't allow any time for passengers to explore. If you do want to stop off and spend some time here, Pevas is a possible base for making river trips more or less independently, at least without going through an Iquitos tour company, though you would need to engage a local guide.

FINDING A RELIABLE GUIDE

In Iquitos you will be approached by a plethora of self-styled guides and touts trying to persuade you to take their tours. Many of them can be unpleasantly persistent, bordering on aggressive, and many work for sub-par establishments for commissions. Check with iPerú to find out whether they are certified, and talk to other travellers and/or your accommodation. Many of the top guides are snapped up by the best jungle lodges.

8

NIGHTLIFE

While mainly an extension of eating out and meeting friends in the main streets, the **nightlife** in Iquitos is vibrant, and there are a number of discos, clubs and bars worth knowing about. They're quite easy to locate, especially after 11pm when things generally get going in the downtown areas, particularly around the Plaza de Armas and nearby Malecón Tarapacá.

Arandú Bar Malecón Maldonado 113; map p.468. Psychedelic wall paintings, an extensive cocktail list (around S/16) and a great people-watching location on the Malecón make this a very popular watering hole. Daily 4pm–late.

Complejo CNI Jr Mariscal Cáceres, block 13; map p.468. More of a covered outdoor arena, this gives a flavour of what the Iquitos youth get up to at weekends, with more than a thousand people dancing all night to mostly live salsa, *chicha* and *cumbia* bands, but with Brazilian influence creeping in. Take a mototaxi (S/4). Thurs–Sat 9pm–4am.

Musmuqui Jr Raimondi 382; map p.468. This lively two-storey bar is very popular with locals and famous for its cocktails that feature all sorts of jungle plants and are served in odd-shaped glasses. Some have alleged aphrodisiac properties, which you may want to put to the test. Mon–Thurs & Sun 5pm–midnight, Fri & Sat 5pm–3am.

Noa Disco Jr Fitzcarrald 298; map p.468. Easily identified after 11.30pm by the huge number of flashy motorbikes lined up outside, this is Iquitos's liveliest club, attracting young and old, expat and *Iquiteño* alike. It has three bars and plays lots of Latino music, including the latest *technocumbia*. S/15 entry. Thurs–Sat 10pm–6am.

La Noche Malecón Maldonado 177; map p.468. Overlooking the waterfront, this bar/restaurant is perfect for people-watching. The food is variable (mains S/30–35), but it's hard to beat the view at sunset from the upstairs balcony and the strong cocktails. Wed–Sun 7.30am–late.

SHOPPING

Centro Artesanal Anaconda Malecón Maldonado s/n; map p.468. The Centro Artesanal Anaconda and surrounding craft stalls on the waterfront sell a really good selection of psychedelic Shipibo embroidery and painted textiles, the designs allegedly inspired by ayahuasca visions. No set hours but typically mid-morning until around 9–10pm; shorter hours on Sun.

Comercial Cardinal Jr Prospero 300; map p.468. Sells fishing tackle, compasses and knives. Daily 9am–6pm.

Mercado Artesanal de Productores San Juan Some 2km east of the airport along the main road; map p.468. A popular souvenir market consisting of a couple of dozen stalls. You can pick up some Shipibo embroidery here; the only other items here that are not mass-produced tat are the vases carved out of beautiful tropical hardwoods, some of them true works of art. Daily roughly 9/10am–6pm.

ANIMAL RESCUE CENTRES

Visiting an **animal rescue centre** is often a core activity of the most popular day trips offered from Iquitos. However, many are insalubrious animal encounters, where you're offered the opportunity to wrap an anaconda or python around yourself or hold a sloth or monkey for that exotic holiday snap. These are nothing more than decrepit zoos and are best avoided, since visiting them perpetuates the **illegal animal trade** in endangered species and dooms the unhappy monkeys, sloths, macaws and snakes to a short life in a cage. Even in the more reputable sanctuaries that give refuge to injured or trafficked creatures rescued by the authorities, animals are rarely rehabilitated and released back into the wild. Although the creatures in question generally live in better conditions than in the places where they were rescued from, visiting tour guides – keen to increase their chance of a tip – may rattle cages or disturb animals to coax them into showing their face for their tour group to photograph. Since all such centres are heavily reliant on the tourist dollar to support their endeavours, it is hard for them to properly regulate visiting tour groups. The exception to the above is the Centro de Rescate Amazónico (see below).

Around Iquitos

The massive river system around Iquitos offers some of the best access to **indigenous villages**, **lodges** and **primary rainforest** in the entire Amazon. For those with ample time and money, the Reserva Nacional Pacaya-Samiria is one of the more distant but rewarding places for eco-safari tours; but there are also towns up and down the river, most notably Pevas, which is en route to Brazil.

8

If you want to go it alone, colectivo boats run up and down the **Río Amazonas** more or less daily, and although you won't get deep into the forest without a **guide**, you can visit some of the larger river settlements on your own.

Many visitors to Iquitos come to stay at one of the **jungle lodges**, which sit either on the Río Amazonas or its tributaries and are a great way of getting to know the rainforest and spotting local wildlife, with the help of experienced guides.

Bellavista and around

5km north of the city centre • 15min by mototaxi (S/5) from the Plaza de Armas

The suburb of **Bellavista**, on the Río Nanay, is the main access point for smaller boats to all the rivers. Bars, shops and stalls are clustered around the Bellavista port, where you can **hire canoes** for short trips at around S/30 an hour. Consider setting out by canoe ferry for **Playa Nanay**, the best beach around Iquitos (when the water is low), popular with locals but not too clean. Alternatively, you could hire a canoe to take you to the confluence of the mud-brown Río Amazonas and the clear blue Río Nanay, just a few minutes away from Bellavista; the abundant fish where the two rivers meet attract **pink river dolphins** and it's easy to spot them.

Centro de Rescate Amazónico

4km southwest of the airport • Daily 9am–3pm • S/20 entry, including tour (in Spanish); show passport on entry • S/12 by mototaxi

Its efforts supported by a Californian aquarium, this hard-working **animal rescue centre** specializes principally in the rehabilitation of orphaned baby **manatees**, whom they take in after their mothers are killed by poachers. The baby manatees are nursed back to health and kept until they are around 2 years old; when they are ready to fend for themselves, they are released into the wild.

Reserva Nacional Pacaya-Samiria

Southwest of Iquitos • S/60 for 2–3 days; S/150 for 4–30 days; pay SERNANP or the park office in Iquitos or at the park entrance in Lagunas • pacaya-samiria.com

The huge **RESERVA NACIONAL PACAYA-SAMIRIA** comprises around two million hectares of lush rainforest (about 1.5 percent of the total landmass of Peru) leading up to the confluence between the ríos Marañón and Huallaga, two of the largest Amazon headwaters and possessing between them the largest protected area of seasonally flooded jungle in the Peruvian Amazon. The reserve is crisscrossed by half a dozen rivers and countless creeks and is dotted with numerous oxbow lakes; it's famous for its abundance of wildlife, particularly pink and grey dolphins, river turtles, manatees, caimans, numerous species of monkey and an astounding 450-plus species of bird. Away from human settlement, there's a good chance of spotting jaguars and other big mammals.

To do the reserve justice you ideally need a week, or at least several days; half-day visits from Iquitos don't even scratch the surface and you're just as likely to spot river dolphins during any short river jaunt.

The reserve is a swampland during the **rainy season** (Dec–May), when the streams and rivers rise; it becomes easier to spot reptiles and there's more bird activity on account of cloudy weather. Mammals are easier to spot during the drier months when they come to the river and creeks to drink; the drier months are also the best time to go fishing. The hottest months are February to June.

This region is home to the **Cocoma**, whose main settlement is **Tipishca**, where the indigenous community is now directly involved in ecotourism, though the community at **Lagunas** is better known. Other indigenous communities, such as Manco Capac and Victoria on the southern side of the park, also carry out tourist-related activities. They can be hired as guides and will provide rustic accommodation, but can only be contacted by asking on arrival. Visitors should be aware that around 50,000 people, mostly **indigenous communities**, still live in the reserve's forest; they are the local residents, and their territory and customs should be respected.

Visiting the park from Lagunas

The cheapest yet most rewarding way to explore the rich wildlife along the mangrove-tangled waterways of Pacaya-Samiria, is to do a tour with one of the four **community tourism** organizations (see page 446) in the small town of **LAGUNAS**, two days upstream from Iquitos towards Yurimaguas. This requires more time and effort, and is not for everyone, since conditions are challenging: you'll be paddled in a narrow **dugout canoe** (often with no seat back) by a Spanish-speaking Cocama guide, and sleep in a combination of rustic huts over water and on a thin mattress or in a hammock over a sheltered wooden platform in the forest. Accommodation varies depending on the water levels within the reserve. Though the guides do their best with the catering, cooking facilities are minimal and the menu is limited to foodstuffs that you can find in Lagunas (often no fruit), and what can fit in the canoe, to be supplemented with the occasional catch of fish. But the rewards for such an adventure are superb:

INDIGENOUS COMMUNITIES AROUND IQUITOS

With all organized visits offered by numerous tour agencies to **indigenous villages** in this area, you can expect the inhabitants to put on a quick show, with a few traditional dances and some singing, before they try to sell you their handicrafts (sometimes over-enthusiastically). Prices range from S/5 to S/35 for necklaces, feathered items (mostly illegal to take out of the country), bark-cloth drawings, string bags (often excellent value) and blowguns; most people buy something, since there's no charge for the visit.

While the experience may leave you feeling somewhat uncomfortable – the men, and particularly the women, only discard Western clothes for the performances – it's arguably an improvement from the times when visits were imposed on communities by unscrupulous tour companies, and it has become a way of preserving the language and traditional costume. Visitors are now these indigenous groups' major source of income, and the Bora and Yaguar have both found a niche within the local tourist industry, though many villagers remain ambivalent about tourism. To ensure more of the money goes directly to the communities, enquire about *turismo vivencial* or *turismo comunitario* at the iPerú office in Iquitos.

SHAMANS AND AYAHUASCA SESSIONS

Ayahuasca is a jungle vine (*Banisteriopsis caapi*) that grows in the Western Amazon region and has been used for thousands of years as a "teacher plant", gaining a worldwide reputation for divination, inspiration and healing of physical, emotional and spiritual ailments. The vine is generally mixed with other jungle plants to enhance its powers and transform it into a bitter-tasting hallucinogenic brew, usually taken in a public session with a shaman.

Each indigenous community in the area around Iquitos has a shaman and ayahuasca **retreats** have long been a booming business here, initially attracting backpackers and hippies when they first appeared on the radar of Western travellers but now popular with well-heeled tourists prepared to spend hundreds of dollars on a spiritual detox. There are dozens of retreats around Iquitos, some of them very upmarket, with plush accommodation and a cleansing superfood diet, others more basic. Few accept visitors who are unable to commit to less than three or four days.

While the vast majority of participants report positive – even life-changing – experiences it's important to be aware that, if ayahuasca is mixed with a particular plant, or if you have an allergic reaction, it can lead to dangerously high blood pressure and even, in rare cases, death. It is at the very least a purging experience (most participants vomit profusely) and since the plant is a powerful **hallucinogen**, stronger than LSD, you may undergo hours of intense and sometimes uncomfortable visions. It's therefore important not only to feel comfortable with the scene and setting, but also with the person leading a session, particularly given the lack of recognized qualifications for practitioners.

Though it's difficult to give specific recommendations, the Temple of the Way of Light (templeofthewayoflight.org), out beyond Iquitos airport, has a good reputation for combining ayahuasca ceremonies with charitable and environmental work; the majority of the shamans are Shipibo women, which is a bonus for female visitors. There are also some well-known local ayahuasca guides, including Francisco Montes and the internationally renowned Agustín Rivas, a famous sculptor who has dedicated more than thirty years to working with ayahuasca. In addition, many if not most of the jungle lodges and camps around Iquitos regularly organize ayahuasca sessions but usually without the customary cleansing and preparations, but talk to fellow travellers about their experience before committing yourself to anything. ayaadvisor.org is a forum dedicated to ayahuasca retreats and a good starting point.

8

total immersion in the rainforest – no outboard motors, few tourists, a chance to get to know your guide(s) well, and **exceptional wildlife-spotting** opportunities. Come prepared with the usual essentials (see page 436).

All four local operators have offices on the main street and charge the same rates for similar packages. Three days is the minimum tour worth taking – five is better, but a couple of the guides have taken tourists for up to twenty days, finishing up at the far end of the park, close to Nauta.

Costs are an affordable S/50 per person per day, including all meals, accommodation, transport and guiding (in Spanish); in addition, bring sufficient cash to cover a night either side of your tour in one of the town's sparse lodgings (doubles around S/60), your onward transport, tip for the guide and the park fee (see page 477) payable to SERNANP at the park entrance, before you start paddling.

ARRIVAL AND INFORMATION — RESERVA NACIONAL PACAYA-SAMIRIA

By boat The slow *lanchas* between Iquitos and Yurimaguas all stop at Lagunas though their timings are unpredictable. Daily *rápidos* from Nauta (10–12hr; S/100) and Yurimaguas (5hr; S/40) also stop at Lagunas.

Tour operators All four community operators have offices along the main street; the more established operators are: ACATUPEL (976 187 364, facebook.com/acatupel) the community cooperative, and Huayruro Tours (965 662 555, peruselva.com), which can also sometimes be contacted in Yurimaguas. Check their website.

Money There is no ATM or bank (and often no electricity) so bring all the cash you will need from Yurimaguas or Iquitos.

ACCOMMODATION

Guided tours require some kind of camp setup or tourist **lodge** facilities. There are two main types of jungle experience available from Iquitos – what Peruvian tour operators describe as "**conventional**" (focusing on lodge stays) and what they describe as "**adventure trips**" (going deeper into the jungle). Bear in mind that during the low-water season some jungle lodges close as they are located on the smaller river tributaries and become inaccessible by boat. Prices given for lodges below are per person, per night. Most of them have a **minimum stay**, though, depending on their distance from Iquitos; check well in advance.

EXPLORAMA LODGES

With over fifty years' experience, Explorama (Av La Marina 340, Iquitos ⊕065 252 530, ⓦexplorama.com) has four lodges set in private reserves, a hotel in Iquitos and an Amazon riverboat.

Explorama ACTS Field Station (Amazon Conservatory for Tropical Studies) Map p.475. Set in primary forest, this place was originally designed for scientific research – so its facilities are slightly more Spartan, though still comfortable, with twenty rooms and shared dining and bathroom facilities. There's a self-guided medicinal plant trail but the real draw is the lengthy canopy walkway, whose topmost platform is 35m high, though tours to the other lodges can include a visit here. For non-scientists, it usually features as part of a multi-day Explorama package that includes other lodges.

Explorama Ceiba Tops Map p.475. The most luxurious of the lodges set in tropical grounds surrounded by forest. located some 40km from Iquitos. Facilities include a swimming pool with water slide, a hammock area, and proper bar and dining areas, surrounded by primary forest. Accommodation is in smart a/c bungalows. This lodge is very popular with families and can be visited in conjunction with other Explorama lodges. US$141

Explorama Lodge Map p.475. Explorama's first, fairly large lodge, 90km from Iquitos, was renovated in 2016 and though well equipped, it retains its rustic charm, and acts as a base camp for long-range programmes. The semi-open bedrooms are simple but attractive, with individual mosquito nets and cold-water showers. You get a chance to swim in the Amazon, go on a night walk and visit a nearby Yaguar community. Can be visited in conjunction with other Explorama lodges. US$176

ExplorNapo Lodge Map p.475. It's similar in style to the *Explorama Lodge* (where you usually spend the first night of a tour) but set deeper in the forest – over 160km from Iquitos, on the Río Sucusari – so wildlife viewing is likely to be better. The lodge's palm-roofed buildings, hammock areas and dining room/bar are linked by a thatch-covered walkway. From here it's an easy 1hr walk to the canopy walkway at the *Explorama ACTS Field Station*. US$250

OTHER LODGES

Heliconia Amazon River Lodge ⊕01 421 9195, ⓦterraverde.com.pe; map p.475. Situated a convenient 80km downriver from Iquitos, in the Reserva Comunal Yanomo, this riverside lodge offers accommodation in en-suite twin or family rooms, or in more private bungalows. The swimming pool set in expansive decking is great for cooling off and activities include jungle hikes, birdwatching, night boat rides, piranha fishing and visits to nearby indigenous communities, though you may want to skip the visit to Isla de los Monos. US$184

★ **Muyuna Lodge** Putumayo 163 ⊕065 242 858, ⓦmuyuna.com; map p.475. Located overlooking the narrow Río Yanayacu, in the Reserva Comunal Tamshiyacu-Tahuayo, *Muyuna* offers attractive, en-suite, mosquito-proof thatched cabins and activities such as forest walks and dolphin-spotting river safaris, and even a little kayaking. The lodge works hard to distinguish itself as a protector of wild animals and most of their guides come from nearby indigenous communities. S/410

★ **Otorongo Lodge** Depto 203, Putumayo 163, Iquitos ⊕065 224 192, ⓦotorongoexpeditions.com; map p.475. Some 100km upriver from Iquitos, down a tributary, this intimate lodge consists of just twelve rooms, with screens and individual mosquito nets. The food is

THE WITOTO AND THE BORA

The **Witoto and the Bora**, largely concentrated around Pevas, arrived here in the 1930s after being relocated from the Colombian Amazon. They are now in virtually everyday contact with the riverine society of Pevas, producing quality goods for sale to passers-by and yet retaining much of their traditional culture of songs, dances and legends, plus significant ethno-pharmacological practice in rainforest medicine. The nearby Bora village of **Puca Urquillo** is a good example, a large settlement based around a Baptist church and school, whose founders moved here from the Colombian side of the Río Putumayo during the hardships of the rubber era rather than be enslaved. A number of local indigenous groups can be visited close to Pevas, including the Bora, the Witoto and the less-known Ocainas. **Costs** are from around US$80 per person per day, with extra for speedboat transport from Iquitos.

INTO BRAZIL AND COLOMBIA: THE THREE-WAY BORDER

Exiting or entering Peru by river via Brazil or Colombia has become increasingly popular in recent years, and inevitably means crossing the **three-way border**. Some boats from Iquitos go all the way to **Leticia (Colombia)** or **Tabatinga (Brazil)**, but most – including the speedboats and the ferry from Iquitos – stop at the small Peruvian frontier settlement and immigration post on **Isla Santa Rosa**. Some of the large *lanchas* pull in at Isla Islandia, opposite Benjamin Constant (on the Brazilian side of the frontier). Santa Rosa accommodation is none too salubrious but since most boats heading upriver to Iquitos leave from here, and before dawn, travellers arriving in Peru tend to bed down here the night before departure to be near the boat.

A lively jungle town with *cumbia* and salsa music blasting out all over the place, Leticia is a much more exciting place to stay than adjacent and unpretty Tabatinga, with a good selection of guesthouses and restaurants, with scope for trekking in relatively pristine jungle or visiting indigenous communities.

CROSSING BY BOAT

You can reach the border from Iquitos by cargo boat, speedboat, or ferry (see page 471). Motorized canoes connect Santa Rosa with Tabatinga and Leticia (15–20min) and also Isla Islandia to Leticia or Tabatinga (40min–1hr).

From Tabatinga Boats sail downriver to Manaus (2–3 times a week; 4 days); tickets cost around R$200 depending on the size and condition of the boat, and whether or not you require a cabin; check departure schedule at the port. If you're coming from Iquitos on a boat that's continuing all the way to Manaus, boats typically stop for the night at Benjamin Constant. Let the captain know whether or not you need to go into Tabatinga to get stamped into Brazil.

From Leticia You can take one of the infrequent boats to Puerto Asís (10–12 days) from where there are buses to Mocoa and Pasto, with onward connections to Popayán, Cali and Bogotá.

CROSSING BY AIR

Tabatinga (Brazil) to Manaus Daily flights (1hr 40min) operate between Tabatinga and Manaus with Azul Linhas Aereas Brasileiras (voeazul.com.br).

Leticia (Colombia) to Bogotá There are one or two daily flights (2hr) between Leticia and Bogotá with LATAM (latam.com) and Avianca (avianca.com).

CUSTOMS AND IMMIGRATION

Get an exit stamp from Peru at Santa Rosa (see above), or get an entry stamp and tourist card if arriving. Brazilian entry and exit formalities are processed at the Policia Federal office, Av da Amizade (097 3412 2180; daily 7am–noon & 2–6pm); if you're entering Brazil you'll usually be asked to show an exit ticket or prove that you have sufficient funds to pay for your stay. Americans need a visa to enter Brazil, which must be obtained in Lima or the US in advance, or online.

To officially enter Colombia, take a short mototaxi ride to Leticia's airport and get a Colombian tourist card from the immigration office there (daily 8am–6pm). There are no border formalities between Leticia and Tabatinga; in fact, you don't even require a Colombian or Brazilian visa if you're not planning on travelling further than Leticia/Tabatinga and intend to turn around and take a boat back to Iquitos.

fantastic and the multilingual, personalized guiding top-notch. Activities range from swimming with river dolphins, canoeing in a flooded forest, fishing for peacock bass and piranha and learning about medicinal plants. The owner also runs birdwatching and extreme fishing trips as well as jungle survival expeditions. US$142

San Pedro Lodge 1hr north of Iquitos by car and boat 955 628 164, sanpedrolodge.com; map p.475. A recommended budget option, this small community-managed lodge lies on the Río Yarapa, close to the Bora community of Padre Cocha, which you can visit. Accommodation for twelve is in very basic wood-and-thatch

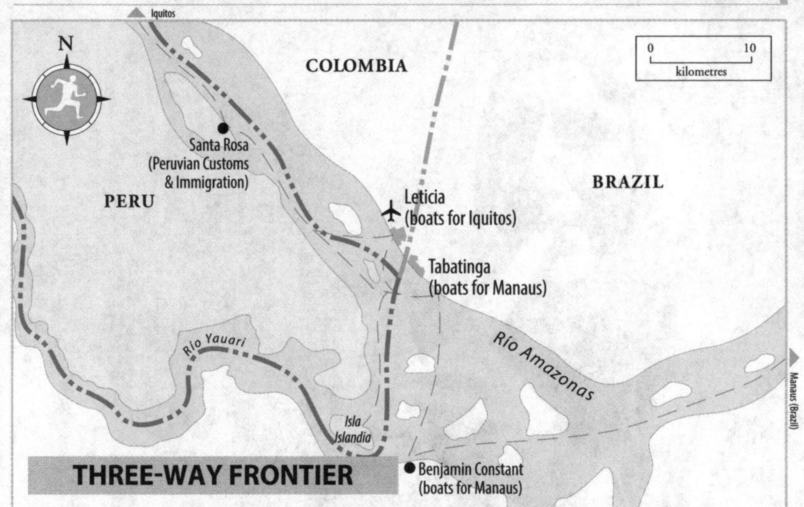

THREE-WAY FRONTIER

cabañas (no electricity) with shared and private cold-water ablutions – or you can choose to sleep in a tent. S/160

★ **Tapiche Lodge** Ricardo Palma 516 065 600 805, tapichejungle.com; map p.475. Located up the Ucayali and Tapiche tributaries, 404km upriver from Iquitos inside the Reserva Tapiche – a new protected area created in 2010 – this fantastic lodge is located further into the rainforest than any other and while the accommodation is not ultra-luxurious (oversized Brazilian hammocks or private, mesh-protected cabins), it's second to none when it comes to proximity to rare and endangered wildlife. Conservation is a priority and human impact is kept to a minimum. Trekking and canoeing are on offer and the emphasis is on animal- and bird-spotting. US$120

8

Downriver to Brazil and Colombia

Few tourists travel south of Iquitos unless they are heading for **Brazil** or **Colombia,** some 400km downriver from Iquitos. However, if you want to escape the ever increasing commercialism of Iquitos, and seek out a more "authentic" Amazonian experience then the midway town of **Pevas** is a good place to start.

Pevas

200km downriver from Iquitos • Access from Iquitos by riverboat or with an organized tour (see page 474). From Iquitos cargo boats take 15hr, the ferry 6hr; speedboats 4hr; from Santa Rosa times are longer

Halfway to the Colombian/Brazilian border, some 200km east of Iquitos, lies attractive, palm-thatched **PEVAS**; it's the oldest town in the Peruvian Amazon and still a frontier settlement populated largely by indigenous folk. The economy here is based primarily on fishing (visit the market where produce is brought in by boat every day), and dugout **canoes** are the main form of transport. Renowned local artist **Francisco Grippa** lives and has a gallery in Pevas, in *La Casa de la Loma* – ask for directions, and for advice on a local hospedaje to spend the night.

The surrounding flood forest is home to hundreds of **caimans** and significant **birdlife,** including several types of parrots, eagles and kingfishers. The area is also good for **butterfly watching**, and November, in particular, is a great time to study orchids and bromeliads in bloom.

PIPE PLAYER, SACRED VALLEY

Contexts

History

The first Peruvians were descendants of the nomadic peoples who crossed into the Americas during the last Ice Age (40,000–15,000 BC), when a combination of ice packs and low sea levels exposed a neck of solid "land" that spanned what's now the Bering Strait. Following herds of game animals from Siberia into what must have been a relative paradise of fertile coast, wild forest, mountain and savanna, successive generations continued south through Central America. Some made their way down along the Andes, into the Amazon, and out onto the more fertile areas of the Peruvian and Ecuadorian coast, while others found their niches en route.

In a number of peoples there seem to be cultural memories of these long migrations, encapsulated in their traditional mythologies. There is archeological evidence of human occupation in Peru dating back to around 20,000–15,000 BC, concentrated in the **Valle de Ayacucho,** where these early Peruvians lived in caves or out in the open. Around 12,000 BC, slightly to the north in the **Valle de Chillón** (just above modern Lima), comes the first evidence of significant craft skills – stone blades and knives for hunting. At this time there were probably similar hunter groups in the mountains and jungle too, but the climatic conditions of these zones make it unlikely that any significant remains will ever be found.

The difficulties of traversing the rugged terrain between the highlands and coast evidently proved little problem for the early Peruvians. From 8000 to 2000 BC, **migratory bands** of hunters and gatherers alternated between camps in the lowlands during the harsh mountain winters, and highland summer "resorts", their actual movements well synchronized with those of wild animal herds. One important mountain encampment from this **Incipient Era** has been discovered at **Lauricocha**, near Huánuco, at an altitude of over 4000m. Here the art of working stone – eventually producing very fine blades and arrow points – seems to have been sophisticated, while at the same time a growing cultural imagination found expression in cave paintings depicting animals, hunting scenes and even dances. Down on the coast at this time other groups were living on the greener *lomas* belts of the desert in places like **Chilca** to the south, and in the mangrove swamps around **Tumbes** to the north.

The emergence of cultism

An awareness of the potential uses of plants began to emerge around **5000 BC** with the **cultivation** of seeds and tubers (the potato being one of the most important "discoveries" later taken to Europe), to be followed over the next two millennia by the introduction, presumably from the Amazon, of gourds and Lima beans, then

20,000–15,000 BC	**12,000 BC**	**8000 BC**
The country's earliest archeological evidence of human occupation dates to this period.	Significant craft skills develop in the Valle de Chillón, not far from modern Lima.	A transhumant population alternates between lowland camps during harsh mountain winters and highland summer "resorts".

THE CHAVÍN CULT

From around 1200 BC to 200 AD – the **Formative Era** – agriculture and village life were established in Peru. Ceramics were invented, and the regions slowly began to integrate, mainly due to the widespread reach of a religious movement – the **Chavín cult**. Remarkable in that it seems to have spread without the use of military force, the cult was based on the worship of nature spirits, and an all-powerful **feline creator-god**. This feline image rapidly exerted its influence over the northern half of Peru and initiated a period of inter-relations between people in fertile basins in the Andes and some of the coastal valleys. How and where the cult originated is uncertain, though it seems probable that it began in the eastern jungles, possibly spreading to the Andes (and eventually the coast) along the upper Río Marañón. There may well have been a significant movement of people and trade goods between these areas and the rainforest regions, too, as evidenced by the many **Amazonian bird feathers** incorporated into capes and headdresses found on the coast. More recent theories, however, suggest that the flow may have been in the opposite direction, starting on the coast. The stone and adobe temples, for instance, in the Sechín area, pre-date the Chavín era, yet seem to be culturally linked.

The Chavín cult was responsible for excellent progress in **stone carving** and **metallurgy** (copper, gold and silver) and, significantly, a ubiquity of temples and pyramids emerged as religious and cultural centres. The most important known centre was the temple complex at **Chavín de Huantar** (see page 337) in Ancash, though a similar one was built at **Kotosh** (see page 306) near Huánuco; the cult's influence seems to have spread over the northern highlands and coast from Chiclayo down as far as the Peninsula de Paracas (where it had a particularly strong impact). There were immense local variations in the expressions of the Chavín Cult: elaborate metallurgy in the far north; adobe buildings on stone platforms in the river valleys; excellent ceramics from Chicama; and the extravagant stone engravings from Chavín itself.

Towards the end of the Chavín phase, an experimental period saw new cultural centres attempting to establish themselves as independent powers with their own distinct cultures. This gave birth to Gallinazo settlements in the Valle del Virú; the Paracas culture on the south coast (with its beautiful and highly advanced textile technology based around a cult of the dead); and the early years of Tiahuanaco development in the Lago Titicaca region. These three cultural upsurges laid the necessary foundations for the flourishing civilizations of the subsequent Classical Era.

squashes, peanuts and eventually cotton. Towards the end of this period a climatic shift turned the coast into a much more arid belt and forced those living there to try their hand at **agriculture** in the fertile riverbeds, a process to some extent paralleled in the mountains.

With a stable agricultural base, permanent settlements sprang up all along the coast, notably at **Chicama**, **Asia** and **Paracas**, and in the sierra at **Kotosh**. The population began to mushroom, and with it came a new consciousness, perhaps influenced by cultural developments within the Amazon Basin to the east: **cultism** – the burial of the dead in mummy form, the capturing of trophy heads and the building of grand religious structures – made its first appearance. At the same time there were also overwhelming technological advances in the spheres of weaving, tool-making and ornamental design.

5000 BC

Plants like cotton are domesticated and stable settlements are characteristic.

2600 BC

Radiocarbon dating proves that the ancient pyramids of Caral were fully functioning for around five hundred years from this date.

1800 BC to 200 AD

The Chavín cult is responsible for progress in stone carving and metallurgy. Temples and pyramids emerge as religious and cultural centres at Chavín de Huantar, Kotosh and Sechín.

Las Pirámides de Caral

Though the German archaeologist Max Uhle apparently came across **Las Pirámides de Caral** as early as 1905, it wasn't until many years later that their extent and significance was fully appreciated, largely because no gold or even ceramics were found there. Yet arguably these stone-built ceremonial structures are, after Machu Picchu, the most important archeological remains to be unearthed in Peru, since they represent human achievements that occurred four thousand years before the Incas appeared, and a hundred years before the Great Pyramid at Giza was built in Egypt.

Located in the Valle de Supe 120km north of Lima, 22km inland from the ocean, the site has been radiocarbon dated as being active for approximately five hundred years, from around 2600 BC. The complex features six stone platform mounds, with **ceremonial plazas** below and irrigation channels serving the surrounding fields. It was, in fact, a pre-ceramic site whose importance resided in another technology, that of the early **domestication of plants**, including cotton, squashes, beans and guava. Some of the best artefacts discovered here, in a ceremonial fire pit by the circular amphitheatre, include 32 flutes made from pelican and animal bones, and engraved with the figures of birds and monkeys, demonstrating a connection with the Amazon region even this long ago.

In its heyday it's thought that at least **three thousand people** were living in Caral. If the other seventeen so far unexcavated sites in the area had held similar-sized populations, then the total population living, working and worshipping in the Valle de Supe around 4600 years ago might have been as high as 20,000 or even more. The complex appears to have been abandoned quite rapidly after about five hundred years of booming occupation; theories as to why include the possibility of drought, which would have forced the inhabitants to move to another valley in search of available water and even more fertile soils.

The Classical Era

A diverse period – and one marked by intense development in almost every field – the **Classical Era** (200–1100 AD) saw the emergence of numerous distinct cultures, both on the coast and in the sierra. The best-documented of these, though not necessarily the most powerful, were the **Mochica and Nazca cultures** (see page 487) – both probably descendants of the coastal Paracas culture – and the **Tiahuanaco**, all forebears of the better-known Inca. In recent years, though, archeological projects in the Valle de Lambayeque on the north coast have revealed important ceremonial centres – particularly the massive sacred complex of truncated pyramids at **Batán Grande** originating from the **Sicán culture** (see page 487).

In the north, the Valle de las Pirámides, or **Túcume** (see page 407), was a major ceremonial centre, covering more than two hundred hectares. Initially begun by the Sicán culture, who started building here around 1100 after abandoning their earlier centre at Batán Grande, it reached its peak in the thirteenth and early fourteenth centuries, during the power vacuum in the Valle de Moche, between the decline of the Mochica and the rise of the Chimú. Archeologists believe that this must have been a time of abundance and population growth in this desert region, with optimum weather

200–1100

Classical cultures emerge throughout the land. The Líneas de Nazca and the Cahuachi complex are developed on the coast.

300

Technological advances in the Valle de Virú and Paracas mean every known form of non-machine weaving is used in textiles.

1200

The Inca Empire is founded by the mysterious Manco Capac. An age of great city building begins.

conditions for agriculture, the improvement of irrigation techniques and plentiful seafood.

Interethnic warfare

An increasing prevalence of **interethnic warfare** characterized the era's later period, culminating in the erection of defensive forts and a multiplication of ceremonial sites, including over sixty large pyramids in the Lima area. The **Huaca Pucllana** (see page 68) is one of these pyramids, a vast pre-Inca adobe mound that can be visited in the suburb of Miraflores, in Lima. It has a hollow core running through its cross-section and is thought to have been constructed in the shape of an enormous frog, a symbol of the rain god, who spoke to priests through a tube connected to the cavern.

Although initially peaceable, the **Tiahuanaco** culture is associated in its decadent phase (900–1000 AD) with militarism. This seems most likely due to conflict with neighbouring powerful peoples, like the **Huari** who were based further north. The ruins at Huari cover some eight square kilometres and include high-walled enclosures of field stones laid and plastered with mud and decorated by just a few stone statues, suggesting that the Huari were warlike, or at least needed to defend their town.

The Chimú era

Eventually Huari-Tiahuanaco influence on the coast was uprooted and overturned by the emergence of three youthful mini-empires – the **Chimú**, the **Cuismancu** and the **Chincha**. In the mountains, its influence mysteriously disappeared to pave the way for the separate growth of relatively large groups of people such as the **Colla** (around Lago Titicaca), the **Inca** (around Cusco) and the **Chanca** (near Ayacucho).

Partly for defensive reasons, this period of isolated development sparked a city-building urge which became almost compulsive by the Imperial Period in the thirteenth century. The most spectacular urban complex was **Chan Chan** (see page 366), near modern Trujillo, built by the Chimú on the side of the river opposite earlier Mochica temples. Indicating a much greater sophistication in social control, the internal structure of the culture's clan-based society was reflected in the complex's intricate layout. By now, with a working knowledge of bronze manufacture, the Chimú had spread their domain from Chan Chan to Tumbes in the north and Paramonga in the south – dominating nearly half the Peruvian coastline. To the south they were bounded by the **Cuismancu**, less powerful, though capable of building similar citadels (such as Cajamarquilla near Lima) and of comparable attainment in craft industries. Further down the coastline, the **Chincha** – known also as the **Ica culture** – also produced fine monuments and administrative centres in the Chincha and Pisco valleys. The lower rainfall on the southern coast, however, didn't permit the Chincha state – or (to an extent) the Cuismancu – to create urban complexes anything near the size of Chan Chan.

The Incas

With the **Inca Empire** (1200–1532 AD) came the culmination of Peru's city-building phase and the beginnings of a kind of Peruvian unity, as the Incas, although originally a people of no more than around 40,000, gradually took over each of the separate

1438–1532

Expansion of the Inca Empire from Cusco, north into Ecuador and south into Chile. The Qhapaq Ñam (Inca Highway) was constructed from Colombia to Chile, parts of which are still in existence.

1513

Spaniard Francisco Pizarro is accompanying explorer Vasco Nuñez de Balboa when he stumbles upon and names the Pacific Ocean while on an expedition in Panama.

CLASSICAL CULTURES

THE MOCHICA CULTURE

The **Mochica culture** has left the fullest evidence of its social and domestic life, all aspects of which, including its work and religion, are vividly represented in the highly realistic imagery of its pottery. The peak of their influence came around 500 to 600 AD, when they had cultural and military control of the coast from Piura in the north to the Valle de Nepeña in the south. The first real urban culture in Peru, its members maintained a firm hierarchy, an elite group combining both secular and sacred power. Ordinary people cultivated land around clusters of dwelling sites, dominated by sacred pyramids – constructed *huacas* dedicated to the gods. The key to the elite's position was probably their organization of large **irrigation projects**, essential to the survival of relatively large population centres in the arid desert of the north coast. In the Mochica region, nature and the world of the ancestors seem the dominant cultural elements; occasional human sacrifices were offered and trophy heads were captured in battle.

THE NAZCA CULTURE

More or less contemporaneous with the Mochica, the **Nazca culture** bloomed for several hundred years on the south coast. The Nazca are thought to be responsible for the astonishing lines and drawings etched into the Pampa de San José (see page 131), though little is known for certain about their society or general way of life. The Nazca did, however, build an impressive temple complex in the desert at **Cahuachi**, and their burial sites have turned up thousands of beautiful ceramics whose abstract designs can be compared only to the quality and content of earlier Paracas textiles.

THE SICÁN CULTURE

Contemporaneous with the Mochica, to the south, there is also strong evidence that the **Sicán culture** revered the same demonic spirit or god, named **Ai-Apaec** in the Mochica language (the "Winged Decapitator"), who kept the world of human life and death in order. Ai-Apaec is also associated with the veritable treasure-trove found in the royal tombs at Sipán, just south of Lambayeque, and those of the **Vicús** culture, to the north, near Piura.

THE TIAHUANACO CULTURE

Contemporaneous with the other classical cultures, but also pre-dating them, the **Tiahuanaco culture** was named after its sacred centre on the shore of Lago Titicaca. The Tiahuanaco culture, and in particular its central site of pilgrimage, was evidently active between 300 BC and 300 AD and then lasted for another 600 years. The last 500 years coincided with the classical Mochica period – with which, initially at least, it peacefully coexisted. Tiahuanaco textiles and pottery spread along the desert, modifying both Mochica and Nazca styles and bending them into more sophisticated shapes and abstract patterns. The main emphasis in Tiahuanaco pottery and stonework was on symbolic elements featuring condors, pumas and snakes – more than likely the culture's main **gods**, representing their respective spheres of the sky, earth and underworld. In this there seem obvious echoes of the deified natural phenomena of the earlier Chavín cult.

coastal empires. One of the last to go – almost bloodlessly, and just sixty years before the Spanish conquest – was the Chimú empire, which for much of this **Imperial Period** was a powerful rival.

1527

Huayna Capac dies of smallpox; civil war breaks out.

1532

Spanish Conquistadors, led by Pizarro, set foot on Peruvian soil for the first time and make their way overland to the Inca town of Cajamarca.

1533

Pizarro brings Atahualpa to trial; the Spanish baptize and then kill him.

Based in the valleys around Cusco, the Incas were, for the first two centuries of their existence, much like any other of the larger mountain ethnic groups. Fiercely protective of their independence, they maintained a somewhat feudal society, tightly controlled by rigid religious tenets, though often disrupted by internal conflict. The founder of the dynasty – around 1200 AD – was **Manco Capac**, who passed into Inca mythology as a cultural hero. Historically, however, little is known about Inca developments or achievements until the accession in 1438 of Pachacuti, and the onset of their great era of expansion.

Inca expansion

Pachacuti, most innovative of all the Inca emperors, was the first to expand the Incas' traditional territory. The beginnings of this expansion were in fact not of his making but in response to a threatened invasion by the powerful, neighbouring Chanca during the reign of his father, **Viracocha**. Viracocha, feeling the odds to be overwhelming, left Cusco under Pachacuti's control, withdrawing to the refuge of Calca along the Río Urubamba. Pachacuti, however, won a legendary victory – Inca chronicles record that the very stones of the battlefield rose up in his defence – and, having vanquished the most powerful force in the region, he shortly took the Inca crown for himself.

Within three decades Pachacuti had consolidated his power over the entire sierra region from Cajamarca to Titicaca, defeating in the process all main imperial rivals except for the Chimú. At the same time the empire's capital at **Cusco** was spectacularly developed, with the evacuation and destruction of all villages within a ten-kilometre radius, a massive programme of agricultural terracing (watched over by a skyline of agro-calendrical towers) and the construction of unrivalled palaces and temples.

Inca territory expanded north into Ecuador, almost reaching Quito, under the next emperor – **Tupac Yupanqui** – who also took his troops down the coast, overwhelming the Chimú and capturing the holy shrine of Pachacamac. Not surprisingly the coastal cultures influenced the Incas perhaps as much as the Incas influenced them, particularly in the sphere of craft industries. Even compared to Pachacuti, Tupac Yupanqui was nevertheless an outstandingly imaginative and able ruler. During the 22 years of his reign (1471–93) he pushed Inca control southwards as far as the Río Maule in Chile; instigated the first proper census of the empire and set up the decimal-based administrative system; introduced the division of labour and land between the state, the gods and the local *ayllus*; invented the concept of "chosen women", or *mamaconas* (see page 504); and inaugurated a new class of respected individuals (the *yanaconas*). An empire had been unified not just physically but also administratively and ideologically.

Huayna Capac and civil war

At the end of the fifteenth century the Inca Empire was thriving, as vital as any civilization before or since. Its politico-religious authority was finely tuned, extracting what it needed from its millions of subjects and giving what was necessary to maintain the status quo – be it brute force, protection or food. The only obvious problem inherent in the Inca system of unification and domination was one of over-extension. When **Huayna Capac** continued Tupac Yupanqui's expansion to the north he created a new Inca city at **Quito**, one which he personally preferred to Cusco and which laid

1535

Foundation of Lima – its colonial architecture draws heavily on Spanish influences, though native craftspeople also leave their mark.

1541

Pizarro is assassinated by displeased Conquistadors; for the next seven years the country is rent by civil war.

1569

Francisco Toledo arrives in Peru as viceroy with a view to reforming the colonial system.

THE INCA EMPERORS

Manco Capac (c.1200 AD) Legendary founder of the Incas and cultural hero; we have little actual information on him or his life.

Sinchi Roca (1230–60) His name means Magnificent Warrior; nevertheless, he was unable to expand the Inca territorial base.

Lloque Yupanqui (1260–90) This Inca failed to expand the Inca Empire and also worsened relations with some of the neighbouring peoples.

Mayta Capac (1290–1320) He inherited the imperial throne at a tender age, and an uncle took command until he reached maturity.

Capac Yupanqui (1320–50) Considered a Machiavellian Inca, since, as the son of Mayta Capac's sister, he was not in direct line to inherit the throne, but nevertheless took it by force.

Inca Roca (1350–80) The first to actually bear the title "Inca". Some of his palace still exists beside the modern Plaza de Armas in Cusco.

Yahuar Huaca (1380–1400) His claim to fame was crying tears of blood after being captured by a neighbouring group when he was eight years old; he managed to escape but did little building in Cusco and was ultimately assassinated.

Viracocha Inca (1400–38) He took the sacred name of the creator-god Viracocha after having a dream. Forced to escape from Cusco when it was taken over briefly by the rival Chanca people from the Abancay region, he later died in isolation.

Pachacuti (1438–71) Also called Pachacutec, he was the Inca who really created the empire; he expanded its territorial base from the Valle de Cusco, began its true megalithic architectural heritage, and developed the social order required to take over and run other parts of Peru and beyond.

Tupac Yupanqui (1471–93) Pachacuti's son, he extended the empire north into Ecuador and took over the Chimú dynasty on Peru's north coast.

Huayna Capac (1493–1525) Much of his reign focused on maintaining the northern end of the empire; in fact, he was in Quito when he first heard of strange sightings of white men in boats off the Peruvian shores. He died of smallpox before naming a successor.

Huascar (1525–32) Huascar was appointed Inca Emperor, but there were many other pretenders, including Atahualpa, who defeated him in battle just before Pizarro landed (see page 490).

Atahualpa (1532–33) The shortest reign of any Inca was terminated by the Conquistadors in Cajamarca (see page 374).

the seed for a division of loyalties within Inca society. At this point in history, the Inca Empire was probably the largest in the world, even though it had neither horses nor wheel technology. The empire was over 5500km long, stretching from southern Colombia right down to northern Chile, with Inca highways covering distances of around 30,000km in all.

Almost as a natural progression from over-extending the empire in this way, divisions in Inca society came to a head even before Huayna Capac's death. Ruling the empire from Quito, along with his favourite son **Atahualpa**, Huayna Capac installed another son, **Huascar**, at Cusco. In the last year of his life he tried to formalize the division – ensuring an inheritance at Quito for Atahualpa – but this was fiercely resisted by Huascar, legitimate heir to the title of Inca Emperor and the whole empire, as well as by many of the influential Cusco priests and nobles. In 1527, when Huayna Capac died of "the white man's disease", smallpox, which had swept down overland from

1572

After fierce fighting and a near escape, Tupac Amaru is captured, brought to trial in Cusco and subsequently beheaded – an act by Toledo that was disavowed by the Spanish Crown.

1742

Juan Santos Atahualpa, a well-travelled *mestizo* from Cusco, rouses indigenous groups in the jungle to rebellion.

1780

Another *mestizo*, José Gabriel Condorcanqui, leads a rebellion around Cusco. Within a year he is executed.

Mexico in the previous seven years, killing over thirty percent of the indigenous population, civil war broke out. Atahualpa, backed by his father's army, was by far the stronger and immediately won a major victory at Ríobamba (in present-day Ecuador) – a battle that, it was said, left the plain littered with human bones for over a hundred years. A still bloodier battle, however, took place along the Río Apurímac at Cotabamba in 1532. This was the decisive victory for Atahualpa, and with his army he retired to relax at the hot baths near Cajamarca. Here, informed of a strange-looking, alien band of men, successors to the bearded adventurers whose presence had been noted during the reign of Huayna Capac, he waited with his followers.

Francisco Pizarro arrives

Francisco Pizarro, along with two dozen soldiers, was accompanying explorer Vasco Nuñez de Balboa, when he stumbled upon and named the Pacific Ocean in 1513 while on an exploratory expedition in modern Panama. From that moment his determination, fired by local tales of a fabulously rich land to the south, was set. Within eleven years he had found himself financial sponsors and set sail down the Pacific coast with the priest Hernando de Luque and Diego de Almagro.

With remarkable determination, having survived several disastrous attempts, the three explorers eventually landed at **Tumbes** in 1532. A few months later, a small, Pizarro-led band of Spaniards (fewer than two hundred men), arrived at the Inca city of **Cajamarca** to meet the leader of what they were rapidly realizing was a mighty empire. En route to Cajamarca, Pizarro had learned of the Inca civil wars and of Atahualpa's recent victory over his brother Huascar. This rift within the empire provided the key to success that Pizarro was looking for.

Pizarro seizes control

The day after their arrival, in what at first appeared to be a lunatic endeavour, Pizarro and his men massacred thousands of **Inca warriors** and captured Atahualpa. Although ridiculously outnumbered, the Spanish had the advantages of surprise, steel, cannons, and – above all – mounted cavalry. The decisive battle was over in a matter of hours; with Atahualpa prisoner, Pizarro was effectively in control of the Inca Empire. Atahualpa was promised his freedom if he could fill the famous Cuarto del Rescate (Ransom Room) at Cajamarca with **gold**. Caravans overladen with the precious metal arrived from all over the land and within six months the room was filled: a treasure worth over 1.5 million pesos, which was already enough to make each of the conquerors extremely wealthy. Pizarro, however, chose to keep the Inca leader as a hostage in case of indigenous revolt, amid growing suspicions that Atahualpa was inciting his generals to attack the Spanish. Atahualpa almost certainly did send messages to his chiefs in Cusco, including orders to execute his brother Huascar, who was already in captivity there. Under pressure from his worried captains, Pizarro brought Atahualpa to trial in July 1533, a mockery of justice in which he was given a free choice: to be burned alive as a pagan or garrotted as a Christian. Since Incas believed the soul would not travel to the afterlife if burned, Atahualpa opted to be baptised, before being killed.

With nothing left to keep him in Cajamarca, Pizarro made his way through the Andes to Cusco where he crowned a puppet emperor, **Manco Inca**, of royal Inca

1819

The first rebel invaders land at Paracas. Ica, Huánuco and the north of Peru and soon opt for independence.

1821

The great liberators – San Martín from the south and Bolívar from the north – enter the capital without a struggle. San Martín proclaims Peruvian independence on July 28.

1824

Spanish resistance to independence is extinguished at the battles of Junín and Ayacucho.

CATHOLIC CULTISM

Despite the evangelistic zeal of the Spanish, religion changed little for the majority of the indigenous population. Although Inca ceremonies, pilgrimages and public rituals were outlawed, their mystical and magical base endured. Each region quickly reverted to the **pre-Inca cults** deep-rooted in their culture and cosmology. Over the centuries the people learnt to absorb symbolic elements of the **Catholic faith** into their beliefs and rituals – allowing them, once again, to worship relatively freely. Magic, herbalism and divination have always managed to continue strongly at the village level, and have successfully pervaded modern Peruvian thought, language and practice (the Peruvian World Cup football squad in 1982 enlisted – in vain – the magical aid of a *curandero*). At the elite level, the Spanish continued their fervent attempts to convert the entire population to their own ritualistic religion. They were, however, more successful with the rapidly growing *mestizo* population, who shared the same cultural aspirations.

Miraculous occurrences became a conspicuous feature in the popular Peruvian Catholic Church, the greatest example being **El Señor des los Milagros (Our Lord of Miracles)**, a cult that originated among the black population of colonial Lima. In the devastating earthquake of 1665, an anonymous mural of the Crucifixion on the wall of a chapel in the poorest quarter was supposedly the only structure left standing. The belief that this was a direct sign from God took hold among the local populace, and El Señor des los Milagros remains the most revered image in Peru. Thousands of devotees process through the streets of Lima and other Peruvian towns every October, and even today many women dress in purple throughout the month to honour the icon.

blood. After all the practice the Spanish had had in imposing their culture on the Aztecs in Mexico, it took them only a few years to replace the Inca Empire with a working colonial mechanism. Now that the Inca civil wars were over, people seemed happy to retire quietly into the hills and get back to the land. However, it was **disease,** rather than battle weariness, that was responsible for the almost total lack of initial reaction to the new conquerors. The indigenous population of Peru had dropped from some 32 million in 1520 to only five million by 1548 – a decline due mainly to new European ailments such as smallpox, measles, bubonic plague, whooping cough and influenza.

Colonial Peru

Peru's vast wealth of resources – beyond treasure – was recognized early on by the Spanish. Between the sixteenth and seventeenth centuries Spain established only two *Virreinatos* (Viceroyalties) in the Americas: first in Mexico, then shortly afterwards in Peru. Queen Isabella indirectly laid the original foundations for the political administration of Peru in 1503 when she authorized the initiation of an **encomienda system**, which meant that successful Spanish conquerors could extract tribute for the Crown and personal service in return for converting people to Christianity. They were not, however, given the titles to the land itself. As governor of Peru, Pizarro used the *encomienda* system to grant large groups of people to his favourite soldier-companions.

1826	1827	1845
Bolívar remains dictator of the Federación de los Andes until 1826.	Within a year of Bolívar's withdrawal Peruvians vote for the liberal General La Mar as president.	Ramón Castilla is the first president to bring any real strength to his office. The country begins to develop on the rising wave of a booming export in guano fertilizer, made of bird droppings.

Colonial society

In 1541 Pizarro was assassinated by a disgruntled faction among the Conquistadors who looked to **Diego de Almagro** as their leader, and for the next seven years the nascent colonial society was struck by civil war. In response, the first **virrey** (viceroy) – Blasco Nuñez de Vela – was sent from Spain in 1544. His task was to act as royal commissioner and to secure the colony's loyalty to Spain; his fate was to be killed by Gonzalo Pizarro, brother of Francisco. But royalist forces, now under Pedro de la Gasca, eventually prevailed – Gonzalo was captured and executed, and Crown control firmly re-established. During the sixteenth and seventeenth centuries, **Peruvian society** was being transformed by the growth of new generations: creoles, descendants of Spaniards born in Peru, and *mestizos*, of mixed Spanish and indigenous blood, created a new class structure. In the coastal valleys where populations had been ravaged by European diseases, slaves were imported from Africa. There were over 1500 black slaves in Lima alone by 1554. At the same time, as a result of the civil wars and periodic indigenous revolts, over a third of the original conquerors had lost their lives by 1550.

In return for the salvation of their souls, the local population were expected to surrender their bodies to the Spanish. Some forms of *mita* (service) were simply continuations of Inca tradition – from keeping the streets clean to working in textile mills. But the most feared was a new introduction, the *mita de minas* – **forced labour in the mines.** With the discovery of the "mountain of silver" at Potosí (now in Bolivia) in 1545, and of mercury deposits at Huancavelica in 1563, it reached new heights. Forced off their smallholdings, few indigenous people who left to work in the mines ever returned. Indeed, the mercury mines at Huancavelica were so dangerous that the quality of their toxic ore could be measured by the number of weekly deaths. Those who were taken to Potosí had to be chained together to stop them from escaping: if they were injured, their bodies were cut from the shackles by sword to save precious time. Around three million labourers toiled in Potosí and Huancavelica alone; some had to walk over 1000km from Cusco to Potosí for the privilege of working themselves to death.

Francisco Toledo becomes viceroy

In 1569, **Francisco Toledo** arrived in Peru to become *virrey*. His aim was to reform the colonial system so as to increase royal revenue while at the same time improving the lot of the local population. Before he could get on with that, however, he had to quash a rapidly developing threat to the colony – the appearance of a **neo-Inca state** (see page 493). Toledo's next task was to firmly establish the viceregal position – something that outlasted him by some two centuries. He toured highland Peru seeking ways to improve Crown control, starting with an attempt to curb the excesses of the *encomenderos* and their tax-collecting *curacas* (hereditary local chieftains) by implementing a programme of **reducciones** – the physical resettlement of indigenous peoples into new towns and villages. Hundreds of thousands of peasants – perhaps millions – were forced to move from remote hamlets into large conglomerations, or *reducciones*, in convenient locations. *Corregidores*, or priests, were placed in charge of them, undercutting the power of the *encomenderos*. Toledo also established a new elected position – the local *varayoc* (or mayor) – in an attempt to displace the *curacas*. The *varayoc*, however, was not necessarily a good colonial tool in that, even more

1856

A new moderate constitution is approved. Castilla begins his second term of office.

1860

Sugar and cotton are exported from coastal plantations and guano exports are also substantial.

1870s

Construction of the high-altitude railway lines and other engineering projects. First exploitation of Amazonian rubber.

REBEL INCAS

After an unsuccessful uprising in 1536, **Manco Inca**, Pizarro's puppet emperor, had disappeared with a few thousand loyal subjects into the remote mountainous regions of Vilcabamba, northwest of Cusco. With the full regalia of high priests, virgins of the sun and the golden idol of Punchau (the sun god), he maintained a **rebel Inca state** and built himself impressive new palaces and fortresses between Vitcos and Espíritu Pampa – well beyond the reach of colonial power. Although not a substantial threat to the colony, Manco's forces repeatedly raided nearby settlements and robbed travellers on the roads between Cusco and Lima.

Manco himself died at the hands of a **Spanish outlaw**, a guest at Vilcabamba who hoped to win himself a pardon from the Crown. But the neo-Inca state continued under the leadership of Manco's son, **Sairi Tupac**, who assumed the imperial fringe at the age of 10. Tempted out of Vilcabamba in 1557, Sairi Tupac was offered a palace and a wealthy life by the Spanish in return for giving up his refuge and subversive aims. He died a young man, only three years after turning to Christianity and laying aside his father's cause. Meanwhile **Titu Cusi**, one of Manco's illegitimate sons, declared himself emperor and took control in Vilcabamba.

Eventually, Titu Cusi began to open his doors. First he allowed two Spanish friars to enter his camp, and then, in 1571, negotiations were opened for a return to Cusco when an emissary arrived from Virrey Toledo. The talks broke down before the year was out and Toledo decided to send an army into Vilcabamba to rout the Incas. They arrived to find that Titu Cusi was already dead and his brother, **Tupac Amaru**, was the new emperor. After fierce fighting and a near escape, Tupac Amaru was captured and brought to trial in Cusco. Accused of plotting to overthrow the Spanish and of inciting his followers to raid towns, Tupac Amaru was quickly **beheaded** – an act by Toledo that was disavowed by the Spanish Crown and which caused much distress in Peru.

than the *curacas*, his interests were rooted firmly in the *ayllu* (extended family or clan, usually village-based) and in his own neighbours, rather than in the wealth of some distant kingdom.

Peruvian independence

The end of the eighteenth century saw profound changes throughout the world. The North American colonies had gained their independence from Britain; France had been rocked by a people's revolution; and liberal ideas were spreading everywhere. Inflammatory newspapers and periodicals began to appear on the streets of Lima, and discontent was expressed at all levels of society. A strong sense of **Peruvian nationalism** emerged in the pages of *Mercurio Peruano* (first printed in the 1790s), a concept that was vital to the coming changes. Even the architecture of Lima had changed in the mid-eighteenth century, as if to welcome the new era. Wide avenues suddenly appeared, public parks were opened, and palatial salons became the focus for the discourse of gentlemen. The philosophy of the Enlightenment was slowly but surely pervading attitudes even in remote Peru.

When, in 1808, Napoleon took control of Spain, the authorities and elites in all the Spanish colonies found themselves in a new and unprecedented position. Was their loyalty to Spain or to its rightful king? And just who was the rightful king now? The

1872	1879	1879–83
Peru's first civilian president – Manuel Pardo – assumes power.	Peru cannot pay off its growing foreign debt.	Chile declares war on Bolivia and Peru over nitrates mined in Bolivia. By 1880 Bolivia had been defeated, and by 1881 the Chilean army occupied Lima, finally defeating Peru in the Battle of Huamachuco in 1884.

INDIGENOUS REBELLION IN THE EIGHTEENTH CENTURY

When the Habsburg monarchy gave way to the Bourbon kings in Spain at the beginning of the eighteenth century, shivers of protest seemed to reverberate deep in the Peruvian hinterland. There were a number of serious **indigenous rebellions** against colonial rule during the next hundred years. One of the most important, though least known, was that led by **Juan Santos Atahualpa**, a *mestizo* from Cusco. Juan Santos had travelled to Spain, Africa and, some say, to England as a young man in the service of a wealthy Jesuit priest. Returning to Peru in 1740 he was imbued with revolutionary fervour and moved into the high jungle region between Tarma and the Río Ucayali where he roused various peoples in the surrounding forests to rebellion. Throwing out the whites, he established a millenarian cult and, with an indigenous army recruited from several communities, successfully repelled all attacks by the authorities. Although never extending his powers beyond Tarma, he lived a free man until his death in 1756.

In 1780, another *mestizo*, José Gabriel Condorcanqui, led a rebellion, calling himself **Tupac Amaru II**. Whipping up the already inflamed peasant opinion around Cusco into a revolutionary frenzy, he imprisoned a local *corregidor* before going on to massacre a troop of nearly six hundred royalist soldiers. Within a year, Tupac Amaru II had been captured and executed but his rebellion had demonstrated both a definite weakness in colonial control and a high degree of popular unrest. Over the next decade several administrative reforms were to alter the situation, at least superficially: the *repartimiento* and the *corregimiento* systems were abolished. In 1784, Charles III appointed a French nobleman – Teodoro de Croix – as the new viceroy to Peru and divided the country into seven *intendencias* containing 52 provinces. This created tighter direct royal control, but also unwittingly provided the pattern for the Republican state of federated *departamentos*.

American War of Independence, the French Revolution and Napoleon's invasion of Spain all pointed towards the opportunity of throwing off the shackles of colonialism, and by the time Ferdinand returned to the Spanish throne in 1814, royalist troops were struggling to maintain order throughout South America. Venezuela and Argentina had already declared their independence, and in 1817 San Martín liberated Chile by force. It was only a matter of time before one of the two great liberators – **José de San Martín** in the south or **Simón Bolívar** in the north – reached Peru.

San Martín was the first to do so. Having already liberated Argentina and Chile, he contracted an English naval officer, Lord Cochrane, to attack Lima. By September 1819 the first rebel invaders had landed at Paracas. Ica, Huánuco and then the north of Peru soon opted for independence, and the royalists, cut off in Lima, retreated into the mountains. Entering the capital without a struggle, San Martín proclaimed Peruvian **independence** on July 28, 1821.

The Republic

Once Peruvian independence had been declared, San Martín immediately assumed political control of the fledgling nation. With the title "Protector of Peru" he set about devising a workable **constitution** for the new nation – at one point even considering importing European royalty to establish a new monarchy. A libertarian as well as a liberator, San Martín declared freedom for slaves' children, abolished the service of

1883	1908	1890–1930
The Treaty of Ancón brings the War of the Pacific to a close. As a result, Bolivia loses access to the sea and Peru's southern border is significantly shortened.	The powerful oligarch Augusto Leguía rises to power and is elected president.	Much modernization in Lima (including the building of the Palacio de Gobierno), and grandiose public buildings are developed elsewhere.

mita (see page 492) and even outlawed the term "Indio". But in practice, with royalist troops still controlling large sectors of the sierra, his approach did more to frighten the establishment than it did to help the slaves and peasants, whose problems remain, even now, deeply rooted in their social and territorial inheritance.

The development of a relatively stable **political system** took virtually the rest of the nineteenth century, although Spanish resistance to independence was finally extinguished at the battles of Junín and Ayacucho in 1824. By this time, San Martín had given up the power game, handing political control over to **Simón Bolívar**, a man of enormous force with definite tendencies towards megalomania. Between them, Bolívar and his right-hand man, Sucre, divided Peru in half, with Sucre first president of the upper sector, renamed Bolivia. Bolívar himself remained dictator of a vast Andean Confederation – encompassing Colombia, Venezuela, Ecuador, Peru and Bolivia – until 1826. Within a year of his withdrawal, however, the Peruvians had torn up his controversial constitution and voted for the liberal **General La Mar** as president.

Political power games

On La Mar's heels raced a generation of *caudillos*, military men, often *mestizos* of middle-class origins who had achieved recognition (on either side) in the battles for independence. Peru was plunged deep into a period of domestic and foreign plotting and counterplotting, while the economy and some of the nation's finest natural resources withered away.

Ramón Castilla was the first president to bring any real strength to his office. After he assumed power in 1845, the country began to develop more positively on the rising wave of a booming export in guano fertilizer (made of bird droppings). In 1856, a new moderate constitution was approved and Castilla began his second term of office in an atmosphere of growth and hope – there was a rail network to be built and the Amazon waterways to be opened up. Sugar and cotton became important exports from coastal plantations and guano deposits alone yielded a revenue of US$15 million in 1860. Castilla abolished the paying of tribute by the indigenous population, and managed to emancipate slaves without socio-economic disruption by buying them from their "owners".

His successors fared less happily. **President Balta** (1868–72) oversaw the construction of most of Peru's rail network, but overspent so freely on these and a variety of other public and engineering works that it left the country on the brink of economic collapse. In the 1872 elections an attempted military coup was spontaneously crushed by a civilian mob, and Peru's first civilian president – the laissez-faire capitalist **Manuel Pardo** – assumed power.

The Peruvian Corporation

Modern Peru is generally considered to have been born in 1895 with the forced resignation of **General Cáceres**, who was twice President of Peru (1886–90 and 1894–95). However, the seeds of industrial development had been laid under his rule, albeit by foreigners. In 1890 an international plan was formulated to bail Peru out of its bankruptcy. The **Peruvian Corporation** was formed in London and assumed the US$50 million national debt in return for "control of the national economy". Foreign companies took over the railways, navigation on Lago Titicaca and vast quantities of

1932

The Trujillo middle class leads a violent uprising against the sugar barons in protest at working conditions on the plantations.

1940s

Inflation is out of control; during the 1940s the cost of living in Peru rises by 262 percent.

1948

General Odría leads a coup d'état from Arequipa and forms a military junta.

THE WAR OF THE PACIFIC

By the late nineteenth century Peru's **foreign debt**, particularly to England, had grown enormously. Even though interest could be paid in guano, there simply wasn't enough. To make matters considerably worse, Peru went to war with Chile in 1879. Lasting over four years, this "**War of the Pacific**" was basically a battle for the rich nitrate deposits located in Bolivian territory. Peru had pressured its ally Bolivia into imposing an export tax on nitrates mined by the Chilean-British Corporation. Chile's answer was to occupy the area and declare war on Peru and Bolivia. Victorious on land and at sea, Chilean forces had occupied Lima by the beginning of 1881 and the Peruvian president had fled to Europe. By 1883 Peru "lay helpless under the boots of its conquerors", and only a diplomatic rescue seemed possible.

The **Treaty of Ancón**, possibly Peru's greatest national humiliation, brought the war to a close in October 1883. Peru was forced to accept the cloistering of an independent Bolivia high up in the Andes, with no land link to the Pacific, and the even harder loss of the nitrate fields to Chile.

guano. They were also given free use of seven Peruvian ports for 66 years as well as the opportunity to start exploiting the rubber resources of the Amazon Basin. Under Nicolás de Piérola (president 1879–81 and 1895–99), some sort of stability had begun to return by the end of the nineteenth century.

The twentieth century

In the early years of the twentieth century, Peru was run by an **oligarchical clan** of big businessmen and great landowners. Fortunes were made in a wide range of enterprises, exploiting above all, sugar along the coast, minerals from the mountains and rubber from the rainforests. Meanwhile, the lot of the ordinary individual worsened dramatically: the lives of the Andean peasants became more difficult, the indigenous groups in the Amazon basin lived like slaves on the rubber plantations; and the owners of sugar plantations were abusing their wealth and power on the coast. In 1932, the Trujillo middle class led a **violent uprising** against the sugar barons and the primitive working conditions on the plantations. It was suppressed by the army, and nearly five thousand lives are thought to have been lost in the revolt.

The rise of the APRA – **the Alianza Popular Revolucionaria Americana** – which had instigated the Trujillo uprising, and the growing popularity of its leader, **Haya de la Torre**, kept the nation occupied during World War II: the unholy alliance between the monied establishment and APRA has been known as the "marriage of convenience" ever since. More radical feeling was aroused in the provinces by **Hugo Blanco**, when his followers created nearly 150 **syndicates,** whose peasant members began to work their own individual plots and refused to work for the hacienda owners. The second phase of Blanco's "reform" was to take physical control of the **haciendas,** mostly in areas so isolated that the authorities were powerless to intervene. Blanco was finally arrested in 1963 but the effects of his peasant revolt outlived him: in the future, Peruvian governments were to take agrarian reform far more seriously.

1963

Revolutionary Hugo Blanco creates nearly 150 *sindicatos* (workers' unions) around Cusco, whose peasant members work their own individual plots.

1968

On October 3, tanks smash into the Palacio de Gobierno; General Velasco and the army seize power.

1969

The new government gives land back to the workers. Great plantations are turned into cooperatives virtually overnight.

In Lima, the **elections** of 1962 had resulted in deadlock; almost inevitably, the army took control. In elections held a year later, Fernando Belaúnde, who had stood for election in the 1962 stalemate, won the vote and remained in power until 1969.

Land reform and the military regime

By the mid-1960s, many intellectuals and government officials saw the agrarian situation as an urgent economic problem as well as a matter of social justice. Even the army believed that **land reform** was a prerequisite for the development of a larger market, without which any genuine industrial development would prove impossible. President Belaúnde didn't agree. On October 3, 1968, tanks smashed through the gates into the courtyard of the Presidential Palace. General Velasco and the army seized power, deporting Belaúnde and ensuring that Haya de la Torre could not even participate in the forthcoming elections.

The new government, revolutionary for a **military regime**, gave the land back to the workers in 1969. The great plantations were turned virtually overnight into **cooperatives**, in an attempt to create a genuinely self-determining peasant class. At the same time guerrilla leaders were brought to trial, political activity was banned in the universities, indigenous banks were controlled, foreign banks nationalized and diplomatic relations established with East European countries. By the end of military rule, in 1980, the land-reform programme had done much to abolish the large capitalist landholding system.

The 1970s and 1980s

After twelve years of military government, the 1980 elections resulted in a centre-right alliance between Acción Popular and the Partido Popular Cristiano. **Belaúnde** resumed the presidency, having become an established celebrity during his years of exile and having built up, too, an impressive array of international contacts. The policy of his government was to increase the pace of development still further, and in particular to emulate Brazilian "success" in opening up the Amazon – building new roads and exploiting the untold wealth in terms of oil, minerals, timber and agriculture, at the cost of the local indigenous populations. But **inflation** continued as an apparently insuperable problem, and Belaúnde fared little better in coming to terms with either the parliamentary Marxists of the United Left or the escalating guerrilla movement led by Sendero Luminoso (see page 498).

The 1980s saw the growth of two major threats to the political and moral backbone of the nation – one through **guerrilla insurgency and terrorism**, the other through the growth of the **cocaine industry**.

Belaúnde lost the 1985 elections, with APRA (see page 496) taking power for the first time and the United Left also getting a large percentage of the votes. Led by a young, highly popular new president, **Alan García**, the APRA government took office riding a massive wave of hope. Sendero Luminoso, however, continued to step up its tactics of anti-democratic guerrilla warfare, and the isolation of Lima and the coast from much of the sierra and jungle regions became a very real threat. By 1985, new urban-based revolutionary groups like the **Movimiento Revolucionario Tupac Amaru** (**MRTA**) began to make their presence felt in the shantytowns around Lima. The

1978

After twelve years of military rule, elections result in a centre-right alliance between Acción Popular and Partido Popular Cristiano. Abimael Guzmán launches the revolutionary wing of Peru's communist party – the Sendero Luminoso (Shining Path).

1982

Alberto Fujimori gains a surprise victory over Mario Vargas Llosa in the presidential elections.

SENDERO LUMINOSO

Sendero Luminoso (the Shining Path), founded in 1980, persistently discounted the possibility of change through the ballot box. In 1976 it adopted armed struggle as the only means to achieve its "anti-feudal, anti-imperial" revolution in Peru. Following the line of the Chinese Gang of Four, Sendero was led by **Abimael Guzmán** (alias Comrade Gonzalo), whose ideas it claimed to be in the direct lineage of Marx, Lenin and Chairman Mao. Originally a brilliant philosophy lecturer from Ayacucho (specializing in the Kantian theory of space), before his capture by the authorities in the early 1990s Gonzalo lived mainly underground, rarely seen even by Senderistas themselves.

Rejecting Belaúnde's style of technological development as imperialist and the United Left as "parliamentary cretins", the group carried out attacks on business interests, local officials, police posts and anything regarded as outside interference with the self-determination of the peasantry. On the whole, members were recruited from the poorest areas of the country and from the **Quechua-speaking population**, coming together only for their paramilitary operations and melting back afterwards into the obscurity of their communities.

Although strategic points in **Lima** were frequently attacked – police stations, petrochemical plants and power lines – Sendero's main centre of activity was in the sierra around **Ayacucho** and **Huanta**, subsequently spreading into the remote regions around the central selva and a little further south in **Vilcabamba** – site of the last Inca resistance, a traditional hideout for rebels, and the centre of Hugo Blanco's activities in the 1960s.

Sendero was very active during the late 1980s and early 1990s, when it had some 10,000–15,000 **secret members**. Guzmán's success lay partly in his use of **Inca millennial mythology** and partly in the power vacuum left after the implementation of the agrarian reform and the resulting unrest and instability. The group's power and popular appeal advanced throughout the 1980s, spreading its wings over most of central Peru, much of the Amazon region, and to a certain extent into many of the northern and southern provincial towns.

Much of Sendero's funding came from the **cocaine trade**. Vast quantities of coca leaves are grown and partially processed all along the margins of Peruvian Amazonia. Much of this is flown clandestinely into Colombia where the processing is completed and the finished product exported to North America and Europe. The thousands of peasants who came down from the Andes to make a new life in the tropical forest throughout the 1980s found that **coca** was by far the most lucrative cash crop. The cocaine barons paid peasants more than they could earn elsewhere and at the same time bought protection from Sendero (some say at a rate of up to US$10,000 per clandestine plane-load).

MRTA had less success than the Senderistas, losing several of their leaders to Lima's prison cells. Their military confidence and capacity were also devastated when a contingent of some 62 MRTA militants was caught in an army ambush in April 1988; only eight survived from among two truckloads. To make things worse, a right-wing death squad – the **Rodrigo Franco Commando (RFC)** – appeared on the scene in 1988, evidently made up of disaffected police officers, army personnel and even one or two Apristas (APRA members). Meanwhile, the once young and popular President García got himself into a financial mess and went into exile, having been accused by the Peruvian judiciary of high-level corruption and possibly even "misplacing" millions of dollars belonging to the people of Peru.

1990s

Fujimori improves roads and takes a firm line with the guerrilla groups Sendero Luminoso and MRTA.

1992

After twelve very bloody years, during which 70,000 were killed, Sendero's leader Abimael Guzmán is captured in a Lima hideout, watching TV in his pyjamas.

THE JAPANESE EMBASSY HOSTAGE CRISIS

The mid-1990s was also the time when the **MRTA** militants battled against Fujimori and his government. On December 17, 1996, the MRTA really hit the headlines when they infiltrated the **Japanese ambassador's residence**, which they held under siege for 126 days, with over three hundred hostages. Some of these were released after negotiation, but Fujimori refused to give in to MRTA demands for the freedom of hundreds of their jailed comrades. Peruvian forces stormed the building in March 1997 – while the guerrillas were playing football inside the residence – massacring them all, though only one hostage perished in the attack. Fujimori's reputation as a hard man and a successful leader shot to new heights.

The 1990s

The year 1990 proved to be a turning point for Peru with the surprise electoral victory by an entirely new party – Cambio 90 (Change 90), formed only months before the election – led by a young college professor of Japanese descent, **Alberto Fujimori**. Fujimori implemented an economic shock strategy and the price of many basics such as flour and fuel trebled overnight. Fujimori did, however, manage to turn the nation around and gain an international confidence in Peru, reflected in the country's stock exchange – one of the fastest-growing and most active in the Americas.

However, the decade's pivotal moment was the capture of Sendero's leader **Abimael Guzmán** in September 1992. He was seized at his Lima hideout (a dance school) by General Vidal's secret anti-terrorist police, DINCOTE; even Fujimori didn't know about the raid until it had been successfully completed. With Guzmán in jail, and presented very publicly on TV as a defeated man, the political tide shifted. The international press no longer described Peru as a country where terrorists looked poised to take over, and Fujimori went from strength to strength, while Sendero's activities were reduced to little more than the occasional car bomb in Lima as they were hounded by the military in their remote hideouts along the eastern edges of the Peruvian Andes. All this was a massive boost to Fujimori's popularity in the elections of 1995, in which he gained over sixty percent of the vote. Perhaps it was also a recognition that his strong policies had paid off as far as the economy was concerned – inflation dipped from a record rate of 2777 percent in 1989 to 10 percent in 1996.

Fujimori continued to grow in popularity, despite Peru going to **war with Ecuador** briefly in January 1995, May 1997 and, more seriously, in 1998 – the border dispute was inflamed by the presence of large **oilfields** in the region. The two countries signed a formal peace treaty later that year. Arguably the most controversial revelations about Fujimori's second term in office concern the mass forced sterilizations between 1995 and 2000, which were inflicted on around 300,000 women – predominantly poor and indigenous – as well as on thousands of men. Fujimori and his health ministers were exonerated of criminal responsibility in 2016, but the women affected continue to fight for justice.

The twenty-first century

The dawn of the new millennium saw Fujimori attempting to stand for an unconstitutional **third term** in office. Even with his firm control of the media

2000

Fujimori insists on standing for a third term of office, despite constitutional term limits. By November, he is forced to resign following revelations of bribery and drug-money laundering, and flees to Japan.

2000–03

The economy is unstable and there are protests over the country's coca eradication programme.

PERU'S WHITE GOLD

Coca, the plant from which cocaine is derived, has come a long way since the Incas distributed this "divine plant" across fourteenth-century Andean Peru. Presented as a gift from the gods, coca was also used to exploit slave labour under Spanish rule: without it Peru's indigenous inhabitants would never have been able to work in the gruelling conditions of colonial mines such as Potosí.

The isolation of the active ingredient in coca, cocaine, in 1859, began an era of intense **medical experimentation**. Its numbing effects have been appreciated by dental patients around the world, and even Pope Leo XIII enjoyed a bottle of the coca wine produced by an Italian physician who amassed a great fortune from its sale in the nineteenth century. On a more popular level, coca was one of the essential ingredients in Coca-Cola until 1906.

Today, **cocaine** is one of the most fashionable – and expensive – illegal drugs. From its humble origins cocaine has become very big business. Unofficially, it may well be the biggest export for countries like Peru and Bolivia, where coca grows best in the Andes and along the edge of the jungle. While most mountain peasants have always cultivated a little for personal use, many have now become dependent on it for obvious economic reasons: coca is still the most profitable cash crop and is readily bought by middlemen operating for extremely wealthy cocaine barons. A constant flow of semi-refined coca paste leaves Peru aboard Amazon riverboats or ocean yachts, or in unmarked light aircraft heading for laboratories in Colombia, bound, ultimately, for markets in North America and Europe. For some rural farmers, it is the most profitable subsistence crop; for others cocaine is a scourge, bringing violence, the mobsters and deforestation in its wake.

(especially TV), he encountered strong opposition in the person of **Alejandro Toledo**, a *serrano* (of Quechua heritage) Perú Posible candidate, representing the interests of Andean cities and communities. Toledo had worked his way up from humble beginnings to become a UN and World Bank economist before standing for president.

Despite Toledo's popularity, Fujimori topped the vote in 2000, amidst unproven allegations of **fraud** and **vote rigging**, and Toledo eventually withdrew from the contest. However, by November the same year Fujimori was forced to resign, following revelations that his head of intelligence, **Vladimiro Montesinos**, had been videotaped bribing politicians before the last election and had also secreted hundreds of millions of dollars (believed to be drug money) in Swiss and other bank accounts around the world. It quickly became clear that Montesinos had exerted almost complete **control** over the president, the army, the intelligence service and the cocaine mafia during the preceding few years. Soon afterwards, Fujimori fled to Japan.

New elections were held in April 2001, which **Toledo** won easily, inheriting a cynical populace and a troubled domestic situation, with slow economic growth and deteriorating social conditions. During his tenure, Peru's Truth and Reconciliation Commission gave its final report on the country's civil conflict; although the Sendero Luminoso was blamed for starting the violence – and for over half of the estimated 70,000 deaths – the state, predominantly through the military, was also held responsible for thousands of deaths and abuses.

Despite dwindling popular support and with little or no backing from Peru's powerful elite business classes, Toledo clung onto his office until the elections of 2006, when he was replaced, amazingly, by an older and much plumper **Alan García**

2003

Political elections are held – ex-president Alan García wins, taking office for the second time. He is seen by many as putting Peru's natural resources out to auction and denies the existence of "uncontacted" indigenous peoples.

2009

After 65 days of protest at exploitation of the Amazon, President García sends in troops to break up a road block by indigenous communities, near Bagua. There are casualties on both sides: at least 32 dead and 200 injured.

– the very same man and ex-president who had left Peru and his first term of office in disgrace back in 1988. Meanwhile, Fujimori returned to South America via Chile in late 2005, and was arrested on arrival. Charged with human rights abuses and corruption (including payments to members of Congress and illegal wiretapping), he was extradited to Peru in 2007. Once back in Lima, he was convicted and sentenced to 25 years in prison until a presidential pardon in December 2017 saw him released on health grounds. However, Montesinos – Fujimori's former right-hand man, who was also convicted – remains locked up.

In the 2011 presidential election, career army officer Ollanta Humala narrowly defeated Keiko Fujimori (the ex-president´s daughter). Following Humala's victory, Peru's stock exchange fell amongst fears of the new president´s socialist and nationalist tendencies. Groundless fears, it turned out, as the president, ever the political chameleon, maintained his predecessors' economic policies and generally toed the line put forward by Miguel Castilla, the minister of economy and the most powerful figure in Humala's government. By the end of his tenure, Humala's initial, socialist policies – increased taxation on foreign mining companies, granting of land titles to indigenous communities, and a pledge to make Peru carbon neutral by 2021 – had all but been forgotten.

Humala's successor, voted into office in 2017, was former World Bank and IMF economist Pablo Pedro Kuczynski – commonly referred to as PPK. By the slenderest of margins, he defeated fellow right-wing opponent Keiko Fujimori, whose Fuerza Popular party holds the majority in Congress. After just over a year in office, PPK was implicated in the **Odebrecht bribery scandal** (or "Lava Jato"; see page 502); the allegations resulted in an impeachment vote in December 2017, which he narrowly survived, thanks to Kenji Fujimori (the ex-president's son) and nine other members of the opposition abstaining. But the suspicion was that PPK had bought Kenji's cooperation in exchange for his father's release – a move which unleashed a wave of protests nationwide, reopening old wounds concerning Alberto Fujimori's role in the atrocities committed by the state during Peru's civil conflict. Fast forward a few months to March 2018, and faced with the prospect of a second impeachment vote in the wake of new evidence, PPK resigned.

While the Odebrecht corruption scandal looks likely to rumble on and claim more scalps from the political and business elite, many of the problems facing ordinary Peruvians remain unaddressed, or are worsening, while social inequalities are all too apparent. Although Peru saw unprecedented economic growth throughout the 2000s, and **poverty levels** overall have decreased this millennium, over half the population still lives in poverty, predominantly in the rural areas of the Andes and the Amazon – especially among indigenous communities – and in the shantytowns of Lima. Successive governments' extractive neo-liberal agendas have prioritised mining and mega-development projects, while paying scant attention to the views or needs of the people most directly affected, and causing untold damage to the environment. The damage of these projects has been compounded by corrupt practices and poor government regulation. People in rural areas, and indigenous communities above all, are finding their lands under increasing threat, be it from drug-trafficking, environmental degradation or violence due to mining and the timber trades (see pages 514 and 515). Underfunding of public services and poor wages have resulted in

2009

Fujimori is sentenced to 25 years in prison on charges of human rights abuses and widespread corruption.

2011

Ollanta Humala wins the presidential elections on a socialist platform, but soon pursues a more right-wing, neoliberal agenda.

2014–16

Solid economic growth from the exploitation of Peru's mineral and timber resources continues to create conflict with local communities.

LAVA JATO – OPERATION "CAR WASH"

Known by its codename Lava Jato (Operation "Car Wash"), what started off as a run-of-the-mill money-laundering sting in Brazil has ballooned into one of the biggest **corporate scandals** in Latin American history, involving the political and business elites of at least twelve countries, including Peru. At the centre of the storm is Brazilian construction behemoth **Odebrecht**, responsible for many of the continent's mega-projects, from dams to highways, power stations to Olympic stadiums, including Lima's metro, the Carretera Interoceánica (connecting the Pacific with Brazil), and the 1000km-long gas pipeline in southern Peru. By way of plea-bargaining, Odebrecht's CEO, who was arrested in 2015, confessed to shelling out millions of dollars in bribes, paying off senior politicians and funding **presidential campaigns**, in return for overpriced contracts. In Peru's case, all four presidents sworn in this century are implicated: Toledo, García, Humala and Kuczynski, as well as Keiko Fujimori, the main opposition figure. Lesser government officials and corporate executives are already behind bars, while Peru's judiciary seeks Toledo's extradition from the US and Humala is awaiting trial. Kuczynski was eventually forced to resign in March 2018. Odebrecht's assets were frozen in 2017, and the company has been banned from any future contracts in Peru, but the fallout is already being felt in the economy: as major construction projects have been halted nationwide, around 150,000 labourers have lost their jobs.

a constant flow of protests and strikes by various public and private sector workers in recent years, as Peruvians become restless for real change. This agitation has led to a few small victories, in particular for some rural communities, with several mega development works being suspended due to sustained public protest.

2016

Andean farmer Maxima Acuña wins prestigious Goldman environmental award for her activism against the giant Conga gold mine.

2017–18

The release of senior Sendero Luminoso figures and pardon of ex-president Fujimori spark widespread protests. The Odebrecht bribery scandal implicates Peru's previous three presidents and forces the latest president, Kuczynski, to resign.

Inca culture

In less than a century, the Incas developed and knitted together a vast empire populated by something like twenty million indigenous people, that was to endure from 1200 to 1532. They established an imperial religion in relative harmony with those of their subject communities; erected monolithic fortresses, salubrious palaces and temples; and, astonishingly, evolved a viable economy – strong enough to maintain a top-heavy elite in almost godlike grandeur. To understand these achievements and get some idea of what they must have meant in Peru five or six hundred years ago, you really have to see for yourself their surviving heritage: the stones of Inca ruins and roads; the cultural objects in the museums of Lima and Cusco; and their living descendants who still work the soil and speak Quechua – the language used by the Incas to unify their empire.

Inca society

The Inca Empire rapidly developed a **hierarchical structure.** At the highest level it was governed by the **Sapa Inca**, son of the sun and direct descendant of the god Viracocha. Under him were the priest-nobles – the royal *ayllu* or kin-group who filled most of the important administrative and religious posts – and, working for them, regional *ayllu* chiefs (*curacas* or *orejones*), responsible for controlling tribute from the peasant base. The Inca nobles were fond of relaxing in thermal baths, of hunting holidays and of conspicuous eating and drinking whenever the religious calendar permitted. *Ayllu* chiefs were often unrelated to the royal Inca lineage, but their position was normally hereditary. As lesser nobles (*curacas*), they were allowed to wear earplugs and special ornate headbands; their task was to both protect and exploit the commoners, and they themselves were free of labour service. One-third of the land belonged to the emperor and the state; another to the high priests, gods and the sun; the last third was for the *ayllu* themselves.

In their conquests, the Incas absorbed **craftsmen** from every corner of the empire: goldsmiths, potters, carpenters, sculptors, masons and *quipumayocs* (accountants) were frequently removed from their homes to work directly for the emperor in Cusco. These skilled men lost no time in developing into a new and entirely separate class of citizen. The work of even the lowest servant in the palace was highly regulated by a rigid division of labour.

Special regulations affected both **senior citizens** and **people with disabilities**. Around the age of fifty, a man was likely to pass into the category of "old". He was no longer capable of undertaking a normal workload, he wasn't expected to pay taxes, and he could always depend on support from the official storehouses. Nevertheless, the community still made small demands by using him to collect firewood and other such tasks, in much the same way the kids were expected to help out around the house and in the fields. In fact, children and old people often worked together, the young learning directly from the old. Disabled people were obliged to work within their potential – the blind, for instance, might de-husk maize or clean cotton. Inca law also bound people with disabilities to marry those with similar disadvantages.

Inca women

Throughout the empire young girls, usually about 9 or 10 years old, were constantly selected for their beauty and serene intelligence. Those deemed perfect enough were taken to an *acllahuasi* – a special sanctuary for the "**chosen women**" – where they were trained in specific tasks, including the spinning and weaving of fine cloth, and the higher culinary arts. Most chosen women were destined ultimately to become *mamaconas* (Virgins of the Sun) or the concubines of either nobles or the Sapa Inca himself. Occasionally some of them were sacrificed by strangulation in order to appease the gods.

For most **Inca women** their allotted role was simply that of peasant/domestic work and rearing children. Women weren't counted in the census; for the Incas, a household was represented by the man and only he was obliged to fulfil tribute duties on behalf of the *ayllu*.

The Inca diet

The Inca diet was essentially **vegetarian**, based on the staple potato but encompassing a range of other foods like quinoa, beans, squash, sweet potatoes, avocados, tomatoes and manioc. In the highlands, emphasis was on root crops like potatoes, which have been known to survive in temperatures as low as 15°C (59°F) at over 5000m. On the valley floors and lower slopes of the Andes, maize cultivation predominated.

The importance of **maize** both as a food crop and for making *chicha* increased dramatically under the Incas; previously it had been grown for ceremony and ritual exchange, as a status rather than a staple crop. The use of **coca** was restricted to the priests and Inca elite. Coca is a mild narcotic stimulant which effectively dulls the body against cold, hunger and tiredness when the leaves are chewed in the mouth with a catalyst such as lime or calcium. The Incas believed its leaves possessed magical properties; they could be cast to divine future events, offered as a gift to the wind, the earth or the mountain *apu*, and they could be used in witchcraft.

As well as coca, their "divine plant", the Incas had their own special hallucinogen: **vilca** (meaning "sacred" in Quechua). The *vilca* tree (probably *Anadenanthera colubrina*) grows in the cloud-forest zones on the eastern slopes of the Peruvian Andes. The Incas used a snuff made from the seeds, which was generally blown up the nostrils of the participant by a helper. Evidently the Inca priests used *vilca* to bring on visions and make contact with the gods and spirit world.

Economy, agriculture and building

The main **resources** available to the Inca Empire were agricultural land and labour, mines (mainly gold, silver or copper) and fresh water, abundant everywhere except along the desert coast. With careful manipulation of these resources, the Incas managed to keep things moving the way they wanted. Tribute in the form of **service** (*mita*) played a crucial role in maintaining the empire and pressuring its subjects into ambitious building and irrigation projects. Some were so grand that they would have been impossible without the demanding whip of a totalitarian state.

Although a certain degree of local barter was allowed, the state regulated the distribution of important products. The astonishing Inca **highways** were one key to this economic success. Some of the tracks were nearly 8m wide and at the time of the Spanish Conquest the main Royal Highway ran some 5000km, from the Río Ancasmayo in Colombia down the backbone of the Andes to the coast, at a point south of the present-day Santiago in Chile. The Incas never used the wheel, but gigantic **llama caravans** were a common sight tramping along the roads, each animal carrying up to 50kg of cargo.

Every corner of the Inca domain was easily accessible via branch roads, all designed or taken over and unified with one intention – to dominate and administer an enormous empire. **Runners** were posted at *chasqui* stations, and *tambo* rest-houses punctuated the road at intervals of between 2km and 15km. Fresh fish was relayed on foot from the coast and messages were sent with runners from Quito to Cusco (2000km) in less than six days. The more difficult mountain canyons were crossed on bridges suspended from cables braided out of jungle lianas (creeping vines) and high passes were – and still are – frequently reached by incredible stairways cut into solid rock cliffs.

Agricultural terracing

The primary sector in the economy was inevitably **agriculture** and in this the Incas made two major advances: large terracing projects created the opportunity for agricultural specialists to experiment with new crops and methods of cultivation, and the transport system allowed a revolution in distribution. Massive agricultural **terracing projects** were going on continuously in Inca-dominated mountain regions. The best examples of these are in the Cusco area at Tipón, Moray, Ollantaytambo, Pisac and Cusichaca. Beyond the aesthetic beauty of Inca stone terraces, they have distinct practical advantages. Terraced hillsides minimize erosion from landslides, and using well-engineered stone channels gives complete control over irrigation.

Inca masonry

Today, however, it is Inca construction that forms their lasting heritage: vast **building projects** masterminded by high-ranking nobles and architects, and supervised by expert masons with an almost limitless pool of peasant labour. Without paper, the architects resorted to imposing their imagination onto clay or stone, making miniature models of the more important constructions – good examples of these can be seen in Cusco museums. More importantly, **Inca masonry** survives throughout Peru, most spectacularly at the fortress of Sacsayhuaman above Cusco, and on the coast in the Acueducto de Achirana, which still brings water down to the Valle de Ica from high up in the Andes.

Arts and crafts

Surprisingly, Inca masonry was rarely carved or adorned in any way. Smaller stone items, however, were frequently ornate and beautiful. High technical standards were achieved, too, in **pottery**. Around Cusco especially, the art of creating and glazing ceramics was highly developed. They were not so advanced artistically, however; Inca designs generally lack imagination and variety, tending to have been mass-produced from models evolved by previous cultures. The most common pottery object was the *aryballus*, a large jar with a conical base and a wide neck, thought to have been used chiefly for storing *chicha*. Its decoration was usually geometric, often associated with the backbone of a fish: the central spine of the pattern was adorned with rows of spikes radiating from either side. Fine plates were made with anthropomorphic handles, and large numbers of cylindrically tapering goblets – *keros* – were manufactured, though these were often of cedar wood rather than pottery.

Refinements in **metallurgy**, as with the ceramics, were mostly developed by craftsmen absorbed from different corners of the empire. The Chimú were particularly respected by the Incas for their superb metalwork. Within the empire, bronze and copper were used for axe-blades and *tumi* knives; gold and silver were restricted to ritual use and for nobles.

Religion

The Inca **religion** was easily capable of incorporating the religious features of most subjugated regions. The Incas merely superimposed their variety of mystical, yet inherently practical, elements onto those they came across. At the very top of the **religio-social hierarchy** was the Villac Uma, the high priest of Cusco, usually a brother of the Sapa Inca himself. Under him were perhaps hundreds of high priests, all nobles of royal blood who were responsible for ceremonies, temples, shrines, divination, curing and sacrifice within the realm, and below them were the ordinary priests and chosen women. At the base of the hierarchy, and probably the most numerous of all religious personalities, were the **curanderos**, local healers practising herbal medicine and magic, and making sacrifices to small regional *huacas* (sacred sites or temples).

Most **religious festivals** were calendar-based and marked by processions, sacrifices and dances. The Incas were aware of lunar time and the solar year, although they generally used the blooming of a special cactus and the stars to gauge the correct time to begin planting. Sacrifices to the gods normally consisted of llamas, *cuys* or *chicha* – only occasionally were chosen women and other adults killed. Once every year, however, young children were apparently sacrificed in the most important sacred centres.

Divination was a vital role played by priests and *curanderos* at all levels of the religious hierarchy. Soothsayers were expected to talk with the spirits and often used a hallucinogenic snuff from the *vilca* tree to achieve a trance-like state. Everything from a crackling fire to the glance of a lizard was seen as a potential omen, and treated as such by making a little offering of coca leaves, coca spittle or *chicha*. There were specific problems which divination was considered particularly accurate in solving: retrieving lost things; predicting the outcome of certain events (including military expeditions); and the diagnosis of illness.

Gods and symbols

The main religious novelty introduced with Inca domination was their demand to be recognized as direct descendants of the creator-god **Viracocha**. A claim to divine ancestry was, to the Incas, a valid excuse for military and cultural expansion. They felt no need to destroy the *huacas* and oracles of subjugated peoples; on the contrary, certain sacred sites were recognized as intrinsically holy, as powerful places for communication with the spirit world. When ancient shrines like Pachacamac, near Lima, were absorbed into the empire they were simply turned over to worship on imperial terms.

The **sun** is the most obvious symbol of Inca belief, a chief deity and the visible head of the state religion. The sun's role was overt, as life-giver to an agriculturally based empire, and its cycle was intricately related to agrarian practice and annual ritual patterns. To think of the Inca religion as essentially sun worship, though, would be far too simplistic. There were distinct **layers** in Inca cosmology: the level of creation, the astral level and the earthly dimension. The first, highest, level corresponds to Viracocha as the creator-god who brought life to the world and society to mankind. Below this, on the astral level, are the celestial gods: the sun itself, the moon and certain stars (particularly the Pleiades, patrons of fertility). The earthly dimension, although that of man, was no less magical, endowed with important *huacas* and shrines which might take the form of unusual rocks or peaks, caves, tombs, mummies and natural springs.

Peruvian music

Latin America's oldest musical traditions are those of the Amerindians of the Andes. Their music is best known outside these countries through the characteristic panpipes of poncho-clad folklore groups. However, there's a multitude of rhythms and popular music alive in Peru that deserve a lot more recognition, including *huayno, chicha, cumbia,* Afro-Peruvian and even reggaeton.

For most people outside Latin America the sound of the Andes is that of bamboo panpipes and *quena* flutes. What is most remarkable is that these instruments have been used to create music in various parts of this large area of mountains – which stretch 7200km from Venezuela down to southernmost Chile – since before the time of the Incas. Pre-Conquest Andean instruments – conch-shell trumpets, shakers which used nuts for rattles, ocarinas, wind instruments and drums – are ever-present in museum collections.

Andean music can be divided roughly into three types: first, that which is of **indigenous origin**, found mostly among rural Amerindian peoples still living very much by the seasons; secondly, music of **European origin**; and thirdly, **mestizo music**, which continues to fuse the indigenous with the European in a whole host of ways. In general, Quechua people have more vocal music than the Aymara.

Traditional music

Panpipes, known by the Aymara as *siku*, by the Quechua as *antara* and by the Spanish as *zampoña*, are ancient instruments, and archeologists have unearthed them tuned to a variety of scales. Simple **notched-end flutes**, or *quenas*, are another independent innovation of the Andean highlands found in both rural and urban areas. The most important pre-Hispanic instrument, they were traditionally made of fragile bamboo (though often these days from plumbers' PVC water pipes) and played in the dry season, with *tarkas* (vertical flutes – like a shrill recorder) taking over in the wet. *Quenas* are played solo or in ritual groups and remain tremendously popular today, with many virtuoso techniques.

MUSIC AT TRADITIONAL FESTIVALS

Peru's many **festivals** are a rewarding source of traditional music. One of the best takes place in January on the island of **Amantani** in Lago Titicaca, its exact date, as is often the case in the Andean highlands, determined by astronomical events. The festival occurs during a period often called the "time of protection", when the rainy season has finally begun. It is related to the cleansing of the pasturage and water sources; stone fences are repaired, walking paths repaved, and the stone effigies and crosses that guard the planting fields replaced or repaired. A single-file "parade" of individuals covers the entire island, stopping to appease the deities and provide necessary maintenance at each site. At the front are local nonprofessional musicians, all male, playing drums and flutes of various types.

Some festivals are celebrated on a larger scale. On the day of the June solstice (midwinter in the Andes) the Inca would ceremonially tie the sun to a stone and coax it to return south, bringing warmer weather and the new planting season. **Inti Raymi**, the Festival of the Sun, is still observed in every nook and cranny in the Andean republics, from the capital city to the most isolated hamlet. The celebration, following a solemn ritual that may include a llama sacrifice, is more of a carnival than anything else. Parades of musicians, both professional bands and thrown-together collages of amateurs, fill the streets. You will be expected to drink and dance until you drop, or hide in your room. This kind of party can run for several days, so be prepared.

Large **marching bands** of drums and panpipes, playing in the cooperative "back and forth" leader/follower style that captivated the Spanish in the 1500s, can still be seen and heard today. The drums are deep-sounding, double-headed instruments known as *bombos* or *wankaras*. These bands exist for parades at life-cycle fiestas, weddings and dances in the regions surrounding the Peruvian–Bolivian frontier and around Lago Titicaca. Apart from their use at fiestas, panpipes are played mainly in the dry season, from April to October.

Folk music festivals to attract and entertain the tourist trade are a quite different experience to music in the village context. While positively disseminating the music, they have introduced the notion of judging and the concept of "best" musicianship – ideas totally at odds with rural community values of diversity in musical repertoire, style and dress.

Charangos and mermaids

The **charango** is another major Andean instrument whose bright, zingy sounds are familiar worldwide. This small guitar – with five pairs of strings – was created in imitation of early guitars and lutes brought by the Spanish colonizers, which Amerindian musicians were taught to play in the churches. Its small size is due to its traditional manufacture from armadillo shells, while its sound quality comes from the indigenous aesthetic that has favoured high pitches from the pre-Columbian period through to the present.

In rural areas in southern Peru, particularly in the Titicaca region and province of Canas, the *charango* is the main instrument – used by young **single men** to woo and court the female of choice. Some villagers construct the sound box in the shape of a **mermaid**, including her head and fish tail, to invest their *charango* with supernatural power. When young men go courting at the weekly markets in larger villages they will not only dress in their finest clothes, but dress up their *charangos* in elaborate coloured ribbons.

Song and brass

Most **singing** in the Andes is done by women, and the preferred style is very high-pitched – almost falsetto to Western ears. There are songs for potato-growing, reaping barley, threshing wheat, marking cattle, sheep and goats, for building houses, for traditional dances and funerals and for many other ceremonies.

Huaynos and orquestas típicas

Visit the Peruvian central sierra and you find a music as lively and energetic as the busy market towns it comes from, and largely unknown outside the country. These songs and dances are **huaynos**, one of the few musical forms that reach back to pre-Conquest times, although the **orquestas típicas** that play them, from sierra towns like Huancayo, Ayacucho and Pucará, include saxophones, clarinets and trumpets alongside traditional instruments like violins, *charangos* and the large Amerindian harp. The buoyant, swinging rhythms of *huayno* songs are deceptive, for the lyrics fuse joy and sorrow; sung in a mixture of Spanish and Quechua, they tell of unhappy love and betrayal, celebrate passion and often deliver homespun philosophy.

Afro-Peruvian music

Afro-Peruvian music has its roots in the communities of black slaves brought to work in the mines along the Peruvian coast. As such, it's a fair way from the Andes, culturally and geographically. However, as it developed, particularly in the twentieth century, it drew on Andean and Spanish, as well as African traditions, while its modern exponents also have affinities with Andean *nueva canción*. The music was little known even in Peru until the 1950s, when it was popularized by the seminal performer Nicomedes Santa Cruz, whose body of work was taken a step further in the 1970s by the group

Perú Negro. Internationally, it has had a recent airing through David Byrne's Luaka Bop label, issuing the compilation, *Perú Negro*, and solo albums by the now world-renowned **Susana Baca**.

Nicomedes Santa Cruz is the towering figure in the development of Afro-Peruvian music. A poet, musician and journalist, he was the first true musicologist to assert an Afro-Peruvian cultural identity through black music and dance, producing books and recordings of contemporary black music and culture in Peru. In 1964 he recorded a four-album set *Cumanana*, now regarded as the bible of Afro-Peruvian music. Santa Cruz himself followed in the footsteps of **Porfirio Vásquez**, who came to Lima in 1920 and was an early pioneer of the movement to regain the lost cultural identity of Afro-Peruvians. A composer of *décimas*, singer, guitarist, *cajonero* (box player) and *zapateador* (dancer), he founded the Academia Folklórica in Lima in 1949. Through Santa Cruz's work and that of the group **Perú Negro** and the singer and composer **Chabuca Granda**, Latin America came to know Afro-Peruvian dances, the names of which were given to their songs, such as *Toro Mata*, *Samba-malató*, *El Alcatraz* and *Festejo*.

Chicha and Cumbia

Chicha, the fermented maize beer, has given its name to a hugely popular brew of Andean tropical music, one which has recently spread to wider Anglophone world music circles. The music's origins lie in the rapidly urbanizing Amazon of the late 1960s, in places like Iquitos and Pucallpa, where bands such as **Los Mirlos** and **Juaneco y Su Combo** fused *cumbia* (local versions of the original Colombian dance), traditional highland *huayno* and Western rock and psychedelia. In the 1970s, mass migration carried *chicha* to Lima, and by the mid-1980s, it had become the most widespread urban music in Peru. Most bands have lead and rhythm guitars, electric bass, electric organ, a *timbales* and conga player, one or more vocalists (who may play percussion) and, if they can, a synthesizer. While most lyrics are about love in all its aspects, nearly all songs actually reveal an aspect of the harshness of the Amerindian experience – displacement, hardship, loneliness and exploitation.

Chicha, and, more recently, the Peruvian version of *cumbia* (which is clearly more *cumbia* than *chicha*), has taken root and also achieved international acclaim. In Peru itself, this belated international recognition has witnessed a resurgence in interest in seminal artists like Juaneco y Su Combo, currently feted by the Lima cognoscenti and the subject of their own recent Barbès retrospective, *Juaneco y Su Combo: Masters of Chicha Volume 1*. The label even has its own in-house band, Chicha Libre, whose excellent debut, *!Sonido Amazónico!*, was released in early 2008. In the last few years, Peruvian *cumbia* artists, like Barreto and also the Hermanos Yaipen, have become very popular. In 2012, during the Selvámonos Festival, a new group of *cumbia* musicians was formed: Cumbia All Stars. Its members are veterans of Peruvian *cumbia* from the 1970s, and their psychedelic brand of *cumbia* hit a chord not only locally but also internationally.

Reggaeton

More rap than reggae, **reggaeton** is popular with the urban youth of Peru today. With Jamaican reggae roots, this sexually explicit and fairly macho genre began life in Panama and Puerto Rico in the late 1980s. Spreading slowly in underground fashion it gradually became popular all over Latin America until breaking through into radio and TV music channels in the twenty-first century. It hit the clubs of Lima between 2007 and 2011, scandalizing the Catholic establishment there with its sexually explicit *el perreo* dancing. If you sample the nightlife in Lima's clubs, you're bound to find this music style thriving in the early hours.

Original material written by Jan Fairley. Adapted from the *Rough Guide to World Music*, Vol 2. with additional contributions by Brendon Griffin.

Natural Peru

Peru's varied ecological niches span an incredible range of climate and terrain; the Amazon region covers 60 percent of Peru's land surface, yet has only nine percent of its population; the highlands cover 28 percent of the land but are home to only 38 percent of the country's people; the desert coast, where 53 percent of Peruvians live, comprises a mere 12 percent of its land area. Between these three major zones, the ecological reality is continuous intergradation, encompassing literally dozens of unique habitats. Humans have occupied Peru for perhaps twenty thousand years, but there has been less disturbance there, until relatively recently, than in most other parts of our planet, which makes it a top-class ecotourism and wildlife photo-safari destination.

The coast

Peru's **coast** is characterized by abundant sea life and by the contrasting scarcity of terrestrial plants and animals. The **Humboldt current** runs virtually the length of Peru, bringing cold water up from the depths of the Pacific Ocean and causing any moisture to condense out over the sea, depriving the mainland coastal strip and lower western mountain slopes of rainfall, thereby maintaining a desert or semi-desert environment. Along with this cold water, large quantities of nutrients are carried up to the surface, helping to sustain a rich planktonic community able to support vast numbers of fish, preyed upon in their turn by a variety of coastal birds: gulls, terns, pelicans, boobies, cormorants and wading birds are always present along the beaches. One beautiful specimen, the **Inca tern**, although usually well camouflaged as it sits high up on inaccessible sea cliffs, is nevertheless very common in the Lima area. The **Humboldt penguin**, with grey rather than black features, is a rarer sight – shyer than its more southerly cousins, it is normally found in isolated rocky coves or on offshore islands. Competing with the birds for fish are schools of dolphins, sea lion colonies and the occasional coastal otter. Dolphins and sea lions are often spotted off even the most crowded of beaches or scavenging around the fishermen's jetty at Chorrillos, near Lima.

One of the most fascinating features of Peruvian birdlife is the number of vast, **high-density colonies**: although the number of species is quite small, their total population is enormous. Many thousands of birds can be seen nesting on islands like the Ballestas, off the Paracas Peninsula, or simply covering the ocean with a flapping, diving carpet of energetic feathers. This huge bird population, and the **Guanay cormorant** in particular, is responsible for depositing mountains of guano (bird droppings), which form a traditional and potent source of natural fertilizer.

The coastal desert

In contrast to these rich waters the **coastal desert** lies stark and barren. Here you find only a few trees and shrubs; you'll need endless patience to find wild animals other than birds. The most common animals are feral **goats**, once domesticated but now living wild, and **burros** (donkeys) introduced by the Spanish. A more exciting sight is the attractively coloured **coral snake** – shy but deadly and covered with black and orange hoops. Most animals are more active after sunset; when out in the desert you can hear the eerily plaintive call of the **huerequeque** (Peruvian thick-knee bird), and the barking

EL NIÑO

In order to understand the Peruvian coastal desert you have to bear in mind the phenomenon of **El Niño**, a periodic climatic shift, of varying strengths, caused by the displacement of the cold Humboldt current by warmer equatorial waters. El Niño causes the plankton and fish communities either to disperse to other locations or to collapse entirely. At such a period, the shore rapidly becomes littered with carrion, since many of the sea mammals and birds are unable to survive in the limited environment. Scavenging condors and vultures, on the other hand, thrive, as does the desert – except where flooding is very severe – where rain falls in deluges along the coast, with a consequent bloom of vegetation and rapid growth in animal populations. When the Humboldt current returns, the desert dries up and its animal populations decline to normal sizes (another temporary feast for the scavengers). While it used to be at least ten years before this cycle was repeated, global warming over the last three decades has witnessed the pattern becoming much more erratic. The most recent extreme El Niño occurred in 2017, resulting in the worst flooding in almost a century in northern Peru; it left around 90 dead and hundreds of thousands homeless, and caused an estimated US$3 billion in damage. Generally considered a freak phenomenon, El Niño is probably better understood as an integral part of coastal ecology; without it the desert would be a far more barren and static environment, virtually incapable of supporting life. At the same time El Niño also needs to be considered in tandem with its antithesis, **La Niña** – which often follows on from an El Niño year. In the case of La Niña, the Humboldt current cools more than usual, resulting in colder temperatures on land, but also greater upwellings in the ocean, and an even greater abundance of plankton for larger marine life to feast on.

of the little **desert fox** – alarmingly similar to the sound of car tyres screeching to a halt. By day you might see several species of small birds, a favourite being the vermilion-headed **Peruvian flycatcher**. Near water – rivers, estuaries and lagoons – desert wildlife is at its most populous. In addition to residents such as **flamingoes**, **herons** and **egrets**, many migrant birds pause in these havens between October and March on their journeys south and then back north.

The mountains

The **Peruvian Andes** possess an incredible variety of habitats. That this is a mountain area of true extremes becomes immediately obvious if you fly across, or along, the Andes towards Lima, the land below shifting from high *puna* to cloud forest to riparian valleys and eucalyptus tracts (trees introduced from Australia in the 1880s). The complexity of the whole makes it incredibly difficult to formulate any overall description that isn't essentially misleading: climate and vegetation vary according to altitude, latitude and local characteristics.

The Andes divides vertically into three main regions, identified by the Incas from top to bottom as the Puna, the Qeswa and the Yunka. The **Puna**, roughly 3800–4300m above sea level, has an average temperature of 3–6°C (37–43°F), and annual rainfall of 500–1000mm. Typical animals here include the main Peruvian cameloids – llamas, alpacas, guanacos and vicuñas – while crops that grow well here include the potato and quinoa grain. At 2500–3500m, the **Qeswa** has average temperatures of around 13°C (55°F), and a similar level of rainfall at 500–1200mm. The traditional forest here, including Andean pine, is not abundant and has been largely displaced by the imported and invasive Australian eucalyptus tree; the main cultivated crops include maize, potatoes and the nutritious *kiwicha* grain. The *ceja de selva* (cloud forest to high forest on the eastern side of the Andes) forms the lower-lying **Yunka**, at 1200–2500m, and has at least twice as much rain as the other two regions and abundant wildlife, including Peru's national bird, the red-crested *gallito de las rocas* (cock-of-the-rock). Plant life, too, is prolific, not least the region's orchids. On the western side of the Andes there is much less rainfall and it's not technically known as the Yunka, but it does share some characteristics: both sides have wild river canes (*caña brava*), and both are suitable for cultivating banana, pineapple, *yuca* and coca.

Mountain flora and fauna

Much of the Andes has been settled for over two thousand years – and there were hunter communities another eight thousand years before this – so larger predators are rare, though still present in small numbers in the more remote regions. Among the most exciting you might actually see are the **mountain cats**, especially the **puma**, which lives at most altitudes and in a surprising number of habitats. Other more remote predators include the shaggy-looking **maned wolf** and the likeable **spectacled bear**, which inhabits the moister forested areas of the Andes and actually prefers eating vegetation to people.

The most visible animals in the mountains, besides sheep and cattle, are the cameloids – the wild **vicuña** and **guanaco**, and the domesticated **llama** and **alpaca**. Although these species are clearly related, zoologists disagree on whether or not the alpaca and llama are domesticated forms of their wild relatives. Domesticated they are, however, and have been so for thousands of years; studies reveal that cameloids appeared in North America some forty to fifty million years ago, crossing the Bering Straits long before any humans did. From these early forms the present species have evolved in Peru, Bolivia, Chile, Argentina and Ecuador, and there are now over three million llamas – 33 percent in Peru and a further 63 percent over the border in Bolivia. The alpaca population is just under four million, with 87 percent in Peru and only 11 percent in Bolivia. Of the two wild cameloids, the vicuña is the smaller and rarer, living only at the highest altitudes (up to 4500m) and with a population of just over 120,000. There are 5000 guanaco in Peru, compared to around 550,000 in Argentina alone.

Andean deer (tarucas) are quite common in the higher valleys and with luck you may even come across the rare **mountain tapir**. Smaller animals tend to be confined to particular habitats – rabbit-like **viscachas**, for example, to rocky outcrops; **squirrels** to wooded valleys; and **chinchillas** (Peruvian chipmunks) to higher altitudes.

Most birds also tend to restrict themselves to specific habitats. The **Andean goose** and **duck** are quite common in marshy areas, along with many species of wader and migratory waterfowl. A particular favourite is the elegant, very pink, **Andean flamingo**, which can usually be spotted from the road between Arequipa and Puno where they turn Lake Salinas into one great red mass. In addition, many species of passerine can be found alongside small streams. Perhaps the most striking of them is the **dipper**, which hunts underwater for larval insects along the stream bed, popping up to a rock every so often for air and a rest. At lower elevations, especially in and around cultivated areas, the **ovenbird** (or horneo) constructs its nest from mud and grasses in the shape of an old-fashioned oven; while in open spaces many birds of prey can be spotted, the comical **caracara**, **buzzard-eagle** and the magical **red-backed hawk** among them. **Andean condors** are actually quite difficult to see up close as, although not especially rare, they tend to soar at tremendous heights for most of the day, landing only on high, inaccessible cliffs, or at carcasses after making sure that no one is around to disturb them. A glimpse of this magnificent bird soaring overhead will come only through frequent searching with binoculars, perhaps in relatively unpopulated areas or at one of the better-known sites such as the Cruz del Cóndor viewing platform in the Cañón del Colca (see page 179).

Tropical rainforest

Descending the eastern edge of the Andes, you pass through the distinct habitats of the Puna, Qeswa and Yunka before reaching the lowland jungle or **rainforest**. In spite of its rich and luxuriant appearance, the rainforest is in fact extremely fragile. Almost all the nutrients are recycled by rapid decomposition (with the aid of the damp climate and a prodigious supply of insect labour) back into the vegetation, thereby creating a nutrient-poor soil that is highly susceptible to large-scale disturbance. When the forest is cleared, for example – usually in an attempt to colonize the area and turn it into viable farmland – there is not only heavy soil erosion to contend with but also a limited amount of nutrients in the earth (only enough for five years of good harvests and twenty years' poorer farming at the most). Indigenous populations of the rainforest have evolved cultural mechanisms by which, on the whole, these problems are avoided: they tend to live in small, dispersed groups, move their cultivations every few years and obey sophisticated social controls to limit the chances of overexploiting any one zone or any particular species.

Around eighty percent of the Amazon rainforest was still intact at the start of the twenty-first century, but for every **hardwood** logged in this forest, an average of 120 other trees are destroyed and left unused or simply burnt. Over an acre per second of this magnificent forest is burnt or bulldozed, equating to an area the size of Great Britain **every year**, even though this makes little economic sense in the long term. According to the late rainforest specialist Dr Alwyn Gentry, just 2.5 acres of primary rainforest could yield up to US$9000 a year from sustainable harvesting of wild fruits, saps, resins and timber – yet the average income for the same area from ranching or plantations in the Amazon is a meagre US$30 a year.

Amazon flora and fauna

The most distinctive attribute of the Amazon Basin is its overwhelming abundance of plant and animal species. Over six thousand species of plants have been reported in one small 250-acre tract of forest, and there are at least a thousand species of birds and dozens of types of monkeys and bats spread about the Peruvian Amazon. There are several reasons for this marvellous **natural diversity** of flora and fauna; most obviously, it is warm, there is abundant sunlight and large quantities of mineral nutrients are washed down from the Andes – ideal conditions for forest growth. Secondly, the rainforest has enormous structural diversity, with layers of vegetation from the forest floor to the canopy 30m above, providing a vast number of niches to fill. Thirdly, since there is such a variety of habitat as you descend the Andes, the changes in altitude mean a great diversity of localized ecosystems. With the rainforest being stable over longer periods of time than temperate areas (there was no Ice Age here, nor any prolonged periods of drought), the fauna has had the freedom to evolve, and to adapt to often very specialized local conditions.

But even though the Amazon Basin boasts Peru's greatest variety of plant and animal species, it is no easy task to see them. Movement through the vegetation is limited to narrow trails and along the rivers in a boat. The riverbanks and flood plains are richly diverse areas: here you are likely to see **caimans**, **macaws**, **toucans**, **oropendulas**, **terns**, **horned screamers** and the primitive **hoatzins** – birds whose young are born with claws at the wrist to enable them to climb up from the water into the branches of overhanging trees. You should catch sight, too, of one of a variety of **hawks** and at least two or three species of **monkeys** (perhaps the **spider monkey**, the **howler** or the **capuchin**). With a lot of luck and more determined observation you may spot a rare **giant river otter**, **river dolphin**, or **capybara**, or maybe even one of the **jungle cats**.

In the rainforest proper you're more likely to find mammals such as the **peccary** (wild pig), **tapir**, **tamandua tree sloth** and the second largest cat in the world, the incredibly powerful **spotted jaguar**. Characteristic of the deeper forest zones, too, are many species of bird, including **hummingbirds** (more common in the forested Andean foothills), **manakins** and **trogons**, though the effects of widespread hunting make it difficult to see these around any of the larger settlements. Logging is proving to be another major problem for the forest fauna – since valuable trees are dispersed among vast areas of other species in the rainforest, a very large area must be disturbed to yield

CONSERVATION AND ENVIRONMENTAL POLITICS IN PERU

Climate change is already having serious impacts on Peru's priceless environment and the country is widely recognized as being extremely vulnerable to the impacts of climate change. Couple this with the long-term effects of a vast, profitable, yet inadequately regulated mining sector, and you have the ingredients for a potent political cocktail.

DIMINISHING GLACIERS

The **glaciers** are retreating fast. South America possesses more than 99 percent of the world's tropical glaciers, with over seventy percent of these located in Peru, where they act as a **reservoir** of meltwater, which provides two vital resources: on the one hand, the meltwater provides water for drinking, hydroelectricity, agriculture and industry across the Andes and along the desert coast, even during the dry season; at the same time, and in the opposite direction, the glaciers feed the main headwaters of the Amazon Basin. With the glaciers diminishing, problems are arising already in both directions – water shortages on the coast and very low dry-season river levels in the Amazon. The Peruvian glaciers, essential stores of the planet's most basic resource, have been described by Lonnie Thompson (an Ohio State University glaciologist) as the "water towers of the world". Nevertheless, Peru's most visited glacier – Pastoruri (see page 318), near the city of Huaraz – and previously its main ski resort, has lost more than half of its surface area since 1995 and some predictions estimate that it will have vanished completely by 2020. To compound matters, as the glaciers retreat, metal-rich rock is exposed and the meltwaters wash lead, arsenic and other **contaminants** into the rivers, causing pollution problems for communities downstream.

GROUND AND WATER POLLUTION

Ground and water **pollution**, among the worst in the world, has become a concern and a source of conflict around many of Peru's Andean mining towns. Just four hours by road from Lima, La Oroya in Junín – home to a smelting plant since 1922 – hit the international headlines when in 2007 it was branded one of the ten most polluted places on the planet; tests found over ninety percent of children had three times the legal limit of **lead** in their blood and on some days sulphur dioxide emissions were ten times over the safe limit. What's more, although the smelter was subsequently closed down, the lead may remain in the soil for centuries, affecting generations to come. Mines in the nearby Mantaro river basin pour contaminated waters downstream, affecting the health of indigenous and settler populations along the Amazon headwaters. These are not isolated problems; with over 200 mines legally operating throughout Peru, and many more planned, pollution is a country-wide concern. Yet the illegal mines – predominantly extracting gold in regions such as Madre de Dios (see page 436) – are arguably causing even greater contamination, through mercury poisoning.

COMMUNITY–MINING CONFLICTS

Protests against the big mining corporations by local communities in mineral-rich areas (and downriver from them) have been escalating over the last two decades; demonstrations or road blocks preventing access to/from the mines have sometimes flared into **violence**, resulting in injuries and occasionally fatalities, especially when riot police and/or the military have been sent in. In addition to concerns about environmental pollution and its attendant health risks, local people are worried about **water availability**. Construction on the gigantic Tia Maria copper mine in the Arequipa region – forecast to be the fifth largest such mine in the world – was suspended in 2015 after violent clashes with protestors, concerned that in this particularly arid area there would insufficient water for agriculture. In 2017, six years after they had started construction, Canadian mining giant Newmont Mining pulled out of the huge Conga Mine, having failed to quell people's anger at their plans to drain three lakes and replace them with reservoirs. Lack of **community consultation**, lack of jobs for local people, companies reneging on promised social development projects, and absent clean-up operations in the case of contamination are just a few instances of the litany of complaints to be laid at the feet of successive Peruvian governments (see page 501).

a relatively small amount of timber. Deeper into the forest, however, and the further you are from human habitation, a glimpse of any of these animals is quite possible.

Most of the bird activity occurs in the canopy, 30 to 40m above the ground, but platforms such as the **canopy walkway** at the Amazon Explorama ACTS Field Station (see page 479) and another, newer one at Inkaterra's Reserva Amazonica (see page 445), on the Río Madre de Dios, make things a little easier.

Deforestation and the timber industry

According to the UN Food and Agriculture Organization (FAO) 2015 forestry survey, around 58 percent of Peru is forested. Of this, over eighty percent is classified as **primary forest**, the most biodiverse and carbon-dense form. Yet **deforestation** is responsible for about half of Peru's carbon dioxide emissions, predominantly to clear land for smallholdings. Alongside this there's the obvious travesty of concomitant destruction of forest habitats and biodiversity – Peru has around 3000 known species of amphibians, birds, mammals and reptiles – and of the homes of many indigenous peoples. According to a study by the Instituto del Bien Común, a Peruvian non-profit organization, between 2001 and 2015 Peru lost almost 200 square kilometres of forest in Amazonia – an area almost the size of Wales (or slightly larger than Washington State). Then there's the insidious threat of **forest degradation,** such as thinning through timber extraction, whose extent is only just beginning to be known thanks to new remote sensing technologies.

Despite Peru's vested interest in mitigating climate change, **logging** of the Amazon region continues apace; a 2012 World Bank report estimated that as much as eighty percent of Peru's logging exports are harvested illegally but whitewashed with fake documents by the time the logs reach Lima and the port of Callao for export. These suspicions were further confirmed in 2014 by Operación Amazonas, a much-publicised investigation into the **illegal timber trade** by the Environment Investigation Agency (EIA; ⓦeia-global.org), an international NGO. The enquiry was coordinated by SUNAT (Peruvian customs), in collaboration with OSINFOR (the Peruvian government's forestry watchdog) and even involved the World Customs Organisation and INTERPOL. Following investigations into the main lumber ship out of Iquitos, the Yacu Kallpa, extensive fieldwork in the forest, and auditing of documents in Callao, the report concluded that on average over ninety percent of the timber leaving Peru was illicit. As a result, millions of dollars of illegal timber was seized, logging permits were cancelled, and rainforest communities at fault were fined. In April 2016, for the first time, nineteen illegal logging gang members – including two police officers and two forestry officials – were arrested.

Yet putting an end to the illegal timber trade in the long-term is not so simple, given the underfunding of the government sectors involved in policing the industry, the complicity of government officials at local, regional and national levels, and the involvement of organized criminal networks in the timber trade, whose tentacles stretch as far as the destination countries in North America and parts of Europe and Asia. Shortly after the EIA exposé was published, loggers whose livelihoods were threatened by the crackdown led angry protests in Iquitos and Pucallpa – major centres of the illegal timber trade – while officials involved in the investigation received death threats. Under pressure from the forestry industry, President Humala sacked the head of OSINFOR, who then fled the country in fear of his life. What's more, the legal documentary requirements that had helped investigators identify the source of illicit timber were dropped by the Peruvian government, making it impossible to carry out similar audits in the future.

Illegal gold mining

Peru's worst example of **illegal gold mining** is found in the southeastern forests of Madre de Dios, home to the Amarakaeri people, where monster-sized machinery is transforming one of the Amazon's most biodiverse regions into a huge muddy scar. A number of gold miners have already moved into the unique Reserva Nacional

MEGADAMS

The Brazilian electricity company Electrobras has an agreement with Peru to build at least six **megadams** to generate electricity in the Peruvian Amazon over the coming years. The plan is that eighty percent of the electricity produced, initially at least, be exported to Brazil to power **aluminium plants** in the western Brazilian Amazon. The dams are so big, however, that their social and environmental impact would be devastating, and the project is seen as another of ex-President García's big thumbs-down to the environment and indigenous Peruvian communities. Currently there are some seventy dams planned for the Amazon basin over the next forty years. In January 2018, however, there were indications that the Brazilian government might shift away from a policy of building megadams, in part due to pressure from environmental and indigenous rights activists; it remains to be seen whether this will impact on Peru. More information on megadam proposals can be found at Ⓦinternationalrivers.org and Ⓦcircleofblue.org.

Tambopata, a protected rainforest area where giant otters, howler monkeys, king vultures, anacondas and jaguars are regularly spotted. An estimated 20,000–30,000 illegal miners are now working in either the adjacent buffer zone, or in the reserve itself. All plant life around each mine is turned into gravel, known in Peru as *cancha*, for just a few ounces of gold a day. Front-loading machines move up to about thirty metres depth of soil, which is then washed on a wooden sluice where high-pressure hoses separate the silt and gold from mud and gravel. **Mercury**, added at this stage to facilitate gold extraction, is later burnt off, causing river and air pollution. The mines are totally unregulated and, since gold prices rocketed following the 2008 global financial crisis, criminal gangs linked to drug trafficking are increasingly running the show; they have the money to import large machines and employ trigger-happy armed guards to ward off unwanted interference.

The **indigenous peoples** are losing control of their territory to an ever-increasing stream of these miners and settlers coming down from the high Andes. As the mercury pollution and suspended mud from the mines upstream kill the life-giving rivers, they have to go deeper and deeper into the forest for fish, traditionally their main source of protein. Beatings and death threats from the miners and police are not uncommon, though many of the miners themselves are exploited.

There is a hope that improved **gold-mining technology** can stem the tide of destruction in these areas; mercury levels in Amazon rivers and their associated food chains are rising at an alarming rate. In a much-publicised health survey across Madre de Dios, over 75 percent of the 1000 people whose hair was tested had levels of mercury above WHO safety limits. However, with raw mercury available for only US$13 a kilo there is little obvious economic incentive to find ways of using less-hazardous materials, although the anti-pollution non-profit organization Pure Earth (Ⓦpureearth.org) is currently training mining families in new mercury-free techniques. Pressure by international **environmental groups**, and the publicity they generate, make some difference, but greater political will and more holistic, inclusive solutions than the current hard-line approach – police and government troops are periodically sent in to torch mining camps and blow up equipment – are needed to truly resolve the issue.

Voluntarily isolated peoples

The Peruvian Amazon is home to approximately fifteen "uncontacted" or **voluntarily isolated** ("*aislados*") ethnic groups comprising up to 15,000 people. But more and more previously uncontacted or voluntarily isolated communities are having their land invaded and/or contaminated by loggers, drug traffickers or oil companies, and the threat of coming into contact with diseases to which they have no resistance is growing. The region of Madre de Dios, in particular, has seen a sharp increase in the number of "encounters" with isolated groups in the past few years. The most notable example to date occurred in 2014, when around two hundred nomadic Mashco-Piro, armed with bows and arrows, raided the village of Monte Salvado, ransacking homes and stealing machetes and other utensils, forcing the population to be evacuated. Such incidents are forcing the Peruvian government to reconsider its no-contact policy with uncontacted groups, which has been in effect since 2006. At the same time, indigenous associations have been lobbying Perúpetro, the body that awards the country's oil prospecting concessions in the Amazon, to either withdraw or modify the boundaries of lots that overlap with territories of isolated groups. Surprisingly, they have succeeded in several cases over the last decade, providing some welcome optimism in an otherwise bleak narrative.

INDIGENOUS RIGHTS AND THE DESTRUCTION OF THE RAINFOREST

Many of the Peruvian Amazon's peoples, like the Ashaninka and Aguaruna-Huambisa, stand firm against exploitation and invasion from outside influences, yet even so, many indigenous communities are being **pushed off their land** by an endless combination of slash-and-burn colonization, megadam builders, big oil companies, gold miners, timber extractors, coca farmers organized by drug-trafficking barons and, at times, "revolutionary" political groups. All along the main rivers and jungle roads, settlers are flooding into the area. In their wake, forcing land-title agreements to which they have no right, are the main timber companies and multinational oil corporations. In large tracts of the rainforest the fragile selva ecology has already been destroyed; in others, communities have been more subtly disrupted as they become dependent on outside consumer goods and trade, or by the imposition of evangelical proselytizing groups, and the indigenous way of life is being destroyed.

In response to the dire situation of indigenous communities, **self-determination groups** sprang up throughout the 1970s and 1980s, such as AIDESEP (Asociación Interétnica de Desarollo de la Selva Peruana) and CONAP (Confederación de Nationalidades Amazónicas de Perú).

In May 2008, Alan García's government very publicly created Peru's first **Ministry of the Environment** during the Lima-based European Union, Latin America and the Caribbean Summit, at which the main focus was climate change. Yet within weeks of the new ministry's creation, the government also announced plans to open up community-owned lands for commercial investment and large-scale agribusiness by making fundamental changes to the law of **land ownership** in the Andes and Amazon regions – a move which was integral to the new free-trade agreement between Peru and the US. This unleashed a wave of protests and road blocks by indigenous communities countrywide, as well as a major march of solidarity in Lima. Matters came to a head on June 5th 2009 in what is known as the "Baguazo" (**Bagua massacre**), Peru's worst case of violence since the Sendero Luminoso insurgency ended. Declaring a state of emergency, the president, seemingly under pressure from the US, sent in the police and army, equipped with tear gas, military-grade weapons and helicopters, to break up a 2000-strong blockade on one of the oil companies' main access routes to the Amazon. Though official numbers are disputed – eye-witnesses said they saw police disposing of civilian bodies to lessen the casualty figures – there were fatalities on both sides: at least 32 dead (included 11 police officers who were kidnapped) and 200 injured or missing. Fifty-three civilians were arrested for the violence – predominantly indigenous protesters, who spent seven years in prison before eventually being declared innocent and released.

On the positive side, Congress has subsequently repealed some of the most controversial land laws, and since 2011 indigenous peoples have a right to be consulted about development projects on their lands – though in practice this frequently means calling a meeting to present a fait accompli rather than engaging in genuine dialogue. A number of indigenous communities have also been granted titles to their land. That said, a land title without a fully supported path to sustainability and protection against illegal loggers, gold-miners and oil companies is mere window-dressing; it also leaves impoverished communities vulnerable to signing agreements with logging companies, in order to derive some benefit from their resources, only to be hoodwinked further down the line.

Books

There are few non-fiction books published in English that deal exclusively with Peru and, until very recently, few works by Peruvian authors ever made it into English. The exception is Nobel Prize-winning author Mario Vargas Llosa, the Colossus of Peruvian literature, whose copious works have been translated into many languages worldwide. Many of the classic works on Peruvian and Inca history are now out of print (o/p), though often available online or in libraries and second-hand bookshops around the world, including in Lima and Cusco. Travel books, coffee-table editions and country guides are also generally for sale in Lima bookshops. Titles marked ★ are especially recommended.

INCA AND PRE-INCA HISTORY

Anthony Aveni *Nasca: Eighth Wonder of the World*. Contains much on the history of the Nazca people and explores the complex relationships between water, worship, social order and the environment. Written by a leading scholar who has spent twenty years excavating here.

Hiram Bingham *Lost City of the Incas*. The classic introduction to the "discovery"of Machu Picchu in 1911: the exploration accounts are interesting but many of the theories should be taken with a pinch of salt. Widely available in Peru.

Peter T. Bradley *The Lure of Peru: Maritime Intrusion into the South Sea 1598–1701*. A historical account of how the worldwide fame of the country's Inca treasures attracted Dutch, French and English would-be settlers, explorers, merchants and even pirates to the seas and shores of Peru. Includes descriptions of naval blockades of Lima and various waves of buccaneers in search of Peru.

Richard Burger *Chavín and the Origins of Andean Civilisation*. A collection of erudite but accessible essays – essential reading for anyone seriously interested in Peruvian prehistory.

★ **Geoffrey Hext Sutherland Bushnell** *Peru* (o/p). A classic, concise introduction to the main social and technological developments in Peru from 2500 BC to 1500 AD; well illustrated, if dated in some aspects.

Pedro de Cieza de León *The Discovery and Conquest of Peru (Latin America in Transition)*. A new paperback version of this classic post-Conquest chronicler account.

★ **John Hemming** *The Conquest of the Incas*. The authoritative narrative of the Spanish Conquest, from Pizarro to the death of the last Inca emperor, a tale of the destruction of a civilisation by a small band of ruthless and greedy men, brought to life from a mass of original sources.

Thor Heyerdahl, Daniel Sandweiss and Alfredo Navárez *Pyramids of Túcume*. A recently published description of the archeological site at Túcume plus the life and society of the civilization that created this important ceremonial and political centre around 1000 years ago. Widely available in Peruvian bookshops.

Kim MacQuarrie *The Last Days of the Incas*. A thoroughly researched and highly dramatic account of Francisco Pizarro's conquest, depicting the Inca rebellion and subsequent guerrilla war. The book also covers the modern search for Vilcabamba. *Life and Death in the Andes: On the Trail of Bandits, Heroes and Revolutionaries* also includes a chapter on Abimael Guzmán, leader of the Sendero Luminoso.

Michael E. Moseley *The Incas and Their Ancestors: The Archeology of Peru*. This revised 2001 edition gives a fine overview of Peru before the Spanish Conquest, making full use of good maps, diagrams, sketches, motifs and photos.

Keith Muscutt *Warriors of the Clouds: A Lost Civilization in the Upper Amazon of Peru*. Some superb photos of the ruins and environment left behind by the amazing Chachapoyas culture of northern Peru.

William Hickling Prescott *History of the Conquest of Peru*. Hemming's main predecessor – a nineteenth-century classic that remains a good read, packed with facts.

Johan Reinhard *Ice Maiden: Mountain Gods, Frozen Mummies and Sacred Sites in the Andes*. The fascinating first-person account of the discovery in 1995 of the mummified body of a young girl (known as Juanita) and ten other human sacrifices. The same author also wrote *Nasca Lines: A New Perspective on Their Origin and Meaning*, giving original theories about the Lines and ancient mountain gods, as well as *Machu Picchu: Exploring an Ancient Sacred Centre*. This last book draws on anthropology, archeology, geography and astronomy to reach highly probable conclusions about the sacred geology and topography of the Cusco region, and how they appear to relate to Inca architecture, in particular Machu Picchu.

Rebecca Stone *Art of the Andes: from Chavín to Inca.* Lavishly illustrated, this tome frequently features on university reading lists as an introduction for students of Pre-Columbian art, covering textiles, ceramics, archeology and painting.

★ **Garcilasco de la Vega** *The Royal Commentaries of the Incas and General History of Peru (abridged).* The most readable and fascinating of contemporary historical sources; written shortly after the conquest by a "Spaniard" of essentially Inca blood, it's the best eyewitness account of Inca life and beliefs from an Inca perspective. *This abridged version includes an excellent, concise introduction and explanatory notes by editor Karen Spalding.*

MODERN HISTORY AND SOCIETY

Catherine J Allen *The Hold Life Has: Coca and Cultural Identity in an Andean Community.* This scholarly ethnography of the Quechua-speaking people of the Andes has been updated, revealing the difficulties of maintaining indigenous culture in a changing world – a world that has changed even since her later fieldwork in 2000.

José María Arguedas *Deep Rivers* and *Yawar Fiesta.* Arguedas is an *indigenista* – writing for and about the indigenous peoples. *Yawar Fiesta* focuses on one of the most impressive (and brutal) Andean peasant ceremonial cycles, involving the annual rite of pitching a condor against a bull (the condor representing the indigenous population and the bull the Spanish Conquistadors).

Jelke Boersten *Intersecting inequalities: Women and Social Policy in Peru 1990–2000.* An academic but accessible text based on research interviews, exploring public policies aimed at bettering women's lot in the areas of poverty relief, reproduction and domestic violence. It shows how programmes often perpetuate the inequalities they purport to address, and how some women are managing to resist the system.

Sally Bowen and Jane Holligan *The Imperfect Spy: the many lives of Vladimiro Montesinos.* Tracing the emergence of Montesinos, who virtually ran Peru throughout the 1990s as head of SIN (Servicio de Inteligencia Nacional), this well-researched book covers his upbringing and career in an engrossing and accessible style. It provides fascinating insights into corruption and power in the CIA and the mafia, as manifested in Peru.

Eduardo Calderón *Eduardo El Curandero: The Words of a Peruvian Healer.* Peru's most famous shaman – El Tuno – outlines his teachings and beliefs in his own words; taken from a transcript of a film documentary.

Catherine M. Conaghan *Fujimori's Peru: Deception in the Public Sphere.* A very readable account of the lesser-known, manipulative side of Fujimori's time in power, his brutalizing of Peru's democratic institutions and eventual downfall.

Carlos Cumes and Romulo Lizarraga Valencia *Pachamama's Children: Mother Earth and Her Children of the Andes in Peru.* A New Age look at the culture, roots and shamanistic aspects of modern Peru.

Holligan de Díaz-Limaco *Peru in Focus.* A good (if short) general reader on Peru's history, politics, culture and environment.

Alberto Flores Galindo *In Search of an Inca: Identity and Utopia in the Andes.* A series of essays that provide an important scholarly investigation of the influence of Peru's Inca past on the identities of Andean peoples and their idealisation of the pre-Conquest period, which has influenced much of their more recent political struggles.

James Higgins *Lima: a Cultural and Literary History.* A scholarly book showing great affection for Lima, carefully weaving together both its culture and social history. It guides the reader through Lima's historical sites with particular emphasis on the colonial era, and culminating with a section on modern-day culture.

Hilaria Supa Huamán *Threads of My Life.* Inspiring autobiographical account of the remarkable life of this tireless activist for indigenous women's rights; from her tough childhood in servitude, through to her election to congress. Its chapters end with questions to provoke reflection.

★ **F. Bruce Lamb and Manuel Córdova-Rios** *The Wizard of the Upper Amazon.* Reconstruction of the true story of Manuel Córdova-Rios – "Ino Moxo" – a famous herbal healer and *ayahuascero* from Iquitos who was kidnapped as a young boy and brought up by an Amawaka community in the early twentieth century. Offers significant insight into indigenous psychedelic healing traditions. For further reading see César Calvo's *The Three Halves of Ino Moxo: Teachings of the Wizard of the Upper Amazon.*

Sewell H. Menzel *Fire in the Andes: U.S. Foreign Policy and Cocaine Politics in Bolivia and Peru.* A good summary of US anti-cocaine activities in these two countries, written by a credible academic.

David Scott Palmer (ed) *Shining Path of Peru.* A modern history compilation of meticulously detailed essays and articles by Latin American academics and journalists on the early and middle phases of Sendero Luminoso's guerrilla campaign in Peru.

William Sater *Fighting the War of the Pacific, 1879–1884.* Focusing mainly on the nitty-gritty of battle, this authoritative account draws on sources from both sides of the battle line to present an even-handed account, revealing a catalogue of blunders and incompetence, and the inevitable unnecessary loss of life.

★ **Orin Starn, Carlos Degregori and Robin Kirk** (eds) *The Peru Reader: History, Culture, Politics.* One of the best overviews yet of Peruvian history and politics, with excerpts from classic texts – by writers as diverse as Mario Vargas Llosa and Abimael Guzmán (imprisoned ex-leader of Sendero Luminoso) – as well as lesser known poems, essays, interviews and photos. Ambitious in scope and vision.

Kimberly Theidon *Intimate Enemies, Violence and Reconciliation in Peru*. The fruits of ten years of ethnographic research in rural Ayacucho, this is an excellent scholarly yet human account of the scars left in Andean communities following the Sendero Luminoso insurgency.

FLORA AND FAUNA

Allen Altman and B. Swift *Checklist of the Birds of Peru*. A useful summary with photos of different habitats.

Clive Byers *Birds of Peru*. Pocket guide covering 250 of the country's most exciting birds, illustrated with colour photos. Perfect for casual birdwatchers.

J.L. Castner, S.L. Timme and **J.A. Duke** *A Field Guide to Medicinal and Useful Plants of the Upper Amazon*. Of interest to enthusiasts and scientists alike, this book contains handy colour illustrations.

L.H. Emmons *Neotropical Rainforest Mammals: A Field Guide*. An excellent paperback with over 250 pages of authoritative text and illustrations.

James Kavanagh *Amazon Wildlife: A Waterproof Pocket Guide to Familiar Species*. A handy pamphlet with over 140 species well illustrated.

David Pearson and Les Baletsky *Peru (Travellers' Wild Life Guide)*. Though it covers over 500 of the more often encountered wildlife (with clear illustrations) – amphibians, birds, reptiles, mammals, insects and other arthropods – it can only serve as a broad introduction to such a species-rich country.

★ **Thomas Schulenberg, Douglas Stotz, Daniel Lane, John O'Neill et al.** *Birds of Peru* (Princeton Field Guide). The most comprehensive and up-to-date guide to the over 1800 species of birds found in Peru, with excellent colour illustrations to aid identification. A hefty tome.

★ **Richard E. Schultes, Albert Hofman and Christian Rätsch** *Plants of the Gods: Their Sacred, Healing and Hallucinogenic Powers*. An updated and superbly illustrated history of the use of psychoactive plants and hallucinogens in shamanic culture.

Thomas Valqui *Where to Watch Birds in Peru*. Published in 2004, it could do with updating but is still useful for twitchers. Covering 151 of the most important birding sites, it features maps, directions to reach the locations, plus where to stay nearby.

Barry Walker *Field Guide to the Birds of Machu Picchu and the Cusco Region, Peru*. Very useful guide with colour illustrations, updated in 2015, which will fit in your pocket. Has a list of the best sites and a checklist, handy for keen birders.

Walter Wust *Manu: el último refugio*. This is an excellent coffee-table book on the wildlife and flora of Manu National Park by one of Peru's foremost wildlife photographers. Available in most good bookshops in Lima and Cusco.

TRAVEL

Mark Adams *Turn Right at Machu Picchu: Rediscovering the Lost City One Step at a Time*. In entertaining self-deprecating style, the author retraces the steps of the original Hiram Bingham expedition, 100 years on, offering an amusing re-evaluation of the explorer. An inexperienced traveller (he had never slept in a tent), Adams' adventures should also provide encouragement for novice hikers on the Inca Trail.

Patricia Chapple Wright *High Moon Over The Andes*. Now a world authority on lemurs, the author recounts the unlikely start to her career as a young, naïve biologist who goes to the Peruvian Amazon to find a mate for her pet owl monkey.

Christopher Isherwood *The Condor and the Cows*. An entertaining diary of Isherwood's South American trip (mostly in Peru) after World War II. Like Paul Theroux, Isherwood eventually arrives in Buenos Aires, to meet Jorge Luis Borges.

John Lane *A Very Peruvian Practice: Travels with La Señora*. This comical autobiographical travel book about Lane's work as adviser to a new ladies' health clinic in Lima paints a colourful picture of life in Peru – from bullfights to funerals, and the rainforest to Andean mountaintops.

Patrick Leigh Fermor *Three Letters from the Andes*. Three long letters in evocative prose written from Peru in 1971, in the days when mountain climbing was the thing for gentlemen to do and tourists were rare.

Dervla Murphy *Eight Feet in the Andes*. An enjoyable account of a rather adventurous journey Dervla Murphy made across the Andes with her young daughter and a mule. It can't compare with her India books, though.

Matthew Parris *Inca Kola, A Traveller's Tale of Peru*. Very amusing description of travelling in Peru with three companions, offering a perspicacious look at Peruvian culture, past and present.

★ **Joe Simpson** *Touching the Void*. Utterly compelling true story which became a blockbuster docu-drama of an attempt to climb the previously unclimbed Siula Grande in the Huayhuash mountains, and the dramatic events that ensued.

Tom Pow *In the Palace of Serpents: An Experience of Peru*. A well-written insight into travelling in Peru, spoilt only by the fact that Tom Pow was ripped off in Cusco and lost his original notes. Consequently he didn't have as wonderful a time as he might have and seems to have missed the beauty of the Peruvian landscapes and the wealth of history and culture.

★ **Hugh Thomson** *The White Rock: An Exploration of The Inca Heartland*. 25 years ago the author set off into the cloud forest in search of a lost Inca city; here he recalls his own adventures while trying to unravel Inca myths from facts. Also by Thompson, *Cochineal Red: Travels through Ancient Peru* is an enthralling mix of travel writing and scholarship exploring recent archeological discoveries in Peru, uncovering layers of Inca and pre-Inca history.

★ **Ronald Wright** *Cut Stones and Crossroads: A Journey in the Two Worlds of Peru*. An enlightened travel book that has stood the test of time, largely due to the author's depth of knowledge on his subject.

PERUVIAN FICTION WRITERS

Martín Adán *The Cardboard House*. A poetic novel based in Lima and written by one of South America's best living poets when he was only twenty.

★ **Daniel Alarcón** *War by Candlelight*. Short stories, mostly set in Peru, examining the effects of political struggle and civil war on ordinary people, written in incisive prose by talented Peruvian–American author. *At Night We Walk in Circles,* a novel set in Peru, traces the history of a man caught up in political upheaval. *Lost City Radio's* protagonist runs a radio show that helps families find their lost loved ones in the wake of civil conflict. An author not to be missed.

Ciro Alegría *Broad and Alien is the World*. Another good book to travel with, this distinguished 1970s novel offers persuasive insight into life in the Peruvian highlands in the early twentieth century.

Susan E. Benner and Kathy S. Leonard (eds) *Fire from the Andes: Short Fiction by Women from Bolivia, Ecuador, and Peru*. A fascinating read, illuminating the lives of women at the turn of the century, often highlighting their feeling of marginalisation.

Alfredo Bryce Echenique *A World for Julius*. A moving semi-autobiographical story of the end of innocence for a young boy growing up in the fifties and sixties in a wealthy family in Lima, who discovers that the world outside his parents' mansion is one of poverty and oppression.

★ **Santiago Roncagliolo** *Red April*. Award-winning political thriller set in 2000; the story follows a prosecutor's pursuit of a serial killer in order to explore the wider societal violence that he suggests is rooted in the officially disbanded Sendero Luminoso and its legacy of corruption and terror.

★ **Claudia Salazar** *Blood of the Dawn*. Prize-winning first novel of an acclaimed short-story writer. A rare foregrounding of female experiences during the Sendero Luminoso period by a female author; in distinctive prose, she focuses on three very different women, spanning both sides of the civil conflict.

César Vallejo *The Complete Poetry: a bilingual edition*. Peru's most internationally renowned poet – and deservedly so. Romantic but highly innovative in style, his writing translates beautifully, though here you can read the poems in Spanish too.

★ **Mario Vargas Llosa** *Death in the Andes*, *A Fish in the Water*, *Aunt Julia and the Scriptwriter*, *The Time of the Hero*, *Captain Pantoja and the Special Service*, *The Green House*, *The Real Life of Alejandro Mayta*, *The War of the End of the World*, *Who Killed Palomino Molero*? The most distinguished and prolific of contemporary Peruvian writers, Nobel prizewinner Vargas Llosa is essentially a novelist but has also written on Peruvian society, run his own current-affairs TV programme in Lima and even made a (rather average) feature film. *Death in the Andes* is a savagely violent story which tells of the effect of the brutality of the Sendero Luminoso and seeks to find the truth behind the bloodshed. His ebullient memoir, *A Fish in the Water*, describes, among other things, Vargas Llosa's experience in unsuccessfully running for the Peruvian presidency. *Aunt Julia and the Scriptwriter*, his best known novel to be translated into English, is a fabulous, comic, semi-autobiographical tale that spirals out of control following the arrival in Lima of a Bolivian scriptwriter for Peruvian radio soap operas, who begins an affair with the protagonist's older aunt by marriage. Essential reading – and perfect for long Peruvian bus journeys. His latest novel – *The Neighbourhood* – is a political detective novel set in nineties Lima high society, teeming with lust and corruption.

FICTION SET IN PERU BY NON-PERUVIAN AUTHORS

Jordan Jacobs *Samantha Sutton and the Labyrinth of Lies*. A great read for young travellers to Peru, this novel is part Nancy Drew, part Indiana Jones, following a teenage girl in a detailed and well-researched adventure with her uncle in the ruins of Chavín de Huantar.

Peter Mathiessen *At Play in the Fields of the Lord*. This celebrated American novel expertly evokes the Peruvian selva, though the indigenous population, whose interactions with modernity are theoretically at the centre of the tale, merely provide the backdrop to the moral agonising of the unloveable foreign protagonists.

Pablo Neruda *The Heights of Machu Picchu (translated by Tomás Q Morín)*. Famous, atmospheric poem by Chile's Nobel prizewinning poet; the Spanish text is included.

Nicholas Shakespeare *The Dancer Upstairs*. Heavily based on the tracking down of Sendero Luminoso leader Abimael Gúzman, this riveting well-crafted thriller gives a fictionalised account of the protagonist-detective's hunt for a Maoist rebel leader.

Geoff Wicks *Inca*. An easy read of early Inca history through the life story of a man who served three Inca emperors and survived the Conquest; well researched and entertaining.

Thornton Wilder *The Bridge of the San Luis Rey*. A classic Pulitzer Prize-winning novella that opens with the collapse of a suspension bridge in Peru in 1714 that plunges five people to their death, prompting the monk who witnesses the scene to attempt make sense of their deaths.

Colin Thubron *To the Lost City*. A tale of travel that follows the varying points of view of an ill-assorted, ill-equipped band of five Europeans trekking to Vilcabamba. The challenging, inhospitable landscape is well evoked; the characters are less inspiring.

SPECIALIST GUIDES

Gastón Acurio *Peru: The Cookbook*. Reflecting the growing international popularity of Peruvian cuisine, this weighty tome features 500 traditional dishes accompanied by glorious glossy photos and explained by Peru's pre-eminent celebrity chef.

John Biggar *The High Andes: A Guide for Climbers*. Expanded 2015 edition of the first comprehensive climbing guide to the Andes' main peaks, focusing mainly on Peru (you can buy these chapters as separate ebooks) but also covering other Andean nations.

Hilary Bradt and Kathy Jarvis *Trekking in Peru: 50 Best Walks and Hikes*. User-friendly and informative, with sketch-maps, covering multi-day hikes in the main. Good background info on flora and fauna.

Nilda Callañaupa Álvarez, Christine Franquemont and Joe Coca *Faces of Tradition: Weaving Elders of the Andes*. Born out of the Centro de Textiles Traditional Tradicionales in Cusco (see page 214), this book narrates (and shows in photos) the personal stories of the weavers; you'll learn as much about the harsh realities of rural Andean life as about the skills of their craft.

Flor Arcaya de Deliot *The Food and Cooking of Peru: traditions, ingredients, tastes & techniques*. A colourful book full of well-illustrated recipes, with alternative ingredients suggested for foods not readily available outside Peru.

★ **Peter Frost** *Exploring Cusco*. A very practical and stimulating site-by-site guide to the whole Cusco area (where it is widely available in bookstores). Unreservedly recommended if you're spending more than a few days in the region, and also for armchair archeologists back home.

Bradley C. Johnson *Classic Climbs of the Cordillera Blanca*. Available in paperback only, this is a must for anyone seriously wanting to climb in Peru's most popular mountaineering destination, and with glorious photos too.

Lynn Meisch *A Traveller's Guide to El Dorado and the Incan Empire*. Good old-fashioned travel journal full of fascinating cultural details – well worth lingering over before visiting Peru.

Alexander Stewart and Henry Stedman *The Inca Trail, Cusco and Machu Picchu*. Regularly updated and expanded, this practical guide answers any question you might have about the famous Inca Trail, but now also covers other routes to and around Machu Picchu.

Mike Torrey *Stone Offerings: Machu Picchu's Terraces of Enlightenment*. Award-winning coffee-table photography book, capturing every angle of the Inca citadel at the June and December solstices; without people, yet without asking anyone to move out of the shot, according to the author.

Ruth Wright and Alfredo Valencia Zegarra *The Machu Picchu Guidebook: a Self-guided Tour*. Updated in 2011, this pocket companion provides accurate detail on the various compounds within the archeological site.

Language

Although Peru is officially a Spanish-speaking nation, a large proportion of its population, possibly more than half, regard Spanish as their second language. When the Conquistadors arrived, Quechua, the official language of the Inca Empire, was widely spoken everywhere but in the Amazon basin. Originally known as Runasimi (from *runa*, "person", and *simis*, "mouth"), it was given the name Quechua – which means "high Andean valleys" – by the Spanish.

Quechua was not, however, the only pre-Columbian tongue. There were, and still are, well over **thirty languages** within Amazonia and, up until the late nineteenth century, **Mochica** had been widely spoken on the north coast for at least 1500 years.

With such a rich linguistic history, it is not surprising to find non-European words intruding constantly into any Peruvian conversation. **Cancha**, for instance, the Inca word for "courtyard", is still commonly used to refer to most sporting areas – *la cancha de basketball*, for example. Other linguistic survivors have even reached the English language: **llama**, **condor**, **puma** and **pampa** among them. Perhaps more interesting is the great wealth of traditional **creole slang** – utilized with equal vigour at all levels of society. This complex speech, much like Cockney rhyming slang, is difficult to catch without almost complete fluency in Spanish.

Once you get into it, **Spanish** is the easiest language there is – and in Peru people are eager to understand even the most faltering attempt. You'll be further helped by the fact that South Americans speak relatively slowly (at least compared with Spanish people in Spain) and that there's no need to get your tongue round the lisping pronunciation.

Pronunciation

The rules of **pronunciation** are pretty straightforward and, once you get to know them, strictly observed. Unless there's an accent, words ending in d, l, r and z are **stressed** on the last syllable, all others on the second last. All **vowels** are pure and short.

A somewhere between the "A" sound of back and that of father

E as in get

I as in police

O as in hot

U as in rule

C is soft before E and I, hard otherwise: **cerca** is pronounced "serka"

G works the same way, a guttural "H" sound (like the ch in loch) before E or I, a hard G elsewhere – **gigante** becomes "higante"

H is always silent

J is the same sound as a guttural G: **jamón** is pronounced "hamon"

LL sounds like an English Y: **tortilla** is pronounced "torteeya"

N is as in English unless it has a tilde (accent) over it, when it becomes NY: **mañana** sounds like "manyana"

QU is pronounced like an English K

R is rolled, RR doubly so

V sounds more like B, **vino** becoming "beano"

X is slightly softer than in English – sometimes almost SH – except between vowels in place names where it has an "H" sound – for example México (Meh-Hee-Ko) or Oaxaca

Z is the same as a soft C, so **cerveza** becomes "servesa"

Below is a list of a few essential words and phrases, though if you're travelling for any length of time a **dictionary** or phrase book is obviously a worthwhile investment – try the *Dictionary of Latin American Spanish* (University of Chicago Press). Bear in mind that in Spanish CH, LL and Ñ count as separate letters and are listed after the Cs, Ls and Ns respectively.

WORDS AND PHRASES

BASICS

Yes Sí
No No
Please Por favor
Thank you Gracias
Where…? ¿Dónde…?
When…? ¿Cuándo…?
What…? ¿Qué…?
How much…? ¿Cuánto…?
Do you have the time? ¿Tiene la hora?
Here Aquí
There Allí
This Este
That Eso
Now Ahora
Later Más tarde
Open Abierto/a
Closed Cerrado/a
With Con
Without Sin
Good Buen(o)/a
Bad Mal(o)/a
Big Gran(de)
Small Pequeño/a
More Más
Less Menos
Today Hoy
Tomorrow Mañana
Yesterday Ayer

GREETINGS AND RESPONSES

Hello Hola
Goodbye Adiós
Good morning Buenos días
Good afternoon/night Buenas tardes/noches
See you later Hasta luego
Sorry Lo siento/discúlpeme
Excuse me Con permiso/perdón
How are you? ¿Como está (usted)?
I (don't) understand (No) Entiendo
Not at all De nada
Do you speak English? ¿Habla (usted) inglés?
I don't speak Spanish No hablo español
My name is … Me llamo …
What's your name? ¿Como se llama usted?

TRANSPORT AND DIRECTIONS

Do you know…? ¿Sabe…?
I don't know No sé
How do I get to…? Por dónde se va a…?
Left, right, straight on Izquierda, derecha, derecho
Where is…? ¿Dónde está…?
…the bus station …la estación de buses/el terminal terrestre
…the train station …la estación de tren
…the nearest bank/ATM …el banco/cajero más cercano
…the post office …el correo
…the toilet ...el baño/sanitario
Where does the bus ¿De dónde sale elto**… leave from?** bus para…?
Is this the train for Lima? ¿Es éste el tren para Lima?
I'd like a (return) Quisiera un boleto (de)**ticket to…** ida y vuelta) para…
What time does it leave ¿A qué hora sale **(arrive in…)?** (llega en…)?

ACCOMMODATION, RESTAURANTS AND SHOPPING

I'd like Quisiera/Me gustaría…
There is (is there)? (¿)Hay(?)
Give me… Deme…
(one like that) (uno así)
Do you have…? Tiene…?
…a room …un cuarto/una habitación
…with two beds/double bed…con dos camas/cama matrimonial
private bathroom baño privado
It's for one person Es para una persona
(two people) (dos personas)
…for one night …para una noche
(one week) (una semana)
It's fine, how much is it? ¿Está bien, cuánto es?
It's too expensive Es demasiado caro
Don't you have anything ¿No tiene algo más **cheaper?** barato?
Can you… ? ¿Se puede…?
…camp (near here?) ¿…acampar aquí (cerca)?
Is there a hotel nearby? ¿Hay un hotel aquí cerca?
What is there to eat? ¿Qué hay para comer?
What's that? ¿Qué es eso?
What's this called ¿Como se llama este en **in Spanish?** castellano?
Breakfast desayuno
Lunch almuerzo
Dinner cena
(cheap) set lunch menu menú del día
Menu carta/menú
Bill cuenta

OTHER USEFUL ACCOMMODATION TERMS

Desk fan or ceiling fan Ventilador
Air-conditioned Aire-acondicionado
Baño colectivo/compartido Shared bathroom

Hot water Agua caliente
Cold water Agua fría
Single bed Sencillo
Single room Cuarto simple
Taxes Impuestos
Check-out time Hora de salida

FOOD AND DRINK

BASICS

Arroz Rice
Avena Oats (porridge)
Galletas Biscuits
Harina Flour
Huevos Eggs
 fritos fried
 duros hard-boiled
 pasados lightly boiled
 revueltos scrambled
Mermelada Jam
Miel Honey
Mostaza Mustard
Pan (integral) Bread (brown)
Picante de… spicy dish of…
Queso Cheese

SOUP (SOPAS) AND STARTERS

Caldo Broth
Caldo de gallina Chicken broth
Causa Mashed potatoes with lime and *ají* (hot sauce) with layered fillings (e.g. tuna, chicken, shrimp)
Conchas a la parmesana Scallops with Parmesan
Huevos a la rusa Egg salad
Inchicapi Appetizing Amazonian soup made from chicken, peanuts, manioc (*yuca*) and fresh coriander herb
Palta (rellena) (stuffed) avocado
Papa a la Huancaína Boiled yellow potatoes in a spicy cheesy sauce served with hard-boiled eggs and olives.
Sopa a la criolla Noodles, vegetables and meat

SEAFOOD (MARISCOS) AND FISH (PESCADO)

Calamares Squid
Camarones Shrimp
Cangrejo Crab
Ceviche Seafood marinated in lime juice, coriander and chilli pepper
Chaufa de mariscos cojinova Chinese rice with seafood
Corvina Sea bass
Erizo Sea urchin
Jalea Large dish of fish with onion
Langosta Lobster
Langostino a lo macho Crayfish in spicy shellfish sauce
Lenguado Sole
Paiche Large Amazonian river fish
Tiradito Ceviche without onion or sweet potato
Tollo Small shark
Zungarro Large Amazonian river fish

MEAT (CARNES)

Adobo Meat/fish in mild chilli sauce
Ají de gallina Chicken in chilli sauce
Anticuchos Skewered heart (usually lamb)
Bifstek (bistek) Steak
Cabrito Goat
Carapulcra Pork, chicken and potato casserole
Carne a lo pobre Steak, fries, egg, rice and plantain
Carne de res Beef
Chicharrones Deep-fried pork crackling
Conejo Rabbit
Cordero Lamb
Cuy Guinea pig (a traditional Andean dish)
Estofado Stewed meat (usually served with rice)
Higado Liver
Jamón Ham
Lechón Pork
Lomo asado Roast beef
Lomo saltado Sautéed beef strips with tomato, onion, fries and rice
Mollejitos Gizzards
Pachamanca Meat and vegetables cooked over hot, buried stones
Parillada Grilled meat
Pato Duck
Pavo Turkey
Pollo (a la brasa) Chicken (spit-roasted)
Tocino Bacon
Venado Venison

VEGETABLES (LEGUMBRES) AND SIDE DISHES

Ají Chilli
Camote Sweet potato
Cebolla Onion
Choclo Corn on the cob
Fideos Noodles
Frijoles Beans
Hongos Mushrooms
Lechuga Lettuce
Papa rellena Fried potato balls, stuffed with olives, egg and mincemeat

Tallarines Spaghetti noodles
Tomates Tomatoes
Yuca a la Huancaina Manioc (like a yam) in spicy cheese sauce

FRUIT

Chirimoya Custard apple (green and fleshy outside, tastes like strawberries and cream)
Lucuma Small nutty fruit (used in ice creams and cakes)
Maracuyá Passion fruit
Palta Avocado
Piña Pineapple
Plátano Plantain (sometimes banana)
Tuna Pear-like cactus fruit (refreshing but full of hard little seeds)

SWEETS (DULCES)

Barquillo Ice cream cone
Churro Sweet stick of deep-fried dough
Flan Crème caramel
Helado Ice cream
Keke Cake
Manjar blanco Thickened, sweetened condensed milk
Mazamorra morada Purple maize and fruit jelly
Panqueques Pancakes
Picarones Doughnuts with syrup

SNACKS (BOCADILLOS)

Castañas Brazil nuts
Chifles Fried plantain crisps
Empanada Pastry stuffed with ground beef, chicken or cheese
Hamburguesa Hamburger
Salchipapas Potatoes, sliced frankfurter sausage and condiments
Sandwich de butifarra Ham and onion sandwich
Sandwich de lechón Pork salad sandwich
Tamale Steamed maize-flour roll stuffed with olives, egg, meat and vegetables in banana leaf/corn husk
Tortilla Omelette-cum-pancake
Tostadas Toast

FRUIT JUICES (JUGOS)

Especial Fruit, milk, sometimes beer
Fresa Strawberry
Higo Fig
Manzana Apple
Melón Melon
Naranja Orange
Papaya Papaya
Piña Pineapple
Surtido Mixed
Toronja Grapefruit
Zanahoria Carrot

BEVERAGES (BEBIDAS)

Agua Water
Água mineral Mineral water
Aguajina Refreshing palm-fruit drink
Algarrobina *Algarrobo*-fruit drink
Café Coffee
Cerveza Beer
Chicha de jora Fermented maize beer
Chicha morada Purple maize soft drink
Chilcano de pisco Pisco with lemonade
Chopp Draught beer
Cuba libre Rum and Coke
Gaseosa Soft carbonated drink
Leche Milk
Limonada Real lemonade
Masato Fermented manioc/cassva/yuca beer
Pisco Pale brandy made from distilled wine
Ponche Punch
Ron Rum
Té Tea
....con leche ....with milk
....de limón ....lemon tea
....hierba luisa ....lemon-grass tea
....manzanilla ....camomile tea

NUMBERS AND DAYS

1 un/uno, una
2 dos
3 tres
4 cuatro
5 cinco
6 seis
7 siete
8 ocho
9 nueve
10 diez
11 once
12 doce
13 trece
14 catorce
15 quince
16 dieciséis
20 veinte
21 veintiuno
30 treinta
40 cuarenta
50 cincuenta
60 sesenta
70 setenta
80 ochenta

90 noventa
100 cien(to)
101 ciento uno
200 doscientos
201 doscientos uno
500 quinientos
1000 mil
2000 dos mil
first primero/a
second segundo/a
third tercero/a
Monday lunes
Tuesday martes
Wednesday miércoles
Thursday jueves
Friday viernes
Saturday sábado
Sunday domingo

GLOSSARY OF PERUVIAN TERMS

Apu Mountain god/villa (also chief/leader in some Amazonian communities)
Ayllu Kinship group, or clan
Barrio Suburb, or sometimes shantytown
Cacique Headman/village chief
Callejón Corridor, or narrow street
Campesino Peasant, country-dweller, someone who works in the fields
Ceja de selva Edge of the rainforest on Andean slopes (800–3800m above sea level), including cloud forest
Chacra Cultivated garden/plot/farmland
Chamba Slang for work
Chaquiras Pre-Columbian stone or coral beads
Chicha Maize beer, or a form of Peruvian music
Chifa Peruvian-Chinese restaurant
Colectivo Shared taxi
Cordillera Mountain range
Criollo/a Creole. Comida criolla is a fusion of Spanish and indigenous cuisine, particularly associated with the coastal regions; música criolla is generally a mix of indigenous, African and Spanish musical influences, again most commonly associated with the coast.
Curaca Chief
Curandero Traditional healer
Grifo Petrol/fuel station
Gringo A European or North American person (sometimes derogatory)
Hacienda Estate
Huaca Sacred spot or object
Huaco Pre-Columbian artefact
Huaquero Someone who digs or looks for *huacos*
INC (Instituto Nacional de Cultura) National Cultural Institute
Jirón Road
Lomas Place where vegetation grows with moisture from the air rather than from rainfall or irrigation
Mamacona Inca Sun Virgin
El monte The forest/bush
Óvalo Roundabout
Pachamama Mother earth
Pakucho Amazonian variant of "gringo"
Paradero Bus stop
Peña Nightclub with live music
Pileta Fountain
Plata Silver; slang for "cash"
Poblado Settlement
Pueblos jóvenes Shantytowns
Puna Barren Andean heights
Selva Jungle/rainforest
Selvático Amazonian-dweller
SERNANP (Servicio Nacional de Áreas Naturales Protegidas por el Estado) State body in charge of protecting the national parks and reserves
Serrano Mountain-dweller
Shushupero "Drunk" or inebriated individual, from the deadly *shushupe* snake
Sierra Mountains
Siete raices Strong medicinal drink
Soroche Altitude sickness
Tambo Inca Highway rest-house
Tipishca Oxbow lake
Varzea Forest which gets regularly flooded

Small print and index

A ROUGH GUIDE TO ROUGH GUIDES

Published in 1982, the first Rough Guide – to Greece – was a student scheme that became a publishing phenomenon. Mark Ellingham, a recent graduate in English from Bristol University, had been travelling in Greece the previous summer and couldn't find the right guidebook. With a small group of friends he wrote his own guide, combining a contemporary, journalistic style with a thoroughly practical approach to travellers' needs.

The immediate success of the book spawned a series that rapidly covered dozens of destinations. And, in addition to impecunious backpackers, Rough Guides soon acquired a much broader readership that relished the guides' wit and inquisitiveness as much as their enthusiastic, critical approach and value-for-money ethos. These days, Rough Guides include recommendations from budget to luxury and cover more than 120 destinations around the globe, from Amsterdam to Zanzibar, all regularly updated by our team of roaming writers.

Browse all our latest guides, read inspirational features and book your trip at **roughguides.com**.

Rough Guide credits

Editors: Rebecca Hallett, Ann-Marie Shaw
Cartography: Carte, Katie Bennett
Managing editors: Rachel Lawrence, Mani Ramaswamy
Picture editor: Aude Vauconsant
Cover photo research: Aude Vauconsant
Senior DTP coordinator: Dan May
Head of DTP and Pre-Press: Rebeka Davies

Publishing information

Tenth edition 2018

Distribution
UK, Ireland and Europe
Apa Publications (UK) Ltd; sales@roughguides.com
United States and Canada
Ingram Publisher Services; ips@ingramcontent.com
Australia and New Zealand
Woodslane; info@woodslane.com.au
Southeast Asia
Apa Publications (SN) Pte; sales@roughguides.com
Worldwide
Apa Publications (UK) Ltd; sales@roughguides.com
Special Sales, Content Licensing and CoPublishing
Rough Guides can be purchased in bulk quantities at discounted prices. We can create special editions, personalised jackets and corporate imprints tailored to your needs. sales@roughguides.com.

roughguides.com
Printed in Poland by Pozkal

A catalogue record for this book is available from the British Library

Help us update

We've gone to a lot of effort to ensure that the tenth edition of **The Rough Guide to Peru** is accurate and up-to-date. However, things change – places get "discovered", opening hours are notoriously fickle, restaurants and rooms raise prices or lower standards. If you feel we've got it wrong or left something out, we'd like to know, and if you can remember the address, the price, the hours, the phone number, so much the better.

Please send your comments with the subject line "**Rough Guide Peru Update**" to mail@uk.roughguides.com. We'll credit all contributions and send a copy of the next edition (or any other Rough Guide if you prefer) for the very best emails.

Reader's updates

Thanks to all the readers who have taken the time to write in with comments and suggestions (and apologies if we've inadvertently omitted or misspelt anyone's name):

Charlotte de Beule; Martin Dormaar; etwn123; Ariel Harroche; Joanne Howard; Megan Kenna; Tim Laslavic; Tom McCormick-Cox; Sally Milius; Leena Pandit; Hans Rossel; Howard Shallard-Brown; Mandy Wright.

ABOUT THE AUTHORS

Steph Dyson moved to South America with little more than a phrasebook and a couple of Rough Guides to keep her company. Since then, she's observed rare giant river otters in the Paraguayan Pantanal, flown mere metres above the Southern Patagonia Ice Field in a GAF Nomad in Chile and appeared live on Bolivian television. A member of the British Guild of Travel Writers, she now spends her time writing for online and print travel publications and can be found somewhere on the road in South America.

Sara Humphreys first went to Peru in 1988, when a flare-up in guerrilla activity meant sharing the wonders of Machu Picchu with only two other tourists. Since then, she has toiled, travelled and tarried in various countries in Latin America. She is the author of the Rough Guide to Namibia and Rough Guide to Panama and co-author of the Rough Guide to Ecuador. When not on the road, she can be found swinging in a hammock in Barbados.

Todd Obolsky's favourite travel experiences include off-roading in Monument Valley, abseiling into New Zealand's Waitomo Caves, and sharing the road with a bear cub in Canada's Yukon. He has previously contributed to Rough Guides to New York City, New England, Chicago, Florida, the USA, Canada and Belize, and wrote and shot images for A Hedonist's Guide to Miami. He can usually be found haunting the bakeries of New York City.

Acknowledgements

Steph Dyson: Thank you to all of the local people I met who offered me their time, wisdom and a pisco sour pick-me-up where necessary; Lucho Hurtado at Incas del Perú; Nuevos Caminos Travel in Chachapoyas; Sara Humphreys for her invaluable help and advice; Rebecca Hallett and Mani Ramaswamy from the RG team for their ongoing assistance; Olivia Richards, for her unwavering optimism and enthusiasm; and Gonzalo Benavides, for his love, support and everything in between.

Sara Humphreys: Appreciation is due to the extremely helpful staff in iPerú offices throughout the country and to various officials from SERNANP, in particular to Anthony Vílchez Rodríguez and Toto Lara in the central office in Lima. Thanks are also due to Iñigo Maneiro, the Coordinador del Turismo Comunitario and to Frank Dither of Ecomundo Ashaninka; also to Americano Cabesilla Gálvez, Director de CENOSEC, and Lyndon Pishagua Chinchuya, Director de ARPI(SC). In the northern Amazon, I'm grateful to Victor Manuel González, who talked me into a very long but worthwhile ride in a peque-peque, and to Orlando Salazar for further explorations in Amazonia. In the UK, thanks go to Ed Aves, who persuaded me to take the job, to Kiki Deere, for providing info and contacts, and to Todd Obolsky and Steph Dyson for being collegial co-authors. Also to Rebecca Hallett and Ann-Marie Shaw for editorial support, and acceptance of missed deadlines, and to Val Humphreys for trawling countless book lists; and last but not least, to Adrian, for all manner of home support.

Todd Obolsky: A tremendous amount of thanks is due to Rex Broekman of The Huaraz Telegraph for his invaluable assistance. Applause also to Alberto Cafferata (Pony's Expeditions), Blanca Rosa Silvia Rios (Museo Pedro de Osma), Aaron Paige Leyton, Giuliani Valle (Promperu), Raul Villacorta, Luke Blezard, Pilar Hoyos, Mani Ramaswamy and Ed Aves from the OG RG, and my super helpful co-authors. Thanks also to Mariella Hoyos and Naty Diaz, who provided a warm introduction to Lima hospitality at Mangos (blanket notwithstanding).

Photo credits

(Key: T-top; C-centre; B-bottom; L-left; R-right)

Abraham Nowitz/Apa Publications 413
Alamy 15T, 17BR, 21B, 109, 152/153, 371
Aurora Photos/AWL Images Ltd 310/311, 451
Getty Images 4, 13TCR 16T, 20TR, 205, 313, 428/429
Hemis/AWL Images 1
iStock 5, 12, 13TL, 14B, 14T, 17T, 18T, 19C, 20TL, 20B, 22, 52/53, 75, 106/107, 125, 175, 233, 249, 278/279, 297, 327, 351, 431
Orient/SIME/4Corners Images 24
Shutterstock 11T, 11B, 14C, 15B, 155, 195, 202/203
Stefano Torrione/SIME/4Corners Images 348/349
Susanne Kremer/4Corners Images 2
Suzanne Porter/Rough Guides 2006 482
Tim Draper/Rough Guides 9, 13C, 13B, 16B, 18B, 19T, 19B, 21T, 55, 95, 141, 213, 273, 281, 389
Treehouse Lodge 17BL

Cover: Peruvian women selling souvenirs at Inca ruins, Sacred Valley **iStock**

Index

A

D

E

F

G

H

I

J

N

O

P

Q

R

S

T

U

W

Z

Map symbols

The symbols below are used on maps throughout the book

- International boundary
- Chapter division boundary
- Highway
- Major road
- Minor road
- Pedestrian road
- 4WD road
- Unpaved road
- Steps
- Railway
- Funicular
- Ferry
- Footpath
- International airport
- Domestic airport
- Transport stop

- Post office
- Hospital
- Information office
- Place of interest
- Internet access
- Telephone office
- Bank
- Campsite
- Golf course
- Viewpoint
- Observatory
- Lodge
- Museum
- Tower
- Monument
- Bird sanctuary

- Mountain range
- Mountain peak
- Spring
- Waterfall
- Cave
- Ruins
- Arch
- Market
- Building
- Church
- Stadium
- Park
- Beach
- Marsh
- Saltpan
- Glacier

Listings key

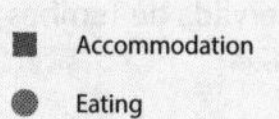

- Accommodation
- Eating

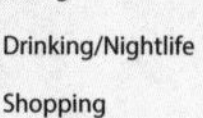

- Drinking/Nightlife
- Shopping